Financial Accounting

Financial Accounting

An Introduction to Concepts, Methods, and Uses

Fourth Edition

Sidney Davidson, Ph.D., CPA
University of Chicago

Clyde P. Stickney, D.B.A., CPA
Dartmouth College

Roman L. Weil, Ph.D., CPA, CMA
University of Chicago

The Dryden Press
Chicago   New York   Philadelphia   San Francisco   Montreal   Toronto
London   Sydney   Tokyo   Mexico City   Rio de Janeiro   Madrid

Acquisitions Editor: Larry Armstrong
Developmental Editor: Judy Sarwark
Project Editor: Russell Hahn, Anne Knowles
Managing Editor: Jane Perkins
Design Director: Alan Wendt
Production Manager: Mary Jarvis

Copy Editor: Lynne Lackenbach
Indexer: Cherie Worman
Compositor: York Graphic Services
Text Type: 10/12 Times Roman

Library of Congress Cataloging in Publication Data

Davidson, Sidney, 1919–
   Financial accounting.

   Includes bibliographical references and index.
   1. Accounting.   I. Stickney, Clyde P., 1944–
II. Weil, Roman L.   III. Title.
HF5635.D228   1985   657   84-8080
ISBN 0-03-071318-8

Printed in the United States of America
567-039-987654321

Address orders:
383 Madison Avenue
New York, NY 10017

Address editorial correspondence:
One Salt Creek Lane
Hinsdale, IL 60521
(800) 323-7437

CBS College Publishing
The Dryden Press
Holt, Rinehart and Winston
Saunders College Publishing

For Katherine, Raymonde, and Sandy, with thanks.

Whatever be the detail with which you cram
your students, the chance of their meeting in
after-life exactly that detail is almost
infinitesimal; and if they do meet it, they will
probably have forgotten what you taught them
about it. The really useful training yields a
comprehension of a few general principles with
a thorough grounding in the way they apply to
a variety of concrete details. In subsequent
practice the students will have forgotten your
particular details; but they will remember by an
unconscious common sense how to apply
principles to immediate circumstances.

Alfred North Whitehead
The Aims of Education and Other Essays

The Dryden Press Series in Accounting

Belkaoui
Cost Accounting: A Multidimensional Emphasis

Davidson, Stickney, and Weil
Financial Accounting: An Introduction to Concepts, Methods, and Uses
Fourth Edition

Davidson, Hanouille, Stickney, and Weil
Intermediate Accounting: Concepts, Methods, and Uses Fourth Edition

Davidson, Maher, Stickney, and Weil
Managerial Accounting: An Introduction to Concepts, Methods, and Uses
Second Edition

Huefner and Largay
Advanced Financial Accounting

Lee
Elementary Accounting

Mueller and Smith
Accounting: A Book of Readings Second Edition

Reynolds, Sanders, and Hillman
Principles of Accounting Third Edition

Slavin, Reynolds, and Sanders
Financial Accounting: A Basic Approach

Titard
Managerial Accounting: An Introduction

Preface

The fourth edition of this book has the same principal objectives as the previous editions. The introductory course in financial accounting has two main purposes:

To help the student develop a sufficient understanding of the basic concepts underlying financial statements so that the concepts can be applied to new and different situations.

To train the student in accounting terminology and methods so that financial statements currently published in corporate annual reports can be interpreted, analyzed, and evaluated.

Most introductory financial accounting textbooks share these, or similar, objectives. The critical differences among textbooks relate to the relative emphases on concepts, methods, and uses.

1. Concepts This book emphasizes the rationale for, and implications of, important accounting concepts. The ability to "conceptualize" material covered is an important part of the learning process. Without such conceptualization, students will have difficulty focusing on relevant issues in new and different situations. Accordingly, important accounting concepts are identified early in each chapter. Following these are several numerical examples illustrating their application. Numerous short exercises are included at the end of each chapter to check the students' ability to apply the concepts to still different problem situations.

2. Methods Sufficient emphasis is placed on accounting procedures so that students can interpret, analyze, and evaluate published financial statements. However, procedures are not emphasized to such an extent that students bog down in detail. The determination of just how much accounting procedure is "enough" is a problem faced by all writers of accounting textbooks. Many feel, as we do, that the most effective way to learn accounting concepts is to work numerous problems and exercises. However, when too much emphasis is placed on accounting procedures, there is a tendency for students to be lulled into the security of thinking they understand accounting concepts when they actually do not. The mixture of concepts and procedures in this book is one with which we have experimented extensively and that we have found effective in classroom use.

Understanding the accounting implications of an event requires that students be able to construct the journal entry for that event. Throughout this book, journal entries are used in describing the nature of accounting events. Moreover, most chapters contain exercises and problems that require the analysis of transactions with debits and credits. Do not conclude, however, by a glance at this text, that it is primarily procedural. The principal objective is that students learn concepts; the procedures are required for learning the concepts.

3. Uses An attempt is made to bridge the gap between the preparation of financial statements and the uses to which the statements might be put. Extensive consideration is given to the effects of alternative accounting principles on the measurement of earnings and financial position and to the types of interpretations that should and should not be made. A complete set of financial statements and related notes appears in Appendix A at the back of the book. Discussion of these financial statements is appropriately integrated into each chapter. Numerous user-oriented cases appear at the end of most chapters.

Changes in This Edition

The major changes in the fourth edition are as follows:

1. The discussion in Chapters 1 through 6 has been structured around three general types of business activities: (1) investing, (2) financing, and (3) operating. Chapter 1 describes these three principal business activities and shows how the results of these activities are reflected in the financial statements.

2. Chapter 5, which discusses the statement of changes in financial position, now defines funds as cash only.

3. Chapter 6 has an expanded discussion of risk analysis, with several new cash-flow ratios introduced.

4. Chapter 7 begins with a discussion of the nature and establishment of generally accepted accounting principles (GAAP), which serves as an introduction to the discussion of GAAP for individual assets and equities in Chapters 7 through 14.

5. Chapter 11 introduces the concept of off-balance sheet financing and the accounting issues it raises.

6. Numerous short exercises emphasizing particular concepts have been added to every chapter.

7. User-oriented analytical and interpretative cases have been added to most chapters.

Organization

This book comprises four major parts. Part One, Overview of Financial Statements, includes Chapter 1; Part Two, Accounting Concepts and Methods, Chapters 2–6;

Part Three, Measuring and Reporting Assets and Equities, Chapters 7–14; and Part Four, Synthesis, Chapter 15. The four parts may be viewed as four tiers, or steps, for coverage of the material. Part One presents a general overview of the principal financial statements. Part Two discusses the basic accounting model used to generate the principal financial statements. Part Three considers the specific accounting principles or methods used in preparing the financial statements. Finally, Part Four serves as a synthesis for the entire book. This organization reflects the view that learning can take place most effectively when the student starts with a broad picture, then breaks up that broad picture into smaller pieces until the desired depth is achieved, and finally synthesizes so that the relationship between the parts and the whole is kept in perspective.

Chapter 1 presents a brief description of the principal activities of a business firm (investing, financing, and operating) and shows how the results of these activities are reported in the three principal financial statements: the balance sheet, the income statement, and the statement of changes in financial position.

Many students feel deluged with the multitude of new terms and concepts after reading Chapter 1. Most of these same students admit later, however, that the broad overview was useful in piecing material together as they later explored individual topics in greater length.

Chapters 2 through 5 present the basic accounting model that generates the three principal financial statements. In each case, the discussion begins with a description of the important concepts underlying each statement. The accounting procedures employed to generate the statements are then described and illustrated. One of the unique features of the book is the integration in Chapter 3 of the accounting entries for transactions during a period with the related adjusting entries at the end of the period. When these two types of entries are discussed in separate chapters, students lose sight of the fact that both kinds of entries are required to measure net income and financial position.

Another unique aspect of the text is the early coverage, in Chapter 5, of the statement of changes in financial position. Two purposes are served by placing it here. First, this placement elevates the statement to its rightful place among the three principal financial statements. Students can thereby integrate the concepts of profitability and cash flow more effectively and begin to understand that one does not necessarily accompany the other. When the funds statement is covered at the end of the course (in many cases, when time is running out), there is a tendency for the student to think it is less important. A second purpose for placing this chapter early in the book is that it serves to cement understanding of the basic accounting model in Chapters 2 through 4: preparing the statement of changes in financial position requires the student to work ''backwards'' from the balance sheet and income statement to reconstruct the transactions that took place.

Chapter 6 introduces the topic of financial statement analysis. This topic is placed here to serve as a partial synthesis of the first five chapters. Students at this point ask how information in the statements might be used. This chapter presents an opportunity to answer some of these questions, even if at only an elementary level. Effective financial statement analysis requires an understanding of the specific accounting methods discussed in Part Three. Chapter 6 therefore serves as a springboard for what is to come.

Chapters 7 through 14 discuss the various ''generally accepted accounting principles'' employed in generating financial statements. Each chapter not only describes and illustrates the application of the various accounting methods but also considers their effects on the financial statements. This approach reflects the view that students should be able to interpret and analyze published financial statements and to understand the effect of alternative accounting methods on such assessments. Some of the more complicated topics have been placed in end-of-chapter appendixes to provide flexibility in coverage. Some instructors may not wish to use this more advanced material.

The students who have used the previous editions of this book have found Chapter 15, which synthesizes much of the material in the first fourteen chapters, in many ways the most useful in the book. Explicit consideration is given to the combined effects of alternative accounting methods on the financial statements and the significance of alternative accounting methods on financial statement analysis. The self-study problem and problems 21 and 22 at the end of Chapter 15 are major review problems for the whole book.

A comprehensive glossary of accounting terms is included at the end of the book. It serves as a useful reference tool for accounting and other business terms and provides additional descriptions of a few topics considered only briefly in the text, such as accounting changes.

Related Materials Accompanying the Text

The following materials have been prepared for use with the text:

Instructor's Manual and Test Bank The instructor's manual, in addition to including responses to all exercises, problems, and cases, presents suggested outlines for courses of varying lengths, a list of chapter objectives, helpful teaching hints, detailed lecture and discussion outlines including the numbers of particularly germane problems, and sample examination questions and problems. The instructor's manual also includes a list of check figures for various problems in the text. These check figures can be photocopied and distributed to students if the instructor so desires.

Study Guide A study guide has been prepared by LeBrone C. Harris, James E. Moon, and William L. Stephens. This study guide includes a listing of highlights from each chapter and is then followed by numerous short true/false, matching, and multiple-choice questions, with answers.

Transparencies A set of transparencies is available for many of the exhibits in the text and the end-of-chapter problems.

Working Papers A set of working papers for the exercises, problems, and cases is also available. These working papers set out the number of each exercise, problem or case, label the columns and rows as appropriate, and provide the necessary working paper (for example, two-column journal, multi-column worksheet).

Practice Set A Practice Set A accompanies the new edition of *Intermediate Accounting,* fourth edition, by Sidney Davidson, Leon Hanouille, Clyde P. Stickney, and Roman L. Weil. This practice set is a review of introductory financial accounting and can be used with *Financial Accounting,* fourth edition, as well.

Acknowledgments

We gratefully acknowledge the helpful criticisms and suggestions of our colleagues and others who reviewed the manuscript at various stages: James A. Largay III, C. L. Mitchell, and Stephen A. Zeff.

Our work on this revision was further aided by reviews from Penelope Sue Campbell, University of Iowa; Howard Felt, Temple University; Stephen Fogg, Temple University; Bruce Johnson, Northwestern University; Patricia King, University of Arizona; John McMichael, University of Pennsylvania; Katherine Schipper, University of Chicago; Bonnie Simmons, North Central College; and John Tracy, University of Colorado. Some of our former students helped us to improve the clarity of the questions and problems and to debug the solutions. We thank them for their help; Stuart Fletcher and Jason Kuehn were especially productive.

Thomas Horton and Daughters, Inc., has graciously given us permission to reproduce material from *Accounting: The Language of Business*. Problems 47–49 in Chapter 3 were adapted from ones prepared by George H. Sorter. These problems involve working backwards from one financial statement to another, and we have found them useful in cementing understanding. Stan Baiman provided us with a series of excellent problems on the statements of changes in financial position for use in Chapters 7 through 13.

We thank the following people for their hard work in helping us to prepare the manuscript for this book: Peg McGann, Sandra Myers, Raymonde Rousselot, and K. Xenophon-Rybowiak. Cherie Worman prepared the Index.

Finally, we thank Larry Armstrong, Russell Hahn, Anne Knowles, and particularly Judy Sarwark of The Dryden Press for their assistance and patience in the preparation of this book.

S.D.
C.P.S.
R.L.W.

Contents

Part One   Overview of Financial Statements

Chapter 1   Introduction to Business Activities and Overview of Principal Financial Statements

Accounting is a system for *measuring* the results of business activities and *communicating* those measurements to interested users. You are about to begin a study of (1) the concepts and procedures used by accountants to make these measurements and (2) the principal financial statements through which the measurements are communicated. You probably will not become an accountant yourself. Rather, you will use accounting as a tool in making production, marketing, investment, or other business decisions. The goal of your study (and this book) is to help you gain sufficient understanding of accounting concepts and procedures so that you can use accounting data effectively.

Distinction Between Managerial and Financial Accounting

The field of accounting divides into two parts: managerial accounting and financial accounting.

Managerial accounting is concerned with the preparation of reports for use by persons within a firm. For example, a corporate treasurer might use a statement of projected cash receipts and disbursements in deciding if short-term borrowing is necessary. A production manager might use a report on the productivity of various employees in deciding how a special order is to be routed through a factory. A sales manager might use a report on the cost of producing and selling different product lines in recommending the prices to be charged and the products to be emphasized by the sales staff. Users of information within a firm can specify the types of information they need for their decisions; managerial accounting reports are designed to satisfy these needs.

In contrast, *financial accounting* is concerned with the preparation of reports for use by persons outside a firm. For example, a bank may desire information on the cash-generating ability of a firm in deciding whether to grant a bank loan. A potential investor may desire information on a firm's profitability before deciding whether to invest in the firm.

The format and content of financial accounting reports are more standardized than those used in managerial accounting. The large number of uses and users of financial accounting reports creates the need for some degree of uniformity in reporting among firms.

The most common reports for external use are the financial statements included in the annual report to shareholders (owners) and potential investors. These financial statements are prepared to conform with "generally accepted accounting principles.'' Such ''principles'' have evolved over time or have been made ''acceptable'' by decree from an official rule-making body. The Financial Accounting Standards Board (FASB), an independent body in the private sector, and the Securities and Exchange Commission (SEC), an agency of the federal government, are the principal rule-making bodies in the United States.

This text discusses the principles that underlie the financial statements prepared by firms for external users. We begin by studying how a typical firm carries out its business activities. We then see how the results of these business activities are measured and reported in the principal financial statements. This chapter introduces material to be covered in greater depth in later chapters. The objective is to develop the ''big picture'' so that a perspective is provided for the concepts and procedures discussed later.

Overview of Business Activities

Financial statements for external users attempt to present in a meaningful way the results of a firm's business activities. Understanding these financial statements requires an understanding of the business activities that they attempt to portray.

Example 1 Bill Marsh and Janet Nelson, while working toward degrees in engineering, developed a computerized mechanism for monitoring automobile engine performance. They received a patent on the device and, having recently graduated, want to set up their own firm to manufacture and sell it. The firm will be called Marnel Corporation.

Some of the more important processes through which Marnel Corporation must go are described below.

Establishing Corporate Goals and Strategies

The *goals* of any firm are the targets, or end results, toward which the energies of the firm are directed. The *strategies* of the firm are the means for achieving these goals.

The detail in which goals and strategies are stated varies among firms. Some firms prefer to state goals and strategies in general terms only. For example, a firm might express its goal as ''be more profitable than our leading competitors.'' Its strategy might be to mechanize production so that it can manufacture quality products at a cost lower than its competitors.

Often firms might be more explicit. The goal might be to achieve a certain rate of profitability. The goals might also be broader than profitability alone and include concerns for employee welfare, environmental protection, and community involvement. Strategies might likewise be spelled out in detail, including step-by-step actions to accomplish the goals.

Marnel Corporation's goal is to develop a continuing stream of quality electronic products that can be manufactured and marketed profitably and thereby increase the value of the firm and the wealth of its owners. Its strategies include the following:

1. All electronic devices will be manufactured by Marnel Corporation, so as to ensure quality and provide some protection against other firms' attempts to imitate the devices.
2. The sales and servicing of the devices will be carried out by the firm's sales staff to provide close working relations with customers.
3. Investments will be made in research and development to ensure the ongoing creation of new products.

Obtaining Financing

Before Marnel Corporation can embark on its business activities, it must obtain the necessary funds. The principal sources of funds are owners and creditors.

Owners Owners provide funds to a firm and in return receive some evidence of their ownership. When a firm is organized as a corporation, ownership is evidenced by shares of common stock and the owners are called *shareholders* or *stockholders*. The firm need not repay the owners at a particular future date. Instead, the owners receive dividends if and when the firm decides to pay them. The owners also have a claim on all increases in the value of the firm resulting from future profitable operations.

Creditors Unlike owners, creditors provide funds but require that the funds be repaid, often with interest, at a specific date. The length of time that elapses until repayment varies. Long-term creditors may provide funds and not require repayment for 20 years or more. Such borrowings are usually evidenced by a *bond*. A bond is simply an agreement in which the borrowing company promises to pay the creditors interest on the amounts borrowed at specific dates in the future and then to repay the amount borrowed at the end of some stated period of years. Banks usually lend for periods between several months and several years. Bank borrowings are usually evidenced by a *note* in which the borrowing company promises to repay the amount borrowed plus interest at some future date. Suppliers of raw materials may not view themselves as sources of funds for a firm. Yet, when they supply raw materials but do not require payment for 30 days, they implicitly provide funds. Likewise, employees who are paid weekly or monthly and governmental units that are paid monthly or quarterly provide funds.

All firms must choose the proportion of funds to be obtained from owners, long-term creditors, and short-term creditors. Finance courses cover such financing decisions.

Making Investments

Once a firm has obtained funds, it usually invests them in various items needed to carry out its business activities, such as the following:

1. Land, buildings, and equipment—Such investments provide a firm with a capacity to manufacture and sell its products and usually take many years to provide all of the potential services for which they were acquired.

2. Patents, licenses, and other contractual rights—Such investments provide a firm with the legal right to use certain property or processes in pursuing its business activities.

3. Common stock or bonds of other firms—A firm might invest in other firms (thereby becoming one of its owners or creditors). Such investments might be made for a few months with temporarily excess cash or for more long-term purposes.

4. Inventories—The principal goal of most business firms is to sell its products to customers. In order to satisfy the needs of customers as they arise, an inventory of products must be on hand. Funds are usually not invested in specific inventory items for very long, because the items will soon be sold to customers. Because a certain amount of inventory must always be on hand, however, firms must continually invest some amount of their funds in inventory items.

5. Accounts receivable from customers—When a firm sells its products to customers who are not required to pay immediately, the firm is providing financing to its customers. Carrying a certain amount of accounts receivable may be in the best interest of the firm if sales and profits are increased accordingly. In extending credit to customers, the firm forgoes collecting its cash right away. Funds to acquire other assets must be obtained elsewhere. Carrying accounts receivable, therefore, requires an investment of funds.

6. Cash—Most firms will leave a portion of their funds in the form of cash in checking or savings accounts so that they can pay their bills currently.

Managerial accounting courses cover the techniques for making proper investment decisions.

Carrying out Operations

A firm obtains financing and invests the funds in various resources in order to generate profit. The following comprises the operating activities of a firm:

1. Purchasing—The purchasing department of a *merchandising* firm acquires the amounts and types of products needed by its retail stores. The purchasing department of a *manufacturing* firm acquires the amounts and types of raw materials needed in production.

2. Production—The production department in a manufacturing firm combines raw materials, labor services, and other manufacturing inputs to produce the products, or outputs, of a firm.

3. Marketing—The marketing department oversees selling the product to customers.

4. Administration—The administrative activity of a firm supports purchasing, production, marketing, and other operating departments. Administration might include data processing, legal services, research and development, and other activities.

Managerial accounting, marketing, and production courses cover the appropriate basis for making operating decisions.

Summary of Business Activities

Figure 1.1 summarizes the four principal business activities discussed in this section. Figure 1.1 distinguishes between the short term and the long term. Although the time line dividing short- from long-term activities varies somewhat among firms, 1 year is generally the dividing line used.

Principal Financial Statements

The annual report to shareholders typically includes a letter from the firm's president summarizing activities of the past year and assessing the firm's prospects for the coming year. Also frequently included are promotional materials, such as pictures of the firm's products and employees. The section of the annual report containing the financial statements comprises the following:

1. Balance sheet.
2. Income statement.
3. Statement of changes in financial position.
4. Notes to the financial statements, including various supporting schedules and notes.
5. Opinion of the independent certified public accountant.

Figure 1.1 Summary of Business Activities

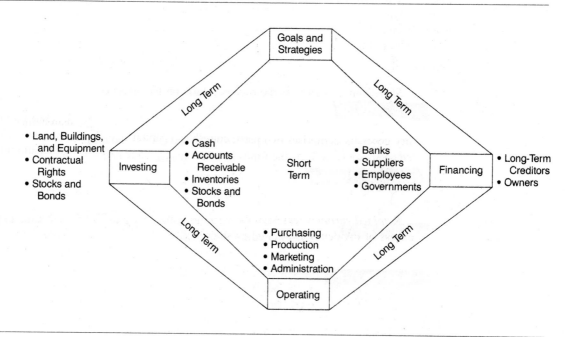

Balance Sheet

The balance sheet presents a snapshot as of a moment in time of the past investing and financing activities of a firm. Exhibit 1.1 presents a comparative balance sheet for Marnel Corporation as of January 1, Year 1, and December 31, Year 1.

The balance sheet on January 1, Year 1, depicts Marnel Corporation on the day it was organized. Owners provided $500,000 of funds, long-term creditors provided $400,000, and suppliers provided $100,000. These funds were invested in inventories, land, building, equipment, and a patent; $70,000 was left in the firm's checking account.

The balance sheet on December 31, Year 1, presents the financial position of Marnel Corporation at the end of the first year. The amounts for most items in the balance sheet changed between the beginning and end of the year.

Note several aspects about the balance sheet.

Concepts of Assets, Liabilities, and Shareholders' Equity The balance sheet presents a listing of a firm's assets, liabilities, and shareholders' equity.

Assets are economic resources. An asset is an item that has the ability or potential to provide future benefits to a firm. For example, cash can be used to purchase inventory or equipment. Inventory can be sold to customers for an amount the firm hopes will be larger than was paid for it. Equipment can be used in transporting inventory to customers.

Liabilities are creditors' claims on the assets of a firm. Marnel Corporation has purchased inventories from its suppliers but has not paid for a portion of the purchases. As a result, these creditors have provided funds to the firm and have a claim on its assets. Labor services have been provided by employees for which payment has not been made as of December 31, Year 1. These employees likewise have provided funds to the firm and have a claim on its assets. Creditors' claims, or liabilities, result from a firm having received benefits (cash, inventories, labor services) previously, and typically have a specified amount and date at which they must be paid.

Shareholders' equity is the owners' claim on the assets of a firm. Unlike creditors, the owners have only a residual interest. That is, owners have a claim on all assets in excess of those required to meet creditors' claims. The shareholders' equity generally comprises two parts: contributed capital and retained earnings. *Contributed capital* reflects the funds invested by shareholders for an ownership interest. The owners initially contributed $500,000 for shares of Marnel Corporation's common stock. They invested an additional $100,000 during Year 1 for more shares of stock.

Retained earnings represent the earnings realized by a firm since its formation in excess of dividends distributed to shareholders. In other words, retained earnings are earnings reinvested by management for the benefit of shareholders. Management directs the use of a firm's assets so that over time more assets are received than are given up in obtaining them. This increase in assets, after any claims of creditors, belongs to the firm's owners. Most firms reinvest a large percentage of the assets generated by earnings for replacement of assets and growth rather than paying dividends.

Exhibit 1.1
MARNEL CORPORATION
Comparative Balance Sheet

	January 1, Year 1	December 31, Year 1
Assets		
Current Assets:		
Cash	$ 70,000	$ 190,000
Accounts Receivable from Customers	—	180,000
Inventories (at manufacturing cost)	100,000	270,000
Total Current Assets	$ 170,000	$ 640,000
Noncurrent Assets (at acquisition cost):		
Land	$ 30,000	$ 30,000
Buildings (net of accumulated depreciation)	400,000	380,000
Equipment (net of accumulated depreciation)	250,000	230,000
Patent (net of accumulated amortization)	150,000	120,000
Total Noncurrent Assets	$ 830,000	$ 760,000
Total Assets	$1,000,000	$1,400,000
Liabilities and Shareholders' Equity		
Current Liabilities:		
Accounts Payable to Suppliers	$ 100,000	$ 130,000
Salaries Payable to Employees	—	30,000
Income Taxes Payable to Federal Government	—	40,000
Total Current Liabilities	$ 100,000	$ 200,000
Noncurrent Liabilities:		
Bonds Payable to Lenders (due Year 20)	400,000	450,000
Total Liabilities	$ 500,000	$ 650,000
Shareholders' Equity:		
Common Stock	$ 500,000	$ 600,000
Retained Earnings	—	150,000
Total Shareholders' Equity	$ 500,000	$ 750,000
Total Liabilities and Shareholders' Equity	$1,000,000	$1,400,000

Equality of Assets and Liabilities Plus Shareholders' Equity   As the balance sheet for Marnel Corporation shows, there is an equality between (1) assets and (2) liabilities plus shareholders' equity. That is,

$$Assets = Liabilities + Shareholders' \ Equity.$$

Assets reflect a firm's past investment decisions, and liabilities plus shareholders' equity reflect a firm's past financing decisions. Every dollar of funds obtained must be invested in something. Thus, we are viewing the same resources from two angles: a listing of the forms in which they are held (assets) and a listing of the parties (creditors and owners) who have provided financing and who, therefore, have a claim on those assets. Thus,

$$\text{Assets} = \text{Liabilities} + \text{Shareholders' Equity,}$$

or

$$\text{Investing} = \text{Financing.}$$

Balance Sheet Classification The balance sheet classifies assets and liabilities as being either current or noncurrent.

Current assets include cash and assets that are expected to be turned into cash, or sold, or consumed within approximately 1 year from the date of the balance sheet. Cash, temporary investments in securities, accounts receivable from customers, and inventories are the most common current assets. *Current liabilities* include liabilities that are expected to be paid within 1 year. Notes payable to banks, accounts payable to suppliers, salaries payable to employees, and taxes payable to governments are examples.

Noncurrent assets, typically held and used for several years, include land, buildings, equipment, patents, and long-term investments in securities. *Noncurrent liabilities* and *shareholders' equity* are a firm's longer-term sources of funds.

Valuation The dollar amount at which each asset and liability appears on the balance sheet is based on one of two valuation bases: (1) cash, or cash equivalent, valuation, or (2) acquisition, or historical, cost valuation.

Cash is stated at the amount of cash on hand or in the bank. Accounts receivable are shown at the amount of cash expected to be collected from customers. Liabilities are generally shown at the present value of the cash required to pay the liabilities. These assets and liabilities are sometimes referred to as *monetary items* because they are valued on a cash, or cash equivalent, basis.

The remaining assets are shown either at acquisition cost or at acquisition cost net of accumulated depreciation or amortization. For example, inventories and land are stated at the amount of cash or other resources that the firm originally sacrificed to acquire those assets. Buildings, equipment, and patents are likewise stated at acquisition cost, but this amount is adjusted downward to reflect the portion of the assets' services that has been used up since acquisition.

Common stock is reported at the amount invested by owners when the firm's common stock was first issued. Retained earnings is the sum of all prior years' earnings in excess of dividends.

Income Statement

The second principal financial statement is the income statement. The income statement presents the results of the operating activities of a firm for a period of time. Exhibit 1.2 presents the income statement for Marnel Corporation for Year 1. This statement indicates the *net income, earnings,* or *profits* of a firm for a period of time. Net income is the difference between revenues and expenses. Note several aspects of the income statement.

Exhibit 1.2
MARNEL CORPORATION
Income Statement for Year 1

Revenues:

Sale of Electronic Devices	$2,250,000
Sale of Engineering Services	140,000
Interest on Accounts Receivable from Customers	10,000
Total Revenues	$2,400,000

Expenses:

Cost of Goods Sold	$1,400,000
Selling Expenses	400,000
Administrative Expenses	200,000
Interest Expense	50,000
Income Tax Expense	150,000
Total Expenses	$2,200,000
Net Income	$ 200,000

Concepts of Net Income, Revenue, and Expense The terms *net income, earnings,* and *profits* are synonyms used interchangeably in corporate annual reports and throughout this text. Generating a profit from operating activities is the primary goal of most business firms. The income statement provides a measure of how successful a firm was in achieving this goal for a given time span. The income statement also reports the sources and amounts of a firm's revenues and the nature and amount of a firm's expenses that net to earnings for the period.

Revenues measure the inflows of assets (or reductions in liabilities) from selling goods and providing services to customers. During Year 1, Marnel Corporation sold electronic devices and provided engineering and financing services. From its customers, Marnel Corporation received either cash or promises to pay cash in the future, called Accounts Receivable from Customers. Both are assets. Thus, revenues were generated and assets increased.

Expenses measure the outflow of assets (or increases in liabilities) used up in generating revenues. *Cost of Goods Sold* (an expense) is a measure of the cost of inventories sold to customers. Selling expenses measure the cash payments made or the liabilities incurred to make future cash payments for marketing services received during the period. For each expense, either an asset decreases or a liability increases.

A firm strives to generate an excess of net asset inflows from revenues over net asset outflows from expenses required in generating the revenues. Net income indicates a firm's accomplishments (revenues) relative to the efforts required (expenses) in pursuing its operating activities. When expenses for a period exceed revenues, a firm incurs a *net loss*.

Classification of Revenues and Expenses The income statement for Marnel Corporation classifies revenues by the nature of the good or service sold (electronic devices, engineering services, financing services) and classifies expenses by the department within the firm that carried out the firm's operating activities (production, marketing, administration). Depreciation and amortization are included in cost of goods sold, selling expenses, and administrative expenses. Interest expense on long-term bonds and income tax expense appear separately. Firms classify revenues and expenses in their income statements in many different ways.

Relationship to Balance Sheet The income statement links the balance sheet at the beginning with that at the end of the period. Recall that retained earnings represent the sum of prior earnings of a firm in excess of dividends. The amount of net income helps explain the change in retained earnings between the beginning and end of the period. During Year 1, Marnel Corporation had net income of $200,000. Dividends declared and paid were $50,000. The change in retained earnings during Year 1 can, therefore, be explained as follows:

Retained Earnings, January 1, Year 1	$ 0
Add Net Income for Year 1	200,000
Subtract Dividends Declared and Paid during Year 1	(50,000)
Retained Earnings, December 31, Year 1	$150,000

Summary of Balance Sheet and Income Statement

Recall that Figure 1.1 summarizes the principal business activities of a firm: financing, investing, and operating. Figure 1.2 now summarizes the relation between these business activities and the balance sheet and income statement.

Statement of Changes in Financial Position

The third principal financial statement is the statement of changes in financial position. This statement reports the sources (inflows) and uses (outflows) of cash during a period of time. Exhibit 1.3 presents a statement of changes in financial position for Marnel Corporation for Year 1. Operations lead to an increase in cash of $50,000. (Recall that not all revenues result in an immediate increase in cash and that not all expenses result in an immediate decrease in cash.) Also, cash was received when bonds and common stock were issued. Cash was used to pay dividends and to acquire equipment. Of what significance is a statement explaining or analyzing the change in cash during a period of time? This might be best understood with an example.

Example 2 Diversified Technologies Corporation began business 4 years ago. In its first 4 years of operations, net income was $100,000, $300,000, $800,000, and $1,500,000, respectively. The company retained all of its earnings for growth. Early in the fifth year, the company learned that despite the retention of all of its earnings, it was running out of cash. A careful study of the problem revealed that the company was expanding accounts receivable, inventories, buildings, and equip-

Figure 1.2 Relationship Between Business Activities and Balance Sheet and Income Statement

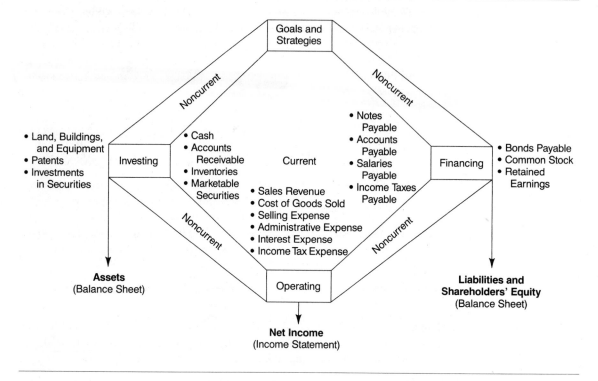

Exhibit 1.3
MARNEL CORPORATION
Statement of Changes in Financial Position for Year 1

Sources of Cash:

Operations.	$ 50,000[a]
New Financing: Issue of Bonds	50,000
Issue of Common Stock	100,000
Sale of Noncurrent Assets.	—
Total Sources	$200,000

Uses of Cash:

Dividends	$ 50,000
Reduction in Financing	—
Acquisition of Noncurrent Assets	30,000
Total Uses.	$ 80,000

Net Increase in Cash for Year 1	$120,000

[a]The computation of cash generated from operations and its relationship to net income are discussed in Chapter 5.

ment so fast that funds were not being generated quickly enough by operations to keep pace with its growth.

This example illustrates a common phenomenon for business firms. Cash may not be generated in sufficient amounts or at the proper times to finance all ongoing or growing operations. If the firm is to continue operating successfully, it must generate more funds than it spends. In some cases the firm can borrow from creditors to replenish its cash, but future operations must generate funds to repay these loans.

Classification of Sources and Uses of Cash   Exhibit 1.3 classifies the sources and uses of cash in parallel with the three principal business activities described earlier in the chapter. Figure 1.3 depicts these various sources and uses graphically.

1. Sources: Operations—The excess of cash received from customers over the amount of cash paid to suppliers, employees, and others in carrying out a firm's operating activities is a primary source of funds for most firms. Although the cash received from customers could be included among the sources and the cash paid to suppliers, employees, and others included among uses, most firms net the sources from operations against the uses from operations.

2. Sources: New Financing—Firms often obtain additional financing by issuing bonds or common stock.

3. Sources: Sale of Noncurrent Assets—The sales of land, buildings, equipment, and other noncurrent assets generate cash. The cash proceeds, however, are seldom sufficient to replace the assets sold.

4. Uses: Dividends—Most firms whose shares are widely held by the public regularly pay dividends. The payment of dividends might be viewed as a reduction in

Figure 1.3 Sources and Uses of Cash

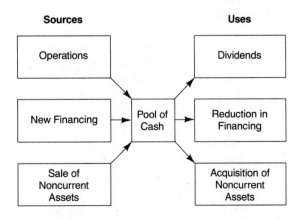

financing, because funds potentially invested by owners (through retained earnings) are now being distributed to them.

5. Uses: Reduction in Financing—Cash is used when a firm repays noncurrent liabilities or reacquires shares of its common stock.

6. Uses: Acquisition of Noncurrent Assets—Firms that expect either to maintain current operating levels or to grow must continually acquire buildings, equipment, and other noncurrent assets.

Relationship to Balance Sheet and Income Statement The statement of changes in financial position explains the change in cash between the beginning and end of the period. The statement also sets forth the major investing and financing activities of the period. Thus, the statement of changes in financial position helps explain changes in various items on the comparative balance sheet.

   The statement of changes in financial position also relates to the income statement in that it shows how operations affected cash for the period.

Other Items in Annual Reports

Notes and Supporting Schedules

The balance sheet, income statement, and statement of changes in financial position shown in the annual report are condensed for easy comprehension by the average reader. Some readers are interested in details omitted from these condensed versions. The annual report, therefore, typically includes schedules that provide more detail for some of the items reported in the three main statements. For example, separate schedules must be provided to explain the change in contributed capital and retained earnings, and may be provided to explain changes in other items in the balance sheet.

   Every set of published financial statements also contains explanatory notes. These notes are an integral part of the statements. As later chapters make clear, a firm must select the accounting methods followed in preparing its financial statements from a set of generally accepted methods. The notes indicate the actual accounting methods used by the firm. The notes also disclose additional information that elaborates on items presented in the three principal statements. To understand fully a firm's balance sheet, income statement, and statement of changes in financial position requires a careful reading of the notes. No such notes are presented for the financial statements of Marnel Corporation because they would not mean much at this stage. Do not conclude, however, that the notes are unimportant merely because they have been omitted from the statements presented in this chapter. See Appendix A, Exhibit A.4, at the back of the book, for examples of notes to the financial statements.

Auditor's Opinion

The annual report to the shareholders contains the opinion of the independent auditor, or Certified Public Accountant, on the financial statements, supporting schedules, and notes.

The auditor's opinion generally follows a standard format, with some variations to meet specific circumstances. An auditor's opinion on the financial statements of Marnel Corporation might be as follows:

> We have examined the comparative balance sheet of Marnel Corporation as of January 1 and December 31, Year 1, and the related statements of net income and changes in financial position for Year 1. Our examination was made in accordance with generally accepted auditing standards, and accordingly included such tests of the accounting records and such other auditing procedures as we considered necessary in the circumstances.
>
> In our opinion, the aforementioned financial statements present fairly the financial position of Marnel Corporation at January 1 and December 31, Year 1, and the results of its operations and changes in financial position for Year 1 in conformity with generally accepted accounting principles applied on a consistent basis.

The opinion usually contains two paragraphs—a *scope* paragraph and an *opinion* paragraph. The scope paragraph indicates the financial presentations covered by the opinion and affirms that auditing standards and practices generally accepted by the accounting profession have been followed unless otherwise noted and described. Exceptions to the statement that the auditor's "examination was made in accordance with generally accepted auditing standards" are seldom seen in published annual reports. There are occasional references to the auditor's having relied on financial statements examined by other auditors, particularly for subsidiaries or for data from prior periods.

The opinion expressed by the auditor in the second paragraph is the heart of the report. The opinion may be *unqualified* or *qualified*. The great majority of opinions are unqualified; that is, there are no exceptions or qualifications to the auditor's opinion that the statements "present fairly the financial position . . . and the results of operations and the changes in financial position . . . in conformity with generally accepted accounting principles applied on a consistent basis."

Qualifications to the opinion result primarily from material uncertainties regarding realization or valuation of assets, outstanding litigation or tax liabilities, or accounting inconsistencies between periods caused by changes in the application of accounting principles. An opinion qualified as to fair presentation is usually noted by the phrase *subject to;* an opinion qualified as to consistency in application of accounting principles is usually noted by *except for,* with an indication of the auditor's approval of the change in principles.

A qualification so material that the auditor feels an opinion cannot be expressed as to the fairness of the financial statements as a whole must result in either a *disclaimer of opinion* or an *adverse opinion*. Adverse opinions and disclaimers of opinion are extremely rare in published reports.

16

Figure 1.4 Summary of Reporting Process and Principal Financial Statements

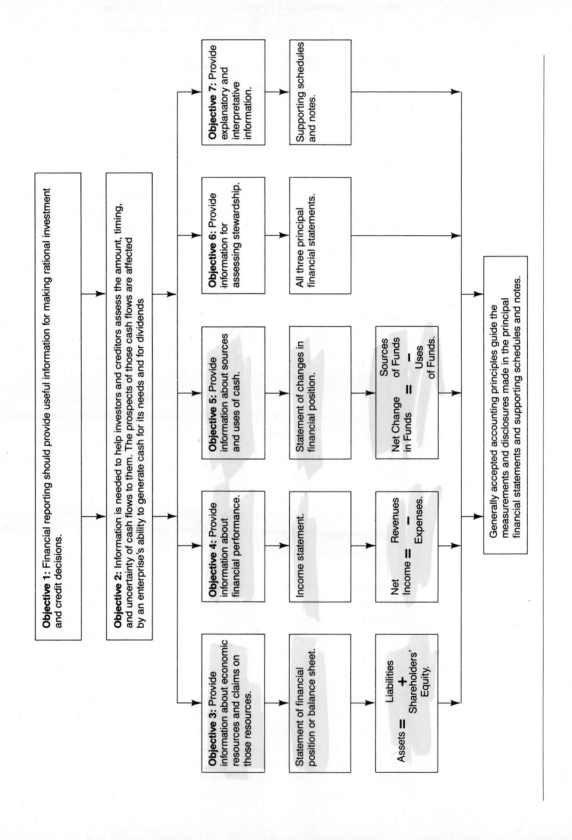

Objectives of Financial Reporting

Financial statements, such as those discussed in this chapter, provide information to investors, creditors, and others who commit funds to a firm. The Financial Accounting Standards Board, the official rule-making body in the private sector, has established a broad set of financial reporting objectives to guide the financial reporting process. Figure 1.4 summarizes these objectives, described briefly below, and their relation to the principal financial statements.

1. Financial reporting should provide information useful for making rational investment and credit decisions. This general-purpose objective states simply that financial reporting should be aimed primarily at investors and creditors and should strive to be useful to these individuals in their decisions.

2. Financial reporting should provide information to help investors and creditors assess the amount, timing, and uncertainty of cash flows. This objective flows from the first by defining "useful" information more fully. It states that investors and creditors are interested primarily in the cash they will receive from investing in a firm. Those cash flows are affected by the ability of the firm to generate cash flows.

3. Financial reporting should provide information about the economic resources of a firm and the claims on those resources. The balance sheet satisfies this objective.

4. Financial reporting should provide information about a firm's operating performance during a period. The income statement accomplishes this objective.

5. Financial reporting should provide information about how an enterprise obtains and uses cash. The statement of changes in financial position accomplishes this objective.

6. Financial reporting should provide information about how management has discharged its stewardship responsibility to owners. Stewardship refers to the prudent use of resources entrusted to a firm. No single statement helps in assessing stewardship. Rather, owners assess stewardship using information from all three financial statements and the notes.

7. Financial reporting should include explanations and interpretations to help users understand the financial information provided. Supporting schedules and notes to the financial statements satisfy this objective.

Summary

This chapter provided an overview of business activities and related them to the principal financial statements included in annual reports to shareholders. Perhaps more questions have been raised than answered. It is helpful, however, to have a broad overview of the various financial statements before examining the concepts and procedures that underlie each statement.

Chapters 2 through 5 discuss and illustrate the concepts and procedures underlying the balance sheet, income statement, and statement of changes in financial position. Chapter 6 considers techniques for analyzing and interpreting these financial statements. Chapters 7 through 14 explore more fully the principles of accounting for individual assets, liabilities, and shareholders' equities. Chapter 15 provides a synthesis for the book.

Now we turn to the study of financial accounting. One of the most effective means of comprehending the concepts and procedures in the book is the careful study of the numerical examples presented in each chapter and the diligent working of several problems, including the self-study problem(s), at the end of each chapter. Frequent reference should also be made to the Glossary of terms at the back of the book as well as to the financial statements and notes for General Products Company presented in Appendix A.

Problem for Self-Study

The accounting records of Digital Electronics Corporation reveal the following:

	December 31	
	Year 1	Year 2
Balance Sheet Items:		
Accounts Payable to Suppliers	$250,000	$295,000
Accounts Receivable from Customers	240,000	320,000
Bonds Payable	100,000	120,000
Buildings (net of accumulated depreciation)	150,000	140,000
Cash	30,000	50,000
Common Stock	100,000	100,000
Equipment (net of accumulated depreciation)	140,000	220,000
Income Taxes Payable	40,000	70,000
Land	60,000	70,000
Merchandise Inventory	380,000	400,000
Retained Earnings	500,000	600,000
Salaries Payable	10,000	15,000
Income Statement Items for Year 2:		
Cost of Merchandise Sold		$ 620,000
Depreciation Expense		40,000
Income Tax Expense		100,000
Insurance Expense		3,000
Interest Expense		10,000
Property Tax Expense		2,000
Rental Revenue (rental of part of building)		30,000
Salary Expense		135,000
Sales Revenue		1,000,000
Dividend Information for Year 2:		
Dividends Declared and Paid		$ 20,000

a. Prepare a comparative balance sheet for Digital Electronics Corporation as of December 31, Year 1 and Year 2. Classify the balance sheet items into the following categories: current assets, noncurrent assets, current liabilities, noncurrent liabilities, and shareholders' equity.

b. Prepare an income statement for Digital Electronics Corporation for Year 2. Separate income statement items into revenues and expenses.

c. Prepare a schedule explaining the changes in retained earnings during Year 2.

Suggested Solution

Exhibit 1.4 presents a comparative balance sheet, Exhibit 1.5 presents an income statement, and Exhibit 1.6 analyzes the change in retained earnings for Digital Electronics Corporation for Year 2.

Exhibit 1.4
DIGITAL ELECTRONICS CORPORATION
Comparative Balance Sheet
December 31, Year 1 and Year 2

	December 31	
	Year 1	Year 2
Assets		
Current Assets:		
Cash	$ 30,000	$ 50,000
Accounts Receivable from Customers.	240,000	320,000
Merchandise Inventory	380,000	400,000
Total Current Assets	$ 650,000	$ 770,000
Noncurrent Assets:		
Land	$ 60,000	$ 70,000
Equipment (net of accumulated depreciation)	140,000	220,000
Buildings (net of accumulated depreciation)	150,000	140,000
Total Noncurrent Assets	$ 350,000	$ 430,000
Total Assets	$1,000,000	$1,200,000
Liabilities and Shareholders' Equity		
Current Liabilities:		
Accounts Payable to Suppliers	$ 250,000	$ 295,000
Salaries Payable	10,000	15,000
Income Taxes Payable	40,000	70,000
Total Current Liabilities	$ 300,000	$ 380,000
Noncurrent Liabilities:		
Bonds Payable	100,000	120,000
Total Liabilities	$ 400,000	$ 500,000
Shareholders' Equity:		
Common Stock	$ 100,000	$ 100,000
Retained Earnings	500,000	600,000
Total Shareholders' Equity	$ 600,000	$ 700,000
Total Liabilities and Shareholders' Equity	$1,000,000	$1,200,000

Exhibit 1.5
DIGITAL ELECTRONICS CORPORATION
Income Statement for Year 2

Revenues:

Sales Revenue	$1,000,000	
Rental Revenue	30,000	
Total Revenues		$1,030,000

Expenses:

Cost of Merchandise Sold	$ 620,000	
Salary Expense	135,000	
Property Tax Expense	2,000	
Insurance Expense	3,000	
Depreciation Expense	40,000	
Interest Expense	10,000	
Income Tax Expense	100,000	
Total Expenses		910,000
Net Income		$ 120,000

Exhibit 1.6
DIGITAL ELECTRONICS CORPORATION
Analysis of Change in Retained Earnings for Year 2

Retained Earnings, December 31, Year 1	$500,000
Plus Net Income	120,000
Less Dividends Declared and Paid	(20,000)
Retained Earnings, December 31, Year 2	$600,000

Questions, Exercises, Problems and Cases

Questions

1. Review the meaning of the following concepts or terms discussed in this chapter.

a.	Managerial accounting.	**m.**	Shareholders' equity.
b.	Financial accounting.	**n.**	Contributed capital.
c.	Generally accepted accounting principles.	**o.**	Retained earnings.
		p.	Cash equivalent value.
d.	Financial Accounting Standards Board.	**q.**	Acquisition cost.
		r.	Net income, earnings, profits.
e.	Securities and Exchange Commission.	**s.**	Net loss.
		t.	Revenue.
f.	Goals and strategies.	**u.**	Expense.
g.	Financing activities.	**v.**	Dividends.
h.	Investing activities.	**w.**	Statement of changes in financial position.
i.	Operating activities.		
j.	Balance sheet.	**x.**	Unqualified, qualified, and adverse opinions.
k.	Assets.		
l.	Liabilities.	**y.**	Financial reporting objectives.

2. Distinguish between financial accounting and managerial accounting. Suggest several ways in which the managers of a firm might use information presented in the three principal externally directed financial statements discussed in this chapter.

3. Suggest reasons why the format and content of financial accounting reports tend to be more standardized than is the case for managerial accounting reports.

4. What purpose is served by having a broad set of financial reporting objectives, such as those issued by the Financial Accounting Standards Board?

5. "Asset valuation and income measurement are closely related." Explain.

6. "Operating activities can be a source of financing." Explain.

7. Does the unqualified or "clean" opinion of a Certified Public Accountant indicate that the financial statements are free of errors and misrepresentations? Explain.

Exercises

8. *Preparation of personal balance sheet.* Prepare a balance sheet of your personal assets, liabilities, and owner's equity. How does the presentation of owner's equity on your balance sheet differ from that in Exhibit 1.1?

9. *Account classification.* Various items are classified on the balance sheet or income statement in one of the following ways:

CA—Current assets.

NA—Noncurrent assets.

CL—Current liabilities.

NL—Noncurrent liabilities.

CC—Contributed capital.

RE—Retained earnings.

NI— Income statement item (revenue or expense).

X— Item would generally not appear on a balance sheet or income statement.

Using the letters above, indicate the classification of each of the following items:
a. Factory.
b. Interest revenue.
c. Common stock issued by a corporation.
d. Goodwill developed by a firm (see Glossary).
e. Automobiles used by sales staff.
f. Cash on hand.
g. Unsettled damage suit against a firm.
h. Commissions earned by sales staff.
i. Supplies inventory.
j. Note payable, due in 3 months.
k. Increase in market value of land held.
l. Dividends.
m. Employee payroll taxes payable.
n. Note payable, due in 6 years.

10. *Balance sheet relations.* Compute the missing balance sheet amounts in each of the four independent cases below.

	a	b	c	d
Noncurrent Assets	$400,000	$500,000	$340,000	?
Shareholders' Equity	?	250,000	290,000	$140,000
Total Assets.	?	?	500,000	?
Current Liabilities	500,000	150,000	?*	?**
Current Assets	600,000	?	?*	?**
Noncurrent Liabilities	100,000	?	?	160,000
Total Liabilities and Shareholders' Equity . . .	?	700,000	?	550,000

*Current assets − current liabilities = $70,000.
**Current assets − current liabilities = $80,000.

11. *Balance sheet relations.* Compute the missing balance sheet amounts in each of the four independent cases below.

	a	b	c	d
Noncurrent Assets	$700,000	$2,000,000	$340,000	?
Shareholders' Equity	?	1,550,000	380,000	$370,000
Total Assets	?	?	500,000	?
Current Liabilities	250,000	400,000	?*	?**
Current Assets.	300,000	?	?*	?**
Noncurrent Liabilities	300,000	?	?	400,000
Total Liabilities and Shareholders' Equity . .	?	2,650,000	?	950,000

*Current assets − current liabilities = $40,000.
**Current assets − current liabilities = $70,000.

12. *Retained earnings relations.* Compute the missing amount affecting retained earnings for Year 2 in each of the independent cases below.

	a	b	c	d	e
Retained Earnings, Dec. 31, Year 1	$80,000	?	$458,000	$120,000	$240,000
Net Income	30,000	$260,000	260,000	?	(60,000)*
Dividends Declared and Paid	10,000	145,000	?	35,000	?
Retained Earnings Dec. 31, Year 2	?	766,000	598,000	110,000	180,000

*Net loss.

13. *Retained earnings relations.* Compute the missing amount affecting retained earnings for Year 2 in each of the independent cases below.

	a	b	c	d	e
Retained Earnings, Dec. 31, Year 1	$150,000	?	$320,000	$75,000	$ 40,000
Net Income	50,000	$125,000	180,000	?	(30,000)*
Dividends Declared and Paid	20,000	75,000	?	30,000	?
Retained Earnings Dec. 31, Year 2	?	500,000	470,000	90,000	10,000

*Net loss.

14. *Relation of net income to balance sheet changes.* The comparative balance sheets of the Sweet Corporation as of December 31, Year 1, and December 31, Year 2, are presented below.

SWEET CORPORATION
Comparative Balance Sheets
December 31, Year 1 and Year 2

	December 31	
	Year 1	Year 2
Total Assets.	$500,000	$800,000
Liabilities	$100,000	$160,000
Common Stock	250,000	290,000
Retained Earnings	150,000	350,000
Total Liabilities and Shareholders' Equity	$500,000	$800,000

Dividends declared and paid during Year 2 were $60,000.

a. Compute net income for the year ending December 31, Year 2, by analyzing the change in retained earnings.

b. Demonstrate that the following relation holds:

$$\frac{\text{Net}}{\text{Income}} = \frac{\text{Increase in}}{\text{Assets}} - \frac{\text{Increase in}}{\text{Liabilities}} - \frac{\text{Increase in}}{\text{Contributed}} + \text{Dividends.}$$
$$\text{Capital}$$

15. *Income statement relations.* Compute the missing amounts affecting the net income for Year 1 in each of the independent cases below.

	a	b	c	d
Sales Revenue.	$500	?	$390	$260
Cost of Goods Sold.	250	$60	?	190
Selling and Administrative Expenses	120	30	70	?
Income Tax Expense	60	20	35	0
Net Income	?	15	35	(15)*

*Net loss.

16. *Statement of changes in financial position relations.* Compute the missing amounts affecting the change in cash for Year 1 in each of the independent cases below.

	a	b	c	d
Sources of Cash:				
Operations.	$500	$250	$600	$(200)*
New Financing	200	100	?	300
Sale of Noncurrent Assets.	50	20	0	100

continued

	a	b	c	d
Use of Cash:				
Dividends	100	75	200	0
Reduction in Financing	80	0	50	50
Acquisition of Noncurrent Assets	550	?	800	120
Change in Cash	?	20	(50)**	?

*Net use of cash for operations.
**Decrease in cash.

17. *Relations between financial statements.* Compute the missing information in each of the independent cases below. The letters in parentheses refer to the following:

BS—Balance sheet.

IS—Income statement.

SCFP—Statement of changes in financial position.

a. Accounts Receivable, Jan. 1, Year 2 (BS) . . . . $ 450
Sales on Account for Year 2 (IS) 1,700
Collections from Customers on Account During Year 2 (SCFP) 1,350
Accounts Receivable, Dec. 31, Year 2 (BS) . . . . ?
b. Salaries Payable, Jan. 1, Year 2 (BS). . . . . $ 120
Salary Expense for Year 2 (IS) . . . . ?
Payments to Salaried Employees During Year 2 (SCFP) 660
Salaries Payable, Dec. 31, Year 2 (BS) 90
c. Equipment (net of depreciation), Jan. 1, Year 2 (BS) . . . . $ 800
Depreciation Expense for Year 2 (IS) . . . . ?
Sales of Equipment During Year 2 (SCFP) 0
Acquisition of Equipment During Year 2 (SCFP) 250
Equipment (net of depreciation), Dec. 31, Year 2 (BS) 900
d. Retained Earnings, Jan. 1, Year 2 (BS) $1,250
Net Income for Year 2 (IS). 300
Dividends Declared and Paid During Year 2 (SCFP) . . . . ?
Retained Earnings, Dec. 31, Year 2 (BS) 1,430

Problems and Cases

18. *Preparation of balance sheet and income statement.* B. Stephens, L. Harris, and G. Winkle, recent graduates, set up a management consulting practice on December 31, Year 1, by issuing common stock for $750,000. The accounting records of the S, H, & W Corporation as of December 31, Year 2, reveal the following.

Balance Sheet Items:

Cash	$ 50,000
Accounts Receivable from Clients	165,000
Supplies Inventory	5,000
Office Equipment (net of depreciation)	85,000
Office Building (net of depreciation)	500,000
Accounts Payable to Suppliers	10,000
Payroll Taxes Payable	5,000
Income Taxes Payable	20,000
Common Stock	750,000

Income Statement Items:

Revenue from Consulting Services	$300,000
Rental Revenue (from renting part of building)	30,000
Salaries Expense	215,000
Property Taxes and Insurance Expense	30,000
Supplies Expense	10,000
Depreciation Expense	25,000
Income Tax Expense	20,000

Dividend Information:

Dividends Declared and Paid	$ 10,000

a. Prepare an income statement for S, H, & W Corporation for the year ending December 31, Year 2. Refer to Exhibit 1.2 for help in designing the format of the statement.

b. Prepare a comparative balance sheet for S, H, & W Corporation on December 31, Year 1, and December 31, Year 2. Refer to Exhibit 1.1 for help in designing the format of the statement.

c. Prepare an analysis of the change in retained earnings during Year 2.

19. *Preparation of balance sheet and income statement.* The accounting records of Laser Sales Corporation reveal the following:

	December 31	
	Year 1	**Year 2**
Balance Sheet Items:		
Accounts Payable	$1,247,000	$1,513,000
Accounts Receivable	740,000	820,000
Bank Loan Payable (due April 10, Year 3)	—	15,000
Bonds Payable (due Year 16)	80,000	100,000
Building (net of accumulated depreciation)	460,000	440,000
Cash	270,000	315,000
Common Stock	1,190,000	1,240,000

continued

	December 31	
	Year 1	Year 2
Equipment (net of accumulated depreciation)	825,000	1,023,000
Income Taxes Payable	25,000	30,000
Land	40,000	50,000
Merchandise Inventory	550,000	610,000
Note Receivable (due June 15, Year 3)	—	20,000
Note Receivable (due December 31, Year 10)	100,000	100,000
Retained Earnings	430,000	470,000
Salaries Payable	28,000	32,000
Supplies Inventory	15,000	22,000

Income Statement Items for Year 2:

Cost of Merchandise Sold	$2,611,000
Depreciation Expense	45,000
Income Tax Expense	55,000
Insurance Expense	8,000
Interest Expense	16,000
Interest Revenue	15,000
Payroll Tax Expense	80,000
Salary Expense	640,000
Sales Revenue	3,500,000

Dividend Information:

Dividends Declared and Paid During Year 2	$ 20,000

a. Prepare a comparative balance sheet for Laser Sales Corporation as of December 31, Year 1 and Year 2. Classify the balance sheet items into one of the following categories: current assets, noncurrent assets, current liabilities, noncurrent liabilities, or shareholders' equity.

b. Prepare an income statement for Laser Sales Corporation for Year 2. Separate income items into revenues and expenses.

c. Prepare a schedule explaining, or accounting for, the change in retained earnings between the beginning and end of Year 2.

20. *Relations between principal financial statements.* The purpose of this problem is to illustrate the relations between the three principal financial statements. Exhibit 1.7 presents a comparative balance sheet for Articulation Corporation as of December 31, Year 1 and Year 2. Exhibit 1.8 presents an income statement and Exhibit 1.9 presents a statement of changes in financial position for Articulation Corporation for Year 2.

Using amounts from these three financial statements, demonstrate that the following relations are correct:

a. Retained earnings at the end of Year 1 plus net income for Year 2 minus dividends declared and paid for Year 2 equal retained earnings at the end of Year 2.

Exhibit 1.7
ARTICULATION CORPORATION
Comparative Balance Sheets
December 31, Year 1 and Year 2

	December 31	
	Year 1	Year 2
Assets		
Current Assets:		
Cash	$ 80	$180
Accounts Receivable from Customers	300	340
Merchandise Inventory	150	160
Total Current Assets	$530	$680
Noncurrent Assets:		
Land	$ 40	$ 55
Buildings and Equipment (net of accumulated depreciation)	130	165
Total Noncurrent Assets	$170	$220
Total Assets	$700	$900
Liabilities and Shareholders' Equity		
Current Liabilities:		
Accounts Payable	$310	$350
Income Taxes Payable	40	60
Total Current Liabilities	$350	$410
Noncurrent Liabilities:		
Bonds Payable	20	25
Total Liabilities	$370	$435
Shareholders' Equity:		
Common Stock	$200	$245
Retained Earnings	130	220
Total Shareholders' Equity	$330	$465
Total Liabilities and Shareholders' Equity	$700	$900

Exhibit 1.8
ARTICULATION CORPORATION
Income Statement for Year 2

Sales Revenue		$1,000
Expenses:		
Cost of Merchandise Sold	$600	
Salary Expense	100	
Depreciation Expense	50	
Interest Expense	20	
Income Tax Expense	120	
Total Expenses		890
Net Income		$ 110

Exhibit 1.9
ARTICULATION CORPORATION
Statement of Changes in Financial Position for Year 2

Sources of Cash:
Operations:

Revenues Increasing Cash	$960	
Expenses Decreasing Cash	790	
Total from Operations	$170	
Issue of Bonds	5	
Issue of Common Stock	45	
Total Sources		$220

Uses of Cash:

Dividends Declared and Paid	$ 20	
Land Acquired	15	
Buildings and Equipment Acquired	85	
Total Uses		120
Net Change in Cash		**$100**

    b. Change in total assets equals change in total liabilities plus change in common stock plus net income minus dividends.

    c. Accounts receivable at the end of Year 1 plus sales (all on account) to customers less cash collections from customers (see statement of changes in financial position) equal accounts receivable at the end of Year 2.

    d. Buildings and equipment at the end of Year 1 plus acquisitions of buildings and equipment minus dispositions of buildings and equipment minus depreciation for Year 2 equal buildings and equipment at the end of Year 2.

    e. Bonds payable at the end of Year 1 plus new bonds issued during Year 2 minus outstanding bonds redeemed during Year 2 equal bonds payable at the end of Year 2.

    f. Common stock at the end of Year 1 plus common stock issued during Year 2 minus outstanding common stock redeemed during year 2 equal common stock at the end of Year 2.

21. *Relations between financial statements. (Adapted from materials prepared by Professor Harvey Mann).* Exhibit 1.10 presents a balance sheet on December 31, Year 1 (columns 1 and 2), an income statement for Year 2 (column 3), a statement of changes in financial position for Year 2 (column 4), and a balance sheet on December 31, Year 2 (columns 5 and 6) for Mann Corporation.

    Compute the amounts for each of the missing items labeled **a** through **j** in the exhibit.

22. *Interpretation of financial statements.* Refer to the financial statements and notes for General Products Company presented in Appendix A at the back of the book. Respond to the following questions.

    a. With respect to the consolidated balance sheet:

        (1) Justify the inclusion of "inventories," and "property, plant, and equipment—net" as assets.

Exhibit 1.10
MANN CORPORATION
Financial Statements for Year 2 (Problem 21)

	Balance Sheet December 31, Year 1 — Assets (1)	Balance Sheet December 31, Year 1 — Liabilities + Shareholders' Equity (2)	Income Statement for Year 2 (3)	Statement of Changes in Financial Position for Year 2 (4)	Balance Sheet December 31, Year 2 — Assets (5)	Balance Sheet December 31, Year 2 — Liabilities + Shareholders' Equity (6)
Accounts Receivable	$ 200		Sales $2,000	Collections from Customers . . . $1,700	a	
Inventories	300		Cost of Goods Sold . b	Purchases of Merchandise . . (1,300)	$ 400	$220
Accounts Payable—Merchandise		$ 180		Change in Accounts Payable . . . 40		40
Salaries Payable		30	Salary Expense . . . (400)	Salaries Paid . . c		10
Interest Payable		d	Interest Expense . . . (20)	Interest Paid . . . (20)		15
Income Taxes Payable		20	Income Tax Expense . (35)	Income Tax Paid . (40)		145
Other Current Liabilities		115	Other Expenses . . . e	Other Expenses Paid . . . (220)		
Land, Building, and Equipment—Net	600		Depreciation Expense . . . (60)	Cash from Operations . . . f	740	400
Bonds Payable		200		Land, Building, and Equipment Acquired . . g		600
Common Stock		h		Bonds Issued . . . 200		i
Retained Earnings		345	Net Income . . . $ 35	Common Stock Issued . . . 300		
Cash	100			Dividend Paid . . . (10)	160	
	$1,200	$1,200		Change in Cash . . $ 60	$1,800	j

(2) Identify the valuation methods used in computing the amounts for the various assets shown on General Products Company's balance sheet. (Note: You must refer to some of General Products Company's notes to respond to this question.)

(3) What justification can you see for excluding General Products Company's investment in a well-trained labor force or its good reputation with customers from its balance sheet?

(4) Liabilities and shareholders' equities represent sources of or claims on the assets of a firm. In what sense are "accounts payable," "taxes payable," and "retained earnings" sources of or claims on the assets of General Products Company?

(5) The "net worth" of a firm has been described as the excess of a firm's assets over its liabilities. Assume that you have agreed to purchase all of the common stock of General Products Company for its net worth as of December 31, 1985. Is $8.2 billion, the total shareholders' equity, a reasonable price to pay? Why or why not?

b. With respect to the consolidated income statement:

(6) Net income is defined as the excess of revenues over expenses. Using only numerical amounts, rearrange the items in General Products Company's income statement for 1985 into the following equation:

$$\text{Net Income} = \text{Revenues} - \text{Expenses}.$$

(7) Revenues are a measure of the inflows of assets (or reductions in liabilities) from selling goods and services to customers. Justify the inclusion of "sales" as revenues.

(8) Expenses are a measure of the outflows of assets (or increases in liabilities) used up in generating revenues. Justify the inclusion of "cost of goods sold," "depreciation," and "income taxes" as expenses.

(9) Net income has been described as a measure of the increase in wealth of a firm for a particular period of time. Do you agree?

c. With respect to the consolidated statement of changes in financial position:

(10) The factors causing a change in cash are depicted graphically in Figure 1.3 in the chapter. Classify each of the sources and uses of cash for General Products Company for 1985 into one of these six categories.

d. Assume that you are a credit officer for a bank contemplating a loan of $500 million to General Products Company as of February 1, 1986. The loan is to be repaid with interest on July 31, 1986. What information from General Products Company's financial statements would you find useful in making this decision?

e. Assume that you are an independently wealthy investor contemplating the purchase of $500 million of General Products Company's common stock. What information from General Products Company's financial statements would you find useful in making this decision?

23. *Relation between net income and cash flows.* The ABC Company started the year in fine shape. The firm made widgets—just what the customer wanted. It made them for $.75 each and sold them for $1.00. The ABC Company kept an inventory equal to shipments of the past 30 days, paid its bills promptly, and collected cash from customers within 30 days after the sale. The sales manager predicted a steady increase of 500 widgets each month beginning in February. It looked like a great year, and it began that way:

January 1	Cash, $875; receivables, $1,000; inventory, $750.
January	In January, 1,000 widgets costing $750 were sold on account for $1,000. Receivables outstanding at the beginning of the month were collected. Production totaled 1,000 units at a total cost of $750. Net income for the month was $250. The books at the end of January showed:
February 1	Cash, $1,125; receivables, $1,000; inventory $750.
February	This month's sales jumped, as predicted, to 1,500 units. With a corresponding step-up in production to maintain the 30-day inventory, ABC Company made 2,000 units at a cost of $1,500. All receivables from January sales were collected. Net income so far, $625. Now the books looked like this:
March 1	Cash, $625; receivables, $1,500; inventory, $1,125.
March	March sales were even better: 2,000 units. Collections: On time. Production, to adhere to the inventory policy: 2,500 units. Operating results for the month, net income of $500. Net income to date: $1,125. The books:
April 1	Cash, $250; receivables, $2,000; inventory, $1,500.
April	In April, sales jumped another 500 units to 2,500, and the manager of ABC Company patted the sales manager on the back. Customers were paying right on time. Production was pushed to 3,000 units, and the month's business netted $625 for a net income to date of $1,750. The manager of ABC Company took off for Miami before the accountant's report was issued. Suddenly a phone call came from the treasurer: "Come home! We need money!"
May 1	Cash, $000; receivables, $2,500; inventory, $1,875.

a. Prepare an analysis that explains what happened to ABC Company. (Hint: Compute the amount of cash receipts and cash disbursements for each month during the period January 1 to May 1.)
b. How can a firm show increasing net income but a decreasing amount of cash?
c. What insights are provided by the problem about the need for all three financial statements: balance sheet, income statement, and statement of changes in financial position?

Part Two   Accounting Concepts and Methods

Chapter 2   Balance Sheet: Presenting the Investments and Financing of a Firm

Chapter 1 introduced the balance sheet, one of the three principal financial statements. Recall that the balance sheet presents a snapshot of the investments of a firm (assets) and the financing of those investments (liabilities and shareholders' equity) as of a specific time. The balance sheet shows the following balance, or equality:

$$\text{Assets} = \text{Liabilities} + \text{Shareholders' Equity.}$$

That is, a firm's assets are in balance with, or equal to, the financing of those assets by creditors and owners. In the balance sheet, we view resources from two angles: a listing of the specific forms in which they are held (for example, cash, inventory, equipment); and a listing of the persons or interests that provided the financing and therefore have a claim on them (for example, suppliers, employees, governments, shareholders). The introduction to the balance sheet in Chapter 1 left several questions unanswered:

1. What limits are set in defining the business entity for which the balance sheet is prepared?
2. Which resources of a firm are recognized as assets?
3. What valuations are placed on these assets?
4. How are assets classified, or grouped, within the balance sheet?
5. Which claims against a firm's assets are recognized as liabilities?
6. What valuations are placed on these liabilities?
7. How are liabilities classified within the balance sheet?
8. What valuation is placed on the owners' equity in a firm, and how is the owners' equity disclosed?

In answering these questions, several accounting concepts underlying the balance sheet must be considered. This discussion not only provides a background for understanding the statement as it is currently prepared, but also permits an assessment of alternative methods of measuring financial position. After this introduction to important accounting concepts, the accounting procedures used in recording transactions and events for presentation in a balance sheet are described and illustrated.

Underlying Concepts

Accounting Entity

Business activities are carried on through various units, or entities. The identification of the business entity is the starting point in designing an accounting system that will provide data for financial statements. Most problems of identifying the business entity are caused by differences between the definition of the entity used in accounting, or the *accounting entity,* and the definition of the entity prescribed by law, or the *legal entity.* In accounting, an attempt is made to emphasize substance over form; that is, the focus is on the unit, or entity, engaged in business activity even though it may not be recognized as a separate legal entity.

Example 1 Joan Webster operates a hardware store in her neighborhood as a sole proprietorship. According to the laws for sole proprietorships in most states, Webster's business assets and personal assets are mingled. That is, suppliers of merchandise to the hardware store can obtain payment for their claims from some or all of her personal assets if business assets are insufficient. Even so, the accounting entity is the hardware store alone, because this is the organizational unit carrying on the business activity.

Example 2 Bill White and Roger Green own and manage an apartment complex, called the Leisure Living Apartments, as a partnership. Under the partnership laws of most states, their personal assets as well as the business assets are subject to the claims of creditors. Even so, the accounting entity is the apartment complex alone, because this is the organizational unit carrying on the business activity.

Example 3 The Wilson Corporation operates through its subsidiaries in 23 states. Each subsidiary is organized as a separate legal corporation under the laws of the state in which it is located. The accounting entity is a combination (or consolidation) of Wilson Corporation and all of its 23 subsidiary corporations, because these legally separate units operate as a single business entity. For purposes of internal performance evaluation by management, however, Wilson Corporation might treat each subsidiary as a separate reporting entity. Thus, the scope of the accounting entity can be related to the purpose to be served by the financial statements.

The accounting entity for which a set of financial statements has been prepared can be ascertained from the heading of each statement. For the three examples above, the headings might read: Webster's Hardware Store, Leisure Living Apartments, and Wilson Corporation and Consolidated Subsidiaries.

Asset Recognition

Assets are resources that have the potential for providing a firm with future economic benefits. That benefit is the ability to generate future cash inflows or to reduce future cash outflows. The resources that are recognized as assets are those (1) for which the firm has acquired rights to their future use as a result of a past transaction or exchange and (2) for which the value of the future benefits can be measured, or quantified, with a reasonable degree of precision.[1]

---

[1]Financial Accounting Standards Board, *Statement of Financial Accounting Concepts No. 3,* ''Elements of Financial Statements of Business Enterprises,'' 1980, par. 19. See Glossary for the Board's specific definition of an asset.

Example 4 Miller Corporation sold merchandise and received a note from the customer who agreed to pay $2,000 within 4 months. This note receivable is an asset of Miller Corporation, because a right has been established to receive a definite amount of cash in the future as a result of the previous sale of merchandise.

Example 5 Miller Corporation acquired manufacturing equipment costing $40,000 and agreed to pay the seller over 3 years. After the final payment, legal title to the equipment will be transferred to Miller Corporation. Even though Miller Corporation does not possess legal title, the equipment is Miller's asset because it has obtained the rights and responsibilities of ownership and can sustain those rights as long as the payments are made on schedule.

Example 6 Miller Corporation plans to acquire a fleet of new trucks next year to replace those wearing out. These new trucks are not now assets, because no exchange has taken place between Miller Corporation and a supplier and, therefore, no right to the future use of the trucks has been established.

Example 7 Miller Corporation has developed a good reputation with its employees, customers, and citizens of the community. This good reputation is expected to provide benefits to the firm in its future business activities. A good reputation, however, is generally *not* recognized as an asset. Although Miller Corporation has made various expenditures in the past to develop the reputation, the future benefits are considered to be too difficult to quantify with a sufficient degree of precision to warrant recognition as an asset.

Most of the difficulties in deciding which items to recognize as assets are related to unexecuted or partially executed contracts. In Example 6, suppose that Miller Corporation entered into a contract with a local truck dealer to acquire the trucks next year at a cash price of $60,000. Miller Corporation has acquired rights to future benefits, but the contract has not been executed. Unexecuted contracts of this nature are generally not recognized as assets in accounting. Miller Corporation will recognize an asset for the trucks when they are received next year.

To take the illustration one step further, assume that Miller Corporation advances the truck dealer $15,000 of the purchase price upon signing the contract. Miller Corporation has acquired rights to future benefits and has exchanged cash. Current accounting practice treats the $15,000 as an advance on the purchase of equipment and reports it as an asset under a title such as Advances to Suppliers. The trucks would not be shown as assets at this time, however, because Miller Corporation is not yet deemed to have received sufficient future rights to justify their inclusion in the balance sheet. Similar asset-recognition questions arise when a firm leases buildings and equipment for its own use under long-term leases or manufactures custom-design products for particular customers. Later chapters discuss these issues more fully.

Asset Valuation Bases

An amount must be assigned to each asset in the balance sheet. Several methods of computing this amount might be used.

Acquisition or Historical Cost The acquisition, or historical, cost of an asset is the amount of cash payment (or cash-equivalent value of other forms of payment) made in acquiring the asset. This amount can generally be found by referring to contracts, invoices, and canceled checks. Because a firm is not compelled to acquire a given asset, it must expect the future benefits from that asset to be at least as large as its acquisition cost. Historical cost then is a lower limit on the amount that a firm considered the future benefits of the asset to be worth at the time of acquisition.

Current Replacement Cost Each asset might be shown on the balance sheet at the current cost of replacing it. Current replacement cost is often referred to as an *entry value,* because it represents the amount required currently to acquire, or "enter" into, the rights to receive future benefits from the asset.

For assets purchased frequently, such as merchandise inventory, current replacement cost can often be calculated by consulting suppliers' catalogs or price lists. The replacement cost of assets purchased less frequently, such as land, buildings, and equipment, is more difficult to ascertain. A major obstacle to implementing current replacement cost is the absence of well-organized secondhand markets for many used assets. Ascertaining current replacement cost in these cases requires finding the cost of a similar new asset and then adjusting that amount downward somehow for the services of the asset already used. There may be difficulties, however, in finding a similar asset. With technological improvements and other quality changes, equipment purchased currently will likely differ from equipment still being used but acquired 10 years previously. Thus, there may be no similar equipment on the market for which replacement cost can be found. Alternatively, the current replacement cost of an asset capable of rendering equivalent services might be substituted when the replacement cost of the specific asset is not readily available. This approach, however, requires subjectivity in identifying assets with equivalent service potential.

Current Net Realizable Value Net realizable value is the net amount of cash (selling price less selling costs) that the firm would receive currently if it sold each asset separately. This amount is often referred to as an *exit value,* because it reflects the amount obtainable if the firm currently disposed of the asset, or "exited" ownership. In measuring net realizable value, one generally assumes that the asset is sold in an orderly fashion, rather than through a forced sale at some "distress" price.

Measuring net realizable value entails difficulties similar to those in measuring current replacement cost. There may be no well-organized secondhand market for used equipment, particularly when the equipment is specially designed for a single firm's needs. In this case, the current selling price of the asset (value in exchange) may be substantially less than the value of the future benefits to the firm from using the asset (value in use).

Present Value of Future Net Cash Flows Another possible valuation basis is the present value of future net cash flows. An asset is a resource that provides a future benefit. This future benefit is the ability of an asset either to generate future net cash receipts or to reduce future cash expenditures. For example, accounts receivable from customers will lead directly to future cash receipts. Merchandise inventory can be sold for cash or promises to pay cash. Equipment can be used to manufacture products that can then be sold for cash. A building that is owned reduces future cash outflows for rental payments. Because these cash flows represent the future services, or benefits, of assets, they might be used in the valuation of assets.

Because cash can be invested to yield interest revenue over time, today's value of a stream of future cash flows, called the *present value,* is worth less than the sum of the cash amounts to be received or saved over time. The balance sheet is to be prepared as of a current date. If future cash flows are to be used to measure an asset's value, then the future net cash flows must be "discounted" to find their present value as of the date of the balance sheet. Chapters 10, 11, and Appendix B discuss the discounting methodology, but the following example presents the general approach.

Example 8 Miller Corporation sold merchandise to a reliable customer, General Models Company, who promised to pay $10,000 one year from the date of sale. General Models Company signed a "promissory note" to that effect and gave the note to Miller Corporation. Miller Corporation judges that the current borrowing rate of General Models Company is 10 percent per year. That is, a loan to General Models Company should yield a return to Miller Corporation of 10 percent. Miller Corporation is to receive $10,000 one year from today. The $10,000 includes both the amount initially lent plus interest on that amount for 1 year. Today's value of the $10,000 to be received 1 year hence is not $10,000 but about $9,100. That is, $9,100 plus 10 percent interest on $9,100 equals $10,000. Hence, the *present value* of $10,000 to be received 1 year from today is $9,100. (Miller Corporation is indifferent between receiving approximately $9,100 today and $10,000 one year from today.) The asset represented by General Models Company's promissory note has a present value of $9,100. If the note were stated on the balance sheet at the present value of the future cash flows, it would be shown at approximately $9,100 on the date of sale.

Using discounted cash flows in the valuation of individual assets requires solving several problems. One is the difficulty caused by the uncertainty of the amounts of future cash flows. The amounts to be received can depend on whether competitors introduce new products, the rate of inflation, and many other factors. A second problem is allocating the cash receipts from selling a single item of merchandise inventory to all of the assets involved in its production and distribution (for example, equipment, buildings, sales staff's automobiles). A third problem is selecting the appropriate rate to be used in discounting the future cash flows to the present. Is the interest rate at which the firm could borrow the appropriate one? Or is the rate at which the firm could invest excess cash the one that should be used? Or is the appropriate rate the firm's cost of capital (a concept introduced in managerial accounting and finance courses)? In the example above, the appropriate rate is General Models' borrowing rate.

Selecting the Appropriate Valuation Basis

The valuation basis selected depends on the financial report being prepared.

Example 9 Miller Corporation is preparing its income tax return for the current year. The Internal Revenue Code and Regulations specify that acquisition or adjusted acquisition cost valuation must be used in most instances.

Example 10 A fire recently destroyed the manufacturing plant, equipment, and inventory of Miller Corporation. The firm's fire insurance policy provides coverage in an amount equal to the cost of replacing the assets that were destroyed. Current replacement cost at the time of the fire is appropriate for supporting the insurance claim.

Example 11 Miller Corporation plans to dispose of one of its manufacturing divisions because it has been operating unprofitably. In deciding on the lowest price to accept for the division, the firm considers the net realizable value of each asset.

Example 12 Brown Corporation is considering the purchase of Miller Corporation. In deciding on the highest price to be paid, Brown Corporation would be interested in the present value of the future net cash flows to be realized from owning Miller Corporation.

Generally Accepted Accounting Asset Valuation Bases

The asset valuation basis appropriate for financial statements issued to shareholders and other investors is perhaps less obvious. The financial statements currently prepared by publicly held firms are based on one of two valuation bases: one for monetary assets and one for nonmonetary assets.

Monetary assets, such as cash and accounts receivable, are generally shown on the balance sheet at their net present value—their current cash, or cash equivalent, value. Cash is stated at the amount of cash on hand or in the bank. Accounts receivable from customers are stated at the amount of cash expected to be collected in the future. If the period of time until a receivable is to be collected spans more than 1 year, then the expected future cash receipt is discounted to a present value. Most accounts receivable, however, are collected within 1 to 3 months. The amount of future cash flows is approximately equal to the present value of these flows, and the discounting process is ignored.

Nonmonetary assets, such as merchandise inventory, land, buildings, and equipment, are stated at acquisition cost, in some cases adjusted downward for depreciation to reflect the services of the assets that have been consumed.

The acquisition cost of an asset includes more than its invoice price. Cost includes all expenditures made or obligations incurred in order to put the asset into usable condition. Transportation cost, costs of installation, handling charges, and any other necessary and reasonable costs incurred in connection with the asset up to the time it is put into service should be considered as part of the total cost assigned to the asset. For example, the cost of an item of equipment might be calculated as follows:

Invoice Price of Equipment	$12,000
Less: 2 Percent Discount for Prompt Cash Payment	240
Net Invoice Price	$11,760
Transportation Cost	326
Installation Costs	735
Total Cost of Equipment	$12,821

The acquisition cost of this equipment to be recorded in the accounting records is $12,821.

Instead of disbursing cash or incurring a liability, other forms of consideration (for example, common stock, merchandise inventory, land) may be given in acquiring an asset. In these cases, acquisition cost is measured by the market value of the consideration given or the market value of the asset received, depending on which market value is more reliably measured.

Foundations for Acquisition Cost Accounting's use of acquisition cost valuations for nonmonetary assets rests on three important concepts or conventions. First, a firm is assumed to be a *going concern*. That is, the firm is assumed to remain in operation long enough for all of its current plans to be carried out. Any increases in the market value of assets held will be realized in the normal course of business when the firm receives higher prices for its products. Current values of the individual assets are therefore assumed to be largely unimportant. Second, acquisition cost valuations are more objective than those obtained from using the other valuation methods. *Objectivity* in accounting refers to the ability of several independent measurers to come to the same conclusion about the valuation of an asset. Obtaining consensus on what constitutes the acquisition cost of an asset is relatively easy. Differences among measurers can arise in ascertaining an asset's current replacement cost, current net realizable value, or present value of future cash flows. Objectivity is necessary if financial statements are to be subject to audits by independent accountants. Third, acquisition cost generally provides more conservative valuations of assets (and measures of earnings) relative to the other valuation methods. Many accountants feel that the possibility of misleading financial statement users will be minimized when assets are stated at lower rather than higher amounts. Thus, *conservatism* has evolved as a convention to justify acquisition-cost valuations.

The preceding description of generally accepted valuation bases does not justify them. The valuation basis—acquisition cost, current replacement cost, current net realizable value, or present value of future cash flows—most relevant to users is an empirical issue for which convincing evidence has not yet been provided. As Chapter 14 discusses, most large, publicly held firms are required to provide supplementary information on the current cost of their inventories, property, plant, and equipment. The required disclosure of such information is, to some extent, a response to the recognized deficiencies of historical cost valuations during periods of changing prices.

Asset Classification

The classification of assets within the balance sheet varies widely in published annual reports. The principal asset categories are described below.

Current Assets   *Current assets* include cash and other assets that are expected to be realized in cash or sold or consumed during the normal operating cycle of the business, usually 1 year. The operating cycle refers to the period of time that elapses for a given firm during which cash is converted into salable goods and services, goods and services are sold to customers, and customers pay for their purchases with cash. Included in current assets are cash, marketable securities held for the short term, accounts and notes receivable, inventories of merchandise, raw materials, supplies, work in process, and finished goods and prepaid operating costs (for example, prepaid insurance and prepaid rent). Prepaid costs, or prepayments, are current assets in that if they were not paid in advance, then current assets would be required within the next operating cycle to acquire those services.

Investments   A second section of the balance sheet, labeled "Investments," includes long-term investments in securities of other firms. For example, a firm might purchase shares of common stock of a supplier to help assure continued availability of raw materials. Or shares of common stock of a firm in another area of business activity might be acquired to permit the acquiring firm to diversify its operations. When one corporation (the parent) owns more than 50 percent of the voting stock in another corporation (the subsidiary), a single set of "consolidated" financial statements is usually prepared. That is, the specific assets, liabilities, revenues, and expenses of the subsidiary are merged, or consolidated, with those of the parent corporation. The securities shown in the Investments section of the balance sheet are therefore investments in firms whose assets and liabilities have *not* been consolidated with the parent or investor firm. Chapter 13 discusses consolidated financial statements.

The holders of a firm's long-term bonds may require that cash be set aside periodically so that sufficient funds will be available to retire the bonds at maturity. The funds are typically given to a trustee, such as a bank or insurance company, which invests the funds received. Funds set aside for this purpose are shown in a Sinking Fund account and classified under Investments on the balance sheet.

Property, Plant, and Equipment   Property, plant, and equipment (sometimes called *plant assets* or *fixed assets*) designates the tangible, long-lived assets used in a firm's operations over a period of years and generally not acquired for resale. This category includes land, buildings, machinery, automobiles, furniture, fixtures, computers, and other equipment. The amount shown on the balance sheet for each of these items (except land) is acquisition cost less accumulated depreciation since the asset was acquired. Frequently, only the net balance, or book value, appears on the balance sheet. Land is shown at acquisition cost.

Intangible Assets Intangible assets include such items as patents, trademarks, franchises, and goodwill. The expenditures made by the firm in developing intangible assets are usually not recognized as assets, because of the difficulty of ascertaining the existence and amount of future benefits. Only intangible assets acquired in market exchanges from other entities are recognized as assets.

Liability Recognition

A liability arises when a firm receives benefits or services and in exchange promises to pay the provider of those goods and services a reasonably definite amount at a reasonably definite future time. The payment is usually in cash but may be made in goods or services.[2]

Example 13 Miller Corporation purchased merchandise inventory and agreed to pay the supplier $8,000 within 30 days. This obligation is a liability, because Miller Corporation has received the goods and must pay a definite amount at a reasonably definite future time.

Example 14 Miller Corporation borrowed $4 million by issuing long-term bonds. Annual interest payments of 10 percent must be made on December 31 of each year, and the $4 million principal must be repaid in 20 years. This obligation is a liability, because Miller Corporation has received the cash and must repay the debt in a definite amount at a definite future time.

Example 15 Miller Corporation provides a 3-year warranty on its products. The obligation to maintain the products under warranty plans creates a liability. The selling price for its products implicitly includes a charge for future warranty services. As customers pay the selling price, Miller Corporation receives a benefit (that is, the cash received). Past experience provides a basis for estimating the proportion of customers who will seek services under the warranty agreement and the expected cost of providing warranty services. Thus, the amount of obligation can be estimated with a reasonable degree of accuracy, and it is shown as a liability.

Example 16 Miller Corporation has signed an agreement with its employees' labor union, promising to increase wages 6 percent and to provide for medical and life insurance. This agreement does not immediately create a liability, because services have not yet been received from employees that would require any payments for wages and insurance. As labor services are received, a liability will arise.

The most troublesome questions of liability recognition relate to unexecuted contracts. The labor union agreement in Example 16 is an unexecuted contract. Other

[2]Financial Accounting Standards Board, *Statement of Financial Accounting Concepts No. 3,* "Elements of Financial Statements of Business Enterprises," 1980, par. 28. See Glossary for the Board's specific definition of a liability.

examples include some leases, pension agreements, purchase order commitments, and employment contracts. Accounting does not currently recognize unexecuted contracts as liabilities, although the issue continues to be controversial.

Liability Valuation

Most liabilities are monetary, requiring payments of specific amounts of cash. Those due within 1 year or less are stated at the amount of cash expected to be paid to discharge the obligation. If the payment dates extend more than 1 year into the future (for example, as in the case of the bonds in Example 14), the liability is stated at the present value of the future cash outflows.

A liability that requires delivering goods or rendering services, rather than paying cash, is nonmonetary. For example, magazine publishers typically collect cash for subscriptions, promising delivery of magazines over many months. Cash is received currently, whereas the obligation under the subscription is discharged by delivering magazines in the future. Theaters and football teams receive cash for season tickets and promise to admit the ticket holder to future performances. Landlords receive cash in advance and promise to let the tenant use the property. Such nonmonetary obligations appear among liabilities. They are stated, however, at the amount of cash received rather than at the expected cost of publishing the magazines or of providing the theatrical or sporting entertainment. The title frequently used for liabilities of this type is Advances from Customers.

Liability Classification

Liabilities in the balance sheet are typically classified in one of the following categories.

Current Liabilities *Current liabilities* include obligations expected to be paid or discharged during the normal operating cycle of the firm, usually 1 year. In general, current liabilities are paid using current assets. Included in this category are liabilities to merchandise suppliers, employees, and governmental units. Notes and bonds payable are also included to the extent that they will require the use of current assets within the next year.

Long-Term Debt Obligations having due dates, or maturities, more than 1 year after the balance sheet date are classified as *long-term debt*. Included are bonds, mortgages, and similar debts, as well as some obligations under long-term leases.

Other Long-Term Liabilities Obligations not properly considered as current liabilities or long-term debt are classified as *other long-term liabilities*. Included are such items as deferred income taxes and some pension obligations.

Owners' Equity Valuation and Disclosure

The owners' equity in a firm is a residual interest.[3] That is, the owners have a claim on all assets not required to meet the claims of creditors.[4] The valuation of the assets and liabilities included in the balance sheet therefore determines the valuation of total owners' equity.

The remaining question concerns the manner of disclosing this total owners' equity. Accounting draws a distinction between contributed capital and earnings retained by a firm. The balance sheet for a corporation generally separates the amounts contributed directly by shareholders for an interest in the firm (that is, common stock) from earnings subsequently realized by the firm in excess of dividends declared (that is, retained earnings).

In addition, the amount received from shareholders is usually further disaggregated into the *par* or *stated value* of the shares and *amounts contributed in excess of par value or stated value*. The par or stated value of a share of stock is a somewhat arbitrary amount assigned to comply with corporation laws of each state and will rarely equal the market price of the shares at the time they are issued. As a result, the distinction between par or stated value and amounts contributed in excess of par or stated value contains little information, but is typically shown nonetheless. (Chapter 12 discusses these fine points of accounting for owners' equity.)

Example 17 Stephens Corporation was formed on January 1, Year 1. It issued 15,000 shares of $10 par value common stock for $10 cash per share. During Year 1, Stephens Corporation had net income of $30,000 and paid dividends of $10,000 to shareholders. The shareholders' equity section of the balance sheet of Stephens Corporation on December 31, Year 1, is as follows:

Common Stock (par value of $10 per share, 15,000 shares issued and outstanding)	$150,000
Retained Earnings.	20,000
Total Shareholders' Equity	$170,000

Example 18 Instead of issuing $10 par value common stock as in Example 17, assume that Stephens Corporation issued 15,000 shares of $1 par value common stock for $10 cash per share. (The market price of a share of common stock depends on the economic value of the firm and not on the par value of the shares.) The shareholders' equity section of the balance sheet of Stephens Corporation on December 31, Year 1, is as follows:

---

[3]Although owners' equity is equal to assets minus liabilities, accounting provides an independent method for computing the amount. This method is presented in this and the next two chapters.

[4]Financial Accounting Standards Board, *Statement of Financial Accounting Concepts No. 3*, "Elements of Financial Statements of Business Enterprises," 1980, par. 43. See Glossary for the Board's specific definition of owners' equity.

Common Stock (par value of $1 per share, 15,000 shares issued and outstanding)	$ 15,000
Capital Contributed in Excess of Par Value	135,000
Retained Earnings.	20,000
Total Shareholders' Equity	$170,000

The balance sheets of firms that are organized as sole proprietorships or partnerships, rather than as corporations, do not distinguish between contributed capital and earnings retained in the business. The designation of par or stated value is also not used, because these forms of organization do not issue capital stock.

Example 19 Joan Webster operates a hardware store as a sole proprietorship. She contributed $20,000 on January 1, Year 1, and used the cash to rent a building, acquire display equipment, and purchase merchandise inventory. During Year 1, she had net income of $15,000 and withdrew $10,000 cash for personal use. The owners' equity section of the balance sheet of Webster's Hardware Store on December 31, Year 1, is as follows:

Joan Webster, Capital	$25,000[a]
Total Owner's Equity	$25,000

[a]$20,000 + $15,000 − $10,000 = $25,000.

Example 20 Bill White and Roger Green own and manage an apartment complex as a partnership. Each partner contributed $50,000 cash to form the partnership on January 1, Year 1. During Year 1, net income from the apartment complex was $40,000, which the partners shared equally. Bill White withdrew $10,000 and Roger Green withdrew $5,000 from the partnership. The owners' equity section of the balance sheet on December 31, Year 1, for the apartment complex is as follows:

Bill White, Capital	$ 60,000[a]
Roger Green, Capital	65,000[b]
Total Owners' Equity	$125,000

[a]$50,000 + (.50 × $40,000) − $10,000 = $60,000.
[b]$50,000 + (.50 × $40,000) − $ 5,000 = $65,000.

Accounting Procedures for Preparing the Balance Sheet

Now that the concepts underlying the balance sheet have been discussed, the manner in which these concepts are applied in preparing the statement can be considered. The objective is to develop a sufficient understanding of the accounting process that generates the balance sheet so that the resulting statement can be interpreted and analyzed.

Dual Effects of Transactions on the Balance Sheet Equation

The equality between total assets and total liabilities plus shareholders' equity in the balance sheet equation is maintained by reporting the effects of *each* transaction in a way that maintains the equation. Any single transaction will have one of the following four effects or some combination of these effects:

1. It increases both an asset and a liability or shareholders' equity.
2. It decreases both an asset and a liability or shareholders' equity.
3. It increases one asset and decreases another asset.
4. It increases one liability or shareholders' equity and decreases another liability or shareholders' equity.

To illustrate the dual effects of various transactions on the balance sheet equation, consider the following selected transactions for Miller Corporation during January.

1. On January 1, 10,000 shares of $10 par value common stock are issued for $100,000 cash.
2. Equipment costing $60,000 is purchased for cash on January 5.
3. Merchandise inventory costing $15,000 is purchased from a supplier on account on January 15.
4. The supplier in **(3)** is paid $8,000 of the amount due on January 21.
5. The supplier in **(3)** accepts 700 shares of common stock at par value in settlement of the $7,000 amount owed.
6. A 1-year insurance premium of $600 for coverage beginning February 1 is paid in cash on January 31.
7. Cash of $3,000 is received from a customer on January 31, for merchandise to be delivered during February.

Exhibit 2.1 illustrates the dual effects of these transactions on the balance sheet equation. Note that after each transaction assets equal liabilities plus shareholders' equity.

The dual effects reported for each transaction may be viewed as an outflow and an inflow. For example, common stock is issued to shareholders and cash is received. A cash expenditure is made and equipment is received. A promise to make a future cash payment is given to a supplier and merchandise inventory is received. Most transactions and events recorded in the accounting system result from exchanges. The accounting records reflect the inflows and outflows arising from these exchanges.

Purpose and Use of Accounts

A balance sheet could be prepared for Miller Corporation as of January 31, using information from the preceding analysis. Total assets are $110,000. To prepare a balance sheet, however, it would be necessary to retrace the effects of each transaction on total assets to ascertain what portion of the $110,000 represents cash, merchandise inventory, and equipment. Likewise, the effects of each transaction on total liabilities and shareholders' equity would have to be retraced to ascertain which liability and shareholders' equity amounts comprise the $110,000 total. Even

Exhibit 2.1
Illustration of Dual Effects of Transactions on Balance Sheet Equation

Transaction	Assets =	Liabilities +	Shareholders' Equity
(1) On January 1, 10,000 shares of $10 par value common stock are issued for $100,000 cash (increase in both an asset and shareholders' equity).	+ $100,000	$ 0 +	$100,000
Subtotal	$100,000 =	$ 0 +	$100,000
(2) Equipment costing $60,000 is purchased for cash on January 5 (increase in one asset and decrease in another asset).	− 60,000 + 60,000		
Subtotal	$100,000 =	$ 0 +	$100,000
(3) Merchandise inventory costing $15,000 is purchased from a supplier on account on January 15 (increase in both an asset and a liability).	+ 15,000	+ 15,000	
Subtotal	$115,000 =	$15,000 +	$100,000
(4) The supplier in (3) is paid $8,000 of the amount due on January 21 (decrease in both an asset and a liability).	− 8,000	− 8,000	
Subtotal	$107,000 =	$ 7,000 +	$100,000
(5) The supplier in (3) accepts 700 shares of common stock at par value in settlement of the $7,000 amount owed (increase in shareholders' equity and decrease in a liability).		− 7,000 +	7,000
Subtotal	$107,000 =	$ 0 +	$107,000
(6) A 1-year fire insurance premium of $600 for coverage beginning February 1 is paid in cash on January 31 (increase in one asset and decrease in another asset).	+ 600 − 600		
Subtotal	$107,000 =	$ 0 +	$107,000
(7) Cash of $3,000 is received from a customer on January 31, for merchandise to be delivered during February (increase in both an asset and a liability).	+ 3,000	+ 3,000	
Total—January 31	$110,000 =	$ 3,000 +	$107,000

with just a few transactions during the accounting period, this approach to preparing a balance sheet would be cumbersome. Considering the thousands of transactions during the accounting period for most firms, some more practical approach to accumulating amounts for the balance sheet is necessary. To accumulate the changes that take place in each balance sheet item, the accounting system uses a device known as an *account*.

Requirement for an Account Because a balance sheet item that changes can only increase or decrease, all an account need do is to provide for accumulating the increases and decreases that have taken place during the period for a single balance sheet item. The balance carried forward from the previous statement is added to the total increases; the total decreases are deducted, and the result is the amount of the new balance for the current balance sheet.

Form of an Account   The account may take many possible forms, and several are commonly used in accounting practice.

Perhaps the most useful form of the account for textbooks, problems, and examinations is the *T-account*. This form of the account is not used in actual practice, except perhaps for memorandums or preliminary analyses. However, it satisfies the requirement of an account and it is easy to use. As the name indicates, the T-account is shaped like the letter T and consists of a horizontal line bisected by a vertical line. The name or title of the account is written on the horizontal line. One side of the space formed by the vertical line is used to record increases in the item and the other side to record the decreases. Dates and other information can appear as well.

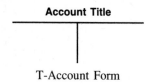

T-Account Form

The form that the account takes in actual records depends on the type of accounting system being used. In manual systems the account may take the form of a single "ledger" sheet with columns for recording increases and decreases; in computer systems it may be a group of similarly coded items in a file. Whatever its form, an account contains the opening balance as well as the increases and decreases in the balance that result from the transactions of the period.

Placement of Increases and Decreases in the Account   Given the two-sided account, we must choose which side will be used to record increases and which, decreases. By long-standing custom, the following rules are used:

1. Increases in assets are entered on the left side and decreases in assets on the right side.
2. Increases in liabilities are entered on the right side and decreases in liabilities on the left side.
3. Increases in shareholders' equity are entered on the right side and decreases in shareholders' equity on the left side.

This custom reflects the fact that a common format for a balance sheet shows assets on the left and liabilities and shareholders' equity on the right. Following this format, asset balances should appear on the left side of accounts; liability and shareholders' equity balances should appear on the right. But asset balances will appear on the left only if asset increases are recorded on the left side of the account. Similarly, right-hand liability and shareholders' equity balances can be produced only by recording liability and shareholders' equity increases on the right. When each transaction is properly analyzed into its dual effects on the accounting equation, and when the above three rules for recording the transaction are followed, then every transaction results in equal amounts in entries on the left- and right-hand sides of various accounts.

Debit and Credit Two terms may now be introduced, *debit* (Dr.) and *credit* (Cr.). These terms are convenient abbreviations: *Debit* is an abbreviation for "record an entry on the left side of an account" when used as a verb and is an abbreviation for "an entry on the left side of an account" when used as a noun or adjective. *Credit* is an abbreviation for "record an entry on the right side of an account" when used as a verb and is an abbreviation for "an entry on the right side of an account" when used as a noun or adjective. Often, however, the word *charge* is used instead of *debit,* both as a noun and as a verb. In terms of balance sheet categories, a debit or charge indicates (1) an increase in an asset, (2) a decrease in a liability, or (3) a decrease in a shareholders' equity item. A credit indicates (1) a decrease in an asset, (2) an increase in a liability, or (3) an increase in a shareholders' equity item.

In order to maintain the equality of the balance sheet equation, the amounts debited to various accounts for each transaction must equal the amounts credited to various accounts. Likewise, the sum of balances in accounts with debit balances at the end of each period must equal the sum of balances in accounts with credit balances.

Summary of Account Terminology and Procedure The conventional use of the account form and the terms debit and credit can be summarized graphically with the use of the T-account form, as follows:

Any Asset Account	
Beginning Balance Increases	Decreases
+	−
Dr.	Cr.
Ending Balance	

Any Liability Account	
Decreases	Beginning Balance Increases
−	+
Dr.	Cr.
	Ending Balance

Any Shareholders' Equity Account	
Decreases	Beginning Balance Increases
−	+
Dr.	Cr.
	Ending Balance

Reflecting the Dual Effects of Transactions in the Accounts

The manner in which the dual effects of transactions change the accounts can now be illustrated. Three separate T-accounts are created: one for assets, one for liabilities, and one for shareholders' equity. The dual effects of the transactions of Miller Corporation for January, described earlier in the chapter, are entered in the T-accounts shown in Exhibit 2.2.

Exhibit 2.2
Summary T-Accounts Showing the Transactions of Miller Corporation

	Assets		= Liabilities		+ Shareholders' Equity	
	Increases (Dr.)	Decreases (Cr.)	Decreases (Dr.)	Increases (Cr.)	Decreases (Dr.)	Increases (Cr.)
(1) Issue of Common Stock for Cash	100,000					100,000
(2) Purchase of Equipment for Cash	60,000	60,000				
(3) Purchase of Merchandise on Account	15,000			15,000		
(4) Payment of Cash to Supplier in (3)		8,000	8,000			
(5) Issuance of Common Stock to Supplier in (3) . .			7,000			7,000
(6) Payment of Insurance Premium in Advance	600	600				
(7) Cash Received from Customer in Advance . . .	3,000			3,000		
Balance	110,000			3,000		107,000

The amount entered on the left side of, or debited to, the accounts for each transaction is equal to the amount entered on the right side of, or credited to, the accounts. Recording equal amounts of debits and credits for each transaction ensures that the balance sheet equation will always be in balance. At the end of January, the assets account has a debit balance of $110,000. The sum of the balances in the liabilities and shareholders' equity accounts is a credit balance of $110,000.

A balance sheet could be prepared for Miller Corporation from the information in the T-accounts. As was the case in the earlier illustration, however, it would be necessary to retrace the entries in the accounts during the period to ascertain which individual assets, liabilities, and shareholders' equity items make up the total assets of $110,000 and the total equities of $110,000.

So that the amount of each asset, liability, and shareholders' equity item can be computed directly, a separate account is used for each balance sheet item, rather than for the three broad categories alone. The recording procedure is the same, except that specific asset or equity accounts are debited and credited.

The transactions of Miller Corporation for January are recorded in Exhibit 2.3, using separate T-accounts for each balance sheet item. The number in parentheses refers to the seven transactions we have been considering for Miller Corporation.

The total assets of Miller Corporation of $110,000 as of January 31 comprise $34,400 in cash, $15,000 in merchandise inventory, $600 of prepaid insurance, and $60,000 in equipment. Total liabilities plus shareholders' equity of $110,000 comprise $3,000 of advances from customers and $107,000 of common stock.

The balance sheet can be prepared using the amounts shown as balances in the T-accounts. The balance sheet of Miller Corporation after the seven transactions of January appears in Exhibit 2.4.

Exhibit 2.3
Individual T-Accounts Showing the Transactions of Miller Corporation

Cash (Asset)			
Increases (Dr.)	Decreases (Cr.)		
(1) 100,000	60,000 (2)		
(7) 3,000	8,000 (4)		
	600 (6)		
Balance 34,400			

Accounts Payable (Liability)			
Decreases (Dr.)	Increases (Cr.)		
(4) 8,000	15,000 (3)		
(5) 7,000			
	0 Balance		

Merchandise Inventory (Asset)	
Increases (Dr.)	Decreases (Cr.)
(3) 15,000	
Balance 15,000	

Advance from Customer (Liability)	
Decreases (Dr.)	Increases (Cr.)
	3,000 (7)
	3,000 Balance

Prepaid Insurance (Asset)	
Increases (Dr.)	Decreases (Cr.)
(6) 600	
Balance 600	

Common Stock (Shareholders' Equity)	
Decreases (Dr.)	Increases (Cr.)
	100,000 (1)
	7,000 (5)
	107,000 Balance

Equipment (Asset)	
Increases (Dr.)	Decreases (Cr.)
(2) 60,000	
Balance 60,000	

An Overview of the Accounting Process

The double-entry recording framework is used in processing the results of various transactions and events through the accounts so that financial statements can be prepared periodically. The accounting system designed around this recording framework generally involves the following operations:

1. Entering the results of each transaction in the *general journal* in the form of a *journal entry,* a process called *journalizing.*
2. Posting the journal entries from the general journal to the accounts in the *general ledger.*
3. Preparing a *trial balance* of the accounts in the general ledger.
4. Making *adjusting* and *correcting* journal entries to accounts listed in the trial balance and posting them to the appropriate general ledger accounts.

Exhibit 2.4
MILLER CORPORATION
Balance Sheet January 31

Assets

Current Assets:

Cash.	$ 34,400
Merchandise Inventory	15,000
Prepaid Insurance	600
Total Current Assets	$ 50,000

Property, Plant, and Equipment:

Equipment	60,000
Total Assets	$110,000

Liabilities and Shareholders' Equity

Current Liabilities:

Advance from Customer	$ 3,000

Shareholders' Equity:

Common Stock	107,000
Total Liabilities and Shareholders' Equity	$110,000

5. Preparing financial statements from a trial balance after adjusting and correcting entries.

Figure 2.1 shows these operations. Each of these operations is described further and illustrated using the transactions of Miller Corporation during January.

Journalizing

Each transaction is initially recorded in the general journal in the form of a *journal entry*. The standard journal entry format is as follows:

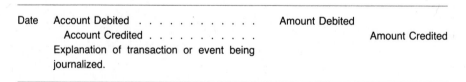

Date	Account Debited	Amount Debited
	Account Credited	Amount Credited
	Explanation of transaction or event being journalized.	

Figure 2.1 Summary of the Accounting Process

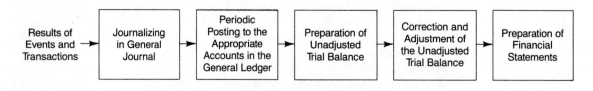

The *general journal* is merely a book or other device containing a listing of journal entries. The general journal is often referred to as the "book of original entry," because transactions initially enter the accounting system through it.

The journal entries for the seven transactions of Miller Corporation during January are presented below.

(1) Jan. 1	Cash	100,000	
	Common Stock		100,000
	10,000 shares of $10 par value common stock are issued for cash.		
(2) Jan. 5	Equipment	60,000	
	Cash		60,000
	Equipment costing $60,000 is purchased for cash.		
(3) Jan. 15	Merchandise Inventory	15,000	
	Accounts Payable		15,000
	Merchandise inventory costing $15,000 is purchased on account.		
(4) Jan. 21	Accounts Payable	8,000	
	Cash		8,000
	Liabilities of $8,000 are paid with cash.		
(5) Jan. 21	Accounts Payable	7,000	
	Common Stock		7,000
	700 shares of $10 par value common stock are issued in settlement of an account payable of $7,000.		
(6) Jan. 31	Prepaid Insurance	600	
	Cash		600
	One-year fire insurance premium of $600 is paid in advance.		
(7) Jan. 31	Cash	3,000	
	Advance from Customer		3,000
	Advance of $3,000 is received from customer for merchandise to be delivered in February.		

Journal entries are useful for indicating the effects of various transactions on a firm's financial statements and in preparing solutions to the problems at the end of each chapter. An accounting event will not be completely understood until it is analyzed into its required debits and credits and the proper journal entry prepared. Consequently, journal entries are used as tools of analysis throughout this text.

Posting

At periodic intervals (for example, weekly or monthly), the transactions journalized in the general journal are entered, or posted, to the individual accounts in the general ledger. In manual systems, the *general ledger* is a book with a separate page for each account. In computerized systems, the general ledger takes the form of an access number in a computer's file. The T-account described earlier serves as a useful surrogate for a general ledger account. The journal entries from the general journal of Miller Corporation would be posted to the general ledger accounts in the manner shown previously in Exhibit 2.3.

As with journal entries, T-accounts are useful tools in preparing solutions to accounting problems and are used throughout this text.

Trial Balance Preparation

A trial balance is a listing of each of the accounts in the general ledger with its balance as of a particular date. The trial balance of Miller Corporation on January 31 appears in Exhibit 2.5.

An equality between the sum of debit account balances and the sum of credit account balances serves as a check on the arithmetic accuracy of the manner in which the dual-entry recording procedure has been carried out during the period. If the trial balance is out of balance, retracing the steps followed in processing the accounting data is necessary to locate the source of the error.

Trial Balance After Adjustment and Correction

Any errors detected in the processing of accounting data must be corrected. A more frequent type of adjustment is often necessary to account for unrecorded events that help to measure net income for the period and financial position at the end of the period. For example, at the end of February, the Prepaid Insurance account will be adjusted downward to reflect the coverage that expired during February. Chapters 3 and 4 discuss this type of adjustment more fully. Most corrections and adjustments are made by preparing a journal entry, entering it in the general journal, and then posting it to the general ledger accounts.

Financial Statement Preparation

The balance sheet and income statement can be prepared from the trial balance after adjustments and corrections. Because correcting or adjusting entries are not required for Miller Corporation, the balance sheet presented in Exhibit 2.4 is correct

Exhibit 2.5
MILLER CORPORATION
Unadjusted Trial Balance January 31

Account	Amounts in Accounts with Debit Balances	Amounts in Accounts with Credit Balances
Cash	$ 34,400	
Merchandise Inventory	15,000	
Prepaid Insurance	600	
Equipment	60,000	
Advance from Customer		$ 3,000
Common Stock		107,000
Totals	$110,000	$110,000

as presented. In subsequent chapters, the accounting procedures for preparing the income statement and the statement of changes in financial position are considered.

The results of various transactions and events are processed through the accounting system in a flow beginning with the journalizing operation and ending with the financial statements.

The audit of the financial statements by the independent auditor typically flows in the opposite direction. The auditor begins with the financial statements prepared by management and then traces various items back through the accounts to the source documents (for example, sales invoices, canceled checks) that support the entries made in the general journal. Thus, it is possible to move back and forth among source documents, journal entries, general ledger postings, and the financial statements.

Balance Sheet Account Titles

The following list shows balance sheet account titles commonly used. The descriptions should help in understanding the nature of various assets, liabilities, and shareholders' equities as well as in selecting appropriate account names for solving problems. Alternative account titles can be easily devised. The list does not show all the account titles used in this book or appearing in the financial statements of publicly held firms.

Assets

Cash on Hand Coins and currency, and such items as bank checks and money orders. The latter items are merely claims against individuals or institutions, but by custom are called "cash."

Cash in Bank Strictly speaking, merely a claim against the bank for the amount deposited. Cash in bank consists of demand deposits, against which checks can be drawn, and time deposits, usually savings accounts and certificates of deposit. In published statements, the two items of Cash on Hand and Cash in Bank usually are combined under the title *Cash*.

Marketable Securities Government bonds, or stocks and bonds of corporations, which the firm plans to hold for a relatively short period of time. The word *marketable* implies that they can be bought and sold readily through a security exchange such as the New York Stock Exchange.

Accounts Receivable Amounts due from customers of a business from the sale of goods or services. The collection of cash occurs some time after the sale. These accounts are also known as "charge accounts" or "open accounts." The general term Accounts Receivable is used in financial statements to describe the figure representing the total amount receivable from all customers but, of course, the firm keeps a separate record for each customer.

Notes Receivable Amounts due from customers or from others to whom loans have been made or credit extended, when the claim has been put into writing in the form of a promissory note.

Interest Receivable Interest on assets such as promissory notes or bonds that has accrued, or come into existence, through the passing of time but that has not been collected as of the date of the balance sheet.

Merchandise Inventory Goods on hand that have been purchased for resale, such as canned goods on the shelves of a grocery store or suits on the racks of a clothing store.

Raw Materials Inventory Unused materials from which manufactured products are to be made.

Finished Goods Inventory Completed but unsold manufactured products.

Work-in-Process Inventory Partially completed manufactured products.

Supplies Inventory Lubricants, cleaning rags, abrasives, and other incidental materials used in manufacturing operations. Stationery, computer disks, pens, and other office supplies. Bags, twine, boxes, and other store supplies. Gasoline, oil, spare parts, and other delivery supplies.

Prepaid Insurance Insurance premiums paid for future coverage.

Prepaid Rent Rent paid in advance for future use of land, buildings, or equipment.

Advances to Suppliers The general name used to indicate payments made in advance for goods to be received at a later date. If no cash is paid by a firm when it places an order, then no asset is recognized.

Investment in Securities The cost of shares of stock in other companies, where the firm's purpose is to hold the shares for relatively long periods of time.

Land Land occupied by buildings or used in operations.

Buildings Factory buildings, store buildings, garages, warehouses, and so forth.

Equipment Lathes, ovens, tools, boilers, computers, motors, bins, cranes, conveyors, automobiles, and so forth.

Furniture and Fixtures Desks, tables, chairs, counters, showcases, scales, and other such store and office equipment.

Accumulated Depreciation This account shows the cumulative amount of the cost of long-term assets (such as buildings and equipment) that has been allocated to the costs of production or to current and prior periods in measuring net income. The amount in this account is subtracted from the acquisition cost of the long-term asset to which it relates in ascertaining the *net book value* of the asset to be shown in the balance sheet.

Leasehold   The right to use property owned by someone else.

Organization Costs   Amounts paid for legal and incorporation fees, for printing the certificates for shares of stock, and for accounting and any other costs incurred in organizing the business so it can begin to function. This asset is seen most commonly on the balance sheets of corporations.

Patents   A right granted for up to 17 years by the federal government to exclude others from manufacturing, using, or selling a certain process or device. Under current generally accepted accounting principles, research and development costs must be treated as an expense in the year incurred rather than being recognized as an asset with future benefits.[5] As a result, a firm that develops a patent will not normally show it as an asset. On the other hand, a firm that purchases a patent from another firm or from an individual will recognize the patent as an asset. Chapter 9 discusses further this inconsistent treatment of internally developed and externally purchased patents.

Goodwill   An amount paid by one firm in acquiring another business enterprise that is greater than the sum of the then-current values assignable to individual, identifiable assets. A good reputation and other desirable attributes are generally not recognized as assets by the firm that creates or develops them. However, when one firm acquires another firm, these desirable attributes are indirectly recognized as assets, because they are a factor in the measurement of goodwill.

Liabilities

Accounts Payable   Amounts owed for goods or services acquired under an informal credit agreement. These accounts are usually payable within 1 or 2 months. The same items appear as Accounts Receivable on the creditor's books.

Notes Payable   The face amount of promissory notes given in connection with loans from a bank or the purchase of goods or services. The same items appear as Notes Receivable on the creditor's books.

Payroll Taxes Payable   Amounts withheld from wages and salaries of employees for federal and state payroll taxes that have not yet been remitted to tax authorities, as well as the employer's share of such taxes.

---

[5]Financial Accounting Standards Board, *Statement of Financial Accounting Standards No. 2,* "Accounting for Research and Development Costs," 1974.

Withheld Income Taxes Amounts withheld from wages and salaries of employees for income taxes that have not yet been remitted to the taxing authority. This is a tentative income tax on the earnings of employees, and the employer acts merely as a tax-collecting agent for the federal and state governments. A few cities also levy income taxes, which the employer must withhold from wages.

Interest Payable Interest on obligations that has accrued or accumulated with the passage of time but that has not been paid as of the date of the balance sheet. The liability for interest is customarily shown separately from the face amount of the obligation.

Income Taxes Payable The estimated liability for income taxes, accumulated and unpaid, based on the taxable income of the business from the beginning of the taxable year to the date of the balance sheet. Because sole proprietorships and partnerships do not pay federal income taxes directly, this term will appear only on the books of a corporation or other taxable entity.

Advances from Customers The general name used to indicate payments received in advance for goods or services to be furnished to customers in the future; a nonmonetary liability. If no cash is received when a customer places an order, then no liability is recorded.

Rent Received in Advance or Advances from Tenants Another example of a nonmonetary liability. The business owns a building that it rents to a tenant. The tenant has prepaid the rental charge for several months in advance. The amount applicable to future months cannot be considered a component of income until the rent is earned as service is rendered with the passage of time. Meanwhile the advance payment results in a liability payable in services (that is, in the use of the building). On the records of the tenant, the same amount would appear as an asset, Prepaid Rent.

Mortgage Payable Long-term promissory notes that have been given greater protection by the pledge of specific pieces of property as security for their payment. If the loan or interest is not paid according to the agreement, the property can be sold for the benefit of the creditor.

Bonds Payable Amounts borrowed by the business for a relatively long period of time under a formal written contract or indenture. The loan is usually obtained from a number of lenders, each of whom receives one or more bond certificates as written evidence of his or her share of the loan.

Convertible Bonds Payable A bond that the holder can *convert* into or "trade in" for shares of common stock. The bond indenture specifies the number of shares to be received when the bond is converted into stock, the dates when conversion can occur, and other details.

Capitalized Lease Obligations The present value of future commitments for cash payments to be made in return for the right to use property owned by someone else.

Deferred Income Taxes Certain income tax obligations are delayed beyond the current accounting period. Chapter 11 discusses this item, which appears on the balance sheet of most U.S. corporations.

Shareholders' Equity

Common Stock Amounts received for the par or stated value of a firm's principal class of voting stock.

Preferred Stock Amounts received for the par value of a class of a firm's stock that has some preference relative to the common stock. This preference is usually with respect to dividends and to assets in the event the corporation is liquidated. Sometimes preferred stock is convertible into common stock.

Capital Contributed in Excess of Par or Stated Value Amounts received from the issuance of common or preferred stock in excess of such shares' par value or stated value. This account is also referred to as *Additional Paid-in Capital* or sometimes as *Premium on Preferred* (or *Common*) *Stock*.

Retained Earnings An account reflecting the increase in net assets since a business was organized as a result of its generating earnings in excess of dividend declarations. When dividends are declared, net assets decrease, and retained earnings decrease by an equal amount.

Treasury Shares This account shows the cost of shares of stock originally issued but subsequently reacquired by the corporation. Treasury shares are not entitled to dividends and are not considered to be ''outstanding'' shares. The cost of treasury shares is almost always shown on the balance sheet as a deduction from the total of the other shareholders' equity accounts. Chapter 12 discusses the accounting for treasury shares.

A balance sheet including many of the accounts described in this section appears in Appendix A, Exhibit A.2, for General Products Company.

Analysis of Balance Sheet

The balance sheet reflects the effects of a firm's investment and financing decisions. In general, firms attempt to balance the term structure of their financing with the term structure of their investments. For example, firms such as retail stores, with large investments in current assets (receivables and inventories), tend to use significant short-term financing. Highly capital-intensive firms, such as electric utilities and steel manufacturers, tend to rely heavily on long-term debt and common stock.

Short-term financing must be paid within approximately 1 year. A firm will want to be sure that it has sufficient cash available within that time period to pay the obligations. Assets classified as "current" will be the assets most likely to generate the cash needed. Likewise, long-term financing is repaid, if at all, over a longer period. Because noncurrent assets tend to generate cash over a longer period of years, long-term financing for these assets is appropriate.

Refer to the balance sheet of General Products Company in Exhibit A.2 in Appendix A at the back of the book. At the end of 1985, current assets represent 53 percent of total assets and current liabilities represent 41 percent of liabilities plus shareholders' equity. At the end of 1984, these percentages were 56 percent and 41 percent, respectively. To provide a cushion, the percentage for current assets tends to be higher than that for current liabilities.

A potential cause for concern occurs when the percentage of short-term financing begins to exceed the percentage of current assets. In this case, the firm is using short-term financing for noncurrent assets. A firm may face difficulties in obtaining sufficient cash from these noncurrent assets to meet required payments on short-term debt.

Summary

The balance sheet comprises three major classes of items—assets, liabilities, and shareholders' equity.

Resources are recognized as assets when a firm has acquired rights to their future use as a result of a past transaction or exchange and when the value of the future benefits can be measured with a reasonable degree of precision. Monetary assets are, in general, stated at their current cash, or cash equivalent, values. Nonmonetary assets are stated at acquisition cost, in some cases adjusted downward for the cost of services that have been consumed.

Liabilities represent obligations of a firm to make payments of a reasonably definite amount at a reasonably definite future time for benefits already received. Shareholders' equity, the difference between total assets and total liabilities, is typically segregated for corporations into contributed capital and retained earnings.

The equality of total assets and total liabilities plus shareholders' equity is maintained by recording the effects of each transaction in a dual manner in the accounts. The double-entry recording framework is summarized as follows:

Asset Accounts		=	Liability Accounts		+	Shareholders' Equity Accounts	
Increases (Debits)	Decreases (Credits)		Decreases (Debits)	Increases (Credits)		Decreases (Debits)	Increases (Credits)

The dual effects of each transaction are initially recorded in journal entry form in the general journal. These journal entries are then posted to the appropriate asset, liability, and shareholders' equity accounts in the general ledger. A trial balance of the ending balances in the general ledger accounts is prepared periodically as a check on the mathematical accuracy of the double-entry recording procedure. Any necessary adjustments or corrections of the account balances in the trial balance are then made in the general journal and posted to the accounts in the general ledger. The financial statements are prepared from the adjusted and corrected trial balance. Chapters 3 and 4 discuss the procedures for preparing the income statement. Chapter 5 discusses the statement of changes in financial position.

When analyzing a balance sheet, one looks for a reasonable balance between the term structure of assets and the term structure of liabilities plus shareholders' equity. The proportion of short- versus long-term financing should bear some relation to the proportion of current versus noncurrent assets.

Problem for Self-Study

The Electronics Appliance Corporation was organized on September 1. The following transactions occurred during the month of September.

1. The firm issues 4,000 shares of $10 par value common stock for $12 cash per share on September 1.

2. The firm's attorney is given 600 shares of $10 par value common stock on September 2 in payment for legal services rendered in the organization of the corporation. The bill for the services is $7,200.

3. A factory building is leased for the 3 years beginning October 1. Monthly rental payments are $5,000. Two months' rent is paid in advance on September 5.

4. Raw materials are purchased on account for $6,100 on September 12.

5. A check for $900 is received on September 15 from a customer as a deposit on a special order for equipment that Electronics plans to manufacture. The contract price is $4,800.

6. Office equipment with a list price of $950 is acquired on September 20. After deducting a discount of $25 for prompt payment, a check is issued in full payment.

7. The company hires three employees to begin work October 1. A cash advance of $200 is given to one of the employees on September 28.

8. Factory equipment costing $27,500 is purchased on September 30. A check for $5,000 is issued, and a long-term mortgage liability is assumed for the balance.

9. The labor costs of installing the new equipment in **(8)** are $450 and are paid in cash on September 30.

   a. Prepare journal entries for each of the nine transactions.
   b. Set up T-accounts and enter each of the nine transactions.
   c. Prepare a balance sheet for Electronics Appliance Corporation as of September 30.

Suggested Solution

The journal entries for the nine transactions are as follows:

(1) Sept. 1	Cash		48,000	
	Common Stock			40,000
	Additional Paid-in Capital			8,000
	Issuance of 4,000 shares of $10 par value common stock for $12 cash per share.			
(2) Sept. 2	Organization Costs		7,200	
	Common Stock			6,000
	Additional Paid-in Capital			1,200
	Issuance of 600 shares of $10 par value common stock in settlement of $7,200 attorney's bill connected with organization of the corporation.			
(3) Sept. 5	Prepaid Rent		10,000	
	Cash			10,000
	Prepayment of rent for October and November on factory building.			
(4) Sept. 12	Raw Material Inventory		6,100	
	Accounts Payable			6,100
	Raw materials costing $6,100 are purchased on account.			
(5) Sept. 15	Cash		900	
	Advances from Customers			900
	An advance of $900 is received from a customer as a deposit on equipment to be manufactured in the future.			
(6) Sept. 20	Equipment		925	
	Cash			925
	Equipment with a list price of $950 is acquired, after a discount, for $925.			
(7) Sept. 28	Advance to Employee		200	
	Cash			200
	A cash advance of $200 is given to an employee beginning work on October 1.			
(8) Sept. 30	Equipment		27,500	
	Cash			5,000
	Mortgage Payable			22,500
	Acquisition of equipment for $5,000 cash and assumption of a $22,500 mortgage for the balance of the purchase price.			
(9) Sept. 30	Equipment		450	
	Cash			450
	Installation cost on equipment acquired in (8) of $450 is paid in cash.			

Exhibit 2.6 presents T-accounts for Electronics Appliance Corporation and shows the recording of the nine entries in the accounts. The letters A, L, and SE are added after the account titles to indicate the balance sheet category of the accounts. Exhibit 2.7 presents a balance sheet as of September 30.

Exhibit 2.6
T-Accounts and Transactions During September for Electronics Appliance Corporation

Cash (A)		Advances to Employees (A)		Raw Materials Inventory (A)		Prepaid Rent (A)	
(1) 48,000	10,000 (3)	(7) 200		(4) 6,100		(3) 10,000	
(5) 900	925 (6)						
	200 (7)						
	5,000 (8)						
	450 (9)						
32,325		200		6,100		10,000	

Equipment (A)		Organization Costs (A)		Accounts Payable (L)		Advances from Customers (L)	
(6) 925		(2) 7,200			6,100 (4)		900 (5)
(8) 27,500							
(9) 450							
28,875		7,200			6,100		900

Mortgage Payable (L)		Common Stock (SE)		Additional Paid-in Capital (SE)	
	22,500 (8)		40,000 (1)		8,000 (1)
			6,000 (2)		1,200 (2)
	22,500		46,000		9,200

Exhibit 2.7
ELECTRONICS APPLIANCE CORPORATION
Balance Sheet September 30

Assets

Current Assets:

Cash	$32,325	
Advances to Employees	200	
Raw Materials Inventory	6,100	
Prepaid Rent	10,000	
Total Current Assets		$48,625

Property, Plant, and Equipment:

Equipment	28,875

Intangibles:

Organization Costs	7,200
Total Assets	$84,700

Liabilities and Shareholders' Equity

Current Liabilities:

Accounts Payable	$ 6,100	
Advances from Customers	900	
Total Current Liabilities		$ 7,000

Long-Term Debt:

Mortgage Payable	22,500
Total Liabilities	$29,500

Shareholders' Equity:

Common Stock, $10 Par Value	$46,000	
Additional Paid-in Capital	9,200	
Total Shareholders' Equity		55,200
Total Liabilities and Shareholders' Equity		$84,700

Questions, Exercises, Problems and Cases

Questions

1. Review the meaning of the following concepts or terms discussed in this chapter.
    a. Accounting entity.
    b. Legal entity.
    c. Sole proprietorship.
    d. Partnership.
    e. Corporation.
    f. Acquisition cost.
    g. Current replacement cost.
    h. Current net realizable value.
    i. Present (discounted) value of future cash flows.
    j. Monetary assets.
    k. Nonmonetary assets.
    l. Going concern.
    m. Objectivity.
    n. Conservatism.
    o. Plant, or fixed, assets.
    p. Intangible assets.
    q. Par value.
    r. Stated value.
    s. Debit.
    t. Charge.
    u. Credit.
    v. Journal entry.
    w. General journal.
    x. General ledger.
    y. T-account.
    z. Trial balance.

2. How can you ascertain from a balance sheet whether the enterprise is a corporation, partnership, or sole proprietorship?

3. Conservatism is generally regarded as a convention in accounting. Indicate who might be hurt by conservatively stated accounting reports.

4. One of the criteria for the recognition of an asset or a liability is that there be a transaction, or exchange. What justification can you see for this requirement?

5. Accounting typically does not recognize either assets or liabilities for mutually unexecuted contracts. What justification can you see for this treatment?

6. Cash discounts taken on the purchase of merchandise or equipment are treated as a reduction in the amount recorded for the assets acquired. What justification can you see for this treatment?

7. A group of investors owns an office building, which is rented unfurnished to tenants. The building was purchased 5 years previously from a construction company and, at that time, was expected to have a useful life of 40 years. Indicate the procedures that might be followed in ascertaining the amount at which the building would be stated under each of the following valuation methods.

    a. Acquisition cost.
    b. Adjusted acquisition cost.
    c. Current replacement cost.
    d. Current net realizable value.
    e. Present value of future cash flows.

8. Some of the assets of one firm correspond to the liabilities of another firm. For example, an account receivable on the seller's balance sheet would be an account payable on the buyer's balance sheet. For each of the following items, indicate whether it is an asset or a liability and give the corresponding account title on the balance sheet of the other party to the transaction.

    a. Advances by Customers.
    b. Bonds Payable.
    c. Interest Receivable.
    d. Prepaid Insurance.
    e. Rental Fees Received in Advance.

Exercises

9. *Asset recognition.* Indicate whether or not each of the following items would be recognized as an asset by a firm according to generally accepted accounting principles.

    a. A patent on a new invention purchased from its creator.
    b. A firm's chief scientist, who has twice won the Nobel prize.
    c. The right to use a building during the coming year. The rent for the period has already been paid.
    d. An automobile acquired with the issue of a note payable. Because the note has not been paid, legal title to the automobile has not yet passed to the firm.
    e. A degree in engineering from a reputable university, awarded to the firm's chief executive.
    f. A contract signed by a customer to purchase $1,000 worth of goods next year.
    g. A favorable reputation.

10. *Asset recognition and valuation.* Indicate whether or not each of the following immediately gives rise to an asset under generally accepted accounting principles. If an asset is recognized, state the account title and amount.

a. A check for $300 has been sent to an insurance company for property insurance. The period of coverage begins next month (consider from the standpoint of the firm making the cash expenditure).

b. A check for $3,000 is issued as a deposit on specially designed equipment. The equipment is to have a total purchase price of $20,000 and will be completed and delivered next year (consider from the standpoint of the firm making the cash expenditure).

c. Shares of common stock of General Electric Company are acquired with temporarily excess cash for $12,000.

d. Merchandise inventory with a list price of $800 is acquired, with payment made in time to secure a 3 percent discount for prompt payment. Cash discounts are treated as a reduction in the acquisition cost of the inventory.

e. A well-known scientist has been hired to manage the firm's research and development activity. Employment begins next month. One-twelfth of the annual salary of $90,000 is payable at the end of each month worked.

f. Bonds with a face value of $200,000 are purchased for $206,000. The bonds mature in 20 years. Interest is payable by the issuer at the rate of 10 percent annually.

g. An order for $700 worth of merchandise is received from a customer.

h. Notice has been received from a manufacturer that raw materials billed at $2,000, with payment due in 30 days, have been shipped by freight. The buyer obtains title to the goods as soon as they are shipped by the seller.

11. *Asset recognition and valuation.* Indicate whether or not each of the following events immediately gives rise to the recognition of an asset under generally accepted accounting principles. If an asset is recognized, state the account title and amount.

a. Raw materials with an invoice price of $4,800 are purchased on account from Greer Wholesalers.

b. Defective raw material purchased in part a for $400 is returned to Greer Wholesalers and full credit is received.

c. The bill of Greer Wholesalers (see parts a and b) is paid promptly. A discount of 2 percent offered by the seller for prompt payment is taken. Cash discounts are treated as a reduction in the acquisition cost of the raw materials.

d. A machine is purchased for $25,000 cash.

e. The cost of transporting the new machine in part d to the plant site is paid in cash, $450.

f. Material and labor costs incurred in installing the machine in part d total $300 and are paid in cash.

12. *Asset recognition and valuation.* Indicate whether or not each of the following events immediately gives rise to an asset under generally accepted accounting principles. If an asset is recognized, state the account title and amount.

a. An investment of $8,000 is made in a government bond. The bond will have a maturity value of $10,000 in 3 years. The firm intends to hold the bond to maturity.

b. A check for $900 is sent to a landlord for 2 months' rent in advance. (Consider from the standpoint of the firm issuing the check.)

   c. A check for $1,000 is written to obtain an option to purchase a tract of land. The price of the land is $32,500. (Consider from the standpoint of the firm issuing the check.)

   d. A firm signs a 4-year employment agreement with its president for $500,000 per year. The contract period begins next month. (Consider from the standpoint of the firm.)

   e. A patent has been purchased from its creator for $40,000.

   f. A patent has been received on a new invention developed by a firm. Expenditures of $40,000 have been made to develop the patented invention.

   g. Notice has been received from a supplier that materials billed at $4,000, with payment due in 30 days, have been shipped by freight. The seller retains title to the materials until received by the buyer.

13. *Asset recognition and valuation.* In each of the following transactions, give the title(s) and amount(s) of the asset(s) that would appear on the balance sheet.

   a. A firm purchases an automobile with a list price of $8,000. The dealer allows a discount of $850 from the list price for payment in cash. Dealer preparation charges on the automobile amount to an extra $200. The dealer collects a 4 percent sales tax on the price paid for the automobile and preparation charges. In addition, the dealer collects a $75 fee to be remitted to the state for this year's license plates and $300 for a 1-year insurance policy provided by the dealer's insurance agency. The firm pays a body shop $75 for painting the firm's name on the automobile.

   b. A firm acquires land that has been appraised at $2 million by a certified real estate appraiser. The firm pays for the land by giving up shares in the Xerox Corporation at a time when equivalent shares traded on the New York Stock Exchange have a market value of $2,100,000.

   c. A firm acquires land that has been appraised at $2 million by a certified real estate appraiser. The firm pays for the land by giving up shares in Small Timers, Inc., whose shares are traded only on the Pacific Stock Exchange. The last transaction in shares of Small Timers, Inc. occurred 4 days prior to this asset swap. Using the prices of the most recent trades, the shares of stock of Small Timers, Inc. given in exchange for the land have a market value of $2,100,000.

14. *Liability recognition.* Indicate whether or not each of the following items is recognized as a liability according to generally accepted accounting principles.

   a. An obligation to provide magazines next year to subscribers who have paid 1 year's subscription fees in advance (consider from the standpoint of the magazine publisher).

   b. The reputation for poor quality control on products manufactured.

   c. An obligation to provide warranty services for 3 years after customers purchase the firm's products.

   d. The outstanding common stock of a corporation.

   e. Unpaid property taxes for the preceding year.

   f. The amount payable by a firm for a television advertisement that has appeared but for which payment is not due for 30 days.

g. A tenant's obligation to maintain a rented warehouse in good repair.

h. The firm's president has an incompetent son who is employed in the business.

15. *Liability recognition and valuation.* Indicate whether or not each of the following events immediately gives rise to the recognition of a liability under generally accepted accounting principles. If a liability is recognized, state the account title and amount.

   a. A company hires its president under a 5-year contract beginning next month. The contract calls for $300,000 compensation per year.

   b. An insurance company receives $2,000 for 6 months' insurance coverage in advance (consider from the standpoint of the insurance company).

   c. A manufacturer agrees to produce a specially designed piece of equipment for $3 million. A down payment of $300,000 is received upon signing the contract, and the remainder is due when the equipment is completed. Consider from the standpoint of the manufacturer.

   d. Additional common stock with a par value of $75,000 is issued for $80,000.

   e. Employees earned wages totaling $6,000 during the last pay period for which they have not been paid. The employer is also liable for payroll taxes of 8 percent of the wages earned.

   f. A firm signs a contract agreeing to sell $6,000 of merchandise to a particular customer.

16. *Liability recognition and valuation.* Indicate whether or not each of the following events immediately gives rise to the recognition of a liability under generally accepted accounting principles. If a liability is recognized, indicate the account title and amount.

   a. A $600 check is received from a tenant for 3 months' rent in advance. (Consider from the standpoint of the lessor, or owner, of the building.)

   b. Utility services received during the past month of $240 have not been paid. (Consider from the standpoint of the firm using the utility services.)

   c. A $10,000 loan has been received from the bank, with the firm signing a note agreeing to repay the loan with interest at 8 percent in 6 months.

   d. A firm has signed an agreement with its employees' labor union agreeing to increase the firm's contribution to the union pension fund by $20,000 per month, beginning next month. (Consider from the standpoint of the firm.)

   e. Income taxes on last year's earnings totaling $15,000 have not been paid.

   f. A firm has signed an employment contract with its controller for a 3-year period beginning next month at a contract price of $200,000 per year. (Consider from the standpoint of the firm.)

17. *Liability recognition and valuation.* Indicate whether or not each of the following events immediately gives rise to a liability under generally accepted accounting principles. If a liability is recognized, state the account title and amount.

   a. A landscaper agrees to improve land owned by a firm. The agreed price for the work is $2,500. (Consider from the standpoint of the firm owning the land.)

b. A check for $36 is received for a 2-year, future subscription to a magazine. (Consider from the standpoint of the magazine publisher.)

c. A construction company agrees to build a bridge for $2 million. A down payment of $200,000 is received upon signing the contract, and the remainder is due when the bridge is completed.

d. Additional common stock with a par value of $60,000 is issued for $80,000.

e. A firm received a 60-day, 10 percent loan of $10,000 from a local bank.

f. A firm signs a contract to purchase at least $6,000 worth of merchandise during the next year.

g. Refer to part **f.** An order for $1,500 of merchandise is placed with the supplier.

18. *Disclosure of owners' equity.* The assets of a business total $700,000, and liabilities total $550,000. Present the owners' equity section of the balance sheet under the following assumptions:

a. The business is a sole proprietorship owned by William Gleason.

b. The business is a partnership. William Gleason has a 35 percent interest, John Morgan has a 40 percent interest, and David Johnson has a 25 percent interest.

c. The business is a corporation. Outstanding common stock was originally issued for $80,000, of which $50,000 represented par value. The remainder of the owners' equity represents accumulated, undistributed earnings.

19. *Balance sheet classification.* Information may be classified with respect to a balance sheet in one of the following ways:

(1) Asset.

(2) Liability.

(3) Shareholders' equity.

(4) Item would not appear on the balance sheet as conventionally prepared.

Using these numbers, indicate the appropriate classification of each of the following items:

a. Salaries payable.

b. Retained earnings.

c. Notes receivable.

d. Unfilled customers' orders.

e. Land.

f. Interest payable.

g. Work-in-process inventory.

h. Mortgage payable.

i. Organization costs.

j. Advances by customers.

k. Advances to employees.

l. Patents.

m. Good credit standing.

n. Common stock.

20. *Balance sheet classification.* Information may be classified with respect to a balance sheet in one of the following ways:

(1) Asset.
(2) Liability.
(3) Shareholders' equity.
(4) Item would not appear on the balance sheet as conventionally prepared.
Using these numbers, indicate the appropriate classification of each of the following items:

   a. Preferred stock.
   b. Furniture and fixtures.
   c. Potential liability under lawsuit (case has not yet gone to trial).
   d. Prepaid rent.
   e. Capital contributed in excess of par value.
   f. Cash on hand.
   g. Goodwill.
   h. Estimated liability under warranty contract.
   i. Raw materials inventory.
   j. Rental fees received in advance.
   k. Bonds payable.
   l. Unexpired insurance.

21. *Working backwards from journal entries*. Presented below are journal entries for a series of transactions. Describe the likely transaction that gave rise to each journal entry.

a. Equipment	10,000	
Cash		2,000
Note Payable		8,000
b. Cash	6,000	
Accounts Receivable		4,000
Advances from Customers		2,000
c. Accounts Payable	2,500	
Merchandise Inventory		2,500
d. Bonds Payable	100,000	
Common Stock		40,000
Additional Paid-in Capital		60,000
e. Cash	800	
Subscription Fees Received in Advance		800
f. Prepaid Rent	2,000	
Cash		2,000

Problems and Cases

22. *Journal entries for various transactions*. Present journal entries for each of the following transactions of Mailor Corporation during April, its first month of operations.

(1) April 2: 250,000 shares of $5 par value common stock are issued for $8 cash per share.

(2) April 3: A building costing $800,000 is acquired. A down payment of $200,000 is made in cash and a 10 percent note maturing in 3 years is signed for the balance.

(3) April 8: A machine costing $15,000 is acquired for cash.

(4) April 15: Merchandise inventory costing $120,000 is acquired on account from various suppliers.

(5) April 18: A check for $400 is issued for insurance coverage for the period beginning May 1.

(6) April 20: A check for $800 is received from a customer for merchandise to be delivered on May 5.

(7) April 26: Invoices totaling $80,000 from the purchases on April 15 are paid, after deducting a 2 percent discount for prompt payment. Cash discounts are treated as a reduction in the acquisition cost of inventory.

(8) April 30: The remaining invoices from the purchases on April 15 are paid after the discount period has lapsed.

23. *Journal entries for various transactions.* Present journal entries for each of the following transactions of Area Corporation. You may omit dates and explanations for the journal entries.

(1) 20,000 shares of $10 par value common stock are issued at par value for cash.

(2) Land and building costing $90,000 are acquired with the payment of $25,000 cash and the assumption of a 20-year, 8 percent mortgage for the balance. The land is to be stated at $30,000 and the building at $60,000.

(3) A used lathe is purchased for $4,620 cash.

(4) Raw materials costing $3,600 are acquired on account.

(5) Defective raw materials purchased in (4) and costing $650 are returned to the supplier. The account has not yet been paid.

(6) The supplier in (4) is paid the amount due, less a 2 percent discount for prompt payment. Cash discounts are treated as a reduction in the acquisition cost of raw materials.

(7) A fire insurance policy providing $100,000 coverage beginning next month is obtained. The 1-year premium of $625 is paid in cash.

(8) A check for $2,000 is issued to Roger White to reimburse him for costs incurred in organizing and promoting the corporation.

(9) A check for $600 is issued for 3 months' rent in advance for office space.

(10) A patent on a machine process is purchased for $35,000 cash.

(11) Office equipment is purchased for $950. A down payment of $250 is made, with the balance payable in 30 days.

(12) $275 is paid to Express Transfer Company for delivering the equipment purchased in (3).

24. *Journal entries for various transactions of a sole proprietorship.* Express the following transactions of the Winkle Grocery Store, a sole proprietorship, in journal entry form. You may omit explanations for the journal entries.

(1) John Winkle contributes $50,000 cash to help set up the grocery store.

(2) A 60-day, 8 percent note is signed in return for a $10,000 loan from the bank.

(3) A building is rented, with the annual rental of $6,000 paid in advance.

(4) Display equipment costing $16,000 is acquired. A check is issued.

(5) Merchandise inventory costing $35,000 is acquired. A check for $8,000 is issued, with the remainder payable in 30 days.

(6) A contract is signed with a nearby restaurant under which the restaurant agrees to purchase $6,000 of groceries each week. A check is received for the first 2 weeks' orders in advance.

25. *Journal entries for various transactions.* Express the following independent transactions in journal entry form. If an entry is not required, indicate the reason. You may omit explanations for the journal entries.

(1) Bonds of the Sommers Company with a face value of $60,000 and annual interest at the rate of 8 percent are purchased for $58,500 cash.

(2) A check for $2,600 is received by a fire insurance company for premiums on policy coverage over the next 2 years.

(3) A corporation issues 20,000 shares of $12 par value common stock in exchange for land, building, and equipment. The land is to be stated at $30,000, the building at $180,000, and the equipment at $75,000.

(4) A contract is signed by a manufacturing firm agreeing to purchase 100 dozen machine tool parts over the next 2 years at a price of $60 per dozen.

(5) 5,000 shares of $1 par value preferred stock are issued to an attorney for legal services rendered in organization of the corporation. The bill for the services is $9,500.

(6) A coupon book, redeemable in future movie viewings, is issued for $60 cash by a movie theatre.

(7) A firm has been notified that it is being sued for $30,000 damages by a customer who incurred losses as a result of purchasing defective merchandise.

(8) Merchandise inventory costing $2,000, purchased on account, is found to be defective and returned to the supplier for full credit.

26. *Effect of transactions on balance sheet equation.* Indicate the effects of the transactions below on the balance sheet equation using the following format:

Transaction Number	Assets	= Liabilities +	Shareholders' Equity
(1)	+$50,000	0	+$50,000
Subtotal	$50,000 =	0 +	$50,000

(1) 5,000 shares of $10 par value common stock are issued at par for cash.

(2) Equipment costing $12,000 is acquired. A down payment of $4,000 is made, with the remainder payable in 6 months with interest at 9 percent.

(3) Raw materials costing $6,000 are acquired on account.

(4) Installation cost of $800 on the equipment in (2) is paid in cash.

(5) The property insurance premium of $420 for the year, beginning on the first day of next month, is paid.

(6) Raw materials acquired in (3) for $700 are found to be defective and returned to the supplier for full credit. The account had not yet been paid.

(7) Invoices from the purchases in (3) totaling $4,000 are paid after deducting a 1 percent discount for prompt payment. Cash discounts are treated as a reduction in the acquisition cost of raw materials.

(8) 100 shares of $10 par value common stock are issued to the firm's attorney for services in organizing the corporation. The attorney's bill was $1,000.

(9) Customers advanced the firm $250 for merchandise to be delivered next month.

27. *Effect of transactions on balance sheet equation.* Indicate the effects of the transactions below on the balance sheet equation using the following format:

Transaction Number	Assets	= Liabilities	+ Shareholders' Equity
(1)	+$30,000	0	+$30,000
Subtotal	$30,000 =	0 +	$30,000

(1) 3,000 shares of $10 par value common stock are issued at par for cash.
(2) Merchandise costing $24,300 is purchased on account.
(3) Store equipment costing $4,800 is acquired. A check for $1,000 is issued and the balance is payable over 3 years under an installment contract.
(4) A check is issued for $900 covering 2 months' rent in advance.
(5) Refer to transaction **(3)**. Common stock with a market value of $3,800 is issued in full settlement of the installment contract.
(6) The merchandise supplier in transaction **(2)** is paid the amount due.

28. *T-account entries for various transactions.* Set up T-accounts for the following accounts. Indicate whether each account is an asset, liability, or shareholders' equity item, and enter the transactions described below:

Cash	Accounts Payable
Merchandise Inventory	Note Payable
Prepaid Insurance	Mortgage Payable
Building	Common Stock—Par Value
Equipment	Additional Paid-in Capital

(1) 30,000 shares of $5 par value stock are issued for $8 cash per share.
(2) A building costing $300,000 is acquired. A cash payment of $60,000 is made, and a long-term mortgage is assumed for the balance of the purchase price.
(3) Equipment costing $5,000 and merchandise inventory costing $7,000 are acquired on account.
(4) A 3-year fire insurance policy is taken out and the $900 premium is paid in advance.
(5) A 90-day, 6 percent note is issued to the bank for a $10,000 loan.
(6) Payments of $8,000 are made to the suppliers in **(3)**.

29. *T-account entries and balance sheet preparation.* The Patterson Manufacturing Corporation is organized on January 1. During January, the following transactions occur:
(1) The corporation issues 15,000 shares of $10 par value common stock for $210,000 in cash.
(2) The corporation issues 28,000 shares of common stock in exchange for land, building, and equipment. The land is to be stated at $80,000, the building at $220,000, and the equipment at $92,000.
(3) The corporation issues 2,000 shares of common stock to an attorney in payment of legal services rendered in obtaining the corporate charter.
(4) Raw materials costing $75,000 are acquired on account from various suppliers.

(5) Manufacturing equipment with a list price of $6,000 is acquired. After deducting a $600 discount, the net amount is paid in cash. Cash discounts are treated as a reduction in the acquisition cost of equipment.

(6) Freight charges of $350 for delivery of the equipment in **(5)** are paid in cash.

(7) Raw materials costing $800 are found to be defective and returned to the supplier for full credit. The raw materials had been purchased on account [see **(4)**], and no payment had been made as of the time that the goods were returned.

(8) A contract is signed for the rental of a fleet of automobiles beginning February 1. The rental for February of $1,400 is paid in advance.

(9) Invoices for $60,000 of raw materials purchased in **(4)** are paid, after deducting a discount of 3 percent for prompt payment. Cash discounts are treated as a reduction in the acquisition cost of raw materials.

(10) Fire and liability insurance coverage is obtained from Southwest Insurance Company. The 2-year policy, beginning February 1, carries a $400 premium, which has not yet been paid.

(11) A contract is signed with a customer for $20,000 of merchandise that Patterson plans to manufacture. The customer advanced $4,500 toward the contract price.

(12) A warehouse costing $60,000 is acquired. A down payment of $7,000 is made, and a long-term mortgage is assumed for the balance.

(13) Raw materials inventory with an original list price of $1,500 is found to be defective and returned to the supplier. This inventory has already been paid for in **(9)**. The returned raw materials are the only items purchased from this particular supplier during January. A cash refund has not yet been received from the supplier.

(14) The firm purchased 6,000 shares of $10 par value common stock of the General Cereal Corporation for $95,000. This investment is made as a short-term investment of excess cash. The shares of General Cereal Corporation are traded on the New York Stock Exchange.

The following assumptions will help you resolve certain accounting uncertainties: (i) Transactions **(2)** and **(3)** occurred on the same day as transaction **(1)**. (ii) The invoices paid in **(9)** are the only purchases for which discounts were made available to the purchaser.

a. Enter these transactions in T-accounts. Indicate whether each account is an asset, liability, or shareholders' equity item. Cross-reference each entry to the appropriate transaction number.

b. Prepare a balance sheet as of January 31.

30. *T-account entries and balance sheet preparation*. The Scott Products Corporation is organized on October 1. During October, the following transactions occur:

(1) The corporation issues 20,000 shares of $5 par value common stock for $7 per share in cash.

(2) The corporation issues 200 shares of $100 par value preferred stock at par value for cash.

(3) The corporation gives $40,000 in cash and 5,000 shares of common stock in exchange for land and building. The land is to be stated at $5,000 and the building at $70,000.

(4) Equipment costing $26,000 is acquired. Cash of $3,000 is paid and an 8 percent note, due in 1 year, is given for the balance.

(5) Transportation costs on the equipment in **(4)** of $800 are paid in cash.

(6) Installation costs on the equipment in **(4)** of $1,100 are paid in cash.

(7) Merchandise inventory costing $45,000 is acquired on account.

(8) License fees for the year beginning November 1 of $800 are paid in advance.

(9) Merchandise costing $1,300 from the acquisition in **(7)** are found to be defective and returned to the supplier for full credit. The account had not been paid.

(10) A patent is purchased from its creator for $15,000.

(11) The corporation signed an agreement to manufacture a specially designed machine for a customer for $60,000, to be delivered in January of next year. At the time of signing, the customer advanced $6,000 of the contract price.

(12) Invoices totaling $30,000 from the purchases in **(7)** are paid, after deducting a 2 percent discount for prompt payment. Cash discounts are treated as a reduction in the acquisition cost of inventory.

   a. Enter the transactions in T-accounts. Indicate whether each account is an asset, liability, or shareholders' equity item. Cross-reference each entry to the appropriate transaction number.

   b. Prepare a balance sheet for Scott Products Corporation as of October 31.

31. *T-account entries and balance sheet preparation.* The Sarwark Corporation is organized on January 1. During January, the following transactions occur:

(1) 10,000 shares of $10 par value common stock are issued for $150,000.

(2) Bonds with a face and maturity value of $100,000 are issued at face value for cash.

(3) Land and building costing $200,000 is acquired. A check for $80,000 is issued, with the remainder payable over 20 years. The land is assigned $20,000 and the building is assigned $180,000 of the acquisition cost.

(4) Equipment costing $40,000 is acquired. After deducting a discount of 2 percent for immediate cash payment, the net amount due is paid.

(5) Merchandise costing $25,000 is acquired on account.

(6) Merchandise costing $2,000 is found to be defective and returned to the supplier. No cash payments have yet been made to this supplier.

(7) An insurance policy for a 1-year period beginning February 1 is obtained. The premium for the 1-year period of $1,200 is paid.

(8) A customer placed an order for $1,500 of merchandise to be delivered in February. The customer sent a check of $300 with the order.

(9) Merchandise suppliers in **(5)** are paid $18,000 of the amounts due. The remaining suppliers will be paid in February.

   a. Enter these transactions in T-accounts. Indicate whether each account is an asset, liability, or shareholders' equity item. Cross reference each entry to the appropriate transaction number.

   b. Prepare a balance sheet as of December 31.

32. *T-account entries and balance sheet preparation for a sole proprietorship*. The following transactions occur during March for Dryden's Book Store, a sole proprietorship, in preparation for its opening for business on April 1.

(1) H. R. Dryden contributes $6,000 in cash, 100 shares of Western Corporation common stock, and an inventory of books to be sold. The stock of Western Corporation is quoted on the New York Stock Exchange at $15 per share on the day it is contributed, and will be sold when additional cash is needed. The books are to be stated at $2,750.

(2) Two months' rent on a store building is paid in advance in cash. The bookstore will occupy the building on April 1. The monthly rental is $400.

(3) Store fixtures are purchased for $4,000, of which $800 is paid in cash. A note, to be paid in 10 equal monthly installments beginning May 1, is signed for the balance.

(4) Books with an invoice price of $2,600 are purchased on account.

(5) A 1-year insurance policy on the store's contents beginning April 1 is purchased. The premium of $160 is paid by check.

(6) A check for $320 is issued to the Darwin Equipment Co. for a cash register and other operating equipment.

(7) Merchandise costing $1,800 is ordered from a publisher. Delivery is scheduled for April 15.

(8) The merchandise purchased in **(4)** is paid for by check. Payment is made in time to obtain a 2 percent cash discount for prompt payment. These are the only purchases for which discounts are available. Cash discounts are treated as a reduction in the acquisition cost of merchandise.

(9) An operating license for the year beginning April 1 is obtained. A fee of $250 is paid by check.

    a. Enter these transactions in T-accounts. Indicate whether each account is an asset, liability, or owner's equity item. Cross-reference each entry to the appropriate transaction number.

    b. Prepare a balance sheet for this sole proprietorship as of March 31.

33. *T-account entries and balance sheet preparation for a partnership*. Priscilla Mullins and Miles Standish form a partnership to operate a laundry and cleaning business to be known as Pilgrim's One Day Laundry and Cleaners. The following transactions occur in late June, prior to the grand opening on July 1.

(1) Standish contributes $400 cash and cleaning equipment that is to be stated at $5,600.

(2) Mullins contributes $3,000 cash and a delivery truck to be stated at $2,500.

(3) The July rent for the business premises of $400 is paid in advance.

(4) Cleaning supplies are purchased on account from the Wonder Chemical Company for $2,500.

(5) Insurance coverage on the equipment and truck for a 1-year period beginning July 1 is purchased for $425 cash.

(6) The firm borrows $2,000 from the First National Bank. A 90-day, 8 percent note is signed, with principal and interest payable at maturity.

(7) The Wonder Chemical Company account is paid in full after deducting a 2 percent discount for prompt payment. Cash discounts are treated as a reduction in the acquisition cost of supplies.

(8) A cash register is purchased for $700. A down payment of $100 is made, and a note is signed for the remainder, payable in 10 equal installments beginning August 1.

   a. Enter these transactions in T-accounts. Indicate whether each account is an asset, liability, or owners' equity item. Cross-reference each entry to the appropriate transaction number.

   b. Prepare a balance sheet for the partnership as of June 30.

34. *Criticism of balance sheet format and disclosure.* Comment on any unusual features of the balance sheet of the Western Sales Corporation shown in Exhibit 2.8.

35. *Effect of recording errors on balance sheet equation.* Using the notation O/S (overstated), U/S (understated), or No (no effect), indicate the effects on assets, liabilities, and shareholders' equity of failing to record each of the following independent transactions or events. For example, a failure to record the issuance of common stock for $10,000 cash would be

Assets—U/S $10,000

Liabilities—No

Shareholders' equity—U/S $10,000

(1) Merchandise costing $6,000 is purchased on account.

(2) A machine costing $10,000 is acquired. A 25 percent down payment is made, with the remainder payable over 5 years.

(3) An order for $3,500 of merchandise is placed with a supplier.

(4) A check for $300 is received from a customer for merchandise to be delivered next month.

(5) A check for $800 was issued to cover rental of a warehouse for the next 2 months.

(6) Common stock with a market value of $1,500 was issued to attorneys for services rendered in setting up the firm.

(7) A note payable for $2,000, which had previously been correctly recorded on the books, was now paid in the amount of $2,000.

(8) A check for $1,000 is issued for an option to purchase a tract of land. The price of the land is $30,000. The option can be exercised within 90 days.

36. *Balance sheet analysis for General Products Company.* Financial analysts typically use information from all three of the principal financial statements discussed in Chapter 1 (that is, balance sheet, income statement, and statement of changes in financial position) in making their analyses and interpretations. It is possible, however, to make some general observations about changes in the structure of a firm's assets and equities by studying comparative balance sheets only. These general observations are then examined further by studying the income statement and statement of changes in financial position.

Exhibit 2.8
WESTERN SALES CORPORATION
Balance Sheet for the Year Ended December 31, Year 5

Assets

Current Assets:

Cash and Certificates of Deposit	$ 86,500	
Accounts Receivable—Net	193,600	
Merchandise Inventory	322,900	$ 603,000

Investments (substantially at cost):

Investment in U.S. Treasury Notes	$ 60,000	
Investment in Eastern Sales Corp.	196,500	256,500

Fixed Assets (at cost):

Land	$225,000	
Buildings and Equipment—Net	842,600	1,067,600

Intangibles and Deferred Charges:

Prepaid Insurance	$ 1,200	
Prepaid Rent	1,500	
Goodwill.	2	2,702
Total Assets		$1,929,802

Liabilities and Shareholders' Equity

Current Liabilities:

Accounts Payable	$225,300	
Accrued Expenses	10,900	
Income Taxes Payable	89,200	$ 325,400

Long-Term Liabilities:

Bonds Payable.	$500,000	
Pensions Payable	40,600	
Contingent Liability	100,000	640,600

Shareholders' Equity:

Common Stock—$10-par value, 50,000 shares issued and outstanding	$625,000	
Earned Surplus	338,802	963,802
Total Liabilities and Shareholders' Equity		$1,929,802

(Problem 36 continued)

Refer to the comparative balance sheet and related notes of General Products Company in Appendix A at the back of the book. Using this financial statement only, describe the most significant changes that occurred in the structure of General Products Company's assets and equities between 1984 and 1985. (Hint: You may want to begin your analysis by expressing various balance sheet components as a percentage of other components. For example, current assets represent 53.4 percent of total assets on December 31, 1985.)

Chapter 3   Income Statement: Reporting the Results of Operating Activities

A second principal financial statement is the income statement. This statement provides a measure of the operating performance of a firm for some particular period of time. *Net income,* or *earnings,* is equal to revenues minus expenses.

Revenues measure the net assets (assets less liabilities) that flow into a firm when goods are sold or services are rendered. *Expenses* measure the net assets used up in the process of generating revenues. As a measure of operating performance, revenues reflect the services rendered by the firm, and expenses indicate the efforts required.

This chapter considers the measurement principles and accounting procedures that underlie the income statement. We begin by considering the concept of an accounting period, the span of time over which operating performance is measured. Next, two common approaches to measuring operating performance, the cash basis and the accrual basis, are described and illustrated. Finally, the accounting procedures used in applying the accrual basis of accounting are illustrated for a merchandising firm. Chapter 4 explores more fully the application of the accrual basis of accounting for manufacturing, construction, and other types of businesses.

The Accounting Period Convention

The income statement reports operating performance for a specific period of time. Years ago, the length of this period varied substantially among firms. Income statements were prepared at the completion of some activity, such as after the round-trip voyage of a ship between England and the Colonies, or at the completion of a construction project.

The operating activities of most modern firms do not so easily divide into distinguishable projects. Instead, the income-generating activity occurs continually. For example, a plant is acquired and used in manufacturing products for a period of 40 years or more. Delivery equipment is purchased and used in transporting merchandise to customers for 4, 5, or more years. If the preparation of the income statement were postponed until all operating activities were completed, the report might be prepared only when the firm ceased to exist and, in any case, would be too late to help a reader appraise operating performance. An accounting period of uniform length facilitates timely comparisons and analyses among firms.

An accounting period of *1 year* underlies the principal financial statements distributed to shareholders and potential investors. Most firms prepare their annual reports using the calendar year as the accounting period. A growing number of firms, however, use a *natural business year*. The use of a natural business year is an attempt to measure performance at a time when most operating activities have been substantially concluded. The ending date of a natural business year varies from one firm to another. For example, J. C. Penney uses a natural business year ending near the end of January, which comes after completion of the Christmas shopping season and before the start of the Easter season. American Motors uses a year ending September 30, the end of its model year. A. C. Nielsen (producers of television ratings and other surveys) uses a year ending August 31, just prior to the beginning of the new television season.

Reports of performance for periods shorter than a year are frequently prepared as indicators of progress during the year. These are known as "interim reports" or "reports for interim periods." Preparing interim reports does not remove the need to prepare an annual report.

Accounting Methods for Measuring Performance

Some operating activities both start and finish within a given accounting period. For example, merchandise might be purchased from a supplier, sold to a customer on account, and the account collected in cash, all within a particular accounting period. Few difficulties are encountered in measuring performance in these cases. The difference between the cash received from customers and the cash disbursed to acquire, sell, and deliver the merchandise represents earnings from this series of transactions.

Many operating activities, however, start in one accounting period and finish in another. Buildings and equipment are acquired in one period but used over a period of several years. Merchandise is sometimes purchased in one accounting period, sold during the next period, with cash collected from customers during a third period. A significant problem in measuring performance for a specific accounting period is measuring the amount of revenues and expenses from operating activities that are in process at the beginning of the period or are incomplete at the end of the period. Two approaches to measuring operating performance are (1) the cash basis of accounting, and (2) the accrual basis of accounting.

Cash Basis of Accounting

Under the *cash basis of accounting*, revenues from selling goods and providing services are recognized in the period when cash is received from customers. Expenses are reported in the period in which expenditures are made for merchandise, salaries, insurance, taxes, and similar items. To illustrate the measurement of performance under the cash basis of accounting, consider the following example.

Donald and Joanne Allens open a hardware store on January 1, Year 1. They contribute $20,000 in cash and borrow $12,000 from a local bank. The loan is repayable on June 30, Year 1, with interest charged at the rate of 12 percent per year. A store building is rented on January 1, and 2 months' rent of $4,000 is paid in advance. The premium of $2,400 for property and liability insurance coverage for the year ending December 31, Year 1, is paid on January 1. During January, mer-

Exhibit 3.1
ALLENS' HARDWARE STORE
Performance Measurement on a Cash Basis
for the Month of January, Year 1

Cash Receipts from Sales of Merchandise		$34,000
Less Cash Expenditures for Merchandise and Services:		
Merchandise	$26,000	
Salaries	5,000	
Rent.	4,000	
Insurance	2,400	
Total Cash Expenditures.		37,400
Excess of Cash Expenditures over Cash Receipts		($ 3,400)

chandise costing $40,000 is acquired, of which $26,000 is purchased for cash and $14,000 is purchased on account. Sales to customers during January total $50,000, of which $34,000 is sold for cash and $16,000 is sold on account. The acquisition cost of the merchandise sold during January is $32,000, and various employees are paid $5,000 in salaries.

Exhibit 3.1 presents a performance report for Allens' Hardware Store for the month of January, Year 1 using the cash basis. Cash receipts from sales of merchandise of $34,000 represent the portion of the total sales of $50,000 made during January that was collected in cash. Whereas merchandise costing $40,000 was acquired during January, only $26,000 cash was disbursed to suppliers, and only this amount is subtracted in measuring performance under the cash basis. Cash expenditures during January for salaries, rent, and insurance are also subtracted in measuring performance, without regard to whether or not the services acquired were fully consumed by the end of the month. Cash expenditures made for merchandise and services exceeded cash receipts from customers during January by $3,400.[1]

As a basis for measuring performance for a particular accounting period (for example, January, Year 1 for Allens' Hardware Store), the cash basis of accounting has two weaknesses. First, the cost of the efforts required in generating revenues is not adequately matched with those revenues. Performance of one period gets mingled with the performance of preceding and succeeding periods. The store rental payment of $4,000 provides rental services for both January and February, but under the cash basis, the full amount is subtracted in measuring performance during January. Likewise, the annual insurance premium provides coverage for the full year, whereas under the cash basis of accounting, none of this insurance cost will be subtracted in measuring performance during the months of February through December.

The longer the period over which future benefits are received, the more serious is this criticism of the cash basis of accounting. Consider, for example, the invest-

---

[1]Note that, under the cash basis, cash received from owners and through borrowing (financing transactions) is not included in the performance report.

Exhibit 3.2
ALLENS' HARDWARE STORE
Income Statement
for the Month of January, Year 1
(Accrual Basis of Accounting)

Sales Revenue		$50,000
Less Expenses:		
Cost of Goods Sold	$32,000	
Salaries Expense	5,000	
Rent Expense	2,000	
Insurance Expense	200	
Interest Expense	120	
Total Expenses		39,320
Net Income		$10,680

ments of a capital-intensive firm in buildings and equipment that might be used for 10, 20, or more years. The length of time between the purchase of these assets and the collection of cash for goods produced and sold can span many years.

Second, the cash basis of accounting postpones unnecessarily the time when revenue is recognized. In most cases, the sale (delivery) of goods or rendering of services is the important event in generating revenue. Collecting cash is relatively routine, or at least highly predictable. In these cases, recognizing revenue at the time of cash collection may result in reporting the effects of operating activities one or more periods after the critical revenue-generating activity has occurred. For example, sales to customers during January by Allens' Hardware Store totaled $50,000. Under the cash basis of accounting, $16,000 of this amount will not be recognized until the cash is collected, during February or even later. If the credit-worthiness of customers has been checked prior to making sales on account, the cash will probably be collected, and there is little reason to postpone recognition of the revenue.

The cash basis of accounting is used principally by lawyers, accountants, and other professional people. These professionals have relatively small investments in multiperiod assets, such as buildings and equipment, and usually collect cash from their clients soon after services are rendered. Most such firms actually use a *modified cash basis of accounting,* under which the costs of buildings, equipment, and similar items are treated as assets when purchased. A portion of the acquisition cost is then recognized as an expense when services of these assets are consumed. Except for the treatment of these long-lived assets, revenues are recognized at the time cash is received and expenses are reported when cash disbursements are made.

Most individuals use the cash basis of accounting for the purpose of computing personal income and personal income taxes. Where inventories are an important factor in generating revenues, such as for a merchandising or manufacturing firm, the Internal Revenue Code prohibits a firm from using the cash basis of accounting in its income tax returns.

Accrual Basis of Accounting

The *accrual basis of accounting* typically recognizes revenue when goods are sold or services are rendered. It reports costs incurred as expenses in the period when the revenues which they helped produce are recognized. Thus, accrual accounting attempts to *match* expenses with associated revenues. Costs incurred that cannot be closely identified with specific revenue streams are treated as expenses of the period in which services of an asset are consumed and the future benefits of an asset disappear.

Exhibit 3.2 presents an income statement for Allens' Hardware Store for January of Year 1 using the accrual basis of accounting. The entire $50,000 of sales during January is recognized as revenue, even though cash in that amount has not yet been received. Because the outstanding accounts receivable will probably be collected, the sale of the goods, rather than the collection of cash from customers, triggers the recognition of revenue. The merchandise sold during January costs $32,000. Recognizing this amount as an expense (cost of goods sold) matches the cost of the merchandise sold with revenue from sales. Of the advance rental payment of $4,000, only $2,000 applies to the cost of services consumed during January. The remaining rental of $2,000 applies to the month of February. Likewise, only $200 of the $2,400 insurance premium represents coverage used up during January. The remaining $2,200 of the insurance premium provides coverage for February through December and will be recognized as an expense during those months. The interest expense of $120 represents 1 month's interest on the $12,000 bank loan at an annual rate of 12 percent (= $12,000 \times .12 \times 1/12$). Although the interest will not be paid until the loan becomes due on June 30, Year 1, the firm benefited from having the funds available for its use during January; an appropriate portion of the total interest cost on the loan should therefore be recognized as an expense of January. The salaries, rental, insurance, and interest expenses, unlike the cost of merchandise sold, cannot be associated directly with revenues recognized during the period. These costs are therefore reported as expenses of January to the extent that services were consumed during the month.

The accrual basis of accounting provides a better measure of operating performance for Allens' Hardware Store for the month of January than does the cash basis for two reasons:

1. Revenues more accurately reflect the results of sales activity during January.
2. Expenses are associated more closely with reported revenues.

Likewise, the accrual basis will provide a superior measure of performance for future periods, because activities of those periods will be charged with their share of the costs of rental, insurance, and other services to be consumed. Thus, the accrual basis focuses on *inflows of net assets* from operations (revenues) and the *use of net assets* in operations (expenses), regardless of whether those inflows and outflows currently produce or use cash.

Most business firms, particularly those involved in merchandising and manufacturing activities, use the accrual basis of accounting. The next section examines the measurement principles of accrual accounting.

Measurement Principles of Accrual Accounting

Recognizing revenues and expenses under the accrual basis of accounting requires considering when revenues and expenses are recognized (timing questions) and how much is recognized (measurement questions).

Timing of Revenue Recognition

The operating process for the acquisition and sale of merchandise might be depicted as shown in Figure 3.1. Revenue could conceivably be recognized at the time of purchase, sale, or cash collection, at some point(s) between these events, or even continuously. Answering the timing question requires a set of criteria for revenue recognition.

Criteria for Revenue Recognition The criteria currently required to be met before revenue is recognized under the accrual basis of accounting are as follows:

1. All, or a substantial portion, of the services to be provided have been performed.
2. Either cash, a receivable, or some other asset susceptible to reasonably precise measurement has been received.

For the vast majority of firms involved in selling goods and services, revenue is recognized at the time of sale (delivery). The goods have been transferred to a buyer or the services have been performed. Future services, such as for warranties, are either insignificant or, if significant, can be estimated with reasonable precision. An exchange between an independent buyer and seller provides an objective measure of the amount of revenue. If the sale is made on account, past experience and an assessment of credit standings of customers provide a basis for predicting the amount of cash that will be collected. Thus, the criteria for revenue recognition are usually met at the time of sale.

Measurement of Revenue

The amount of revenue recognized is measured by the cash or cash-equivalent value of other assets received from customers. As a starting point, this amount is the agreed-upon price between buyer and seller at the time of sale. Some adjustments to

Figure 3.1 Operating Process for the Acquisition and Sale of Merchandise this amount may be necessary, however, if revenue is recognized in a period prior to the collection of cash.

Uncollectible Accounts If some portion of the sales for a period is not expected to be collected, the amount of revenue recognized for that period must be adjusted for estimated uncollectible accounts arising from those sales. This adjustment of revenue occurs in the period when revenue is recognized and not in a later period when specific customers' accounts are found to be uncollectible. If the adjustment were postponed, reported income of subsequent periods would be affected by earlier decisions to extend credit to customers. Thus, the performance of the firm for both the period of sale and the period when the account is judged uncollectible would be measured inaccurately. Chapter 7 considers these problems further.

Sales Discounts and Allowances Customers may take advantage of discounts for prompt payment; the seller may grant allowances for unsatisfactory merchandise. In these cases, the amount of cash eventually to be received can be expected to be less than the stated selling price. Appropriate reductions should therefore be made at the time of sale in measuring the amount of revenue to be recognized.

Delayed Payments When the period between the sale of the goods or services and the time of cash collection extends over a year or more and there is no provision for explicit interest payments, the selling price probably includes an interest charge for the right to delay payment. Under the accrual basis of accounting, this interest element is recognized as interest revenue during the periods between sale and collection when the loan is outstanding. To recognize all potential revenue entirely in the period of sale would be to recognize too soon the return for services rendered over time in lending money. Thus, when cash collection is to be delayed beyond 1 year, the measure of revenue for the current period is the selling price reduced to account for interest during future periods. Only the *present value* at the time of sale of the amount to be received should be recognized as revenue during the period of sale. For most accounts receivable, the period between sale and collection spans only 2 to 3 months. The interest element is likely to be relatively insignificant in these cases. As a result, in accounting practice no reduction for interest on delayed payments is made for receivables to be collected within 1 year or less. This procedure is a practical expedient rather than a strict adherence to the underlying accounting theory.

Timing of Expense Recognition

Assets provide future benefits to the firm. *Expenses* are a measurement of the assets consumed in generating revenue. Assets are *unexpired costs* and expenses are *expired costs* or ''gone assets.'' Our attention focuses on *when* the asset expiration takes place. The critical question is ''When have asset benefits expired—leaving the balance sheet—and become expenses—entering the income statement as reductions in owners' equity?'' Thus:

Balance Sheet	**Income Statement**

Assets or Unexpired Costs → Expenses or Expired Costs (which reduce owners' equity on the balance sheet).

Expense Recognition Expenses are recognized as follows:

1. Asset expirations associated directly with particular types of revenue are expenses in the period in which the revenues are recognized. This treatment is called the *matching convention,* because cost expirations are matched with revenues.
2. Asset expirations not associated with revenues are expenses of the period in which services are consumed in operations.

Product Costs The cost of goods or merchandise sold is perhaps the easiest expense to associate with revenue. At the time of sale, the asset physically changes hands. Revenue is recognized, and the cost of the merchandise transferred is an expense.

A *merchandising firm* purchases inventory and later sells it without changing its physical form. The inventory appears as an asset stated at acquisition cost on the balance sheet. Later, when the inventory is sold, the same amount of acquisition cost appears as an expense (cost of goods sold) on the income statement.

A *manufacturing firm,* on the other hand, incurs various costs in changing the physical form of the goods it produces. There are three types of cost: (1) direct material, (2) direct labor, and (3) manufacturing overhead (sometimes called indirect manufacturing costs). Direct material and direct labor costs are associated directly with particular products manufactured. Manufacturing overhead includes a mixture of costs that provide a firm with a capacity to produce. Examples of manufacturing overhead costs are expenditures for utilities, property taxes, and insurance on the factory, as well as depreciation on manufacturing plant and equipment. The services of each of these items are used up during the period while the firm is creating new assets—the inventory of goods being worked on or held for sale. Benefits from direct material, direct labor, and manufacturing overhead are transferred to, or become embodied in, the asset represented by units of inventory. Because the inventory items are assets until sales are made to customers, the various direct material, direct labor, and manufacturing overhead costs incurred in producing the goods are included in the manufacturing inventory under the titles Work-in-Process Inventory and Finished Goods Inventory. Such costs, which are assets transformed from one form to another, are called *product costs*. Product costs are assets; they become expenses only when the goods in which they are embodied are sold. Chapter 4 discusses more fully the accounting for manufacturing costs.

Selling Costs In most cases, the costs incurred in selling, or marketing, a firm's products relate to the units sold during the period. For example, salaries and commissions of the sales staff, sales literature used, and most advertising costs are incurred in generating revenue currently. Because these selling costs are associated with the revenues of the period, they are reported as expenses in the period when their services are used. It can be argued that some selling costs, such as advertising and other sales promotion, provide future-period benefits for a firm and should continue to be treated as assets. However, distinguishing the portion of the cost relating to the current period (to be recognized as an expense) from the portion relating to future periods (to be treated as an asset) can be extremely difficult. Accountants, therefore, treat selling and other marketing activity costs as expenses of the period when the services are used. These selling costs are treated as *period expenses* rather than as assets, even though they may enhance the future marketability of a firm's products.

Administrative Costs The costs incurred in administering the activities of the firm cannot be closely associated with units produced or sold and, like selling costs, are treated as period expenses. Examples include the president's salary, accounting and data processing costs, and the costs of conducting various supportive activities, such as legal services and corporate planning.

Measurement of Expenses

Expenses represent assets consumed during the period. The amount of an expense is therefore the cost of the expired asset. Thus, the basis for expense measurement is the same as for asset valuation. Because assets are stated primarily at acquisition cost on the balance sheet, expenses are measured by the acquisition cost of the assets that were either sold or used during the period.

Summary

The *amount* of income from operating activities is equal to the difference between the cash received from customers and the amount of cash paid to suppliers, employees, and other providers of goods and services. However, cash receipts from customers do not always occur in the same accounting period as the related cash expenditures to the providers of goods and services. To obtain a measure of operating performance in which outflows are matched more effectively with inflows, the accrual basis of accounting is used.

The accrual basis determines the *timing* of income recognition. Revenue is typically recognized at the time of sale under the accrual basis. Costs that can be associated directly with particular revenues become expenses in the period when revenues are recognized. The cost of acquiring or manufacturing inventory items is treated in this manner. Costs that cannot be closely associated with particular revenue streams become expenses of the period when goods or services are consumed in operations. Most selling and administrative costs are treated in this manner.

The accounting procedures for preparing the income statement are considered next.

Overview of Accounting Procedures

Relationship Between Balance Sheet and Income Statement

Net income, or earnings, for a period measures the excess of revenues (net asset inflows) over expenses (net asset outflows) from selling goods and providing services. Dividends measure the net assets distributed to shareholders. The Retained Earnings account on the balance sheet measures the cumulative excess of earnings over dividends since the firm began operations. The following disaggregation of the balance sheet equation shows the relation of revenues, expenses, and dividends to the components of the balance sheet.

Purpose and Use of Individual Revenue and Expense Accounts

Revenue and expense amounts could be recorded directly in the Retained Earnings account. For example, the sale of merchandise on account results in an increase in assets (accounts receivable) and retained earnings (sales revenue) and a decrease in assets (merchandise inventory) and retained earnings (cost of goods sold). Measuring the *amount* of net income would be relatively simple if revenues and expenses were recorded directly in the Retained Earnings account. Net income would be computed from the following equation:

$$\text{Net Income} = \frac{\text{Retained Earnings}}{\text{End of Period}} - \frac{\text{Retained Earnings}}{\text{Beginning of Period}} + \text{Dividends.}$$

The income statement is not designed merely to report net income. As the equation above indicates, the amount of net income can be deduced from the change in the Retained Earnings account. Rather, the income statement is designed to report the sources and amounts of a firm's revenues and the nature and amounts of a firm's expenses that sum to income for the period. Knowledge of the components of a firm's net income is helpful both in appraising past performance and in forecasting future performance.

To help in preparing the income statement, individual revenue and expense accounts are maintained during the accounting period. These accounts begin the accounting period with a zero balance. During the period, revenues and expenses are recorded in the accounts as they arise. At the end of the period, the balance in each revenue and expense account represents the cumulative revenues and expenses *for the period*. These amounts are reported in the income statement, which shows the net income of the period.

Because revenues and expenses are basically components of retained earnings, the balance in each revenue and expense account is transferred at the end of the period to the Retained Earnings account. Each revenue and expense account will then have a zero balance after the transfer. Retained earnings will be increased by the amount of net income (or decreased by the net loss) for the period.

The end result of maintaining separate revenue and expense accounts during the period and transferring their balances to the Retained Earnings account at the end of the period is the same as if revenues and expenses were initially recorded directly in the Retained Earnings account. Using separate revenue and expense accounts facilitates preparation of the income statement, which shows specific types of revenues and expenses. Once this purpose has been served, the need for separate revenue and expense accounts *for a given accounting period* has ended. Having been reduced to a zero balance at the end of the accounting period, these accounts begin the following accounting period with a zero balance and are therefore ready for entry of the revenue and expense amounts of the following period.

The process of transferring the balances in revenue and expense accounts to retained earnings is referred to as the *closing process,* because each revenue and expense account is closed, or reduced to a zero balance. Revenue and expense accounts accumulate amounts for only a single accounting period, and are therefore *temporary accounts*. On the other hand, the accounts on the balance sheet reflect the cumulative changes in each account from the time the firm was first organized, and are not closed each period. The balances in these accounts at the end of one period are carried over as the beginning balances of the following period. Balance sheet accounts are *permanent accounts*.

Debit and Credit Procedures for Revenues, Expenses, and Dividends

Because revenues, expenses, and dividends are components of retained earnings, the recording procedures for these items are the same as for any other transaction affecting shareholders' equity accounts.

Shareholders' Equity	
Decreases (Debit)	Increases (Credit)
	Issues of Capital Stock
Expenses	Revenues
Dividends	

The transaction giving rise to revenue results in an increase in net assets (increase in assets or decrease in liabilities) and an increase in shareholders' equity. The usual journal entry to record a revenue transaction is therefore

Asset (A) Increase or Liability (L) Decrease	Amount
Revenue (SE)	Amount
Typical entry to recognize revenue.	

The transaction giving rise to expense results in a decrease in net assets (decrease in assets or increase in liabilities) and a decrease in shareholders' equity. The usual journal entry to record an expense is therefore

Expense (SE)	Amount
Asset (A) Decrease or Liability (L) Increase	Amount
Typical entry to record expense.	

Dividends result in a decrease in net assets and a decrease in shareholders' equity. As we discuss in Chapter 12, dividends may be paid either in cash or in other assets. Although the accounting procedures for dividends are similar regardless of the form of the distribution, we assume that cash is used unless information is provided to the contrary. The usual entry to record the declaration of a dividend by the board of directors of a corporation is

Retained Earnings (SE)	Amount
Dividends Payable (L)	Amount
Typical entry to record dividend declaration.	

When the dividend is paid, the journal entry is

Dividends Payable (L)	Amount
Cash (A)	Amount
Typical entry to record dividend payment.	

A conceptual error sometimes made is that of treating dividends as an expense on the income statement. *Dividends are not expenses.* They are not costs incurred in *generating* revenues. Rather, they represent *distributions* of assets arising from current and prior years' operations to the owners of the firm.[2]

---

[2]An alternative method for recording dividends is to debit an account, Dividends Declared. At the end of the accounting period, the balance in the Dividends Declared account is closed to the Retained Earnings account, thereby reducing the balance of Retained Earnings. The end result is a debit to Retained Earnings and a credit to Dividends Payable for the amount of dividends declared during the period. Because the account, Dividends Declared, is closed in a manner similar to an expense account at the end of the accounting period, this method of recording the dividend sometimes leads to the erroneous treatment of dividends as expenses. In this book, declarations of dividends are debited directly to Retained Earnings.

Before illustrating the recording procedures for revenues and expenses, it may be helpful to review briefly the steps in the accounting process.

Review of the Accounting Process

The steps in the accounting process, discussed in Chapter 2, are as follows:

Journalizing Each transaction or series of transactions during the period is recorded in journal entry form in the general journal (or in a special journal that supplements the general journal).

Posting At periodic intervals, the entries in the general journal are posted to the accounts in the general ledger.

Trial Balance At the end of the accounting period, the balance in each general ledger account is calculated and a trial balance is prepared. A trial balance is a listing of all accounts in the general ledger and their balances. If the recording process has been carried out properly, the total amount in accounts having debit balances must equal the total amount in accounts having credit balances.

Adjusting Entries During the period, some accounting events may be only partially recorded, not recorded at all, or recorded incorrectly. Before the financial statements can be prepared at the end of the period, the omissions must be accounted for and the errors corrected. The entries to do this are known as *adjusting entries*. These entries are made so that revenues and expenses are reported in appropriate accounts with correct amounts and so that balance sheet accounts show correct amounts of assets and equities at the end of the period. The income statement can be prepared after adjusting entries have been made.

Closing Entries The revenue and expense accounts are closed at the end of the accounting period by transferring the balance in each account to Retained Earnings.

Statement Preparation The balance sheet, statement of changes in financial position, and any desired supporting schedules (for example, an analysis of changes in the Cash, Buildings and Equipment, or Retained Earnings accounts) are then prepared.

Illustration of the Accounting Process for a Merchandising Firm

Stephen's Shoe Store, Inc., has been in business since Year 1. A trial balance taken from its general ledger accounts on January 1, Year 4, the first day of an accounting period, is shown in Exhibit 3.3. To facilitate understanding, in this illustration the asset accounts are designated (A), the liability accounts (L), and the shareholders' equity (including revenue and expense) accounts (SE). Trial balances do not usually contain such designations.

Exhibit 3.3
STEPHEN'S SHOE STORE, INC.
Trial Balance
January 1, Year 4

	Accounts with Debit Balances	Accounts with Credit Balances
Cash (A)	$ 30,000	
Accounts Receivable (A)	63,000	
Merchandise Inventory (A)	175,000	
Land (A)	100,000	
Building and Equipment (A)	525,000	
Accumulated Depreciation (XA)		$ 85,000
Accounts Payable (L)		135,000
Bonds Payable (L)		100,000
Common Stock (SE)		250,000
Additional Paid-in Capital (SE)		200,000
Retained Earnings (SE)		123,000
Total	$893,000	$893,000

Note that the revenue and expense accounts do not appear in this trial balance; they have zero balances at the beginning of an accounting period. One of the accounts in the trial balance, Accumulated Depreciation, has not previously been considered. This account is presented on the balance sheet as a deduction from Building and Equipment. (See Exhibit 3.9 for balance sheet presentation of this account.) Because of this manner of disclosure, this account is referred to as a *contra account*. A contra account accumulates amounts that are subtracted from the amount in another account. The nature and use of these contra accounts are discussed later in this illustration. An asset contra account is designated XA in the trial balance.

Journalizing

The transactions of Stephen's Shoe Store during Year 4 and the appropriate journal entries at the time of the transactions follow.

1. The firm purchases merchandise on account costing $355,000.

(1) Merchandise Inventory (A)	355,000	
Accounts Payable (L)		355,000

2. Sales during the year are $625,000, of which $225,000 are for cash collected at the time of sale and the remainder are on account.

(2) Cash (A)	225,000	
Accounts Receivable (A)	400,000	
Sales Revenue (SE)		625,000

3. The cost of merchandise sold during Year 4 is $390,000.

(3) Cost of Goods Sold (SE)	390,000	
Merchandise Inventory (A)		390,000

4. The firm pays salaries in cash of $110,000 during the year.

(4) Salaries Expense (SE)	110,000	
Cash (A)		110,000

5. The firm collects cash of $325,000 from customers who had purchased on account.

(5) Cash (A)	325,000	
Accounts Receivable (A)		325,000

6. The firm makes payments of $270,000 to merchandise suppliers for purchases on account.

(6) Accounts Payable (L)	270,000	
Cash (A)		270,000

7. The firm makes a premium payment of $1,500 on January 1, Year 4, for a 3-year property and liability insurance policy.

(7) Prepaid Insurance (A)	1,500	
Cash (A)		1,500

The debit in this entry, made on January 1, Year 4, is to an asset account, because the insurance provides 3 years of coverage beginning on that date. The entry to reduce the Prepaid Insurance account and to record the insurance expense for Year 4 is one of the adjusting entries made at the end of the accounting period and is illustrated later.

8. Warehouse space not needed in the company's operations is rented out for 1 year beginning December 1, Year 4. The firm receives the annual rental of $600 at that time.

(8) Cash (A)	600	
Advances from Tenants (L)		600

9. On December 31, Year 4, the firm pays annual interest at 8 percent on the long-term bonds outstanding; .08 × $100,000 = $8,000.

(9) Interest Expense (SE)	8,000	
Cash (A)		8,000

10. A customer who had purchased merchandise on account for $10,000 has experienced financial difficulty and has been unable to pay for the goods on time. The customer now promises to pay $10,000 in 90 days with interest at 9 percent per year. As evidence of that promise, the customer gives a promissory note. On November 1, Year 4, Stephen's Shoe Store accepts the 90-day note for $10,000 bearing interest at 9 percent in settlement of the open account receivable.

(10) Notes Receivable (A)	10,000	
Accounts Receivable (A).		10,000

11. The board of directors declared a cash dividend of $15,000 on December 28, Year 4. The dividend is to be paid on January 20, Year 5.

(11) Retained Earnings (SE)	15,000	
Dividends Payable (L)		15,000

Posting

The entries in the general journal are posted to the appropriate general ledger accounts. In this illustration, the posting operation takes place on December 31, Year 4. The T-accounts in Exhibit 3.4 show the opening balances from the trial balance in Exhibit 3.3 and the effects of transactions (**1**) through (**11**).

Exhibit 3.4
STEPHEN'S SHOE STORE, INC.
T-Accounts Showing Beginning Balances, Transactions During Year 4, and Ending Balance Before Adjusting Entries

Cash (A)

Bal. 1/1	30,000		
(2)	225,000	110,000	(4)
(5)	325,000	270,000	(6)
(8)	600	1,500	(7)
		8,000	(9)
Bal. 12/31	191,100		

Accounts Receivable (A)

Bal. 1/1	63,000		
(2)	400,000	325,000	(5)
		10,000	(10)
Bal. 12/31	128,000		

Notes Receivable (A)

Bal. 1/1	0		
(10)	10,000		
Bal. 12/31	10,000		

Merchandise Inventory (A)

Bal. 1/1	175,000		
(1)	355,000	390,000	(3)
Bal. 12/31	140,000		

Land (A)

Bal. 1/1	100,000	
Bal. 12/31	100,000	

Building and Equipment (A)

Bal. 1/1	525,000	
Bal. 12/31	525,000	

Prepaid Insurance (A)

Bal. 1/1	0		
(7)	1,500		
Bal. 12/31	1,500		

Accumulated Depreciation (XA)

	85,000	Bal. 1/1
	85,000	Bal. 12/31

Accounts Payable (L)

	135,000 Bal. 1/1
(6) 270,000	355,000 (1)
	220,000 Bal. 12/31

Bonds Payable (L)

	100,000 Bal. 1/1
	100,000 Bal. 12/31

Retained Earnings (SE)

(11) 15,000	123,000 Bal. 1/1
	108,000 Bal. 12/31

Cost of Goods Sold (SE)

Bal. 1/1 0	
(3) 390,000	
Bal. 12/31 390,000	

Dividends Payable (L)

	0 Bal. 1/1
	15,000 (11)
	15,000 Bal. 12/31

Common Stock (SE)

	250,000 Bal. 1/1
	250,000 Bal. 12/31

Sales Revenue (SE)

	0 Bal. 1/1
	625,000 (2)
	625,000 Bal. 12/31

Salaries Expense (SE)

Bal. 1/1 0	
(4) 110,000	
Bal. 12/31 110,000	

Advances from Tenants (L)

	0 Bal. 1/1
	600 (8)
	600 Bal. 12/31

Additional Paid-In Capital (SE)

	200,000 Bal. 1/1
	200,000 Bal. 12/31

Interest Expense (SE)

Bal. 1/1 0	
(9) 8,000	
Bal. 12/31 8,000	

Trial Balance Preparation

The trial balance prepared at the end of the accounting period before adjusting and closing entries is called an *unadjusted trial balance*. The unadjusted trial balance of Stephen's Shoe Store as of December 31, Year 4, appears in Exhibit 3.5. The amounts in the unadjusted trial balance are taken directly from the ending balances in the T-accounts in Exhibit 3.4.

Adjusting and Correcting Entries

The entries in the general journal made during the year result from transactions between the firm and outsiders (for example, suppliers, employees, customers, and governmental units). Other events continually occur, however, for which no specific transaction signals the requirement for a journal entry, but which must be considered in measuring net income for the period and financial position at the end of the period. For example, building and equipment are continually used in the process of generating revenue. Because the services of these assets are consumed during the period, a portion of their acquisition cost must be recorded as an expense. Similarly, insurance coverage expires continually throughout the year. Because the

Exhibit 3.5
STEPHEN'S SHOE STORE, INC.
Unadjusted Trial Balance
December 31, Year 4

	Accounts with Debit Balances	Accounts with Credit Balances
Cash (A).	$ 191,100	
Accounts Receivable (A)	128,000	
Notes Receivable (A)	10,000	
Merchandise Inventory (A)	140,000	
Prepaid Insurance (A)	1,500	
Land (A)	100,000	
Building and Equipment (A)	525,000	
Accumulated Depreciation (XA)		$ 85,000
Accounts Payable (L)		220,000
Dividends Payable (L)		15,000
Advances from Tenants (L)		600
Bonds Payable (L)		100,000
Common Stock (SE)		250,000
Additional Paid-in Capital (SE)		200,000
Retained Earnings (SE)		108,000
Sales Revenue (SE)		625,000
Cost of Goods Sold (SE)	390,000	
Salaries Expense (SE)	110,000	
Interest Expense (SE)	8,000	
Totals	$1,603,600	$1,603,600

services of the asset are gradually consumed, a portion of the asset, Prepaid Insurance, must be recorded as an expense.

Other kinds of events occur that affect the revenues and expenses of the period but for which a cash transaction with an outsider will not occur until a subsequent period. For example, salaries and wages are earned by administrative employees during the last several days of the current accounting period, but they will not be paid until the following accounting period. Such salaries and wages, although payable in the next period, are expenses of the current period when the labor services are consumed. Similarly, interest accrues on a firm's notes receivable or payable. Interest will be collected or paid in a subsequent period, but a portion of the interest should be recognized as revenue or expense in the current period.

Adjusting entries are prepared at the end of the accounting period. These entries change the balances in the general ledger accounts in order to recognize all revenues and expenses for the proper reporting of net income and financial position. The following sections illustrate several examples of adjusting entries for Stephen's Shoe Store.

Recognition of Accrued Revenues and Receivables   Revenue is earned as services are rendered. For example, rent is earned as a tenant uses the property. Interest, a "rent" for the use of money, is earned from a loan as time passes. Recording these amounts as they accrue day by day is usually not convenient, however. At the end of the accounting period, there may be some situations in which revenue has been earned but for which no entry has been made, either because cash has not been received or the time has not arrived for a formal invoice to be sent to the customer. A claim has come into existence that, although it may not be due immediately, should appear on the balance sheet as an asset and be reflected in the revenues of the period. The purpose of the adjusting entry for interest eventually receivable by the lender is to recognize on the balance sheet the right to receive cash in an amount equal to the interest already earned and to recognize the same amount as revenue on the income statement for the period.

Stephen's Shoe Store received a 90-day note from a customer on November 1, Year 4. At year-end, the note already appears on the trial balance. Interest earned during November and December, however, does not appear in the unadjusted trial balance. The note earns interest at the rate of 9 percent per year. By convention in business practice, interest rates stated on loans are almost always stated as annual interest rates. Also, by convention, a year equal to 12 months of 30 days each, or 360 days, is usually assumed to simplify the calculation of interest earned. Interest of $150 is earned by Stephen's Shoe Store, Inc., during November and December. This amount is equal to the $10,000 principal times the 9 percent annual interest rate times the elapsed 60 days divided by 360 days ($150 = $10,000 × .09 × 60/360). The adjusting entry to recognize the asset, Interest Receivable, and the interest earned, is

(12) Interest Receivable (A)	150	
Interest Revenue (SE)		150

Recognition of Accrued Expenses and Payables As various services are received, their cost should be reflected in the financial statements, whether or not payment has been made or an invoice received. Here, also, recording these amounts day by day is frequently not convenient. Some adjustment of expenses and liabilities will probably be necessary at the end of the accounting period.

Salaries and wages earned during the last several days of the accounting period, which will not be paid until the following accounting period, illustrate this type of adjustment. According to payroll records, employees of Stephen's Shoe Store earned salaries of $6,000 during the last several days of Year 4 that were not recorded at year-end. The adjusting entry is

(13) Salaries Expense (SE)	6,000	
Salaries Payable (L).		6,000

Other examples of this type of adjusting entry include costs incurred for utilities, taxes, and interest.

Allocation of Prepaid Operating Costs Another type of adjustment arises because assets are acquired for use in the operations of the firm but are not completely used during the accounting period in which they are acquired. For example, Stephen's Shoe Store paid $1,500 on January 1, Year 4, for a 3-year insurance policy. During Year 4, one-third of the coverage expired, so $500 of the premium should be removed from the asset account and reflected as insurance expense. The balance sheet on December 31, Year 4, should show only $1,000 of prepaid insurance as an asset, because this portion of the premium is a future benefit—the asset of insurance coverage to be received over the next 2 years.

The nature of the adjusting entry to record an asset expiration as an expense depends on the recording of the original payment. If the payment resulted in a debit to an asset account, the adjusting entry must reduce the asset and increase the expense for the services used up during the accounting period. Stephen's Shoe Store had recorded in entry (7), as discussed on page 94, the payment of the insurance premium on January 1, Year 4, as follows:

(7) Prepaid Insurance (A)	1,500	
Cash (A)		1,500

The adjusting entry is, therefore,

(14) Insurance Expense (SE)	500	
Prepaid Insurance (A)		500

Insurance expense for Year 4 is $500, and prepaid insurance of $1,000 appears as an asset on the balance sheet on December 31, Year 4.

Alternative Procedure Instead of debiting an asset account at the time the premium is paid, some firms debit an expense account. For example, Stephen's Shoe Store might have recorded the original premium payment as follows:

(7a) Insurance Expense (SE)	1,500	
Cash (A)		1,500

Because many operating costs become expenses in the period in which the expenditure is made (for example, monthly rent), this second procedure for recording expenditures during the year sometimes reduces the number of adjusting entries that must be made at year-end. In the situation with the insurance policy, however, not all of the $1,500 premium paid is an expense of Year 4. If the original journal entry had been (7a), the adjusting entry would then be

(14a) Prepaid Insurance (A)	1,000	
Insurance Expense (SE)		1,000

After the original entry in (7a) and the adjusting entry in (14a), insurance expense for Year 4 is reflected in the accounts at $500, and prepaid insurance at $1,000. The *end result* of these two approaches to recording the original payment of the premium is the same. The *adjusting entries,* however, are quite different. (See Problem 3 for Self-Study at the end of the chapter.)

Recognition of Depreciation When assets such as buildings, machinery, furniture, and trucks are purchased, their acquisition cost is debited to appropriate asset accounts. Although these assets may provide services for a number of years, their future benefits expire as time passes. The portion of an asset's cost that will expire is spread systematically over its estimated useful life. The charge made to the current operations for the portion of the cost of such assets consumed during the current period is called *depreciation*. Depreciation involves nothing new in principle; it is identical with the procedure for prepaid operating costs presented previously. For example, the cost of a building is a prepayment for a series of future services, and depreciation allocates the cost of the services to the periods in which services are received and used.

Various accounting methods are used in allocating the acquisition cost of long-lived assets to the periods of benefit. The most widely used method is the *straight-line method*. Under this procedure, an equal portion of the acquisition cost less estimated salvage value is allocated to each period of the asset's estimated useful life. The depreciation charge for each period is computed as follows:

$$\frac{\text{Acquisition Cost} - \text{Estimated Salvage Value}}{\text{Estimated Useful Life in Periods}} = \frac{\text{Depreciation Charge for}}{\text{Each Period.}}$$

Internal records indicate that the Building and Equipment account of Stephen's Shoe Store comprises a store building with an acquisition cost of $400,000 and a group of items of equipment with an acquisition cost of $125,000. At the time the building was acquired, it had an estimated 40-year useful life and a zero salvage value. Depreciation expense for each year of the building's life is calculated to be

$$\frac{\$400,000 - \$0}{40 \text{ years}} = \$10,000 \text{ per year.}$$

At the time the equipment was acquired, it had an estimated useful life of 6 years and an estimated salvage value of $5,000. Annual depreciation is, therefore,

$$\frac{\$125,000 - \$5,000}{6 \text{ years}} = \$20,000 \text{ per year.}$$

The adjusting entry to record depreciation of $30,000 (= $10,000 + $20,000) for Year 4 is

(15) Depreciation Expense (SE)	30,000	
Accumulated Depreciation (XA)		30,000

The credit in entry (15) could have been made directly to the Building and Equipment account, because the credit records the portion of the asset's cost that has expired, or become an expense, during Year 4. The same end result is achieved by crediting the Accumulated Depreciation account, a contra-asset account, and then deducting the balance in this account from the acquisition cost of the assets in the Building and Equipment account on the balance sheet. Using the contra account enables the financial statements to show both the acquisition cost of the assets in use and the portion of that amount that has previously been recognized as an expense. Showing both acquisition cost and accumulated depreciation amounts separately provides a rough indication of the relative age of the firm's long-lived assets. (See Exercise 29 at the end of the chapter.)

Note that the Depreciation Expense account includes only depreciation for the current accounting period, whereas the Accumulated Depreciation account includes the cumulative depreciation charges since acquisition. The Accumulated Depreciation account is sometimes referred to as Allowance for Depreciation.

Valuation of Liabilities When a firm receives cash from customers before it sells merchandise or renders services, it incurs a liability. For example, Stephen's Shoe Store received $600 on December 1, Year 4, as 1 year's rent on warehouse space. When the cash was received, the liability account, Advances from Tenants, was credited. One month's rent has been earned as of December 31, Year 4. The adjusting entry is

(16) Advances from Tenants (L)	50	
Rent Revenue (SE)		50
To reduce liability from $600 to $550.		

The remaining $550 of the collections for rent is yet to be earned and appears on the December 31, Year 4, balance sheet as a liability.

Correction of Errors Various errors and omissions may be discovered at the end of the accounting period as the process of checking, reviewing, and auditing is carried out. For example, the sales for 1 month during the year might have been recorded as $38,700 instead of $37,800. Or the sale to a specific customer might not have been recorded. Entries must be made at the end of the accounting period to correct for these errors. There were no such errors in the accounts of Stephen's Shoe Store.

Trial Balance After Adjusting Entries The adjusting entries are posted or entered in the general ledger in the same manner as entries made during the year. A trial balance of the general ledger accounts after adjusting entries are made is called an *adjusted trial balance* and helps in preparing the financial statements. Exhibit 3.6 presents the trial balance data before and after adjusting entries for Stephen's Shoe Store. The exhibit indicates the effect of the adjustment process on the various accounts. The parenthetical number identifies the debit and credit components of each adjusting entry.

Preparing Income Statement The adjusted trial balance shows all revenue and expense accounts with their correct amounts for the period. The income statement can be prepared by listing all the revenue accounts, listing all the expense accounts, and showing the difference between the sum of the revenues and the sum of the expenses as net income. Revenue and expense accounts are temporary labels for portions of retained earnings. Once the adjusted trial balance has been prepared, the revenue and expense accounts have served their purpose for the current period and are closed.

Closing of Temporary Accounts

The closing process transfers the balances in the temporary revenue and expense accounts to Retained Earnings. A temporary account with a debit balance is closed by crediting it with the amount equal to its balance at the end of the period and debiting Retained Earnings. The usual closing entry for a temporary account with a debit balance is

Retained Earnings (SE)	X	
Account with Debit Balance (SE) (use specific account title) . . .		X

A temporary account with a credit balance is closed by debiting the temporary account and crediting Retained Earnings. The usual closing entry for a temporary account with a credit balance is

Exhibit 3.6
STEPHEN'S SHOE STORE, INC.
Trial Balance Before and After Adjusting Entries[a]
December 31, Year 4

Accounts	Unadjusted Trial Balance Debit	Unadjusted Trial Balance Credit	Adjusting Entries Debit	Adjusting Entries Credit	Adjusted Trial Balance Debit	Adjusted Trial Balance Credit
Cash (A)	$ 191,100				$ 191,100	
Accounts Receivable (A)	128,000				128,000	
Notes Receivable (A)	10,000				10,000	
Interest Receivable (A)			$ 150 (12)		150	
Merchandise Inventory (A)	140,000				140,000	
Prepaid Insurance (A)	1,500			$ 500 (14)	1,000	
Land (A)	100,000				100,000	
Building and Equipment (A)	525,000				525,000	
Accumulated Depreciation (XA)		$ 85,000		30,000 (15)		$ 115,000
Accounts Payable (L)		220,000				220,000
Salaries Payable (L)				6,000 (13)		6,000
Dividends Payable (L)		15,000				15,000
Advances from Tenants (L)		600	50 (16)			550
Bonds Payable (L)		100,000				100,000
Common Stock (SE)		250,000				250,000
Additional Paid-in Capital (SE)		200,000				200,000
Retained Earnings (SE)		108,000				108,000
Sales Revenue (SE)		625,000				625,000
Interest Revenue (SE)				150 (12)		150
Rent Revenue (SE)				50 (16)		50
Cost of Goods Sold (SE)	390,000				390,000	
Salaries Expense (SE)	110,000		6,000 (13)		116,000	
Interest Expense (SE)	8,000				8,000	
Insurance Expense (SE)			500 (14)		500	
Depreciation Expense (SE)			30,000 (15)		30,000	
Totals	$1,603,600	$1,603,600	$36,700	$36,700	$1,639,750	$1,639,750

[a]This convenient tabular form is often called a *work sheet.*

Account with Credit Balance (SE) (use specific account title)	X	
Retained Earnings (SE)		X

After closing entries, the balances in all temporary accounts are zero. The former debit (credit) balances in temporary accounts become debits (credits) in the Retained Earnings account.

Each temporary revenue and expense account could be closed by a separate entry. Some recording time is saved, however, by closing all revenue and expense accounts in a single entry as follows:

(17) Sales Revenue (SE)	625,000	
Interest Revenue (SE)	150	
Rent Revenue (SE)	50	
Cost of Goods Sold (SE)		390,000
Salaries Expense (SE)		116,000
Interest Expense (SE)		8,000
Insurance Expense (SE)		500
Depreciation Expense (SE)		30,000
Retained Earnings (SE)		80,700

The amount credited to Retained Earnings is the difference between the amounts debited to revenue accounts and the amounts credited to expense accounts. This amount is the net income for the period.[3]

Alternative Closing Procedure An alternative closing procedure uses a temporary "Income Summary" account. Individual revenue and expense accounts are first closed to the Income Summary account. The income statement is prepared using information on the individual revenues and expenses in the Income Summary account. The balance in the Income Summary account, representing net income for the period, is then closed to Retained Earnings.

For example, the entry to close the Sales Revenue account under this alternative procedure is

(17a) Sales Revenue (SE)	625,000	
Income Summary (SE)		625,000

---

[3]The amount credited to Retained Earnings in the closing entry is called a *plug*. When making some journal entries in accounting, often all debits are known, as are all but one of the credits (or vice versa). Because double-entry recording procedure requires equal debits and credits, the unknown quantity can be found by subtracting the sum of the known credits from the sum of all debits (or vice versa). This process is known as *plugging*.

The entry to close the Cost of Goods Sold account is

(17b) Income Summary (SE)	390,000	
Cost of Goods Sold (SE)		390,000

Similar closing entries are made for the other revenue and expense accounts. The Income Summary account will have a credit balance of $80,700 after all revenue and expense accounts have been closed. The balance in the Income Summary account is then transferred to Retained Earnings:

(17c) Income Summary (SE)	80,700	
Retained Earnings (SE)		80,700

The end result of both closing procedures is the same. Revenue and expense accounts, as well as the Income Summary account if one is used, have zero balances after closing entries, and the Retained Earnings account is increased by the net income for the period of $80,700. Exhibit 3.7 shows the Income Summary account for Stephen's Shoe Store after all revenue and expense accounts have been closed at the end of the period.

Financial Statement Preparation

The income statement, balance sheet, and any desired supporting schedules can be prepared from information in the adjusted trial balance. Exhibit 3.8 presents the income statement of Stephen's Shoe Store for Year 4. Exhibit 3.9 presents the comparative balance sheets for December 31, Year 3 and Year 4. Exhibit 3.10 presents an analysis of changes in retained earnings.

Exhibit 3.7
Illustration of Income Summary Account for Stephen's Shoe Store, Inc.

Income Summary Account (SE)				Retained Earnings (SE)		
Cost of Goods Sold	390,000	625,000	Sales Revenue		123,000	Beginning Balance
Salaries Expense	116,000	150	Interest Revenue			
Interest Expense	8,000	50	Rent Revenue	Dividends 15,000	80,700	Net Income
Insurance Expense	500	625,200				
Depreciation Expense	30,000				188,700	Ending Balance
To Close Income Summary Account	80,700					
	625,200					

Exhibit 3.8
STEPHEN'S SHOE STORE, INC.
Income Statement for the
Year Ending December 31, Year 4

Revenues:

Sales Revenue	$625,000	
Interest Revenue	150	
Rent Revenue	50	
Total Revenues		$625,200

Less Expenses:

Cost of Goods Sold	$390,000	
Salaries Expense	116,000	
Interest Expense	8,000	
Insurance Expense	500	
Depreciation Expense	30,000	
Total Expenses		544,500
Net Income		$ 80,700

Summary

Measurements of net income *for the period* and of financial position *at the end of the period* are interrelated. Revenues result from selling goods or rendering services to customers and lead to increases in assets or decreases in liabilities. Expenses indicate that services have been used in generating revenue and result in decreases in assets or increases in liabilities. Because revenues represent increases in shareholders' equity, revenue transactions are recorded by crediting (increasing) a shareholders' equity account for the specific type of revenue and by debiting either an asset or liability account. Expenses represent decreases in shareholders' equity and are recorded by debiting (decreasing) a shareholders' equity account for the specific type of expense and crediting either an asset or a liability account. The revenue and expense accounts accumulate the revenues earned and expenses recognized during the period. After an adjusted trial balance has been prepared, the balances in these temporary accounts are transferred, or closed, to the Retained Earnings account.

Some events will not be recorded as part of the regular day-to-day recording process during the period because no explicit transaction between the firm and some external party (such as a customer, creditor, or governmental unit) has taken place to signal the requirement for a journal entry. Such events require an adjusting entry at the end of the period so that periodic income and financial position can be properly reported on an accrual basis.

Exhibit 3.9
STEPHEN'S SHOE STORE, INC.
Comparative Balance Sheet
December 31, Year 3 and Year 4

		December 31, Year 3		December 31, Year 4
Assets				
Current Assets				
Cash.		$ 30,000		$191,100
Accounts Receivable		63,000		128,000
Notes Receivable		—		10,000
Interest Receivable		—		150
Merchandise Inventory.		175,000		140,000
Prepaid Insurance.		—		1,000
Total Current Assets.		$268,000		$470,250
Property, Plant, and Equipment				
Land.		$100,000		$100,000
Building and Equipment—at acquisition cost	$525,000		$525,000	
Less: Accumulated Depreciation . . .	85,000		115,000	
Building and Equipment—net.		440,000		410,000
Total Property, Plant, and Equipment		$540,000		$510,000
Total Assets		$808,000		$980,250
Liabilities and Shareholders' Equity				
Current Liabilities				
Accounts Payable		$135,000		$220,000
Salaries Payable		—		6,000
Dividends Payable		—		15,000
Advances from Tenants		—		550
Total Current Liabilities		$135,000		$241,550
Long-Term Debt				
Bonds Payable		100,000		100,000
Total Liabilities		$235,000		$341,550
Shareholders' Equity:				
Common Stock—at par value		$250,000		$250,000
Additional Paid-in Capital		200,000		200,000
Retained Earnings.		123,000		188,700
Total Shareholders' Equity		$573,000		$638,700
Total Liabilities and Shareholders Equity		$808,000		$980,250

Exhibit 3.10
STEPHEN'S SHOE STORE, INC.
Analysis of Changes in Retained Earnings for the
Year Ending December 31, Year 4

Retained Earnings, December 31, Year 3		$123,000
Net Income.	$80,700	
Less Dividends	15,000	
Increase in Retained Earnings		65,700
Retained Earnings, December 31, Year 4		$188,700

Problem 1 for Self-Study

Harris Equipment Corporation was organized on January 2, Year 2, with the issuance of 10,000 shares of $10-par value common stock for $15 cash per share. The
following transactions occurred during Year 2:

(1) January 2, Year 2: The firm acquired a building costing $80,000 and equipment
costing $40,000. It paid cash in the amount of $60,000 and assumed a 10
percent mortgage for the balance of the purchase price. Interest is payable on
January 2 of each year, beginning 1 year after the purchase.

(2) January 2, Year 2: The firm bought a 2-year fire insurance policy on the building and equipment. It paid the insurance premium of $1,200 for the 2-year
period in advance (debit an asset account).

(3) During Year 2: Merchandise acquired on account totaled $320,000. Payments
to these suppliers during Year 2 totaled $270,000.

(4) During Year 2: Sales of merchandise totaled $510,000, of which $80,000 was
for cash and $430,000 was on account. Collections from credit customers dur-
ing Year 2 totaled $360,000.

(5) During Year 2: Salaries paid to employees totaled $80,000.

(6) During Year 2: Utility bills totaling $1,300 were paid.

(7) November 1, Year 2: A customer advanced $600 toward the purchase price of
merchandise to be delivered during January, Year 3.

(8) November 1, Year 2: A customer gave a $1,000, 9 percent, 90-day note to settle
an open account receivable.

(9) December 1, Year 2: The firm rented out a portion of the building for a 3-month
period. It received the rent for the period of $900 in advance (credit a revenue
account).

Give the journal entries to record these nine transactions *during Year 2*. (Adjusting entries at the end of Year 2 are analyzed in the next self-study problem.) Omit
explanations for the journal entries.

Suggested Solution

(1) Jan. 2, Year 2	Building		80,000	
	Equipment		40,000	
	Cash			60,000
	Mortgage Payable			60,000
(2) Jan. 2, Year 2	Prepaid Insurance		1,200	
	Cash			1,200
(3) During Year 2	Merchandise Inventory		320,000	
	Accounts Payable			320,000
During Year 2	Accounts Payable		270,000	
	Cash			270,000
(4) During Year 2	Cash		80,000	
	Accounts Receivable		430,000	
	Sales Revenue			510,000
During Year 2	Cash		360,000	
	Accounts Receivable			360,000
(5) During Year 2	Salary Expense		80,000	
	Cash			80,000
(6) During Year 2	Utilities Expense		1,300	
	Cash			1,300
(7) Nov. 1, Year 2	Cash		600	
	Advances from Customers			600
(8) Nov. 1, Year 2	Note Receivable		1,000	
	Accounts Receivable			1,000
(9) Dec. 1, Year 2	Cash		900	
	Rent Revenue			900

Problem 2 for Self-Study

Refer to the data for Harris Equipment Corporation in the preceding self-study problem. Give the adjusting entries on December 31, Year 2, to reflect the following items. You may omit explanations to the journal entries.

(10) The building acquired on January 2, Year 2, has a 20-year estimated life and zero salvage value. The equipment has a 7-year estimated life and $5,000 salvage value. The straight-line depreciation method is used.

(11) After a physical inventory is taken at the end of the year, the cost of merchandise sold during Year 2 is found to be $180,000.

(12) Interest expense on the mortgage liability for Year 2 is recognized.

(13) Salaries earned by employees during the last three days of December total $800 and will be paid on January 4, Year 3.

(14) Interest revenue is recognized on the note receivable [see transaction **(8)** in the preceding self-study problem].

(15) An adjusting entry is made to record the proper amount of rent revenue for Year 2 [see transaction **(9)** in the preceding self-study problem].

(16) Dividends of $25,000 are declared. The dividend will be paid on January 15, Year 3 (debit Retained Earnings).

Suggested Solution

(10) Depreciation Expense	9,000	
Accumulated Depreciation		9,000
($80,000 − $0)/20 = $4,000; ($40,000 − $5,000)/7 = $5,000.		
(11) Cost of Goods Sold	180,000	
Merchandise Inventory		180,000
(12) Interest Expense	6,000	
Interest Payable		6,000
$60,000 × .10 = $6,000.		
(13) Salary Expense	800	
Salaries Payable		800
(14) Interest Receivable	15	
Interest Revenue		15
$1,000 × .09 × 60/360.		
(15) Rent Revenue	600	
Advances from Tenants		600
(16) Retained Earnings	25,000	
Dividends Payable		25,000

Problem 3 for Self-Study

To achieve efficient recording of day-to-day cash receipts and disbursements relating to operations, a firm may credit *all* cash receipts to revenue accounts and debit *all* cash disbursements to expense accounts. The efficiency stems from treating all receipts in the same way and from treating all disbursements in the same way. As a result, lower-paid clerks can be employed to make the routine and repetitive entries for receipts and disbursements. In the day-to-day recording of transactions, the clerk need not be concerned with whether a specific cash transaction reflects settlement of a past accrual, a revenue or expense correctly assigned to the current period, or a prepayment relating to a future period. Higher-paid accountants need be employed only at the end of the period to analyze the existing account balances and to construct the adjusting entries required to correct them. This process results in temporarily incorrect balances in some balance sheet and income statement accounts *during* the accounting period.

Construct the adjusting entry required for each of the following scenarios.

   a. On September 1, Year 2, a tenant paid $24,000 rent for the 1-year period starting at that time. The tenant debited the entire amount to Rent Expense and credited Cash. The tenant made no adjusting entries for rent between September 1 and December 31. Construct the adjusting entry to be made on December 31, Year 2, to recognize the proper balances in the Prepaid Rent and Rent Expense accounts.

   b. The tenant's books for December 31, Year 2, after adjusting entries, show a balance in the Prepaid Rent account of $16,000. This amount represents rent for the period January 1 through August 31, Year 3. On September 1, Year 3, the tenant paid $30,000 for rent for the 1-year period starting September 1, Year 3. The tenant debited this amount to Rent Expense and credited Cash, but made no adjusting entries for rent during Year 3. Construct the adjusting entry required on December 31, Year 3.

c. The tenant's books for December 31, Year 3, after adjusting entries, show a balance in the Prepaid Rent account of $20,000. This amount represents rent for the period January 1 through August 31, Year 4. On September 1, Year 4, the tenant paid $18,000 for rent for the *6-month* period starting September 1, Year 4. The tenant debited this amount to Rent Expense and credited Cash, but made no adjusting entries during Year 4. Construct the adjusting entry required on December 31, Year 4.

d. Whenever the firm makes payments for wages, it debits Wage Expense. At the start of April, the Wages Payable account had a balance of $5,000, representing wages earned but not paid during the last few days of March. During April, the firm paid $30,000 in wages, debiting the entire amount to Wage Expense. At the end of April, analysis of amounts earned since the last payday indicates that wages of $4,000 have been earned but not yet paid. Construct the required adjusting entry.

e. A firm purchased an insurance policy providing 1 year's coverage from May 1, Year 1, and debited the entire amount to Insurance Expense. After the firm made adjusting entries, the balance sheet for December 31, Year 1, correctly showed Prepaid Insurance of $3,000. Construct the adjusting entry that must be made on January 31, Year 2, if the books are closed monthly and a balance sheet is to be prepared for January 31, Year 2.

f. The record-keeping system for an apartment building instructs the bookkeeper always to credit rent revenue when a payment is received from tenants. At the beginning of Year 3, the liability account, Advances from Tenants, had a credit balance of $25,000 representing collections from tenants for rental services to be received during Year 3. During Year 3, collections from tenants of $250,000 were all debited to Cash and credited to Rent Revenue. No adjusting entries were made during Year 3. At the end of Year 3, analysis of the individual accounts indicates that of the amounts already collected, $30,000 represents collections for rental services to be provided to tenants during Year 4. Present the required adjusting entry.

g. When the firm acquired new equipment costing $10,000 on January 1, Year 1, the bookkeeper debited Depreciation Expense and credited Cash for $10,000, but made no further entries for this equipment during Year 1. The equipment has an expected service life of 5 years and an estimated salvage value of zero. Construct the adjusting entry required before a balance sheet for December 31, Year 1, can be prepared.

Suggested Solution

a. The Prepaid Rent account on the year-end balance sheet should represent 8 months of prepayments. The rent per month is $2,000 (= $24,000/12), so the balance required in the Prepaid Rent account is $16,000 (= 8 × $2,000).

Prepaid Rent	16,000	
Rent Expense		16,000
To increase the balance in the Prepaid Rent account, reducing the amount in the Rent Expense account.		

b. The Prepaid Rent account on the balance sheet for the end of Year 3 should represent 8 months of prepayments. The rent per month is $2,500 (= $30,000/12), so the required balance in the Prepaid Rent account is $20,000 (= 8 × $2,500). The balance in that account is already $16,000, so the adjusting entry must increase it by $4,000 (= $20,000 − $16,000).

Prepaid Rent	4,000	
Rent Expense		4,000
To increase the balance in the Prepaid Rent account, reducing the amount in the Rent Expense account.		

The Rent Expense account will have a balance at the end of Year 3 before closing entries of $26,000 (= $30,000 − $4,000). This amount comprises $16,000 (= $2,000 × 8) for rent from January through August and $10,000 (= $2,500 × 4) for rent from September through December.

c. The Prepaid Rent account on the balance sheet at the end of Year 4 should represent 2 months of prepayments. The rent per month is $3,000 (= $18,000/6), so the required balance in the Prepaid Rent account is $6,000 (= 2 × $3,000). The balance in that account is $20,000, so the adjusting entry must reduce it by $14,000 (= $20,000 − $6,000).

Rent Expense	14,000	
Prepaid Rent		14,000
To reduce the balance in the Prepaid Rent account, increasing the amount in the Rent Expense account.		

The Rent Expense account will have a balance at the end of Year 3 before closing entries of $32,000 (= $18,000 + $14,000). This amount comprises $20,000 (= $2,500 × 8) for rent from January through August and $12,000 (= $3,000 × 4) for rent from September through December.

d. The Wages Payable account should have a credit balance of $4,000 at the end of April, but it has a balance of $5,000 carried over from the end of March. The adjusting entry must reduce the balance by $1,000, which requires a debit to the Wages Payable account.

Wages Payable	1,000	
Wage Expense.		1,000
To reduce the balance in the Wages Payable account, reducing the amount in the Wage Expense account.		

e. The Prepaid Insurance account balance of $3,000 represents 4 months of coverage. Thus, the cost of insurance is $750 (= $3,000/4) per month. The adjusting entry for a single month is

Insurance Expense	750	
Prepaid Insurance		750

f. The Advances from Tenants account has a balance of $25,000 carried over from the start of the year. At the end of Year 3, it should have a balance of $30,000. Thus, the adjusting entry must increase the balance by $5,000, which requires a credit to the liability account.

Rent Revenue	5,000	
Advances from Tenants		5,000
To increase the balance in the Advances from Tenants account, reducing the amount in the Rent Revenue account.		

g. The Depreciation Expense for the year should be $2,000 (= $10,000/5). The balance in the Accumulated Depreciation account should also be $2,000 and, thus, the Depreciation Expense account must be reduced (credited) by $8,000 (= $10,000 − $2,000). The adjusting entry not only reduces recorded Depreciation Expense, but sets up the asset account and its accumulated depreciation contra account.

Equipment.	10,000	
Accumulated Depreciation		2,000
Depreciation Expense		8,000
To reduce Depreciation Expense, setting up the asset and its contra account.		

Questions, Exercises, Problems and Cases

Questions

1. Review the meaning of the following concepts or terms discussed in this chapter.

a. Revenue.	**k.** Product cost.
b. Expense.	**l.** Period expense.
c. Net income or net loss.	**m.** Expense versus dividend.
d. Accounting period.	**n.** Temporary and permanent accounts.
e. Natural business year or fiscal period.	**o.** General journal entries.
f. Cash basis of accounting.	**p.** Adjusting entries.
g. Accrual basis of accounting.	**q.** Closing entries.
h. Unexpired costs.	**r.** Unadjusted trial balance.
i. Expired costs.	**s.** Adjusted trial balance.
j. Matching convention.	**t.** Contra account.

2. What factors would a firm likely consider in its decision to use the calendar year versus a fiscal (natural business) year as its accounting period?

3. Which of the following types of businesses are likely to have a natural business year different from the calendar year?
  a. A ski resort in Vermont.
  b. A professional basketball team.
  c. A grocery store.

4. Distinguish between a revenue and a cash receipt. Under what conditions will they be the same?

5. Distinguish between an expense and a cash expenditure. Under what conditions will they be the same?

6. "Cash flows determine the *amount* of revenue and expense but not the *timing* of their recognition." Explain.

7. "Accrual accounting focuses on the use, rather than the financing, of assets." Explain.

8. "Depreciation on equipment may be a product cost or a period expense depending on the type of equipment." Explain.

9. "Revenue and expense accounts are useful accounting devices, but they could be dispensed with." What is an alternative to using them?

10. Why are revenue and expense accounts closed at the end of each accounting period?

11. Before the books have been closed for an accounting period, what types of accounts will have nonzero balances? After the books have been closed, what types of accounts will have nonzero balances?

12. If each transaction occurring during an accounting period has been recorded properly, why is there a need for adjusting entries at the end of the period?

13. What is the purpose of using contra accounts? What is the alternative to using them?

Exercises

14. *Relation between cash flows and revenues and expenses.* Under the accrual basis of accounting, cash receipts and disbursements may precede, coincide with, or follow the period in which revenues and expenses are recognized. Give an example of each of the following:

    a. A cash receipt that precedes the period in which revenue is recognized.

    b. A cash receipt that coincides with the period in which revenue is recognized.

    c. A cash receipt that follows the period in which revenue is recognized.

    d. A cash disbursement that precedes the period in which expense is recognized.

    e. A cash disbursement that coincides with the period in which expense is recognized.

    f. A cash disbursement that follows the period in which expense is recognized.

15. *Revenue recognition.* Assume that the accrual basis of accounting is used and that revenue is recognized at the time the goods are sold or services are rendered. How much revenue is recognized during the month of May in each of the following transactions?

    a. Collection of cash from customers during May for merchandise sold and delivered in April, $8,200.

    b. Sales of merchandise during May for cash, $9,600.

    c. Sales of merchandise during May to customers to be collected in June, $2,400.

    d. A store building is rented to a toy shop for $800 a month, effective May 1. A check for $1,600 for 2 months' rent is received on May 1.

    e. Data in part **d**, except that collection is received from the tenant in June.

16. *Revenue recognition.* Assume that the accrual basis of accounting is used and that revenue is recognized at the time goods are sold or services are rendered. Indicate the amount of revenue recognized in each of the months of April, May, and June relating to the following cash receipts during May.

    a. $4,600 collected from customers for merchandise sold and delivered in April.

    b. $8,900 collected from customers for merchandise sold and delivered in May.

    c. $1,800 collected from customers for merchandise to be delivered in June.

    d. $3,600 collected from subscribers for subscription fees to magazines for the 1-year period beginning April 1.

e. Same as part **d**, except that the subscription period begins May 1.

f. Same as part **d**, except that the subscription period begins June 1.

17. *Revenue recognition.* Indicate the amount of revenue recognized, if any, from each of the following related events, assuming that the accrual basis of accounting is used.

a. A firm receives purchase orders from regular customers for $8,400 of merchandise. A 2 percent discount is allowed, and generally taken, for prompt payment.

b. The customers' orders are filled and shipped by way of the company's trucking division.

c. The firm sends invoices totaling $8,400 to the customers.

d. The merchandise is received by customers in the correct quantities and according to specifications.

e. The firm receives checks in the amount of $8,232 (= .98 × $8,400) from customers in payment of the merchandise.

f. Upon reinspection, several days later, merchandise with a gross invoice price of $600 is found to be defective by customers and returned for appropriate credit.

18. *Revenue recognition.* Indicate which of the following transactions or events immediately gives rise to the recognition of revenue under the accrual basis of accounting.

a. The receipt of an order from a customer for merchandise.

b. The shipment of goods that have been paid for in advance.

c. The issue of additional shares of common stock.

d. The completion of a batch of men's suits by a clothing factory.

e. The sale of tickets by a major league baseball team for a game in 2 weeks.

f. Same as part **e**, except that sale was made by Ticketron, a ticket agent.

g. The interest earned on a savings account between interest dates.

h. A collection of cash from accounts receivable debtors.

i. The rendering of accounting services to a customer on account.

19. *Expense recognition.* Give the amount of expense recognized, if any, from each of the following related events, assuming that the accrual basis of accounting is used.

a. The purchasing department notifies the stockroom that the supply of $\frac{1}{2}$-inch plywood has reached the minimum point and should be reordered.

b. The firm sends a purchase order to Central Lumber Company for $10,000 of the material.

c. The firm receives an acknowledgment of the order. It indicates that delivery will be made in 15 days but that the price has been raised to $10,200.

d. The shipment of plywood arrives and is checked by the receiving department. The correct quantity has been delivered.

e. The purchase invoice arrives. The amount of $10,200 is subject to a 2 percent discount if paid within 10 days. Cash discounts are treated as a reduction in the acquisition cost of inventory.

     f. Upon reinspection, the firm finds plywood with a gross invoice price of $200 to be defective and returns it to the supplier.

     g. The balance of the amount due the Central Lumber Company is paid in time to obtain the discount.

     h. The firm sells the plywood to customers for $12,000.

20. *Expense recognition.* Assume that the accrual basis of accounting is used and that revenue is recognized at the time goods are sold or services are rendered. Indicate the amount of expense recognized during March, if any, from each of the following transactions or events.

     a. An insurance premium of $1,800 is paid on March 1 for 1 year's coverage beginning on that date.

     b. On April 3, a utilities bill totaling $460 for services during March is received.

     c. $700 worth of supplies was purchased on account during March. $500 of these purchases on account was paid in March and the remainder was paid in April. On March 1, supplies were on hand that cost $300. At March 31, supplies that cost $350 were still on hand.

     d. Data of **c**, except that $200 of supplies was on hand at March 1.

     e. Property taxes of $4,800 on an office building for the year were paid in January.

     f. An advance of $250 on the April salary is paid to an employee on March 29.

21. *Expense recognition.* Assume that the accrual basis of accounting is used and that revenue is recognized at the time goods are sold or services are rendered. Indicate the amount of expense recognized in each of the months of April, May, and June relating to the following cash expenditures during May.

     a. $1,900 for advertising that appeared on television programs during April.

     b. $3,200 for sales commissions on sales made during May.

     c. $500 for rent on delivery equipment for the month of June.

     d. $600 for an insurance premium for coverage from May 1 until October 30.

     e. $800 as a deposit on equipment to be delivered during June.

     f. $1,200 for property taxes on an office building for the current calendar year.

22. *Income recognition.* Feltham Company acquired used machine tools costing $75,000 from various sources. These machine tools were then sold to Mock Corporation. Delivery costs paid by Feltham Company totaled $4,500. Mock Corporation had agreed to pay $100,000 cash for these tools. Finding itself short of cash, however, Mock Corporation offered some of its bonds to Feltham Company. The bonds have a face value of $110,000 and mature in 5 years. The bonds promise 8 percent interest per year. At the time the offer was made, the bonds could have been sold in public bond markets for $98,000.

    Feltham Company accepted the offer and held the bonds for 3 years. During the 3 years, it received interest payments of $8,800 per year, or $26,400 total. At the end of the third year, Feltham Company sold the bonds for $95,000.

     a. What profit or loss did Feltham Company recognize at the time of sale of machine tools to Mock Corporation?

     b. What profit or loss would Feltham Company have recognized at the time of the sale of machine tools if it had sold the bonds for $98,000 immediately upon receiving them?

   c. What profit or loss would Feltham Company have recognized at the time of the sale of machine tools if it had held the bonds to maturity, receiving $8,800 each year for another 5 years and $110,000 at the time the bonds matured?

23. *Identifying missing half of journal entries.* In the business world, many transactions are routine and repetitive. Because accounting records business transactions, many accounting entries are also routine and repetitive. Knowing one-half of an entry in the double-entry recording system often permits a reasoned guess about the other half. The items below give the account name for one-half of an entry. Indicate your best guess as to the nature of the transaction being recorded and the name of the account of the *routine* other half of the entry. Also indicate whether the other account is increased or decreased by the transaction.

   a. Debit: Cost of Goods Sold.
   b. Debit: Accounts Receivable.
   c. Credit: Accounts Receivable.
   d. Debit: Accounts Payable.
   e. Credit: Accounts Payable.
   f. Credit: Accumulated Depreciation.
   g. Debit: Retained Earnings.
   h. Credit: Prepaid Insurance.
   i. Debit: Property Taxes Payable.
   j. Debit: Merchandise Inventory.

24. *Asset versus expense recognition.* Give the journal entry that should be made upon the receipt of each of the following invoices by the South Appliance Company, assuming that no previous entry has been made.

(1) From Western Electric Supply Company, $385, for repair parts purchased.
(2) From Touch & Rose, certified public accountants, $800, for services in filing income tax returns.
(3) From the General Electric Company, $12,365, for refrigerators purchased.
(4) From the White Stationery Company, $250, for office supplies purchased.
(5) From the Showy Sign Company, $540, for a neon sign acquired.
(6) From Schutheis and Schutheis, attorneys, $1,000, for legal services in changing from the corporate to the partnership form of organization.
(7) From the Bell Telephone Company, $65, for telephone service for next month.
(8) From the Madison Avenue Garage, $43, for gasoline and oil used by the delivery truck.
(9) From the Municipal Electric Department, $105, for electricity used for lighting last month.

25. *Journal entries for notes receivable and notes payable.* The General Supply Company received a $10,000, 3-month, 9 percent promissory note, dated December 1, Year 6, from Widen Stores to apply on its open accounts receivable.

   a. Present journal entries for the General Supply Company from December 1,

Year 6, through collection at maturity. The books are closed quarterly. Include the closing entry.

    b. Present journal entries for Widen Stores from December 1, Year 6, through payment at maturity. The books are closed quarterly. Include the closing entry.

26. *Journal entries for notes payable.* Selected transactions of the Burlson Company are described below. Present dated journal entries for these transactions and adjusting entries at the end of each month from January 15, Year 2, through July 1, Year 2. Assume that only the notes indicated were outstanding during this period. The accounting period is 1 month.

(1) The company issued a $6,000, 2-month, 10 percent promissory note on January 15, Year 2, in lieu of payment on an account due that date to the Grey Wholesale Company.

(2) The note in **(1)** and interest were paid at maturity.

(3) The company issued a $2,000, 3-month, 9 percent promissory note to the Grey Wholesale Company on the date of purchase of merchandise, April 1, Year 2.

(4) The note in **(3)** and interest were paid at maturity.

27. *Journal entries for office supply inventories.* On January 1, Year 4, the Office Supplies Inventory account of the Harris Company had a balance of $4,200. During the ensuing quarter, supplies were acquired on account in the amount of $9,000. On March 31, Year 4, the inventory was taken and calculated to amount to $2,500.

    Present journal entries to record the above acquisition and adjustments at the end of March in accordance with each of the following sets of instructions, which might be established in an accounting systems manual:

    a. An expense account is to be debited at the time supplies are acquired.

    b. An asset account is to be debited at the time supplies are acquired.

28. *Journal entries for rental receipts and payments.* The Florida Realty Company rents office space to Maddox Consultants at the rate of $600 per month. Collections have been made for rental through April 30, Year 3. The following transactions occurred on the dates indicated:

(1) May 1, Year 3: Collection, $600.

(2) June 1, Year 3: Collection, $1,200.

(3) August 1, Year 3: Collection, $1,800.

Present journal entries for the above transactions and for adjusting and closing entries from May 1 to August 31, inclusive, as they relate to both companies, assuming that each company closes its books monthly.

29. *Using accumulated depreciation to estimate asset age.*

    a. Machine A costs $10,000, has accumulated depreciation of $4,000 as of year-end, and is being depreciated on a straight-line basis over 10 years with an estimated salvage value of zero. How long ago was machine A acquired?

    b. Machine B has accumulated depreciation (straight-line basis) of $6,000 at year-end. The depreciation charge for the year is $2,000. The estimated salvage value of the machine at the end of its useful life is $1,000. How long ago was machine B acquired?

30. *Effect of recording errors on financial statements.* In recording transactions of Rogow Corporation during Year 7, the following errors were made:

(1) An expenditure of $2,000 to acquire a tract of land was debited to Administrative Expenses.

(2) Cash collections during Year 7 of $1,500 relating to sales made during Year 6 were credited to Sales Revenue of Year 7.

(3) An expenditure of $1,200 for insurance coverage from October 1, Year 7 to September 30, Year 8, was debited to Administrative Expenses on October 1, Year 7.

(4) Cash collections during Year 7 of $1,000 for goods to be delivered during Year 8 were credited to Sales Revenue of Year 7.

Indicate the effect (exclusive of income tax implications) of these errors on the following items in the financial statements prepared on December 31, Year 7.

    a. Current assets.
    b. Property, plant, and equipment.
    c. Current liabilities.
    d. Sales Revenue.
    e. Administrative expenses.
    f. Net income.
    g. Retained earnings.

31. *Effect of recording errors on financial statements.* In recording the adjusting entries of the Hammond Sales Company, Inc., at the end of Year 7, the following adjustments were omitted:

(1) Depreciation on the delivery truck of $3,000.
(2) Insurance expired on the delivery truck of $600.
(3) Interest accrued on notes payable of $150.
(4) Interest accrued on notes receivable of $330.

Indicate the collective effect (exclusive of income tax implications) of these omissions on the following items in the financial statements prepared on December 31, Year 7.

    a. Current assets.
    b. Property, plant, and equipment.
    c. Current liabilities.
    d. Selling and administrative expenses.
    e. Net income.
    f. Retained earnings.

32. *Effect of recording errors on financial statements.* Using the notation O/S (overstated), U/S (understated), and NO (no effect), indicate the effects on assets, liabilities, and shareholders' equity as of December 31, Year 5, of the following independent errors or omissions. Ignore income tax implications.

    a. An expenditure of $1,200 for insurance coverage for the 1-year period beginning September 1, Year 5, was debited to Administrative Expenses.
    b. Sales commissions earned and paid during December Year 5 were debited to Interest Expense.

   c. Depreciation on delivery equipment for Year 5 of $1,500 was not recorded.

   d. A check for $900 was received from a customer during December Year 5 for merchandise to be delivered during January Year 6. Sales Revenue was credited when the cash was received.

   e. Interest accrued on Notes Payable of $400 as of December 31, Year 5, was not recorded.

   f. Interest accrued on Notes Receivable of $560 as of December 31, Year 5, was recorded as $650.

33. *Effect of recording errors on financial statements.* Using the notation O/S (overstated), U/S (understated), and NO (no effect), indicate the effects on assets, liabilities, and shareholders' equity as of December 31, Year 3, of the following independent errors or omissions. Ignore income tax implications.

   a. An expenditure of $600 made on December 1, Year 3, for 6 months rent on an automobile was debited to Prepaid Rent. No adjusting entry was made on December 31, Year 3.

   b. A microcomputer acquired on July 1, Year 3, for $6,000 was debited to Administrative Expenses. The microcomputer has an expected useful life of 3 years and zero estimated salvage value.

   c. The company rented out excess office space for the 6-month period beginning January 1, Year 3. A rental check for this period of $600 was received on December 26, *Year 2,* and correctly credited to Rental Fees Received in Advance. No further journal entries were made relating to this rental during Year 3.

   d. Interest accrued on Notes Receivable of $500 as of December 31, Year 3, was not recorded.

   e. A check for $250 was received from a customer on December 31, Year 3, in settlement of an account receivable. No journal entries have been made to record this check.

   f. An expenditure of $740 for travel during December 31, Year 3, was recorded as $470.

Problems and Cases

34. *Cash versus accrual basis of accounting.* J. Thompson opened a hardware store on January 1, Year 5. Thompson invested $10,000 and borrowed $8,000 from a local bank. The loan is repayable on June 30, Year 5, with interest at the rate of 9 percent per year.

Thompson rented a building on January 1, and paid 2 months' rent in advance in the amount of $2,000. Property and liability insurance coverage for the year ending December 31, Year 5, was paid on January 1 in the amount of $1,200.

Thompson purchased $28,000 of merchandise inventory on account on January 2 and paid $10,000 of this amount on January 25. The cost of merchandise on hand on January 31 was $15,000.

During January, cash sales to customers totaled $20,000 and sales on account totaled $9,000. Of the sales on account, $2,000 had been collected as of January 31.

Other costs incurred and paid in cash during January were as follows: utilities, $400; salaries, $650; taxes, $350.

a. Prepare an income statement for January, assuming that Thompson uses the accrual basis of accounting with revenue recognized at the time goods are sold (delivered).

b. Prepare an income statement for January, assuming that Thompson uses the cash basis of accounting.

c. Which basis of accounting do you feel provides a better indication of the operating performance of the hardware store during January? Why?

35. *Cash versus accrual basis of accounting.* Management Consultants, Inc., opened a consulting business on July 1, Year 2. Roy Bean and Sarah Bower each contributed $7,000 cash for shares of the firm's common stock. The corporation borrowed $8,000 from a local bank on August 1, Year 2. The loan is repayable on July 31, Year 3, with interest at the rate of 9 percent per year.

Office space was rented on August 1, with 2 months' rent paid in advance. The remaining monthly rental fees of $900 per month were made on the first of each month, beginning October 1. Office equipment with a 4-year life was purchased for cash on August 1 for $4,800.

Consulting services rendered for clients between August 1 and December 31, Year 2, were billed at $15,000. Of this amount, $9,000 was collected by year-end.

Other costs incurred and paid in cash by the end of the year were as follows: utilities, $450; salary of secretary, $7,500; supplies, $450. Unpaid bills at year-end are as follows: utilities, $80; salary of secretary, $900; supplies, $70. All supplies acquired were used.

a. Prepare an income statement for the 5 months ended December 31, Year 2, assuming that the corporation uses the accrual basis of accounting, with revenue recognized at the time services are rendered.

b. Prepare an income statement for the 5 months ended December 31, Year 2, assuming that the corporation uses the cash basis of accounting.

c. Which basis of accounting do you feel provides a better indication of operating performance of the consulting firm for the period? Why?

36. *Cash versus accrual basis of accounting.* J. Hennessey opened a retail store on January 1, Year 8. Hennessey invested $20,000 and borrowed $10,000 from a local bank. The loan is repayable on December 31, Year 9, with interest at the rate of 12 percent per year.

Hennessey purchased $84,000 of merchandise on account during Year 8 and paid $76,000 of the amount by the end of Year 8. The cost of merchandise on hand on December 31, Year 8, was $12,000.

During Year 8, cash sales to customers were $30,000 and sales on account totaled $70,000. Of the sales on account, $62,000 was collected by December 31, Year 8.

Other costs incurred and paid in cash were salaries, $20,000; utilities, $1,500. Unpaid bills at year-end are as follows: salaries, $1,200; utilities, $120.

    a. Prepare an income statement for Year 8 assuming that the company uses the accrual basis of accounting, with revenue recognized at the time of sale.

    b. Prepare an income statement for Year 8 assuming that the company uses the cash basis of accounting.

    c. Which basis of accounting do you feel provides a better indication of operating performance for the retail store during Year 8? Why?

37. *Miscellaneous transactions and adjusting entries.* Present journal entries for each of the following separate sets of data:

    a. On January 15, Year 2, a $6,000, 2-month, 12 percent note was received by the company. Present adjusting entries at the end of each month and the entry for collection at maturity.

    b. The company uses one Merchandise Inventory account to record the beginning inventory and purchases during the period. The balance in this account on December 31, Year 2, was $580,000. The inventory of merchandise on hand at that time was $60,000. Present the adjusting entry.

    c. The company rents out part of its building for office space at the rate of $900 a month, payable in advance for each calendar quarter of the year. The quarterly rental for the first quarter was received one month late on February 1, Year 2. Present collection and adjusting entries for the quarter. Assume that the books are closed monthly.

    d. The company leases branch office space at $3,000 a month. Payment is made by the company on the first of each 6-month period. Payment of $18,000 was made on July 1, Year 2. Present payment and adjusting entries through August 31, Year 2. Assume that the books are closed monthly.

    e. The balance of the Prepaid Insurance account on October 1, Year 2, was $400. On December 1, Year 2, the company renewed its only insurance policy for another 2 years, beginning on that date, by payment of $3,000. Present journal entries for renewal and adjusting entries through December 31, Year 2. Assume that the books are closed quarterly.

    f. The Office Supplies on Hand account had a balance of $400 on December 31, Year 2. Purchases of supplies in the amount of $580 were recorded in the Office Supplies Expense account during the month. The physical inventory of office supplies on December 31, Year 2, was $340. Present any necessary adjusting entry at December 31, Year 2.

    g. An office building was constructed at a cost of $560,000. It was estimated that it would have a useful life of 50 years from the date of occupancy, October 31, Year 2, and a residual value of $80,000. Present the adjusting entry for the depreciation of the building in Year 2. Assume that the books are closed annually at December 31.

38. *Miscellaneous transactions and adjusting entries.* Give the journal entry to record each of the transactions below as well as any necessary adjusting entries on December 31, Year 6, assuming that the accounting period is the calendar year and the books are closed on December 31.

    a. Harrison's Supply Company received a 90-day note from a customer on December 1, Year 6. The note in the face amount of $3,000 replaced an open account receivable of the same amount. The note is due with interest at 9 percent per year on March 1, Year 7.

b. Thompson's Wholesale Company purchased a 2-year insurance policy on September 1, Year 6, paying the 2-year premium of $9,600 in advance.

c. William's Products Company acquired a machine on July 1, Year 6, for $20,000 cash. The machine is expected to have a $4,000 salvage value and a 4-year life.

d. Greer Electronics Company acquired an automobile on September 1, Year 5, for $5,000 cash. The automobile is expected to have $1,400 salvage value and a 4-year life.

e. Devine Company rented out excess office space for the 3-month period beginning December 15, Year 6. The first month's rent of $6,400 was received on this date.

f. Prentice Products Corporation began business on November 1, Year 6. It acquired office supplies costing $5,000 on account. Of this amount, $4,000 was paid by year-end. A physical inventory indicates that office supplies costing $2,400 were on hand on December 31, Year 6.

39. *Preparation of T-account entries and adjusted trial balance.* A corporation known as the Kirby Collection Agency is organized by Betty Kirby and Charles Stevens on January 1, Year 3. The business of the firm is to collect overdue accounts receivable of various clients on a commission basis. The following transactions occurred during January:

(1) Kirby contributes office supplies worth $3,000 and cash of $12,000. She is issued stock certificates for 500 shares with a par value of $30 a share.

(2) Stevens contributes $3,000 in cash and office equipment valued at $9,000. He is issued stock certificates for 400 shares.

(3) The Kirby agency collects $400 on an account that was turned over to it by the Jiggly Market. The commission earned is 50 percent of the amount collected.

(4) The stenographer's salary during the month, $600, is paid.

(5) A bill is received from Lyband and Linn, certified public accountants, for $400 to cover the cost of installing a computer system.

(6) The amount due the Jiggly Market [see **(3)**] is paid.

(7) An office is leased for the year beginning February 1, Year 3, and the rent for 2 months is paid in advance. A check is drawn for $900.

(8) An automobile is purchased on January 30 for $4,500; $2,500 is paid by check, and an installment contract, payable to the Scotch Automobile Sales Company, is signed for the balance.

    a. Open T-accounts and record the transactions during January.

    b. Prepare an adjusted, preclosing trial balance as of January 31, Year 3. Indicate, by "R" or "E," accounts that are revenue or expense accounts.

40. *Preparation of T-account entries and adjusted trial balance.* Bill Wilson operates a restaurant that he has rented fully equipped from its owner. The trial balance of the restaurant on November 1, Year 6, the first day of an accounting period, is as follows:

Cash	$ 6,975	
Food on Hand	5,400	
Accounts Payable, Barry Meat Company		$ 2,050
Accounts Payable, Conell Wholesale Grocery		2,378
Bill Wilson, Capital		7,947
	$12,375	$12,375

A summary of the transactions for the month of November is as follows:

(1) Cash received for meals served, $26,550.
(2) November rent paid by check, $4,050.
(3) Food purchased on account from the Conell Wholesale Grocery, $7,650.
(4) Maintenance to equipment paid in cash, $450.
(5) Food purchased on account from the Barry Meat Company, $4,725.
(6) Payment to Barry Meat Company, $5,650.
(7) Payment to Conell Wholesale Grocery, $8,228.
(8) Salaries for the month totaling $6,273 are paid.
(9) Cost of food used, $11,925.

  a. Open T-accounts for the accounts in the trial balance and enter the beginning balances. Record the transactions for the month of November in the T-accounts, opening additional T-accounts for individual revenues and expenses as needed.
  b. Prepare an adjusted, preclosing trial balance to check the accuracy of your entries.

41. *Preparation of T-account entries, adjusted trial balance, income statement, and balance sheet.* The trial balance of Safety Cleaners and Dyers at February 28, Year 6, is shown below. The books have not been closed nor have adjusting entries been made since December 31, Year 5.

Cash	$ 3,400	
Accounts Receivable	15,200	
Supplies on Hand	4,800	
Prepaid Insurance	1,200	
Equipment	65,000	
Accumulated Depreciation		$ 9,680
Accounts Payable		7,900
P. O. Grey, Capital		60,000
Sales Revenue		46,060
Salaries and Wages Expense	26,600	
Cost of Outside Work	2,040	
Advertising Expense	400	
Repairs Expense	500	
Rent Expense	1,200	
Power, Gas, and Water Expense	880	

Supplies Used	—	
Depreciation Expense	—	
Miscellaneous Expense	2,420	
	$123,640	$123,640

A summary of the transactions for the month of March Year 6 is as follows:

(1) Sales: For cash, $14,000; on account, $5,800.
(2) Collections on account, $10,000.
(3) Purchases of outside work (cleaning done by wholesale cleaners), $800, on account.
(4) Purchases of supplies, on account, $2,800.
(5) Payments on account, $4,000.
(6) March rent paid, $600.
(7) Supplies used (for the quarter), $5,340.
(8) Depreciation (for the quarter), $2,420.
(9) March salaries and wages of $11,120 are paid.
(10) Bills received but not recorded or paid by the end of the month: advertising, $200; Maintenance on equipment, $60; power, gas, and water, $380.
(11) Insurance expired (for the quarter), $400.

    a. Open T-accounts and enter the trial balance amounts.
    b. Record the transactions for the month of March in the T-accounts, opening additional T-accounts as needed. Cross-number the entries.
    c. Prepare an adjusted, preclosing trial balance at March 31, Year 6, an income statement for the 3 months ending March 31, Year 6, and a balance sheet as of March 31, Year 6.
    d. Enter closing entries in the T-accounts using an Income Summary account.

42. *Preparation of T-account entries, adjusted trial balance, income statement, and balance sheet.* The balance sheet accounts of Hanover Camera Repair Shop at June 30, Year 8, are as follows:

Cash	$1,920	
Repair Parts Inventory	600	
Office Supplies Inventory	80	
Equipment	2,200	
Accumulated Depreciation		$ 300
Accounts Payable		2,500
B. Greer, Capital		2,000
	$4,800	$4,800

A summary of the transactions during July is as follows:

(1) Performed repair services, for which $900 in cash was received immediately.
(2) Performed additional repair work, $200, and sent bills to customers for this amount.

(3) Paid creditors, $400.

(4) Took out insurance on equipment on July 1, and issued a check to cover 1 year's premium of $96.

(5) Paid $60 for a series of advertisements that appeared in the local newspaper during July.

(6) Issued a check for $130 for rent of shop space for July.

(7) Paid telephone bill for the month, $35.

(8) Collected $100 of the amount charged to customers in item **(2)**.

Adjusting entries required at the end of July relate to the following:

(9) The insurance expired during July is calculated at $8.

(10) Cost of repair parts used during the month, $180.

(11) Cost of office supplies used during July, $40.

(12) Depreciation of equipment for the month is $30.

  a. Open T-accounts and insert the July 1 balances. Record the transactions for the month in the T-accounts, opening additional T-accounts for individual revenue and expense accounts as needed.

  b. Prepare an adjusted, preclosing trial balance at July 31, Year 8.

  c. Enter closing entries in the T-accounts using an Income Summary account.

  d. Prepare an income statement for the month of July and a balance sheet as of July 31, Year 8.

43. *Preparation of T-account entries, adjusted trial balance, income statement, and balance sheet.* The trial balance of Jones Shoe Repair Shop at February 28, Year 2, is shown below. The books have not been closed since December 31, Year 1.

Cash	$ 6,060	
Accounts Receivable	15,200	
Supplies Inventory	4,800	
Prepaid Insurance	900	
Equipment	65,000	
Accumulated Depreciation		$ 11,460
Accounts Payable		6,120
W. R. Jones, Capital		62,360
Sales Revenue		46,060
Salaries and Wages Expense	26,600	
Cost of Outside Work	2,040	
Advertising Expense	900	
Rent Expense	1,200	
Power, Gas, and Water Expense	880	
Supplies Used	—	
Depreciation Expense	—	
Miscellaneous Expense	2,420	
	$126,000	$126,000

A summary of the transactions during the month of March, Year 2 is as follows:

(1) Sales: for cash, $26,000; on account, $17,600.
(2) Collections on account, $22,000.
(3) Purchases of outside work (repair work done by another shoe repair shop for Jones), $1,600, on account.
(4) Purchases of supplies, on account, $2,800.
(5) Payments on account, $6,000.
(6) March rent paid, $1,200.
(7) March salaries and wages of $13,290 are paid.

Adjusting entries required at the end of March relate to the following:

(8) Supplies used (for the quarter), $4,960.
(9) Depreciation (for the quarter), $3,820.
(10) Bills received but not yet recorded or paid by the end of the month: advertising, $300; power, gas, and water, $620.
(11) Insurance expired (for the quarter), $300.

a. Open T-accounts and enter the trial balance amounts.
b. Record the transactions for the month of March in the T-accounts, opening additional T-accounts as needed. Cross-number the entries.
c. Enter closing entries in the T-accounts using an Income Summary account.
d. Prepare an adjusted, preclosing trial balance at March 31, Year 2, an income statement for the 3 months ending March 31, Year 2, and a balance sheet as of March 31, Year 2.

44. *Preparation of journal entries, T-accounts, adjusted trial balance, income statement, and balance sheet.* The post-closing trial balance of Cunningham's Hardware Store on September 30, Year 4, is as follows:

Cash	$ 88,400	
Accounts Receivable	54,500	
Merchandise Inventory	136,300	
Prepaid Insurance	800	
Equipment	420,000	
Accumulated Depreciation		$168,000
Accounts Payable		66,200
Note Payable		10,000
Salaries Payable		2,500
Capital Stock		300,000
Retained Earnings		153,300
Total	$700,000	$700,000

Transactions during October and additional information are as follows:

(1) Sales, all on account, total $170,000.
(2) Merchandise inventory purchased on account from various suppliers is $92,600.

(3) Rent for the month of October of $23,500 is paid.

(4) Salaries paid to employees during October are $41,200.

(5) Accounts receivable of $68,300 are collected.

(6) Accounts payable of $77,900 are paid.

(7) Miscellaneous expenses of $6,400 are paid in cash.

(8) The premium on a 1-year insurance policy was paid on June 1, Year 4.

Adjusting entries required at the end of October relate to the following:

(9) Equipment is depreciated over a 10-year life. Estimated salvage value of the equipment is considered to be negligible.

(10) Employee salaries earned during the last two days of October but not paid are $3,200. These are the only unpaid salaries at the end of October.

(11) The note payable is a 90-day, 12 percent note issued on September 30, Year 4.

(12) Merchandise inventory on hand on October 31, Year 4, totals $155,900.

a. Prepare general journal entries to reflect the transactions and other events during October. Indicate whether each entry records a transaction during the month (T) or is an adjusting entry at the end of the month (A).

b. Set up T-accounts and enter the opening balances in the accounts on September 30, Year 4. Record the entries from part **a** in the T-accounts, creating additional accounts as required.

c. Prepare an adjusted, preclosing trial balance as of October 31, Year 4.

d. Prepare an income statement for the month of October.

e. Enter the appropriate closing entries at the end of October in the T-accounts, assuming that the books are closed each month. Use an Income Summary account. Prepare a balance sheet as of October 31, Year 4.

45. *Preparation of adjusting entries.* The following unadjusted trial balance is taken from the books of the Kathleen Clothing Company at July 31, Year 3. The company closes its books monthly.

Accounts Payable		$ 12,952
Accounts Receivable	$ 18,257	
Accumulated Depreciation		8,214
Advances by Customers		540
Capital Stock		40,000
Cash	9,000	
Equipment	2,640	
Depreciation Expense	—	—
Dividends Payable	—	—
Furniture and Fixtures	12,000	
Income Tax Expense	—	—
Income Tax Payable		3,500
Insurance Expense	—	—
Leasehold	10,800	
Merchandise Cost of Goods Sold	—	—
Merchandise Inventory	49,500	

Miscellaneous Expense.	188	
Prepaid Insurance	450	
Rent Expense	—	—
Retained Earnings		14,294
Salaries and Commissions Expense	2,020	
Salaries and Commissions Payable		500
Sales.		25,000
Supplies Inventory	145	
	$105,000	$105,000

Additional data:

(1) Depreciation on equipment is to be calculated at 10 percent of cost per year (assume zero salvage value).
(2) Depreciation on furniture and fixtures is to be calculated at 20 percent of cost per year (assume zero salvage value).
(3) The leasehold represents long-term rent paid in advance by Kathleen. The monthly rental charge is $600.
(4) One invoice of $420 for the purchase of merchandise from the Peoria Company on account was recorded during the month as $240. The account has not yet been paid.
(5) Commissions unpaid at July 31, Year 3, are $340. All salaries have been paid. The balance in the Salaries and Commissions Payable account represents the amount of commissions unpaid at July 1.
(6) Merchandise with a sales price of $350 was recently delivered to a customer, and charged to Accounts Receivable, although the customer had paid $350 in advance.
(7) The balance in the Prepaid Insurance account relates to a 3-year policy that went into effect on January 1, Year 3.
(8) A dividend of $3,000 was declared on July 31, Year 3.
(9) The inventory of merchandise on July 31, Year 3, was $33,600.
Present adjusting journal entries at July 31, Year 3. Use only ⸏e accounts listed in the trial balance.

46. *Preparation of closing entries.* The adjusted trial balance of Life Photographers, Inc., at June 30, Year 2, is presented in Exhibit 3.11.
   a. Present the journal entries to close the revenue and expense accounts directly to Retained Earnings as of June 30, Year 2.
   b. Set up in T-account form the revenue, expense, and retained earnings accounts. Insert the trial balance amounts and record the closing entries from part **a**.

47. *Working backwards to balance sheet at beginning of period.* (Problems **47** through **49** are adapted from problems by George H. Sorter.) The following data relate to the Prima Company:

(1) Post-closing trial balance at December 31, Year 2.

Exhibit 3.11
LIFE PHOTOGRAPHERS, INC.
Adjusted Trial Balance
June 30, Year 2
(Problem 46)

Accounts Payable		$ 3,641
Accounts Receivable	$ 3,900	
Accumulated Depreciation		1,995
Advertising Expense	1,500	
Cameras and Equipment	15,500	
Cash	2,994	
Common Stock		10,000
Depreciation Expense—Cameras and Equipment	180	
Depreciation Expense—Furniture and Fixtures	105	
Electricity Expense	300	
Equipment Repairs Expense	180	
Furniture and Fixtures	9,600	
Insurance Expense	330	
Photographic Supplies Expense	1,950	
Photographic Supplies on Hand	3,390	
Prepaid Insurance	270	
Rent Expense	1,425	
Retained Earnings		14,138
Revenue—Commercial Photography		18,090
Revenue—Printing Service		4,680
Salaries Expense	10,800	
Telephone Expense	120	
	$52,544	$52,544

(Problem 47 continued.)

Debits

Cash	$ 10,000
Marketable Securities	20,000
Accounts Receivable	25,000
Merchandise Inventory	30,000
Prepayments for Miscellaneous Services	3,000
Land, Buildings, and Equipment	40,000
Total Debits	$128,000

Credits

Accounts Payable (for merchandise)	$ 25,000
Interest Payable	300
Taxes Payable	4,000
Notes Payable (6 percent, long-term)	20,000
Accumulated Depreciation	16,000
Capital Stock	50,000
Retained Earnings	12,700
Total Credits	$128,000

(2) Income and retained earnings data for Year 2:

Sales		$200,000
Less Expenses:		
Cost of Goods Sold	$130,000	
Depreciation Expense	4,000	
Taxes Expense	8,000	
Other Operating Expenses	47,700	
Interest Expense	1,200	
Total Expenses		190,900
Net Income		$ 9,100
Less Dividends		5,000
Increase in Retained Earnings		$ 4,100

(3) Summary of cash receipts and disbursements in Year 2:

Cash Receipts

Cash Sales	$ 47,000	
Collection from Credit Customers	150,000	
Total Receipts		$197,000

Cash Disbursements

Payment to Suppliers of Merchandise	$128,000	
Payment to Suppliers of Miscellaneous Services	49,000	
Payment of Taxes	7,500	
Payment of Interest	1,200	
Payment of Dividends	5,000	
Purchase of Marketable Securities	8,000	
Total Disbursements		198,700
Excess of Disbursements over Receipts		$ 1,700

(4) Purchases of merchandise during the period, all on account, were $127,000. All "Other Operating Expenses" were credited to Prepayments.

Prepare a balance sheet for January 1, Year 2. (*Hint:* Set up T-accounts for each of the accounts in the trial balance and enter the *ending* balances in the T-accounts. Starting with information from the income statement and statement of cash receipts and disbursements, reconstruct the transactions that took place during the year and enter the amounts in the appropriate T-accounts.)

48. *Working backwards to cash receipts and disbursements.* The Secunda Company's trial balance at the beginning of Year 2 and the adjusted, preclosing trial balance at the end of Year 2 are presented below.

	1/1/Year 2	12/31/Year 2
Debits		
Cash	$ 20,000	$ 9,000
Accounts Receivable	36,000	51,000
Merchandise Inventory	45,000	60,000
Prepayments	2,000	1,000
Land, Buildings, and Equipment	40,000	40,000
Cost of Goods Sold	—	50,000
Interest Expense	—	3,000
Other Operating Expenses	—	29,000
Total Debits	$143,000	$243,000
Credits		
Accumulated Depreciation	$ 16,000	$ 18,000
Interest Payable	1,000	2,000
Accounts Payable	30,000	40,000
Mortgage Payable	20,000	17,000
Capital Stock	50,000	50,000
Retained Earnings	26,000	16,000
Sales	—	100,000
Total Credits	$143,000	$243,000

All goods and services acquired during the year were purchased on account. The Other Operating Expenses account includes depreciation charges and expirations of prepayments. Dividends declared during the year were debited to Retained Earnings.

Prepare a schedule showing all cash transactions for Year 2. (*Hint:* Set up T-accounts for each of the accounts listed in the trial balance and enter the amounts shown as of January 1, Year 2, and December 31, Year 2. Starting with the entries in revenue and expense accounts, reconstruct the transactions that took place during the year and enter the amounts in the appropriate T-accounts. The effect of earnings activities is not yet reflected in the Retained Earnings account because the trial balance is preclosing.)

49. *Working backwards to income statement.* Tertia Company presents the following incomplete post-closing trial balances, as well as a statement of cash receipts and disbursements:

	1/1/Year 2	12/31/Year 2
Debits		
Cash	$?	$?
Accounts and Notes Receivable	36,000	41,000
Merchandise Inventory	55,000	49,500

Interest Receivable	1,000	700
Prepaid Miscellaneous Services	4,000	5,200
Building, Machinery, and Equipment	47,000	47,000
Total Debits	$?	$?

Credits

Accounts Payable (miscellaneous services)	$ 2,000	$ 2,500
Accounts Payable (merchandise)	34,000	41,000
Property Taxes Payable	1,000	1,500
Accumulated Depreciation	10,000	12,000
Mortgage Payable	35,000	30,000
Capital Stock	25,000	25,000
Retained Earnings	76,000	?
Total Credits	$183,000	$211,200

	Year 2

Cash Receipts

1. Collection from Credit Customers	$144,000
2. Cash Sales	63,000
3. Collection of Interest	1,000
	$208,000

Less: Cash Disbursements

4. Payment to Suppliers of Merchandise	$114,000
5. Repayment on Mortgage	5,000
6. Payment of Interest	500
7. Prepayment to Suppliers of Miscellaneous Services . . .	57,500
8. Payment of Property Taxes	1,200
9. Payment of Dividends	2,000
	$180,200
Increase in Cash Balance for Year	$ 27,800

Prepare a combined statement of income and retained earnings for Year 2. (*Hint:* Set up T-accounts for each of the balance sheet accounts listed in the trial balance and enter the amounts shown as of January 1, Year 2, and December 31, Year 2. Starting with the cash receipts and disbursements for the year, reconstruct the transactions that took place during the year and enter them in the appropriate T-accounts. The effect of earnings activities for the year is already reflected in the Retained Earnings account, because the trial balance shown is post-closing.)

50. *Analyses of General Products Company.* Refer to the Consolidated Statements of Income and Retained Earnings for General Products Company in Appendix A at the back of the book. Prepare a common-size (see Glossary) income statement for each of the years 1983, 1984, and 1985 in which each income statement account is expressed as a percentage of sales revenue (that is, sales revenue equals 100 percent). What changes in the profitability of General Products Company can be observed over this 3-year period?

Chapter 4   Income Statement: Extensions of the Accrual Concept

Chapter 3 points out that most business firms use an accrual, rather than a cash, basis of accounting. The two distinguishing features of the accrual basis are the following:

1. Revenue is recognized when all, or a substantial portion, of the services to be provided have been performed and cash, a receivable, or some other asset whose cash equivalent value can be measured objectively, has been received.
2. Expenses are recognized in the period when related revenues are recognized or, if not associated with a particular revenue stream, expenses are recognized in the period when goods or services are consumed in operations.

For most merchandising firms, revenue is recognized in the period when goods are sold. Expenses are then matched either directly with the revenue or with the period when goods or services are consumed. This chapter explores the application of the accrual concept to other types of businesses: firms involved in manufacturing, firms involved in long-term contract activities, and firms selling goods on an installment basis.

Accrual Basis for Manufacturers

A manufacturing firm incurs various costs in changing the physical form of the goods it produces. Figure 4.1 depicts the operating process for a typical manufacturing firm. A firm acquires productive facilities (plant and equipment) to provide capacity to manufacture goods. Raw materials for use in production are also acquired. Converting raw materials into a salable product requires labor and other manufacturing services (for example, utilities, insurance, taxes, and depreciation on production facilities) during the period of production. The finished product is held in inventory until sold. When the good is sold, either cash is collected or a receivable from the customer arises.

Most manufacturing firms recognize revenue at the time goods are sold. At this time, the production activity has been completed, a customer has been identified and a selling price agreed upon, and an assessment of the customer's credit standing provides a reasonable basis for estimating the amount of cash that will be collected.

Accounting for Manufacturing Costs

As Chapter 3 points out, a merchandising firm acquires inventory items in finished form ready for sale. The acquisition cost of these items remains in the asset account, Merchandise Inventory, until the units are sold. At the time of sale, the cost of the

Period of Production

Figure 4.1 Operating Process for Manufacturing Firm

items sold is transferred from the asset account, Merchandise Inventory, to the expense account, Cost of Goods Sold.

A manufacturing firm, in contrast, incurs various costs in transforming raw materials into finished products. These manufacturing costs are generally classified into direct material (or raw material), direct labor, and manufacturing overhead. Manufacturing overhead includes a variety of indirect costs that provide a firm with productive capacity (depreciation, insurance, and taxes on manufacturing facilities, supervisory labor, and supplies for factory equipment). Until the units are sold and revenue is recognized, manufacturing costs are treated as product costs—assets— and accumulated in various inventory accounts.

A manufacturing firm, like a merchandising firm, also incurs various selling costs (commissions for the sales staff, depreciation, insurance and taxes on the sales staff's automobiles) and administrative costs (salary of president, depreciation on computer facilities). Selling and administrative costs are treated as period expenses by both merchandising and manufacturing firms. Figure 4.2 summarizes the nature and flow of various costs for a manufacturing firm.

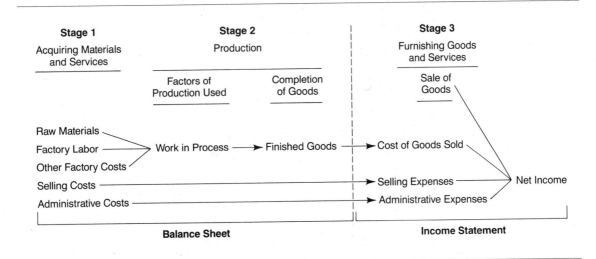

Figure 4.2 Diagram of Cost Flows

Figure 4.3 Flow of Manufacturing Costs through the Accounts

Raw Materials Inventory (A)

Cost of Raw Materials Purchased | Raw Materials Costs Incurred in Manufacturing

Cash (A) or Wages Payable (L)

| Direct Labor Costs Incurred in Manufacturing

Cash (A), Accumulated Depreciation (XA), Other Accounts

| Overhead Costs Incurred in Manufacturing

Work-In-Process Inventory (A)

→ Raw Materials Costs Incurred in Manufacturing | Manufacturing Cost of Units Completed and Transferred to Storeroom

→ Direct Labor Costs Incurred in Manufacturing

→ Overhead Costs Incurred in Manufacturing

Finished Goods Inventory (A)

→ Manufacturing Cost of Units Transferred from Factory | Manufacturing Cost of Units Sold

Cost of Goods Sold (SE)

→ Manufacturing Cost of Units Sold

Separate inventory accounts are maintained by a manufacturing firm for product costs incurred at various stages of completion. The Raw Materials Inventory account includes the cost of raw materials purchased but not yet transferred to production. The balance in the Raw Materials Inventory account indicates the cost of raw materials on hand in the raw materials storeroom or warehouse. When raw materials are issued to producing departments, the cost of the materials is transferred from the Raw Materials Inventory account to the Work-in-Process Inventory account. The Work-in-Process Inventory account accumulates the costs incurred in producing units during the period. The Work-in-Process Inventory account is debited for the cost of raw materials transferred from the raw materials storeroom, the cost of direct labor services used, and the manufacturing overhead costs incurred. The Work-in-Process Inventory account is credited for the total manufacturing cost of units completed in the factory and transferred to the finished goods storeroom. The Finished Goods Inventory account includes the total manufacturing cost of units completed but not yet sold. The cost of units sold during the period is transferred from the Finished Goods Inventory account to the Cost-of-Goods-Sold account. Figure 4.3 shows the flow of manufacturing costs through the various inventory and other accounts.

Illustration of the Accounting Process for a Manufacturing Firm

The accounting process for a manufacturing firm is illustrated with information about the operations of the Moon Manufacturing Company. The Company was formed on January 1, with the issuance of 10,000 shares of $10-par value common stock for $30 per share. Transactions during January are described below, and the appropriate journal entries are provided.

1. A building costing $200,000 and equipment costing $50,000 are acquired for cash.

(1) Building (A)	200,000	
Equipment (A)	50,000	
Cash (A)		250,000

2. Raw materials costing $25,000 are purchased on account.

(2) Raw Materials Inventory (A)	25,000	
Accounts Payable (L)		25,000

3. Raw materials costing $20,000 are issued to producing departments.

(3) Work-in-Process Inventory (A)	20,000	
Raw Materials Inventory (A)		20,000

4. The total payroll for January is $60,000. Of this amount, $40,000 is paid to factory workers, and $20,000 is paid to selling and administrative personnel.

(4) Work-in-Process Inventory (A)	40,000	
Salaries Expense (SE)	20,000	
Cash (A)		60,000

Recall that nonmanufacturing costs are recorded as expenses of the period in which the services are consumed, because these costs rarely create assets with future benefits. Journal entry (4) [as well as entries (5) and (6) below] illustrates the difference between the recording of a product cost and a period expense.

5. The expenditures for utilities during January are $1,200. Of this amount, $1,000 is attributable to manufacturing, and $200 to selling and administrative activities.

(5) Work-in-Process Inventory (A)	1,000	
Utilities Expense (SE)	200	
Cash (A)		1,200

6. Depreciation on building and equipment during January is as follows: factory, $8,000; selling and administrative, $2,000.

(6) Work-in-Process Inventory (A)	8,000	
Depreciation Expense (SE)	2,000	
Accumulated Depreciation (XA)		10,000

7. The manufacturing cost of units completed during January and transferred to the finished goods storeroom is $48,500.

(7) Finished Goods Inventory (A)	48,500	
Work-in-Process Inventory (A)		48,500

8. Sales during January total $75,000, of which $25,000 is on account.

(8) Cash (A)	50,000	
Accounts Receivable (A)	25,000	
Sales Revenue (SE)		75,000

9. The cost of the goods sold during January is $42,600.

(9) Cost of Goods Sold (SE)	42,600	
Finished Goods Inventory (A)		42,600

Exhibit 4.1 shows how the various manufacturing and other costs incurred flow through the accounts. Exhibit 4.2 presents an income statement for Moon Manufacturing Company for January.

Summary of the Accounting for Manufacturing Operations

The accounting procedures for the selling and administrative costs of manufacturing firms resemble those for merchandising firms. These costs are expenses of the period in which services are consumed. The accounting procedures for a manufacturing firm differ from those of a merchandising firm primarily in the treatment of inventories. A manufacturing firm incurs various costs in transforming raw materials into finished products. Until the units produced are sold, manufacturing costs are accumulated in inventory accounts—the Work-in-Process Inventory account or the Finished Goods Inventory account—depending on the stage of completion of each unit being produced. Product costs are therefore debited to inventory (asset) accounts until the time of sale.

Accrual Basis for Long-Term Contractors

The operating process for a long-term contractor (for example, building construction, shipbuilding) differs from that of a manufacturing firm (depicted in Figure 4.1) in three important respects:

1. The period of construction (production) may span several accounting periods.
2. A customer is identified and a contract price agreed upon in advance (or at least in the early stages of construction).
3. Periodic payments of the contract price are often made by the buyer as work progresses.

The criteria for the recognition of revenue from long-term contracts are often satisfied during the period of construction. The existence of a contract indicates that a buyer has been identified and a price agreed upon. Either cash is collected in advance or an assessment of the customer's credit standing leads to a reasonable expectation that the contract price will be received in cash after construction is completed. Although future services required on these long-term construction contracts can be substantial at any given time, the costs to be incurred in providing these services can often be estimated with reasonable precision. In agreeing to a

Exhibit 4.1
MOON MANUFACTURING COMPANY
T-Accounts Showing Transactions During January

Raw Materials Inventory (A)	
(2) 25,000	20,000 (3))
Bal. 1/31 5,000	

Work-in-Process Inventory (A)	
→(3) 20,000	48,500 (7))
(4) 40,000	
(5) 1,000	
(6) 8,000	
Bal. 1/31 20,500	

Finished Goods Inventory (A)	
→(7) 48,500	42,600 (9))
Bal. 1/31 5,900	

Cost of Goods Sold (SE)	
→(9) 42,600	
Bal. 1/31 42,600	

Cash (A)	
Bal. 1/1 300,000	250,000 (1)
(8) 50,000	60,000 (4)
	1,200 (5)
Bal. 1/31 38,800	

Accounts Receivable (A)	
(8) 25,000	
Bal. 1/31 25,000	

Building (A)	
(1) 200,000	
Bal. 1/31 200,000	

Equipment (A)	
(1) 50,000	
Bal. 1/31 50,000	

Accumulated Depreciation (XA)	
	10,000 (6)
	10,000 Bal. 1/31

Salaries Expense (SE)	
(4) 20,000	
Bal. 1/31 20,000	

Sales Revenue (SE)	
	75,000 (8)
	75,000 Bal. 1/31

Accounts Payable (L)	
	25,000 (2)
	25,000 Bal. 1/31

Utilities Expense (SE)	
(5) 200	
Bal. 1/31 200	

Depreciation Expense (SE)	
(6) 2,000	
Bal. 1/31 2,000	

Exhibit 4.2
MOON MANUFACTURING COMPANY
Income Statement for the Month of January

Sales Revenue		$75,000
Less Expenses:		
Cost of Goods Sold	$42,600	
Salaries Expense	20,000	
Utilities Expense	200	
Depreciation Expense	2,000	
Total Expenses		64,800
Net Income		$10,200

contract price, the firm must have some confidence in its estimates of the total costs to be incurred on the contract.

When the criteria for revenue recognition are met as construction progresses, revenue is usually recognized during the period of construction using the *percentage-of-completion method*. Under the percentage-of-completion method, a portion of the total contract price, based on the degree of completion of the work during the period, is recognized as revenue for the period. This proportion is based either on engineers' or architects' estimates of the degree of completion or on the ratio of costs incurred to date to the total expected costs for the contract. The actual schedule of cash collections is *not* significant for the revenue recognition process when the percentage-of-completion method is used. Even if all of the contract price is collected at completion of construction, the percentage-of-completion method may still be used as long as reasonable estimates of the amount of cash to be collected and of the costs remaining to be incurred can be made as construction progresses.

As portions of the contract price are recognized as revenues, corresponding proportions of the total estimated costs of the contract are recognized as expenses. Thus, the percentage-of-completion method follows the accrual basis of accounting, because expenses are matched with related revenues.

To illustrate the percentage-of-completion method, assume that a firm agrees to construct a bridge for $5,000,000. Estimated costs are as follows: Year 1, $1,500,000; Year 2, $2,000,000; Year 3, $500,000. Thus, the expected profit from the contract is $1,000,000 (= $5,000,000 − $1,500,000 − $2,000,000 − $500,000).

Assuming that the degree of completion is based on the percentage of total costs incurred and that actual costs are incurred as anticipated, revenue and expense from the contract are as follows:

Year	Degree of Completion	Revenue	Expense	Profit
1	$1,500,000/$4,000,000 = 37.5%	$1,875,000	$1,500,000	$ 375,000
2	$2,000,000/$4,000,000 = 50.0%	2,500,000	2,000,000	500,000
3	$500,000/$4,000,000 = 12.5%	625,000	500,000	125,000
		$5,000,000	$4,000,000	$1,000,000

Some firms involved with construction contracts postpone the recognition of revenue until the construction project and the sale are completed. This method is the same as the completed sale basis, but is often referred to as the *completed contract method* of recognizing revenue. If the completed contract method were used in the example above, no revenue or expense from the contract would be recognized during Year 1 or Year 2. In Year 3, contract revenue of $5,000,000 and contract expenses of $4,000,000 would be recognized in measuring net income.

In some cases, the completed contract method is used because the contracts are of such short duration (such as a few months) that earnings reported with the percentage-of-completion method and the completed contract method are not significantly different. In these cases, the completed contract method is used because it is generally easier to implement. Firms use the completed contract method in situations when a specific buyer has not been obtained during the periods while construction is progressing, as is sometimes the case in constructing residential housing. In these cases, future selling efforts are required and substantial uncertainty may exist regarding the contract price ultimately to be established and the amount of cash to be received.

The primary reason for a contractor's not using the percentage-of-completion method when a contract exists is the uncertainty of total costs to be incurred in carrying out the project. If total costs cannot be reasonably estimated, the percentage of total costs incurred by a given date also cannot be estimated, and the percentage of services already rendered (revenue) cannot be measured.

Accrual Basis When Cash Collectibility Is Extremely Uncertain

Occasionally, estimating the amount of cash or cash equivalent value of other assets that will be received from customers is difficult. This may occur because the future financial condition of the buyer is highly uncertain. Therefore, an objective measure of the present value of the cash to be received cannot be made at the time of the sale. Under these circumstances, revenue is recognized at the time of cash collection using either the installment method or the cost-recovery-first method. Unlike the cash method of accounting, however, there is an attempt to match expenses with revenues.

Installment Method

Under the installment method, revenue is recognized as parts of the selling price are collected in cash. At the same time, corresponding parts of the cost of the good or service sold are recognized as expenses. For example, assume that merchandise costing $60 is sold for $100. The buyer agrees to pay (ignoring interest) $20 per month for 5 months. Under the installment method, revenue of $20 is recognized each month as cash is received. Likewise, cost of goods sold is $12 (= $20/$100 × $60) each month. By the end of 5 months, total income of $40 [= 5 × ($20 − $12)] would be recognized.

The installment method is sometimes used by land development companies. These companies typically sell undeveloped land and promise to develop it over several future years. The buyer makes a nominal down payment and agrees to pay the remainder of the purchase price in installments over 10, 20, or more years. In these cases, future development of the land is a significant aspect of the earnings process. Also, substantial uncertainty often exists as to the ultimate collectibility of the installment notes, particularly those not due until several years in the future. The customer can always elect to stop making payments, merely losing the right to own the land.

Cost-Recovery-First Method

Under circumstances where there is such great uncertainty about cash collection, the *cost-recovery-first method* of income recognition can also be used. Under this method, costs of generating revenues are matched dollar for dollar with cash receipts until all such costs are recovered. Revenues and expenses are equal in each period until all costs are recovered. Only when cumulative cash receipts exceed total costs will profit (that is, revenue without any matching expenses) be shown in the income statement.

To illustrate the cost-recovery-first method, refer to the example above relating to the sale of merchandise for $100. During the first 3 months, revenue of $20 and expenses of $20 would be recognized. By the end of the third month, cumulative cash receipts of $60 would be exactly equal to the cost of the merchandise sold. During the fourth and fifth months, revenue of $20 per month would be recognized but without an offsetting expense. For the 5 months as a whole, total income of $40 would again be recognized, but in a different pattern than under the installment method.

Use of Installment and Cost-Recovery-First Methods

Generally accepted accounting principles permit the installment method and the cost-recovery-first method only when great uncertainty exists about cash collection. For most sales of goods and services, past experience and an assessment of customers' credit standings provide a sufficient basis for estimating the amount of cash to be received. If a reasonable estimate of the amount of cash to be received can be made, the installment method and the cost-recovery-first method are not allowed for financial reporting and revenue must be recognized no later than the time of sale.[1]

The installment method is allowed for income tax reporting under most circumstances, even when cash collections are assured. Retailers and other firms selling on extended payment plans often use the installment method for income tax reporting

---

[1]Accounting Principles Board, *Opinion No. 10,* "Omnibus Opinion—1966," par. 12, footnote 8. When cash collection is sufficiently uncertain that either of these methods is allowed by generally accepted accounting principles, the cost-recovery-first method seems to reflect more accurately the substance of the uncertainty. The installment method assumes that all cash will eventually be received or, if not, then when payments cease, the goods can be repossessed while still having substantial value.

(while recognizing revenue at the time of sale for financial reporting). The cost-recovery-first method is sometimes used in tax reporting, but only in special circumstances, such as for pension benefits received.

Recognition of Revenue Between Purchase and Sale

The period between the acquisition or production of inventory items and the sale of the items to customers is referred to as a *holding period*. The current market prices of these assets could change during this holding period while the items are held in inventory. Such changes are described as *unrealized holding gains and losses,* because a transaction or exchange has not taken place.

Unrealized holding gains could be recognized as they occur. Accountants typically wait, however, until the asset is sold or exchanged in an arm's-length transaction before recognizing any gain. At that time, an inflow of net assets subject to objective measurement takes place. Because the accountant assumes that the firm is a going concern, the unrealized gain will eventually be recognized as revenue in the ordinary course of business in a future period. The recognition of revenue and the valuation of assets are therefore closely associated. Nonmonetary assets are typically stated at acquisition cost until sold. At the time of sale, an inflow of net assets occurs (for example, cash, accounts receivable), and revenue reflecting the previously unreported unrealized gain is recognized. This treatment of unrealized holding gains has the effect of shifting income from periods when the asset is held and the market price increases to the later period of sale. The longer the holding period (as, for example, land held for several decades), the more is reported income likely to be shifted to later periods.

Current accounting practices do not treat all unrealized holding losses in the same way as unrealized holding gains. If the current market prices of inventory items or marketable securities decrease below acquisition cost during the holding period, the asset is usually written down with a credit to the asset account. The matching debit recognizes the unrealized loss in the period of price decline. This treatment of losses rests on the convention that earnings should be reported conservatively. Considering the estimates and predictions required in measuring revenues and expenses, some accountants prefer to provide a conservative measure of earnings so that statement users will not be misled into thinking the firm is doing better than it really is.

The inconsistent treatment of unrealized gains and unrealized losses does not seem warranted. The arguments used against recognizing unrealized gains apply equally well to unrealized losses. If gains cannot be measured objectively prior to sale, then how can losses be measured prior to sale? If losses can be measured objectively prior to sale, then why cannot gains? The accounting treatment of unrealized holding gains and losses is considered further in Chapters 7, 8, and 13.

Summary Illustration of Income Recognition Methods

Exhibit 4.3 illustrates various methods of income recognition discussed in Chapters 3 and 4. The illustration relates to a contract for the construction of a bridge for

Exhibit 4.3
Comprehensive Illustration of
Revenue and Expense Recognition
(all dollar amounts in thousands)

Period	Cash Basis of Accounting[a]		
	Revenue	Expense	Income
1	$ 1,000	$1,600	$ (600)
2	1,000	4,000	(3,000)
3	2,000	4,000	(2,000)
4	4,000	—	4,000
5	4,000	—	4,000
Total	$12,000	$9,600	$2,400

Period	Percentage-of-Completion Method			Completed Contract Method		
	Revenue	Expense	Income	Revenue	Expense	Income
1	$ 2,000[d]	$1,600	$ 400	$ —	$ —	$ —
2	5,000[e]	4,000	1,000	—	—	—
3	5,000[e]	4,000	1,000	12,000	9,600	2,400
4	—	—	—	—	—	—
5	—	—	—	—	—	—
Total	$12,000	$9,600	$2,400	$12,000	$9,600	$2,400

Period	Installment Method[b]			Cost-Recovery-First Method[c]		
	Revenue	Expense	Income	Revenue	Expense	Income
1	$ 1,000	$ 800[f]	$ 200	$ 1,000	$1,000	$ 0
2	1,000	800[f]	200	1,000	1,000	0
3	2,000	1,600[g]	400	2,000	2,000	0
4	4,000	3,200[h]	800	4,000	4,000	0
5	4,000	3,200[h]	800	4,000	1,600	2,400
Total	$12,000	$9,600	$2,400	$12,000	$9,600	$2,400

[a]The cash basis is not allowed for tax or financial reporting if inventories are a material factor in generating income.

[b]The installment method is allowed for financial reporting only if extreme uncertainty exists as to the amount of cash to be collected from customers. Its use for tax purposes is independent of the collectibility of cash.

[c]The cost-recovery-first method is allowed for financial reporting only if extreme uncertainty exists as to the amount of cash to be collected from customers. It is sometimes used for tax purposes.

[d]$1,600/$9,600 × $12,000.

[e]$4,000/$9,600 × $12,000.

[f]$1,000/$12,000 × $9,600.

[g]$2,000/$12,000 × $9,600.

[h]$4,000/$12,000 × $9,600.

$12 million. The expected and actual pattern of cash receipts and disbursements under the contract is as follows:

Period	Expected and Actual Cash Receipts	Expected and Actual Cash Expenditures
1	$ 1,000,000	$1,600,000
2	1,000,000	4,000,000
3	2,000,000	4,000,000
4	4,000,000	—
5	4,000,000	—
Total	$12,000,000	$9,600,000

The bridge was completed in period 3. Exhibit 4.3 indicates the revenues, expenses, and income recognized each period under the contract using the cash basis of accounting, the percentage-of-completion method, the completed contract (completed sale) method, the installment method, and the cost-recovery-first method. Not all five methods of income recognition could be justified for financial reporting. They are presented merely for illustrative purposes. Note that the total revenues, expenses, and income recognized for the 5 years are the same for all methods. In historical cost accounting over long enough time periods, income is equal to cash inflows less cash outflows. The patterns of annual income significantly differ, however, depending on the accounting method.

Format and Classification Within the Income Statement

The income statement might contain some or all of the following sections or categories, depending on the nature of the firm's income for the period:

1. Income from continuing operations.
2. Income, gains, and losses from discontinued operations.
3. Adjustments for changes in accounting principles.
4. Extraordinary gains and losses.
5. Earnings per share.

The great majority of income statements include only the first and fifth sections. The other sections are added if necessary.

Income from Continuing Operations   Revenues, gains, expenses, and losses from the continuing areas of business activity of a firm appear in the first section of the income statement.

Income, Gains, and Losses from Discontinued Operations   If a firm sells a major division or segment of its business during the year or contemplates its sale within a short time after the end of the accounting period, any income, gains, and losses related to that segment must be disclosed separately from ordinary, continuing operations in a section of the income statement entitled "Income, Gains, and Losses from Discontinued Operations."[2] This section follows the section presenting Income from Continuing Operations.

Adjustments for Changes in Accounting Principles   A firm that changes its principles, or methods, of accounting during the period is required in some cases to disclose the effects of the change on current and prior years' net income.[3] This information is presented in a separate section, after Income, Gains, and Losses from Discontinued Operations.

Extraordinary Gains and Losses   Extraordinary gains and losses are presented in a separate section of the income statement. For an item to be extraordinary, it must generally meet both of the following criteria:

1. Unusual in nature.
2. Infrequent in occurrence.[4]

An example of an item likely to be extraordinary for most firms would be a loss from expropriation or confiscation of assets by a foreign government. Such items are likely to be rare. Since 1973, when Accounting Principles Board *Opinion No. 30* was issued, extraordinary items have seldom been seen in published annual reports (except for gains or losses on bond retirements,[5] which are discussed in Chapter 10).

Earnings per Share   Earnings-per-share data must be shown in the body of the income statement by publicly held firms in order to receive an unqualified accountant's opinion.[6] Earnings per common share is conventionally calculated by dividing net income minus preferred stock dividends by the average number of outstanding common shares during the accounting period. For example, assume that a firm had net income of $500,000 during the year. Dividends declared and paid on outstanding preferred stock were $100,000. The average number of shares of outstanding common stock during the year was 1 million shares. Earnings per common share would be $.40 [= ($500,000 − $100,000)/1,000,000].

If a firm has securities outstanding that can be converted into common stock (for example, convertible bonds) or exchanged for common stock (for example, stock options), it may be required to present two sets of earnings-per-share amounts: primary earnings per share and fully diluted earnings per share.[7] Chapter 6 discusses the calculation of primary and fully diluted earnings per share.

---

[2]Accounting Principles Board, *Opinion No. 30,* "Reporting the Results of Operations," 1973.
[3]Accounting Principles Board, *Opinion No. 20,* "Accounting Changes," 1971.
[4]Accounting Principles Board, *Opinion No. 30.*
[5]Financial Accounting Standards Board, *Statement of Financial Accounting Standards No. 4,* "Reporting Gains and Losses from Extinguishment of Debt," 1975.
[6]Accounting Principles Board, *Opinion No. 15,* "Earnings per Share," 1969.
[7]Accounting Principles Board, *Opinion No. 15.*

Problem 1 for Self-Study

The following data relate to the manufacturing activities of the Haskell Corporation during March.

	March 1	March 31
Raw Materials Inventory	$42,400	$ 46,900
Work-in-Process Inventory	75,800	63,200
Finished Goods Inventory	44,200	46,300
Factory Costs Incurred During the Month:		
Raw Materials Purchased		$ 60,700
Labor Services Received		137,900
Heat, Light, and Power		1,260
Rent		4,100
Expirations of Previous Factory Acquisitions and Prepayments:		
Depreciation of Factory Equipment		$ 1,800
Prepaid Insurance Expired		1,440
Other Data Relating to the Month:		
Sales		$400,000
Selling and Administrative Expenses		125,000

a. Calculate the cost of raw materials used during March.
b. Calculate the cost of units completed during March and transferred to the finished goods storeroom.
c. Calculate the cost of goods sold during March.
d. Calculate income before taxes for March.

Suggested Solution

The transactions and events relating to manufacturing activities are shown in the appropriate T-accounts in Exhibit 4.4.
a. The cost of raw materials used is $56,200.
b. The cost of units completed during March is $215,300.
c. The cost of units sold during March is $213,200.
d. Income before taxes is $61,800 (= $400,000 − $213,200 − $125,000).

Problem 2 for Self-Study

The Brennan Construction Company contracted on May 15, Year 2, to build a bridge for the city for $4,500,000. Brennan estimated the cost of constructing the bridge would be $3,600,000. Brennan incurred $1,200,000 in construction costs during Year 2, $2,000,000 during Year 3, and $400,000 during Year 4 in completing the bridge. The city paid $1,000,000 during Year 2, $1,500,000 during Year 3,

Exhibit 4.4
T-Accounts and Transactions
for Haskell Corporation

Raw Materials Inventory			
Bal.	42,400		
(1)	60,700	56,200	(2)ᵃ
Bal.	46,900		

Work-in-Process Inventory			
Bal.	75,800		
(2)	56,200	215,300	(8)ᵃ
(3)	137,900		
(4)	1,260		
(5)	4,100		
(6)	1,800		
(7)	1,440		
Bal.	63,200		

Finished Goods Inventory			
Bal.	44,200		
(8)	215,300	213,200	(9)ᵃ
Bal.	46,300		

Cost of Goods Sold	
(9)	213,200

Cash or Various Liabilities		
	60,700	(1)
	137,900	(3)
	1,260	(4)
	4,100	(5)

Prepaid Insurance	
1,440	(7)

Accumulated Depreciation	
1,800	(6)

ᵃAmounts calculated by plugging.

and the remaining $2,000,000 of the contract price at the time the bridge was completed and approved in Year 4.

a. Calculate the net income (revenue less expenses) of Brennan on the contract during Year 2, Year 3, and Year 4, assuming that the percentage-of-completion method is used.

b. Repeat part **a**, assuming that the completed contract method is used.

c. Repeat part **a**, assuming that the installment method is used.

d. Repeat part **a**, assuming that the cost-recovery-first method is used.

Suggested Solution

a. Percentage-of-completion method:

Year	Incremental Percentage Complete	Revenue Recognized	Expenses Recognized	Net Income
2	12/36 (.333)	$1,500,000	$1,200,000	$300,000
3	20/36 (.556)	2,500,000	2,000,000	500,000
4	4/36 (.111)	500,000	400,000	100,000
Total	36/36 (1.000)	$4,500,000	$3,600,000	$900,000

b. Completed contract method:

Year	Revenue Recognized	Expenses Recognized	Net Income
2	\$ 0	\$ 0	\$ 0
3	0	0	0
4	4,500,000	3,600,000	900,000
Total	\$4,500,000	\$3,600,000	\$900,000

c. Installment method:

Year	Cash Collected (= revenue)	Fraction of Cash Collected	Expenses (= fraction × total cost)	Net Income
2	\$1,000,000	2/9	\$ 800,000	\$200,000
3	1,500,000	3/9	1,200,000	300,000
4	2,000,000	4/9	1,600,000	400,000
Total	\$4,500,000	1.0	\$3,600,000	\$900,000

d. Cost-recovery-first method:

Year	Cash Collected (= revenue)	Expenses Recognized	Net Income
2	\$1,000,000	\$1,000,000	\$ 0
3	1,500,000	1,500,000	0
4	2,000,000	1,100,000	900,000
Total	\$4,500,000	\$3,600,000	\$900,000

Questions, Exercises, Problems and Cases

Questions

1. Review the meaning of the following concepts or terms discussed in this chapter.

a. Product cost.
b. Period expense.
c. Direct material.
d. Direct labor.
e. Manufacturing overhead.
f. "Flow of costs."
g. Raw materials inventory.
h. Work-in-process inventory.
i. Finished goods inventory.
j. Percentage-of-completion method.
k. Completed sales, or completed contract, method.
l. Installment method.
m. Cost-recovery-first method.
n. Unrealized holding gain or loss.

o. Conservatism.

p. Income from continuing operations.

q. Income, gains, and losses from discontinued operations.

r. Adjustments for changes in accounting principles.

s. Extraordinary gains and losses.

t. Primary earnings per share.

u. Fully diluted earnings per share.

2. "Depreciation on equipment may be a product cost or a period expense, depending on the type of equipment." Explain.

3. Compare and contrast the Merchandise Inventory account of a merchandising firm and the Finished Goods Inventory account of a manufacturing firm.

4. The percentage-of-completion method is often used by construction companies. Why isn't this method of income recognition used by a typical manufacturing firm?

5. Under both the installment method and the cost-recovery-first method, revenue is recognized when cash is received. Why, then, is the pattern of income (that is, revenues minus expenses) over time different under these two methods?

6. Compare and contrast the installment method and the cash basis of accounting.

7. "When the *total* amount of cash to be collected from a customer is highly uncertain, the cost-recovery-first method seems more appropriate than the installment method." Explain.

8. Economists typically define income as an increase in value, or wealth, while assets are held. Accountants typically recognize income when the criteria for revenue recognition are satisfied. Why does the accountants' approach to income recognition differ from that of the economists?

9. Why do income statements separate income relating to continuing operations from income relating to discontinued operations?

Exercises

10. *Identifying product costs and period expenses.* Indicate whether each of the following types of wages and salaries are (1) product costs or (2) period expenses:

a. Cutting-machine operators.

b. Delivery labor.

c. Factory janitors.

d. Factory payroll clerks.

e. Factory superintendent.

f. General office secretaries.

g. Guards at factory gate.

h. Inspectors in factory.

i. Maintenance workers who service factory machinery.

j. Nightwatch force at the factory.

k. General office clerks.

l. Operator of a lift truck in the shipping room.

m. President of the firm.

n. Sales manager.

o. Shipping room workers.

p. Sweepers who clean retail store.

q. Traveling salespersons.

11. *Identifying product costs and period expenses.* Indicate whether each of the following types of materials and supplies are (1) product costs or (2) period expenses:

a. Cleaning lubricants for factory machines.
b. Paper for central office computer.
c. Glue used in assembling products.
d. Supplies used by factory janitor.
e. Gasoline used by salespersons.
f. Sales promotion pamphlets distributed.
g. Materials used in training production workers.

12. *Identifying product costs, period expenses, and assets.* Indicate whether each of the following costs are (1) period expenses, (2) product costs, or (3) some balance sheet account other than those for product costs.
a. Office supplies used.
b. Salary of factory supervisor.
c. Purchase of a fire insurance policy on the store building for the 3-year period beginning next month.
d. Expiration of 1 month's protection of the insurance in **c**.
e. Property taxes for the current year on the factory building.
f. Wages of truck drivers who deliver finished goods to customers.
g. Wages of factory workers who install a new machine.
h. Wages of mechanics who repair and service factory machines.
i. Salary of the president of the company.
j. Depreciation of office equipment.
k. Factory supplies used.

13. *Raw materials inventory transactions.* Compute the missing item in each of the independent cases below.

	a	b	c	d
Raw Materials Inventory, Jan. 1	$ 15,000	$ 76,900	$ 28,700	?
Purchases of Raw Materials	$297,000	$696,000	?	$76,700
Raw Materials Used	$290,000	?	$467,300	$71,700
Raw Materials Inventory, Dec. 31	?	$ 72,100	$ 37,900	$12,300

14. *Work-in-process inventory transactions.* Compute the missing item in each of the independent cases below.

	a	b	c	d
Work-in-Process Inventory, Jan. 1 . . .	$ 26,000	$ 55,600	$ 39,400	?
Raw Materials Used	$290,000	$700,800	$ 467,300	$ 71,700
Direct Labor Costs.	$260,000	$675,800	?	$ 87,300
Manufacturing Overhead Costs . . .	$180,000	$267,900	$ 136,900	$ 42,900
Cost of Units Completed	$724,000	?	$1,206,600	$193,400
Work-in-Process Inventory, Dec. 31 . .	?	$ 72,300	$ 35,900	$ 41,700

15. *Finished goods inventory transactions.* Compute the missing item in each of the independent cases below.

	a	b	c	d
Finished Goods Inventory, Jan. 1 . .	$ 71,000	$ 189,300	$ 110,300	?
Cost of Units Completed	$724,000	$1,627,800	?	$193,400
Costs of Units Sold	$701,000	?	$1,197,900	$187,200
Finished Goods Inventory, Dec. 31 .	?	$ 179,600	$ 119,000	$ 22,100

16. *Income computation for a manufacturing firm.* The following data relate to a manufacturing firm for a period:

Sales	$250,000
Cost of Units Completed	240,000
Cost of Units Sold	210,000
Selling and Administrative Expenses	30,000

Compute net income for the period.

17. *Income computation for a manufacturing firm.* The following data relate to the United Manufacturing Corporation for the month of April.

	April 1	April 30
Raw Materials Inventory	0	$10,000
Work-in-Process Inventory	0	25,000
Finished Goods Inventory	0	22,000

Manufacturing costs (direct material used, direct labor, manufacturing overhead) incurred during April totaled $65,000. Sales revenue for April was $25,000 and selling and administrative expenses were $2,000.

Compute net income for April.

18. *Percentage-of-completion and completed contract methods of income recognition.* A construction company agreed to build a warehouse for $2,500,000. Expected and actual costs to construct the warehouse were as follows: Year 1, $600,000; Year 2, $1,000,000; Year 3, $400,000. The warehouse was completed in Year 3.

Compute revenue, expense, and net income for Year 1, Year 2, and Year 3 using the percentage-of-completion method and the completed contract method.

19. *Installment and cost-recovery-first methods of income recognition.* A real estate firm sold a tract of land costing $80,000 to a manufacturing firm for $100,000. The manufacturing firm agreed to pay $25,000 per year for 4 years (plus interest).

Compute revenue, expense, and net income for each of the 4 years using the installment method and the cost-recovery-first method. Ignore interest.

Problems and Cases

20. *Preparation of journal entries and income statement for a manufacturing firm.* Westside Products showed the following amounts in its inventory accounts on January 1.

Raw Materials Inventory	$15,000
Work-in-Process Inventory	65,000
Finished Goods Inventory	32,000

The following transactions occurred during January:

(1) Raw materials costing $28,500 were acquired on account.
(2) Raw materials costing $31,600 were issued to producing departments.
(3) Salaries and wages paid during January for services received during the month were as follows:

Factory Workers	$46,900
Sales Personnel	14,300
Administrative Officers	20,900

(4) Depreciation on buildings and equipment during January were as follows:

Manufacturing Facilities	$12,900
Selling Facilities	2,300
Administrative Facilities	1,800

(5) Other operating costs incurred and paid in cash were as follows:

Manufacturing	$15,600
Selling	4,900
Administrative	3,700

(6) The cost of goods manufactured and transferred to the finished goods storeroom totaled $85,100.

(7) Sales on account during January totaled $150,000.

(8) A physical inventory taken on January 31 revealed a finished goods inventory of $35,200.

    a. Present journal entries to record the transactions and events during January.

    b. Prepare an income statement for Westside Products for January.

21. *Preparation of journal entries and an income statement for a manufacturing firm*. Southside Products showed the following amounts in its inventory accounts on January 1.

Raw Materials Inventory	$40,000
Work-in-Process Inventory	96,000
Finished Goods Inventory	73,000

The following transactions occurred during January.

(1) Raw materials costing $122,700 were acquired on account.

(2) Raw materials costing $119,200 were issued to production.

(3) Salaries and wages paid during January for services received during the month were as follows:

Factory Workers	$87,600
Sales Personnel	18,900
Administrative Personnel	27,400

(4) Depreciation on buildings and equipment during January were as follows:

Manufacturing Facilities	$14,700
Selling Facilities	2,400
Administrative Facilities	2,900

(5) Other operating costs incurred and paid in cash were as follows:

Manufacturing	$18,200
Selling	7,300
Administrative	4,400

(6) The cost of goods completed and transferred to the finished goods storeroom totaled $234,000.

(7) Sales on account during January totaled $325,000.

(8) A physical inventory taken on January 31 revealed a finished goods inventory of $68,000.

a. Present journal entries to record the transactions and events during January.

b. Prepare an income statement for Southside Products for January.

22. *Flow of manufacturing costs through the accounts.* The following data relate to the manufacturing activities of the Cornell Company during June.

	June 1	June 30
Raw Materials Inventory	$ 46,900	$ 43,600
Factory Supplies Inventory	7,600	7,700
Work-in-Process Inventory	110,900	115,200
Finished Goods Inventory.	76,700	71,400

Factory costs incurred during the month:

Raw Materials Purchased	$429,000
Supplies Purchased	22,300
Labor Services Received.	362,100
Heat, Light, and Power	10,300
Insurance	4,200

Expirations of previous factory acquisitions and prepayments:

Depreciation on Factory Equipment	$36,900
Prepaid Rent Expired	3,600

a. Calculate the cost of raw materials and factory supplies used during June.

b. Calculate the cost of units completed during June and transferred to the finished goods storeroom.

c. Calculate the cost of goods sold during June.

23. *Flow of manufacturing costs through the accounts.* The following data relate to the activities of Myers Corporation during April.

	April 1	April 30
Raw Materials Inventory	$18,700	$16,400
Work-in-Process Inventory	66,800	72,400
Finished Goods Inventory.	32,900	29,800

Factory costs incurred during the month:

Raw Materials Purchased	$87,300
Labor Services Received	66,100
Heat, Light, and Power	2,700
Depreciation	15,600

Other data relating to the month:

Sales	$250,000
Selling and Administrative Expenses	38,100

    a. Calculate the cost of raw materials used during April.

    b. Calculate the cost of units completed during April and transferred to the finished goods storeroom.

    c. Calculate net income for April.

24. *Preparing T-account entries, adjusted trial balance, income statement, and balance sheet for a manufacturing firm.* On July 1, the accounts of the Tampa Manufacturing Company contained the following balances:

Debit Balances		Credit Balances	
Cash	$ 110,000	Accumulated Depreciation .	$ 30,000
Accounts Receivable . . .	220,000	Accounts Payable	56,000
Raw Materials Inventory .	80,000	Wages Payable	24,000
Work-in-Process Inventory .	230,000	Capital Stock	1,000,000
Finished Goods Inventory .	170,000	Retained Earnings	200,000
Factory Supplies Inventory .	20,000		
Manufacturing Equipment .	480,000		
Total	$1,310,000	Total	$1,310,000

Transactions for the month of July are listed below in summary form:

    (1) Sales, all on account, were $310,000.

    (2) Labor services furnished by employees during the period (but as yet unpaid) amounted to $80,000. All labor is employed in the factory.

    (3) Factory supplies were purchased for $8,500; payment was made by check.

    (4) Raw materials purchased on account, $100,000.

    (5) Collections from customers, $335,000.

    (6) Payment of $108,000 was made to raw materials suppliers.

    (7) Payments to employees total $78,500.

    (8) Rent of the factory building for the month, $8,000, was paid.

    (9) Depreciation of manufacturing equipment for the month, $12,000.

(10) Other manufacturing costs incurred and paid, $40,000.

(11) All selling and administrative services are furnished by Clark and Company for $10,000 per month. Their bill was paid by check.

(12) Raw materials used during month, $115,000.

(13) Factory supplies used during month, $8,000.

(14) Cost of goods completed during month, $258,000.

(15) Goods costing $261,500 were shipped to customers during the month.

    a. Open T-accounts and record the July 1 amounts. Record transactions **(1)** through **(15)** in the T-accounts, opening additional accounts as needed.

    b. Prepare an adjusted, preclosing trial balance as of July 31.

    c. Prepare a combined statement of income and retained earnings for July.

    d. Enter closing entries in the T-accounts using an Income Summary account.

    e. Prepare a balance sheet as of July 31.

25. *Preparing T-account entries and adjusted trial balance for a manufacturing firm.* Melton Plastics Company was incorporated on September 16. By September 30, the firm was ready to begin operations. The trial balance at that date was as follows:

Cash	$387,200	
Raw Materials Inventory	19,200	
Factory Equipment	136,000	
Accounts Payable		$ 22,400
Capital Stock		520,000
	$542,400	$542,400

The following data relate only to the manufacturing operations of the firm during October:

(1) Materials purchased on account, $161,600.

(2) Wages and salaries earned during the month, $148,000.

(3) Raw materials requisitioned and put into process during the month, $168,800.

(4) Equipment was acquired during the month at a cost of $112,000. A check for $40,000 was issued, and an equipment contract payable in eight equal monthly installments was signed for the remainder.

(5) Additional payments by check:

Raw Materials Suppliers	$140,000
Payrolls	112,420
Building Rent	6,000
Utilities	2,920
Insurance Premiums (for 1 year from October 1)	9,600
Miscellaneous Factory Costs	26,400
	$297,340

(6) Invoices received but unpaid at October 31:

City Water Department.	$ 120
Hoster Machine Supply Company, for additional equipment	2,400

(7) Depreciation on equipment for the month, $1,200.

(8) One month's insurance expiration is recorded.

(9) The cost of parts finished during October was $281,750.

    a. Open T-accounts and enter the amounts from the opening trial balance.

    b. Record the transactions during the month in the T-accounts, opening additional accounts as needed.

    c. Prepare an adjusted trial balance at October 31.

26. *Preparing T-account entries and financial statements for a manufacturing firm.* This problem is a continuation of Problem 25, Melton Plastics Company. In addition to the manufacturing activities described in that problem, the following transactions relating to selling and administrative activities occurred during October.

(10) Sales, on account, $340,600.

(11) Collections from customers, $330,000.

(12) Salaries earned during the month: sales, $30,800; office, $31,200.

(13) Payments by check:

Sales Salaries	$27,630
Office Salaries	27,550
Advertising during October	7,200
Rent of Office and Office Equipment for October	2,200
Office Supplies	1,600
Miscellaneous Office Costs	1,400
Miscellaneous Selling Costs	2,800
Total.	$70,380

(14) The inventory of office supplies on October 31 is $800.

(15) The inventory of finished goods on October 31 is $59,000.

    a. Employing the T-accounts of Problem 25 and additional accounts as needed, record the selling and administrative activities for the month in the T-accounts.

    b. Enter closing entries in the T-accounts, using an Income Summary account.

    c. Prepare a combined statement of income and retained earnings for the month.

    d. Prepare a balance sheet as of October 31.

27. *Income recognition for shipbuilder.* Maine Shipbuilding Company agreed on June 15, Year 2, to construct an oil tanker for Global Petroleum Company. The contract price of $80 million is to be paid as follows: at the time of signing, $8 million; December 31, Year 3, $32 million; at completion on June 30, Year 4, $40 million. Maine Shipbuilding Company incurred the following costs in constructing the tanker: Year 2: $21.6 million; Year 3: $36 million; Year 4: $14.4 million. These amounts conformed to original expectations.

Calculate the amount of revenue, expense, and net income for Year 2, Year 3, and Year 4 under each of the following revenue recognition methods.

    a. Percentage-of-completion method.

    b. Completed contract method.

    c. Installment method.

    d. Cost-recovery-first method.

    e. Which method do you feel provides the best measure of Maine Shipbuilding Company's performance under the contract? Why?

28. *Income recognition for contractor*. The Humbolt Electric Company received a contract late in Year 1 to build a small electricity-generating unit. The contract price was $700,000 and it was estimated that total costs would be $600,000. Estimated and actual construction time was 15 months and it was agreed that payments would be made by the purchaser as follows:

March 31, Year 2	$ 70,000
June 30, Year 2	105,000
September 30, Year 2	203,000
December 31, Year 2	161,000
March 31, Year 3	161,000
	$700,000

Estimated and actual costs of construction incurred by the Humbolt Electric Company were as follows:

January 1–March 31, Year 2	$120,000
April 1–June 30, Year 2	120,000
July 1–September 30, Year 2	180,000
October 1–December 31, Year 2	120,000
January 1–March 31, Year 3	60,000
	$600,000

The Humbolt Electric Company prepares financial statements quarterly at March 31, June 30, and so forth.

Calculate the amount of revenue, expense, and net income for each quarter under each of the following methods of revenue recognition:

    a. Percentage-of-completion method.

    b. Completed contract method.

    c. Installment method.

    d. Cost-recovery-first method.

    e. Which method do you feel provides the best measure of Humbolt's perform-ance under this contract? Why?

    f. Under what circumstances would the methods not selected in part **e** provide a better measure of performance?

29. *Point-of-sale versus installment method of income recognition.* The Freda Company begins business on January 1, Year 8. Activities of the company for the first 2 years are summarized below.

	Year 8	Year 9
Sales, All on Account	$100,000	$150,000
Collections from Customers		
On Year 8 Sales	45,000	55,000
On Year 9 Sales		60,000
Purchases of Merchandise	90,000	120,000
Inventory of Merchandise at 12/31	30,000	57,000
All Expenses Other than Merchandise, Paid in Cash.	16,000	22,000

    a. Prepare income statements for Year 8 and Year 9, assuming that the com-pany uses the accrual basis of accounting and revenue is recognized at the time of sale.

    b. Prepare income statements for Year 8 and Year 9, assuming that the com-pany uses the installment method of accounting.

30. *Income recognition over 2-year period.* The Webster Corporation produces a single product at a cost of $5 each, all of which is paid in cash when the unit is produced. The selling cost consists of a sales commission of $3 a unit and is paid in cash at the time of shipment. The selling price is $10 a unit; all sales are made on account. No uncollectible accounts are expected, and no costs are incurred at the time of collection.

    During Year 2, the firm produced 200,000 units, shipped 150,000 units, and collected $1 million from customers. During Year 3, the firm produced 125,000 units, shipped 160,000 units, and collected $2 million from customers.

    Calculate the amount of net income for Year 2 and Year 3:

    a. If revenue and expense are recognized at the time of production.

    b. If revenue and expense are recognized at the time of shipment.

    c. If revenue and expense are recognized at the time of cash collection.

    d. A firm experiencing growth in its sales volume will often produce more units during a particular period than it sells. In this way, inventories can be built up in anticipation of an even larger sales volume during the next pe-riod. Under these circumstances, will recognition of revenue and expense at the time of production, shipment, or cash collection generally result in the largest reported net income for the period? Explain.

    e. A firm experiencing decreases in its sales volume will often produce fewer units during a period than it sells in an effort to reduce the amount of inventory on hand for next period. Under these circumstances, will recognition of revenue and expense at the time of production, shipment, or cash collection generally result in the largest reported net income for a period? Explain.

31. *Classifying items in income statement.* The results of various transactions and events are usually classified within the income statement in one of the following three sections: (1) income from continuing operations, (2) income, gains, and losses from discontinued operations, and (3) extraordinary items. Using the appropriate number, identify the classification of each of the transactions or events below. State any assumptions you feel are necessary.

    a. Depreciation expense for the year on a company's automobile used by its president.

    b. Uninsured loss of a factory complex in Louisiana as a result of a hurricane.

    c. Gain from the sale of marketable securities.

    d. Loss from the sale of a delivery truck.

    e. Loss from the sale of a division that conducted all of the firm's research activities.

    f. Earnings during the year up to the time of sale of the division in part **e.**

    g. Loss in excess of insurance proceeds on an automobile destroyed during an accident.

    h. Loss of plant, equipment, and inventory held in a South American country when confiscated by the government of that country.

32. *Classifying items in income statement.* Comment on any unusual features of the income statement of Nordic Enterprises, Inc., shown in Exhibit 4.5.

33. *Revenue recognition for various types of businesses.* Discuss when revenue is likely to be recognized by firms in each of the following types of businesses:

    a. A shoe store.

    b. A shipbuilding firm constructing an aircraft carrier under a government contract.

    c. A real estate developer selling lots on long-term contracts with small down payments.

    d. A barber shop.

    e. A citrus-growing firm.

    f. A producer of television movies, where the rights to the movies for the first 3 years are sold to a television network and all rights thereafter revert to the producer.

    g. A residential real estate developer who constructs only "speculative" houses and then later sells the houses to buyers.

    h. A producer of fine whiskey that ages from 6 to 12 years before sale.

    i. A savings and loan association lending money for home mortgages.

    j. A travel agency.

    k. A printer who prints only custom-order stationery.

    l. A seller of trading stamps to food stores redeemable by food store customers for various household products.

    m. A wholesale food distributor.

    n. A livestock rancher.

Exhibit 4.5
NORDIC ENTERPRISES, INC.
Income Statement
December 31, Year 5

Revenues and Gains:

Sales Revenue	$1,964,800	
Rental Revenue	366,900	
Interest Revenue	4,600	
Gain on Sale of Equipment	2,500	
Gain on Sale of Subsidiary	643,200	$2,982,000
Expenses and Losses:		
Cost of Goods Sold	$1,432,900	
Depreciation Expense	226,800	
Salaries Expense	296,900	
Interest Expense	6,600	
Loss of Plant Due to Fire	368,800	
Income Tax Expense	200,000	
Dividends Expense	100,000	2,632,000
Net Income		$ 350,000

o. A shipping company that loads cargo in one accounting period, carries cargo across the ocean in a second accounting period, and unloads the cargo in a third period. The shipping is all done under contract, and cash collection of shipping charges is relatively certain.

34. *Revenue recognition for franchise.* Pickin Chicken, Incorporated, and Country Delight, Incorporated, both sell franchises for their chicken restaurants. The franchisee receives the right to use the franchisor's products and to benefit from national training and advertising programs. The franchisee agrees to pay $50,000 for exclusive franchise rights in a particular city. Of this amount, $20,000 is paid upon signing the franchise agreement and the remainder is payable in five equal annual installments of $6,000 each.

Pickin Chicken, Incorporated, recognizes franchise revenue as franchise agreements are signed, whereas Country Delight, Incorporated, recognizes franchise revenue on an installment basis. In Year 2, both companies sold eight franchises. In Year 3, they both sold five franchises. In Year 4, neither company sold a franchise.

a. Calculate the amount of revenue recognized by each company during Year 2, Year 3, Year 4, Year 5, Year 6, Year 7, and Year 8.

b. When do you feel that franchise revenue should be recognized? Why?

Chapter 5   Statement of Changes in Financial Position: Reporting the Effects of Investing, Financing, and Operating Activities on Cash Flows

Chapter 1 pointed out that three major financial statements are useful to those interested in understanding the financial activities of a business. Chapter 2 discussed the balance sheet, a snapshot of the *investments* and *financing* of a firm at a moment in time. Chapters 3 and 4 considered the income statement, a report on the revenues and expenses related to *operations* for a period of time. This chapter discusses a third major statement, the statement of changes in financial position. The statement of changes in financial position reports the flows of cash into and out of a business during a period of time. This statement is also sometimes referred to as the ''funds statement.''

Rationale for the Statement of Changes in Financial Position

Recall from Chapter 1 the relation between the principal activities of a business and the two financial statements already discussed, the balance sheet and the income statement. These relations are as follows:

These three business activities might be thought of as three interconnected cogwheels, each turning on its own, yet connected in important ways with the other activities.

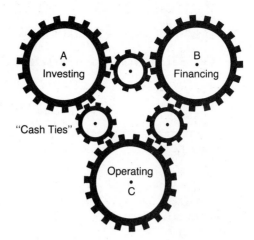

Cash ties these three activities together and keeps them running smoothly. If cash cannot be generated in sufficient amounts and at the right times, then a firm faces financial difficulty and even bankruptcy.

Example Solinger Electric Corporation was formed during January, Year 1, to operate a retail electrical supply business. It obtained financing from creditors and owners and invested the funds in buildings and equipment. The firm operated profitably since opening, with net income increasing from $3,000 in Year 1 to $20,000 in Year 4. The firm has had increasing difficulty, however, paying its monthly bills as they become due. Management is puzzled as to how net income could be increasing while, at the same time, the firm continually finds itself strapped for cash.

Relationship Between Income Flows and Cash Flows

Revenues and expenses reported in the income statement for a period differ in amount from cash receipts and disbursements for the period. The differences arise for two principal reasons.

1. The accrual basis of accounting is used in measuring net income. Thus, the recognition of revenues does not necessarily coincide with receipts of cash from customers. Likewise, the recognition of expenses does not necessarily coincide with disbursements of cash to suppliers, employees, and other creditors. As Chapter 3 pointed out, the accrual basis of accounting focuses on the use of assets in generating earnings and not on their associated cash receipts and disbursements.

2. The firm receives cash from sources that are not related directly to operations, such as issuing capital stock or bonds. Similarly, the firm makes cash disbursements for such things as dividends and the acquisition of equipment that are not related directly to operations during the current period.

To illustrate the differences between income flows and cash flows, refer to the data for Solinger Electric Corporation for Year 4 in Exhibit 5.1. Sales revenue

Exhibit 5.1
SOLINGER ELECTRIC CORPORATION
Income Statement and Statement of
Cash Receipts and Disbursements for the Year 4

	Income Statement	Statement of Cash Receipts and Disbursements	
Sales Revenue	$125,000	$ 90,000	. . . Collections from Customers
Less Expenses:			*Less Disbursements:*
Cost of Goods Sold .	$ 60,000	$ 50,000	. . . To Merchandise Suppliers
Salaries	20,000	19,000	. . . To Employees
Depreciation	10,000	0	. . . —
Other	15,000	13,000	. . . To Other Suppliers
Total Expenses . .	$105,000	$ 82,000	. . . Total Disbursements to Suppliers and Employees
Net Income	$ 20,000	$ 8,000	. . . Net Cash Inflow from Operations
		100,000	. . . Receipts from Issuing Long-Term Bonds
		$108,000	. . . Total Receipts from Operations and Bond Issue
		$ 8,000	. . . Disbursements for Dividends
		125,000	. . . Disbursements for Equipment
		$133,000	. . . Total Disbursements for Dividends and Equipment
		$ 25,000	. . . Net Decrease in Cash

reported in the income statement totaled $125,000. However, only $90,000 was collected in cash from customers. The remaining amount of sales was not collected by the end of the year and is reflected in the increase in the Accounts Receivable account on the balance sheet.[1] Likewise, the cost of goods sold shown on the income statement totaled $60,000. Only $50,000 cash was disbursed to suppliers during the year. Similar differences between income flows and cash flows can be seen for salaries and for other expenses. Note that there is no specific cash flow associated with depreciation expense during Year 4. Cash was used in some earlier period for the acquisition of buildings and equipment, but the amount of cash spent earlier was not reported then as an expense in accrual accounting. Rather, it was reflected in the balance sheet as an increase in the asset account for buildings and equipment and shown in the statement of changes in financial position as a use of

---

[1]This example has been simplified for purpose of illustration. In a realistic situation, some of the receipts would have been from collection of receivables existing at the start of the year. Similarly, some of the payments would have been for liabilities existing at the start of the year.

funds. Now, as the buildings and equipment are being used, the cost of the assets' services used is reported as an expense of the period even though there is now no outflow of cash. Although the operating activities generated $20,000 in net income, these activities led to an increase in cash of only $8,000 during Year 4.

Solinger Electric Corporation engaged in other activities affecting cash during Year 4, as is reported in the lower portion of Exhibit 5.1. Cash in the amount of $100,000 was received from the issue of bonds, $8,000 was disbursed for dividends, and $125,000 was disbursed for the acquisition of new equipment. The result of all of the firm's activities is a decrease in cash of $25,000.

The experience of Solinger Electric Corporation is not unusual. Many firms, particularly those growing rapidly, discover that their cash position is deteriorating despite an excellent earnings record. The statement of changes in financial position explains how the financing, investing, and operating activities of a firm affect cash for a period.

Objective of the Statement of Changes in Financial Position

The statement of changes in financial position reports the major sources and uses of cash flowing through a firm during a period of time. Figure 5.1 shows the major sources and uses, which are described below.

Sources—Operations The net amount of cash generated from selling goods and providing services is one of the most important sources of funds for a financially healthy company. When assessed over several years, cash provided by operations indicates the extent to which the operating or earnings activities have generated more cash than is used up. The excess from operations can then be used for dividends, acquisition of buildings and equipment, or repayment of long-term debt as necessary.

Figure 5.1 Sources and Uses of Cash

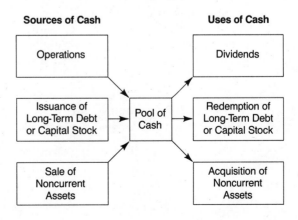

Sources—Issuance of Long-Term Debt or Capital Stock In the long run, a firm must generate most of its cash from operating activities. Potential shareholders are not willing to invest in unprofitable firms. Neither are banks willing to lend large amounts of cash to firms that do not generate profits. A potentially profitable firm finds that it can raise cash by issuing shares to owners or by borrowing. The amount of cash that can be generated by issuing stock or by borrowing is limited, however, by the marketplace's assessment of the firm's prospects.

Sources—Sales of Noncurrent Assets The sale of buildings, equipment, and other noncurrent assets increases cash. These sales generally are not a major source of financing for an ongoing firm. The amounts received from the sales are not likely to be sufficient to replace the assets sold.

Uses—Dividends Dividends are generally a recurring use of cash. Most publicly held firms are reluctant to omit the payment of dividends, even during a year of poor earnings performance. Because dividends use cash that might otherwise be retained and used elsewhere, they generally increase the need for other forms of financing.

Uses—Redemption of Long-Term Debt or Capital Stock In most instances, publicly held firms redeem or pay long-term debt at maturity with the proceeds of another debt issue. Thus, these redemptions often have little effect on the *net* change in cash. Some firms also occasionally reacquire, or redeem, their own capital stock for various reasons (discussed in Chapter 12).

Uses—Acquisition of Noncurrent Assets The acquisition of noncurrent assets, such as buildings and equipment, usually represents the most important ongoing use of cash. Such assets must be replaced as they wear out, and additional noncurrent assets must be acquired if a firm is to grow.

Firms sometimes issue long-term debt or capital stock directly to the seller in acquiring buildings, equipment, or other noncurrent assets. These transactions technically do not affect cash. However, the transaction is reported in the statement of changes in financial position as though two transactions took place: the issuance of long-term debt or capital stock for cash and the immediate use of that cash in the acquisition of noncurrent assets. This is called the *dual transactions assumption*. Such a transaction would normally be disclosed in the statement of changes in financial position as both a source and use of cash of equal amounts.

Uses of Information in the Statement of Changes in Financial Position

The statement of changes in financial position provides information that may be used in:

1. Assessing changes in a firm's liquidity, and
2. Assessing changes in the structure of a firm's assets and equities.

Liquidity Perhaps the most important factor not reported on either the balance sheet or income statement is how the operations of a period affected the liquidity of a firm. It is easy to conclude that increased earnings mean increased cash or other liquid assets. Such a conclusion may not be valid. The successful firm may acquire a new plant, so that it has less cash after a good year than before. On the other hand, increased liquidity can accompany reduced earnings. Consider, for example, a firm that is gradually reducing the scope of its operations. Such a firm is likely to report reduced net income or even losses over time. But because it is not replacing plant and equipment, it is likely to be accumulating cash or other liquid assets.

Structure of Assets and Equities In addition to providing information about changes in a firm's liquidity during a period, the statement of changes in financial position indicates the major transactions causing changes in the structure of a firm's assets (investments) and its liabilities and shareholders' equity (financing). For example, acquisitions and sales of specific types of assets (buildings, equipment, patents) are reported. Likewise, issues and redemptions of long-term debt and common stock are disclosed. These transactions are difficult to observe by looking at the income statement or the balance sheet or both. For example, the change in the account, Buildings and Equipment—Net of Accumulated Depreciation, could be attributable to depreciation charges, to acquisition of new buildings and equipment, to disposition of old buildings and equipment, or to a combination of these. The income statement and comparative balance sheets do not provide sufficient information about these three items individually for the reader to disaggregate the net change in the account during the period. A statement of changes in financial position is required to report this information.

Analysis of the Effects of Transactions on Cash

Algebraic Formulation

The effects of various transactions on cash might be seen by reexamining the accounting equation. In doing so, the following notation is used:

C—cash

NCA—noncash assets

L—liabilities

SE—shareholders' equity

Δ—the change in an item, whether positive (an increase) or negative (a decrease) from the beginning of a period to the end of the period.

The accounting equation states that:

$$\text{Assets} = \text{Liabilities} + \text{Shareholders' Equity}$$
$$\text{C} + \text{NCA} = \text{L} + \text{SE}.$$

Furthermore, this equation must be true for balance sheets constructed at both the start of the period and the end of the period. If the start-of-the-period and end-of-the-period balance sheets maintain the accounting equation, then the following equation must also be valid:

$$\Delta C + \Delta NCA = \Delta L + \Delta SE.$$

Rearranging terms in this equation, we obtain the equation for changes in cash:

$$\Delta C = \Delta L + \Delta SE - \Delta NCA.$$

The left-hand side of the above equation represents the change in cash. The right-hand side of the equation, reflecting changes in all noncash accounts, must also be equal in amount to the net change in cash. The equation states that increases in cash (left-hand side) are equal to, or caused by, the increases in liabilities plus the increases in shareholders' equity less the increases in noncash assets (right-hand side). Next, we illustrate how the changes in the accounts on the right-hand side bring about the change in cash on the left-hand side.

Illustration of Transactions Analysis

We can analyze some typical transactions to demonstrate how the equation is maintained and how cash is affected.

   Assume that the following events occur during Year 4 for the Solinger Electric Corporation, considered earlier in Exhibit 5.1.

 1. Merchandise costing $70,000 is acquired on account.
 2. Merchandise costing $60,000 is sold to customers on account for $125,000.
 3. Salaries of $19,000 are paid in cash.
 4. Other expenses of $13,000 are paid in cash.
 5. Cash collections of customers' accounts total $90,000.
 6. Cash payments to suppliers of merchandise total $50,000.
 7. Salaries earned but not paid as of December 31, Year 4, are accrued, $1,000.
 8. Other expenses not paid as of December 31, Year 4, are accrued, $2,000.
 9. Depreciation for Year 4 is recorded, $10,000.
10. Long-term debt is issued for cash, $100,000.
11. Dividends of $8,000 are declared and paid.
12. Equipment costing $125,000 is acquired for cash.

The effects of these transactions on cash are analyzed in Exhibit 5.2. Cash decreased by $25,000 during Year 4. Both sides of the equation show this net change. The net change in cash during a period (left-hand side of the equation) can therefore be explained, or analyzed, by focusing on the changes in noncash accounts (right-hand side of the equation). For Solinger Electric Corporation, the net decrease in cash of $25,000 is explained as follows:

Exhibit 5.2

Analysis of the Effects of Solinger Electric Corporation's Transactions
During Year 4 on Cash and Noncash Accounts

Transactions	Changes in Cash ΔC	=	ΔL	+	Changes in Noncash Accounts ΔSE	−	ΔNCA
					Effect on Cash		
(1) Merchandise costing $70,000 is acquired on account, increasing a noncash asset and a noncash liability	$ 0	=	$ 70,000	+	0	−	(+$ 70,000)
(2) Merchandise costing $60,000 is sold to customers on account for $125,000, increasing a noncash asset, accounts receivable, by $125,000, decreasing the noncash asset, inventory, by $60,000, and increasing shareholders' equity by $65,000	0	=	0	+	$65,000	−	(+$125,000) (−$ 60,000)
(3) Salaries of $19,000 are paid in cash, decreasing cash and shareholders' equity	(−$ 19,000)	=	0	+	(−$19,000)	−	0
(4) Other expenses of $13,000 are paid in cash, decreasing cash and shareholders' equity	(−$ 13,000)	=	0	+	(−$13,000)	−	0
(5) Cash collections of customers' accounts total $90,000, increasing cash and decreasing the noncash asset, accounts receivable	$ 90,000	=	0	+	0	−	(−$ 90,000)
(6) Payments to suppliers of merchandise total $50,000, decreasing cash and a liability . . .	(−$ 50,000)	=	(−$ 50,000)	+	0	−	0
(7) Salaries of $1,000 earned but not paid as of December 31, Year 4, are accrued, increasing a liability and decreasing shareholders' equity	0	=	$ 1,000	+	(−$ 1,000)	−	0
(8) Other expenses of $2,000 not paid as of December 31, Year 4, are accrued, increasing a liability and decreasing shareholders' equity	0	=	$ 2,000	+	(−$ 2,000)	−	0
(9) Depreciation for Year 4 of $10,000 is recorded, decreasing shareholders' equity and noncash assets	0	=	0	+	(−$10,000)	−	(−$ 10,000)
Total from operations	$ 8,000	=	$ 23,000	+	$20,000	−	$ 35,000
(10) Long-term debt is issued for $100,000, increasing cash and a liability	$100,000	=	$100,000	+	0	−	0
(11) Dividends of $8,000 are declared and paid, decreasing cash and shareholders' equity	(−$ 8,000)	=	0	+	(−$ 8,000)	−	0
(12) Equipment costing $125,000 is acquired for cash, decreasing cash and increasing noncash assets	(−$125,000)	=	0	+	0	−	$125,000
Net change in cash and noncash accounts	−$25,000	=	$123,000	+	$12,000	−	$160,000

Increases in Cash:

From Operations	$ 8,000
From Issuing Long-Term Debt	100,000
Total Increases	$108,000

Decreases in Cash:

For Dividends	$ 8,000
For Acquisition of Equipment	125,000
Total Decreases	$133,000

Net Decrease in Cash	$ 25,000

Note that the recording of depreciation for the period does not affect cash. A noncash asset is decreased and shareholders' equity is decreased. Cash is not affected. (Cash was reduced in an earlier period when the noncurrent asset was purchased.)

The information necessary to prepare the statement of changes in financial position could be developed using the transactions analysis approach illustrated in Exhibit 5.2. This approach quickly becomes cumbersome, however, as the number of transactions increases. The next section describes an alternative procedure for preparing the statement of changes in financial position that uses the T-account discussed in previous chapters.

Preparation of the Statement of Changes in Financial Position

As with the balance sheet and income statement, knowing how to prepare a statement of changes in financial position is not essential in order to use it effectively. Nevertheless, learning how to construct this statement facilitates understanding its rationale and content. This section presents a step-by-step procedure for preparing the statement of changes in financial position. This procedure is then illustrated, using the transactions of Solinger Electric Corporation for Year 4.

Unlike the balance sheet and income statement, the statement of changes in financial position is not generated as a regular output of a firm's record-keeping system. The statement of changes in financial position is usually prepared with a work sheet or other analysis after the balance sheet and income statement have been prepared.

The Procedure and an Illustration

Step 1 Obtain balance sheets for the beginning and end of the period covered by the statement of changes in financial position. Exhibit 5.3 presents the comparative balance sheets of Solinger Electric Corporation for December 31, Year 3 and Year 4.

Exhibit 5.3
SOLINGER ELECTRIC CORPORATION
Comparative Balance Sheets for
December 31, Year 3 and Year 4

	December 31,	
	Year 3	**Year 4**
Assets		
Current Assets:		
Cash	$ 30,000	$ 5,000
Accounts Receivable	20,000	55,000
Merchandise Inventory	40,000	50,000
Total Current Assets	$ 90,000	$110,000
Noncurrent Assets:		
Buildings and Equipment (cost)	$100,000	$225,000
Accumulated Depreciation	(30,000)	(40,000)
Total Noncurrent Assets	$ 70,000	$185,000
Total Assets	$160,000	$295,000
Equities		
Current Liabilities:		
Accounts Payable—Merchandise Suppliers	$ 30,000	$ 50,000
Accounts Payable—Other Suppliers	10,000	12,000
Salaries Payable	5,000	6,000
Total Current Liabilities	$ 45,000	$ 68,000
Noncurrent Liabilities:		
Bonds Payable	$ 0	$100,000
Shareholders' Equity:		
Common Stock	$100,000	$100,000
Retained Earnings	15,000	27,000
Total Shareholders' Equity	$115,000	$127,000
Total Equities	$160,000	$295,000

Step 2 Prepare a T-account *work sheet*. An example of such a T-account work sheet appears in Exhibit 5.4. At the top of the work sheet is a master T-account titled Cash. Note that this T-account has sections labeled Operations, Financing, and Investing. Transactions affecting cash during the period are classified under one of these headings to aid in the preparation of the statement of changes in financial position. This procedure is explained later in this section. The beginning and ending amounts of cash are then entered in the master T-account. The beginning and ending amounts of cash for Solinger Electric Corporation are $30,000 and $5,000, respectively. The check marks indicate that the figures are balances. The number at the top of the T-account is the opening balance; the one at the bottom is the closing balance. Note that the master T-account, Cash, is another means of expressing the left-hand side of the equation for changes in cash in Exhibit 5.2.

Exhibit 5.4
T-Account Work Sheet for
Solinger Electric Corporation

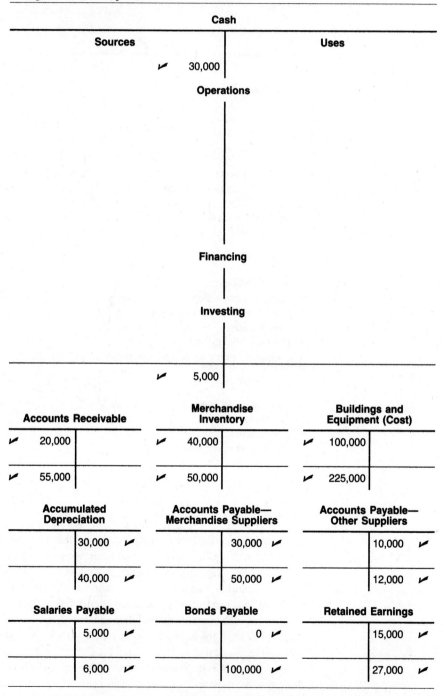

Cash	
Sources	**Uses**
✓ 30,000	
Operations	
Financing	
Investing	
✓ 5,000	

Accounts Receivable		Merchandise Inventory		Buildings and Equipment (Cost)	
✓ 20,000		✓ 40,000		✓ 100,000	
✓ 55,000		✓ 50,000		✓ 225,000	

Accumulated Depreciation		Accounts Payable—Merchandise Suppliers		Accounts Payable—Other Suppliers	
	30,000 ✓		30,000 ✓		10,000 ✓
	40,000 ✓		50,000 ✓		12,000 ✓

Salaries Payable		Bonds Payable		Retained Earnings	
	5,000 ✓		0 ✓		15,000 ✓
	6,000 ✓		100,000 ✓		27,000 ✓

After the master T-account for Cash has been prepared (as at the top of Exhibit 5.4), the work sheet is completed by preparing T-accounts for *each* noncash asset, liability, and shareholders' equity account. Enter the beginning and ending balances in each account for the period as given in Exhibit 5.3. The lower portion of Exhibit 5.4 shows the T-accounts for each noncash account. Note that the sum of the changes in these individual T-accounts is another means of expressing the right-hand side of the equation for changes in cash in Exhibit 5.2.

Step 3 Explain the change in the master cash account between the beginning and end of the period by explaining, or accounting for, the change in the balance of each noncash account during the period. This step is accomplished by *reconstructing the entries originally recorded in the accounts during the period*. The reconstructed entries are written in the appropriate T-accounts on the work sheet. Once the net change in each of the noncash accounts has been accounted for, sufficient information will have been generated to account for the net change in cash. That is, if the changes in the right-hand side of the cash equation have been explained, the causes of the changes in cash itself on the left-hand side will also have been explained.

The process of reconstructing the transactions during the year is usually easiest if information supplementary to the balance sheet is accounted for first. Assume the following information concerning the Solinger Electric Corporation for Year 4:

1. Net income is $20,000.
2. Depreciation expense is $10,000.
3. Dividends declared and paid total $8,000.

The analytic entry to record the information concerning net income is

```
(1) Cash (Operations—Net Income) . . . . . . . . . . . . . .     20,000
        Retained Earnings . . . . . . . . . . . . . . . . . . .            20,000
    Entry recorded in T-account work sheet.
```

To understand this entry, review the process of recording revenues and expenses and the closing entries for those temporary accounts from Chapter 3. All of the journal entries that together record the process of earning $20,000 net income are equivalent to the following single journal entry:

```
Net Assets (= All Assets − All Liabilities) . . . . . . . . . . .     20,000
    Retained Earnings . . . . . . . . . . . . . . . . . . . . . .            20,000
Summary entry equivalent to recording earnings of $20,000.
```

The summary journal entry debits Net Assets. The initial assumption at this stage of preparing the statement of changes in financial position is that all of the net assets generated by the earnings process were cash. Thus, in the analytic entry (1) above, the debit results in showing a provisional increase in cash from operations in an amount equal to net income for the period.

Not all of the items recognized as expenses and deducted in calculating net income, however, decrease cash (refer to Exhibit 5.1). The portion of the expenses that does not affect cash is added to the provisional increase in cash to calculate the net amount of cash from operations. One expense not using cash is depreciation, illustrated in entry (2).

---

(2) Cash (Sources: Operations—Depreciation Expense Addback) .   10,000
     Accumulated Depreciation.   10,000
    Entry recorded in T-account work sheet.

Because depreciation expense was deducted in calculating net income but did not reduce cash, the amount of depreciation expense must be added back to net income in calculating the amount of cash provided by operations.

The supplementary information concerning dividends of $8,000 declared and paid is recorded as follows:

---

(3) Retained Earnings   8,000
    Cash (Uses: Financing—Dividends)   8,000
    Entry recorded in T-account work sheet. Dividends reduce re-
    tained earnings and cash.

Because paying dividends generally increases the need for other forms of financing, they are classified on the statement of changes in financial position as a "financing" activity.

Once the supplementary information has been reflected in the T-account work sheet, it is necessary to make inferences about the reasons for the remaining changes in the noncash accounts on the balance sheet. (If the statement of changes in financial position were being prepared for an actual firm, such inferences might not be necessary, because sufficient information regarding the change in each account is likely to be available from the firm's accounting records.) The changes in noncash accounts are explained in the order of their appearance.

The Accounts Receivable account shows an increase of $35,000. The analytic entry to record this assumed information in the work sheet is

---

(4) Accounts Receivable   35,000
    Cash (Uses: Operations—Subtractions)   35,000
    Entry recorded in T-account work sheet.

The operations of the period generated sales. Not all of these sales resulted in an increase in cash. Some of the sales resulted in an increase in Accounts Receivable. Because we start the statement of changes in financial position with net income, in deriving the amount of cash from operations we must *subtract that portion of revenues not producing cash* (that is, the excess of sales on account over cash collections from customers).

The next noncash account showing a change is that for Merchandise Inventory. That account shows an increase during the year of $10,000. As the operations of the firm have expanded, so has the amount carried in inventory. The analytic entry in the work sheet to explain the change in Merchandise Inventory is

---

(5) Merchandise Inventory   10,000
     Cash (Uses: Operations—Subtractions)   10,000
     Entry recorded in T-account work sheet.

Solinger Electric Corporation found it necessary to increase the amount of inventory carried to make possible increased future sales. An increase in inventory is ordinarily an operating use of cash. Because we start the statement of changes in financial position with net income, in deriving cash from operations we must subtract from net income the incremental investment in inventories during the year (that is, the excess of purchases over the cost of goods sold).

The next noncash account showing a change is that for Buildings and Equipment (Cost). The Buildings and Equipment (Cost) account shows a net increase of $125,000 (= $225,000 − $100,000). Because we have no other information, we must assume that buildings and equipment costing $125,000 were acquired during the year. The analytic entry is

---

(6) Buildings and Equipment (Cost)   125,000
     Cash (Uses: Investing—Acquisitions of Buildings
       and Equipment)   125,000

The next noncash account showing a change is that for Accounts Payable—Merchandise Suppliers. As the amounts carried in inventory have increased, so have the amounts owed to suppliers of inventory. The analytic entry to explain the increase in the amount of Accounts Payable—Merchandise Suppliers is

---

(7) Cash (Sources: Operations—Additions)   20,000
     Accounts Payable—Merchandise Suppliers   20,000
     Entry recorded in T-account work sheet.

Ordinarily, acquiring inventory requires cash. Suppliers who allow a firm to pay later for goods (and services) received now are effectively supplying the firm with cash. Thus an increase in the amount of accounts payable for inventory results from a transaction where inventory increased but cash did not decrease, which is equivalent to saying that an increase in payables provides cash, even if only temporarily.

The increase in cash resulting from increased payables for inventory is an operating source of funds.

The next noncash account showing a change is Accounts Payable—Other Suppliers. As the scope of operations has increased, so has the amount owed to others. The analytic entry to explain the increase in the amount of Accounts Payable— Other Suppliers is

---

(8) Cash (Sources: Operations—Additions)   2,000
       Accounts Payable—Other Suppliers   2,000
     Entry recorded in T-account work sheet.

The reasoning behind this entry is the same as for entry (7). Creditors who permit a firm to owe them more effectively provide cash. The same reasoning applies to an increased amount of Salaries Payable, the next noncash account showing a change. The analytic entry to record the increase in Salaries Payable is

---

(9) Cash (Sources: Operations—Additions)   1,000
      Salaries Payable   1,000
     Entry recorded in T-account work sheet.

Employees who do not demand immediate payment for salaries earned have provided their employer with cash, at least temporarily.

The final noncash account showing a change not yet explained is Bonds Payable. It shows a net increase of $100,000 for the year. Because no other information is given, it must be assumed that long-term bonds were issued during the year. The analytic entry is

---

(10) Cash (Sources: Financing—Long-Term Bond Issue)   100,000
      Bonds Payable   100,000

Exhibit 5.5 presents the completed T-account work sheet for Solinger Electric Corporation for Year 4. All changes in the noncash T-accounts have been explained with the 10 entries. If the work is correct, the causes of the change in the Cash account will have been presented in the entries in the master Cash account.

Step 4 The final step is the preparation of a formal statement of changes in financial position. Exhibit 5.6 presents the statement for Solinger Electric Corporation. The statement is prepared directly from the information provided in the master T-account for Cash in the completed work sheet.

Exhibit 5.5
T-Account Work Sheet for
Solinger Electric Corporation

	Cash	
Sources		**Uses**
	✔ 30,000	

Operations

Net Income	(1) 20,000	35,000 (4) Increased Accounts Receivable
Depreciation Expense Addback	(2) 10,000	10,000 (5) Increased Merchandise Inventory
Increased Accounts Payable to Merchandise Suppliers	(7) 20,000	
Increased Accounts Payable to Other Suppliers	(8) 2,000	
Increased Salaries Payable	(9) 1,000	

Financing

Long-Term Bond Issue	(10) 100,000	8,000 (3) Dividends

Investing

		125,000 (6) Acquisition of Buildings and Equipment
	✔ 5,000	

Accounts Receivable		**Merchandise Inventory**		**Buildings and Equipment (Cost)**	
✔ 20,000		✔ 40,000		✔ 100,000	
(4) 35,000		(5) 10,000		(6) 125,000	
✔ 55,000		✔ 50,000		✔ 225,000	

Accumulated Depreciation		**Accounts Payable Merchandise Suppliers**		**Accounts Payable Other Suppliers**	
	30,000 ✔		30,000 ✔		10,000 ✔
	10,000 (2)		20,000 (7)		2,000 (8)
	40,000 ✔		50,000 ✔		12,000 ✔

Salaries Payable		**Bonds Payable**		**Retained Earnings**	
	5,000 ✔		0 ✔		15,000 ✔
	1,000 (9)		100,000 (10)	(3) 8,000	20,000 (1)
	6,000 ✔		100,000 ✔		27,000 ✔

Exhibit 5.6
SOLINGER ELECTRIC CORPORATION
Statement of Changes in Financial Position for Year 4

Sources of Cash

Operations:

Net Income.	$20,000	
Additions:		
Depreciation Expense Not Using Cash	10,000	
Increased Accounts Payable:		
To Suppliers of Merchandise	20,000	
To Other Suppliers	2,000	
Increased Salaries Payable	1,000	
Subtractions:		
Increased Accounts Receivable.	(35,000)	
Increased Merchandise Inventory	(10,000)	
Cash Provided by Operations		$ 8,000
Proceeds of Long-Term Bonds Issue		100,000
Total Sources of Cash.		$108,000

Uses of Cash

Dividends	$ 8,000
Acquisition of Buildings and Equipment	125,000
Total Uses of Cash	$133,000
Net (Decrease) in Cash for Year: Sources − Uses	**($ 25,000)**

The first item disclosed in the statement is the amount of cash generated by operations. In deriving cash from operations, published annual reports typically start with net income. Expenses not using cash are then added to net income, and revenues not providing cash are subtracted to obtain cash from operations. Exhibit 5.6 illustrates this format. Because depreciation expense is added to net income to calculate cash provided by operations, some readers of financial statements incorrectly conclude that depreciation expense is a source of cash. As Exhibit 5.2 illustrated, the recording of depreciation expense does not affect cash. A noncash asset is decreased and a shareholders' equity account is decreased. Cash is not affected. Cash from operations results from selling goods and services to customers. If no sales are made, then there will be no cash provided by operations regardless of how large the depreciation charge may be.

Depreciation Is Not a Source of Funds To demonstrate that depreciation is not a source of funds, refer to the income statement of Solinger Electric Corporation (Exhibit 5.1) and the cash flow from the operations section of the statement of changes in financial position (Exhibit 5.6). Exhibit 5.7 reproduces them in condensed form. Ignore income taxes for a moment. Suppose that depreciation for Year 4 had been $25,000 rather than $10,000. Then the condensed income statement and cash flow from operations would appear as in Exhibit 5.8. Note that the

Exhibit 5.7
SOLINGER ELECTRIC CORPORATION
Year 4
Depreciation $10,000

Income Statement		Cash Flow from Operations	
Revenues.	$125,000	Net Income	$20,000
Expenses Except Depreciation.	(95,000)	Additions:	
	$ 30,000	Depreciation.	10,000
Depreciation Expense	(10,000)	Other.	23,000
		Subtractions:	(45,000)
		Cash Flow Provided by	
Net Income	$ 20,000	Operations	$ 8,000

Exhibit 5.8
SOLINGER ELECTRIC CORPORATION
Year 4
Depreciation $25,000

Income Statement		Cash Flow from Operations	
Revenues.	$125,000	Net Income	$ 5,000
Expenses Except Depreciation.	(95,000)	Additions:	
	$ 30,000	Depreciation.	25,000
Depreciation Expense	(25,000)	Other.	23,000
		Subtractions:	(45,000)
		Cash Flow Provided by	
Net Income	$ 5,000	Operations	$ 8,000

total cash flow from operations remains $30,000, which is the difference between receipts from revenues and all expenses that did use cash. The only effects on cash of transactions involving long-term assets are that (1) cash is typically used when a long-term asset is acquired, and (2) cash is provided when the asset is sold.

At a more sophisticated level, however, when income taxes are a factor, depreciation does affect funds flow. Depreciation is a factor in the calculation of net income reported in the financial statements. Depreciation is also a deduction from otherwise taxable income on tax returns. The larger is depreciation on tax returns, the smaller is taxable income, and the smaller is the current payment for income taxes. Chapters 9 and 11 discuss the effect of depreciation on income taxes.

An alternative procedure for deriving cash flow from operations is to list all revenue items that provide cash and then to subtract all expense items that use cash. The right-hand column of Exhibit 5.1 illustrates this approach. This alternative presentation is appealing because depreciation expense does not appear as an element in the calculation of cash flow provided by operations. The latter presentation, although acceptable, is rarely used in published financial statements.

Extension of the Illustration

The illustration for Solinger Electric Corporation considered so far in this chapter is simpler than the typical published statement of changes in financial position in at least four respects:

1. There are only a few balance sheet accounts whose changes are to be explained.
2. Several types of more complex transactions that affect the sources of cash from operations are not involved.
3. Each transaction recorded in step 3 involves only one debit and one credit.
4. Each explanation of a noncash account change involves only one analytic entry on the work sheet, except for the Retained Earnings account.

Most of the complications that arise in interpreting published statements of changes in financial position relate to accounting events that are not discussed until later chapters. As these transactions are discussed, their effects on the statement of changes in financial position will be illustrated. One complication caused by supplementary disclosure can be illustrated at this time, however. Suppose that the firm sold some of its buildings and equipment during the year. For now, and until the issue is addressed again in Chapter 9, assume that the firm disposes of existing buildings and equipment at their book value; the cash proceeds from disposition are equal to acquisition cost less accumulated depreciation of the assets. With this assumption, there will be no gain or loss on disposition.

Reconsider the Solinger Electric Corporation example with the following new information. Solinger Electric Corporation sold some equipment during Year 4. This equipment cost $10,000 and was sold for $3,000 at a time when accumulated depreciation on the equipment sold was $7,000. The actual entry made during the year to record the sale of the equipment was as follows:

Cash	3,000	
Accumulated Depreciation	7,000	
Buildings and Equipment (Cost)		10,000
Journal entry for sale of equipment.		

Assume that the comparative balance sheets as shown in Exhibit 5.3 are correct and thus that the net decrease in cash for Year 4 is still $25,000. The entries in the T-accounts must be altered to reflect this new information. The following entry in the work sheet T-account is required to recognize the effect of the sale of equipment:

(1a) Cash (Sources: Sale of Equipment)	3,000	
Accumulated Depreciation	7,000	
Buildings and Equipment (Cost)		10,000
Entry recorded in T-account work sheet.		

The debit to Cash (Sources: Sale of Noncurrent Assets) shows the proceeds of the sale.

As a result of entry (1a), the T-accounts for Buildings and Equipment (Cost) and Accumulated Depreciation would appear as follows:

Buildings and Equipment (Cost)				Accumulated Depreciation		
✔ 100,000					30,000	✔
	10,000	(1a)	(1a)	7,000		
✔ 225,000					40,000	✔

When the time comes to explain the change in the account, Buildings and Equipment (Cost), the T-account indicates that there is an increase of $125,000 and a credit entry (1a) of $10,000 to recognize the sale of equipment. The net increase in the Buildings and Equipment (Cost) account can be accounted for, given the decrease already entered, only by assuming that new buildings and equipment have been acquired during the period for $135,000.

The reconstructed entry to complete the explanation of the change in this account would be as follows:

(6a) Buildings and Equipment (Cost)   135,000
        Cash (Uses: Acquisition of Buildings and Equipment)   135,000
        Entry recorded in T-account work sheet.

Likewise, when the change in the T-account for Accumulated Depreciation is explained, there is a net credit change of $10,000 and a debit entry (1a) of $7,000 to recognize the sale. Thus, the depreciation charge for Year 4 must have been $17,000. The reconstructed entry to complete the explanation of the change in the Accumulated Depreciation account would be as follows:

(2a) Cash (Operations—Depreciation Expense Addback)   17,000
        Accumulated Depreciation   17,000
        Entry recorded in T-account work sheet.

Exhibit 5.9 presents a revised T-account work sheet for Solinger Electric Corporation incorporating the new information on the sale of equipment.

Alternative Definitions of Funds

The illustrations thus far in this chapter have defined funds as cash. That is, the statement of changes in financial position reports the sources and uses of cash during the period.

Exhibit 5.9
Revised T-Account Work Sheet for
Solinger Electric Corporation

Cash

Sources		Uses
✔	30,000	

Operations

Net Income	(1)	20,000	35,000 (4)	Increased Accounts Receivable
Depreciation Expense Addback	(2a)	17,000	10,000 (5)	Increased Merchandise Inventory
Increased Accounts Payable to Merchandise Suppliers	(7)	20,000		
Increased Accounts Payable to Other Suppliers	(8)	2,000		
Increased Salaries Payable	(9)	1,000		

Financing

Long-Term Bond Issue	(10)	100,000	8,000 (3)	Dividends

Investing

Sale of Equipment	(1a)	3,000	135,000 (6a)	Acquisition of Buildings and Equipment
✔		5,000		

Accounts Receivable			Merchandise Inventory			Buildings and Equipment (Cost)		
✔	20,000		✔	40,000		✔	100,000	
(4)	35,000		(5)	10,000		(6a)	135,000	10,000 (1a)
✔	55,000		✔	50,000		✔	225,000	

Accumulated Depreciation			Accounts Payable Merchandise Suppliers			Accounts Payable Other Suppliers		
		30,000 ✔			30,000 ✔			10,000 ✔
(1a)	7,000	17,000 (2a)			20,000 (7)			2,000 (8)
		40,000 ✔			50,000 ✔			12,000 ✔

Salaries Payable			Bonds Payable			Retained Earnings		
		5,000 ✔			0 ✔			15,000 ✔
		1,000 (9)			100,000 (10)	(3)	8,000	20,000 (1)
		6,000 ✔			100,000 ✔			27,000 ✔

The term "funds" is, however, a general one, which can be defined differently. The following definitions of "funds" can be found in published statements of changes in financial position:

1. Cash only.
2. Cash plus marketable securities.
3. Cash plus marketable securities net of short-term borrowing.
4. Current assets net of current liabilities, called working capital.

Prior to 1980, most firms defined funds as working capital (= current assets minus current liabilities). Transactions that caused working capital to change were reported as a source or use of "funds." For example, the sale of merchandise on account would be reported as a source of working capital (that is, accounts receivable increases), even though no cash is received. When funds are defined as cash, the sale of merchandise on account is not reported as a source of funds.

Since 1980, firms have increasingly used a more restrictive definition of funds, such as one of the first three definitions above. These more restrictive definitions of funds focus on the most liquid assets of a firm. This shift to a narrower definition of funds reflects the importance of liquidity during periods of high interest and inflation rates.

The illustrations and problems in this book define funds as cash only.

Analysis of Statement of Changes in Financial Position

The principal questions that the statement of changes in financial position is designed to answer include the following:

1. What is the relation between the various sources of cash (operations, new financing, sale of noncurrent assets)?
2. What is the relation between the various uses of cash (dividends, reduction in financing, acquisition of noncurrent assets)?
3. What is the relation between the total sources and the total uses of cash?

In analyzing the statement of changes in financial position, it is often useful to express each source as a percentage of total sources and each use as a percentage of total uses. Such an analysis appears in Exhibit 5.10 for General Products Company, whose financial statements appear in Appendix A. Because the percentages for any particular year can be significantly affected by a large debt or common stock issue in that year, it is often useful to combine the data for several years as is done in the far-right column of Exhibit 5.10.

Note the following regarding General Products Company.

1. Approximately 85 percent of the funds needed over the 3-year period were generated from operations. Such a percentage is characteristic of a financially healthy firm.
2. Approximately 60 percent of the funds used were for the acquisition of plant, equipment, and other noncurrent assets. Such percentages are likewise typical of a manufacturing firm experiencing significant growth.

Exhibit 5.10
GENERAL PRODUCTS COMPANY
Statement of Changes in Financial Position
(amounts in millions)

	1985		1984		1983		Combined	
Sources								
Operations	$1,930	80.7%	$2,233	88.6%	$2,185	84.5%	$6,348	84.5%
New Financing . . .	289	12.1	198	7.5	258	10.0	745	9.9
Sale of Noncurrent Assets and Other .	173	7.2	102	3.9	143	5.5	418	5.6
Total Sources . .	$2,392	100.0%	$2,533	100.0%	$2,586	100.0%	$7,511	100.0%
Uses								
Dividends	$ 570	25.8%	$ 624	24.9%	$ 670	22.6%	$1,864	24.6%
Reduction in Financing	582	26.4	253	13.6	214	7.2	1,049	13.8
Acquisition of Noncurrent Assets and Other	1,055	47.8	1,543	61.5	2,077	70.2	4,675	61.6
Total Uses	$2,207	100.0%	$2,420	100.0%	$2,961	100.0%	$7,588	100.0%

3. More funds were obtained from operations than were paid out as dividends. Thus, the firm is not liquidating itself, or shrinking. Instead, the excess cash generated from operations is being used for replacement and growth of assets.

General Products Company is a sound, financially healthy company. For a contrast, refer to Problem 24 at the end of the chapter, which involves analysis of the statement of changes in financial position for a financially troubled company.

Summary

The statement of changes in financial position (funds statement) reports the effects of a firm's investing, financing, and operating activities on funds. Funds are typically defined as cash, although some firms use a broader definition.

The statement of changes in financial position helps explain the major reasons for a change in a firm's liquidity. In particular, it shows the relation between net income and cash generated by operations. The statement also reports the reasons for significant shifts in the structure of a firm's assets (changes in receivables, inventories, plant and equipment) and in the structure of a firm's liabilities and shareholders' equity (changes in accounts payable, bonds payable, common stock, retained earnings). These types of information are difficult to observe from a balance sheet or income statement alone.

The statement of changes in financial position is basically derived from an analysis of changes in balance sheet accounts during the accounting period. If the double-entry recording process has been applied properly, the net change in cash (or other definition of funds) should equal the net change in all noncash (nonfund) accounts.

By reconstructing the entries made in noncash accounts and explaining their net change during the period, the net change in cash will also be explained.

The statement of changes in financial position usually begins with net income for the period. Adjustments are then made for revenues not providing cash and expenses not using cash. The result is cash generated by operations. Other sources (new financing, sale of noncurrent assets) are then shown. From the total sources are subtracted the uses of cash (dividends, reductions in financing, acquisition of noncurrent assets) to derive the net change in cash for the period.

When analyzing a statement of changes in financial position, the focus is on the relation between the various sources, the relations among the various uses, and the relation between the total sources and total uses. A financially healthy firm typically obtains a majority of its funds from operations and invests a large percentage in plant and equipment.

Problem 1 for Self-Study

Exhibit 5.11 presents a comparative balance sheet for Robbie Corporation as of December 31, Year 1 and Year 2. During Year 2, no plant and equipment was sold and no dividends were declared or paid.

Prepare a T-account work sheet for the preparation of a statement of changes in financial position.

Exhibit 5.11
ROBBIE CORPORATION
Comparative Balance Sheet
December 31, Year 1 and Year 2
(Problem 1 for Self-Study)

Assets	December 31, Year 1	Year 2	Liabilities and Shareholders' Equity	December 31, Year 1	Year 2
Current Assets:			**Current Liabilities:**		
Cash	$10	$ 25	Accounts Payable	$30	$ 40
Accounts Receivable	15	20	Total Current Liabilities	$30	$ 40
Merchandise Inventories	20	25	**Long-Term Debt:**		
Total Current Assets.	$45	$ 70	Bonds Payable	$10	$ 15
			Total Liabilities	$40	$ 55
Property, Plant, and Equipment. .	$50	$ 60			
Less Accumulated Depreciation .	(25)	(30)	**Shareholders' Equity:**		
Total Property, Plant, and Equipment	$25	$ 30	Common Stock	$10	$ 20
Total Assets	$70	$100	Retained Earnings	20	25
			Total Shareholders' Equity	$30	$ 45
			Total Liabilities and Shareholders' Equity	$70	$100

Suggested Solution

Exhibit 5.12 presents a completed T-account work sheet for Robbie Corporation.

Exhibit 5.12
T-Account Work Sheet for Robbie Corporation
Funds Defined as Cash
(amounts in 000's)

	Cash		
Sources			**Uses**
✔ 10			
	Operations		
(4) 5		5 (1)	
(5) 10		5 (2)	
(8) 5			
	Financing		
(6) 5			
(7) 10			
	Investing		
		10 (3)	
✔ 25			

Accounts Receivable		Merchandise Inventories		Property, Plant, and Equipment		Accumulated Depreciation	
✔ 15		✔ 20		✔ 50			25 ✔
(1) 5		(2) 5		(3) 10			5 (4)
✔ 20		✔ 25		✔ 60			30 ✔

Accounts Payable		Bonds Payable		Common Stock		Retained Earnings	
	30 ✔		10 ✔		10 ✔		20 ✔
	10 (5)		5 (6)		10 (7)		5 (8)
	40 ✔		15 ✔		20 ✔		25 ✔

Problem 2 for Self-Study

Exhibit 5.13 presents a comparative balance sheet for Gordon Corporation as of December 31, Year 1 and Year 2. The following information pertains to Gordon Corporation for Year 2.

1. Net income was $200,000.
2. Dividends declared and paid were $120,000.
3. Depreciation expense totaled $80,000.

Exhibit 5.13
GORDON CORPORATION
Comparative Balance Sheet
December 31, Year 1 and Year 2
(amounts in 000's)
(Problem 2 for Self-Study)

	December 31, Year 1	December 31, Year 2
Assets		
Current Assets:		
Cash	$ 70	$ 40
Accounts Receivable	320	420
Merchandise Inventories	360	470
Prepayments	50	70
Total Current Assets	$ 800	$1,000
Property, Plant, and Equipment:		
Land	$ 200	$ 250
Buildings and Equipment (net of accumulated depreciation of $800 and $840)	1,000	1,150
Total Property, Plant, and Equipment	$1,200	$1,400
Total Assets	$2,000	$2,400
Liabilities and Shareholders' Equity		
Current Liabilities:		
Accounts Payable	$ 320	$ 440
Income Taxes Payable	60	80
Other Current Liabilities	170	360
Total Current Liabilities	$ 550	$ 880
Noncurrent Liabilities:		
Bonds Payable	250	200
Total Liabilities	$ 800	$1,080
Shareholders' Equity:		
Common Stock	$ 500	$ 540
Retained Earnings	700	780
Total Shareholders' Equity	$1,200	$1,320
Total Liabilities and Shareholders' Equity	$2,000	$2,400

4. Buildings and equipment originally costing $50,000 and with accumulated depreciation of $40,000 were sold for $10,000.

a. Prepare a T-account work sheet for the preparation of a statement of changes in financial position.

b. Prepare a formal statement of changes in financial position.

Suggested Solution

Exhibit 5.14 presents a completed T-account work sheet for Gordon Corporation. Exhibit 5.15 presents a formal statement of changes in financial position.

Exhibit 5.14
T-Account Work Sheet for Gordon Corporation
Funds Defined as Cash
(amounts in 000's)

Sources			Cash		Uses
	✔	70			
			Operations		
(1)	200	100	(5)		
(3)	80	110	(6)		
(10)	120	20	(7)		
(11)	20				
(12)	190				
			Financing		
(14)	40	120	(2)		
		50	(13)		
			Investing		
(4)	10	50	(8)		
		240	(9)		
	✔	40			

continued

Exhibit 5.14 *continued*
T-Account Work Sheet for Gordon Corporation
Funds Defined as Cash
(amounts in 000's)

Accounts Receivable

✔	320		
(5)	100		
✔	420		

Merchandise Inventories

✔	360		
(6)	110		
✔	470		

Prepayments

✔	50		
(7)	20		
✔	70		

Land

✔	200		
(8)	50		
✔	250		

Buildings and Equipment—Net

✔	1,000		
(4)	40	80	(3)
(9)	240	50	(4)
✔	1,150		

Accounts Payable

		320	✔
		120	(10)
		440	✔

Income Taxes Payable

		60	✔
		20	(11)
		80	✔

Other Current Liabilities

		170	✔
		190	(12)
		360	✔

Bonds Payable

		250	✔
(13)	50		
		200	✔

Common Stock

		500	✔
		40	(14)
		540	✔

Retained Earnings

		700	✔
(2)	120	200	(1)
		780	✔

Exhibit 5.15
GORDON CORPORATION
Statement of Changes in Financial Position
For Year 2

Sources of Cash

Operations:

Net Income	$200	
Additions:		
Depreciation Expense	80	
Increase in Accounts Payable	120	
Increase in Income Taxes Payable	20	
Increase in Other Current Liabilities	190	
Subtractions:		
Increase in Accounts Receivable	(100)	
Increase in Merchandise Inventories	(110)	
Increase in Prepayments	(20)	
Cash Provided by Operations		$380
Common Stock Issued		40
Buildings and Equipment Sold		10
Total Sources		$430

continued

Exhibit 5.15 *continued*
GORDON CORPORATION
Statement of Changes in Financial Position
For Year 2

Uses of Cash

Dividends	$120
Repayment of Bonds	50
Acquisition of Land	50
Acquisition of Buildings and Equipment	240
Total Uses	$460
Net Change in Cash	$ (30)

Questions, Exercises, Problems and Cases

Questions

1. Review the meaning of the following concepts or terms discussed in this chapter.
   a. Relation between income flows and cash flows.
   b. Cash provided by operations.
   c. Liquidity.
   d. Dual transactions assumption.
   e. T-account work sheet.
   f. Depreciation is not a source of funds.
   g. Alternative definitions of funds.

2. "The reporting objective of the income statement under the accrual basis of accounting and the reporting objective of the statement of changes in financial position could be more easily accomplished by issuing a single income statement using the cash basis of accounting." Evaluate this proposal.

3. The text indicates that the statement of changes in financial position provides information about changes in the structure of a firm's assets and equities. Of what value is information about the structure of a firm's assets and equities?

4. The text states that the statement of changes in financial position can be used for assessing changes in both (1) liquidity and (2) the structure of assets, liabilities, and shareholders' equity. The acquisition of equipment by assuming a noncurrent liability is a transaction that must be disclosed (using the dual transactions assumption) even though it does not involve cash. This disclosure is made primarily for the second rather than the first use of the statement of changes in financial position listed above. Explain.

5. One writer stated that:

Depreciation expense is the chief source of cash for growth in industries.

A reader criticized this statement by replying:

The fact remains that if the companies listed had elected, in any year, to charge off $10 million more depreciation than they did charge off, they would not thereby have added one dime to the total of their cash available for plant expansion or for increasing inventories or receivables. Therefore, to speak of depreciation expense as a source of cash has no significance in a discussion of fundamentals.

Comment on these statements, including income tax effects.

6. A firm generated net income for the current year, but cash flow relating to operations was negative. How can this happen?

7. A firm operated at a net loss for the current year, but cash flow relating to operations was positive. How can this happen?

Exercises

8. *Effect of various transactions on cash.* Prepare a work sheet with the following headings.

Effect of Transaction or Event on:

Transaction or Event	Cash	Other Current Assets	Noncurrent Assets	Current Liabilities	Noncurrent Liabilities	Shareholders' Equity

 a. For each of the transactions or events listed below, indicate the effect on the balance sheet categories shown in the work sheet.

 (1) Purchase of merchandise on account, $5,000.
 (2) Payment of $4,000 of amount due for purchases in **(1)**.
 (3) Sale of merchandise to customers on credit. Selling price is $7,000; cost of goods sold is $3,500.
 (4) Collection of $5,500 of amount due from customers from sales in **(3)**.
 (5) Depreciation expense for the period is $600.
 (6) Employees earn salaries of $1,200 [also see transaction **(7)**].
 (7) Employees are paid $1,100 of amount due in **(6)**.
 (8) Insurance premium of $200 is paid for coverage to begin next accounting period.
 (9) Income taxes for the period are accrued, $900 [also see transaction **(10)**]
 (10) Income taxes of $600 are paid.
 (11) Bonds payable are issued, $200.
 (12) Equipment costing $1,500, and on which $1,000 of depreciation had been taken, is sold for $500.
 (13) Equipment costing $300 is acquired for cash.
 (14) Equipment costing $200 is acquired and a noncurrent liability of $200 is assumed for the purchase price.
 (15) Dividends of $700 are declared and paid.

b. Indicate whether each of the transactions or events affecting cash relates to an operating, financing, or investing activity.

9. *Calculating cash provided by operations.* The following items were found in the financial statements of Maher Company for Year 2:

Sales	$90,000
Depreciation Expense.	45,000
Income Taxes	10,000
Other Expenses	20,000
Common Stock Issued During Year	17,500

The changes in current asset and current liability accounts were as follows:

Accounts Receivable	$45,000 Increase
Merchandise Inventories	30,000 Increase
Prepayments	5,000 Decrease
Accounts Payable	15,000 Increase
Income Taxes Payable	7,500 Decrease

Compute the amount of cash provided by operations.

10. *Calculating cash provided by operations.* Compute the amount of cash provided by operations in each of the independent cases below.

	a	b	c	d
Net Income (Loss)	$100	$50	$70	$(40)
Depreciation Expense	15	10	12	18
Increase (Decrease) in:				
Accounts Receivable.	20	15	(10)	12
Merchandise Inventories	25	(10)	15	15
Prepayments	10	(3)	4	(6)
Accounts Payable	15	10	(20)	14
Income Taxes Payable	18	(8)	14	(16)
Other Current Liabilities	12	(9)	(7)	11

11. *Working backwards from changes in buildings and equipment account.* The comparative balance sheet of the Kanodia Company showed a balance in the Buildings and Equipment account at December 31, Year 5, of $24,600,000; at December 31, Year 4, the balance was $24,000,000. The Accumulated Depreciation account showed a balance of $8,600,000 at December 31, Year 5, and $7,600,000 at December 31, Year 4. The statement of changes in financial position reports that expenditures for buildings and equipment for the year totaled $1,300,000. The

income statement indicates a depreciation charge of $1,200,000 for the year. Buildings and equipment were sold during the year at their book value.

Calculate the acquisition cost and accumulated depreciation of the buildings and equipment retired during the year and the proceeds from their disposition.

12. *Preparing statement of changes in financial position; working backwards from changes in plant asset accounts.* The balance in the Property, Plant, and Equipment (Cost) account was $200 on January 1 and $260 on December 31. The balance in the Accumulated Depreciation account was $120 on January 1 and $140 on December 31. During the year, equipment costing $25 and with accumulated depreciation of $15 was sold for $10. No dividends were paid during the year, nor were there any changes in the Bonds Payable or the Common Stock accounts. Cash provided by operations totaled $80, and the net change in cash for the year was an increase of $5.

Prepare a statement of changes in financial position for the year.

13. *Preparing statement of changes in financial position using changes in balance sheet accounts.* The accounting records of Kropp Corporation reveal the following for the current year.

Account	Amount	Change
Cash	$120	Increase
Accounts Receivable	15	Increase
Merchandise Inventories	20	Decrease
Property, Plant, and Equipment	50[a]	Increase
Accumulated Depreciation	10	Increase
Accounts Payable	25	Increase
Bonds Payable	20	Increase
Common Stock	30	Increase
Retained Earnings	80[b]	Increase

[a]There were no dispositions of property, plant, and equipment during the year.
[b]Net income was $130; dividends were $50.

Prepare a statement of changes in financial position, explaining the change in cash for the year.

14. *Preparing statement of changes in financial position using changes in balance sheet accounts.* The accounting records of Baker Corporation reveal the following for the current year.

Account	Amount	Change
Cash	$75	Decrease
Accounts Receivable	40	Increase
Merchandise Inventories	30	Increase
Property, Plant, and Equipment	60[a]	Increase

continued

continued

Accumulated Depreciation	20[a]	Increase
Accounts Payable	25	Decrease
Bonds Payable	35[b]	Decrease
Common Stock.	45	Increase
Retained Earnings	50[c]	Increase

[a]Equipment costing $15 and with accumulated depreciation of $12 was sold for $3 during the year.
[b]Bonds with a face value and book value of $50 were retired during the year at no gain or loss.
[c]Dividends declared and paid totaled $20 during the year.

Prepare a statement of changes in financial position, explaining the change in cash for the year.

15. *Reformating statement of changes in financial position.* Guerrero Corporation has prepared the statement of changes in financial position appearing in Exhibit 5.16. Recast this statement into a properly formated statement of changes in financial position.

Exhibit 5.16
GUERRERO CORPORATION
Statement of Changes in Financial Position
For the Current Year
(Exercise 15)

Sources of Cash

Proceeds from Issue of Bonds	$ 20,000
Proceeds from Issue of Common Stock	30,000
Proceeds from Sale of Equipment.	4,000
Net Income	40,000
Depreciation Expense	10,000
Increase in Accounts Payable	15,000
Total Sources	$119,000

Uses of Cash

Acquisition of Equipment[a]	$ 60,000
Payment of Dividends	12,000
Repayment of Bonds Payable	8,000
Increase in Accounts Receivable	16,000
Increase in Merchandise Inventory	11,000
Total Uses	$107,000
Net Change in Cash	$ 12,000

[a]In addition, equipment costing $25,000 was acquired and a noncurrent liability assumed for the purchase price.

16. *Effect of various transactions on statement of changes in financial position.* Exhibit 5.17 shows a simplified statement of changes in financial position for a period. Eleven of the lines in the statement are numbered. Other lines are various subtotals and grand totals; these are to be ignored in the remainder of the problem. Assume that the accounting cycle is complete for the period and that all of the financial statements have been prepared. Then it is discovered that a transaction has

Exhibit 5.17
Simplified Statement of
Changes in Financial Position
(Exercise 16)

Sources of Cash

From Operations:

Net Income	(1)
Addback for Expenses and Losses Not Using Working Capital	+ (2)
Additions for Decreases in Current Asset Accounts Other than Cash	
and for Increases in Current Liability Accounts	+ (3)
Subtractions for Revenues and Gains Not Producing Working Capital	
from Operations	− (4)
Subtractions for Increases in Current Asset Accounts Other than	
Cash and for Decreases in Current Liability Accounts	− (5)
Total Cash Provided by Operations [= (1) + (2) + (3) − (4) − (5)]	S1
Other Sources:	
Increases in Debt or Capital Stock	(6)
Proceeds from Dispositions of Noncurrent Assets	(7)
Total "Other" Sources of Cash [= (6) + (7)]	S2
Total Sources of Cash (= S1 + S2)	S3

Uses of Cash

Dividends	(8)
Reduction in Debt or Common Stock	(9)
Acquisition of Noncurrent Assets	(10)
Total Uses of Cash [= (8) + (9) + (10)]	S4
Sources of Cash Minus Uses of Cash = Change in Cash for the Period	
(= S3 − S4)	(11)

been overlooked. That transaction is recorded in the accounts and all of the financial statements are corrected. For each of the following transactions, indicate which of the numbered lines of the statement of changes in financial position are affected. Define funds as cash. If net income, line (1), is affected, be sure to indicate whether it decreases or increases. Ignore income tax effects.

  a. Depreciation expense on office computer.
  b. Purchase of machinery for cash.
  c. Declaration of a cash dividend on common stock; the dividend was paid by the end of the fiscal year.
  d. Issue of common stock for cash.
  e. Proceeds of sale of common stock investment, a noncurrent asset, for cash. The investment was sold for book value.
  f. Amortization of patent, treated as an expense.
  g. Amortization of patent, charged to production activities. The items being produced have not yet been completed.
  h. Acquisition of a factory site by issue of capital stock.
  i. Purchase of inventory on account.
  j. Uninsured fire loss of merchandise inventory.
  k. Collection of an account receivable.

    l. Issue of bonds for cash.

    m. Proceeds from sale of equipment. The equipment was sold for its book value.

Problems and Cases

17. *Preparing statement of changes in financial position.* Exhibit 5.18 presents a comparative balance sheet for Bragg Corporation as of the beginning and end of the current year. During the year, there were no dispositions of property, plant, and equipment, and no dividends were declared or paid.

    Prepare a statement of changes in financial position for Bragg Corporation for the current year, supporting the statement with a T-account work sheet.

Exhibit 5.18
BRAGG CORPORATION
Comparative Balance Sheet
(Problem 17)

	January 1	December 31
Assets		
Current Assets:		
Cash	$ 6,000	$ 10,000
Accounts Receivable	72,000	82,000
Merchandise Inventories	95,000	110,000
Total Current Assets	$173,000	$202,000
Property, Plant, and Equipment	$350,000	$425,000
Less Accumulated Depreciation	(123,000)	(135,000)
Total Property, Plant, and Equipment	$227,000	$290,000
Total Assets	$400,000	$492,000
Liabilities and Shareholders' Equity		
Current Liabilities:		
Accounts Payable	$ 95,000	$121,000
Income Taxes Payable	10,000	15,000
Total Current Liabilities	$105,000	$136,000
Long-Term Debt:		
Bonds Payable	50,000	75,000
Total Liabilities	$155,000	$211,000
Shareholders' Equity:		
Common Stock	$105,000	$106,000
Retained Earnings	140,000	175,000
Total Shareholders' Equity	$245,000	$281,000
Total Liabilities and Shareholders' Equity	$400,000	$492,000

18. *Preparing statement of changes in financial position.* Condensed financial statement data for the Harris Company for the current year appear in Exhibits 5.19 and 5.20. During the current year, equipment costing $10,000 and with $8,000 of accumulated depreciation was sold for $2,000.

Exhibit 5.19
HARRIS COMPANY
Comparative Balance Sheets
(Problem 18)

	January 1	December 31
Assets		
Cash	$ 20,000	$ 24,000
Accounts Receivable	52,000	58,000
Inventory	79,000	81,000
Land	15,000	15,000
Buildings and Equipment (Cost)	400,000	415,000
Less Accumulated Depreciation	(240,000)	(252,000)
Total Assets	$326,000	$341,000
Liabilities and Shareholders' Equity		
Accounts Payable for Inventory	$ 62,000	$ 65,000
Interest Payable	6,000	4,000
Mortgage Payable	60,000	55,000
Common Stock.	120,000	130,000
Retained Earnings	78,000	87,000
Total Liabilities and Shareholders' Equity	$326,000	$341,000

Exhibit 5.20
HARRIS COMPANY
Statement of Income and Retained Earnings
For the Current Year

Revenues		$200,000
Expenses:		
Cost of Goods Sold	$80,000	
Wages and Salaries	26,000	
Depreciation	20,000	
Interest	8,000	
Income Taxes	27,000	
Total		161,000
Net Income.		$ 39,000
Dividends on Common Stock.		30,000
Addition to Retained Earnings for Year		$ 9,000
Retained Earnings, January 1		78,000
Retained Earnings, December 31		$ 87,000

Prepare a statement of changes in financial position for the year, supporting the statement with a T-account work sheet. Define funds as cash.

19. *Preparing statement of changes in financial position.* Financial statement data for the Perkerson Supply Company for the current year appear in Exhibit 5.21.

Additional information:

(1) Net income for the year was $324,000; dividends declared and paid were $70,000.
(2) Depreciation expense for the year was $305,000 on buildings and machinery.
(3) Machinery originally costing $125,000 and with accumulated depreciation of $110,000 was sold for $15,000.

Exhibit 5.21
PERKERSON SUPPLY COMPANY
Comparative Balance Sheets
(Problem 19)

	January 1	December 31
Assets		
Current Assets:		
Cash.	$ 179,000	$ 162,000
Accounts Receivable	473,000	526,000
Inventory	502,000	604,000
Total Current Assets.	$1,154,000	$1,292,000
Noncurrent Assets:		
Land.	297,000	$ 315,000
Buildings and Machinery	4,339,000	4,773,000
Less Accumulated Depreciation.	(1,987,000)	(2,182,000)
Total Noncurrent Assets	$2,649,000	$2,906,000
Total Assets	$3,803,000	$4,198,000
Liabilities and Shareholders' Equity		
Current Liabilities:		
Accounts Payable	$ 206,000	$ 279,000
Taxes Payable	137,000	145,000
Other Short-Term Payables.	294,000	363,000
Total Current Liabilities.	$ 637,000	$ 787,000
Noncurrent Liabilities:		
Bonds Payable	992,000	967,000
Total Liabilities	$1,629,000	$1,754,000
Shareholders' Equity:		
Common Stock	836,000	$ 852,000
Retained Earnings.	1,338,000	1,592,000
Total Shareholders' Equity	$2,174,000	$2,444,000
Total Liabilities and Shareholders' Equity	$3,803,000	$4,198,000

Prepare a statement of changes in financial position for the Perkerson Supply Company for the year with funds defined as cash. Support the statement with a T-account work sheet.

20. *Preparing income statement and statement of changes in financial position.* Condensed financial statement data for the Victoria Company for the year appear in Exhibit 5.22.

Expenditures on new plant and equipment for the year amounted to $121,000. Old plant and equipment that had cost $94,000 were sold during the year. It was sold for cash at book value.

Exhibit 5.22
VICTORIA COMPANY
Post-closing Trial Balance
Comparative Data
(Problem 20)

	January 1	December 31
Debits:		
Cash	$ 62,000	$ 55,000
Accounts Receivable	135,000	163,000
Merchandise Inventory	247,000	262,000
Plant and Equipment (cost)	1,362,000	1,389,000
Total Debits	$1,806,000	$1,869,000
Credits:		
Accounts Payable	$ 72,000	$ 75,000
Accumulated Depreciation	508,000	573,000
Long-Term Debt	200,000	215,000
Capital Stock	509,000	509,000
Retained Earnings	517,000	497,000
Total Credits	$1,806,000	$1,869,000
Income Statement Data		
Sales.		$1,338,000
Cost of Goods Sold (excluding depreciation)		932,000
Selling and Administrative Expenses.		298,000
Depreciation Expense		93,000
Interest Expense		20,000
Other Expenses		15,000

    a. Prepare an income statement (including a reconciliation of retained earnings) for the year.

    b. Prepare a statement of changes in financial position for the Victoria Company for the year, defining funds as cash. Support the statement of changes in financial position with a T-account work sheet.

21. *Preparing statement of changes in financial position.* Exhibit 5.23 presents a comparative balance sheet for Psilos Corporation as of the beginning and end of the current year. Additional information related to the year is as follows:

Net Income	$40,000
Dividends Declared and Paid	50,000
Property, Plant, and Equipment Acquired:	
For Cash	40,000
By Assuming Long-Term Debt	15,000
Proceeds from Sale of Property, Plant, and Equipment Sold at Book Value . . .	5,000

Prepare a statement of changes in financial position for Psilos Corporation for the current year, supporting the statement with a T-account work sheet.

Exhibit 5.23
PSILOS CORPORATION
Comparative Balance Sheet
(Problem 21)

	January 1	December 31
Assets		
Current Assets:		
Cash	$ 28,000	$ 16,000
Accounts Receivable	125,000	109,000
Merchandise Inventories	147,000	163,000
Total Current Assets	$300,000	$288,000
Property, Plant, and Equipment	$210,000	$240,000
Less Accumulated Depreciation	(87,000)	(85,000)
Total Property, Plant, and Equipment	$123,000	$155,000
Total Assets	$423,000	$443,000
Liabilities and Shareholders' Equity		
Current Liabilities:		
Accounts Payable	$177,000	$175,000
Income Taxes Payable	23,000	30,000
Total Current Liabilities	$200,000	$205,000
Long-Term Debt:		
Bonds Payable	50,000	75,000
Total Liabilities	$250,000	$280,000
Shareholders' Equity:		
Common Stock	$ 10,000	$ 10,000
Retained Earnings	163,000	153,000
Total Shareholders' Equity	$173,000	$163,000
Total Liabilities and Shareholders' Equity	$423,000	$443,000

22. *Preparing statement of changes in financial position over 2-year period.* Condensed financial statement data of the Alberta Company for the years ending December 31, Year 1, Year 2, and Year 3, are presented in Exhibits 5.24 and 5.25.

Exhibit 5.24
ALBERTA COMPANY
Post-closing Trial Balance
Comparative Data
(Problem 22)

	12/31/Year 1	12/31/Year 2	12/31/Year 3
Debits:			
Cash	$ 55,000	$ 87,000	$ 97,000
Accounts Receivable	110,000	120,000	105,000
Merchandise Inventories.	125,000	115,000	140,000
Total Current Assets	$ 290,000	$ 322,000	$ 342,000
Property, Plant, and Equipment	1,616,000	1,679,000	1,875,000
Total Debits	$1,906,000	$2,001,000	$2,217,000
Credits:			
Accounts Payable	$ 81,000	$ 80,000	$ 83,000
Accumulated Depreciation	697,000	720,000	745,000
Bonds Payable	106,000	90,000	135,000
Common Stock	377,000	423,000	514,000
Retained Earnings	645,000	688,000	740,000
Total Credits	$1,906,000	$2,001,000	$2,217,000

Exhibit 5.25
ALBERTA COMPANY
Income and Retained Earnings
Statement Data

	Year 2	Year 3
Sales	$910,000	$970,000
Interest and Other Revenue.	5,000	7,000
Cost of Goods Sold (excluding depreciation)	370,000	413,000
Selling and Administrative Expenses	320,000	301,000
Depreciation.	87,000	98,000
Federal Income Taxes	55,000	66,000
Dividends Declared	40,000	47,000

a. Prepare a statement of changes in financial position for Year 2. Support the statement with a T-account work sheet. The original cost of the property, plant, and equipment sold during Year 2 was $108,000. These assets were sold for cash at their net book value.

b. Prepare a T-account work sheet and a statement of changes in financial position for Year 3. Property, plant, and equipment were sold during the year at book value. Expenditures on new property, plant, and equipment amounted to $318,000 during Year 3.

23. *Working backwards through statement of changes in financial position.* The Quinta Company presents the post-closing trial balance shown in Exhibit 5.26 and statement of changes in financial position shown in Exhibit 5.27 for Year 5.

Investment, equipment, and land were sold for cash at their net book value. The accumulated depreciation of the equipment sold was $20,000.

Prepare a balance sheet for the beginning of the year, January 1, Year 5.

Exhibit 5.26
QUINTA COMPANY
Post-closing Trial Balance
December 31, Year 5
(Problem 23)

Debit Balances:

Cash	$ 25,000
Accounts Receivable	220,000
Merchandise Inventories	320,000
Land	40,000
Buildings and Equipment	500,000
Investments (noncurrent)	100,000
Total Debits	$1,205,000

Credit Balances:

Accumulated Depreciation	$ 200,000
Accounts Payable	280,000
Other Current Liabilities	85,000
Bonds Payable	100,000
Common Stock	200,000
Retained Earnings	340,000
Total Credits	$1,205,000

Exhibit 5.27
QUINTA COMPANY
Statement of Changes in Financial Position
For Year 5
(Problem 23)

Sources of Cash

From Operations:

Net Income	$200,000

Additions:

Depreciation Expense	60,000
Increase in Accounts Payable	25,000

Subtractions:

Increase in Accounts Receivable	(30,000)
Increase in Merchandise Inventories	(40,000)
Decrease in Other Current Liabilities	(45,000)
Total Sources from Operations	$170,000

continued

Exhibit 5.27 *continued*
QUINTA COMPANY
Statement of Changes in Financial Position
For Year 5
(Problem 23)

Proceeds from Issues of Securities and Debt:

Common Stock Issue	$60,000	
Bond Issue	40,000	
Total Proceeds		100,000

Proceeds of Disposition of Noncurrent Assets:

Sale of Investments	$40,000	
Sale of Buildings and Equipment	15,000	
Sale of Land	10,000	
Total Proceeds		65,000
Total Sources of Cash		$335,000

Uses of Cash

Dividends	$200,000
Acquisition of Buildings and Equipment	130,000
Total Uses of Cash	$330,000
Increase in Cash During the Year (sources minus uses) . . .	$ 5,000

24. *Interpretative case using statement of changes in financial position (adapted from a problem by Leonard Morrissey).* RV Suppliers, Incorporated, founded in January, Year 1, manufactures "Kaps." A "Kap" is a relatively low-cost camping unit attached to a pickup truck. Most units consist of an extruded aluminum frame and a fiberglass skin.

After a loss in its initial year, the company was barely profitable in Year 2 and Year 3. More substantial profits were realized in Years 4 and 5, as indicated in the financial statements shown in Exhibits 5.28 and 5.29.

Exhibit 5.28
RV SUPPLIERS, INCORPORATED
Income Statements
(amounts in 000's)
(Problem 24)

	Year 4	Year 5	Year 6
Net Sales	$266.4	$424.0	$247.4
Cost of Goods Sold	191.4	314.6	210.6
Gross Margin	$ 75.0	$109.4	$ 36.8
Operating Expenses[a]	35.5	58.4	55.2
Income (loss) Before Income Taxes	$ 39.5	$ 51.0	$ (18.4)
Income Taxes	12.3	16.4	5.0
Net Income (loss)	$ 27.2	$ 34.6	$ (13.4)

[a]Includes depreciation expense of $1.7 in Year 4, $4.8 in Year 5, and $7.6 in Year 6.

Exhibit 5.29
RV SUPPLIERS, INCORPORATED
Balance Sheet
(amounts in 000's)
(Problem 24)

	Dec. 31 Year 4	Dec. 31 Year 5	Dec. 31 Year 6
Assets			
Current Assets:			
Cash	$ 14.0	$ 12.0	$ 5.2
Accounts Receivable	28.8	55.6	24.2
Inventories	54.0	85.6	81.0
Tax Refund Receivable	0	0	5.0
Prepayments	4.8	7.4	5.6
Total Current Assets	$101.6	$160.6	$121.0
Property, Plant, Equipment—Net (Note 1)	30.2	73.4	72.2
Total Assets	$131.8	$234.0	$193.2
Liabilities and Shareholders' Equity			
Current Liabilities:			
Bank Notes Payable	$ 10.0	$ 52.0	$ 70.0
Accounts Payable	31.6	53.4	17.4
Income Taxes Payable	5.8	7.0	0
Other Current Liabilities.	4.2	6.8	4.4
Total Current Liabilities	$ 51.6	$119.2	$ 91.8
Shareholders' Equity:			
Capital Stock	$ 44.6	$ 44.6	$ 44.6
Retained Earnings	35.6	70.2	56.8
Total Shareholders' Equity	$ 80.2	$114.8	$101.4
Total Liabilities and Shareholders' Equity	$131.8	$234.0	$193.2

Note 1	Year 4	Year 5	Year 6
Acquisitions	$ 13.4	$ 48.4	$ 11.8
Depreciation Expense	(1.7)	(4.8)	(7.6)
Book Value and Sales Proceeds from Retirements . . .	(.4)	(.4)	(5.4)
Net Change in Property, Plant, and Equipment	$ 11.3	$ 43.2	$ (1.2)

However, in Year 6, ended just last month, the company suffered a loss of $13,400. Sales dropped from $424,000 in Year 5 to $247,400 in Year 6. The outlook for Year 7 is not encouraging. Potential buyers continue to shun pickup trucks in preference to more energy-efficient small foreign and domestic automobiles.

How did the company finance its rapid growth during the year ended December 31, Year 5? What were the sources and uses of cash during the year? Similarly, how did the company manage its financial affairs during the abrupt contraction in business during the year just ended last month?

Chapter 6

Introduction to Financial Statement Analysis

Chapters 1 through 5 have considered the three principal financial statements needed to understand the financial activities of a business: the balance sheet, the income statement, and the statement of changes in financial position. For each financial statement, we have examined its purpose, its underlying concepts, the procedures for preparing it, and some of the uses that can be made of information contained in the statement.

Chapters 7 through 14 explore the "generally accepted accounting principles" used in preparing these financial statements. Before embarking on a study of generally accepted accounting principles, it will be useful to pause and introduce some of the techniques that can be used in analyzing financial statements. Such analysis can be done at only an elementary level at this point; effective financial statement interpretation and analysis require a fuller understanding of the impact of accounting principles on the reported amounts. Introducing the tools and techniques of financial statement analysis at this time, however, provides an opportunity to synthesize the material in the preceding five chapters.

Objectives of Financial Statement Analysis

The first question likely to be raised in analyzing a set of financial statements is "What do I look for?" The response to this question requires an understanding of investment decisions.

To illustrate, assume that you recently inherited $25,000 and must decide what to do with the bequest. You have narrowed the investment decision to purchasing either a certificate of deposit at a local bank or shares of common stock of Horrigan Corporation, currently selling for $40 per share. Your decision will be based on the *return* anticipated from each investment and the *risk* associated with that return.

The bank is currently paying interest at the rate of 10 percent annually on certificates of deposit. Because it is unlikely that the bank will go out of business, you are virtually certain of earning 10 percent each year.

The return from investing in the shares of common stock of Horrigan Corporation has two components. First, the firm paid a cash dividend in their most recent year of $.625 per share, and it is anticipated that this dividend will continue in the future. Second, the market price of the stock is likely to change between the date the shares are purchased and the date in the future when they are sold. The difference between the eventual selling price per share and the $40 purchase price, often called a *capital gain*, is a second component of the return from buying the stock.

The return from the common stock investment is more risky than the interest on the certificate of deposit. Future dividends and market price changes are likely to be associated, at least partially, with the profitability of the firm. Future income might be less than is currently anticipated if competitors introduce new products that erode Horrigan Corporation's share of its sales market. Future income might be greater than currently anticipated if Horrigan Corporation makes important discoveries or introduces successful new products.

The market price of Horrigan Corporation's shares will probably also be affected by economy-wide factors such as inflation and changes in international tensions. Also, specific industry factors, such as raw materials shortages or government antitrust actions, may influence the market price of the shares. Because most individuals prefer less risk to more risk, you will probably demand a higher expected return from the purchase of Horrigan Corporation's shares than if you invest the inheritance in a certificate of deposit.

Theoretical and empirical research has shown that the expected return from investing in a firm is, in part, related to the expected profitability of the firm.[1] A firm's past operating, or earnings, performance is analyzed as a basis for forecasting its future profitability.

Investment decisions also require that the risk associated with the expected return be assessed.[2] A firm may find itself with a shortage of cash and be unable to repay a short-term loan coming due. Or the amount of long-term debt in the capital structure may be so large that the firm has difficulty meeting the required interest and principal payments. The financial statements provide information for assessing how these and other elements of risk affect expected return.

Most financial statement analysis, therefore, is directed at some aspect of a firm's *profitability* or its *risk*.

Usefulness of Ratios

The various items in financial statements may be difficult to interpret in the form in which they are presented. For example, the profitability of a firm may be difficult to assess by looking at the amount of net income alone. It is helpful to compare earnings with the assets or capital required to generate those earnings. This relation, and other important ones between various items in the financial statements, can be expressed in the form of ratios. Some ratios compare items within the income statement; some use only balance sheet data; others relate items from more than one of the three principal financial statements. Ratios are useful tools of financial statement analysis because they conveniently summarize data in a form that is more easily understood, interpreted, and compared.

Ratios are, by themselves, difficult to interpret. For example, does a rate of return on common stock of 8.6 percent reflect a good performance? Once calculated, the ratios must be compared with some standard. Several possible standards might be used:

1. The planned ratio for the period being analyzed.
2. The corresponding ratio during the preceding period for the same firm.

---

[1]Ray Ball and Phillip Brown, ''An Empirical Evaluation of Accounting Income Numbers,'' *Journal of Accounting Research,* Autumn 1968, pp. 159–178.

[2]Modern finance makes a distinction between systematic (market) risk and nonsystematic (firm-specific) risk. The discussion in this chapter does not differentiate between these two dimensions of risk.

3.   The corresponding ratio for a similar firm in the same industry.
4.   The average ratio for other firms in the same industry.

Difficulties encountered in using each of these bases for comparison are discussed later.

The sections that follow describe several ratios useful for assessing profitability and various dimensions of risk. To demonstrate the calculation of various ratios, we use data for Horrigan Corporation for Years 2 through 4 as shown in Exhibit 6.1 (comparative balance sheets), Exhibit 6.2 (comparative income statements), and Exhibit 6.3 (comparative statements of changes in financial position). Our analysis for Horrigan Corporation is based on a study of the changes in its various ratios over the 3-year period. Such an analysis is referred to as *time-series analysis*. Comparison of a given firm's ratios with those of other firms for a particular period is referred to as *cross-section analysis*. Cross-section analysis requires an understanding of the accounting principles used by different firms and is considered in Chapter 15.

Exhibit 6.1
HORRIGAN CORPORATION
Comparative Balance Sheets
(amounts in millions)

	December 31			
	Year 1	Year 2	Year 3	Year 4
Assets				
Cash	$ 10	$ 14	$ 8	$ 12
Accounts Receivable (net).	26	36	46	76
Inventories	14	30	46	83
Total Current Assets	$ 50	$ 80	$100	$171
Land	$ 20	$ 30	$ 60	$ 60
Building	150	150	150	190
Equipment.	70	192	276	313
Less Accumulated Depreciation	(40)	(52)	(66)	(84)
Total Noncurrent Assets.	$200	$320	$420	$479
Total Assets	$250	$400	$520	$650
Liabilities and Shareholders' Equity				
Accounts Payable	$ 25	$ 30	$ 35	$ 50
Salaries Payable	10	13	15	20
Income Taxes Payable	5	7	10	20
Total Current Liabilities	$ 40	$ 50	$ 60	$ 90
Bonds Payable.	50	50	100	150
Total Liabilities	$ 90	$100	$160	$240
Common Stock ($10 par value)	$100	$150	$160	$160
Additional Paid-in Capital	20	100	120	120
Retained Earnings	40	50	80	130
Total Shareholders' Equity.	$160	$300	$360	$410
Total Liabilities and Shareholders' Equity	$250	$400	$520	$650

Exhibit 6.2
HORRIGAN CORPORATION
Comparative Income Statements
(amounts in millions)

	Years Ended December 31		
	Year 2	Year 3	Year 4
Sales Revenue	$210	$310	$475
Less Expenses:			
Cost of Goods Sold	$119	$179	$280
Selling	36	38	46
Administrative	12	13	15
Depreciation	12	14	18
Interest	5	10	16
Total	$184	$254	$375
Net Income Before Taxes	$ 26	$ 56	$100
Income Tax Expense	10	22	40
Net Income	$ 16	$ 34	$ 60

Analysis of Profitability

The operating activities of a firm are carried out in order to generate net income. Three measures of profitability discussed in this section are

1. Rate of return on assets.
2. Rate of return on common shareholders' equity.
3. Earnings per common share.

Rate of Return on Assets

The rate of return on assets is a measure of a firm's performance in using assets to generate earnings independent of the financing of those assets. In terms of the three principal business activities (investing, financing, and operating) discussed in previous chapters, the rate of return on assets relates the results of *operating* performance to the *investments* that a firm has made without regard to how the acquisition of those investments was *financed*.

The rate of return on assets is calculated as follows:

$$\frac{\text{Net Income Plus Interest Expense}}{\text{Average Total Assets}} \cdot$$

Net of Income Tax Savings

Because the rate of return on assets measures a firm's performance in using assets independent of the financing of those assets, the earnings figure used in calculating the rate of return on assets is income before deducting any payments or distributions to the providers of capital. Because interest is a payment to a furnisher of capital,

Exhibit 6.3
HORRIGAN CORPORATION
Comparative Statements of
Changes in Financial Position
(amounts in millions)

	For the Year Ended December 31		
	Year 2	Year 3	Year 4
Sources of Cash			
Operations:			
Net Income.	$ 16	$ 34	$ 60
Additions:			
Depreciation Expense	12	14	18
Increase in Accounts Payable	5	5	15
Increase in Salaries Payable	3	2	5
Increase in Income Taxes Payable	2	3	10
Subtractions:			
Increase in Accounts Receivable	(10)	(10)	(30)
Increase in Inventories	(16)	(16)	(37)
Cash Provided by Operations.	$ 12	$ 32	$ 41
Issuance of Bonds	—	50	50
Issuance of Common Stock	130	30	—
Total Sources	$142	$112	$ 91
Uses of Cash			
Dividends.	$ 6	$ 4	$ 10
Purchase of Land	10	30	—
Purchase of Building.	—	—	40
Purchase of Equipment	122	84	37
Total Uses	$138	$118	$ 87
Increase (Decrease) in Cash	$ 4	$ (6)	$ 4

interest expense should not be deducted in measuring the return on total assets. To derive income before interest charges, it is usually easier to start with net income and add to that figure. The amount added to net income is not, however, the interest expense shown on the income statement. Because interest expense is deductible in calculating taxable income, interest expense does not reduce *aftertax* net income by the full amount of interest expense. The amount added back to net income is interest expense reduced by income tax savings.

For example, interest expense for Horrigan Corporation for Year 4, as shown in Exhibit 6.2, is $16 million. The income tax rate is assumed to be 40 percent of pretax income. The income taxes saved, because interest is deductible in computing taxable income, is $6.4 million (= .40 × $16 million). The amount of interest expense net of income tax savings that is added back to net income is therefore $9.6 million (= $16 million − $6.4 million). There is no need to add back dividends paid to shareholders, because they are not deducted as an expense in calculating net income.

Because the earnings rate *during the year* is being computed, the measure of investment should reflect the average amount of assets in use during the year. A crude, but usually satisfactory, figure for average total assets is one-half the sum of total assets at the beginning and at the end of the year.

The calculation of rate of return on assets for Horrigan Corporation for Year 4 is as follows:[3]

$$\frac{\text{Net Income Plus Interest Expense Net of Income Tax Savings}}{\text{Average Total Assets}} = \frac{\$60 + (\$16 - \$6.4)}{\frac{1}{2}(\$520 + \$650)} = 11.9 \text{ percent.}$$

Thus, for each dollar of assets used, the management of Horrigan Corporation was able to earn $.119 during Year 4 before payments to the suppliers of capital. The rate of return on assets was 5.8 percent in Year 2 and 8.7 percent in Year 3. Thus, the rate of return has increased steadily during this 3-year period.

One might question the rationale for a measure of return that is independent of the means of financing. After all, the assets must be financed and the cost of that financing must be covered if the firm is to be profitable.

The rate of return on assets is of particular concern to lenders, or creditors, of a firm. These creditors have a senior claim on earnings and assets relative to common shareholders. Creditors receive their return in the form of interest. This return typically comes from earnings generated from assets before any other suppliers of capital receive a return (for example, dividends). When extending credit or providing debt capital to a firm, creditors would want to be sure that the return generated by the firm on that capital (assets) exceeded its cost.

The rate of return on assets is also useful to common shareholders in assessing financial leverage, a topic discussed later in this chapter.

Disaggregating the Rate of Return on Assets

One means of studying changes in the rate of return on assets is to disaggregate the ratio into two other ratios as follows:

$$\begin{array}{ccc} \text{Rate of} & & \text{Profit Margin Ratio} & \text{Total Assets} \\ \text{Return} & = & \text{(before interest expense} \times & \text{Turnover} \\ \text{on Assets} & & \text{and related income tax effects)} & \text{Ratio,} \end{array}$$

or

$$\frac{\text{Net Income Plus Interest Expense Net of Income Tax Savings}}{\text{Average Total Assets}} = \frac{\text{Net Income Plus Interest Expense Net of Income Tax Savings}}{\text{Revenues}} \times \frac{\text{Revenues}}{\text{Average Total Assets}}.$$

---

[3]Throughout the remainder of this chapter, we omit reference to the fact that the amounts for Horrigan Corporation are in millions of dollars.

The profit margin ratio is a measure of a firm's ability to control the level of costs, or expenses, relative to revenues generated. By holding down costs, a firm will be able to increase the profits from a given amount of revenue and thereby improve its profit margin ratio. The total assets turnover ratio is a measure of a firm's ability to generate revenues from a particular level of investment in assets, or to put it another way, the total assets turnover measures a firm's ability to control the level of investment in assets for a particular level of revenues.

Exhibit 6.4 shows the disaggregation of the rate of return on assets for Horrigan Corporation for Year 2, Year 3, and Year 4 into profit margin and total assets turnover ratios. Much of the improvement in the rate of return on assets between Year 2 and Year 3 results from an increase in the profit margin ratio from 9.1 percent to 12.9 percent. The total assets turnover ratio remained relatively stable between these two years. On the other hand, most of the improvement in the rate of return on assets between Year 3 and Year 4 can be attributed to the increased total assets turnover. The firm was able to generate $.81 of sales from each dollar invested in assets during Year 4 as compared to $.67 of sales per dollar of assets in Year 3. The increased total assets turnover, coupled with an improvement in the profit margin ratio, permitted Horrigan Corporation to increase its rate of return on assets during Year 4. We must analyze the changes in the profit margin ratio and total assets turnover ratio in greater depth to pinpoint the causes of the changes in Horrigan Corporation's profitability over this 3-year period. We return to this analysis shortly.

Exhibit 6.4
Disaggregation of Rate of Return
on Assets for Horrigan Corporation
For Year 2, Year 3, and Year 4

	Net Income Plus Interest Expense Net of Income Tax Savings / Average Total Assets	=	Net Income Plus Interest Expense Net of Income Tax Savings / Revenues	×	Revenues / Average Total Assets
Year 2:	$\dfrac{\$16 + (\$5 - \$2)}{\frac{1}{2}(\$250 + \$400)}$	=	$\dfrac{\$16 + (\$5 - \$2)}{\$210}$	×	$\dfrac{\$210}{\frac{1}{2}(\$250 + \$400)}$
	5.8%	=	9.1%	×	.65
Year 3:	$\dfrac{\$34 + (\$10 - \$4)}{\frac{1}{2}(\$400 + \$520)}$	=	$\dfrac{\$34 + (\$10 - \$4)}{\$310}$	×	$\dfrac{\$310}{\frac{1}{2}(\$400 + \$520)}$
	8.7%	=	12.9%	×	.67
Year 4:	$\dfrac{\$60 + (\$16 - \$6.4)}{\frac{1}{2}(\$520 + \$650)}$	=	$\dfrac{\$60 + (\$16 - \$6.4)}{\$475}$	×	$\dfrac{\$475}{\frac{1}{2}(\$520 + \$650)}$
	11.9%	=	14.7%	×	.81

Improving the rate of return on assets can be accomplished by increasing the profit margin ratio, the rate of asset turnover, or both. Some firms, however, may have little flexibility in altering one of these components. For example, a firm committed under a 3-year labor union contract may have little control over wage rates paid. Or a firm operating under market- or government-imposed price controls may not be able to increase the prices of its products. In these cases, the opportunities for improving the profit margin ratio may be limited. In order to increase the rate of return on assets, the level of investment in assets such as inventory, plant, and equipment must be reduced or, to put it another way, revenues per dollar of assets must be increased.

Analyzing Changes in the Profit Margin Ratio

Profit, or net income, is measured by subtracting various expenses from revenues. To identify the reasons for a change in the profit margin ratio, changes in a firm's expenses relative to revenues must be examined. One approach is to express individual expenses and net income as a percentage of revenues. Such an analysis is presented in Exhibit 6.5 for Horrigan Corporation. Note that we have altered somewhat the conventional income statement format in this analysis by subtracting interest expense (net of its related income tax effects) as the last expense item. The percentages on the line, Income Before Interest and Related Income Tax Effect, correspond (except for rounding) to the profit margin ratios (before interest and related tax effects) shown in Exhibit 6.4.

Exhibit 6.5
Net Income and Expenses as a Percentage of
Revenues for Horrigan Corporation for
Year 2, Year 3, and Year 4

	Years Ended December 31		
	Year 2	**Year 3**	**Year 4**
Sales Revenue	100.0%	100.0%	100.0%
Less Operating Expenses:			
Cost of Goods Sold	56.7%	57.7%	58.9%
Selling	17.1	12.3	9.7
Administrative	5.7	4.2	3.2
Depreciation	5.7	4.5	3.8
Total	85.2%	78.7%	75.6%
Income Before Income Taxes and Interest	14.8%	21.3%	24.4%
Income Taxes at 40 percent	5.7	8.4	9.7
Income Before Interest and Related Income Tax Effect	9.1%	12.9%	14.7%
Interest Expense Net of Income Tax Effect	1.5	1.9	2.1
Net Income	7.6%	11.0%	12.6%

The analysis in Exhibit 6.5 indicates that the improvement in the profit margin ratio over the 3 years for Horrigan Corporation can be attributed primarily to decreases in selling, administrative, and depreciation expenses as a percentage of sales. The reasons for these decreasing percentages should be explored further with management. Does the decrease in selling expenses as a percentage of sales reflect a reduction in the rate of advertising expenditures that could hurt future sales? Does the decrease in depreciation expense as a percentage of sales reflect a failure to expand plant and equipment as sales have increased? On the other hand, do these decreasing percentages merely reflect the realization of economies of scale as fixed selling, administrative, and depreciation expenses are being spread over a larger number of units?[4] The amount or trend in a particular ratio cannot, by itself, be the basis for investing or not investing in a firm. Ratios merely indicate areas where additional analysis is required. For example, the increasing percentage of cost of goods sold to sales should be explored further. It may reflect a successful, planned pricing policy of reducing gross margin (selling price less cost of goods sold) in order to increase the volume of sales. On the other hand, the replacement cost of inventory items may be increasing without corresponding increases being made in selling prices. Or the firm may be accumulating excess inventories that are physically deteriorating or becoming obsolete.

Analyzing Changes in the Total Assets Turnover Ratio

The total assets turnover ratio depends on the turnover ratios for its individual asset components. Three turnover ratios are commonly calculated: accounts receivable turnover, inventory turnover, and fixed asset turnover.

Accounts Receivable Turnover   The rate at which accounts receivable turn over gives an indication of their nearness to being converted into cash. The accounts receivable turnover is calculated by dividing net sales on account by average accounts receivable. For Horrigan Corporation, the accounts receivable turnover for Year 4, assuming that all sales are on account (that is, none are for immediate cash), is calculated as follows:

$$\frac{\text{Net Sales on Account}}{\text{Average Accounts Receivable}} = \frac{\$475}{\frac{1}{2}(\$46 + \$76)} = 7.8 \text{ times per year.}$$

The concept of accounts receivable turnover is often expressed in terms of the average number of days that receivables are outstanding before cash is collected. The calculation is to divide the accounts receivable turnover ratio into 365 days. The average number of days that accounts receivable are outstanding for Horrigan Corporation for Year 4 is 46.8 days (= 365 days/7.8 times per year). Thus, on average, accounts receivable are collected approximately $1\frac{1}{2}$ months after the date of sale. The interpretation of this average collection period depends on the terms of sale. If the terms of sale are "net 30 days," the accounts receivable turnover

---

[4]This phenomenon is called *operating leverage* and is discussed more fully in managerial economics textbooks.

indicates that collections are not being made in accordance with the stated terms. Such a ratio would warrant a review of the credit and collection activity for an explanation and for possible corrective action. If the firm offers terms of "net 45 days," then the results indicate that accounts receivable are being handled better.

Inventory Turnover The inventory turnover ratio is considered to be a significant indicator of the efficiency of operations for many businesses. It is calculated by dividing cost of goods sold by the average inventory during the period. The inventory turnover for Horrigan Corporation for Year 4 is calculated as follows:

$$\frac{\text{Cost of Goods Sold}}{\text{Average Inventory}} = \frac{\$280}{\frac{1}{2}(\$46 + \$83)} = 4.3 \text{ times per year.}$$

Thus, inventory is typically on hand an average of 84.9 days (= 365 days/4.3 times per year) before it is sold.

The interpretation of the inventory turnover figure involves two opposing considerations. Management would like to sell as many goods as possible with a minimum of capital tied up in inventories. An increase in the rate of inventory turnover between periods would seem to indicate more profitable use of the investment in inventory. On the other hand, management does not want to have so little inventory on hand that shortages result and customers are turned away. An increase in the rate of inventory turnover in this case may mean a loss of customers and thereby offset any advantage gained by decreased investment in inventory. Some trade-offs are therefore required in deciding the optimum level of inventory for each firm, and thus the desirable rate of inventory turnover.

The inventory turnover ratio is sometimes calculated by dividing sales, rather than cost of goods sold, by the average inventory. As long as there is a relatively constant relationship between selling prices and cost of goods sold, changes in the *trend* of the inventory can usually be identified with either measure. It is inappropriate to use sales in the numerator if the inventory turnover ratio is to be used to calculate the average number of days inventory is on hand until sale.

Plant Asset Turnover The plant asset turnover ratio is a measure of the relationship between sales and the investment in plant assets such as property, plant, and equipment. It is calculated by dividing revenues by average plant assets during the year. The plant assets turnover ratio for Horrigan Corporation for Year 4 is

$$\frac{\text{Revenues}}{\text{Average Plant Assets}} = \frac{\$475}{\frac{1}{2}(\$420 + \$479)} = 1.1 \text{ times per year.}$$

Thus, for each dollar invested in plant assets during Year 4, $1.10 was generated in revenues.

Changes in the plant asset turnover ratio must be interpreted carefully. Investments in plant assets (for example, production facilities) are often made several periods before the time when sales are generated from products manufactured in the plant. Thus, a low or decreasing rate of plant asset turnover may be indicative of an expanding firm preparing for future growth. On the other hand, a firm may cut back its capital expenditures if the near-term outlook for its products is poor. Such action could lead to an increase in the plant asset turnover ratio.

Exhibit 6.6
Asset Turnover Ratios for
Horrigan Corporation for
Year 2, Year 3, and Year 4

	Year 2	Year 3	Year 4
Total Assets Turnover	.65	.67	.81
Accounts Receivable Turnover	6.8	7.6	7.8
Inventory Turnover	5.4	4.7	4.3
Plant Asset Turnover	.8	.8	1.1

We noted earlier that the total assets turnover for Horrigan Corporation was relatively steady between Year 2 and Year 3 but increased dramatically in Year 4. Exhibit 6.6 presents the four turnover ratios we have discussed for Horrigan Corporation over this 3-year period. The accounts receivable turnover ratio increased steadily over the 3 years, indicating either more careful screening of credit applications or more effective collection efforts. The inventory turnover ratio decreased during the 3 years. Coupling this result with the increasing percentage of cost of goods sold to sales shown in Exhibit 6.5 indicates that there may be excessive investments in inventories that are physically deteriorating or becoming obsolete.

Most of the increase in the total assets turnover between Year 3 and Year 4 can be attributed to an increase in the plant assets turnover. We note in the statement of changes in financial position for Horrigan Corporation in Exhibit 6.3 that total capital expenditures on land, building, and equipment have decreased over the 3-year period, possibly accounting for the increase in the plant assets turnover. The reasons for this decrease should be investigated.

Summary of the Analysis of the Rate of Return on Assets

This section began by stating that the rate of return on assets is a useful measure for assessing a firm's performance in using assets to generate earnings. The rate of return on assets was then disaggregated into profit margin and total assets turnover components. The profit margin ratio was, in turn, disaggregated by relating various expenses and net income to sales. The total assets turnover was further analyzed by calculating turnover ratios for accounts receivable, inventory, and plant assets.

The analysis revealed the following:

1. The rate of return on assets increased steadily over the 3-year period from Year 2 to Year 4.

2. The improved rate of return on assets can be attributed to an increasing profit margin over all 3 years and an improved total asset turnover during Year 4.

3. The improved profit margin is in large measure attributable to a decrease in the percentage of selling expenses to sales. The reason for this decrease should be explored further to ascertain whether advertising and selling efforts are being curtailed currently that might adversely affect future sales.

4. The changes in the total assets turnover reflect the effects of increasing accounts receivable and plant asset turnovers and a decreasing inventory turnover. The increasing plant asset turnover might be attributable to a reduction in the level of investment in new property, plant, and equipment that could hurt future productive capacity and should be explored further. The decreasing rate of inventory turnover coupled with the increasing percentage of cost of goods sold to sales may be indicative of inventory control problems (build-up of obsolete inventory) and should likewise be explored further.

Rate of Return on Common Shareholders' Equity

A second measure of profitability is the *rate of return on common shareholders' equity*. The rate of return on common shareholders' equity measures a firm's performance in using assets to generate earnings but, unlike the rate of return on assets, explicitly considers the financing of those assets. Thus, this measure of profitability incorporates the results of operating, investing, and financing decisions. This measure of profitability is of primary interest to investors in a firm's common stock. The rate of return on common shareholders' equity is calculated as follows:

$$\frac{\text{Net Income} - \text{Dividends on Preferred Stock}}{\text{Average Common Shareholders' Equity}}.$$

To calculate the amount of earnings assignable to common shareholders' equity, the earnings allocable to any preferred stock equity—usually the dividends on preferred stock declared during the period—must be deducted from net income. The capital provided during the period by common shareholders can be calculated by averaging the aggregate par value of common stock, capital contributed in excess of par value on common stock, and retained earnings (or by deducting the equity of preferred shareholders from total shareholders' equity) at the beginning and end of the period.

The rate of return on common shareholders' equity of Horrigan Corporation for Year 4 is calculated as

$$\frac{\text{Net Income} - \text{Dividends on Preferred Stock}}{\text{Average Common Shareholders' Equity}} = \frac{\$60 - \$0}{\frac{1}{2}(\$360 + \$410)} = 15.6 \text{ percent.}$$

The rate of return on common shareholders' equity was 7.0 percent in Year 2 and 10.3 percent in Year 3. Thus, like the rate of return on assets, the rate of return on common shareholders' equity increased dramatically over the 3 years.

Relationship Between Return on Assets and Return on Common Shareholders' Equity

Figure 6.1 graphs the two measures of rate of return discussed thus far for Horrigan Corporation for Year 2, Year 3, and Year 4. In each year, the rate of return on common shareholders' equity exceeded the rate of return on assets. What accounts for this relation?

Figure 6.1 Rates of Return for Horrigan Corporation

Recall that the rate of return on assets measures the profitability of a firm *before* any payments to the suppliers of capital. This return on assets must then be allocated among the various providers of capital. Creditors are allocated an amount equal to any contractual interest to which they have a claim. Preferred shareholders, if any, are allocated an amount equal to the stated dividend rate on the preferred stock. *Any remaining return* belongs to the common shareholders. That is, common shareholders have a residual claim on all earnings after creditors and preferred shareholders have received amounts contractually owed them. Thus,

$$\text{Rate of Return on Assets} \rightarrow \begin{array}{c} \text{Return to} \\ \text{Creditors} \\ \text{(interest)} \end{array} + \begin{array}{c} \text{Return to} \\ \text{Preferred} \\ \text{Shareholders} \\ \text{(dividends)} \end{array} + \begin{array}{c} \text{Return to} \\ \text{Common} \\ \text{Shareholders} \\ \text{(residual)}. \end{array}$$

We can now see how the rate of return on common shareholders' equity can be larger than the rate of return on assets. The rate of return on assets must exceed the aftertax cost of debt capital (Horrigan Corporation has no preferred stock outstanding). For Year 4, the rate of return on assets was 11.9 percent and the aftertax cost of debt was 4.8 percent [= (1 − .4)($16)/.5($160 + $240); see Exhibits 6.1 and 6.2]. This excess return belongs to the common shareholders.

The common shareholders earned a higher return only because the shareholders undertook more risk in their investment. They were placed in a riskier position because the firm incurred debt obligations with fixed payment dates. The phenomenon of common shareholders trading extra risk for a potentially higher return is called financial leverage and is described next.

Financial Leverage: Trading on the Equity

Financing with debt and preferred stock to increase the potential return to the resid-ual common shareholders' equity is referred to as *financial leverage* or *trading on the equity*. So long as a higher rate of return can be earned on assets than is paid for the capital used to acquire those assets, the rate of return to common shareholders can be increased. Exhibit 6.7 explores this phenomenon. Leveraged Company and No-Debt Company both have $100,000 of assets. Leveraged Company borrows $40,000 at a 10 percent annual rate. No-Debt Company raises all its capital from common shareholders. Both companies pay income taxes at the rate of 40 percent.

Consider first a "good" earnings year. Both companies earn $10,000 before interest charges (but after taxes except for tax effects of interest charges).[5] This represents a rate of return on assets for both companies of 10 percent (= $10,000/$100,000). Leveraged Company's net income is $7,600 [= $10,000 − (1 − .40 tax rate) × (.10 interest rate × $40,000 borrowed)], representing a rate of return on common shareholders' equity of 12.7 percent (= $7,600/$60,000). Net income of No-Debt Company is $10,000, representing a rate of return on sharehold-ers' equity of 10 percent. Leverage increased the rate of return to shareholders of Leveraged Company, because the capital contributed by the long-term debtors earned 10 percent but required an aftertax interest payment of only 6 percent [= (1 − .40 tax rate) × (.10 interest rate)]. This additional 4 percent return on each dollar of assets increases the return to the common shareholders.

Although leverage increased the return to the common stock equity during the "good" earnings year, the increase would be larger if a larger proportion of the assets were financed with long-term borrowing and the firm were made more risky. For example, assume that the assets of $100,000 were financed with $50,000 of long-term borrowing and $50,000 of shareholders' equity. Net income of Lever-aged Company in this case would be $7,000 [= $10,000 − (1 − .40 tax rate) × (.10 × $50,000 borrowed)]. The rate of return on common stock equity would be 14 percent (= $7,000/$50,000). This rate compares with a rate of return on com-mon stock equity of 12.7 percent when long-term debt was only 40 percent of the total capital provided.

Financial leverage increases the rate of return on common stock equity when the rate of return on assets is higher than the aftertax cost of debt. The greater the proportion of debt in the capital structure, however, the greater the risk borne by the common shareholders. Debt cannot, of course, be increased without limit. As more debt is added to the capital structure, the risk of default or insolvency becomes greater. Lenders, including investors in a firm's bonds, will require a higher and higher return (interest rate) to compensate for this additional risk. A point will be reached when the aftertax cost of debt will exceed the rate of return that can be earned on assets. At this point, leverage can no longer increase the potential rate of

---

[5]That is, income before taxes and before interest charges is $16,667; $10,000 = (1 − .40) × $16,667.

Exhibit 6.7
Effects of Financial Leverage on Rate of Return of Shareholders' Equity
(income tax rate is 40 percent of pretax income)

	Long-Term Equities		Income After Taxes but before Interest Charges[a]	Aftertax Interest Charges[b]	Net Income	Rate of Return on Total Assets[c] (Percent)	Rate of Return on Common Shareholders' Equity (Percent)
	Long-Term Borrowing at 10 Percent per Year	Shareholders' Equity					
Good Earnings Year							
Leveraged Company .	$40,000	$ 60,000	$10,000	$2,400	$ 7,600	10.0%	12.7%
No-Debt Company ..	—	100,000	10,000	—	10,000	10.0	10.0
Neutral Earnings Year							
Leveraged Company .	40,000	60,000	6,000	2,400	3,600	6.0	6.0
No-Debt Company ..	—	100,000	6,000	—	6,000	6.0	6.0
Bad Earnings Year							
Leveraged Company .	40,000	60,000	4,000	2,400	1,600	4.0	2.7
No-Debt Company ..	—	100,000	4,000	—	4,000	4.0	4.0

[a]But not including any income tax savings caused by interest charges. Income before taxes and interest for *good* year is $16,667; for *neutral* year is $10,000; for *bad* year is $6,667.
[b]$40,000 (borrowed) × .10 (interest rate) × [1 − .40 (income tax rate)]. The numbers shown in the preceding column for aftertax income do not include the effects of interest charges on taxes.
[c]In each year, the rate of return on assets is the same for both companies as the rate of return on common shareholders' equity for No-Debt Company: 10 percent, 6 percent, and 4 percent, respectively.

return to common stock equity. For most large manufacturing firms, liabilities represent between 30 percent and 60 percent of total capital.

Exhibit 6.7 also demonstrates the effect of leverage in a "neutral" earnings year and in a "bad" earnings year. In the "neutral" earnings year, the rate of return to common shareholders is neither increased nor decreased by leverage, because the return on assets is 6 percent and the aftertax cost of long-term debt is 6 percent. In the "bad" earnings year, the return on assets of 4 percent is less than the aftertax cost of debt of 6 percent. The return on common stock equity therefore drops—to only 2.7 percent—below the rate of return on assets. Clearly, financial leverage can work in two ways. It can enhance owners' rate of return in good years, but owners run the risk that bad earnings years will be even worse than they would be without the borrowing.

Disaggregating the Rate of Return on Common Shareholders' Equity

The rate of return on common shareholders' equity can be disaggregated into several components in a manner similar to the disaggregation of the rate of return on assets. The rate of return on common shareholders' equity might be disaggregated as follows:

$$\begin{array}{c}\text{Rate of Return} \\ \text{on Common} \\ \text{Shareholders'} \\ \text{Equity}\end{array} = \begin{array}{c}\text{Profit Margin Ratio} \\ \text{(after interest} \\ \text{expense and} \\ \text{preferred dividends)}\end{array} \times \begin{array}{c}\text{Total} \\ \text{Assets} \\ \text{Turnover} \\ \text{Ratio}\end{array} \times \begin{array}{c}\text{Leverage} \\ \text{Ratio.}\end{array}$$

The profit margin percentage indicates the portion of the revenue dollar left over for the common shareholders after all operating costs have been covered and all claims of creditors and preferred shareholders have been subtracted. The total assets turnover, as discussed earlier, indicates the revenues generated from each dollar of assets. The leverage ratio indicates the extent to which capital (= total assets) has been provided by common shareholders. The larger is the leverage ratio, the smaller is the portion of capital provided by common shareholders and the larger the proportion provided by creditors and preferred shareholders. Thus, the larger the leverage ratio, the greater will be the extent of financial leverage.

The disaggregation of the rate of return on common shareholders' equity ratio for Horrigan Corporation for Year 4 is as follows:

$$\frac{\$60}{\frac{1}{2}(\$360 + \$410)} = \frac{\$60}{\$475} \times \frac{\$475}{\frac{1}{2}(\$520 + \$650)} \times \frac{\frac{1}{2}(\$520 + \$650)}{\frac{1}{2}(\$360 + \$410)}$$

$$15.6 \text{ percent} = 12.6 \text{ percent} \times \quad .81 \quad \times \quad 1.5.$$

Exhibit 6.8 shows the disaggregation of the rate of return on common shareholders' equity for Horrigan Corporation for Year 2, Year 3, and Year 4. Most of the increase in the rate of return on common shareholders' equity can be attributed to an increasing profit margin over the 3-year period plus an increase in total assets turnover in Year 4. The leverage ratio remained reasonably stable over this period.

Earnings per Share of Common Stock

A third measure of profitability is earnings per share of common stock. This ratio is computed by dividing net income attributable to common stock by the average number of common shares outstanding during the period.

Exhibit 6.8
Disaggregation of Rate of Return
on Common Shareholders' Equity for Horrigan Corporation

Year	Rate of Return on Common Shareholders' Equity =	Profit Margin ×	Total Assets Turnover ×	Leverage Ratio
Year 2	7.0%	= 7.6% ×	.65 ×	1.4
Year 3	10.3%	= 11.0% ×	.67 ×	1.4
Year 4	15.6%	= 12.6% ×	.81 ×	1.5

Earnings per share for Horrigan Corporation for Year 4 is calculated as follows:

$$\frac{\text{Net Income} - \text{Preferred Stock Dividend}}{\substack{\text{Weighted Average} \\ \text{Number of Common Shares} \\ \text{Outstanding} \\ \text{During the Period}^6}} = \frac{\$60 - \$0}{16 \text{ shares}} = \$3.75 \text{ per share.}$$

Earnings per share were $1.28 (= $16/12.5) for Year 2 and $2.19 (= $34/15.5) for Year 3.

If a firm has securities outstanding that can be converted into or exchanged for common stock, it may be required to present two earnings-per-share amounts: *primary earnings per share* and *fully diluted earnings per share*. For example, some firms issue convertible bonds or convertible preferred stock that can be exchanged directly for shares of common stock. Also, many firms have employee stock option plans under which shares of the company's common stock may be acquired by employees under special arrangements. If these convertible securities were converted or stock options were exercised and additional shares of common stock were issued, the amount conventionally shown as earnings per share would probably decrease, or become *diluted*. When a firm has outstanding securities that, if exchanged for shares of common stock, would decrease earnings per share by 3 percent or more, a dual presentation of primary and fully diluted earnings per share is required.[7]

Primary Earnings per Share In calculating earnings per share, adjustments may be made to the conventionally calculated amount for securities that are nearly the same as common stock. These securities are called *common stock equivalents*. Common stock equivalents are securities whose principal value arises from their capability of being exchanged for, or converted into, common stock rather than only for their own periodic cash yields over time. Stock options and warrants are always common stock equivalents. Convertible bonds and convertible preferred stock may or may not be common stock equivalents. A test is employed to ascertain if the return from these convertible securities at the date of their issue is substantially below the return available from other debt or preferred stock investments. If so, the presumption is that the securities derived their value primarily from their conversion privileges and are therefore common stock equivalents. Adjustments are made in calculating primary earnings per share for the dilutive effects of securities classified as common stock equivalents.

Fully Diluted Earnings per Share As the title implies, fully diluted earnings per share indicates the maximum possible dilution that would occur if all options, warrants, and convertible securities outstanding at the end of the accounting period were exchanged for common stock. This amount, therefore, represents the maxi-

---

[6]Exhibit 6.1 indicates that the par value of a common share is $10 and that the common stock account has a balance of $160 million throughout Year 4. The shares outstanding were therefore 16 million.

[7]Accounting Principles Board, *Opinion No. 15*, "Earnings per Share," 1969.

mum limit of possible dilution that could take place on the date of the balance sheet. All securities convertible into or exchangeable for common stock, whether or not classified as common stock equivalents, enter into the calculation of fully diluted earnings per share.

Firms that do not have convertible or other potentially dilutive securities outstanding compute earnings per share in the conventional manner. Firms with outstanding securities that have the potential for materially diluting earnings per share, as conventionally computed, must present dual earnings-per-share amounts.

Interpreting Earnings per Share Earnings per share has been criticized as a measure of profitability because it does not consider the amount of assets or capital required to generate that level of earnings. Two firms with the same earnings and earnings per share will not be equally profitable if one of the firms requires twice the amount of assets or capital to generate that earnings than does the other firm.

Earnings-per-share amounts are also difficult to interpret when comparing firms. For example, assume that two firms have identical earnings, common shareholders' equity, and rates of return on common shareholders' equity. One firm may have a lower earnings per share simply because it has a larger number of shares outstanding (due perhaps to the use of a lower par value for its shares or to different earnings retention policies; see Problem 21 at the end of this chapter).

Price-Earnings Ratio Earnings-per-share amounts are often compared with the market price of the stock. This is usually expressed as a *price-earnings ratio* (= market price per share/earnings per share). For example, the common stock of Horrigan Corporation is selling for $40 per share at the end of Year 4. The price-earnings ratio, often called the P/E ratio, is 10.67 to 1 (= $40/$3.75). This ratio is often presented in tables of stock market prices and in financial periodicals. The relationship is sometimes expressed by saying that ''the stock is selling at 10.7 times earnings.''

The relation between earnings and market price per share might be expressed as a rate (= earnings per share/market price per share). This calculation, 9.4 percent (= $3.75/$40) for Horrigan Corporation, is seen less often than the price-earnings ratio.

Summary of Profitability Analysis

Three broad measures for assessing a firm's profitability have been discussed in this chapter. Because the rate of return on assets and rate of return on common shareholders' equity relate earnings to some measure of the capital required to generate those earnings, most of our attention has been focused on the two profitability measures.

Exhibit 6.9 summarizes the analysis discussed. On the most general level, the concern is with overall measures of profitability and the effectiveness of financial leverage. On the next level, the overall measures of profitability are disaggregated into profit margin, asset turnover, and leverage components. On the third level, the

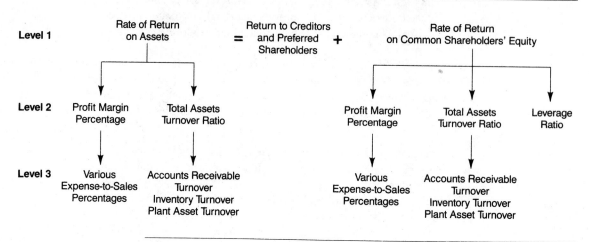

Exhibit 6.9 Profitability Ratios

profit margin and asset turnover ratios are further disaggregated to gain additional insights into reasons for changes in profitability. The depth of analysis required in any particular case depends on the differences or changes in profitability observed.

Analysis of Risk

The second parameter in investment decisions is risk. There are various factors that affect the risk of business firms:

1. Economy-wide factors, such as increased inflation or interest rates, unemployment, or recessions.
2. Industry-wide factors, such as increased competition, lack of availability of raw materials, changes in technology, or increased government antitrust actions.
3. Firm-specific factors, such as labor strikes, loss of facilities due to fire or other casualty, or poor health of key managerial personnel.

The ultimate risk is that a firm will be forced into bankruptcy and creditors and investors will lose the capital they provided to the firm.

When assessing risk, the focus is generally on the relative *liquidity* of a firm. Cash and near-cash assets provide a firm with the resources needed to adapt to these various dimensions of risk as potential losses arise. That is, liquid resources provide a firm with *financial flexibility*. Cash is also the connecting link that permits the operating, investing, and financing activities of a firm to continue operating smoothly and effectively.

When assessing liquidity, time is of critical importance. Consider the following three questions:

1. Does a firm have sufficient cash to repay a loan due tomorrow?
2. Will the firm have sufficient cash to repay a note due in 6 months?
3. Will the firm have sufficient cash to repay bonds due in 5 years?

In answering the first question, the analysis would probably focus on the amount of cash on hand and in the bank relative to obligations coming due tomorrow. In answering the second question, consideration would be given to the amount of cash expected to be generated from operations during the next 6 months, as well as to any new borrowing, relative to obligations coming due during that period. In answering the third question, the focus would shift to the longer-run cash-generating ability of a firm relative to the amount of long-term debt that would become due.

Measures of Short-Term Liquidity Risk

This section discusses four measures for assessing short-term liquidity risk: (1) current ratio, (2) quick ratio, (3) operating cash flow to current liabilities ratio, and (4) working capital turnover ratio.

Current Ratio

The *current ratio* is calculated by dividing current assets by current liabilities. It is commonly expressed as a ratio such as ''2 to 1'' or ''2 : 1,'' meaning that current assets are twice as large as current liabilities. The current ratio of Horrigan Corporation on December 31, Year 1, Year 2, Year 3, and Year 4, is

	Current Ratio $=$ $\dfrac{\text{Current Assets}}{\text{Current Liabilities}}$	
December 31, Year 1	$\dfrac{\$ 50}{\$ 40}=$	1.25 to 1.0
December 31, Year 2	$\dfrac{\$ 80}{\$ 50}=$	1.60 to 1.0
December 31, Year 3	$\dfrac{\$100}{\$ 60}=$	1.67 to 1.0
December 31, Year 4	$\dfrac{\$171}{\$ 90}=$	1.90 to 1.0

This ratio is presumed to indicate the ability of the concern to meet its current obligations, and is therefore of particular significance to short-term creditors. Although an excess of current assets over current liabilities is generally considered desirable from the creditor's viewpoint, changes in the trend of the ratio may be difficult to interpret. For example, when the current ratio is larger than 1 to 1, an increase of equal amount in both current assets and current liabilities results in a decline in the ratio, whereas equal decreases result in an increased current ratio.

In a recession period, business is contracting, current liabilities are paid, and even though the current assets may be at a low point, the ratio may go to high levels. In a boom period, just the reverse effect might occur. In other words, a very high current ratio may accompany unsatisfactory business conditions, whereas a falling ratio may accompany profitable operations.

Furthermore, the current ratio is susceptible to "window dressing"; that is, management can take deliberate steps to produce a financial statement that presents a better current ratio at the balance sheet date than the average or normal current ratio. For example, toward the close of a fiscal year normal purchases on account may be delayed. Or loans to officers, classified as noncurrent assets, may be collected and the proceeds used to reduce current liabilities. These actions may be taken so that the current ratio will appear as favorable as possible in the annual financial statements at the balance sheet date.

Although the current ratio is probably the most common liquidity ratio presented in statement analysis, there are limitations in its use as discussed above. Its trends are difficult to interpret and, if overemphasized, it can easily lead to undesirable business practices as well as misinterpretation of financial condition.

Quick Ratio

A variation of the current ratio, usually known as the *quick ratio* or *acid test ratio,* is computed by including in the numerator of the fraction only those current assets that could be converted quickly into cash. The numerator customarily includes cash, marketable securities, and receivables, but it would be better to make a study of the facts in each case before deciding whether or not to include receivables and to exclude inventories. In some businesses, the inventory of merchandise might be converted into cash more quickly than the receivables of other businesses.

Assuming that the accounts receivable of Horrigan Corporation are included but that the inventory is excluded, the quick ratio on December 31, Year 1, Year 2, Year 3, and Year 4, is

	Quick Ratio $=$	Cash, Marketable Securities, Accounts Receivable / Current Liabilities
December 31, Year 1	$\dfrac{\$36}{\$40} =$	.90 to 1.0
December 31, Year 2	$\dfrac{\$50}{\$50} =$	1.0 to 1.0
December 31, Year 3	$\dfrac{\$54}{\$60} =$	.90 to 1.0
December 31, Year 4	$\dfrac{\$88}{\$90} =$	.98 to 1.0

Whereas the current ratio increased steadily over the period, the quick ratio remained relatively constant. The increase in the current ratio resulted primarily from a build-up of inventories.

Operating Cash Flow to Current Liabilities

Both the current ratio and quick ratio can be criticized in that they are calculated using amounts at a specific point in time. If financial statement amounts at that particular time are unusually large or small, the resulting ratios will not reflect more normal conditions.

To overcome these deficiencies, the operating cash flow to current liabilities ratio can be calculated. The numerator of this ratio is cash provided by operations for the year. The denominator is average current liabilities for the year. The operating cash flow to current liabilities ratios for Horrigan Corporation for Year 2, Year 3, and Year 4 are as follows:

	$\dfrac{\text{Operating Cash Flow}}{\text{to Current Liabilities}} = \dfrac{\text{Cash Provided by Operations}}{\text{Average Current Liabilities}}$		
Year 2	$\dfrac{\$12}{\frac{1}{2}(\$40 + \$50)}$	=	26.7 percent
Year 3	$\dfrac{\$32}{\frac{1}{2}(\$50 + \$60)}$	=	58.2 percent
Year 4	$\dfrac{\$41}{\frac{1}{2}(\$60 + \$90)}$	=	54.7 percent

A ratio of 40 percent or more[8] is common for a healthy firm. Thus, the liquidity of Horrigan Corporation improved dramatically between Year 2 and Year 3. The decrease between Year 3 and Year 4 is due primarily to a build-up in current liabilities (which, in turn, is probably related to the build-up in inventories noted above).

Working Capital Turnover Ratio

The *operating cycle* of a firm is a sequence of activities in which:

1. Inventory is purchased on account from suppliers.
2. Inventory is sold on account to customers.
3. Customers pay amounts due.
4. Suppliers are paid amounts due.

---

[8]Cornelius Casey and Norman Bartczak, ''Operating Cash Flow Data and Financial Distress: Some Empirical Evidence,'' *Journal of Accounting Research* (forthcoming).

This cycle occurs continually for most business firms. The longer the cycle, the longer is the time that funds are tied up in receivables and inventories. The interest cost on funds required to carry receivables and inventory reduces net income and hurts profitability. Funds tied up in receivables and inventory also have negative effects on the short-run liquidity of a firm. The more quickly inventory and receivables are turned into cash, the more liquid is a firm.

The working capital turnover ratio is a measure of the length of the operating cycle. It is calculated by dividing sales by the average working capital for the year. Working capital is equal to current assets minus current liabilities. The working capital turnover ratio for Horrigan Corporation is as follows:

	$\frac{\text{Working Capital}}{\text{Turnover Ratio}} = \frac{\text{Sales}}{\text{Average Working Capital}}$
Year 2	$\frac{\$210}{\frac{1}{2}(\$10 + \$30)} = $ 10.5 times
Year 3	$\frac{\$310}{\frac{1}{2}(\$30 + \$40)} = $ 8.9 times
Year 4	$\frac{\$475}{\frac{1}{2}(\$40 + \$81)} = $ 7.9 times

The turnover rate has decreased over the 3-year period, primarily because inventories net of current liabilities increased faster than sales.

The working capital turnover ratio is often converted to the number of days required for one revolution of the operating cycle by dividing the turnover ratio into 365 days. Thus, working capital turned over an average every 34.8 days (= 365/10.5) during Year 2. The corresponding amounts for Year 3 and Year 4 were 41.0 days and 46.2 days, respectively.

The working capital turnover ratio varies significantly across firms depending on the nature of their businesses. The working capital turnover for grocery stores is approximately 12 times per year, whereas for a construction company the turnover is sometimes less than one. When using the working capital turnover ratio to evaluate short-term liquidity, the analyst must be aware of the type of business in which the firm is involved.

Summary of Short-Term Liquidity Analysis

The current and quick ratios give snapshot measures of liquidity at particular points in time. These ratios for Horrigan Corporation are at reasonably adequate levels at the end of each year, although they indicate a build-up of inventories in Year 4.

The cash flow from operations to current liabilities and the working capital turnover ratios provide measures of short-term liquidity for a period of time. Both ratios indicate a significant improvement in liquidity between Year 2 and Year 3, due primarily to increased cash flow from operations. Both ratios decreased during Year 4 due to the build-up of inventory. However, the levels of the ratios during

Year 4 do not yet indicate serious short-term liquidity problems for Horrigan Corporation. Given the growth rate in sales during the past 2 years (approximately 50 percent per year), a build-up of inventories may be justified.

Measures of Long-Term Liquidity Risk

Measures of long-term liquidity risk are used in evaluating the firm's ability to meet interest and principal payments on long-term debt and similar obligations as they become due. If the payments cannot be made on time, the firm becomes *insolvent* and may have to be reorganized or liquidated.

Perhaps the best indicator for assessing long-term liquidity risk is a firm's ability to generate profits over a period of years. If a firm is profitable, it will either generate sufficient cash from operations or be able to obtain needed capital from creditors and owners. The measures of profitability discussed previously are therefore applicable for this purpose as well. Three other measures of long-term liquidity risk are debt ratios, the cash flow from operations to total liabilities ratio, and the number of times that interest charges are covered.

Debt Ratios

There are several variations of the debt ratio, but the one most commonly encountered in financial analysis is the *long-term debt ratio*. It reports the portion of the firm's long-term capital that is furnished by debt holders. To calculate this ratio, divide total long-term debt by the sum of total long-term debt and total shareholders' equity.

Another form of the debt ratio is the *debt-equity ratio*. To calculate the debt-equity ratio, divide total liabilities (current and noncurrent) by total equities (liabilities plus shareholders' equity = total assets).

Exhibit 6.10 shows the two forms of the debt ratio for Horrigan Corporation on December 31, Year 1, Year 2, Year 3, and Year 4. In general, the higher these ratios, the higher the likelihood that the firm may be unable to meet fixed interest and principal payments in the future. The decision for most firms is how much financial leverage, with its attendant risk, they can afford to assume. Funds obtained from issuing bonds or borrowing from a bank have a relatively low interest cost but require fixed, periodic payments that increase the likelihood of bankruptcy.

In assessing the debt ratios, analysts customarily vary the standard in direct relation to the stability of the firm's earnings and cash flows from operations. The more stable the earnings and cash flows, the higher the debt ratio that is considered acceptable or safe. The debt ratios of public utilities are customarily high, frequently on the order of 60 to 70 percent. The stability of public utility earnings and cash flows makes these ratios acceptable to many investors who would be dissatisfied with such high leverage for firms with less stable earnings and cash flows. The debt ratios of Horrigan Corporation are about average for an industrial firm.

Because several variations of the debt ratio appear in corporate annual reports, care in comparing debt ratios among firms is necessary.

Exhibit 6.10
HORRIGAN CORPORATION
Debt Ratios

$\dfrac{\text{Long-Term}}{\text{Debt Ratio}} = \dfrac{\textbf{Total Long-Term Debt}}{\begin{array}{c}\textbf{Total Long-Term Debt}\\\textbf{Plus Shareholders'}\\\textbf{Equity}\end{array}}$		Debt-Equity Ratio $= \dfrac{\textbf{Total Liabilities}}{\begin{array}{c}\textbf{Total Liabilities Plus}\\\textbf{Shareholders'}\\\textbf{Equity}\end{array}}$	
Dec. 31, Year 1 . .	$\dfrac{\$\,50}{\$210} = 24$ percent	Dec. 31, Year 1 . .	$\dfrac{\$\,90}{\$250} = 36$ percent
Dec. 31, Year 2 . .	$\dfrac{\$\,50}{\$350} = 14$ percent	Dec. 31, Year 2 . .	$\dfrac{\$100}{\$400} = 25$ percent
Dec. 31, Year 3 . .	$\dfrac{\$100}{\$460} = 22$ percent	Dec. 31, Year 3 . .	$\dfrac{\$160}{\$520} = 31$ percent
Dec. 31, Year 4 . .	$\dfrac{\$150}{\$560} = 27$ percent	Dec. 31, Year 4 . .	$\dfrac{\$240}{\$650} = 37$ percent

Cash Flow from Operations to Total Liabilities Ratio

The debt ratios give no recognition to the varying liquidity of assets for covering various levels of debt. The cash flow from operations to total liabilities ratio overcomes this deficiency. This cash flow ratio is similar to the one used in assessing short-term liquidity risk, but here all liabilities (both current and noncurrent) are included in the denominator. The cash flow from operations to debt ratio for Horrigan Corporation is

	$\dfrac{\textbf{Cash Flow from Operations}}{\textbf{to Debt Ratio}} = \dfrac{\textbf{Cash Flow from Operations}}{\textbf{Average Total Liabilities}}$		
Year 2	$\dfrac{\$12}{\frac{1}{2}(\$90 + \$100)}$	=	12.6 percent
Year 3	$\dfrac{\$32}{\frac{1}{2}(\$100 + \$160)}$	=	24.6 percent
Year 4	$\dfrac{\$41}{\frac{1}{2}(\$160 + \$240)}$	=	20.5 percent

A ratio of 20 percent or more is normal for a financially healthy company. Thus, the long-term liquidity risk decreased significantly between Year 2 and Year 3 but increased again in Year 4. The level of the ratio in Year 4, though, is still adequate.

Interest Coverage: Times Interest Charges Earned

Another measure of long-term liquidity risk is the *number of times that interest charges are earned,* or covered. This ratio is calculated by dividing net income before interest and income tax expenses by interest expense. For Horrigan Corporation, the times interest earned ratios for Year 2, Year 3, and Year 4, are

	Times Interest Charges Earned =	Net Income Before Interest and Income Taxes
		Interest Expense
Year 2	$\dfrac{\$16 + \$5 + \$10}{\$5} =$	6.2 times
Year 3	$\dfrac{\$34 + \$10 + \$22}{\$10} =$	6.6 times
Year 4	$\dfrac{\$60 + \$16 + \$40}{\$16} =$	7.3 times

Thus, whereas the bonded indebtedness increased sharply during the 3-year period, the growth in net income before interest and income taxes was sufficient to provide increasing coverage of the fixed interest charges.

The purpose of this ratio is to indicate the relative protection of bondholders and to assess the probability that the firm will be forced into bankruptcy by a failure to meet required interest payments. If periodic repayments of principal on long-term liabilities are also required, the repayments might also be included in the denominator of the ratio. The ratio would then be described as the *number of times that fixed charges were earned,* or covered.

The times interest or fixed charges earned ratios can be criticized as measures for assessing long-term liquidity risk because the ratios use earnings rather than cash flows in the numerator. Interest and other fixed payment obligations are paid with cash, and not with earnings. When the value of the ratio is relatively low (for example, two to three times), some measure of cash flows, such as cash flows from operations, may be preferable in the numerator.

Summary of Long-Term Liquidity Analysis

The focus of long-term liquidity analysis is on the amount of debt, particularly long-term debt, in the capital structure and the adequacy of earnings and cash flows for debt service—making interest and principal payments as they become due. Although both short- and long-term debt of Horrigan Corporation have increased over the 3-year period, increases in sales, earnings, and cash flows from operations all appear to be increasing sufficiently to cover the current levels of debt.

Limitations of Ratio Analysis

For convenient reference, Exhibit 6.11 summarizes the calculation of the ratios discussed in this chapter.

The analytical computations discussed in this chapter have a number of limitations that should be kept in mind when preparing or using them. Several of the more important limitations are the following:

1. The ratios are based on financial statement data and are therefore subject to the same criticisms as the financial statements (for example, use of acquisition cost rather than current replacement cost or net realizable value; the latitude permitted firms in selecting from among various generally accepted accounting principles).

Exhibit 6.11
Summary of Financial Statement Ratios

Ratio	Numerator	Denominator
Profitability Ratios		
Rate of Return on Assets . .	Net Income + Interest Expense (net of tax effects)[a]	Average Total Assets During the Period
Profit Margin Ratio (before interest effects) . .	Net Income + Interest Expense (net of tax effects)[a]	Revenues
Various Expense Ratios . . .	Various Expenses	Revenues
Total Assets Turnover Ratio	Revenues	Average Total Assets During the Period
Accounts Receivable Turnover Ratio	Net Sales on Accounts	Average Accounts Receivable During the Period
Inventory Turnover Ratio . .	Cost of Goods Sold	Average Inventory During the Period
Plant Asset Turnover Ratio	Revenues	Average Plant Assets During the Period
Rate of Return on Common Shareholders' Equity . . .	Net Income − Preferred Stock Dividends	Average Common Shareholders' Equity During the Period
Profit Margin Ratio (after interest expense and preferred dividends)	Net Income − Preferred Stock Dividends	Revenues
Leverage Ratio	Average Total Assets During the Period	Average Common Shareholders' Equity During the Period
Earnings per Share of Stock[b]	Net Income − Preferred Stock Dividends	Weighted-Average Number of Common Shares Outstanding During the Period

continued

2. Changes in many ratios are highly associated with each other. For example, the changes in the current ratio and quick ratio between two different times are often in the same direction and approximately proportional. It is therefore not necessary to compute all the ratios to assess a particular factor.

3. When comparing the size of a ratio between periods for the same firm, one must recognize conditions that have changed between the periods being compared (for example, different product lines or geographic markets served, changes in economic conditions, changes in prices).

4. When comparing ratios of a particular firm with those of similar firms, one must recognize differences between the firms (for example, use of different methods of accounting, differences in the method of operations, type of financing, and so on).

Exhibit 6.11 *continued*
Summary of Financial Statement Ratios

Ratio	Numerator	Denominator
Short-Term Liquidity Ratios		
Current Ratio.	Current Assets	Current Liabilities
Quick or Acid Test Ratio . .	Highly Liquid Assets (ordinarily, cash, marketable securities, and receivables)[c]	Current Liabilities
Cash Flow from Operations to Current Liabilities Ratio	Cash Provided by Operations	Average Current Liabilities During the Period
Working Capital Turnover Ratio	Revenues	Average Working Capital During the Period
Long-Term Liquidity Ratios		
Long-Term Debt Ratio. . . .	Total Long-Term Debt	Total Long-Term Debt Plus Shareholders' Equity
Debt-Equity Ratio	Total Liabilities	Total Equities (liabilities plus shareholders' equity)
Cash Flow from Operations to Total Liabilities Ratio	Cash Provided by Operations	Average Total Liabilities During the Period
Times Interest Charges Earned	Net Income Before Interest and Income Taxes	Interest Expense

[a]If a consolidated subsidiary is not owned entirely by the parent corporation, the minority interest share of earnings must also be added back to net income. See the description in Chapter 13.

[b]This calculation can be more complicated when there are convertible securities, options, or warrants outstanding.

[c]Receivables could conceivably be excluded for some firms and inventories included for others. Such refinements are seldom employed in practice.

Results of financial statement analyses cannot be used by themselves as direct indications of good or poor management. Such analyses merely indicate areas that might be investigated further. For example, a decrease in the turnover of raw materials inventory, ordinarily considered to be an undesirable trend, may reflect the accumulation of scarce materials that will keep the plant operating at full capacity during shortages when competitors have been forced to restrict operations or to close down. Ratios derived from financial statements must be combined with an investigation of other facts before valid conclusions can be drawn.

Summary

This chapter began with the question, ''Should you invest your inheritance in a certificate of deposit or in the shares of common stock of Horrigan Corporation?'' Analysis of Horrigan Corporation's financial statements indicates that it has been a growing, profitable company with few indications of either short-term or long-term liquidity problems. At least three additional inputs are necessary before making the investment decision. First, consideration must be given to other sources of information besides the financial statements to ascertain if information relevant for projecting rates of return or for assessing risk needs to be considered. Second, you must decide your attitude toward, or willingness to assume, risk. Third, you must decide if you think the stock market price of the shares makes them an attractive purchase.[9] It is at this stage in the investment decision that the analysis becomes particularly subjective.

Problem 1 for Self-Study

Exhibit 6.12 presents a comparative balance sheet for Cox Corporation as of December 31, Year 1 and Year 2, and Exhibit 6.13 presents an income statement for Year 2. Using information from these financial statements, compute the following ratios. The income tax rate is 40 percent. Cash provided by operations totals $3,300.

continued on page 242

Exhibit 6.12
COX CORPORATION
Comparative Balance Sheet
December 31, Year 1 and Year 2

	December 31	
	Year 1	Year 2
Assets		
Current Assets:		
Cash	$ 600	$ 750
Accounts Receivable	3,600	4,300
Merchandise Inventories	5,600	7,900
Prepayments	300	380
Total Current Assets	$10,100	$13,330
Property, Plant, and Equipment:		
Land	$ 500	$ 600
Buildings and Equipment (net)	9,400	10,070
Total Property, Plant, and Equipment	$ 9,900	$10,670
Total Assets	$20,000	$24,000

continued

---

[9]Other important factors cannot be discussed here, but are in finance texts. Perhaps the most important question of all is how a particular investment fits in with the investor's entire portfolio. Modern research suggests that the suitability of a potential investment depends more on the attributes of the other components of an investment portfolio and the risk attitude of the investor than it does on the attributes of the potential investment itself.

Exhibit 6.12 *continued*
COX CORPORATION
Comparative Balance Sheet
December 31, Year 1 and Year 2

	December 31 Year 1	Year 2
Liabilities and Shareholders' Equity		
Current Liabilities:		
Notes Payable	$ 2,000	$ 4,000
Accounts Payable	3,500	3,300
Other Current Liabilities.	1,500	1,900
Total Current Liabilities	$ 7,000	$ 9,200
Noncurrent Liabilities:		
Bonds Payable	4,000	2,800
Total Liabilities.	$11,000	$12,000
Shareholders' Equity:		
Preferred Stock	$ 1,000	$ 1,000
Common Stock	2,000	2,500
Additional Paid-in Capital	1,500	1,800
Retained Earnings	4,500	6,700
Total Shareholders' Equity	$ 9,000	$12,000
Total Liabilities and Shareholders' Equity	$20,000	$24,000

Exhibit 6.13
COX CORPORATION
Income and Retained Earnings Statement
For Year 2

Sales Revenue		$30,000
Less Expenses:		
Cost of Goods Sold	$18,000	
Selling	4,500	
Administrative	1,800	
Interest	700	
Income Taxes	2,000	
Total Expenses		27,000
Net Income		$ 3,000
Less Dividends:		
Preferred	$ 100	
Common	700	800
Increase in Retained Earnings for Year 2		$ 2,200
Retained Earnings, December 31, Year 1.		4,500
Retained Earnings, December 31, Year 2.		$ 6,700

a. Rate of return on assets.
b. Profit margin ratio (before interest and related tax effects).
c. Cost of goods sold to sales percentage.
d. Selling expense to sales percentage.
e. Total assets turnover.
f. Accounts receivable turnover.
g. Inventory turnover.
h. Plant asset turnover.
i. Rate of return on common shareholders' equity.
j. Profit margin (after interest).
k. Leverage ratio.
l. Current ratio (both dates).
m. Quick ratio (both dates).
n. Cash flow from operations to current liabilities.
o. Working capital turnover.
p. Long-term debt ratio (both dates).
q. Debt-equity ratio (both dates).
r. Cash flow from operations to total liabilities.
s. Time interest charges earned.

Suggested Solution

a. Rate of return on assets $= \dfrac{\$3,000 + (1 - .40)(\$700)}{.5(\$20,000 + \$24,000)} = 15.5$ percent.

b. Profit margin ratio $= \dfrac{\$3,000 + (1 - .40)(\$700)}{\$30,000} = 11.4$ percent.

c. Cost of goods sold to sales percentage $= \dfrac{\$18,000}{\$30,000} = 60.0$ percent.

d. Selling expense to sales percentage $= \dfrac{\$4,500}{\$30,000} = 15.0$ percent.

e. Total assets turnover $= \dfrac{\$30,000}{.5(\$20,000 + \$24,000)} = 1.4$ times per year.

f. Accounts receivable turnover $= \dfrac{\$30,000}{.5(\$3,600 + \$4,300)} = 7.6$ times per year.

g. Inventory turnover $= \dfrac{\$18,000}{.5(\$5,600 + \$7,900)} = 2.7$ times per year.

h. Plant asset turnover $= \dfrac{\$30,000}{.5(\$9,900 + \$10,670)} = 2.9$ times per year.

i. Rate of return on common shareholders' equity $= \dfrac{\$3,000 - \$100}{.5(\$8,000 + \$11,000)} = 30.5$ percent.

j. Profit margin (after interest) $= \dfrac{\$3,000 - \$100}{\$30,000} = 9.7$ percent.

k. Leverage ratio $= \dfrac{.5(\$20,000 + \$24,000)}{.5(\$8,000 + \$11,000)} = 2.3$.

l. Current ratio

December 31, Year 1: $\dfrac{\$10,100}{\$7,000} = 1.4:1.$

December 31, Year 2: $\dfrac{\$13,330}{\$9,200} = 1.4:1.$

m. Quick ratio

December 31, Year 1: $\dfrac{\$4,200}{\$7,000} = .6:1.$

December 31, Year 2: $\dfrac{\$5,050}{\$9,200} = .5:1.$

n. Cash flow from operations to current liabilities $= \dfrac{\$3,300}{.5(\$7,000 + \$9,200)} = 40.7$ percent.

o. Working capital turnover $= \dfrac{\$30,000}{.5(\$3,100 + \$4,130)} = 8.3$ times per year.

p. Long-term debt ratio

December 31, Year 1: $\dfrac{\$4,000}{\$13,000} = 30.8$ percent.

December 31, Year 2: $\dfrac{\$2,800}{\$14,800} = 18.9$ percent.

q. Debt-equity ratio

December 31, Year 1: $\dfrac{\$11,000}{\$20,000} = 55.0$ percent.

December 31, Year 2: $\dfrac{\$12,000}{\$24,000} = 50.0$ percent.

r. Cash flow from operations to total liabilities $= \dfrac{\$3,300}{.5(\$11,000 + \$12,000)} = 28.7$ percent.

s. Times interest charges earned $= \dfrac{\$3,000 + \$2,000 + \$700}{\$700} = 8.1$ times.

Problem 2 for Self-Study

Exhibit 6.14 presents a ratio analysis for Abbott Corporation for Year 1 to Year 3.
a. What is the likely explanation for the decreasing rate of return on assets?
b. What is the likely explanation for the increasing rate of return on common shareholders' equity?
c. What is the likely explanation for the behavior of the current and quick ratios?
d. What is the likely explanation for the decreases in the two cash flow from operations to liabilities ratios?

Suggested Solution

a. Given that the profit margin (before interest expense and related tax effects) is stable over the 3 years, the decreasing rate of return on assets is attributable to a

Exhibit 6.14
Ratio Analysis for Abbott Corporation

	Year 1	Year 2	Year 3
Rate of Return on Assets	10.0%	9.6%	9.2%
Profit Margin (before interest and related tax effects)	6.0%	6.1%	6.1%
Total Assets Turnover	1.7	1.6	1.5
Cost of Goods Sold/Revenues	62.5%	62.3%	62.6%
Selling Expenses/Revenues	10.3%	10.2%	10.4%
Interest Expense/Revenues.	1.5%	2.0%	2.5%
Accounts Receivable Turnover	4.3	4.3	4.2
Inventory Turnover	3.2	3.4	3.6
Plant Asset Turnover	.8	.7	.6
Rate of Return on Common Shareholders' Equity	14.0%	14.2%	14.5%
Profit Margin (after interest)	5.1%	4.9%	4.6%
Leverage Ratio	1.6	1.8	2.1
Current Ratio	1.4	1.3	1.2
Quick Ratio.	1.0	.9	1.0
Cash Flow from Operations to Current Liabilities	38.2%	37.3%	36.4%
Working Capital Turnover	4.8	5.0	5.2
Long-term Debt Ratio	37.5%	33.8%	43.3%
Debt-Equity Ratio	37.5%	44.4%	52.4%
Cash Flow from Operations to Total Liabilities	16.3%	13.4%	11.1%
Times Interest Charges Earned	6.7	5.1	4.1

decreasing total assets turnover. The decreasing total assets turnover is caused primarily by a decreasing plant asset turnover (the accounts receivable turnover is stable while the inventory turnover increased). Explanations for a decreasing plant asset turnover include (1) acceleration of capital expenditures in anticipation of higher sales in the future, and (2) decreasing use of plant capacity so that depreciation expense must be covered by fewer units sold.

b. Given that the rate of return on assets is decreasing, the increasing rate of return on common shareholders' equity must be due to increased financial leverage. The increased financial leverage is evident from the leverage ratio, as well as the percentage of interest expense to sales and the difference between the profit margin measures before and after interest expense.

c. Because the primary difference between the current and quick ratios relates to inventories, the decreasing current ratio coupled with a stable quick ratio must be caused by more efficient inventory management. This explanation is supported by the increasing inventory turnover.

d. Given the stability of the profit margin (before interest expense and related tax effects) and the accounts receivable turnover and given the increased inventory turnover, we must look to the impact of interest expense on operating cash flows for the explanation. The increasing debt load has decreased the profit margin (after interest) and drained greater and greater amounts of cash for interest payments. These drains on operating cash flows coupled with increasing amounts of debt, particularly long-term debt, have driven the cash flow ratios down.

Questions, Exercises, Problems and Cases

Questions

1. Review the meaning of the following concepts or terms discussed in this chapter.

    a. Return and risk.

    b. Profitability.

    c. Short-term liquidity risk.

    d. Long-term liquidity risk.

    e. Time-series analysis.

    f. Cross-section analysis.

    g. Rate of return on assets.

    h. Profit margin and expense ratios.

    i. Total assets turnover ratio.

    j. Accounts receivable turnover ratio.

    k. Inventory turnover ratio.

    l. Plant asset turnover ratio.

    m. Rate of return on common stock equity.

    n. Financial leverage.

    o. Leverage ratio.

    p. Earnings per share.

    q. Primary and fully diluted earnings per share.

    r. Current ratio.

    s. Quick ratio.

    t. Cash flow from operations to current liabilities ratio.

    u. Working capital turnover ratio.

    v. Long-term debt ratio.

    w. Debt-equity ratio.

    x. Cash flow from operations to total liabilities ratio.

    y. Times interest charges earned.

2. Describe several factors that might limit the comparability of a firm's financial statement ratios over several periods.

3. Describe several factors that might limit the comparability of one firm's financial statement ratios with those of another firm in the same industry.

4. "I can understand why interest expense is added back to net income in the numerator of the rate of return on assets, but I don't see why an adjustment is made for income taxes." Provide an explanation.

5. One company president stated: "The operations of our company are such that we must turn inventory over once every 4 weeks." Another company president in a similar industry stated: "The operations of our company are such that we can live comfortably with a turnover of four times each year." Explain what these two company presidents probably had in mind.

6. It has been suggested that for any given firm at a particular time there is an optimal inventory turnover ratio. Explain.

7. Under what circumstances will the rate of return on common shareholders' equity be greater than the rate of return on assets? Under what circumstances will it be less?

8. A company president recently stated: "The operations of our company are such that we can effectively use only a small amount of financial leverage." Explain.

9. Define financial leverage. As long as a firm's rate of return on assets exceeds its aftertax cost of borrowing, why doesn't the firm increase borrowing to as close to 100 percent of financing as possible?

10. Illustrate with amounts how a decrease in working capital can accompany an increase in the current ratio.

Exercises

11. *Calculation and disaggregation of rate of return on assets.* The following data are taken from the most recent annual reports of Alabama Company and Carolina Company.

	Alabama Co.	Carolina Co.
Revenues	$2,000,000	$2,400,000
Expenses Other than Interest and Income Taxes	1,700,000	2,150,000
Interest Expense	100,000	50,000
Income Tax Expense at 40 percent	80,000	80,000
Net Income	120,000	120,000
Average Total Assets During the Year	1,500,000	1,000,000

   a. Calculate the rate of return on assets for each company.
   b. Disaggregate the rate of return in part **a** into profit margin and total assets turnover components.
   c. Comment on the relative profitability of the two companies.

12. *Profitability analysis for two types of retailers.* The following information is taken from the annual reports of two companies, one of which is a retailer of quality men's clothes and the other of which is a discount household goods store. Neither company had any interest-bearing debt during the year. Identify which of these companies is likely to be the clothing retailer and which is likely to be the discount store. Explain.

	Company A	Company B
Sales	$3,000,000	$3,000,000
Net Income	60,000	300,000
Average Total Assets	600,000	3,000,000

13. *Analysis of accounts receivable for two companies.* The following information relates to the activities of Tennessee Corporation and Kentucky Corporation for the current year.

	Tennessee Corp.	Kentucky Corp.
Sales on Account	$4,050,000	$2,560,000
Accounts Receivable, January 1	960,000	500,000
Accounts Receivable, December 31	840,000	780,000

    a. Compute the accounts receivable turnover of each company.
    b. Compute the average number of days that accounts receivable are outstanding for each company.
    c. Which company is managing its accounts receivable more efficiently?

14. *Analysis of inventories over 4 years.* The following information relates to the activities of Carlson Corporation.

	Year 1	Year 2	Year 3	Year 4
Sales	$1,000	$2,500	$5,000	$8,000
Cost of Goods Sold	600	1,550	3,150	5,120
Average Inventory	200	550	1,170	2,050

    a. Compute the inventory turnover for each year.
    b. Compute the average number of days that inventories are held for each year.
    c. How well has Carlson Corporation been managing its inventories?

15. *Analysis of plant assets over 4 years.* The following information relates to Steele Company.

	Year 1	Year 2	Year 3	Year 4
Sales	$500	$800	$1,500	$3,000
Average Plant Assets.	400	670	1,290	2,630
Expenditures on Plant Assets	250	500	1,200	2,700

    a. Compute the plant asset turnover for each year.
    b. How well has Steele Company been managing its investment in plant assets?

16. *Calculation and disaggregation of rate of return on common shareholders' equity.* The following data are taken from the financial statements of Maine Corporation.

	Year 1	Year 2	Year 3	Year 4
Revenues	$2,000	$2,250	$2,500	$2,750
Net Income	160	180	200	220
Average Total Assets	500	592	694	809
Average Common Shareholders' Equity	1,000	1,160	1,333	1,517

    a. Calculate the rate of return on common shareholders' equity.

    b. Disaggregate the rate of return on common shareholders' equity into profit margin, total assets turnover, and leverage components.

    c. How has the profitability of Maine Corporation changed over the 4 years?

17. *Profitability analysis for three companies.* The data below show five items from the financial statements for three companies for a recent year.

	Company A	Company B	Company C
For Year			
Revenues	$28,947,200	$13,639,900	$9,716,900
Income Before Interest and Related Taxes[a]	4,295,800	824,600	156,400
Net Income to Common Shareholders[b] . .	2,915,800	522,600	148,600
Average During Year			
Total Assets	77,107,200	10,885,000	1,532,400
Common Shareholders' Equity	29,769,200	5,118,800	743,830

[a]Net Income + Interest Charges $\times$ (1 − Tax Rate).
[b]Net Income − Preferred Stock Dividends.

    a. Compute the profit margin (after interest) ratio for each company. Which company seems to be the most successful according to this ratio?

    b. How many dollars of sales on average does each of the companies make for each dollar's worth of average assets held during the year?

    c. Compute the rate of return on assets for each company. Which company seems to be the most successful according to this ratio?

    d. Compute the rate of return on common shareholders' equity for each company. Which company seems to be the most successful according to this ratio?

    e. The three companies are American Telephone & Telegraph, Safeway Stores, and Sears, Roebuck and Company. (Dollar amounts shown are actually in thousands.) Which of the companies corresponds to A, B, and C? What clues did you use in reaching your conclusion?

18. *Relation of profitability to financial leverage.*

    a. Compute the ratio of return on common shareholders' equity in each of the following independent cases.

	Total Assets	Interest- Bearing Debt	Common Share- holders' Equity	Rate of Return on Assets	Aftertax Cost of Interest- Bearing Debt
Case					
A	$200	$100	$100	6%	6%
B	$200	$100	$100	8%	6%
C	$200	$120	$ 80	8%	6%
D	$200	$100	$100	4%	6%
E	$200	$ 50	$100	6%	6%
F	$200	$ 50	$100	5%	6%

      b. In which cases is leverage working to the advantage of the common share-
         holders?

19. *Analysis of financial leverage.* The Borrowing Company has total assets of
$100,000 during the year. It has borrowed $20,000 at a 10 percent annual rate and
pays income taxes at a rate of 40 percent of pretax income. Shareholders' equity is
$80,000.

      a. What must net income be for the rate of return on shareholders' equity to
         equal the rate of return on assets?

      b. What is the rate of return on common shareholders' equity for the net in-
         come determined in part **a**?

      c. What must income before interest and income taxes be to achieve this net
         income?

      d. Repeat parts **a, b,** and **c,** assuming borrowing of $80,000 and common
         shareholders' equity of $20,000.

      e. Compare the results from the two different debt-equity relations. What gen-
         eralizations can be made?

20. *Ratio analysis of profitability and risk.* Refer to the data below for the
Adelsman Company.

	Year 1	Year 2	Year 3
Rate of Return on Common Shareholders' Equity	8%	10%	11%
Earnings per Share	$3.00	$4.00	$4.40
Net Income/Total Interest Expense[a]	10	5	4
Debt-Equity Ratio (liabilities/all equities)	20%	50%	60%

[a]Note that this computation does not represent "times interest earned" as defined in the chapter.

The income tax rate was 40 percent in each year and 100,000 common shares were
outstanding throughout the period.

      a. Did the company's profitability increase over the 3-year period? How can
         you tell? (*Hint:* Compute the rate of return on assets.)

b. Did risk increase? How can you tell?

c. Are shareholders better off in Year 3 than in Year 1?

21. *Interpreting changes in earnings per share.* Company A and Company B both start Year 1 with $1 million of shareholders' equity and 100,000 shares of common stock outstanding. During Year 1, both companies earn net income of $100,000, a rate of return of 10 percent on common shareholders' equity. Company A declares and pays $100,000 of dividends to common shareholders at the end of Year 1, whereas Company B retains all its earnings, declaring no dividends. During Year 2, both companies earn net income equal to 10 percent of shareholders' equity at the beginning of Year 2.

   a. Compute earnings per share for Company A and for Company B for Year 1 and for Year 2.

   b. Compute the rate of growth in earnings per share for Company A and Company B, comparing earnings per share in Year 2 with earnings per share in Year 1.

   c. Using the rate of growth in earnings per share as the criterion, which company's management appears to be doing a better job for its shareholders? Comment on this result.

22. *Working backwards from profitability ratios to financial statement data.* The revenues of Lev Company were $1,000 for the year. A financial analyst computed the following ratios for Lev Company, using the year-end balances for balance sheet amounts. The Lev Company has no preferred shares outstanding.

Debt-Equity Ratio (all liabilities/all equities)	73⅓ percent
Income Tax Expense as a Percentage of Pretax Income	40 percent
Net Income as a Percentage of Revenue	12 percent
Rate of Return on Common Shareholders' Equity.	10 percent
Rate of Return on Assets	6 percent

From this information, compute each of the following items.

   a. Interest expense.

   b. Income tax expense.

   c. Total expenses.

   d. Net income.

   e. Total assets.

   f. Total liabilities.

23. *Effect of financing strategy on earnings per share (CMA adapted).* The Virgil Company is planning to invest $10 million in an expansion program that is expected to increase income before interest and taxes by $2.5 million. Currently, Virgil Company has total equities of $40 million, 25 percent of which is debt and 75 percent of which is shareholders' equity, represented by 1 million shares. The expansion can be financed with the issuance of 200,000 new shares at $50 each or by issuing long-term debt at an annual interest rate of 10 percent. The following is an excerpt from the most recent income statement.

Earnings Before Interest and Taxes	$10,500,000
Less: Interest Charges	500,000
Earnings Before Income Taxes.	$10,000,000
Income Taxes (at 40 percent)	4,000,000
Net Income	$ 6,000,000

Assume that Virgil Company maintains its current earnings on its present assets, achieves the planned earnings from the new program, and that the tax rate remains at 40 percent.

    a. What will be earnings per share if the expansion is financed with debt?

    b. What will be earnings per share if the expansion is financed by issuing new shares?

    c. At what level of earnings before interest and taxes will earnings per share be the same, whichever of the two financing programs is used?

    d. At what level of earnings before interest and taxes will the rate of return on shareholders' equity be the same, whichever of the two financing plans is used?

24. *Relation between book and market rates of return.* Net income attributable to common shareholders' equity of Florida Corporation during the current year was $250,000. Earnings per share were $.50 during the period. The average common shareholders' equity during the year was $2,500,000. The market price at year-end was $6.00.

    a. Calculate the rate of return on common shareholders' equity for the year.

    b. Calculate the rate of return currently being earned on the market price of the stock (the ratio of earnings per common share to market price per common share).

    c. Why is there a difference between the rates of return calculated in parts **a** and **b**?

25. *Calculation and interpretation of short-term liquidity ratios.* The following data are taken from the financial statements of Maloney Corporation.

For the Year	Year 2	Year 3	Year 4
Revenues	$245	$270	$281
Cash Flow from Operations	79	105	137

On December 31	Year 1	Year 2	Year 3	Year 4
Quick Assets	$200	$225	$330	$350
Current Assets	320	375	420	455
Current Liabilities	200	250	300	350

    a. Compute the current and quick ratios as of December 31 of each of the Years 1 through 4.

      b. Compute the cash flow from operations to current liabilities ratio and the working capital turnover ratio for each of the Years 2 through 4.

      c. How has the short-term liquidity risk of Maloney Corporation changed over the 3-year period?

26. *Calculating changes in current ratio and working capital.* Merchandise inventory costing $30,000 is purchased on account. Indicate the effect (increase, decrease, no effect) of this transaction on (1) working capital and (2) the current ratio, assuming that current assets and current liabilities immediately prior to the transaction were as follows:

      a. Current assets, $120,000; current liabilities, $120,000.

      b. Current assets, $120,000; current liabilities, $150,000.

      c. Current assets, $120,000; current liabilities, $80,000.

27. *Relation of profitability to short-term liquidity.* Following is a schedule of the current assets and current liabilities of the Lewis Company:

	December 31	
	Year 2	Year 1
Current Assets:		
Cash	$ 355,890	$ 212,790
Accounts Receivable	389,210	646,010
Inventories.	799,100	1,118,200
Prepayments.	21,600	30,000
Total Current Assets	$1,565,800	$2,007,000
Current Liabilities:		
Accounts Payable	$ 152,760	$ 217,240
Accrued Payroll, Taxes, etc.	126,340	318,760
Notes Payable	69,500	330,000
Total Current Liabilities	$ 348,600	$ 866,000

    During Year 2, the Lewis Company operated at a loss of $100,000. Depreciation expense during Year 2 was $30,000.

      a. Calculate the current ratio for each date.

      b. Calculate the amount of cash provided by operations for Year 2.

      c. Explain how the improved current ratio is possible under the Year 2 operating conditions.

28. *Calculation and interpretation of long-term liquidity ratios.* The following data are taken from the financial statements of Michigan Corporation.

For the Year	Year 2	Year 3	Year 4
Net Income Before Interest and Income Taxes	$ 200	$ 325	$ 360
Cash Flow from Operations	115	155	184
Interest Expense	40	50	60

On December 31	Year 1	Year 2	Year 3	Year 4
Current Liabilities	$ 200	$ 250	$ 304	$ 362
Total Liabilities	500	650	822	1,018
Total Assets	1,000	1,250	1,522	1,818

   a. Compute the long-term debt ratio and the debt-equity ratio at the end of each of the Years 1 through 4.

   b. Compute the cash flow from operations to total liabilities ratio and the times interest charges earned ratio for each of the Years 2 through 4.

   c. How has the long-term liquidity risk of Michigan Corporation changed over this 3-year period?

29. *Effect of various transactions on financial statement ratios.* Indicate the immediate effects (increase, decrease, no effect) of each of the independent transactions below on (1) rate of return on common shareholders' equity, (2) current ratio, and (3) debt-equity ratio. State any necessary assumptions.

   a. Merchandise inventory costing $205,000 is purchased on account.

   b. Merchandise inventory costing $120,000 is sold on account for $150,000.

   c. Collections from customers on accounts receivable total $100,000.

   d. Payments to suppliers on accounts payable total $160,000.

   e. A machine costing $40,000, on which $30,000 of depreciation had been taken, is sold for $10,000.

   f. Dividends of $80,000 are declared. The dividends will be paid during the next accounting period.

   g. Common stock is issued for $75,000.

   h. A machine costing $60,000 is acquired. Cash of $10,000 is given and a note for $50,000 payable 5 years from now is signed for the balance of the purchase price.

30. *Effect of various transactions on financial statement ratios.* Indicate the effects (increase, decrease, no effect) of the independent transactions below on (1) earnings per share, (2) working capital, and (3) quick ratio, where accounts receivable are *included* but merchandise inventory is *excluded* from "quick assets." State any necessary assumptions.

   a. Merchandise inventory costing $240,000 is sold on account for $300,000.

   b. Dividends of $160,000 are declared. The dividends will be paid during the next accounting period.

   c. Merchandise inventory costing $410,000 is purchased on account.

   d. A machine costing $80,000, on which $60,000 depreciation had been taken, is sold for $20,000.

   e. Merchandise inventory purchased for cash in the amount of $7,000 is returned to the supplier because it is defective. A cash reimbursement is received.

   f. 10,000 shares of $10 par value common stock were issued on the last day of the accounting period for $15 per share. The proceeds were used to acquire the assets of another firm composed of the following: accounts receivable, $30,000; merchandise inventory, $60,000; plant and equipment, $100,000. The acquiring firm also agreed to assume current liabilities of $40,000 of the acquired company.

Problems and Cases

31. *Calculation of profitability and risk ratios.* The following data are taken from the financial statements of the Press Company:

	January	December
Current Assets	$180,000	$210,000
Noncurrent Assets	255,000	275,000
Current Liabilities	85,000	78,000
Long-Term Liabilities	30,000	75,000
Common Stock (10,000 shares)	300,000	300,000
Retained Earnings	20,000	32,000

	Operations
Net Income	$72,000
Interest Expense	3,000
Income Taxes (40 percent rate)	48,000
Cash Provided by Operations	30,970
Dividends Declared	60,000

Calculate the following ratios:
   a. Rate of return on assets.
   b. Rate of return on common shareholders' equity.
   c. Earnings per share of common stock.
   d. Current ratio (both months).
   e. Cash flow from operations to current liabilities.
   f. Debt-equity ratio (both months).
   g. Cash flow from operations to total liabilities.
   h. Times interest charges earned.

32. *Calculation of profitability and risk ratios.* The comparative balance sheets, income statement, and statement of changes in financial position of Solinger Electric Corporation for the current year are shown in Exhibits 6.15, 6.16, and 6.17.
   a. Calculate the ratios listed in Exhibit 6.11 in the chapter for Solinger Electric Corporation for the current year. You may omit expense ratios. Balance sheet ratios should be computed at both the beginning and end of the year.

b. Was Solinger Electric Corporation successfully leveraged during the current year?

c. Assume that the bonds were issued on November 1. At what annual interest rate were the bonds apparently issued?

d. If Solinger Electric Corporation earns the same rate of return on assets next year as it realized this year, and issues no more debt, will the firm be successfully leveraged next year?

Exhibit 6.15
SOLINGER ELECTRIC CORPORATION
Comparative Balance Sheets
(Problem 32)

	January 1	December 31
Assets		
Current Assets:		
Cash	$ 30,000	$ 3,000
Accounts Receivable	20,000	55,000
Merchandise Inventory	40,000	50,000
Total Current Assets	$ 90,000	$108,000
Noncurrent Assets:		
Buildings and Equipment (cost)	$100,000	$225,000
Accumulated Depreciation	(30,000)	(40,000)
Total Noncurrent Assets	$ 70,000	$185,000
Total Assets	$160,000	$293,000
Liabilities and Shareholders' Equity		
Current Liabilities:		
Accounts Payable—Merchandise Suppliers	$ 30,000	$ 50,000
Accounts Payable—Other Suppliers	10,000	12,000
Salaries Payable	5,000	6,000
Total Current Liabilities	$ 45,000	$ 68,000
Noncurrent Liabilities:		
Bonds Payable	0	100,000
Total Liabilities	$ 45,000	$168,000
Shareholders' Equity:		
Common Stock ($10 par value)	$100,000	$100,000
Retained Earnings	15,000	25,000
Total Shareholders' Equity	$115,000	$125,000
Total Liabilities plus Shareholders' Equity	$160,000	$293,000

Exhibit 6.16
SOLINGER ELECTRIC CORPORATION
Income Statement for the Current Year
(Problem 32)

Sales Revenue	$125,000
Less Expenses:	
Cost of Goods Sold	$ 60,000
Salaries	19,667
Depreciation	10,000
Interest.	2,000
Income Taxes.	13,333
Total Expenses	$105,000
Net Income	$ 20,000

Exhibit 6.17
SOLINGER ELECTRIC CORPORATION
Statement of Changes in Financial Position
for the Current Year
(Problem 32)

Sources of Cash		
Net Income	$20,000	
Additions:		
Depreciation Expense.	10,000	
Increase in Accounts Payable:		
Merchandise Suppliers	20,000	
Other Suppliers	2,000	
Increase in Salaries Payable	1,000	
Subtractions:		
Increase in Accounts Receivable.	(35,000)	
Increase in Merchandise Inventory	(10,000)	
Cash Provided by Operations		$ 8,000
Proceeds from Long-Term Bonds Issued		100,000
Total Sources of Cash		$108,000
Uses of Cash		
Dividends		$ 10,000
Acquisition of Buildings and Equipment		125,000
Total Uses of Cash		$135,000
Net Decrease in Cash during the Year		
(Sources minus Uses)		$ 27,000

33. *Calculation of profitability and risk ratios.* Comparative balance sheets, income statement, and statement of changes in financial position of Nykerk Electronics Corporation for the current year are presented in Exhibits 6.18, 6.19, and 6.20, respectively.

a. Calculate the ratios listed in Exhibit 6.11 in the chapter for Nykerk Electronics Corporation for the current year. You may omit expense ratios. Balance sheet ratios should be computed at both the beginning and end of the year.

b. Was Nykerk Electronics Corporation successfully leveraged during the year?

Exhibit 6.18
NYKERK ELECTRONICS CORPORATION
Comparative Balance Sheets
(Problem 33)

	(In 000's of dollars)	
	December 31	January 1
Assets		
Current Assets:		
Cash	$ 1,600	$ 1,400
Accounts Receivable (net).	2,600	2,500
Inventories.	7,300	6,900
Total Current Assets	$11,500	$10,800
Noncurrent Assets:		
Plant and Equipment	$ 5,200	$ 4,500
Less Accumulated Depreciation	1,300	1,000
Net Plant and Equipment	$ 3,900	$ 3,500
Land	1,200	1,200
Total Noncurrent Assets.	$ 5,100	$ 4,700
Total Assets	$16,600	$15,500
Liabilities and Shareholders' Equity		
Current Liabilities:		
Accounts Payable	$ 1,600	$ 1,700
Accrued Payables	800	900
Income Taxes Payable	300	200
Notes Payable	1,900	1,200
Total Current Liabilities	$ 4,600	$ 4,000
Long-Term Liabilities:		
Bonds Payable (8 percent)	$ 2,000	$ 2,100
Mortgage Payable	200	200
Total Long-Term Liabilities.	$ 2,200	$ 2,300
Total Liabilities	$ 6,800	$ 6,300
Shareholders' Equity:		
Preferred Stock (6 percent, $100 par)	$ 2,000	$ 2,000
Common Stock ($1 par).	500	500
Additional Paid-in Capital	2,500	2,500
Total Contributed Capital	$ 5,000	$ 5,000
Retained Earnings	4,800	4,200
Total Shareholders' Equity.	$ 9,800	$ 9,200
Total Liabilities and Shareholders' Equity	$16,600	$15,500

Exhibit 6.19
NYKERK ELECTRONICS CORPORATION
Statement of Income and Retained Earnings
for the Current Year
(Problem 33)

	(in 000's of dollars)
Revenues:	
Sales	$26,500
Less Sales Allowances, Returns, and Discounts	600
Net Sales	$25,900
Interest and Other Revenues	200
Total Revenues	$26,100
Expenses:	
Cost of Goods Sold	$20,500
Selling and Administrative Expenses:	
Selling Expenses $2,120	
Administrative Expenses 1,000	
Depreciation 300	
Total Selling and Administrative Expenses	3,420
Interest Expense	180
Income Tax Expense	800
Total Expenses	$24,900
Net Income	$ 1,200
Dividends:	
Dividends on Preferred Shares $ 120	
Dividends on Common Shares 480	
Total Dividends	600
Addition to Retained Earnings for Year	$ 600
Retained Earnings, January 1	4,200
Retained Earnings, December 31	$ 4,800

34. *Calculation of profitability and risk ratios.* Refer to the financial statements for General Products Company in Appendix A at the back of the book.

a. Calculate the rate of return on assets for 1985. Assume an income tax rate of 46 percent in computing the tax effect of interest expense. In computing income before distributions to providers of capital, add to net income the $21 million shown as the minority interest in earnings of consolidated affiliates. Chapter 13 explains minority interest.

b. Disaggregate the rate of return on assets for 1985 into profit margin (before interest) and asset turnover components. Note that "Other Income" should be included in revenues.

Exhibit 6.20
NYKERK ELECTRONICS CORPORATION
Statement of Changes in Financial Position
for the Current Year
(Problem 33)

	(in 000's of dollars)
Sources of Cash	
Operations:	
Net Income	$1,200
Additions:	
Depreciation Expense	300
Increase in Income Taxes Payable	100
Subtractions:	
Increase in Accounts Receivable	(100)
Increase in Inventories	(400)
Decrease in Accounts Payable	(100)
Decrease in Accrued Payables	(100)
Cash Provided by Operations	$ 900
New Financing by Bank Note	700
Total Sources of Cash	$1,600
Uses of Cash	
Preferred Stock Dividend	$ 120
Common Stock Dividend	480
Purchase of Plant and Equipment	700
Redemption of Bonds Payable	100
Total Uses of Cash	$1,400
Increase in Cash for the Year	$ 200

   c. Calculate the accounts receivable turnover, inventory turnover, and plant asset turnover ratios for 1985. The numerator of the accounts receivable and plant asset turnover should include sales revenue but exclude "Other Income."
   d. Calculate the rate of return on common shareholders' equity for 1985.
   e. Disaggregate the rate of return on common shareholders' equity for 1985 into profit margin (after interest), asset turnover, and leverage components.
   f. Calculate the current and quick ratios as of December 31, 1984 and 1985, and the cash flow to current liabilities and working capital turnover ratios for 1985. Include "Other Income" in the numerator of the working capital turnover ratio.
   g. Calculate the long-term debt and debt-equity ratios as of December 31, 1984 and 1985, and the cash flow from operations to total liabilities and times

interest charges earned ratios for 1985. Include "Other (noncurrent) Liabilities" in long-term debt. Include "Minority Interest in Equity of Consolidated Affiliates" in the denominator of the long-term debt ratio. Include "Minority Interest in Earnings of Consolidated Affiliates" in the numerator of the times interest charges earned ratio.

35. *Analysis of profitability and risk for two companies.* Exhibits 6.21 and 6.22 present the income statements and balance sheets of Illinois Corporation and Ohio Corporation.

Exhibit 6.21
Income Statements for the Current Year
(Problem 35)

	Illinois Corp.	Ohio Corp.
Sales .	$4,300,000	$3,000,000
Less Expenses:		
Costs of Goods Sold .	$2,800,000	$1,400,000
Selling and Administrative Expenses .	330,000	580,000
Interest Expense.	100,000	200,000
Income Tax Expense.	428,000	328,000
Total Expenses	$3,658,000	$2,508,000
Net Income .	$ 642,000	$ 492,000

Exhibit 6.22
Balance Sheets December 31
(Problem 35)

	Illinois Corp.	Ohio Corp.
Assets		
Cash .	$ 100,000	$ 50,000
Accounts Receivable (net)	700,000	400,000
Merchandise Inventory .	1,200,000	750,000
Plant and Equipment (net)	4,000,000	4,800,000
Total Assets.	$6,000,000	$6,000,000
Liabilities and Shareholders' Equity		
Accounts Payable .	$ 572,000	$ 172,000
Income Taxes Payable .	428,000	328,000
Long-Term Bonds Payable (10 percent)	1,000,000	2,000,000
Common Stock .	2,000,000	2,000,000
Retained Earnings .	2,000,000	1,500,000
Total Liabilities and Shareholders' Equity .	$6,000,000	$6,000,000

Cash flow provided by operations was $600,000 for Illinois Corporation and $550,000 for Ohio Corporation.

Assume that the balances in asset and equity accounts at year-end approximate the average balances during the period. The income tax rate is 40 percent. On the basis of this information, which company is

    a. More profitable?

    b. Less risky in terms of short-term liquidity?

    c. Less risky in terms of long-term liquidity?

Use financial ratios, as appropriate, in doing your analysis.

36. *Detective analysis: identify company.* In this problem, you become a financial analyst/detective. The condensed financial statements in Exhibit 6.23 are constructed on a percentage basis. In all cases, total sales revenues are shown as 100.00%. All other numbers were divided by sales revenue for the year. The 13 companies (all corporations except for the accounting firm) shown here represent the following industries:

  (1) Advertising and public opinion survey firm.

  (2) Beer brewery.

  (3) Department store chain (that carries its own receivables).

  (4) Distiller of hard liquor.

  (5) Drug manufacturer.

  (6) Finance company (lends money to consumers).

  (7) Grocery store chain.

  (8) Insurance company.

  (9) Manufacturer of tobacco products, mainly cigarettes.

(10) Public accounting (CPA) partnership.

(11) Soft drink bottler.

(12) Steel manufacturer.

(13) Utility company.

Use whatever clues you can to match the companies in Exhibit 6.23 with the industries listed above. You may find it useful to refer to average industry ratios compiled by Dun & Bradstreet, Prentice-Hall, Robert Morris Associates, and the Federal Trade Commission. Copies of these documents can be found in most libraries.

37. *Interpretation of ratio analysis.* Exhibit 6.24 presents a ratio analysis for Sarwark Company.

    a. What is the likely explanation for the stable rate of return on assets coupled with the decreasing rate of return on common shareholders' equity?

    b. What is the likely reason for the increasing plant asset turnover?

38. *Interpretation of ratio analysis.* Exhibit 6.25 presents a ratio analysis for Widdicombe Corporation for Year 1 through Year 3.

    a. What is the likely explanation for the increasing rate of return on assets coupled with the decreasing rate of return on shareholders' equity?

    b. How effectively has the firm been managing its inventories?

    c. What is the likely explanation for the increasing total assets turnover?

Exhibit 6.23
Data for Ratio Detective Exercise
(Problem 36)

| | Company Numbers | | | | | | |
	(1)	(2)	(3)	(4)	(5)	(6)	(7)
Balance Sheet at End of Year							
Current Receivables	0.31%	29.11%	6.81%	25.25%	3.45%	38.78%	17.64%
Inventories	7.80	0.00	3.14	0.00	6.45	14.94	20.57
Net Plant and Equipment*	8.50	9.63	11.13	19.88	49.87	15.59	37.60
All Other Assets	2.16	7.02	25.59	32.93	24.05	15.54	30.07
Total Assets	18.77%	45.76%	46.67%	78.06%	83.82%	84.85%	105.88%
*Cost of Plant and Equipment (gross)	14.64%	14.80%	19.57%	29.03%	79.03%	24.80%	59.73%
Current Liabilities	6.08%	9.82%	6.41%	17.49%	14.83%	35.28%	27.68%
Long-Term Liabilities	2.12	7.96	0.00	0.00	0.00	8.33	1.33
Owners' Equity	10.58	27.98	40.25	60.57	69.00	41.24	76.86
Total Equities	18.78%	45.76%	46.66%	78.06%	83.83%	84.85%	105.87%
Income Statement for Year							
Revenues	100.00%	100.00%	100.00%	100.00%	100.00%	100.00%	100.00%
Cost of Goods Sold (excluding depreciation) or Operating Expenses[a]	78.97	53.77	48.21	59.07	68.62	60.88	33.29
Depreciation	1.04	1.39	1.72	2.07	4.07	1.09	3.02
Interest Expense	0.16	0.52	0.00	0.08	0.02	1.35	0.73
Advertising Expense	3.72	0.00	11.43	0.06	4.39	2.93	2.28
Research and Development Expense	0.00	1.00	0.00	0.00	0.15	0.00	9.06
Incomes Taxes	1.28	0.53	9.59	6.52	7.87	3.78	8.55
All Other Items (net)	13.34	18.88	18.58	24.52	6.40	24.39	27.66
Total Expenses	98.51%	76.09%	89.53%	92.32%	91.52%	94.42%	84.59%
Net Income	1.50%	23.92%	10.47%	7.68%	8.49%	5.59%	15.41%

continued

Exhibit 6.24
Ratio Analysis for Sarwark Company
(Problem 37)

	Year 1	Year 2	Year 3
Rate of Return on Assets	10.1%	10.2%	9.9%
Profit Margin (before interest and related tax effects) . . .	11.9%	10.0%	9.6%
Total Assets Turnover	0.85	1.02	1.03
Cost of Goods Sold/Revenues	72.4%	73.9%	73.8%
Selling and Administrative/Revenues	10.5%	10.4%	10.5%
Interest Expense/Revenues	2.1%	3.5%	4.0%
Income Tax Expense/Revenues	4.2%	4.1%	3.8%
Accounts Receivable Turnover	4.6	4.7	4.6
Inventory Turnover	3.7	3.6	3.7
Plant Asset Turnover	1.2	1.5	1.7
Rate of Return on Common Shareholders' Equity	15.5%	15.2%	14.7%

continued

Exhibit 6.23 *continued*
Data for Ratio Detective Exercise
(Problem 36)

	Company Numbers					
	(8)	(9)	(10)	(11)	(12)	(13)
Balance Sheet at End of Year						
Current Receivables	12.94%	9.16%	25.18%	27.07%	13.10%	653.94%
Inventories	15.47	56.89	79.53	0.00	1.62	0.00
Net Plant and Equipment*	70.29	28.36	19.22	2.64	251.62	2.88
All Other Assets	18.37	26.42	24.72	223.91	23.68	200.37
Total Assets	117.07%	120.83%	148.65%	253.62%	290.02%	857.19%
*Cost of Plant and Equipment (gross)	167.16%	42.40%	35.08%	4.45%	320.90%	3.81%
Current Liabilities	19.37%	33.01%	20.42%	161.37%	28.01%	377.56%
Long-Term Liabilities	20.62	34.07	36.09	10.62	115.50	280.79
Owners' Equity	77.09	53.74	92.13	81.63	146.51	198.83
Total Equities	117.08%	120.82%	148.64%	253.62%	290.02%	857.18%
Income Statement for Year						
Revenues	100.00%	100.00%	100.00%	100.00%	100.00%	100.00%
Cost of Goods Sold (excluding depreciation) or Operating Expenses[a]	81.92	57.35	42.92	82.61	45.23	47.69
Depreciation	5.81	1.90	1.97	0.05	14.55	0.00
Interest Expense	1.23	2.69	3.11	1.07	7.15	24.33
Advertising Expense	0.00	6.93	13.04	0.00	0.00	0.00
Research and Development Expense	0.76	0.00	0.00	0.00	0.71	0.00
Income Taxes	2.15	7.47	10.63	3.92	8.73	12.89
All Other Items (net)	3.81	14.82	17.99	2.97	11.51	−5.57
Total Expenses	95.68%	91.16%	89.66%	90.62%	87.88%	79.34%
Net Income	4.32%	8.84%	10.34%	9.38%	12.11%	20.65%

[a]Represents operating expenses for the following companies: Advertising/public opinion survey firm, insurance company, finance company, and the public accounting partnership.

Exhibit 6.24 *continued*
Ratio Analysis for Sarwark Company
(Problem 37)

	Year 1	Year 2	Year 3
Current Ratio	1.6:1	1.4:1	1.2:1
Quick Ratio	.9:1	.7:1	.5:1
Total Liabilities/Total Liabilities and Shareholders' Equity	42.0%	48.0%	60.0%
Long-Term Liabilities/Total Liabilities and Shareholders' Equity	25.0%	26.0%	25.0%
Revenues as Percentage of Year 1 Revenues	100%	115%	130%
Assets as Percentage of Year 1 Assets	100%	113%	125%
Capital Expenditures as Percentage of Year 1 Capital Expenditures	100%	112%	120%

Exhibit 6.25
Ratio Analysis for Widdicombe Corporation
(Problem 38)

	Year 1	Year 2	Year 3
Rate of Return on Assets	10%	11%	12%
Profit Margin (before interest and related taxes)	18%	16%	14%
Total Asset Turnover	.56	.69	.86
Cost of Goods Sold/Revenues	62%	63%	65%
Selling and Administrative/Revenues	8%	10%	10%
Interest Expense/Revenues	16%	12%	8%
Income Tax Expense/Revenues.	4%	5%	7%
Accounts Receivable Turnover	2.6	2.5	2.4
Inventory Turnover	3.2	2.8	2.5
Fixed Asset Turnover	.3	.5	.7
Rate of Return on Common Shareholders' Equity.	18%	16%	14%
Profit Margin (after interest)	10%	10%	10%
Asset Turnover	.56	.69	.86
Leverage Ratio	3.2	2.3	1.6
Revenues as Percentage of Year 1 Revenues	100%	102%	99%
Assets as Percentage of Year 1 Assets	100%	104%	105%
Net Income as Percentage of Year 1 Net Income.	100%	102%	99%
Capital Expenditures as Percentage of Year 1 Capital Expenditures.	100%	90%	85%

39. *Case analysis of bankruptcy.* On October 2, 1975, W. T. Grant Company filed for bankruptcy protection under Chapter XI of the Bankruptcy Act. At that time, it reported assets of $1.02 billion and liabilities of $1.03 billion. The company had operated at a profit for most years prior to 1974, but reported an operating loss of $177 million for its fiscal year January 31, 1974, to January 31, 1975.

The accompanying Exhibits 6.26–6.29 contain:

(1) Balance sheets, income statements, and statements of changes in financial position for W. T. Grant Company for the 1971 through 1975 fiscal periods.
(2) Additional financial information about W. T. Grant Company, the retail industry, and the economy for the same period as above.

Prepare an analysis that explains the major causes of Grant's collapse. You may find it useful to refer to financial and nonfinancial data presented in other sources, such as *The Wall Street Journal,* in addition to that presented here. Assume an income tax rate of 48 percent.

Exhibit 6.26
W. T. GRANT COMPANY
Comparative Balance Sheets
(Problem 39)

	January 31				
	1971	**1972**	**1973**	**1974**	**1975**
Assets					
Cash and Marketable Securities	$ 34,009	$ 49,851	$ 30,943	$ 45,951	$ 79,642
Accounts Receivable	419,731	477,324	542,751	598,799	431,201
Inventories	260,492	298,676	399,533	450,637	407,357
Other Current Assets	5,246	5,378	6,649	7,299	6,581
Total Current Assets.	$719,478	$831,229	$ 979,876	$1,102,686	$ 924,781
Investments	23,936	32,367	35,581	45,451	49,764
Property, Plant, and Equipment (net)	61,832	77,173	91,420	100,984	101,932
Other Assets	2,382	3,901	3,821	3,862	5,790
Total Assets	$807,628	$944,670	$1,110,698	$1,252,983	$1,082,267
Equities					
Short-Term Debt	$246,420	$237,741	$ 390,034	$ 453,097	$ 600,695
Accounts Payable	118,091	124,990	112,896	103,910	147,211
Current Deferred Taxes	94,489	112,846	130,137	133,057	2,000
Total Current Liabilities	$459,000	$475,577	$ 633,067	$ 690,064	$ 749,906
Long-Term Debt	32,301	128,432	126,672	220,336	216,341
Noncurrent Deferred Taxes.	8,518	9,664	11,926	14,649	—
Other Long-Term Liabilities	5,773	5,252	4,694	4,195	2,183
Total Liabilities	$505,592	$618,925	$ 776,359	$ 929,244	$ 968,430
Preferred Stock	$ 9,600	$ 9,053	$ 8,600	$ 7,465	$ 7,465
Common Stock	18,180	18,529	18,588	18,599	18,599
Additional Paid-in Capital	78,116	85,195	86,146	85,910	83,914
Retained Earnings	230,435	244,508	261,154	248,461	37,674
Total.	$336,331	$357,285	$ 374,488	$ 360,435	$ 147,652
Less Cost of Treasury Stock	(34,295)	(31,540)	(40,149)	(36,696)	(33,815)
Total Shareholders' Equity	$302,036	$325,745	$ 334,339	$ 323,739	$ 113,837
Total Equities	$807,628	$944,670	$1,110,698	$1,252,983	$1,082,267

Exhibit 6.27
W. T. GRANT COMPANY
Statement of Income and Retained Earnings
(Problem 39)

	Years Ended January 31				
	1971	**1972**	**1973**	**1974**	**1975**
Sales.	$1,254,131	$1,374,811	$1,644,747	$1,849,802	$1,761,952
Concessions	4,986	3,439	3,753	3,971	4,238
Equity in Earnings	2,777	2,383	5,116	4,651	3,086
Other Income	2,874	3,102	1,188	3,063	3,376
Total Revenues	$1,264,768	$1,383,735	$1,654,804	$1,861,487	$1,772,652
Cost of Goods Sold	$ 843,192	$ 931,237	$1,125,261	$1,282,945	$1,303,267
Selling, General, and Administration	329,768	373,816	444,377	518,280	540,953
Interest	18,874	16,452	21,127	51,047	199,238
Taxes: Current	21,140	13,487	9,588	(6,021)	(19,439)
Deferred	11,660	13,013	16,162	6,807	(98,027)
Other Expenses	557	518	502	—	24,000
Total Expenses	$1,225,191	$1,348,523	$1,617,017	$1,853,058	$1,949,992
Net Income	$ 39,577	$ 35,212	$ 37,787	$ 8,429	$ (177,340)
Dividends	(20,821)	(21,139)	(21,141)	(21,122)	(4,457)
Other.	—	—	—	—	(28,990)
Change in Retained Earnings	$ 18,756	$ 14,073	$ 16,646	$ (12,693)	$ (210,787)
Retained Earnings—Beg. of Period	211,679	230,435	244,508	261,154	248,461
Retained Earnings—End of Period	$ 230,435	$ 244,508	$ 261,154	$ 248,461	$ 37,674

Exhibit 6.28
W. T. GRANT COMPANY
Statement of Changes in Financial Position
(Problem 39)

| | Years Ended January 31 | | | | |
	1971	1972	1973	1974	1975
Sources of Cash					
New Financing:					
Short-Term Bank Borrowing	$ 64,288	—	$152,293	$ 63,063	$147,898
Issue of Long-Term Debt	—	$100,000	—	100,000	—
Sale of Common Stock:					
To Employees	5,218	7,715	3,492	2,584	886
On Open Market	—	2,229	174	260	—
Other Sources (net)	—	—	2,307	—	—
Total Sources of Cash	$ 69,506	$109,944	$158,266	$165,907	$148,784
Uses of Cash					
Net Income	$ 39,577	$ 35,212	$ 37,787	$ 8,429	$(177,340)
Additions:					
Depreciation and Other	9,619	10,577	12,004	13,579	14,587
Decrease in Accounts Receivable	—	—	—	—	121,351
Decrease in Inventories	—	—	—	—	43,280
Increase in Accounts Payable	13,947	6,900	—	—	42,028
Increase in Deferred Taxes	14,046	18,357	17,291	2,920	—
Subtractions:					
Equity in Earnings and Other	(2,470)	(1,758)	(1,699)	(1,344)	(16,993)
Increase in Accounts Receivable	(51,464)	(57,593)	(65,427)	(56,047)	—
Increase in Inventories	(38,365)	(38,184)	(100,857)	(51,104)	—
Increase in Prepayments	(209)	(428)	(1,271)	(651)	(11,032)
Decrease in Accounts Payable	—	—	(12,093)	(8,987)	—
Decrease in Deferred Taxes	—	—	—	—	(101,078)
Cash Used by Operations	$ 15,319	$ 26,917	$114,265	$ 93,205	$ 85,197
Reduction in Financing:					
Repayment of Short-Term Borrowing (net) . . .	—	$ 8,680	—	—	—
Retirement of Long-Term Debt	$ 1,538	5,143	$ 1,760	$ 6,336	$ 3,995
Reacquisition of Preferred Stock	948	308	252	618	—
Reacquisition of Common Stock	13,224	—	11,466	133	—
Dividends	20,821	21,138	21,141	21,122	4,457
Total for Reductions in Financing	$ 36,531	$ 35,269	$ 34,619	$ 28,209	$ 8,452
Investments in Noncurrent Assets:					
Property, Plant, and Equipment	$ 16,141	$ 25,918	$ 26,250	$ 23,143	$ 15,535
Investments in Securities	436	5,951	2,040	5,700	5,182
Total for Investments	$ 16,577	$ 31,869	$ 28,290	$ 28,843	$ 20,717
Other Uses (net)	$ 47	$ 47	—	$ 642	$ 727
Total Uses of Cash	$ 68,174	$ 94,102	$177,174	$150,899	$115,093
Increase (decrease) in Cash	$ 1,332	$ 15,842	$ (18,908)	$ 15,008	$ 33,691

Exhibit 6.29
Additional Information
(Problem 39)

	Fiscal Years Ending January 31				
	1971	1972	1973	1974	1975
W. T. Grant Company					
Range of Stock Price, Dollar per Share[a]	$41\frac{7}{8}$–$70\frac{5}{8}$	$34\frac{3}{4}$–$48\frac{3}{4}$	$9\frac{7}{8}$–$44\frac{3}{8}$	$9\frac{5}{8}$–41	$1\frac{1}{2}$–12
Earnings per Share in Dollars	$2.64	$2.25	$2.49	$ .76	$(12.74)
Dividends per Share in Dollars	$1.50	$1.50	$1.50	$1.50	$ .30
Number of Stores	1,116	1,168	1,208	1,189	1,152
Total Store Area, Thousands of Square Feet	38,157	44,718	50,619	53,719	54,770

	1970	1971	1972	1973	1974
Retail Industry[b]					
Total Chain Store Industry Sales in Millions of Dollars	$6,969	$6,972	$7,498	$8,212	$8,714

	1970	1971	1972	1973	1974
Aggregate Economy[c]					
Gross National Product in Billions of Dollars	$1,075.3	$1,107.5	$1,171.1	$1,233.4	$1,210
Bank Short-Term Lending Rate	8.48%	6.32%	5.82%	8.30%	11.28%

[a]Source: Standard and Poor's Stock Reports.
[b]Source: Standard Industry Surveys.
[c]Source: Survey of Current Business.

Part Three

Measuring and Reporting Assets and Equities Using Generally Accepted Accounting Principles

Chapter 7

Cash, Marketable Securities, and Receivables: The Liquid Assets

Overview of Part Three

By now, most of the basic concepts and procedures of financial accounting have been introduced. The purpose of accounting, its theoretical framework, and some of its procedures have been discussed. Tools for analyzing financial statements have been presented. From this point onward, generally accepted accounting principles (GAAP) will be considered in approximate balance sheet order: liquid assets in Chapter 7, inventories in Chapter 8, noncurrent assets in Chapter 9, liabilities and owners' equity in Chapters 10, 11, and 12. Chapter 13, somewhat out of "balance sheet order," focuses on accounting for certain long-term investments in securities of other companies. Before examining GAAP for liquid assets, it will be helpful to explore the nature and development of accounting principles.

Nature and Development of Generally Accepted Accounting Principles

Generally accepted accounting principles, or GAAP, are the accounting methods and procedures used by firms in preparing their financial statements. This section considers the nature of these principles and the process through which they are developed.

Nature of Accounting Principles To understand the nature of principles in accounting, contrast them with principles in fields such as physics and mathematics. In physics and other natural sciences, a principle (or theory) is evaluated by asking how well the predictions of the principle correspond with physically observed phenomena. Mathematicians evaluate a principle (or theorem) by comparing its internal consistency with the structure of definitions and underlying axioms. In accounting, principles stand or fall on their general acceptability to preparers and users of accounting reports. Unlike those in the physical sciences, principles in accounting do not exist naturally, merely awaiting discovery. Unlike mathematics, accounting has no structure of definitions and concepts that can be used unambiguously to develop accounting principles. For example, one generally accepted accounting principle requires land to be stated at its acquisition cost as long as it is held by a firm. Changes in the market value of the land are not reflected in the financial statements until the land is sold. This accounting principle cannot be "proven" to be correct. It has simply been judged to be the generally acceptable method of accounting for land. Accounting principles might more aptly be called "accounting conventions."

Development of Accounting Principles Accounting principles result from an essentially political process. Various persons or groups have power, or authority, in the decision process that yields generally accepted accounting principles. The next few paragraphs describe the most important participants in this process.

Congress By enacting the Securities Act of 1933, the Congress accepted the ultimate legal authority to prescribe the methods of accounting used in preparing financial statements for shareholders of publicly owned corporations. Congress has delegated its authority to the Securities and Exchange Commission (SEC), an agency of the federal government. Whereas the SEC has *legal* authority to prescribe accounting principles, since 1938 it has delegated most of the responsibility for developing accounting principles to the accounting profession.[1] Typically, the SEC serves as an advisor or consultant on proposed accounting principles. In a few instances, the SEC has effectively exerted its legal authority by disagreeing with positions taken within the accounting profession.

In recent years, the pronouncements of the SEC have been concerned primarily with format and disclosure in the financial statements rather than with valuation and measurement. The SEC requires that certain financial statement information be included in the annual report to shareholders. The financial statements for General Products Company in Appendix A appear in the required format. The annual report to shareholders, along with certain supplementary information, must then be included in the annual report submitted to the SEC (known as the *10-K report*).[2]

Accounting Profession The accounting profession is composed of practicing public accountants, financial executives, controllers, academics, and others. Most accounting principles have been developed by officially appointed committees or boards within the accounting profession.

Between 1938 and 1959, the Committee on Accounting Procedure of the American Institute of Certified Public Accountants issued *Bulletins* on various topics. Between 1959 and 1973, the Accounting Principles Board (APB) of the American Institute of Certified Public Accountants issued *Opinions*. These *Bulletins* and *Opinions,* unless superceded, still constitute generally accepted accounting principles. The APB consisted of individuals from the accounting profession, with many representatives from public accounting firms.

Since 1973, the Financial Accounting Standards Board (FASB) has been the major agency outside the federal government responsible for developing accounting

---

[1]Securities and Exchange Commission, *Accounting Series Release No. 4,* 1938. The SEC reaffirmed its delegation of responsibility by recognizing the Financial Accounting Standards Board in *Accounting Series Release No. 150,* 1973. Reissued in Section 101 of *Codification of Financial Reporting Policies.*

[2]Securities and Exchange Commission, *Accounting Series Releases No. 279, 280, and 281,* 1980. Reissued in Sections 101 and 102 of *Codification of Financial Reporting Policies.*

principles. The FASB includes substantial representation from several groups of statement preparers and users in addition to members from the public accounting profession. The members of the FASB serve on a full-time basis, having severed all relations with their previous firms or universities. This independence of Board members reduces chances for undue influence by previous employers and adds credibility to the standard-setting process. The FASB issues *Statements of Financial Accounting Standards,* which represent generally accepted accounting principles. In contrast to the SEC's emphasis on disclosure, pronouncements of the FASB tend to deal more with valuation and measurement issues.

The process by which the FASB sets accounting principles has two noteworthy attributes. First, the FASB follows a due process procedure in its deliberations and, second, it attempts to relate specific *Standards* to general-purpose financial statement objectives.

The FASB generally follows the procedures listed below:

1. The FASB identifies a reporting issue and places it on the agenda.

2. The technical staff of the FASB, in consultation with a group of knowledgeable persons in the accounting and business community (formed in a "task force"), prepares a *Discussion Memorandum (DM)* on the reporting issue. The *DM* is intended to be an impartial discussion of the major questions to be considered by the Board.

3. The *DM* is "exposed" to the public for a period of at least 60 days.

4. The FASB holds a public hearing on the contents of the *DM*. Individuals and organizations have an opportunity to comment on the questions raised and to indicate support for particular positions.

5. The FASB, after considering the oral and written comments received, prepares an *Exposure Draft* of a Proposed Financial Accounting Standard. The *Exposure Draft* takes a definitive position on the major issues under consideration.

6. The *Exposure Draft* is "exposed" to the public for a period of at least 30 days.

7. A second public hearing is frequently held. The comments this time are directed at the content of the Proposed Standard.

8. After additional consideration of the comments received, the FASB either (a) adopts the Proposed Standard as an official *Statement of Financial Accounting Standard,* (b) revises the Proposed Standard before making it official, in some cases allowing additional opportunities for public comment (in effect, returning to step **6**), (c) delays issuance of an official Standard but keeps the issue on its active agenda, or (d) decides not to issue an official Standard and takes the issue off its agenda.

The FASB's due process procedure recognizes that the standard-setting process is political and that all constituents must be given an opportunity to speak. It also recognizes that accounting standards are judged according to their acceptability to several groups. By involving the various preparer and user groups in the deliberation process, the FASB hopes that these groups will be able to make more informed recommendations and be more tolerant of viewpoints that differ from their own.

A second attribute of the FASB's standard-setting process is its effort to relate specific accounting Standards to more general-purpose financial statement objectives. These objectives are discussed in Chapter 1. This approach results from criticisms directed at the FASB's predecessors that they attempted to solve problems without a conceptual framework. Unless accounting pronouncements derive from some underlying set of objectives or purposes of financial statements, the pronouncements can become internally inconsistent. Time will tell whether the FASB can be more successful in relating its pronouncements to a conceptual framework for financial reporting than were its predecessors.

Other Participants Income tax legislation and administration also have had a substantial impact on adequate accounting and reporting. Although the income tax requirements do not establish principles and practices for general external reporting, they influence the choice of acceptable procedures. Individual users of financial statements can offer their own opinions on proposed standards to the FASB and thereby influence the standard-setting process.

Future Development of Accounting Principles Unless Congress or the SEC unexpectedly decides to exert its legal authority, there is little reason to anticipate that the future development of accounting principles will differ from the past. The process will continue to be political, with opposing interests attempting to exert influence on the decision process. Positions taken or opinions rendered by participants in this process must be carefully developed and marketed if the positions are to become generally acceptable to others.

The rest of this chapter presents the generally accepted accounting principles for liquid assets.

Liquidity and Moneylike Assets

Chapters 5 and 6 point out that liquidity is essential for business operations. An insolvent company, one that cannot pay its bills and meet its commitments as they mature, will not survive no matter how large its owners' equity. Most bankrupt companies show positive owners' equity on their balance sheets at the time of bankruptcy. Bankruptcy is usually caused by an inability to meet debts as they become due. One of the largest bankruptcies occurred in 1970 when the Penn Central Transportation Company was placed into bankruptcy by its parent holding company, the Penn Central Company. At that time, Penn Central Transportation Company had almost $2 billion of shareholders' equity, including some $500 million of retained earnings. Nevertheless, the company became insolvent because it could not meet "only" a few hundred million dollars in obligations due at that time.

Moneylike assets are an important determinant of a firm's liquidity. Cash, marketable securities, accounts receivable, and notes receivable are the principal liquid assets of a business. These assets are generally stated at their current cash, or cash equivalent, values on the balance sheet. This chapter explores various inclusion and valuation questions related to each of these liquid assets. The objective of the chapter is to present the methods of accounting and reporting for moneylike assets so that assessments can be made of a firm's liquidity at a moment in time and changes in that liquidity over time.

Cash

Cash is the most liquid asset. It is also the most vulnerable because of its susceptibility to theft or embezzlement. This section considers cash inclusions and valuation as well as cash management and control.

Cash Inclusions and Valuation

To be counted as Cash on the balance sheet, an item should be freely available for use as a medium of exchange. Coins, currency, travelers' checks, and undeposited checks qualify. Most cash is cash in the bank in the form of demand deposits, savings accounts, and certificates of deposit. Although banks can restrict the immediate withdrawal of funds from savings accounts and certificates of deposit, these items are usually sufficiently available for use as a medium of exchange to be included in cash. Cash includes foreign currency unless a firm's ability to use the currency is severely restricted. For example, foreign currency held by a division located in a country that forbids the outflow of funds would not be included. Also, funds set aside or restricted for a particular purpose would not be included. For example, firms are often required to establish "sinking funds" to retire outstanding debt. The cash in a sinking fund appears as Investments, rather than as Cash, on the balance sheet.

Compensating balances are frequently excluded from Cash. A compensating balance generally takes the form of a minimum checking account balance that must be maintained in connection with a borrowing arrangement with a bank. For example, a firm might borrow $5 million from a bank and agree to maintain a 10 percent (= $500,000) compensating balance in an interest-free checking account. This arrangement results in a reduction of the amount effectively borrowed and an increase in the interest rate effectively paid by the borrower. Unless compensating balances are adequately disclosed, incorrect assessments of a firm's liquidity can occur.

The SEC requires that legally restricted deposits held as compensating balances against short-term borrowing arrangements be separated from Cash but included among current assets. Compensating balances held against long-term borrowing arrangements should be included under noncurrent assets, preferably Investments. When compensating balance arrangements exist but the firm may legally use the cash, the nature of the arrangements and the amounts involved should be disclosed in a note to the financial statements.[3]

---

[3]Securities and Exchange Commission, *Accounting Series Release No. 148,* "Amendments to Regulations S-X and Related Interpretations and Guidelines Regarding the Disclosure of Compensating Balances and Short-Term Borrowing Arrangements," 1973. Reissued in Section 203 of *Codification of Financial Reporting Policies.*

Once an item meets the criteria to be included in cash, there are few valuation problems. Cash is normally stated at its face amount. Foreign currency must be translated to its U.S. dollar-equivalent amount, using the exchange rate in effect on the date of the balance sheet.

Cash Management

The management of cash involves two distinct goals. First, a firm establishes a system of internal controls to ensure that cash is safeguarded from theft or embezzlement. Typical internal control procedures include separating duties of individuals handling cash receipts and disbursements, depositing cash receipts immediately, disbursing cash only by authorized checks, and preparing bank account reconciliations regularly. The appendix to this chapter describes some of the internal control procedures for cash.

Second, management wants to regulate cash balances so that neither too much nor too little cash is available at any time. Cash on hand or in checking accounts generally does not earn interest. During inflationary periods, idle cash loses purchasing power and decreases in real value. A firm does not want to maintain excessive cash balances. On the other hand, a firm does not want to be short of cash and unable to meet its obligations as they become due or unable to take advantage of cash discounts.

A weekly or monthly budget of cash receipts and disbursements aids cash management. Such a budget indicates both the amounts and times when excess cash will be available for investment or when additional borrowing will become necessary.

Appendix 7.1 presents some of the procedures used by most firms to control and account for cash.

Marketable Securities

A business may find itself with more cash than it needs for current and near-term business purposes. Rather than allow cash to remain unproductive, the business may invest some of its currently excess cash in income-yielding securities, such as U.S. government bonds or stocks or bonds of other companies. Such liquid assets appear under the caption Marketable Securities in the Current Assets section of the balance sheet.

A business may also acquire securities intending to hold them for a longer period. Such securities are treated as long-term investments. This section considers the classification and valuation of securities held either temporarily as current assets or as long-term investments.

Classification of Securities

Securities appear as "marketable securities" among current assets as long as they can be readily converted into cash *and* management intends to do so when it needs cash. Securities that do not meet both of these criteria appear under Investments on the balance sheet.

Example 1 Morrissey Manufacturing Corporation invested $150,000 of temporarily excess funds in U.S. Treasury notes. The notes mature in 3 months. This investment appears among marketable securities because the notes can be sold at any time and even if not sold, the cash will be collected within 3 months.

Example 2 Suppose that Morrissey Manufacturing Corporation had acquired 20-year bonds of Greer Electronics Company instead of the U.S. Treasury notes. Its intent in acquiring the bonds was the same as before, the investment of temporarily excess cash. These bonds would similarly appear as marketable securities.

Example 3 West Corporation acquired 10 percent of the outstanding shares of Xerox Corporation on the open market for $10 million. West Corporation plans to hold these shares as a long-term investment. Even though the shares of Xerox Corporation are readily marketable, they would not be classified as marketable securities, because West Corporation does not intend to turn the securities into cash within a reasonably short period. These securities appear as long-term Investments on the balance sheet.

In published financial statements, all securities properly classified as the current asset, Marketable Securities, appear together on a single line on the balance sheet. As discussed below, however, the accounting for *marketable debt securities* and *marketable equity securities* may differ.

Valuation of Marketable Securities as Temporary Investments

Marketable securities are initially recorded at acquisition cost. Acquisition cost includes the purchase price plus any commissions, taxes, and other costs incurred. For example, if marketable securities are acquired for $10,000 plus $300 for commissions and taxes, the entry is

Marketable Securities	10,300	
Cash		10,300

Dividends on marketable securities become revenue when declared. Interest revenue is recognized when earned. Assuming that $250 of dividends was declared and $300 of interest was earned on marketable securities and these amounts were immediately received in cash, the entry is

Cash	550	
Dividend Revenue		250
Interest Revenue		300

There is nothing unusual about the valuation of marketable securities at date of acquisition or the recording of dividends and interest. The valuation of marketable securities after acquisition, however, departs from strict historical cost accounting.

Marketable Equity Securities Financial Accounting Standards Board *Statement of Financial Accounting Standards No. 12* (1975) requires that the *portfolio* of marketable equity securities (that is, common stock, preferred stock, stock options, and warrants) classified as current assets be stated at the lower of acquisition cost or market value at the end of each period.[4] Under the *lower-of-cost-or-market method*, decreases in the market value of a portfolio of marketable equity securities are recognized as holding losses each period as the decreases occur, even though a market transaction or exchange has not taken place. Subsequent increases in the market value of the portfolio up to the original acquisition cost are recognized as holding gains. The FASB decided that showing marketable securities at acquisition cost when their objectively observable market value declines *below* cost distorts the income and financial position of the firm. When market values rise *above* acquisition cost, the amounts are just as objectively observable, but the FASB does not permit increasing income and asset amounts above cost and recognizing income for unrealized holding gains. The FASB thinks that doing so departs too much from historical cost accounting. The FASB chose to apply lower of cost or market to the entire portfolio, rather than security by security, because "many enterprises regard their portfolios of marketable equity securities . . . as collective assets . . ." and the security-by-security approach would "be unduly conservative and at variance with the manner in which enterprises generally view their investment in marketable equity securities."[5]

The credit to reduce the carrying amount of the current asset, Marketable Equity Securities, is made to a contra account usually called the Allowance for Excess of Cost of Marketable Securities over Market Value. Using a separate contra account enables the simultaneous identification of both the acquisition cost and the amount of decline in the market value of the portfolio. This is necessary to enable subsequent write-ups to original acquisition cost, but no further. The portfolio cannot be stated at an amount greater than the original acquisition cost; that is, the allowance account can never have a debit balance. The following sections illustrate the procedures for applying the lower-of-cost-or-market method.

Example 4 Wolfson Company acquired various marketable equity securities during Year 1 as shown in Exhibit 7.1.[6] The entry to record the acquisition of securities during Year 1 is

Marketable Securities	100,000	
Cash		100,000

---

[4] "Market value," as defined by Financial Accounting Standards Board, *Statement No. 12,* "Accounting for Certain Marketable Securities," is the quoted market price for both buyers and sellers excluding brokerage commissions, taxes, and similar costs.

[5] Financial Accounting Standards Board, *Statement No. 12,* par. 31.

[6] In reality, a firm holding these securities for 4 years would probably classify them as investments, not as current assets. For purposes of illustration, we have shown the accounting for a portfolio of marketable securities over several years.

Exhibit 7.1
Data for Illustration of Accounting
for Marketable Equity Securities of Wolfson Company

			Market Value			
Security	Date Acquired	Acquisition Cost	Dec. 31, Year 1	Dec. 31, Year 2	Dec. 31, Year 3	Dec. 31, Year 4
A Company. .	4/1/Year 1	$ 50,000	$53,000	$54,000	$52,000	$43,000
B Company. .	6/1/Year 1	30,000	27,000	22,000	—a	—
C Company. .	8/1/Year 1	20,000	16,000	23,000	24,000	—b
Total		$100,000	$96,000	$99,000	$76,000	$43,000

[a]Holdings of Company B sold during Year 3 for $32,000.
[b]Holdings of Company C sold during Year 4 for $17,000.

Unrealized Holding Loss   At the end of Year 1, the portfolio of marketable equity securities had an aggregate acquisition cost of $100,000 (= $50,000 + $30,000 + $20,000) and an aggregate market value of $96,000 (= $53,000 + $27,000 + $16,000). A write-down of $4,000 recognizes the unrealized holding loss.

Unrealized Holding Loss on Valuation of Marketable Securities . . .	4,000	
Allowance for Excess of Cost of Marketable Securities over		
Market Value		4,000
Entry to adjust credit balance in allowance account to $4,000.		

The loss account appears in the income statement for Year 1 among the expenses.[7] The allowance account appears as a contra account to marketable securities on the balance sheet at the end of Year 1. Exhibits 7.2 and 7.7 illustrate the required disclosures.

Because the lower-of-cost-or-market method applies to the entire portfolio, rather than security by security, the amount of the decline in market value below cost is not recorded separately for each security. As in this example, gains on some securities may offset losses on others.

Recovery of Unrealized Holding Loss   Assume no acquisitions or dispositions of marketable equity securities during Year 2 and that the market value of the portfolio at the end of Year 2 increased to $99,000. The valuation of the portfolio of securities is increased (but never to an amount greater than original acquisition cost). The entry is:

---

[7]For income tax purposes, losses (or gains) are reported only when realized, generally by sale.

Allowance for Excess of Cost of Marketable Securities over Market Value	3,000	
Recovery of Unrealized Holding Loss on Valuation of Marketable Securities		3,000
To increase valuation of marketable securities by reducing allowance account.		

The debit entry above decreases the credit balance in the allowance account to $1,000. The Recovery of Unrealized Holding Loss on Valuation of Marketable Securities account appears in the income statement for Year 2 as a revenue, or gain. See Exhibit 7.2 for illustrative disclosures.

Realized Gain or Loss Through Sale Upon selling an individual marketable equity security, the realized gain or loss is the difference between the selling price and the *original acquisition cost* of the individual security, regardless of the related balance in the allowance account. For example, if the securities of B Company were sold during Year 3 for $32,000, the entry to record the sale during Year 3 is

Cash	32,000	
Realized Holding Gain on Sale of Marketable Securities		2,000
Marketable Securities		30,000
To recognize realized holding gain of $2,000 (= $32,000 proceeds of sale − $30,000 original cost).		

The realized holding gain appears in the income statement for Year 3; see Exhibit 7.2.[8] The aggregate acquisition cost of the portfolio at the end of Year 3 decreases to $70,000 (= $50,000 + $20,000). The aggregate market value of the portfolio at the end of Year 3 is $76,000 (= $52,000 + $24,000). Because aggregate market value exceeds aggregate cost, the allowance account should have a zero balance so that the portfolio appears at cost on the balance sheet. Because the allowance account has a $1,000 credit balance carried over from Year 2, the following entry at the end of Year 3 reduces the allowance account to zero.

Allowance for Excess of Cost of Marketable Securities over Market Value	1,000	
Recovery of Unrealized Holding Loss on Valuation of Marketable Securities		1,000
To increase valuation of marketable securities by reducing the allowance.		

The securities appear at $70,000 on the December 31, Year 3, balance sheet in Exhibit 7.2. Income for Year 3 increases by $1,000 plus the realized gain of $2,000.

[8]The gain would also be taxable.

Exhibit 7.2
Items in Income Statement and Balance Sheet
of Wolfson Company Illustrating Transactions in Marketable
Equity Securities as *Temporary Investments*—Current Assets

	Year 1	Year 2	Year 3	Year 4
Excerpts from Income Statement for Year				
Other Items (assumed) Before Taxes	$300,000	$300,000	$300,000	$300,000
Realized Gain (Loss) on Sale of Marketable Equity Securities	—	—	2,000	(3,000)
Unrealized Holding Loss on Valuation of Marketable Equity Securities	(4,000)	—	—	(7,000)
Recovery of Unrealized Holding Loss on Valuation of Marketable Equity Securities	—	3,000	1,000	—
Income Before Taxes	$296,000	$303,000	$303,000	$290,000
Balance Sheet Items at Year-End				
Marketable Securities at Cost.	$100,000	$100,000	$ 70,000	$ 50,000
Less Allowance for Excess of Cost of Marketable Equity Securities over Market Value	(4,000)	(1,000)	—	(7,000)
Marketable Equity Securities at Lower of Cost or Market[a]	$ 96,000	$ 99,000	$ 70,000	$ 43,000

[a]Notes to the financial statements must disclose separately the unrealized gains on all securities with gains and the unrealized losses on securities with losses. Exhibit 7.7 illustrates these disclosures. Consider, for example, the first column shown here and the underlying data reported in the preceding exhibit. Unrealized gains on securities with gains (A Company) total $3,000, whereas unrealized losses on securities with losses (B Company and C Company) total $7,000 [= ($30,000 − $27,000) + ($20,000 − $16,000)]. Both the amounts of the unrealized gains of $3,000 and the unrealized losses of $7,000 appear in notes, whereas the net unrealized loss of $4,000 (= $7,000 − $3,000) appears in the Allowance account for the year. For the third year shown here, the notes disclose that the aggregate market value of the securities exceeds their cost by $6,000.

Realized Loss and Unrealized Loss The data for Year 4 illustrate the simultaneous realization of a loss on sale of one security and further unrealized holding losses on securities still held. Holdings of Company C that had cost $20,000 are sold for $17,000. The journal entry is

Cash	17,000	
Realized Holding Loss on Sale of Marketable Securities	3,000	
Marketable Securities		20,000
Sale of holding of Company C for $3,000 less than original cost.		

Securities held at the end of Year 4 have an aggregate cost of $50,000 and an aggregate market value of $43,000. Thus, the ending balance in the allowance

Exhibit 7.3
Items in Income Statement and Balance Sheet of
Wolfson Company Illustrating Transactions in Long-Term
Investments in Marketable Equity Securities

	Year 1	Year 2	Year 3	Year 4
Excerpts from Income Statement for Year				
Other Items (Assumed) Before Taxes	$300,000	$300,000	$300,000	$300,000
Realized Gain (Loss) on Sale of Investments in Marketable Equity Securities.	—	—	2,000	(3,000)
Income Before Taxes	$300,000	$300,000	$302,000	$297,000
Excerpts from Balance Sheet Items at Year-End				
Asset Section				
Investments in Marketable Equity Securities at Cost	$100,000	$100,000	$ 70,000	$ 50,000
Less Allowance for Excess of Cost of Investments in Marketable Equity Securities over Market Value	(4,000)	(1,000)	—	(7,000)
Marketable Equity Securities at Lower of Cost or Market . . .	$ 96,000	$ 99,000	$ 70,000[a]	$ 43,000
Owners' Equity Section				
Net Unrealized Loss on Investments in Marketable Equity Securities (Debit Balance)	($ 4,000)	($ 1,000)	—	($ 7,000)

[a]The captions on the balance sheet or the notes must disclose that the market value on December 31, Year 3, is $76,000. See Exhibit 7.1.

account must be $7,000. Because it had a zero balance at the start of the year, the journal entry is

---

Unrealized Holding Loss on Valuation of Marketable Securities . . .	7,000	
Allowance for Excess of Cost of Marketable Securities over Market Value		7,000
Adjustment of balance in allowance account from zero to $7,000.		

Income for Year 4 is decreased for the realized loss of $3,000 and for the unrealized holding loss of $7,000. See Exhibit 7.2.

Marketable Debt Securities FASB *Statement No. 12* addressed only marketable *equity* securities. The accounting for marketable *debt* securities follows *Accounting Research Bulletin No. 43* (Chapter 3A), which prescribes acquisition cost as the valuation method except "where market value is less than cost by a substantial amount . . . , the amount to be included as a current asset should not exceed the market value."

As a practical matter, many firms use lower of cost or market for marketable debt securities as well.

Valuation of Marketable Securities as Long-Term Investments

Businesses may acquire equity securities of another firm as a long-term investment. The motive for acquisition may be either passive or active. With a passive investment, the owning firm hopes to accumulate wealth by receiving dividends and realizing capital gains on selling the equity securities. The owning firm does not, however, actively control or significantly influence the activities of the other firm. (In this sense, an individual's purchase of shares of stock is usually passive.) In contrast, a firm can acquire shares of another company with hope of controlling or significantly influencing the other company's activities.

Chapter 13 discusses the criteria used for judging whether investments are active or passive and the accounting for active investments. The general rule is that an investment of less than 20 percent of the outstanding shares is presumed to be passive, but when the ownership is 20 percent or more, the investment is presumed to be active.

The accounting for passive investments differs from the accounting for active investments. Passive investments are accounted for with a lower-of-cost-or-market method similar to that explained above for temporary holdings, but with important differences. The decrease in the market value of a portfolio of equity securities classified as Investments is not recognized as a loss in calculating net income during the period when the decrease occurs, as is done for marketable securities classified as current assets. Instead, the debit is to an account such as Net Unrealized Loss on Investments in Marketable Equity Securities, which is an owners' equity contra account. The account appears in the owners' equity section, usually between Additional Paid-in Capital and Retained Earnings. The account always has a debit (or zero) balance and reduces the other amounts (credit balances) of owners' equity. The difference in accounting treatments results from the FASB's view that "the present concepts of income require authoritative clarification with respect to the recognition of unrealized gains and losses on long-term assets. Such clarification is beyond the scope of this Statement."[9]

Exhibit 7.3 illustrates the accounting for long-term investments in marketable securities. It uses the same data as in the illustration of accounting for temporary investments. The amounts shown in Exhibits 7.2 and 7.3 differ primarily because of the treatment of unrealized holding losses and recoveries of unrealized holding losses. In Exhibit 7.3, these items do not affect net income as they arise but appear separately in owners' equity, reducing it. Exhibit 12.1 in Chapter 12 illustrates the balance sheet presentation of the owners' equity contra account.

---

[9]Financial Accounting Standards Board, *Statement No. 12,* par. 30.

Transfer of Securities Between Current and Noncurrent Portfolios

The same holding of equity securities may be classified either as a current asset or as a noncurrent asset, depending on the owner's intentions. The owner can transfer a security from the current asset portfolio to the noncurrent asset portfolio or vice versa. If the market price of the security is less than cost on the date of transfer, generally accepted accounting principles require a "dual transaction assumption." FASB *Statement No. 12* (paragraph 10) requires that a transfer between portfolios of a security whose cost exceeds market value be treated as though the security were sold for cash equal to market value at the time of transfer and immediately repurchased at the same price. Thus, the transfer between portfolios establishes a realized loss and a new cost basis. Assume, for example, that equity securities had been purchased for $50,000 and held as a current asset while the market price declined to $40,000. The investment has been accounted for using the lower-of-cost-or-market basis. If the firm decides to reclassify the investment as a long-term investment, the following entry is made:

Realized Loss on Reclassification of Marketable Security as a Noncurrent Asset	10,000	
Investments (Noncurrent Asset)	40,000	
Marketable Securities (Current Asset)		50,000

The loss appears on the income statement for the year;[10] the cost basis of the noncurrent asset is $40,000; subsequent increases in market value, even to $50,000, are not recognized in the accounts.

Order of Procedures for Lower-of-Cost-or-Market Method

Students often find the treatment of the various events relating to investments in marketable securities confusing: the recording of realized gains or losses (through sale or reclassification from current to noncurrent or vice versa), the recording of unrealized losses, the recovery of unrealized losses, and the valuation of the allowance account. To minimize the chance for error, analyze and record transactions in the following order:

1. Record any *realized* gains or losses, from whatever source (sale, reclassification from current to noncurrent portfolio, or vice versa).

2. Compare the market value of the portfolio at the end of the period with its acquisition cost to ascertain the required credit balance in the Allowance account (= cost less market value if cost exceeds market value and zero otherwise).

3. Prepare a journal entry to adjust the Allowance account from its zero or credit balance at the start of the period to its required credit or zero balance at the end of the period.

---

[10]The loss would not be deductible in computing taxable income until the securities were *actually* sold.

    a. If the adjustment requires a credit to the Allowance account, then the debit is to the Unrealized Loss account, which appears in the income statement if the securities are current assets but only in the owners' equity section of the balance sheet if the securities are long-term investments.

    b. If the adjustment requires a debit to the Allowance account, the credit for current assets is to the Recovery of Unrealized Loss account, which appears on the income statement, and for long-term investments is to the Unrealized Loss account, which appears only on the balance sheet.

Individual securities are valued at cost, not at the lower of cost or market with separate valuation allowances; only the portfolio is valued at lower of cost or market.

The Marketable Securities and Investment accounts are "controlling accounts" showing the sum of all of the recorded acquisition costs of all the individual securities in the portfolios. When a security is removed from a portfolio, its acquisition cost must be taken out of the Marketable Securities or Investment account.

Evaluation of Lower of Cost or Market

For many years, some accounting theorists have argued that marketable securities should be shown at market value, whether greater or less than cost. Their very marketability makes valuing them on a current basis reasonably objective. The market value of the securities is the most relevant value for assessing a firm's liquidity. The FASB has taken the position, however, that it will not permit the write-up of marketable securities to an amount greater than acquisition cost until it establishes an acceptable conceptual framework of accounting.

Keep in mind that the total gain (or loss) on the holding of a security is the difference between the cash received on disposal less the original cash cost; over long enough time spans, income equals cash-in less cash-out. The write-downs and write-ups, if any, merely allocate that income to the various accounting periods between the dates of purchase and sale as market conditions change.

Accounts Receivable

The third liquid asset this chapter considers is accounts receivable. Trade accounts receivable typically arise when goods or services are sold on account. The entry is

Accounts Receivable	250	
Sales Revenue		250

Receivables sometimes also arise from transactions other than sales. For example, advances might be made to officers or employees, deposits might be made to guarantee performance or cover potential damages, or claims may be made against insurance companies, governmental bodies, common carriers, or others. These receivables are classified as either current assets or investments, depending on the expected collection date. This section focuses on trade accounts receivable, considering both their valuation and their management.

Accounts Receivable Valuation

Individual accounts receivable are initially recorded at the amount owed by each customer. The recording is made either in a subsidiary ledger (manual accounting system) or in a separately coded section of a computer memory bank. The sum of the amounts in individual customers' accounts appears in the master, or ''control,'' account for Accounts Receivable. The Accounts Receivable account records the total of the amounts in individual customers' accounts.

The amount in the master account for Accounts Receivable is reduced for estimated uncollectible accounts, sales discounts, and sales returns and allowances. The reporting objective is to state accounts receivable at the amount expected to be collected in cash. The difference between the amounts owed by customers and the amounts expected to be collected in cash must be charged against income. The charge against income for expected uncollectible amounts, sales discounts, and sales returns and allowances is preferably made in the period when the sales occur. In this way, revenue and net income for a period will reflect the amounts expected to be collected for services rendered during the period.

Uncollectible Accounts

Whenever credit is extended to customers, some accounts will almost certainly never be collected. Most businesses should even prefer to have some customers who do not pay their bills: For most firms, the optimal amount of uncollectibles is not zero. If a firm is to have no uncollectible accounts, it must screen credit customers carefully, which is costly. Furthermore, the firm would deny credit to many customers who would pay their bills even though they could not pass a credit check designed to weed out all potential uncollectibles. Some of the customers who are denied credit will take their business elsewhere and sales will be lost. So long as the amount *collected* from credit sales to a given class of customers exceeds the cost of goods sold and the other costs of serving that class of customers, the firm will be better off selling to that class rather than losing the sales. The rational firm should prefer granting credit to a class of customers who have a high probability of paying their bills, rather than losing their business, even though there may be some uncollectible accounts within the class.

For example, if gross margin—selling price less cost of goods sold—on new credit sales is 20 percent of credit sales, then a firm could afford uncollectible accounts of up to 20 percent of the new credit sales and still show increased net income, so long as all other costs of serving customers remain constant.

This does not suggest, of course, that a firm grant credit indiscriminately or ignore collection efforts for uncollected accounts receivable. A cost/benefit analysis of credit policy should dictate a strategy that results in some amount of uncollectible accounts, an amount that is reasonably predictable before any sales are made.

Firms use two methods of accounting for uncollectible accounts: (1) the direct charge-off method and (2) the allowance method.

Direct Charge-off Method

The direct charge-off method recognizes losses from uncollectible accounts in the period in which a specific customer's account is determined to be uncollectible. The method is sometimes called the "direct write-off method." For example, if it is decided that the account receivable of John Mahoney for $200 has become uncollectible, the following entry would be made:

Bad Debt Expense	200	
Accounts Receivable.		200
To record loss from an uncollectible customer's account.		

The direct charge-off method has three important shortcomings. First, the loss from uncollectible accounts is usually not recognized in the period in which the sale occurs and revenue is recognized. Too much income is recognized in the period of sale and too little in the period of write-off. Second, the amount of losses from uncollectible accounts recognized in any period is susceptible to intentional misrepresentation, because it is difficult to ascertain just when a particular account becomes uncollectible. Third, the amount of accounts receivable on the balance sheet does not reflect the amount of cash expected to be collected. The direct charge-off method is not appropriate when such losses are significant in amount, occur frequently, and are reasonably predictable, as in retail stores.

Allowance Method

When amounts of uncollectibles can be estimated with reasonable precision, accounting requires an alternative procedure, the allowance method. The allowance method involves:

1. Estimating the amount of uncollectible accounts that will occur over time in connection with the sales of each period.

2. Making an adjusting entry reducing income of the period for the estimated uncollectible amount.

3. Making a corresponding adjustment to the amount of accounts receivable so that the balance sheet figure reports the amount expected to be collected.

The entry involves a debit to reduce income and a credit to Allowance for Uncollectible Accounts, which is an account contra to the total of Accounts Receivable. The credit must be made to a contra account rather than to Accounts Receivable because no specific, individual account is being written off at the time of entry. Because the Allowance for Uncollectible Accounts is a contra to Accounts Receivable, its balance at the end of the period appears on the balance sheet as a deduction from Accounts Receivable.

Views differ as to the type of account—expense or revenue contra—debited when providing for estimated uncollectibles. Many firms debit Bad Debt Expense and include its amount among total expenses on the income statement. Their rationale is that a certain amount of bad debts is a necessary "cost" of generating revenues. Advocates of using a revenue contra account point out that its use permits net sales to be shown at the amount of cash expected to be collected. When the provision is debited to an expense account and included among total expenses on the income statement, net sales will overstate the amount of cash expected to be received. More important, though, advocates of using a revenue contra account point out that uncollectible accounts cannot be an expense. An expense is a gone asset. Accounts that, at the time of recording, were not expected to be collected were never assets to begin with. Although the arguments for using a revenue contra account may be persuasive, Bad Debt Expense is the account debited in this book because that account is more widely used in practice.

To illustrate the allowance method, assume that 2 percent of the credit sales made during the present period are estimated never to be collected. If sales on account are $90,000, then the entry to reduce the amount of Accounts Receivable to the amount expected to be collected would be

Bad Debt Expense	1,800	
Allowance for Uncollectible Accounts		1,800
To record estimate of uncollectible accounts arising from current period's sales (.02 × $90,000).		

When a particular customer's account is judged uncollectible, it is written off against the Allowance for Uncollectible Accounts. If, for example, it is decided that a balance of $200 due from John Mahoney will not be collected, the entry to charge off the account is

Allowance for Uncollectible Accounts	200	
Accounts Receivable.		200
To write off John Mahoney's account.		

The entry to write off specific accounts may be made during the period, as information about specific customers' accounts is obtained, or at the end of the period as an adjusting entry.

Under the allowance method, the income for the period of sale is reduced by the amount of uncollectibles that is estimated to arise from that period's sales. Some time later, when the attempts at collection are finally abandoned, the specific account is written off. Net assets are not affected by writing off the specific account. The reduction in net assets took place earlier, when the Allowance for Uncollectible Accounts was credited in the entry recognizing the estimated amount of eventual uncollectibles.

Estimating Uncollectibles

Accountants use two basic methods for calculating the amount of the adjustment for uncollectible accounts: the *percentage-of-sales method* and the *aging-of-accounts-receivable method*. The first requires fewer computations than the second, but the second method provides a useful check on the first.

Percentage-of-Sales Method The easiest method in most cases is to multiply the total sales on account during the period by an appropriate percentage, because it seems reasonable to assume that uncollectible account amounts will vary directly with the volume of credit business. (The example on page 287 used the percentage-of-sales method.) The percentage to be used is estimated by studying the experience of the business or by inquiring into the experience of similar enterprises. The rates found in use will generally be within the range of $\frac{1}{4}$ percent to 2 percent of credit sales.

   To illustrate, assume that sales on account total $1,500,000, and experience indicates that the appropriate percentage of uncollectible accounts is 2 percent. The entry is

---

Bad Debt Expense   30,000
   Allowance for Uncollectible Accounts   30,000
To provide for estimate of uncollectibles computed as a percentage of sales.

If cash sales occur in a relatively constant proportion to credit sales, the estimated uncollectibles percentage, proportionately reduced, can be applied to the total sales for the period. The total amount of all sales may be more readily available than that for sales on account.

Aging-of-Accounts-Receivable Method A more costly but more accurate method of calculating the amount of the adjustment, called *aging the accounts*, involves classifying each customer's account as to the length of time for which the account has been uncollected. Common intervals used for classifying individual accounts receivable are

1. Not yet due.

2. Past due 30 days or less.

3. Past due 31 to 60 days.

4. Past due 61 to 180 days.

5. Past due more than 180 days.

The accountant presumes that the balance in the Allowance for Uncollectible Accounts should be large enough to cover substantially all accounts receivable past due for more than 6 months and smaller portions of the more recent accounts. The actual portions are estimated from experience.

Exhibit 7.4
Illustration of Aging Accounts Receivable

Classification of Accounts	Amount	Estimated Uncollectible Percentage	Estimated Uncollectible Amounts
Not yet due	$680,000	0.5 percent	$ 3,400
1–30 days past due	60,000	6.0	3,600
31–60 days past due	30,000	25.0	7,500
61–180 days past due	50,000	50.0	25,000
More than 180 days past due	30,000	95.0	28,500
	$850,000		$68,000

As an example of the adjustment to be made, assume that the present balance in the Accounts Receivable account is $850,000 and the balance in the Allowance for Uncollectible Accounts before the adjusting entry for the period is $36,000. An aging of the accounts receivable balance ($850,000), shown in Exhibit 7.4, results in an estimate that $68,000 of the accounts will probably become uncollectible. The adjustment requires that the Allowance for Uncollectible Accounts balance be $68,000, an increase of $32,000. The adjusting entry at the end of the period is

Bad Debt Expense	32,000	
Allowance for Uncollectible Accounts		32,000
To increase Allowance account to $68,000 computed by an aging analysis; $68,000 − $36,000 = $32,000.		

Even when the percentage-of-sales method is used, aging the accounts should be done periodically to check on the accuracy of the percentage being used. If the aging analysis shows that the balance in the Allowance for Uncollectible Accounts is apparently too large or too small, the percentage of sales to be charged to the Bad Debt Expense account can be lowered or raised.

When the percentage-of-sales method is used, the periodic provision for uncollectible accounts (for example, $30,000) is merely added (credited) to the amounts provided in previous periods in the account, Allowance for Uncollectible Accounts. When the aging method is used, the balance in the account, Allowance for Uncollectible Accounts, is adjusted (for example, by $32,000) to reflect the desired ending balance. If the percentage used under the percentage-of-sales method reasonably reflects collection experience, the *balance* in the allowance account should be approximately the same at the end of each period under these two methods of estimating uncollectible accounts.

Exhibit 7.5 illustrates the operation of the allowance method for uncollectibles over two periods. In the first period the percentage method is used. In the second period the aging method is used. Normally, a firm would use the same method in all periods.

Exhibit 7.5
Review of the Allowance Method
of Accounting for Uncollectible Accounts

Transactions in the First Period:
(1) Sales are $1,000,000.
(2) Cash of $937,000 is collected from customers in payment of their accounts.
(3) At the end of the first period, it is estimated that uncollectibles will be 2 percent of sales; .02 × $1,000,000 = $20,000.
(4) Specific accounts totaling $7,000 are written off as uncollectible.
(5) The revenue and expense accounts are closed.

Transactions in the Second Period:
(6) Sales are $1,200,000.
(7) Specific accounts totaling $22,000 are written off during the period as information on their uncollectibility becomes known. The debit balance of $9,000 will remain in the Allowance account until the adjusting entry is made at the end of the period; see (9).
(8) Cash of $1,100,000 is collected from customers in payment of their accounts.
(9) An aging of the accounts receivable shows that the amount in the Allowance account should be $16,000. The amount of the adjustment is $25,000. It is computed as the difference between the desired $16,000 credit balance and the current $9,000 debit balance in the Allowance account.
(10) The revenue and expense accounts are closed.

Cash		Accounts Receivable		Allowance for Uncollectible Accounts	
		(1) 1,000,000			20,000 (3)
(2) 937,000			937,000 (2)		
			7,000 (4)	(4) 7,000	
Bal. ?		Bal. 56,000			13,000 Bal.
		(6) 1,200,000			
			22,000 (7)	(7) 22,000	
(8) 1,100,000			1,100,000 (8)		
					25,000 (9)
Bal. ?		Bal. 134,000			16,000 Bal.

Bad Debt Expense		Sales Revenue	
(3) 20,000			1,000,000 (1)
	Closed (5)	(5) Closed	
(9) 25,000			1,200,000 (6)
	Closed (10)	(10) Closed	

Sales Discounts

Often the seller of merchandise offers a reduction from its invoice price for prompt payment. Such reductions are called *sales discounts* or *cash discounts*.[11] There is

[11]See Glossary at the back of the book for the definition of a *discount* and a summary of the various contexts where this word is used in accounting.

nothing incongruous in the proposition that goods may have two prices: a cash price or a higher price if goods are sold on credit. The seller offers a cash discount, not only as an interest allowance on funds paid before the bill is due—the implied interest rate is unreasonably large—but also as an incentive for prompt payment so that additional bookkeeping and collection costs can be avoided.

The goods are sold for a certain price if prompt payment is made, and a penalty is added in the form of a higher price if the payment is delayed. The bills rendered by some public utilities illustrate this approach. The amount of sales discount made available to customers, then, should be considered as an adjustment in measuring net sales revenue.

The need to prepare income statements for relatively short periods leads to alternative possibilities for recording sales discounts and computing the amount of sales discounts reported for a period. The issue is whether the amount of cash discount should be deducted from sales revenue in the period when the sales revenue is recognized or in the period of cash collection. In computing the amount of sales discounts recognized for a period, the major alternatives are the following:

1. To recognize discounts when taken by the customer, without regard to the period of sale (called the *gross price method*).
2. To estimate the total amount of discounts that will be taken on the sales made during the period (called the *allowance method*).
3. To record sales amounts reduced by all discounts made available to customers and to recognize additional revenue when a discount lapses (called the *net price method*).

Intermediate accounting texts discuss these methods.

Sales Returns

When a customer returns merchandise, the sale has been canceled, and an entry to reverse the sale would be appropriate. In analyzing sales activities, however, management may be interested in the amount of goods returned. If so, a sales contra account is used to accumulate the amount of returns for a particular period.

A cash refund, such as might be made in a retail store when a customer returns merchandise that had been purchased for cash, would be entered as

Sales Returns.	23	
Cash on Hand		23

This treatment assumes that the return occurred before entries have been made to recognize the reduction in inventory and the related cost of goods sold. If the return occurred after cost of goods sold has been recognized, then the following entry must also be made:

Merchandise Inventory	16	
Cost of Goods Sold		16

To reduce cost of goods sold by the cost (or net realizable value, if lower) of returned goods.

Return of goods by a customer who buys ''on account'' would usually involve the preparation of a credit memorandum, which is the reverse of a sales invoice. The credit memorandum lists the goods that have been returned and indicates the amount that is to be allowed the customer. The entry to record the issuance of the credit would normally be a debit to the Sales Returns and a credit to the Accounts Receivable account.

Misleading sales and income amounts can result if goods are returned in a period after the one of sale. If there is no adjustment in the period of sale for estimated returns, the sales and income amounts for the period of sale are overstated, because they reflect transactions that are later canceled. Further, income statement amounts of sales and income are correspondingly understated in the period when the goods are returned. An allowance method for estimated returns similar to that for estimated uncollectible accounts could be used. Because the amounts of sales returns for most businesses are usually relatively small, however, an allowance method is not often used.

Sales Allowances

A *sales allowance* is a reduction in price granted to a customer, usually after the goods have been delivered and found to be unsatisfactory or damaged. Again, as for sales returns, the effect is a reduction in the sales revenue, but it may be desirable to accumulate the amount of such adjustments as a separate item. An account, Sales Allowances, may be used for this purpose, or a combined account title, Sales Returns and Allowances may be used. The record-keeping problems are similar to those caused by sales returns.

Presentation of Sales Adjustments in the Income Statement

In discussing the complications that accompany accounts receivable, several adjustments to sales have been introduced. All these adjustments—for uncollectible accounts, for discounts, for returns, and for allowances—are illustrated in the Alexis Company's income statement, Exhibit 7.6, which appears later in this chapter.

Turning Receivables into Cash

A firm may find itself temporarily short of cash and unable to borrow from its usual sources. In such instances, accounts receivable can be used to obtain funds. A firm may *assign* its accounts receivable to a bank or finance company to obtain a loan. The borrowing company physically maintains control of the accounts receivable, collects amounts remitted by customers, and then forwards the proceeds to the lending institution. Alternatively, the firm may *pledge* its accounts receivable to the lending agency. If the borrowing firm is unable to make loan repayments when due, the lending agency has the power to sell the accounts receivable in order to obtain payment. Finally, the accounts receivable may be *factored* to a bank or finance company to obtain cash. In this case, the accounts receivable are sold to the lending institution, which physically controls the receivables and collects payments from customers. If accounts receivable have been assigned or pledged, a footnote to the financial statements should indicate this fact: The collection of such accounts receivable will not increase the liquid resources available to the firm to pay general trade creditors. Accounts receivable that have been factored will not appear on the balance sheet, because they have been sold.

Notes Receivable

The last liquid asset considered in this chapter is notes receivable. Many business transactions involve written promises to pay sums of money at a future date. These written promises are called *promissory notes*. The holder of a promissory note has a liquid asset, notes receivable. A promissory note is a written contract in which one person, known as the *maker,* promises to pay to another person, known as the *payee,* a definite sum of money. The money may be payable either on demand or at a definite future date. A note may or may not provide for the payment of interest in addition to the principal amount.

Promissory notes are used most commonly in connection with obtaining loans at banks or other institutions, the purchase of various kinds of property, and as a temporary settlement of an open or charge account balance when payment cannot be made within the usual credit period. A note may be *secured* by a mortgage on real estate (land and buildings) or personal property (machinery and merchandise), or by the deposit of specific collateral (stock certificates, bonds, and so forth). If the secured note is not collected at maturity, the lender can take possession of the real estate, personal property, or other collateral, sell it, and apply the proceeds to the repayment of the note. Any proceeds in excess of the amount due under the note are then paid to the borrower. Alternatively, the note may be *unsecured,* in which case it has about the same legal position as an account receivable.

Calculation of Interest Revenue

Interest is the price paid for the use of borrowed funds. From the lender's point of view, it is revenue. The interest price is usually expressed as a percentage rate of the principal, with the rate being stated on an annual basis. Thus, a 2-month, 12 percent note would have interest equal to 2 percent of the principal; a 4-month, 15 percent note would have interest equal to 5 percent of principal, and so on. Because interest is a payment for the use of borrowed funds for a period of time, it accrues with the passage of time. Although interest accrues every day (indeed, every time the clock ticks), firms usually record interest only at the time of payment or at the end of an accounting period.

Most short-term notes receivable from customers are based on *simple interest* calculations.[12] The general formula for the calculation of simple interest is

Interest = Base (Principal or Face) × Interest Rate × Elapsed Time.

The calculation of simple interest for any multiple or fraction of a year is an elementary arithmetic computation. For example, the interest at the rate of 12 percent a year on $20,000 is $200 for 1 month, $400 for 2 months, $1,200 for 6 months, and so on. The calculation for shorter periods, although still not an involved mathematical problem, is complicated by the odd number of days in a year and the variations in the number of days in a month. Simple interest at the rate of 12 percent a year on $20,000 for 90 days would be $20,000 × .12 × 90/365, or $592, if an exact computation were made. For many purposes, especially the calculation of accrued interest, a satisfactory approximation of the correct interest can be obtained by assuming that the year has 360 days and that each month is one-twelfth of a year. Thus, 30 days is the equivalent of 1 month, and 60 days is the equivalent of 2 months, or one-sixth of a year. Under this method, the interest at 12 percent on $20,000 for 90 days would be the same as the interest for 3 months, or one-quarter of a year, or $600. Keep in mind that nearly all quotations of simple interest rates state the rate per year, unless some other period is specifically mentioned. In the formula for simple interest, Principal × Rate × Elapsed Time, "time" should be expressed in terms of years, or portions of a year, because the rate is the rate per year.

For the sake of uniformity and simplicity, the following rules are used for the calculation of interest throughout the text and problems:

1. When the maturity terms are given in months, consider 1 month to be one-twelfth of a year; 3 months to be one-fourth of a year; 6 months to be one-half of a year, and so on, regardless of the actual number of days in the period. This is equivalent to regarding any 1-month period as being 30 days in a 360-day year.
2. When the maturity terms are given in days, use the 360-day year. Consider 30 days to be one-twelfth of a year, 60 days to be one-sixth of a year, 17 days to be 17/360 of a year, and so on. Calculate maturity dates and elapsed time by using the actual number of days.

Accounting for Interest-Bearing Notes Receivable

The notes to be discussed in this section, so-called interest-bearing notes, are those that indicate a face, or principal, amount together with explicit interest at a stated fair market rate for the time period stated in the note.[13] For example, the basic elements of such a note might read: "Two months after date (June 30), the Suren Company promises to pay to the order of the Mullen Company $3,000 with interest from date at the rate of 12 percent per annum." At the maturity date, August 31, the

---

[12]Most long-term notes involve *compound interest,* which Appendix B discusses.

[13]Both non-interest-bearing notes, where the face amount is the same as the maturity value, and notes where the stated rate differs from the fair market rate, involve compound interest calculations; Chapters 10 and 11 discuss them.

maturity value would be the face amount of $3,000 plus interest of $60 calculated in accordance with the preceding discussion ($60 = $3,000 × .12 × 2/12), or a total of $3,060.

The transactions related to a note receivable discussed in this section are the following: receipt of note, interest recognition at an interim date, transfer prior to maturity, and collection at maturity date.

Receipt of Notes and Collection at Maturity Promissory notes usually are received from customers in connection with sales or with the settlement of an open account receivable. The customer is usually the maker, but the customer may transfer a note that has been received from another. It is common practice to allow the customer full credit for the face value and accrued interest, if any, although a different value might be agreed upon in some instances.

If, on June 30, the Mullen Company were to receive a 60-day, 12 percent note for $3,000, dated June 30 from the Suren Company, to apply on its account, the entry would be

June 30 Notes Receivable	3,000	
Accounts Receivable—Suren Company		3,000

Assuming the accounting period of the Mullen Company to be the calendar year, the entry upon collection at maturity would be

Aug. 31 Cash	3,060	
Notes Receivable		3,000
Interest Revenue		60

Assuming, instead, that the accounting period of the Mullen Company is 1 month, the interest adjustment at the interim date, July 31, would be

July 31 Interest Receivable	30	
Interest Revenue		30
($3,000 × .12 × 30/360 = $30.)		

The entry upon collection at maturity would then be

Aug. 31 Cash	3,060	
Notes Receivable		3,000
Interest Receivable		30
Interest Revenue		30

Exhibit 7.6
Income Statement Illustration of Sales and Sales Adjustments
Alexis Company
Partial Income Statement
for the Year Ended June 30, 1985

Revenues:

Sales—Gross		$515,200
Less Sales Adjustments:		
Discounts Taken[a]	$23,600	
Allowances	11,000	
Estimated Uncollectibles[b]	10,300	
Returns	8,600	
Total Sales Adjustments		53,500
Net Sales		$461,700

[a]The gross price method is used. If the net price method were used, discounts taken would not be shown and there would be an *addition* to revenue for the amount of sales discounts that lapsed.
[b]Most companies would call this account Bad Debt Expense and list it among the expenses.

At the maturity date, the note may be collected, as illustrated above, renewed, partially collected with renewal of the balance, or dishonored by the maker. These other possibilities involve more advanced accounting procedures and are not discussed in this book.

Transfer of Notes Receivable To obtain cash, a note may be transferred to another party *without recourse*. This procedure is equivalent to a sale of the note, because the transferor has no further liability even if the maker fails to pay at maturity.

If Mullen Company transferred without recourse the 2-month, 12 percent, $3,000 note to Lane Trust Company for $3,030 one month after the date of the note, the entry would be

July 31 Cash	3,030	
Notes Receivable		3,000
Interest Revenue		30
To record transfer of note without recourse.		

Most businesses that "purchase" notes are, however, unwilling to acquire them without recourse. Such firms do not want to be responsible for investigating the creditworthiness of the maker or for any collection efforts required for dishonored notes. Consequently, most notes that are transferred are done so *with recourse*.

A transfer with recourse places a potential or "contingent" obligation on the transferor if the maker fails to pay at maturity. Such a transfer is not a completed transaction because of the possibility that the endorser will have to pay the note in case the maker defaults at maturity.

Chapter 10 discusses contingent obligations, such as those for notes transferred with recourse or for the potential loss arising from an unsettled damage suit. Contin-

Exhibit 7.7
Detailed Illustration of Current Assets
Alexis Company Balance Sheet (Excerpts)
June 30, 1985 and 1984

	June 30, 1985		June 30, 1984	
Current Assets:				
Cash in Change and Petty Cash Funds		$ 1,000		$ 800
Cash in Bank		13,000		11,000
Cash Held as Compensating Balances		1,500		1,500
Certificates of Deposit		8,000		7,500
Marketable Securities Acquisition Cost	$30,000		$25,000	
Less: Allowance for Excess of Cost of Marketable Securities over Market Value (on June 30, 1984, market value of $31,000 exceeds cost)	(3,000)		—	
Marketable Securities at Lower of Cost or Market (see Note A).		27,000		25,000
Notes Receivable (see Note B)		12,000		10,000
Interest and Dividends Receivable		500		400
Accounts Receivable, Gross.	$58,100		$57,200	
Less: Allowance for Uncollectible Accounts	(3,600)		(3,500)	
Accounts Receivable, Net		54,500		53,700
Merchandise Inventory[a]		72,000		67,000
Prepayments		4,800		4,300
Total Current Assets		$194,300		$181,200

Note A. Gross unrealized holding gains and gross unrealized holding losses on Marketable Securities are as follows:

	June 30, 1985	June 30, 1984
Gross Unrealized Holding Gains	$7,000	$7,000
Gross Unrealized Holding Losses	(10,000)	(1,000)
Net Unrealized Holding Gain (loss)	($3,000)	$6,000

Note B. The amount shown for Notes Receivable does not include notes with a face amount of $2,000 that have been discounted with recourse at The First National Bank. The company is contingently liable for these notes, should the makers not honor them at maturity. The estimated amount of our liability is zero.

[a]Additional, required disclosures for this item omitted here. See Chapter 8.

gent obligations do not appear in the accounts, but are disclosed in notes to the balance sheet.

If Mullen Company transferred with recourse the 60-day, 12 percent, $3,000 note to Lane Trust Company 1 month after the date of the note, the entry would be the same as if the note was transferred without recourse. If Mullen Company prepared financial statements before Lane Trust Company collected from the maker, however, the notes to Mullen's balance sheet would contain a statement such as the following:

Contingencies. The firm is contingently liable for a note transferred and accrued interest thereon to the Lane Trust Company. The face value of the transferred note is $3,000.

Illustration of Balance Sheet Presentation

The balance sheet accounts discussed in this chapter include Cash, Certificates of Deposit, Marketable Securities, Notes Receivable, Accounts Receivable, and the Allowance for Uncollectible Accounts. Exhibit 7.6 shows how transactions affecting these accounts appear in the income statement. Exhibit 7.7 illustrates the presentation of these items in the balance sheet, which includes all of the current assets for the Alexis Company as of June 30, 1985.

Effect of Transactions Involving Liquid Assets on the Statement of Changes in Financial Position

Marketable Securities

One issue in the design of a statement of changes in financial position is whether purchases and sales of marketable securities should be classified as *operating* activities or as *investing* activities.

Proponents of treating such transactions as operating activities argue that marketable securities are purchased when there is excess cash not needed for regular operations and later sold when the cash is so needed. Thus, the decisions to purchase and to sell are driven by operating considerations. Opponents argue that such transactions are not operating because they do not involve purchases and sales of the firm's products or services. Purchases and sales of marketable securities should therefore be classified as investing activities.

Both treatments can be found in corporate annual reports. This book treats transactions involving purchases and sales of marketable securities as investing activities. Dividends received from holding of securities are operating revenues under either treatment, just as are revenues generated by investments in plant and equipment.

A write-down of the portfolio of marketable securities in applying the lower-of-cost-or-market method results in a loss that does not use cash. The funds statement shows an addition to net income for the loss in computing cash provided by operations.

Accounts Receivable

Unlike purchases and sales of marketable securities, transactions changing accounts receivable clearly involve operations. Because the change in accounts receivable is added to or subtracted from net income to derive cash provided by operations, no special entry need be made in preparing the funds statement.

Summary

This chapter has examined the accounting for cash and other liquid, or cashlike, assets. Among the questions addressed were the following:

1. What items are included in each of the liquid asset accounts?
2. At what amount are they stated?
3. Are there any restrictions on the use of particular liquid assets?

The appendix to this chapter discusses internal control procedures for protecting cash.

Appendix 7.1: Controlling Cash

Of all assets, cash is the most vulnerable—the most difficult to safeguard from theft. This appendix discusses the usual procedures of accounting for and controlling cash. For internal control purposes, most firms maintain two cash accounts, Cash on Hand and Cash in Bank.

Controlling Cash Receipts and Disbursements

The system for controlling cash receipts should be designed to ensure that all money collected for the firm benefits the firm. In most businesses, collections are received primarily through the mail in the form of bank checks or in currency for cash sales. The need to control the collections of currency and coins is obvious. All collections for cash sales should be recorded promptly, either in a cash register or some other device that both records the receipts and locks in the amount of the collection. Other kinds of collections are more susceptible to mishandling because they occur less often. These include receipts from the sale of assets not normally intended to be sold, receipts from dividends and interest on investments, collections on notes receivable, proceeds of bank loans, and proceeds of stock or bond issues.

One way to provide effective control of cash receipts would be to maintain duplicate sets of records, each under separate supervision. But doing so would be expensive. The business need not undertake this expensive control device, however, if it (1) designs its cash-handling techniques so that the monthly statement received from its bank effectively serves as a duplicate record and (2) separates the functions of cash handling and record keeping. To use the bank statement as an effective cash-controlling device requires prompt depositing of *all* receipts and making all disbursements by check.

Undeposited Cash If a firm follows the desirable practice of depositing all receipts intact each day, disbursements will usually be made only from checking accounts. Any balance in the Cash on Hand account will represent cash received since the last deposit. A daily record of cash on hand is desirable. Cash registers facilitate the accumulation of such cash data. There are many types, but the usual cash register is a combination of a cash drawer and a multiple-register adding machine. The transactions are entered by hand. Then they are recorded and accumulated by the register so that at the end of the day the totals are available for each of several divisions of the day's activities—the total cash sales (sometimes classified according to products or departments), total collections on account, and total sales of each salesperson.

Cash in Bank—Deposits   A deposit ticket provides the information for preparing the journal entry to record the deposit of cash funds in the checking account. The deposit ticket should be prepared in duplicate; the bank keeps the original and the firm keeps the duplicate. The duplicate is often initialed by the bank teller and used as a receipt for the deposit of the funds. The total on the deposit ticket is entered in a journal as a debit to Cash in Bank and a credit to Cash on Hand.

Cash in Bank—Issuance of Checks   The information for the entry to record checks drawn in payment of bills comes from the document authorizing the payment. The customary entry will be a debit to Accounts Payable and a credit to Cash in Bank.

Control of Disbursements by Check   All cash payments except for those of very small amounts should be made by check. The firm can thereby restrict the authority for payments to a few employees. Firms often provide further control by requiring that all checks be signed by two employees. Another control device is the use of a Cash Disbursements Journal or Check Register in which all checks issued are recorded. Using such a journal provides control because a single person, who is not allowed to authorize payments or to sign checks, is responsible for recording all payments.

In any case, control over payments should ensure that:

1. Payments are made only by authorized persons.
2. Adequate records support each payment. Such records attest that payment was for goods and services procured by proper authority and actually received by the business. The records attest that payment is made in accordance with the purchase contract.
3. The transaction is entered properly in the formal accounting records.
4. Authorization of payment is separate from making payment, and record keeping is separate from both.

The Bank Statement

At the end of each month (or other regular interval), the bank sends a statement together with the canceled checks that have been paid and deducted from the depositor's account, and memorandums of any other additions or deductions that have been made by the bank. When the bank statement is received, it should be compared promptly with the record of deposits, checks drawn, and other bank items on the records of the firm.

The balance shown on the bank statement will rarely correspond to the balance of the Cash in Bank account. The two basic causes of the difference are time lag and errors. In the normal course of business activities, some items will have been recorded by either the bank or the firm without having reached the recording point on the other set of records, hence a *time lag* difference. Causes of such differences include: checks outstanding (that is, checks recorded by the drawing firm but not yet received by the bank on which they were drawn); deposits made just before the bank statement date that do not appear on the bank statement; and transactions (such as

Exhibit 7.8
SARWARK COMPANY
Bank Reconciliation Schedule—State National Bank
April 1

Balance Shown on Bank Statement, April 1		$3,941.43
Deposits of March 30 and 31, Not Yet Recorded by Bank		753.25
Check of J. Sarwark Deducted by Bank in Error		102.00
		$4,796.68
Outstanding Checks:		
#2443	$ 79.67	
#2459	242.53	
#2471	131.26	
#2472	32.44	
#2473	243.55	
Less: Total Outstanding Checks		(729.45)
Adjusted Bank Balance[a]		$4,067.23
Balance Shown on Books, April 1.		$3,588.23
Items Unrecorded on Books:		
Collection of Note of J. B. Ball:		
Face Amount of Note	$500.00	
Less Collection Charge	(15.00)	485.00
Less: Bank Service Charge for March		(24.00)
Adjusted Book Balance Before Correction of Errors		$4,049.23
Check #2467 for $268.81 was entered in the check register as $286.81. It was issued in March to pay a bill for office equipment		18.00
Adjusted Book Balance[a]		$4,067.23

[a]This is the amount that would be shown in the Cash in Bank account if a balance sheet were prepared as of April 1.

service charges and collections of notes or drafts) that have not been recorded on the firm's books. The other basic difference is caused by errors in record keeping by either the firm or the bank. The process of comparing the bank statement with the books is known as *reconciling* the bank account, and the schedule that is prepared to demonstrate the results of the comparing is called a *bank reconciliation*. Exhibit 7.8 shows a typical reconciliation schedule.

Preparing the Bank Reconciliation Schedule The bank reconciliation explains the difference between the book balance of Cash in Bank and the bank's statement of the firm's cash on deposit. It indicates the required adjustments of the firm's accounts. If the bank statement is used as a control device, the bank reconciliation is the final step in the monthly procedure for controlling cash receipts and disbursements. The bank reconciliation provides a convenient summary of the adjusting entries that must be made by the firm to account for previous errors in recording cash-related transactions or for cash transactions that have not yet been recorded.

Preparing the bank reconciliation schedule typically involves the following steps:

1. Enter at the top of the reconciliation schedule the balance as shown on the bank statement.

2. Enter next any deposits that have not been recorded on the bank statement. Such items usually occur because the bank has prepared the statement before the deposits for the last day or two have been recorded. If there are any time or date breaks in the list of deposits for the period, the bank should be notified promptly.

3. Enter any other adjustments of the bank's balance, such as errors in recording canceled checks or deposits, or the return of checks belonging to some other customer of the bank. Errors on bank statements are infrequent.

4. Obtain a total.

5. List the outstanding checks. A list should be prepared, beginning with the checks still outstanding from the previous period and continuing with the checks outstanding that were drawn during the current period.

6. Deduct the sum of the outstanding checks from the total obtained in step **4**. The balance is the adjusted bank balance—the balance that would be shown on the bank statement if all deposits had been entered, all checks written had been returned, and no errors had been made; it is the final figure for this first section of the statement.

These steps will frequently conclude the reconciliation because this balance should correspond to the balance of the Cash in Bank account as of the bank statement date when there are no unrecorded transactions or errors. If these two amounts are not equal at this point, the following steps must be taken and shown in a second section of the reconciliation schedule.

7. Enter the Cash in Bank account balance as shown on the books as of the bank statement date.

8. Add or deduct any errors or omissions that have been disclosed in the process of reviewing the items returned by the bank. These will include such items as errors in recording deposits or checks, unnumbered checks that have not been entered in the check register, and service charges and collection fees deducted by the bank.

9. The net result is the adjusted book balance, and it must correspond to the adjusted bank balance derived in the first section. If it does not, the search must be continued for other items that have been overlooked.

Adjusting Entries from Bank Reconciliation Schedule   The bank reconciliation schedule shows two distinct kinds of differences:

1.   Differences between the balance shown on the bank statement and the adjusted bank balance.
2.   Differences between the account balance on the firm's books and the adjusted book balance.

Only the second type of difference requires entries on the firm's books. Any deposits not credited by the bank will presumably have been recorded by the time the reconciliation is prepared and, in any event, represent funds that the depositor may assume are in the bank and available for use.

Entries must be made for all of the differences between the firm's account balance on the books and the adjusted book balance, because they represent errors or omissions.

The reconciliation illustrated in Exhibit 7.8 requires adjustments for bank service charges, for the collection of a note, and for the check whose amount was incorrectly recorded. (The bank must, of course, correct any error on its books when the mistake is called to its attention.) The entries would be

---

Bank Service Charge Expense	24	
Cash in Bank		24
Service charges for month of March.		
Cash in Bank	485	
Collection Expense	15	
Note Receivable, J. B. Ball		500
Note collected by bank.		
Cash in Bank	18	
Accounts Payable		18
To correct entry of check #2467.		

Summary of Accounting for Cash

Cash is an enterprise's most vulnerable resource. An internal control system is essential to the proper management of cash. One way to provide control is to maintain duplicate and independent records of cash flows, but the monthly bank statement can serve as the duplicate record. Using the bank statement as an effective control device requires depositing receipts daily and making all disbursements by check. By this means the bank reconciliation serves as a control device, because the bank record will reflect the cash inflows and outflows of the enterprise.

Problem 1 for Self-Study

Refer to the data in Exhibits 7.1 and 7.2 showing transactions in marketable securities for the Wolfson Company over 4 years. Assume that in addition to those transactions, Wolfson Company purchased 1,000 shares of D Company on October 1, Year 1, for $40 per share, $40,000 in total. Shares of D Company had a market value of $45 per share at the end of Year 1, $35 per share at the end of Year 2, $30 per share at the end of Year 3, and $50 per share at the end of Year 4.

a. What are the amounts of each of the following at the end of each of the 4 years: Marketable Securities at Cost, Allowance for Excess of Cost of Marketable Securities over Market Value, and Marketable Securities at Lower of Cost or Market? What is the Unrealized Loss (or Recovery of Unrealized Loss) for each of the 4 years?

b. If, early in Year 2, Wolfson Company sells 900 shares of D Company at $30 each, $27,000 in total, what is the realized gain or loss for Year 2 and the Unrealized Holding Loss or Recovery of Unrealized Holding Loss for Year 2?

c. Ignore the information in part **b**. During Year 2, Wolfson Company transferred all 1,000 shares of D Company to its noncurrent asset portfolio of Investments at a time when these shares had an aggregate market value of $38,000. What is income before taxes for Year 2?

d. Ignore information in parts **b** and **c**. Now assume that the securities of all four companies have been classified as the noncurrent asset Investments from the time of acquisition. During Year 3, Wolfson Company sold 400 shares of D Company for $38 per share and transferred the remaining 600 shares to a current asset account, Marketable Securities, at a time when the share price was $35 each. What is income before taxes for Year 3?

e. Ignore information in parts **b**, **c**, and **d**. Assume, now, that Wolfson Company left its holdings of D Company intact until the last day of Year 2, when it sold some shares for $35 per share. If the correct balance on the balance sheet at the end of Year 2 for marketable securities valued at lower of cost or market is $109,500, how many shares were sold on December 31, Year 2?

Suggested Solution

a. See Exhibit 7.9.

b. Realized Loss = $900 \times (\$40 - \$30) = \$9,000$. December 31 valuation of remaining portfolio is as follows:

At Cost: $100,000 + (100 × $40)	$104,000
At Market: $ 99,000 + (100 × $35)	$102,500
Required Allowance	$ 1,500
Allowance at Start of Year	$ 0
Unrealized Holding Loss for Year	$ 1,500

c. Other Items Before Taxes	$300,000
Realized Loss on Transfer of Securities Between Portfolios (= $40,000 − $38,000)	(2,000)
Unrealized Holding Loss of Securities A, B, and C	(1,000)
Income Before Taxes	$297,000

d. Other Items Before Taxes	$300,000
Realized Loss on Sales 400 × ($40 − $38)	(800)
Realized Loss on Transfer 600 × ($40 − $35)	(3,000)
Income Before Taxes	$296,200

Exhibit 7.9
Problem 1 for Self-Study
(Suggested Solution to Part **a**)

Marketable Securities	Year 1	Year 2	Year 3	Year 4
At Cost	$140,000	$140,000	$110,000	$90,000
Allowance	—	(6,000)	(4,000)	—
At Lower of Cost or Market	$140,000	$134,000	$106,000	$90,000
Unrealized Loss for Year.	—	$ (6,000)	—	—
Recovery of Unrealized Loss for Year	—	—	$ 2,000	$ 4,000

e. Let *x* represent number of shares of D Company remaining, so that:

Marketable Securities (December 31, Year 2):	
At Cost	$100,000 + $40x
Allowance	(1,000 + 5x)
At Lower of Cost or Market	$ 99,000 + $35x

If the correct balance is $109,500, then $35x is $10,500 and x is 300 shares; 700 (= 1,000 − 300) shares were sold.

Problem 2 for Self-Study

Refer to the data in Exhibit 7.5 showing sales and collection activities for two periods. At the end of the third period, the *unadjusted* trial balance included the following accounts and amounts: Accounts Receivable—$75,000 debit; Allowance for Uncollectible Accounts—$8,000 debit; Bad Debt Expense—zero (adjusting entries have not yet been made); Sales Revenue—$1,300,000. No further specific accounts receivable need be written off for the period.

a. Reconstruct the transactions of the third period, assuming that all sales were made on account.

b. What were the total cash collections for the third period from customers who paid their accounts?

c. Reconstruct the transactions of the third period, assuming that only $1 million of the $1.3 million total sales were made on account.

d. What were the total cash collections for the third period, including collections both from customers who paid cash and from customers who paid their accounts?

e. Does one need to know the actual split of sales between cash sales and sales on account to know the total amount of cash collected from customers, that is, the sum of cash sales and collections on account? Why or why not?

f. Assume that 2 percent of all sales for the third period is estimated to be uncollectible. What is the adjusting entry to be made at the end of the third period for estimated uncollectibles? What net balance of Accounts Receivable will appear on the balance sheet at the end of the third period?

g. Independent of the answer to the preceding part, assume that an aging of accounts receivable indicates that the amount in the Allowance for Uncollectibles appropriate for the status of outstanding accounts at the end of the third period is $20,000. What is the adjusting entry to be made at the end of the third period for estimated uncollectibles? What amount of sales less bad debt expense will be reported for the third period?

Suggested Solution

a. Sales were $1,300,000, debited to Accounts Receivable. Specific accounts receivable of $24,000 (= $16,000 credit at start of period plus $8,000 debit by the end of period) were written off with debits to the Allowance for Uncollectibles account and credits to Accounts Receivable. Thus, the balance in accounts receivable before cash collections was $1,410,000 (= $134,000 + $1,300,000 − $24,000). Because the ending balance is actually $75,000, the cash collections from customers who bought on account are $1,335,000 (= $1,410,000 − $75,000).

b. $1,335,000, as derived above.

c. Sales were $1,300,000, debited $300,000 to Cash and $1,000,000 to Accounts Receivable. Specific accounts receivable of $24,000 were written off with debits to the Allowance for Uncollectibles account and credits to Accounts Receivable. The amount is derived as in part **a.** The write-off of specific accounts left a balance of $1,110,000 (= $134,000 + $1,000,000 − $24,000), but the actual ending balance was $75,000, so $1,035,000 (= $1,110,000 − $75,000) of accounts must have been collected in cash.

d. $1,335,000 = $300,000 cash sales plus $1,035,000 from collections on account.

e. No. Once cash from a sale on account has been collected, the overall effect of the sale on the financial statements is identical with a cash sale. Thus, cash sales and collected credit sales have the same effects on the financial statements.

---

f. | Bad Debt Expense . . . . | 26,000 | |
| Allowance for Uncollectibles . . . . | | 26,000 |

Amount is equal to .02 × $1,300,000. Ending balance in the allowance account is $18,000 (= $26,000 credit less $8,000 debit).

The net Accounts Receivable balance at the end of the third period is $57,000 (= $75,000 − $18,000).

---

g. Bad Debt Expense   28,000
   Allowance for Uncollectibles   28,000
   A $28,000 credit is required to establish a $20,000 credit balance
   in an account with a tentative $8,000 debit balance.

Sales less bad debt expense are $1,272,000 (= $1,300,000 gross sales less $28,000 adjustment for uncollectibles). The net Accounts Receivable balance at the end of the third period is $55,000 (= $75,000 − $20,000).

Questions, Exercises, Problems and Cases

Questions

1. Review the meaning of the following concepts or terms discussed in this chapter.

a. Generally accepted accounting principles.
b. SEC.
c. FASB.
d. Liquidity.
e. Insolvent.
f. Cash.
g. Demand deposits.
h. Certificate of deposit.
i. Foreign currency.
j. Compensating balance.
k. Marketable securities.
l. Investments (noncurrent).
m. Marketable debt securities.
n. Marketable equity securities.

o. Lower of cost or market.
p. Unrealized loss on marketable securities.
q. Recovery of unrealized loss on marketable securities.
r. Realized gain or loss on marketable securities.
s. Aging of accounts receivable.
t. Sales Contra, Discounts.
u. Sales Contra, Returns and Allowances.
v. Simple interest.
w. Recourse.
x. Factoring.
y. Contingent obligation.

2. What purpose is served by having a broad set of financial reporting objectives, such as those issued by the FASB?

3. Generally accepted accounting principles are the methods of accounting used by publicly held firms in preparing their financial statements. A principle in physics, such as the law of gravity, serves as a basis for developing theories and explaining the relations among physical objects. In what ways are generally accepted accounting principles similar to and different from principles of physics?

4. The text states that the standard-setting process is essentially political in nature. Yet the FASB is striving to relate its pronouncements to a broad set of financial reporting objectives. Do you see any inconsistency between these two approaches to standard setting?

5. Distinguish between a *Discussion Memorandum,* an *Exposure Draft* of a Proposed Financial Accounting Standard, and a *Financial Accounting Standard.*

6. What evidence of cash control have you observed in a cafeteria? A department store? A theater? A gasoline station?

7. The Tastee Delight ice cream stores prominently advertise on signs in the stores that the customer's purchase is free if the clerk does not present a receipt. Oakland's Original hot dog stand says that the customer's purchase is free if the cash register receipt contains a red star. What control purposes do such policies serve?

8. Current assets are defined as those assets that are expected to be turned into cash, or sold, or consumed within the next operating cycle. Cash is not always classified as a current asset, however. Explain.

9. Does application of the lower-of-cost-or-market valuation method to the portfolio of marketable equity securities or to each marketable equity security individually result in the most conservative asset values and net income amounts?

10. Which of the two methods for treating uncollectible accounts (direct write-off or allowance) implies recognizing income reductions earlier rather than later? Why?

11. a. An old wisdom in tennis holds that if your first serves are always good, then you are not hitting them hard enough. An analogous statement in business might be that if you have no uncollectible accounts, then you probably are not selling enough on credit. Comment on the validity of this statement.
  b. When are more uncollectible accounts better than fewer uncollectible accounts?
  c. When is a higher percentage of uncollectible accounts better than a lower one?

12. The customary method of accounting for sales results in adequate reporting for the returned sales when the goods are returned in the same period in which they are sold. If the goods are returned in a period subsequent to that of the sale, distortion of the reported income results. Explain how sales returns may produce each of the described effects.

13. Under what circumstances will the Allowance for Uncollectible Accounts have a debit balance during the accounting period? The balance sheet figure for the Allowance for Uncollectible Accounts at the end of the period should never show a debit balance. Why?

14. What is the effect on the financial statements of discounting, or transferring, a note with recourse versus without recourse?

Exercises

15. *Inclusions in Cash account.* Indicate if each of the following items should be included in "cash" on the balance sheet. If not, indicate how the item should be reported.
  a. Cash that has been collected from customers and is awaiting deposit in the firm's checking account.
  b. Cash left in cash registers each day, which serves as a change fund.

    c. Cash set aside in a special savings account to accumulate funds to replace equipment as it wears out. The firm is not legally obligated to use the funds for this purpose.

    d. Cash set aside in a special savings account to accumulate funds to retire debt as it becomes due. The firm is legally obligated to use the funds for this purpose.

    e. A postdated check received from a customer. The check is dated 60 days after the date of the balance sheet.

    f. A money order received from a customer.

    g. Postage stamps.

    h. Cash held for small miscellaneous expenditures, such as freight charges and executive lunches.

    i. Cash in a checking account that must be maintained at a certain minimum level in accordance with a written loan agreement for a 6-month loan.

16. *Inclusions in Cash account.* You are asked to compute the amount that should be shown as Cash on the balance sheet as of December 31 for Zeff Transportation Company from the following information.

    a. Coins, currency, and checks received from customers on December 31, but not yet deposited, $6,500.

    b. Cash held for making small miscellaneous cash expenditures. The fund normally has a balance of $100, but expenditures of $22 were made on December 31.

    c. The firm's postage meter was "filled" on December 31 and contains $500 of postage.

    d. The books indicate that the balance in the firm's checking account on December 31 is $45,800. When the bank statement is received on the next January 10, it is learned that one customer's check for $800, which was deposited on December 28, was returned for insufficient funds. In addition, during December the bank collected $2,200 for a note receivable from one of Zeff's customers and added the amount to Zeff's bank account. The note had a face value of $2,000 and interest of $200.

    e. Certificate of deposit for a face value of $10,000. The certificate was acquired on July 1 of this year and matures on June 30 of next year. Simple interest of 12 percent per year accumulates on the note and is payable at maturity with the principal.

    f. British sterling currency, £10,000. The exchange rate on December 31 is $1.60 per pound sterling.

17. *Effect of compensating balances on effective interest rate.* Davidoff Corporation borrowed $1 million from the local bank on July 1. The bank charged Davidoff Corporation interest at its prime lending rate of 13.5 percent. The principal and interest on the loan are repayable on the following June 30. Davidoff Corporation must maintain a $100,000 compensating balance in an interest-free checking account at the bank during the term of the loan.

    a. What is the effective annual interest rate that Davidoff Corporation is paying on this loan?

b. What message to Davidoff Corporation is implicit in the bank's requirement that a compensating balance be maintained?

18. *Bank reconciliation.*

a. Arrange the following data related to the Antle Company in bank reconciliation form.

Adjusted Bank Balance	$6,713
Adjusted Book Balance	6,713
Balance per Bank Statement, October 31	7,873
Balance per Books, October 31	6,028
Error in Deposit of October 28; $457 Deposit Entered on Books as $547	90
Outstanding Checks	1,305
Payroll Account Check Deducted from This Account in Error	145
Proceeds on Note of W. Y. Smith, Taken by the Bank for Collection, Less Collection Fee of $25	775

b. Present journal entries on the books of the Antle Company to record the adjustments indicated in the bank reconciliation schedule.

19. *Bank reconciliation.*

a. Prepare a bank reconciliation schedule at July 31 for the Home Appliance Company from the following information:

Balance per Bank Statement, July 29	$1,240
Balance per Ledger, July 31	714
Deposit of July 30 Not Recorded by Bank	280
Debit Memo—Service Charges	8
Credit Memo—Collection of Note by Bank	300

An analysis of canceled checks returned with the bank statement reveals the following: Check #901 for purchase of supplies on account was correctly drawn for $58 but was recorded as $85. The manager wrote a check for traveling expenses of $95 while out of town. The check was not recorded. The following checks are outstanding:

#650	$120
#721	162
#728	300
	$582

b. Journalize the adjusting entries required by the information revealed in the bank reconciliation schedule.

20. *Bank reconciliation*. On May 31, the books of the Griffin Company show a debit balance in the Cash in Bank account of $4,720. The bank statement at that date shows a balance of $6,000. The deposit of May 31 of $250 is not included in the bank statement. Notice of collections made by the bank on mortgages of the company in the amount of $350, including interest of $250, and of bank service charges of $20 have not previously been received. Outstanding checks at May 31 total $1,200.

    a. Prepare a bank reconciliation for the Griffin Company at May 31.

    b. Journalize the entries required upon preparation of the bank reconciliation schedule.

21. *Classify marketable securities*. Indicate the classification of each of the securities below in the balance sheet of Bower Corporation on December 31.

    a. U.S. Treasury Bills, acquired on October 15. The bills mature next April 15.

    b. Shares of Brazil Coffee Corporation, a major supplier of raw materials for Bower Corporation's products.

    c. Shares of Overland Transportation Company. The shares were originally acquired as a temporary investment of excess cash. Overland Transportation Company has been so profitable that Bower Corporation plans to increase its ownership percentage, eventually obtaining 51 percent of the outstanding shares.

    d. American Telephone and Telegraph Company bonds that mature in 3 years. The bonds were acquired with a cash advance from a customer on a contract for the manufacture of machinery and will be sold, as needed, to pay costs of manufacturing. The manufacturing process will take 3 years.

22. *Journal entries for holdings of marketable equity securities*. The following list gives all events for Germont Company's actions with respect to its current asset portfolio of marketable equity securities during the period August, Year 1, through January, Year 2.

  8/21   Germont Company purchases 1,000 shares of Grenvil Company for $15 per share. In addition, it pays $150 in brokerage commissions to its stockbroker.

   9/1   The stockbroker calls Germont Company to report that Grenvil Company shares closed on the preceding day at $18 per share.

  9/30   Grenvil Company declares a dividend of $.25 per share.

 10/25   Germont Company receives a dividend check for $250.

 12/31   The stockbroker calls Germont Company to report that Grenvil Company shares closed the year at $11 per share. The books are closed for the year.

  1/31   Germont Company sells 600 shares for $13 per share, the closing price for the day. Brokerage commissions, deducted from the proceeds, are $100.

  1/31   Germont Company prepares an up-to-date balance sheet as part of an application for a loan.

Prepare dated journal entries as required by the events described above. Ignore income taxes.

23. *Journal entries for portfolio of marketable equity securities.* The aggregate cost and aggregate market value of the portfolio of marketable equity securities, current assets, of Elson Corporation at various dates appear below:

Date	Aggregate Cost	Aggregate Market Value
December 31, Year 1.	$150,000	$130,000
December 31, Year 2.	160,000	144,000
December 31, Year 3.	170,000	185,000
December 31, Year 4.	180,000	168,000

Give the journal entry required at the end of each year, assuming that the accounting period is the calendar year.

24. *Journal entries for the allowance method.* The trial balance of the Walker Company at the end of its first year of operations included $20,000 of outstanding customers' accounts. An analysis reveals that 80 percent of the total credit sales of the year had been collected and that no accounts had been charged off as uncollectible.

The auditor estimated that 2 percent of the total credit sales would be uncollectible. On the next January 31, the account of H. J. Williams, who had owed a balance of $300 for 6 months, was judged uncollectible and was written off.

On July 1, the amount owed by H. J. Williams, previously written off, was collected in full.

Present dated journal entries to record the following:

    a. Adjustment for estimated uncollectible accounts on December 31.

    b. Write-off of the H. J. Williams account on January 31.

    c. Collection of the H. J. Williams account on July 1. Assume that it is felt that there is evidence that the account should never have been written off as uncollectible, and that total uncollectibles are likely not to be different from the original estimates.

25. *Reconstructing events when allowance method is used.* The balance sheets of Wilton Corporation on December 31, Year 1 and Year 2, showed gross accounts receivable of $8,300,000 and $9,700,000, respectively. The balances in the Allowance for Uncollectible Accounts account at the beginning and end of Year 2, after closing entries, were credits of $750,000 and $930,000, respectively. The income statement for Year 2 shows that the expense for estimated uncollectible accounts was $300,000, which was 1 percent of sales. All sales are made on account. There were no recoveries during Year 2 of accounts written off in previous years.

Give all the journal entries made during Year 2 that have an effect on Accounts Receivable and Allowance for Uncollectible Accounts.

26. *Aging accounts receivable.* Love Company's accounts receivable show the following balances by ages:

Age of Accounts	Balance Receivable
0–30 Days	300,000
31–60 Days	75,000
61–120 Days	30,000
More than 120 Days	15,000

The credit balance in the Allowance for Uncollectible Accounts is now $6,000.

Love Company's independent auditors suggest that the following percentages be used to compute the estimates of amounts that will eventually prove uncollectible: 0–30 days, .5 of 1 percent; 31–60 days, 1 percent; 61–120 days, 10 percent; more than 120 days, 60 percent.

Prepare a journal entry that will carry out the auditor's suggestion.

27. *Aging accounts receivable.* Rozay Company's accounts receivable show the following balances:

Age of Accounts	Balance Receivable
0–30 Days	500,000
31–60 Days	175,000
61–120 Days	80,000
More than 120 Days	40,000

An adjusting entry based on the percentage-of-sales method has already been made for the period. The credit balance in the Allowance for Uncollectible Accounts is now $30,000. The Bad Debt Expense account has a balance of $35,000.

Analysis of recent collection experience suggests that the following percentages be used to compute the estimates of amounts that will eventually prove uncollectible: 0–30 days, .5 of 1 percent; 31–60 days, 1 percent, 61–120 days, 10 percent; more than 120 days, 40 percent.

Prepare the indicated adjusting entry.

28. *Simple interest computations.* Calculate simple interest on a base of $6,000 for the following intervals and rates, using a 360-day year.
   a. 60 days at 12 percent.
   b. 90 days at 9 percent.
   c. 60 days at 16 percent.
   d. 15 days at 16 percent.
   e. 5 months, 15 days at 12 percent.

29. *Journal entries for notes.* On May 10, the Dukes Company receives a note from one of its customers, Salk Builders, Inc., to apply on its account. The 6-

month, 12 percent note for $6,000, issued on May 10, is valued at its face amount, $6,000.

On July 25, the Dukes Company endorses the note and transfers it with recourse to the Beaver Company to settle an account payable. The note is valued at its face amount plus accrued interest.

On November 12, the Dukes Company is notified that the note was paid at maturity.

   a. Present dated entries on the books of the Dukes Company, assuming that it closes its books quarterly on March 31, June 30, and so on.

   b. Present dated entries on the books of the Beaver Company, assuming that it closes its books quarterly on March 31, June 30, and so on.

Problems and Cases

30. *Bank reconciliation and journal entries.* The bank reconciliation of the Clovis Company at March 31 was as follows:

Balance per Bank Statement, March 31	$3,965
Unrecorded Deposit	475
Outstanding Checks	820
Adjusted Bank and Book Balance, March 31	3,620

The bank statement, returned checks, and other documents received from the bank at the end of April provide the following information:

Balance, April 29	$ 3,800
Deposit of March 31	475
Deposits of April 1–29 Including a Credit Memo for a Collection of a Note, $860	16,160
Canceled Checks Issued Prior to April 1	600
Canceled Checks Issued During April	16,200

The Cash in Bank account of the Clovis Company for the month of April shows deposits of $16,140 and checks drawn of $17,015. The credit memo has not as yet been recorded on the books of the company; it represents the collection of a note with $800 face value on which $40 of the $60 total interest had already been accrued as of March 31.

   a. Prepare a bank reconciliation for the Clovis Company at April 30.

   b. Present in journal entry form any adjustment of the company's books resulting from the information generated by the bank reconciliation.

31. *Journal entries and financial statement presentation of marketable equity securities.* The information below summarizes data about the marketable equity securities of Albion Corporation.

Security	Date Acquired	Acquisition Cost	Date Sold	Selling Price	Market Value Dec. 31, Year 1	Market Value Dec. 31, Year 2
A	1/5/Year 1	$40,000	11/5/Year 2	$50,000	$45,000	—
B	6/12/Year 1	85,000	—	—	75,000	$82,000
C	2/22/Year 2	48,000	—	—	—	46,000
D	3/25/Year 2	25,000	11/5/Year 2	18,000	—	—
E	4/25/Year 2	36,000	—	—	—	40,000

    a. Give all journal entries relating to these marketable equity securities during Year 1 and Year 2, assuming that the accounting period is the calendar year.

    b. Indicate the manner in which marketable securities would be presented in the balance sheet and related notes on December 31, Year 1.

    c. Indicate the manner in which marketable securities would be presented in the balance sheet and related notes on December 31, Year 2.

32. *Financial statement presentation of marketable equity securities.* Exhibit 7.10 gives data on holdings of marketable securities of Sprouse Company for Year 1 and Year 2. There were no sales of securities during Year 1. During Year 2, Sprouse Company purchased new shares in Security F. During Year 2, the following sales of securities took place:

	Net Proceeds of Sale	Cost	Realized Gain (Loss)
Security A	$125,000	$100,000	$ 25,000
Security B	65,000	100,000	(35,000)
	$190,000	$200,000	$(10,000)

The valuation allowances required at December 31, Year 2, are as follows:

	Charged Against Income	Charged Against Equity
In Current Assets:		
Cost $900,000 Less Market $850,000	$50,000	
In Noncurrent Assets:		
Cost $650,000 Less Market $540,000		$110,000

Ignore income taxes.

    a. Prepare in parallel columns for year-end Year 2 and Year 1 the data that appear in the December 31, Year 2, balance sheet.

Exhibit 7.10
Data on Marketable Securities for Sprouse Company
(Problem 32)

	Year 2		Year 1	
	Cost	Market	Cost	Market
In Current Assets:				
Security A	$100,000	$100,000	$200,000	$250,000
B	200,000	150,000	300,000	250,000
C	200,000	175,000	200,000	150,000
D	150,000	100,000	150,000	200,000
E	50,000	100,000	50,000	75,000
F	200,000	225,000	—	—
Total of Portfolio	$900,000	$850,000	$900,000	$925,000
In Noncurrent Assets:				
Security G	$300,000	$200,000	$300,000	$200,000
H	100,000	190,000	100,000	250,000
I.	250,000	150,000	250,000	250,000
Total of Portfolio	$650,000	$540,000	$650,000	$700,000

    b. Prepare a suitable footnote to accompany the balance sheet for December 31, Year 2.

33. *Effects of applying lower of cost or market to entire portfolios, rather than security by security.* Information relating to the marketable equity securities of TSS Company is shown below:

					Market Value	
Security	Date Acquired	Acquisition Cost	Date Sold	Selling Price	Dec. 31, Year 1	Dec. 31, Year 2
H	4/26/Year 1	$18,000	2/9/Year 2	$15,000	$16,000	—
I.	5/25/Year 1	25,000	8/10/Year 2	26,000	24,000	—
J	11/24/Year 1	12,000	—	—	14,000	$15,000
K	2/26/Year 2	34,000	—	—	—	33,500
L	12/17/Year 2	8,000	—	—	—	7,800

    a. Compute both the realized and the unrealized gain or loss for Year 1, applying lower of cost or market to the entire portfolio.

    b. Compute both the realized and the unrealized gain or loss for Year 2, applying lower of cost or market to the entire portfolio.

    c. Repeat steps **a** and **b**, but assume that lower of cost or market is applied individually to each security, rather than to the portfolio of securities. This treatment does *not* conform to generally accepted accounting principles.

d. Does application of lower of cost or market at the level of the portfolio or at the level of individual securities result in the more conservative asset values and measures of earnings?

34. *Allowance method; working "backwards."* The sales, all on account, of the Needles Company in Year 1, its first year of operations, were $600,000. Collections totaled $500,000. On December 31, Year 1, it was estimated that 1.5 percent of all sales would probably be uncollectible. On that date, specific accounts in the amount of $3,000 were written off.

The company's *unadjusted* trial balance (but after all nonadjusting entries were made) on December 31, Year 2, included the following accounts and balances:

Accounts Receivable (Dr.)	$60,000
Allowance for Uncollectible Accounts (Dr.)	4,000
Bad Debt Expense	—
Sales (Cr.)	$700,000

In Year 2, Needles Company switched to the aging method for estimating uncollectibles. It estimated that the Year 2 ending balance of accounts receivable contained $12,000 of probable uncollectibles. You may assume, although it is not necessary to do so (why?), that all sales in Year 2 were made on account.

Present journal entries for the following:

    a. Transactions and adjustments of Year 1 related to sales and customers' accounts.

    b. Transactions of Year 2 resulting in the above trial balance amounts.

    c. Adjustment for estimated uncollectibles for Year 2.

35. *Reconstructing events when allowance method is used.* The amounts in certain accounts on January 1, and before adjusting entries on December 31, appear below:

	January 1	December 31
Accounts Receivable.	$400,000 Dr.	$ 500,000 Dr.
Allowance for Uncollectible Accounts	30,000 Cr.	20,000 Dr.
Bad Debt Expense	0	0
Sales	0	2,000,000 Cr.

During the year, 90 percent of sales were on account and 3 percent of credit sales are judged to be uncollectible. During the year one account for $1,500 was collected, although it had been written off as uncollectible during the preceding year. When the written-off account was reinstated, the credit was to the Allowance account.

    a. Give the journal entries made during the year that explain the changes in the four accounts as listed above.

    b. Give any adjusting entries required on December 31.

36. *Estimating percentage of uncollectibles.* The data in the following schedule pertain to the first 8 years of the Glidden Company's credit sales and experiences with uncollectible accounts.

Year	Credit Sales	Related Uncollectible Accounts	Year	Credit Sales	Related Uncollectible Accounts
1	$200,000	$5,100	5	$500,000	$6,000
2	300,000	6,450	6	550,000	5,400
3	400,000	7,450	7	560,000	5,750
4	450,000	8,000	8	580,000	5,950

Glidden Company has not previously used an Allowance for Uncollectible Accounts but has merely charged accounts written off directly to Bad Debt Expense.

What percentage of credit sales for a year would you recommend that Glidden Company charge to the sales contra account if the allowance method were to be adopted at the end of year 8?

37. *Decision to extend credit to a new class of customers.* The Feldman Company has a gross margin on credit sales of 30 percent. That is, cost of goods sold on account is 70 percent of sales on account. Uncollectible accounts amount to 2 percent of credit sales. If credit is extended to a new class of customers, credit sales will increase by $10,000, 8 percent of the new credit sales will be uncollectible, and all other costs, including interest to finance extra inventories, will increase by $1,000.

    a. Would Feldman Company be better or worse off if it extended credit to the new class of customer and by how much?

    b. How would your answer to part **a** differ if $3,000 of the $10,000 increase in credit sales had been made anyway as sales for cash? (Assume that the uncollectible amount on new credit sales is $800.)

38. *Decision to extend credit; working backwards to uncollectible rate.* The Hanrahan Company has credit sales of $100,000, a gross margin on those sales of 25 percent, with 3 percent of the credit sales uncollectible. If credit is extended to a new class of customers, sales will increase by $40,000, other expenses will increase by $2,500, and uncollectibles will be 5 percent of *all* credit sales. Verify that Hanrahan Company will be $3,500 better off if it extends credit to the new customers. What percentage of the new credit sales are uncollectible?

39. *Journal entries for notes.* On November 1, Year 1, the Atlas Company receives a note from one of its customers to apply on its open account receivable. The 9-month, 18 percent note for $8,000, issued November 1, Year 1, is valued at its face amount.

On January 31, Year 2, the Atlas Company endorses the note and transfers it with recourse to First National Bank in return for a cash payment of $8,100. The company's checking account at this bank is increased for the proceeds, $8,100.

On August 1, Year 2, the Atlas Company is notified by the bank that the note was collected from the customer at maturity.

Atlas Company closes its books annually on December 31.

Present dated journal entries on the books of Atlas Company relating to this note.

40. *Reconstructing events from journal entries.* Give the likely transaction or event that would result in making each of the independent journal entries below:

a. Notes Receivable	300	
Accounts Receivable		300
b. Marketable Securities	10,000	
Cash		10,000
c. Bad Debt Expense	2,300	
Allowance for Uncollectible Accounts		2,300
d. Unrealized Loss on Valuation of Marketable Equity Securities . .	4,000	
Allowance for Excess of Cost of Marketable Equity Securities over Market Value		4,000
e. Cash	295	
Notes Receivable		285
Interest Revenue		10
f. Cash	1,200	
Loss on Sale of Marketable Securities	200	
Marketable Securities		1,400
g. Allowance for Uncollectible Accounts	450	
Accounts Receivable		450
h. Allowance for Excess of Cost of Marketable Equity Securities over Market Value	1,000	
Recovery of Unrealized Loss on Valuation of Marketable Equity Securities		1,000
i. Bad Debt Expense	495	
Accounts Receivable		495
j. Accounts Receivable	285	
Allowance for Uncollectible Accounts		285

41. *Funds statement effects.* Refer to the Simplified Statement of Changes in Financial Position for a Period in Exhibit 5.17 on page 201. Eleven of the lines in the statement are numbered. Ignore the unnumbered lines in responding to the questions below.

Assume that the accounting cycle is complete for the period and that all of the financial statements have been prepared. Then it is discovered that a transaction has been overlooked. That transaction is recorded in the accounts, and all of the financial statements are corrected. Define *funds* as *cash.*

For each of the following transactions or events, indicate which of the numbered lines of the funds statement is affected and by how much. Ignore income tax effects.

    a. Estimated uncollectibles equal to 1 percent of the year's sales of $1 million are recognized. An entry is made increasing the Allowance for Uncollectible Accounts.

b. The specific account receivable of Eli Worman in the amount of $2,000 is written off by a firm using the allowance method.

c. The specific account receivable of Eli Worman in the amount of $3,000 is written off by a firm using the direct write-off method.

d. A firm owns short-term marketable securities. Dividends of $30,000 are declared on the shares owned. The payment will be received next period.

e. The portfolio of short-term marketable securities acquired this period has a market value of $60,000 less than their net amount shown on the balance sheet at the end of the current accounting period. An entry is made changing the allowance account contra to the current asset, marketable securities.

f. The market value of the same portfolio of marketable securities referred to in part **e** has increased $40,000 by the end of the next period. An entry is made changing the allowance account for marketable securities.

42. *Prepare funds statement; adapted from a problem by Stan Baiman.* Exhibit 7.11 shows comparative balance sheets and an income statement of Trimolet Company for Year 2.

Prepare the Year 2 statement of changes in financial position with funds defined as cash.

43. *Analysis of financial statement disclosures of marketable equity securities held as investments.* A recent annual report of Warner Communications, Inc. (WCI), contained the following information about its investments in marketable equity securities (noncurrent assets). Dollar amounts appear in thousands.

	Year 2	Year 1
Noncurrent Asset Section of Balance Sheet		
Marketable equity securities carried at lower of cost or market	$44,143	$96,571
Owners' Equity Section of Balance Sheet		
Net unrealized loss on marketable equity securities	(3,887)	(18,736)

a. What was the cost of marketable securities on hand at the end of Year 1?

b. Is the amount shown for these securities on hand at the end of Year 2 their cost or their market value? How do you know?

c. Assume that no new securities were acquired during Year 2. What was the cost of securities sold during Year 2?

d. Assume that on December 31, Year 2, WCI decided to sell its entire portfolio of securities early in Year 3 and, in anticipation of that event, reclassified the entire portfolio as a current asset. Give the journal entries that WCI would make and indicate the effect of these entries on both the income statement for Year 2 and total owners' equity at the end of Year 2.

Exhibit 7.11
TRIMOLET COMPANY
Comparative Balance Sheets and Income Statement
(Problem 42)

	December 31	
Balance Sheets	**Year 1**	**Year 2**
Cash	$ 50,000	$130,000
Accounts Receivable	100,000	110,000
Less: Allowance for Uncollectibles	(20,000)	(25,000)
Inventory	100,000	90,000
Prepaid Rent	220,000	250,000
Total Assets	$450,000	$555,000
Accounts Payable	$ 20,000	$ 40,000
Capital Stock	200,000	135,000
Retained Earnings	230,000	380,000
Total Equities	$450,000	$555,000
Year 2 Income Statement		
Gross Sales		$500,000
Less: Sales Discounts		5,000
Net Sales		$495,000
Cost of Goods Sold		$200,000
Bad Debt Expense		15,000
Rent Expense		30,000
Income Tax Expense		100,000
Total Expenses		$345,000
Net Income		$150,000

Note: During Year 2, $6,000 in specific accounts receivables were defaulted upon and written off as uncollectible.

44. *Analysis of financial statement disclosures for marketable equity securities.* Exhibit 7.12 reproduces the marketable equity securities note of Sunshine Mining Company for a recent year, with dates changed for convenience. Assume that no holdings of current marketable securities were held at the end of Year 1, that no current marketable securities were sold during Year 2, and that no noncurrent marketable securities were purchased or transferred to the current portfolio during Year 2. The income statement for Year 2 shows a realized loss on sale of noncurrent marketable securities of $3,068,000.

    a. What amount for net unrealized gain or loss on noncurrent marketable securities appears on the balance sheet for the end of Year 1?

    b. What amount for net unrealized gain or loss on noncurrent marketable securities appears on the balance sheet for the end of Year 2?

    c. What were the proceeds of sale of noncurrent marketable securities sold during Year 2?

    d. What amount for unrealized loss on holdings of marketable securities appears on the income statement for Year 2?

45. *Analysis of opportunity to manage income with selective sales from portfolio of marketable equity securities.* Insurance companies report holdings of marketable

Exhibit 7.12
SUNSHINE MINING COMPANY
Data on Marketable Equity Securities
(dollar amounts in thousands)
(Problem 44)

Marketable Equity Securities	Cost	Market Value	Balance Sheet Carrying Value
At December 31, Year 2:			
Current Marketable Securities	$ 7,067	$ 4,601	$ 4,601
Noncurrent Marketable Securities	$ 6,158	$ 8,807	$ 6,158
At December 31, Year 1:			
Noncurrent Marketable Securities	$21,685	$11,418	$11,418

equity securities at market value on the balance sheet, but only *realized* gains and losses in the income statement. Unrealized gains (losses) are credited (debited) directly to a balance sheet owners' equity account. The treatment of *both gains and losses* on all an insurance company's equity holdings is like that required by FASB *Statement No. 12* for *losses* on long-term investments in equity securities by noninsurance companies.

Assume that an insurance company has been in business long enough to hold a portfolio of equity securities, some of which have unrealized holding gains (market price increases since acquisition), whereas others have unrealized losses (market price decreases since acquisition). Its income can be manipulated as follows: If more income is wanted, sell securities with unrealized gains; if less income is wanted, sell securities with unrealized losses. Over long time spans, income can be smoothed, even if it cannot be managed arbitrarily. Limits to income management are imposed by the overall portfolio performance.

Sears, Roebuck and Co. owns 100 percent of Allstate Insurance Company. Sears' reported income includes only the *realized* gains and losses on Allstate's investments.

Exhibit 7.13 shows data for a recent decade for various items reported by Sears and Allstate. Column (1) shows Sears' income as reported and column (3) shows Allstate's realized gains and losses, after taxes, on its investments in equity securities.

Columns (5)–(7) show the magnitude of Sears/Allstate's opportunity for managing earnings. Examine Year 4, for example. At the end of Year 4, Allstate had $140.0 million of unrealized gains in its portfolio. Presumably, Allstate's and, hence, Sears' income could have been larger by up to $140.2 million (about 20 percent) before taxes. Similarly, at the end of Year 4, Allstate had $211.8 million of unrealized losses in its portfolio. Presumably, Allstate's income could have been smaller by $211.0 million (about 30 percent) before taxes.[14] Of course, these oppor-

---

[14]These percentages are calculated before allowing for the effect of any income tax assessed against the gains and losses, once they are realized. The effective income tax rate on such gains and losses is difficult to estimate prior to realization, and it is possible, by timing the realization of gains and losses judiciously, that the effective rate could be far below the statutory rate.

Exhibit 7.13
Data on Income, Realized Holding Gains, and Unrealized Holding Gains
of Sears, Roebuck and Co. and Allstate Insurance Company
(dollar amounts in millions)
(Problem 45)

	In Reported Income (Loss) Items				Size of Manageable Income Pool at Year-End (Pretax)		
	Reported Total[a]		Allstate's Aftertax Realized Investment Gains (Losses) for Year	Allstate's Unrealized Gains (Losses) for Year	Unrealized Gains on Securities With Gains	Unrealized (Losses) on Securities With Losses	Net Unrealized Pretax Gains (Losses)
Year	Dollars (1)	Percent Change (2)	(3)	(4)	(5)	(6)	(7)
Year 1 .	$679.9		$26.1	$(258.7)	NR	NR	$ (63.2)
Year 2 .	511.4	−24.8	10.8	(422.1)	NR	NR	(498.8)
Year 3 .	522.6	2.2	11.8	271.8	$104.3	$(304.6)	(200.3)
Year 4 .	694.5	32.9	8.0	129.6	140.2	(211.0)	(70.8)
Year 5 .	838.0	20.7	1.7	26.2	128.4	(172.2)	(43.8)
Year 6 .	921.5	10.0	16.0	36.5	156.2	(162.0)	(5.8)
Year 7 .	810.1	−12.1	24.9	79.5	234.6	(121.1)	113.5
Year 8 .	606.0	−25.2	52.5	76.5	391.0	(118.4)	272.6
Year 9 .	650.1	7.3	58.0	(103.8)	227.8	(159.7)	68.1
Year 10 .	861.2	32.5	31.5	123.0	374.7	(133.8)	240.9

[a]As originally reported, not as restated in subsequent reports for accounting changes.
NR: Not reported or disclosed.
Column (1): Taken from Sears' income statements; includes amounts in column (3), but not amounts in column (4).
Columns (3), (4), (5), and (6): Taken from Allstate's financial statements and notes thereto in the Sears' annual reports.
Column (7) = column (5) + column (6), if not separately reported.

tunities for income management implicit in the data in columns (5)–(7) are not independent of each other. If, for example, Allstate had realized all of the gains available at the end of Year 4, there would have been substantially smaller (perhaps zero) unrealized gains at the end of Year 5.

    a. Compute the year-to-year changes in Sears' income *before* realized gains.

    b. Compare these changes with the year-to-year changes in Sears' reported net income; analyze Sears' use of unrealized gains and losses in the Allstate portfolio of marketable equity securities to smooth income over time.

46. *Management of marketable securities portfolios to affect income and financial statement ratios.* The chief financial officer (CFO) of Easton Company is nervous about the state of the company's financial affairs, as reflected in its tentative post-closing trial balance at the end of the current year, which appears in Exhibit 7.14. The CFO worries that the current ratio is too low.

    Several years ago, the company borrowed $6 million in the form of a long-term bond issue, maturing 15 years from now, carrying an interest rate of 7.5 percent per year. Interest rates have increased substantially since then, and comparable borrowings would now cost the firm more than 10 percent per year. The CFO worries about

Exhibit 7.14
EASTON COMPANY
Tentative Post-Closing Trial Balance at Current Year-End
(dollar amounts in thousands)
(Problem 46)

	Dr.	Cr.
Allowance for Excess of Cost of Marketable Securities over Market Value (current asset contra)		$ 2,500
Current Liabilities		5,500
Investments in Marketable Equity Securities (noncurrent assets)	$ 3,000	
Marketable Equity Securities (current assets), at Cost.	3,500	
Noncurrent Liabilities		6,000
Other Current Assets	5,000	
Other Noncurrent Assets, Net	12,000	
Owner's Equity Accounts		9,500
Totals	$23,500	$23,500

Holdings of Equity Securities

	Cost	Year-End Market Value
Current Assets:		
Company A	$ 2,000	$ 600
Company B	1,500	400
Total.	$ 3,500	$ 1,000
Noncurrent Assets:		
Company C	$ 1,000	$ 5,000
Company D	2,000	1,600
Total.	$ 3,000	$ 6,600

terms of the bond agreement that require the firm to maintain a ratio of current assets to current liabilities of at least 1.20 to 1.00. If the current ratio falls below that amount, then the bond issue becomes due immediately, rather than maturing at its original maturity date, which is still 15 years in the future. The CFO knows it will be costly to borrow new funds to replace the old and ponders the company's recent success in holding down its amounts of receivables and inventories, both sound management practices that reduce current assets but also reduce the current ratio.

Over the past several years Easton Company has acquired various holdings of marketable equity securities, some as current assets and some as noncurrent assets. Data on these holdings appear in Exhibit 7.14. The holdings of any one company were acquired in a single transaction. The CFO wonders what, if anything, can be done with the holdings of marketable equity securities to keep the call provision of the bond issue from being triggered.

The chief executive officer (CEO) of Easton Company has discussed these problems with the CFO and raises another issue. The CEO's compensation package contains a bonus clause. As things now stand, the CEO will not receive a bonus because income for the year is $1.5 million short of the minimum for a bonus to be earned. Neither the CFO nor the CEO want the firm to incur any extra income tax payments, as will become payable at a rate of 40 percent on any gains realized on sale of securities. Both the CEO and the CFO seek your advice.

a. Is the bond issue in danger of being declared due for current payment? Why or why not?

b. What actions, if any, can management of Easton Company undertake to protect the outstanding bond issue from coming due at the end of the current year without having to pay additional income taxes? Provide journal entries that record the actions you suggest. What is the effect on income? On owner's equity?

c. What actions, if any, can management undertake to boost reported income sufficiently so that the CEO will receive a bonus? Provide journal entries that record the actions you suggest. How will these actions affect the current ratio?

Chapter 8

Inventories:
The Source of Operating Profits

In the last decade many major U.S. corporations changed their accounting for inventories and cost of goods sold. As a result, these corporations reported net income smaller by hundreds of millions of dollars than would have been reported without the change. Paradoxically, perhaps, these firms made themselves better off by changing. This chapter shows how a firm can be better off reporting smaller, rather than larger, net income. Income tax effects cause the result. This chapter introduces the choices that a firm must make in accounting for inventories and shows the impact of these decisions on reported expenses and net income for the period. The choices made in accounting for inventories can make two companies that are basically alike appear to be quite different.

Inventory Terminology

The term *inventory* means a stock of goods or other items owned by a firm and held for sale, or for processing before being sold, as part of a firm's ordinary business operations. Tools, for example, are inventory in the hands of a tool manufacturer or hardware store, but not in the hands of a carpenter. Marketable securities are inventory in the hands of a securities dealer, but not in the hands of a manufacturer.

Goods held for sale by a retail or wholesale business are called *merchandise inventory;* goods held for sale by a manufacturing concern are called *finished goods inventory.* The inventories of manufacturing firms also include *raw materials* (materials being stored that will become part of goods to be produced) and *work in process* (partially completed products in the factory). The balance sheet may also include inventories of supplies to be consumed in administrative, selling, and manufacturing operations.

To "inventory" a stock of goods means to prepare a list of the items on hand at some specified date, to assign a unit cost to each item, and to calculate the total cost of the goods.

Significance of Accounting for Inventories

Financial accounting attempts to measure periodic income. Accounting for inventories affects income measurement by assigning costs to various accounting periods as expenses. The total cost of goods available for sale during a period must be allocated between the current period's use (cost of goods sold, an expense) and the amounts carried forward to future periods (end-of-period inventory, an asset now, but later an expense).

Inventory Equation

The inventory equation aids understanding of accounting for inventory. In the following equation, all quantities are measured in physical units.

$$\underbrace{\frac{\text{Beginning}}{\text{Inventory}} + \text{Additions}}_{\substack{\text{Goods Available for} \\ \text{Use or Sale}}} - \text{Withdrawals} = \frac{\text{Ending}}{\text{Inventory}}.$$

If we begin a period with 2,000 lb of sugar (beginning inventory) and if we purchase (add) 4,500 lb during the period, then there are 6,500 (= 2,000 + 4,500) lb available for use. If we use (withdraw) 5,300 lb during the period, then there should be 1,200 lb of sugar left at the end of the period (ending inventory).

The inventory equation can also be rewritten as

$$\underbrace{\frac{\text{Beginning}}{\text{Inventory}} + \text{Additions}}_{\substack{\text{Goods Available for} \\ \text{Use or Sale}}} - \frac{\text{Ending}}{\text{Inventory}} = \text{Withdrawals}.$$

If we begin the period with 2,000 lb of sugar, if we purchase 4,500 lb of sugar, and if we observe 1,200 lb of sugar on hand at the end of the period, then we know that 5,300 (= 2,000 + 4,500 − 1,200) lb of sugar were used, or otherwise withdrawn from inventory, during the period. The sum of Beginning Inventory plus Additions is usually called "Goods available for use or sale." In this example, there are 6,500 lb of sugar available for use.

If accounting were concerned merely with tracing physical quantities, no conceptual problems in accounting would arise for inventories. But, of course, accounting reports are stated in dollar amounts, not physical quantities. When prices remain constant, inventory accounting problems are minor, because all items carry the same per-unit cost. Any variation in values of inventories results only from changes in quantities. The major problems in inventory accounting arise because the unit acquisition costs of inventory items fluctuate over time.

To illustrate, suppose that an appliance store had a beginning inventory of one television set, "TV set 1," which cost $250. Suppose, further, that two TV sets are purchased during the period, TV set 2 for $290 and TV set 3 for $300, and that one TV set is sold for $550. The three TV sets are exactly alike in all physical respects; only their costs differ. Assume that there is no way to know which TV set was sold.

The inventory equation can be written as follows, with all quantities measured in dollars of cost:

$$\underbrace{\frac{\text{Beginning}}{\text{Inventory}} + \frac{\text{Net}}{\text{Purchases}}}_{\substack{\text{Cost of Goods} \\ \text{Available for Sale} \\ \$840}} - \frac{\text{Ending}}{\text{Inventory}} = \frac{\text{Cost of}}{\text{Goods Sold.}}$$

$$\underbrace{\$250 \quad + \quad \$590}_{\substack{\text{Cost of Goods} \\ \text{Available for Sale} \\ \$840}} - \quad ? \quad = \quad ?$$

If financial statements are prepared with amounts measured in dollar terms, then some assumption must be made about which TV set was sold. There are at least four assumptions that can be made in applying the inventory equation to compute the Cost of Goods Sold expense for the income statement and the ending inventory for the balance sheet. Exhibit 8.1 shows these assumptions. As the inventory equation and the TV set example both show, the higher the Cost of Goods Sold, the lower must be the Ending Inventory. Which particular pair of numbers appears—one in the income statement and one in the balance sheet—reflects the *cost flow assumption,* a major accounting issue discussed below.

Problems of Inventory Accounting

The remainder of this chapter discusses four problems of inventory accounting:

1. The costs to be included in acquisition cost.
2. The valuation basis to be used for items in inventory.
3. The frequency of carrying out inventory computations, periodically or "perpetually."
4. The cost flow assumption used to trace the movement of costs into and out of inventory, which may not parallel the physical movement of goods.

Because income tax laws affect some of a firm's choices in accounting for inventories, income taxes are discussed at appropriate places.

The following discussion can be divided into four distinct sections: computation of acquisition cost, subsequent valuation, timing of inventory computations, and cost flow assumptions. These four distinct problems should be kept in mind as the discussion proceeds.

Problem 1:
Costs Included in Inventory at Acquisition

Components of Inventory Cost

The amount on a balance sheet for inventory includes all costs incurred to acquire goods and prepare them for sale. For a merchandising firm, such costs should include purchasing, transportation, receiving, unpacking, inspecting, and shelving costs, as well as any bookkeeping and office costs for recording purchases.[1] The

---

[1]Because the amounts involved are often relatively small, and because it is difficult to assign a definite dollar amount for many of these costs to specific purchases, practice tends to restrict the actual additions to a few significant items that can easily be identified with particular goods, such as transportation costs. The costs of operating a purchasing department, the salaries and expenses of buyers, the costs of the receiving and warehousing departments, and the costs of handling and shelving are usually treated as expenses of the period in which they are incurred, even though they must be incurred to make merchandise ready for sale.

Exhibit 8.1
Assumptions for Inventory Illustrations

Assumed Item Sold	Cost of Goods Available for Sale (beginning inventory plus purchases)[a]	= Cost of Goods Sold (for income statement)	+ Ending Inventory (for balance sheet)
TV Set 1	$840	$250	$590
TV Set 2	840	290	550
TV Set 3	840	300	540
"Average" TV Set	840	280[b]	560[b]

[a]Cost of goods available for sale = cost of (TV set 1 + TV set 2 + TV set 3) = ($250 + $290 + $300) = $840.
[b]Average cost of a TV set = $840/3 = $280.

example on page 40 (in Chapter 2), showing the computation of the cost of some equipment, applies to inventory as well.

For a manufacturing firm, inventory costs include direct materials, direct labor, and manufacturing overhead. In a manufacturing firm, *all* production costs are debited to Work-in-Process Inventory. The process of recording *all* manufacturing costs in Work-in-Process Inventory is straightforward. The later allocation of costs in Work-in-Process Inventory to individual items transferred to the Finished Goods Inventory is not conceptually difficult, but requires special techniques of cost accounting, beyond the scope of this book. See the Glossary at "flow of costs." The procedure followed is called *absorption* (or *full*) *costing* and is required for both external financial and income tax reporting.[2]

The Purchase Transaction

The purchase transaction includes receiving goods, inspecting them, and recording the purchase. Legally, purchases should be recorded in the formal accounting records when title to the goods passes. The timing of title passage is often a technical

---

[2]An alternative procedure, known as *variable costing* (or, sometimes, *direct costing*), may be superior for internal management purposes.

In the variable costing procedure, product costs are classified into variable manufacturing costs (those that tend to vary with output) and fixed manufacturing costs (those that tend to be relatively unaffected in the short run by the number of units produced). Nonvariable (fixed) manufacturing costs are treated in the same way as selling and administrative costs; that is, they are treated as expenses assigned to the period of incurrence rather than as costs assignable to the product produced. Nonvariable manufacturing costs are charged in their entirety against revenues in calculating net income for the period.

When absorption costing is used, unit costs of product manufactured tend to vary inversely with the total number of units produced because a given amount of fixed costs is allocated to all the units produced. The larger is the number of units produced, the smaller is the per-unit cost.

Generally accepted accounting principles prohibit the issuing of financial statements based on variable costing. Because variable costing is not a generally accepted accounting principle, managerial accounting courses discuss the criticism of absorption costing and suggested benefits of variable costing for internal management uses.

question, whose answer depends on many circumstances of the transaction. For convenience, the accountant usually recognizes purchases only after the invoice and the goods are received and inspected. Adjustments may be made at the end of the accounting period to reflect the legal formalities for goods in transit that belong to the purchaser or for goods on hand that still belong to the seller.

Merchandise Purchases Adjustments

The invoice price of goods purchased seldom measures the total acquisition cost. Additional costs are incurred in transporting and handling the goods; deductions may be required for cash discounts, goods returned, and other adjustments of the invoice price. All of these adjustments could be debited or credited to the Merchandise Inventory account. Frequently, however, a number of contra and adjunct accounts are used for these adjustments so that a more complete analysis of the cost of purchases is available. Purchase Discounts, Freight-in, Purchase Returns, and Purchase Allowances accounts are used to provide the needed detail. The accounting for purchase adjustments closely parallels the accounting for sales adjustments discussed in Chapter 7.

The largest adjustment to the invoice price of merchandise is likely to be that for purchase discounts. Sellers often offer a discount from the invoice price for prompt payment. For example, the terms of sale ''2/10, net/30'' mean that a 2 percent discount from invoice price is offered if payment is made within 10 days and, otherwise, the full invoice price is due within 30 days.[3] Purchase discounts become a reduction in the purchase price. Two methods for recording purchases and the later treatment at time of payment (depending on whether the discount is actually taken) are the *gross price method* and the *net price method*. Problem 28 at the end of the chapter describes and illustrates these methods of record keeping.

Problem 2: Bases of Inventory Valuation

The basis for valuing inventory—the rule for assigning a cost to a physical unit—affects both periodic net income and the amount at which inventories appear on the balance sheet. At least five valuation bases are used for one purpose or another: acquisition cost, current cost measured by replacement cost, current cost measured by net realizable value, lower of (acquisition) cost or market, and standard cost. Some of the following discussion reviews fundamentals considered in Chapter 2. Generally accepted accounting principles require the use of the lower-of-cost-or-market basis for most purposes.

---

[3]Problem 28 at the end of Appendix B demonstrates that the interest rate implied in these terms of sales is about *45 percent per year*. That is, a purchaser who does not take such a discount is borrowing money at an interest rate of about 45 percent per year. Most purchasers find it advantageous to take such discounts and to borrow elsewhere at lower rates.

Acquisition Cost Basis

The acquisition cost basis values units in inventory at their historical cost until sold. In accounting, the terms *acquisition cost* and *historical cost* mean the same thing.

Using acquisition costs implies using the *realization convention:* Gains (or losses) caused by increases (or decreases) in the market value of assets do not appear in income until the particular assets are sold. When the acquisition cost basis is used, only sales transactions affect income. Any changes in the value of inventory items occurring between the time of acquisition and the time of sale are not recognized. The figure shown on the balance sheet for inventory becomes out of date to the extent that prices have changed since the items were acquired. The longer the time since acquisition, the more likely the current value of the inventory will differ from its acquisition cost.

Current Cost Basis

A current cost basis values units in inventory at a current market price. Two current cost bases discussed below are (1) current entry value, often called *replacement cost,* and (2) current exit value, often called *net realizable value*. When inventories are stated at current cost, gains and losses from changes in prices are recognized during the holding period that elapses between acquisition (or production) and the time of sale.

Whereas acquisition cost for inventory shows objective, verifiable information that may be out of date, current cost shows up-to-date information, which can be more useful, but the amount shown may be more difficult to measure and to audit.

Replacement Cost (Entry Value) The replacement cost of an item at a given time is the amount a firm would have to pay to acquire the item at that time. In computing replacement cost, one assumes a fair market (or arm's-length) transaction between a willing buyer and a willing seller. One also assumes that the inventory is bought in the customary fashion in the customary quantities. Replacement cost does not imply the forced purchase of inventory by a frantic buyer from a hoarding seller (which probably implies a premium price) or purchases of abnormally large quantities (which often can be bought at a lower-than-normal price) or purchases of abnormally small quantities (which usually cost more per unit to acquire).

Net Realizable Value (Exit Value) The amount that a firm could realize as a willing seller (not a "distressed seller") in an arm's-length transaction with a willing buyer in the ordinary course of business is *net realizable value*. The measurement of net realizable value can present problems for items of inventory not yet ready for sale (for example, partially complete inventory in a manufacturing firm). Additional manufacturing costs will have to be incurred before the item can be sold. Also, a sales commission and other selling costs, such as packaging and freight costs, will probably be incurred. In these cases, net realizable value is the estimated final selling price of the inventory less the estimated costs necessary to make the item ready for sale and to sell it. Consider as examples, agricultural products and precious metals on hand at the close of an accounting period. These are often stated at net realizable value. It may be easier to estimate a market price less selling costs than to measure the historical cost of a bushel of apples harvested from an orchard.

Lower-of-Cost-or-Market Basis

The lower-of-cost-or-market valuation basis is the lesser of the two amounts; acquisition cost or "market value," the latter generally measured as replacement cost.[4]

A decline of $5,000 in the market value of inventory is recognized with the following entry:

Loss from Decline in Value of Inventory	5,000	
Inventory		5,000

The entry directly credits the Inventory account, not a contra account as is done for marketable securities (explained in Chapter 7), because subsequent recoveries in market value are not recorded as gains. Under some approaches to inventory accounting, the above entry is not recorded explicitly; instead, the loss appears as a higher cost of goods sold. Consider, for example, the calculation in Exhibit 8.2 of cost of goods sold when beginning inventory is $19,000, purchases are $100,000, and ending inventory has a cost of $25,000 but has a market value of $20,000.

Note that cost of goods sold is $5,000 larger under the lower-of-cost-or-market basis than under the acquisition cost basis. The loss of $5,000 is not reported separately, but income will be $5,000 smaller than when the acquisition cost basis is used. If the amount of the write-down to market is so large that the reader of the

Exhibit 8.2
Calculating Cost of Goods Sold Illustrating
Different Bases of Inventory Valuation

	Cost Basis	Lower-of-Cost-or-Market Basis
Beginning Inventory	$ 19,000	$ 19,000
Purchases	100,000	100,000
Goods Available for Sale.	$119,000	$119,000
Less Ending Inventory	(25,000)	(20,000)
Cost of Goods Sold	$ 94,000	$ 99,000

[4]Actually, the definition of "market value" in the computation of lower of cost or market is more complex than mere replacement cost. Market value is replacement cost but no more than net realizable value nor less than the quantity net realizable value reduced by a "normal profit margin" on sales of items of this type.

statements will be misled without separate disclosure of the decline in market value, then the write-down can be shown as an adjustment to cost of goods sold or as a loss, separately reported as part of operating activities.

The lower-of-cost-or-market basis for inventory valuation is called a "conservative" policy because (1) losses from decreases in market value are recognized before goods are sold, but gains from increases in market value are not recorded before a sale takes place; and (2) inventory figures on the balance sheet are never greater, but may be less, than acquisition cost. That is, *holding losses* are reported currently, whereas *holding gains* are not reported until the goods are sold.

Over long enough time spans, however, income equals cash-in less cash-out. For any one unit, there is only one total gain or loss figure—the difference between its selling price and its acquisition cost; the valuation rule merely determines how this gain or loss is spread over the accounting periods between acquisition and final disposition. When the lower-of-cost-or-market basis is used, the net income of the present period may be "conservatively" lower than if the acquisition cost basis were used, but if so, the net income of a later period, when the unit is sold, will be higher.

Standard Costs

Standard cost is a predetermined estimate of what items of *manufactured* inventory *should* cost. Studies of past and estimated future cost data provide the basis for standard costs. Manufacturing firms frequently use standard cost systems for internal performance measurement and control. Managerial and cost accounting texts discuss these uses. Standard cost is also used occasionally as the valuation basis for preparing financial statements. Units in inventory may be valued at standard cost, especially in the preparation of monthly or quarterly statements.[5]

Generally Accepted Accounting Basis for Inventory Valuation

Accounting uses a historical cost basis for most assets. Because the "market value" of some inventory items can be significantly less than acquisition cost, either because of price changes for this kind of inventory generally or because of physical deterioration of the particular items in an inventory, generally accepted accounting principles require lower of cost or market for inventory.[6] This is the same as saying that "market values" must be used in some cases. Computing market value requires both replacement cost and net realizable value amounts. Thus, generally accepted accounting principles for inventory valuation and measurement of cost of goods sold require a combination of three valuation bases: acquisition cost, replacement cost, and net realizable value. In a period of rising prices, replacement cost and net

---

[5]If so, any excess of actual cost over standard cost (called an *unfavorable variance*) is usually debited to cost of goods sold or to other expenses of the period. If actual cost is less than standard cost, the favorable variance is usually credited to cost of goods sold.

[6]Committee on Accounting Procedure, *Accounting Research Bulletin No. 43,* "Inventory Pricing," Chapter 4, Statements 5 and 6, AICPA, 1953.

realizable value are likely to be higher than acquisition cost, so valuation at cost and the lower of cost or market usually give the same valuation.

The FASB requires disclosure by large firms of the current replacement cost of beginning inventory, ending inventory, and cost of goods sold in notes to the financial statements even though the financial statements are based on lower-of-cost-or-market values.[7] Chapter 14 discusses these disclosures more fully.

Problem 3: Timing of Computations

Two principal approaches to calculating the physical quantity and dollar amount of an inventory are the *periodic* inventory system and the *perpetual* inventory system. The periodic inventory system is less expensive to use than the perpetual inventory system because it involves fewer accounting computations, but the perpetual inventory system provides useful information not provided by the periodic inventory system.

Periodic Inventory System

In a periodic inventory system, the ending inventory figure results from making a physical count of units on hand at the end of an accounting period and multiplying the quantity on hand by the cost per unit. Then the inventory equation calculates the withdrawals that represent the cost-of-goods-sold expense. The following form of the inventory equation computes the cost of goods sold under a periodic system:

$$\underbrace{\begin{matrix} \text{Beginning} \\ \text{Inventory} \\ \text{(known)} \end{matrix} + \begin{matrix} \text{Purchases} \\ \text{(known)} \end{matrix}}_{\begin{matrix}\text{Goods Available} \\ \text{for Use or Sale}\end{matrix}} - \begin{matrix} \text{Ending} \\ \text{Inventory} \\ \text{(counted} \\ \text{and costed)} \end{matrix} = \begin{matrix} \text{Cost of} \\ \text{Goods Sold} \\ \text{(solved for).} \end{matrix}$$

When a periodic system is used, no entry is made for withdrawals (cost of goods sold) until the inventory on hand at the end of the accounting period is counted and costed.

To illustrate the periodic system, assume that sales during the year amounted to $165,000. The entries made to record sales during the year would have the combined effect of the following entry:

Cash and Accounts Receivable	165,000	
Sales.		165,000

Sales recorded for the entire year have this effect.

---

[7]Financial Accounting Standards Board, *Statement of Financial Accounting Standards No. 33,* "Financial Reporting and Changing Prices," 1979.

At the end of the year, a physical count is taken, inventory costs are assigned, and the cost of the withdrawals is computed from the inventory equation. Exhibit 8.2 derives cost of goods sold for the lower-of-cost-or-market basis embedded in a periodic inventory system. We assume that all purchases have been debited to the Merchandise Inventory account. The cost-of-goods-sold expense is recognized in a single entry:

Cost of Goods Sold	99,000	
Merchandise Inventory		99,000

Cost of goods sold recognized under a periodic inventory system.

A periodic inventory system generates no separate information to aid in controlling the amount of inventory shrinkage (the general name for losses from such causes as breakage, theft, evaporation, and waste). All goods not in the physical ending inventory count are assumed to have been either sold or used. Any losses from shrinkage appear in the cost of goods sold amount. Furthermore, physically counting the inventory at the end of the accounting period can seriously interfere with normal business operations for several days. Some firms using the periodic inventory system even close down and engage a large staff in physically counting the items on hand. Preparing income statements more frequently than once a year is expensive when the inventory figures result only from physically counting inventories.[8]

Perpetual Inventory System

In a *perpetual (continuous)* inventory system, cost of goods sold is calculated and recorded whenever an item is taken from inventory. A perpetual inventory system requires a constant tracing of costs as items move into and out of inventory. Such entries as the following may be made from day to day:

Accounts Receivable.	800	
Sales.		800
Cost of Goods Sold	475	
Finished Goods Inventory		475

To record the cost of goods withdrawn from inventory and sold for $800.

After postings for a period have been completed, the balance in the Merchandise Inventory account is the cost of the goods that should be on hand. Statements can be prepared without carrying out a physical count of inventory. In a perpetual inven-

---

[8]The gross margin method and retail inventory methods provide for approximating ending inventory costs when counts cannot easily be taken. Intermediate accounting texts discuss these methods, but Problems 30 and 31 at the end of this chapter introduce them.

tory system, the following form of the inventory equation computes goods expected to remain in the ending inventory after each acquisition or withdrawal:

$$\underbrace{\begin{matrix} \text{Beginning} \\ \text{Inventory} \\ \text{(known)} \end{matrix} + \begin{matrix} \text{Purchases} \\ \text{(known)} \end{matrix}}_{\substack{\text{Goods Available} \\ \text{for Use or Sale}}} - \begin{matrix} \text{Withdrawals} \\ \text{(recorded)} \end{matrix} = \begin{matrix} \text{Ending} \\ \text{Inventory} \\ \text{(solved for).} \end{matrix}$$

Using a perpetual inventory system does not eliminate the need to take a physical inventory in which the items of inventory on hand are counted and costed. A physical count and assigning of costs to remaining items enable measurement of any loss from shrinkage. The loss is the difference between the amounts in the Inventory account and the cost of the goods actually on hand. To illustrate, assume a book balance for inventory of $10,000 and an amount based on a physical count of $9,200. The entry to record the shrinkage is

---

Loss from Inventory Shrinkage	800	
Merchandise Inventory		800

To write down inventory from book amount of $10,000 to actual amount of $9,200.

The credit reduces the book amount of inventory from its recorded amount, $10,000, to the correct amount, $9,200. The debit is to a Loss account or, if immaterial, to Cost of Goods Sold. In either case, it reduces net income for the current period.

Some businesses using a perpetual approach make a complete physical check at the end of the accounting period, in the same way as when a periodic inventory is used. A more effective procedure is available. Rather than taking the inventory of all items at one time, the count may be staggered throughout the period. For example, a college bookstore may check actual physical amounts of textbooks and inventory account amounts at the end of the school year, whereas the comparison for beach wear might be done in November. All items should be counted at least once during every year, but not all items need be counted at the same time. The count of a particular item should be scheduled for a time when the stock on hand is near its low point for the year.

Choosing Between Periodic and Perpetual Inventory Systems

A perpetual inventory system helps maintain up-to-date information on quantities actually on hand. It is justified when being "out of stock" may lead to costly consequences, such as customer dissatisfaction or the need to shut down production lines. In such cases, a perpetual inventory system might keep track of the physical quantities of inventory but not the dollar amounts. Controlling losses is easier under a perpetual system because inventory records always indicate the goods that should remain. A periodic inventory system usually costs less than a perpetual inventory system, but it provides no data on shrinkages.

As with other choices that have to be made in business, costs should be compared with benefits. A periodic inventory system is likely to be cost-effective when being out of stock will not be extremely costly, when there is a large volume of items with a small value per unit, or when items are hard to steal or pilfer. Perpetual inventory systems are cost-effective when there is a small volume of high-value items or when running out of stock is costly.

As the cost of record keeping with computers declines, the cost of perpetual inventories declines. Their use, therefore, increases over time.

Problem 4: Cost Flow Assumptions

Specific Identification and the Need for a Cost Flow Assumption

Individual units sold can sometimes be physically matched with a specific purchase. If so, then no special problems arise in ascertaining the acquisition cost of the units withdrawn from inventory and the cost of the units still on hand. For example, cost can be marked on the unit or on its container, or the unit can be traced back to its purchase invoice or cost record. The inventory and cost of goods sold of an automobile dealer or of a dealer in diamonds or fur coats might be computed using specific identification of costs.

In most cases, however, new items are mixed with old units on shelves, in bins, or in other ways, and physical identification is impractical. Accounting traces cost flows, not flows of goods. Moreover, to assume that cost flows differ from physical flows of goods may be desirable (for reasons to be discussed in this section).

Flow of Historical Costs

The inventory *costing* problem arises because of *two* unknowns in the inventory equation:

$$\underbrace{\begin{array}{cc} \text{Beginning} & \text{Net} \\ \text{Inventory} + \text{Purchases} \\ \text{(known)} & \text{(known)} \end{array}}_{\begin{array}{c} \text{Goods Available} \\ \text{for Use or Sale} \end{array}} = \begin{array}{cc} \text{Cost of} & \text{Ending} \\ \text{Goods Sold} + \text{Inventory} \\ \text{(unknown)} & \text{(unknown)}. \end{array}$$

We know the costs of the beginning inventory and net purchases but not the amounts for cost of goods sold and for ending inventory. The question is whether to compute amounts for the units in ending inventory using the most recent costs, the oldest costs, the average cost, or some other choice. Of course, the question could have been put in terms of computing amounts for the cost of goods sold, for once we place an amount on one unknown quantity, the inventory equation automatically determines the amount of the other. The sum of the two unknowns, Cost of Goods Sold and Ending Inventory, must equal the cost of goods available for sale (= beginning inventory plus net purchases). The higher the cost assigned to one unknown, the lower must be the cost assigned to the other.

When prices are changing, no historical cost-based accounting method for costing ending inventory and cost of goods sold allows the accountant to show recent costs on both the income statement and the balance sheet. For example, in a period of rising prices, if recent, higher acquisition prices are used in measuring cost of goods sold for the income statement, then older, lower acquisition prices must be used in costing the ending inventory for the balance sheet. As long as cost of goods sold and ending inventory are based on acquisition costs, financial statements can present current amounts in the income statement or the balance sheet, but not in both. Of course, combinations of current and out-of-date information can appear in both statements.

If more than one purchase is made of the same item at different prices and specific identification is not feasible, then some assumption must be made about the flow of costs. Using a cost flow assumption, the accountant computes the acquisition cost applicable to the units remaining in the inventory. One of three cost flow assumptions is typically used for this purpose. These cost flow assumptions are

1. First-in, first-out (FIFO),
2. Last-in, first-out (LIFO), and
3. Weighted average.

The following demonstrations of each of these methods use the TV set example introduced earlier and repeated at the top of Exhibit 8.3. The example of the three TV sets illustrates most of the important points about the cost flow assumption required in accounting for inventories and cost of goods sold. The first problem for self-study at the end of this chapter illustrates the techniques more realistically, but contains no new concepts.

First-In, First-Out

The first-in, first-out cost flow assumption, abbreviated FIFO, assigns the cost of the earliest units acquired to the withdrawals and the cost of the most recent acquisitions to the ending inventory. This cost flow assumes that the oldest materials and goods are used first. This cost flow assumption conforms to good business practice in managing physical flows, especially in the case of items that deteriorate or become obsolete. Column (1) of Exhibit 8.3 illustrates FIFO. TV set 1 is assumed to be sold, whereas TV sets 2 and 3 are assumed to remain in inventory. The designation FIFO refers to the cost flow of units sold. A parallel description for ending inventory is last-in, still-here, or LISH.

Last-In, First-Out

The last-in, first-out cost flow assumption, abbreviated LIFO, assigns the cost of the latest units acquired to the withdrawals and the cost of the oldest units to the ending inventory. Some theorists argue that LIFO matches current costs to current revenues and therefore that LIFO better measures income. Column (3) of Exhibit 8.3 illustrates LIFO. The $300 cost of TV set 3 is assumed to leave, whereas the costs of TV sets 1 and 2 are assumed to remain in inventory. The designation of

Exhibit 8.3
Comparison of Cost Flow Assumptions
Historical Cost Basis

Assumed Data

Beginning Inventory: TV Set 1 Cost	$250
Purchases: TV Set 2 Cost	290
TV Set 3 Cost	300
Cost of Goods Available for Sale	$840
Sales: One TV set	$550

Financial Statements	Cost Flow Assumption		
	FIFO (1)	Weighted Average (2)	LIFO (3)
Sales	$550	$550	$550
Cost of Goods Sold	250[a]	280[b]	300[c]
Gross Margin on Sales	$300	$270	$250
Ending Inventory	$590[d]	$560[e]	$540[f]

[a]TV set 1 costs $250.
[b]Average TV set costs $280 (= $840/3).
[c]TV set 3 costs $300.
[d]TV sets 2 and 3 cost $290 + $300 = $590.
[e]Two average TV sets cost 2 × $280 = $560.
[f]TV sets 1 and 2 cost $250 + $290 = $540.

LIFO refers to the cost flow for units sold. A parallel description for ending inventory is first-in, still-here, or FISH.

Firms have increasingly used LIFO since it first became acceptable for income tax reporting in 1939. In a period of consistently rising prices, LIFO results in a higher cost of goods sold, a lower reported periodic income, and lower current income taxes than either FIFO or weighted-average cost flow assumptions.

LIFO usually does not reflect physical flows but is used because it produces a cost-of-goods-sold figure based on more up-to-date prices. In a period of rising prices, LIFO's higher (than FIFO's) cost-of-goods-sold figure reduces reported income and income taxes. Income tax factors are discussed below.

Weighted Average

Under the weighted-average cost flow assumption, the average of the costs of all goods available for sale (or use) during the accounting period, including the cost applicable to the beginning inventory, must be calculated.[9] The weighted-average cost is applied to the units on hand at the end of the month. Column (2) in Exhibit

---

[9]This description is technically correct only when a periodic inventory system is used. The first problem for self-study at the end of this chapter explores the procedures for applying the weighted-average method in a perpetual inventory system.

8.3 illustrates the weighted-average cost flow assumption. The weighted-average cost of TV sets available for sale during the period is $280 [= $\frac{1}{3}$ × ($250 + $290 + $300)]. Cost of Goods Sold is thus $280 and ending inventory is $560 (= 2 × $280).

Comparison of Cost Flow Assumptions

FIFO results in balance sheet figures that are closest to current cost, because the latest purchases dominate the ending inventory amounts. Remember LISH—last-in, still-here. The cost-of-goods-sold expense tends to be out of date, however, because FIFO assumes that the earlier prices of the beginning inventory and the earliest purchases are charged to expense. When prices rise, FIFO usually leads to the highest reported net income of the three methods, and to the smallest when prices are falling.

Because LIFO ending inventory can contain cost of items acquired many years previously, LIFO produces balance sheet figures usually much lower than current costs. LIFO's cost-of-goods-sold figure closely approximates current costs. Exhibit 8.4 summarizes the differences between FIFO and LIFO. Of the cost flow assumptions, LIFO usually implies the smallest net income when prices are rising (highest cost of goods sold), and the largest when prices are falling (lowest cost of goods sold). Also, LIFO results in the least fluctuation in reported income in businesses where selling prices tend to change as current prices of inventory items change.

The weighted-average cost flow assumption falls between the other two in its effect on both the balance sheet and the income statement. It is, however, much more like FIFO than like LIFO in its effects on the balance sheet. When inventory turns over rapidly, the weighted-average inventory costs reflect present prices almost as much as FIFO.

A Closer Look at LIFO's Effects on Financial Statements

As discussed above, LIFO usually presents a cost-of-goods-sold figure that reflects current costs. It also generally has the practical advantage of deferring income taxes. If a firm uses a LIFO flow assumption in its income tax return, it must also use LIFO in its financial reports to shareholders. This is the one major choice of accounting principles where the tax laws require conformity between the financial statements and the tax return. This "LIFO conformity rule" of the Internal Revenue Service is under attack in Congress and by some members of the U.S. Treasury Department. The outcome is uncertain. By the time you read this, LIFO conformity may no longer be required. Because LIFO conformity is required as this book goes to press, the discussions and illustrations assume it.

In the last decade, many firms, including Du Pont, General Motors, Eastman Kodak, and Sears, Roebuck, switched from FIFO to LIFO. Given the rapid rate of price increases over the past decade, the switch from FIFO to LIFO has resulted in substantially lower cash payments for income taxes. For example, when Du Pont

Exhibit 8.4
Age of Information About Inventory Items

Cost Flow Assumption	Income Statement	Balance Sheet	Inventory-on-Hand Assumption
FIFO	Old Prices	Current Prices	LISH
LIFO	Current Prices	Very[a] Old Prices	FISH

[a]The oldest prices on the FIFO income statement are just over 1 year old in nearly all cases and the *average* price on the FIFO income statement (for a year) is slightly more than $\frac{1}{2}$ year old. The larger the rate of inventory turnover, the closer the average age on the income statement is to $\frac{1}{2}$ year. LIFO balance sheet items are generally much older than the FIFO income statement items, with some costs from the 1940s in many cases.

and General Motors switched from FIFO to LIFO, they each lowered current income taxes by about $150 million. At the same time, these firms reported lower net income to shareholders than would have been reported if FIFO had still been used.[10]

LIFO Layers In any year when purchases exceed sales, the quantity of units in inventory increases. The amount added to inventory for that year is called a *LIFO layer*. For example, assume that a firm acquires 10 TV sets each year and sells 8 TV sets each year for 4 years. Then, its inventory at the end of the fourth year would be 8 units. The cost of the 8 units under LIFO is the costs of sets numbered 1 and 2 (from the first year), 11 and 12 (from the second year), 21 and 22 (from the third year), and 31 and 32 (from the fourth year). Common terminology would say that this firm has four LIFO layers, each labeled with its year of acquisition. The physical units on hand would almost certainly be the most recently acquired units in Year 4, but they would appear on the balance sheet at prices paid during each of the 4 years.

Dipping into LIFO Layers One problem of LIFO results from "dipping" into old LIFO layers. LIFO reduces current taxes in periods of rising prices and rising inventory quantities. If inventory quantities decline, however, the opposite effect occurs in the year of the decline: Older, lower costs per unit of prior years' LIFO layers leave the balance sheet and are charged to expense.

If a firm must for some reason reduce end-of-period physical inventory quantities below what they were at the beginning of the period, then cost of goods sold will be based on the current period's purchases plus a portion of the older and lower costs in the beginning inventory. Such a firm will have larger reported income and income taxes in that period than if the firm had been able to maintain its ending inventory at beginning-of-period levels.

Example of Dip into LIFO Layers Assume that LIFO inventory at the beginning of Year 5 consists of 460 units with a total cost of $34,200; see Exhibit 8.5.

[10]Thus, the apparent "paradox" in the introduction to this chapter is explained.

Exhibit 8.5
Data for Illustration of LIFO Dips
(Inventory at January 1, Year 5)

LIFO Layers		Cost	
Year Purchased	**Number of Units**	**Per Unit**	**Total Cost**
Year 1	100	$ 50	$ 5,000
Year 2	110	60	6,600
Year 3	120	80	9,600
Year 4	130	100	13,000
	460		$34,200

Assume that the cost at the end of Year 5 is $120 per unit. If, however, the Year 5 ending inventory drops to 100 units, then all the 360 units purchased in Year 2 through Year 4 will also enter cost of goods sold. These 360 units cost $29,200 (= $6,600 + $9,600 + $13,000), but the current cost of comparable units is $43,200 (= 360 units × $120 per unit). Cost of goods sold will be $14,000 (= $43,200 − $29,200) smaller than if quantities had not declined because of the "dip into old LIFO layers" of inventory. Income subject to income taxes will be $14,000 larger than if inventory had been purchased so that quantities had not declined from 460 to 100 units.

Annual Report of Disclosure of Dip into LIFO Layers Many actual LIFO firms have inventory layers built up since the 1940s, and the costs of the early units are often as little as 10 percent of the current cost. For these firms, a dip into old layers will substantially increase income. A footnote from an earlier annual report of the U.S. Steel Corporation illustrates this phenomenon:

> Because of the continuing high demand throughout the year, inventories of many steel-making materials and steel products were unavoidably reduced and could not be replaced during the year. Under the LIFO system of accounting, used for many years by U.S. Steel, the net effect of all the inventory changes [reductions] was to increase income for the year by about $16 million [about 5 percent].

In recent years, U.S. Steel has shortened its explanation; for example, in a year when U.S. Steel reported a loss of $360 million, it said:

> Cost of sales has been reduced and income from all operations increased by $621 million . . . from the liquidations of LIFO inventories.

LIFO's Effects on Purchasing Behavior Consider the quandary faced by a purchasing manager of a LIFO firm nearing the end of a year when the quantity sold for the year has exceeded the quantity purchased so far during the year. If the year ends with sales greater than purchases, the firm will dip into old LIFO layers and will have to pay increased taxes. Assume that the purchasing manager thinks current prices for the goods are abnormally high and prefers to delay purchasing until prices drop, presumably in the next year. Waiting implies, however, dips into old LIFO layers during this period and higher taxes. Buying now may entail higher inventory and carrying costs. LIFO can induce firms to manage LIFO layers and cost of goods sold in a way that would be unwise in the absence of tax effects. LIFO also gives management the opportunity to manipulate income: Under LIFO, end-of-year purchases, which can be manipulated, affect net income for the year.

LIFO Balance Sheet LIFO usually leads to a balance sheet amount for inventory so much less than current costs as possibly to confuse readers of financial statements. For example, in recent years U.S. Steel has reported that the cost of its ending inventory based on LIFO is about one-half of what it would have been had FIFO been used. U.S. Steel's inventory on the balance sheet, reported assuming LIFO cost flow, comprises about 10 percent of total assets. Using FIFO cost flow, inventory would be about 25 percent of total assets.

Consider the current ratio (= current assets/current liabilities). Some financial statement analysts use the current ratio to assess the short-term liquidity of a company. If LIFO is used in periods of rising prices while inventory quantities are increasing, the amount of inventory included in the numerator will be much smaller than if the inventory were valued at current prices. Hence, the unwary reader may underestimate the liquidity of a company that uses a LIFO cost flow assumption.

Similarly, the calculation of inventory turnover (= cost of goods sold/average inventory during the period) can be drastically affected by using LIFO. Again referring to the U.S. Steel example, the inventory turnover ratio from the financial statements constructed assuming LIFO cost flow is about twice as large as would result from FIFO cost flow. One of the self-study problems at the end of this chapter explores this phenomenon.

Supplementary LIFO Disclosure When a company uses LIFO, the SEC requires that it disclose in notes the current value of beginning and ending inventory. Appendix A for General Products Company illustrates these disclosures. See Note 10 in Appendix Exhibit A.4.

FIFO Versus LIFO Impact on Financial Statements: An Illustration

No accounting method for inventories based on historical cost can simultaneously report current data in both the income statement and the balance sheet. If a firm reports current prices in the income statement under LIFO, then its balance sheet amount for ending inventory contains some *very* old costs. The SEC is concerned that readers of financial statements not be misled by out-of-date information. It requires firms using LIFO to disclose in notes to the financial statements the amounts by which LIFO inventories would have increased if they had been recorded at FIFO or current cost.[11] From this disclosure and the inventory equation, we can

---

[11]The excess of current cost over LIFO cost of inventories is referred to by some managers as the "LIFO reserve." For reasons discussed in the Glossary at the back of the book, the term *reserve* is among the most objectionable, although it continues to be used. A term such as "inventory valuation allowance" is as descriptive as "LIFO reserve," and is less likely to mislead.

compute what a LIFO firm's income would have been had it been using FIFO instead. In this way, the financial statements of firms using LIFO can be made more comparable with the financial statements of firms using FIFO.

Note 10 to the financial statements of General Products Company in Appendix A states, in part:

If the FIFO method of inventory accounting had been used to value all inventories, they would have been $2,240 [million] higher than reported at December 31, 1985 ($1,950 [million] higher at year-end 1984).

General Products' beginning inventories under LIFO (see Note 10) amounted to $3,161 million, its ending inventory amounted to $3,343 million, and its cost of goods sold totaled $17,751 million. Exhibit 8.6 demonstrates the calculation of cost of goods sold on a FIFO basis. Recall from the inventory equation:

$$\frac{\text{Beginning}}{\text{Inventory}} + \text{Purchases} - \frac{\text{Ending}}{\text{Inventory}} = \frac{\text{Cost of}}{\text{Goods Sold.}}$$

FIFO's higher beginning inventory increases the reported cost of goods available for sale and the cost of goods sold by $1,950 million, relative to LIFO. FIFO's higher ending inventory decreases cost of goods sold by $2,240 million, relative to LIFO. Hence, the cost of goods sold is $2,240 million minus $1,950 million, or $290 million less under FIFO than it was under LIFO. General Products' pretax income would be $290 million more under FIFO than under the LIFO flow assumption actually used.

The choice of cost flow assumption can significantly affect financial statements and their interpretation. During periods of substantial price change, no other choice between generally accepted financial accounting principles affects financial statements for most companies as much as the cost flow assumption for inventory.

Identifying Operating Margin and Holding Gains

The reported net income under FIFO is generally larger than under LIFO during periods of rising prices. This higher reported net income is caused by including a larger *realized holding gain* in reported net income under FIFO than under LIFO. This section illustrates the significance of holding gains in the calculation of net income under FIFO and LIFO.

The conventionally reported gross margin (sales minus cost of goods sold) consists of:

1. An operating margin, and
2. A realized holding gain (or loss).

(Unrealized holding gains and losses do not appear in income, but can be computed from information in notes to the financial statements.)

The difference between the selling price of an item and its replacement cost at the time of sale is called an *operating margin*. This operating margin gives some indication of the relative advantage that a particular firm has in the market for its goods,

Exhibit 8.6
GENERAL PRODUCTS COMPANY
Inventory Data from Financial Statements and Footnotes
(amounts in millions)

(Amounts shown in **boldface** appear in
General Products Company's financial
statements. Other amounts are computed
as indicated.)

	LIFO Cost Flow Assumption (actually used)	+	Excess of FIFO over LIFO Amount	=	FIFO Cost Flow Assumption (hypothetical)
Beginning Inventory	**$ 3,161**		**$ 1,950**		$ 5,111
Purchases	17,933[a]		0		17,933
Cost of Goods Available for Sale .	$21,094		**$ 1,950**		$23,044
Less Ending Inventory	**3,343**		**2,240**		5,583
Cost of Goods Sold	**$17,751**		$ (290)		$17,461
Sales	**$24,959**		0		**$24,959**
Less Cost of Goods Sold	**17,751**		$ (290)		17,461
Gross Margin on Sales	**$ 7,208**		$ 290		**$ 7,498**

[a]Computation of Purchases not presented in GP's financial statements:

Purchases = Cost of Goods Sold + Ending Inventory − Beginning Inventory,
  $17,933 =   **$17,751**   +   **$3,343**   −   **$3,161.**

such as a reputation for quality or service. The difference between the current replacement cost of an item and its acquisition cost is called a *holding gain* (or *loss*). The holding gain (or loss) reflects the change in cost of an item during the period while the inventory item is held. Holding gains indicate increasing prices and the skill (or luck) of the purchasing department in timing acquisitions.

To demonstrate the calculation of the operating margin and holding gain, consider the TV set example discussed in this chapter. The acquisition cost of the three items available for sale during the period is $840. Assume that one TV set is sold for $550. The replacement cost of the TV set at the time it was sold is $320. The current replacement cost at the end of the period for each item in ending inventory is $350. The top portion of Exhibit 8.7 illustrates the separation of the conventionally reported gross margin into the operating margin and the realized holding gain.

The operating margin is the difference between the $550 selling price and the $320 replacement cost at the time of sale. The operating margin of $230 is the same under both the FIFO and LIFO cost flow assumptions. The *realized holding gain* is the difference between cost of goods sold based on replacement cost and cost of goods sold based on acquisition cost. The realized holding gain under FIFO is larger than under LIFO, because the earlier purchases at lower costs are charged to cost of goods sold under FIFO. The larger realized holding gain under FIFO explains why net income under FIFO is typically larger than under LIFO during periods of rising prices. In conventional financial statements, the realized holding gain does *not* appear separately, as in Exhibit 8.7. Sometimes the realized holding gain on inventory is called *inventory profit*.

Exhibit 8.7
Reporting of Operating Margins
and Holding Gains for TV Sets
Using the Periodic Inventory Method

	Cost Flow Assumption			
	FIFO		LIFO	
Sales Revenue	$550		$550	
Less Replacement Cost of Goods Sold	320		320	
Operating Margin on Sales		$230		$230
Realized Holding Gain on TV Sets:				
Replacement Cost (at time of sale) of Goods Sold	$320		$320	
Less Acquisition Cost of Goods Sold (FIFO—TV set 1; LIFO—TV set 3)	250		300	
Realized Holding Gain on TV Sets (inventory profit) . . .		70		20
Conventionally Reported Gross Margin[a]		$300		$250
Unrealized Holding Gain:				
Replacement Cost of Ending Inventory (2 × $350)	$700		$700	
Less Acquisition Cost of Ending Inventory (FIFO—TV sets 2 and 3; LIFO—TV sets 1 and 2) . . .	590		540	
Unrealized Holding Gain on TV Sets		110		160
Economic Profit on Sales and Holding Inventory of TV Sets (not reported in financial statements)		$410		$410

[a]Note that Exhibit 8.3 stops here.

The calculation of an unrealized holding gain on units in ending inventory also appears in Exhibit 8.7. The *unrealized holding gain* is the difference between the current replacement cost of the ending inventory and its acquisition cost.[12] This unrealized holding gain on ending inventory is not reported in the income statement as presently prepared. The unrealized holding gain under LIFO is larger than under FIFO, because earlier purchases with lower costs remain in ending inventory under LIFO. The sum of the operating margin plus all holding gains (both realized and unrealized), called "Economic Profit" in Exhibit 8.7, is the same under FIFO and LIFO. Most of the holding gain under FIFO, that is, the realized portion, is recognized in computing net income each period, whereas most of the holding gain under LIFO, that is, the unrealized portion, is not currently recognized in the income statement. Instead, under LIFO the unrealized holding gain remains unreported, so long as the older acquisition costs are shown on the balance sheet as ending inventory.

[12]The unrealized holding gain for a *given year* on items on hand both at the beginning and at the end of the year is the difference between year-end current cost and beginning-of-year current cost. The examples in this chapter do not illustrate this complication; all items on hand at the end of the year are purchased during the year. See the Glossary at *inventory profit* for an illustration of the computation of holding gains for the year where there is a beginning inventory that includes unrealized holding gains from preceding periods.

The total increase in wealth for a period includes both realized and unrealized holding gains. That total increase, $410 in the example, is independent of the cost flow assumption, but does not appear in financial statements under currently accepted accounting principles.

The FASB requires disclosure in notes of the realized and unrealized holding gains on inventory (and plant) under certain conditions. See the discussion in Chapter 14.

Current Cost Basis Removes the Need for a Cost Flow Assumption

The preceding sections illustrate the difficulty in constructing useful financial statements in historical cost accounting for inventory in times of changing prices. If a FIFO cost flow assumption is used, then the income statement reports out-of-date cost of goods sold. If a LIFO cost flow assumption is used, then the balance sheet reports out-of-date ending inventory. (See Exhibit 8.4.)

A current cost basis for inventory allows up-to-date information to be shown on both statements, eliminating the need for a cost flow assumption. But using a current cost basis eliminates the realization convention from accounting and requires the accountant to make estimates of current costs. Some accountants find the resulting loss of objectivity and verifiability outweighs the potential benefits from using current cost data. Other accountants think that the benefits of current data outweigh the costs of having less auditable numbers.

Exhibit 8.8 illustrates the TV set example when both cost of goods sold and ending inventory are valued at replacement cost.

The first income figure, $230, is labeled *Operating Margin*. This figure shows selling price less replacement cost of goods sold at the time of sale. This number may have significance for companies operating in unregulated environments. The significance can perhaps be understood by considering the following assertion. If the retailer of the TV sets pays out more than $230 in other expenses, taxes, and dividends, then there will be insufficient funds retained in the firm for it to replace inventory and to allow it to continue in business carrying out the same physical operations next period as it did this period. On the date of sale, a new TV set costs $320; the historical cost of the TV set sold, whether $250 or $230 or some amount in between, does not help the retailer to understand the costs required to maintain its productive assets intact, given the *current* economic conditions.

The second income item shown in Exhibit 8.8 is called *Holding Gains*. Holding gains of $180 occurred during the period on the TV sets held in inventory. At the time of sale, the replacement cost of TV sets had increased to $320. Thus, the holding gain on three TV sets, on the date of sale of one of them, was $120 [= $3 \times $320 - ($250 + $290 + $300)]. By the end of the accounting period there was another $60 [= $2 \times ($350 - $320)] holding gain on the two TV sets still held in inventory as the replacement cost increased to $350 from $320.

The $410 income figure shown after the inclusion of holding gains may also be significant. It represents the increase in wealth of the firm without regard to the realization convention. Some economists define income as the change in

Exhibit 8.8
Using Replacement Cost Data to
Analyze Components of Income

Assumed Data

Beginning Inventory: TV Set 1 Cost	$250
Purchases: TV Set 2 Cost	290
TV Set 3 Cost	300
Historical Cost of Goods Available for Sale	$840
Sales: One TV Set for	$550
Replacement Cost of TV Sets on:	
Date of Sale.	$320
At End of Period	$350

Income Statement

Sales	$550
Replacement Cost of Goods Sold	320
Operating Margin	$230
Holding Gains for Year[a] (see calculation below)	180
Economic Income	$410

Calculation of Holding Gains for Year

Replacement Cost at Time of Sale[a]	$ 320
Replacement Cost of Ending Inventory (2 × $350).	700
Total Replacement Cost	$1,020
Historical Cost of Goods Available for Sale	840
Total Holding Gains for Year	$ 180
Ending Inventory (two TV sets, $350 current cost each)	$ 700

[a]To give some recognition to the realization convention, the total holding gain might be divided into realized and unrealized portions. To do so requires knowing the acquisition cost of the TV set sold, and that requires a cost flow assumption. As Exhibit 8.7 indicates, if a LIFO assumption is made, then the realized holding gain is $20 and the realized income of $250 could be shown intermediate between the operating margin of $230 and the economic income of $410.

wealth during the period. They judge realization through arm's-length transactions to be unimportant. Economic income, including all holding gains, is $410 in the example.

In recent years, generally accepted accounting principles have required major corporations to disclose the current cost of goods sold computed at the time of sale and the current cost of ending inventory. Such information makes possible measuring operating margin and holding gains. Chapter 14 discusses current costs more fully.

Effects of Transactions Involving Inventory on the Statement of Changes in Financial Position

Inventory is a current asset and, hence, part of working capital. Thus all transactions involving inventory affect the operations section of the statement of changes in financial position. None of the transactions involving inventory discussed in this chapter requires special adjustments in deriving cash provided by operations, because insofar as they do not change cash they do change other working capital accounts.

Consider, for example, the adjusting entry to recognize cost of goods sold in a perpetual inventory system:

Cost of Goods Sold	12,000	
Inventory		12,000

Although this entry recognizes an expense that does not use cash, it does reduce the net balance in the Inventory account. Reductions in Inventory, like other reductions in current assets, appear in the operating section of the statement of changes in financial position as a source of cash. Refer to Exhibit 5.17 on page 201. The expense reduces income and cash from operations; the reduction in Inventory increases cash from operations. The total leaves cash from operations unchanged, which is correct because cash did not change.

Or, consider the entry recognizing the acquisition of inventory:

Inventory	140,000	
Accounts payable		140,000

The current asset for Inventory increases, absorbing cash from operations, but the current liability for Accounts Payable also increases, providing cash from operations. The net effect is that cash provided by operations does not change. Later, when the payable is paid, the entry is

Accounts Payable	140,000	
Cash		140,000

The current liability Accounts Payable declines, absorbing cash from operations.

Summary

Inventory measurements affect both the cost-of-goods-sold expense on the income statement for the period and the amount shown for the asset, inventory, on the balance sheet at the end of the period. The sum of the two must be equal to the beginning inventory plus the cost of purchases, at least in accounting based on acquisition costs and market transactions. The allocation between expense and asset depends primarily on the valuation basis and the cost flow assumption used.

Additional inventory problems include dealing with the inclusions (absorption and variable costing, with absorption costing required for financial reporting) and timing inventory computations (periodic and perpetual approaches).

Common business terminology often inhibits clear thinking about the four problems because the term "inventory method" is so often used. For example, the terms "absorption costing method," "acquisition cost method," "perpetual method," and "LIFO method" are often used, but these are not alternatives to one another. An inventory method results from a combination of choices, one from each of the following:

1. Inclusion: absorption or variable costing.
2. Basis: historical cost, lower of cost or market, current cost, or standard cost, among others.
3. Frequency of computations: periodic or perpetual.
4. Cost flow assumption: FIFO, LIFO, or weighted average.

Be prepared for the ambiguous use of the term "inventory method," realizing that one of several distinctions may be at issue.

Problem 1 for Self-Study

Exhibit 8.9 presents data on beginning amounts of, additions to, and withdrawals from the inventory of item X during June. Beginning inventory is assumed to be 100 units, costing $10 each, in all cases.[13]

a. Compute cost of goods sold and ending inventory using a FIFO cost flow assumption. Note that periodic and perpetual approaches give the same results.

Exhibit 8.9
Data for Illustration
of Inventory Calculations

Item X	Units	Unit Cost	Total Cost
Beginning Inventory, June 1	100	$10.00	$1,000
Purchases, June 7	400	11.00	4,400
Purchases, June 12	100	12.50	1,250
Total Goods Available for Sale at Cost	600		$6,650
Withdrawals, June 5	25		?
Withdrawals, June 10	10		?
Withdrawals, June 15	200		?
Withdrawals, June 25	260		?
Total Withdrawals During June	495		?
Ending Inventory, June 30	105		?
Replacement Cost per Unit, June 30		$13.60	

---

[13]To simplify the problem, beginning inventory is shown as having the same opening valuation of $1,000 under all cost flow assumptions. If costs had varied in the past, then the opening unit costs would differ across cost flow assumption.

b. Compute cost of goods sold and ending inventory using a LIFO cost flow assumption with a periodic inventory.

c. Compute cost of goods sold and ending inventory using a LIFO cost flow assumption with a perpetual inventory.

d. Compute cost of goods sold and ending inventory using a weighted-average cost flow assumption in a periodic inventory.

e. Compute cost of goods sold and ending inventory using a weighted-average cost flow assumption in a perpetual inventory.

Suggested Solution

a. See Exhibit 8.10. $\qquad$ **d.** See Exhibit 8.13.

b. See Exhibit 8.11. $\qquad$ **e.** See Exhibit 8.14.

c. See Exhibit 8.12.

Exhibit 8.10
Ending Inventory and Cost-of-Goods-Sold Computation
Using a Periodic Inventory and a FIFO Cost Flow Assumption

Item X

Ending Inventory Computation

100 units @ $12.50 (from June 12 purchase)	$1,250
5 units @ $11.00 (from June 7 purchase)	55
Ending Inventory, June 30	$1,305

Cost-of-Goods-Sold Computation

Cost of Goods Available for Sale	$6,650
Less Ending Inventory	1,305
Cost of Goods Sold	$5,345

Exhibit 8.11
Ending Inventory and Cost-of-Goods-Sold Computation
Using a Periodic Inventory and a LIFO Cost Flow Assumption

Item X

Ending Inventory Computation

100 units @ $10.00 (from beginning inventory)	$1,000
5 units @ $11.00 (from first purchase, June 7)	55
Ending Inventory at Cost	$1,055

Cost-of-Goods-Sold Computation

Cost of Goods Available for Sale	$6,650
Less Ending Inventory	1,055
Cost of Goods Sold	$5,595

Exhibit 8.12
Ending Inventory and
Cost-of-Goods-Sold Computation
Using a Perpetual Inventory
and a LIFO Cost Flow Assumption

Item X

Cost-of-Goods-Sold Computation

Date	Received			Issued			Balance		
	Units	Cost	Amount	Units	Cost	Amount	Units	Cost	Amount
6/1							100	$10.00	$1,000
6/5				25	$10.00	$ 250	75	10.00	750
6/7	400	$11.00	$4,400				75	10.00	750
							400	11.00	4,400
6/10				10	11.00	110	75	10.00	750
							390	11.00	4,290
6/12	100	12.50	1,250				75	10.00	750
							390	11.00	4,290
							100	12.50	1,250
6/15				100	12.50	1,250	75	10.00	750
				100	11.00	1,100	290	11.00	3,190
6/25				260	11.00	2,860	75	10.00	750
							30	11.00	330
Cost of Goods Sold						$5,570			

Ending Inventory Computation

75 units @ $10.00	$ 750
30 units @ $11.00	330
Ending Inventory	$1,080

Alternative Cost-of-Goods-Sold Computation

Cost of Goods Available for Sale	$6,650
Less Ending Inventory	1,080
Cost of Goods Sold	$5,570

Exhibit 8.13
Ending Inventory and Cost-of-Goods-Sold Computation
Using Periodic Inventory and a
Weighted-Average Cost Flow Assumption

Ending Inventory Computation

6/1	100 units @ $10.00	$1,000
6/7	400 units @ $11.00	4,400
6/12	100 units @ $12.50	1,250
	600 units @ $11.08 (= $6,650/600).	$6,650
Ending Inventory (105 units @ $11.08)		$1,163

Cost-of-Goods-Sold Computation

Cost of Goods Available for Sale	$6,650
Less Ending Inventory	1,163
Cost of Goods Sold	$5,487[a]

[a]Because of rounding error, this number is *not* 495 (= 600 − 105) units × $11.08 = $5,485. In general, the weighted-average unit price should be applied either to ending inventory or to cost of goods sold. After being applied to one, the other is found from the inventory equation.

Exhibit 8.14
Ending Inventory and Cost-of-Goods-Sold Computation
Using a Perpetual Inventory and a
Moving-Average Cost Flow Assumption

Item X

Cost-of-Goods-Sold and Ending Inventory Computation

	Received			Issued			Balance		
Date	Units	Cost	Amount	Units	Cost	Amount	Units	Total Cost	Unit Cost[a]
6/1							100	$1,000	$10.00
6/5				25	$10.00	$ 250	75	750	10.00
6/7	400	$11.00	$4,400				475	5,150	10.84
6/10				10	10.84	108	465	5,042	10.84
6/12	100	12.50	1,250				565	6,292	11.14
6/15				200	11.14	2,228	365	4,064	11.13[b]
6/25				260	11.13	2,894	105	1,170	11.14
Cost of Goods Sold						$5,480			

Alternative Cost-of-Goods-Sold Computation

Cost of Goods Available for Sale	$6,650
Less Ending Inventory	1,170
Cost of Goods Sold	$5,480

[a]Unit cost = total cost/units.
[b]Note how the rounding effects change the unit cost even though no new units were acquired.

Exhibit 8.15
Reporting of Operating Margins
and Holding Gains for Item X

	Cost Flow Assumption			
	FIFO		LIFO	
Periodic Inventory Method				
Sales Revenue from Item X (495 × $15.00). . . .	$7,425		$7,425	
Less Replacement Cost of Goods Sold [(25 × $10.00) + (10 × $11.00) + (460 × $12.50)]	6,110		6,110	
Operating Margin on Sales of Item X.		$1,315		$1,315
Realized Holding Gain on Item X:				
Replacement Cost of Goods Sold	$6,110		$6,110	
Less Acquisition Cost of Goods Sold (FIFO—Exhibit 8.10; LIFO—Exhibit 8.11). . . .	5,345		5,595	
Realized Holding Gain on Item X		765		515
Conventionally Reported Gross Margin		$2,080		$1,830
Unrealized Holding Gain on Item X:				
Replacement Cost of Ending Inventory (105 × $13.60; see Exhibit 8.9)	$1,428		$1,428	
Less Acquisition Cost of Ending Inventory (FIFO—Exhibit 8.10; LIFO—Exhibit 8.11). . . .	1,305		1,055	
Unrealized Holding Gain on Item X		123		373
Economic Profit on Sales and Holding Inventory of Item X.		$2,203		$2,203

Problem 2 for Self-Study

Refer to the data for item X in Exhibits 8.10 and 8.11, showing cost of goods sold and ending inventory in a periodic inventory, using FIFO and LIFO cost flow assumptions, respectively. Assume that the 495 units withdrawn from inventory were sold for $15 each, $7,425 in total. Construct a schedule that both separates operating margin from holding gains and separates *realized* holding gains from *unrealized* holding gains. Show the results for FIFO and LIFO in parallel columns. The total of operating margin and realized holding gain should be equal to the gross margin reported in historical cost income statements. The total of operating margin and all holding gains should be the same for LIFO as for FIFO.

Suggested Solution

See Exhibit 8.15.

Problem 3 for Self-Study

American Steel Company uses a LIFO cost flow assumption for inventories. Its year-end financial statements show the following amounts.

Balance Sheet Inventories:

Beginning of Year	$1,500,000
End of Year.	$1,700,000

Income Statement Amounts:

Cost of Goods Sold	$8,000,000
Income Before Taxes	800,000
Net Income (40 percent tax rate)	480,000

Supplementary Information in Notes on Inventory Provide Data on the Excess of FIFO Cost over Reported LIFO Cost of Inventory:

Beginning of Year	$1,650,000
End of Year.	$1,850,000

a. Compute the inventory turnover ratio from the published financial statements based on LIFO cost flow.

b. Compute the income before taxes assuming FIFO cost flow.

c. Compute the net income assuming FIFO cost flow and an income tax rate of 40 percent.

d. Compute the inventory turnover ratio computed from the financial statements as they would appear using FIFO cost flow.

Suggested Solution

a. Inventory Turnover $= \dfrac{\text{Cost of Goods Sold}}{\text{Average Inventory During Year}}$

$$= \dfrac{\$8,000,000}{.5(\$1,500,000 + \$1,700,000)}$$

$$= 5 \text{ times per year.}$$

b. Pretax income would be larger by the amount that cost of goods sold would be smaller. Cost of goods sold would be smaller by $200,000 = \$1,850,000 - \$1,650,000$. See Exhibit 8.6.

c. Net income would be larger by the amount found in part **b** multiplied by (1 − income tax rate) = $200,000 \times .60 = \$120,000$.

d. $\dfrac{\text{Inventory}}{\text{Turnover}} = \dfrac{\text{Cost of Goods Sold}}{\text{Average Inventory During Year}}$

$$= \dfrac{\$8,000,000 - \$200,000}{.5[(\$1,500,000 + \$1,650,000) + (\$1,700,000 + \$1,850,000)]}$$

$$= \dfrac{\$7,800,000}{\$3,350,000}$$

$$= 2.33 \text{ times per year.}$$

Questions, Exercises, Problems and Cases

Questions

1. Review the meaning of the following concepts or terms discussed in this chapter.

a.	Inventory (as both a noun and a verb).	**m.**	Standard cost.
b.	Inventory equation.	**n.**	Absorption (full) costing.
c.	Purchases.	**o.**	Variable (direct) costing.
d.	Purchase returns.	**p.**	Cost flow assumption.
e.	Purchase discounts.	**q.**	FIFO.
f.	Shrinkages.	**r.**	LIFO.
g.	Periodic inventory.	**s.**	Weighted average.
h.	Perpetual inventory.	**t.**	LIFO inventory layer contrasted to LIFO reserve.
i.	Acquisition cost basis.	**u.**	LIFO conformity.
j.	Replacement cost.	**v.**	Realized holding gain.
k.	Net realizable value.	**w.**	Unrealized holding gain.
l.	Lower-of-cost-or-market basis.	**x.**	Inventory profit.

2. Under what circumstances would the perpetual and periodic inventory systems both yield the same inventory amount if the weighted-average flow assumption were used?

3. During a period of rising prices, will the FIFO or LIFO cost flow assumption result in the higher ending inventory amount? The lower inventory amount? Assume no changes in physical quantities during the period.

4. Refer to the preceding question. Which cost flow assumption will result in the higher ending inventory amount during a period of declining prices? The lower inventory amount?

5. a. During a period of rising prices, will a FIFO or LIFO cost flow assumption result in the higher cost of goods sold? The lower cost of goods sold? Assume no changes in physical quantities during the period.

b. Which cost flow assumption, LIFO or FIFO, will result in the higher cost of goods sold during a period of declining prices? The lower cost of goods sold?

6. ''Cost flow assumptions for inventory are required only because specific identification of items sold is costly. Specific identification is theoretically superior to any cost flow assumption and eliminates the possibility for income manipulation available with some cost flow assumptions.''
Comment.

7. Assume that a steel manufacturer and a retailing firm have identical sales and income and that the costs of their purchased inputs of goods and services increase at the same rate. The steel company has inventory turnover of about four times per year, whereas the retailer has inventory turnover of about 10 times per year.

Which of the two firms is more likely to benefit from switching from FIFO to LIFO? Explain.

8. "LIFO provides a more meaningful income statement than FIFO, even though it provides a less meaningful balance sheet."

Does it ever? Does it always?

9. Assume that the cost basis for inventory is changed from historical cost to current cost, that current costs exceed historical costs at the end of the year of change, and that all year-end inventory is sold during the following year. Ignore income tax effects.

What will be the impact of the change on net income for the year of change? On income for the following year? On total income over the 2 years?

10. Would you expect to find a periodic or perpetual inventory system used in each of the following situations?

    a. The greeting card department of a retail store.
    b. The fur coat department of a retail store.
    c. Supplies storeroom for an automated production line.
    d. Automobile dealership.
    e. Wholesale dealer in bulk salad oil.
    f. Grocery store.
    g. College bookstore.
    h. Diamond ring department of a jewelry store.
    i. Ballpoint pen department of a jewelry store.

11. A noted accountant once claimed that firms which use a LIFO cost flow assumption will find that historical cost of goods sold is *greater than* replacement cost of goods sold computed as of the time of sale. Under what circumstances is this assertion likely to be true? (*Hint:* Compare the effects of periodic and perpetual approaches on LIFO cost of goods sold.) Do you agree that the assertion is likely to be true?

Exercises

12. *Journal entries for periodic and perpetual inventories.* Goods that cost $1,500 are sold for $2,000 cash. Present the normal journal entries at the time of the sale:

    a. When a periodic inventory is used.
    b. When a perpetual inventory is used.

13. *Computations involving different cost flow assumptions.* The inventory at September 1 and the purchases during September of Hanna Company's raw material were as follows:

9/1 Inventory	1,000 lb	$ 4,500
9/5 Purchased	3,000 lb	13,500
9/14 Purchased	3,500 lb	17,500
9/27 Purchased	3,000 lb	16,500
9/29 Purchased	1,000 lb	8,000

The inventory at September 30 is 1,800 lb.

Assume a periodic inventory system. Compute the cost of the inventory on September 30 under each of the following cost flow assumptions:
   a. FIFO.
   b. Weighted average.
   c. LIFO.

14. *Compute acquisition cost of inventory and record sales transaction using perpetual inventory.* Ducru Company ordered from an overseas supplier 10,000 shirts that had a list price of $12 each, requesting the normal trade discount. The invoice arrived showing a discount of 40 percent from list price. Ducru Company paid its customs broker $750 for taxes and paid a trucking company $250 to deliver the goods. Later, it sold 1,000 shirts for $12 each on account. Ducru Company uses a perpetual inventory.

Prepare journal entries to record the sales transaction.

15. *Over long enough time spans, income is cash-in less cash-out; cost flow assumptions.* Gazin Company was in business for 4 years. Exhibit 8.16 shows its purchases and sales during that 4-year period. Ignore income taxes.

Exhibit 8.16
GAZIN COMPANY
Purchases and Sales
(Exercise 15)

	Purchases		Sales	
	Units	Unit Cost	Units	Unit Price
Year 1	12,000	$10	9,000	$15
Year 2	11,000	11	10,000	17
Year 3	10,000	12	11,000	19
Year 4	9,000	13	12,000	21
Totals	42,000		42,000	

   a. Compute income for each of the 4 years assuming FIFO cost flow.
   b. Compute income for each of the 4 years assuming LIFO cost flow.
   c. Compare total income over the 4-year period. Does the cost flow assumption matter?

16. *Over long enough time spans, income is cash-in less cash-out; cost basis for inventory.* The Sales Company began business on January 1, Year 1. Information concerning merchandise inventories, purchases, and sales for the first 3 years of operations follows:

	Year 1	Year 2	Year 3
Sales	$300,000	$330,000	$450,000
Purchases	280,000	260,000	350,000

continued

	Year 1	Year 2	Year 3
Inventories, Dec. 31:			
At cost	80,000	95,000	95,000
At market	75,000	80,000	100,000

    a. Compute the gross margin on sales (sales minus cost of goods sold) for each year, using the lower-of-cost-or-market basis in valuing inventories.

    b. Compute the gross margin on sales (sales minus cost of goods sold) for each year, using the acquisition cost basis in valuing inventories.

    c. Indicate your conclusion whether the lower-of-cost-or-market basis of valuing inventories is "conservative."

17. *When goods available for sale exceed sales, income can be manipulated, even when specific identification is used.* Langoa Company has 300 identical TV sets available for sale during December, when it expects to sell 200 sets for $500 each. These TV sets were acquired as follows: 100 in June for $200 each, 100 in August for $300 each, and 100 in November for $250 each. Assume that sales for December are 200 units at $500 each.

    a. Compute gross margin for December assuming FIFO.

    b. Compute gross margin for December assuming specific identification of sales and sets sold to minimize reported income for tax purposes.

    c. Compute gross margin for December assuming specific identification of sales and sets sold to maximize reported income, so as to increase the store manager's profit-sharing bonus for the year.

18. *Computations involving cost flow assumptions and periodic or perpetual approaches.* The following information concerning Arpesfeld Company's inventory of raw materials is available:

Nov. 2 Inventory	4,000 lb @ $5
9 Issued	3,000 lb
16 Purchased	7,000 lb @ $6
23 Issued	3,000 lb
30 Issued	3,000 lb

Compute the cost of goods sold and the cost of ending inventory on November 30 for each of the following combinations of inventory systems and cost flow assumptions.

    a. Periodic FIFO.

    b. Periodic weighted average.

    c. Periodic LIFO.

    d. Perpetual FIFO.

    e. Perpetual weighted average.

    f. Perpetual LIFO.

19. *Computing cost of goods sold under various treatments of cost flows with periodic and perpetual systems.* The Central Supply Company has in its inventory on May 1 three units of item K, all purchased on the same date at a price of $60 per unit. Information relative to item K is as follows:

Date	Explanation	Units	Unit Cost	Tag Number
May 1	Inventory	3	$60	K–515,516,517
3	Purchase	2	65	K–518,519
12	Sale	3		K–515,518,519
19	Purchase	2	76	K–520,521
25	Sale	1		K–516

Compute the cost of units sold in accordance with the following:
  a. Specific identification of units sold.
  b. FIFO cost flow assumption and periodic inventory system.
  c. FIFO cost flow assumption and perpetual inventory system.
  d. LIFO cost flow assumption and periodic inventory system.
  e. LIFO cost flow assumption and perpetual inventory system.
  f. Weighted-average cost flow assumption and perpetual inventory system.
  g. Weighted-average cost flow assumption and periodic inventory system.

20. *LIFO provides opportunity for income manipulation.* Lagrange Company began the year with 20,000 units of product on hand that cost $10 each. During the year, it produced another 30,000 units at a cost of $18 each. Sales for the year were expected to total 50,000 units. During November, the company had to make a decision about production for the remainder of the year. No additional units need be produced this year beyond the 30,000 units already produced. Up to 60,000 additional units could be produced; the cost would be $22 per unit regardless of the quantity produced. The company uses a periodic LIFO inventory. Assume that sales are 50,000 units for the year at an average price of $25 per unit.
  a. What production for the remainder of the year gives the largest cost of goods sold for the year? What is that cost of goods sold?
  b. What production for the remainder of the year gives the smallest cost of goods sold for the year? What is that cost of goods sold?
  c. Compare the gross margins implied by the two production plans devised in the preceding parts.

21. *Calculations combining cost basis and cost flow assumptions.* The Sanlex Company started the year with no inventories on hand. It manufactured two batches of inventory, 100 units each, which were identical except that the variable costs of producing the first batch were $120 and the variable costs of producing the second batch were $200 because of rising prices. By the end of the year, Sanlex Company had sold 75 units from the first batch for $300 and none of the second batch. The ending inventory had a market value of $305. Total fixed manufacturing costs for the year were $160. Under the absorption costing procedure, $100 of fixed manufacturing costs allocated to units produced remained in inventory at the close of the year. Selling and administrative expenses for the year were $40.

Prepare a statement of pretax income for the Sanlex Company for the year under each of the following sets of assumptions.

   a. FIFO, acquisition cost basis.
   b. LIFO, acquisition cost basis.
   c. FIFO, lower-of-cost-or-market basis.

22. *Analysis of annual report; usage of LIFO.* The notes to the financial statements in a recent report of Sears, Roebuck and Company contain the following statement.

> If the physical quantity of goods in inventory at [year-end and the beginning of the year] . . . were to be replaced, the estimated expenditures of funds required would exceed the amounts reported by approximately $670 million and $440 million, respectively.

Sears uses LIFO.

   a. How much higher or lower would Sears' pretax reported income have been if its inventories had been valued at current costs, rather than with a LIFO cost flow assumption?
   b. Sears reported $606 million net income for the year. Assume tax expense equal to 46 percent of pretax income. By what percentage would Sears' net income increase if a FIFO flow assumption had been used?

23. *Effects on funds statement.* Indicate the effect on Cash Provided by Operations of the following independent transactions. Include the effects of income taxes, assuming a rate of 40 percent of pretax income, that the accounting methods used on the tax return are the same as on the financial statements, and that taxes have been paid in cash.

   a. A firm using the lower-of-cost-or-market basis for inventories writes ending inventory down by $100,000.
   b. A firm has been using FIFO. It switches to LIFO at the end of the current year and finds that the cost of goods sold is $200,000 larger than it would have been under FIFO.

24. *Reconstructing financial statement data from information on effects of liquidations of LIFO layers.* The inventory footnote to the annual report of the Alcher Company reads in part as follows:

> Because of continuing high demand throughout the year, inventories were unavoidably reduced and could not be replaced. Under the LIFO system of accounting, used for many years by Alcher Company, the net effect of all the inventory changes was to increase pretax income by $600,000 over what it would have been had inventories been maintained at their physical levels at the start of the year.

The price of Alcher Company's merchandise purchases was $18 per unit during the year, after having risen erratically over past years. Alcher Company uses a periodic inventory method. Alcher Company's inventory positions at the beginning and end of the year are summarized as follows:

Date	Physical Count of Inventory	LIFO Cost of Inventory
January 1	300,000 units	$?
December 31	200,000 units	$2,600,000

    a. What was the average cost per unit of the 100,000 units removed from the January 1 LIFO inventory?

    b. What was the January 1 LIFO cost of inventory?

25. *Separating operating margin from holding gains.* On January 1, the merchandise inventory of Revsine Appliance Store consisted of 1,000 units acquired for $450 each. During the year, 2,500 additional units were acquired at an average price of $600 each while 2,300 units were sold for $900 each. The replacement cost of these units at the time they were sold averaged $600 during the year. The replacement cost of units on December 31 was $750 per unit.

    a. Calculate cost of goods sold under both FIFO and LIFO cost flow assumptions.

    b. Prepare partial statements of income showing gross margin on sales as revenues less cost of goods sold with both FIFO and LIFO cost flow assumptions.

    c. Prepare partial income statements separating the gross margin on sales into operating margins and realized holding gains under both FIFO and LIFO.

    d. Append to the bottom of the statements prepared in part **c** a statement showing the amount of unrealized holding gains and the total of realized income plus unrealized holding gains.

    e. If you did the above steps correctly, the totals in part **d** are the same for both FIFO and LIFO. Is this equality a coincidence? Why or why not?

Problems and Cases

26. *Effect of inventory errors.* On December 30, Year 1, merchandise amounting to $1,000 was received by the Warren Company and was counted in its December 31 listing of all inventory items on hand. The invoice was not received until January 4, Year 2, at which time the acquisition was recorded as a Year 2 acquisition. The acquisition should have been recorded for Year 1. Assume that the error was not ever discovered by the firm. Warren Company uses a periodic inventory system. Indicate the effect (overstatement, understatement, none) on each of the following amounts. Ignore income taxes.

    a. Inventory, 12/31/Year 1.

    b. Inventory, 12/31/Year 2.

    c. Cost of goods sold, Year 1.

    d. Cost of goods sold, Year 2.

    e. Net income, Year 1.

    f. Net income, Year 2.

      g. Accounts payable, 12/31/Year 1.
      h. Accounts payable, 12/31/Year 2.
      i. Retained earnings, 12/31/Year 2.

27. *Analysis of adjunct and contra accounts used for purchases and sales.* The accounts listed below might appear in the records of a retail store. Their use is never required, but accounts such as these often provide details about purchase activity useful to management. From the name of the account and your understanding of the accounting for purchase and sales, indicate:

    a. Whether the account is a permanent account (to appear as such on the balance sheet) or a temporary account (to be closed at the end of the accounting period).
    b. The normal balance, debit or credit, in the account. If the account is a temporary one, give the normal balance prior to closing.
    c. If the account is a temporary one, the kind of account it is closed to—balance sheet asset, balance sheet liability, balance sheet owners' equity through a revenue account, or balance sheet owners' equity through an expense (or revenue contra) account.

      (1) Merchandise Purchases.
      (2) Merchandise Purchase Allowances.
      (3) Merchandise Purchase Returns.
      (4) Purchase Returns.
      (5) Sales Tax on Purchases.
      (6) Freight-in on Purchases.
      (7) Sales Allowances.
      (8) Allowance for Sales Discounts.
      (9) Federal Excise Taxes Payable on Sales.

    (The next three items should not be attempted until Problem 28 has been read.)

      (10) Purchase Discounts.
      (11) Purchase Discounts Taken.
      (12) Purchase Discounts Lost.

28. *Gross and net price methods for treating purchase discounts.* The chapter mentions two alternatives for treating discounts on merchandise purchases often used in practice: (1) the gross price method, which recognizes the amount of discounts taken on payments made during the period, without regard to the period of purchase, and (2) the net price method, which deducts all discounts made available from the gross purchase invoice prices at the time of purchases. This problem explains the two methods.

Alternative 1: Gross Price Method The gross price method of accounting for purchases records invoices at the gross price and accumulates the amount of discounts taken on payments made. Suppose that goods with a gross invoice price of $1,000 are purchased, 2/10, net/30. (That is, a 2 percent discount from invoice price is offered if payment is made within 10 days and the full invoice price is due, in any case, within 30 days.) The entries to record the purchase and the payment (1) under the assumption that the payment is made in time to take the discount, and (2) under the assumption that the payment is too late to take advantage of the discount, are as follows:

Gross Price Method	(1) Discount Taken		(2) Discount Not Taken	
Purchases (or Inventory)	1,000		1,000	
Accounts Payable		1,000		1,000
To record purchase.				
Accounts Payable	1,000		1,000	
Cash		980		1,000
Purchase Discounts (or Inventory)		20		—
To record payment.				

The balance in the Purchase Discounts account is deducted from the balance in the Purchases account in calculating net purchases for a period. Such a deduction approximates the results achieved by treating purchase discounts as a reduction in purchase price at the time of purchase. It is only an approximation because the total adjustment includes discounts taken on payments made this period, without regard to the period of purchase.

An accurate adjustment would require eliminating the discounts taken related to purchases of previous periods while including the amount of discounts available at the end of the accounting period that are expected to be taken during the following period. This refinement in the treatment of purchase discounts is seldom employed in practice.

Alternative 2: Net Price Method In recording purchases, the purchase discount is deducted from the gross purchase price immediately upon receipt of the invoice, and the net invoice price is used in the entries. The example used previously of a $1,000 invoice price for goods subject to a 2 percent cash discount would be recorded as follows under the net price method:

Net Price Method	(1) Discount Taken		(2) Discount Not Taken	
Purchases (or Inventory)	980		980	
Accounts Payable		980		980
To record purchase.				
Accounts Payable	980		980	
Purchase Discounts Lost		—		20
Cash		980		1,000
To record payment.				

The balance in the Purchase Discounts Lost account could be added to the cost of the merchandise purchased and, therefore, viewed as an additional component of goods available for sale. Most accountants believe, however, that discounts lost should be shown as a general operating expense rather than as an addition to the cost of purchases, because lost discounts may indicate an inefficient office force or inadequate financing. In this text, we treat purchase discounts lost as an expense unless an explicit contrary statement is made.

a. Attempt to decide which of these two alternatives is preferable and why. You might find working part **b**, below, helpful in making your decision.

b. Prepare a journal form with two pairs of columns, one headed Net Price Method and the other headed Gross Price Method. Using this journal form, show summary entries for the following events in the history of Evans and Foster, furniture manufacturers.

(1) During the first year of operations, materials with a gross invoice price of $60,000 are purchased. All invoices are subject to a 2 percent cash discount if paid within 10 days.

(2) Payments to creditors during the year amount to $53,000, settling $54,000 of accounts payable at gross prices.

(3) Of the $6,000, gross, in unpaid accounts at the end of the year, the discount time has expired on one invoice amounting to $400. It is expected that all other discounts will be taken. This expectation is reflected in the year-end adjustment.

(4) During the first few days of the next period, all invoices are paid in accordance with expectations.

29. *Gross and net price methods for recording purchase discounts.* (This problem should not be attempted until Problem 28 has been read.) The following are selected transactions of the Skousen Appliance Store:

(1) A shipment of refrigerators is received from the Standard Electric Company, $15,000. Terms 2/30, n/60.

(2) Part of the shipment of (1) is returned. The gross invoice price of the returned goods is $1,200, and a credit memorandum for this amount is received from the Standard Electric Company.

(3) The invoice of the Standard Electric Company is paid in time to take the discount.

   a. Give entries on the books of the Skousen Appliance Store, assuming that the net price method is used.

   b. Give entries on the books of the Skousen Appliance Store, assuming that the gross price method is used.

30. *Fundamentals of the gross margin method for approximating inventory amounts.* The merchandise inventory of Parks Store was destroyed by fire on July 4. The accounting records were saved and provided the following information:

Cost of Merchandise Inventory on Hand, January 1	$45,000
Purchases of Merchandise, January 1 to July 4	125,000
Sales, January 1 to July 4	180,000

The average retail markup over cost of the goods sold during the year before the fire was 50 percent of the acquisition cost. That is, selling price equals 150 percent of cost.

a. Estimate the cost of the goods on hand at the time of the fire.
b. Give the journal entry to record the loss, assuming that it was uninsured.
c. Give the journal entry to record the loss, assuming that all goods were fully insured for their acquisition cost.

31. *Fundamentals of the retail inventory method for approximating inventory amounts.* Refer to the data in the preceding problem. Assume that the store owner does not know the average retail markup over cost for the destroyed goods. The accounting records show that the total sales revenue during the 4 years preceding the fire amounted to $1,000,000 and the total cost of goods sold over the same period was $650,000.

a. Assume that the ratio of sales prices to cost of goods sold for the last 4 years reflects this year's operations as well. Estimate the cost of the goods destroyed in the fire.
b. Assume the same facts as above, except that the $1,000,000 represents the original selling price of the goods sold during the last 4 years. Certain goods were marked down before sale so that the actual sales revenue was only $975,000. Assuming that the same percentage of goods were marked down by the same price percentage during the first 6 months of this year as in the previous 4 years, estimate the cost of the goods destroyed by the fire.

32. *Detailed comparison of various choices for inventory accounting.* The Harrison Corporation was organized and began retailing operations on January 1, Year 1. Purchases of merchandise inventory during Year 1 and Year 2 were as follows:

	Quantity Purchased	Unit Price	Acquisition Cost
1/10/Year 1	1,000	$10	$10,000
6/30/Year 1	400	15	6,000
10/20/Year 1	200	16	3,200
Total Year 1	1,600		$19,200

	Quantity Purchased	Unit Price	Acquisition Cost
2/18/Year 2	300	$18	$ 5,400
7/15/Year 2	100	20	2,000
12/15/Year 2	500	22	11,000
Total Year 2	900		$18,400

The number of units sold during Year 1 and Year 2 was 900 units and 1,100 units, respectively. Harrison Corporation uses a periodic inventory system.

    a. Calculate the cost of goods sold during Year 1 under the FIFO cost flow assumption.

    b. Calculate the cost of goods sold during Year 1 under the LIFO cost flow assumption.

    c. Calculate the cost of goods sold during Year 1 under the weighted-average cost flow assumption.

    d. Calculate the cost of goods sold during Year 2 under the FIFO cost flow assumption.

    e. Calculate the cost of goods sold during Year 2 under the LIFO cost flow assumption.

    f. Calculate the cost of goods sold during Year 2 under the weighted-average cost flow assumption.

    g. For the 2 years taken as a whole, will FIFO or LIFO result in reporting the larger net income? What is the difference in net income for the 2-year period under FIFO as compared to LIFO? Assume an income tax rate of 40 percent for both years.

    h. Which method, LIFO or FIFO, should Harrison Corporation probably prefer and why?

33. *Continuation of preceding problem introducing current cost concepts.* (This problem should not be attempted until Problem 32 has been done.) Assume the same data for the Harrison Corporation as given in the previous problem. In addition, assume the following:

Selling Price per Unit:	
Year 1	$25
Year 2	30
Average Current Replacement Cost:	
Year 1	$15
Year 2	20
Current Replacement Cost:	
December 31, Year 1	$17
December 31, Year 2	22

    a. Prepare an analysis for Year 1 that identifies operating margins, realized holding gains and losses, and unrealized holding gains and losses for the FIFO, LIFO, and weighted-average cost flow assumptions.

    b. Repeat part **a** for Year 2.

    c. Demonstrate that over the 2-year period, the income plus holding gains before taxes of Harrison Corporation are independent of the cost flow assumption.

34. *Impact on financial statements of the choice between a FIFO and a LIFO flow assumption.* Take 12 pieces of paper and mark each one with a number between 1 and 12 inclusive. Sort the pieces of paper into a pile with the numbers in consecutive order facing up, so that number 1 is on top and number 12 is on bottom. These

12 pieces of paper are to represent 12 identical units of merchandise purchased over three periods at prices increasing from $1 to $12. Assume that four of the units are purchased each period for three periods, that three units are sold each period, and that a periodic inventory system is used.

   a. Compute the cost-of-goods-sold and ending inventory amounts for each of the three periods under a FIFO flow assumption.

   b. Compute the cost-of-goods-sold and ending inventory amounts for each of the three periods under a LIFO flow assumption.

   c. Re-sort the 12 pieces of paper into decreasing order to represent declining prices for successive purchases. Compute the cost-of-goods-sold and ending inventory amounts for each of the three periods under a FIFO flow assumption.

   d. Repeat part **c** using a LIFO flow assumption.

   e. Convince yourself that the following are all true statements.

   (1) In periods of rising prices and increasing physical inventories, FIFO implies higher reported income than does LIFO.

   (2) In periods of declining prices and increasing physical inventories, LIFO implies higher reported income than does FIFO.

   (3) Under FIFO, current prices are reported on the balance sheet and old prices are reported on the income statement.

   (4) Under LIFO, current prices are reported on the income statement and very old prices are reported on the balance sheet.

   (5) In periods of rising prices and increasing physical inventories, the difference between FIFO and LIFO balance sheet amounts for inventory at the end of each period after the first one is larger than the differences between FIFO and LIFO reported net income for each period after the first one.

   f. Assume that in period 4, only one unit (number 13) is purchased for $13, but three are sold. What additional "truth" can you deduce from comparing LIFO and FIFO cost of goods sold when physical quantities are declining and prices are rising?

   g. The LIFO portion of Figure 8.1 represents a periodic inventory. In this part of the question, assume that in each period the first item is acquired before any sales occur. Then one item is sold; then the two items are purchased; then one more item is sold; then the last purchase is made and the last sale occurs. (If P represents purchase and S represents sale, the events of each period are PSPPSPS.) Draw a figure similar to those in Figure 8.1 to represent a LIFO cost flow assumption coupled with a perpetual inventory system. Convince yourself that in times of rising prices the LIFO cost-of-goods-sold figure with a periodic inventory exceeds LIFO cost of goods sold computed with a perpetual inventory.

35. *Exploring the relation between replacement cost of goods sold and historical LIFO cost of goods sold.* The points to grasp in this problem are as follows:

(1) LIFO cost of goods sold is generally larger in a periodic inventory than in a perpetual inventory.

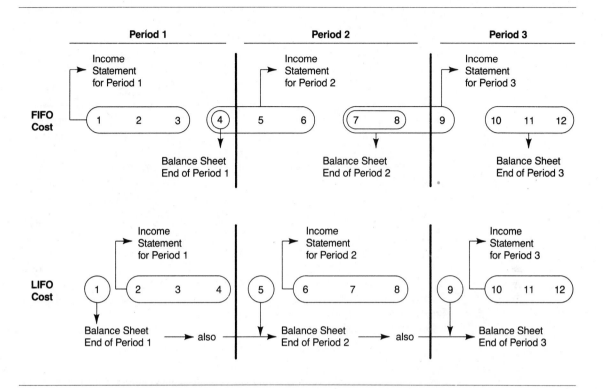

Figure 8.1 To Aid in Understanding Problem 34

(2) LIFO cost of goods sold for most companies is insignificantly different from replacement cost of goods sold using replacement costs as of the time of sale.

(3) Historical LIFO cost of goods sold in a periodic inventory is likely to be larger (although not significantly) than the replacement cost of goods sold using replacement cost at the time of sale.

The data in Exhibit 8.17 are hypothetical. They are constructed from ratios of an actual retailing firm selling grocery products. Sales revenue for the year is $2,820,000. All expenses (including income taxes) other than cost of goods sold are $144,000 for the year. Exhibit 8.17 shows cost of goods available for sale. The costs of the grocery items for this company increase during the year at a steady rate of about 1 percent per month. The company starts the year with an inventory equal to $1\frac{1}{2}$ months' sales. These items were acquired at the end of December of Year 1 for $300,000. At the end of each month during Year 2, the firm is assumed to acquire inventory in physical quantities equal to the next month's sales requirements. We assume that all sales occur at mid-month during each month and that all purchases occur at the end of a month to be sold during the next month. (These artificial assumptions capture the reality of a firm acquiring inventory on average $\frac{1}{2}$ month before it is sold and an inventory turnover rate of about eight times per year.) Identical physical quantities are purchased and sold each month.

Exhibit 8.17
Data for Problem 35

	Replacement Cost of Goods Measured at	
	Sales Dates (mid-month)	Purchases Dates (end of month)
December Year 1	—	$ 300,000
January Year 2	$ 201,000	202,000
February Year 2	203,000	204,000
March Year 2	205,000	206,000
April Year 2	207,000	208,000
May Year 2	209,000	210,000
June Year 2	211,000	212,000
July Year 2	213,000	214,000
August Year 2	215,000	216,000
September Year 2	217,000	218,000
October Year 2	219,000	220,000
November Year 2	221,000	222,000
December Year 2	223,000	224,000
Replacement Cost of Goods Sold at Times of Sale .	$2,544,000	
Cost of Goods Available for Sale		$2,856,000

Exhibit 8.17 shows the actual cost of the items purchased at the end of each month and the replacement cost of those items if they had been acquired at mid-month.

At the end of the year, ending physical inventory is equal in amount to $1\frac{1}{2}$ months' sales, which is the same as the physical quantity on hand at the start of the year.

   a. Compute LIFO historical cost of goods sold and net income for Year 2 using a periodic inventory system.

   b. Compute LIFO historical cost of goods sold and net income for Year 2 using a perpetual inventory system.

   c. Compute net income for Year 2 using replacement cost of goods sold at the time of sale.

   d. What is the percentage difference between the largest and smallest cost-of-goods-sold figures computed in the preceding 3 parts?

   e. What is the percentage error in using LIFO costs of goods sold to approximate replacement cost of goods sold? (Compute percentage errors for both LIFO periodic and LIFO perpetual calculations.)

   f. Would you expect that most companies that use LIFO for tax purposes do so with a periodic inventory system or with a perpetual inventory system? Why?

36. *Comparing LIFO and FIFO with declines in inventory quantities.* The LIFO Company and the FIFO Company both manufacture paper and cardboard products. Prices of timber, paper pulp, and finished paper products have generally increased by about 5 percent per year through the *start of this year*. Inventory data for the beginning and end of the year are shown below:

	Inventory Amounts	
	January 1	December 31
LIFO Company Inventory (last-in, first-out; historical cost)	$19,695,000	$15,870,000
FIFO Company Inventory (first-in, first-out; lower of cost or market)	46,284,000	38,250,000

Income statements for the two companies for the year ending December 31 are as follows:

	LIFO Company	FIFO Company
Sales	$57,000,000	$129,000,000
Expenses:		
Cost of Goods Sold	$44,580,000	$108,000,000
Depreciation	5,400,000	12,000,000
General Expenses	2,220,000	5,400,000
Income Taxes (40 percent of pretax income)	1,920,000	1,440,000
Total Expenses	$54,120,000	$126,840,000
Net Income	$ 2,880,000	$ 2,160,000

    a. Assuming that the prices for timber, paper pulp, and finished paper had remained unchanged during the year, how would the two companies' respective inventory choices affect the interpretation of their financial statements for the year?

    b. How would the answer to part **a** differ if prices at the end of the year had been lower than at the beginning of the year?

    c. How would the answer to part **a** differ if prices at the end of the year had been higher than at the beginning of the year?

37. *LIFO layers influence purchasing behavior and provide opportunity for income manipulation.* The Wilson Company sells chemical compounds made from expensium. The company has used a LIFO inventory flow assumption for many years. The inventory of expensium on December 31, 1984, consisted of 4,000 lb from 1975 through 1981 at prices ranging from $30 to $52 per pound. Exhibit 8.18 shows the layers of 1984 ending inventory.

Expensium costs $62 per pound during 1985, but the purchasing agent expects its price to fall back to $52 per pound in 1986. Sales for 1985 require 7,000 lb of expensium. Wilson Company wants to carry a stock of 4,000 lb of inventory. The purchasing agent suggests that the inventory of expensium be allowed to decrease from 4,000 to 600 lb by the end of 1985 and to be replenished to the desired level of 4,000 lb early in 1986.

Exhibit 8.18
WILSON COMPANY
Layers of 1984 Year-End Inventory
(Problem 37)

Year Acquired	Purchase Price per Pound	1984 Year-End Inventory	
		Pounds	Cost
1975	$30	2,000	$ 60,000
1980	46	200	9,200
1981	48	400	19,200
1984	52	1,400	72,800
		4,000	$161,200

The controller argues that such a policy would be foolish. If inventories are allowed to decrease to 600 lb, then the cost of goods sold will be extraordinarily low (because the older LIFO layers will be consumed) and income taxes will be extraordinarily high. He suggests that 1985 purchases should be planned to maintain an end-of-year inventory of 4,000 lb.

Assume that sales for 1985 do require 7,000 lb of expensium, that the prices for 1985 are as forecast, and that the income tax for Wilson Company is 40 percent.

    a. Calculate the cost of goods sold and end-of-year LIFO inventory for 1985, assuming that the controller's advice is followed and inventory at the end of 1985 is 4,000 lb.

    b. Calculate the cost of goods sold and end-of-year LIFO inventory for 1985, assuming that the purchasing agent's advice is followed and inventory at the end of 1985 is 600 lb.

    c. Assuming that the controller's, not the purchasing agent's, advice is followed, calculate the tax savings for 1985 and the extra cash costs for inventory.

    d. What should Wilson Company do?

    e. Management of Wilson Company wants to know what discretion it has to vary income for 1985 by planning its purchases of expensium. If the controller's policy is followed, aftertax income for 1985 will be $50,000. What is the range, after taxes, of income that can be achieved by the purposeful management of expensium purchases?

38. *Reconstructing underlying events from ending inventory amounts (adapted from CPA examination).* The Burch Corporation began a merchandising business on January 1, Year 1. It acquired merchandise costing $100,000 in Year 1, $125,000 in Year 2, and $135,000 in Year 3. Exhibit 8.19 shows information about Burch Corporation's inventory as it would appear on the balance sheet under different inventory methods.

Exhibit 8.19
BURCH CORPORATION
Inventory Valuations for Balance Sheet Under Various Assumptions
(Problem 38)

December 31,	LIFO Cost	FIFO Cost	Lower of FIFO Cost or Market
Year 1	$40,200	$40,000	$37,000
Year 2	36,400	36,000	34,000
Year 3	41,800	44,000	44,000

In answering each of the following questions, indicate how the answer is deduced. You may assume that in any one year, prices moved only up or down, but not both.

   a. Did prices go up or down in Year 1?
   b. Did prices go up or down in Year 3?
   c. Which inventory method would show the highest income for Year 1?
   d. Which inventory method would show the highest income for Year 2?
   e. Which inventory method would show the highest income for Year 3?
   f. Which inventory method would show the lowest income for all 3 years combined?
   g. For Year 3, how much higher or lower would income be on the FIFO cost basis than it would be on the lower-of-cost-or-market basis?

39. *Reconstructing accounting policies from financial statement data.* Data for Company A and Company B in Exhibit 8.20 are taken from the annual reports of two actual companies for a recent year. One of these companies uses a LIFO cost flow assumption for 100 percent of its inventories, and the other uses LIFO for about 45 percent of its inventories. Answer the following questions, making explicit the reasoning used in each case.

   a. From the cost-of-goods-sold data alone, which of the companies appears to be the 100 percent LIFO company? The 45 percent LIFO company?
   b. From the ending inventory data alone, which of the companies appears to be the 100 percent LIFO company? The 45 percent LIFO company?
   c. From your answers to parts **a** and **b**, draw a conclusion as to which of the companies appears to be which.
   d. Note that Company A earned net income equal to 2.1 percent of sales, whereas Company B earned net income equal to 7.6 percent of sales. Can you conclude that Company A is less profitable than Company B? Why or why not?
   e. Which of the two companies is more likely to be involved in retailing, and which is more likely to be involved in manufacturing? Explain.

40. *Cost flow assumptions and financial statement ratios.* The financial statements of the General Products Company (GP) are included in Appendix A at the back of this book. Refer to the data for 1985.

Exhibit 8.20
Data for Analysis of LIFO and FIFO
Effects on Financial Statements
(Problem 39)

	Dollar Amounts in Millions	
	Company A	Company B
Sales Revenue	$5,151	$5,042
Cost of Goods Sold:[a]		
Historical Cost Basis.	3,638	3,720
Replacement Cost Basis	3,675	3,720
Net Income	108	383
Ending Inventory:		
Historical Cost Basis.	1,026	1,245
Replacement Cost Basis	1,056	2,169
Ratio of Net Income to Revenue	2.1 percent	7.6 percent

[a]Excludes depreciation charges.

    a. GP uses a LIFO cost flow assumption. There is sufficient information given in the notes for you to construct hypothetical financial statements assuming both that GP used a FIFO cost flow assumption and that GP used a current cost basis for inventories, without any cost flow assumption. Some of this is done in Exhibit 8.6. For each of these treatments—LIFO, FIFO, current cost—compute each of the following ratios (ignoring income tax effects):

    (1) Current ratio.
    (2) Inventory turnover ratio.
    (3) Rate of return on shareholders' equity.

    (Make current cost adjustments only for effects on inventory, ignoring effects for property, plant, and equipment. When assuming a FIFO cost flow assumption or a current value basis for inventory, be sure to increase owners' equity by the same amount that you increase ending inventory. When you hypothetically debit ending inventory to increase it, you must also credit owners' equity.)

    b. What inferences can you draw from the computations done in part **a** about comparing the financial statements of a company using LIFO with ones of a company using FIFO? What inferences can you draw about the comparison of financial statements using historical cost accounting for inventories with those based on current values measured by replacement cost?

41. *Analysis of financial statement ratios affected by cost flow assumptions.* A recent annual report of General Motors Corporation contained the following in the section "Financial Review: Management's Discussion and Analysis." (Dates have been changed for convenience.)

    General Motors' liquidity can be measured by its current ratio (ratio of current assets to current liabilities). For the years ended December 31, Year 2 and Year 1, the current ratio, based on LIFO inventories, was 1.13 and 1.09, respectively. The LIFO method, while improving Corporate cash flow, adversely affects the current ratio. . . . If inventories were valued at FIFO, the current ratio would be 1.21 and 1.18, at the ends of Year 2 and Year 1, respectively.

Assume an income tax rate of 46 percent and that current assets were $14,043 million and $13,714 million at the end of Year 2 and Year 1, respectively.

   a. Compute the difference between FIFO and LIFO inventories at the ends of Year 2 and Year 1.
   b. How did the use of LIFO affect cash flow for Year 2?
   c. By how much has the use of LIFO improved cash flow since the time it was adopted?

42. *Analysis of disclosures from published financial reports on effects of changing from average cost to LIFO.* The following is adapted from various disclosures in the annual reports of E. I. duPont de Nemours & Company in the year it switched from average cost to LIFO for most of its inventories and the 2 following years. Assume an income tax rate of 48 percent.

Year 1. During the year, the Company changed its cost flow assumption for most of its inventories from average cost to LIFO to achieve a better matching of current costs with revenues. Net income was reduced by $249.6 million, 27 percent, for the year.

Year 2. During the year, inventory quantities were reduced from the abnormally high levels at the start of the year. This resulted in liquidation of LIFO inventory quantities carried at costs lower than those prevailing during the year. The effect was to increase net income by approximately $36.4 million.

Year 3. If inventory had been valued at current cost, rather than at historical cost using a LIFO cost flow assumption, then the amounts on the balance sheet would have exceeded the amounts reported by $490 million at end of the year and by $410 million at the beginning of the year.

   a. By how much did LIFO cost of goods sold in Year 1 differ from the amount computed with an average-cost flow assumption?
   b. Why does a liquidation of LIFO layers, such as in Year 2, increase net income?
   c. By how much did cost of goods sold for Year 2 differ from the amount that would have been reported had the layers not been liquidated? Give the amount and whether this represents an increase or decrease in cost of goods sold.
   d. Why might the company not have changed back to average cost for Year 2?
   e. Assume that an average-cost flow assumption gives ending inventory amounts approximately the same as current costs. What were the savings in taxes for Year 3 from the Company's using LIFO rather than average cost?
   f. Why might the Company choose a cost flow assumption for inventory that reduces reported income?

43. *Effects of cost flow assumptions on reported income.* Exhibit 8.21 shows data for the General Electric Company's inventories (excluding uranium subsidiaries) for a period of years under the LIFO assumption as actually used and under FIFO, as they would have been if it had been used.

    a. Compute the pretax income for Years 2 through 6, assuming that a FIFO cost flow assumption had been used.

    b. Calculate the percentage change in pretax income for each of the years 3 through 6 under both LIFO and FIFO (that is, the increase in pretax income in Year 3 relative to Year 2, the increase in pretax income in Year 4 relative to Year 3, and so on).

    c. Calculate the percentage change in pretax income between Year 2 and Year 6 (that is, the 5-year period taken as a whole) under both LIFO and FIFO.

    d. Did the quantity of items in inventory increase or decrease during each of the Years 3 through 6? How can you tell?

Exhibit 8.21
GENERAL ELECTRIC COMPANY
(amounts in millions)
(Problem 43)

End of Year	LIFO Ending Inventory	FIFO Ending Inventory
1	$1,611.7	$1,884.5
2	1,759.0	2,063.1
3	1,986.2	2,415.9
4	2,257.0	3,040.7
5	2,202.9	3,166.6
6	2,354.4	3,515.2

For the Year	Pretax Operating Income Using LIFO
2	$ 897.2
3	1,011.6
4	1,000.7
5	1,174.0
6	1,627.5

End of Year	Amounts in Millions	
	Current Assets	Current Liabilities
2	$3,979.3	$2,869.7
3	4,485.4	3,492.4
4	5,222.6	3,879.5
5	5,750.4	4,163.0
6	6,685.0	4,604.9

   e. Did the acquisition cost of items in inventory increase or decrease during each of the Years 3 through 6? How can you tell?

   f. Assume for this part that the inventory value under LIFO at the end of Year 1 of $1,611.7 is the initial LIFO layer. This layer may be viewed as the bottom layer on a cake. Construct a figure showing the addition or subtraction of LIFO layers for each of the Years 2 through 6.

   g. The current assets and current liabilities of the General Electric Company at the end of Years 2 through 6 using a LIFO cost flow assumption are shown in Exhibit 8.21. Compute General Electric's current ratio for each year using the data given.

   h. Recompute General Electric's current ratio for each year using a FIFO cost flow assumption for inventories. Although it is unrealistic to do so, assume for this part that there are no changes in income taxes payable or in current liabilities. (To make the figures realistic after taxes, ending LIFO inventory should be increased by about *one-half* the difference between FIFO and LIFO ending inventory amounts. Why?)

44. *Analysis of statement of changes in financial position; change definition of funds to exclude inventories.* For many years, General Motors Corporation (GM) defined funds as working capital (= current assets − current liabilities) in its statement of changes in financial position. Exhibit 8.22 presents condensed excerpts of GM's funds statements for several recent years with funds defined as working capital. During this 5-year period GM changed the definition of funds to cash and marketable securities. Increasingly, companies present the funds statement with funds defined as cash or cash plus marketable securities. One implication of the difference is that changes in inventories become sources or uses of funds, rather than mere alterations of the components of funds.

   Derive funds provided by operations for GM, defining funds as cash plus marketable securities. Treat changes in working capital accounts other than cash and marketable securities as *operating* sources and uses of funds. Analyze the apparent differences in changes in liquidity by comparing your statements to those in Exhibit 8.22. Try to form an opinion as to which funds statement you as an analyst would prefer to use.

Exhibit 8.22
GENERAL MOTORS CORPORATION
Excerpts from Statement of Changes in Financial Position
with Working Capital Definition of Funds
(dollar amounts in millions)
(Problem 44)

	Year 5	Year 4	Year 3	Year 2	Year 1
Total Working Capital Provided by Current Operations	$5,589.0	$4,807.6	$3,726.7	$5,758.8	$6,479.7
Increase (Decrease) in Working Capital Items by Element:					
Cash and Marketable Securities	$1,805.5	($2,394.5)	$ 728.8	($1,068.4)	$ 814.8
Accounts and Notes Receivable	(778.8)	(125.1)	(1,262.0)	(608.3)	957.6
Inventories	(1,038.5)	(72.3)	(844.1)	499.6	401.0
Prepaid Expenses and Deferred Income Taxes . . .	341.1	820.6	243.1	(266.8)	(131.1)
Accounts Payable	99.0	268.0	(586.4)	307.0	893.3
Loans Payable	545.3	(51.3)	(752.4)	466.2	(57.3)
Accrued Liabilities	(474.3)	(498.7)	(1,065.9)	(590.0)	(1,567.3)
Increase (Decrease) in Working Capital Items	$ 499.3	($2,053.3)	($3,538.9)	($1,260.7)	$1,311.0

Chapter 9   Plant, Equipment, and Intangible Assets: The Source of Operating Capacity

Assets are future benefits, short-lived or long-lived. A business acquires a short-lived asset, such as insurance coverage, in one period and uses up its benefits within a year. A long-lived asset is different: To reap its benefits, the owner uses it for several years. In these cases, the accountant allocates the cost of the asset over the several accounting periods of benefit. This general process is called *amortization*. Amortization of *plant assets,* which include the fixtures, machinery, equipment, and physical structures of a business, is called *depreciation*.

In addition to its plant assets, companies such as Exxon and Santa Fe Industries own natural resources, called *wasting assets*. Oil wells, coal mines, uranium deposits, and other natural resources are eventually used up. Amortization of the cost of these wasting assets is called *depletion*.

Businesses may also acquire *intangible assets* and, although there are many examples, some of the best-known ones are everyday words such as Coca-Cola, Kleenex, and Kodak, all famous trademarks. A firm may purchase a McDonald's or Kentucky Fried Chicken franchise. Other intangible assets are goodwill, copyrights, and patents. Although such intangibles may have indefinite economic lives, the accountant generally amortizes their costs to the periods of benefit. There is no specific term for the amortization of intangibles; the general term *amortization* is used to describe the process of writing off the cost of all intangibles.

Most of this chapter treats depreciation, because plant assets are the most common long-lived assets and depreciation problems are typical of almost all other amortization problems.[1]

The problems of plant asset valuation and depreciation measurement conveniently divide into the consideration of four separate kinds of events:

1. Recording the acquisition of the asset.
2. Recording its use over time.
3. Recording adjustments for changes in capacity or efficiency and for repairs or improvements.
4. Recording its retirement or other disposal.

---

[1] The terms *plant assets* and *fixed assets* are often used interchangeably. They refer to long-lived assets used in the operations of trading, service, and manufacturing enterprises, and include land, buildings, machinery, and equipment. The ordinary usage of the terms *plant assets* and *fixed assets* often does not adequately encompass the class of long-lived assets that includes all land, buildings, machinery, and equipment. *Plant assets* is sometimes used too narrowly to mean only items in a factory or plant. *Fixed assets* is sometimes used too narrowly to mean only items such as land and buildings that are immovable.

Acquisition of Plant Assets

The cost of a plant asset includes all charges necessary to prepare it for rendering services, and it is often recorded in a series of transactions. Thus, the cost of a piece of equipment will be the sum of the entries to recognize the invoice price (less any discounts), transportation costs, installation charges, and any other costs incurred before the equipment is ready for use. See the example on page 40.

Computing the acquisition cost of an asset acquired in a trade-in transaction presents special problems. A trade-in transaction involves both the retirement of an old asset and the acquisition of a new one. Although its problems might be discussed with acquisitions, this chapter discusses trade-in transactions in the section on retirements. Computing the acquisition cost of a self-constructed asset presents other problems, discussed next.

Self-Constructed Asset

When a firm constructs its own buildings or equipment, many entries to record the labor, material, and overhead costs will normally be required before the total cost is recorded. FASB *Statement No. 34*[2] requires the firm also to include interest paid during the construction period as part of the cost of the asset being constructed. The amount of interest included is based on the entity's actual borrowings and interest payments. It is intended to be the interest cost incurred during the assets' acquisition periods that in principle could have been avoided if the assets had not been acquired.

If there is a specific new borrowing in connection with the asset being constructed, the interest rate on that borrowing is used. If the expenditures on plant exceed such specific new borrowings, the interest rate to be applied to such excess is the weighted average of rates applicable to other borrowings of the enterprise. There need not be specific new borrowings; then the average interest rate on old borrowings is used to compute the total amount to be capitalized. The total amount of interest included cannot exceed total interest costs for the period. The capitalization of interest into plant during construction reduces otherwise reportable interest expense and increases income during periods of construction. In later periods, the plant will have higher depreciation charges, reducing income.

Example Assume the following long-term debt structure:

Construction Loan at 15 Percent on Building Under Construction	$1,000,000
Other Borrowings at 12 Percent Average Rate	3,600,000
Total Long-Term Debt	$4,600,000

[2]Financial Accounting Standards Board, *Statement of Financial Accounting Standards No. 34,* "Capitalization of Interest Cost," 1979.

The account Building Under Construction has an average balance during the year of $3,000,000. The amount of interest to be capitalized is based on all of the new construction-related borrowings, $1,000,000, and enough of the older borrowings, $2,000,000, to bring the total to $3,000,000. The interest capitalized, $390,000, is computed as

$1,000,000 × .15	$150,000
$2,000,000 × .12	240,000
$3,000,000	$390,000

The entries to record interest and then to capitalize the required amounts might be

Interest Expense	582,000	
Interest Payable		582,000
To record all interest as expense: $582,000 = (.15 × $1,000,000) + (.12 × $3,600,000) = $150,000 + $432,000.		

Building Under Construction	390,000	
Interest Expense		390,000
The amount capitalized reduces interest expense and increases the recorded cost of the building.		

The preceding two entries might be combined as one:

Interest Expense	192,000	
Building Under Construction	390,000	
Interest Payable		582,000
The amount for Interest Expense is a plug.		

Both total interest for the year, $582,000, and the amount capitalized, $390,000, must be disclosed in notes. The income statement will report interest expense, $192,000, in the example. The amount shown in future years for depreciation of the plant will be larger than otherwise because of interest capitalization in earlier years. Over the life of the asset, from construction through retirement, total income is unaffected by capitalizing interest, because the increased income in the construction period is later exactly offset with larger depreciation charges. Over long enough time spans, total expense must equal total cash expenditure.

Depreciation—Fundamental Concepts

Purpose of Depreciation

Most plant assets can be kept intact and in usable operating condition for more than a year, but, except for land, eventually they must be retired from service. Depreciation systematically allocates the cost of these assets to the periods of their use.

Allocation of Cost The cost of a depreciating asset is the price paid for a series of future services. The asset account is like a prepayment, similar to prepaid rent or insurance—a payment in advance for services to be received. As the asset is used in each accounting period, a portion of the investment in the asset is treated as the cost of the service received and is recognized as an expense of the period or as part of the cost of goods produced during the period.

Depreciation is a process of cost allocation, not one of valuation. This chapter discusses the problems of *allocating* assets' costs to the periods of benefit. A depreciation problem will exist whenever (1) funds are invested in services to be rendered by a plant asset, and (2) at some date in the future, the asset must be retired from service with a residual value less than its original cost.

No uniquely correct amount for the periodic charge for depreciation can be computed. The cost of the plant asset is a *joint cost* of the several benefited periods. That is, each of the periods of the asset's use benefits from its services. There is usually no single correct way to allocate a joint cost. The depreciation process assigns periodic charges that reflect systematic calculations.

Return of Capital A business attempts to earn both a return *of* capital and a return *on* capital. Before there can be a return *on* capital (as measured by accounting profits), all costs must be recovered. The purpose of amortization is to charge against revenues the cost of noncurrent assets. To understand the role of amortization in this process, reconsider the installment method and the cost-recovery-first method of recognizing revenue, introduced in Chapter 4. In the cost-recovery-first method, there is no accounting income until all costs are recovered. The accounting under cost recovery first charges to expense an amount equal to cash collections so that there is no accounting income until all anticipated costs have been debited to expense. In contrast, under the installment method, costs are allocated over the time of cash collections so that each dollar collected represents identical proportions of cost recovery and profits. In accounting for noncurrent assets, one might, in principle, debit expense and credit plant assets so that there is no profit until the costs of plant assets have been written off. The early periods of a noncurrent asset's life could have no income but the later periods would show no expense for plant and, consequently, larger net income. Instead, accounting estimates the life of the noncurrent asset and writes off its cost over its life, in principle allowing each period to show both cost recovery and income. The amortization process provides for the gradual return of the investment in a noncurrent asset. In historical cost accounting, the process is designed to provide a return of the cost of the asset, no more and no less.[3] But the return of costs is designed to occur over the asset's life, not all in the early periods of its life.

Depreciation Is Not a Decline in Value

In ordinary conversation, "depreciation" frequently means a decline in value. Over the entire service life of a plant asset, there is a decline in value of the asset from acquisition until it is retired from service. The charge made to the operations of each accounting period does not result from declines in value during that period but, rather, from the process of ensuring a return of capital invested. If, in a given period, an asset increases in value, there will still be depreciation during that period. There have been two partially offsetting processes: (1) a holding gain on the asset, which usually is not recognized in historical cost-based accounting, and (2) depreciation of the asset's historical cost to achieve a return of investment.

The Causes of Depreciation

The causes of depreciation are the causes of decline in an asset's service potential and of its ultimate retirement. Unless the asset must eventually be retired from its planned use, there is no depreciation. When the services provided by land do not diminish over time, land is not depreciated; all costs are recovered when the land is sold. Many factors lead to the retirement of assets from service, but the causes of decline in service potential can be classified as either *physical* or *functional*. The physical factors include such things as ordinary wear and tear from use, chemical action such as rust or electrolysis, and the effects of wind and rain. The most important functional (nonphysical) cause is *obsolescence*. Inventions, for example, may result in new processes that reduce the unit cost of production to the point where continued operation of old equipment is not economical, even though it may be relatively unimpaired physically. Retail stores often replace display cases and storefronts long before they are worn out in order to make the appearance of the store more attractive. Changed economic conditions may also become functional causes of depreciation, such as when an old airport becomes inadequate and must be abandoned, and a new, larger one is built to meet the requirements of heavier traffic, or when an increase in the cost of gasoline causes a reduction in demand for automobile products, which results in a reduced scale of operations in automobile manufacturing.

---

[3]As inflation has become a major economic problem, accountants increasingly recognize that basing depreciation charges on acquisition costs will not, in most cases, charge amounts to expense that are sufficient to maintain the productive capacity of the business. Basing depreciation on acquisition costs will enable a business to recover its initial cash investment but not necessarily enough to replace the physical productive capacity purchased with the cash.

Financial Accounting Standards Board, *Statement of Financial Accounting Standards No. 33,* "Financial Reporting and Changing Prices," 1979, requires major corporations to disclose as supplemental information depreciation charges based on current costs. The formal financial statements continue to report acquisition cost measured in nominal dollars. Chapter 14 describes the calculation and reporting of depreciation to reflect the effect of changing prices.

Identifying the specific causes of depreciation is not essential for measuring it. Almost any physical asset will eventually have to be retired from service, and in some cases the retirement will become necessary at a time when physical deterioration is negligible. Understanding the specific causes can, nevertheless, help in estimating an asset's useful life.

Depreciation Accounting Problems

The three principal accounting problems in allocating the cost of an asset over time are

1. Measuring the depreciable basis of the asset.
2. Estimating its useful service life.
3. Deciding on the pattern of expiration of asset cost over the useful service life.

Depreciable Basis of Plant Assets—Cost Less Salvage Value

Depreciation charges in historical cost accounting are based on the acquisition cost of the asset less the estimated residual value—the amount to be received when the asset is retired from service. The amounts invested in an asset that will be recovered when the asset is retired need not be recovered through depreciation charges. Recall that land is not depreciated because its cost will be recovered at the time of sale. Similarly, the amount estimated to be recovered from a depreciating plant asset at its retirement need not be depreciated; that portion of the initial investment is recovered at retirement.

Estimating Salvage Value Depreciation charges are based on the difference between acquisition cost and the asset's estimated salvage value or net residual value. The terms *salvage value* and *net residual value* refer to estimated proceeds on disposition of an asset less all removal and selling costs. Salvage value must be an estimate at any time before the asset is retired. Hence, before retirement, the terms *salvage value* and *estimated salvage value* are synonymous.

For buildings, common practice assumes a zero salvage value. This treatment rests on the assumption that the cost to be incurred in tearing down the building will approximate the sales value of the scrap materials recovered. For other assets, however, the salvage value may be substantial and should be taken into account in making the periodic depreciation charge. For example, a car rental firm will replace its automobiles at a time when other owners can use the cars for several years more. The rental firm will be able to recover a substantial part of acquisition cost (and return of part of the capital invested) from the sale of used cars. Past experience usually forms the best basis for estimating salvage value. (Salvage value can be negative. Consider, for example, the cost of dismantling a nuclear electricity-generating plant.)

Estimates of salvage value are necessarily subjective. Disputes over estimated salvage value have led to many disagreements between Internal Revenue Service agents and taxpayers. Partly to reduce such controversy, the Internal Revenue Code has been amended to provide that salvage value may be ignored entirely in calculating depreciation for tax reporting. In calculating depreciation in problems in this text, take the entire salvage value into account unless explicit contrary instructions are given.

Unit of Account Whenever feasible, depreciation should be computed for individual items such as a single building, machine, or automobile. Where similar items are in use and each one has a relatively small cost, individual calculations may be impractical and the depreciation charge is usually calculated for the group as a whole. Furniture and fixtures, tools, and telephone poles are examples of assets that are usually depreciated in groups. Group depreciation techniques are treated in more advanced financial accounting courses. The basic principles of depreciating individual items discussed here apply, however, to group depreciation situations.

Estimating Service Life

The depreciation calculation requires an estimate of the economic service life of the asset. In making the estimate, both the physical and the functional causes of depreciation must be considered. Experience with similar assets, corrected for differences in the planned intensity of use or alterations in maintenance policy, is usually the best guide for this estimate.

Despite abundant data from experience, estimating service lives for financial reporting is the most difficult task in the entire depreciation calculation. Allowing for obsolescence is particularly difficult because most obsolescence results from forces outside the firm. Estimates will probably prove to be incorrect. For this reason, estimates of useful service life of assets are reconsidered every few years.

Income tax laws allow shorter lives to be used in computing depreciation for tax reporting, but when these lives are shorter than the economic lives of the assets, they should not be used for financial reporting.

In 1981, Congress passed income tax legislation that brought into use the Accelerated Cost Recovery System (ACRS). Under ACRS, almost all assets are grouped into one of four classes: those to be depreciated over 3 years for tax purposes (such as automobiles and light trucks), those to be depreciated over 5 years for tax purposes (such as most machinery and equipment), those to be depreciated over 10 years for tax purposes (such as railroad tank cars), and those to be depreciated over 15 years for tax purposes (such as buildings and some property of public utilities).

Pattern of Expiration of Costs

Once the cost is measured and both salvage value and service life are estimated, the total of depreciation charges for the whole life of the asset has been determined. If salvage value is assumed to be zero, then the entire cost will be depreciated. The problem remains of selecting the pattern for allocating those charges to the specific years of the life. Depreciation based on the passage of time follows one of five basic patterns. They are labeled E, A, S, D, and N in Figures 9.1 and 9.2.

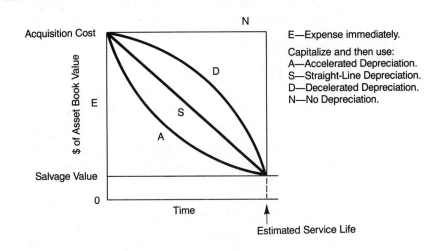

Figure 9.1 Patterns of Writing off Costs: Book Value over Economic Life of Asset

Figure 9.2 Patterns of Annual Depreciation Charge over Economic Life of Asset

The next section discusses the patterns in more detail. A represents *accelerated* depreciation; S, *straight-line* depreciation; D, *decelerated* depreciation. (Understanding the terms "accelerated" and "decelerated" is easier if you compare the depreciation charges in the early years to straight-line depreciation. See Figure 9.2.) Pattern D is not used in financial reporting, but is useful for certain managerial accounting problems. Pattern E represents immediate expensing of the item. All costs are charged to the period when the cost is incurred. The section on intangibles discusses this pattern. Pattern N represents the situation, such as for land, where there are no periodic amortization charges. The asset is shown on the books at acquisition cost until sold or otherwise retired.

Depreciation Methods

All depreciation methods systematically allocate the cost of the asset minus its estimated salvage value to the periods in which it is used. The methods discussed here are as follows:

1. Straight-line (time) method (pattern S).
2. Production or use (straight-line use) method.
3. Declining-balance methods (pattern A).
4. Sum-of-the-years'-digits method (pattern A).
5. Accelerated Cost Recovery System for tax reporting (pattern A).

When a depreciable asset is acquired or retired during an accounting period, depreciation should be calculated only for that portion of the period during which the asset is used.

The Straight-Line (Time) Method

The allocation method most commonly used for financial reporting is the *straight-line* method. Under the straight-line method, the cost of the asset, less any estimated salvage value, is divided by the number of years of its expected life in order to arrive at the annual depreciation:

$$\text{Annual Depreciation} = \frac{\text{Cost Less Estimated Salvage Value}}{\text{Estimated Life in Years}}.$$

For example, if a machine costs $12,000, has an estimated salvage value of $1,000, and has an expected useful life of 5 years, the annual depreciation will be $2,200 [= ($12,000 − $1,000)/5]. Occasionally, instead of a positive salvage value, the cost of removal exceeds the gross proceeds on disposition. This excess of removal costs over gross proceeds should be added to the cost of the asset in making the calculation. Thus, if a building is constructed for $3,700,000, and it is estimated that it will cost $500,000 to remove it at the end of 25 years, the annual depreciation would be $168,000 [= ($3,700,000 + $500,000)/25].

Production or Use (Straight-Line Use) Method

Many assets are not used uniformly over time. Manufacturing plants often have seasonal variations in operation so that certain machines may be used 24 hours a day at one time and 8 hours or less a day at another time of year. Trucks are not likely to receive the same amount of use in each year of their lives. The straight-line (time) method of depreciation may result in depreciation patterns unrelated to usage patterns.

When the rate of usage varies over periods and when the total usage of an asset over its life can be estimated, a depreciation charge based on actual usage during the period may be used. For example, depreciation of a truck for a period could be based on the ratio of miles driven during the period to total miles expected to be driven over the truck's life. The depreciation cost per unit (mile) of use is

$$\text{Depreciation Cost per Unit} = \frac{\text{Cost Less Estimated Salvage Value}}{\text{Estimated Number of Units}}.$$

Assume that a truck costs \$24,000, has an estimated salvage value of \$1,200, and is expected to be driven 100,000 miles before it is retired from service. The depreciation per mile is \$.228 [= (\$24,000 − \$1,200)/100,000]. If the truck is operated 2,000 miles in a given month, the depreciation charge for the month is 2,000 × \$.228 = \$456.

Accelerated Depreciation

The earning power of some plant assets declines as the assets grow older. Cutting tools lose some of their precision; printing presses must be shut down more frequently for repairs; rent receipts from an old office building are lower than those from a new one. Some assets provide more and better services in the early years of their lives while requiring increasing amounts of maintenance as they grow older. Where this is the case, methods that recognize larger depreciation charges in early years and progressively smaller depreciation charges later may be justified. Such methods are referred to as *accelerated depreciation* methods because the depreciation charges in the early years of the asset's life are larger than in later years. Accelerated depreciation leads to a pattern such as A in Figures 9.1 and 9.2.

Declining-Balance Methods

The *declining-balance* method is one accelerated depreciation method. In this method, the depreciation charge is calculated by multiplying the *net book value* of the asset (cost less accumulated depreciation) at the start of each period by a fixed rate. The estimated salvage value is not subtracted from the cost in making the depreciation calculation, but the asset cannot be written down below its estimated salvage value. Because the net book value declines from period to period, the result is a declining periodic charge for depreciation throughout the life of the asset.[4] A

---

[4]Under the declining-balance method, as strictly applied, the fixed depreciation rate used is one that will charge the cost less salvage value of the asset over its service life. The formula for computing the rate is

$$\text{Depreciation Rate} = 1 - \sqrt[n]{\frac{s}{c}} = 1 - \left(\frac{s}{c}\right)^{1/n}.$$

In this formula n = estimated periods of service life, s = estimated salvage value, and c = cost.

   Estimates of salvage value have a profound effect on the rate. Unless a positive salvage value is assumed, the rate is 100 percent—that is, all depreciation is charged in the first period. For an asset costing \$10,000, with an estimated life of 5 years, the depreciation rate is 40 percent per period if salvage value is \$778, but it is 60 percent if salvage value is \$102.

   The effect of small changes in salvage value on the rate and the seeming mathematical complexity of the formula have resulted in widespread use of approximations or rules of thumb instead of the formula.

Exhibit 9.1
150 Percent Declining-Balance Depreciation
Asset with 5-Year Life

Year	Acquisition Cost (1)	Accumulated Depreciation as of Jan. 1 (2)	Net Book Value as of Jan. 1 = (1) − (2) (3)	Depreciation Rate (4)	Depreciation Charge for the Year = (3) × (4) (5)
1 . . .	$5,000	$ 0	$5,000	.30	$1,500
2 . . .	5,000	1,500	3,500	.30	1,050
3 . . .	5,000	2,550	2,450	a	817
4 . . .	5,000	3,367	1,633	a	817
5 . . .	5,000	4,184	816	a	816

aThe firm switches to straight-line write-off of the remaining balance over the remaining life, or $817 (= $2,450/3), during the last 3 years.

method sometimes used is the *150 percent declining-balance* method. (This method underlies ACRS, used in income tax reporting.) An asset with an estimated 10-year life would be depreciated at a rate of 15 percent (= $\frac{1}{10}$ × 1.5) per year of the book value at the start of the year. Under declining-balance methods, the firm switches to straight-line depreciation of the remaining book value at the time when straight line provides higher depreciation charges. If a machine costing $5,000 is purchased on January 1, Year 1, and it is estimated to have a 5-year life, a 30 percent (= $\frac{1}{5}$ × 1.5) rate would be used for 2 years and then the firm would switch to straight-line depreciation. The depreciation charges, assuming zero salvage value, would be calculated as shown in Exhibit 9.1.

Sum-of-the-Years'-Digits Method

Another accelerated depreciation method is the *sum-of-the-years'-digits* method. Under this method, the depreciation charge is calculated by applying a fraction, which diminishes from year to year, to the cost less estimated salvage value of the asset. The numerator of the fraction is the number of years of remaining life at the beginning of the year for which the depreciation calculation is being made. The denominator is the sum of all such numbers, one for each year of estimated service life; if the service life is n years, the denominator for the sum-of-the-years'-digits method is $1 + 2 + \cdots + n$.[5]

Consider an asset costing $5,000 purchased January 1, Year 1, which has an estimated service life of 5 years and an estimated salvage value of $200. The sum of the years' digits is 15 (= 1 + 2 + 3 + 4 + 5).[6] The depreciation charges appear in Exhibit 9.2.

---

[5]A formula useful for summing the numbers 1 through n is $1 + 2 + \cdots + n = n(n + 1)/2$.
[6]That is, according to the formula given in the previous footnote, $1 + 2 + 3 + 4 + 5 = 5 \times 6/2 = 15$.

Exhibit 9.2
Sum-of-the-Years'-Digits Depreciation
Asset with 5-Year Life, $5,000 Cost,
and $200 Estimated Salvage Value

Year	Acquisition Cost Less Salvage Value (1)	Remaining Life in Years (2)	Fraction = (2)/15 (3)	Depreciation Charge for the Year = (3) × (1) (4)
1	$4,800	5	5/15	$1,600
2	4,800	4	4/15	1,280
3	4,800	3	3/15	960
4	4,800	2	2/15	640
5	4,800	1	1/15	320
				$4,800

Accelerated Cost Recovery System for Income Tax Reporting

For income tax reporting, firms generally use the Accelerated Cost Recovery System (ACRS), which specifies depreciation charges accelerated in three distinct ways. First, the depreciable lives themselves are generally shorter than economic lives. (Straight-line depreciation for a shorter period will produce depreciation charges accelerated when compared to straight-line over a longer period.) Second, ACRS provides for depreciation over the specified life based on the 150 percent declining-balance depreciation method, which is more rapid than straight-line. ACRS assumes, however, that each asset is acquired at mid-year of the year of acquisition, so the first-year percentage represents only a half-year of depreciation. Third, ACRS allows the entire depreciable basis to be written off over the depreciation period; salvage value is ignored. Exhibit 9.3 shows the percentage of the asset's cost to be depreciated under ACRS for tax reporting for various classes of property.

An automobile with a 5-year economic life (for financial reporting) is in the 3-year property class for ACRS. If it costs $12,000 and has $2,000 estimated salvage value, the ACRS deductions for the tax return would be $3,000 (= .25 × $12,000) in the first year, $4,560 (= .38 × $12,000) in the second year, $4,440 (= .37 × $12,000) in the third year, and zero in the fourth and fifth years of service. Note that ACRS ignores salvage value, so if the asset is retired for $2,000, there will be a taxable gain on retirement of $2,000. Only rarely would depreciation based on ACRS be appropriate for financial reporting.[7]

Compound Interest Methods

Compound interest methods are seldom used in financial accounting, but they are theoretically sound for many management decisions. For plant assets producing equal annual net inflows of cash, compound interest depreciation leads to a pattern

---

[7]For financial reporting under the straight-line method, this automobile would have depreciation charges of $2,000 [= ($12,000 − $2,000)/5] per year for 5 years and would have a book value of $2,000 at the end of the fifth year.

Exhibit 9.3
Accelerated Cost Recovery System
Percentage of Depreciable Cost
Allowed by Year of Asset's Life

Recovery Year	Property Class			
	3-Year	5-Year[b]	10-Year	15-Year
1[a]	25%	15%	8%	5%
2	38	22	14	10
3	37	21	12	9
4		21	10	8
5		21	10	7
6			10	7
7			9	6
8			9	6
9			9	6
10			9	6
11				6
12				6
13				6
14				6
15				6
Total	100%	100%	100%	100%

[a]Assets are assumed to be acquired at mid-point of first year, independent of actual acquisition dates.
[b]ACRS is generally based on the 150 percent declining-balance method. For an asset with a 5-year life acquired at mid-year, the implied percentages would be 15, 26, 20, 20, 19. The numbers in this column do not follow the general rule.

like D in Figures 9.1 and 9.2. This text does not illustrate compound interest methods, but see Problem 40 at the end of this chapter.

Factors in Choosing the Depreciation Method

Depreciation affects both income reported in the financial statements and taxable income on tax returns. A firm need not choose the same depreciation method for both financial and tax reporting purposes. If it chooses different methods for the two purposes, the difference between depreciation in the financial statements and on the tax return leads to a problem in accounting for income taxes, discussed in Chapter 11.

Financial Reporting Financial reporting for long-lived assets seeks an income statement that realistically measures the expiration of their benefits and provides a "reasonable" pattern of cost recovery. No one knows, however, just what portion of the service potential of a long-lived asset expires in any one period. The cost of the plant asset is a joint cost of the several periods of use, and no uniquely correct way of allocating joint costs exists. All that can be said is that financial statements should report depreciation charges based on reasonable estimates of asset expirations. Chapter 15 discusses more fully the firm's selection from alternative accounting principles, including the choice of depreciation methods.

Tax Reporting It seems clear that in selecting depreciation methods for tax reporting, the goal of the firm should be to maximize the present value of the reductions in tax payments from claiming depreciation. Earlier deductions are worth more than later ones, because a dollar saved today is worth more than a dollar saved tomorrow. Congress has presented business firms with several permissible alternatives under ACRS to follow in determining the amount of depreciation to be deducted each year. A firm will generally choose that alternative which meets the general goal of paying the least amount of tax, as late as possible, within the law. This goal is sometimes called the *least and latest rule*.

Accounting for Periodic Depreciation

The debit made in the entry to record periodic depreciation is usually either to an expense account or to a product cost account. In a manufacturing concern, the depreciation of factory buildings and equipment is a product cost, a part of the cost of work-in-process and finished goods. Depreciation on sales equipment is a selling expense. Depreciation on office equipment is a general or administrative expense. The matching credit for periodic depreciation could, in principle, be made directly to the asset account affected, such as buildings or equipment. Although such an entry is sometimes made, usually the credit is to a contra-asset account. This leaves the acquisition cost of the asset undisturbed and permits easy computation of the total amount written off through depreciation. The effect, however, is precisely the same as a direct credit to the asset account. The contra-asset account, Accumulated Depreciation, is the title of the account credited.

The entry to record periodic depreciation of office facilities, a period expense, is

Depreciation Expense	1,500	
Accumulated Depreciation		1,500

The entry to record periodic depreciation of manufacturing facilities, a product cost, is:

Work-in-Process Inventory	1,500	
Accumulated Depreciation		1,500

The Depreciation Expense account is closed at the end of the accounting period as a part of the regular closing-entry procedure. The Work-in-Process Inventory account is an asset. Product costs, such as depreciation on manufacturing facilities, accumulate in the Work-in-Process account until the goods being produced are completed and transferred to Finished Goods Inventory. The Accumulated Depreciation account remains open at the end of the period and appears on the balance sheet as a deduction from the asset account to which it refers. The balance in the Accumulated Depreciation account usually represents the total charges to accounting periods prior to the balance sheet date for the depreciation on assets currently in use. The difference between the balance of the asset account and the balance of its accumulated depreciation account is called the *book value* of the asset.

In the statement of changes in financial position, the periodic depreciation charge is an addback in the "operations" section. It represents an expense that does not use funds but instead uses a noncurrent asset.

Changes in Periodic Depreciation

The original depreciation schedule for a particular asset may require changing. Estimates of useful life (and of salvage value as well) may be judged incorrect in the light of new information, which may become apparent at any time during its life. The accuracy of the estimates improves as retirement approaches. If the misestimate has a material impact, corrective action must be taken. The generally accepted procedure is to make no adjustment for the past misestimate, but to spread the remaining undepreciated balance less the revised estimate of salvage value over the new estimate of remaining service life of the asset.

To illustrate the accounting for changes in periodic depreciation, assume the following facts. An office machine was purchased on January 1, Year 1, for $9,200. It was estimated that the machine would be operated for 15 years with a salvage value of $200. The depreciation charge recorded for each of the years from Year 1 through Year 5 under the straight-line method would have been $600 [= ($9,200 − $200)/15]. On December 31, Year 6, before the books are closed for the year, it is decided that a total useful life of 10 years is more likely, but the salvage estimate of $200 is still reasonable.

The accepted procedure for recognizing this substantial decrease in service life is to revise the future depreciation so that the correct total will be accumulated in the Accumulated Depreciation account at the end of the revised service life. No adjustments of amounts previously recorded may be made. In our example, the total amount of acquisition cost yet to be depreciated before the Year 6 adjustments is $6,000 [= ($9,200 − $200) − (5 × $600)]. The new estimate of the *remaining* life is 5 years (the year just ended plus the next 4), so the new annual depreciation charge is $1,200 (= $6,000/5). The only change in the accounting procedure is to substitute the new amount of $1,200 for the former annual depreciation of $600. The depreciation entry on December 31, Year 6, and each year thereafter would be

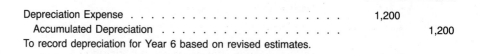

Depreciation Expense	1,200	
Accumulated Depreciation		1,200

To record depreciation for Year 6 based on revised estimates.

Figure 9.3 illustrates the revised depreciation path.

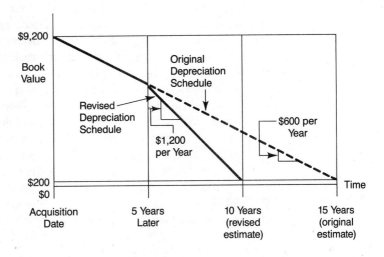

Figure 9.3 Illustration of Revised Depreciation Schedule. Asset's Service Life Estimate Is Decreased from 15 to 10 Years at the Start of Year 6. The Straight-Line Method Is Used. Asset Cost Is $9,200 and Has Estimated Salvage Value of $200.

Repairs and Improvements

Depreciation is not the only cost of using a plant asset. Repair and maintenance costs during the life of the asset will be incurred. The repair policy adopted by the business will often affect the depreciation rate. If, for example, machinery, trucks, and other plant assets are checked and repaired frequently, such assets will have a longer useful life, and therefore a lower depreciation rate than otherwise. The more commonly used estimates of service life and depreciation rates assume that normal repairs will be made during the life of an asset.

Repairs must be distinguished from improvements (sometimes called *betterments*). *Repairs* do not extend estimated service life materially or otherwise increase productive capacity. They restore future benefits to originally estimated levels. *Improvements* involve making an asset substantially better, improving its productive capacity. Repairs maintain or restore service potential; improvements and betterments extend service beyond that originally anticipated.

Whether a particular expenditure is a repair, treated as a period expense, or is an improvement, treated as an asset, can be difficult to decide. The line between maintaining service and improving or extending it is not distinct. Some expenditures may both restore and extend service potential. Consider, for example, an aircraft engine repair during which improved alloy materials are installed where inferior alloy parts had been used before. There is frequent disagreement between the Internal Revenue Service and taxpayers, as well as among accountants, over this question in specific situations.

Unit of Account Sometimes Distinguishes Repair from Improvement Some assets are actually composites of assets. Consider, for example, a truck, which might simplistically be thought of as a chassis, an engine, and a set of tires.

Although some major parts of a composite asset may have shorter lives than the asset as a whole, accounting for them with separate asset accounts is frequently impractical. Thus, the cost of a replacement set of tires is usually charged to repairs expense, although the tires could be treated as a separate asset. In some cases, composite assets are disaggregated for the purposes of depreciation. Exhibit 9.4 illustrates the effects on the timing and amounts of depreciation and repair expense of treating a truck either as a single asset or as a group of assets. At the time the truck is acquired, replacing the tires every second year and the engine after 3 years was anticipated. The repair to the windows in Year 5 was not. The truck has a 6-year life and zero estimated salvage value. When the truck is depreciated as a single asset, replacement of tires or the engine is a repair. When separate accounts are used, replacing the tires is an improvement, the acquisition of a new asset.

Retirement of Assets

When an asset is retired from service, the cost of the asset and the related amount of accumulated depreciation must be removed from the books. As part of this entry, the amount received from the sale or trade-in and any difference between that amount and book value must be recorded. The difference between the proceeds received on retirement and book value is a gain (if positive) or a loss (if negative). Before making the entry to write off the asset and its accumulated depreciation, an entry is made to bring the depreciation up to date; that is, the depreciation that has occurred between the start of the current accounting period and the date of disposition is recorded.

To illustrate the retirement of an asset, assume that sales equipment which cost $5,000, was expected to last 4 years, and had an estimated salvage value of $200, is depreciated on a straight-line basis at $1,200 [= ($5,000 − $200)/4] per year. Depreciation has been recorded for 2 years, and the equipment is sold at mid-year in the third year. The depreciation from the start of the accounting period to the date of sale of $600 [= $\frac{1}{2}$ × ($5,000 − $200)/4] is recorded:

Depreciation Expense	600	
Accumulated Depreciation		600
To record depreciation charges up to the date of sale.		

The book value of the asset is now its cost less $2\frac{1}{2}$ years of straight-line depreciation of $1,200 per year or $2,000 (= $5,000 − $3,000). The entry to record the retirement of the assets depends on the amount of the selling price.

Exhibit 9.4
Unit of Account Influences Depreciation and Maintenance Charges
Truck: Cost $48,000; 6-Year Life
Engine: Cost $9,000; 3-Year Life
Tires: Cost $1,200; 2-Year Life
Windows: Repair Cost $800 in Year 5
(straight-line depreciation)

| | Depreciation of | | | | |
	Truck	Engine	Tires	Maintenance	Total Expense
Separate Asset Accounts					
Year 1	$ 6,300[a]	$ 3,000[b]	$ 600[c]	—	$ 9,900
Year 2	6,300	3,000	600	—	9,900
Year 3	6,300	3,000	600[c]	—	9,900
Year 4	6,300	3,000[b]	600	—	9,900
Year 5	6,300	3,000	600[c]	$ 800[d]	10,700
Year 6	6,300	3,000	600	—	9,900
	$37,800	$18,000	$3,600	$ 800	$60,200
Single Asset Account					
Year 1	$ 8,000[e]	—	—	—	$ 8,000
Year 2	8,000	—	—	$ 1,200[f]	9,200
Year 3	8,000	—	—	9,000[g]	17,000
Year 4	8,000	—	—	1,200[f]	9,200
Year 5	8,000	—	—	800[d]	8,800
Year 6	8,000	—	—	—	8,000
	$48,000			$12,200	$60,200

[a]Truck: ($48,000 − $9,000 − $1,200)/6.
[b]Engine: $9,000/3.
[c]Tires: $1,200/2.
[d]Window repair.
[e]$48,000/6.
[f]Tires.
[g]Engine.

1. Suppose that the equipment were sold for $2,000 cash. The entry to record the sale would be

Cash	2,000	
Accumulated Depreciation	3,000	
Equipment		5,000

2. Suppose that the equipment were sold for $2,300. The entry to record the sale would be

Cash	2,300	
Accumulated Depreciation	3,000	
Equipment		5,000
Gain on Retirement of Equipment		300

3. Suppose that the equipment were sold for $1,500. The entry to record the sale would be

Cash	1,500	
Accumulated Depreciation	3,000	
Loss on Retirement of Equipment	500	
Equipment		5,000

Retirement Entries in the Statement of Changes in Financial Position The cash received from the disposition of a plant asset is a nonoperating source of funds. It appears on the funds statement as a source, "Proceeds from Disposition of Noncurrent Assets." The loss on retirement of equipment reduces net income but does not use cash. Thus, in deriving cash from operations, the amount of the loss is an addback to net income. Its presentation is similar to that for depreciation expense.

If there is a gain on retirement of equipment, two alternative treatments are possible and found in practice. One shows the entire proceeds from disposition of the asset as a nonoperating source of funds and thus requires treating the gain on retirement as a subtraction in computing cash from operations. The subtraction would be classified under the general heading of revenues not producing cash from operations, because all cash produced is shown under the heading of proceeds from disposition of noncurrent assets. The alternative treatment shows only the book value of the asset disposed of as a nonoperating source of funds and includes the gain in cash from operations. (That is, there is no subtraction in the operating section.) The first approach is preferred and used throughout this book.[8]

Trade-in Transactions

Instead of being sold when it is retired from service, the asset may be traded in on a new unit, a common practice for automobiles. The trade-in transaction can best be viewed as a sale of the old asset followed by a purchase of the new asset. The accounting for trade-in transactions determines simultaneously the gain or loss on disposal of the old asset and the acquisition cost recorded for the new asset. The procedures depend on the data available about the market value of the asset traded in and the cash equivalent cost of the new asset.

---

[8]See American Institute of Certified Public Accountants, *Technical Practice Aids*, 1984, Section 1300.09.

Using Market Value of Old Asset If the fair market value of the old asset traded in can be found, that amount plus the cash given up generally determines the valuation of the new asset. Assume that used equipment originally costing $5,000 with $3,000 of accumulated depreciation has a fair market value of $1,300 and is traded in on a new piece of equipment, along with an additional $5,500 of cash. The entries could be

Accumulated Depreciation	3,000	
Trade-in Allowance	1,300	
Loss on Disposition of Equipment	700	
Equipment		5,000

To record disposition of old equipment; plug for loss.

Equipment	6,800	
Trade-in Allowance		1,300
Cash		5,500

To record acquisition of new equipment; plug for cost of new equipment. The Trade-in Allowance account is not required but is used to split the transaction into two components: the sale of the old asset and purchase of the new.

Note that the *list* price of the new equipment does not affect the entries shown above. Valuation of the used asset in established secondhand markets almost always offers more reliable information than quoted list prices.

Using Market Value of New Asset If, however, a reliable valuation of the used asset is not available, then the lowest available cash price for the new asset (which is sometimes the list price) will determine the valuation of the new asset as well as the gain or loss on disposition of the old asset. If the list price of the new equipment in the preceding example were $7,000 and there were no other reliable information available, the entries would be

Equipment	7,000	
Cash		5,500
Trade-in Allowance		1,500

To record acquisition at list price; plug for trade-in allowance.

Accumulated Depreciation	3,000	
Trade-in Allowance	1,500	
Loss on Disposition of Equipment	500	
Equipment		5,000

To record disposition of old equipment. Loss is determined by list price of new equipment.

Income Tax Rules The income tax regulations do not permit the recognition of a gain or loss on the trade-in of an old asset in acquiring a new, similar asset. Instead, the cost of the new asset is assumed to be the book value of the used asset plus the cash paid. The tax rules are designed to reduce opportunity for manipulation of taxable income in trade-in transactions where, typically, the list price of new assets and offsetting trade-in allowances are subject to arbitrary offsetting adjustments. In the illustration used in this section, the entries for tax purposes would be

Accumulated Depreciation	3,000	
Trade-in Allowance	2,000	
Equipment		5,000
To record disposition of old equipment at book value; no gain or loss can be recognized. Plug for trade-in allowance.		
Equipment	7,500	
Cash		5,500
Trade-in Allowance		2,000
To record acquisition of new equipment. Cost of new equipment is a plug.		

The three illustrations use a two-step approach to facilitate discussion. In each case, the two entries could be combined into one, removing the need for a Trade-in Allowance account.

Gain on Trade-in The same analysis and same type of entries would be made if there were a *gain* on disposition. An exception to the concept that the cash equivalent price of the new asset is recorded occurs where this would result in a gain from the trade-in of a *similar* asset. In that case, no gain is recognized and the new asset is recorded at the book value of the old asset plus the cash paid in the trade-in transaction.[9] The rule is designed to reduce opportunity for manipulating reported income with trade-in transactions.

The Investment Tax Credit

In order to stimulate investment in machinery and equipment, Congress has passed tax laws that permit the purchaser of machinery and equipment to claim a credit against income taxes otherwise payable. The credit reduces the purchaser's income tax liability to the federal government. The rate of the credit and the property eligible for the credit have varied through the years as Congress has amended the tax

---

[9]In the highly unlikely situation where cash is received by the party making the trade-in, some gain is recognized; Accounting Principles Board, *Opinion No. 29,* "Accounting for Nonmonetary Transactions," 1973. (See *trade-in transaction* in the Glossary at the back of the book.)

laws. The examples in this section assume a 10 percent tax credit on all equipment purchases.[10]

If a firm buys $200,000 of equipment with an economic service life of 8 years (ACRS 5-year property class) this year, it will receive a $20,000 (= .10 × $200,000) investment tax credit. If its income tax liability shown on the tax return before the investment tax credit is $600,000, the following entry would be made:

Income Tax Expense	600,000	
Income Tax Payable		600,000
To record income taxes before the investment tax credit.		

The investment credit will reduce income taxes payable by $20,000 in the year the credit is earned, independent of the financial accounting treatment of the credit. There are two generally accepted methods of recording the investment tax credit for financial reporting—the flow-through method and the deferral method.[11]

Under the flow-through method, the entire investment credit realized during the year by all asset acquisitions is recorded as a reduction in income tax expense of the year. (It all "flows through" to income this year.) The entry would be

Income Tax Payable	20,000	
Income Tax Expense		20,000
To record the investment credit (= .10 × $200,000) for the year.		

The deferral method spreads the reduction in income tax expense over the years of the service life of the equipment acquired. The entire investment credit reduces the amount of income taxes payable in the year of acquisition, even though the reported reductions in income tax expense are spread over the years of service life. In the example, the entry in the year of acquisition, using the deferral method, would be

---

[10]The investment credit provisions are much more complex. The eligibility of property for the credit depends on its service life. Sixty percent of the cost of equipment with an ACRS life of 3 years is eligible. Only if the ACRS life is 5 years or more is the entire cost of the asset fully eligible for the investment tax credit. In addition, when the maximum investment credit is taken, the depreciable basis for tax purposes is reduced by one-half the amount of the investment credit. The credit may not exceed a stated percentage of the tax liability, with appropriate carrybacks and carryforwards of benefits.

[11]Accounting Principles Board, *Opinion No. 4*, "Accounting for the 'Investment Credit,'" 1964. Problem 31 at the end of this chapter explores the theoretical possibilities one might consider in choosing the methods in practice.

Income Tax Payable	20,000	
Income Tax Expense		2,500
Deferred Investment Credit		17,500

Part ($\frac{1}{8}$ × $20,000) of investment credit reduces expense in first year. The remaining portion will reduce expense in later years. The entire effect on taxes payable occurs in the first year.

The Deferred Investment Credit account appears on the balance sheet either as an asset contra or among the noncurrent liabilities, although it is not a liability.[12] At the end of each of the 7 following years, the following entry would be made:

Deferred Investment Credit	2,500	
Income Tax Expense		2,500

To amortize the deferred investment credit. Recorded income tax expense is reduced by $2,500 in each year 2 through 8. Income taxes payable were reduced by $20,000 in Year 1.

Effects over Time

Income taxes payable are always reduced in the year the investment tax credit is realized. Income tax expense is reduced by the full amount of the investment credit under both methods, but over different time periods.

If the deferral approach is used, the credit to income tax expense includes not only a part of this year's investment credit but also portions of the investment credit relating to earlier years that are still being amortized. For a firm in equilibrium (and assuming no change in the tax law with regard to the investment credit), income tax expense and net income will be the same under the flow-through and deferral approaches. For a growing firm, the flow-through method produces higher reported net income in all years during the growth period.

Funds Statement Effects

The flow-through method requires no adjustments to net income in deriving cash provided by operations.

If the deferral method is used, income tax expense for a growing firm will be greater than taxes paid or taxes currently payable. This excess represents an expense that does not use cash. It is added to net income in the operating section of the statement of changes in financial position to derive cash provided by operations.

[12]See Financial Accounting Standards Board, *Statement of Financial Accounting Concepts No. 3,* "Elements of Financial Statements of Business Enterprises," 1980, par. 166–168. Although APB Opinion No. 2 (1962) and *SFAC No. 3* appear to express a preference for treatment as an asset contra, most firms using the deferral method show deferred investment credits among the liabilities. The majority of nonregulated firms use the flow-through method for the investment credit, and so the issue of balance sheet presentation of deferred investment credits rarely arises.

Wasting Assets and Depletion

The costs of finding natural resources and preparing to extract them from the earth should be capitalized and amortized. Whether all costs of exploration or the costs of only the successful explorations are capitalized into the asset accounts remains an open accounting question. Generally accepted accounting principles allow two treatments. Under *full costing,* the costs of all explorations (both successful and unsuccessful) are capitalized so long as the expected benefits from the successful explorations will more than cover the cost of all explorations. Under *successful efforts costing,* only the cost of the successful efforts is capitalized; the costs of unsuccessful exploration efforts become expenses of the period when the fact becomes apparent that the efforts will not result in productive sites.[13]

Amortization of wasting assets, or natural resources, is called *depletion.* The depletion method most often used is the *units-of-production* method. For example, if $4.5 million in costs are incurred to discover an oil well that contains an estimated 1.5 million barrels of oil, then the costs of $4.5 million would be amortized (depleted) at the rate of $3 (= $4,500,000/1,500,000) for each barrel of oil removed from the well. The major accounting problem of extractive industries stems from uncertainty about the eventual total of units that will result from exploratory efforts.

Percentage Depletion Allowances

In some special circumstances, the tax laws permit computation of depletion in measuring taxable income as a percentage of the revenues secured from the sale of the minerals each year. The total of depletion charges over the life of the asset is not limited to costs incurred if this method, known as *percentage depletion,* is used. In financial accounting, depletion allocates the cost of natural resources to the periods when the resources are used. The percentage depletion allowances are a device instituted by the Congress to make the search for natural resources more attractive than it otherwise would be. The effect of percentage depletion is to allow some firms to deduct, on income tax returns over the life of the asset, amounts larger than the total of costs incurred. Financial statement expense over the life of the asset must be equal to the acquisition cost of the asset in a historical cost system.

Intangible Assets and Amortization

Assets can provide future benefits without having physical form. Such assets are called *intangibles.* Examples are research costs, advertising costs, patents, trade secrets, know-how, trademarks, and copyrights. The first problem with intangibles is to decide:

---

[13]Financial Accounting Standards Board, *Statement of Financial Accounting Standards No. 25,* "Suspension of Certain Accounting Requirements for Oil and Gas Producing Companies," 1979.

1. Whether expenditures made to acquire or develop intangibles have future benefits and can be quantified with a sufficient degree of precision so that they should be "capitalized" (set up as assets) and amortized over time; or

2. Whether they have no future benefits and thus are expenses of the period in which the costs are incurred.

If the latter, the immediate expensing of the asset's cost appears as pattern E in Figures 9.1 and 9.2.

The second problem to solve is how to amortize the costs if they have been capitalized. Deciding the period of amortization (the estimated service life) is a difficult question. Amortization of capitalized intangibles is usually recorded using the straight-line method, but other methods can be used if they seem appropriate. This section discusses some common intangibles and the issues involved in deciding whether to expense or to capitalize their costs. In generally accepted accounting principles, no intangible assets acquired after 1970 can be amortized over a period longer than 40 years.[14] Notes 2 and 13 of the General Products Company in Appendix Exhibit A.4 illustrate the typical disclosure for amortization of intangibles.

Research and Development

One common intangible is the benefit provided by expenditures on research and development (R&D). Such costs are incurred for various reasons. Perhaps the firm seeks to develop a technological or marketing advance in order to have an edge on competition. Or it might wish to explore possible applications of existing technology to design a new product or improve an old one. Other research may be undertaken in response to a government contract, in preparing for bids on potential contracts, or in pursuit of "discoveries," with no specific product in mind. Whatever the reason, practically all research costs will yield their benefits, if any, in future periods. Herein lies the accounting issue: Should research and development costs be charged to expense immediately as they are incurred, or should they be capitalized and amortized over future periods?

Generally accepted accounting principles[15] require immediate expensing of research and development costs. (Note 2 of the financial statements of General Products Company in Appendix Exhibit A.4 illustrates the required disclosures.) This requirement is based on arguments that the future benefits from most R&D efforts are too uncertain to warrant capitalization and that writing them off as soon as possible is more conservative. Nevertheless, some accountants feel that there must be future benefits in many cases or else R&D efforts would not be pursued. They think that R&D costs should be matched with the benefits produced by the R&D expenditures through the capitalization procedure with amortization over the benefited periods. This procedure is not allowed.

---

[14]Accounting Principles Board, *Opinion No. 17,* "Intangible Assets," 1970.
[15]Financial Accounting Standards Board, *Statement of Financial Accounting Standards No. 2,* "Accounting for Research and Development Costs," 1974.

Advertising

Advertising expenditures are designed to increase sales, currently and in the future, but there is a lag between the incurrence of these costs and their impact. The impact of advertising probably extends into subsequent periods.

Although generally accepted accounting principles allow capitalizing and then amortizing advertising costs, common practice immediately expenses all advertising costs, regardless of the timing of their impact (see pattern E in Figures 9.1 and 9.2). Those supporting this practice argue that (1) it is more conservative to do so; (2) it is almost impossible to quantify the future effects and timing of benefits derived from these costs; and (3) when these costs remain stable from year to year, income is not affected by the capitalization policy after the first few years. Nevertheless, some accountants support the capitalization treatment because doing so will better report assets and match costs with resulting benefits.

Patents

A patent is a right obtained from the federal government to exclude others from the benefits of an invention. The legal life of patent protection may be as long as 17 years, although the economic life of the patent may be considerably less. The accounting for patent costs depends on whether the patent was purchased from another party or developed internally. If the former, the purchase price is capitalized. If the latter, the total cost of product development and patent application is expensed as required for all R&D costs.[16] Purchased patent costs are usually amortized over the shorter of (1) the remaining legal life, or (2) its estimated economic life. If for some reason the patent becomes worthless, the remaining capitalized cost is recognized immediately as an expense of that period.

Goodwill

Goodwill is an intangible asset that will be mentioned here only briefly. More details follow in Chapter 13. Goodwill arises from the purchase of one company or operating unit by another company and is measured as the difference between the amount paid for the acquired company as a whole and the sum of the current value of its individual assets less its liabilities. Thus, goodwill will appear in the financial statements of the company making the acquisition. Under present practice, goodwill (and other intangibles) acquired after October 1970 must be amortized over a time period not longer than 40 years.[17]

---

[16]*SFAS No. 2* does not give reasoning to justify this distinction in accounting treatments of purchased versus developed patents.

[17]APB, *Opinion No. 17.*

Summary

Three major classes of long-lived operating assets are plant assets, wasting assets (nonrenewable natural resources), and intangibles. The major accounting problems for each class are the same: (1) calculating the cost of the asset to be capitalized as an asset, (2) estimating the total period of benefit or the amount of expected benefits, and (3) assigning the cost to the benefited periods or units produced in a systematic and reasonable fashion so that investment in the asset is recovered through charges to income.

The chapter emphasized depreciable plant assets and their depreciation. The cost to be charged off is reduced by any salvage value. The period (or number of units) of benefit is based on experience or, for tax reporting, by relying on guidelines set down by the Internal Revenue Service. The pattern of depreciation charges over the asset's life is usually based on some conventional method—the most common method in practice is straight line.

If the asset is retired before the end of the estimated service life for an amount different from its book value, a gain or loss will be recognized. If the asset is traded in on another asset, a gain or loss may or may not be recognized depending on the terms of the transaction.

Intangibles such as trademarks, copyrights, patents, and computer programs are among the most valuable resources owned by some firms. The accounting treatment of *purchased* intangibles is the same as for tangible assets. For most intangibles developed within a firm, accounting requires the immediate expensing of the development costs. The firms most likely to be affected are service, rather than manufacturing, companies.

Problem 1 for Self-Study

Purdy Company acquires two used trucks from Foster Company. Although the trucks are not identical, they both cost $15,000. Purdy Company knew when it negotiated the purchase price that the first truck required extensive engine repair, expected to cost about $4,000. The repair was made the week after acquisition and actually cost $4,200. Purdy Company thought the second truck was in normal operating condition when it negotiated the purchase price but discovered upon taking possession of the truck that certain bearings needed replacing. The cost of this repair, made the week after acquisition, was $4,200.

a. What costs should be recorded in the accounts for the two trucks?

b. If the amounts recorded above are different, distinguish between the two "repairs."

Suggested Solution

a. First truck recorded at $19,200. Second truck recorded at $15,000, with $4,200 debited to expense or loss.

b. At the time the first truck was acquired, Purdy Company knew it would have to make the "repair." The purchase price was presumably reduced because of the known cost to be incurred. At the time of acquisition, the cost was anticipated to be required in order to produce the expected service potential of the asset. The fact that the cost is $4,200, rather than "about $4,000," seems not to violate the Purdy Company's expectations at the time it acquired the truck. If the repair had cost significantly more than $4,000—say, $7,000—then the excess would be loss or expense.

The second truck was assumed to be operable when the purchase price was agreed. The cost of the repair is incurred to bring about the level of service potential already thought to have been acquired. There are no more future benefits after the repair than had been anticipated at the time of acquisition. Therefore, the $4,200 is expense or loss.

Problem 2 for Self-Study

Jensen Company purchased land with a building standing on it as the site for a new plant it planned to construct. The company received bids from several independent contractors for demolition of the old building and construction of the new one. It rejected all bids and undertook demolition and construction using company labor, facilities, and equipment.

All transactions relating to these properties were debited or credited to a single account, Real Estate. Various items in the Real Estate account are described below. The Real Estate account is to be closed. All amounts in it should be taken out and reclassified into one of the following accounts:

(1) Land account.
(2) Buildings account.
(3) Revenue, gain, or expense contra account.
(4) Expense, loss, or revenue contra account.
(5) Some other account.

You may reclassify amounts of the following transactions into two or more of the above. If you use **(5)**, some other account, indicate the nature of the account.
a. Cost of land, including old building.
b. Legal fees paid to bring about purchase of land and to transfer its title.
c. Invoice cost of materials and supplies used in construction.
d. Direct labor and materials cost incurred in demolition of old building.
e. Direct costs of excavating raw land to prepare it for the foundation of the new building.
f. Discounts earned for prompt payment of item **c**.
g. Interest for year on notes issued to finance construction.
h. Amounts equivalent to interest on Jensen Company's own funds used in construction that would have been invested in marketable securities if an independent contractor had been used. The amount was debited to Real Estate and credited to Interest Revenue so that the cost of the real estate would be comparable to its cost if it had been built by an independent contractor.
i. Depreciation for period of construction on trucks that were used both in construction and regular company operations.
j. Proceeds of sale of materials salvaged from old buildings were debited to Cash and credited to Real Estate.

   k. Cost of building permits.

   l. Salaries of certain corporate engineering executives can be allocated between Salary Expense and Real Estate. The portion debited to Real Estate represents an estimate of the portion of the time spent during the year on planning and construction activities for the new building.

   m. Payments for property taxes on plant site owed by its former owner but assumed by Jensen Company.

   n. Payments for property taxes on plant site for construction period.

   o. Insurance premiums to cover workers engaged in demolition and construction activities. The insurance policy contains various deductible clauses, requiring the company to pay the first $5,000 of damages from any accident.

   p. Cost of injury claims for $2,000 paid by the company because the amount was less than the deductible amount in the policy.

   q. Costs of new machinery to be installed in building.

   r. Installation costs for the machinery above.

   s. Profit on construction of new building (computed as the difference between lowest independent contractor's bid and the actual construction cost) was debited to Real Estate and credited to Construction Revenue.

Suggested Solution

(1) a, b, d, j, l, m, o, p.
(2) c, e, f, g, i, k, l, n, o, p.
(3) —.
(4) h, i, s.
(5) i, q, r.

Comments and Explanations

   f. The reduction in cost of materials and supplies will reduce the cost of the buildings. The actual accounting entries depend on the method used to record the potential discount. These issues are not discussed in this book, but see Problem 28 at the end of Chapter 8.

   h. Although one capitalizes explicit interest, one may not capitalize opportunity-cost interest or interest imputed on one's own funds used. The adjusting entry credits Real Estate and debits Interest Revenue or its contra. In any case, the debit reduces income, removing the revenue that had been recognized by the company.

   i. Computation of the amounts to be allocated requires an estimate. Once the amounts are estimated, they are debited to Building or to Depreciation Expense and Work-in-Process Inventory, as appropriate, for the regular company operations.

   j. Credit to Land account, reducing its cost.

   l. Allocate to Land and Building based on estimate of how time was spent. Given the description, most of these costs are probably for the building. If all of the salaries had been debited to Real Estate, then some must be reclassified as Salary Expense.

m. Part of the cost of the land.

n. Capitalized as part of the Building account for the same reasons that interest during construction is capitalized. Some accountants would treat this item as expense. In any case, this item can be an expense for tax reporting.

p. Most accountants would treat this as an expense or loss for the period. Others would treat it as part of the cost of the building for the same reason that the explicit insurance cost is capitalized. If, however, the company was irrational in acquiring insurance policies with deductible clauses, then this item is expense or loss. Accounting usually assumes that most managements make rational decisions most of the time. In any case, this item can be treated as an expense or loss for tax reporting.

q. Debit to Machine and Equipment account, an asset account separate from Building.

r. Treat the same as preceding item; installation costs are part of the cost of the asset. See Chapter 2, page 40.

s. The effect of recognizing revenue is reversed. The Real Estate account is credited and Construction Revenue or its contra is debited.

Problem 3 for Self-Study

Central States Electric Company constructed a nuclear generating power plant at a cost of $200 million. The plant is expected to last 50 years before being retired from service. The company estimates that at the time the plant is retired from service, $20 million in "decommissioning costs" (costs to dismantle the plant and dispose of the radioactive materials) will be incurred. Straight-line depreciation is computed and charged once per year, at year-end.

During the eleventh year of operation, new regulations governing nuclear waste disposal are enacted. The estimated decommissioning costs increase from $20 million to $24 million.

During the thirty-first year of operation, the life of the plant is revised. It will last 60 years in total, not 50 years.

At the end of the thirty-fifth year, the plant is sold to another utility company for $80 million.

a. What is the depreciation charge for the first year?

b. What is the depreciation charge for the eleventh year?

c. What is the depreciation charge for the thirty-first year?

d. Record the journal entry for the sale of the plant at the end of the thirty-fifth year.

Suggested Solution

(Dollar amounts in millions.)

a. $4.4 per year = ($200 + $20)/50 years.

b. $4.5 per year = ($200 + $20 + $4 − $4.4 per year × 10 years)/40 years remaining life,

= ($224 − $44)/40,

= $180/40.

c. $3.0 per year = ($180 − $4.5 × 20 years)/30 years remaining life,
$$= (\$180 - \$90)/30,$$
$$= \$90/30.$$
d. Accumulated depreciation
   at time of sale
$$= (\$4.4 \times 10) + (\$4.5 \times 20) + (\$3.0 \times 5) = \$149.0.$$

December 31 of Year 35

Cash	80.0	
Accumulated Depreciation on Power Plant	149.0	
Power Plant.		200.0
Gain on Disposal of Plant		29.0

Problem 4 for Self-Study

Widdicomb Company is considering changing from the flow-through method to the deferral method of accounting for the investment credit. It expects to acquire assets subject to increasing dollar amounts of investment credits each year for the foreseeable future. Indicate the effect on each of the following items in the financial statements 2 years hence if the deferral, rather than the flow-through, method is used, starting now and continuing for the indefinite future.
a. Recorded Cost of Assets Acquired.
b. Income Taxes Payable.
c. Income Tax Expense.
d. Deferred Investment Credits on balance sheet.
e. Depreciation Expense.
f. Net Income for year.
g. Retained Earnings.
h. Total Equities.

Suggested Solution

Larger under the deferral method than under the flow-through method: **c, d**.
Smaller under the deferral method than under the flow-through method: **f, g**.
The same under both methods: **a, b, e, h**.

Questions, Exercises, Problems and Cases

Questions

1. Review the meaning of the following concepts or terms discussed in this chapter.
   a. Amortization.
   b. Plant assets and depreciation.
   c. Interest during construction.
   d. Wasting assets and depletion.
   e. Percentage depletion allowance.
   f. Intangibles.

g. Capitalize.
h. Improvements.
i. Repairs.
j. Maintenance.
k. Joint cost.
l. Value.
m. Residual or salvage value.
n. Service or depreciable life.
o. Asset depreciation range.
p. Straight-line (time and use) methods.
q. Declining-balance methods.

r. Sum-of-the-years'-digits method.
s. Book value.
t. Treatment of changes in estimates of useful lives and residual values of long-lived assets.
u. Trade-in transaction.
v. Research and development.
w. Goodwill.
x. Investment credit.
y. Flow-through method.
z. Deferral method.

2. **a.** "Accounting for depreciating assets would be greatly simplified if accounting periods were only long enough or the life of the assets short enough." What is the point of the quotation?

b. "The major purpose of depreciation accounting is to provide funds for the replacement of assets as they wear out." Do you agree? Explain.

3. "Showing both acquisition cost and accumulated depreciation amounts separately provides a rough indication of the relative age of the firm's long-lived assets."

a. Assume that the Poyfer Company acquired an asset with a depreciable cost of $100,000 several years ago. Accumulated depreciation as of December 31, recorded on a straight-line basis, is $60,000. The depreciation charge for the year is $10,000. What is the asset's depreciable life? How old is the asset?

b. Assume straight-line depreciation. Devise a formula that, given the depreciation charge for the year and the asset's accumulated depreciation, can be used to determine the age of the asset.

4. **a.** What is the effect of capitalizing interest on reported net income summed over all the periods of the life of a given self-constructed asset, from building through use, until eventual retirement? Contrast with a policy of expensing interest as incurred.

b. Consider a company engaging in increasing dollar amounts of self-construction activity each period over periods when interest rates do not decline. What is the effect on reported income each year of capitalizing interest in contrast to expensing interest as incurred?

Exercises

5. *Classification of expenditures as asset or expense.* For each of the following expenditures or acquisitions, indicate the type of account debited. Classify the accounts as asset other than product cost, product cost (Work-in-Process Inventory), or expense. If the account debited is an asset account, then specify whether it is current or noncurrent.

    a. $150 for repairs of office machines.
    b. $1,500 for emergency repairs to an office machine.
    c. $250 for maintenance of delivery trucks.
    d. $5,000 for a machine acquired in return for a 3-year note.
    e. $4,200 for research and development staff salaries.
    f. $3,100 for newspaper ads.
    g. $6,400 for wages of factory workers engaged in production.
    h. $3,500 for wages of factory workers engaged in installing equipment.
    i. $2,500 for salaries of office work force.
    j. $1,000 for legal fees in acquiring an ore deposit.
    k. $1,200 for a 1-year insurance policy beginning next month.
    l. $1,800 for U.S. Treasury Notes, to be sold to pay the next installment due on income taxes.
    m. $4,000 for royalty payment on a patent used in manufacturing.
    n. $10,000 for purchase of a trademark.
    o. $100 filing fee for copyright registration application.

6. *Journal entries for trade-in transactions and depreciation.* On April 30, Year 6, the Tico Wholesale Company acquired a new machine with a fair market value of $14,000. The seller agreed to accept the company's old machine, $7,000 in cash, and a 12 percent, 1-year note for $4,000 in payment.

    The old machine was purchased on January 1, Year 1, for $10,000. It was estimated that the old machine would be useful for 8 years, after which it would have a salvage value of $400. It is estimated that the new machine will have a service life of 10 years and a salvage value of $800.

    Assuming that the Tico Company uses the straight-line method of depreciation and closes its books annually on December 31, give the entries that were made in Year 6.

7. *Computations and journal entries for retirement of plant.* On July 1, 1962, a building and land were purchased for $96,000 by The Hub, a retail clothing store. Of this amount, $40,000 was allocated to the land and the remainder to the building. The building is depreciated on a straight-line basis.

    On July 1, 1984 (no additions or retirements having been recorded in the meanwhile), the net book value of the building was $25,200. On March 31, 1985, the building and site were sold for $60,000. The fair market value of the land was $50,000 on this date.

    The firm closes its books annually at June 30. Give the entries required on March 31, 1985. (*Hint:* First compute what the annual depreciation charges must be, based on the facts given.)

8. *Journal entries for plant acquisition, depreciation, and retirement.* Journalize the following transactions:

    a. A piece of office equipment is purchased for $850 cash.
    b. Depreciation for 1 year of $170 is recorded.
    c. The equipment is sold for $400. At the time of the sale, the Accumulated Depreciation shows a balance of $340. Depreciation of $170 for the year of the sale has not yet been recorded.

9. *Journal entries for revising estimate of life.* Give the journal entries for the following selected transactions of the Eagle Manufacturing Company. The company uses the straight-line method of calculating depreciation and closes its books annually on December 31.

    a. A machine is purchased on November 1, 1979, for $30,000. It is estimated that it will be used for 10 years and that it will have a salvage value of $600 at the end of that time. Give the journal entry for the depreciation at December 31, 1979.

    b. Record the depreciation for the year ending December 31, 1980.

    c. In August 1985, it is decided that the machine will probably be used for a total of 12 years and that its salvage value will be $400. Record the depreciation for the year ending December 31, 1985.

    d. The machine is sold for $1,000 on March 31, 1990. Record the entries of that date, assuming that depreciation is recorded as indicated in part **c**.

10. *Straight-line depreciation, working backwards.* On March 1, one of the buildings owned by the Metropolitan Storage Company was destroyed by fire. The cost of the building was $100,000. The balance in the Accumulated Depreciation account at January 1 was $38,125. A service life of 40 years with a zero salvage value had been estimated for the building. The company uses the straight-line method. The building was not insured.

    a. Give the journal entries made at March 1.

    b. If there have been no alterations in the service life estimate, how many years previously was the building acquired?

11. *Journal entries to correct accounting errors.* Give correcting entries for the following situations. In each case, the firm uses the straight-line method of depreciation and closes its books annually on December 31. Recognize all gains and losses currently.

    a. A cash register was purchased for $300 on January 1, 1980. It was depreciated at a rate of 10 percent of original cost per year. On June 30, 1985, it was sold for $200 and a new cash register was acquired for $500. The bookkeeper made the following entry to record the transaction:

Store Equipment	300	
Cash in Bank		300

    b. A used truck was acquired for $4,000. Its cost, when new, was $6,000, and the bookkeeper made the following entry to record the purchase:

Truck	6,000	
Accumulated Depreciation		2,000
Cash		4,000

c. A testing mechanism was purchased on April 1, 1983, for $600. It was depreciated at a 10 percent annual rate. On June 30, 1985, it was stolen. The loss was not insured, and the bookkeeper made the following entry:

Theft Loss	600	
Testing Mechanism		600

12. *Journal entries for acquisition of asset with a note and subsequent recognition of depreciation and interest.* The Grogan Manufacturing Company started business on January 1, 1983. At that time it acquired machine A for $20,000, payment being made by check.

Because of an expansion in the volume of business, machine B, costing $25,000, was acquired on September 30, 1984. A check for $15,000 was issued, with the balance to be paid in annual installments of $2,000 plus interest at the rate of 12 percent on the unpaid balance. The first installment is due on September 30, 1985.

On June 30, 1985, machine A was sold for $13,000 and a larger model, machine C, was acquired for $30,000.

All installments are paid on time.

All machines have an estimated life of 10 years with an estimated salvage value equal to 10 percent of acquisition cost. The company closes its books on December 31. The straight-line method is used.

Prepare dated journal entries to record all transactions through December 31, 1985, including year-end adjustments but excluding closing entries.

13. *Cost of self-constructed assets.* The Dickhaut Manufacturing Company purchased a plot of land for $90,000 as a plant site. There was a small office building on the plot, conservatively appraised at $20,000, which the company will continue to use with some modification and renovation. The company had plans drawn for a factory and received bids for its construction. It rejected all bids and decided to construct the plant itself. Below are listed additional items that management feels should be included in plant asset accounts:

(1) Materials and Supplies	$200,000
(2) Excavation	12,000
(3) Labor on Construction	140,000
(4) Cost of Remodeling Old Building into Office Building	13,000
(5) Interest on Money Borrowed by Dickhaut[a]	6,000
(6) Interest on Dickhaut's Own Money Used	9,000
(7) Cash Discounts on Materials Purchased	7,000
(8) Supervision by Management	10,000
(9) Workman's Compensation Insurance Premiums	8,000
(10) Payment of Claims for Injuries Not Covered by Insurance	3,000
(11) Clerical and Other Expenses of Construction	8,000
(12) Paving of Streets and Sidewalks	5,000

(13) Architect's Plans and Specifications.	4,000
(14) Legal Costs of Conveying Land	2,000
(15) Legal Costs of Injury Claim	1,000
(16) Income Credited to Retained Earnings Account, Being the Difference Between the Foregoing Cost and the Lowest Contractor's Bid	11,000

^aThis interest is the entire amount of interest paid during the construction period.

Show in detail the items to be included in the following accounts: Land, Factory Building, Office Building, and Site Improvements. Explain why you excluded any items that you did not include in the four accounts.

14. *Calculations for various depreciation methods.* Calculate the depreciation charge for the first and second years of the asset's life in each of the following cases.

Asset	Cost	Estimated Salvage Value	Life (years)	Depreciation Method
a. Blast Furnace	$800,000	$25,000	20	150% Declining-Balance
b. Hotel	500,000	50,000	45	Straight-Line
c. Typewriter	800	80	8	Sum-of-the-Years'-Digits
d. Tractor	18,000	1,500	10	Double-Declining-Balance (use twice the straight-line rate)
e. Delivery Truck	22,000	5,200	6	Sum-of-the-Years'-Digits
f. Delivery Truck	22,000	5,200	3	Accelerated Cost Recovery System

15. *Calculations for various depreciation methods.* On January 1, 1985, the Central Production Company acquired a new turret lathe for $36,000. It was estimated to have a useful life of 4 years and no salvage value. The company closes its books annually on December 31. Indicate the amount of the depreciation charge for each of the 4 years under:

  a. The straight-line method.
  b. The declining-balance method at twice the straight-line rate.
  c. The sum-of-the-years'-digits method.
  d. ACRS depreciation assuming that the lathe belongs to the 3-year property class.
  e. Assume now that the lathe was acquired on April 1, 1985. Indicate the amount of the depreciation charge for each of the years from 1985 to 1989, using the sum-of-the-years'-digits method. (*Hint:* Depreciation charges for a year, however they are computed, are allocated on a straight-line basis to periods *within* a year.)

16. *Amount of interest capitalized during construction.* Chan Company builds some of its own chemical processing plants. At the start of the year the Construction-in-Process account had a balance of $1 million. Construction activity occurred uniformly throughout the year. At the end of the year the balance was $5 million. The borrowings of the company during the year were as follows:

New Construction Loans at 20 Percent per Year	$ 2,000,000
Old Bond Issues Maturing at Various Times, Averaging 10 Percent Rate . .	8,000,000
Total Interest-Bearing Debt	$10,000,000

a. Compute the amount of interest to be capitalized into the Construction-in-Process account for the year.

b. Present journal entries for interest for the year.

17. *Calculations for various depreciation methods.* A machine is acquired for $8,900. It is expected to last 8 years and to be operated for 25,000 hours during that time. It is estimated that its salvage value will be $1,700 at the end of that time. Calculate the depreciation charge for each of the first 3 years using:

a. The straight-line (time) method.

b. The sum-of-the-years'-digits method.

c. The declining-balance method using a 25 percent rate.

d. The units-of-production method. Operating times are as follows: first year, 3,500 hours; second year, 2,000 hours; third year, 5,000 hours.

18. *Revision of estimated service life changes depreciation schedule.* The Slowpoke Shipping Company buys a new car for $10,000 on January 1, 1984. It is estimated that it will last 6 years and have a salvage value of $1,000. Early in 1986, it is discovered that the car will last only an additional 2 years, or 4 years in total. The company closes its books on December 31. Present a table showing the depreciation charges for each year from 1984 to 1987 and give the adjusting entry made in 1986. Follow the instructions for each of the depreciation methods listed below:

a. The straight-line method.

b. The sum-of-the-years'-digits method.

19. *Retirement of plant assets.* The Lindahl Manufacturing Company acquires a new machine for $7,200 on July 1, 1981. It is estimated that it will have a salvage value of $900. The company closes its books annually on June 30.

a. Compute the depreciation charges for each year of the asset's life assuming the straight-line method.

b. If the machine were sold for $700 on October 30, 1986, give the journal entries that would be made on that date.

20. *Trade-in transactions.* The Twombly Company purchased a new panel truck in May 1983. The truck cost $18,600. It was estimated that the truck would be driven for 100,000 miles before being traded in and that its salvage value at that time would be $2,600.

Odometer readings are as follows:

December 31, 1983	12,000
December 31, 1984	50,000
December 31, 1985	82,000
June 16, 1986	98,000

On June 16, 1986, the truck was traded in for a new one with a list price of $22,000. The old truck had a fair market of $2,600, but the dealer allowed $3,000 on it toward the list price of the new one. The balance of the purchase price was paid by check.

    a. Compute the depreciation charges for each year through 1985, using a ''production'' or ''use'' method.

    b. Record the entries for June 16, 1986, assuming that the list price of the new truck is unreliable, whereas the fair market value of the old is reliable.

    c. Record the entries for June 16, 1986, assuming that there were no reliable estimates for the fair market value of the old truck.

21. *Funds statement; loss on disposal of plant.* Refer to the data in Problem 18 at the end of Chapter 5 on page 203 for the Harris Company. Assume that the proceeds of sale of the equipment amount to $400 rather than $2,000. As a result, net income declines from $39,000 to $37,400, and dividends are reduced from $30,000 to $28,400. All other items remain unchanged. Prepare a statement of changes in financial position for Year 5, using a cash definition of funds.

22. *Funds statement; gain on disposal of plant.* Refer to the data in Problem 18 at the end of Chapter 5 on page 203 for the Harris Company. Assume that the proceeds of sale of the equipment amount to $3,000 rather than $2,000. As a result, net income increases from $39,000 to $40,000, and dividends are increased from $30,000 to $31,000. All other items remain unchanged. Prepare a statement of changes in financial position for Year 5, using a cash definition of funds.

23. *Journal entries for investment tax credit.* The Libby Company has income tax expense, before any investment credits, of $50,000 each year. At the start of the first year, it acquires an asset with a depreciable life of 4 years belonging to the ACRS 3-year property class. Assume that the asset qualifies for an investment credit of $4,000.

    a. Record income taxes and the entries related to the investment credit for the 4 years of the asset's life using the flow-through method.

    b. Record entries related to income taxes and the investment credit for the 4 years of the asset's life using the deferral method.

24. *Whether a single asset account or separate asset accounts are used affects classification of expenditures as repairs or improvements.* Lafleur Company purchased a delivery truck for $20,000 at the start of Year 1. The truck is expected to last for 4 years, but the engine is expected to be replaced at the end of Year 2 at a cost of $6,000. Lafleur Company must choose between depreciating the truck as a single unit or as two separate assets—the engine and the rest of the truck. The company uses straight-line depreciation for financial reporting.

   a. Compute total expense for each of the 4 years of the truck's life, depreciating the entire cost of $20,000 in a single asset account.
   b. Compute total expense for each year of the truck's life, depreciating the engine and the rest of the truck in separate asset accounts.

Problems and Cases

25. *Allocation of cost in "basket" purchases.* In each of the following situations, compute the amounts of gain or loss to be shown on the income statement for the year, as well as the amount of asset to be shown on the balance sheet as of the end of the year. Show the journal entry or entries required, and provide reasons for your decisions.

   a. A company wishes to acquire a 5-acre site for a new warehouse. The land it wants is part of a 10-acre site that the owner insists be purchased as a whole for $18,000. The company purchases the land, spends $2,000 in legal fees for rights to divide the site into two 5-acre plots, and immediately offers half of the land for resale. The two best offers are

   (1) $12,000 for the east half, and
   (2) $13,000 for the west half.

   The company sells the east half.
   b. The same data as in part **a**, except the two best offers are

   (1) $5,000 for the east half, and
   (2) $12,000 for the west half.

   The company sells the west half.

26. *Composite depreciation versus individual-item depreciation.* The Alexander Company acquired three used machine tools for a total price of $49,000. Costs to transport the machine tools from the seller to Alexander Company's factory were $1,000. The machine tools were renovated, installed, and put to use in manufacturing the firm's products. The costs of renovation and installation were as follows:

	Machine Tool A	Machine Tool B	Machine Tool C
Renovation Costs	$1,700	$800	$950
Installation Costs	300	550	250

The machine tools have the following estimated lives: tool A—4 years; tool B—10 years; tool C—6 years.

   a. Assume that each machine tool is capitalized in a separate asset account and that the remaining life of each machine tool is used as the basis for allocating the joint costs of acquisition. Compute the depreciable cost of each of the three machine tools.

b. Present journal entries to record depreciation charges for years 1, 5, and 8, given the assumption in part **a**. Use the straight-line method.

c. Assume that the three machine tools are treated as one composite asset in the accounts. If management decides to depreciate the entire cost of the composite asset on a straight-line basis over 10 years, what is the depreciation charge for each year?

d. Which treatment, **a** or **c**, should management of the Alexander Company probably prefer for tax purposes and why?

27. *Funds statement effects.* Refer to the Simplified Statement of Changes in Financial Position for a Period in Exhibit 5.17 on page 201. Eleven lines in the statement are numbered. Ignore the unnumbered lines in responding to the questions below.

Assume that the accounting cycle is complete for the period and that all of the financial statements have been prepared. Then it is discovered that a transaction has been overlooked. That transaction is recorded in the accounts and all of the financial statements are corrected. Define *funds* as *cash*. For each of the following transactions, indicate which of the numbered lines of the funds statement is affected and by how much. Ignore income tax effects.

a. A machine that cost $10,000 and that has $7,000 of accumulated depreciation is sold for $4,000 cash.

b. A machine that cost $10,000 and that has $7,000 of accumulated depreciation is sold for $2,000 cash.

c. A machine that cost $10,000 and that has $7,000 of accumulated depreciation is traded in on a new machine. The new machine has a cash price of $12,000. A trade-in allowance for the old machine of $4,000 is given, so that $8,000 cash is paid.

d. A fire destroys a warehouse. The loss is uninsured. The warehouse cost $80,000 and at the time of the fire had accumulated depreciation of $30,000.

e. Refer to the facts of part **d**. Inventory costing $70,000 was also destroyed. The loss was uninsured. Record the effects of only these new facts.

28. *Effects of investment credit on funds statement.* Refer to the instructions in the preceding question. Follow the instructions for the transactions or events below relating to the investment credit. During the year, qualifying assets with a 10-year depreciable life are acquired, and investment credits of $10,000 are realized. Ignore asset acquisition itself; focus on the investment tax credit.

a. The flow-through method of accounting is used. Record the effects for the year the assets are acquired.

b. The flow-through method of accounting is used. Record the effects for the year after the assets are acquired.

c. The deferral method is used. Record the effects for the year the assets are acquired.

d. The deferral method is used. Record the effects for the year after the assets are acquired.

29. *Preparing funds statements (adapted from a problem by Stan Baiman).* Exhibit 9.5 shows comparative balance sheets, an income statement of Ormes Company for Year 2, and supplementary notes.

Prepare the Year 2 statement of changes in financial position with funds defined as cash.

Exhibit 9.5
ORMES COMPANY
Comparative Balance Sheets and Income Statement
(Problem 29)

	December 31	
	Year 1	Year 2
Balance Sheets		
Cash	$ 30,000	$130,000
Accounts Receivable	100,000	120,000
Less: Allowance for Uncollectibles	(20,000)	(25,000)
Inventory	100,000	80,000
Plant and Equipment	700,000	750,000
Accumulated Depreciation	(380,000)	(500,000)
Total Assets	$530,000	$555,000
Accounts Payable	$ 20,000	$ 30,000
Capital Stock.	200,000	145,000
Retained Earnings	310,000	380,000
Total Equities	$530,000	$555,000
Year 2 Income Statement		
Net Sales		$495,000
Gain on Sale of Equipment		110,000
		$605,000
Cost of Goods Sold.		$200,000
Bad Debt Expense		15,000
Depreciation Expense.		140,000
Income Tax Expense		100,000
Total Expenses.		$455,000
Net Income		$150,000

Notes: (1) During Year 2, Ormes acquired property, plant, and equipment at a cost of $200,000.
(2) During Year 2, Ormes did not collect on any accounts receivable that had previously been written off.
(3) All depreciation charges are expensed.
(4) Dividends declared have been paid in cash.

30. *Investment credits for a firm growing to equilibrium.* Refer to the data in Exercise 23 for the Libby Company. Assume that each year the Libby Equilibrium Company acquires an asset with a depreciable life of 4 years. Each year the asset acquired qualifies for an investment credit of $4,000, and income tax expense before any investment credits is $50,000.

    a. Record entries related to income taxes and the investment credit for each of the first 5 years using the flow-through method.

    b. Record entries related to income taxes and the investment credit for each of the first 5 years using the deferral method.

    c. Assuming that Libby Equilibrium Company's income taxes, asset acquisitions, and investment credits continue in the following years as in the first 4 years, describe the effects on the financial statements of the two methods of accounting for the investment credit.

    d. Assume the same data as in part **c**, but that the new asset's cost increases by 10 percent each year and that the amount of the investment credit earned increases by 10 percent each year. Describe the effects on the financial statements of the two methods of accounting for the investment credit.

31. *Choosing between the deferral and flow-through methods for the investment credit.* Three companies have each recently made investments in equipment designed to save fuel. The equipment purchased by each company costs $200,000 and has a 10-year service life. In all three cases, the company was entitled to a $10,000 investment tax credit when it purchased the asset during the current year. The income taxes otherwise payable of all three companies were reduced by $10,000 during the current year. In all three companies, management had made careful studies of the costs and benefits of acquiring the new equipment.

    Management of Company A decided that the equipment purchased would provide operating cost savings with a present value of $250,000. The company is delighted to acquire the asset.

    Management of Company B decided that the equipment it purchased would provide operating cost savings with a present value of $190,000. The equipment was worth acquiring only because of the investment credit.

    Management of Company C decided that the equipment it purchased provided operating cost savings with a present value of $196,000. The equipment was acquired only because the investment credit made the investment worthwhile.

    a. Discuss the considerations the management of each of these companies might give to accounting for the investment credit.

    b. What can you conclude from this problem about the method of accounting for the investment credit that reflects managerial decisions?

32. *Capitalizing versus expensing advertising costs: effects on financial statements and rate of return.* The Consumer Products Company has $300,000 of total assets. The Consumer Products Company has been earning $45,000 per year and generating $45,000 per year of cash flow from operations. Each year the Consumer Products Company distributes its earnings by paying cash of $45,000 to owners. Management of the Consumer Products Company believes that a new advertising campaign now will lead to increased sales over the next 4 years. The anticipated net cash flows of the project are as follows:

Beginning of Year	Net Cash Inflow (outflow)
1	($24,000)
2, 3, and 4	10,000 each year

Assume that the advertising campaign is undertaken, that cash flows are as planned, and that the Consumer Products Company makes payments to owners of $45,000 at the end of the first year and $47,000 at the end of each of the next 3 years. Assume that there are no interest expenses in any year. Ignore any income tax effects.

  a. Compute net income and the rate of return on assets of the Consumer Products Company for each of the 4 years, assuming that advertising expenditures are expensed as they occur. Use the year-end balance of total assets in the denominator of the rate-of-return calculation.

  b. Compute net income and the rate of return on assets of the Consumer Products Company for each year of the project, assuming that advertising costs are capitalized and then amortized on a straight-line basis over the last 3 years. Use the year-end balance of total assets in the denominator of the rate of return on assets.

  c. How well has the management of the Consumer Products Company carried out its responsibility to its owners? On what basis do you make this judgment? Which method of accounting seems to reflect performance more adequately?

33. *Accounting for intangibles.* In Year 1, Epstein Company acquired the assets of Falk Company. The assets of Falk Company included various intangibles. Discuss the accounting for the acquisition in Year 1, and in later years, for each of the following items.

  a. Registration of the trademark Thyrom® for thyristors expires in 3 years. Epstein Company thought that the trademark had a fair market value of $100,000. It expects to continue making and selling Thyrom thyristors indefinitely.

  b. The design patent covering the ornamentation of the containers for displaying Thyrom thyristors expires in 5 years. The Epstein Company thought that the design patent had a fair market value of $30,000 and expects to continue making the containers indefinitely.

  c. An unpatented trade secret on a special material used in manufacturing thyristors was viewed as having a fair market value of $200,000.

  d. Refer to the trade secret in part **c**. Suppose that in Year 2 a competitor discovers the trade secret, but does not disclose the secret to other competitors. How should the accounting policies be changed?

  e. During Year 1, the Epstein Company produced a sales promotion film, *Using Thyristors for Fun and Profit,* at a cost of $45,000. The film is licensed to purchasers of thyristors for use in training their employees and customers. The film is copyrighted.

34. *Expensing versus capitalizing advertising costs for firm advertising every year.* Equilibrium Company plans to spend $60,000 at the beginning of each of the next several years advertising the company's brand names and trademarks. As a result of the advertising expenditure for a given year, aftertax income (not counting advertising expense) is expected to increase by $24,000 a year for 3 years, including the year of the expenditure itself. Equilibrium Company has other aftertax income of $20,000 per year. The controller of Equilibrium Company wonders what will be the effect on the financial statements of following one of two accounting policies with respect to advertising expenditures:

(1) Expensing the advertising costs in the year of expenditures.
(2) Capitalizing the advertising costs and amortizing them over 3 years, including the year of the expenditure itself.

Assume that the Company does spend $60,000 at the beginning of each of 4 years and that the planned increase in income occurs. Ignore income tax effects.

   a. Prepare a 4-year condensed summary of net income, assuming that policy **(1)** is followed and advertising costs are expensed as incurred.
   b. Prepare a 4-year condensed summary of net income, assuming that policy **(2)** is followed and advertising costs are capitalized and amortized over 3 years. Compute also the amount of Deferred Advertising Costs (asset) to be shown on the balance sheet at the end of each of the 4 years.
   c. In what sense is policy **(1)** a conservative policy?
   d. What will be the effect on net income and on the balance sheet if Equilibrium Company continues to spend $60,000 each year and the effects on aftertax income continue as in the first 4 years?

35. *Improvements versus repairs or maintenance.* The balance sheet of Woolf's Department Store shows a building with an original cost of $800,000 and accumulated depreciation of $660,000. The building is being depreciated on a straight-line basis over 40 years. The remaining depreciable life of the building is 7 years. On January 2 of the current year, an expenditure of $28,000 was made on the street-level display windows of the store. Indicate the accounting for the current year if the expenditure of $28,000 was made under each of the following circumstances. Each of these cases is to be considered independently of the others, except where noted. Ignore income tax effects.

   a. Management decided that improved display windows would make the store's merchandise seem more attractive. The windows are a worthwhile investment.
   b. A violent hailstorm on New Year's Day destroyed the display windows previously installed. There was no insurance coverage for this sort of destruction. The new windows installed are physically identical to the old windows. The old windows had a book value of $28,000 at the time of the storm.
   c. Vandals destroyed the display windows on New Year's Day. There was no insurance coverage for this sort of destruction. The new windows installed are physically identical to the old windows. The old windows had a book value of $28,000 at the time of the destruction.

d. The old displays contained windows constructed of nonshatterproof glass. Management had previously considered replacing its old nonshatterproof windows with new ones but had decided that there was *zero* benefit to the firm in doing so. New shatterproof windows are installed because a new law was passed requiring that all stores must have shatterproof windows on the street level. The alternative to installing the new windows was to shut down the store. In responding to this part, assume *zero* benefits result from the new windows. Part **e** below considers the more realistic case of some benefits.

e. Management had previously considered replacing its old, nonshatterproof windows with new ones, but decided that the new windows would produce future benefits of only $7,000 and so were not a worthwhile investment. However, a new law (see part **d**) now requires them to do so (or else shut down), and the new windows are installed.

36. *Capitalizing versus expensing; if capitalized, what amortization period?* In each of the following situations, compute the amounts of revenue, gain, expense, and loss to be shown on the income statement for the year and the amount of asset to be shown on the balance sheet as of the end of the year. Show the journal entry or entries required, and provide reasons for your decisions. Straight-line amortization is used. The reporting period is the calendar year. The situations are independent of each other, except where noted.

a. Because of a new fire code, a department store must install an additional fire escape on its building. Management had previously considered installing the additional fire escape. It had rejected the idea because it had already installed a modern sprinkler system, which was even more cost-effective, instead. The new code gives management no alternative except to close the store. The fire escape is acquired for $28,000 cash on January 1. The building is expected to be demolished 7 years from the date the fire escapes were installed.

b. Many years ago, a firm acquired shares of stock in the General Electric Company for $100,000. On December 31, the firm acquired a building with an appraised value of $1 million. The company paid for the building by giving up its shares in the General Electric Company at a time when equivalent shares traded on the New York Stock Exchange for $1,050,000.

c. Same data as part **b**, except that the shares of stock represent ownership in Small Timers, Inc., whose shares are traded on a regional stock exchange. The last transaction in shares of Small Timers, Inc., occurred on December 27. Using the prices of the most recent trades, the shares of stock of Small Timers, Inc., given in exchange for the building have a market value of $1,050,000.

d. A company decides that it can save $3,500 a year for 10 years by switching from small panel trucks to larger delivery vans. To do so requires remodeling costs of $18,000 for various garages. The first fleet of delivery vans will last for 5 years, and the garages will last for 20 years. The garages are remodeled on January 1.

e. A company drills for oil. It sinks 10 holes during the year at a cost of $1 million each. Nine of the holes are dry, but the tenth is a gusher. By the end of the year, the oil known to be recoverable from the gusher has a net realizable value of $40 million, and Amoco has offered to buy the well for $40 million. No oil was extracted during the year.

f. A company manufactures aircraft. During the current year, all sales were to the government under defense contracts. The company spent $400,000 on institutional advertising to keep its name before the business community. It expects to resume sales of small jet planes to corporate buyers in 2 years.

g. A company runs a large laboratory that has, over the years, found marketable ideas and products worth tens of millions of dollars. On average, the successful products have a life of 10 years. Expenditures for the laboratory this year were $1,500,000.

h. A textile manufacturer gives $250,000 to the Textile Engineering Department of a local university for basic research in fibers. The results of the research, if any, will belong to the general public.

i. On January 1, an automobile company incurs costs of $6 million for specialized machine tools necessary to produce a new model automobile. Such tools last for 6 years, on average, but the new model automobile is expected to be produced for only 3 years.

j. On January 1, an airline purchased a fleet of airbuses for $100 million cash. The airbuses have an expected useful life of 10 years and no salvage value. At the same time the airline purchased for cash $20 million of spare parts for use with those airbuses. The spare parts have no use, now or in the future, other than replacing broken or worn-out airbus parts. During the first year of operation, no spare parts were used.

k. Refer to the data in the preceding part. In the second year of operation, $1 million of spare parts were used.

37. *Effect on net income of changes in estimates for depreciable assets.* A major airline has $3 billion of assets, including airplanes costing $2.5 billion with net book value of $1.6 billion. It earns income equal to approximately 6 percent of total assets. Airplanes have been depreciated for financial reporting purposes on a straight-line basis over 10-year lives to a salvage value equal to 10 percent of original cost. The airline has announced a change in depreciation policy; it will use 14-year lives and salvage values equal to 12 percent of original cost. Assume that the airplanes are all 4 years old and an income tax rate of 46 percent.

What will be the approximate impact on net income of the change in depreciation policy? Compute both dollar and percentage effects.

38. *Analysis of financial statements and supplemental disclosures; effect of depreciation method on financial statement ratios.* Exhibit 9.6 reproduces information from a recent annual report of the General Electric Company (GE). GE discloses that it uses the sum-of-the-years'-digits method of depreciation for financial reporting. Assume that GE depreciates all of its assets using a 16-year life with zero estimated salvage value and the assets are $4\frac{1}{2}$ years old.

Exhibit 9.6
GENERAL ELECTRIC COMPANY
Condensed Balance Sheet at Year-End
(dollar amounts in millions)
(Problem 38)

Current Assets	$10,356	Current Liabilities	$ 8,153
Plant and Equipment at Cost	13,843	Noncurrent Liabilities and	
Accumulated Depreciation .	(6,535)	Owners' Equity	13,462
Other Assets	3,951		$21,615
	$21,615		

Other Data for Year

Depreciation Charge for Year	$ 964
Additions to Plant and Equipment During the Year	1,608
Plant and Equipment, Beginning of Year	12,705
Accumulated Depreciation, Beginning of Year	5,861
Income Before Interest Charges (net of income tax effects)	2,040

a. Demonstrate that the data in the balance sheet are approximately consistent with GE's using sum-of-the-years'-digits depreciation and assumptions that assets have 16-year lives and are $4\frac{1}{2}$ years old.

b. Compute the depreciation charge for the year and the amount of accumulated depreciation that would appear on the balance sheet if GE used straight-line depreciation.

c. Reconstruct GE's balance sheet for year-end as it would appear if GE used straight-line depreciation. Assume no change in income tax expense.

d. Compute GE's rate of return on assets [= income before interest charges (net of tax effects) divided by end-of-year assets]. First, use the financial statements as reported and then use the financial statements as they would appear if GE used straight-line depreciation.

e. What was the cost and the accumulated depreciation on plant and equipment retired during the year?

39. *Analysis of financial statement disclosure of effects of depreciation policy.* A recent annual report of Caterpillar Tractor Company contained the following statement of depreciation policy:

> Depreciation is computed principally using accelerated methods for both income tax and financial reporting purposes. These methods result in a larger allocation of the cost of buildings, machinery, and equipment to operations in the early years of the lives of assets than does the straight-line method.

Then Caterpillar discloses the amounts for "Buildings, Machinery, and Equipment—Net" as they would appear if the straight-line method had always been used. Exhibit 9.7 shows these amounts and other data from the financial statements for three recent years.

Exhibit 9.7
Excerpts from Annual Report of Caterpillar Tractor Company
(dollar amounts in millions)
(Problem 39)

	Year 3	Year 2	Year 1
Buildings, Machinery, and Equipment—Net:			
As Reported	$3,339	$3,300	$2,928
If Straight-Line Depreciation Were Used	4,020	3,894	3,431
Depreciation Expense Reported.	505	448	370

    a. What amounts would be reported for depreciation expense for Years 2 and 3 if the straight-line method had always been used?

    b. Now assume a 40 percent tax rate, that straight-line depreciation had been used always for both income tax and financial reporting purposes, and that Buildings, Machinery, and Equipment—Net on the balance sheet amounted to $4,020 at the end of Year 3. What other items on the balance sheet for the end of Year 3 would probably change and by how much?

40. *Straight-line depreciation is probably too "conservative"; it usually writes off an asset's cost faster than future benefits disappear.* (This problem requires material from Appendix B.) Assets are acquired for their future benefits—the future cash flows they produce, either cash inflows or savings of cash outflows. As the near-term cash flows are received, the future benefits decline, but the future cash flows come closer to being received, *increasing* the value of the future benefits. The present value of future cash flows may, in total, increase or decrease during any one year. This problem explores changes in the present value of future cash flows with the passage of time and illustrates the phenomenon that for many business projects the present value of future benefits (that is, future cash flows) declines at a rate much slower than implied by straight-line depreciation.

    Pasteur Company plans to acquire an asset that will have a 10-year life and promises to generate cash flows of $10,000 per year at the end of each of the 10 years of its life. Given the risk of the project that uses the asset, Pasteur Company judges that a 12 percent rate is appropriate for discounting its future cash flows. Using a 12 percent discount rate, the present value of $1 received at the end of each of the next 10 years is $5.65022 (see Table 4 at the back of the book; 10-period row, 12 percent column). Because the project is expected to generate $10,000 per year, the present value of the cash flows is $56,502 (= $10,000 × 5.65022). Assume that Pasteur Company purchases the asset for exactly $56,502 at the beginning of Year 1. Exhibit 9.8 shows for each year the present value of the cash flows remaining at the beginning of each year of the asset's life. The numbers in column (3) are $10,000 multiplied by the number appearing in Table 4, 12 percent column, for the number of periods remaining in the asset's life. Column (4) shows the percentage of the asset's present value of the cash flows remaining, and column (5) shows the percentage loss in present value of cash flows during the preceding year.

Exhibit 9.8

Pattern of Expiration of Future Benefits Measured as the
Net Present Value of Future Cash Flows
(Problem 40)

Asset Cost $56,502 and Has 10-Year Life
Asset Yields $10,000 per Year of Cash Inflow
Discount Rate = 12 Percent per Year

Beginning of Year (1)	Years Remaining (2)	Present Value of Remaining Cash Flows (3)	Percentage of Present Value of Cash Flows Remaining (4)	Percentage of Loss in Value During Preceding Year (5)	Straight-line Depreciation for Preceding Year (6)
1	10	$56,502	100%		
2	9	53,282	94	6%	10%
3	8	49,676	88	6	10
4	7	45,638	81	7	10
5	6	41,114	73	8	10
6	5	36,048	64	9	10
7	4	30,373	54	10	10
8	3	24,018	43	11	10
9	2	16,901	30	13	10
10	1	8,929	16	14	10
11	0	0	0	16	10
Total . .				100%	100%

Column (3) from Table 4 (at back of book), 12 percent column, row corresponding to number in column (2) here multiplied by $10,000.
Column (4) = number in column (3)/$56,502.
Column (5) = column (4) preceding year − column (4) this year.

Column (6) shows the percentage write-off in cost each year using straight-line depreciation—10 percent per year. Note that the decline in present value of cash flows is less that straight-line in the first 5 years, but greater in the last 4 years.

    a. Construct an exhibit similar to Exhibit 9.8 for an asset with a 5-year life promising $10,000 of cash flows at the end of each year. Use a discount rate of 15 percent per year. The asset cost is $33,522. Compare the resulting decline in present value with straight-line depreciation.

    b. Now consider another asset with a 5-year life with risk appropriate for a 15 percent discount rate. This asset also has net present value of cash flows of $33,522, but the expected cash flows are $11,733 at the end of the first year, $10,767 at the end of the second year, $9,722 at the end of the third year, $8,716 at the end of the fourth year, and $7,710 at the end of the fifth year. Construct an exhibit similar to Exhibit 9.8 for this asset. You should find that the present value of future cash flows disappears at the rate of 20 percent per year of $33,522, the initial present value.

    c. Using the results of your work above, comment on the nature of conservatism of straight-line depreciation.

41. *Analysis of financial statements to compute the change in property and plant assets required to sustain sales growth* (*developed from a suggestion by Katherine Schipper*). Exhibit 9.9 shows data from several recent years for the General Electric Company (GE). Assume that analysis of GE's markets indicates that GE can sustain sales growth of 10 percent per year for the next several years. The corporate treasurer must plan ways to raise the new funds that will be required to finance the expansion of assets needed to support such increased sales. Assume that GE's financial policy calls for financing of new property and plant with long-term financing, owners' equity (including earnings and retentions), and long-term borrowings, whereas financing for current assets, such as receivables and inventory, can be generated with current liabilities, such as increases in payables and short-term bank borrowings.

Exhibit 9.9
GENERAL ELECTRIC COMPANY
Data on Sales, Plant/Equipment, and Total Assets
(dollar amounts in millions)

			Plant and Equipment				Total Assets			
Year (1)	Sales (2)	Dollar Change from Preceding Year (3)	Balance Sheet Total Net of Accumulated Depreciation December 31 (4)	Dollar Change from Preceding Year (5)	New Acquisitions for Year (6)	Balance Sheet Total December 31 (7)	Dollar Change from Preceding Year (8)	Turnover Ratios Fixed Assets (9)	Total Assets (10)
---	---	---	---	---	---	---	---	---	---
12 . . .	$27,240	$2,281	$6,844	$1,064	$2,025	$20,942	$2,431	4.32	1.38
11 . . .	24,959	2,498	5,780	1,167	1,948	18,511	1,867	4.80	1.42
10 . . .	22,461	2,807	4,613	590	1,262	16,644	1,608	5.20	1.42
9 . . .	19,654	2,135	4,023	439	1,055	15,036	1,339	5.17	1.37
8 . . .	17,519	1,822	3,584	228	823	13,697	1,647	5.05	1.36
7 . . .	15,697	1,592	3,356	175	740	12,050	1,309	4.80	1.38
6 . . .	14,105	187	3,181	565	588	10,741	1,372	4.87	1.40
5 . . .	13,918	1,973	2,616	255	813	9,369	1,045	5.59	1.57
4 . . .	11,945	1,471	2,361	224	735	8,324	922	5.31	1.52
3 . . .	10,474	917	2,137	111	501	7,402	514	5.03	1.47
2 . . .	9,557	723	2,026	277	711	6,888	689	5.06	1.46
1 . . .	8,834		1,749		685	6,199			
Weighted average								4.94	1.42

Columns (2), (4), (6), (7): taken from annual reports.

Columns (3), (5), (8): amount for a given year computed by subtracting amount for preceding year from amount for given year, using data in preceding column.

$$\text{Column (9)} = \frac{\text{Column (2)}}{.5 \times [\text{Column (4)} + \text{Column (4), Preceding Year}]}.$$

$$\text{Column (10)} = \frac{\text{Column (2)}}{.5 \times [\text{Column (7)} + \text{Column (7), Preceding Year}]}.$$

Past relations appear in Exhibit 9.9; note the computation of the fixed asset turnover ratio and the total asset turnover ratio. These ratios show the average amount of sales per dollar of investment in plant and equipment and the average amount of sales per dollar of investment in total assets. The total asset turnover ratio averages 1.42, indicating that $1.42 of sales requires about $1.00 of total assets. Putting it another way, about $.70 (= $1/1.42) of assets is required for each dollar of sales. The average fixed asset turnover ratio of 4.94 indicates that about $1 of net property and plant is required for $4.94 of sales, or that $1 of sales requires about $.20 (= $1/4.94) of property and plant. From these data, management has tentatively concluded that to increase sales by $1 will require about $.70 of new assets, of which about $.20 will be invested in new property and plant, with the remaining $.50 invested in current assets such as receivables and inventories. Thus, to increase sales by 10 percent, or $2.7 billion, will require about $1.9 (= .70 × $2.7) billion of new funds, with about $540 million (= .20 × $2.7 billion) required from long-term sources.

Can you sharpen and improve this analysis? Consider the *incremental* sales achieved by past incremental investments in both property/plant and total assets. Consider that turnover ratios deal with average relations, whereas the questions at issue require analysis of incremental relations—how much additional investment is required for additional sales.

42. *Analysis of effects of capitalization of interest and other funds into construction work in progress.* Regulated public utilities capitalize into their plant assets under construction not only explicit interest costs, but also an amount for the cost of funds provided by owners. These amounts are often called AFUDC—allowance for funds used during construction; see the Glossary for an explanation of the term and an indication of why this is done.

Exhibit 9.10 reproduces excerpts from the recent financial statements of Commonwealth Edison, a regulated producer of electricity. The balance sheet amount for Construction Work in Progress includes amounts for interest and owners' equity capitalized as AFUDC. The income statement shows credits to income each year for the amounts of AFUDC.

   a. Compute the rate of return on common shareholders' equity, using the average of beginning- and end-of-year balances.
   b. Compute the net income to common shareholders before AFUDC and the implied rates of return on common shareholders' equity, as in the preceding part.
   c. Estimate the average construction period for Commonwealth Edison's plant by dividing the average balance of Construction Work in Progress by the Construction Expenditures for the year.
   d. Independent of your answer to the preceding part, assume that the average construction period is 3.75 years. Assume that expenditures for new construction occur evenly throughout the year. Estimate the amount of AFUDC included in the Construction Work in Progress at the end of Year 4. Ignore income tax considerations (which is appropriate because the amounts shown for AFUDC are net of income tax effects). What would Retained Earnings be at the end of Year 4 without the capitalization of AFUDC into Construction in Progress for the last 3.75 years?

Exhibit 9.10
COMMONWEALTH EDISON
Financial Statement Excerpts
(dollars in millions)

	Year 4	Year 3	Year 2	Year 1
Balance Sheet at December 31				
Construction Work in Progress.	$ 4,876	$ 5,103	$ 4,148	$3,296
Utility Plant (net)	6,907	5,551	5,583	5,419
Other Assets (net)	799	669	446	458
Total Assets	$12,582	$11,323	$10,177	$9,173
Liabilities and Deferred Credits	$ 7,513	$ 7,005	$ 6,152	$5,563
Preferred Stock Equity	1,165	1,100	1,112	1,076
Common Stock Equity:				
Contributed Capital	3,094	2,517	2,251	1,904
Retained Earnings	810	701	662	630
Total Equities	$12,582	$11,323	$10,177	$9,173
Income Statement for Year				
Electric Operating Income	$ 654	$ 597	$ 493	$ 335
Total Interest Expense (before capitalization into plant)	(602)	(544)	(451)	(335)
Amounts Capitalized into Construction Work in Progress	420	303	254	222
Other (net)	35	(4)	(9)	(7)
Net Income to Common Shares	$ 507	$ 352	$ 287	$ 215
Statement of Changes in Financial Position				
Construction Expenditures (including amounts capitalized into construction work in progress)	$ 1,426	$ 1,304	$ 1,180	$1,317
Interest Rate Used for Capitalization	9.5%	8.6%	7.7%	7.3%

Chapter 10   Liabilities: Introduction

This chapter and the next two examine the accounting concepts and procedures for the right-hand side of the balance sheet, which shows the sources of a firm's financing. The funds used to acquire assets come from two sources: owners and nonowners. Chapter 12 discusses owners' equity. This chapter and Chapter 11 discuss obligations incurred by a business that result from raising funds from nonowners. Banks and creditors providing debt on a long-term basis understand their role as providers of funds. Suppliers and employees, who do not require immediate cash payment for goods provided or services rendered, usually do not think of themselves as contributing to a firm's funds, but they do. Likewise, customers who advance cash to a firm prior to delivery of a good or service provide funds to the firm. The obligations of a business to these nonowning contributors of funds are *liabilities*.

A thorough understanding of liabilities requires knowledge of compound interest and present value computations. In these computations, payments made at different times are made comparable by taking into account the interest that cash can earn over time. Appendix B at the back of the book introduces the computations.

Basic Concepts of Liabilities

In accounting, an obligation is generally recognized as a liability of an entity if it has three essential characteristics:[1]

1. The obligation involves a probable future sacrifice of resources—a future transfer of cash, goods, or services or the forgoing of a future cash receipt—at a specified or determinable date. The cash equivalent value of resources to be sacrificed must be measurable with reasonable precision.
2. The entity has little or no discretion to avoid the transfer.
3. The transaction or event giving rise to the entity's obligation has already occurred.

Example 1 Miller Corporation's employees have earned wages and salaries that will not be paid until the next payday, 2 weeks after the end of the current accounting period. Miller Corporation's suppliers are owed substantial amounts for goods sold to Miller Corporation, but these debts are not due for 10 to 30 days after the end

---

[1]Financial Accounting Standards Board, *Statement of Financial Accounting Concepts No. 3,* "Elements of Financial Statements of Business Enterprises," 1980, par. 29.

of the period. Miller Corporation owes the federal and state governments for taxes, but the payments are not due until the 15th of next month. Each of these items meets the three criteria to be a liability. Thus, they are shown as liabilities under titles such as Wages Payable, Salaries Payable, Accounts Payable, and Taxes Payable.

Example 2 When Miller Corporation sells television sets, it gives a warranty to repair or replace any faulty parts or faulty sets within 1 year after sale. This obligation meets the three criteria of a liability. Because some television sets will surely need repair, the future sacrifice of resources is probable. The obligation to make repairs is Miller Corporation's. The transaction giving rise to the obligation, the sale of the television set, has already occurred.

The amount is not known with certainty, but Miller Corporation has had sufficient experience with its own television sets to be able to estimate with reasonable precision what the expected costs of repairs or replacements will be. The repairs or replacements will occur within a time span, 1 year, known with reasonable precision. Miller Corporation will thus show Estimated Liability for Warranty Payments on its balance sheet.

Example 3 Miller Corporation signs a binding contract to supply certain goods to a customer within the next 6 months. In this case, there is an obligation, definite time, and definite amount (of goods, if not cash), but there has been no past or current transaction. Chapter 2 pointed out that accounting does not recognize assets or liabilities for executory contracts—the mere exchange of promises where there is no mutual performance. Without some mutual performance, there is no current or past benefit. Thus no liability is shown in this case.

Example 4 Facts are the same as in Example 3, except that the customer made a $10,000 cash deposit upon signing the order. Here, there has been more than an exchange of promises. The customer has paid cash and Miller Corporation has accepted it. It will show a liability called Advances from Customers in the amount of $10,000. The remainder of the order is still executory and is not recognized in accounting. Such arrangements are called "partially executory contracts."

Example 5 Miller Corporation has signed a 3-year, noncancelable lease with the IBM Corporation to make payments of $3,000 per month for the use of a computer system with a 3-year life. Definite amounts are due at definite times, and a transaction has occurred—a computer system has been received. Miller Corporation will show a liability called Present Value of Future Payments Under Capital Leases on its balance sheet.

Example 6 Miller Corporation is defendant in a class action lawsuit alleging damages of $10 million. The lawsuit was filed by customers who claim to have been injured by misleading advertising about Miller Corporation's television sets. Lawyers retained by the corporation think that there is an adequate defense to the charges. Because there is no obligation to make a payment at a reasonably definite time, there is no liability. The notes to the financial statements will disclose the existence of the lawsuit, but no liability will appear on the balance sheet.

Example 7 Miller Corporation has signed a contract promising to employ its president for the next 5 years and to pay the president a salary of $250,000 per year. The salary is to be increased in future years at the same rate as the Consumer Price Index, published by the U.S. government, increases. Miller Corporation has an obligation to make payments (although the president may quit at any time without penalty). The payments are of reasonably certain amounts and are to be made at definite times. At the time the contract is signed, no mutual performance has occurred. The contract is purely executory. Because a transaction is deemed not to have taken place, no liability appears on the balance sheet. A liability will, of course, arise as the president performs services over time.

Example 8 Miller Corporation has signed a contract with Interstate Oil Pipe Line Company to ship at least 10,000 barrels of crude oil per month for the next 3 years. Miller Corporation must pay for the shipping services, whether or not it actually ships oil. An arrangement such as this, called a *throughput contract,* is not recorded as a liability, because the event giving rise to the obligation is viewed as being actual shipment, which has not yet occurred. Such an obligation is merely disclosed in notes. Similarly, long-term obligations for so-called take-or-pay contracts, where the "purchaser" is obligated to pay for certain quantities or goods, whether or not the purchaser actually takes delivery of the goods, is not a formal liability, but must be disclosed.[2] Both throughput and take-or-pay contracts are viewed as executory.

Valuation

In *historical* cost accounting, liabilities appear on the balance sheet as the present value of payments to be made in the future. The interest rate used in computing the present value amount throughout the life of a liability is the interest rate that the specific borrower was required to pay at the time the liability was initially incurred. That is, the *historical* interest rate is used.

As Chapter 2 mentions, most current liabilities appear at the amount payable because the difference between the amount ultimately payable and its present value is immaterial.

Classification

Liabilities are generally classified on the balance sheet as *current* or *noncurrent.* The criterion generally used for dividing current from noncurrent liabilities is the length of time that will elapse before payment must be made. The dividing line between the two is the length of the operating cycle, usually 1 year.

---

[2]Financial Accounting Standards Board, *Statement of Financial Accounting Standards No. 47,* "Disclosure of Long-Term Obligations," 1981.

Contingencies—Potential Obligations

One of the criteria used by accountants to recognize a liability is that there be a probable future sacrifice of resources. The world of business and law is full of uncertainties. At any given time a firm may find itself potentially liable for events that have occurred in the past. Contingencies of this nature are not recognized as accounting liabilities. They are potential future obligations rather than current obligations. The potential obligations arise from events that occurred in the past but whose outcome is not now known. Whether an item becomes a liability, and how large a liability it will become, depends on a future event, such as the outcome of a lawsuit.

Suppose that the company is sued for damages in a formal court proceeding for an accident involving a customer who was visiting the company. The suit is not scheduled for trial until after the close of the accounting period. If the company's lawyers and auditors agree that the outcome is likely to be favorable for the company or that, if unfavorable, the amount of the damage settlement will not be large, then no liability will be recognized on the balance sheet. The notes to the financial statements must disclose, however, significant contingencies.

The FASB has said that an estimated loss from a contingency should be recognized in the accounts only if both of the following conditions are met:[3]

(a) Information available prior to the issuance of the financial statements indicates that it is probable that an asset had been impaired or that a liability had been incurred. . . .
(b) The amount of the loss can be reasonably estimated.

An example suggested by the FASB *Statement* is that of a toy manufacturer who has sold products for which a safety hazard has been discovered. The toy manufacturer thinks it likely that liabilities have been incurred. Test (b) would be met if experience or other information enabled the manufacturer to make a reasonable estimate of the loss. The journal entry would be

Loss on Damage Claim	50,000	
Estimated Liability for Damages		50,000
To recognize estimated liability for expected damage arising from safety hazard of toys sold.		

The debit in the above entry is to a loss account (presented among other expenses on the income statement), and the credit is to an estimated liability, which should be

[3]Financial Accounting Standards Board, *Statement of Financial Accounting Standards No. 5,* "Accounting for Contingencies," 1975. When information indicates that it is probable that an asset has been impaired or a liability has been incurred and an estimate of the amount has been made, but the estimate is a range, then the lower end of the range is to be used. For example, if the estimated loss is a range from $1 million to $1.5 million, then the amount $1 million would be used.

treated as a current liability, similar to the Estimated Warranty Liability account, on the balance sheet. In practice, an account with the title "Estimated Liability for Damages" would seldom, if ever, appear in published financial statements, because it would be perceived as an admission of guilt. Such an admission is likely to adversely affect the outcome of the lawsuit. The liability account would be combined with others for financial statement presentation.

The term *contingency,* or sometimes *contingent liability,* is used only when the item is not recognized in the accounts but, rather, in the footnotes. (Notes receivable sold *with* recourse, described in Chapter 7, are another example of a contingency.) A recent annual report of General Motors illustrates the disclosure of contingencies as follows.

> **Note 14. Contingent Liabilities** There are various claims and pending actions against the Corporation and its subsidiaries with respect to commercial matters, including warranties and product liability, governmental regulations including environmental and safety matters, civil rights, patent matters, taxes and other matters arising out of the conduct of business. Certain of these actions purport to be class actions, seeking damages in very large amounts. The amounts of liability on these claims and actions at . . . [year-end] were not determinable but, in the opinion of the management, the ultimate liability resulting will not materially affect the consolidated financial position or results of operations of the Corporation and its consolidated subsidiaries.

Current Liabilities

Current liabilities are those due within the current operating cycle, normally 1 year. They include accounts payable to creditors, payroll accruals, short-term notes payable, taxes payable, and a few others. Current liabilities are continually discharged and replaced with new ones in the course of business operations.

These obligations will not be paid for several weeks or months after the current balance sheet date. Their present value is therefore less than the amount that will be paid. Nevertheless, these items are shown at the full amount to be paid, because the difference is usually so small that separate accounting for the difference and subsequent interest expense is judged not worth the trouble.

Accounts Payable to Creditors

Companies seldom pay for goods and services when received. Payment is usually deferred until a bill is received from the supplier. Even then, the bill might not be paid immediately, but instead, accumulated with other bills until a specified time of the month when all bills are paid. Because explicit interest is not paid on these accounts, management tries to obtain as much capital as possible from its creditors by delaying payment as long as possible. Failure to keep promises to creditors according to schedule can, however, lead to poor credit ratings and to restrictions on future credit.

Wages, Salaries, and Other Payroll Items

When employees earn wages, they owe part of their earnings to governments for income and other taxes. Employees may also owe other amounts for union dues and insurance plans. The amounts, although wage expense of the employer, are not paid directly to employees, but are paid on their behalf to the governments, unions, and insurance companies.

In addition, the employer must pay various payroll taxes and may have agreed to pay for other fringe benefits because wages were earned. Employers owe federal Social Security taxes (called FICA taxes, for Federal Insurance Contributions Act) for each employee as well as both federal and state unemployment compensation taxes (called FUTA taxes, for Federal Unemployment Tax Act). The rates for FICA and FUTA taxes vary over time; the amounts used in this book are approximately correct.[4]

Employers often provide paid vacations to employees who have worked for more than 6 months or a year. The employer must accrue the costs of the earned but unused vacations (including the payroll taxes and fringe benefits on them) at the time the employees earn them, not the later time when employees take vacations and are paid. In this way, the accountant will charge each quarter of the year with a portion of the cost of vacations, rather than allocating all to the summer when most employees take the majority of their vacation days.

Example 9 Assume that employees earn $100,000, that the employees' withholding rates for federal income taxes average 20 percent, that the employees' withholding rates for state income taxes average 4 percent, and that employees owe 8 percent of their wages for Social Security taxes. In addition, employees, in aggregate, owe $500 for union dues to be withheld by the employer and $3,000 for health insurance plans.

The employer must pay FICA taxes of 8 percent of gross wages and FUTA taxes of 3.5 percent on the first $40,000 of gross wages. Part (2.7 percent) of the FUTA tax is payable to the state government and part (0.8 percent) is payable to the federal government. The employer owes $4,500 for payments to provide life and health insurance coverage. Employees have earned vacation pay estimated to be $4,000; estimated employer payroll taxes and fringe benefits are 18 percent of the gross amount.

The journal entries below record these wages. If some of the wages were earned by production workers, some of the debits would be to Work-in-Process Inventory, rather than to Wage and Salaries Expense. Although three journal entries are used (one for payments to employees, one for employer payroll taxes, and one for the accrual for estimated vacation pay), in practice these might be prepared as 11 separate entries or even as a single entry.

---

[4]Readers interested in exact tax rates should consult a current tax manual, such as those published by Commerce Clearing House, Prentice-Hall, and others.

Wages and Salaries Expense	100,000	
U.S. Withholding Taxes Payable		20,000
State Withholding Taxes Payable		4,000
FICA Taxes Payable		8,000
Withheld Dues Payable to Union		500
Insurance Premiums Payable		3,000
Wages and Salaries Payable		64,500

Record wage expense; plug for $64,500 actually payable to employees.

Wages and Salaries Expense	13,900	
FICA Taxes Payable		8,000
FUTA Taxes Payable to U.S. Government		320
FUTA Taxes Payable to State Government		1,080
Insurance Premiums Payable		4,500

Employer's expense for amounts not payable directly to employees. The debit is a plug.

Wages and Salaries Expense	4,720	
Estimated Vacation Wages and Fringes Payable		4,720

Estimate of vacation pay and fringes thereon earned during the current period; .18 × $4,000 = $720.

On payday, the employer pays $64,500 to employees, discharging the direct liability to them. The employer writes checks at various times to the federal government, the state government, the union, and the insurance companies. Such checks may be sent as often as twice a week (for withheld income and FICA taxes if the amounts are sufficiently large), or as seldom as once or twice per year (for life insurance). The insurance might be paid in advance with the debit being made to Prepaid Insurance; if so, the credits when wages are recorded will be to the Prepaid Insurance account. The amounts paid to employees taking vacation are debited to the liability account, Estimated Vacation Wages and Fringes Payable, not to an expense account.

Short-Term Notes and Interest Payable

Businesses obtain interim financing for less than a year from banks or other creditors in return for a short-term note called a *note payable*. Chapter 7 discusses such notes from the point of view of the lender, or note holder. The treatment of these notes by the borrower is the mirror image of the treatment by the lender. Where the lender records an asset, the borrower records a liability. When the lender records interest receivable and revenue, the borrower records interest payable and expense.

Income Taxes Payable

Businesses organized as corporations must pay federal income taxes based on their taxable income from business activities. In contrast, businesses organized as partnerships or sole proprietorships do not pay income taxes. Instead, the income of the business entity is taxed to the individual partners or sole proprietor. Each partner or sole proprietor adds his or her share of business income to income from all other (nonbusiness) sources in preparing an individual income tax return.

The details of the income tax on corporations are subject to change. The rates and schedules of payments mentioned below should not be taken as an indication of the exact procedure in force at any particular time, but rather as an indication of the type of accounting procedures that are involved. Throughout the remainder of the text, an income tax rate of 40 percent is used in almost all illustrations for ease of calculation. The accounting for state and local income taxes follows the same general pattern as that for federal income taxes, except for rates and dates of payment.

Corporations must make an estimate of the amount of taxes that will be due for the year and make quarterly payments equal to one-fourth of the estimated tax. This is frequently described as "pay-as-you-go" taxation. For a corporation on a calendar-year basis, and using 1985 as an example, 25 percent of the estimated tax for 1985 must be paid by April 15, 1985, 50 percent by June 15, 1985, 75 percent by September 15, 1985, and the entire estimated tax for 1985 must be paid by December 15, 1985.

The estimated income and, hence, the estimated tax may change as the year passes. The corporation must report such changed estimates quarterly. The amount of the quarterly payment is revised to reflect the new estimated tax and takes into account the cumulative payments made during previous quarters of the year. The final income tax return for the year is due by March 15, 1986. Any difference between the actual tax liability for 1985 and the cumulative tax payments during 1985 must be paid by March 15, 1986. The law provides for penalties if the amount estimated is substantially less than the actual tax liability.

If income statements are prepared more often than quarterly, or the end of the reporting period does not coincide with the tax payment period, estimating the income tax for the reporting period becomes necessary so that a more accurate measurement can be made of the net income for the period. Monthly or other short-period estimates of the tax are likely to be undependable, because there are various special provisions in the tax law. During the early quarters of the year, it is not clear which of the special provisions the corporation will ultimately be able to use. One can only prepare the best possible estimate of tax in the light of earnings of the year to date and the prospects for the remainder of the year.

Illustration of Income Tax Computations Exhibit 10.1 illustrates the procedures over several quarterly payments. The related journal entries are of two types and could be combined:

Income Tax Expense	100,000	
Income Taxes Payable		100,000
To accrue quarterly payment.		
Income Taxes Payable	100,000	
Cash		100,000
To make payment.		

Exhibit 10.1
Estimating Quarterly Income Tax Payments
and Final Payments of Actual Taxes

Date	Estimates of Taxable Income for Year 1	Amounts Payable for Income Taxes of Year 1
Year 1		
April 15	$1,000,000	$100,000[a]
June 15	1,000,000	100,000[b]
September 15	1,000,000	100,000[c]
December 15	1,000,000	100,000[d]
Year 2		
March 15	1,100,000[e]	40,000[f]

[a] $.25 \times [.40 \times (\$1,000,000)]$.
[b] $.50 \times [.40 \times (\$1,000,000)] - \$100,000$.
[c] $.75 \times [.40 \times (\$1,000,000)] - \$200,000$.
[d] $1.00 \times [.40 \times (\$1,000,000)] - \$300,000$.
[e] Actual income for Year 1 was $1,100,000.
[f] $.40 \times (\$1,100,000) - \$400,000$.

Deferred Performance Liabilities

Another current liability arises when customers make advance payments for goods or services to be delivered in the future. This liability, unlike the preceding ones, is discharged by delivering goods or services rather than by paying cash. This liability represents "unearned" and, therefore, unrecognized, revenue; that is, cash is received before the goods or services are furnished to the customer.

An example of this type of liability is the advance sale of theater tickets, say, for $200. Upon the sale, the following entry is made:

Cash	200	
Advances from Customers		200
Tickets are sold for cash, but there is no revenue until service is rendered.		

These deferred performance obligations qualify as liabilities. The account credited is called Advances from Customers or Liability for Advance Sales. After the theater performance, or after the tickets have expired, revenue is recognized and the liability is removed:

Advances from Customers	200	
Performance Revenue		200
Service has been rendered and revenue is recognized.		

Deferred performance liabilities also arise in connection with the sale of magazine subscriptions, transportation tickets, and service contracts.

A related type of deferred performance liability arises when a firm provides a warranty for free service or repairs for some period after the sale. At the time of sale, the firm can only estimate the likely amount of warranty liability. If sales during the accounting period were $28,000, and the firm estimated that an amount equal to 4 percent of the sales revenue will eventually be used to satisfy warranty claims, the entry is

Accounts Receivable	28,000	
Warranty Expense	1,120	
Sales		28,000
Estimated Warranty Liability		1,120

To record sales and estimated payment to be made for warranties on items sold.

Note that this entry recognizes the warranty expense in the period when revenue is recognized, even though the repairs may be made in a later period. Thus, warranty expense is matched with associated revenues. Because the expense is recognized, the liability is created. In this case, neither the amount nor the due date of the liability is definite, but they are reasonably certain. FASB *Statement No. 5,* discussed earlier, requires the accrual of the expense and related warranty liability when the amounts can be "reasonably estimated."

As expenditures of, say, $175 are made next period for repairs under the warranty, the entry is

Estimated Warranty Liability	175	
Cash (or other assets consumed for repairs)		175

Repairs made. No expense is recognized now; all expense was recognized in the period of sale.

With experience, the firm will adjust the percentage of sales it charges to Warranty Expense. Its goal is to achieve a credit balance in the Estimated Warranty Liability account at each balance sheet date that reasonably estimates the actual cost of repairs to be made under warranties outstanding at that time. The accounting for warranties is an "allowance method," similar in many ways to the allowance method for uncollectibles, discussed in Chapter 7.

Long-Term Liabilities

The principal long-term liabilities are mortgages, notes, bonds, and leases. The significant differences between long-term and short-term liabilities are that (1) interest on long-term liabilities is ordinarily paid at regular intervals during the life of a long-term obligation, whereas interest on short-term debt is usually paid in a lump sum at maturity; (2a) the principal of long-term obligations is often paid back in installments, or (2b) special funds are accumulated by the borrower for retiring long-term liabilities.

Accounting for all long-term liabilities generally follows the same procedures. Those procedures are outlined next and illustrated throughout the rest of this chapter and the next.

Procedures for Recording Long-Term Liabilities

Long-term liabilities are initially recorded at the present value of all promised payments using the market interest rate at the time the liability is incurred. This market interest rate is also used to compute the amount of interest expense throughout the life of the liability. A portion (perhaps all) of each cash payment represents interest expense. Any excess of cash payment over interest expense is used to reduce the liability itself (often called the *principal*). If a given payment is not sufficient to discharge the entire interest expense that has accrued since the last payment date, then the liability principal increases by the excess of interest expense over cash payment.

Retirement of long-term liabilities can occur in several ways, but the process is the same. The net amount shown on the books for the obligation is debited, the asset given up in return (usually cash) is credited, and any difference is recognized as a gain or loss on retirement of the debt.

Mortgages and Interest-Bearing Notes

In a mortgage contract, the lender takes legal title to certain property of the borrower, with the provision that the title reverts to the borrower when the loan is repaid in full. (In a few states, the lender merely acquires a lien on the borrower's property rather than legal title to it.) The mortgaged property is collateral for the loan.[5] The customary terminology designates the lender as the "mortgagee" and the borrower as the "mortgagor."[6]

As long as the mortgagor meets the obligations under the mortgage agreement, the mortgagee does not have the ordinary rights of an owner to possess and use the property. If the mortgagor defaults on either the principal or interest payments, the mortgagee can usually arrange to have the property sold for his or her benefit through a process called *foreclosure*. The mortgagee has first rights to the proceeds from the foreclosure sale for satisfying any unpaid claim. If there is an excess, it is

---

[5]Accountants are generally careful to use the word *collateral*, rather than *security*, in this context. Whether the loan is "secured" is a matter of legal judgment; moreover, accountants do not wish to imply that the value of the collateral will be sufficient to be able to satisfy the debt, as "secured" might imply.

[6]When you borrow money to finance a home purchase, you give the bank a mortgage, not vice versa.

paid to the mortgagor. If the proceeds are insufficient to pay the remaining loan, the lender becomes an unsecured creditor of the borrower for the unpaid balance.

A note is similar to a mortgage except that no property is typically pledged as collateral.

Accounting for Mortgages and Interest-Bearing Notes

Some of the more common problems in accounting for mortgages are presented in the following illustration.

On October 1, Year 1, the Western Company borrows $125,000 for 5 years from the Home Savings and Finance Company to obtain funds for additional working capital. As collateral, Western Company pledges to Home Savings and Finance Company several parcels of land that it owns and that are on its books at a cost of $50,000. Interest is charged on the unpaid balance of the loan principal at an interest rate of 12 percent per year compounded semiannually. Payments are due on April 1 and October 1 of each year. Western agrees to make 10 payments over the 5 years of the mortgage so that when the last payment is made on October 1, Year 6, the loan and all interest will have been paid. The first nine payments are to be $17,000 each. The tenth payment is to be just large enough to discharge the balance of the loan. The Western Company closes its books annually on December 31. (The derivation of the semiannual payment of $17,000 appears in Example 11 in Appendix B at the end of the book.)

The entries from the time the mortgage is issued through December 31, Year 2, assuming annual closings on December 31, are as follows:

10/1/Year 1	Cash	125,000	
	Mortgage Payable		125,000
	Loan obtained from Home Savings and Finance Company for 5 years at 12 percent compounded semiannually.		

As Example 11 in Appendix B shows, $125,000 is approximately equal to the present value of 10 semiannual cash payments of $17,000, each discounted at 12 percent compounded semiannually.

12/31/Year 1	Interest Expense	3,750	
	Interest Payable		3,750
	Adjusting entry: Interest expense on mortgage from 10/1/Year 1 to 12/31/Year 1.		

Interest expense on the loan for the first 6 months is $7,500 (= .06 × $125,000). To simplify the calculations, accounting typically assumes that the interest accrues evenly over the 6-month period. Thus, interest expense for October, November, and December is one-half of the $7,500, or $3,750.

4/1/Year 2	Interest Expense	3,750	
	Interest Payable.	3,750	
	Mortgage Payable	9,500	
	Cash.		17,000

Cash payment made requires an entry. Interest expense on mortgage from 1/1/Year 2 to 4/1/Year 2, payment of 6 months' interest, and reduction of loan by the difference, $17,000 − $7,500 = $9,500.

After the cash payment on April 1, Year 2, the unpaid principal of the loan is $115,500 (= $125,000 − $9,500). Interest expense during the second 6-month period is based on this unpaid principal amount.

10/1/Year 2	Interest Expense	6,930	
	Mortgage Payable	10,070	
	Cash		17,000

Cash payment made requires an entry. Interest expense for the period 4/1/Year 2 to 10/1/Year 2 is $6,930 [= .12 × ($125,000 − $9,500) × 1/2]. The loan is reduced by the difference, $17,000 − $6,930 = $10,070.

| 12/31/Year 2 | Interest Expense . . . . | 3,163 | |
| | Interest Payable . . . . | | 3,163 |

Adjusting entry: Interest expense from 10/1/Year 2 to 12/31/Year 2 = [.12 × ($125,000 − $9,500 − $10,070) × 3/12].

Amortization Schedule

Exhibit 10.2 presents an "amortization schedule" for this mortgage. For each period it shows the balance at the beginning of the period, the interest for the period, the payment for the period, the reduction in principal for the period, and the balance at the end of the period. (The last payment, $16,782 in this case, often differs slightly from the others because of the cumulative effect of rounding errors.) *All* long-term liabilities have analogous amortization schedules, which aid in understanding the timing of payments to discharge the liability. Amortization schedules for various long-term liabilities appear throughout this chapter and the next.

Bonds

When funds can be borrowed from one lender, the firm usually issues mortgages or notes. When larger amounts are needed, the firm may have to borrow from the general investing public with a bond issue. Bonds are used primarily by corporations and governmental units. The distinctive features of a bond issue are as follows.

Exhibit 10.2
Amortization Schedule for
$125,000 Mortgage (or note), Repaid in 10
Semiannual Installments of
$17,000, Interest Rate of 12 Percent,
Compounded Semiannually

Semiannual Journal Entry

Dr. Interest Expense . . . .   Amount in Column (3)
Dr. Mortgage (or Note) Payable . . . .   Amount in Column (5)
    Cr. Cash . . . .   Amount in Column (4)

6-Month Period (1)	Loan Balance Start of Period (2)	Interest Expense for Period (3)	Payment (4)	Portion of Payment Reducing Principal (5)	Loan Balance End of Period (6)
0					$125,000
1	$125,000	$7,500	$17,000	$ 9,500	115,500
2	115,500	6,930	17,000	10,070	105,430
3	105,430	6,326	17,000	10,674	94,756
4	94,756	5,685	17,000	11,315	83,441
5	83,441	5,006	17,000	11,994	71,448
6	71,448	4,287	17,000	12,713	58,734
7	58,734	3,524	17,000	13,476	45,259
8	45,259	2,715	17,000	14,285	30,974
9	30,974	1,858	17,000	15,142	15,832
10	15,832	950	16,782	15,832	0

Note: In preparing this table, calculations were rounded to the nearest cent. Then, for presentation, results are rounded to the nearest dollar.
Column (2) = column (6) from previous period.
Column (3) = .06 × column (2).
Column (4) is given, except row 10, where it is the amount such that column (4) = column (2) + column (3).
Column (5) = column (4) − column (3).
Column (6) = column (2) − column (5).

1. A *bond indenture,* or agreement, is drawn up that shows in detail the terms of the loan and the rights and duties of the borrower and other parties to the contract. Bond indentures typically limit the borrower's right to declare dividends and to make other distributions to owners in order to provide better protection to bondholders.

2. *Bond certificates* are used. Engraved certificates are prepared, each one representing a portion of the total loan. The usual minimum denomination in business practice is $1,000, although smaller denominations are occasionally used. Government bonds have been issued in denominations as small as $50.

3. If property is pledged as collateral for the loan (as in a mortgage bond), then a *trustee* is named to hold title to the property serving as collateral. The trustee acts as the representative of the bondholders and is usually a bank or trust company.

4. An agent is appointed, usually a bank or trust company, to act as *registrar* and *disbursing agent*. The borrower deposits interest and principal payments with the disbursing agent, who distributes the funds to the bondholders.

5. Most bonds are *coupon bonds*. Coupons attached to the bond certificate represent promises to make interest payments throughout the life of the bond. When a coupon comes due, the bondholder cuts it off and deposits it with a bank. The bank sends the coupon through the bank clearing system to the disbursing agent for payment, which is deposited in the bondholder's account at the bank.

6. The entire bond issue is usually issued by the borrower to an investment banking firm, or to a group of investment bankers known as a *syndicate,* which takes over responsibility for reselling the bonds to the investing public. Members of the syndicate usually bear the risks and rewards of interest rate fluctuations during the period while the bonds are being sold to the public.

Types of Bonds

Mortgage bonds carry a mortgage on real estate as collateral for the repayment of the loan. *Collateral trust bonds* are usually collateralized by stocks and bonds of other corporations. The most common type of corporate bond, except in the railroad and public utility industries, is the *debenture bond*. This type carries no special collateral; instead, it is issued on the general credit of the business. To give added protection to the bondholders, provisions are usually included in the bond indenture that limit the dividends that can be declared or the amount of subsequent long-term debt that can be incurred. *Convertible bonds* are debentures that the holder can exchange, possibly after some specific period of time has elapsed, for a specific number of shares of common stock.

Almost all bonds provide for the payment of interest at regular intervals, usually semiannually. The amount of interest is typically expressed as a percentage of the principal. For example, a 12 percent, 10-year, semiannual coupon bond with face amount of $1,000 promises to pay $60 every 6 months. Here, we assume, the first payment occurs 6 months after the issue date. A total of 20 payments are made. At the time of the final $60 coupon payment, the $1,000 principal is also due. The coupon rate is 12 percent in this case. The principal amount of a bond is its face, or par, value. The terms *face value* and *par value* are synonymous in this context. In general, the par amount multiplied by the coupon rate equals the amount of cash paid per *year,* whether in quarterly, semiannual, or annual installments. By far the majority of corporate bonds provide for semiannual coupon payments. A bond can be issued and subsequently traded in the marketplace for amounts below par, at par, or above par.

Proceeds of a Bond Issue

The amount received by the borrower will usually differ from the par value of the bonds issued. The difference arises because the coupon rate printed on the bond certificates differs from the interest rate the market requires given the risk of the borrower, the general level of interest rates in the economy, and other factors. Whatever the market rate, at time of issue or at any time thereafter, the annual cash payments for a bond remain the product of the face value multiplied by the coupon rate. If the coupon rate is less than the rate the market requires the firm to pay, then the bonds will sell for less than par. The difference between par and selling price is called the *discount* on the bond. The issuer will pay the full amount at maturity. The difference between the face amount and the initial issue proceeds is part of the interest the market requires the borrower to pay. Even though the payment occurs at maturity, the accounting procedures are designed to record that interest systematically over the life of the bond. If the coupon rate is larger than the rate the market requires, the bonds will sell above par. The difference between selling price and par is called the *premium* on the bond.

The presence of a discount or premium in and of itself indicates nothing about the credit standing of the borrower. A firm with a credit standing that would enable it to borrow funds at 11 percent might issue 10 percent bonds that would sell at a discount, whereas another firm with a lower credit standing, which would require it to pay 11.5 percent on loans, might issue bonds at 12 percent that would sell at a premium.

Issued at Par The Macaulay Corporation issues $100,000 face value of 12 percent semiannual coupon debenture bonds. The bonds are dated July 1, Year 1. The principal amount is repayable on July 1, Year 6, or 5 years later. Interest payments (coupons) are due on July 1 and January 1 of each year. The coupon payments promised at each interest payment date total $6,000. Figure 10.1 presents a time line for the two sets of cash flows associated with this bond. Assuming that the issue was taken by Penman & Company, investment bankers, on July 1, Year 1, at a rate to yield exactly 12 percent compounded semiannually, the calculation of the proceeds to Macaulay would be as follows. (Appendix B at the back of the book explains the present value calculations.)

(a) Present Value of $100,000 to Be Paid at the End of 5 Years	$ 55,839
(Appendix Table 2 at the back of the book shows the present value of $1 to be received in 10 periods at 6 percent per period to be $.55839; $100,000 × .55839 = $55,839.)	
(b) Present Value of $6,000 to Be Paid Each 6 Months for 5 Years	44,161
(Appendix Table 4 shows the present value of an ordinary annuity of $1 per period for 10 periods discounted at 6 percent to be $7.36009; $6,000 × 7.36009 = $44,161.)	
Total Proceeds	$100,000

The issue price would be stated as 100.0 (that is, 100 percent of par), which implies that the market interest rate was 12 percent compounded semiannually, the same as the coupon rate.

Issued at Less than Par Assume that these same bonds were issued at a price to yield 14 percent compounded semiannually. The promised cash flows after July 1, Year 1, associated with these bonds (payment of periodic interest plus repayment of

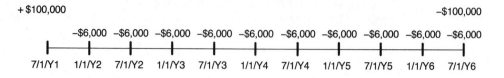

Figure 10.1 Time Line for 5-Year Semiannual Coupon Bonds, 12 Percent Annual Coupons. $100,000 Par Value Issued at Par.

principal) are identical to those in the time line shown in Figure 10.1. These future cash flows would be discounted to their present value using a 14 percent discount rate compounded semiannually. The calculation of the issue proceeds (that is, initial market price) would be as follows. (Why it is that ''12-percent'' bonds can be issued to yield 14 percent is discussed on page 451.)

(a) Present Value of $100,000 to Be Paid at the End of 5 Years $50,835
(Present value of $1 to be received in 10 periods at 7 percent per period is $0.50835; $100,000 × 0.50835 = $50,835.)

(b) Present Value of $6,000 to Be Paid Each 6 Months for 5 Years 42,141
(Present value of an ordinary annuity of $1 per period for 10 periods, discounted at 7 percent per period = $7.02358; $6,000 × 7.02358 = $42,141.)

Total Proceeds $92,976

If the issue price were stated on a conventional pricing basis in the market at 92.98 (92.98 percent of par), the issuing price would be $92,980. This amount implies a market yield of slightly less than 14 percent compounded semiannually.

Issued at More than Par Assume that the bonds were issued at a price to yield 10 percent compounded semiannually. The cash flows, after July 1, Year 1, would again be identical to those shown in Figure 10.1. They would be discounted at 10 percent compounded semiannually to calculate their present value. The calculation of the proceeds would be as follows:

(a) Present Value of $100,000 to Be Paid at the End of 5 Years . . . . . . $ 61,391
(Present value of $1 to be received in 10 periods at 5 percent per period is $0.61391; $100,000 × 0.61391 = $61,391.)

(b) Present Value of $6,000 to Be Paid Each 6 Months for 5 Years 46,330
(Present value of an ordinary annuity at $1 per period for 10 periods, discounted at 5 percent per period = $7.72173; $6,000 × 7.72173 = $46,330.)

Total Proceeds $107,721

If the issue price were stated on a conventional pricing basis in the market at 107.72 (107.72 percent of par), the issuing price would be $107,720.[7] The price would imply a market yield of slightly more than 10 percent compounded semiannually.

Bond Tables

These tedious calculations need not be made every time a bond issue is analyzed. *Bond tables* show the results of calculations like those just described. Examples of such tables are Tables 5 and 6 at the back of the book. Table 5 shows the price for 10 percent, semiannual coupon bonds as a percent of par for various market interest rates (yields) and years to maturity. Table 6 shows market rates and implied prices for 12 percent, semiannual coupon bonds. (Some modern calculators make the calculations represented by these tables in a few seconds.)

The percentages of par shown in these tables represent the present value of the bond indicated. Because the factors are expressed as a percent of par, they have to be multiplied by 10 to find the price of a $1,000 bond. If you have never used bond tables before now, turn to Table 6 after Appendix B at the back of the book and find in the fifth-year row the three different prices for the three different market yields used in the preceding examples. Notice further that a bond will sell at par if, and only if, it has a market yield equal to its coupon rate.

These tables are useful whether a bond is being issued by a corporation or resold later by an investor. The approach to computing the market price will be the same in either case, although the years to maturity will be less than the original term of the bond when it is resold. The following generalizations can be made regarding bond prices:

1. When the market interest rate equals the coupon rate, the market price will equal par.
2. When the market interest rate is greater than the coupon rate, the market price will be less than par.
3. When the market interest rate is less than the coupon rate, the market price will be greater than par.

Accounting for Bonds Issued at Par

The following illustration covers the more common problems associated with bonds issued at par.

---

[7]In many contexts, bond prices are quoted in dollars plus thirty-seconds of a dollar. A bond selling for about $107\frac{23}{32}$ percent of par would be quoted at $107\frac{23}{32}$, which would be written as 107.23. In order to read published bond prices, you must know whether the information after the "decimal" point refers to fractions expressed in one-hundredths or in thirty-seconds. (If you are reading published bond prices and see any number larger than 31 after the decimal point, then you can be sure that one-hundredths are being used. If you see many prices, but none of the numbers shown after the point is larger than 31, then you can be reasonably sure that thirty-seconds are being used.)

We use the data presented in the previous sections for the Macaulay Corporation, where the bonds were issued at par and we assume that the bonds are closed semiannually on June 30 and December 31. The entry at the time of issue would be

7/1/Year 1	Cash.	100,000	
	Debenture Bonds Payable		100,000
	$100,000 of 12 percent, 5-year bonds issued at par.		

The entries for interest would be made at the end of the accounting period and on the interest payment dates. Entries through January 1, Year 2, would be

12/31/Year 1	Interest Expense	6,000	
	Interest Payable		6,000
1/1/Year 2	Interest Payable	6,000	
	Cash		6,000
	To record payment of 6 months' interest.		

Bond Issued Between Interest Payment Dates   The actual date that a bond is issued seldom coincides with one of the payment dates. Assuming these same bonds were actually brought to market on September 1, rather than July 1, and were issued at par, the purchasers of the bonds would be expected to pay Macaulay Corporation for 2 months' interest in advance. After all, on the first coupon Macaulay Corporation promises a full $6,000, for 6 months' interest, but would have had the use of the borrowed funds for only 4 months. The purchasers of the bonds would pay $100,000 plus 2 months' interest of $2,000 (= .12 × $100,000 × $\frac{2}{12}$) and would get the $2,000 back when the first coupons are redeemed. The journal entry made by Macaulay Corporation, the issuer, would be

9/1/Year 1	Cash.	102,000	
	Bonds Payable		100,000
	Interest Payable.		2,000
	To record issue of bonds at par between interest payment dates. The purchasers pay an amount equal to interest for the first 2 months but will get it back when the first coupons are redeemed.		

Accounting for Bonds Issued at Less than Par

The following illustrates the more common problems associated with bonds issued for less than par.

Assume the data presented for the Macaulay Corporation, where 12 percent, $100,000-par value, 5-year bonds were issued to yield 14 percent compounded semiannually. The issue price was shown previously to be $92,976. The journal entry at the time of issue would be

| 7/1/Year 1 | Cash. . . . . | 92,976 | |
| | Debenture Bonds Payable . . . . | | 92,976 |

The issuance of these bonds for $92,976, instead of the $100,000 par value, indicates that 12 percent is not a sufficiently high rate of interest for the bonds to induce purchasers to pay the full par value in the open market. If purchasers of these bonds paid the full $100,000 par value, they would earn only 12 percent compounded semiannually, the coupon rate. Purchasers desiring a rate of return of 14 percent will postpone their purchases until the market price drops to $92,976. At this price, purchasers of the bonds will earn the 14 percent return they require. The return will be composed of ten $6,000 coupon payments over the next 5 years plus $7,024 (= $100,000 − $92,976) as part of the payment at maturity.

For Macaulay Corporation, the total interest expense over the life of the bonds is equal to $67,024 (periodic interest payments totaling $60,000 plus $7,024 paid at maturity). Two methods of allocating the total interest expense of $67,024 to the periods of the loan are the effective interest method and the straight-line method.

Interest Expense Under the Effective Interest Method

Under the effective interest method, interest *expense* each period is equal to the market interest rate at the time the bonds were initially issued (14 percent compounded semiannually in this example) multiplied by the *book value* of the liability at the beginning of the interest period. For example, interest expense for the period from July 1, Year 1, to December 31, Year 1, the first 6-month period, is $6,508 (= .07 × $92,976). The bond indenture provides that only $6,000 (= .06 × $100,000) need be paid on January 1, Year 2. This amount is equal to the coupon rate times the par value of the bonds. The difference between the interest expense of $6,508 and the interest currently payable of $6,000 is added to the book value of the bond and will be paid as part of the principal amount at maturity. The journal entry made on December 31, Year 1, to recognize interest for the last 6 months of Year 1 is

12/31/Year 1	Interest Expense	$6,508	
	Interest Payable		6,000
	Debenture Bonds Payable		508
	To recognize interest expense for 6 months.		

The Interest Payable account would be shown as a current liability on the balance sheet at the end of Year 1. Debenture Bonds Payable of $93,484 (= $92,976 + $508) will appear on the balance sheet as a noncurrent liability.

On January 1, Year 2, the first periodic cash payment is made.

1/1/Year 2	Interest Payable.	$6,000	
	Cash.		6,000
	To record payment of interest for 6 months.		

Interest expense for the second 6 months, from January 1, Year 2, through June 30, Year 2, is $6,544 (= .07 × $93,484). Interest expense for the second 6 months of $6,544 is larger than the $6,508 for the first 6 months because the recorded book value of the liability at the beginning of the second 6 months is larger. The journal entry on June 30, Year 2, to record interest expense is

6/30/Year 2	Interest Expense	$6,544	
	Interest Payable		6,000
	Debenture Bonds Payable		544
	To recognize interest expense for 6 months.		

An amortization schedule for these bonds over their 5-year life appears in Exhibit 10.3. Column (3) shows the periodic interest expense, and column (6) shows the book value that appears on the balance sheet at the end of each period.

The effective interest method of recognizing interest expense on a bond has the following financial statement effects.

1. On the income statement, interest expense will be a constant percentage of the recorded liability at the beginning of each interest period. This percentage will be equal to the market interest rate for these bonds when they were initially issued. When bonds are issued for less than par value, the *dollar amount* of interest expense will increase each period as the recorded book value amount increases.

2. On the balance sheet at the end of each period, the bonds will be stated at the present value of the *remaining* cash outflows discounted at the market rate of interest when the bonds were initially issued. For example, on June 30, Year 2, the present value of the remaining cash payments is as follows:

Present Value of July 1, Year 2, Interest Payment	$ 6,000
Present Value of 8 Remaining Semiannual Interest Payments Discounted at 14 Percent, Compounded Semiannually (Appendix Table 4 shows the present value of an ordinary annuity of $1 per period for 8 periods discounted at 7 percent to be $5.97130; $6,000 × 5.97130 = $35,827)	35,827
Present Value of $100,000 to Be Paid at the End of 4 Years (Appendix Table 2 shows the present value of $1 to be paid at the end of 8 periods discounted at 7 percent to be $.58201; $100,000 × .58201 = $58,201)	58,201
Total Present Value	$100,028
Less Amount Shown as Current Liability for Interest Payable	6,000
Equals Amount Shown for Debenture Bonds Payable	$ 94,028

The amount $94,028 appears in column (6) of Exhibit 10.3 for the liability at the end of the second 6-month period.

Exhibit 10.3
Effective Interest Amortization Schedule for $100,000 of
12 Percent, 5-Year Bonds Issued for 92.976 Percent of Par
to Yield 14 Percent, Interest Payable Semiannually

Semiannual Journal Entry

Dr. Interest Expense	Amount in Column (3)
Cr. Cash	Amount in Column (4)
Cr. Debenture Bonds Payable	Amount in Column (5)

Period (6-month intervals) (1)	Liability at Start of Period (2)	Effective Interest: 7 Percent per Period (3)	Coupon Rate: 6 Percent of Par (4)	Increase in Recorded Book Value of Liability (5)	Liability at End of Period (6)
0					$92,976
1	$92,976	$ 6,508	$ 6,000	$ 508	93,484
2	93,484	6,544	6,000	544	94,028
3	94,028	6,582	6,000	582	94,610
4	94,610	6,623	6,000	623	95,233
5	95,233	6,666	6,000	666	95,899
6	95,899	6,713	6,000	713	96,612
7	96,612	6,763	6,000	763	97,375
8	97,375	6,816	6,000	816	98,191
9	98,191	6,873	6,000	873	99,064
10	99,064	6,936	6,000	936	100,000
Total		$67,024	$60,000	$7,024	

Note: In preparing this table, calculations were rounded to the nearest cent. Then, for presentation, results were rounded to the nearest dollar.
Column (2) = column (6) from previous period.
Column (3) = .07 × column (2).
Column (4) is given.
Column (5) = column (3) − column (4).
Column (6) = column (2) + column (5).

Discount on Bonds Payable Account

The preceding description of the recording of bonds issued below par value shows the book value of the bonds directly in the Bonds Payable account. Accountants have sometimes shown Bonds Payable at par value with a liability contra account, Discount on Bonds Payable, carrying the amount by which par value must be reduced to show book value. If the Discount on Bonds Payable account were used, the balance sheet on June 30, Year 2, after two semiannual interest periods would show:

Bonds Payable—Par Value	$100,000
Less: Discount on Bonds Payable	(5,972)
Bonds Payable—Net Book Value.	$ 94,028

Interest Expense Under
the Straight-Line Method

The second method for recording interest expense over the life of the bond issue is the straight-line method. Under the straight-line method, total interest expense (periodic coupon payments plus any amount paid at the time of maturity) is spread evenly over the life of the bonds. In the example for Macaulay Corporation, total interest expense is $67,024 [= ($6,000 × 10) + ($100,000 − $92,976)]. Interest expense each 6 months will therefore be $6,702.40 (= $67,024/10). The journal entry to record interest expense at the end of each 6 months is

Interest Expense	6,702.40	
Interest Payable		6,000.00
Debenture Bonds Payable		702.40
To recognize interest expense for 6 months.		

The straight-line method of computing interest expense is computationally easier than the effective interest method. It has two theoretical weaknesses, however:

1. When bonds are issued for less than par value, interest expense will be a decreasing percentage of the bond liability at the beginning of each period. That is, interest expense (numerator) will be constant but the bond liability (denominator) will increase as the maturity date approaches. In contrast, the effective interest method provides an amount for interest expense that is a constant percentage (the interest rate at time of issue) of the beginning-of-the-period liability.

2. The amount at which the bonds are stated on the balance sheet each period will not equal the present value of the bond's remaining cash flows discounted at the historical interest rate.

Preferred Method of Recognizing Interest Expense

Generally accepted accounting principles require the effective interest method.[8] The straight-line method is allowed only when its results do not differ materially from the effective interest method.

Interest on Bonds Issued for Less than Par
and the Statement of Changes in Financial Position

Recognizing interest expense on bonds issued for less than par requires special treatment in computing cash provided by operations in the statement of changes in financial position. Interest expense reported for the first 6 months is $6,508: $6,000

---

[8]Accounting Principles Board, *Opinion No. 21,* "Interest on Receivables and Payables," 1971, par. 15.

in coupon payments and $508 in increased principal amount. Notice that only $6,000 of cash was used for the expense. There was an increase in Interest Payable of $6,000 followed by discharge of that current liability with cash payment. The remainder of the interest expense, $508, is an increase in the noncurrent liability, Debenture Bonds Payable. Consequently, there must be an addition to net income in computing "cash provided by operations" in the statement of changes in financial position. The amount of the addback is the amount of the expense that did not use working capital, $508.

Accounting for Bonds
Issued for More than Par

The following discussion illustrates the more common problems associated with bonds issued for more than par.

Assume the data presented for the Macaulay Corporation, in which 12 percent, $100,000-par value, 5-year bonds were issued to yield approximately 10 percent compounded semiannually. The issue price, derived previously, is $107,721. The journal entry at the time of issue would be

7/1/85	Cash	107,721	
	Debenture Bonds Payable		107,721

The firm borrows $107,721. The issuance of these bonds for $107,721, instead of the $100,000 par value, indicates that 12 percent is a higher rate of interest for the bonds than the purchasers demand. If purchasers of these bonds paid the $100,000 par value, they would earn 12 percent compounded semiannually, the coupon rate. Purchasers requiring a rate of return of only 10 percent will bid up the market price to $107,721. At this price, purchasers of the bonds will earn only the 10 percent demanded return. The return comprises ten $6,000 coupon payments over the next 5 years reduced by $7,721 (= $107,721 − $100,000) lent but not repaid at maturity.

For Macaulay Corporation, the total interest expense over the life of the bonds is equal to $52,279 (periodic interest payments totaling $60,000 less $7,721 of principal not repaid at maturity). Two methods of allocating the total interest expense of $52,279 to the periods of the loan are the effective interest method and the straight-line method.

Interest Expense Under
the Effective Interest Method

Under the effective interest method, interest *expense* each period is equal to the market interest rate at the time the bonds were initially issued (10 percent compounded semiannually in this example) multiplied by the recorded book value of the liability at the beginning of the interest period. For example, interest expense for the period from July 1, Year 1, to December 31, Year 1, the first 6-month period, is

$5,386 (= .05 \times \$107,721)$. The bond indenture provides that $6,000 (= .06 \times \$100,000)$ be paid on January 1, Year 2. This amount equals the coupon rate times the face value of the bonds. The difference between the payment of $6,000 and the interest expense of $5,386 reduces the amount of the liability. The journal entry made on December 31, Year 1, to recognize interest for the last 6 months of Year 1 is

12/31/Year 1	Interest Expense	5,386	
	Debenture Bonds Payable	614	
	Interest Payable		6,000
	To recognize interest expense for 6 months.		

The Interest Payable account appears as a current liability on the balance sheet at the end of Year 1. Debenture Bonds Payable of $107,107 (= $107,721 − $614) appears as a noncurrent liability.

On January 1, Year 2, the first periodic cash payment is made:

1/1/Year 2	Interest Payable.	6,000	
	Cash.		6,000
	To record payment of interest for 6 months.		

Interest expense for the second 6 months, from January 1, Year 2, through June 30, Year 2, is $5,355 (= .05 × $107,107). Interest expense for the second 6 months of $5,355 is smaller than the $5,386 for the first 6 months because the unpaid balance of the liability at the beginning of the second 6 months is smaller. The journal entry on June 30, Year 2, to record interest expense is

6/30/Year 2	Interest Expense	5,355	
	Debenture Bonds Payable	645	
	Interest Payable		6,000
	To recognize interest expense for 6 months.		

An amortization schedule for these bonds over their 5-year life appears in Exhibit 10.4. Column (3) shows the periodic interest expense and column (6) shows the book value that appears on the balance sheet at the end of the period.

The effective interest method of recognizing interest expense on a bond has the following financial statement effects.

1. On the income statement interest expense will be a constant percentage of the recorded liability at the beginning of each interest period. This percentage will be equal to the market interest rate when the bonds were initially issued. When bonds are issued for more than par value, the *dollar amount* of interest expense will decrease each period as the unpaid liability decreases to the amount to be paid at maturity.

Exhibit 10.4
Effective Interest Amortization Schedule for $100,000 of
12 Percent, 5-Year Bonds Issued for 107.721 Percent of Par
to Yield 10 Percent, Interest Payable Semiannually

Semiannual Journal Entry

Dr. Interest Expense . . . . Amount in Column (3)
Dr. Debenture Bonds Payable . . . . . Amount in Column (5)
   Cr. Cash . . . . Amount in Column (4)

Period (6-month Intervals) (1)	Liability at Start of Period (2)	Effective Interest: 5 Percent per Period (3)	Coupon Rate: 6 Percent of Par (4)	Decrease in Recorded Book Value of Liability (5)	Liability at End of Period (6)
0					$107,721
1	$107,721	$ 5,386	$ 6,000	$ 614	107,107
2	107,107	5,355	6,000	645	106,462
3	106,462	5,323	6,000	677	105,785
4	105,785	5,289	6,000	711	105,074
5	105,074	5,254	6,000	746	104,328
6	104,328	5,216	6,000	784	103,544
7	103,544	5,177	6,000	823	102,721
8	102,721	5,136	6,000	864	101,857
9	101,857	5,093	6,000	907	100,950
10	100,950	5,050	6,000	950	100,000
Total		$52,279	$60,000	$7,721	

Column (2) = column (6) from previous period.
Column (3) = .05 × column (2).
Column (4) is given.
Column (5) = column (4) − column (3).
Column (6) = column (2) − column (5).

2. On the balance sheet at the end of each period, the bonds will be stated at the present value of the *remaining* cash flow discounted at the market rate of interest when the bonds were initially issued. For example, on June 30, Year 2, the present value of the remaining cash payments is as follows:

Present Value of July 1, Year 2, Interest Payment	$ 6,000
Present Value of 8 Remaining Semiannual Interest Payments Discounted at 10 Percent, Compounded Semiannually (Appendix Table 4 shows the present value of an ordinary annuity of $1 per period for 8 periods discounted at 5 percent to be $6.46321; $6,000 × 6.46321 = $38,779)	38,779
Present Value of $100,000 to Be Paid at the End of 4 Years (Appendix Table 2 shows the present value of $1 to be paid at the end of 8 periods discounted at 5 percent to be $.67684; $100,000 × .67684 = $67,684)	67,684
Total Present Value	$112,463
Less Amount Shown as Current Liability for Interest Payable	6,000
Equals Amount Shown for Debenture Bonds Payable	$106,463

The amount $106,462, different because of rounding effects, appears in column (6) of Exhibit 10.4 for the liability at the end of the second 6-month period.

Premium on Bonds Payable Account

The preceding description of the recording of bonds issued above par value shows the book value of the bonds directly in the Bonds Payable account. Accountants have sometimes shown Bonds Payable at par value with a liability adjunct account, Premium on Bonds Payable, carrying the amount added to par value to show book value. If the Premium on Bonds Payable account were used, the balance sheet on June 30, Year 2, after two semiannual interest periods would show:

Bonds Payable—Par Value	$100,000
Plus: Premium on Bonds Payable	6,462
Bonds Payable—Net Book Value	$106,462

Interest Expense Under the Straight-Line Method

Under the straight-line method, total interest expense (periodic coupon payments reduced by the excess of initial issue proceeds over amounts paid at maturity) is spread evenly over the life of the bonds. In the example for Macaulay Corporation, total interest expense is $52,279 [= ($6,000 × 10) − ($107,721 − $100,000)]. Interest expense each 6 months will therefore be $5,227.90 (= $52,279/10). The journal entry to record interest expense at the end of each 6 months is

Interest Expense	5,227.90	
Debenture Bonds Payable	772.10	
Interest Payable		6,000.00
To recognize interest expense for 6 months.		

The straight-line method of computing interest expense is computationally easier than the effective interest method. It has two theoretical weaknesses:

1. When bonds are issued for more than par value, interest expense will be an increasing percentage of the bond liability at the beginning of each period. That is, interest expense (numerator) will be constant but the bond liability (denominator) will decrease as the maturity date approaches. In contrast, the effective interest method provides an amount for interest expense that is a constant percentage of the beginning-of-the-period liability.

2. The amount at which the bonds are stated on the balance sheet each period will not equal the present value of the remaining cash flows relating to the bond discounted at the historical interest rate.

Effects on Statement of Changes in Financial Position

Interest expense on bonds originally issued above par is less than the periodic amounts of cash disbursed. The excess of cash disbursed (or current liability for Interest Payable recorded) over interest expense is a repayment of a portion of the bond liability to the lenders. This payment can be interpreted in either of two ways.

1. It is an operating use of cash. Because the amount of cash disbursed exceeds interest expense, there must be a subtraction in the statement of changes in financial position in deriving ''cash provided by operations.'' The amount subtracted is the excess of cash disbursed over interest expense.

2. It is a nonoperating use of cash and appears as a (partial) retirement of debt in the section showing uses of cash for financing.

The problems and examples in this book use the first interpretation, although the second is supportable.

Bond Retirement

Many bonds remain outstanding until the stated maturity date. Refer to Exhibit 10.3, the Macaulay example, where the 12 percent coupon bonds were issued to yield 14 percent. The company pays the final coupon, $6,000, and the face amount, $100,000, on the stated maturity date. The entries are

7/1/Year 6	Interest Expense	6,936	
	Cash.		6,000
	Debenture Bonds Payable		936
	See row 10 of Exhibit 10.3.		
	Debenture Bonds Payable	100,000	
	Cash.		100,000
	Retirement at maturity of bonds.		

Retirement Before Maturity A firm sometimes purchases its own bonds on the open market before maturity. Because market interest rates constantly change, the purchase price will seldom equal the recorded book value of the bonds. Assume that Macaulay Corporation originally issued its 12 percent coupon bonds to yield 14 percent compounded semiannually. Assume that 3 years later, on July 1, Year 4, interest rates in the marketplace have increased so that the market then requires a 15 percent interest rate to be paid by Macaulay Corporation. Refer to Table 6 at the back of the book, 2-year row, 15 percent column, which shows that 12 percent bonds with 2 years until maturity will sell in the marketplace for 94.9760 percent of par if the current interest rate is 15 percent compounded semiannually.

The marketplace is not constrained by the principles of historical cost accounting. Even though Macaulay Corporation shows the Debenture Bonds Payable on the balance sheet at $96,612 (see row 6 of Exhibit 10.3), the marketplace puts a price of only $94,976 on the entire bond issue. From the point of view of the marketplace, these bonds are the same as 2-year bonds issued on July 1, Year 4, at an effective yield of 15 percent and, so, carry a discount of $5,024 (= $100,000 − $94,976).

If, on July 1, Year 4, Macaulay Corporation purchases $10,000 of par value of its own bonds, it would have to pay only $9,498 (= .94976 × $10,000) for those bonds, which have book value of $9,661. The journal entries it would make at the time of purchase are

7/1/Year 4	Interest Expense	6,713	
	Interest Payable.		6,000
	Debenture Bonds Payable		713
	See row 6 of Exhibit 10.3.		
	Interest Payable.	6,000	
	Cash.		6,000
	To record payment of coupons, as usual.		
	Debenture Bonds Payable	9,661	
	Cash.		9,498
	Gain on Retirement of Bonds.		163
	To record purchase of bonds for less than the current amount shown in the accounting records.		

If the bonds are shown at face value, offset with a separate Discount on Bonds Payable account, the entry to record retirement would be

Debenture Bonds Payable	10,000	
Discount on Bonds Payable		339
Cash		9,498
Gain on Retirement of Bonds		163
The discount account is "retired" along with the bonds themselves; book value of bonds retired is $9,661 (= $10,000 − $339).		

The adjustment to give equal debits and credits in the retirement entry is a gain. The gain arises because the firm is able to retire a liability recorded at one amount, $9,661, for a smaller cash payment, $9,498. This gain actually occurred as interest rates increased between Year 1 and Year 4. In historical cost accounting, the gain is reported only when realized—in the period of bond retirement. This phenomenon is analogous to a firm's purchasing marketable securities, holding those securities as prices increase, selling the securities in a subsequent year, and reporting all the gain in the year of sale. It is caused by the historical cost accounting convention of recording amounts at historical cost and not recording increases in wealth until those increases are realized in arm's-length transactions with outsiders.

During the 1970s, interest rates jumped upward from their levels in the 1960s. Many companies had issued bonds at prices near par with coupon rates of only 3 or 4 percent per year in the 1960s. When interest rates in the 1970s jumped to 12 or 15 percent per year, these bonds traded in the market for substantial discounts from face value. Many companies repurchased their own bonds, recording substantial gains in the process. (In one year Pan American World Airlines was able to report profits after 7 consecutive years of losses. Pan Am had gains on bond retirement that year in excess of the entire amount of reported net income.)

Because there is no alternative in historical cost accounting to showing a gain (or loss) on bond retirement (the debits must equal the credits) and because the FASB is reluctant to let companies manage their own reported income by timing the repurchase of bonds, it generally requires that gains and losses on bond retirements be reported in the income statement as extraordinary items.[9] Such items are included in net income, but with a separate caption. See the discussion in Chapter 4. Because bond retirements are financing transactions, the gains (or losses) do not produce (or use) cash from operations. Adjustments must therefore be made to net income for gains (subtractions) and for losses (additions) in deriving cash provided by operations.

Serial Bonds   The bond indenture may require the issuing firm to make a special provision for retiring the bond issue. There are two major types of retirement provisions. One provides that certain portions of the principal amount will come due on a succession of maturity dates; the bonds of such issues are known as *serial bonds*. (The bonds considered so far in this chapter are not serial bonds.)

Sinking Fund Bonds   The other major type of retirement provision in bond indentures requires the firm to accumulate a fund of cash or other assets that will be used to pay the bonds when the maturity date arrives or to reacquire and retire portions of the bond issue.[10] Funds of this type are commonly known as *sinking funds*, although *bond retirement funds* would be a more descriptive term. The trustee of the bond issue usually holds the sinking fund. It appears on the balance sheet as a noncurrent asset in the ''Investments'' section.

Refunded Bonds   Some bond indentures make no provision for installment repayment or for accumulating sinking funds for the payment of the bonds when they come due. Such bonds are usually well protected with property held by trustees as collateral or by the high credit standing of the issuer. Under these circumstances, the entire bond liability may be paid at maturity out of cash in the bank at that time. Quite commonly, however, this procedure is not followed. Instead the bond issue is *refunded*—a new set of bonds is issued to obtain the funds to retire the old ones when they come due.

---

[9]Financial Accounting Standards Board, *Statement of Financial Accounting Standards No. 4,* ''Reporting Gains and Losses from Extinguishment of Debt,'' 1975. The exception is mentioned in the next footnote.

[10]Gain or loss on bond retirement is part of ordinary income when it results from bond retirement in accord with sinking fund provisions; FASB *Statement of Financial Accounting Standards No. 4.* The gain or loss, like the gain or loss on voluntary bond retirement, does not produce or use funds from operations. Similarly, it requires an adjustment to net income in deriving funds from operations in the statement of changes in financial position.

Callable Bonds   A common provision gives the issuing company the right to retire portions of the bond issue before maturity if it so desires, but does not require it do so. To facilitate such reacquisition and retirement of the bonds, the bond indenture can provide that the bonds be *callable*. That is, the issuing company has the right to reacquire its bonds at prices specified in the bond indenture. When the bonds are called, the trustee will not immediately pay a subsequent coupon presented for redemption. Rather, the trustee will notify the holder to present all remaining coupons and the bond principal for payments equal to the call price plus accrued interest.

The *call price* is usually set a few percentage points above the par value and declines as the maturity date approaches. Because the call provision may be exercised by the issuing company at a time when the market rate of interest is less than the coupon rate, callable bonds usually are sold in the marketplace for something less than otherwise similar, but noncallable, bonds.

Assume, for example, that a firm had issued 12 percent semiannual coupon bonds at a discount, implying a borrowing rate higher than 12 percent. Later, market interest rates and the firm's credit standing allow it to borrow at 10 percent. If $100,000-par value bonds issued with book value of $98,000 are called at 105, the entry, in addition to the one to record the accrued interest expense, would be

Debenture Bonds Payable	98,000	
Loss on Retirement of Bonds	7,000	
Cash		105,000

Bonds called and retired. The loss is an extraordinary item unless the retirement results from a sinking fund provision.

The loss recognized on bond retirement, like the analogous gain, is generally classified as an extraordinary item in the income statement.

The market rate of interest a firm must pay to borrow depends on two factors: the general level of interest rates and its own creditworthiness. If the market rate of interest has risen since bonds were issued (or the firm's credit rating has declined), the bonds will sell in the market at less than issue price. A firm that wanted to retire such bonds would not *call* them, because the call price is typically greater than the face value. Instead the firm would probably purchase its bonds on the open market and realize a gain on the retirement of bonds.

Unifying Principles of Accounting for Long-Term Liabilities

Long-term liabilities are obligations to pay fixed amounts at definite future times more than 1 year in the future. The obligations appear on the balance sheet at the present value of the future payments. The present value computations use the historical rate of interest—the market interest rate on the date the obligation was incurred.

The methods of accounting for all long-term liabilities and related expenses are conceptually and procedurally identical—the effective interest method. The liability is initially recorded at the cash equivalent value received, which will equal the present value of the future contractual payments using the interest rate relevant for the borrower on the date the loan begins. At any subsequent interest accrual or interest payment date, Interest Expense is computed by multiplying the book value of the liability by the historical interest rate. The amount of interest expense increases liabilities. The amount of any cash payment made reduces the liabilities. The difference between interest expense and the cash payment increases or decreases the book value of the liability for the next accounting period.

Amortization schedules, such as those in Exhibits 10.2, 10.3, 10.4, 10.5, and in Chapter 11, illustrate this unchanging procedure for a variety of long-term liabilities.

Summary

A liability is an obligation by an entity involving a probable future sacrifice of resources. The amount of the obligation and the timing of its payment can be estimated with reasonable certainty. The transaction causing the obligation to arise has already occurred.

Accounting for long-term liabilities is accomplished by recording these obligations at their present value at the date the obligation is incurred (which equals the cash equivalent value received at the time of the borrowing) and then showing the change in that present value as the maturity date of the obligation approaches. In historical cost accounting, the interest rate used throughout the life of the liability is the firm's borrowing rate at the time the liability was originally incurred. Retirement of long-term liabilities can be brought about in a variety of ways, but in each case, the process is the same. The net obligation is offset against what is given in return, usually cash, with gain or loss on retirement recognized as appropriate.

Problem 1 for Self-Study

Avner Company issues a 3-year, $100,000 note bearing interest at the rate of 15 percent per year. That is, Avner Company promises to pay $15,000 at the end of 1 year, $15,000 at the end of 2 years, and $115,000 at the end of 3 years. The market rate of interest on the date the note is issued is 10 percent.

a. Compute the proceeds Avner Company receives for its note.

b. Prepare an amortization schedule similar to Exhibit 10.2 for the life of the note.

c. Prepare journal entries that would be made on three dates: the date of issue, 6 months after the date of issue (assuming the books were closed then), and 1 year after the date of issue, assuming an interest payment is made then.

Suggested Solution

a. Present Value of 3 Payments of $15,000, Discounted at 10 percent (see
Table 4, 3-period row, 10 percent column: $15,000 × 2.48685) . . . . $ 37,303

Present Value of 1 Payment of $100,000, Discounted at 10 percent for 3
Periods (see Table 2, 3-period row, 10 percent column:
$100,000 × .75131) 75,131

Net Proceeds from Issue of Note $112,434

b. Exhibit 10.5
Amortization Schedule for Note with Face Value
of $100,000 Issued for $112,434, Bearing Interest at the
Rate of 15 Percent of Face Value per Year, Issued to Yield 10 Percent
(Problem 1 for Self-Study)

Yearly Periods (1)	Loan Balance Start of Period (2)	Interest Expense for Period (3)	Payment (4)	Portion of Payment Reducing Book Value of Liability (5)	Loan Balance End of Period (6)
0					$112,434
1	$112,434	$11,243	$ 15,000	$ 3,757	108,677
2	108,677	10,868	15,000	4,132	104,545
3	104,545	10,455	115,000	104,545	0

Column (2) = column (6) from previous period.
Column (3) = .10 × column (2).
Column (4) is given.
Column (5) = column (4) − column (3).
Column (6) = column (2) − column (5).

c. Cash 112,434
    Note Payable 112,434
Proceeds of issue of note.

Interest Expense 5,622
    Interest Payable 5,622
See Exhibit 10.5; accrual of 6 months' interest = $11,243/2.

Interest Expense 5,621
Interest Payable 5,622
Notes Payable 3,757
    Cash 15,000
Interest expense for the remainder of the first year and cash pay-
ment made. Excess of cash payment over interest expense re-
duces note principal.

Problem 2 for Self-Study

Generally accepted accounting principles require that long-term monetary liabilities be stated at the present value of the future cash flows discounted at the market rate of interest appropriate to the monetary items at the time they were initially recorded. APB *Opinion No. 21* specifically excludes from present value valuation those obligations that arise from warranties. Warranties, being nonmonetary liabilities, are stated at the estimated cost of providing warranty goods and services in the future.

Assume that the estimated future costs of a 3-year warranty plan on products sold during Year 1 are as follows:

Year	Expected Cost
2	$ 500,000
3	600,000
4	900,000
Total	$2,000,000

Actual costs coincided with expectations both as to timing and amount.

a. Prepare the journal entries for each of the years 1 through 4 for this warranty plan following current generally accepted accounting principles.

b. Now, assume that generally accepted accounting principles allow these liabilities to be shown at their present value. Prepare the journal entries for each of the years 1 through 4 for this warranty plan assuming that the warranty liability is stated at the present value of the future costs discounted at 10 percent. To simplify the calculations, assume that all warranty costs are incurred on December 31 of each year.

c. What theoretical arguments can be offered for the valuation basis in part b?

Suggested Solution

a. Year 1	Warranty Expense.	2,000,000	
	Estimated Warranty Liability		2,000,000
Year 2	Estimated Warranty Liability	500,000	
	Cash and Other Accounts		500,000
Year 3	Estimated Warranty Liability	600,000	
	Cash and Other Accounts		600,000
Year 4	Estimated Warranty Liability	900,000	
	Cash and Other Accounts		900,000

b. The present value of the future cost amounts on December 31, Year 1, discounted at 10 percent, is $1,626,594, computed as follows:

Year 2	$500,000 × .90909	$ 454,545
Year 3	$600,000 × .82645	495,870
Year 4	$900,000 × .75131	676,179
Total		$1,626,594

Year 1	Warranty Expense	1,626,594	
	Estimated Warranty Liability		1,626,594
Year 2	Interest Expense	162,659	
	Estimated Warranty Liability		162,659
	.10 × $1,626,594 = $162,659.		
Year 2	Estimated Warranty Liability	500,000	
	Cash and Other Accounts		500,000
Year 3	Interest Expense	128,925	
	Estimated Warranty Liability		128,925
	.10 × ($1,626,594 + $162,659 − $500,000) = $128,925.		
Year 3	Estimated Warranty Liability	600,000	
	Cash and Other Accounts		600,000
Year 4	Interest Expense	81,818	
	Estimated Warranty Liability		81,818
	.10 × (1,626,594 + $162,659 − $500,000 + $128,925 − $600,000) = .10 × $818,178 = $81,818.		
Year 4	Estimated Warranty Liability	899,996	
	Interest Expense	4	
	Cash		900,000

There is a rounding error of $4 in the Estimated Warranty Liability account at the end of Year 4. Interest expense for Year 4 is, therefore, increased by $4.

c. The goods and services provided under the warranty plan must first be acquired for cash. Thus, even though customers will receive goods and services, the firm must expend cash at some point. To be consistent with monetary liabilities, these amounts would be discounted to their present value.

Questions, Exercises, Problems and Cases

Questions

1. Review the meaning of the following concepts or terms discussed in this chapter.
   a. Liability.
   b. Executory contract.
   c. FICA.
   d. FUTA.
   e. Contingent liability and estimated liability.
   f. Mortgage, mortgagee, mortgagor.
   g. Collateral.
   h. Bond indenture.
   i. Coupon bond.
   j. Debenture bond.

k. Convertible bond.
l. Yield or effective rate of bond.
m. Bond tables.
n. Amortization of bonds using the straight-line and effective interest methods.

o. Sinking fund.
p. Serial bonds.
q. Bond refunding.
r. Call price.

2. For each of the following items, indicate whether the item meets all of the criteria of a liability. If so, how is it valued?

a. Interest accrued but not paid on a note.
b. Advances from customers for goods and services to be delivered later.
c. Firm orders from customers for goods and services to be delivered later.
d. Mortgages payable.
e. Bonds payable.
f. Product warranties.
g. Fifteen-year cancelable lease on an office building.
h. Damages the company must pay if a pending lawsuit is lost.
i. Cost of restoring strip-mining sites after mining operations are completed.
j. Contractual promises to purchase natural gas for each of the next 10 years.

3. Describe the similarities and differences between the allowance method for uncollectibles (see Chapter 7) and the allowance method for estimated warranty costs.

4. Generally accepted accounting principles specifically require the accrual of earned but unpaid wages and fringe benefits thereon. Generally accepted accounting principles specifically require the accrual of earned but unused vacation pay under most circumstances. Generally accepted accounting principles do not mention fringe benefits (such as FICA, FUTA, insurance, and pensions) attached to vacation pay. Explain why the text might say that accrual of these items is required even though there is no specific pronouncement that mentions such a requirement.

5. A noted accountant once remarked that the optimal number of faulty TV sets for the General Electric Company to sell is "not zero," even if GE promises to repair all faulty GE sets that break down, for whatever reason, within 2 years of purchase. Why could the optimal number be "not zero"?

6. A private school has a reporting year ending June 30. It hires teachers for the 10-month period, September of one year through June of the following year. It contracts to pay teachers in 12 monthly installments over the period September of one year through August of the next year. For the current academic year, the total contractual salaries to be paid to teachers is $360,000. How should this amount be accounted for in the financial statements issued June 30, at the end of the academic year?

7. While shopping in a store on July 5, 1983, a customer slipped on the floor and sustained back injuries. On January 15, 1984, the customer sued the store for $1 million. The case came to trial on April 30, 1984. The jury's verdict was rendered on June 15, 1984, with the store found guilty of gross negligence. A damage award of $400,000 was granted to the customer. The store, on June 25, 1984, appealed the decision to a higher court on the grounds that certain evidence had not been admitted by the lower court. The higher court ruled on November 1, 1984, that the evidence should have been admitted. The lower court reheard the case beginning on March 21, 1985. Another jury, on April 20, 1985, again found the store guilty of gross negligence and awarded $500,000. On May 15, 1985, the store paid the $500,000 judgment. When should a loss from these events be recognized by the supermarket? Explain your reasoning.

8. What factors determine the amount of money a firm actually receives when it offers a bond issue to the market?

9. A call premium is the difference between the call price of a bond and its par value. What is the purpose of such a premium?

10. Why does a company that gives trading stamps to its customers usually not have a problem of estimating a liability for the cost of goods to be given to customers who redeem their stamps?

11. If a company borrows $1,000,000 by issuing, at par, 20-year, 10 percent bonds with semiannual coupons, the total interest expense over the life of the issue is $2,000,000 (= 20 × .10 × $1,000,000). If a company undertakes a 20-year mortgage or note with an implicit borrowing rate of 10 percent, the annual payments are $1,000,000/8.51356 = $117,460. (See Table 4 at the end of the book, 20-period row, 10 percent column.) The total mortgage payments are $2,349,200 (= 20 × $117,460), and the total interest expense over the life of the note or mortgage is $1,349,200 (= $2,349,200 − $1,000,000).

Why are the amounts of interest expense different for these two means of borrowing for the same length of time at identical interest rates?

12. The following questions compare the effective interest method and the straight-line method of accounting for interest expense on bonds.
   a. Which method gives higher interest expense in the first year for a bond issued at less than par value?
   b. Which method gives higher interest expense in the first year for a bond issued at more than par value?
   c. Which method gives higher interest expense in the last year for a bond issued at less than par value?
   d. Which method gives higher interest expense in the last year for a bond issued at more than par value?
   e. Which method involves the larger adjustment to net income in deriving funds provided by operations in the first year for a bond issued at more than par value?
   f. Which method involves the larger adjustment to net income in deriving funds provided by operations in the first year for a bond issued at less than par value?
   g. What are the relative advantages and disadvantages of the straight-line method versus the effective interest method of accounting for interest expense on a bond?

13. Are high-quality, long-term bonds always sound investments? A friend has $20,000 to invest to pay for a child's education expenses. The funds will be needed in 4 years. The friend believes that the 10 percent semiannual coupon bonds of the U.S. government maturing in the year 2010 would be as safe and sound an investment as any available. What advice can you give?

14. Critics of historical cost accounting for long-term debt argue that the procedures give management unreasonable opportunity to "manage" income with the timing of bond retirements. What phenomenon do these critics have in mind?

15. What purposes do restrictions placed on borrowing firms by bond indentures serve?

Exercises

16. *Journal entries for payroll.* During the current period, office employees earned wages of $200,000. Fifteen percent of this amount must be withheld from payments for federal income taxes, 4 percent must be withheld for state income taxes, and 8 percent must be deducted for Social Security taxes. The employer must pay 8 percent of gross wages for Social Security taxes, 2 percent for state FUTA taxes, and 1 percent for federal FUTA taxes. The employer has promised to contribute 4 percent of gross wages to a profit-sharing fund, whose proceeds are used to pay workers when they retire. Employees earned vacation pay estimated to be $9,000; estimated fringes are 20 percent of that amount.
  a. Prepare journal entries for these wage-related items.
  b. What is total wage and salary expense?

17. *Journal entries for payroll.* Prepare journal entries for the following wages, fringes, and accruals of Bages Company. Factory employees earned $90,000 and office employees earned $60,000. Employers must pay 15 percent of employees' wages to the federal government for withheld income taxes, 3 percent to the state government for withheld income taxes, and 8 percent to the federal government for withheld Social Security taxes. The employer also owes 8 percent for Social Security taxes and 3 percent for FUTA taxes, 2 percent to the state government and 1 percent to the federal government. The employer pays all costs of insurance plans; it owes $5,000 for health and life insurance premiums. The employer awards paid vacations to employees who have been working for a year or more. During the current period, employees earning 90 percent of the gross wages are expected to earn paid vacations, which is estimated to be 4 percent of their gross wages. Payroll taxes and fringe benefits are estimated to be 20 percent of vacation pay.

18. *Computations and journal entries for income taxes payable.* The Siegal Company files its income tax returns on a calendar-year basis and issues financial statements quarterly as of March 31, June 30, and so on. All income taxes are estimated or paid at the rate of 40 percent of taxable income. The following data are applicable to the company's income tax for Year 1.

Year 1

Mar. 31	It is estimated that total taxable income for Year 1 will be about $15 million. The first quarter's financial statements are prepared.
April 15	The first payment on estimated taxes is made.
June 15 . . .	It is now estimated that total taxable income for the year will be about $17 million. The second payment on estimated taxes is made.
June 30 . . .	The second quarter's financial statements are prepared.
Sept. 15 . . .	It is now estimated that total taxable income for the year will be about $16 million. The third payment on estimated taxes is made.
Sept. 30 . . .	The third quarter's financial statements are prepared.
Dec. 15	It is now estimated that total taxable income for the year will be about $17.5 million. The fourth payment on estimated taxes is made.
Dec. 31	Income for the year is $17,750,000. Financial statements for the year are prepared.

Year 2

Mar. 15	The balance of taxes for Year 1 is paid.

a. Prepare schedules showing

(1) For tax returns: estimated taxes for year, cumulative payments due, and payment made for each payment date.

(2) For financial statements: tax expenses for the quarterly reports and annual report.

b. Record the transactions related to Year 1 income taxes in journal entry form.

c. Present the T-accounts for Cash, Prepaid Income Taxes (if necessary), Income Taxes Payable, and Income Tax Expense.

19. *Journal entries for estimated warranty liabilities and subsequent expenditures.* A new product introduced by Junn Company carries a 2-year warranty against defects. The estimated warranty costs as a percentage of dollar sales are 3 percent in the year of sale and 5 percent in the next year. Sales (all on account) and actual warranty expenditures (all paid in cash) for the first 2 years of the product's life were as follows:

	Sales	Actual Warranty Expenditures
Year 1	$400,000	$10,000
Year 2	500,000	35,000

a. Prepare journal entries for the events of Year 1 and Year 2. Closing entries are not required.

b. What is the balance in the Estimated Warranty Liability account at the end of Year 2?

20. *Using bond tables.* The Gonedes Company issues 12 percent semiannual coupon bonds maturing in 10 years. The face amount of the bonds is $1 million. The net cash proceeds to Gonedes Company from the bond issue amounts to $944,907.

What interest rate will be used in applying the effective interest method over the life of this bond issue?

21. *Using bond tables.* Refer to Table 6 for 12 percent semiannual coupon bonds issued to yield 13 percent per year compounded semiannually. All of the questions below refer to $1 million face value of such bonds.

    a. What are the initial issue proceeds for bonds issued to mature in 30 years?

    b. What is the book value of those bonds after 5 years?

    c. What is the book value of the bonds when they have 20 years until maturity?

    d. What are the initial issue proceeds of bonds issued to mature in 20 years? (Compare to your answer above.)

    e. Write an expression for interest expense for the last 6 months before maturity.

    f. If the market rate of interest on the bonds is 14 percent, what is the market value of the bonds when they have 20 years to maturity?

    g. When the bonds have 10 years until maturity, they trade in the market for 112.46 percent of par. What is the effective market rate at that time?

22. *Using bond tables; computing interest expense.* Refer to Table 5 in the back of the book for 10 percent semiannual coupon bonds. On January 1, Year 1, Souverain Company issued $1 million of face-value, 10 percent semiannual coupon bonds maturing in 20 years (on December 31, Year 20) at a price to yield 14 percent per year, compounded semiannually. Use the effective interest method of computing interest expense.

    a. What were the proceeds of the original issue?

    b. What was the interest expense for the first half of Year 1?

    c. What was the interest expense for the second half of Year 1?

    d. What was the book value of the bonds on January 1, Year 6 (when the bonds have 15 years until maturity)?

    e. What was the interest for the first half of Year 6?

23. *Funds statement effects; gain or loss on bond retirement.* Refer to the data in the preceding exercise for Souverain Company.

    a. By what amount did cash used for debt service differ from interest expense, and how does this amount affect the fund statement's derivation of cash provided by continuing operations for Year 1?

    b. On January 1, Year 11 (when bonds have 10 years to maturity), $100,000 face value of bonds are purchased in the open market and retired. The market rate of interest at the time of purchase is 12 percent compounded semiannually. What gain or loss will Souverain Company report?

24. *Journal entry for short-term note payable.* On December 1, the O'Brien Company obtained a 90-day loan for $15,000 from the Twin City State Bank at an annual interest rate of 12 percent. On the maturity date the note was renewed for another 30 days, with a check being issued to the bank for the accrued interest. The O'Brien Company closes its books annually at December 31.

    a. Present entries on the books of the O'Brien Company to record the issue of the note, the year-end adjustment, the renewal of the note, and the payment of cash at maturity of the renewed note.

   b. Present entries at maturity date of the original note for the following variations in the settlement of the note of the O'Brien Company.

   (1) The original note is paid at maturity.
   (2) The note is renewed for 30 days; the new note bears interest at 15
   percent per annum. Interest on the old note was not paid at maturity.

25. *Partial amortization schedule for note.* The Holmes Sales Company sells a
building lot to N. Wolfe on September 1 for $27,000. The down payment is $3,000,
and minimum payments of $265 a month are to be made on the contract. Interest at
the rate of 12 percent per annum on the unpaid balance is deducted from each
payment, and the balance is applied to reduce the principal. Payments are made as
follows: October 1, $265; November 1, $265; December 1, $600; January 2, $265.
   Prepare a partial amortization schedule showing payments, interest and principal,
and remaining liability at each of these dates. Round amounts to the nearest dollar.

26. *Partial amortization schedule for mortgage.* Lynne Michals secures a mortgage
loan of $112,000 from the Oakley National Bank. The terms of the mortgage re-
quire monthly payments of $1,660. The interest rate to be applied to the unpaid
balance is 9 percent per year.
   Prepare a partial amortization schedule showing payments, interest and principal,
and remaining liability for the first 4 months of the loan. Round amounts to the
nearest dollar.

27. *Journal entries for effective interest and straight-line methods of computing
bond interest.* On October 1, Year 1, Howell Stores, Inc., issues 20-year, first
mortgage bonds with a face value of $1,000,000. The proceeds of the issue are
$1,060,000. The bonds bear interest at the rate of 10 percent per year, payable
semiannually at April 1 and October 1. Howell Stores, Inc., closes its books annually at December 31. Round amounts to the nearest dollar.
   a. Present dated journal entries related to the bonds from October 1, Year 1,
   through October 1, Year 2, inclusive. Assume that Howell Stores, Inc., uses
   the straight-line method to recognize interest expense.
   b. Repeat instructions for part **a** but assume that the company uses the effective
   interest method. The effective interest rate to be used is 9.3 percent, compounded semiannually.

28. *Amortization schedule for bonds.* Hanouille Company issues 10 percent semiannual coupon bonds maturing 5 years from the date of issue. Interest of 5 percent
of the face value of $100,000 is payable January 1 and July 1. The bonds are issued
to yield 12 percent, compounded semiannually.
   a. What are the initial issue proceeds received by Hanouille Company?
   b. Construct an amortization schedule for this bond issue, similar to Exhibit
   10.3.
   c. By how much does interest expense for the first year (note *year,* not first
   6-month period) of the bond's life under the effective interest method differ
   from that under the straight-line method?
   d. Assume that at the end of the third year of the bond's life, $10,000 face
   value of bonds are called and retired for 103 percent of par. Give the journal
   entry to record the retirement.

29. *Accounting for bond issue and subsequent interest including journal entries.* The Central Power Company issued $2 million bonds in two series, A and B. Each series had face amount of $1 million and was issued at prices to yield 11 percent. Issue A contained semiannual 10 percent coupons. Issue B contained 12 percent semiannual coupons. Issues A and B both mature 30 years from issue date.

Answer the following questions for issue A. Round amounts to the nearest dollar.

- **a.** What is the issuing price of the bonds?
- **b.** Make the journal entry for the date of bond issue.
- **c.** Using the effective interest method, show the journal entries made on the first semiannual interest payment date.
- **d.** Repeat part **c** for the second and third payment dates.
- **e.** Show the semiannual entry if straight-line method is used.

30. *Accounting for bond issue and subsequent interest including journal entries.* Refer to the data in Exercise **29.** Work the problem for issue B.

Problems and Cases

31. *Allowance method for warranties; reconstructing transactions.* Colantoni Company sells appliances, all for cash. All acquisitions of appliances during a year are debited to the Merchandise Inventory account. The company provides warranties on all its products, guaranteeing to make repairs within 1 year of the date of sale as required for any of its appliances that break down. The company has many years of experience with its products and warranties.

The schedule shown in Exhibit 10.6 contains trial balances for the Colantoni Company at the ends of Year 1 and Year 2. The trial balances for the end of Year 1 are the Adjusted Preclosing Trial Balance (after all adjusting entries have been properly made) and the final Post-Closing Trial Balance. The trial balance shown for the end of Year 2 is taken before any adjusting entries of any kind, although entries have been made to the Estimated Liability for Warranty Repairs account during Year 2, as repairs have been made. Colantoni Company closes its books once each year.

At the end of Year 2, the management of Colantoni Company analyzes the appliances sold within the preceding 12 months. All appliances in the hands of customers that are still covered by warranty are classified as follows: those sold on or before June 30 (more than 6 months old), those sold after June 30, but on or before November 30 (more than 1 month, but less than 6 months old), and those sold on or after December 1. One-half of 1 percent of the appliances sold more than 6 months ago are estimated to require repair, 5 percent of the appliances sold 1 to 6 months before the end of the year are estimated to require repair, and 8 percent of the appliances sold within the last month are assumed to require repair. From this analysis, management estimated that $5,000 of repairs still would have to be made in Year 3 on the appliances sold in Year 2. Ending inventory on December 31, Year 2, is $120,000.

- **a.** What were the total acquisitions of merchandise inventory during Year 2?
- **b.** What is the cost of goods sold for Year 2?

Exhibit 10.6
COLANTONI COMPANY
(Problem 31)

Trial Balances—End of Year 1	Adjusted Preclosing		Post-Closing	
	Dr.	Cr.	Dr.	Cr.
Estimated Liability for Warranty Repairs		$ 6,000		$ 6,000
Merchandise Inventory	$ 100,000		$100,000	
Sales		800,000		
Warranty Expense	18,000			
All Other Accounts	882,000	194,000	110,000	204,000
Totals	$1,000,000	$1,000,000	$210,000	$210,000

Trial Balance—End of Year 2	Unadjusted Trial Balance	
	Dr.	Cr.
Estimated Liability for Warranty Repairs	$ 15,000	
Merchandise Inventory	820,000	
Sales		$1,000,000
Warranty Expense	—	—
All Other Accounts	265,000	100,000
Totals	$1,100,000	$1,100,000

c. What was the dollar amount of repairs made during Year 2?

d. What is the Warranty Expense for Year 2?

e. Give journal entries for repairs made during Year 2, for the warranty expense for Year 2, and for cost of goods sold for Year 2.

32. *Nonmonetary liabilities; reconstructing transactions.* The Myrtle Lunch sells coupon books that patrons may use later to purchase meals. Each coupon book sells for $17 and has a face value of $20. That is, each book can be used to purchase meals with menu prices of $20. On July 1, redeemable unused coupons with face value of $1,500 were outstanding. During July, 250 coupon books were sold; during August, 100; during September, 100. Cash receipts exclusive of coupons were $1,200 in July, $1,300 in August, and $1,250 in September. Coupons with a face value of $2,700 were redeemed by patrons during the 3 months.

a. If the Myrtle Lunch had a net income of $500 for the quarter ending September 30, how large were expenses?

b. What effect, if any, do the July, August, and September coupon sales and redemptions have on the right-hand side of the September 30 balance sheet?

33. *Nonmonetary liabilities; journal entries.* The Lambert Company sells service contracts to repair copiers at $300 per year. When the contract is signed, the $300 fee is collected and the Service Contract Fees Received in Advance account is credited. Revenues on contracts are recognized on a quarterly basis during the year in which the coverage is in effect. On January 1, 1,000 service contracts were outstanding. Of these, 500 expired at the end of the first quarter, 300 at the end of the second quarter, 150 at the end of the third quarter, and 50 at the end of the fourth quarter. Sales and service during the year came to these amounts (assume that all sales occurred at the beginning of the quarter):

	Sales of Contracts	Service Expenses
First Quarter	$120,000 (400 contracts)	$50,000
Second Quarter	240,000 (800 contracts)	60,000
Third Quarter. . . . . . ·	90,000 (300 contracts)	45,000
Fourth Quarter	60,000 (200 contracts)	55,000

    a. Prepare journal entries for the first three quarters of the year for the Lambert Company. Assume that quarterly reports are prepared on March 31, June 30, and September 30.

    b. What is the balance in the Service Contract Fees Received in Advance account on December 31?

34. *Journal entries for purchase with existing mortgage; subsequent interest entries.* On June 1, the Loebbecke Company purchases a warehouse from F. S. Brandon for $600,000, of which $100,000 is assigned to the land and $500,000 to the building. There is a mortgage on the property payable to the Dixie National Bank, which, together with the accrued interest, will be assumed by the purchaser. It bears interest at the rate of 12 percent per year. The balance due on the mortgage is $240,000. The principal of the mortgage will be paid on April 1 and October 1 of each year in installments of $20,000 each. The principal payments of $20,000 are in addition to the interest of 6 percent per six-month period on the outstanding balance. A 10-year second mortgage for $150,000 is issued to F. S. Brandon; it bears interest at the rate of 15 percent per year, payable on June 1 and December 1. A check is drawn to complete the purchase.

    Loebbecke Company closes its books once a year on December 31. Prepare journal entries for June 1, October 1, and December 1.

35. *Accounting for investment in bonds.* On April 1, Year 1, the Oliver Company acquired $1,000,000 par value of bonds of the Bret Company for $1,398,000. Costs of acquisition amounted to an additional $2,000. The bonds bear interest at 15 percent per year payable on March 31 and September 30 and mature on March 31, Year 10. Use the straight-line method to recognize interest revenue.

    a. Present journal entries on the books of the Oliver Company from April 1, Year 1, through March 31, Year 2, inclusive. Assume that the books are closed annually on December 31.

    b. Present the journal entry (or entries) for the sale of the bonds on August 1, Year 4, at 103.5 plus accrued interest.

36. *Operations of a syndicate and risk of interest rate fluctuations.* During October 1979, IBM arranged with a syndicate of investment bankers to borrow $1 billion. IBM and the syndicate reached agreement on IBM's borrowing rate and the amounts the syndicate would pay to IBM on a Friday. Over the weekend, the Federal Reserve System took actions that drastically increased interest rates. The members of the syndicate were responsible for any difference between the amount they had obligated themselves to pay to IBM and the amount for which they could sell the bonds during the following week.

   a. Did the syndicate gain or lose by the change in interest rates over the weekend?

   b. What sorts of actions might members of the syndicate take to insulate themselves from involuntary speculation in interest rates over the weekend?

37. *Preparing funds statement (adapted from a problem by Stan Baiman).* Exhibit 10.7 shows comparative balance sheets, an income statement for Year 2, and supplementary notes of Branaire Company.

Prepare the Year 2 statement of changes in financial position with funds defined as cash.

38. *Funds statement effects.* Refer to the Simplified Statement of Changes in Financial Position for a Period in Exhibit 5.17 on page 201. Eleven of the lines in the statement are numbered. Ignore the unnumbered lines in responding to the questions below.

Assume that the accounting cycle is complete for the period and that all of the financial statements have been prepared. Then it is discovered that a transaction has been overlooked. That transaction is recorded in the accounts and all of the financial statements are corrected. Define *funds* as *cash*. For each of the following transactions, indicate which of the numbered lines of the funds statement is affected and by how much. Ignore income tax effects.

   a. Bonds are issued for $100,000 cash.

   b. Bonds with a fair market value of $100,000 are issued for a building.

   c. Bonds with a book value of $100,000 are retired for $90,000 cash.

   d. Bonds with a book value of $100,000 are called for $105,000 cash and retired.

   e. Interest expense for half a year on bonds is recorded using the effective interest method. The bonds have a face value of $100,000 and a current book value of $90,000. The coupon rate is 10 percent, paid semiannually, and the bonds were originally issued to yield 12 percent, compounded semiannually.

   f. Interest expense for half a year on bonds is recorded using the effective interest method. The bonds have a face value of $100,000 and a book value of $105,000. The coupon rate is 12 percent paid semiannually, and the bonds were originally issued to yield 10 percent, compounded semiannually.

39. *Managing income and the debt-equity ratio through bond retirement.* Meyney Company issued $40 million of 5 percent semiannual coupon bonds many years ago at par. The bonds now have 20 years until scheduled maturity. Because market

Exhibit 10.7
BRANAIRE COMPANY
Comparative Balance Sheets and Income Statement
(Problem 37)

	December 31	
	Year 1	Year 2
Balance Sheets		
Cash	$ 30,000	$130,000
Accounts Receivable	100,000	120,000
Less: Allowance for Uncollectibles	(20,000)	(25,000)
Inventory	140,000	150,000
Plant and Equipment	800,000	855,000
Accumulated Depreciation	(380,000)	(500,000)
Total Assets	$670,000	$730,000
Accounts Payable	$ 20,000	$ 25,000
Bonds Payable	100,000	110,000
Premium on Bonds Payable	40,000	44,000
Capital Stock.	200,000	206,000
Retained Earnings	310,000	345,000
Total Equities	$670,000	$730,000
Year 2 Income Statement		
Net Sales		$495,000
Gain on Sale of Equipment		110,000
		$605,000
Cost of Goods Sold		$200,000
Bad Debt Expense		15,000
Depreciation Expense		140,000
Income Tax Expense		100,000
Total Expenses		$455,000
Income Before Extraordinary Items		$150,000
Extraordinary Loss on Bond Retirement		4,000
Net Income		$146,000

Notes:
(1) During Year 2, Branaire sold property, plant, and equipment that had originally cost $200,000.
(2) All depreciation charges are expensed.
(3) Dividends declared have been paid in cash.
(4) New bonds due in 15 years were issued for $10,000 more than face value.
(5) Bonds with face value of $20,000 and unamortized premium of $6,000 were retired at a loss (which has no income tax effects).

(Problem 39 continued)
interest rates have risen to 12 percent, the market value of the bonds has dropped to 63 percent of par. Meyney Company has $5 million of current liabilities and $35 million of owners' equity in addition to the $40 million of long-term debt in its financial structure. The debt-equity ratio is 56% [= ($40 + $5)/($5 + $40 + $35)]. (Owners' equity includes an estimate of the current year's income.) The

(Problem 39 continued)

president of Meyney Company is concerned about boosting reported income for the year, which is about $8 million for the year in the absence of any other actions. Also, the debt-equity ratio appears to be larger than that of other firms in the industry. The president wonders what would be the impact on net income and the debt-equity ratio of issuing at par new 12 percent semiannual coupon bonds to mature in 20 years and using the proceeds to retire the outstanding bond issue. Assume that such action is taken and that any gain on bond retirement is taxable at the rate of 40 percent.

    a. Prepare the journal entries for the issue of new bonds in amount required to raise funds to retire the old bonds, retirement of the old bonds, and income tax effects.

    b. What is the effect on income for the year? Give both dollar and percentage amounts.

    c. What is the debt-equity ratio after the transaction?

40. *Comparison of straight-line and effective interest methods of amortizing bond discount.* IBM established the IBM Credit Corporation (IBMCC) on May 1, 1981. On July 1, 1981, IBMCC issued $150 million of "zero coupon notes" due July 1, 1988. Zero coupon notes promise to pay a single amount, in this case $150 million, at maturity—in this case, 7 years after issue date. The issue was marketed at a price to yield 14 percent, compounded semiannually. The notes are redeemable at the option of IBMCC at any time, in whole or in part, at 100 percent of the principal amount.

Interest expense on IBMCC's financial statements is computed with the effective interest method, and on IBMCC's tax return using the straight-line method. Assume an income tax rate of 46 percent.

The financial statements of IBMCC present the following data about long-term debt for December 31, 1981:

	(dollars in thousands)
14⅜% Notes Due July, 1986	$100,000
Zero Coupon Notes Due July, 1988	150,000
	$250,000
Less: Unamortized Discount, Related Principally to the Zero Coupon Notes	87,762
	$162,238

    a. What were the proceeds to IBMCC from issue of the zero coupon notes?

    b. What interest expense was reported on the income statement for the 6-month period ending December 31, 1981, for these notes?

    c. What was the interest deduction on the tax return for 1981 for these notes?

    d. What was the amount of "Unamortized Discount. . ." that relates only to the zero coupon notes on the balance sheet at year-end 1981?

    e. A news story in 1982 reported:

. . . [T]he Treasury wants to plug a tax loophole that has enabled companies to borrow billions of dollars cheaply. . . . At issue is a tax break granted to

companies issuing . . . "zero-coupon" bonds . . . and other deeply discounted debt instruments, which pay very low interest rates.

Describe the advantages to issuers and purchasers of zero coupon bonds. Give your
interpretation of the "tax loophole" alleged by the Treasury. Be specific in your
response by indicating the dollar amount of "loophole" used by IBMCC in 1981.
What tax policy with respect to zero coupon bonds would you recommend?

41. *Financial institutions holding bonds of issuers in financial difficulties may find
the book value and the market of the bonds to be quite different; should this change
be recognized in accounting; troubled debt restructuring.* On January 1, 1979, First
National Bank (FNB) acquired $10 million of face value bonds issued on that date
by the Occidental Oceanic Power Systems (OOPS). The bonds carry 12 percent,
semiannual coupons and were to mature 20 years from the issue date. The bonds
were issued by OOPS, and purchased by FNB, at par.

By 1984, OOPS was in severe financial difficulty and threatened to default on the
bonds. After much negotiation with FNB (and other creditors), it agreed to repay
the bond issue, but only on less burdensome terms. OOPS agreed to pay 5 percent
per year, semiannually, for 25 years and to repay the principal on January 1, 2009,
or 25 years after the negotiation. FNB will receive $250,000 each 6 months starting
with July 1, 1984, and $10 million on January 1, 2009. By January 1, 1984, OOPS
was being charged 20 percent per year, compounded semiannually, for its new
long-term borrowings.

   a. What is the value of the bonds that FNB holds? That is, what is the present
   value of the newly promised cash payments when discounted at OOPS'
   current borrowing rate?

   b. Consider two accounting treatments for this negotiation (called a "troubled
   debt restructuring" by the FASB in *SFAS No. 15*).

   (1) Write down the bonds to the value computed in the preceding part and
   base future interest revenue computations on that new book value and
   the new historical interest rate of 20 percent per year, compounded
   semiannually. (What loss would FNB recognize?)
   (2) Make no entry to record the negotiation and record interest revenue as
   the amount of cash, $250,000, received semiannually.

   Over the new life of the bond issue, how will total income vary as a function
   of the method chosen?

   c. Which of these two methods would you recommend and why? (In *SFAS No.
   15*, the FASB chose the second method for troubled debt restructurings like
   those in this problem. In some troubled debt restructurings, those where the
   future undiscounted cash flows are less than the book value of the debt on
   the creditor's books, the creditor must recognize a loss equal to the excess of
   book value over the sum of the undiscounted future promised cash flows.)

42. *Financial statement analysis involving consideration of leverage and valuation
of bond liabilities* (*adapted from a problem by C. L. Mitchell*). Condensed financial
statements of Feltham, Inc., and Mattessich Company for 1984 appear in Exhibit
10.8.

Exhibit 10.8
FELTHAM, INC., and MATTESSICH COMPANY
Condensed Financial Statements
(Problem 42)

Balance Sheets
December 31, 1984
(dollars in thousands)

	Feltham, Inc.	Mattessich Company		Feltham, Inc.	Mattessich Company
Current Assets	$ 542	$ 268	Current Liabilities	$ 268	$ 133
Plant and			Bonds Payable	800	400
Equipment			Bond Discount	(77)	—
(net)	2,051	1,027	Bond Premium	—	28
			Shareholders' Equity	1,602	734
	$2,593	$1,295		$2,593	$1,295

Income Statements
Year Ended December 31, 1984
(dollars in thousands except per-share amounts)

	Feltham, Inc.	Mattessich Company
Sales	$2,398	$1,204
Less Cost of Sales	(1,439)	(722)
Gross Margin	$ 959	$ 482
Less Selling and Administrative Expenses	(501)	(253)
Operating Profit	$ 458	$ 229
Less Bond Interest	(56)	(30)
Net Income Before Income Tax	$ 402	$ 199
Less Income Tax Expense (at 40 percent)	(161)	(80)
Net Income	$ 241	$ 119
Earnings per Share	$2.41	$1.19

The operations of the two companies are similar and, except for their size, there appears to be no apparent difference between them except their financing activities. The financial statements appear to reflect the operating similarities. The companies own similar productive assets of the same age.

The one difference between the two companies is their bond financing. On January 1, 1975, both companies issued bonds with interest payable annually on December 31. Feltham, Inc., issued at par $800,000, 7 percent annual coupon bonds maturing on December 31, 1984, and Mattessich Company issued at 110.59, $400,000, 8 percent annual coupon bonds maturing on December 31, 1994. On December 31, 1984, Feltham, Inc., redeemed the 7 percent issue primarily from the proceeds of a new issue at 90.33 of $800,000, 14 percent annual coupon bonds maturing on December 31, 1994, yielding a return of 16 percent. On December 31,

1984, the market interest rate on Mattessich Company's 8 percent annual coupon bonds was 16 percent and the market value was $245,337.

Both companies compute interest expense and amortize bond premium or discount with the effective interest method.

The shares of Feltham, Inc., currently trade at $15.00 per share, and the shares of Mattessich Company at $7.40 per share.

Which company is more conservatively financed? On the basis of the information presented here, which company appears to be a more attractive investment?

Chapter 11 Liabilities: Interest Imputation, Leases, Off-Balance-Sheet Financing, Deferred Income Taxes, and Pensions

The preceding chapter discussed the concept of an accounting liability and described the accounting for current liabilities, long-term notes, and long-term bonds. This chapter examines more advanced issues in liability recognition, valuation, and accounting. The chapter treats the accounting for long-term notes payable where the historical interest rate must be imputed, the accounting for leases and pensions, problems in accounting for income taxes, and off-balance-sheet financing.

Contracts and Long-Term Notes: Interest Imputation

Real estate is often purchased on a *land contract*. Equipment is frequently acquired on the installment plan, and the liability is called an *equipment contract*. Such contracts usually require periodic payments. Sometimes the contract provides for an explicit interest rate. Many contracts, however, do not state an explicit interest rate. Instead, so-called *carrying charges* are added to the purchase price, and the total is divided over a certain number of months without any specific charge being indicated for interest. The "principal" or "face" in this case includes *implicit* interest.

Generally accepted accounting principles require that all long-term liabilities, including those carrying no explicit interest, be stated at the present value of the future cash payments. The interest rate used in discounting is the rate appropriate for the particular borrower given the amount and terms of the borrowing arrangement. It is called the *imputed interest rate*. The difference between the present value and the face value of the liability represents interest to be recognized over the period of the loan. The next two sections discuss two acceptable ways to compute the present value of the liability and the amount of imputed interest.

Base Interest Rate on Market Value of Asset

The first approach uses the market value of the assets acquired as a basis for computing the present value of the liability. For example, assume that a piece of equipment can be bought for $10,500 cash. The equipment is purchased in return for a single-payment note with face amount of $16,000 payable in 3 years. The implied interest rate is about 15 percent per year. (That is, $1.15^3 \times $10,500$ is approximately equal to $16,000.) The journal entry using this approach would be

Equipment	10,500	
Note Payable		10,500

To record purchase of equipment using the known cash price. The amount for the note is inferred from the known cash price of the equipment.

At the end of each accounting period that intervenes between the acquisition of the equipment and repayment of the note, journal entries would be made for depreciation of the equipment. These are not shown. Journal entries must also be made to recognize interest expense. Assume that the note was issued at the beginning of a year. The entries for the 3 years would be

(1) Interest Expense	1,575	
Note Payable		1,575

Entry made 1 year after issuance of note. Interest is .15 × $10,500. The amount is not paid in cash but is added to the principal amount of the liability.

(2) Interest Expense	1,811	
Note Payable		1,811

Entry made 1 year after entry above, 2 years after issuance of note. Interest is .15 × ($10,500 + $1,575).

(3) Interest Expense	2,114	
Note Payable		2,114

Entry made 1 year after entry (2) at maturity of note to increase liability to its maturity amount, $16,000. Interest = $16,000 − ($10,500 + $1,575 + $1,811) which is approximately equal to .15 × ($10,500 + $1,575 + $1,811); the difference is the accumulated rounding error caused by using 15 percent as the implicit interest rate, rather than the exact rate, which is 15.074 percent.

(4) Note Payable	16,000	
Cash		16,000

To repay note at maturity.

Of the $16,000 paid at maturity, $5,500 represents interest accumulated on the note since its issue.

Use of Market Interest Rate to Establish Market Value of Asset and Present Value of Note

If the firm purchased used equipment with the same 3-year note, it might be unable to establish a reliable estimate of the current market value of the asset acquired. The firm would then use the interest rate it would have to pay for a similar loan in the open market to find the present value of the note. This is the second acceptable method for quantifying the amount of the liability and computing the imputed interest. Suppose that the market rate for notes such as the one above is 12 percent compounded annually, rather than 15 percent. The present value at 12 percent per year of the $16,000 note due in 3 years is $11,388 (= $16,000 × .71178; Appendix Table 2 at the back of the book, 3-period row, 12 percent column). The entry to record the purchase of used equipment and payment with the note would be

---

Equipment	11,388
Note Payable	11,388

To record purchase of equipment. Cost of equipment is inferred from known interest rate.

Entries would be made at the end of each period to recognize interest expense, using the 12 percent borrowing rate, and to increase the principal amount of the liability. After the third period, the principal amount of the liability would be $16,000. See Exercise 19 at the end of the chapter.

Funds Statement Effects of Interest Imputation

The process just described for imputing interest on a long-term, single-payment note results in the recognition of interest expense even though no cash is disbursed (at least until the last period when the note is discharged). In deriving cash provided by operations, there must be an addback to net income in the amount of expense that is credited to the long-term liability account, rather than to the Cash account.

Total Expense Is Independent of Interest Rate

In the first case, the equipment is recorded at $10,500 and there is $5,500 of imputed interest. In the second case, the equipment is recorded at $11,388 and there is $4,612 of imputed interest. The total expense over the combined lives of the note and the equipment—interest plus depreciation—is the same, $16,000, no matter which interest rate is used. Over long enough time periods, total expense equals the total cash expenditure; accrual accounting affects only the timing of the expense recognition.

Long-Term Notes Held as Receivables

A note that is the long-term liability of the borrower is a long-term asset of the lender. Generally accepted accounting principles require the lender to show the asset in the Long-Term Note Receivable account at its present value. The rate at which the lender discounts the note should in theory be the same as that used by the borrower, but in practice the two rates sometimes differ. The lender's accounting mirrors the borrower's: The lender has interest revenue where the borrower has interest expense.

Leases

Many firms acquire rights to use assets through long-term noncancelable leases. A company might, for example, agree to lease an office suite for 5 years or an entire building for 40 years, promising to pay a fixed periodic fee for the duration of the lease. Promising to make an irrevocable series of lease payments commits the firm just as surely as a bond indenture or mortgage, and the accounting is similar in many cases.

This section examines two methods of accounting for long-term, noncancelable leases: the operating lease method and the capital lease method.

To illustrate these two methods, suppose that Myers Company wants to acquire a computer that has a 3-year life and costs $45,000. Assume that Myers Company can borrow money for 3 years at 15 percent per year. The computer manufacturer is willing to sell the equipment for $45,000 or to lease it for 3 years. Myers Company is responsible for property taxes, maintenance, and repairs of the computer whether leased or purchased.

Assume that the lease is signed on January 1, Year 1, and that payments on the lease are due on December 31, Year 1, Year 2, and Year 3. In practice, lease payments are usually made in advance, but the computations in the example are simpler if we assume payments at the end of the year. Compound interest computations show that each lease payment must be $19,709. (The present value of $1 paid at the end of this year and each of the next 2 years is $2.28323 when the interest rate is 15 percent per year. See Table 4 at the end of the book. Because the lease payments must have present value of $45,000, each payment must be $45,000/2.28323 = $19,709.)

Operating Lease Method

In an *operating lease,* the owner, or lessor, transfers only the rights to use the property to the lessee for specified periods of time. At the end of the lease period, the property is returned to the lessor. For example, car rental companies lease cars by the day or week on an operating basis. If the Myers Company lease is cancelable and Myers Company can stop making payments and return the computer at any time, then the lease is considered an *operating lease*. No entry would be made on January 1, Year 1, when the lease is signed, and the following entry would be made on December 31, Year 1, Year 2, and Year 3:

Rent Expense.	19,709	
Cash.		19,709
To recognize annual expense of leasing computer.		

Capital Lease Method

If this lease is noncancelable, then the arrangement is a form of borrowing to purchase the computer. It would be accounted for as a *capital lease*.[1] This treatment recognizes the signing of the lease as the simultaneous acquisition of a long-term asset, called a *leasehold*, and the incurring of a long-term liability for lease payments. At the time the lease is signed, both the leasehold and the liability are recorded on the books at the present value of the liability, $45,000 in the example.

The entry made at the time Myers Company signed its 3-year noncancelable lease would be

Asset—Computer Leasehold	45,000	
Liability—Present Value of Lease Obligation		45,000
To recognize acquisition of asset and the related liability.		

At the end of the year, two separate entries must be made. The leasehold is a long-term asset and, like most long-term assets, it must be amortized over its useful life. The first entry made at the end of each year recognizes the amortization of the leasehold asset. Assuming that Myers Company uses straight-line amortization of its leasehold, the entries made at the end of Year 1, Year 2, and Year 3 would be

Amortization Expense (on Computer Leasehold)	15,000	
Asset—Computer Leasehold		15,000

(An alternative treatment credits a contra-asset account, Accumulated Amortization of Computer Leasehold.) The second entry made at the end of each year recognizes the lease payment, which is part payment of interest on the liability and part reduction in the liability itself. The entries made at the end of each of the 3 years would be

December 31, Year 1:		
Interest Expense	6,750	
Liability—Present Value of Lease Obligation	12,959	
Cash		19,709
To recognize lease payment, interest on liability for year (.15 × $45,000 = $6,750) and the plug for reduction in the liability. The present value of the liability after this entry is $32,041 = $45,000 − $12,959.		
December 31, Year 2:		
Interest Expense	4,806	
Liability—Present Value of Lease Obligation	14,903	
Cash		19,709

(continued on next page)

---

[1] Financial Accounting Standards Board, *Statement of Financial Accounting Standards No. 13,* "Accounting for Leases," 1976, reissued and reinterpreted, 1980.

To recognize lease payment, interest on liability for year (.15 ×
$32,041 = $4,806) and the plug for reduction in the liability. The present value of the liability after this entry is $17,138 = $32,041 −
$14,903.

December 31, Year 3:

Interest Expense	2,571	
Liability—Present Value of Lease Obligation	17,138	
Cash		19,709

To recognize lease payment, interest on liability for year (.15 ×
$17,138 = $2,571) and the plug for reduction in the liability. The present value of the liability after this entry is zero (= $17,138 − $17,138).

Exhibit 11.1 shows the amortization schedule for this lease. Note that its form is
exactly the same as in the mortgage amortization schedule shown in Exhibit 10.2.
The underlying principle uses the effective interest method of computing interest
each period.

Accounting Method Determines
Timing, But Not Amount, of Total Expense

Notice that, in the capital lease method, the total expense over the 3 years is
$59,127, consisting of $45,000 (= $15,000 + $15,000 + $15,000) for amortization expense and $14,127 (= $6,750 + $4,806 + $2,571) for interest expense.

Exhibit 11.1
Amortization Schedule for $45,000 Lease Liability,
Repaid in Three Annual Installments of $19,709 Each,
Interest Rate 15 Percent, Compounded Annually

Annual Journal Entry

Dr. Interest Expense	Amount in Column (3)
Dr. Liability—Present Value of Lease Obligations.	Amount in Column (5)
Cr. Cash	Amount in Column (4)

Year (1)	Lease Liability Start of Year (2)	Interest Expense for Year (3)	Payment (4)	Portion of Payment Reducing Lease Liability (5)	Lease Liability End of Year (6)
0					$45,000
1	$45,000	$6,750	$19,709	$12,959	32,041
2	32,041	4,806	19,709	14,903	17,138
3	17,138	2,571	19,709	17,138	0

Column (2) = column (6), previous period.
Column (3) = .15 × column (2).
Column (4) is Given.
Column (5) = column (4) − column (3).
Column (6) = column (2) − column (5).

Exhibit 11.2
Comparison of Expense
Recognized Under Operating and
Capital Lease Methods

| | Expense Recognized Each Year Under | |
Year	Operating Lease Method	Capital Lease Method
1	$19,709	$21,750 (= $15,000 + $ 6,750)
2	19,709	19,806 (= 15,000 + 4,806)
3	19,709	17,571 (= 15,000 + 2,571)
Total	$59,127[a]	$59,127 (= $45,000[b] + $14,127[c])

[a]Rent expense.
[b]Amortization expense.
[c]Interest expense.

This is exactly the same as the total expense recognized under the operating lease method described above ($19,709 × 3 = $59,127). The capital lease method recognizes expense sooner than does the operating lease method, as summarized in Exhibit 11.2. But, over long enough time periods, expense is equal to the cash expenditure. One difference between the operating lease method and the capital method is the *timing* of the expense recognition. The other difference is that the capital lease method recognizes both the asset (leasehold) and the liability on the balance sheet.

Choosing the Accounting Method

When a journal entry debits an asset account and credits a liability account, the debt-equity ratio increases, making the company appear more risky. Thus, given a choice, most managements prefer not to show an asset and a related liability on the balance sheet. These managements prefer an operating lease to either an installment purchase or capital lease, where both the asset and liability appear on the balance sheet. Many managements would also prefer to recognize expenses later rather than sooner for financial reporting. These preferences have led managements to structure asset acquisitions so that the financing takes the form of an operating lease.

Conditions Requiring Capital Lease Accounting   The FASB has provided detailed rules of accounting for long-term noncancelable leases. A lease must be accounted for as a capital lease if it meets any one of four conditions.[2]

A lease is a capital lease if it extends for at least 75 percent of the asset's life, or if it transfers ownership to the lessee at the end of the lease term, or if it seems likely that ownership will be transferred to the lessee because of a "bargain purchase" option. A bargain purchase option gives the lessee the right to purchase the asset for

[2]FASB, *Statement of Financial Accounting Standards No. 13*, par. 7.

a price less than the fair market value of the asset expected when the option is exercised. These three conditions for a capital lease are relatively easy to avoid in lease contracts if a firm prefers to treat a lease as an operating rather than a capital lease.

The most difficult of the four conditions to avoid compares the contractual lease payments discounted at an ''appropriate'' market interest rate with 90 percent of the fair market value of the asset at the time the lease is signed. (The interest rate must be appropriate given the creditworthiness of the lessee.) If the present value of the contractual lease payments equals or exceeds 90 percent of the fair market value of the asset at the time the lease is signed, then the lease is a capital lease. Many lessors do not wish to lease assets where they have more than 10 percent of the asset's value at risk. The major risks and rewards of ownership have therefore been transferred from the lessor (landlord) to the lessee. In economic substance, the lessee has acquired an asset and agreed to pay for it under a long-term contract, to be recognized as a liability.

Effects on Lessor

The lessor (landlord) generally uses the same criteria for classifying a lease as a capital lease or an operating lease as does the lessee (tenant). At the time that a capital lease is signed, the lessor recognizes revenue in an amount equal to the present value of all future lease payments and recognizes expense (analogous to cost of goods sold) in an amount equal to the book value of the leased asset. The difference between the revenue and expense is the lessor's gain on the ''sale'' of the asset. The lease receivable is recorded like any other long-term receivable at the present value of the future cash flows. Interest revenue is then recognized over the collection period of the payments. Lessors tend to prefer capital lease accounting for financial reporting because it enables the recognition of a gain on the ''sale'' of the asset on the date the lease is signed. Under the operating lease method, all lease revenue is recognized gradually over time as lease payments are received.

Off-Balance-Sheet Financing[3]

Firms generally obtain debt financing either directly from banks and other financial institutions or by issuing bonds to investors. These arrangements result in a debit to cash and a credit to a liability account, and increase the debt-equity ratio. Under some other financing arrangements, the resulting obligations do not have to be recorded on the balance sheet as liabilities.

---

[3]This section was developed from materials by Richard Dieter, David L. Landsittel, John E. Stewart, and Arthur R. Wyatt, all of Arthur Andersen & Co. See Landsittel and Stewart, ''Off-Balance Sheet Financing; Commitments and Contingencies,'' in *Handbook of Modern Accounting,* 3rd ed., edited by S. Davidson and R. L. Weil, McGraw-Hill Book Company, New York; 1983, chap. 26.

Keeping Debt off the Balance Sheet

To be an accounting liability, an obligation must be incurred for a past or current benefit received—the event or transaction giving rise to the obligation must already have happened. If the obligation arises from an executory contract, in which both parties have exchanged only promises but there has been no event in which economic risk is transferred, accounting typically does not recognize a liability. The FASB's criterion for recognizing a long-term liability focuses on the transfer of risks and rewards of ownership, not just on the undertaking of commitments to make fixed payments.

Example (Land Option) Miller Corporation desires to acquire land costing $25 million, on which it will build a shopping center. It could borrow the $25 million from its bank, paying interest at 12 percent, and buy the land outright from the seller. If so, both an asset and a liability will appear on the balance sheet. Instead, it borrows $5 million and purchases for $5 million from the seller an option to buy the land from the seller at any time within the next 6 years for a price of $20 million. The option costs Miller Corporation $5 million immediately and provides for continuing "option" payments of $2.4 million per year, which is just equal to Miller Corporation's borrowing rate multiplied by the remaining purchase price of the land: $2.4 million = .12 × $20 million. Although Miller Corporation need not continue payments and can let the option lapse at any time, it also has an obligation to begin developing on the site immediately. Because Miller Corporation has invested a substantial sum in the option, will invest more, and will begin immediately developing the land, Miller Corporation is almost certain to exercise its option before it expires. The seller of the land can take the option contract to the bank and borrow $20 million, paying interest at Miller Corporation's borrowing rate, 12 percent per year. The continuing option payments from Miller Corporation will be sufficient to enable the seller to make its payments to the bank. Generally accepted accounting principles view Miller Corporation as having acquired an option for $5 million, rather than having acquired land costing $25 million in return for $5 million cash and a liability of $20 million. As a result, Miller Corporation keeps $20 million of "debt" off the balance sheet until it borrows more funds to exercise the option.

The techniques for off-balance-sheet financing generally exploit the requirement that to be a liability in accounting, there must have been mutual performance. That is, benefits must have been received in the past obligating the firm to make payments in the future. When the mutual performance will occur in the future (as in executory contracts), accounting typically does not recognize a liability. In the example above, the buyer is viewed as not yet having performed beyond having purchased an option, even though the terms of the option make its eventual exercise by Miller Corporation a virtual certainty.

Why Remove Debt from the Balance Sheet?

When debt is left off the balance sheet, ratios (such as the debt-equity ratio) that have proved useful to analysts for many years will appear more favorable to the borrower. One motive may be to prevent an adverse debt-equity ratio from developing later. The entity may foresee reaching the danger point in its debt-equity relations based on historical standards. Future credit ratings might be lowered and future borrowing costs might increase.

Accounting's Response

The accounting profession has begun to recognize that certain off-balance-sheet financing arrangements have the economic substance of notes or bonds and should be recognized as accounting liabilities. For leases (discussed earlier in this chapter) the accounting profession attempted for more than 10 years to develop a set of criteria that specify clearly which lease obligations must be recognized as liabilities.[4] The FASB has dealt with the transactions on a case-by-case basis, without having promulgated principles to deal with all such transactions. Some accountants think that there will never be a satisfactory solution until accounting requires the recording of a liability whenever there is an obligation to pay a reasonably definite amount at a reasonably definite time, independent of the executory nature of the contract.

Income Tax Accounting and Deferred Income Taxes

As discussed throughout this book, a firm often selects different methods of accounting for financial and tax reporting. In most cases, the *total amount* of revenue or expense recognized over the life of an asset or other item will be the same for these two purposes. However, the *timing* of recognition may differ. For example, the total depreciation recognized for both financial and tax reporting over an asset's life is its acquisition cost. In the early years, tax depreciation for an asset will exceed depreciation recognized for financial reporting, so that taxable income will be less than financial statement income before taxes. In later years, depreciation for tax reporting is less than that for financial reporting, so that taxable income will exceed income before taxes.[5]

The use of different accounting methods for financial and tax reporting creates a problem in measuring income tax *expense* each period:

---

[4]In any lease contract, the lessee promises to make future payments. If the payments are sufficiently large in present value relative to the value of the asset leased, the FASB judges that the risks and rewards of ownership have been transferred from the lessor to the lessee; the lessee will record both an asset and a liability. If the contractual lease payments have sufficiently small relative present value, even though they are material in amount, the FASB views the contract as executory: The lessor has an obligation to provide future services and the lessee will pay for those services as used.

[5]The term *financial statement income,* although descriptive, is somewhat cumbersome. Throughout this section, the term *book income* is used to refer to net income before taxes reported in the financial statements and *taxable income* is used to refer to the amount reported on the income tax return. Similarly, the terms *book purposes* and *tax purposes* differentiate the financial statements from the income tax return.

1. Should income tax expense be equal to the income taxes actually payable each period based on taxable income, or
2. Should income tax expense be equal to the income taxes that would have been payable had the methods of accounting used for financial reporting also been used for tax reporting?

Illustration

Assume that Burns, Inc., pays income taxes at the rate of 40 percent of taxable income. Burns purchased a plant asset for $100,000 that has a 5-year estimated service life and an estimated salvage value of zero. This asset produces an excess of revenues over operating expenses (other than depreciation and taxes) of $30,000 a year. That is, after paying for the costs of running and maintaining the asset, the firm enjoys a $30,000-per-year excess of revenue over expenses (except depreciation and taxes). Burns uses straight-line depreciation for financial reporting and ACRS for taxes.

As Chapter 9 indicated, ACRS classifies plant assets into four cost recovery periods: 3, 5, 10, and 15 years. The ACRS cost recovery period is not determined by the estimated service life of the plant asset but instead by the defined plant asset categories. Assume for purposes of this illustration that the asset being considered is the 3-year recovery property. The cost recovery (depreciation) deductions for assets in this category are 25 percent the first year, 38 percent the second, and 37 percent the third.

Thus, in the first year the new plant asset is used, depreciation for financial reporting will be $20,000 (= $100,000/5) and on the tax return will be $25,000 (= $100,000 × .25). In addition to the $30,000 from the plant asset, other pretax income for each year is $70,000.

Exhibit 11.3 summarizes the computation of taxes for tax purposes and for financial reporting.

The first column in Exhibit 11.3 shows the tax return for the first, second, and fifth years. Note that nothing changes over time other than the depreciation deduction and taxes payable. As depreciation increases from Year 1 to Year 2, taxes payable decrease. As depreciation decreases from Year 2 to Year 5, taxes payable increase. The middle column shows book income resulting from an income statement (not allowed by GAAP) where income tax expense is equal to income taxes payable. Note that pretax book income is the same, $80,000, in all years, but that aftertax net income increases from $50,000 in Year 1 to $55,200 in Year 2, and then declines to $40,000 by Year 5. The pattern results from fluctuations in income taxes over the 5 years: $30,000; $24,800; $25,200; $40,000; $40,000. [All five of these numbers appear in column (8) of Exhibit 11.4, discussed later.] Those who set generally accepted accounting principles are uncomfortable with the notion that reported income (as in the middle column) will fluctuate merely because different accounting methods are used for tax and for book purposes. Consequently, in this case, generally accepted accounting principles require that the income tax expense for financial reporting be based on pretax *book* income, not on taxes actually payable. The third column of Exhibit 11.3 shows the required accounting. Note that

Exhibit 11.3
Deferred Income Tax
Computations for Burns, Inc.

	Tax Return	Book Income Using Taxes Payable (not acceptable)	Financial Reporting (required)
First Year			
Other Pretax Income	$ 70,000	$70,000	$70,000
Excess of Revenues over Expenses Except			
Depreciation from Plant Asset	30,000	30,000	30,000
Depreciation	(25,000)	(20,000)	(20,000)
Income Before Taxes	$ 75,000	$80,000	$80,000
Income Taxes Currently Payable			
(at 40 percent)	$ 30,000		
Income Tax Expense (at 40 percent):			
On Taxable Income.		(30,000)	
On Pretax Book Income.			(32,000)
Net Income	$ 45,000	$50,000	$48,000
Second Year			
Other Pretax Income	$ 70,000	$70,000	$70,000
Excess of Revenues over Expenses Except			
Depreciation from Plant Asset	30,000	30,000	30,000
Depreciation	(38,000)	(20,000)	(20,000)
Income Before Taxes	$ 62,000	$80,000	$80,000
Income Taxes Currently Payable			
(at 40 percent)	$ 24,800		
Income Tax Expense (at 40 percent):			
On Taxable Income.		(24,800)	
On Pretax Book Income.			(32,000)
Net Income		$55,200	$48,000
Fifth Year			
Other Pretax Income	$ 70,000	$70,000	$70,000
Excess of Revenues over Expenses Except			
Depreciation from Plant Asset	30,000	30,000	30,000
Depreciation	—	(20,000)	(20,000)
Income Before Taxes	$100,000	$80,000	$80,000
Income Taxes Currently Payable			
(at 40 percent)	$ 40,000		
Income Tax Expense (at 40 percent):			
On Taxable Income.		(40,000)	
On Pretax Book Income.			(32,000)
Net Income		$40,000	$48,000

aftertax net income in each year equals that of the first year, just as pretax income in each year equals that of the first year.

Rationale for Deferred Tax Accounting

Relative to straight-line depreciation, ACRS "borrows" income tax deductions in the early years from later years. The fluctuation in taxable income is predictable during the first year, because it results from a difference in the depreciation methods used in financial statements and the tax return. The tax reduction in the first 3 years, relative to the last 2 years, is a difference that will reverse with the mere passage of time. Generally accepted accounting principles require that the reported net income be the same in each year, because pretax income on the financial statements is the same each year.[6] The required accounting matches income tax expense and pretax book income rather than income tax expense and taxable income. The rationale is that income taxes will become payable in future years when the difference between book and taxable income reverses. This future cash outflow is an expense of the current period to be matched against pretax book income much the same as future warranty costs are an expense of the period when the warranteed product is sold.

Timing Differences Versus Permanent Differences

In general, the problem of accounting for income taxes arises from differences in timing between financial reporting of revenues and expenses and tax reporting of these items. A *timing difference* is any item of revenue or expense that appears on the financial statements in one period but on the tax return in a different period. The total amounts appearing over time on the financial statements and the tax return are identical. Only the timing differs. The following list shows some of the ways in which the timing differences can arise.

1. Depreciation for tax purposes is different from that shown in the financial records in a given period because ACRS is used for taxes and a different method is used for books. Total depreciation over the asset's entire life is generally the same for book and for tax purposes.

2. Income from credit sales is recognized for financial reporting in the year of sale, but recognized for tax purposes in the year when cash is collected from customers. Total income from the credit sale is the same for book and for tax; the timing of income recognition differs.

3. Income from long-term construction projects is recognized for financial reporting on the percentage-of-completion basis but on tax returns under the completed contract basis. Total income is again the same for book and for tax, but its timing differs.

4. Expenses for estimated warranty costs appear on the financial statements in the year of sale, but tax deductions are allowed only later, when expenditures for

---

[6]Accounting Principles Board, *Opinion No. 11,* "Accounting for Income Taxes," 1967.

repairs are made. In this case, unlike the preceding ones, financial statement income is *less* than taxable income in the year the timing difference originates.

Some differences between reported income and taxable income will never reverse, because the tax laws single them out for special treatment. These include items of revenue that are never taxed or expenses that are never deductible in computing income taxes payable. An example is interest revenue on tax-exempt municipal bonds held as assets. Such tax-exempt interest is part of reported income but is never part of taxable income. Differences between reported income and taxable income that never reverse are called *permanent differences*. Although permanent differences appear in financial statement income, they do not affect income tax expense.

Permanent differences do, however, cause a difference between the effective income tax rate (income tax expense divided by pretax income on the financial statements) and the statutory income tax rate (generally, 46 percent for corporations). Consider, for example, a firm with book income before taxes of $1 million which includes $100,000 of interest from holdings of tax-exempt municipal bonds. The taxable income is $900,000 (= $1,000,000 − $100,000) and the income tax expense is equal to $414,000 (= .46 × $900,000). The effective income tax rate is 41.4 percent (= $414,000/$1,000,000), even though the statutory income tax rate is 46 percent. The SEC requires firms to disclose the causes for the effective tax rate's differing from the statutory tax rate. The third schedule in Note 6 of the annual report of the General Products Company (in Appendix A at the back of the book) illustrates the required disclosure.

Accounting Procedures for Income Taxes Where Timing Differences Exist

Where there are timing differences for depreciation because straight-line is used for financial reporting but ACRS is used for taxes, generally accepted accounting principles require that income tax *expense* on the financial statements be computed as though straight-line depreciation over estimated service life were used on the tax return. Under such an assumption, income tax expense in the Burns, Inc. example would be $32,000 each year. Because only $30,000 is payable in the first year and $24,800 in the second year, the following entries would be made:

Income Tax Expense	32,000	
Income Tax Payable		30,000
Deferred Income Tax Liability		2,000

First year income tax entry; expense exceeds cash payment; liability is created.[7]

(continued on page 497)

---

[7]APB *Opinion No. 11* states that the account credited should be viewed as a "deferred credit" and not as a liability. The issue of whether deferred income taxes is a liability is discussed later in this section.

Exhibit 11.4
Summary of Deferred Income Tax Liability Account for Burns, Inc.

Annual Journal Entry

	Dr. Income Tax Expense	Amount in Column (5)
or {	Dr. Deferred Income Tax Liability . . .	Amount in Column (9)
	Cr. Deferred Income Tax Liability . . .	Amount in Column (10)
	Cr. Income Taxes Payable	Amount in Column (8)

Year (1)	Financial Statements				Tax Returns			Deferred Income Tax Liability Account		
	Income Before Depreciation and Tax Expenses (2)	Depreciation Expense (3)	Pretax Income (4)	Tax Expense (5)	Depreciation Deduction (6)	Pretax Income (7)	Taxes Payable (8)	Debit (9)	Credit (10)	Credit Balance at Year-End (11)
1	$100,000	$ 20,000	$ 80,000	$ 32,000	$ 25,000	$ 75,000	$30,000		$2,000	$ 2,000
2	100,000	20,000	80,000	32,000	38,000	62,000	24,800		7,200	9,200
3	100,000	20,000	80,000	32,000	37,000	63,000	25,200		6,800	16,000
4	100,000	20,000	80,000	32,000	0	100,000	40,000	$8,000		8,000
5	100,000	20,000	80,000	32,000	0	100,000	40,000	8,000		0
		$100,000	$400,000	$160,000	$100,000	$400,000	$160,000			

Column (4) = column (2) − column (3).

Column (5) = .40 × $80,000.

Column (6) = ACRS: 25 percent, 38 percent, 37 percent of $100,000 for 3 years, zero for fourth and fifth years.

Column (7) = column (2) − column (6).

Column (8) = column (7) × .40.

Column (9) and (10) = column (5) − column (8); if positive, appears in column (10); if negative, appears in column (9).

Column (11) = Sum of entries in column (10) reduced by column (9).

Income Tax Expense	32,000	
Income Taxes Payable		24,800
Deferred Income Taxes Liability		7,200

Second year income tax entry; expense exceeds cash payment; liability is increased.

For this one asset, the $2,000 tax not paid in the first year and the $7,200 not paid in the second year are not forgiven by the government. Instead, these payments are merely delayed. If Burns had only this one asset, the additional taxes would be paid in later years. The bottom panel of Exhibit 11.3 shows the computation of Income Taxes Payable in the fifth year to be $40,000. Because the financial statements will have Income Tax Expense computed under the assumption that straight-line depreciation is used on the tax return, the reported Income Tax Expense will remain $32,000. Because the actual tax payment must be $40,000, however, the journal entry to recognize the income tax expense for the fifth year is

Income Tax Expense	32,000	
Deferred Income Tax Liability	8,000	
Income Tax Payable		40,000

Fifth-year income tax entry; expense is less than cash payment; liability is reduced.

The amounts of expense not paid in cash in the early years are credited to the Deferred Income Tax Liability account. Later, when cash payments exceed reported expense, the liability account is debited and its balance reduces. Exhibit 11.4 shows a summary of the entries in Burns' Deferred Income Tax Liability account for the 5 years during which it uses the plant asset. Observe that the total tax expense in column (5) shown on the financial statements over the asset's life is the same as the total taxes payable on the tax returns in column (8), but that using the accelerated method on the tax returns defers payment and thus leads to a lower present value of taxes paid.

Funds Statement Effects In the first year, income tax expense exceeds income taxes payable by $2,000. That $2,000 of tax expense did not use cash, so an addback to net income is required in the statement of changes in financial position in deriving "cash provided by operations." The $2,000 of expense increases the non-current liability for deferred income taxes. The statement of changes in financial position of General Products Company for 1985, in Exhibit A.3, illustrates the addback to net income for deferred taxes in arriving at cash provided by operations.

In the fifth year more cash ($40,000) is used than the amount of the expense ($32,000) reported in the income statement. Consequently, there must be a subtraction of $8,000 in the statement of changes in financial position to derive "cash provided by operations." See the 1984 column of Exhibit A.3 for General Products Company.

Summary of Income Tax Accounting for Timing Differences

Income tax *expense* always refers to the financial statements; income taxes *payable* refers to the amount on the tax return.

Income taxes payable computed on the tax return result from accounting principles selected by the firm to minimize the present value of the cash burden for income taxes. Income tax *expense* shown in the financial statements results from a measure of taxable income computed using the financial statement's accounting principles for timing differences, rather than the tax return's accounting principles. The excess of income tax expense over income taxes payable, if any, is credited to the Deferred Income Taxes balance sheet account. The excess of income taxes payable over income tax expense, if any, is debited to the Deferred Income Taxes balance sheet account. If the Deferred Income Taxes account has a credit balance, then it appears on the balance sheet among the equities, usually as a liability. If the Deferred Income Taxes account has a debit balance, then it appears on the balance sheet among the assets.

Disclosure of Deferred Income Taxes in Financial Statements

Notes to financial statements contain a wealth of information about income taxes. Among the items of information included is the amount of deferred tax expense for the year caused by each of the several important timing differences. Note 6 of Exhibit A.4 in Appendix A for General Products Company illustrates this disclosure.

Typically, the financial statements do not disclose the amount of deductions claimed on the tax return. The information in the notes about deferred taxes can be used to deduce many of them. For example, the financial statements of Burns, Inc., for the first year in our example, show depreciation expense of $20,000. The notes disclose both that the deferred tax expense caused by depreciation timing differences is $2,000 and that the income tax rate is 40 percent of pretax income. From these data, we can deduce that depreciation claimed on the tax return exceeded depreciation expense on the financial statements by $5,000 (= $2,000/.40). Thus, depreciation claimed on the tax return must have been $25,000 (= $20,000 + $5,000).

Criticisms of the Accounting for Deferred Income Taxes

The accounting for deferred income taxes has been subject to criticism for many years. The FASB is currently considering changing the requirements for accounting for timing differences because of the following criticisms.

Benefits Ignored Deferred tax accounting for timing differences conceals the benefit conveyed by tax rules that delay tax payments. Note that the income statements of Burns, Inc., would look the same as the third column in Exhibit 11.3 if it were to use straight-line depreciation on the tax return. (In fact, Income Tax Expense on Burns' financial statement is computed *assuming* that straight-line depreciation is used on the tax return.) Taxes paid later are less burdensome than taxes paid sooner, but deferred tax accounting conceals this exploitation of the benefit.

Payments Deferred Indefinitely A going concern using accelerated cost recovery on the tax return may be able to defer payment of deferred taxes indefinitely. Taxes are levied on overall operations, not on individual assets. Although timing differences for earlier timing differences do reverse, new acquisitions create new timing differences that offset the reversals if asset acquisitions at least remain level over time in dollar amounts. If increasing amounts are spent each year on new assets, the new timing differences will exceed the reversing timing differences and the credit balance in the deferred tax account will grow. If the firm continues to acquire depreciable assets each year (in dollar amounts no less than it acquired in the preceding year), then in every year Income Taxes Payable will *be less than or equal to* Income Tax Expense computed as generally accepted accounting principles require. In no year will there be a net debit entry to the Deferred Income Tax account on the balance sheet.

Tax payments will exceed tax expense (as in years 4 and 5 of the Burns example) only when the firm stops acquiring new assets while it continues to earn taxable income. Few firms shrink in size (as is required for the income taxes payable to exceed income tax expense) and at the same time remain profitable. Most shrinking firms owe no taxes because they fail to earn taxable income.

The deferred tax is probably not going to be paid, and if it is, the time when payment is finally made is uncertain.[8]

---

[8]Whether timing differences actually reverse remains a controversial question among accounting writers. A majority agree with generally accepted accounting principles on the matter of computing and recognizing deferred income taxes. They argue that the reasons offered against recognizing deferred income tax liabilities also support a conclusion that Accounts Payable are not liabilities either. After all, accounts payable are never paid off in the aggregate for a going concern; in fact, the amount of Accounts Payable usually grows over time.

The critical difference between accounts payable and income taxes, however, is that income taxes are levied on the income of a firm as a whole. Losses or deductions from one project can offset gains or income from another. The government does not tax a firm asset by asset. If a firm shrinks and becomes bankrupt, having no taxable income, then the government does not ask for income tax payments; creditors (those who are due to be paid for the Accounts Payable) will be entitled to payment (or partial payment) from the remaining assets as the firm winds down its business. Accounts Payable do have significance as liabilities even though they may increase year after year. There has been empirical work on this issue of whether there are any, many, or few firms that find taxes payable exceeding tax expense because of reversals of depreciation timing differences. The interested reader can refer to the data presented in the *Journal of Accountancy,* April 1977, pages 53–59. The data show that for 3,100 companies over 19 years (nearly 60,000 company-years), there are about 700 cases (slightly more than 1 percent) of a firm's remaining profitable while its depreciable assets shrink in size for the year.

To avoid facing the question of whether the liability will ever be paid, APB *Opinion No. 11* refers to the item as a "deferred credit" rather than as a liability.

Not an Obligation The amount on the balance sheet for deferred income taxes is not an obligation (to the federal government or to anyone else). The government levies taxes on taxable income as shown on the tax return and only as it is earned. It does not automatically levy a tax because depreciation deductions decline. The government does not suggest to Burns, Inc., in Years 1, 2, and 3 that the firm will also be profitable in Years 4 and 5 or that it has in Years 1, 2, and 3 a liability for taxes due in Years 4 and 5.

Uncertain Amount Another, but less important, criticism of deferred tax accounting is that if the firm does find at some future date that it has income taxes payable larger than income tax expense, it is unlikely that the tax rate on the income will be the same as the rate at the time the deferred tax expense was originally computed. Tax rates change periodically. Even if aggregate timing differences eventually reverse at a time when the firm has taxable income, the tax rate for that period is currently not estimable with reasonable precision in most cases.

Undiscounted Amount Finally, note that obligations for deferred income taxes are shown as undiscounted amounts, not at the present value of those amounts. All other long-term obligations reported on the balance sheet are shown at the present value of the future cash payments. The present value is computed using the historical interest rate appropriate for the firm, as borrower, on the date the obligation is first recorded. The valuation method to be used for deferred income taxes is also under study by the FASB.

Pensions

Under a pension plan, an employer promises to make payments to employees after retirement. Private pension plan systems have grown in number and size over the last several decades so rapidly that the major asset of many individuals is the present value of their pension benefits and a significant obligation of many firms results from their pension promises. The basic operations of a pension plan are simple, but the concepts can be lost in a variety of details. In a pension plan:

1. The employer sets up a pension plan, specifying the eligibility of employees, the types of promises to employees, the method of funding, and the pension plan administrator.[9]

2. The employer computes a pension expense each period according to some formula. The employer debits Pension Expense for that amount and credits Pension Liability. This process is called "expensing pension obligations."

3. The employer transfers cash to the plan each period according to some formula. The employer debits Pension Liability and credits Cash. This process is called

---

[9]Pension law distinguishes the *plan administrator* (who has the fiduciary responsibility for the plan) from the *funding agent* (which receives cash payments and invests them). This discussion does not distinguish between the functions of these two agents in the pension process.

"funding pension liabilities." The amounts funded in this step are usually, but *not* necessarily, the same as the amounts expensed each period in step 2.

The preceding steps comprise the employer's accounting for pensions. The employer is sometimes called the "plan sponsor." The following steps are carried out by the pension plan.

1. The plan receives cash each period from the plan sponsor. In the accounting records of the pension plan, Cash is debited and Liability for Payments to Employees is credited.

2. Funds received are invested to generate income. The income is not part of the employer's (sponsor's) income for the period, but is reported in separate financial statements of the pension plan. The fund debits its Investment asset account and credits Investment Revenue.

3. The plan makes payments to those entitled to receive them. The plan debits Liability for Payments to Employees and credits Cash.

Accounting Principles Board *Opinion No. 8* (1966) and FASB *Statement No. 36* (1980) govern the *employer's* accounting and reporting for the pension plan. FASB *Statement No. 35* (1980) governs the *administrator's* accounting and reporting for the pension plan.

Introduction to Pension Plans

There are almost as many different kinds of pension plans as there are employers who have them. The basic variables of a pension plan are the following:

1. Its requirement for contributions by employers and employees.
2. Vesting provisions.
3. Funding provisions.
4. The kinds of promises made by the employer.
5. Treatment of past service obligation, if any.

Each of these variables is explained and discussed.

Contributions Under a *noncontributory* plan, the employee makes no explicit contribution of funds to the pension plan; only the employer contributes. Under a *contributory* plan both the employee and the employer contribute, but they do not necessarily contribute equal amounts. Employees retain a claim to their explicit contributions under virtually all plans. The employee's rights to the employer's contributions are determined by the *vesting* provisions. The rest of this section considers noncontributory plans or, if the plan is contributory, only the employer's contributions.

Vesting Provisions An employee's rights under a pension plan may be fully vested or partially vested. When the rights are *fully vested,* the pension benefits purchased with the employer's contributions cannot be taken away from the employee. (These benefits are partially insured by an agency of the federal government.) If the rights are not vested, the employee will lose rights to the employer's contributions if he or she leaves the company. Under *partially vested* (or "graded vesting") plans, rights vest gradually. For example, an employee in the fifth year of work might have no vested rights, but by the time he or she has been employed for 15 years, all rights will be vested. The nature of vesting provisions will influence the present value of the expected pension liabilities generated during an accounting period. If employees leave their jobs, then their rights, and therefore the employer's liabilities, are less if the benefits are only partially vested than when the benefits are fully vested.

Federal pension law (the Pension Reform Act of 1974, called the *Employee Retirement Income and Security Act* or *ERISA*) requires that an employee's benefits from contributions by the employer must become vested according to one of several formulas. These generally provide for full vesting by the time the employee has worked for the employer for 15 years.

Funding Provisions A pension plan may be *fully funded* or *partially funded*. Under a fully funded plan, the employer pays cash to an outside trustee, such as an insurance company, equal to the present value of all expected pension liabilities. Partially funded plans have cash available in an amount less than the present value of all pension obligations. ERISA mandates certain minimum funding requirements for corporate pension plans.

Employer Promises

Employers make essentially two different kinds of pension promises to employees:

1. Some employers make promises about the amounts to be contributed to the pension plan without specifying the benefits to be received by retired employees. Such plans are *defined-contribution* plans. Employer inputs, or contributions to the plan, are defined. The amounts eventually received by employees depend on the investment performance of the pension fund.

2. Most employers make promises about the amount each employee will receive during retirement based on wages earned and number of years of employment. The plan does not specify the amounts the employer will contribute to the plan. Such plans are called *defined-benefit* plans. Payments to employees are defined. The employer must make contributions to the plan so that those amounts plus their earnings are large enough to make the promised payments.

Defined-Contribution Plans In a defined-contribution plan, the employer promises to contribute an amount determined by formula to each employee's pension account. Zenith Radio Corporation, for example, promises to contribute between 6 and 12 percent of income before the contribution (the exact amount depending on some other factors) to the pension plan each year. An employee's share in the company's pension fund depends on his or her annual compensation. Another employer might agree to contribute an amount equal to 5 percent of an employee's salary to a pension fund. Subject to reasonable investment risks, the funds are managed to produce as large a series of payments as is possible during the employee's retirement. No specific promises are made to employees about the amount of the eventual pension. Inputs are defined; total outputs depend on investment performance.

The accounting for defined-contribution plans is straightforward. If the employer contributes $75,000 to a trustee to be managed for employees' retirement benefits, the journal entry is

Pension Expense	75,000	
Cash		75,000

Other than periodically overseeing the activities of the plan administrator to ensure that investment policies are being carried out prudently, the employer's obligation under the pension plan is largely completed once the cash is paid to the plan administrator. Neither the assets of the pension plan nor the amounts expected to be paid to retired employees appear in the employer's financial statements. The income from pension fund investments each period is not included in the net income of the employer, but in separate financial statements of the plan.

Defined-Benefit Plans Under a defined-benefit plan, the employer promises the employee a series of retirement payments based on a formula. The typical formula takes into account the employee's length of service and some measure of average earnings. For example, the employer might promise to pay during retirement an annual pension equal to a stated percentage of the average annual salary earned during the 5 highest-paid working years for all employees. The percentage might increase by 2 percentage points for each year of service, so that an employee with 40 years of service would get a pension equal to 80 percent of his or her average salary during the 5 highest-paid working years. The defined-benefit formula is

$$\text{Pension Benefit per Year During Retirement} = .02n \times \text{Average Salary for the 5 Highest-Paid Years of Employment}$$

where n is the number of years of the employee's employment. Payments are defined by formula; the exact amount to be paid later to employees is not known currently and therefore must be estimated. This amount depends on factors such as mortality, inflation, and future wages.

The employer must set aside funds to fulfill its pension obligations to employees and report expenses for these amounts. The amount depends on, among other factors, the rate of return to be earned on pension fund investments. Because defined-benefit pension plans are based on numerous estimates, accounting for such plans must be able to cope with misestimates as they become apparent.

Comparison of Types of Promises Most corporate pension plans are defined-benefit plans. Federal pension law, known as ERISA, makes defined-contribution plans relatively more attractive than they had been previously. The number of defined-contribution plans is increasing, but such plans remain a minority. Some employees prefer a defined-benefit plan because it reduces the employee's risk in planning for retirement. Employers tend to prefer defined-contribution plans because of the reduced uncertainty of pension expenses and contributions and because defined-benefit plans are more highly regulated by governments than are defined-contribution plans. The plan used in any given firm is likely to be the result of labor-management negotiations.

Generally Accepted Accounting Principles by Employers for Defined-Benefit Plans

Current Service Benefits: Normal Costs Generally accepted accounting principles[10] require the employer with a defined-benefit plan to show as a cost of the period the present value of the pension liabilities generated by employees' service during the period. The expense for pensions earned during a given period is called the *normal cost* of that period. ERISA generally requires that the liabilities generated during the period for normal costs be funded in the current period. For example, if actuarial calculations show the expected present value of pension obligations arising from labor services for the year to be $500,000, the entry to recognize the expense is[11]

Pension Expense (Normal Costs)	500,000	
Pension Liability		500,000
To recognize pension expense for current service and related liability.		

When the pension plan is funded, the entry, assuming that $500,000 is paid to the plan administrator, is

Pension Liability	500,000	
Cash		500,000
To fund pension liability.		

Because federal law generally requires companies to fund pension expense for normal costs in the same year that it is recognized, most companies show no Pension Liability account for current service on their balance sheets. In these cases, the effect of the two entries shown above is often recorded in a single entry:

---

[10]Accounting Principles Board, *Opinion No. 8,* "Accounting for the Cost of Pension Plans," 1966.

[11]If the wages of the workers involved were debited to product cost accounts (such as Work-in-Process Inventory), then the pension costs would be product costs, not period expenses. In the rest of this chapter we assume that all pension costs are debited to Pension Expense to simplify the illustrations.

Pension Expense (Normal Costs)	500,000
Cash	500,000

To recognize pension expense for current service and its immediate funding.

Past Service Benefits

When a pension plan is adopted, current employees will usually receive retroactive credit for years of work performed before the plan's adoption. Moreover, from time to time, the pension plan may be made more generous; that is, the benefits promised to employees during retirement may be "sweetened." At the time the plan is made more generous, employees will usually be given credit for those prior years when the defined-benefit formula is applied.

Consider, for example, the defined benefit formula introduced earlier: Pension = $.02n \times$ Average Salary for 5 Highest Paid Years. Assume that after an employee has been working for ten years, the plan is sweetened, so that the first factor in the formula is changed to .025 from .02. A question arises as to which n will be used in applying the new formula. Shall n be the number of years between the time of sweetening and retirement, or shall it be the total number of years the employee will have worked by retirement, which will be 10 larger than the first number? Most plan adoptions and sweetenings use the total work life, not just the time between adoption (or sweetening) and retirement. As a result, the creating or sweetening of a pension plan usually creates employer obligations to pay pensions for prior years' work. These obligations have been called various things at various times.[12] In this discussion, the obligations are called *costs for past service* or *past service obligations*.

The present value of the unfunded past service obligation is *not* recognized as a liability in the accounting records, but its amount must be disclosed in the notes to the financial statements.

The cost for obligations for past service is disclosed in notes on the date the obligation is incurred either because of a plan's adoption or a plan's sweetening. In subsequent periods, the obligation is gradually recognized in the formal accounting records. The recognition takes the form of a journal entry debiting Pension Expense and crediting Pension Liability. (The liability is usually funded in the same period, with cash paid to the pension plan administrator.)

This process of gradually recognizing the obligations as a formal liability is called *amortizing* costs for past service. The amortizing results in debits to expense—decreasing owners' equity—and credits to liability—creating (or increasing) a balance sheet liability. Eventually a cash payment discharges the liability.

---

[12]*Actuarial accrued liability* is the term used by actuaries since 1981. Before that time, the terms *past service cost, prior service cost,* and *supplemental actuarial value* were used. These terms had different meanings depending on the context. See the discussion in the Glossary at "actuarial accrued liability."

Generally accepted accounting principles and federal law permit amortization and funding of past service obligations over a time span chosen by the individual firm, subject to minimum and maximum limitations not discussed here.

Illustration Assume that the sweetening of an existing plan creates an obligation for past service with present value of $1 million. If an obligation of $1,000,000 is to be amortized and funded over 30 years using a discount rate of 8 percent, then the annual expense and funding payment would be $88,827.[13] The annual journal entry to recognize the expense would be

Pension Expense (Past Service)	88,827	
Pension Liability		88,827

To recognize pension expense for past service of $1,000,000 being amortized over 30 years.

The above entry recognizes the pension expense. Its effect is to remove part of the obligation for pension payments from the footnotes, where it is not recognized as a liability, and to transfer the obligation to the balance sheet where it appears as an actual long-term liability. When the revenue and expense accounts for the period are closed, the Pension Expense account is closed to income, reducing it, and then to the Retained Earnings account, reducing it. The overall balance sheet effect of this entry is to recognize an increase in a liability and a decrease in owners' equity.

Most corporate pension plans provide for funding of pension liabilities as they are recognized. Thus the corporation making the journal entry just above is likely to make a funding payment of cash of $88,827 to a pension fund and to make the following journal entry:

Pension Liability	88,827	
Cash		88,827

To fund liability.

Note that the entries recognizing the liability and then funding it could be combined as follows:

Pension Expense (Past Service)	88,827	
Cash		88,827

To recognize and fund pension expense for actuarial accrued liability of $1,000,000 being amortized and funded over 30 years.

From the point of view of accrual accounting, the funding via cash payment is not required. Accounting merely requires that the obligation for both normal costs and

---

[13]The present value of a $1 annuity for 30 years discounted at 8 percent per year is $11.25778; $1,000,000/11.25778 = $88,827.

past service obligations be recognized as expense and recognized as liabilities on a systematic basis. As the obligation is funded, the liability is reduced. ERISA, however, requires periodic funding of these liabilities.

Funds Statement Effects When pension expense is recorded, income decreases and a liability for pensions increases. When pension liabilities are funded, cash and liabilities are both reduced. Thus, when pension funding is the same amount each period as pension expense, no pension-related adjustments to net income are required in deriving cash provided by continuing operations. If pension expense exceeds pension funding, an addback of the excess is required in deriving funds provided by continuing operations. (When pension expense differs from pension funding, other issues arise that are beyond the scope of this discussion.)

FASB Proposals to Change Generally Accepted Accounting Principles for Costs of Past Service

Recall that a liability results from a past transaction that creates an obligation to make a payment at a future time. Some think that the obligation to employees for benefits based on their prior work meets these criteria. The timing of payments can be reasonably estimated because of demographic data on retirement ages and actuarial data on length of life. The amounts of payments can also be estimated. Actuaries can estimate mortality (both before and after retirement) as well as wage rates. The obligation results from employment contracts and federal law. Thus, when a pension plan is brought into existence with retroactive benefits promised for past service or when a plan is sweetened with the sweetenings applying retroactively for prior service, then some think that a liability has been created. The FASB is currently considering requiring the recognition of that liability and a related intangible asset representing the employee "goodwill" resulting from providing retroactive benefits.

Summary of Corporate Pension Accounting by Employer

Total corporate pension expense for a period under a defined-benefit plan is the sum of the charge for current service benefits earned during the period (normal cost) plus the charge for the gradual recognition of costs for past service.

Generally accepted accounting principles require certain minimum disclosures for pension plans by the employer. Note 3 of Exhibit A.4 in Appendix A at the back of the book illustrates the required disclosure for the General Products Company.

Generally Accepted Accounting Principles by the *Plan* for Defined-Benefit Pensions

The pension plan receives the cash paid by the employer/sponsor and invests it until paid to retired employees. The plan keeps its own accounting records and makes disclosures according to rules in FASB *Statement No. 35*. Note 3 of Exhibit A.4 in

Appendix A illustrates the required disclosures for the separate pension plan of the General Products Company.

The plan reports its assets, usually investments of various sorts, at fair market value. The fluctuations in market value each year are part of the earnings or losses of the pension plan.

Problem 1 for Self-Study

The Chang Company purchased a truck from Guttman's Auto Agency. The truck had a list price of $25,000, but discounts of 10 to 15 percent from list price are common in purchases of this sort. Chang Company paid for the truck by giving a noninterest-bearing note due 2 years from the date of purchase. The note had a maturity value of $28,730. The rate of interest that Chang Company paid to borrow on secured 2-year loans ranged from 10 to 15 percent during the period when the purchase occurred.

  a. Record the acquisition of the truck on Chang Company's books, assuming that the fair market value of the truck was computed using a 10 percent discount from list price.

  b. What imputed interest rate will be used throughout the loan for computing interest expense if the acquisition is recorded as in part **a**?

  c. Record the acquisition of the truck on Chang Company's books, assuming that the estimated interest rate Chang Company must pay to borrow is deemed reliable and is 12 percent per year.

  d. Record the acquisition of the truck on Chang Company's books, assuming that the interest rate Chang Company must pay to borrow is 1 percent per month.

  e. Prepare journal entries to record the loan and to record interest over 2 years, assuming that the truck is recorded at $23,744 and the interest rate implicit in the loan is 10 percent per year.

  f. Throughout, this book has stressed that over long enough time periods, total expense is equal to cash outflow. In what sense is the total expense for this transaction the same, independent of the interest rate (and, therefore, the interest expense)?

Suggested Solution

a. Truck	22,500	
Note Payable		22,500
.90 × $25,000 = $22,500.		

  b. $28,730/$22,500 = 1.27689. The truck has fair market value of $22,500 (= .90 × $25,000); $(1 + r)^2 = 1.27689$ implies that $r = \sqrt{1.27689} - 1 = .13$ or 13 percent per year. That is, $22,500 grows to $28,730 in 2 years when the interest rate is 13 percent per period.

c. Truck	22,903	
Note Payable		22,903
$(1.12)^{-2} = .79719; .79719 \times \$28,730 = \$22,903.$		

d. $(1.01)^{-24} = .78757.$ (See Table 2, 24-column row, 1 percent column.) $.78757 \times \$28,730 = \$22,627.$

Truck	22,627	
Note Payable		22,627

e. Truck	23,744	
Note Payable		23,744
Year 1:		
Interest Expense (= .10 × $23,744)	2,374	
Note Payable		2,374
Year 2:		
Interest Expense [= .10 × ($23,744 + $2,374)]	2,612	
Note Payable		2,612
Balance in Note Payable Account at End of Year 2		$28,730

f. Total expense equals interest expense on note *and* depreciation on truck. Interest expense is $28,730 less the amount at which the truck is recorded. Depreciation expense is equal to the amount at which the truck is recorded less estimated salvage value. Thus, over the life of the truck, or 2 years, whichever is longer, the total expense equals $28,730 less salvage value of the truck.

Problem 2 for Self-Study

Landlord Company, as lessor, entered into a long-term lease agreement with Tenant Company, as lessee. The present value of the lease payments exceeded the lessor's cost of manufacturing the asset. Both companies accounted for the lease as an operating lease, whereas both companies should have accounted for it as a capital lease. What effect—understated, overstated, or none—does this error have on each of the following items in the financial statements of each of the companies for the first year of the lease?

a. Current assets.

b. Liabilities.

c. Revenue.

d. Expense.

e. Net income.

f. Retained earnings.

Suggested Solution

		Tenant Company	Landlord Company
a. Current Assets		None	Understated[a]
b. Liabilities		Understated	None
c. Revenue		None	Understated[b]
d. Expense		Understated	Understated[b]
e. Net Income		Overstated	Understated[b]
f. Retained Earnings		Overstated	Understated[b]

[a]Lease receivables are part current and part noncurrent. Asset is all noncurrent.

[b]In a capital lease, the lessor treats the signing of the lease as an installment sale. The lessor has sales revenue, cost of goods sold, and a new asset, the long-term receivable.

Problem 3 for Self-Study

The accounting records of Wilson Company disclose the following data on book and taxable income for Year 1 through Year 4.

	Year 1	Year 2	Year 3	Year 4
(1) Pretax Book Income	$90,000	$90,000	$90,000	$90,000
(2) Timing Differences (Reducing) or Increasing Book Income to Taxable Income	($20,000)	($10,000)	$15,000	$ 5,000
(3) Permanent Differences Increasing (or Decreasing) Taxable Income	($ 8,000)	$ 6,000	($ 4,000)	$ 2,000

The income tax rate is 40 percent of taxable income.

a. Compute taxable income on which income taxes are payable.

b. Compute the book amount on which income tax expense is based for each year.

c. Give the journal entries to record income tax expense, income taxes payable, and deferred income taxes for each year.

d. Compute aftertax net income for each year.

e. What is the balance in the Deferred Income Taxes account on the balance sheet at the end of Year 4?

Suggested Solution

a. Taxable income on the tax return each year is line (1) plus or minus line (2) plus or minus line (3): Year 1—$62,000; Year 2—$86,000; Year 3—$101,000; Year 4—$97,000.

Exhibit 11.5
WILSON COMPANY
(Suggested Solution to Problem 3 for Self-Study)

	Year 1	Year 2	Year 3	Year 4
Journal Entries				
Income Tax Expense[a]	32,800	38,400	34,400	36,800
Deferred Income Taxes	—	—	6,000	2,000
Income Taxes Payable[b]. . .	24,800	34,400	40,400	38,800
Deferred Income Taxes . . .	8,000	4,000	—	—

[a].40 of amounts in answer to part **b**.
[b].40 of amounts in answer to part **a**.

Income Statement				
Pretax Book Income	$90,000	$90,000	$90,000	$90,000
Income Tax Expense	(32,800)	(38,400)	(34,400)	(36,800)
Net Income	$57,200	$51,600	$55,600	$53,200

b. Income tax expense for each year is based on line (1) plus or minus line (3): Year 1—$82,000; Year 2—$96,000; Year 3—$86,000; Year 4—$92,000.
c. See Exhibit 11.5.
d. See Exhibit 11.5.
e. $4,000 credit = $8,000 credit + $4,000 credit − $6,000 debit − $2,000 debit.

Problem 4 for Self-Study

The Dominiak Company reports the following information about its financial statements and tax return for a year:

Depreciation Expense from Financial Statements	$270,000
Financial Statement Pretax Income	160,000
Income Tax Expense from Financial Statements	36,000
Income Taxes Payable from Tax Returns	24,000

Taxable income is taxed at a rate of 40 percent. Permanent differences result from interest on municipal bonds that is revenue in the financial statements but is exempt from income taxes. Timing differences result from the use of accelerated depreciation for tax returns and straight-line depreciation for financial reporting.

Reconstruct the financial statements and the tax return for the year, identifying the components of timing differences and permanent differences.

Suggested Solution

Exhibit 11.6
DOMINIAK COMPANY
Illustration of Timing Differences and Permanent Differences
(Suggested Solution to Problem 4 for Self-Study)

	Financial Statements	Type of Difference	Income Tax Return
Operating Income Except Depreciation	$360,000 (6)	—	$360,000 (4)
Depreciation	(270,000) (g)	Timing	(300,000) (3)
Municipal Bond Interest	70,000 (5)	Permanent	—
Taxable Income	—		$ 60,000 (2)
Pretax Income	$160,000 (g)		
Income Taxes Payable at 40 Percent . . .			$ 24,000 (g)
Income Tax Expense at 40 Percent of $90,000 = $160,000 − $70,000, Which Is Book Income Excluding Permanent Differences	(36,000) (g)		
Net Income	$124,000 (1)		

Order and derivation of computations:

(g) Given.

(1) $124,000 = $160,000 − $36,000.

(2) $60,000 = $24,000/.40.

(3) Timing difference for depreciation is ($36,000 − $24,000)/.40 = $30,000. Because income taxes payable are less than income tax expense, we know that depreciation deducted on tax return exceeds depreciation expense on financial statements. Thus, the depreciation deduction on the tax return is $300,000 = $270,000 + $30,000.

(4) $360,000 = $300,000 + $60,000.

(5) Taxable income on financial statements is $90,000 = $36,000/.40. Total financial statement income before taxes, including permanent differences, is $160,000. Hence permanent differences are $160,000 − $90,000 = $70,000.

(6) $160,000 + $270,000 − $70,000 = $360,000. See also (4), for check.

Problem 5 for Self-Study

Edwards Company adopted a defined-benefit pension plan at the beginning of Year 1. The normal pension costs for Year 1 and Year 2 are $40,000 and $45,000, respectively. These amounts are expensed and funded in full each year.

The plan grants retroactive credit to all employees for their years of work preceding Year 1. The present value of the prior service obligation created on adoption of the pension plan was $324,000. This amount is to be recognized as an expense and a liability over 20 years. The interest rate used in computing the present value is 8 percent per year. Pension expenses are recognized and funded on the last day of each year. The amounts paid to the pension plan are equal to the amounts expensed. Assume that the pension fund actually earns 9 percent during Year 2.

a. Give journal entries made by Edwards Company for Year 1 and Year 2.
b. What is the dollar value of the investments in the pension fund at the end of Year 2 before the Year 2 contribution is recorded?
c. Assuming that the pension fund was expected to earn only 8 percent in each year, what is the dollar amount of actual earnings in excess of the projected earnings for Year 2?

Suggested Solution

a. The present value of $1 paid at the end of each of the next 20 years is $9.81815 when the discount rate is 8 percent per year; see Table 4, 20-payment row, 8 percent column. The annual amount to amortize $324,000 over 20 years at 8 percent is $33,000 (= $324,000/9.81815). Thus, the journal entries are

	Year 1		Year 2	
Pension Expense (Normal Costs).	40,000		45,000	
Pension Expense (Prior Service)	33,000		33,000	
Pension Liability		73,000		78,000
To recognize expense.				
Pension Liability	73,000		78,000	
Cash		73,000		78,000
To fund liability with payments to pension plan.				

b. $79,570 = 1.09 × $73,000.
c. $730 = $73,000 × (1.09 − 1.08).

Questions, Exercises, Problems and Cases

Questions

1. Review the meaning of the following concepts or terms discussed in this chapter.
   a. Interest-bearing note.
   b. Noninterest-bearing note.
   c. Implicit interest.
   d. Imputed interest rate.
   e. Capital lease.
   f. Operating lease.
   g. Off-balance-sheet financing.
   h. Deferred income tax expense and liability.
   i. Timing difference.
   j. Permanent difference.
   k. Effective income tax rate.
   l. Statutory income tax rate.
   m. Pension plan.
   n. Defined-benefit plan.
   o. Defined-contribution plan.
   p. Normal costs.
   q. Past service obligation.

2. In what sense is the historical cost accounting for noncurrent liabilities subsequent to the date of issuance based on historical costs?

3. Brealey Company negotiated a 5-year loan for $1 million with its bank. The terms of the loan require that the interest rate can be changed as the bank chooses, but that the company can repay the loan at any time. Interest is to be paid quarterly. How should Brealey Company classify this note on its balance sheet?

4. Demonstrate that the amortization schedule in Exhibit 11.1 conforms to the "unifying principles of accounting for long-term liabilities" described on pages 462 and 463 of Chapter 10.

5. Why is the question, "Who enjoys the potential rewards and bears the risks of an asset?" important for lease accounting?

6. In what ways is the economic substance of a capital lease by a lessee similar to, and different from, that of an installment purchase?

7. Distinguish between the lessee's accounting for a capital lease and for an installment purchase.

8. In what sense is the total expense from a lease independent of the method of accounting for it by the lessee?

9. "Deferred income taxes might be viewed as an interest-free loan from the government." Do you agree? Why or why not?

10. Most large firms report income tax expense that is a lower percentage of book, pretax income than the statutory income tax rate. One cause of this difference is the investment credit. What is another cause?

11. Why do many managements find off-balance-sheet financing attractive?

12. How should the deferred income tax liability be treated by an analyst who wishes to study the debt-equity ratio of a business?

13. Under what circumstances will the Deferred Income Taxes account reduce to a zero balance?

14. You have been called to testify before a Congressional committee on income taxation. One committee member states: "My staff has added up the amounts shown for Deferred Income Taxes on the balance sheets of the largest 500 U.S. Corporations. If we collected these amounts immediately, we could reduce the national deficit by billions of dollars. After all, I have to pay my taxes as they become due each year. Why shouldn't corporations have to do the same?" How would you respond?

15. What are the economic and accounting differences between a defined-benefit pension plan and a defined-contribution plan?

16. Why does the amendment ("sweetening") of a defined-benefit plan ordinarily increase the past service obligation, whereas a change with the same cost in a defined-contribution plan does not?

17. The Hicks Company is adopting a defined-benefit pension plan. Who, the employee or the Hicks Company, is more likely to bear the risks and rewards of fluctuating market returns on funds invested to pay the pension?

Exercises

18. *Nature of liabilities.*

   a. For each of the following items, indicate if the item meets all of the criteria of the accountant's usual definition of a liability.

   b. If the item is recognized as a liability, how is the amount of the liability computed?

(1) Fifteen-year cancelable lease on an office building.

(2) Twenty-year noncancelable lease on a factory building.

(3) Deferred income taxes.

(4) Anticipated future cost of restoring strip-mining sites after mining operations are completed.

(5) Obligation to pay pensions under defined-benefit formula for labor services during current year.

(6) Obligation to pay pensions under defined-benefit formula with retroactive credit given to employees for labor services provided before the plan was adopted.

19. *Journal entries for land contract with imputed interest.* Refer to the example on page 482 of the chapter where equipment is acquired in exchange for a single-payment note for $16,000 due in 3 years. The issuer of the note pays 12 percent interest for borrowings of this sort. The present value of the note on the date of issue is $11,388. Assume the note is issued on January 1, Year 1, and that the firm closes its books annually.

   Provide adjusting entries for the end of Years 1, 2, and 3 and an entry for the payment of the note at maturity.

20. *Funds statement effects of leases.* Refer to the Simplified Statement of Changes in Financial Position for a Period in Exhibit 5.17 on page 201. Eleven of the lines in the statement are numbered. Ignore the unnumbered lines in responding to the questions below.

   Assume that the accounting cycle is complete for the period and that all of the financial statements have been prepared. Then it is discovered that a transaction has been overlooked. That transaction is recorded in the accounts and all of the financial statements are corrected. Define *funds* as *cash*. For each of the following transactions, indicate which of the numbered lines of the funds statement is affected and by how much. Ignore income tax effects except where taxes are explicitly mentioned.

   For the following questions, assume that an asset with an economic life of 10 years, costing $100,000, is leased for $19,925 per year, paid at the end of each year.

   a. The lessor, using the operating lease method, records depreciation for the year.

   b. The lessor, using the operating lease method, records receipt of a cash payment for the year. Revenue has not previously been recognized.

   c. The lessee, using the operating lease method, records payment of cash for the year. Expense has not previously been recognized.

   d. The lessor, using the capital lease method, records receipt of cash at the end of the first year and uses an interest rate of 15 percent per year. $15,000 is interest and $4,925 is receipt of principal. No entries have previously been made recognizing revenue.

e. The lessee, using the capital lease method, records payment of cash for the first year and uses an interest rate of 15 percent per year. $15,000 is interest and $4,925 is payment of principal.

21. *Funds statement effects of income taxes.* Refer to the instructions in the preceding exercise. For each of the following transactions, indicate which of the numbered lines of the funds statement is affected and by how much. Assume an income tax rate of 40 percent of taxable income.

a. Pretax financial statement income is $200,000. Depreciation claimed on the tax return exceeds depreciation expense on the financial statements by $50,000. An entry is made to record income tax expense and *accrual* of amounts payable, because no previous entry for taxes had been made.

b. Pretax financial statement income is $300,000 and the income tax rate is 40 percent of taxable income. Warranty deductions allowed on the tax return are less than warranty expense on the financial statements by $40,000. An entry is made to record income tax expense and *payment* of amounts payable, because no previous entry for taxes had been made.

c. Nontaxable municipal bond interest of $10,000 is received. No previous entry had been made for this interest. All effects of this transaction, including income tax effects, if any, are recorded.

22. *Funds statement effects of pensions.* Refer to the instructions in the two preceding exercises. For each of the following transactions, indicate which of the numbered lines of the funds statement is affected and by how much. Ignore income tax effects.

a. A pension plan is adopted with credit given for past service; an obligation of $100,000 arises.

b. A past service obligation is expensed and funded in the amount of $100,000.

c. Normal costs of $40,000 are recognized and funded.

23. *Amortization schedule for note where explicit interest differs from market rate of interest.* Garstka Company acquires a computer from Berney's Computer Store. The cash price (fair market value) of the computer is $50,568. Garstka Company gives a 3-year, interest-bearing note with maturity value of $60,000. The note requires annual interest payments of 9 percent of face value, $5,400 per year. The interest rate implicit in the note is 16 percent per year.

a. Prepare an amortization schedule for the note.

b. Prepare journal entries for Garstka Company over the life of the note.

24. *Operating lease accounting (adapted from CPA Examination).* The Jackson Company manufactured a piece of equipment at a cost of $7 million, which is held for resale from January 1 to June 30 at a price of $8 million. On July 1, Jackson leased the equipment to the Crystal Company. The lease. is appropriately recorded as an operating lease for accounting purposes. The lease is for a 3-year period. Equal monthly payments under the lease are $115,000 and are due on the first of the month. The first payment was made on July 1. The equipment is being depreciated on a straight-line basis over an 8-year period with no residual value expected.

    a. What expense should Crystal record as a result of the above facts for the current year ended December 31? Show supporting computations in good form.

    b. What income or loss before income taxes should Jackson record as a result of the above facts for the year ended December 31? Show supporting computations in good form.

25. *Computations and journal entries for income taxes with both timing and permanent differences.* Joyce Company reported the following amounts for book and tax purposes for its first 3 years of operations:

	Year 1	Year 2	Year 3
Pretax Book Income	$300,000	$280,000	$440,000
Taxable Income	240,000	320,000	340,000

The differences between book and taxable income are attributable to the use of different depreciation methods. The income tax rate was 40 percent during all years.

    a. Give the journal entry to record income tax expense for each year.

    b. Assume, for this part, that $10,000 of interest on state and municipal bonds was included in the pretax book income amounts shown above for each year but properly excluded from taxable income. Give the journal entry to record income tax expense for each year.

26. *Income tax timing differences from differing methods of revenue recognition.* Refer to the data in Exhibit 4.3 on page 149 showing income over a 5-year period under various methods of revenue and income recognition. Use the methods of accounting indicated below for financial statements and for tax returns. Assume an income tax rate of 40 percent. Compute income tax expense, income taxes payable, and deferred income taxes for each period. Put this information into journal entry form.

    a. Use the percentage-of-completion method on the financial statements and the completed contract method on the tax return.

    b. Use the cost-recovery-first method on the financial statements and the installment method on the tax return.

27. *Deriving permanent and timing differences from financial statement disclosures.* Gigondas Company reports the following information for a year:

Financial Statement Pretax Income	$106,000
Income Tax Expense	52,000
Income Taxes Payable for This Year	16,000
Income Tax Rate on Taxable Income	40 Percent

The company has both permanent and timing differences between book and taxable income.

    a. What is the amount of timing differences for the year? Give the amount and whether the effect is to make reported income larger or smaller than taxable income.

    b. What is the amount of permanent differences for the year? Give the amount and whether the effect is to make reported income larger or smaller than taxable income.

28. *Journal entries for pension plan including amortization of past service obligations.* On January 1, Year 1, Kayco Company instituted a defined-benefit pension plan with credit given to employees for prior years' work. The present value of the past service benefits awarded to current employees is $1,200,000. The present value of the benefits earned by employees during both Year 1 and Year 2 is $700,000 at the end of each of those years. Kayco Company designates the Retirement Insurance Company as the trustee of the pension plan and deposits all funding payments with the insurance company at the end of each year. Interest on unfunded liabilities is accrued at a rate of 8 percent per year. Kayco Company plans to fund an amount each year equal to the pension expense recognized for the year.

    Show the journal entries that Kayco Company would make on December 31, Year 1 and Year 2, for its pension plan and related expenses under the following two assumptions:

    a. Past service obligations are amortized over 10 years.

    b. Past service obligations are amortized over 30 years.

29. *Computation of unfunded past service obligation.* (This problem should not be attempted until the previous one has been worked.) Refer to the data on past service obligations for Kayco Company presented in the preceding problem. Assume that the amount is amortized over 10 years, that all expenses are funded as recognized, and that interest on the unfunded amount of past service obligations is charged at the rate of 8 percent per year.

    a. What amount of unfunded obligation for past service obligations will be disclosed in the footnotes to Kayco Company's financial statements issued for December 31, Year 1?

    b. What amount of unfunded obligation for past service obligations would be disclosed in the footnotes to Kayco Company's financial statements issued for December 31, Year 2?

Problems and Cases

30. *Comparing expense for operating lease with capital lease.* Maher Company has calculated that the annual payment in arrears to amortize a $1 million loan over 25 years at 15 percent interest is $154,700.

    a. What is rent expense for the first year of an operating lease when the rent payment is $154,700.

    b. What is lease expense for the first year of a 25-year capital lease for use of an asset costing $1 million requiring annual payments in arrears of $154,700? Use straight-line amortization of leasehold.

c. How much larger in percentage terms is the lessee's expense in the first year under the capital lease than under the operating lease?

31. *Criteria for classifying leases as operating or capital.* Assume that Rich's Department Stores is about to sign four separate leases for stores in four separate shopping centers. Each of the stores would cost $20 million if purchased outright and has an economic life of 20 years. Assume that the company currently must pay interest at the rate of 15 percent per year on long-term borrowing when sound collateral backs the loan. The lease payments are to be made at the end of each year in all four cases.

Based on the information given here, decide whether each of the four leases requires accounting as operating leases or as capital leases. Give your reasoning.

	Lease Term	Annual Lease Payment
a. Cumberland Mall	16 Years	$2,500,000
b. Normandale Center	16 Years	2,600,000
c. Eastbrook Haven	12 Years	3,300,000
d. Peachtree Parkview	12 Years	3,400,000

32. *Comparison of borrow/buy with operating and capital leases.* The Carom Company plans to acquire, as of January 1, Year 1, a computerized cash register system that costs $100,000 and has a 5-year life and no salvage value. The company is considering two plans for acquiring the system.

(1) Outright purchase. To finance the purchase, $100,000 of par value, 10 percent semiannual coupon bonds will be issued January 1, Year 1, at par.

(2) Lease. The lease requires 5 annual payments to be made on December 31, Year 1, Year 2, Year 3, Year 4, and Year 5. The lease payments are such that they have a present value of $100,000 on January 1, Year 1, when discounted at 10 percent per year.

Straight-line amortization methods will be used for all depreciation and amortization computations for assets.

a. Verify that the amount of the required lease payment is $26,380 by constructing an amortization schedule for the 5 payments. Note that there will be a $2 rounding error in the fifth year. Nevertheless, you may treat each payment as being $26,380 in the rest of the problem.

b. What balance sheet amounts will be affected if plan **(1)** is selected? If plan **(2)** is selected, the lease is cancelable, and the operating lease treatment is used? If plan **(2)** is selected, the lease is noncancelable, and the capital lease treatment is used?

c. What will be the total depreciation and interest expenses for the 5 years under plan **(1)**?

d. What will be the total expenses for the 5 years under plan **(2)** if the lease is accounted for as an operating lease? As a capital lease?

    e. Why are the answers in part **d** the same? Why are the answers in part **c** different from those in part **d**?

    f. What will be the total expenses for Year 1, under plan **(1)**? Under plan **(2)** accounted for as an operating lease? Under plan **(2)** accounted for as a capital lease?

    g. Repeat part **f** for the fifth year, Year 5.

33. *Analysis of risks and rewards of lease contracts.* Pan American World Air Lines (Pan Am) leased three Boeing 707 aircraft in 1963 from Sally Leasing Company (Sally). The aircraft had a purchase price of $6.64 million each. The leases covered 13-year terms, were noncancelable, contained no purchase options, and required monthly payments of $71,115. The rental cost per month of $71,115 was several hundred dollars less than Pan Am would have had to pay for conventional financing at the then-prevalent interest rate.

    a. What, if anything, did Pan Am give up in return for its savings of several hundred dollars per month for 13 years? What, if anything, did Sally Leasing Company get for giving up several hundred dollars per month for 13 years?

    b. Who bore the risks and rewards of ownership in these leases?

    c. Verify that the interest rate implicit in the lease contract is about three-fourths of 1 percent per month.

    d. Assume that FASB *Statement No. 13* had been in effect when these leases were signed. To ascertain how the leases would be accounted for, what further information would you need?

34. *Behavior of deferred income tax account when new assets are acquired every year.* Equilibrium Company adopted a program of purchasing a new machine each year. It uses ACRS on its income tax return and straight-line depreciation on its financial statements. Each machine costs $10,000 installed, has an economic life of 5 years for financial reporting, and is in the 3-year property class for ACRS. ACRS deductions are 25, 38, and 37 percent of cost in each of the first 3 years, respectively.

    a. Calculate the total depreciation deduction on the tax return for each of the first 6 years in accordance with ACRS.

    b. Calculate depreciation for each year using the straight-line method of depreciation.

    c. Calculate the annual difference in depreciation charges using the results from parts **a** and **b**.

    d. Calculate the annual increase in the Deferred Income Taxes account for the balance sheet by multiplying the tax rate, 40 percent, by the amount found in the preceding part.

    e. Calculate year-end balances for the Deferred Income Taxes account on the balance sheet.

    f. If Equilibrium Company continues to follow its policy of buying a new machine every year for $10,000, what will happen to the balance in the Deferred Income Taxes account on the balance sheet?

35. *Accounting for deferred income taxes using net present values of payments expected to be made.* The FASB is considering changing the requirements and procedures for accounting for deferred income taxes. Assume that it were to require that firms record income tax expense and liability for the *present value* of payments to be made when timing differences reverse. In all respects, the methods were to conform to the principles of historical cost accounting for liabilities.

Describe the estimates firms would have to make, the journal entries that would be required on first recording the deferred tax liability, and the subsequent entries in subsequent periods as the reversal approaches and occurs.

36. *Possible accounting treatments for past service obligations.* When a company adopts a defined-benefit pension plan giving credit to current employees for past service, an obligation, perhaps in large amounts, arises. This amount is currently disclosed in notes and is only gradually recognized in the balance sheet. The FASB is considering the recognition of this obligation as a liability.

Assume that the amount is immediately credited to a liability when it comes into existence. What accounts might be debited? Give justifications for debiting an asset account or an expense account, or directly debiting Retained Earnings.

37. *Interpreting financial statement disclosure about timing differences.* Refer to Note 6 of the financial statements of General Products Company shown in Appendix A at the back of the book.

   a. What is the combined average federal, state, and local income tax rate that General Products Company appeared to pay in 1985?

In the remainder of this problem, assume that the marginal income tax rate is 40 percent of pretax income. That is, if General Products Company were to earn another $1, it would have additional income tax expense of $.40.

   b. By how much did depreciation claimed on the tax return exceed depreciation expense reported in the financial statements for the year 1985?

   c. Warranty costs are not deductible on the tax return until actual repairs or replacements are made. Estimated warranty expenses are shown in the financial statements whenever they can be computed with a reasonable degree of precision. Did warranty expense on the financial statements exceed deductions for warranty costs on the tax return or vice versa in 1985? How can you tell? By how much?

38. *Deferred taxes arising from using different methods of amortizing bond discount on financial statements and tax return; funds statement effects (adapted from a case by James M. Patell and Roman L. Weil).* Refer to Problem **40** in Chapter 10 concerning the zero coupon notes of IBM Credit Corporation (IBMCC). Exhibit 11.7 reproduces the funds statement and income tax footnote from IBMCC's annual report.

   a. Assume an income tax rate of 46 percent. What was the deferred tax for 1981 arising ''from the timing differences between financial and tax reporting of the amortization of the original issue discount on Zero Coupon Notes?'' Did this amount increase or decrease the credit balance for deferred taxes on the balance sheet?

   b. Refer to the statement of funds flow for IBMCC. What lines of this statement were affected by the issue of the zero coupon notes, by the interest expense on them, and by the related income taxes, including the effects of timing differences? By how much were these lines affected?

Exhibit 11.7
IBM CREDIT CORPORATION
(Problem 38)
Statement of Funds Flow for the Period May 1, 1981, to December 31, 1981

	(dollars in thousands)
Funds (cash and cash equivalents) at May 1	$ —
Provided by:	
Operations	
Net Earnings	$ 9,867
Increase in Amounts Due to IBM Corporation	97,162
Change in Deferred Charges and Other Assets, Taxes, and Other Accruals	7,392
	114,421
Financings	
Commercial Paper	318,426
Long-Term Debt	162,238
	480,664
Capital Contributions	95,000
Total	$690,085
Used for:	
Purchase of Installment Payment Agreement Receivables, Net of Collections	689,553
Funds (cash and cash equivalents) at December 31	$ 532

Income Tax Footnote Concerning 8-Month Period, May 1–December 31, 1981
   Taxes: The components of the provision for income taxes, in thousands of dollars, are as follows:

U.S. Federal:	
Current	$2,548
Deferred	1,033
	$3,581
State and Local:	
Current	$1,269
Deferred	225
	$1,494
Total Provision	$5,075

Deferred taxes arise primarily from timing differences between financial and tax reporting of the amortization of original issue discount on the Zero Coupon Notes.

39. *Analysis of data on operating leases; hypothetical capitalization of contractual lease payments.* FASB *SFAS No. 13* does not require the capitalization onto the balance sheet of assets and liabilities relating to contractual lease payments when the lease qualifies as an operating lease. Although a lessee (tenant) commits itself for a substantial amount of minimum lease payments, because the length of the lease term is sufficiently short and the present value of the lease payments sufficiently small, the resulting leases are viewed as executory contracts. That is, the lessor will provide services in the future and the lessee will pay for those services as used. In this regard, contractual payments under operating leases are treated in the

Exhibit 11.8
Financial Statement Excerpts for J. C. Penney Company, Inc.,
and Sears, Roebuck and Co. (Merchandising Group)
(dollar amounts in millions)
(Problem 39)

	J. C. Penney	Sears
Balance Sheet Data at End of Year 0		
Current Liabilities	$2,070	$2,181
Long-Term Debt.	1,384	188
Owners' Equity	3,228	4,318
Total	$6,682	$6,687
Minimum Payments Due Under Operating Leases		
Year 1	$ 195	$ 212
Year 2	186	181
Year 3	172	138
Year 4	167	110
Year 5	157	89
Thereafter	1,855	604
Total	$2,732	$1,334
Amounts Representing Interest	(1,832)	?
Net Present Value.	$ 900	$?

same way as employment contracts, which also commit the firm to fixed payments in the future in return for future services.

Some retailing companies own their stores or acquire their premises under capital leases. Other retailing companies acquire the use of store facilities under operating leases, contracting to make future payments. An analyst comparing the potential long-term solvency of retailing companies (particularly those who own versus those who rent) may wish to make adjustments to published financial statements to account for the fixed payments the renting firm has promised to make.

Exhibit 11.8 reproduces information from recent annual reports of J. C. Penney Company, Inc., and the Sears, Roebuck Merchandising Group. The data include the disclosures mandated by *SFAS No. 13* for operating leases. J. C. Penney goes beyond the minimal requirement to report the present value of the future contractual payments on operating leases. Assume that Sears' fixed payments after Year 5 are $50 million per year for 12 years and that all payments for operating leases occur at year-end.

    a. Compute both the debt-equity ratio (total liabilities/total equities) and the long-term debt ratio [= long-term debt/(long-term debt + owners' equity)] for both Penney and Sears from the published financial statements.

    b. Estimate the present value of Sears' minimum rent payments under operating leases. Assume a 12 percent annual discount rate.

    c. Recompute the ratios in part **a**, assuming that the present values of the minimum contractual payments under operating leases are capitalized. What would be the implied journal entry for this capitalization?

40. *Deducing pretax effects of accounting transaction from aftertax data.* The footnote disclosure on inventories from a recent annual report of Deere & Company appears below.

> Substantially all inventories owned by Deere & Company and its United States subsidiaries are valued at cost on the "last-in, first-out" (LIFO) method.
>
> During the fourth quarter, the company's inventories declined due to the lower level of production. As a result, lower costs which prevailed in prior years were matched against current year revenues, the effect of which was to increase net income by $20.8 million or 31 cents per share.
>
> During the fourth quarter, in conjunction with an examination completed by the Internal Revenue Service of certain prior years' United States Federal income tax returns, the company increased the valuation of its slow-moving service parts inventories. As a result net income was increased by $13.2 million or 20 cents per share.
>
> If all the company's inventories had been valued on a current cost basis, which approximates FIFO, inventories at year-end were estimated to be $1,885 million compared with approximately $1,941 million at the beginning of the year.

The balance sheet reported inventories of $760.9 million at the end of the year and $872.0 million at the beginning of the year. Assume an income tax rate of 46 percent.

    a. The second paragraph refers to inventory declines caused by lower production levels. By how much did the costs of the older inventories "matched against current year revenues" differ from current costs? Give the amount and whether larger or smaller.

    b. How much did the dip into old LIFO layers cost Deere in extra income tax payments for 1982?

    c. The extract refers to resolution of a dispute with the IRS. What was the most likely cause of the dispute?

    d. As a result of the settlement with the IRS, Deere changed the balance sheet amount of its inventories. What was the amount of the change? Indicate whether increase or decrease.

    e. How much has Deere reduced its income taxes payable since it adopted LIFO?

41. *Different depreciation methods, cost flow assumptions for inventories, and different policies for interest capitalization for financial and tax reporting generate timing differences.* Northwest Industries is organized as a group of separate legal corporations, such as Acme Boot Company, General Battery Corporation, Lone Star Steel Company, Microdot, Inc., and Velsicol Chemical Corporation, whose shares are owned by Northwest Industries. (Chapter 13 discusses the reasons why a company organizes as a group of separate legal corporations.) The separate corporations each file individual tax returns. The parent (a holding company) issues financial statements, which report on the group as a whole, to its shareholders, the general investing public.

In recent years, several corporations, including Northwest Industries, have used the separate corporate identities of the subsidiaries to challenge the "LIFO conformity" rule of the Internal Revenue Service, which requires firms using LIFO for tax reporting to use LIFO in financial statements to shareholders. Northwest Industries has each of its subsidiaries file tax returns, using LIFO, and report to its shareholder (which is Northwest, the parent) using LIFO. But when Northwest reports to its public shareholders, it uses FIFO for many of these inventories.* A recent annual report of Northwest Industries contains the following excerpts.

[From the Summary of Significant Accounting Policies.] For financial reporting purposes, inventory amounts are determined using the last-in, first-out (Lifo), the first-in first-out (Fifo) and the average cost methods. For federal income tax purposes, substantially all inventory amounts are determined using the Lifo cost method.

[From the note on Income Taxes.] Deferred income taxes result from reporting certain items for tax purposes in different periods than in the statement of earnings. The effects of such items [on deferred income tax expense for the current year] were as follows (in thousands of dollars) . . .

Depreciation and amortization	$21,700
Inventory valuation	8,000
Interest capitalized	4,600

[From the note on Inventories.] Lifo inventory costs represented approximately 48% of total inventory costs [at year end] and 34% [at the beginning of the year]. If the Fifo cost method had been used to value inventories for which the Lifo method was used, such inventories would have been $119 million and $100 million higher [than reported at year end and the beginning of the year respectively].

Northwest Industries reported net income for the year of $184.6 million. Assume an income tax rate of 46 percent.

   a. By how much did depreciation and amortization claimed on the tax return exceed the expense on the financial statements for the year?

   b. Assume that all deferred income taxes for "inventory valuation" result from Northwest's using LIFO on the tax return and other cost flow assumptions on the financial statements. If Northwest Industries had been required to use LIFO conformity, what would have been the impact on reported income? Do you think this represents a material impact?

   c. By how much did the capitalization of interest into plant under construction affect income reported for the year? Give the amount and whether an increase or a decrease. Northwest Industries reported that interest capitalized during the year amounted to $15 million. Reconcile Northwest's disclosure with your answer.

42. *Preparing funds statement (adapted from a problem by Stan Baiman).* Exhibit 11.9 shows comparative balance sheets and income statement of Hermitage Company for Year 2, and supplementary notes.

---

*The 1984 tax law prohibits this practice.

Exhibit 11.9
HERMITAGE COMPANY
Comparative Balance Sheets and Income Statement
(Problem 42)

Balance Sheets	December 31	
	Year 1	Year 2
Cash	$ 30,000	$130,000
Accounts Receivable (net)	80,000	95,000
Inventory	140,000	150,000
Plant and Equipment	800,000	875,000
Accumulated Depreciation	(380,000)	(520,000)
Total Assets	$670,000	$730,000
Accounts Payable	$ 20,000	$ 25,000
Taxes Payable	60,000	76,000
Deferred Investments Credits	10,000	13,000
Deferred Income Taxes	40,000	64,000
Capital Stock.	200,000	210,000
Retained Earnings	340,000	342,000
Total Equities	$670,000	$730,000

Year 2 Income Statement	
Net Sales	$605,000
Cost of Goods Sold.	$200,000
Bad Debt Expense	15,000
Depreciation Expense	140,000
Income Tax Expense	
Current	76,000
Deferred	24,000
Total Expenses.	$455,000
Net Income	$150,000

Notes:

(1) All depreciation charges are expensed.

(2) Dividends declared have been paid in cash.

(3) During Year 2, Hermitage acquired property, plant, and equipment to be depreciated over 10 years for financial reporting. The items are eligible for an investment credit of $7,500; income taxes for Year 2 are already decreased by this amount.

(4) Hermitage uses the deferral method for the investment credit and deferred 90 percent of the investment tax credit earned during Year 2. Current income tax expense was reduced by $4,500 because of the investment tax credit.

    a. How much of the $7,500 investment tax credit earned during Year 2 was deferred? Why does the Deferred Investment Credits account increase by only $3,000, an amount smaller than this?

    b. Prepare the Year 2 statement of changes in financial position with funds defined as cash.

43. *Analysis of attempts to achieve off-balance-sheet financing* [*adapted from "Off-Balance-Sheet Financing," Case 4.1 in* Accounting and Auditing Case Studies (*The Trueblood Professors' Seminar*), *The Touche Ross Foundation and The American Accounting Association, 1983, pp. 21–22*]. Container Company has developed a process for manufacturing plastic bottles at a cost lower than any competitor's. Gigantic Drugs, Inc., has offered to purchase enough of the bottles so that Container will have to build a new plant just to fill Gigantic's orders. The new plant will be built next to Gigantic's plant, with a conveyor belt to carry the bottles into Gigantic's plant. Container will operate the plant. The problem is that Container does not have, and is unable to raise, sufficient funds to finance construction of the new plant. Gigantic is willing to provide its financial backing to raise the necessary funds but has insufficient cash to finance the project. Moreover, it is unwilling to borrow the funds if doing so increases the recorded debt on its balance sheet because of potential default on some of its own debt covenants and some other new plans it has to raise funds by borrowing. The financial executives of Container and Gigantic have devised two plans to finance the plant while attempting to satisfy Gigantic's requirements. Under both plans, Container will create a subsidiary, Borrower Company, to borrow all the funds required from a bank to build the plant.

Plan 1. Borrower will lease the plant to Gigantic for 40 years with lease payments matched in size and timing to Borrower's debt service payments to the bank. Gigantic is sufficiently solvent and profitable that its promised lease payments and the plant itself will induce a bank to provide 100 percent financing at Gigantic's borrowing rate. Borrower would contract with Container to manage the new plant.

Plan 2. Gigantic will sign a contract to purchase bottles from the new plant. It will buy all the bottles produced by the plant when it operates at normal capacity. Contractual payments will cover all variable manufacturing costs, debt service on the bank loan, and the payments to Container to manage the new plant. If Gigantic does not wish to purchase the entire output of the plant and if Borrower is unable to sell the bottles to other bottle users, then Gigantic will agree to make a cash payment to Borrower for the difference so that Borrower can meet all its cash obligations. Any cash that Borrower can generate from selling bottles to other bottle users for amounts larger than variable manufacturing costs will reduce the payments Gigantic makes to Borrower.

Discuss these two plans from two perspectives.
  a. Consider the auditor who must decide whether each arrangement requires recognition on the balance sheet or whether footnote disclosure is enough.
  b. Consider an investment banker who is planning to bid on the new bond issue Gigantic will use to raise funds for a different purpose. The banker must take into account, among other things, Gigantic's entire financial structure.

44. *Analysis of take-or-pay contract including capitalization of future payments and possible losses.* Natural gas pipelines sign take-or-pay contracts with producers of natural gas. Under these contracts the pipelines agree to purchase the natural gas in fixed (or computable) quantities at fixed (or computable) prices or to pay for the gas even if they do not take delivery. By the mid-1980s, there was a large quantity of natural gas contracted for relative to the amounts that could be sold by the pipelines. A *Business Week* article on the subject said:

Most of the unfavorable contracts were hastily signed after the cold winters of 1977 and 1978, when the gas shortage assumed crisis proportions. The pipeline industry faced the prospect of . . . lawsuits over its inability to supply contracted-for fuel. . . . Aggressively bidding for new supplies, the pipelines bought their way out of the problem—and into an even greater mess. They now find themselves stuck with massive numbers of "take-or-pay" agreements. . . . The fear of another icy, gasless winter, some say, drove pipeline executives to close one bad deal after another. Tenneco . . . had 4 billion cu. ft. per day of gas available for delivery and sales of just over 2 billion cu. ft. per day. . . . [The] costs [of natural gas had] soared to $3.48 per thousand cu. ft. . . . and price escalators in many contracts threaten to keep costs rising, especially after [price] controls expire. . . .

The financial statements of Tenneco showed total assets of $17.4 billion, current liabilities of $6.9 billion, long-term debt of $5.0 billion, and owners' equity of $5.5 billion. Notes to the statements indicate that some of Tenneco's take-or-pay contracts extend 25 years into the future.

    a. Compute the long-term debt ratio [= long-term debt/(long-term debt + owners' equity)] from the financial statement data.

    b. Compute the present value of the obligation to take 4 billion cubic feet of gas per day for 10 years. Assume a price of $3.50 per thousand cubic feet, a year of 300 business days, and a discount rate of 15 percent per year. Payments occur at year-end.

    c. Assume that these contractual payments are capitalized on the balance sheet and that an asset is recorded in the same amount. Compute the long-term debt ratio.

    d. Now assume that Tenneco will be able to sell only 60 percent of the contracted-for gas. The other 40 percent will be paid for, but because it is not taken, there is no offsetting asset for this amount, only a loss. Assume that the loss is tax deductible and an income tax rate of 46 percent. Recompute owners' equity and the long-term debt ratio for the financial statements excerpted above.

45. *Attempts to achieve off-balance-sheet financing (adapted from materials by Richard Dieter, David L. Landsittel, John E. Stewart, and Arthur R. Wyatt).* Brion Company wishes to raise $50 million cash but, for various reasons, does not wish to do so in a way that results in a newly recorded liability. It is sufficiently solvent and profitable that its bank is willing to lend up to $50 million at the prime interest rate. Brion Company's financial executives have devised six different plans, described below.

Transfer of Receivables with Recourse Brion Company will transfer to Credit Company its long-term accounts receivable, which call for payments over the next 2 years. Credit Company will pay an amount equal to the present value of the receivables less an allowance for uncollectibles and a discount because it is paying now, but will collect cash later. Brion Company must repurchase from Credit Company at face value any receivables that become uncollectible in excess of the allowance. In addition, Brion Company may repurchase any of the receivables not yet due at face value less a discount specified by formula and based on the prime rate at the time of transfer. (This option permits Brion Company to benefit if an unexpected drop in interest rates occurs after the transfer.) The accounting issue is whether the transfer is a sale (where Brion Company debits Cash, credits Accounts Receivable, and debits expense or loss on transfer) or whether the transfer is merely a loan collateralized by the receivables (where Brion Company debits Cash and credits Notes Payable at the time of transfer).

Product Financing Arrangement Brion Company will transfer inventory to Credit Company, who will store the inventory in a public warehouse. Credit Company may use the inventory as collateral for its own borrowings, whose proceeds will be used to pay Brion Company. Brion Company will pay storage costs and will repurchase all the inventory within the next 4 years at contractually fixed prices plus interest accrued for the time elapsed between the transfer and later repurchase. The accounting issue is whether the inventory is sold to Credit Company, with later repurchases treated as new acquisitions for Brion's inventory, or whether the transaction is merely a loan, with the inventory remaining on Brion's balance sheet.

Throughput Contract Brion Company requires a branch line of a railroad to be built from the main rail line to carry raw material directly to its own plant. It could, of course, borrow the funds and build the branch line itself. Instead, it signs an agreement with the railroad to ship specified amounts of material each month for 10 years. Even if it does not ship the specified amounts of material, it will pay the agreed shipping costs. The railroad will take the contract to its bank and, using it as collateral, borrow the funds to build the branch line. The accounting issue is whether Brion Company would debit asset for future rail services and credit liability for payments to the railroad. The alternative is to make no accounting entry except when Brion makes payments to the railroad.

Construction Partnership Brion Company and Mission Company will jointly undertake to build a plant to manufacture chemicals both need in their own production processes. Each will contribute $5 million to the project, called Chemical. Chemical will borrow another $40 million from a bank, with Brion, only, guaranteeing the debt. Brion and Mission are each to contribute equally to future operating expenses and debt service payments of Chemical, but, in return for its guaranteeing the debt, Brion will have an option to purchase Mission's interest for $20 million 4 years hence. The accounting issue is whether Brion Company would recognize a liability for the funds borrowed by Chemical; because of the debt guarantee, debt service payments will ultimately be the responsibility of Brion Company. Alternatively, the debt guarantee is a commitment merely to be disclosed in notes to Brion Company's financial statements.

Research and Development Partnership Brion Company will contribute a laboratory and preliminary finding about a potentially profitable gene-splicing discovery to a partnership, called Venture. Venture will raise funds by selling the remaining interest in the partnership to outside investors for $2 million and borrowing $48

Exhibit 11.10
Alcoa, General Electric, and U.S. Steel Pension and Other Data
(dollar amounts in millions)
(Problem 46)

	Alcoa		General Electric		U.S. Steel	
	SFAS No. 35 (decelerated)	Inside Company (accelerated)	SFAS No. 35 (decelerated)	Inside Company (accelerated)	SFAS No. 35 (decelerated)	Inside Company (accelerated)
End of Year						
Present Value of Pension Plan Benefits as Based on Actuarial Cost Method . . .	$ (1)	$ (2)	$ (4)	$ (5)	$ (7)	$ (8)
Current Market Value of Assets in Pension Fund . . .	773	(3)	4,968	(6)	5,100	(9)
Unfunded Obligation of Pension Plan . . .	$ 305	$492	$ 840	$1,036	$ 0	$1,000
Owner's Equity . . .	$2,529		$7,362		$4,895	
For Year						
Net Income (loss) . . .	$ 505		$1,409		$ (293)	

million from a bank, with Brion Company guaranteeing the debt. Although Venture will operate under the management of Brion Company, it will be free to sell the results of its further discoveries and development efforts to anyone, including Brion Company. Brion Company is not obligated to purchase any of Venture's output. The accounting issue is whether the liability would be recognized by Brion Company. (Would it make any difference if Brion Company has either the *option* to purchase or an *obligation* to purchase the results of Venture's work?)

Hotel Financing Brion Company owns and operates a profitable hotel. Brion could use the hotel as collateral for a conventional mortgage loan. Instead, it considers selling the hotel to a partnership for $50 million cash. The partnership will sell ownership interests to outside investors for $5 million and borrow $45 million from a bank on a conventional mortgage loan, using the hotel as collateral. Brion Company guarantees the debt. The accounting issue is whether Brion Company would record the liability for the guaranteed debt of the partnership.

Consider each of these proposed arrangements from the viewpoint of the auditor (who must decide whether the transaction will result in a liability to be recorded or whether footnote disclosure will suffice) and from the viewpoint of an investment banker (who must assess the financing structure of Brion Company in order to make a competitive bid on a proposed new underwriting of Brion Company common shares).

46. *Analyzing pension disclosure; changes in cost methods.* The employer's costs of a single employee's pension is the amount required to fund the pension promises over the employee's retirement years measured on the date the pension payments start. Assume that number can be estimated at any time with reasonable precision. Once the accountant estimates that number, the problem remains of allocating the costs to the individual years when the employee works. Various methods of allocating that cost, called "actuarial cost methods," can be used. The choosing of an actuarial cost method is much like choosing a depreciation method. The method can be straight-line, accelerated, or decelerated. In 1980, in order to achieve more uniformity in pension reporting, the FASB (in *SFAS No. 35*) required all pension plans to use a specific decelerated method. Many companies had been using accelerated or straight-line methods, which recognize the pension expenses faster than the decelerated method. Alcoa, General Electric, and U.S. Steel, among others, disclosed for several years the fact that for financial reporting and internal purposes, they used a method different (and more conservative) than the FASB-required method. Exhibit 11.10 reproduces data from the annual reports of these companies, based on the FASB-required method and the more conservative method used inside the companies.

    a. Fill in the missing numbers **(1)** through **(9)** in Exhibit 11.10. Keep in mind that changing the method for allocating costs to specific periods has no effect on the current market value of the assets in the pension fund.

    b. By how much does the change in cost methods change expense for the year for these companies? Does the change in cost methods appear to be material for the companies?

Chapter 12   Owners' Equity

The economic resources of a firm come from two major sources. Nonowners provide funds to a firm; the sources of these funds appear on the balance sheet as *liabilities*, discussed in Chapters 10 and 11. Owners provide funds; the sources of these funds appear on the balance sheet as *owners' equity*.

The accounting equation states that:

$$\text{Assets} = \text{Liabilities} + \text{Owners' Equity,}$$

or

$$\text{Assets} - \text{Liabilities} = \text{Owners' Equity.}$$

Many readers of financial statements think of owners' equity as being calculated as assets minus liabilities. Double-entry record keeping provides, however, a continuous, independent calculation of owners' equity.

This chapter discusses corporate owners' equity. The corporate organization is used for at least three reasons:

1. The corporate form provides the owner (shareholder) with limited liability. That is, should the corporation become insolvent, creditors' claims are limited to the assets of the corporate entity. The corporation's creditors cannot claim the assets of the individual owners. On the other hand, creditors of partnerships and sole proprietorships have a claim on both the owners' personal and business assets to settle such firms' debts.

2. The corporate form allows the raising of funds by the issuing of shares. The general public can acquire the shares in varying amounts. Individual investments can range from a few dollars to hundreds of millions of dollars.

3. The corporate form makes transfer of ownership interests relatively easy, because individual shares can be sold by current owners to others without interfering with the ongoing operations of the business. Ongoing changes in ownership do not affect the continuity of the management and of operations.

This chapter discusses the accounting for capital contributed by owners; the accounting for income earned by the firm, which may be retained or distributed to owners; and other changes in owners' equity accounts.

Capital Contributions

The corporation is a legal entity separate from its owners. Individuals or other entities make capital contributions under a contract between themselves and the corporation.[1] Because those who contribute funds receive certificates for shares of stock, they are known as "stockholders" or "shareholders." The rights and obligations of a shareholder are governed by:

1. The corporation laws of the state in which incorporation takes place.

2. The articles of incorporation or *charter*. This is a contract between the firm and the state in which the business is incorporated. The state grants to the firm the privilege of operating as a corporation for certain stated purposes and of obtaining its capital through the issue of shares of stock.

3. The bylaws of the corporation. The board of directors adopts bylaws, which are the rules and regulations governing the internal affairs of the corporation.

4. The stock contract. Each type of capital stock has its own provisions as to such matters as voting, sharing in earnings, distribution of earnings, and sharing in assets in case of dissolution.

Some "closely held" corporations have a small number of shareholders and operate much like a partnership. The few people involved agree to the amount of capital to be contributed, elect each other to be members of the board of directors and officials of the firm, and agree on policies regarding dividends and salaries. They may restrict the transfer of shares to outsiders, and may even become liable for debts of the corporation by endorsing its notes and bonds.

Issue of Shares of Stock

The accounting for the initial issue of shares of stock for cash is

Cash	1,250,000	
Capital Stock		1,250,000
Issue of shares of capital stock.		

In addition to exchanges for cash, stock is sometimes issued in exchange for property, for personal services rendered, or in settlement of a liability. The entry in these cases is the same as the one illustrated above, but the debit will be made to the accounts for property or services received or the liability settled. The amount for the entry should be the fair market value of the product, property, or services received, or, if this amount is not reasonably estimable, the fair market value of the stock issued.[2]

---

[1]In accounting for owners' equity, the term *contribution* almost never means a gift; capital given to the corporation as a gift is specifically called *donated capital*.

[2]Accounting Principles Board, *Opinion No. 29,* "Accounting for Nonmonetary Transactions," 1973.

Classes of Shares

Corporations are often authorized to issue more than one class of shares, each representing ownership in the business. Most shares issued are either *common* or *preferred*. Occasionally, there may be several classes of common or preferred shares, each with different rights and privileges. All corporations have at least one class of shares. They are usually called "common shares," but they may be designated by another name, such as class A shares. Preferred shares may, but need not be, issued by a corporation.

Common shares have the claim to earnings of the corporation after commitments to creditors and preferred shareholders have been satisfied. Frequently, common shares are the only voting shares of the company. In the event of corporate dissolution, all of the proceeds of asset disposition, after settling the claims of creditors and required distributions to preferred shareholders, are distributed to the common shareholders.

Preferred shares have special privileges. Although these privileges vary considerably from issue to issue, a preferred share usually entitles its holder to dividends at a certain rate, which must be paid before dividends can be paid to common shareholders. Sometimes, though, these dividends may be postponed or omitted. If the provisions of the stock contract designate the preferred dividends as *cumulative,* then all current and previously postponed dividends must be paid before any dividends on common shares can be paid.

Many preferred shares issued by corporations in recent years have been *callable.* Callable preferred shares can be reacquired by the corporation at a specified price, which may vary according to a preset time schedule. Callability is commonly thought to benefit the corporation. If financing becomes available at a lower cost than the rate fixed for the preferred shares, a corporation may wish to reduce the relatively fixed commitment of preferred dividends (as compared to common). It can do so by exercising its option to call the preferred shares. This option is valuable to the corporation but makes the shares less attractive to potential owners. Other things being equal, noncallable shares will be issued for a higher price than callable shares. Thus, the degree to which the corporation benefits by making shares callable is not clear-cut.

Preferred shares with a conversion feature have also become increasingly popular. Convertible preferred shares may be converted by their owner into a specified amount of common shares at specified times. The conversion privilege may appear advantageous to both the individual shareholder and the corporation. The preferred shareholder enjoys the security of a relatively assured dividend as long as the shares are held. The shareholder also has the opportunity to realize capital appreciation by converting the shares into common stock if the market price of the common shares rises sufficiently. Because of this feature, the change in the market price of convertible preferred shares will often parallel changes in the market price of the common shares.

The firm may also benefit from the conversion option. By including it in the issue, the company is usually able to specify a lower dividend rate on the preferred than otherwise would have been required to issue the shares for a given price.

In recent years, some firms have issued redeemable preferred shares. The holder of these shares is allowed under specified conditions to trade these shares in for cash. Because such shares have some characteristics of debt, the SEC requires separate disclosure of them.[3]

Separate accounts are used for each class of shares. On the balance sheet, each class of shares appears separately, often with a short description of the major features of the shares. Customarily, preferred shares appear before common shares on the balance sheet.

Par Value and No-Par Shares

Shares of capital stock often have either a *par* or a *stated* value. The articles of incorporation specify the amount, which is printed on the face of the stock certificates. The par value of common stock has some legal significance but little economic substance. For legal reasons, accountants separate par value from other contributed capital amounts.[4] The par value rarely denotes the market value of the shares, except perhaps at the date of original issue. Readers of financial statements can usually assume merely that the shareholders in the corporation have invested an amount at least equal to the par value of all common shares. Par value of preferred stock is more meaningful. The dividend rate specified in the preferred stock contract (for example, 9 percent) is almost always based on par value. Any preference as to assets in liquidation that preferred shareholders may have is usually related to the par value of the preferred shares, although some preferred stock contracts may specify a liquidation value different from par value.

Although preferred shares usually have a par value, common shares without a par value are widely used. When no-par-value shares are issued, the amount actually contributed can be credited directly to the capital stock account.

The *book value of a share of common stock*—the total common shareholders' equity divided by the number of shares outstanding—is almost always greater than the par value of the shares. The excess results from retained earnings and from capital contributions in excess of par or stated value.

Contributions in Excess of Par Value

Shares are usually issued for amounts greater than par. Typically, individuals who purchase newly issued shares from the corporation some years after the corporation began operations pay a higher price per share to compensate current shareholders

---

[3]Securities and Exchange Commission, *Accounting Series Release No. 268*, "Presentation in Financial Statements of 'Redeemable Preferred Stock,'" 1979. Reissued in Section 101 of *Codification of Financial Reporting Policies*.

[4]The original legal concept was that par value represented an investment to be maintained by the corporation for the protection of creditors. The investment level was called "legal" or "statutory" or "stated" capital, and many states have prohibited corporations from declaring dividends out of such capital. The concept is now obsolete, because creditors have found more effective ways to protect themselves, such as through specific limitations in debt contracts on corporate financing behavior.

for the additional assets provided by the retention of earnings. The corporation credits its capital stock account with only the par value of the shares issued. The excess of issue proceeds over par (or stated) value is credited to an account called Additional Paid-in Capital. The title ''Capital Contributed in Excess of Par (Stated) Value'' is more descriptive but too cumbersome to be widely used. Sometimes the title used is ''Premium on Capital Stock.''

If par-value shares are used, the credit to the Additional Paid-in Capital account is always the difference between the amount received and the par value of the shares issued to the shareholders. Thus, the entry to record the issue of 100 shares with a par value of $10 per share, for $10,000, would be

Cash	10,000	
Capital Stock—Par Value		1,000
Additional Paid-in Capital		9,000
Issue of shares for amount greater than par value.		

Treasury Shares

Shares of stock reacquired by the issuing corporation are called *treasury stock* or *treasury shares*. The firm may reacquire its own shares for later distribution under stock option plans or for stock dividends. (Stock option plans and stock dividends are discussed later in this chapter.) The firm may also consider treasury shares a worthwhile use for idle funds. Treasury shares are not entitled to dividends nor to vote, because they are not considered to be ''outstanding'' shares for these purposes. Treasury shares held may be reissued, or resold, on the market.

Accounting for Treasury Shares   The fundamental principle of accounting for treasury shares is that a corporation does not report profit or loss on transactions involving its own shares. Even though the firm may ''sell'' (technically, reissue) the shares for more than their acquisition cost, the ''gain'' is not reported in income. Similarly, the firm may subsequently reissue shares for less than their acquisition cost. Even so, the ''loss'' is not part of net income. The adjustments for reissue of treasury shares are made directly to the contributed capital accounts, bypassing the income statement and, generally, the Retained Earnings account.

When common shares are reacquired, a Treasury Shares—Common account is debited with the total amount paid to reacquire the shares.

Treasury Shares—Common	11,000	
Cash		11,000
$11,000 paid to reacquire 1,000 common shares.		

If the treasury shares are later reissued by the corporation, Cash is debited with the amount received and the Treasury Shares account credited with the cost of the shares. The reissue price will usually differ from the amount paid to acquire the treasury shares. If the reissue price is greater than the acquisition price, the Additional Paid-in Capital account is credited to make the entry balance. Assuming that the 1,000 shares reacquired in the entry illustrated above were reissued for $14,000, the entry would be

Cash	14,000	
Treasury Shares—Common		11,000
Additional Paid-in Capital		3,000
Reissue of 1,000 shares of treasury stock at a price greater than acquisition cost.		

If the reissue price is less than the amount paid, the debit to make the entry balance is usually to Additional Paid-in Capital, as long as there is a sufficient credit balance in that account. If there is not, the additional balancing debit is made directly to Retained Earnings. This debit to Retained Earnings is viewed similarly to a dividend, not an expense or loss reported in the income statement.

Disclosure of Treasury Shares The Treasury Shares account is contra to total shareholders' equity. Chapter 7 introduced the direct debits to shareholders' equity required for declines in market value of the portfolio of investments in marketable equity securities. The debits for such price declines are generally shown as a negative number either before or after Retained Earnings. An annual report of Warner Communications, Inc., illustrates the disclosures of these two deductions from shareholders' equity; see Exhibit 12.1.

Exhibit 12.1
Presentation of Owners' Equity in Balance Sheet for
Warner Communications, Inc.
(amounts in 000's)

Shareholders' Equity

Convertible Preferred Shares Issued, Par Value $1 per Share, 20,000,000 Shares Authorized	—
Common Shares Issued, Par Value $1 per Share, 40,000,000 Shares Authorized	$ 28,407
Paid-in Capital	136,373
Retained Earnings	487,568
Net Unrealized Loss on Marketable Equity Securities	(3,887)
	$648,461
Less Common Shares in Treasury, at Cost	33,540
Total Shareholders' Equity	$614,921

Should a Firm Raise New Funds by Issuing Shares or Bonds?

A major consideration in the issue of common or preferred shares is that dividends are not deductible in calculating taxable income. Bond interest is, however, deductible. Thus, the aftertax accounting cost of borrowing may be less than the aftertax accounting cost of issuing shares, even though the interest rate on the bonds is higher than the dividend rate. Exhibit 12.2 illustrates this phenomenon. The accounting figures, however, do not reflect the economic costs of risk. When bonds are issued, both preferred and common shares become more risky, because bondholders have a claim on future cash flows senior to the claim of shareholders. When preferred shares are issued, common shares become more risky. When shares become more risky, all else being equal, the rate of return on those shares required by the market increases. (For a given dollar amount of return from an investment in a share, this means that the price of the share must fall.) Even though a project financed with a bond issue may result in a larger earnings-per-share increase than one financed by a common stock issue, one cannot conclude that raising new funds by borrowing is better than raising new funds with share issues. As Chapter 6

Exhibit 12.2
Accounting Benefit of Raising New Funds by
Borrowing Rather than by Issuing Common Shares (financial leverage)

Assumptions (before new Funds are raised)
Income Tax Rate: 40 Percent
Net Income: $216,000
Shares Outstanding: 90,000
Market Price per Share: $20.00
Earnings per Share: $2.40 (= $216,000/90,000 shares)

Assumptions About New Project
Requires New Funds of $1,000,000
Generates Income Before Financing Charges and Taxes of $200,000 per Year

Assumptions About New Financing Options
Issue $1,000,000 of Bonds at Par with Annual Coupon Rate of 12.5 Percent
or Issue 50,000 New Common Shares at $20 Each

Pro Forma Income Statements After New Financing

	Issue Bonds	Issue Shares
Income from New Project Before Interest and Taxes . . .	$200,000	$200,000
Less Interest Expense (= .125 × $1,000,000)	(125,000)	—
Less Additional Income Taxes at 40 Percent	(30,000)	(80,000)
Additional Income	$ 45,000	$120,000
Previously Earned Income	216,000	216,000
Net Income	$261,000	$336,000
Shares Outstanding	90,000	140,000
Earnings per Share	$2.90	$2.40
Rate of Return on Market Value of Share of $20	14.5%	12.0%

pointed out, leverage (the raising of funds by borrowing) is a two-edged sword. Corporate finance texts discuss whether there is an optimal way to raise new funds.

If the new project undertaken by the firm illustrated in Exhibit 12.2 has the same risk characteristics as the other, older projects of the firm, it is likely that the market value after either form of financing will remain at about $20 per share. If so, the return required by the market of the bond-financed firm increases from 12.0 percent to 14.5 percent. Although projected earnings per share increase, so does risk.

Retained Earnings

After a new business has become established and profitable, it usually generates additional owners' equity from undistributed earnings. These undistributed earnings represent the accumulated periodic net income remaining after dividends have been declared. Retaining earnings increase shareholders' equity and provide capital for expansion or for replacing assets at higher costs.

Net Income and Cash Position

One misconception about net income is that it represents a fund of cash available for distribution or expansion. Earnings from operations usually involve cash at some stage: Goods are sold to customers, the cash is collected, more goods are acquired, bills are paid, more sales are made, and so on. Assets generated by earnings do not, however, remain in the form of cash.[5] Only under most unlikely conditions, where net plant and equipment, inventories, receivables, and liabilities remain at constant amounts, would earnings correspond to the increase in cash. The statement of changes in financial position shows how the cash provided by operations (and other sources) is used during a period.

A well-managed firm keeps its cash at a reasonable minimum. If cash starts to accumulate, the firm may pay some obligations, increase its inventory, buy more equipment, or declare dividends. Thus, there is no way of knowing how retaining earnings affects the individual asset and liability accounts. The only certain statement is that an increase in retained earnings results in increased *net assets* (that is, an increase in the excess of all assets over all liabilities).

Cash Dividends

The shareholders of a corporation do not directly control distributions of corporate assets generated by net income. State laws and corporation bylaws almost always

---

[5]For many businesses, increased net income is frequently associated with decreased cash, whereas contraction of net income may be accompanied by an increase in cash. In the first stages of a business decline, cash may start to build up from the liquidation of inventories and receivables that have not been replaced, as well as from postponing replacement or expansion of plant. When conditions improve, inventories and receivables are expanded, new plant is acquired, and a cash shortage may develop.

delegate the authority to declare dividends to the board of directors. When a dividend is declared, the entry is

Retained Earnings	150,000	
Dividends Payable		150,000

To record declaration of dividends. (Sometimes an account called Dividends or Dividends Declared is debited. The Dividends account is a temporary account and is closed to Retained Earnings at the end of the period.)

Once the board of directors declares a dividend, the dividend becomes a legal liability of the corporation. Dividends Payable is shown as a current liability on the balance sheet if the dividends have not been paid at the end of the accounting period. When the dividends are paid, the entry is

Dividends Payable	150,000	
Cash		150,000

A distribution of a corporation's assets other than cash to its shareholders is called a *dividend in kind* or a *property dividend*. Such dividends are accounted for just like cash dividends, except that when the dividend is paid, the asset given up, rather than cash, is credited. The amount debited to Retained Earnings is the fair market value of the assets distributed. Any gain or loss is part of income for the period.

Stock Dividends

The retention of earnings may lead to a substantial increase in shareholders' equity, which represents a relatively permanent commitment by shareholders to the business. The commitment is relatively permanent because the net assets generated have been invested in operating assets such as inventories and plant. To indicate such a permanent commitment of reinvested earnings, the board of directors may declare a *stock dividend*. The accounting involves a debit to Retained Earnings and a credit to the contributed capital accounts. When a stock dividend is declared, shareholders receive additional shares of stock in proportion to their existing holdings. If a 5 percent stock dividend is issued, each shareholder receives one additional share for every 20 shares held before the dividend.

Generally accepted accounting principles require that the valuation of the newly issued shares be based on the market value of the shares issued. For example, the directors of a corporation may decide to declare a stock dividend of 10,000 additional shares of common stock with a par value of $10 per share at a time when the market price of a share is $40. The entry would be

Retained Earnings	400,000	
Common Stock—Par		100,000
Additional Paid-in Capital		300,000

Declaration of a stock dividend—recorded using market price of shares to quantify the amounts: $40 \times 10,000$ shares = \$400,000.

The stock dividend relabels a portion of the retained earnings that had been legally available for dividend declarations as a more permanent form of owners' equity. A stock dividend formalizes the fact that some of the funds represented by past earnings have been used for plant expansion, to replace assets at increased prices, or to retire bonds. Such funds are therefore unavailable for cash dividends.

Stock dividends have little economic substance for shareholders: The same ownership is spread over more pieces of paper. If the distributed shares are of the same type as those held before, each shareholder's proportionate interest in the capital of the corporation and proportionate voting power have not changed. Although the book value per common share (total common shareholders' equity divided by number of common shares outstanding) decreases, a proportionately larger number of shares will be held, so the total book value of each shareholder's interest will remain unchanged. The market value per share should decline, but, all else being equal, the total market value of an individual's shares will not change. To describe such a distribution of shares as a "dividend"—meaning a distribution of earnings—is potentially misleading. It is, nevertheless, generally accepted terminology.

Dividend Policy

The directors, in considering whether to declare cash dividends, must conclude both (1) that declaring a dividend is legal and (2) that it is financially expedient.

Statutory Limits on Dividends

State corporation laws limit directors' freedom to declare dividends. These limitations are designed to protect creditors whose interests might be jeopardized because neither shareholders nor directors are liable for debts of the corporation.

Generally, the laws provide that dividends "may not be paid out of capital" but must be "paid out of earnings." The wording and interpretation of this rule varies among states. "Capital" is usually defined to be equal to the total amount paid in by shareholders. Some states allow dividends to be declared out of the earnings of the current period even though Retained Earnings are negative because of accumulated losses from previous periods.

For most companies, statutory limits have little influence on the accounting for shareholders' equity and dividends. A balance sheet does not spell out all the legal details of amounts available for dividends, but it ought to disclose information necessary for the user to apply the legal rules of the state in which the business is incorporated. For example, state statutes can provide that "treasury shares may be acquired only with retained earnings." That is, dividends cannot exceed the amount of Retained Earnings reduced by the cost of treasury shares. If treasury shares are acquired under these circumstances, then the amount of this limit on dividends should appear in a footnote to the balance sheet.[6]

The statutory requirements for declaring dividends can be met by building up a balance in retained earnings. Such a balance does not mean that a fund of cash is available for the dividends. Managing cash is a specialized problem of corporate finance; cash for dividends must be anticipated just as well as cash for the purchase of equipment, the retirement of debts, and so on. Borrowing from the bank to pay the regular dividend is not unsound if the corporation's financial condition justifies the resulting increase in liabilities.

Contractual Limits on Dividends

Contracts with bondholders, other lenders, and preferred shareholders often limit dividend payments and thereby compel the retention of earnings. A bond contract might provide that the retirement of the debt be made "out of earnings." Such a provision involves curtailing dividends so that the necessary debt service payments, plus any dividends, will not exceed the amount of net income for the period. Such a provision forces the shareholders to increase their investment in the business by limiting the amount of dividends that might otherwise be made available to them. Financial statement notes must disclose significant limitations on dividend declarations. The notes to a recent financial statement of Holiday Inns, Inc., contain the following disclosure:

> The company's various loan and credit agreements require certain defined current ratio levels and restrict both the amount of retained earnings available for dividends and the borrowing capacity of the company. . . . Under the most restrictive of these agreements, . . . $282,391,000 [of retained earnings of $671,000,000] was available for dividends.

Dividends and Corporate Financial Policy

Dividends are generally less than the legal maximum. The directors may allow the retained earnings to increase as a matter of corporate financial policy for several reasons:

1. Earnings are not reflected in a corresponding increase of available cash.
2. Restricting dividends in prosperous years may permit continued dividend payments in poor years.
3. Funds may be needed for expansion of working capital or plant and equipment.
4. Reducing the amount of borrowings, rather than paying dividends, may seem prudent.

---

[6]Accounting Principles Board, *Opinion No. 6*, "Status of Accounting Research Bulletins," 1965.

The statement of changes in financial position helps the reader understand how cash provided by earnings and other sources has been used.

Stabilization of Dividends Many corporate shareholders want to receive a predictable cash return. To accommodate such shareholders and to create a general impression of stability, directors commonly attempt to declare a regular dividend. They try to maintain the regular dividend through good years and bad. When earnings and financial policy permit, they may declare ''extra'' dividends.

Financial Policy Some shareholders prefer a policy that restricts dividends in order to finance expansion. When dividends are declared, such shareholders use the funds received to acquire an equivalent amount of the new shares issued to finance the expansion. These shareholders will be saved transaction costs if earnings are retained. If the corporation pays dividends, the shareholders must pay income taxes on the receipts before they can be reinvested. If the funds are reinvested directly by the corporation, there is a deferral of, and possibly a permanent avoidance of, personal income taxes.

Other shareholders may want a steady flow of cash but do not wish to sell a portion of their shares to raise cash. Such shareholders will resent being forced to reinvest in the corporation when expansion is financed through the curtailing of dividends. They may change their investment to corporations that declare regular dividends.

How to finance expansion is a problem of managerial finance, not accounting. Research in finance suggests that, within wide limits, what a firm does makes little difference so long as it tends to follow the same policy over time. Shareholders who want earnings reinvested can invest in shares of firms that finance expansion with earnings, whereas others who want a steady cash flow can invest in shares of firms that regularly pay dividends.

Other Changes in Owners' Equity Accounts

Stock Splits

Stock splits (or, more technically, *splitups*) are like stock dividends. Additional shares of stock are issued to shareholders in proportion to their existing holdings. No additional assets are brought into the firm. In a stock split, the par value of all the stock in the issued class is reduced. A corporation may, for example, have 1,000 shares of $10-par-value stock outstanding, and, by a stock split, exchange those shares for 2,000 shares of $5-par-value stock (a two-for-one split), or 4,000 shares of $2.50-par-value stock (a four-for-one split), or any number of shares of no-par stock. If the shares outstanding have no par value, then the shareholders keep the existing certificates and receive the new ones.

A stock split generally does not require a journal entry. The amount of retained earnings is not reduced. The amount shown in the capital stock account represents a larger number of shares. Of course, the additional number of shares held by each shareholder must be recorded in the subsidiary capital stock records. Sometimes stock splits are accounted for as stock dividends—with a transfer from Retained

Earnings to the Contributed Capital account. If so, the amounts are based on the market value of the shares on the date of the split. There is no easy way to distinguish stock splits from stock dividends. Usually, small percentage distributions are treated as stock dividends and larger ones as stock splits.

A stock split (or a stock dividend) usually reduces the market value per share, all other factors remaining constant, in inverse proportion to the split (or dividend). Thus a two-for-one split could be expected to result in a 50 percent reduction in the market price per share. Stock splits have, therefore, usually been used to keep the market prices per share from rising to a price level unacceptable to management. For example, the board of directors might think that a market price of $30 to $40 is an effective trading range for its stock. (This is a purely subjective estimate, and it is almost never supported by convincing evidence.) If the share prices have risen to $60 in the market, then the board of directors may declare a two-for-one split. The only certain result of stock splits and dividends is increased record-keeping costs. Stock splits and stock dividends are used primarily by corporations whose stocks are currently, or soon to be, traded in a public market.

Stock Options

Stock options are often a part of employee compensation plans. Under such plans, employees are granted an option to purchase shares in their company. Stock options present two kinds of accounting problems: (1) recording the granting of the option and (2) recording its exercise or lapse.

Granting the Option   The generally accepted accounting treatment[7] for options usually results in no entry being made at the time the options are granted. The *exercise price of an option* is the price the option holder will have to pay to acquire a share of stock. If the exercise price is equal to the market price of the stock on the date the option is granted, then the granting of the option is not viewed as resulting in compensation to the employee or expense to the employer, and no entry is made. If the exercise price is less than the market price of the stock on the date of the grant, then compensation expense may have to be recognized under some circumstances, which may have adverse income tax consequences.

Exercise or Lapse   When the option is exercised, the conventional entry treats the transaction simply as an issue of shares at the option price:

Cash	35,000	
Common Shares—Par		5,000
Additional Paid-in Capital		30,000

To record issue of 1,000 shares of $5-par-value stock upon exercise of options and receipt of $35,000 cash.

If the option lapses or expires without being exercised, no entry is required.

---

[7]Accounting Principles Board, *Opinion No. 25,* "Accounting for Stock Issued to Employees," 1972.

Disclosure of Options Generally accepted accounting principles require that the terms of options granted, outstanding, and exercised during a period be disclosed in text or notes accompanying the financial statements. For example, Note 20 to the financial statements of General Products Company in Appendix A, Exhibit A.4, discloses data on stock options.

Stock Rights and Warrants

Opportunities to buy shares of stock may be granted through *stock rights* and *stock warrants*.

Stock Rights Stock rights are similar to stock options, but differ in some respects. Stock options are granted to employees, are nontransferable, and are a form of compensation. In contrast, stock rights are granted to current shareholders and can usually be traded in public markets. They are generally exercisable for only a limited period but occasionally are good indefinitely. Stock rights are ordinarily associated with attempts to raise new capital for a firm from current shareholders. Journal entries are not necessary when stock rights are granted to current shareholders. When the rights are exercised, the entry is like the one to record the issue of new shares at the price paid.

Stock Warrants Stock warrants are issued to the general investing public for cash. They are exercisable for a limited period in most cases. Assume that a corporation issues warrants for $15,000 cash. The holders are allowed to purchase 10,000 shares for $20 each. The entry would be

Cash	15,000	
Common Stock Warrants		15,000

To record issue of warrants to the public. The Common Stock Warrants account would normally be included with Additional Paid-in Capital for balance sheet presentation.

When the rights contained in these warrants are exercised and 10,000 shares of $5-par-value common stock are issued in exchange for the warrants plus $200,000, the entry would be

Cash	200,000	
Common Stock Warrants	15,000	
Common Stock—Par Value		50,000
Additional Paid-in Capital		165,000

To record the issue of 10,000 shares for $200,000 cash and the redemption of warrants. (The amount originally received for the warrants is transferred to Additional Paid-in Capital.)

If the warrants expire without having been exercised, the entry would be

Common Stock Warrants	15,000	
Additional Paid-in Capital		15,000
To record expiration of common stock warrants and the transfer to permanent contributed capital.		

Convertible Bonds

Convertible bonds are, typically, semiannual coupon bonds like the ones discussed in Chapter 10—with one added feature. The holder of the bond can *convert* the bond into shares of stock. The bond indenture specifies the number of shares to be received when the bond is converted into stock, the dates when conversion can occur, and other details. Convertible bonds are usually callable.

Investors often find convertible bonds attractive. The owner is promised a regular interest payment. In addition, should the company business be so successful that its share prices rise on the stock market, then the holder of the bond can convert the investment from debt into equity. The creditor has become an owner and can share in the good fortune of the company.[8] Of course, an investor does not get something for nothing. Because of the potential participation in the earnings of the company once the bonds are converted into common shares, an investor in the bonds must accept a lower interest rate than would be received if the bonds were not convertible into stock. From the company's point of view, convertible bonds allow borrowing at lower rates of interest than is required on ordinary debt, but the company must promise to give up an equity interest if the bonds are converted. The purchaser of the convertible bond is paying something for the option to acquire common stock later. Thus, a portion of the proceeds from the issue of convertible bonds actually represents a form of capital contribution, even though it is not so recorded.

Issue of Convertible Bonds   Suppose, for example, that the Johnson Company's credit rating would allow it to issue $100,000 of ordinary 10-year, 14-percent semiannual coupon bonds at par. The firm prefers to issue convertible bonds with a lower coupon rate. Assume that Johnson Company issues at par $100,000 of 10-year, 10-percent semiannual coupon bonds, but each $1,000 bond is convertible into 50 shares of Johnson Company $5-par-value common stock. (The entire issue is convertible into 5,000 shares.) The following entry is required:

Cash	100,000	
Convertible Bonds Payable		100,000
Issue of convertible bonds at par.		

[8]In recent years, the brokers' commission fees for trading convertible bonds have often been less than those for comparable dollar amounts of trades in the underlying common shares.

This entry effectively treats convertible bonds just like ordinary, nonconvertible bonds and records the value of the conversion feature at zero. (Generally accepted accounting principles do recognize the potential issue of common stock implied by the conversion feature in the calculations of earnings-per-share figures.)

Recognizing the Value of the Conversion Feature Is Not Permitted Appendix Table 5 (for 10-percent coupon bonds) indicates that 10-percent, 10-year semi-annual (nonconvertible) coupon bonds sell for about 79 percent of par when the market rate of interest is 14 percent. Thus, if the 10-percent convertible bonds can be issued at par, then the conversion feature must be worth about 21 (= 100 − 79) percent of par. Then 21 percent of the proceeds from the bond issue is actually a capital contribution by the bond buyers for the right to acquire common stock later. The entry to record the substance of the issue of these 10-percent convertible bonds at par would be

Cash	100,000	
Convertible Bonds Payable		79,000
Additional Paid-in Capital		21,000

Issue of 10-percent semiannual coupon convertible bonds at a time when ordinary 10-percent bonds could be issued for 79 percent of par.

Notice that the calculation of the amounts for this entry requires knowing the proceeds of an issue of nonconvertible bonds that are otherwise similar to the convertible bonds. Because auditors often feel that they are unable to ascertain this information in a reasonably objective manner, generally acceptable accounting principles do not allow the journal entry above.[9] The entry is simply a debit to Cash and a credit to Convertible Bonds Payable for $100,000.

Conversion of Bonds Assume that the common stock of the Johnson Company increases in the market to $30 a share, so that one $1,000 bond, which is convertible into 50 shares, can be converted into shares with a market value of $1,500. If the entire convertible issue were converted into common shares at this time, then 5,000 shares of $5-par-value stock would be issued on conversion.

The usual entry to record the conversion of bonds into shares ignores current market prices in the interest of simplicity and merely shows the swap of shares for bonds at their book value.

---

[9]Accounting Principles Board, *Opinion No. 14,* ''Accounting for Convertible Debt and Debt Issued with Stock Purchase Warrants,'' 1969. The APB stated that, in reaching its conclusions, less weight was given to the practical difficulties than to some other considerations, spelled out in the *Opinion.* The dissent to this *Opinion,* expressed by several members of the Board, expressed preference for the treatment recognizing the implied capital contribution.

Convertible Bonds Payable	100,000	
Common Shares—$5 Par		25,000
Additional Paid-in Capital		75,000

To record conversion of 100 convertible bonds with book value of $100,000 into 5,000 shares of $5-par-value stock.

An allowable alternative treatment recognizes that market prices provide information useful in quantifying the market value of the shares issued. Under the alternative treatment, when the market price of a share is $30 and the fair market value of the 5,000 shares issued on conversion is $150,000, the journal entry made would be

Convertible Bonds Payable	100,000	
Loss on Conversion of Bonds	50,000	
Common Shares—$5 Par		25,000
Additional Paid-in Capital		125,000

To record conversion of 100 convertible bonds into 5,000 shares of $5-par-value stock at a time when the market price is $30 per share.

The alternative entry results in the same total owners' equity: smaller retained earnings (because the Loss on Conversion of Bonds will reduce current net income and thus Retained Earnings), but larger contributed capital. It is equivalent to the following two entries:

Cash	150,000	
Common Shares—$5 Par		25,000
Additional Paid-in Capital		125,000

To record issue of 5,000 shares of $5-par-value stock at $30 per share.

Convertible Bonds Payable	100,000	
Loss on Retirement of Bonds	50,000	
Cash		150,000

Retirement by purchase for $150,000 of 100 convertible bonds carried on the books at $100,000.

Potential Dilution of Earnings per Share

Chapter 6 explained that earnings per share of common stock is conventionally calculated by dividing net income attributable to the common shareholders by the weighted-average number of shares of common stock outstanding during the period. When a firm has outstanding securities that, if exchanged for common stock, would decrease earnings per share as conventionally calculated, then the earnings-per-share calculations become somewhat more complicated. Stock options, stock rights, warrants, and convertible bonds all have the potential of reducing earnings per share and must be taken into account in calculating earnings per share. These complications are discussed in intermediate accounting books, but are introduced in Problem 41 at the end of this chapter.

Reported Income and Retained Earnings Adjustments

The Income Statement Reconsidered

What is the purpose of the income statement? It is *not* just to show net income for the period. The reader of the financial statements can generally ascertain net income by subtracting the beginning balance of Retained Earnings from its ending balance and adding dividends. The purpose of the income statement is to show the *causes* of income.[10] Then, a company's performance can be compared with other companies or with itself over time, and more informed projections can be made about the future.

To help the reader understand the causes of income, generally accepted accounting principles require the separate reporting of various income components:

1. Income from continuing operations,
2. Income from operations to be discontinued,
3. Gain or loss from disposal of discontinued operations,
4. Income from extraordinary items, and
5. Adjustments to income resulting from changes in accounting principles.

Items **2** and **3** appear on the income statement under the combined heading of "Discontinued Operations." The Financial Accounting Standards Board has defined criteria for the classification of items into these five categories.

Analysts of financial statements often focus on income from continuing operations in making projections and buy/sell recommendations. As a result, some managements have attempted to report "good" news in the operating section of the income statement and "bad" news elsewhere. For example, before Accounting Principles Board *Opinion No. 30,* issued in 1973, prescribed rules for classifying an item as extraordinary, most extraordinary items found in published income statements were losses ("bad news"). Managements found ways to justify including nearly all gains ("good news") in income before extraordinary items.

The FASB continued to refine the exceptional cases for items to be excluded from operating income in order to make the income statement more useful to readers and less susceptible to management whim.

---

[10]Parallel statements can be made about the funds statement. The purpose of the statement of changes in financial position is *not* to report the change in cash for the period. That can be deduced by subtracting the balance in the Cash account at the start of the period from that at the end of the period. The purpose is to report the *causes* of the change in the Cash account.

Direct Adjustments to Retained Earnings

Nearly all items that cause the total of retained earnings to change during a period result from transactions reported in the income statement for that period. The major exception to this general rule is dividend declarations. Dividend declarations are distributions that reduce the balance in the Retained Earnings account but do not affect reported income. Two other exceptions to the general rule that changes in retained earnings arise from transactions reported in the income statement are the *correction of errors* and *prior-period adjustments*.

Correction of Errors Errors result from such actions as miscounting inventories, arithmetic mistakes, and misapplications of accounting principles. Such errors, if they are material, are corrected with direct debits or credits to the Retained Earnings account. Assume, for example, that merchandise inventory is discovered to be $10,000 less than was reported at the end of the previous period, and that cost of goods sold was computed last period using a periodic inventory method:

$$\frac{\text{Cost of}}{\text{Goods Sold}} = \frac{\text{Beginning}}{\text{Inventory}} + \text{Purchases} - \frac{\text{Ending}}{\text{Inventory}}$$

Then the following entry (ignoring income tax effects) would be made this period:

Retained Earnings	10,000	
Merchandise Inventory		10,000
Correction of inventory error. Last period's cost of goods sold was too small; income was overstated.		

Prior-Period Adjustments Assume that the Internal Revenue Service disallowed certain deductions on the firm's tax return of 4 years ago, increasing income tax expense for that year and reducing income for that year. Two treatments of this and similar events are worth considering. Some accountants believe that the income statement for the current period will be more useful if the resulting decrease in Retained Earnings is shown only in the statement reconciling the changes in retained earnings and not in the current income statement. They argue that the time-series trend in reported income will be more meaningful if net income for the prior period is adjusted and the current period's income is unaffected. Other accountants believe that users of financial statements may overlook disclosures of this sort that do not appear in the current income statement, which they feel is the most closely studied of the financial statements. These accountants think that all revenues, gains, expenses, and losses relating to the earnings activity of a firm should be reported in current and future income statements. If a loss is treated as a direct adjustment of retained earnings at the beginning of the period, it will not have appeared in the income statement originally issued for any period.

The FASB requires the latter treatment: Nearly "all items of profit and loss recognized during a period, including accruals of estimated losses from loss contingencies, shall be included in the determination of net income for that period."[11] The rarely occurring exceptions relate to income tax loss carryforwards of purchased subsidiaries.

New Information About Accounting Estimates Does Not Result in Direct Adjustments of Retained Earnings New information often becomes available that helps refine estimates required to apply accounting principles, such as the amount of uncollectible accounts or the service life of depreciable assets. Earlier chapters have pointed out that this information is incorporated by current and future adjustments to reported revenues and expenses, not with direct adjustments of retained earnings. Refer, for example, to Figure 9.3, which illustrates the use of information about a long-term asset's service life. Although, in principle, the accounting rules might require an adjustment of previously reported expenses with direct adjustments of the Retained Earnings account, the FASB generally takes the position that items affecting retained earnings should appear in the income statement for some current or future period. Otherwise, management might be tempted to be optimistic in current reporting, with later direct reductions in the Retained Earnings account.

Disclosure of Changes in Owners' Equity

The changes in all owners' equity accounts must be explained in the annual reports to shareholders.[12] As previous chapters have pointed out, the reconciliation of retained earnings may appear in the balance sheet, in a statement of income and retained earnings, or in a separate statement. The financial statements of General Products Company in Appendix A show the reconciliation of retained earnings at the bottom of the combined statement of income and retained earnings (Exhibit A.1) and the causes of all other changes in owners' equity accounts in a separate schedule in Note 18 (Exhibit A.4).

Journal Entries for Changes in Owners' Equity

To review the accounting for owners' equity, Exhibit 12.3 reconstructs the journal entries made for 1984 and 1985 that resulted in the changes in owners' equity disclosed for General Products Company in Exhibits A.1 and Note 18 of Exhibit A.4. The amounts in the entries in Exhibit 12.3 represent millions of dollars.

Changes in Owners' Equity Reported in the Statement of Changes in Financial Position

The transactions affecting owners' equity generally affect cash and are reported in the statement of changes in financial position. Exhibit A.3 in Appendix A presents the statement of changes in financial position for General Products Company. The

---

[11]Financial Accounting Standards Board, *Statement of Financial Accounting Standards No. 16*, "Prior Period Adjustments," 1977, par. 10.
[12]Accounting Principles Board, *Opinion No. 12*, "Omnibus Opinion—1967," 1967.

Exhibit 12.3
Journal Entries Illustrating Transactions Involving
Owners' Equity for General Products Company, 1984–1985

Entry and Explanation	Millions of Dollars			
	1985		1984	
(1) Income Summary	1,514		1,409	
Retained Earnings		1,514		1,409
Net income for the year, recorded assuming that an Income Summary account is used. This entry, in effect, closes all temporary revenue and expense accounts, with the credit balance being reported as income for the year.				
(2) Retained Earnings	670		624	
Dividends Payable—Common Stock		670		624
Cash dividends declared on preferred and common stock.				
(3) Treasury Shares, at Cost	145		156	
Cash		145		156
Acquisitions of treasury shares in market transactions with outsiders.				
(4) Cash	139		146	
Capital in Excess of Par Value ("Loss")	—		2	
Treasury Shares, at Cost		136		148
Capital in Excess of Par Value ("Gain")		3		—
Issue of shares to employees under stock plan and savings and stock ownership, incentive compensation and stock option plans. The shares issued in 1984 had market value on date of reissue of $2 million less than their cost. The "loss" is debited to the Capital in Excess of Par Value account. The shares issued in 1985 had market value on date of reissue of $3 million more than their cost. The "gain" is credited to the Capital in Excess of Par Value account, which GP calls "Amounts Received for Stock in Excess of Par Value."				

effects of net income can be seen in the statement of changes in financial position. The "Sources" section also shows the amounts for "Newly Issued Common Shares" and "Disposition of Treasury Shares" for the various compensation and savings plans. The section "Application of Funds" shows lines for Dividend Declarations and Purchase of Treasury Shares.

Summary

Accounting for owners' equity in a corporation is based on the premise that there should be a separate account for each source of capital contributed by owners. The sources of capital from shareholders include:

1. Receipts from issues of stock at par or stated value.
2. Receipts in excess of par or stated value of stock issues.
3. Earnings retentions.

Most changes in retained earnings are reported in the income statement. Dividend declarations are the major exception.

Problem 1 for Self-Study

Exhibit 12.4 shows the owners' equity accounts for Lorla Corporation at the end of Year 1 and Year 2. During Year 2, Lorla Corporation issued new shares of stock for $40 a share and reacquired 60 shares for the treasury at $42 per share. Still later in the year, it sold some of the treasury shares. Revenues for Year 2 were $90,000, and net income was $10,000.

Reconstruct all of the transactions involving owners' equity accounts for Year 2, and show the journal entries for those transactions.

Exhibit 12.4
LORLA CORPORATION
Owners' Equity Accounts
(Problem for Self-Study)

	December 31	
	Year 1	Year 2
Common Stock ($5 par value)	$ 5,000	$ 5,500
Additional Paid-in Capital	30,000	33,620
Net Unrealized Loss on Investments in Marketable Equity Securities.	(900)	(800)
Retained Earnings	60,000	67,300
	$94,100	$105,620
Less: Cost of Treasury Shares	—	(840)
Total Owners' Equity	$94,100	$104,780

Suggested Solution

Cash	4,000	
Common Stock ($5 par value)		500
Additional Paid-in Capital		3,500

Because the Common Stock account went up by $500 and the par value is $5 per share, 100 shares (= $500/$5 per share) must have been issued. The issue price was $40 per share; hence the cash raised was $4,000 (= $40 × 100 shares).

Treasury Shares.	2,520	
Cash		2,520

Acquisition of 60 shares for the treasury at $42 per share; 60 × $42 = $2,520.

Cash	1,800	
Treasury Shares.		1,680
Additional Paid-in Capital		120

Because the year-end balance in the treasury shares account is $840, 20 shares (= $840/$42 per share) must remain in the treasury. Thus, 40 (= 60 − 20) shares were resold. Because the year-end Additional Paid-in Capital account is $120 [= $33,620 − ($30,000 + $3,500)] larger than is explained by the issue of new shares, a "gain" of $120 must have been realized on the resale of the shares from the treasury. Because 40 shares were resold, the total "gain" was $120, and the "gain" per share must have been $3 (= $120/40 shares). Thus, the total resale price per share must have been $45 (= $42 + $3). Cash raised must have been $1,800 = $45 per share × 40 shares.

Allowance for Excess of Cost over Market Value of Investments in Marketable Equity Securities	100	
Recovery of Unrealized Loss on Investment in Marketable Equity Securities		100

Market value of the portfolio of investments in marketable equity securities has increased by $100 during the year.

Revenue Accounts.	90,000	
Expense Accounts		80,000
Retained Earnings		10,000

Closing entries for revenue and expense accounts, given that revenues were $90,000 and net income was $10,000 for the year.

Retained Earnings	2,700	
Dividends Payable		2,700

The Retained Earnings account increased by only $7,300 for the year. Dividends must have been $10,000 − $7,300 = $2,700.

Problem 2 for Self-Study

Patell Company owns 100,000 shares of the General Electric Corporation, which it has held as an investment. The shares had cost $2 million, $20 each, and now have a fair market value of $50 each. Patell Company declares a dividend in kind, distributing the shares of the General Electric Company to its shareholders.

a. Prepare the journal entry to record the declaration. Under generally accepted accounting principles, dividends in kind are recorded at the market value, not the cost, of the assets distributed.

b. Prepare a journal entry that would record the dividend using the cost of the shares. This treatment is not generally acceptable.

c. Compare the effects on net income, retained earnings, and total owners' equity of the two treatments.

Suggested Solution

a. Retained Earnings	5,000,000	
Investments		2,000,000
Gain on Disposition of Investments.		3,000,000
The gain appears on the income statement and is closed to Retained Earnings.		
b. Retained Earnings	2,000,000	
Investments		2,000,000

c. Net income is larger when the dividend is recorded at fair market value. In both cases, Retained Earnings and total owners' equity decline by $2 million. The difference is that in the former treatment, income is increased by $3 million, the holding gain on the shares, which offsets the larger debit to retained earnings for the larger amount of dividend recognized.

Questions, Exercises, Problems and Cases

Questions

1. Review the meaning of the following concepts or terms discussed in this chapter.

a. Corporation.	**j.** Treasury shares.
b. Corporate charter.	**k.** Earnings are not cash.
c. Corporate bylaws.	**l.** Convertible bond.
d. Capital stock, common stock, preferred shares.	**m.** Stock dividend.
	n. Stock split.
e. Cumulative preferred shares.	**o.** Stock option.
f. Callable preferred shares.	**p.** Stock right.
g. Convertible preferred shares.	**q.** Stock warrant.
h. Par or stated value.	**r.** Correction of error.
i. Additional paid-in capital.	**s.** Prior-period adjustment.

2. Under what circumstances would you expect par value stock to be issued at a price in excess of par? What is the entry to record such an issue?

3. A construction corporation is attempting to borrow money on a note secured by some of its property. A bank agrees to accept the note, provided that the president of the corporation will personally endorse it. What is the point of this requirement?

4. "Par value of preferred stock is frequently a significant figure, but par value of common stock possesses little significance." Why may par value of preferred stock be significant?

5. Why is the amount in the Retained Earnings account for a profitable, growing company that has been in business for several decades unlikely to be of much value for predicting future dividend declarations?

6. What is treasury stock? How is it reported on the balance sheet?

7. A certain corporation retained almost all of its earnings, only rarely paying a cash dividend. When some of the shareholders objected, the reply of the president was "Why do you want cash dividends? You would just have to go to the trouble of reinvesting them. Where can you possibly find a better investment than our own company?" Comment.

8. Compare the position of a shareholder who receives a cash dividend with that of one who receives a stock dividend.

9. At the annual shareholders' meeting, the president of the Santa Cris Corporation made the following statement: "The net income for the year, after taxes, was

$1,096,000. The directors have decided that the corporation can afford to distribute only $500,000 as a cash dividend.'' Are the two sentences of this statement compatible?

10. The text says, ''Convertible bonds are usually callable.'' The call feature is included so that the issuer can force conversion of the bonds. Explain.

11. Are accumulated, but unpaid, dividends to preferred shareholders, which must be paid before dividends can be declared on common shares, liabilities? Explain.

12. What are prior-period adjustments? Why do some accountants think that GAAP should only rarely allow them?

13. Interest on bonds is deductible for tax purposes. Dividends on preferred stock issues are not. Assume that a company can raise $100 million either by issuing bonds promising 12 percent annual interest or by issuing preferred shares, convertible in common stock shares promising 12 percent annual dividends. The firm expects to continue to have income (in excess of all interest payments) taxable at the rate of 40 percent per year.
  a. Which of the two financing methods will show a larger income available for common shares?
  b. Why does this book suggest that, in spite of the answer above, one financing method is not necessarily preferred to the other?

Exercises

14. *Effects of transactions involving owners' equity.* Indicate whether each of the following statements is true or false and justify your response. Ignore the effects of income taxes.
  a. Cash dividends reduce the book value per share of capital stock.
  b. A stock dividend does not affect the Retained Earnings account.
  c. Investing 50 percent of net income in government bonds has no effect on the amount legally available for dividends.
  d. Stock dividends reduce the book value per share of capital stock.
  e. The declaration of a cash dividend does not reduce the amount of the shareholders' equity.
  f. The distribution of a stock dividend tends to reduce the market value per share of capital stock.
  g. A stock split generally does not affect the Retained Earnings account.
  h. A stock dividend declaration is usually accompanied by a reduction in par or stated value per share.

15. *Effects of transactions on Retained Earnings and owners' equity.* Indicate the effect of each of the following transactions on **(1)** the balance in the Retained Earnings and **(2)** the total shareholders' equity.
  a. Bonds are issued at a discount.
  b. A check is written to the Internal Revenue Service for additional income taxes levied on past years' income (no previous entry).

    c. A stock split is voted by the directors. The par value per share is reduced from $20 to $5, and each shareholder is given four new shares in exchange for each old share.

    d. The manager is voted a bonus of $35,000 by the directors.

    e. Notes payable in the face amount of $50,000 are paid by check.

    f. A dividend in preferred stock is issued to common shareholders (no previous entry).

    g. Securities held as a long-term investment are sold at book value.

    h. A building site is received as a donation by the company from the local chamber of commerce.

    i. A building is sold for less than its book value.

16. *Journal entries for transactions involving owners' equity.* Present the journal entries for each of the following transactions. These transactions do not relate to the same set of records.

    a. The shares of no-par stock of a corporation are selling on the market at $100 a share. In order to bring the market value down to a "more popular" figure, the board of directors votes to issue four shares to shareholders in exchange for each share already held by them. The shares are issued.

    b. The treasurer of the corporation reports that cash on hand exceeds normal requirements by $300,000. Pending a decision by the board of directors on the final disposition of the funds, investments in marketable securities in the amount of $299,600 are made.

    c. The net income for the year is $150,000. The directors vote to issue 1,000 shares of 10 percent, $100-par-value preferred stock as a stock dividend on the 2,500 shares of no-par common stock outstanding. The preferred's market price is $102 a share. The common's market price is $50 a share.

    d. After the books are closed and the financial statements are issued, it is discovered that an arithmetic error was made in calculating depreciation on office equipment for the preceding period. The depreciation expense was $8,000 too large.

17. *Analyzing changes in owners' equity accounts.* The comparative balance sheet of the Forty-Misty Company shows the following data:

	Dec. 31, Year 1	Dec. 31, Year 2
Common Stock.	$1,200,000	$1,320,000
Retained Earnings	460,000	400,000
Total Shareholders' Equity.	$1,660,000	$1,720,000

During Year 2, common shareholders received $60,000 in cash dividends and $120,000 in stock dividends. A refund on Year 0 taxes of $30,000 was received on March 1, Year 2, and was credited directly to Retained Earnings. A loss on retirement of plant assets of $5,600 occurred during the year and was debited directly to Retained Earnings.

a. What net income is reported for Year 2, after the accounting was done as described?

b. What net income should actually be reported for Year 2? Show your calculations.

18. *Analyzing changes in owners' equity accounts.* The comparative balance sheet of the Royal Corporation shows the following information:

	Dec. 31, Year 1	Dec. 31, Year 2
Preferred Stock (6 percent)	$ 750,000	$ 600,000
Common Stock	1,400,000	1,550,000
Retained Earnings	324,000	372,000
Total Shareholders' Equity	$2,474,000	$2,522,000

During Year 2, stock dividends of $150,000 were issued to common shareholders. In addition, common shareholders received $70,000 in cash dividends; the preferred shareholders received $36,000 in cash dividends. On July 1, Year 2, preferred stock with a par value of $150,000 was called at 104; that is, $156,000 was paid to retire the shares. The call premium was debited to the Common Stock account.

What net income is reported to shareholders for Year 2?

19. *Journal entries for transactions involving owners' equity.* Give journal entries for the following transactions.

a. Outstanding shares of stock are acquired by the issuing corporation for its treasury at a cost of $100,000.

b. Dividends are declared on preferred stock, $220,000.

c. A dividend is paid to common shareholders consisting of shares of preferred stock in the same corporation with a par value of $200,000.

d. A dividend is paid to common shareholders consisting of shares of no-par common stock in the same corporation. The amount assigned to these shares of stock is $600,000.

e. The building is mortgaged for $100,000, and this amount is distributed to the common shareholders as a cash dividend.

20. *Journal entries for transactions involving owners' equity and other accounts.* Give journal entries, if required, for the following transactions, which are unrelated unless otherwise specified.

a. The regular quarterly dividend is declared on the 10 percent, $100-par-value preferred stock. There are 10,000 shares authorized, 8,000 shares issued, of which 1,600 shares have been reacquired and are held in the treasury.

b. The dividend on the preferred stock (see part **a**) is paid.

c. A stock dividend of $250,000 of no-par common stock is issued to common shareholders.

d. A building replacement fund of $125,000 is created. The fund is to be used to purchase a new building when the present one becomes inadequate.

    e. Bonds with $500,000 par value are retired at par out of the sinking fund created for that purpose.

    f. The shares of no-par stock of the corporation are selling on the market at $300 a share. In order to bring the market value down to a more popular price and thereby broaden the distribution of its stockholdings, the board of directors votes to issue four extra shares to shareholders for each share already held by them. The shares are issued.

21. *Journal entries for transactions involving owners' equity.* Journalize the following transactions.

    a. A cash dividend of $2 a share is declared on the outstanding preferred stock. There are 5,000 shares authorized, 3,000 shares issued, and 100 shares reacquired and held in the treasury.

    b. A cash dividend of $1 a share is declared on the no-par common stock, of which there are 10,000 shares authorized, 7,000 shares issued, and 1,000 shares reacquired and held in the treasury.

    c. The dividend on the preferred stock is paid.

    d. The dividend on the common stock is paid.

22. *Restrictions on dividend declarations.* Daley Company has total retained earnings of $100 million and has acquired treasury shares at a cost of $25 million. Its loan agreements limit dividend declarations that would reduce retained earnings below $60 million. The corporation laws of the state of Daley Company's incorporation do not allow dividend declarations if the amount of retained earnings is less than the cost of treasury shares held.

    What is the maximum amount of dividends that Daley Company can declare?

23. *Stock splits and stock splits accounted for as stock dividends.* The Horngren Company has 5 million common shares outstanding with par value of $5 per share and retained earnings of $600 million. The common shares have a market price of $80 each. The board of directors wishes to increase the number of shares in circulation to 10 million either by declaring a two-for-one stock split or by declaring a 100 percent stock dividend to be accounted for as a stock split.

    a. Give journal entries for each of these treatments.

    b. Explain the relative advantages and disadvantages of each.

24. *Transactions to incorporate and run a business.* The following events relate to shareholders' equity transactions of the Richardson Copper Company during the first year of its existence. Present journal entries for each of the transactions.

    a. January 2. Articles of incorporation are filed with the State Corporation Commission. The authorized capital stock consists of 5,000 shares of $100-par-value, preferred stock which offers an 8 percent annual dividend, and 50,000 shares of no-par common stock. The original incorporators are issued 100 shares of common stock at $20 per share; cash is collected for the shares. A stated value of $20 per share is assigned to the common stock.

    b. January 6. 1,600 shares of common stock are issued for cash at $20 per share.

    c. January 8. 3,000 shares of preferred stock are issued at par.

    d. January 9. Certificates for the shares of preferred stock are issued.

    e. January 12. The tangible assets and goodwill of Richardson Copper Works, a partnership, are acquired in exchange for 600 shares of preferred stock and 10,000 shares of common stock. The tangible assets acquired are valued as follows: inventories, $40,000; land, $45,000; buildings, $80,000; and equipment, $95,000.

    f. July 3. The semiannual dividend on the preferred stock outstanding is declared, payable July 25, to shareholders of record on July 12.

    g. July 5. Operations for the first 6 months have been profitable, and it is decided to expand. The company issues 20,000 shares of common stock for cash at $33 per share.

    h. July 25. The preferred stock dividend declared on July 3 is paid.

    i. October 2. The directors declare a dividend of $1 per share on the common stock, payable October 25, to shareholders of record on October 12.

    j. October 25. The dividend on common stock declared on October 2 is paid.

25. *Transactions to incorporate and run a business.* The following data are selected from the records of capital stock and retained earnings of the Wheellock Company. Present journal entries for these transactions.

    a. July 5, Year 1. Articles of incorporation are filed with the secretary of state. The authorized capital stock consists of 1,000 shares of 6 percent preferred stock with a par value of $100 per share and 10,000 shares of no-par common stock.

    b. July 8, Year 1. The company issues 3,000 shares of common stock for cash at $60 per share.

    c. July 9, Year 1. The company issues 6,000 shares of common stock for the assets of the partnership of Wheellock and Wheellock. Their assets are valued as follows: accounts receivable, $30,000; inventories, $60,000; land, $80,000; buildings, $90,000; and equipment, $100,000.

    d. July 13, Year 1. 750 shares of preferred stock are issued at par for cash.

    e. December 31, Year 1. The balance in the Income Summary account, after closing all expense and revenue accounts, is $300,000 credit. The account is to be closed to the Retained Earnings account.

    f. January 4, Year 2. The regular semiannual dividend on the preferred stock and a dividend of $2 per share on the common stock are declared. The dividends are payable on February 1.

    g. February 1, Year 2. The dividends declared on January 4 are paid.

    h. July 2, Year 2. The regular semiannual dividend on the preferred stock is declared. The dividend is payable on August 1.

    i. August 1, Year 2. The dividend declared on July 2 is paid.

26. *Accounting for convertible bonds.* On January 2, Year 1, the Oklahoma Corporation issues $1 million of 20-year, $1,000-par-value, 10 percent semiannual coupon bonds at par. Each $1,000 bond is convertible into 40 shares of $1-par-value common stock. The Oklahoma Corporation's credit rating is such that it would have to issue 15-percent semiannual coupon bonds if the bonds were not convertible and if they were to be issued at par. On January 2, Year 5, the bond issue is converted into common stock. The common stock has a market price of $45 a share on January 2, Year 5.

Present the journal entries made on January 2, Year 1 and Year 5, under generally accepted accounting principles, to record the issue and conversion of the issue.

Problems and Cases

27. *Granting stock options to executives involves an element of compensation.* Assume that accounting were to require recognition of compensation expense on the date that stock options were granted to an employee. A precise measure of the amount of the compensation expense would not be possible, but various approximations could be made. How might the accountant put a dollar amount on the compensation expense granted through stock options? You may assume that the exercise price is the market price on the date the option is granted.

28. *Market reaction to stock dividends.* Chapter 7 of *Accounting Research Bulletin No. 43,* issued in 1953, presented the rules of accounting for stock dividends and stock splits. Paragraph 10 provides reasons for the rules; it says that the rules are justified by ''. . . those instances, which are by far the most numerous, where the issuances [of stock dividends] are so small in comparison with the shares previously outstanding that they do not have any apparent effect upon the share market price and, consequently, the market value of the shares previously held remains substantially unchanged.''
    Comment.

29. *Reconstructing transactions involving owners' equity.* The Chelex Company began business on January 1. Its balance sheet on December 31 contains the shareholders' equity section shown in Exhibit 12.5.

Exhibit 12.5
CHELEX COMPANY
Shareholders' Equity as of December 31
(Problem 29)

Capital Stock ($10 par value)	$ 50,000
Additional Paid-in Capital	78,000
Retained Earnings	10,000
Less: 300 Shares Held in Treasury	(6,000)
Total Shareholders' Equity	$132,000

During the year, Chelex Company engaged in the following capital stock transactions:

(1) Issued shares for $25 each.
(2) Acquired a block of 500 shares for the treasury in a single transaction.
(3) Reissued some of the treasury shares.

Assuming that these were all of the capital stock transactions during the year, answer the following questions:
    a. How many shares were issued for $25?

b. What was the price at which the treasury shares were acquired?
c. How many shares were reissued from the block of treasury shares?
d. What was the price at which the treasury shares were issued?
e. What journal entries must have been made during the year?

30. *Reconstructing transactions involving owners' equity.* The Worman Company began business on January 1. Its balance sheet on December 31 contains the shareholders' equity section shown in Exhibit 12.6.

Exhibit 12.6
WORMAN COMPANY
Shareholders' Equity as of December 31
(Problem 30)

Capital Stock ($5 par value)	$ 50,000
Additional Paid-in Capital	254,800
Retained Earnings	25,000
Less: 600 Shares Held in Treasury	(16,800)
Total Shareholders' Equity	$313,000

During the year, Worman Company engaged in the following capital stock transactions:

(1) Issued shares for $30 each.
(2) Acquired a block of 1,000 shares for the treasury in a single transaction.
(3) Reissued some of the treasury shares.

Assuming that these were the only capital stock transactions during the year, answer the following questions:

a. How many shares were issued for $30 each?
b. What was the price at which the treasury shares were acquired?
c. How many shares were reissued from the block of treasury shares?
d. What was the price at which the treasury shares were reissued?
e. What journal entries must have been made during the year?

31. *Funds statement effects.* Refer to the Simplified Statement of Changes in Financial Position for a Period in Exhibit 5.17 on page 201. Eleven of the lines in the statement are numbered. Ignore the unnumbered lines in responding to the questions below.

Assume that the accounting cycle is complete for the period and that all of the financial statements have been prepared. Then it is discovered that a transaction has been overlooked. The transaction is recorded in the accounts and all of the financial statements are corrected. Define *funds* as *cash*. For each of the following transactions, indicate which of the numbered lines of the funds statement is affected and by how much. Ignore income tax effects.

a. Common shares are issued for $200,000.
b. Common shares originally issued for $50,000 are repurchased for $75,000 and retired.

c. Convertible bonds with a book value of $100,000 and a market value of $240,000 are converted into common shares with a par value of $10,000 and a market value of $240,000.

d. Treasury shares acquired for $20,000 are reissued for $15,000.

e. A stock dividend is declared. The par value of the shares issued is $1,000 and their market value is $300,000.

f. A cash dividend of $70,000 is declared and paid.

g. A previously declared cash dividend of $70,000 is paid.

h. Stock rights are exercised. The shares have a par value of $1,000 and market value of $35,000 on the date of exercise. The exercise price is $20,000, and $20,000 cash is received.

32. *Dilutive effects of stock options.* Refer to the schedule reproduced in Exhibit 12.7, which shows employee stock option data for the International Products Company (IP). At December 31, Year 3, there were 2.7 million options outstanding to purchase shares at an average of $54 per share. Total shareholders' equity at December 31, Year 3, was about $2.5 billion.

Exhibit 12.7
INTERNATIONAL PRODUCTS COMPANY
Disclosure of Employee Stock Options
(Problem 32)

Stock Options	Shares Subject to Option	Average per Share Option Price	Market Price
Balance at December 31, Year 1 . . .	2,388,931	$45	$72
Options Granted	475,286	77	77
Options Exercised	(297,244)	42	76
Options Terminated	(90,062)	45	—
Balance at December 31, Year 2 . . .	2,476,911	50	83
Options Granted	554,965	75	75
Options Exercised	(273,569)	42	74
Options Terminated	(58,307)	52	—
Balance at December 31, Year 3 . . .	2,700,000	54	77

a. If IP were to issue 2.7 million shares in a public offering at the market price per share on December 31, Year 3, what would be the proceeds of the issue?

b. If IP were to issue 2.7 million shares to employees who exercised all outstanding stock options, what would be the proceeds of the issue?

c. Are IP's shareholders better off under a or under b?

d. The text accompanying the stock option data in the IP annual report reads, in part, as follows:

Option price under these plans is the full market value of International Products common stock on date of grant. Therefore, participants in the plans do not benefit unless the stock's market price rises, thus benefiting all share owners. . . .

IP seems to be saying that shareholders are not harmed by these options, whereas your answers to parts **a** and **b** show shareholders are worse off when options are exercised than when shares are issued to the public. Attempt to reconcile IP's statement with your own analysis in parts **a** and **b**.

33. *Dividends in kind.* In the mid-1970s, before *SFAS No. 12* on marketable equity was in force, American Express Company held shares of Donaldson, Lufkin & Jenrette, Inc. (DLJ), as an investment. These shares had cost about $27 million but had a market value of about $6 million. The shares were carried on the books as a long-term investment at cost. During a year when its income was about $200 million, American Express distributed the shares of DLJ as a dividend in kind to its own shareholders. The annual report of American Express said that in management's opinion the difference between the cost and the market value of the DLJ investment "did not represent a permanent impairment in value. . . . Accordingly, the entire carrying value of the DLJ investment . . . was charged to retained earnings." Ignore income tax effects.
    a. What journal entry did American Express apparently make?
    b. What journal entries would have been made had the dividend in kind been recorded at market value of the assets distributed?
    c. What are the differences in these two treatments on net income and retained earnings?

34. *Reporting nonrecurring gains in the income statement.* After American Airlines lost a DC-10 in a Chicago crash, it collected about $37 million in insurance payments. The original cost of the DC-10 was $18 million, and at the time of the crash its net book value was $11 million. Ignore income tax effects.
    a. Give the journal entry American Airlines made on loss of the plane.
    b. How do you think this transaction, which represented a significant fraction of American Airline's income for the period, should be reported in the financial statements?

35. *Dividend policy and dividend reinvestment plans.* Many companies have "automatic dividend reinvestment plans." Shareholders notify the company that they wish to reinvest all cash dividends in common shares. The company arranges to have common shares purchased at current market value for the accounts of the shareholders.
    General Products Company, whose financial statements appear in Appendix A, has such an automatic dividend reinvestment plan. At the end of 1985 it declared and paid a dividend of $2 per share. Holders of 10 percent of the shares have elected the automatic dividend reinvestment option. The market price of a share on the date of reinvestment is $60. General Products Company instructs a stockbroker to purchase the required shares on the New York Stock Exchange.
    a. Give the journal entries, if any, that General Products Company makes for the dividend declaration and for the automatic reinvestment of dividends.
    b. A shareholder complained that if the company would refrain from paying dividends, only to have them reinvested, it would save paperwork and the shareholders would save income taxes. Comment.

36. *Dilution of earnings per share.* In May of Year 1, the A-Tat Company issued 100,000 shares of no-par, convertible preferred stock for $50 a share. The shares promised a dividend of $6. All shares were issued for cash. These shares were convertible into common stock (par value $1 per share) at a rate of 5 shares of common stock for each share of preferred. The preferred shares are *not* regarded as equivalent to common shares in the calculation of earnings per share.

The company's earnings increased sharply during the next 4 years, and during January of Year 5, all shares of preferred were converted into common shares. One million common shares were outstanding before conversion of the shares. If the conversion had not taken place, the net income to common for Year 5 would have been $3,000,000. Other data are as follows:

	May Year 1	Jan. Year 5
Market Prices:		
A-Tat Common Stock	$10	$ 20
A-Tat $6 Preferred Stock	50	100
Book Value per A-Tat Common Share (before conversion of preferred)	14	18

    a. Prepare journal entries to record the issuance and conversion of the preferred stock.

    b. Compute earnings per common share before conversion of the shares. What was the effect of the conversion on book values and on earnings per common share?

    c. Did the conversion of the preferred shares into common stock lead to a dilution of the common shareholders' equity? Explain your reasoning.

37. *Accounting for detachable warrants.* After several years of rapid expansion, the Alcher Company approached the State National Bank for a $1 million, 5-year loan. The bank was willing to lend the money at an interest rate of 12 percent per year. Alcher Company then approached an individual investor who was willing to provide the same funds for only 8 percent per year, provided that the Alcher Company gave the investor an option to purchase 20,000 shares of Alcher Company $5-par-value common stock for $20 per share at any time within 5 years of the initial date of the loan.

Alcher weighed both opportunities and decided to borrow from the investor. At the time of the loan, the common shares had a market price of $15 per share. Five years after the initial date of the loan, the investor exercised the option and purchased 20,000 shares for $20 each. At that time, the market price of the common shares was $45 each.

    a. Did the use of the "detachable warrants" (the technical name for the option granted to the investor) reduce the Alcher Company's cost of borrowing?

    b. How should the loan and annual interest payments of $80,000 be recorded in the books of the Alcher Company to reflect the economic reality of the transaction?

c. How might the exercise of the warrants (and the purchase of the 20,000 shares) be recorded?

d. Did exercise of the option dilute the owners' equity of the other shareholders on the date the option was exercised?

e. What disclosures during the life of the loan do you think appropriate? Why?

38. *Comprehensive review of accounting for owners' equity.* The shareholders' equity section of the balance sheet of the Reis Corporation at December 31 is shown below.

Shareholders' Equity

Common Stock—$10 Par Value, 500,000 Shares Authorized and 100,000 Shares Outstanding	$1,000,000
Additional Paid-in Capital	500,000
Retained Earnings	3,000,000
Total Shareholders' Equity	$4,500,000

a. Calculate the total book value and the book value per common share as of December 31.

b. For each of the following transactions or events, give the appropriate journal entry and determine the total book value and the book value per common share of the Reis Corporation after the transaction. The transaction and events are independent of each other, except where noted.

(1) A 10 percent stock dividend is declared when the market price of Reis Corporation's common stock is $60 per share.

(2) A two-for-one stock split is declared, and the par value of the common stock is reduced from $10 to $5 per share. The new shares are issued immediately.

(3) Ten thousand shares of Reis Corporation's common stock are purchased on the open market for $50 per share and held as treasury stock.

(4) Ten thousand shares of Reis Corporation's common stock are purchased on the open market for $30 per share and held as treasury stock.

(5) The shares acquired in (3) are sold for $70 per share.

(6) The shares acquired in (3) are sold for $40 per share.

(7) The shares acquired in (3) are sold for $30 per share.

(8) Options to acquire 10,000 shares of Reis Corporation stock are exercised by officers for $15 per share.

(9) Same as (8), except that the exercise price is $50 per share.

(10) Convertible bonds with a book value of $300,000 and a market value of $340,000 are exchanged for 10,000 shares of common stock having a market value of $34 per share. No gain or loss is recognized on the conversion of bonds.

(11) Same as (10), except that gain or loss is recognized on the conversion of bonds into stock. Ignore income tax effects.

c. Using the results from part **b**, summarize the transactions and events that result in a reduction in:

(1) Total book value.

(2) Book value per share.

39. *Evaluation of various financing alternatives* (*adapted from a case by C. L. Mitchell*). In early January, B. R. Baine, President of Franco Incorporated, a diversified public company, faced the problem of determining the means of financing a major project recently approved by the board of directors. This project requires an investment of $1,000,000 and is expected to produce an operating income before financing costs and income taxes of $200,000 a year, with the principal returned at the end of the fifth year. Franco Incorporated is subject to an income tax rate of 40 percent.

The corporate treasurer has advised B. R. that the following alternative sources of financing are available:

(1) Issue new common shares at $20 per share.

(2) Arrange a 5-year bank loan with 14 percent interest payable annually in arrears.

(3) Issue 5-year convertible bonds at par with 10 percent interest payable annually. Each $1,000 bond would be convertible into 45 common shares.

(4) Issue cumulative, redeemable, convertible $1.75 preferred shares. The preferred shares are redeemable in 5 years at their issue price and convertible into common shares on the basis of one common share for each preferred share. The preferred shares would be issued at $25 per share. Other income is expected to be $420,000 per year with earnings per share of $2.10.

Analyze the forms of financing and their impact on earnings per share.

40. *Reconstructing events affecting owners' equity.* Exhibit 12.8 reproduces the statement of changes in owners' equity accounts for Granof Company for Year 2.

    a. Identify the most likely events or transaction for each of the events numbered **(1)** to **(6)** in the exhibit.

    b. Prepare journal entries for each of these events or transactions.

41. *Case introducing earnings-per-share calculations for a complex capital structure.* The Layton Ball Corporation has a relatively complicated capital structure. In addition to common shares, it has issued stock options, warrants, and convertible bonds. Exhibit 12.9 summarizes some pertinent information about these items. Net income for the year is $9,500, and the income tax rate used in computing income tax expense is 40 percent of pretax income.

    a. First, ignore all items of capital except for the common shares. Calculate earnings per common share.

    b. In past years, employees have been issued options to purchase shares of stock. Exhibit 12.9 indicates that the price of the common stock throughout the year was $25, but that the stock options could be exercised at any time for $15 each. The holder of an option is allowed to surrender it along with $15 cash and receive one share in return. Thus, the number of shares would be increased, which would decrease the earnings-per-share figure. The company would, however, have more cash. Assume that the holders of options were to tender their options, along with $15 each, to purchase shares.

Exhibit 12.8
GRANOF COMPANY
Statement of Changes in Owners' Equity Accounts for Year 2
(Problem 40)

| | Common Shares | | | | | |
	Market Value per Share[a]	Number of Shares	Par Value	Additional Paid-in Capital	Retained Earnings	Total Owners' Equity
Balances, Dec. 31, Year 1	$100	2,000,000	$12,000,000	$48,000,000	$40,000,000	$100,000,000
Events Causing Changes						
Event (1)	$105	4,000,000	—	—	—	—
Event (2)	$ 40	600,000	1,200,000	22,800,000	(24,000,000)	—
Event (3)	$ 45	100,000	200,000	4,300,000	—	4,500,000
Event (4)	$ 48	50,000	100,000	1,400,000	—	1,500,000
Event (5)	$ 50	—	—	—	45,000,000	45,000,000
Event (6)	$ 53	—	—	—	(6,750,000)	(6,750,000)
Balances, Dec. 31, Year 2		6,750,000	$13,500,000	$76,500,000	$54,250,000	$144,250,000

[a]Before event.

Exhibit 12.9
LAYTON BALL CORPORATION
Information on Capital Structure
for Earnings-per-Share Calculation
(Problem 41)

Assume the following data about the capital structure and earnings for the Layton Ball Corporation for the year:

Number of Common Shares Outstanding Throughout the Year	2,500 shares
Market Price per Common Share Throughout the Year	$25
Options Outstanding During the Year:	
Number of Shares Issuable on Exercise of Options	1,000 shares
Exercise Price per Share	$15
Warrants Outstanding During the Year:	
Number of Shares Issuable on Exercise of Warrants	2,000 shares
Exercise Price per Share	$30
Convertible Bonds Outstanding:	
Number (issued 15 years ago)	100 bonds
Proceeds per Bond at Time of Issue (= par value)	$1,000
Shares of Common Issuable on Conversion (per bond)	10 shares
Coupon Rate (per year)	$4\frac{1}{8}$ percent

Assume that the company would use the cash to purchase shares for the treasury at a price of $25 each. Compute a new earnings-per-share figure. (Treasury shares are *not* counted in the denominator of the earnings-per-share calculation.)

c. Exhibit 12.9 indicates that there are also warrants outstanding in the hands of the public. Anyone who owns such a warrant is allowed to turn in that warrant along with $30 cash and to purchase one share. If the warrants are exercised, then there would be more shares outstanding, which would reduce earnings per share. The company would, however, have more cash, which it could use to purchase shares for the treasury, reducing the number of shares outstanding. Assume that all holders of warrants were to exercise them. Assume that the company were to use the cash to purchase outstanding shares for the treasury. Compute a new earnings-per-share figure. (Ignore the information about options and the calculations in part **b** at this point.) Note that a rational warrant holder would *not* exercise his or her warrants for $30 when a share can be purchased for $25.

d. There are convertible bonds outstanding. A holder of a convertible bond is entitled to trade in that bond for 10 shares. If a bond is converted, the number of shares would increase, which would tend to reduce earnings per share. On the other hand, the company would not have to pay interest and thus would have no interest expense on the bond, because it would no longer be outstanding. This would tend to increase income and earnings per share. Assume that all holders of convertible bonds were to convert their bonds into shares. Compute a new net income figure (do not forget income tax effects on income of the interest saved) and a new earnings-per-share figure. (Ignore the information about options and warrants and the calculations in parts **b** and **c** at this point.)

e. Now consider all the above calculations. Which sets of assumptions from parts **b**, **c**, and **d** would lead to the lowest possible earnings per share when they are all made simultaneously? Compute a new earnings per share under the most restrictive set of assumptions about reductions in earnings per share.

f. Accountants publish several earnings-per-share figures for companies with complicated capital structures and complicated events during the year. *The Wall Street Journal,* however, publishes only one figure in its daily columns (where it reports the price-earnings ratio—the price of a share of stock divided by its earnings per share). Which of the figures computed above for earnings per share do you think should be reported by *The Wall Street Journal* as *the* earnings-per-share figure? Why?

Chapter 13   Long-Term Investments in Corporate Securities

For a variety of reasons, corporations often acquire the securities (bonds, capital stock) of other corporations. For example, a corporation may temporarily hold excess cash that is not needed for operations. Rather than permit the cash to remain idle in its bank account, the corporation may acquire the bonds or capital stock of another corporation. Relatively short-term holdings of corporate securities are usually classified as Marketable Securities and are shown in the Current Assets section of the balance sheet. Chapter 7 discusses the accounting for marketable securities.

A corporation may acquire another corporation's capital stock for some more long-term purpose.[1] For example, a firm may acquire shares of common stock of a major raw materials supplier to help assure continued availability of raw materials. Or a firm may wish to diversify its operations by acquiring a controlling interest in an established firm in some new area of business. Long-term investments in corporate securities are typically classified on the asset side of the balance sheet in a separate section called "Investments." The accounting for long-term investments in capital stock is discussed in both Chapter 7 and this chapter.

Types of Long-Term Investments

The accounting for long-term investments depends on the purpose of the investment and on the percentage of voting stock that one corporation owns of another. Refer to Figure 13.1. Three types of long-term investments can be identified:

1. Minority, passive investments—Shares of capital stock of another corporation are viewed as a good long-term investment and are acquired for the dividends and capital gains (increases in the market price of the shares) anticipated from owning the shares. The percentage owned of the other corporation's shares is not so large that the acquiring company can control or exert significant influence over the other company. Generally accepted accounting principles view investments of less than 20 percent of the voting stock of another company as minority, passive investments, in most cases.[2]

2. Minority, active investments—Shares of another corporation are acquired so that the acquiring corporation can exert significant influence over the other com-

---

[1]Industrial firms seldom acquire bonds of other corporations as long-term investments. Consequently, this chapter focuses on long-term investments in capital stock.

[2]Accounting Principles Board, *Opinion No. 18,* "The Equity Method of Accounting for Investments in Common Stock," 1971.

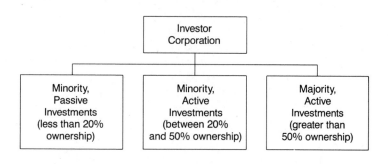

Figure 13.1 Types of Intercorporate Investments in Capital Stock

pany's activities. This significant influence is usually at a broad policy-making level through representation on the other corporation's board of directors. Because the shares of capital stock of most publicly held corporations are widely dispersed among numerous individuals, many of whom do not vote their shares, significant influence can be exerted over another corporation with ownership of less than a majority of the voting stock. Generally accepted accounting principles view investments of between 20 percent and 50 percent of the voting stock of another company as minority, active investments "unless evidence indicates that significant influence cannot be exercised."[3]

3. Majority, active investments—Shares of another corporation are acquired so that the acquiring corporation can control the other company. This control is typically at both the broad policy-making level and at the day-to-day operational level. Ownership of more than 50 percent of the voting stock of another company implies an ability to control, unless there is evidence to the contrary.[4]

The sections that follow discuss the accounting for these three types of investments. Throughout the chapter, the acquiring corporation is designated P, for *purchaser* or for *parent,* depending on the context, and the acquired corporation is designated S, for *seller* or for *subsidiary.*

Minority, Passive Investments

If a firm does not own a sufficient percentage of the voting stock of another corporation to control or significantly influence it (assumed to be 20 percent or more under generally accepted accounting principles), the management of the investment in-

---

[3]APB, *Opinion No. 18;* Financial Accounting Standards Board, *Interpretation No. 35,* "Criteria for Applying the Equity Method of Accounting for Investments in Common Stock," 1981.

[4]A corporation may be unable to exercise its control over another corporation, despite the ownership of a majority of the voting stock, if the other corporation is in bankruptcy proceedings and under the control of a court.

volves two activities: (1) awaiting the receipt of dividends and (2) deciding when the investment should be sold for a capital gain or loss. Minority, passive investments must be accounted for by using the *lower-of-cost-or-market method*. Chapter 7 describes and illustrates the lower-of-cost-or-market method for both marketable securities classified as Current Assets (that is, those planned to be sold within a short period when cash is needed) and minority, passive investments classified as Investments (that is, those held for some long-term purpose). To summarize the lower-of-cost-or-market method for minority, passive investments:

1. Investments are initially recorded at acquisition cost.

2. Dividends received or receivable each period are recognized as dividend revenue.

3. At the end of each period, the market value of the portfolio of noncurrent marketable equity securities is compared to the acquisition cost of the portfolio. The amount shown on the balance sheet for these investments is the lower-of-acquisition-cost or current market value.

Assume that a portfolio of marketable equity securities held as long-term investments had an acquisition cost of $100,000. The portfolio has a market value of $95,000 at the end of a firm's first year of operations. The following entry would be made at year-end:

Unrealized Holding Loss on Valuation of Marketable Equity Investments.	5,000	
Allowance for Excess of Cost of Investments over Market Value		5,000

The account debited, Unrealized Holding Loss on Valuation of Marketable Equity Investments, is included as a negative amount in the shareholders' equity section of the balance sheet, typically between Additional Paid-in Capital and Retained Earnings. See Exhibit 12.1 on page 537. The unrealized loss is not included in the calculation of net income for the period. The suggested rationale is that these investments are acquired for their long-term capital gains (plus dividends). Short-term changes in market value, therefore, should not affect periodic earnings. The account credited, Allowance for Excess of Cost of Investments over Market Value, is a contra account to the Investments in Securities account. Using it permits the net investments to be shown at the lower of cost or market while retaining the amount of acquisition cost in the Investment in Securities account.

Subsequent increases in the market value of the portfolio up to, but not exceeding, the original cost of the investments in the portfolio are debited to the asset contra and credited to the balance sheet shareholders' equity account for unrealized losses.

4. When a particular minority, passive investment is sold, the difference between the selling price and the acquisition cost of the investment is recognized as a gain or loss. Thus, all changes in market value between the time an investment is acquired and when it is sold are reflected in net income in the period of sale. The net amount shown for investments on the asset side of the balance sheet reflects the *potential* future holding loss on the portfolio of such investments.

You may find it helpful to review the illustration of the lower-of-cost-or-market method for minority, passive investments in Chapter 7.

Minority, Active Investments

When less than a majority of the voting stock of another corporation is owned, judgment is required in ascertaining when significant influence can be exercised. For the sake of uniformity, generally accepted accounting principles presume that one company can significantly influence another company when 20 percent or more of the voting stock of the other company is owned. Significant influence may be present when less than 20 percent is owned, but in these cases management must demonstrate to the independent accountants that it exists.

Minority, active investments, those where ownership is between 20 percent and 50 percent, must be accounted for using the *equity method*. Under the equity method, the firm owning shares in another firm recognizes as revenue (expense) each period its share of the net income (loss) of the other firm. Dividends received from S are not recognized as income but as a return of investment. In the discussion that follows, we designate the firm owning shares as P and the firm whose shares are owned as S.

Equity Method: Rationale

The rationale for using the equity method when significant influence is present can be best understood by considering the financial statement effects of using the lower-of-cost-or-market method in these circumstances. Under the lower-of-cost-or-market method, P recognizes income or loss on the income statement only when it receives a dividend or sells all or part of the investment. Suppose, as often happens, that S follows a policy of financing its own growing operations through retention of earnings and consistently declares dividends significantly less than its net income. The market price of S's shares will probably increase to reflect the retention of assets generated by earnings. Under the lower-of-cost-or-market method, P will continue to show the investment at acquisition cost and P's only reported income from the investment will be the modest dividends received. P, because of its ownership percentage, can influence the dividend policy of S and thereby the amount of income recognized under the lower-of-cost-or-market method. Under these conditions, the lower-of-cost-or-market method may not reasonably reflect the earnings of S generated under P's influence. The equity method is designed to provide a better measure of a firm's earnings and of its investment when, because of its ownership interest, significant influence can be exerted over the operations of another firm.

Equity Method: Procedures

Under the equity method, the initial purchase of an investment is recorded at acquisition cost, the same as under the lower-of-cost-or-market method. Company P treats as revenue, each period, its proportionate share of the periodic earnings, not the dividends, of Company S. Dividends declared by S are then treated by P as a reduction in its Investment in S.

Suppose that P acquires 30 percent of the outstanding shares of S for $600,000. The entry to record the acquisition would be:

---

(1) Investment in Stock of S   600,000
    Cash   600,000
    Investment made in 30 percent of Company S.

Between the time of the acquisition and the end of P's next accounting period, S reports income of $80,000. P, using the equity method, would record:

---

(2) Investment in Stock of S   24,000
    Revenue from Investments   24,000
    To record 30 percent of income earned by investee, accounted for
    using the equity method. Revenue account title often used in prac-
    tice is Equity in Earnings of Unconsolidated Affiliates.

If S pays a dividend of $30,000 to holders of common stock, P would be entitled to receive $9,000 and would record:

---

(3) Cash   9,000
    Investment in Stock of S   9,000
    To record dividends received from investee, accounted for using
    the equity method, and the resulting reduction in the investment
    account.

Notice that the credit is to the Investment in S account. P records income earned by S as an *increase* in investment. The dividend becomes a return of investment and *decreases* the Investment account.[5]

Suppose that S subsequently reports earnings of $100,000 and also pays dividends of $40,000. P's entries would be:

---

[5]Students often have difficulty understanding journal entry (3), particularly the credit by the investor when a dividend is paid by the investee company. The transactions and entries are analogous to an individual's ordinary savings account at a local bank. Assume that you put $600,000 in a savings account, that later interest of 4 percent (or $24,000) is added by the bank to the account, and that still later you withdraw $9,000 from the savings account. Journal entries (1)–(3) in the text could be recorded for these three events, with slight changes in the account titles: Investment in S changes to Savings Account, and Revenue from Investments changes to Interest Revenue. The cash withdrawal reduces the amount invested in the savings account. Similarly, the declaration of a cash dividend by an investee company accounted for with the equity method reduces the investor's investment in the company.

(4) Investment in Stock of S	30,000	
Revenue from Investments		30,000
(5) Cash	12,000	
Investment in Stock of S		12,000
To record revenue and dividends from investee, accounted for using equity method.		

P's Investment in S account now has a balance of $633,000 as follows:

Investment in Stock of S

(1)	600,000	9,000	(3)
(2)	24,000	12,000	(5)
(4)	30,000		
Bal.	633,000		

If P now sells one-fourth of its shares for $165,000, P's entry to record the sale would be:

Cash	165,000	
Investment in Stock of S		158,250
Gain on Sale of Investment in S		6,750
$(\frac{1}{4} \times \$633,000 = \$158,250.)$		

The equity method as described above is simple enough to use. To make financial reports that use the equity method more realistic, generally accepted accounting principles require some modification of the entries under certain circumstances, described next.

Even though S does not declare all of its earnings in dividends, P reports its proportionate share of S's earnings as income. But this income to P is not currently taxable. Consequently, there will sometimes be an entry in the deferred tax account. Calculating the amount of the deferred tax charge presents issues too complex for this introductory text.

An additional complication in using the equity method arises when the acquisition cost of P's shares exceeds P's proportionate share of the book value of the net assets (= assets minus liabilities), or shareholders' equity, of S at the date of acquisition. For example, assume that P acquires 25 percent of the stock of S for $400,000, when the total shareholders' equity of S is $1 million. The excess of P's cost over book value acquired is $150,000 (= $400,000 − .25 × $1,000,000). Under the equity method, the excess is generally *goodwill*. Goodwill must be amortized over a period not greater than 40 years.[6] Accounting for goodwill, including its amortization, is discussed later in the appendix to this chapter.

---

[6]Accounting Principles Board, *Opinion No. 17,* "Intangible Assets," 1970.

On the balance sheet, an investment accounted for with the equity method is shown in the Investments section. The amount shown will generally be equal to the acquisition cost of the shares plus P's share of S's undistributed earnings since the date the shares were acquired. On the income statement, P shows its share of S's income as a revenue each period. (The financial statements of the investee, S, are not affected by the accounting method used by the investor, P.)

Equity Method and the Statement of Changes in Financial Position

When Company P uses the lower-of-cost-or-market method to account for its investment in Company S, all dividend revenues recognized in computing net income also generally produce cash. No adjustment to net income is therefore normally required in calculating Cash Provided by Operations.

Accounting for investments using the equity method requires, however, an adjustment to net income to compute Cash Provided by Operations. Suppose that Company P prepares its financial statements at the end of a year during which transactions (1)–(5), above, occurred. P's revenue from its investment in S is $54,000. This amount is the sum of the revenue recognized in transactions (2) and (4). P's income (ignoring income tax effects) increased $54,000 because of its investment. However, P's cash increased by only $21,000 [transactions (3) and (5)] as a result of S's dividends. Consequently, there must be a *subtraction* from net income of $33,000 (= $54,000 − $21,000) in computing Cash Provided by Operations to show that cash did not increase by as much as the amount of revenue recognized under the equity method.

In preparing P's statement of changes in financial position using the T-account method, the following change in a noncurrent asset account would have to be explained:

**Investment in
Stock of S**

Bal.	0	
Bal.	633,000	

The entries to explain this debit change of $633,000 would be

Investment in Stock of S	600,000	
Cash (Use—Acquisition of Investment)		600,000
To recognize use of cash for an investment in a noncurrent asset.		
Investment in Stock of S	33,000	
Cash (Subtraction—Undistributed Income Under Equity Method) .		33,000
To recognize that cash was not increased by the full amount of revenue recognized under the equity method.		

Keep in mind that these two entries are not formally made in the accounting records, but are made only in the work sheet used for preparing the statement of changes in financial position.

Equity Method Illustrated

The equity method can be illustrated using information for General Products Company found in Appendix A. The balance sheet (Exhibit A.2) indicates that investments were $1,691 million on December 31, 1984, and $1,820 million on December 31, 1985. Note 12 to the financial statements indicates that the investment in General Products Credit Corporation, a wholly owned, unconsolidated finance affiliate, is included in investments on the balance sheet. Because General Products Company owns all of General Products Credit Corporation's outstanding common stock, but chooses not to consolidate it, the equity method of accounting is used.

The change in the Investment in General Products Credit Corporation account during 1985 is as follows (amounts in millions):

Investment in General Products Credit Corporation, Dec. 31, 1984 (Note 12) . . .	$817
Plus: Equity in Earnings of General Products Credit Corporation for 1985 (Note 4).	115
Additional Investments (change in capital stock account on balance sheet of General Products Credit Corporation—Note 12)	92
Less: Dividends Received (see statement of current and retained earnings—Note 12)	(93)
Investment in General Products Credit Corporation, Dec. 31, 1985 (Note 12) . . .	$931

Income generated from this investment totaled $115 million during 1985. However, only $93 million was received in cash. Thus, the statement of changes in financial position must show a subtraction of $22 (= $115 − $93) million for income that did not produce cash. Also included among other uses of cash will be $92 million for additional investments in the credit subsidiary. (For an explanation as to why a subsidiary would pay a dividend of $93 million and require the parent to reinvest $92 million immediately, see Authors' Note 61 in Appendix A.)

Majority, Active Investments

When one firm, P, owns more than 50 percent of the voting stock of another company, S, P can control the activities of S. This control can be both at a broad policy-making level and at a day-to-day operational level. The majority investor in this case is called the *parent* and the majority-owned company is called the *subsidiary*. Generally accepted accounting principles permit majority-owned active investments to be accounted for in one of two ways. In most cases, the financial statements of the majority-owned subsidiary are combined, or *consolidated*, with those of the parent. In some instances, however, consolidated financial statements are not prepared. Instead, the investment is reported using the equity method. Whether consolidated statements are prepared or the equity method is used depends on the consolidation policy of the firm, which is discussed later in this section.

Reasons for Legally Separate Corporations

There are many reasons why a business firm prefers to operate as a group of legally separate corporations, rather than as a single legal entity. From the standpoint of the parent company, the more important reasons for maintaining legally separate subsidiary companies include the following:

1. To reduce financial risk. Separate corporations may be used for mining raw materials, transporting them to a manufacturing plant, producing the product, and selling the finished product to the public. If any one part of the total process proves to be unprofitable or inefficient, losses from insolvency will fall only on the owners and creditors of the one subsidiary corporation.

2. To meet more effectively the requirements of state corporation laws and tax legislation. If an organization does business in a number of states, it is often faced with overlapping and inconsistent taxation, regulations, and requirements. Organizing separate corporations to conduct the operations in the various states may be more economical.

3. To expand or diversify with a minimum of capital investment. A firm may absorb another company by acquiring a controlling interest in its voting stock. The result may be accomplished with a substantially smaller capital investment, as well as with less difficulty, inconvenience, and risk, than if a new plant had been constructed or the firm had geared up for a new line of business.

Purpose of Consolidated Statements

For a variety of reasons, then, a single *economic entity* may exist in the form of a parent and several legally separate subsidiaries. (The General Electric Company, for example, consists of about 150 legally separate companies.) A consolidation of the financial statements of the parent and each of its subsidiaries presents the results of operations, financial position, and changes in financial position of an affiliated group of companies under the control of a parent, essentially as if the group of companies were a single entity. The parent and each subsidiary are legally separate entities, but they operate as one centrally controlled *economic* entity. Consolidated financial statements generally provide more useful information to the shareholders of the parent corporation than would separate financial statements of the parent as investor and each subsidiary as an operating company.

Consolidated financial statements also generally provide more useful information than does use of the equity method. The parent, because of its voting interest, can effectively control the use of all of the subsidiary's assets. Consolidation of the individual assets, liabilities, revenues, and expenses of both the parent and the subsidiary provides a more realistic picture of the operations and financial position of the single economic entity.

In a legal sense, consolidated statements merely supplement, and do not replace, the separate statements of the individual corporations, although it is common practice to present only the consolidated statements in published annual reports.

Consolidation Policy

Consolidated financial statements are generally prepared when all of the following three criteria are met:

1. The parent owns more than 50 percent of the voting stock of the subsidiary.
2. There are no important restrictions on the ability of the parent to exercise control of the subsidiary.
3. The asset and equity structure of the subsidiary is not significantly different from that of the parent.

Ownership of more than 50 percent of the subsidiary's voting stock implies an ability to exert control over the activities of the subsidiary. For example, the parent can control the subsidiary's corporate policies and dividend declarations. There may be situations, however, where control of the subsidiary's activities cannot be carried out effectively, despite the ownership of a majority of the voting stock. For example, the subsidiary may be located in a foreign country that has severely restricted the withdrawal of funds from that country. Or the subsidiary may be in bankruptcy and under the control of a court-appointed group of trustees. In these cases, the financial statements of the subsidiary probably will not be consolidated with those of the parent. When the parent owns more than 50 percent of the shares and can exercise control, but consolidated statements are not prepared, then the equity method must be used.

If the asset and equity structure of the subsidiary is significantly different from that of the parent, the subsidiary's financial statements are frequently not consolidated with those of the parent and the equity method is used. For example, a consolidated statement might not be prepared if the parent is a manufacturing concern with heavy investments in property, plant, and equipment, whereas the subsidiary is a finance or insurance company with large holdings of cash, receivables, and marketable securities. The presentation of consolidated financial statements of corporations with significantly different asset and equity structures is sometimes thought to submerge potentially important information about the individual corporations. This is particularly true when the assets of the subsidiary are not, by law, fully available for use by the parent, such as when the subsidiary is a bank or an insurance company.

Example 1 General Motors, General Electric, and Westinghouse, among others, have wholly owned finance subsidiaries. These subsidiaries make many of their loans to customers who wish to purchase the products of the parent company. The financial statements of these subsidiaries are not consolidated with those of the parent company. The assets of these subsidiaries are largely receivables. It is argued that statement readers might be misled as to the relative liquidity of these firms if consolidated statements were prepared and the assets of the parent—largely noncurrent manufacturing plant and equipment—were combined with the more liquid assets of the finance subsidiary.

Example 2 Sears, Roebuck & Co. and J. C. Penney Company are large retailers. Each has organized a separate subsidiary to finance customers' purchases and another separate subsidiary to sell insurance. Sears consolidates both its finance subsidiary and its insurance subsidiary. Penney consolidates neither, but uses the equity method for both.

Example 3 A major mining corporation owns a mining subsidiary in South America. The government of the country enforces stringent control over cash payments outside the country. The company is not able to control the use of all the assets, despite the ownership of a majority of the voting shares. Therefore, it does not prepare consolidated statements with the subsidiary.

Disclosure of Consolidation Policy

The summary of significant accounting principles in financial statements includes a statement about the consolidation policy of the parent. If a significant majority-owned subsidiary is not consolidated, then its financial statements are often included in the notes to the financial statements. For example, the note on page 718 for the General Products Company indicates that all significant majority-owned subsidiaries are consolidated, with the exception of its finance company. For this subsidiary, the equity method is required and used. The financial statements of the finance company appear in Note 12 on pages 732 and 734.

Understanding Consolidated Statements

This section discusses three concepts essential for understanding consolidated financial statements:

1. The need for intercompany eliminations.
2. The meaning of consolidated net income.
3. The nature of the external minority interest.

Need for Intercompany Eliminations State corporation laws typically require each legally separate corporation to maintain its own set of books. Thus, during the accounting period, the accounting records of each corporation will record transactions of that entity with all other entities (both affiliated and nonaffiliated). At the end of the period, each corporation will prepare its own set of financial statements. The consolidation of these financial statements basically involves summing the amounts for various financial statement items across the separate company statements. The amounts resulting from the summation must be adjusted, however, to eliminate double counting resulting from intercompany transactions. Consolidated financial statements are intended to reflect the results that would be achieved if the affiliated group of companies were a single company. Consolidated financial statements reflect only the transactions between the consolidated entity and others.

The eliminations to remove intercompany transactions are typically made on a consolidation work sheet and are not recorded on the books of any of the legal entities being consolidated. The consolidated financial statements are then prepared directly from the work sheet. There are generally no separate books for the consolidated entity.

To illustrate the need for, and the nature of, elimination entries, refer to the data for Company P and Company S in Exhibit 13.1. Column (1) shows the balance sheet and income statement data for Company P taken from its separate company books. Column (2) shows similar data for Company S. Column (3) sums the amounts from columns (1) and (2). The amounts in column (3) include the effects of several intercompany items and, therefore, do not represent the correct amounts for *consolidated* assets, equities, revenues, or expenses.

For example, separate company records indicate that $12,000 of Company S's accounts receivable represent amounts payable by Company P. The funds underlying this transaction are effectively counted twice in column (3): once as part of Accounts Receivable on Company S's books and a second time as Cash (Other Assets) on Company P's books. Also, the liability shown on Company P's books is included in the combined amount for Accounts Payable in column (3), even though the amount is not payable to an entity external to the consolidated group. To eliminate double counting on the asset side and to report Accounts Payable at the amount payable to external entities, an elimination entry must be made to reduce the amounts for Accounts Receivable and Accounts Payable in column (3) by $12,000.

To take a more complex example, Company P's balance sheet shows an asset, Investment in Stock of Company S. The subsidiary's balance sheet shows its individual assets. When the two balance sheets are added together in column (3), the sum shows both Company P's investment in Company S's assets and the assets themselves. Company P's account, Investment in Stock of Company S, must therefore be eliminated from the sum of the balance sheets. Because the consolidated balance sheet must maintain the accounting equation, corresponding eliminations must be made on the right-hand, or equities, side in this case.

To understand the eliminations from the right-hand side of the balance sheet, recall that the right-hand side shows the sources of the firm's financing. Company S is financed by creditors (liabilities) and by owners (shareholders' equity). In this case, Company P owns 100 percent of Company S's voting shares. Thus, the assets on the consolidated balance sheet of the single economic entity are financed by the creditors of both companies and by Company P's shareholders. That is, the equities of the consolidated entity are the liabilities of both companies but the shareholders' equity of Company P alone. If the shareholders' equity accounts of Company S were added to those of Company P, then the financing from Company P's shareholders would be counted twice (once on the parent's books and once on the subsidiary's books). Hence, when Company P's investment account is eliminated from the sum of the two companies' assets, the accounting equation is maintained by eliminating the shareholders' equity accounts of Company S.

Similarly, certain intercompany items must be eliminated from the sum of income statement accounts, so that the operating performance of the consolidated entity can be meaningfully presented. Company P's accounts show Equity in Earnings of Company S of $48,000. Company S's records show individual revenues and

Exhibit 13.1
Illustrative Data for Preparation of Consolidated Financial Statements

| | Single-Company Statements | | |
	Company P (1)	Company S (2)	Combined (3) = (1) + (2)
Condensed Balance Sheets on December 31			
Assets:			
Accounts Receivable	$ 200,000	$ 25,000	$ 225,000
Investment in Stock of Company S (at equity)	705,000	—	705,000
Other Assets	2,150,000	975,000	3,125,000
Total Assets	$3,055,000	$1,000,000	$4,055,000
Equities:			
Accounts Payable	$ 75,000	$ 15,000	$ 90,000
Other Liabilities	70,000	280,000	350,000
Common Stock	2,500,000	500,000	3,000,000
Retained Earnings	410,000	205,000	615,000
Total Equities	$3,055,000	$1,000,000	$4,055,000
Condensed Income Statement for Current Year			
Revenues:			
Sales	$ 900,000	$ 250,000	$1,150,000
Equity in Earnings of Company S	48,000	—	48,000
Total Revenues	$ 948,000	$ 250,000	$1,198,000
Expenses:			
Cost of Goods Sold (excluding depreciation)	$ 440,000	$ 80,000	$ 520,000
Depreciation Expense	120,000	50,000	170,000
Administrative Expenses	80,000	40,000	120,000
Income Tax Expense	104,000	32,000	136,000
Total Expenses	$ 744,000	$ 202,000	$ 946,000
Net Income	$ 204,000	$ 48,000	$ 252,000
Dividend Declarations	50,000	13,000	63,000
Increase in Retained Earnings for the Year	$ 154,000	$ 35,000	$ 189,000

expenses which net to $48,000. If the revenues and expenses of the two companies were merely summed, as is done in column (3) of Exhibit 13.1, the earnings of Company S would be double-counted. The account, Equity in Earnings of Company S, must, therefore, be eliminated in preparing consolidated statements (illustrated later in the chapter).

Another example of an intercompany item involves intercompany sales of inventory. Separate company records indicate that Company S sold merchandise to Company P for $40,000 during the year. None of this inventory remains in Company P's inventory on December 31. The merchandise inventory items sold are included in Sales Revenue on both Company S's books (sale to Company P) and on Company P's books (sale to external entity). Thus, sales are overstated from the standpoint of the consolidated entity. Likewise, Cost of Goods Sold of both companies includes the separate company cost of the goods sold. To eliminate double counting, the intercompany sale from Company S to Company P must be eliminated (illustrated later).

To complete the above example, suppose that the subsidiary sells to the parent but that the parent has not yet sold the goods to the public. The subsidiary will have recorded profits on the sale, but from the standpoint of the overall economic entity, no profits for shareholders have actually been realized, because the items are still in the inventory of the overall economic entity. Consequently, profits from the subsidiary's sales to the parent that have not been realized by subsequent sales to outsiders are eliminated from consolidated net income and balance sheet amounts. The consolidated income statement attempts to show sales, expenses, and net income figures that report the results of operations of the group of companies as though they were a single company.

A later section illustrates the adjustment to convert column (3) of Exhibit 13.1 to a consolidated basis.

Consolidated Income The amount of consolidated net income for a period is the same as the amount that the parent would show on its separate company books from applying the equity method. That is, consolidated net income is equal to:

Parent Company's Net Income from Its Own Activities + Parent Company's Share of Subsidiary's Net Income − Profit (or Plus Loss) on Intercompany Transactions.

The principal difference between a consolidated income statement and an income statement where the equity method has been used is in the components of the income presented. When the equity method is used for an unconsolidated subsidiary, the parent's share of the subsidiary's net income minus gain (or plus loss) on intercompany transactions is shown on a single line, Equity in Earnings of Unconsolidated Subsidiary. When a consolidated income statement is prepared, the individual revenues and expenses of the subsidiary (less intercompany adjustments) are combined with those of the parent, and the account, Equity in Earnings of Unconsolidated Subsidiary, shown on the parent's books, is eliminated.[7]

External Minority Interest in Consolidated Subsidiary In many cases, the parent will not own 100 percent of the voting stock of a consolidated subsidiary. The owners of the remaining shares of voting stock are called *external minority shareholders,* or the *minority interest.*[8] These shareholders continue to have a proportion-

---

[7]The equity method is sometimes referred to as a "one-line consolidation" because the individual revenues and expenses of the subsidiary are netted in the one account, Equity in Earnings of Unconsolidated Subsidiary.

[8]Do not confuse this minority interest in a consolidated subsidiary with a firm's own minority investments, discussed earlier. The minority *interest* belongs to others outside the parent and its economic entity. The parent's minority *investments* are merely those for which the parent owns less than 50 percent of the shares.

ate interest in the net assets (= total assets minus total liabilities) of the subsidiary as shown on the subsidiary's separate corporate records. They also have a proportionate interest in the earnings of the subsidiary.

An issue in the generally accepted accounting principles for consolidated statements is whether the statements should show only the parent's share of the assets and liabilities of the subsidiary or whether they should show all of the subsidiary's assets and liabilities along with the minority interests in them. The generally accepted accounting principle is to show all of the assets and liabilities of the subsidiary, because the parent, with its controlling voting interest, can effectively direct the use of all the assets and liabilities, not merely an amount equal to the parent's percentage of ownership. The consolidated balance sheet and income statement in these instances must, however, disclose the interest of the minority shareholders in the subsidiary that has been consolidated.

The amount of the minority interest shown on the balance sheet is generally the result of multiplying the common stockholders' equity of the subsidiary by the minority's percentage of ownership. For example, if the common shareholders' equity (or assets minus liabilities) of a consolidated subsidiary totals $500,000 and the minority owns 20 percent of the common stock, then the minority interest shown on the consolidated balance sheet is $100,000 (= .20 × $500,000).

The minority interest is typically presented among the equities on the consolidated balance sheet between the liabilities and shareholders' equity. See, for example, the General Products Company's consolidated balance sheet in Exhibit A.2 on page 714. Note that "Minority Interest" is shown among the liabilities but is not clearly labeled as one. This presentation is typical of many published financial statements. The right-hand side of the balance sheet contains only liabilities and owners' equity items, so that the minority interest should appear as one or the other. Because the minority interest has no maturity date, it does not meet the criteria to be a liability discussed in Chapter 10. It is therefore classified as part of owners' equity in this text.

The amount of the minority interest in the subsidiary's income, shown on the consolidated income statement, is generally the result of multiplying the *subsidiary's* net income by the minority's percentage of ownership. The consolidated income is allocated to show the portions applicable to the parent company and the portion of the subsidiary's income applicable to the minority interest. Refer again to General Products Company's consolidated income statement, shown in Exhibit A.1. Notice the deduction of $21 million for the "Minority Interest in Earnings of Consolidated Affiliates" before the consolidated net income figure for 1985. The consolidated net income includes only that portion of net income of subsidiary companies allocable to the shareholders of General Products Company. Typically, the minority interest in the subsidiary's income is shown as a deduction in calculating consolidated net income.

The minority interest share of earnings is deducted in calculating consolidated net income. This deduction did not require the use of cash. Consequently, there must be an addback to derive cash provided by operations. General Products Company shows the addback of $21 million in its statement of changes in financial position, Exhibit A.3, as "Minority Interest in Earnings of Consolidated Affiliate."

Limitations of Consolidated Statements

The consolidated statements do not replace those of individual corporations; rather, they supplement those statements and aid in their interpretation. Creditors must rely on the resources of one corporation and may be misled if forced to rely entirely on a consolidated statement that combines the data of a company in good financial condition with those of one verging on insolvency. Dividends can legally be declared only from the retained earnings of one corporation. Where the parent company does not own all of the shares of the subsidiary, the outside or minority shareholders can judge the dividend constraints, both legal and financial, only by an inspection of the subsidiary's statements.

Preparing Consolidated Financial Statements

This section illustrates the preparation of consolidated financial statements for Company P and Company S. Knowing how to construct consolidated financial statements is not essential for learning how to interpret and to analyze them, but it helps.

Data for the Illustration

The single-company financial statements of Company P and Company S appear in Exhibit 13.1 on page 582. The following additional information is to be considered in preparing the consolidated financial statements.

1. Company P acquired 100 percent of the outstanding shares of Company S for $650,000 cash on January 1, Year 1. At the time of acquisition, the book value of the shareholders' equity of Company S was $650,000, comprised of the following balances:

Company S, January 1, Year 1	
Common Stock	$500,000
Retained Earnings.	150,000
Total Shareholders' Equity	$650,000

Company P made the following journal entry on its books at the time of acquisition:

Investment in Stock of Company S	650,000	
Cash		650,000

2. Company P records its investment in the shares of Company S using the equity method. The increase in Retained Earnings of Company S since January 1, Year 1, the date of acquisition, has been $55,000 (= $205,000 − $150,000). This increase

Exhibit 13.2
Work Sheet to Derive Consolidated Financial Statements for Company P and Company S
Based on Data from Preclosing Trial Balances for Year 4

	Company P		Company S		Adjustments and Eliminations		P and S Consolidated	
	Debit	Credit	Debit	Credit	Debit	Credit	Debit	Credit
Trial Balance Accounts								
Accounts Receivable.	$ 200,000		$ 25,000				$ 213,000	
Investment in Stock of Company S.	705,000		—			(1) 705,000		
Other Assets	2,150,000		975,000				3,125,000	
Accounts Payable		$ 75,000		$ 15,000	(2) $ 12,000			$ 78,000
Other Liabilities		70,000		280,000				350,000
Common Stock		2,500,000		500,000	(1) 500,000			2,500,000
Retained Earnings, January 1, Year 4:								
Company P		256,000						256,000
Company S				170,000	(1) 170,000			
Sales		900,000		250,000	(3) 40,000			1,110,000
Equity in Earnings of Company S		48,000		—	(1) 48,000			
Cost of Goods Sold	440,000		80,000			(3) 40,000	480,000	
Depreciation Expense	120,000		50,000				170,000	
Administrative Expenses	80,000		40,000				120,000	
Income Taxes.	104,000		32,000				136,000	
Dividends Declared	50,000		13,000			(1) 13,000	50,000	
Totals	$3,849,000	$3,849,000	$1,215,000	$1,215,000	$770,000	$770,000	$4,294,000	$4,294,000

has been reflected in the Investment in Company S account on Company P's books: $705,000 = $650,000 + $55,000.

3. At December 31, Year 4, $12,000 of Company S's accounts receivable represent amounts payable by Company P.

4. During Year 4, Company S sold merchandise to Company P for $40,000. None of that merchandise remains in Company P's inventory as of December 31, Year 4.

Work Sheet Preparation

In preparing consolidated statements for Company P and Company S, the following steps, characteristic of the consolidation procedure, are illustrated.

A. Elimination of the parent company's investment account.

B. Elimination of intercompany receivables and payables.

C. Elimination of intercompany sales and purchases.

The preparation of consolidated statements illustrated here starts with single-company, preclosing trial balances. These data appear in the first two pairs of columns of the work sheet in Exhibit 13.2, which contain the same information as the first two columns of Exhibit 13.1. Note that the amounts shown for Retained Earnings are the balances as of January 1, Year 4. Revenue, expense, and dividend declaration accounts for Year 4 have not yet been closed to Retained Earnings. The fourth pair of columns in Exhibit 13.2 shows the amounts on a consolidated basis for Company P and Company S. The amounts in the last pair of columns horizontally sum the amounts in the other columns—Company P items, Company S items, as well as adjustments and eliminations. The adjustments and eliminations are discussed below. Keep in mind that these adjustments and eliminations are recorded only on a work sheet to prepare consolidated statements—not in the accounting records of either company.

A. Elimination of Parent Company's Investment Account Company P acquired the shares of Company S for a price equal to their book value ($650,000). Since acquisition, Company P has used the equity method and has recorded the increase in Retained Earnings of Company S ($55,000) in its investment account. To avoid double counting the net assets of Company S, the investment account must be eliminated. The elimination is as follows:

(1) Common Stock (Company S) 500,000	
Retained Earnings, January 1, Year 4 (Company S) 170,000	
Equity in Earnings of Company S (Company P) 48,000	
Dividends Declared (Company S)	13,000
Investment in Stock of Company S (Company P)	705,000

Aside from the minority interest, if any, the owners' equity of the consolidated entity is provided by the shareholders of the parent. There is no minority interest in

$$\text{Cost of Goods Sold} = \text{Beginning Inventory} + \text{Purchases} - \text{Ending Inventory}$$
$$= \quad \text{Goods Available for Sale} \quad - \text{Ending Inventory.}$$

Therefore, the offsetting credit to eliminate intercompany sales must be to the Cost of Goods Sold account.

---

(3) Sales	40,000	
Cost of Goods Sold		40,000
To eliminate intercompany sales and purchases.		

Company S sold goods to Company P and Company P sold the goods outside the consolidated pair of companies. In the absence of the elimination of intercompany sales, these sales would be counted twice. The profits on the sales would be computed properly, but the amount of gross sales and purchases (Cost of Goods Sold) would be inflated. To see that profits are computed properly, even without the elimination, assume that the goods cost Company S $30,000 and that Company P sold them for $45,000. In the single-company income statements, Company S profits are $10,000 (= $40,000 − $30,000) as a result of the sale to Company P. Company P profits are $5,000 (= $45,000 − $40,000) as a result of its sales to others. Total profits of the consolidated group from these transactions are $15,000, or Company P's revenue of $45,000 less Company S's cost of $30,000. The elimination of intercompany sales does not change the consolidated sales to outsiders or the consolidated cost of goods sold to outsiders.

If either company holds bonds or long-term notes of the other, then there would be a similar elimination of the "borrower's" interest expense and of the "lender's" interest revenue.

Statement Preparation

Once the consolidation work sheet has been completed, the consolidated statements can be prepared. Column (2) of Exhibit 13.3 presents a consolidated balance sheet on December 31, Year 4, and a consolidated income statement for Year 4 for Company P and Company S. As a basis for comparison, column (1) of Exhibit 13.3 repeats the balance sheet and income statement for Company P alone, assuming that Company S is *not* consolidated and the Investment in Stock of Company S is accounted for using the equity method. Note the following aspects of using the equity method for an unconsolidated subsidiary versus fully consolidating that subsidiary.

1. When a subsidiary is not consolidated, the parent's balance sheet will show the investment in the subsidiary's net assets in a single investment account. When the subsidiary is consolidated, the investment account is replaced with the individual assets and liabilities of the subsidiary.

2. *Consolidated* retained earnings are the same amount as those that result when the parent uses the equity method for an *unconsolidated* subsidiary.

Exhibit 13.3
Balance Sheet and Income Statement Assuming that
Company S Is Not Consolidated and that Company S Is Consolidated

	Company P Unconsolidated (Equity Method) (1)	Company P and Company S Consolidated (2)
Balance Sheet		
Assets:		
Accounts Receivable	$ 200,000	$ 213,000
Investment in Stock of S Company	705,000	—
Other Assets	2,150,000	3,125,000
Total Assets.	$3,055,000	$3,338,000
Equities:		
Accounts Payable	$ 75,000	$ 78,000
Other Liabilities	70,000	350,000
Common Stock	2,500,000	2,500,000
Retained Earnings	410,000	410,000
Total Equities	$3,055,000	$3,338,000
Income Statement		
Revenues:		
Sales.	$ 900,000	$1,110,000
Equity in Earnings of Company S	48,000	—
Total Revenues	$ 948,000	$1,110,000
Expenses:		
Cost of Goods Sold	$ 440,000	$ 480,000
Depreciation Expense	120,000	170,000
Administrative Expenses	80,000	120,000
Income Taxes	104,000	136,000
Total Expenses	$ 744,000	$ 906,000
Net Income	$ 204,000	$ 204,000

3. When a subsidiary is not consolidated, the parent's interest in the earnings of the subsidiary appears on the single line, Equity in Earnings of Company S, on the parent's income statement. When the subsidiary is consolidated, the individual revenues and expenses of the subsidiary replace the Equity in Earnings of S account.

4. *Consolidated* net income is the same amount as that which results when the parent uses the equity method for an *unconsolidated* subsidiary.

Consolidated Statement of Changes in Financial Position

The consolidated statement of changes in financial position is prepared from consolidated balance sheets for the beginning and end of the period, plus additional information from the consolidated income statement. Because the preparation of a consolidated statement of changes in financial position for Company P and Company S would involve no new concepts, it is not illustrated.

The illustration, now complete, for Company P and Company S is simpler than typical consolidation problems in several respects. More complex consolidation problems are discussed in Appendix 13.1.

Summary

Businesses acquire stock in other businesses for a variety of reasons and in a variety of ways. The acquisition of stock of another company as a long-term investment is generally recorded as follows:

Investment in S	X	
Cash or Other Consideration Given		X

The investment account is recorded at the amount of cash given or the market value of other consideration exchanged.

The accounting for the investment subsequent to acquisition depends on the ownership percentage. The lower-of-cost-or-market method is used when the parent owns less than 20 percent. The equity method is used when the parent owns at least 20 percent, but not more than 50 percent, of the stock of another company. Consolidated statements are generally prepared when the parent owns more than 50 percent of the voting shares of another company, but the equity method may be used. Exhibit 13.4 summarizes the accounting for investments subsequent to the acquisition.

Under the lower-of-cost-or-market method, income is recognized only when dividends become receivable by the investor or when the securities are sold.

Consolidated statements and the equity method both have the same effect on net income. The parent shows as income its proportional share of the acquired firm's periodic income after acquisition. Income statement amounts of revenues and expenses will be larger under the consolidation method, however, because the revenues and expenses of the acquired company are combined with those of the parent. Balance sheet components will be larger under the consolidation method than under the equity method, because the individual assets and liabilities of the acquired company will be substituted for the investment balance on the parent company's books.

Appendix 13.1: Some Complexities in Consolidation

The illustrations in Exhibits 13.1 and 13.2 were simplified. This appendix considers two situations encountered in consolidated statements not illustrated in this chapter. These are:

1. Acquisition price of subsidiary exceeds book value acquired.

Exhibit 13.4

Effects of Various Methods of Accounting for Long-Term Investments in Corporate Securities

Method of Accounting	Balance Sheet	Income Statement	Statement of Changes in Financial Position
Lower-of-cost-or-market method (generally when ownership percentage is less than 20 percent).	Investment account shown at lower of acquisition cost or current market value as a noncurrent asset. Unrealized losses resulting from decline in market value below cost are credited to an asset contra and debited to an unrealized loss account that is shown as a negative component of owners' equity.	Dividends declared by investee shown as revenue of investor. Gains and losses (from original cost) are reported in income only as realized in arm's-length transactions with outsiders.	Dividends received by investee included in cash provided by operations of investor.
Equity method (generally when ownership percentage is at least 20 percent but not more than 50 percent).	Investment account shown at cost plus share of investee's net income less share of investee's dividends since acquisition.	Equity in investee's net income shown as revenue in period that investee earns income.	Equity in investee's undistributed earnings is subtracted from net income to derive cash provided by operations of investor. Cash from operations is thus increased only by the amount of dividend received.
Consolidation (generally when ownership percentage is greater than 50 percent).	Investment account is eliminated and replaced with individual assets and liabilities of subsidiary. Minority interest in subsidiary's net assets shown among equities.	Individual revenues and expenses of subsidiary are combined with those of parent. Minority interest in subsidiary's net income shown as a subtraction.	Individual sources and uses of cash of subsidiary are combined with those of parent. Minority interest in net income is added to net income to obtain cash provided by operations.

2. Less than 100 percent of the subsidiary's stock is acquired, resulting in a minority interest.

Refer to the data in Exhibits 13.1 and 13.2, and to steps A–C listed on page 587.

Acquisition Price Exceeds Book Value Acquired

Suppose that Company P had paid $700,000, rather than $650,000, for its 100 percent investment in Company S. The $50,000 difference in purchase price represents the amount paid for Company S's assets in excess of their book value, for goodwill, or for both. Assume that on the date of acquisition, January 1, Year 1, the book value of Company S's recorded assets and liabilities equaled their market values at that time. The fact that Company P was willing to pay $700,000 for recorded assets having book values and market values equal to $650,000 means that Company S must have had *unrecorded* assets of $50,000 on January 1, Year 1. The $50,000 of unrecorded assets represents goodwill. Generally accepted accounting principles[9] require that goodwill be amortized over a period not exceeding 40 years.

---

[9]Accounting Principles Board, *Opinion No. 17.*

Assume that Company P chose a 40-year amortization period. On its separate company books, Company P would have made the following entry during each of the Years 1 through 4:

Amortization Expense	1,250	
Investment in Stock of Company S		1,250
To recognize amortization of goodwill; $1,250 = ($700,000 − $650,000)/40.		

In preparing the consolidation work sheet at the end of Year 4, entry (1) would be the same as that shown in Exhibit 13.2. After entry (1), the Investment in Stock of Company S would still have a debit balance of $45,000 [= $50,000 − (4 × $1,250)]. This amount represents the *unamortized* goodwill arising from the acquisition. A work sheet entry should be made to reclassify this amount from the investment account to goodwill. The entry is

Goodwill	45,000	
Investment in Stock of Company S		45,000
To reclassify goodwill.		

The consolidated balance sheet on December 31, Year 4, will show goodwill of $45,000 [= $50,000 − (4 × $1,250)]. Consolidated net income for Year 4 will now be $202,750 (= $204,000 − $1,250) to reflect amortization expense for Year 4. Consolidated retained earnings will be $405,000 [= $410,000 − (4 × $1,250)]. The statement of changes in financial position will show an addback of $1,250 for amortization expense that did not use cash.

Recognizing External, Minority Interest

Now assume that Company P had acquired only 90 percent of the capital stock of Company S on January 1, Year 1, at its book value. In this case, other individuals or entities own the remaining 10 percent of the shares. These individuals or entities represent an external minority interest in the earnings and net assets of Company S.

The net assets, or shareholders' equity, of Company S is allocable to Company P and to the minority shareholders as shown in Exhibit 13.5. Assuming that Company P has acquired its 90 percent interest in Company S for book value, it would have paid $585,000 (= .90 × $650,000) on January 1, Year 1. The Investment in Stock of Company S account would have been recorded initially at this amount on Company P's books. Between Year 1 and Year 4, Company P would have increased the investment account for 90 percent of Company S's earnings and decreased the investment account for 90 percent of Company S's dividends. Thus, the Investment in Stock of Company S account would show a balance of $634,500 on December

Exhibit 13.5
Allocation of Shareholders' Equity of Company S
to Company P and Minority Interest Shareholders

	Total (1)	To Company P (90 percent) (2)	To Minority Shareholders (10 percent) (3)
January 1, Year 1: Common Stock . . .	$500,000	$450,000	$50,000
Retained Earnings . .	150,000	135,000	15,000
Increase in Retained Earnings, January 1, Year 1–December 31, Year 3	20,000	18,000	2,000
Subtotal	$670,000	$603,000	$67,000
Net Income for Year 4	48,000	43,200	4,800
Dividends Declared for Year 4	(13,000)	(11,700)	(1,300)
December 31, Year 4	$705,000	$634,500	$70,500

31, Year 4 [see column (2) of Exhibit 13.5]. The work sheet elimination entry for the investment account would be as follows:

Common Stock (Company S)	450,000	
Retained Earnings, January 1 (Company S)	153,000	
Equity in Earnings of Company S (Company P)	43,200	
Dividends Declared (Company S)		11,700
Investment in Stock of Company S (Company P)		634,500

The remaining balances in Company S's shareholders' equity accounts are the minority interest. The work sheet entry to recognize the minority interest is

Common Stock (Company S)	50,000	
Retained Earnings (Company S)	17,000	
Minority Interest in Earnings of Company S	4,800	
Dividends Declared (Company S)		1,300
Minority Interest in Net Assets of Company S		70,500

The account, Minority Interest in Earnings of Company S, is "created" on the consolidation work sheet. It does not appear as an account on either of the separate-company books. It represents the external minority interest in the earnings of Company S and is shown as a deduction in calculating consolidated net income. Consolidated net income is, therefore, $199,200 (= $204,000 − $4,800).

The account Minority Interest in Net Assets of Company S is, likewise, created on the consolidation work sheet. It represents the external minority interest in the net assets of Company S, a *consolidated* subsidiary. It is shown on the right-hand side of the consolidated balance sheet, usually between liabilities and shareholders' equity.

The consolidated statement of changes in financial position starts with the net income of $199,200 to shareholders of Company P. Amounts are added back for the minority interest in S's undistributed earnings for the year of $3,500 (= $4,800 − $1,300) and for depreciation ($170,000), neither of which uses cash. The only use of cash is the $50,000 of dividends paid by the parent. Parts **f** through **i** of the Problem for Self-Study review the material in this appendix.

Appendix 13.2:
Accounting for Corporate Acquisitions

When one corporation acquires all, or substantially all, of another corporation's common stock in a single transaction, the transaction is referred to as a corporate acquisition. Two methods of accounting for corporate acquisitions are permitted under generally accepted accounting principles, depending on the manner in which the acquisition is structured: (1) the purchase method and (2) the pooling-of-interests method.

Purchase Method

The purchase method uses acquisition cost accounting. The Investment in Subsidiary account on the parent's books is recorded initially at the amount of cash or market value of other consideration given in the exchange. When the consolidation work sheet is prepared, any difference between the amount in the investment account on the date of acquisition and the book value of the net assets acquired is allocated to individual assets and liabilities to write them up or down to their market values. Any excess of the purchase price over the market values of the individual assets and liabilities is then allocated to goodwill. Thus, under the purchase method, the assets and liabilities of the acquired company are reported in the consolidated balance sheet at the date of acquisition at their market values. The consolidated income statement in subsequent periods will show expenses (depreciation and amortization) based on these market values. The principles of the purchase method have implicitly been used throughout this chapter.

Pooling-of-Interests Method

The pooling-of-interests method accounts for a corporate acquisition as the uniting of ownership interests of two companies by exchange of equity (common stock) securities. The exchange of equity interests is viewed as a change in *form,* not in *substance.* That is, the shareholders of the predecessor companies become shareholders in the new combined enterprise. Each of the predecessor companies continues carrying out its operations as before. Because there is no change in the substance of either the ownership interest or the nature of the activities of the enterprises involved, no new basis of accountability arises. That is, the book values of the assets and liabilities of the predecessor companies are carried over to the new combined, or consolidated, enterprise. Unlike the purchase method, assets and liabilities do not reflect market values at the date of acquisition on the consolidated balance sheet.

Illustration of Purchase and Pooling-of-Interests Methods

To illustrate the purchase and pooling-of-interests methods, assume that Company P and Company S decide to combine operations. Management estimates that the combination will save $50,000 a year in expenses of running the combined businesses. Columns (1) and (2) in Exhibit 13.6 show abbreviated single-company financial statements for Company P and Company S before combination. Company S has 20,000 shares of stock outstanding that sell for $84 per share in the market. The market value of Company S as a going concern is, therefore, $1,680,000. As shown in column (3), S's shareholders have $1,230,000 of equity not recorded on the books. Of this $1,230,000, $400,000 is attributable to undervalued noncurrent assets, and $830,000 is attributable to goodwill. Company P has 100,000 shares outstanding, which have a $5 par value and sell for $42 each in the market. Income taxes are ignored.

Purchase Method To carry out the acquisition, P issues (sells) 40,000 additional shares on the market for $42 each, or $1,680,000 in total, and uses the proceeds to purchase all shares of S for $84 each. (Each share of S is, in effect, "sold" for two shares of P.) P has acquired 100 percent of the shares of S and now owns S.

P's acquisition of S will be accounted for using the purchase method. Under these conditions, P will amortize the revalued asset costs over 5 years and the goodwill over 40 years. Consolidated financial reports under the purchase method are shown in column (4). The consolidated balance sheet is the sum of columns (1) and (3) except for the shareholders' equity section. Since P issued 40,000 new shares for $42 each, the Common Stock account shows 140,000 shares at $5 par value. The Additional Paid-in Capital account shows P's former Additional Paid-in Capital plus the addition arising from the new stock issue: $200,000 + [40,000 × ($42 − $5)] = $1,680,000. The retained earnings of the consolidated enterprise are equal to P's retained earnings.

The consolidated income statement, when the acquisition is treated as a purchase, starts with the combined incomes before consolidation. To that amount is added the cost savings of $50,000 resulting from the more efficient operations of the combination. Then both the additional depreciation expense arising from the asset revaluations and the goodwill amortization expense are subtracted. The reported consolidated net income, as projected, is $409,250.

Pooling of Interests Now, examine the accounting for the acquisition, as shown in column (5), assuming that it qualifies for the pooling-of-interests method. Assume that P issued the 40,000 shares of stock directly to the owners of S in return for their shares. The balance sheet items, except for the individual shareholders' equity accounts, are merely the sum of the single-company amounts shown in columns (1)

Exhibit 13.6
Consolidated Statements Comparing Purchase and Pooling-of-Interests Methods

	Historical Cost P (1)	S (2)	S Shown at Current Values (3)	Companies P & S Consolidated at Date of Acquisition Purchase (4)	Pooling of Interests (5)
Balance Sheets					
Assets					
Current Assets	$1,500,000	$450,000	$ 450,000	$1,950,000	$1,950,000
Long-Term Assets Less Accumulated Depreciation	1,700,000	450,000	850,000	2,550,000	2,150,000
Goodwill.	—	—	830,000	830,000	—
Total Assets	$3,200,000	$900,000	$2,130,000	$5,330,000	$4,100,000
Equities					
Liabilities	$1,300,000	$450,000	$ 450,000	$1,750,000	$1,750,000
Common Stock ($5 par).	500,000	100,000	100,000	700,000[a]	700,000[a]
Additional Paid-in Capital	200,000	150,000	150,000	1,680,000[b]	250,000[e]
Retained Earnings	1,200,000	200,000	200,000	1,200,000[c]	1,400,000[d]
Unrecorded Equity at Current Valuation	—	—	1,230,000	—	—
Total Liabilities and Shareholders' Equity	$3,200,000	$900,000	$2,130,000	$5,330,000	$4,100,000
Income Statements (ignoring income taxes)[h]					
Precombination Income	$ 300,000	$160,000		$ 460,000	$ 460,000
From Combination:					
Cost Savings (projected)	—	—		50,000	50,000
Extra Depreciation Expense	—	—		(80,000)[f]	—
Amortization of Goodwill	—	—		(20,750)[g]	—
Net Income	$ 300,000	$160,000		$ 409,250[h]	$ 510,000[h]
Number of Common Shares Outstanding . . .	100,000	20,000		140,000	140,000
Earnings per Share.	$3.00	$8.00		$2.92	$3.64

Assumptions: (1) Company S has 20,000 shares outstanding that sell for $84 each in the market.
           (2) Company P's shares sell for $42 each in the market. Company P issues 40,000 shares for the purpose of acquiring Company S.

[a]P's 100,000 original shares plus 40,000 new shares at $5 par.
[b]P's $200,000 original additional paid-in capital plus 40,000 × ($42 − $5).
[c]P's retained earnings.
[d]Sum of P's and S's retained earnings.
[e]Plug to equate pooled shareholders' equity to the sum of all the shareholders' equity accounts of the combining companies before combination.
[f]1/5 × ($850,000 − $450,000).
[g]1/40 × $830,000.
[h]As projected.

and (2). The shareholders' equity after pooling must then equal total shareholders' equity before pooling.

The common stock of the pooled enterprise must, of course, equal the par value of the shares outstanding after pooling. After pooling there are 140,000 shares outstanding with a par value of $700,000. The general rule is that the pooled retained earnings balance is the sum of the retained earnings before pooling. The example illustrates the general rule. The total paid-in capital (par value plus additional paid-in capital) after pooling will generally equal the sum of the paid-in capital accounts of the firms before pooling. Thus, the additional paid-in capital of the pooled firm is, ordinarily, the plug to equate the pooled paid-in capital with the sum of the paid-in capital accounts before pooling.

The income statement resulting from a pooling of interests shows the same revenues and cost savings as those following a purchase. There are, however, no extra depreciation and amortization expenses resulting from increased asset valuations and the recognition of goodwill. Consequently, the pooled enterprise projects net income of $510,000 and shareholders' equity of $2,350,000 (a rate of return on shareholders' equity of 22 percent), whereas the identical acquisition accounted for using the purchase method projects smaller income, $409,250, and larger shareholders' equity of $3,580,000 (a rate of return on shareholders' equity of 11 percent). Notice that the earnings-per-share figure—one often scrutinized by financial analysts—under the pooling-of-interests method is 25 percent larger than under the purchase method.

This example, if anything, understates the difference between the purchase and pooling methods. Notice that S's market value before the merger is less than four times ($1,680,000/$450,000 = 3.7) its book value. In practice, poolings of interests have occurred when the ratio of market value to book value was as high as 10 or more to one. Thus, the amortization charges of the "purchased" subsidiary's assets can be many times larger than the amortization of the "pooled" subsidiary's assets.

Managing Earnings

Pooling of interests not only keeps reported expenses from increasing after the merger, it may also allow management of the pooled companies to manage the reported earnings in an arbitrary way. Suppose, as has happened, that Company P merges with an old, established firm, Company F, which has produced commercial movie films. These films were made in the 1940s and 1950s and were amortized so that by the early 1980s the book value of these films is close to zero. But the market value of the films is much larger than zero, because television stations and cable networks find that old movies please their audiences. If Company P purchases Company F, then the old films will be shown on the consolidated balance sheet at the films' current market value. If Company P merges with Company F using the pooling-of-interests method, the films will be shown on the consolidated balance sheet at their near-zero book values. Then, when Company P wants to boost reported earnings for the year, it can sell some old movies to a television or cable network, and report a large gain. Actually, of course, the owners of Company F enjoyed this gain when their stock was "sold to" (or exchanged with) Company P for current asset values, not the obsolete book values.

Those who defend pooling-of-interests accounting argue that the management of the pooled enterprise has no more opportunity to manage earnings than did the management of Company F before the pooling. Management of Company F can sell old movies any time it chooses and then report handsome gains. The problem is caused by the historical cost basis of accounting, which recognizes gains only when there has been a market transaction. Defenders of pooling argue that there is no reason to penalize the management of a merged company relative to the management of an established company with many assets undervalued on its books. Opponents of pooling reply that it was the management of Company F that earned the holding gains, whereas the management of Company P will be able to report them as realized gains under pooling.

In summary, if the acquisition qualifies as a purchase, then the reported income of the combined enterprise may be reduced by additional depreciation and amortization expenses. The extra depreciation and amortization expenses result from recognizing increased asset valuations and, perhaps, goodwill. If the acquisition qualifies as a pooling of interests, reported income for the consolidated enterprise will ordinarily be larger than for the same consolidated enterprise accounted for as a purchase.

Problem for Self-Study

Reynolds Corporation acquired shares of common stock of Company R, Company S, and Company T on January 2, as long-term investments. These are the only long-term investments in securities of Reynolds Corporation. Data relating to the acquisitions are shown below.

Company	Percentage Acquired	Book Value and Market Value of Total Net Assets on January 2	Acquisition Cost	Net Income for Year	Dividends Declared for Year	Market Value of Shares Owned on December 31
R	10%	$5,000,000	$ 540,000	$1,000,000	$400,000	$ 520,000
S	30	5,000,000	1,700,000	1,000,000	400,000	1,710,000
T	100	5,000,000	5,000,000	1,000,000	400,000	5,200,000

Any goodwill arising from the acquisitions is amortized over 10 years.

a. Give the journal entries made to acquire the shares of Company R and to account for the investment during the year, using the lower-of-cost-or-market method.

b. Give the journal entries made to acquire the shares of Company S and to account for the investment during the year, using the equity method.

c. Give the journal entries made to acquire the shares of Company T and to account for the investment during the year, using the equity method.

d. Give the consolidation work sheet entry to eliminate the Investment in Stock of Company T account at the end of the year, assuming that the equity method is used and that the work sheet is based on preclosing trial balance amounts. Company T had $2,000,000 in its Common Stock account throughout the year and a zero balance in Additional Paid-in Capital.

e. Repeat part **d**, but assume that the work sheet is based on post-closing trial balance amounts.

Parts **f** through **i** should not be worked until Appendix 13.1 has been read.

f. Assume that the shares of Company T had been acquired for $5,500,000, instead of $5,000,000. Give the journal entries made during the year to acquire the shares of Company T and to account for the investment, using the equity method. Any excess of cost over book value is considered goodwill and is amortized over 10 years.

g. Refer to Part **f**. Give the consolidation work sheet entry to eliminate the Investment in Stock of Company T account, assuming the work sheet is based on preclosing trial balance data.

h. Assume that Reynolds Corporation had paid $4,000,000 for 80 percent of the shares of Company T on January 2. Give the journal entries made during the year to acquire the shares of Company T and to account for the investment, using the equity method.

i. Refer to Part **h**. Give the consolidation work sheet entries to eliminate the Investment in Stock of Company T account and to recognize the external minority interest in Company T, assuming the work sheet is based on preclosing trial balance data.

Suggested Solution

a. Investment in Stock of Company R 540,000
  Cash 540,000
  To record acquisition of shares of Company R.

Cash and Dividends Receivable 40,000
  Dividend Revenue 40,000
  To record dividends received or receivable.

Unrealized Holding Loss on Valuation of Marketable Equity
  Investments 20,000
    Allowance for Excess of Cost of Investments over
      Market Value 20,000
  To write down portfolio (Company R only) of minority, passive investments to market value; $20,000 = $540,000 − $520,000.

b. Investment in Stock of Company S 1,700,000
  Cash 1,700,000
  To record acquisition of shares of Company S.

Investment in Stock of Company S 300,000
  Equity in Earnings of Company S 300,000
  To accrue share of Company S's earnings, $300,000 = .30 × $1,000,000.

| Cash and Dividends Receivable . . . . | 120,000 | |
| Investment in Stock of Company S . . . . | | 120,000 |

To record dividends received or receivable.

| Amortization Expense . . . . | 20,000 | |
| Investment in Stock of Company S . . . . | | 20,000 |

To record amortization of goodwill implicit in purchase price, $20,000 = ($1,700,000 - $1,500,000)/10.

---

c.
| Investment in Stock of Company T. . . . . | 5,000,000 | |
| Cash . . . . | | 5,000,000 |

To record acquisition of shares of Company T.

| Investment in Stock of Company T. . . . . | 1,000,000 | |
| Equity in Earnings of Company T . . . . | | 1,000,000 |

To accrue earnings of Company T; $1,000,000 = 100% × $1,000,000.

| Cash and Dividends Receivable . . . . | 400,000 | |
| Investment in Stock of Company T. . . . . | | 400,000 |

To record dividends received or receivable.

---

d.
Common Stock	2,000,000	
Retained Earnings (January 2)	3,000,000	
Equity in Earnings of Company T	1,000,000	
Dividends Declared.		400,000
Investment in Stock of Company T.		5,600,000

To eliminate investment account on consolidation work sheet.

---

e.
Common Stock	2,000,000	
Retained Earnings (December 31)	3,600,000	
Investment in Stock of Company T.		5,600,000

To eliminate investment account on consolidation work sheet.

---

f.
| Investment in Stock of Company T. . . . . | 5,500,000 | |
| Cash . . . . | | 5,500,000 |

To record acquisition of shares of Company T.

| Investment in Stock of Company T. . . . . | 1,000,000 | |
| Equity in Earnings of Company T . . . . | | 1,000,000 |

To accrue earnings of Company T.

| Cash and Dividends Receivable . . . . | 400,000 | |
| Investment in Stock of Company T. . . . . | | 400,000 |

To record dividends received or receivable.

| Amortization Expense . . . . | 50,000 | |
| Investment in Stock of Company T. . . . . | | 50,000 |

To record amortization of goodwill implicit in purchase price; $50,000 = ($5,500,000 - $5,000,000)/10.

g. Common Stock 2,000,000
Retained Earnings 3,000,000
Equity in Earnings of Company T 1,000,000
Goodwill 450,000
   Dividends Declared. 400,000
   Investment in Stock of Company T. 6,050,000
To eliminate investment account on consolidation work sheet;
$6,050,000 = $5,500,000 + $1,000,000 − $400,000 − $50,000.

h. Investment in Stock of Company T. 4,000,000
   Cash 4,000,000
To record acquisition of shares of Company T.

Investment in Stock of Company T. 800,000
   Equity in Earnings of Company T 800,000
To accrue share of Company T's earnings; $800,000 = .80 ×
$1,000,000.

Cash and Dividends Receivable 320,000
   Investment in Stock of Company T. 320,000
To record dividends received or receivable; $320,000 = .80 ×
$400,000.

i. Common Stock 1,600,000
Retained Earnings 2,400,000
Equity in Earnings of Company T 800,000
   Dividends Declared. 320,000
   Investment in Stock of Company T. 4,480,000
To eliminate investment account on consolidation work sheet;
$4,480,000 = $4,000,000 + $800,000 − $320,000.

Common Stock 400,000
Retained Earnings 600,000
Minority Interest in Earnings of Company T 200,000
   Dividends Declared. 80,000
   Minority Interest in Net Assets of Company T 1,120,000
To recognize external minority interest in Company T.

Questions, Exercises, Problems and Cases

Questions

1. Review the meaning of the following concepts or terms discussed in this chapter.

   a. Marketable securities classified as current assets or as long-term investments.
   b. Minority, passive investments.
   c. Minority, active investments.
   d. Majority, active investments.
   e. Lower-of-cost-or-market method for long-term investments.

   f. Significant influence by an investor over an investee.
   g. Equity method.
   h. Parent.
   i. Subsidiary.
   j. Consolidated financial statements.
   k. Consolidation policy.

l. Economic entity versus legal entity.	**n.** Intercompany transactions.
m. Adjustments and eliminations in a consolidation work sheet.	**o.** Minority interest in a consolidated subsidiary.
	p. Goodwill.

2. Unrealized holding losses from price declines of marketable equity securities classified as current assets are recognized as they arise in calculating net income. Similar unrealized holding losses from long-term investments accounted for using the lower-of-cost-or-market method are not recognized as they arise in calculating net income. What is the rationale for this difference in accounting treatment?

3. Compare and contrast each of the following pairs of accounts.
  a. Unrealized Holding Loss on Valuation of Marketable Equity Securities, and Unrealized Holding Loss on Valuation of Marketable Equity Investments.
  b. Allowance for Excess of Cost of Marketable Securities over Market Value, and Allowance for Excess of Cost of Investments over Market Value.
  c. Dividend Revenue, and Equity in Earnings of Unconsolidated Affiliates.
  d. Equity in Earnings of Unconsolidated Affiliate, and Minority Interest in Earnings of Consolidated Subsidiary.
  e. Minority Interest in Earnings of Consolidated Subsidiary, and Minority Interest in Net Assets of Consolidated Subsidiary.

4. "Dividends received or receivable from another company may be either an item of revenue in calculating net income or a return of investment, depending on the method of accounting used." Explain.

5. Why is the equity method sometimes called a *one-line consolidation*? Consider both the balance sheet and the income statement in your response.

6. Distinguish between minority investments in other companies and the minority interest in a consolidated subsidiary.

7. "Net income will be the same independent of whether an investment in a subsidiary is accounted for using the equity method and not consolidated or whether the subsidiary is consolidated. Total assets will be different, however, depending on whether or not the subsidiary is consolidated." Explain.

Exercises

8. *Amount of income recognized under various methods of accounting for investments.* On January 1, Buyer Company acquired common stock of X Company. At the time of acquisition, the book value and fair market value of X Company's net assets were $200,000. During the year, X Company earned $50,000 and declared dividends of $40,000. How much income would Buyer Company report for the year from its investment under the assumption that Buyer Company:
  a. Paid $30,000 for 15 percent of the common stock and uses the lower-of-cost-or-market method for its investment in X Company?
  b. Paid $40,000 for 15 percent of the common stock and uses the lower-of-cost-or-market method for its investment in X Company?
  c. Paid $60,000 for 30 percent of the common stock and uses the equity method to account for its investment in X Company?

d. Paid $80,000 for 30 percent of the common stock and uses the equity method to account for its investment in X Company? Give the maximum income that Buyer Company can report from the investment.

9. *Balance sheet and income effects of alternative methods of accounting for investments.* On January 1, P acquired common stock of S. At the time of acquisition, the book value and market value of S's net assets were $400,000. During the current year, S earned $80,000 and declared dividends of $50,000. Indicate the amount shown for Investment in S on the balance sheet on December 31 and the amount of income P would report for the year from its investment under the assumption that P:

a. Paid $40,000 for a 10 percent interest in S and uses the lower-of-cost-or-market method. The market value of S on December 31 was $400,000.

b. Same as part **a**, except that the market value of S on December 31 was $390,000.

c. Paid $45,000 for a 10 percent interest in S and uses the lower-of-cost-or-market method. The market value of S on December 31 was $450,000.

d. Paid $160,000 for a 40 percent interest in S and uses the equity method.

e. Paid $180,000 for a 40 percent interest in S and uses the equity method. Goodwill is amortized over 40 years.

10. *Journal entries under various methods of accounting for investments.* Johnson Corporation made three long-term intercorporate investments on January 2. Data relating to these investments for the year are as follows:

Company	Percentage Acquired	Book Value and Market Value of Net Assets on January 2	Acquisition Cost	Net Income for the Year	Dividends Declared During the Year
X	20%	$2,000,000	$ 400,000	$200,000	$ 80,000
Y	25	3,000,000	800,000	300,000	120,000
Z	30	4,000,000	1,300,000	400,000	160,000

Give the journal entries to record the acquisition of these investments and to apply the equity method during the year. Goodwill is amortized over 20 years.

11. *Journal entries under various methods of accounting for investments.* Maddox Corporation made three long-term intercorporate investments on January 2. Data relating to these investments are as follows:

Company	Percentage Acquired	Book Value and Market Value of Net Assets on January 2	Acquisition Cost	Net Income for Year	Dividends Declared During the Year	Market Value of Shares Held on December 31
A.	10%	$1,800,000	$ 200,000	$100,000	$40,000	$ 180,000
B.	25	1,800,000	500,000	100,000	40,000	510,000
C	60	1,800,000	1,400,000	100,000	40,000	1,431,000

Assume that these were the only three intercorporate investments of Maddox Corporation. Goodwill is amortized over 40 years.

a. Give the journal entries on Maddox Corporation's books to record these acquisitions of common stock and to account for the intercorporate investments under generally accepted accounting principles. The investment in Company C is not consolidated. Be sure to include any required year-end adjusting entries.

b. Assuming that the financial statements of Company C are consolidated with those of Maddox Corporation, that the investment in Company C is accounted for using the equity method, and that the consolidation work sheet is based on preclosing trial balance data, give the work sheet entry to eliminate the Investment in Stock of Company C account on December 31. The Common Stock account of Company C has a balance of $1,000,000, and Additional Paid-in Capital has a zero balance.

c. Refer to Part b. Give the consolidation work sheet entry to recognize the minority interest in Company C on December 31.

12. *Consolidation policy and principal consolidation concepts.* The CAR Corporation manufactures computers in the United States. It owns 75 percent of the voting stock of Charles of Canada, 80 percent of the voting stock of Alexandre de France (in France), and 90 percent of the voting stock of R Credit Corporation (a finance company). The CAR Corporation prepares consolidated financial statements consolidating Charles of Canada, using the equity method for R Credit Corporation, and using the lower-of-cost-or-market method for its investment in Alexandre de France. Data from the annual reports of these companies are given below.

	Percentage Owned	Net Income	Dividends	Accounting Method
CAR Corporation Consolidated	—	$1,000,000	$ 70,000	—
Charles of Canada	75%	100,000	40,000	Consolidated
Alexandre de France[a]	80	80,000	50,000	Lower of Cost or Market
R Credit Corporation	90	120,000	100,000	Equity

[a]Market value of shares exceeds cost.

a. Which, if any, of the companies is incorrectly accounted for by CAR according to generally accepted accounting principles?

Assuming the accounting for the three subsidiaries shown above to be correct, answer the following questions.

b. How much of the net income reported by CAR Corporation Consolidated is attributable to the operations of the three subsidiaries?

c. What is the amount of the minority interest now shown on the income statement, and how does it affect net income of CAR Corporation Consolidated?

d. If all three subsidiaries had been consolidated, what would have been the net income of CAR Corporation Consolidated?

e. If all three subsidiaries had been consolidated, what would be the minority interest shown on the income statement?

13. *Equity method and consolidation elimination entries.* The Hart Company acquired control of the Keller Company on January 2 by purchasing 80 percent of its outstanding stock for $700,000. The entire excess of cost over book value acquired is attributed to goodwill, which is amortized over 40 years. The shareholders' equity accounts of the Keller Company appeared as follows on January 2 and December 31 of the current year.

	Jan. 2	Dec. 31
Common Stock	$600,000	$600,000
Retained Earnings	200,000	420,000

Keller Company had earnings of $250,000 and declared dividends of $30,000 during the year. The accounts receivable of the Hart Company at December 31 include $4,500 that is due it from the Keller Company. Hart Company accounts for its investment in Keller Company on its single-company books using the equity method.

a. Give the journal entries to record the acquisition of the shares of Keller Company and to apply the equity method during the year on the books of Hart Company.

b. Give the required elimination entries for a consolidation work sheet at the end of the year, assuming that the work sheet is based on preclosing trial balance data.

14. *Equity method and consolidation elimination entries.* The Roe Company purchased 80 percent of the common stock of Danver Company on January 2 at book value, $480,000. The total common stock of Danver Company at this date was $450,000, and the retained earnings balance was $150,000. During the year, net income of the Danver Company was $90,000; dividends declared were $36,000. The Roe Company uses the equity method to account for the investment.

a. Give the journal entry made by Roe Company during the year to account for its investment in Danver Company.

b. Give the elimination entry for the investment account, assuming that the consolidation work sheet is based on preclosing trial balance data.

15. *Equity method and consolidation work sheet entries.* The Little Company is a subsidiary of the Butler Company and is accounted for using the equity method on the single-company books of the Butler Company.

a. Present journal entries for the following selected transactions. Record the set of entries on the books of the Little Company separately from the set of entries on the books of the Butler Company.

(1) On January 2, the Butler Company acquired on the market, for cash, 80 percent of all the common stock of the Little Company. The outlay was $325,000. The total contributed capital of the stock outstanding was

$300,000; the retained earnings balance was $80,000. The excess of cost over book value acquired is all attributed to goodwill and is amortized over 10 years.

(2) The Little Company purchased materials from the Butler Company on account at the latter's cost, $23,000.

(3) The Little Company obtained an advance of $9,000 from the Butler Company. The funds were deposited in the bank.

(4) The Little Company paid $19,000 on the purchases in (2).

(5) The Little Company repaid $7,500 of the loan received from the Butler Company in (3).

(6) The Little Company declared and paid a dividend of $24,000 during the year.

(7) The net income of the Little Company for the year was $40,000.

   b. Prepare the adjustment and elimination entries which would be necessary in the preparation of the December 31 consolidated balance sheet, recognizing the effects of only the above transactions. Assume that the work sheet is based on preclosing financial statement data.

16. *Intercompany inventory transactions between consolidated entities.* Company P owns 70 percent of a consolidated subsidiary, Company S. During the year, Company P's sales to Company S amounted to $50,000. The cost of those sales was $35,000. The following data are taken from the two companies' income statements:

	Company P	Company S
Sales	$120,000	$250,000
Cost of Goods Sold	70,000	150,000

   a. Compute consolidated sales and consolidated cost of goods sold for the year, assuming that Company S sold all the goods purchased from Company P.

   b. Compare the consolidated sales, cost of goods sold, and gross margin on sales to the sum of the sales, cost of goods sold, and gross margins of the separate companies.

17. *Working backwards to consolidation relationships.* A parent company owns shares in one other company. It has owned them since the other company was formed. The parent company has retained earnings from its own operations independent of intercorporate investments of $100,000. The consolidated balance sheet shows no goodwill and retained earnings of $160,000. Consider each of the following questions independently of the others.

   a. If the parent owns 80 percent of its consolidated subsidiary, what are the retained earnings of the subsidiary?

   b. If the subsidiary has retained earnings of $96,000, what fraction of the subsidiary does the parent own?

   c. If the subsidiary had not been consolidated but instead had been accounted for by the equity method, how much revenue in excess of dividends received would the parent have recognized over the life of the investment?

18. *Working backwards from consolidated income statements.* Sealco Enterprises published the consolidated income statement for the year that is shown in Exhibit 13.7. The unconsolidated affiliate retained 20 percent of its earnings of $100,000 during the year, having paid out the rest as dividends. The consolidated subsidiary earned $200,000 during the year and declared no dividends.

Exhibit 13.7
SEALCO ENTERPRISES
Consolidated Income Statement
(Problem 18)

Revenues:		
Sales		$1,000,000
Equity in Earnings of Unconsolidated Affiliate.		40,000
Total Revenues		$1,040,000
Expenses:		
Cost of Goods Sold (excluding depreciation)		$ 650,000
Administrative Expenses		100,000
Depreciation Expense		115,000
Amortization of Goodwill		5,000
Income Tax Expenses:		
Currently Payable	$42,000	
Deferred	10,000	52,000
Total Expenses		$ 922,000
Income of the Consolidated Group		$ 118,000
Less Minority Interest in Earnings of Consolidated		
Subsidiary		30,000
Net Income to Shareholders		$ 88,000

a. What percentage of the unconsolidated affiliate does Sealco Enterprises own?

b. What dividends did Sealco Enterprises receive from the unconsolidated affiliate during the year?

c. What percentage of the consolidated subsidiary does Sealco Enterprises own?

19. *Working backwards from the statement of changes in financial position.* Lesala Corporation purchased most of the common stock of its subsidiary in Year 1. The subsidiary earned $1 million in Year 3 but declared no dividends. Exhibit 13.8 is an excerpt from Lesala Corporation's financial statements issued for Year 3.

a. What percentage of the consolidated subsidiary does Lesala Corporation own?

b. Goodwill arising from the acquisition of the consolidated subsidiary is being amortized, using the straight-line method, to show the minimum charges allowed by generally accepted accounting principles. What was the excess of the subsidiary's market value as a going concern over the market value of the actual assets shown on its books as of the date of acquisition? Assume that the acquisition occurred on January 1, Year 1.

Exhibit 13.8
LESALA CORPORATION
Consolidated Statement of
Changes in Financial Position
for the Year 3

Sources of Cash:		
Consolidated Net Income.		$3,000,000
Additions:		
Depreciation of Plant.	$150,000	
Amortization of Goodwill Arising from Acquisition of Consolidated Subsidiary	10,000	
Minority Interest in Earnings of Consolidated Subsidiary	200,000	
Increases in Current Liabilities	75,000	
Subtractions:		
Increases in Current Assets Other than Cash.	(90,000)	345,000
Cash Provided by Operations		$3,345,000

20. *Effect of transactions on the statement of changes in financial position.* Refer to the Simplified Statement of Changes in Financial Position for a Period in Exhibit 5.17 on page 201. Eleven of the lines in the statement are numbered. Ignore the unnumbered lines in responding to the questions below.

Assume that the accounting cycle is complete for the period and that all of the financial statements have been prepared. Then it is discovered that a transaction has been overlooked. The transaction is recorded in the accounts, and all of the financial statements are corrected. Define *funds* as *cash*. For each of the following transactions or events, indicate which of the numbered lines of the statement of changes in financial position is affected and by how much. Ignore income tax effects.

    a. A 100 percent-owned affiliate accounted for on the equity method earns $10,000 and pays dividends of $4,000.

    b. A 100 percent-owned affiliate accounted for on the equity method reports a loss for the year of $5,000.

    c. Minority interest in income of a consolidated subsidiary is recognized in the amount of $20,000.

    d. Minority interest in the losses of a consolidated subsidiary is recognized in the amount of $8,000.

    e. A 100 percent-owned consolidated subsidiary sold merchandise to the parent company for $10,000. The subsidiary's cost of the goods sold was $6,000. The parent sold the merchandise for $12,000. An elimination of the intercompany transactions is made.

    f. The *investment* in the portfolio of equity securities accounted for with the lower-of-cost-or-market method is written down from $10,000 to $8,000.

    g. A dividend of $7,000 is received on shares held as an *investment* and accounted for with the lower-of-cost-or-market method.

    h. The market value of the portfolio of equity securities accounted for as *current assets* (Marketable Securities) is $5,000 less than the net amount shown for the same portfolio on the balance sheet at the end of the previous accounting period. The amount in the allowance contra to the Marketable Securities account is changed.

   i. The market value of the portfolio of marketable equity securities in part **h** increases $3,000 by the end of the next accounting period. The amount in the allowance contra to the Marketable Securities account is changed.

21. *Effect of errors on financial statements.* Using the notation O/S (overstated), U/S (understated), or No (no effect), indicate the effects on assets, liabilities, and net income of each of the independent errors below. Ignore income tax effects.

   a. In applying the lower-of-cost-or-market method to the portfolios of marketable equity investments, dividends received were incorrectly credited to the Investment account.

   b. The market value of the portfolio of marketable equity investments at the end of a firm's first year of operations was $5,000 less than its cost. The firm neglected to make the required journal entry in applying the lower-of-cost-or-market method.

   c. In applying the equity method, P correctly accrued its share of S's net income for the year. However, when a dividend was received, Dividend Revenue was credited.

   d. P acquired 30 percent of S on January 1 of the current year for an amount in excess of the market value of S's net assets. P correctly accounted for its share of S's net income and dividends for the year but neglected to amortize any of the excess purchase price.

   e. During the current year, P sold inventory items to S, its wholly owned subsidiary, at a profit. These inventory items were sold by S and P has paid for them before the end of the year. No elimination entry was made for this intercompany sale on the consolidation work sheet. Indicate the effect of this error on consolidated assets, liabilities, and net income.

   f. Refer to part **e.** Assume that one-fourth of these goods were not sold by S during the year and therefore remain in ending inventory.

   g. Refer to part **e.** Assume that S owes P $10,000 for intercompany purchases at year-end. No elimination entry is made for this intercompany debt. Indicate the effect on consolidated assets, liabilities, and net income.

   h. P owns 90 percent of S. The minority interest in consolidated subsidiaries is treated as part of shareholders' equity. In preparing a consolidated work sheet, no entry was made to accrue the minority interest's share of S's net income or of S's net assets.

Problems and Cases

22. *Consolidation work sheet for wholly owned subsidiary purchased at book value.* The trial balances of High Company and Low Company on December 31 of the current year are shown in Exhibit 13.9.

Exhibit 13.9
HIGH COMPANY and LOW COMPANY
Preclosing Trial Balances
(Problems 22 and 23)

	High Company	Low Company
Debits:		
Cash	$ 50,000	$ 5,000
Accounts Receivable	80,000	15,000
Investment in Stock of Low Company (at equity)	90,000	—
Other Assets	360,000	100,000
Cost of Goods Sold	160,000	60,000
Selling and Administrative Expenses	50,000	20,000
Income Tax Expense	40,000	10,000
Totals	$830,000	$210,000
Credits:		
Accounts Payable	$ 70,000	$ 30,000
Bonds Payable	100,000	—
Common Stock	150,000	50,000
Retained Earnings	200,000	30,000
Sales Revenue	300,000	100,000
Equity in Earnings of Low Company	10,000	—
Totals	$830,000	$210,000

High Company acquired all of the common stock of Low Company on January 1 of this year for $80,000. The receivables of High Company and the liabilities of Low Company contain $5,000 of advances from High Company to Low Company. Prepare a consolidation work sheet for High Company and Low Company for the year. The adjustments and eliminations columns should contain entries to:

(1) Eliminate the investment account.
(2) Eliminate intercompany receivables and payables.

23. *Consolidation work sheet entries for less than wholly owned subsidiary purchased for more than book value.* Refer to the data for High Company and Low Company in Problem **22**. Give the consolidation work sheet adjustment and elimination entries under each of the following independent situations:

a. High Company paid $100,000, instead of $80,000, for all of the common stock of Low Company on January 1. The market values of Low Company's recorded assets and liabilities equaled their book values. Goodwill is amortized over 10 years.

b. High Company paid $64,000 for 80 percent of the common stock of Low Company on January 1. The Investment in Stock of Low Company account showed a balance of $72,000 on December 31.

24. *Consolidation work sheet for less than wholly owned subsidiary purchased for book value.* The preclosing trial balances of Company L and Company M on December 31, Year 2, are shown in Exhibit 13.10. Company L acquired 90 percent of the common stock of Company M on January 2, Year 1, for $270,000. On this date, the shareholders' equity accounts of Company M were as follows:

Common Stock	$100,000
Retained Earnings.	200,000
Total	$300,000

During Year 2, Company L sold merchandise costing $30,000, on account, to Company M for $40,000. Of the amount, $10,000 remains unpaid at year-end. Company M sold all of the merchandise during Year 2.

Exhibit 13.10
COMPANY L and COMPANY M
Preclosing Trial Balances
(Problem 24)

	Company L	Company M
Debits:		
Receivables	$ 60,000	$130,000
Investment in Stock of Company M	319,500	—
Other Assets	761,500	285,000
Cost of Goods Sold	550,000	150,000
Other Expenses	120,000	10,000
Dividends Declared	30,000	15,000
Totals	$1,841,000	$590,000
Credits:		
Accounts Payable	$ 80,000	$ 20,000
Other Liabilities	90,000	40,000
Common Stock	400,000	100,000
Retained Earnings	435,000	230,000
Sales Revenue	800,000	200,000
Equity in Earnings of Company M	36,000	—
Totals	$1,841,000	$590,000

    a. Prepare a consolidation work sheet for Company L and Company M for Year 2. The adjustments and eliminations columns should contain entries to:

      (1) Eliminate the investment account.
      (2) Eliminate intercompany sales.
      (3) Eliminate intercompany receivables and payables.
      (4) Recognize the minority interest.

    b. Prepare a consolidated statement of income and retained earnings for Year 2 and a consolidated balance sheet as of December 31, Year 2.

25. *Consolidation work sheet for less than wholly owned subsidiary purchased for more than book value.* The condensed balance sheets of the Ely Company and the Sims Company at December 31 are shown in Exhibit 13.11.

Exhibit 13.11
ELY COMPANY and SIMS COMPANY
Balance Sheet Data
(Problem 25)

	Ely Company	Sims Company
Assets		
Cash	$ 60,000	$ 5,000
Receivables	120,000	15,000
Investment in Sims Company Stock (at equity)	88,200	—
Other Assets.	540,000	100,000
	$808,200	$120,000
Liabilities and Shareholders' Equity		
Current Liabilities.	$250,000	$ 30,000
Common Stock	400,000	50,000
Retained Earnings	158,200	40,000
	$808,200	$120,000

The receivables of the Ely Company and the liabilities of the Sims Company contain an advance from the Ely Company to the Sims Company of $5,500. The Ely Company acquired 85 percent of the capital stock of the Sims Company on the market at January 2 of this year for $80,000. At that date, the balance in the Retained Earnings account of the Sims Company was $30,000. Amortize goodwill, if any, over 40 years.

Prepare a consolidation work sheet for Ely Company and Sims Company. The adjustment and elimination columns should contain entries to:

(1) Eliminate the Investment in the Sims Company account.
(2) Eliminate intercompany obligations.
(3) Recognize the minority interest.

26. *Consolidation work sheet subsequent to year of acquisition.* The condensed balance sheets of Companies R and S on December 31, Year 2, are shown in Exhibit 13.12.

Additional information:

Company R owns 90 percent of the capital stock of Company S. The stock of Company S was acquired on January 1, Year 1, when Company S's retained earnings amounted to $20,000.

Company R holds a note issued by Company S in the amount of $8,200.

Excess of cost over book value acquired is all attributable to goodwill, to be amortized over 40 years.

Prepare a work sheet for a consolidated balance sheet.

Exhibit 13.12
COMPANY R and COMPANY S
Balance Sheet Data
(Problem 26)

	Company R	Company S
Assets		
Cash	$ 18,000	$ 13,000
Accounts and Notes Receivable	90,000	25,000
Inventories	220,000	125,000
Investment in Stock of Company S (at equity)	312,450	—
Plant Assets	300,000	212,000
Total Assets	$940,450	$375,000
Liabilities and Shareholders' Equity		
Accounts and Notes Payable	$ 55,000	$ 17,000
Dividends Payable	—	12,500
Other Liabilities	143,000	11,000
Common Stock	600,000	250,000
Capital Contributed in Excess of Stated Value	—	50,000
Retained Earnings	142,450	34,500
Total Liabilities and Shareholders' Equity	$940,450	$375,000

27. *Purchase versus pooling: balance sheet.* Marmee Company and Small Enterprises agree to merge at a time when the balance sheets of the two companies are as shown below.

	Marmee Company	Small Enterprises
Assets	$700,000	$312,000
Liabilities	$150,000	$100,000
Common Stock ($1 par)	160,000	64,000
Additional Paid-in Capital	120,000	34,000
Retained Earnings	270,000	114,000
Total Equities	$700,000	$312,000

Marmee issues 50,000 shares with market value of $800,000 to the owners of Small in return for their 64,000 shares, which represent equity of $212,000 (= $312,000 of assets − $100,000 of liabilities). The excess of Marmee's cost ($800,000) over the book value of Small's assets acquired ($212,000) results from Small's book value of assets being $448,000 less than their current value and from $140,000 of goodwill ($800,000 − $212,000 = $448,000 + $140,000).

Prepare consolidated balance sheets as of the merger date, assuming that the merger is treated as a:

a. Purchase.

b. Pooling of interests.

28. *Purchasing versus pooling: income statement.* Refer to the data in Problem **27**. Partial single-company income statements for Marmee Company and Small Enterprises are shown below for the first year after the merger.

	Marmee Company	Small Enterprises
Sales.	$2,000,000	$1,500,000
Other Revenues	50,000	10,000
Total Revenues	$2,050,000	$1,510,000
Expenses Except Income Taxes.	1,700,000	1,300,000
Pretax Income	$ 350,000	$ 210,000

Make the following assumptions:

(1) The income tax rate for the consolidated firm is 40 percent.

(2) Where necessary, the extra asset costs that must be recognized in the consolidated statement are amortized over 5 years, and the goodwill is amortized over 40 years.

(3) Amortization of asset costs and goodwill arising from the purchase are not deductible from taxable income in calculations for tax returns.

(4) Small Enterprises declared no dividends.

Prepare consolidated income statements and consolidated earnings per share for the first year following the merger. Assume that the merger is treated as a

a. Purchase.

b. Pooling of interests.

29. *Effect of accounting methods for investments on financial statements.* General Manufacturing (G.M.) Company manufactures heavy-duty industrial equipment and consumer durable goods. In order to enable its customers to make convenient credit arrangements, G.M. Company organized General Manufacturing Credit Corporation several years ago. G.M. Credit Corporation is 100 percent owned by G.M. Company. G.M. Company accounts for its investment in G.M. Credit Corporation using the *equity method*. G.M. owns shares of many other companies, and consolidates several of them in its financial statements. Refer to the comparative balance sheets and income statements for the two companies in Exhibits 13.13 and 13.14.

a. Given that G.M. Company accounted for its investment in G.M. Credit Corporation on the equity method, identify, for Year 3, the components of G.M. Company's income that are attributable to the Credit Corporation's dividends and earnings.

b. Assume that G.M. Company had accounted for its investment in the Credit Corporation using the lower-of-cost-or-market method, and market value has exceeded acquisition cost at all times since acquisition.

Exhibit 13.13
GENERAL MANUFACTURING COMPANY AND
CONSOLIDATED AFFILIATES
(Problems 29, 30, 31)

Balance Sheet	(In millions of $) December 31		
	Year 3	Year 2	Year 1
Investment in G.M. Credit Corporation.	$ 260.0	$ 231.9	$ 190.0
Other Assets	7,141.8	6,655.9	6,008.5
Total Assets	$ 7,401.8	$6,887.8	$6,198.5
Total Liabilities	$ 4,317.2	$4,086.0	$3,644.9
Shareholders' Equity	3,084.6	2,801.8	2,553.6
Total Equities	$ 7,401.8	$6,887.8	$6,198.5

Income Statement	For the Years		
	Year 3	Year 2	Year 1
Sales	$10,387.6	$9,546.4	$8,813.6
Equity in Net Earnings of Credit Corporation	41.1	30.9	19.9
Total Revenues	$10,428.7	$9,577.3	$8,833.5
Expenses	(9,898.7)	(9,105.5)	(8,505.0)
Net Income	$ 530.0	$ 471.8	$ 328.5

Exhibit 13.14
GENERAL MANUFACTURING CREDIT CORPORATION
(Problems 29, 30, 31)

Balance Sheet	(In millions of $) December 31		
	Year 3	Year 2	Year 1
Total Assets	$2,789.5	$2,358.7	$2,157.0
Total Liabilities	$2,529.5	$2,126.8	$1,967.0
Capital Stock	$ 110.0	$ 90.0	$ 55.0
Retained Earnings	150.0	141.9	135.0
Shareholders' Equity	$ 260.0	$ 231.9	$ 190.0
Total Equities	$2,789.5	$2,358.7	$2,157.0

Statement of Income and Retained Earnings	For the Year		
	Year 3	Year 2	Year 1
Revenues	$ 319.8	$ 280.0	$ 247.5
Less: Expenses	278.7	249.1	227.6
Net Income	$ 41.1	$ 30.9	$ 19.9
Less: Dividends	33.0	24.0	15.0
Earnings Retained for Year	$ 8.1	$ 6.9	$ 4.9
Retained Earnings at January 1	141.9	135.0	130.1
Retained Earnings at December 31	$ 150.0	$ 141.9	$ 135.0

(1) Show the components of G.M. Company's income from the Credit Corporation, and compute how much larger or smaller G.M. Company's income would have been for Year 3 than was reported.

(2) Identify any G.M. Company balance sheet accounts that would have different balances, and calculate the differences from what is shown in the actual statements and what would be shown had the alternative treatment been used.

c. Assume that G.M. Company had accounted for its investment in the Credit Corporation by *consolidating* it. Perform the same computations as required in **(1)** and **(2)** of part **b** for Year 3. Notice that when a 100 percent-owned affiliate—accounted for with the equity method—is consolidated, the effect on balance sheet totals and subtotals can be summarized as follows:

(i) Total owners' equity on the parent's books remains unchanged.

(ii) Total liabilities on the parent's books increases by the amount of the affiliate's total liabilities (assuming that there are no intercompany receivables and payables).

(iii) Total assets on the parent's books increase net by an amount equal to the affiliate's liabilities. (All of the affiliate's assets are put onto the parent's books, but the parent's investment in the affiliate, an amount equal to the affiliate's owners' equity, is removed. The net effect is to increase assets by the amount of the affiliate's total assets − affiliate's owners' equity = affiliate's liabilities.)

d. Compute the following ratios for G.M. from the annual report as published for Year 3. (Refer to Exhibit 6.11 if you have forgotten how to compute these ratios.)

(1) Rate of return on assets. (Insufficient information is given to allow an addback to the numerator for interest payments net of tax effects; ignore that adjustment to net income that is ordinarily required. Use the year-end balance of total assets for the year's average.)

(2) Debt-equity ratio.

e. For Year 3, compute the two ratios required in part **d**, assuming that G.M. had consolidated the Credit Corporation, rather than accounting for it with the equity method. Use the information derived in part **c**.

f. Compare the results in parts **d** and **e**. What conclusions can you draw from this exercise about comparing financial ratios for companies that consolidate their subsidiaries with those of companies that do not?

30. Repeat Problem **29** for Year 2.

31. Repeat Problem **29** for Year 1.

32. *Impact of consolidation policy on debt ratios.* This problem illustrates the impact that consolidation policy can have on financial statements and financial statement analysis. Sears, Roebuck & Co. and J. C. Penney Company are large retailers who have similar operations. Both companies have organized financing subsidiaries. Each subsidiary borrows funds in credit markets and lends the funds to customers who purchase goods or services from the retailers. Each subsidiary is 100 percent owned by its parent company. Sears consolidates its financing subsidiary (Sears, Roebuck Acceptance Corp.) in published financial statements. Penney's uses the equity method for its financing subsidiary (J. C. Penney Financial Corporation) and shows the separate financial statements of the financing subsidiary in notes to the published financial statements.

In this problem we focus on the debt ratio, because the effects are easy to illustrate. Other ratios could be used as well. Throughout this text, the debt-equity ratio has been defined as

$$\text{Debt-Equity Ratio} = \frac{\text{Total Liabilities}}{\text{Total Equities}}.$$

Many financial analysts prefer to use a form of the debt ratio such as

$$\text{Debt Ratio} = \frac{\text{Total } \textit{Long-Term} \text{ Debt}}{\text{Total Shareholders' Equity}}.$$

Such analysts feel that this version of the debt ratio focuses more attention on the risk of companies being analyzed. (The notion is that the percentage of current liabilities to total equities is, to a large degree, determined by the nature of the business and that so long as current assets are as large as current liabilities, the percentage of current liabilities in total equities is not important.)

The accompanying Exhibit 13.15 shows pertinent data from recent financial statements for both Sears and Penney's. Both versions of the debt ratio mentioned above are presented. The data for Sears are taken directly from the financial statements. For Penney's, the exhibit shows data from the published balance sheet in column (1), data from the statements of the financing subsidiary in column (2), and presents a column for Penney's hypothetical financial statements, assuming consolidation of the financing subsidiary. Column (3) represents the accounting for Penney's that is analogous to Sears' accounting.

   a. Complete column (3) for Penney's. (The ratios shown are correct; you can check your work from them.) You may find the summary in part **c** of Problem **29** to be useful.
   b. As measured by the debt ratios (and ignoring other factors—see Problem **20** in Chapter 15), which company appears to be the more risky? Which company do you think is more risky and why?
   c. Assume that the managements of Penney's and Sears are both considering additional long-term financing to raise funds. Managements of both companies are concerned about how the marketplace will react to new debt financing on the one hand or new common share issues on the other. How are financial analysts who are concerned with risk (as measured in part by debt ratios) likely to react to these two companies? How are managements of the two companies likely to react in making their financing decisions if they anticipate the reaction of financial analysts?

Exhibit 13.15
Effect of Consolidation Policy
(all dollar amounts in millions)
(Problem 32)

	J. C. Penney Company			Sears, Roebuck & Co.
	Financial Statements as Issued (1)	Financing Subsidiary Statements as Shown in Notes (2)	Hypothetical Financial Statements if Subsidiary Were Consolidated (3)	Financial Statements as Issued (4)
Total Assets	$3,483.8	$1,458.1	?	$12,711.5
Total Liabilities	1,567.2	1,078.9	?	6,774.6
Long-Term Debt	355.5	517.0	?	1,563.5
Shareholders' Equity	1,916.6	379.2	?	5,936.9
Debt-Equity Ratio (Total Liabilities/ Total Equities)	45.0%	72.3%	58.0%	53.3%
Long-Term Debt/Shareholders' Equity	18.5%	136.3%	45.5%	26.3%

33. *Preparation of statement of changes in financial position (adapted from problem by Stan Baiman).* Exhibit 13.16 presents a comparative balance sheet for Cherry Corporation for Year 6. The following additional information is obtained.

Additional Information:

(1) For the year ended December 31, Year 6, Cherry reported net income of $496,000.

(2) Uncollectible accounts receivable of $4,500 were written off as a result of defaults.

(3) Bad debt expense on Year 6 sales on account is estimated to be $5,000.

(4) On January 3, Year 6, Cherry acquired 90 percent of the outstanding common stock of Zuber Co. To consummate this transaction, Cherry paid $72,000 cash and issued 3,500 shares of its preferred stock and 2,400 shares of its common stock. The market price of Cherry's preferred stock on January 3, Year 6, was $3 a share and the market price of its common stock was $12 a share. The market value of the cash and stock given up by Cherry was equal to its share of Zuber's net book value.

Zuber Co. is considered to be an unrelated business and not compatible with Cherry's operations. Therefore Zuber is not consolidated with Cherry. Rather the investment in Zuber is accounted for on Cherry's financial statement using the equity method. For the year ended December 31, Year 6, Zuber Co. reported $160,000 of net income and declared and paid cash dividends of $10,000.

(5) Cherry's investment in the common stock of Roy Co. was made in Year 2 and represented a 3 percent interest. On January 1, Year 6, Cherry sold this investment

Exhibit 13.16
CHERRY CORPORATION
Comparative Balance Sheets
December 31
(Problem 33)

	Year 6	Year 5
Assets		
Current Assets		
Cash.	$ 450,000	$ 287,000
Accounts Receivable (net of allowance for doubtful accounts).	645,000	550,000
Inventories	460,000	298,000
Total Current Assets.	$1,555,000	$1,135,000
Investments:		
Common Stock of Roy Co. (3 percent)	$ 0	$ 39,000
Common Stock of Zuber Co. (90 percent)	246,300	0
Plant Assets	455,000	381,000
Less: Accumulated Depreciation	(193,000)	(144,000)
Patents (net)	26,000	19,000
Total Assets	$2,089,300	$1,430,000
Liabilities and Shareholders' Equity		
Current Liabilities:		
Dividends Payable	$ 181,000	$ 0
Accounts Payable	170,000	70,000
Accrued Liabilities	24,800	41,800
Total Current Liabilities	$ 375,800	$ 111,800
Long-Term Bonds Payable	223,000	180,000
Less: Unamortized Bond Discount	(49,000)	(47,000)
Total Liabilities	$ 549,800	$ 244,800
Preferred Stock at Par ($2).	$ 60,000	$ 53,000
Additional Paid-in Capital—Preferred	6,000	2,500
Common Stock at Par ($10)	752,000	700,000
Additional Paid-in Capital—Common	20,000	9,600
Retained Earnings.	701,500	420,100
Total Shareholders' Equity	$1,539,500	$1,185,200
Total Liabilities and Shareholders' Equity	$2,089,300	$1,430,000

for $46,000. In addition, Cherry acquired new plant assets at a cost of $81,000. Plant assets with a cost of $22,000 and accumulated depreciation of $17,600 were sold for $3,200. The remaining increase in plant assets resulted from major repairs that were accounted for properly as capital expenditures.

(6) Amortization of patents for Year 6 was $3,000. A new patent was acquired for cash.

(7) On January 2, Year 6 (before the purchase of Zuber), Cherry declared and issued a 4 percent stock dividend on its common stock. The market price of the

common stock on that date was $12 a share. On December 31, Year 6, cash dividends of $145,000 on the common stock and $36,000 on the preferred stock were declared.

(8) During Year 6, bonds with a face value of $20,000 and unamortized bond discount of $3,000 were repurchased for $17,000. During Year 6, bond discount of $4,000 was amortized against interest expense. During Year 6, new bonds were issued at a discount.

   a. Prepare a T-account work sheet for a statement of changes in financial position, defining funds as cash.
   b. Prepare a statement of changes in financial position for Cherry Corporation for Year 6.

Chapter 14 Accounting for the Effects of Changing Prices

One of the most persistent and significant criticisms of the conventional accounting model based on historical costs is that it ignores the economic facts of life. Throughout the world, a steady and rapid upward movement in prices has been occurring during the last decade. Yet, until recently, this important economic phenomenon largely went unrecognized under generally accepted accounting principles. FASB *Statement No. 33* (1979), however, requires that the conventional financial statements of larger firms be supplemented with certain information about the impact of changing prices. This chapter discusses the accounting problems associated with changing prices and illustrates techniques for dealing with them.

Impact of Changing Prices on Conventional Financial Statements

The accounting problems associated with changing prices might be separated into those related to *changes in general price levels* and those associated with *changes in prices of specific goods and services*. This distinction might be grasped most easily by considering the manner in which a price index is constructed.

Nature and Construction of Price Indices

A *price index* measures the prices of a group, or "basket," of goods and services at one date relative to prices at some other date. For example, assume that we wish to construct a price index for food to measure the change in overall prices between January 1 and December 31 of a particular year. We begin by constructing a typical market basket of food items. To keep the illustration simple, suppose we specify that a typical market basket includes meat, starch, vegetable, beverage, and bread. We ascertain the price of a specific commodity in each of these food groupings at the beginning and end of a year. The prices of the individual commodities at each date are summed to obtain the aggregate market price of the basket of goods. The aggregate market price at one date is then compared to the aggregate price at the other date to obtain the average change in prices for the basket of goods. Exhibit 14.1 illustrates the construction of a price index.[1]

---

[1] A price series is a set of index numbers, such as 100 and 110 in Exhibit 14.1, that represent the price levels at different times. The absolute numbers are not important. The percentage change in the numbers from one period to the next provides the information about the change in relative prices. Thus, a price index series of 50 and 55 represents the same price increase, of 10 percent, as does a price index series of 100 and 110. Similarly, a price index series of 200 and 220 represents a price increase of 10 percent. By convention, the time period for which the price index is 100 is called the "base period" of a given price series.

Exhibit 14.1
Illustration of the Construction of a Price Index

Commodity	January 1	December 31	Percentage Change in Market Price of Individual Commodities
Sirloin Steak (pound)	$3.64	$ 4.00	+10 percent
Rice (32 ounces)	1.95	1.79	−8
Frozen Vegetables (package) .	.60	.69	+15
Beer (six-pack)	2.27	2.89	+27
Bread (loaf)	.83	.85	+2
Total	$9.29	$10.22	
Price Index, Where January 1 Prices Equal 100	100	110 (= $10.22/$9.29)	

Prices for this group of commodities increased an average of 10 percent between the beginning and end of the year. The prices of the individual commodities, however, changed at different rates. The price of bread remained relatively stable, while the price of rice decreased. The prices of sirloin steak, frozen vegetables, and beer increased significantly, but only that of the frozen vegetables and the beer increased more than the average 10 percent for the group.

Price indices are constructed by the federal government for many different groupings, or baskets, of commodities. Some of these indices are based on a wide assortment of goods and services and are intended as measures of price changes in general. The two most important *general price indices* are the Gross National Product Implicit Price Deflator Index (issued quarterly) and the Consumer Price Index (issued monthly). Other price indices are constructed for specific groupings of goods and services, such as women's apparel, men's shoes, automobiles, and refrigerators. Even these more *specific price indices,* however, contain an assortment of goods of various qualities, dimensions, and styles within the particular product category.

Accounting Problems Associated with General Price Changes

The conventional accounting model uses as a measuring unit the *actual,* or *nominal,* dollars expended or received over time in recording transactions or events in the accounts. Implicit in the use of nominal dollars is the assumption that the dollar represents a constant, or uniform, measuring unit over time. That is, the measuring unit (the dollar) used in recording the acquisition of a machine costing $10,000 five years ago is assumed to have the same economic significance as the measuring unit used in recording the acquisition of merchandise inventory one week ago for $10,000.

As general price levels change, however, the purchasing power of the dollar, or its command over goods and services, changes. The general purchasing power sacrificed to acquire the machine 5 years ago is not equivalent to the purchasing power sacrificed last week to acquire the merchandise inventory. In terms of general purchasing power, therefore, the dollar does not represent a constant, or uniform, measuring unit through time.

Because the conventional financial statements do not recognize the changing purchasing power of the dollar, the amounts assigned to individual assets in the balance sheet cannot be meaningfully summed to measure the total purchasing power sacrificed to acquire assets. Likewise, the dollars sacrificed to acquire the various assets consumed as expenses differ in purchasing power from the dollars generated by the revenues of the period. The income statement therefore matches dollar amounts measured in different purchasing powers.

Accounting Problems Associated with Specific Price Changes

The conventional accounting model also rests on *historical cost valuations*. Increases in the market prices of individual assets are not reflected in the valuation of assets on the balance sheet or as gains in measuring net income until the assets are sold. Only at the time of sale is the measurement of the gain considered to be sufficiently objective to warrant recognition in the accounts.

Management, however, bases many decisions on information about changes in the prices of individual assets and liabilities. In pricing decisions, management considers the current cost of replacing the goods and services sold. In plant asset replacement decisions, management considers the current market values of individual assets held relative to the acquisition prices of assets with similar operating characteristics. In refinancing decisions, management considers the current market rates of interest on outstanding debt relative to the cost of issuing new debt. By using historical cost valuations and the realization convention, the conventional financial statements fail to reflect the results of management's decisions in the firm's current economic environment.

Official Pronouncement on Accounting for Changing Prices

Recognizing the deficiencies of the conventional accounting model based on nominal dollars and historical cost valuations, the FASB requires large, publicly held firms to report certain supplementary information about the impact of changing prices.[2] The types of information disclosed are described and illustrated in the remaining sections of the chapter under the following headings:

1. Historical cost/constant dollar accounting—Conventional financial statement data is restated to a constant dollar basis to obtain a uniform measuring unit.
2. Current cost/nominal dollar accounting—Historical cost valuations are replaced with current cost valuations.

---

[2]Financial Accounting Standards Board, *Statement of Financial Standards No. 33,* "Financial Reporting and Changing Prices," 1979.

3. Current cost/constant dollar accounting—Current cost valuations are restated to a constant dollar basis.

The illustrations in this chapter present complete balance sheets and income statements under each of these three approaches to accounting for changing prices. The FASB, however, requires only that certain financial data prepared under these three approaches be reported. The Board's reasoning is that the disclosures are sufficiently new and complex that a period of education and experimentation is required. After studying the uses made of the various supplemental disclosures, the FASB expects to issue another pronouncement that will narrow somewhat the type of information reported. The illustrations in this chapter should provide sufficient conceptual background for understanding both current supplemental disclosures and any new reporting formats the FASB may subsequently require.

The illustrations of the three approaches to accounting for changing prices are based on data for Aliber Corporation for the current year. The following transactions and events take place.

1. January 2. The firm is organized by issuing common stock for $400 cash. The Consumer Price Index (CPI), a measure of the general price level, is 200 on this date.

2. January 2. Aliber Corporation purchases two widgets for $100 each and equipment with a 5-year life for $100 (CPI = 200).

3. January 2 to June 30. The CPI increases 5 percent during the 6-month period, from 200 to 210.

4. June 30. The firm sells one widget for $240. It replaces it with a new widget costing $115. It also pays other operating expenses of $100 (CPI = 210).

5. July 1 to December 31. The CPI increases 10 percent during this 6-month period, from 210 to 231.

6. December 31. At the end of the year, the current cost of replacing one widget is $140, and the current cost of replacing the equipment in new condition is $120 (CPI = 231).

Exhibit 14.2 summarizes these data.

Historical Cost/Constant Dollar Accounting

Objective of Historical Cost/Constant Dollar Accounting

The objective of historical cost/constant dollar accounting is to state all financial statement amounts in dollars of uniform general purchasing power, thereby obtaining a constant, or uniform, measuring unit. The general approach is to convert the actual, or nominal, dollars received or expended over time to an equivalent number of dollars on some constant dollar date. For example, consider the equipment ac-

Exhibit 14.2
Data for Inflation Accounting Illustration—Aliber Corporation

Balance Sheet as of January 2
Cash: $400   Contributed Capital: $400

	January 2		June 30		December 31
Consumer Price Index (CPI)	200	$\left(\begin{array}{c}5\%\\ \text{increase}\end{array}\right)\!\!\rightarrow$	210	$\left(\begin{array}{c}10\%\\ \text{increase}\end{array}\right)\!\!\rightarrow$	231
Cost of One Widget	$100		$115		$140
Cost of Equipment	$100		$110		$120
Transactions	(1) Buy 2 Widgets at $100 Each, $200.		(1) Sell 1 Widget for $240; Replace Widget at $115.		(1) Close Books and Prepare Statements.
	(2) Purchase Equipment (5-year life) for $100.		(2) Pay Other Expenses of $100.		

quired on January 2 by Aliber Corporation for $100. This acquisition cost amount represents a sacrifice of 100 January 2 dollars. That sacrifice in purchasing power can be restated in several different ways, as illustrated next.

1. The purchasing power of $100 on January 2 is equal to the purchasing power of 50 base-year dollars, because

$$\frac{\$100 \times 100}{200} = \$50.00.$$

2. The purchasing power of $100 on January 2 is equal to the purchasing power of 105.00 June 30 dollars, because

$$\frac{\$100 \times 210}{200} = \$105.00.$$

3. The purchasing power of $100 on January 2 is equal to the purchasing power of 115.50 December 31 dollars, because

$$\frac{\$100 \times 231}{200} = \$115.50.$$

In words, 100 dollars of January 2 purchasing power have 50 dollars of base-year purchasing power or 105 dollars of June 30 purchasing power or 115.50 dollars of December 31 purchasing power.

Using the constant dollar notation, we can write

$$C\$_{1/2}100.00 = C\$_{\text{Base}}50.00 = C\$_{6/30}105.00 = C\$_{12/31}115.50.$$

These four amounts are economically equivalent because they represent equal amounts of general purchasing power. The notation "C$" denotes that constant, instead of nominal, dollars underlie the measurements made.[3]

The constant dollar date used for restating financial statement amounts is an arbitrary choice. Some have suggested that the date ought to be the base year of the price index used for restatement. Others have suggested using the end of the current year. Still others, including the FASB for certain disclosures, advocate mid-year dollars of the most recent year being reported. The restatement procedures are analogous, whatever date is used. In the illustrations in this chapter, constant dollars of December 31 purchasing power are used.

It should be noted that the historical cost/constant dollar amounts do not equal the market prices of individual assets. The market price of the equipment of Aliber Corporation, for example, could have changed in an entirely different direction and pattern from that of the general price change (just as the prices of the individual food items in Exhibit 14.1 changed at a different rate than the average of 10 percent for the group). Historical cost/constant dollar accounting makes the measuring unit used in acquisition cost-based accounting systems more comparable over time. It is not intended to reflect current market prices of individual assets and equities.

Restatement of Monetary and Nonmonetary Items

An important distinction is made in the constant dollar restatement procedure between monetary items and nonmonetary items.

Monetary Items A *monetary item* is a claim receivable or payable in a specified number of dollars, regardless of changes in the general purchasing power of the dollar. Examples of monetary items are cash; accounts, notes, and interest receivable; accounts, notes, and interest payable; income taxes payable; and bonds. In preparing a constant dollar-restated balance sheet, the valuation of monetary items at the number of dollars due on the date of the balance sheet automatically states them in terms of the general purchasing power of the dollar at that time. No restatement is therefore necessary, and the conventionally reported and restated amounts are the same. For example, Aliber Corporation has $125 of cash on December 31. On the conventionally prepared balance sheet, this item would be stated at $125, the amount of cash on hand. On the constant dollar-restated balance sheet, this item would also be reported at C$125, representing $125 of December 31 general purchasing power.

---

[3]In principle, the notation "C$" is incomplete. To be completely unambiguous, there should be a subscript indicating which date's purchasing power is being used. Because the constant dollar date is fixed for a given set of financial statements, the typical accounting disclosure indicates the constant dollar date in some fashion less clumsy than by putting a subscript on the C$. (See, for example, the notes of General Products Company in Exhibit A.4 near the notations "84" and "86" on pages 748 and 750.) In the paragraph above, however, the subscripts on the C$ notation have been used to indicate the different dates that might be used in stating the purchasing power given up to acquire the asset.

Because monetary items are receivable or payable in a specified number of dollars rather than in terms of a given amount of general purchasing power, holding monetary items over time while the general purchasing power of the dollar changes gives rise to *purchasing power gains and losses*. During a period of inflation, holders of monetary assets lose general purchasing power. For example, a firm with outstanding notes receivable incurs a purchasing power loss, because the dollars loaned out are worth more in terms of general purchasing power than the dollars to be received when the account is collected. Likewise, a holder of monetary liabilities gains in general purchasing power during periods of inflation, because the dollars required to repay the debt represent less purchasing power than the dollars originally borrowed.[4] The gain or loss from holding monetary items is reported as an element of constant dollar net income but is not included in conventionally reported nominal dollar net income.

Nonmonetary Items   A *nonmonetary item* is an asset or equity that does not represent a claim to or for a specified number of dollars. That is, if an item is not a monetary item, then it must be nonmonetary. Examples of nonmonetary items are inventory, land, buildings, equipment, capital stock, revenues, and expenses. In conventionally prepared financial statements, nonmonetary items are stated in terms of varying amounts of general purchasing power depending on the date the nonmonetary assets were acquired and nonmonetary equities arose. These conventionally reported amounts must be restated to an equivalent number of dollars as of the constant dollar restatement date. The amount of this restatement does not represent a gain or loss, but is merely an adjustment to equalize the measuring unit being used.

Illustration of the Restatement Procedure

Column (1) of Exhibit 14.3 presents an income statement for the year and a balance sheet on December 31 for Aliber Corporation as conventionally reported, based on historical cost/nominal dollars. Column (2) shows these historical cost amounts restated to constant dollars of December 31 purchasing power.

Income Statement   Consider first the income statement. The sale of the widget for $240 occurred on June 30, when the CPI was 210. The equivalent number of constant December 31 dollars is C$264 (= $240 × 231/210). The widget that was sold had an historical cost in nominal dollars of $100 on January 2, when the CPI was 200. The equivalent number of constant December 31 dollars is C$115.50

---

[4]The purchasing power gain on long-term debt is conceptually an offset to interest expense. In setting an interest rate on long-term borrowing, lenders recognize that the dollars to be received when the debt is repaid will be worth less in terms of general purchasing power than the dollars loaned out. Lenders will, therefore, set a higher interest rate to compensate for this expected loss in purchasing power. To the borrower, the purchasing power gain has effectively been "paid for" as part of the higher interest cost on the debt. As long as the actual rate of inflation coincides with that anticipated in setting the interest rate, the borrower is not better off as a result of reporting a purchasing power gain. The borrower is better (worse) off only if the actual rate of inflation is greater (less) than the anticipated rate.

Exhibit 14.3
ALIBER CORPORATION
Financial Statements Reflecting Accounting for Changing Prices

	(1) Historical Cost/ Nominal Dollars		(2) Historical Cost/ Constant Dollars		(3) Current Cost/ Nominal Dollars		(4) Current Cost/ Constant Dollars	
Income Statement								
Sales		$240		C$264.0[a]		$240		C$264.0[a]
Cost of Goods Sold.	$100		C$115.5[b]		$115		C$126.5[n]	
Depreciation	20		23.1[c]		22[i]		24.2[o]	
Other Expenses	100	220	110.0[d]	248.6	100	237	110.0[d]	260.7
Operating Income		$ 20		C$ 15.4		$ 3		C$ 3.3
Realized Holding Gains:								
Goods Sold		—		—		15[j]		11.0[p]
Depreciable Assets Used .		—		—		2[k]		1.1[q]
Unrealized Holding Gains:								
Inventory		—		—		65[l]		38.0[r]
Depreciable Assets		—		—		16[m]		3.6[s]
Purchasing Power Loss . . .		—		(18.0)[e]		—		(18.0)[e]
Net Income		$ 20		C$ (2.6)		$101		C$ 39.0
Balance Sheet								
Cash		$125		C$125.0		$125		C$125
Inventory		215		242.0[f]		280		280
Equipment	$100		C$115.5[g]		$120		C$120	
Accumulated Depreciation . .	(20)	80	(23.1)	92.4	(24)[t]	96	(24)[t]	96
Total Assets		$420		C$459.4		$501		C$501
Contributed Capital		$400		C$462.0[h]		$400		C$462[h]
Retained Earnings		20		(2.6)		101		39
Total Equities		$420		C$459.4		$501		C$501

Notes to Exhibit 14.3:

[a]$240 × (231/210) = C$264.0.
[b]$100 × (231/200) = C$115.5.
[c]$100 × (231/200) = C$115.5;
C$115.5/5 = C$23.1.
[d]$100 × (231/210) = C$110.
[e][$100 × (10/200) × (231/210) +
$125 × (21/210)]
= C$5.50 + C$12.50 = C$18.
[f]$100 × (231/200) + $115 ×
(231/210) = C$242.
[g]$100 × (231/200) = C$115.5.
[h]$400 × (231/200) = C$462.

[i]$110/5 = $22.
[j]$115 − $100 = $15.
[k]$22 − $20 = $2.
[l]$280 − $215 = $65.
[m]$96 − $80 = $16.
[n]$115 × (231/210) = C$126.5.
[o]$22 × (231/210) = C$24.2.
[p]C$126.5 − $115.5 = C$11.
[q]C$24.2 − $23.1 = C$1.1.
[r]C$280 − $242 = C$38.
[s]C$96 − $92.4 = C$3.6.

[t]The amount shown for accumulated depreciation differs from the amount shown for depreciation expense at the end of Aliber Corporation's first year of operations. The difference arises because depreciation expense is measured in terms of *average* current cost and accumulated depreciation is measured in terms of *end-of-year* current cost, as required by FASB *Statement No. 33*. Because a full set of financial statements adjusted for the effect of changing prices is not required by *Statement No. 33*, this articulation problem between the income statement and balance sheet was not dealt with by the FASB.

(= $100 \times 231/200$). The restatement of depreciation and other operating expenses likewise reflects the cumulative change in the CPI between the date the original historical cost measurements were made (January 2 and June 30, respectively) and the end of the year.

Operating income measured in constant dollars will typically be less than operating income measured in nominal dollars, as is the case for Aliber Corporation. Sales and operating expenses will typically be restated for approximately one-half year of general price change. Cost of goods sold will usually reflect either somewhat less (LIFO cost flow assumption) or somewhat more (FIFO cost flow assumption) than one-half year of price change. Depreciation expense, however, will reflect cumulative inflation since the depreciable assets were acquired. The restatement of depreciation expense for Aliber Corporation for the current year reflects only 1 year of general price change. The restatement of depreciation expense on the equipment for next year will reflect changes in the general price level for both this year and next year. In later years, still more cumulative inflation will be reflected in the restatements. Firms with relatively large amounts of old depreciable assets find that depreciation expense stated in constant dollars is much larger than depreciation expense stated in nominal dollars.

Also shown in column (2) is the purchasing power loss for the year. Aliber Corporation held cash during the year, its only monetary item, and incurred a loss in general purchasing power of C$18. The calculation of this loss appears in Exhibit 14.4.

Exhibit 14.4
Calculation of Purchasing Power Gain or Loss for Aliber Corporation

	Historical Cost/ Nominal Dollars	Restatement	Historical Cost/ Constant Dollars
Net Monetary Asset Position, Jan. 1	—		—
Increases in Net Monetary Assets:			
Issue of Common Stock for Cash	$400	231/200	C$462.00
Sale of Widget.	240	231/210	264.00
Decreases in Net Monetary Assets:			
Purchase of 2 Widgets on Jan. 1	(200)	231/200	(231.00)
Purchase of Equipment	(100)	231/200	(115.50)
Purchase of 1 Widget on June 30	(115)	231/210	(126.50)
Payment of Operating Expenses	(100)	231/210	(110.00)
Net Monetary Asset Position, Dec. 31	$125		C$143.00

Purchasing Power Loss: $125 − C$143 = C$18.

The first column in Exhibit 14.4 shows the sources and uses of net monetary assets measured in nominal dollars. In the third column, these nominal dollar amounts are restated to equivalent December 31 dollars. In order for Aliber Corporation to have maintained the purchasing power of its net monetary assets, a net monetary asset position of $143 would be required at year end. Because the actual net monetary asset position is only $125, Aliber Corporation has lost $18 of purchasing power during the year.

Most publicly held firms are in a net monetary liability position because of outstanding long-term debt. Therefore, they experience purchasing power gains instead of losses during periods of inflation. These purchasing power gains sometimes more than offset the lower operating income resulting from the restatement of depreciation.

Balance Sheet Column (2) of Exhibit 14.3 also shows the restatement of the balance sheet to a constant dollar basis. Cash is the only monetary item. It is shown at C$125, the same amount as in the nominal dollar balance sheet. Ending inventory is composed of two units, one purchased for $100 on January 2 and the other purchased for $115 on June 30. The December 31 constant dollar equivalent of these amounts is

January 2 Purchase: $100 × 231/200	C$115.50
June 30 Purchase: $115 × 231/210.	126.50
Total.	C$242.00

The cost of the equipment purchased for $100 on January 31 is restated to C$115.50 December 31 dollars (= $100 × 231/200). Accumulated depreciation is equal to one-fifth of the constant dollar cost, or C$23.10. Contributed capital is likewise restated for 1 year of general price change; $400 × 231/200 = C$462. Constant dollar retained earnings is equal to the constant dollar net loss for the year.

Summary of Constant Dollar Restatement Procedure The constant dollar restatement procedure can be summarized as follows:

1. Select the constant dollar date to which all financial statement items will be restated.

2. Restate revenues and expenses on the income statement from the nominal dollars underlying their measurement in the conventional income statement to dollars of the desired constant general purchasing power. The numerator of the restatement factor is the Consumer Price Index on the desired constant dollar date. The denominator is the Consumer Price Index on the date of the underlying nominal dollar measurements.

3. Calculate the purchasing power gain or loss. Begin with a listing of the sources and uses of net monetary items during the period. This listing of inflows and outflows should fully account for the change in the net monetary position between the beginning and end of the period. Then restate the beginning net monetary position and all sources and uses of net monetary items from the price level in which the monetary item is measured in nominal dollars to the price level on the constant dollar date. The difference between the actual and constant dollar net monetary position at the end of the period is the purchasing power gain or loss for the period.

4. Restate each balance sheet item to its constant-dollar equivalent. If dollars of end-of-the-year purchasing power are selected as the constant dollar, monetary items are automatically stated in year-end dollars, and no restatement is required. Nonmonetary items must be restated from the nominal dollars underlying their measurement in the conventional financial statements to the equivalent number of constant dollars.

Evaluation of Historical Cost/Constant Dollar Accounting

The procedures for restating financial statements to a constant dollar basis can be traced back to before 1920.[5] Yet it was not until 1979 that disclosure of constant dollar information, even as supplementary disclosure, became a part of generally accepted accounting principles. The usefulness of constant dollar information has been, and continues to be, controversial.

The Case for Constant Dollar Accounting   Proponents of constant dollar accounting offer the following arguments:

1. Constant dollar accounting makes the results of arithmetic operations more meaningful. If the measuring unit (the dollar) varies over time because of changes in the general purchasing power of the dollar, then additions and subtractions of recorded amounts cannot be made meaningfully.

2. Constant dollar accounting makes interperiod comparisons more meaningful. Changes in the amount of an item (sales, cost of goods sold) are difficult to interpret if the measuring unit used is not the same over time.

3. Constant dollar accounting improves the meaning and measurement of net income. Revenues and expenses are matched in terms of a constant measuring unit. Also, a gain or loss is explicitly recognized for the change in the general purchasing power of monetary assets and liabilities held. Income before the purchasing power gain or loss must exceed any loss of purchasing power of net monetary assets if the purchasing power of the monetary, or financial, capital of the firm is to be maintained.

4. No additional judgments are required in that government-prepared price indices are used to restate audited historical cost amounts.

---

[5]See Livingston Middleditch, Jr., "Should Accounts Reflect the Changing Value of the Dollar?" *Journal of Accountancy,* February 1918, pp. 114–120. This article was "rediscovered" and reprinted by Stephen A. Zeff (ed.) in *Asset Appreciation, Business Income and Price-Level Accounting: 1918–1935,* Arno Press, New York, 1976. Generally, however, the credit for developing constant dollar accounting is given to Henry W. Sweeney for his *Stabilized Accounting,* Harper & Brothers, New York, 1936.

The Case Against Constant Dollar Accounting Opponents of constant dollar accounting argue that it fails to measure the economically significant effects of changing prices on a firm. They argue as follows:

1. With respect to nonmonetary items, the strategies that firms follow in coping with inflation focus on changes in the prices of the specific goods and services that the firm normally acquires and not on changes in the prices of a broad market basket of consumer goods and services. Raw materials are purchased early in anticipation of increased acquisition costs. A capital-intensive plant is constructed in anticipation of increased labor costs. Yet, under constant dollar accounting, the results of these decisions are judged against a standard based on changes in the general purchasing power of the dollar.

2. With respect to monetary items, the purchasing power gain or loss is based on an inappropriate index of purchasing power. Users of financial statements are interested in a firm's ability to maintain the purchasing power of its monetary assets for the particular kinds of goods and services that it normally purchases.

Current Cost/Nominal Dollar Accounting

Objective of Current Cost/Nominal Dollar Accounting

The objective of current cost/nominal dollar accounting is to report the effects of specific price changes on the operating performance and financial position of a firm.[6] The FASB defines current cost as the amount a firm would have to pay currently to replace the service potential embodied in its specific assets. It takes into account the inherent technological capabilities and levels of obsolescence of the existing assets. For example, if a firm owned a 2-year-old automobile, it would base its current replacement cost valuation on the prices of similar 2-year-old automobiles in the used car market. If replacement cost amounts for identical, used assets are not available, then the replacement cost of new assets with similar service potential would be used. The replacement cost of the new asset would be adjusted downward, however, for both the used condition of the existing asset and any technological changes that have occurred.

---

[6]Several alternative approaches to reflecting changes in specific prices have been suggested by various writers. These include:

1. *Current reproduction cost*—The cost of material, labor, and overhead that would be required currently to reproduce an asset identical to that now owned.
2. *Current replacement cost*—The cost of acquiring an asset that has the same service potential or operating capacity as an asset now owned.
3. *Net realizable value*—The net amount that would be received if an asset were sold currently.
4. *Present value of future cash flows*—The present value of the future cash inflows and cash outflows expected from an asset.

The arguments for and against each of these alternative valuation bases are beyond the scope of this book, but are considered in intermediate accounting texts.

Measuring Current Cost Amounts

There are several sources of information that might be consulted in ascertaining the current cost of a particular asset.

1. *Used asset market.* For automobiles, furniture, office machines, and similar items, active used asset markets exist that can help to measure the current cost of such assets.
2. *Suppliers' catalogs.* For inventories of raw materials, supplies, and standardized equipment, suppliers' catalogs can be consulted.
3. *Appraisals.* The current cost of land and building might be estimated by real estate appraisers.
4. *Specific price indices.* The federal government prepares specific price indices for a wide assortment of goods and services. These price indices indicate the change over time in the price of particular classes of items. These indices typically indicate the current cost of items in new condition. To use the price indices to measure the current cost of existing assets, some recognition must be given to their used condition.

Illustration of Current Cost/Nominal Dollar Accounting

Column (3) of Exhibit 14.3 on page 629 shows the income statement and balance sheet of Aliber Corporation on a current cost/nominal dollar basis.

Income Statement Sales revenue is stated at the amount of cash received (or expected to be received) from the sale of inventory items; the amount is the same as in the conventional financial statements. Matched against sales revenue is the current cost of inventory sold, equipment services used, and other goods and services consumed. When the widget was sold on June 30, it had a replacement cost of $115. The current cost of goods sold is, therefore, stated at this amount. The equipment of Aliber Corporation had an average current cost of $110 during the year. Based on a 5-year life and the straight-line depreciation method, depreciation expense on a current cost basis is $22 (= $110/5). Other expenses incurred during the year are already stated in terms of current cost.

Operating income indicates the extent to which selling prices were set sufficiently high to cover the current cost of replacing goods and services sold or consumed during the period. If a firm is to maintain its operating capacity, it must be able to replace assets as they are used up. Cash generated from sales is the primary means for doing so. Thus, operating income on a current cost basis indicates the extent to which a firm has maintained its operating capacity during the period.

The income statement also shows realized and unrealized holding gains and losses on nonmonetary assets. Recall from the discussion of inventories in Chapter 8 that a holding gain arises when an asset is held while its current cost increases. Consider, for example, the widget purchased on January 1 for $100 and sold on June 30 for $240. The current cost of replacing the widget on June 30 was $115. While the widget was held, its current cost increased $15 (= $115 − $100). Because this widget was sold during the year, the holding gain has been realized. The conventional gross margin on the sale of $140 (= $240 − $100) is separated in column (3) into an operating margin of $125 (= selling price − current cost of goods sold = $240 − $115) and a realized holding gain of $15 (= current cost of goods sold − historical cost of goods sold = $115 − $100). There is also a realized holding gain of $2 on the equipment used. The gain is equal to the difference between the current cost of the equipment's services used during the year of $22 and the historical cost of those services of $20. Note that operating income plus realized holding gains on a current cost/nominal dollar basis are equal to net income in the conventional financial statements: $3 + $15 + $2 = $20.

The income statement in column (3) also includes unrealized holding gains on inventory and equipment not yet sold or used. The current cost of replacing the two widgets at the end of the year is $280 (= $140 × 2). The historical cost of these widgets is $215 (= $100 + $115). Thus, the unrealized holding gain is $65 (= $280 − $215). Similarly, the current cost of replacing the equipment in new condition at the end of the year is $120. If the equipment has a 5-year life, the current cost of replacing the equipment in its existing 1-year-old condition is $96 (= $\frac{4}{5}$ × $120). The difference between the current cost of the equipment of $96 and the historical cost of the same service potential of $80 (= $\frac{4}{5}$ × $100) is an unrealized holding gain.

Net income on a current cost/nominal dollar basis is composed of operating income, realized holding gains and losses, and unrealized holding gains and losses.[7]

Balance Sheet Cash is stated at its face amount in the current cost balance sheet. If Aliber Corporation had other monetary items (accounts receivable, accounts payable, bonds payable), they should, at least theoretically, also be revalued to a current cost basis. The approach is to ascertain the current interest rate appropriate to the monetary item. The future cash flows associated with the monetary item should be discounted to their present value using the current interest rate. As a practical matter, probably only *long-term* receivables and *long-term* debt would be revalued. FASB *Statement No. 33* does not currently require the revaluation of monetary items in its current cost disclosures.

The inventory and equipment, both nonmonetary items, are stated at their current cost on December 31. Contributed capital is stated at its historical cost/nominal dollar amount, because it is not feasible to measure the current cost of such contributed capital at the end of the year. The current market value of the outstanding capital stock might appear to be an appropriate basis for such a current cost valuation. This market value is for the firm's entire net assets (contributed capital plus retained earnings), not just the contributed capital portion. Retained earnings for Aliber Corporation is equal to current cost net income for the year.

---

[7]Considerable controversy exists in accounting as to whether holding gains and losses, both realized and unrealized, should be included in net income. Advocates of a *financial capital maintenance* viewpoint argue that they should be included, whereas advocates of a *physical capital maintenance* viewpoint argue that they should not be included. The issues involved in this controversy are beyond the scope of this book.

Evaluation of Current Cost/Nominal Dollar Accounting

Current cost/nominal dollar accounting continues to be controversial.

The Case for Current Cost/Nominal Dollar Accounting   Advocates of current cost/nominal dollar accounting offer the following arguments.

1. Management's actions to cope with changing prices are based on expected changes in the prices of the particular goods and services normally acquired by a firm. Current cost financial statements provide a consistent basis on which to evaluate management's actions and performance.
2. Current cost income is separated into operating margin and holding gains and losses, permitting statement users to assess the impact of changing prices on the profitability of the firm.
3. Current cost balance sheets provide a more realistic indication of the current economic value of assets and liabilities than do the balance sheets based on historical costs.

The Case Against Current Cost/Nominal Dollar Accounting   Opponents of current cost/nominal dollar accounting offer the following arguments.

1. Current cost amounts are often difficult to calculate, particularly for specialized used assets, raising questions about the reliability and comparability of current cost data between firms.

2. Current cost net income, which includes holding gains and losses, must be interpreted cautiously. Unrealized holding gains do not produce cash or claims to cash. Basing dividends on current cost net income may result in impairing the operating capacity of the firm.[8]

3. Current cost accounting in nominal dollars fails to recognize that the measuring unit used to calculate current cost amounts is not of the same dimension over time. Changes in the general purchasing power of the dollar make current cost amounts on the balance sheet at the beginning and end of the period noncomparable. Likewise, net income amounts over time, using current costs, are not based on a constant measuring unit.

4. Changes in current costs relative to changes in the general price level are not considered in measuring holding gains and losses under current cost/nominal dollar accounting. A holding gain of 8 percent on a tract of land on a current cost basis has one meaning when the general price level increases 6 percent and another meaning when general prices increase by 10 percent.

5. Current cost accounting fails to recognize purchasing power, or inflation, gains or losses on monetary items. As discussed earlier in this chapter, monetary items gain or lose purchasing power as they are held over time. These gains and losses are often equally as important as holding gains and losses on inventories, depreciable assets, and similar items.

---

[8]For this reason, advocates of a physical capital maintenance concept of income would exclude holding gains and losses. See footnote 7.

The last three arguments are overcome with current cost/constant dollars, which is discussed next.

Current Cost/Constant Dollar Accounting

Objective of Current Cost/Constant Dollar Accounting

The objective of current cost/constant dollar accounting is to report in a constant measuring unit the effects of specific price changes on the operating performance and financial position of a firm. Because constant dollar accounting deals with the measuring unit and current cost accounting deals with the valuation basis, there are no theoretical obstacles to combining the two approaches.

Illustration of Current Cost/Constant Dollar Accounting

Column (4) of Exhibit 14.3 on page 629 shows the income statement and balance sheet of Aliber Corporation on a current cost/constant dollar basis. The constant dollar date is December 31.

Income Statement Sales revenue, cost of goods sold, depreciation, and other expenses are stated in column (3) at their current cost on June 30, measured in terms of June 30 dollars. To measure them in terms of December 31 dollars requires that they be restated using the factor 231/210.

The realized holding gains must be recomputed to reflect a constant measuring unit. Recall that the realized holding gain on the widget sold in column (3) is equal to the current cost of the widget on June 30 of $115, minus the historical cost on January 1, of $100. These two amounts are expressed in different measuring units. Both amounts must be restated to constant December 31 dollars as follows:

Current Cost of Widget Sold: $115 × 231/210	C$126.50
Historical Cost of Widget Sold: $100 × 231/200	115.50
Realized Holding Gain on Inventory Sold	C$ 11.00

Similarly, the realized holding gain on depreciable assets shown in column (3) is the difference between the average current cost of the services used during the year of $22 and the historical cost of the services of $20. Both amounts must be expressed in constant December 31 dollars as follows:

Current Cost of Depreciable Assets Used: $22 × 231/210	C$24.2
Historical Cost of Depreciable Assets Used: $20 × 231/200	23.1
Realized Holding Gain on Depreciable Assets Used	C$ 1.1

The unrealized holding gains must also be recalculated to place all measurements in terms of constant December 31 dollars.

Current cost/constant dollar net income is composed of operating income, realized and unrealized holding gains and losses on nonmonetary items, and purchasing power gains and losses on monetary items.

Balance Sheet   The amounts on the asset side of the balance sheet in column (3) reflect current costs on December 31. Because these amounts are already stated in terms of December 31 dollars, no restatement is necessary. Contributed capital is restated from January 1 to December 31 dollars using the factor 231/200.

Evaluation of Current Cost/Constant Dollar Accounting

A careful reading of the arguments for and against historical cost/constant dollar accounting and current cost/nominal dollar accounting reveals that most of the criticisms of these two approaches are overcome by combining them. An added difficulty arises, however. The computations may be so complex that readers of the financial statements will be unable to understand and interpret the disclosures made. An educational effort is required to inform statement readers as to the kinds of interpretations that should and should not be made.

Required Disclosures Under *Statement No. 33*

The FASB recognizes that opinions vary widely on the usefulness of information generated by each of the three approaches to accounting for changing prices discussed in this chapter [that is, the information of columns (2), (3), and (4) of Exhibit 14.3]. Rather than require that a full set of supplemental financial statements be prepared under only one of these three approaches, the FASB in *Statement No. 33* requires certain minimum disclosures using each of the three approaches. This approach provides statement users with time to educate themselves as to the nature of the disclosures made and to assess their relative usefulness. The FASB will continue to monitor the reporting process to determine if the required disclosures should be altered.

The following minimum disclosures are required by *Statement No. 33*.

1. Income from continuing operations for the current fiscal year on an historical cost/constant dollar basis. This amount is analogous to Operating Income in column (2) of Exhibit 14.3.

2. The purchasing power gain or loss on net monetary items for the current fiscal year. *Statement No. 33* requires that the purchasing power gain or loss be excluded from income from continuing operations. Thus, unlike the presentation in column (2) of Exhibit 14.3, the income from continuing operations of C$15.4 would need not be netted with the purchasing power loss of C$18 to obtain a constant dollar net income figure.

3. Income from continuing operations for the current fiscal year on a current cost/nominal dollar basis. This amount is analogous to Operating Income in column (3) of Exhibit 14.3.

4. Increases or decreases for the current fiscal year in the current cost amounts of inventory and property, plant, and equipment, net of inflation. These items were referred to as holding gains and losses in Exhibit 14.3. The amounts to be disclosed are those in column (4), the amounts net of general price inflation. These holding gains and losses must be disclosed separately. They need not be added to income from continuing operations to obtain a current cost net income.

5. Current cost of inventory and property, plant, and equipment at the end of the current fiscal year. Other assets and equities on the balance sheet need not be stated at current cost.

6. For each of the five most recent fiscal years, the following items must be disclosed:

    a. Historical cost/constant dollar information:

        (1) Net sales and other operating revenue.

        (2) Income from continuing operations.

        (3) Income per common share from continuing operations.

        (4) Purchasing power gain or loss on monetary items.

        (5) Net assets at fiscal year-end.

        (6) Cash dividends declared per common share.

        (7) Market price per common share at year end.

    b. Current cost information:

        (8) Income from continuing operations.

        (9) Income per common share from continuing operations.

       (10) Increases or decreases in current cost amounts of inventory and property, plant, and equipment, net of inflation.

       (11) Net assets at fiscal year-end.

The notes to the financial statements of General Products Company in Appendix A illustrate the supplementary disclosures required by FASB *Statement No. 33*.

Changing Prices and the Statement of Changes in Financial Position

Of the three principal financial statements, the statement of changes in financial position is the least affected by changing prices. Most transactions affecting cash flow occur during the period being reported. Any adjustment of these amounts for either general or specific price changes would reflect price changes for approximately 1 year or less.

    As is the case in preparing the statement of changes in financial position in historical cost/nominal dollars, the restated statement reflecting either general or specific price changes can be most easily prepared after the balance sheet and income statement have been restated for price changes. The amounts included in the restated statement of changes in financial position can usually be obtained from either the restated balance sheet or the restated income statement.

FASB *Statement No. 33* does not require the disclosure of information about the effects of inflation on the statement of changes in financial position.

Summary

Accounting for changing prices is currently in a period of transition and experimentation. Financial statement preparers and users have recognized for many years that changing prices, either in general or for specific goods and services, bring to question the validity and meaningfulness of conventional financial statements based on historical cost and nominal dollars. The pronouncement by the Financial Accounting Standards Board allows firms considerable flexibility in the way changing prices are accounted for and disclosed. Whether constant dollar accounting, current cost accounting, or some other approach replaces or regularly supplements the historical cost/nominal dollars financial statements will depend on the benefits of the disclosures as perceived by users, relative to the cost of generating the necessary data. It is, as yet, too early to evaluate effectively these benefits and costs.

Problem for Self-Study

The Whitmyer Corporation was formed on January 2 to conduct an office rental business. Listed below are various transactions and other events of the firm during the year. The assumed values of the Consumer Price Index (CPI) are shown in parentheses.

(1) January 2 (CPI = 200). Common stock is issued at par value, $1,000,000.

(2) January 2, (CPI = 200). Land costing $100,000 and a building costing $1,500,000 are acquired. A cash payment of $900,000 is made for the land and building with a long-term, 10 percent note signed for the remainder of the purchase price. Interest on the note is payable on December 31 of each year, and the principal is repayable in 10 years.

(3) January 2 to December 31 (average CPI = 212). Rentals totaling $300,000 for the year are collected in cash.

(4) January 2 to December 31 (average CPI = 212). Operating costs incurred evenly over the year total $60,000, of which $40,000 are paid in cash and the remainder are on account. All of these costs are expenses of the current year.

(5) January 2 to December 31 (average CPI = 212). Interest costs are accrued monthly on the mortgage payable and are paid on December 31.

(6) December 31 (CPI = 224). Depreciation on the building is calculated using the straight-line method, a 30-year life, and zero salvage value.

(7) December 31 (CPI = 224). A cash dividend of $75,000 is declared and paid.

On December 31 the land had a current cost of $150,000. A similar new office building had a current cost in new condition of $1,560,000, whereas a similar 1-year-old office building had a current cost of $1,508,000. The amounts reported as operating and interest expenses in the conventional financial statements closely approximate their average current costs during the year.

Prepare an income statement for the current year and a balance sheet as of December 31 for Whitmyer Corporation under each of the following (round all amounts to the nearest dollar).

a. Historical cost/nominal dollars.
b. Historical cost/constant dollars of December 31 purchasing power.
c. Current cost/nominal dollars.
d. Current cost/constant dollars of December 31 purchasing power.

Suggested Solution

Exhibit 14.5 presents income statements and balance sheets for Whitmyer Corporation for the current year. The computations are shown in the notes to Exhibit 14.5 and in Exhibit 14.6.

Questions, Exercises, Problems and Cases

Questions

1. Review the meaning of the following concepts or terms discussed in this chapter.

a. General price level changes.
b. Specific price level changes.
c. Price index.
d. Nominal dollars.
e. Constant dollars.
f. Acquisition cost.
g. Current cost.
h. Constant dollar date.
i. Monetary item.

j. Nonmonetary item.
k. Purchasing power gain or loss on monetary items.
l. Realized holding gain or loss on nonmonetary items.
m. Unrealized holding gain or loss on nonmonetary items.
n. Holding gains and losses net of inflation.

2. Refer to the income statements and balance sheets of Aliber Corporation in Exhibit 14.3 in the chapter.

a. Under what conditions will the amounts in column (1) (historical cost/nominal dollars) and column (3) (current cost/nominal dollars) be the same?
b. Under what conditions will the amounts in column (2) (historical cost/constant dollars) and column (4) (current cost/constant dollars) be the same?
c. Under what conditions will the amounts in column (2) (historical cost/constant dollars) and column (3) (current cost/nominal dollars) be the same?

Exhibit 14.5
WHITMYER CORPORATION
Financial Statements Reflecting Accounting for Changing Prices

	Historical Cost/ Nominal Dollars	Historical Cost/ Constant Dollars	Current Cost/ Nominal Dollars	Current Cost/ Constant Dollars
Income Statement				
Rent Revenue	$ 300,000	C$ 316,981[a]	$ 300,000	C$ 316,981[a]
Depreciation Expense	(50,000)	(56,000)[b]	(51,000)[j]	(53,887)[o]
Operating Expenses	(60,000)	(63,396)[c]	(60,000)	(63,396)[c]
Interest Expense	(70,000)	(73,962)[d]	(70,000)	(73,962)[d]
Operating Income	$ 120,000	C$ 123,623	$ 119,000	C$ 125,736
Realized Holding Gain:				
Building	—	—	1,000[k]	(2,113)[p]
Unrealized Holding Gain:				
Land	—	—	50,000[l]	38,000[q]
Building	—	—	58,000[m]	(116,000)[r]
Purchasing Power Gain	—	62,377[e]	—	62,377[e]
Net Income	$ 120,000	C$ 186,000	$ 228,000	C$ 108,000
Less Dividends Declared	(75,000)	(75,000)	(75,000)	(75,000)
Retained Earnings, December 31	$ 45,000	C$ 111,000	$ 153,000	C$ 33,000
Balance Sheet				
Assets:				
Cash	$ 215,000	C$ 215,000	$ 215,000	C$ 215,000
Land	100,000	112,000[f]	150,000	150,000
Building—Cost	1,500,000	1,680,000[g]	1,560,000	1,560,000
Less Accumulated Depreciation	(50,000)	(56,000)[h]	(52,000)[n]	(52,000)
Total Assets	$1,765,000	C$1,951,000	$1,873,000	C$1,873,000

Liabilities and Shareholders' Equity:

Accounts Payable	$ 20,000	C$ 20,000	$ 20,000	C$ 20,000
Note Payable	700,000	700,000	700,000	700,000
Common Stock	1,000,000	1,120,000[i]	1,000,000	1,120,000[i]
Retained Earnings	45,000	111,000	153,000	33,000
Total Equities	$1,765,000	C$1,951,000	$1,873,000	C$1,873,000

Notes to Exhibit 14.5:

[a] $300,000 × 224/212 = C$316,981.
[b] $50,000 × 224/200 = C$56,000.
[c] $60,000 × 224/212 = C$63,396.
[d] $70,000 × 224/212 = C$73,962.
[e] See Exhibit 14.6.
[f] $100,000 × 224/200 = C$112,000.
[g] $1,500,000 × 224/200 = C$1,680,000.
[h] C$1,680,000/30 = C$56,000.
[i] $1,000,000 × 224/200 = C$1,120,000.
[j] ($1,500,000 + $1,560,000)/2 = $1,530,000; $1,530,000/30 = $51,000.
[k] $51,000 − $50,000 = $1,000.
[l] $150,000 − $100,000 = $50,000.
[m] ($1,560,000 − $52,000) − ($1,500,000 − $50,000) = $1,508,000 − $1,450,000 = $58,000.
[n] $1,560,000/30 = $52,000.
[o] $51,000 × 224/212 = C$53,887.
[p] ($51,000 × 224/212) − ($50,000 × 224/200) = C$53,887 − C$56,000 = C$(2,113).
[q] $150,000 − ($100,000 × 224/200) = C$150,000 − C$112,000 = C$38,000.
[r] C$1,508,000 − C$1,624,000 = C$(116,000).

Exhibit 14.6
WHITMYER CORPORATION
Calculation of Purchasing Power Gain or Loss for Current Year

	Historical Cost/ Nominal Dollars	Restatement	Historical Cost/ Constant Dollars
Net Monetary Position, Jan. 1	—	—	—
Increases in Net Monetary Assets:			
Issue of Common Stock for Cash	$1,000,000	224/200	C$1,120,000
Accrual of Rent Receivable.	300,000	224/212	316,981
Decreases in Net Monetary Assets:			
Disbursement of Cash in Acquisition of Land and Building	(900,000)	224/200	(1,008,000)
Issuance of Note Payable in Acquisition of Land and Building	(700,000)	224/200	(784,000)
Accrual of Operating Costs	(60,000)	224/212	(63,396)
Accrual of Interest Costs	(70,000)	224/212	(73,962)
Declaration of Dividend	(75,000)	224/224	(75,000)
Net Monetary Liability Position, Dec. 31	$(505,000)		C$(567,377)

Purchasing Power Gain: C$567,377 − C$505,000 = C$62,377.

3. When historical cost/constant dollar financial statements are prepared, under what conditions will a firm incur:
   a. A purchasing power gain?
   b. A purchasing power loss?
   c. Neither a purchasing power gain nor a purchasing power loss?

4. Why is there no purchasing power gain or loss on nonmonetary items in historical cost/constant dollar financial statements?

5. "Financial statements prepared under the conventional accounting model reflect dollars of mixed purchasing power." Explain the meaning of this statement in relation to the balance sheet, income statement, and statement of changes in financial position.

6. For which types of asset and equity structures would you expect:
   a. Significant differences between net income as conventionally reported and as restated to a constant dollar basis (including the purchasing power gain or loss)?
   b. Insignificant differences between the two earnings measures?

7. "The amount of income from continuing operations for any given year on a historical cost/constant dollar basis will differ depending on which constant dollar date is selected." Explain.

8. "Operating income on a current cost/nominal dollar basis indicates the extent to which a firm has maintained its operating capacity during a period." Explain.

9. "All realized holding gains or losses were once unrealized holding gains or losses." Do you agree? Why or why not?

10. A firm reports a realized holding gain on land in its current cost/nominal dollar income statement but a realized holding loss in its current cost/constant dollar income statement. What is the likely explanation for this difference?

11. "The LIFO cost flow assumption for inventories and accelerated depreciation methods for plant and equipment are only partial solutions to the accounting problems associated with specific price changes." Explain.

Exercises

12. *Calculating the gain on sale of land under various approaches to accounting for changing prices.* Rockness Corporation acquired a parcel of land on January 2 for $50,000. The parcel was sold on July 1 of the same year for $65,000. An index of the general price level and the current cost of the land on various dates are as follows:

	General Price Index	Current Cost
January 2	160	$50,000
July 1	185	65,000
December 31	200	75,000

Calculate the amount of income or loss relating to this land for the year under each of the following bases (round amounts to the nearest dollar).
   a. Historical cost/nominal dollars.
   b. Historical cost/constant dollars of December 31 purchasing power.
   c. Current cost/nominal dollars.
   d. Current cost/constant dollars of December 31 purchasing power.

13. *Disaggregating the gross margin into operating margin and holding gains.* The merchandise inventory of Scoggin's Appliance Store on January 1 consists of 1,000 units acquired for $250 each. During the year, 2,500 units are purchased at a unit price of $300, while 2,400 units are sold for $400 each. The average current cost per unit during the year is $300, whereas the current cost on December 31 is $360 per unit.
   a. Using historical cost and nominal dollars, calculate the gross margin (sales minus cost of goods sold) for the year using the FIFO and the LIFO cost flow assumptions.
   b. Using current cost and nominal dollars, disaggregate the gross margin in part **a** into the operating margin and realized holding gain. Compute unrealized holding gains and the sum of operating margin plus all holding gains.

14. *Restating equipment and depreciation to a constant dollar basis.* Sunder Equipment Corporation depreciates its machinery using the straight-line method over a 10-year life with zero estimated salvage value. A full year's depreciation is taken in the year of acquisition and none in the year of disposal. Acquisitions, which took place evenly over the appropriate years, were as follows: Year 1, $400,000; Year 2, $200,000; Year 3, $300,000. An index of the average general price level during Year 1 was 180, during Year 2 was 220, and during Year 3 was 240. The general price index on December 31, Year 3, is 250.

   a. Calculate the amount of depreciation expense for Year 3 and the book value of the machinery on December 31, Year 3, using the historical costs and nominal dollars.

   b. Repeat part **a** using the historical costs and constant dollars of December 31, Year 3, purchasing power. Round all amounts to the nearest dollar.

15. *Calculating the purchasing power gain or loss.* The Cunningham Drug Store had a net monetary asset position of $300,000 on January 1, at which time an index of the general price level was 200. Transactions during the year and associated indices of the general price level (GPI) are listed below.

(1) Purchases, all on account, totaled $400,000 (GPI = 210).
(2) Sales, all on account, totaled $600,000 (GPI = 210).
(3) Collections from customers for sales on account, $450,000 (GPI = 215).
(4) Payments to suppliers for purchases on account, $300,000 (GPI = 215).
(5) Declaration of a $200,000 dividend, payable during January of next year (GPI = 250). The general price index on December 31 is 230.

   a. Calculate the amount of the purchasing power gain or loss for the year stated in terms of constant December 31 dollars. Round all amounts to the nearest dollar.

   b. Repeat part **a** assuming a net monetary liability position of $300,000 on January 1.

16. *Calculating the purchasing power gain or loss.* On January 1 the Bill Langston family had $800 in its checking account and $4,000 in a savings account. The unpaid balance for the mortgage on their home totaled $25,000, and unpaid bills relating to purchases during December of last year amounted to $600. An index of the general price level on January 1 was 210. During the current year, the following transactions occurred (general price index is shown in parentheses):

(1) Bill Langston's take-home salary was $25,000 (average GPI = 225).
(2) The unpaid bills of $600 on January 1 were paid (GPI = 213).
(3) Principal repayments of $2,000 were made on the home mortgage loan (average GPI = 225).
(4) Food, clothing, interest, and other costs incurred by the family totaled $20,500 of which $19,700 was paid in cash (average GPI = 225).
(5) Interest earned and added to the savings account totaled $300 (average GPI = 225).
(6) In addition to the interest earned in **(5)**, $1,500 was transferred from the checking to the savings account (GPI = 158). The general price index on December 31 is 240.

Calculate the purchasing power gain or loss for the year for the family stated in terms of constant December 31 dollars. Round conversion factors used to two decimal places—for example, 240/225 = 1.07.

17. *Preparing income statement and balance sheet under four measurement and valuation approaches.* Straus Corporation is organized on January 2 with the issuance of common stock for $200. The following transactions occur during the year.

(1) January 2. Two widgets are purchased for $50 each.
(2) January 2. Furniture with a 5-year life and zero estimated salvage value is acquired for $50. The straight-line depreciation method is used.
(3) June 30. One widget is sold for $120.
(4) June 30. One new widget is purchased for $80.
(5) June 30. Other expenses of $50 are paid in cash.

An index of the general price level was 100 on January 1, 120 on June 30, and 132 on December 31. On December 31, the current cost of a widget was $90. On this same date, the current cost of replacing the furniture in new condition was $60.

   a. Prepare a four-column income statement and balance sheet as of December 31 for Straus Corporation using the following headings:

   (1) Historical cost/nominal dollars.
   (2) Historical cost/constant dollars of December 31 purchasing power.
   (3) Current cost/nominal dollars.
   (4) Current cost/constant dollars of December 31 purchasing power.

   b. How successful was Straus Corporation in coping with inflation during the year?

18. *Graphical illustration of changing prices relationships.* The Bulova Corporation acquired two tables on January 1. One of these tables was sold on June 30. The other table was still in inventory on December 31. Figure 14.1 depicts various selling price and cost relationships relating to these tables during the year. Point A is the acquisition cost of each table. Using the letters shown in Figure 14.1, indicate the computation of the following items.
   a. Gross margin on sale in historical cost/nominal dollars.
   b. Gross margin on sale in historical cost/constant dollars of June 30 purchasing power.
   c. Gross margin on sale in historical cost/constant dollars of December 31 purchasing power.
   d. Operating margin before holding gains and losses in current cost/nominal dollars.
   e. Realized holding gain in current cost/nominal dollars.
   f. Unrealized holding gain in current cost/nominal dollars.
   g. Operating margin before holding gains and losses in current cost/constant dollars of June 30 purchasing power.
   h. Operating margin before holding gains and losses in current cost/constant dollars of December 31 purchasing power.
   i. Realized holding gain or loss in current cost/constant dollars of June 30 purchasing power.

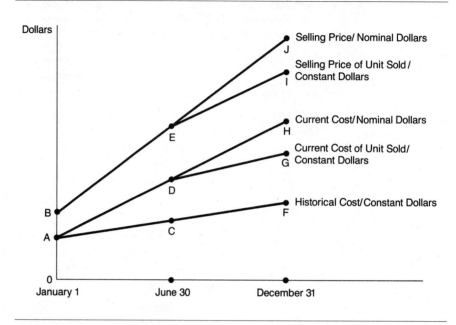

Figure 14.1 Selling Price and Cost Relationships for Bulova Corporation

    j. Realized holding gain or loss in current cost/constant dollars of December 31 purchasing power.

    k. Unrealized holding gain or loss in current cost/constant dollars of December 31 purchasing power.

Problems and Cases

19. *Preparing historical cost/constant dollar financial statements—Year 1.* The financial statements of the Hargrave Corporation for Year 1, its first year of operations, are presented in Exhibits 14.7 and 14.8.

    Indices of the general price level on various dates were as follows (round dollar amounts to the nearest dollar).

(1) On January 1, Year 1, When Common Stock Was Issued.	200
(2) When Store Equipment Was Acquired	205
(3) When Merchandise Inventory Was Acquired	210
(4) When Sales Were Made.	220
(5) When Selling and Administrative Costs Were Incurred	215
(6) On December 31, Year 1	240

    a. Restate the balance sheet on December 31, Year 1, to the general purchasing power of the dollar on December 31, Year 1.

Exhibit 14.7
HARGRAVE CORPORATION
Balance Sheet
December 31, Year 1
(Problem 19)

Assets

Cash	$ 70,000
Accounts Receivable	200,000
Merchandise Inventory	350,000
Store Equipment	400,000
Less Accumulated Depreciation	(40,000)
Total Assets	$980,000

Equities

Accounts Payable	$480,000
Common Stock	250,000
Additional Paid-in Capital	50,000
Retained Earnings	200,000
Total Equities	$980,000

Exhibit 14.8
HARGRAVE CORPORATION
Income Statement
for Year 1
(Problem 19)

Sales Revenue	$800,000
Less Expenses:	
Cost of Goods Sold	$450,000
Depreciation Expense	40,000
Selling and Administrative Expenses	110,000
Total Expenses	$600,000
Net Income	$200,000

b. Restate the income statement for Year 1 to the general purchasing power of
the dollar on December 31, Year 1. Include a separate calculation of the
monetary gain or loss.

20. *Preparing current cost financial statement in nominal and constant dollars.*
Refer to the data for Hargrave Corporation in Problem **19**. Assuming the following
additional information about current cost for Year 1:

	December 31, Year 1
Merchandise Inventory	$410,000
Store Equipment (net)	396,000

	For Year 1
Cost of Goods Sold	$490,000
Depreciation Expense	42,000

    a. Prepare an income statement for Year 1 and a balance sheet as of December 31, Year 1, for Hargrave Corporation in terms of current cost and nominal dollars.

    b. Repeat part **a**, but state all amounts in terms of constant December 31, Year 1, dollars. Assume that sales were made evenly over the year.

21. *Preparing historical cost/constant dollar financial statements—Year 2.* The financial statements of the Hargrave Corporation (see Problem **19**) for Year 2, its second year of operations, are presented in Exhibits 14.9 and 14.10.

Exhibit 14.9
HARGRAVE CORPORATION
Balance Sheet
December 31, Year 2
(Problem 21)

Assets

Cash	$ 110,000
Accounts Receivable	210,000
Merchandise Inventory (based on FIFO)	500,000
Store Equipment	400,000
Accumulated Depreciation	(80,000)
Total Assets	$1,140,000

Equities

Accounts Payable	$ 490,000
Common Stock	250,000
Additional Paid-in Capital	50,000
Retained Earnings	350,000
Total Equities	$1,140,000

Exhibit 14.10
HARGRAVE CORPORATION
Income Statement for Year 2
(Problem 21)

Sales Revenue	$1,000,000
Less Expenses:	
Cost of Goods Sold	$ 550,000
Depreciation Expenses	40,000
Selling and Administrative Expenses	150,000
Total Expenses	$ 740,000
Net Income	$ 260,000

Indices of the general price level on various dates during Year 2 were as follows (round conversion factors to two decimal places; for example, 225/200 = 1.13).

(1) On January 1, Year 2 240
(2) When Merchandise Inventory Was Acquired 245
(3) When Sales Were Made. 260
(4) When Selling and Administrative Costs Were Incurred 255
(5) When Dividend Was Declared and Paid. 280
(6) On December 31, Year 2 280

 a. Restate the balance sheet on December 31, Year 2, in terms of constant dollars of December 31, Year 2, purchasing power.
 b. Restate the income statement for the year ending December 31, Year 2, in terms of constant dollars of December 31, Year 2, purchasing power. Include a separate calculation of the purchasing power gain or loss.
 c. Prepare an analysis of changes in retained earnings for the year ending December 31, Year 2, before and after restatement to a constant dollar basis. The January 1, Year 2, balance in retained earnings, restated to constant dollars of December 31, Year 2, purchasing power is C$293,375.

22. *Interpreting income statements restated for changing prices.* Exhibit 14.11 presents a skeleton four-column income statement under four accounting valuation and measurement bases. Various lines of these income statements are denoted by letter. Using these letters, identify the line or lines on the income statement being described in each of the following cases.
 a. A firm wishes to know whether its selling prices are sufficiently high to cover the cost of replacing goods and services consumed during the period.
 b. A firm wishes to know how much of its conventional net income is due to operating advantages in the markets it serves and how much is due to acquiring assets prior to increases in their replacement cost.

Exhibit 14.11
(Problem 22)

	Historical Cost/ Nominal Dollars (1)	Historical Cost/ Constant Dollars (2)	Current Cost/ Nominal Dollars (3)	Current Cost/ Constant Dollars (4)
Sales	A	E	J	P
Expenses	B	F	K	Q
Operating Income.	C	G	L	R
Realized Holding Gains and Losses	—	—	M	S
Unrealized Holding Gains and Losses	—	—	N	T
Purchasing Power Gain or Loss . .	—	H	—	U
Net Income	D	I	O	V

   c. A firm wishes to know whether the costs of replacing its inventory and depreciable assets have increased faster or slower during the current period than changes in the general price level.

   d. A firm's dividend policy is to pay out the maximum dividend without impairing operating capacity. Which item in Exhibit 14.11 should form the basis for this firm's dividend decisions?

   e. When there have been no changes in either specific or general prices, these net income amounts will be the same.

   f. When specific prices have changed at the same rate as the general price level, these measures of operating income will be the same.

   g. When specific prices of inventory, property, plant, and equipment have increased at a faster rate than the general price level, what will be the relation between M and S?

   h. Respond to part **g**, assuming that specific prices have increased at a slower rate than the general price level.

   i. Respond to part **g**, assuming that specific prices have increased at the same rate as the general price level.

   j. If sales and cost incurrences occur evenly over the year and the constant dollar date is mid-year dollars, what should be the relation between L and R?

   k. If sales and cost incurrences occur evenly over the year and the constant dollar date is year-end dollars, what should be the relation between L and R, assuming both are positive?

   l. During inflation, a firm with a relatively large net debt-equity ratio will find this item to be a positive amount.

23. *Interpreting financial statements restated for changing prices.* Refer to the supplementary information on the impact of changing prices presented for General Products Company in Appendix A. Respond to each of the following questions.

   a. Was General Products Company likely to have been in a net monetary asset position or a net monetary liability position during 1985? Explain.

   b. How much of the conventional income before income taxes, as reported in historical cost/nominal dollars of $2,493 million for 1985, is composed of realized holding gains on inventory items sold and depreciable assets used?

   c. With respect to inventory items sold during 1985, did the general price level increase at a faster or a slower rate than the specific prices of the inventory items since the inventory items were acquired? Explain.

   d. With respect to depreciable assets used during 1985, did the general price level increase at a faster or a slower rate than the specific prices of depreciable assets since the depreciable assets were acquired? Explain.

   e. What is the amount of unrealized holding gain or loss for the year 1985 on inventory, property, plant, and equipment measured in current cost/nominal dollars?

   f. What is the amount of unrealized holding gain or loss for the year 1985 on inventory, property, plant, and equipment measured in current cost/constant average 1985 dollars?

Part Four   Synthesis

Chapter 15   Significance and Implications of Alternative Accounting Principles

The independent accountant expresses an unqualified opinion on a firm's financial statements by stating that the statements were prepared in accordance with "generally accepted accounting principles." Previous chapters have described and illustrated the important accounting principles currently employed in preparing financial statements. This chapter focuses on the following questions:

1. What criteria should a firm employ in selecting its accounting principles from among those that are considered "generally acceptable"?
2. What are the effects of using alternative accounting principles on the principal financial statements?
3. What are the effects of using alternative accounting principles on investors' decisions to invest their capital resources?

One who understands the significance and implications of alternative generally accepted accounting principles is a more effective reader and interpreter of published financial statements. Throughout this chapter, the terms *accounting principles, methods,* and *procedures* are used interchangeably.

Summary of Generally Accepted Accounting Principles

This section lists the major currently acceptable accounting principles, most of which have been discussed in previous chapters. These accounting principles might be classified into three broad groups based on the flexibility permitted to firms in selecting alternative methods of accounting for a specific item. In some instances, the firm has wide flexibility in choosing among alternative methods, such as in selecting depreciation methods. In other instances, the specific conditions associated with a transaction or event dictate the method of accounting that must be used. For example, the method of accounting for investments in the common stock of other firms depends partly on the ownership percentage. In still other instances, the firm has wide flexibility in selecting accounting principles for purposes of preparing its income tax return but limited flexibility in selecting methods for its financial statements. For example, a retail merchandising firm selling goods or services on an installment basis may use the installment basis of recognizing revenue in its tax return but generally cannot use this method in its financial statements. Thus, a particular firm does not have wide flexibility in selecting its accounting methods in all instances.

Revenue Recognition Revenue may be recognized at the time goods are sold or services are rendered, as is typically done under the accrual basis of accounting, at the time cash is collected (installment method or cost-recovery-first method), or as production progresses (percentage-of-completion method for long-term contracts).

Uncollectible Accounts A firm may recognize expense for uncollectible accounts in the period when revenue is recognized (allowance method) or, if the amount of uncollectibles is unpredictable, in the period when specific accounts are found to be uncollectible (direct write-off method).

Inventories A firm may cost inventories on one of several bases: acquisition cost, lower of acquisition cost or market, standard cost, and, in the case of some by-products and precious minerals, net realizable value. When the cost of the specific goods cannot be ascertained, the firm must make a cost flow assumption. The cost flow assumption may be FIFO, LIFO, or weighted average, although LIFO must generally be used for financial reports if it is used for income tax returns.

Investments in Securities A firm accounts for investments in the common stock securities of other firms using either the lower-of-cost-or-market method or the equity method, or else prepares consolidated statements. The method used depends primarily on the percentage of outstanding shares that are held.

Machinery, Equipment, and Other Depreciable Assets These plant assets may be depreciated using the straight-line, double-declining-balance, sum-of-the-years'-digits, or units-of-production method. Estimates of service lives for similar assets may differ among firms.

Leases A firm may set up as an asset and subsequently amortize (capital lease method) the rights to the use of property acquired under lease or give no recognition to the lease except at the time that lease payments are due each period (operating lease method). Likewise, the lessor can set up the rights to receive future lease payments as a receivable at the inception of the lease (capital lease method), or give no recognition to the lease except to the extent that lease payments become due each period (operating lease method). Whether the capital or operating lease method is used depends on such factors as the life of the lease relative to the life of the leased asset and the present value of the lease payments relative to the market value of the leased property. The facts of each lease agreement determine the method to be used. Both the lessor and the lessee will generally use the same method for any lease.

Interest Revenue and Expense on Long-Term Investments and Debt A firm recognizes interest revenue and expense on long-term investments and debt using the effective interest method, although the straight-line method is acceptable if the results are not materially different.

Investment Tax Credits The Internal Revenue Code allows a credit, or reduction, in income taxes payable for investments in certain depreciable assets, such as equipment, furniture, automobiles, and similar property.[1] The maximum credit is currently 10 percent of the cost of the property, although the rate has been changed several times by Congress. The credit reduces the amount of income tax that the firm must pay in the year the assets are acquired. For financial reporting purposes, the firm can recognize the credit as an immediate reduction in income tax expense (flow-through method), or the credit can be deferred and amortized over the life of the property that gave rise to the credit (deferral method).

The preceding list of alternative acceptable accounting principles is not exhaustive. Also, remember that a firm does not always have a choice of methods. The factors that a firm might consider in selecting its accounting principles are discussed next.

The Firm's Selection of Alternative Accounting Principles

The methods of accounting used for income tax and financial reporting purposes generally do not have to be the same. (An exception is the requirement that if LIFO is used for income tax purposes, it must in general also be used for financial reporting.) Because the firm might pursue different objectives for financial and tax reporting, the selection of accounting principles for the two types of reports is discussed separately.

Financial Reporting Purposes

Accurate Presentation One of the criteria for assessing the usefulness of accounting information is *accuracy in presentation* of the underlying events and transactions. This criterion might be used by the firm as a basis for selecting its methods of accounting. For example, assets have been defined as resources having future service potential and expenses as a measurement of the cost of services consumed during the period. In applying the accuracy criterion, the firm would select the inventory cost flow assumption and depreciation method that most accurately measured the pattern of services consumed during the period and the amount of services still available at the end of the period. As a basis for selecting an accounting method, this approach has at least one serious limitation. The accountant can seldom directly observe the services consumed and the service potential remaining. Without this information the accountant cannot ascertain which accounting principles lead to the most accurate presentation of the underlying events. This criterion can serve only as a normative criterion toward which the development and selection of accounting principles should be directed.

---

[1]See footnote 10 in Chapter 9 on page 401, regarding the specific tax rules relating to the investment credit.

Conservatism In choosing among alternative, generally acceptable, methods, the firm might select the set that provides the most conservative measure of net income. Considering the uncertainties involved in measuring benefits received as revenues and services consumed as expenses, some have suggested that a conservative measure of earnings should be provided, thereby reducing the possibility of unwarranted optimism by users of financial statements. As a criterion for selecting accounting principles, *conservatism* implies that methods should be chosen that minimize cumulative reported earnings. That is, expenses should be recognized as quickly as possible, and the recognition of revenue should be postponed as long as possible. This reporting objective would lead to selecting the double-declining-balance or sum-of-the-years'-digits depreciation method, selecting the LIFO cost flow assumption if periods of rising prices are anticipated, and expensing intangible development costs in the year incurred.

The rationale for conservatism as a reporting objective has been challenged. Over the whole life of the firm, income is equal to cash receipts minus cash expenditures. Thus, to the extent that net income of earlier periods is smaller, earnings of later periods must be larger. The "later" periods when income must be larger may, however, be many periods later, sometimes even the last period of the firm's existence. Also, some statement users may be misled by earnings reports based on conservative reporting principles. Consider, for example, investors who sell shares because they feel that the firm is not operating in a sufficiently profitable manner with the resources available, when earnings reported in a less conservative manner would not have induced the sale. Or consider the potential investors who do not purchase securities because they are misled by the published "conservative" statement of earnings.

Profit Maximization A reporting objective having an effect opposite to conservatism might be employed in selecting among alternative generally accepted accounting principles. Somewhat loosely termed *reported profit maximization,*[2] this criterion suggests the selection of accounting methods that maximize cumulative reported earnings. That is, revenue should be recognized as quickly as possible, and the recognition of expense should be postponed as long as possible. For example, the straight-line method of depreciation would be used and, when periods of rising prices are anticipated, the FIFO cost flow assumption would be selected. The use of profit maximization as a reporting objective is an extension of the notion that the firm is in business to generate profits and the firm should present as favorable a report on performance as possible within currently acceptable accounting methods. Profit maximization is subject to a similar, but mirror-image, criticism as the use of conservatism as a reporting objective. Reporting income earlier under the profit maximization criterion must mean that smaller income will be reported in some later period.

---

[2]The concept of profit maximization as a reporting objective is not the same as the profit maximization dictum of microeconomics.

Income Smoothing A final reporting objective that might be used in selecting accounting principles is called *income smoothing*. This criterion suggests selecting accounting methods that result in the smoothest earnings trend over time. As discussed later in this chapter, empirical research has shown that changes in stock prices are related to changes in earnings. Advocates of income smoothing suggest that if a company can minimize fluctuations in earnings, then the perceived risk of investing in shares of its stock will be reduced and, all else being equal, its stock price will be higher. Note that this reporting criterion suggests that net income, not revenues and expenses individually, is to be smoothed. As a result, the firm must consider the total pattern of its operations before selecting the appropriate accounting methods. For example, the straight-line method of depreciation may provide the smoothest amount of depreciation expense on a machine over its life. If, however, the productivity of the machine declines with age so that revenues decrease in later years, net income using the straight-line method may not provide the smoothest net income stream.

Summary The principal message of this section is that accurate presentation, although perhaps a desirable reporting objective, is not operational for selecting accounting principles. As a result, firms may select from among the methods included in the set of generally acceptable accounting principles using whatever reporting criterion they choose.

Where does this flexibility permitted in selecting accounting principles leave the user of financial statements? Accounting Principles Board *Opinion No. 22*[3] requires firms to disclose the accounting principles used in preparing financial statements, either in a separate statement or as a note to the principal statements. An example of such disclosure for General Products Company appears at the beginning of Exhibit A.4 in Appendix A. The effect of alternative accounting principles on investment decisions is discussed later in the chapter.

Income Tax Reporting Purposes

In selecting accounting procedures for income tax purposes, the corporation's objective should be to select those methods that minimize the present value of the stream of income tax payments. The operational rule, sometimes called the *least and latest rule,* is to pay the least amount of taxes as late as possible within the law. The least and latest rule generally translates into a policy of recognizing expenses as quickly as possible and postponing the recognition of revenue as long as possible. This policy might be altered somewhat if income tax rates are expected to change, if the firm had losses in earlier years, or if the firm is a small corporation, a sole proprietorship, or a partnership where earnings are subject to graduated income tax rates of the owners.

The desire to recognize expenses as quickly as possible suggests the adoption of the LIFO inventory cost flow assumption, accelerated cost recovery system, and immediate expensing of research and development, advertising, and similar costs.

---

[3]Accounting Principles Board, *Opinion No. 22,* "Disclosure of Accounting Policies," 1972.

Using the installment basis of recognizing revenue is generally desirable for income tax purposes where permitted by the Internal Revenue Code and Regulations, because it results in postponing the recognition of revenue and the resulting income tax payments until cash is collected.

An Illustration of the Effects of Alternative Accounting Principles on a Set of Financial Statements

This section illustrates the effects of using different accounting principles on a set of financial statements. The illustration has been constructed so that the accounting principles used create significant differences in the financial statements. Therefore, inferences about the usual magnitude of the effects of alternative methods should not be drawn from this example.

The Scenario

On January 1, two corporations are formed to operate merchandising businesses. The two firms are alike in all respects except for their methods of accounting. Conservative Company chooses the accounting principles that will minimize its reported net income. High Flyer Company chooses the accounting principles that will maximize its reported net income. The following events occur during the year.

1. Both corporations issue 2 million shares of $10-par-value stock on January 1, for $20 million cash.
2. Both firms acquire equipment on January 1 for $14 million cash. The equipment is estimated to have a 10-year life and zero salvage value.
3. Both firms make the following purchases of merchandise inventory:

Date	Units Purchased	Unit Price	Cost of Purchases
January 1	170,000	@$60	$10,200,000
May 1	190,000	@$63	11,970,000
September 1	200,000	@$66	13,200,000
Total	560,000		$35,370,000

4. During the year, both firms sell 420,000 units at an average price of $100 each. All sales are made for cash.
5. During the year, both firms have selling, general, and administrative expenses, excluding depreciation, of $2.7 million.
6. The income tax rate is assumed to be 46 percent.

Accounting Principles Used

The methods of accounting used by each firm in preparing its financial statements are described below.

Inventory Cost Flow Assumption Conservative Company makes a LIFO cost flow assumption, whereas High Flyer Company makes a FIFO assumption. The method chosen by each firm is used for both its financial reports and income tax returns. Because the beginning inventory is zero, the cost of goods available for sale by each firm is equal to the purchases during the year of $35,370,000. Both firms have 140,000 units in ending inventory. Conservative Company therefore reports a cost of goods sold of $26,970,000 [= $35,370,000 − (140,000 × $60)], whereas High Flyer Company reports a cost of goods sold of $26,130,000 [= $35,370,000 − (140,000 × $66)]. Income tax regulations generally require a firm to use LIFO in its financial reports if it uses LIFO for its tax return. High Flyer Company desires not to use LIFO in its financial reports and therefore forgoes the tax savings opportunities from using it for tax purposes.

Depreciation Conservative Company decides to depreciate its equipment using the double-declining-balance method in its financial statements whereas High Flyer Company decides to use the straight-line method. Conservative Company therefore reports depreciation expense of $2.8 million (= $2 \times \frac{1}{10} \times$ $14,000,000), whereas High Flyer Company reports depreciation expense of $1.4 million (= $\frac{1}{10} \times$ $14,000,000) to shareholders. Both companies compute depreciation for tax purposes using the Accelerated Cost Recovery System (ACRS). Depreciation on the tax return is $2.1 million for the year.

Investment Tax Credit Because both firms purchased long-term, depreciable equipment costing $14 million, each is entitled to a tax reduction or credit of $1.4 million (= .10 × $14,000,000) in the taxes otherwise payable for the year. On its financial statements to shareholders, Conservative Company chooses to report the benefits of the tax reduction over the 10-year life of the equipment that gave rise to the tax reduction (deferral method), whereas High Flyer Company reports the entire benefit of the tax reduction in computing net income reported to shareholders (flow-through method) for the current year.

Comparative Income Statements

Exhibit 15.1 presents comparative income statements for Conservative Company and High Flyer Company for the year ending December 31. For each company, the revenues and expenses (except for depreciation) reported in the financial statements are the same as reported in the income tax return.

Conservative Company reports $700 million (= $2,800 − $2,100) more depreciation in the financial statements than in the tax return. The $700 million difference is viewed as a timing difference. Income taxes payable currently (before considering the investment tax credit) of $4,705.8 million exceed income tax expense (be-

Exhibit 15.1
Comparative Income Statements Based on Different Accounting
Principles for the Year Ending December 31
(amounts in 000's, except for per-share amounts)

	Conservative Company		High Flyer Company	
	Financial Statement	Tax Return	Financial Statement	Tax Return
Sales Revenue.	$42,000.0	$42,000.0	$42,000.0	$42,000.0
Expenses:				
Cost of Goods Sold.	$26,970.0	$26,970.0	$26,130.0	$26,130.0
Depreciation on Equipment[a] . . .	2,800.0	2,100.0	1,400.0	2,100.0
Other Selling, General, and Administrative	2,700.0	2,700.0	2,700.0	2,700.0
Expenses Before Income Taxes . .	$32,470.0	$31,770.0	$30,230.0	$30,930.0
Net Income Before Income Taxes	$ 9,530.0	$10,230.0	$11,770.0	$11,070.0
Income Tax Expense[b].	4,243.8		4,014.2	
Net Income	$ 5,286.2		$ 7,755.8	
Earnings per Share (2,000,000 shares outstanding) .	$2.64		$3.88	

[b]Computation of Income Tax Expense:

Income Before Taxes	$ 9,530.0	$10,230.0	$11,770.0	$11,070.0
Income Tax on Current Income (at 46 percent)	$ 4,383.8	$ 4,705.8	$ 5,414.2	$ 5,092.2
Less: Tax Credit for Investment in Equipment	140.0	1,400.0	1,400.0	1,400.0
Income Tax Expense.	$ 4,243.8		$ 4,014.2	
Income Tax Currently Payable . .		$ 3,305.8		$ 3,692.2
Deferred Investment Tax Credit ($1,400 − $140)	$ 1,260.0			
[a]Income Taxes Deferred by Timing Differences for Depreciation:				
Dr. = .46 ($2,100 − $2,800) .	$ (322.0)			
Cr. = .46 ($2,100 − $1,400) .			$ 322.0	

fore considering the investment tax credit) of $4,383.8. The $322.0 difference
(= $4,705.8 − $4,383.8) is debited to Prepaid Income Taxes on the balance sheet.

For tax purposes, the $1,400 investment tax credit on the equipment purchases
immediately reduces taxes payable by Conservative Company. For the financial
statements, the credit will be deferred and amortized to income over the life of the
equipment. Thus, income tax expense is reduced by $140 thousand in the current
year and the unamortized investment tax credit of $1,260 (= $1,400 − $140) ap-
pears on the balance sheet.

High Flyer Company reports $700 (= $1,400 − $2,100) thousand less deprecia-
tion in the financial statements than in the tax return. This $700 thousand difference
is likewise a timing difference. Because taxes payable currently (before considering

the investment tax credit) are less than income tax expense (before the investment credit), a deferred tax credit appears on the equities side of the balance sheet. Because High Flyer recognizes the full investment credit realized as an immediate reduction in income tax expense, it will not show a Deferred Investment Tax Credit account on the balance sheet.

Note in this illustration that reported net income and earnings per share of High Flyer Company are significantly larger than for Conservative Company.

Comparative Balance Sheets

Exhibit 15.2 presents comparative balance sheets for Conservative Company and High Flyer Company as of December 31. Merchandise inventory and equipment (net) as well as total assets of Conservative Company are stated at lower amounts than those of High Flyer Company. The only real difference between the economic positions of each company is the amount of cash. The difference in the amount of cash is attributable to the payment of different amounts of income taxes by the two firms. Note that Conservative Company has more cash because it paid smaller income taxes. One could argue that it is better off than High Flyer Company.

The differences in the amounts at which merchandise inventory and equipment (net) are stated result from the different accounting methods used by the two companies. The amounts shown for Conservative Company are smaller than the corresponding amounts for High Flyer Company because a larger portion of the costs incurred during the period by Conservative Company has been recognized as an expense. Conservative Company also shows Prepaid Income Taxes of $322 arising from differences in depreciation for financial and tax reporting.

Exhibit 15.2
Comparative Balance Sheets Based on Alternative
Accounting Principles, December 31
(amounts in 000's)

	Conservative Company	High Flyer Company
Assets		
Cash	$ 6,624.2	$ 6,237.8
Merchandise Inventory	8,400.0	9,240.0
Equipment (at acquisition cost)	14,000.0	14,000.0
Less: Accumulated Depreciation	(2,800.0)	(1,400.0)
Prepaid Income Taxes	322.0	—
Total Assets	$26,546.2	$28,077.8
Equities		
Deferred Investment Tax Credits	$ 1,260.0	—
Deferred Income Taxes	—	$ 322.0
Common Stock	20,000.0	20,000.0
Retained Earnings	5,286.2	7,755.8
Total Equities	$26,546.2	$28,077.8

In the equities portion of the balance sheet, Conservative Company shows deferred investment tax credits, reflecting its decision to recognize the current reduction in income taxes payable as a reduction of expense over the life of the property. High Flyer Company reports deferred income taxes on the balance sheet resulting from differences in the timing of depreciation on equipment in the financial statements and income tax return.

Note the effect of using alternative accounting principles on the ratio, rate of return on total assets (= net income/total assets). Conservative Company reports a smaller amount of net income but also a smaller amount of total assets. One might expect, then, the rate of return on total assets of the two firms to approximate each other more closely than either net income or total assets individually. Significant differences in the ratio for the two firms are still observable, however, in this illustration. The rate of return on total assets of Conservative Company is 22.7 percent [= $5,286,200/($20,000,000 + $26,546,200)/2] and of High Flyer Company is 32.3 percent [= $7,755,800/($20,000,000 + $28,077,800)/2].

Exhibit 15.3 presents comparative statements of changes in financial position for Conservative Company and High Flyer Company. The amount of cash provided by operations of Conservative Company is larger than for High Flyer Company. The difference of $386.4 million (= $624.2 − $237.8) is attributable to the difference in the amount of income taxes paid. These companies paid different amounts of income taxes because they used different cost flow assumptions for inventories on their tax returns, as shown below:

Conservative Company: LIFO Cost of Goods Sold	$26,970
High Flyer Company: FIFO Cost of Goods Sold	26,130
Difference in Cost of Goods Sold and Taxable Income	$ 840
Tax Rate	46%
Difference in Cash Flow	$ 386.4

Note that the use of different depreciation methods *on the financial statements* does not affect cash flows and the statement of changes in financial position. As long as these firms use the same depreciation method on their tax returns, cash flows will be the same. Thus, the statement of changes in financial position tends to be affected much less by alternative generally accepted accounting principles than are the balance sheet and income statement.

Moral of the Illustration

In order to interpret published financial statements, the analyst must be aware of which accounting principles from the set of alternative generally accepted accounting principles are used. When reports of several companies are compared, the amounts shown should be adjusted where possible for the different accounting methods used. The techniques for making some of these adjustments were illustrated in previous chapters (for example, LIFO to FIFO cost flow assumption,

Exhibit 15.3
Comparative Statements of Changes
in Financial Position for the Year Ending December 31
(amounts in 000's)

	Conservative Company	High Flyer Company
Sources of Cash		
Operations:		
Net Income	$ 5,286.2	$ 7,755.8
Additions:		
Depreciation Expense	2,800.0	1,400.0
Excess of Investment Tax Credit Reducing Income Taxes Payable over Credit Recognized in Computing Net Income ($1,400 − $140) . .	1,260.0	—
Deferred Tax Credit	—	322.0
Subtractions:		
Deferred Tax Debit	(322.0)	
Increase in Merchandise Inventory	(8,400.0)	(9,240.0)
Cash Provided by Operations	$ 624.2	$ 237.8
Issue of Common Stock	20,000.0	20,000.0
Total Sources of Cash	$20,624.2	$20,237.8
Uses of Cash		
Acquisition of Equipment	14,000.0	14,000.0
Change in Cash	$ 6,624.2	$ 6,237.8

equity method to consolidated statements). The notes to the financial statements will disclose the accounting methods used, but not necessarily the data required to make appropriate adjustments.

Assessing the Effects of Alternative Accounting Principles on Investment Decisions

Previous sections of this chapter emphasized the flexibility that firms have in selecting accounting procedures and the possible effects of using different accounting procedures on the financial statements. We now focus briefly on a related and important question: Do investors accept financial statement information as presented, or do they somehow filter out all or most of the differences in the financial statements of various firms resulting from differences in the methods of accounting employed? If investors accept financial statement information as presented, without adjustments for the methods of accounting used, then two firms, otherwise identical except for the accounting procedures employed, might receive a disproportionate amount of capital funds. Thus, the use of alternative accounting principles could lead to a misallocation of resources in the economy. On the other hand, if investors make adjustments for the different accounting procedures in analyzing the financial statements of various firms, perhaps the policy maker need not be concerned over the variety of acceptable accounting principles. If investors do make such adjustments, then increased disclosure of the procedures followed may be more important than greater uniformity in accounting principles.

The question as to the effect of alternative accounting principles on investment decisions has been the subject of extensive debate among public accountants, academics, personnel in government agencies, and financial statement users.

Those who believe that investors can be misled point to examples where the market prices of particular firms' shares of stock have decreased dramatically after the effects of using specific accounting procedures have been carefully analyzed and reported in the financial press.[4] In these examples it is often difficult, however, to judge if the price change is attributable to the disclosure of the effects of using particular accounting procedures or to other, more temporary factors affecting the specific firm, its industry, or all firms in the economy. Also, it is difficult to generalize on the effects of using alternative accounting principles on investment decisions from isolated and anecdotal examples.

An expanding number of empirical research studies, on the other hand, have provided support for the view that investors at the aggregate market level are rarely misled by the accounting methods employed. This research has developed from the theory and empirical evidence that the stock market is efficient, in the sense that market prices adjust quickly and in an unbiased manner to new information.[5] Unlike the examples supporting the view that investors are misled, these empirical studies have been based on data for a large number of firms over long time periods. Also, an effort is made in these studies to control for the effects of economy-wide and industry effects on market price changes.

Several studies have shown that changes in earnings and changes in market prices are associated and, therefore, indicate that information contained in the financial statements is used by investors in making their resource allocation decisions.[6] Several studies have examined the effects of *changes* in the methods of accounting on

---

[4]For several examples see Abraham J. Briloff, *More Debits Than Credits,* Harper & Row, New York, 1976. For an analysis of these examples see George Foster, "Briloff and the Capital Market," *Journal of Accounting Research,* Spring 1979, pp. 262–274.

[5]See Eugene F. Fama, "Efficient Capital Markets: A Review of Theory and Empirical Work," *Journal of Finance,* May 1970, pp. 383–417.

[6]See, for example, Ray Ball and Philip Brown, "An Empirical Evaluation of Accounting Income Numbers," *Journal of Accounting Research,* Autumn 1968, pp. 159–178; William H. Beaver, "The Information Content of Annual Earnings Announcements," *Empirical Research in Accounting: Selected Studies, 1968,* Supplement to Vol. 6, *Journal of Accounting Research,* pp. 67–92; Robert G. May, "The Influence of Quarterly Earnings Announcements on Investor Decisions as Reflected in Common Stock Price Changes," *Empirical Research in Accounting: Selected Studies, 1971,* Supplement to Vol. 9, *Journal of Accounting Research,* pp. 119–163.

market prices,[7] and a third group of studies looked at *differences* in the methods of accounting across firms.[8] The results of these last two groups of studies have been mixed, with several studies supporting the position that investors are misled and several studies supporting the position that they are not misled. The methodology employed in many of these studies has been extensively criticized, so the full implications are not clear.[9]

Research into the question regarding the effects of alternative accounting principles on investment decisions has not progressed sufficiently for any consensus to have been reached. The research that has been conducted has been described here briefly to emphasize an important point. It is not obvious, as it might first appear, that the current flexibility permitted firms in selecting accounting principles necessarily misleads investors and results in a misallocation of resources.[10]

Development of Principles in Accounting

Chapter 7 indicated that the development of "generally accepted accounting principles" is essentially a political process. Various persons or groups have power or authority in the decision process, including Congress and the Securities and Exchange Commission, the courts, professional accounting organizations and their members, business firms, and financial statement users. Although Congress has the

---

[7]See, for example, Ray Ball, "Changes in Accounting Techniques and Stock Prices," *Empirical Research in Accounting: Selected Studies, 1972,* Supplement to Vol. 10, *Journal of Accounting Research,* pp. 1–38; Robert S. Kaplan and Richard Roll, "Investor Evaluation of Accounting Information: Some Empirical Evidence," *Journal of Business,* April 1972, pp. 225–257; Shyam Sunder, "Relationships Between Accounting Changes and Stock Prices: Problems of Measurement and Some Empirical Evidence," *Empirical Research in Accounting: Selected Studies, 1973,* Supplement to Vol. 11, *Journal of Accounting Research,* pp. 1–45.

[8]See, for example, Robert E. Jensen, "An Experimental Design for Study of Effects of Accounting Variations in Decision Making," *Journal of Accounting Research,* Autumn 1966, pp. 224–238; Thomas R. Dyckman, "On the Investment Decision," *The Accounting Review,* April 1964, pp. 285–295; John L. O'Donnell, "Relationships Between Reported Earnings and Stock Prices in the Electric Utility Industry," *The Accounting Review,* January 1965, pp. 135–143.

[9]For a review of these studies, see Ray Ball and George Foster, "Corporate Financial Reporting: A Methodological Review of Empirical Research," *Studies in Current Methodologies in Accounting: A Critical Evaluation,* Supplement to Vol. 20 (1982), *Journal of Accounting Research,* pp. 117–148; Baruch Lev and James A. Ohlson, "Market-Based Empirical Research: A Review, Interpretation, and Extension," *Ibid.,* pp. 249–322.

[10]For a description of the theoretical framework and a summary of the empirical work behind this position, see Nicholas J. Gonedes and Nicholas Dopuch, "Capital Market Equilibrium, Information-Production, and Selecting Accounting Techniques: Theoretical Framework and Review of Empirical Work," *Studies on Financial Accounting Objectives: 1974,* Supplement to Vol. 12, *Journal of Accounting Research,* pp. 48–129; and Robert S. Kaplan, "Information Content of Financial Accounting Numbers: A Survey of Empirical Evidence," in *Symposium of Impact of Accounting Research in Financial Accounting and Disclosure on Accounting Practice,* edited by T. Keller and R. Abdel-khalik, Duke University Press, Durham, N.C., 1978.

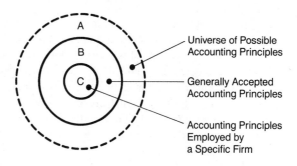

Figure 15.1 Structure of Accounting Principles

ultimate authority to specify acceptable accounting methods, it has delegated that authority in almost all cases to the Securities and Exchange Commission. The commission has indicated that it will generally accept the pronouncements of the Financial Accounting Standards Board on accounting principles. The role of the private sector versus the public sector in setting accounting principles and regulating professional accounting practice continues, however, to be the subject of extensive debate.

Summary

The structure of accounting principles might be depicted as shown in Figure 15.1. The *universe* of possible accounting principles is encircled by a dashed line because of the difficulty in defining the relative size, or boundaries, of circle A. The process of specifying the principles designated as *generally acceptable* (the subset of principles from circle A represented by circle B) is political in nature. Congress and the Securities and Exchange Commission have the legal authority to make the selection, but most of the responsibility for doing so has, in effect, been delegated to the Financial Accounting Standards Board. The individual firm's selection of accounting principles (the subset of principles from circle B represented by circle C) might be based on a criterion of accurate presentation. However, because benefits received and services consumed are seldom observable events and are therefore difficult to measure, reaching consensus on which generally accepted accounting principles provide an accurate or fair presentation is difficult. This chapter suggests that a firm might pursue a specific reporting objective, such as conservatism, profit maximization, or income smoothing, in selecting its accounting principles.

Before we can know whether circle B should be widened or narrowed, we must learn whether investors accept financial statement information as presented or whether investors make adjustments to recognize the effects of using alternative accounting principles. This question has been, and continues to be, the subject of extensive research.

Master Review Problem for Self-Study

Presented below are a set of financial statements for Kaplan Corporation, including a consolidated income statement (Exhibit 15.4) and a consolidated statement of changes in financial position (Exhibit 15.5) for Year 2, and a comparative consolidated balance sheet (Exhibit 15.6) on December 31, Year 1 and Year 2. Following the financial statements is a series of notes providing additional information on certain items in the financial statements. Respond to each of the questions on page 673, using information from the financial statements and notes. It is suggested that you study the statements and notes carefully before attempting to respond to the questions.

Exhibit 15.4
KAPLAN CORPORATION
Consolidated Income Statement for Year 2
(amounts in 000's)

Revenues:	
Sales	$12,000
Equity in Earnings of Unconsolidated Affiliates	300
Dividend Revenue	20
Gain on Sale of Marketable Securities	30
Total Revenues	$12,350
Expenses:	
Cost of Goods Sold	$ 7,200
Selling and Administrative	2,689
Loss on Sale of Equipment	80
Unrealized Loss from Price Decline of Marketable Equity Securities	20
Interest (Notes 7 and 8)	561
Total Expenses	$10,550
Net Income Before Income Taxes and Minority Interest	$ 1,800
Income Tax Expense	720
Net Income Before Minority Interest	$ 1,080
Minority Interest in Earnings of Heimann Corporation	40
Net Income	$ 1,040

Note 1: Summary of Accounting Policies

Basis of consolidation. The financial statements of Kaplan Corporation are consolidated with Heimann Corporation, an 80 percent-owned subsidiary acquired on January 2, Year 1.

Marketable securities. Marketable securities are stated at the lower of acquisition cost or market.

Accounts receivable. Uncollectible accounts of customers are accounted for using the allowance method.

Exhibit 15.5
KAPLAN CORPORATION
Consolidated Statement of Changes in Financial Position for Year 2
(amounts in 000's)

Sources of Cash and Marketable Securities:

Operations:

Net Income	$1,040	
Additions:		
Depreciation	560	
Deferred Taxes	120	
Loss on Sale of Equipment	80	
Minority Interest in Undistributed Earnings of Consolidated Subsidiaries	34	
Amortization of Discount on Bonds	28	
Amortization of Goodwill	10	
Increase in Notes Payable	1,000	
Increase in Accounts Payable	1,355	
Increase in Interest Payable	100	
Increase in Income Taxes Payable	125	
Subtractions:		
Equity in Earnings of Affiliates and Subsidiaries in Excess of Dividends Received	(180)	
Amortization of Premium on Bonds	(28)	
Increase in Accounts Receivable	(550)	
Increase in Inventories	(520)	
Increase in Prepayments	(170)	
Decrease in Salaries Payable	(200)	
Cash Provided by Operations		$2,804
New Financing:		
Common Stock Issued	$ 500	
Treasury Shares Sold	15	
Cash Provided by Financing		515
Sale of Equipment		150
Total Sources of Cash and Marketable Securities		$3,469

Uses of Cash and Marketable Securities:

Dividends		$ 250
Acquisition of Assets:		
Investment in Johnson Corporation	$ 50	
Land	100	
Building	300	
Equipment	1,400	
Total Used for Acquisition of Assets		1,850
Total Uses of Cash		$2,100
Change in Cash and Marketable Securities		$1,369

Exhibit 15.6
KAPLAN CORPORATION
Consolidated Balance Sheets
December 31, Year 1 and Year 2
(amounts in 000's)

	December 31, Year 1	December 31, Year 2
Assets		
Current Assets:		
Cash	$ 1,470	$ 2,739
Marketable Securities (Note 2).	450	550
Accounts Receivable (net; Note 3)	2,300	2,850
Inventories (Note 4)	2,590	3,110
Prepayments.	800	970
Total Current Assets	$ 7,610	$10,219
Investments (Note 5):		
Investment in Maher Corporation (10 percent)	$ 200	$ 185
Investment in Johnson Corporation (30 percent)	310	410
Investment in Burton Credit Corporation (100 percent) .	800	930
Total Investments	$ 1,310	$ 1,525
Property, Plant, and Equipment:		
Land	$ 400	$ 500
Buildings	800	940
Equipment.	3,300	3,800
Total Cost	$ 4,500	$ 5,240
Less Accumulated Depreciation	(1,200)	(930)
Net Property, Plant, and Equipment	$ 3,300	$ 4,310
Goodwill (Note 6)	90	80
Total Assets	$12,310	$16,134

continued

Inventories. Inventories are determined using a last-in, first-out (LIFO) cost flow assumption.

Investments. Investments of less than 20 percent of the outstanding common stock of other companies are accounted for using the lower-of-cost-or-market method. Investments of greater than or equal to 20 percent of the outstanding common stock of unconsolidated affiliates and subsidiaries are accounted for using the equity method.

Buildings and equipment. Depreciation for financial reporting purposes is calculated using the straight-line method. For income tax purposes, ACRS is used.

Goodwill. Goodwill is amortized over a period of 10 years.

Interest on long-term debt. Interest expense on bonds payable is recognized using the effective interest method.

Deferred income taxes. Deferred income taxes are provided for timing differences between book income and taxable income.

Investment tax credit. The investment tax credit is accounted for using the flow-through method.

Exhibit 15.6 *(continued)*

Liabilities and Shareholders' Equity

Current Liabilities:

Note Payable (Note 7)	$ —	$ 1,000
Accounts Payable	1,070	2,425
Salaries Payable	800	600
Interest Payable	300	400
Income Taxes Payable	250	375
Total Current Liabilities	$ 2,420	$ 4,800
Long-Term Liabilities:		
Bonds Payable (Note 8).	$ 6,209	$ 6,209
Deferred Income Taxes	820	940
Total Long-Term Liabilities.	$ 7,029	$ 7,149
Minority Interest	$ 180	$ 214
Shareholders' Equity:		
Common Shares ($10 par value).	$ 500	$ 600
Additional Paid-in Capital	800	1,205
Unrealized Loss on Valuation of Investments	(25)	(40)
Retained Earnings	1,436	2,226
Total	$ 2,711	$ 3,991
Less Treasury Shares (at cost)	(30)	(20)
Total Shareholders' Equity.	$ 2,681	$ 3,971
Total Liabilities and Shareholders' Equity	$12,310	$16,134

Note 2: Marketable securities are shown net of an allowance for market price declines below acquisition cost of $50,000 on December 31, Year 1, and $70,000 on December 31, Year 2.

Note 3: Accounts receivable are shown net of an allowance for uncollectible accounts of $200,000 on December 31, Year 1, and $250,000 on December 31, Year 2. Bad debt expense of $120,000 is included in Selling and Administrative Expenses.

Note 4: Inventories consist of the following:

	December 31, Year 1	December 31, Year 2
Raw Materials	$ 330,000	$ 380,000
Work in Process	460,000	530,000
Finished Goods	1,800,000	2,200,000
Total	$2,590,000	$3,110,000

The current cost of inventories exceeded the amounts determined on a LIFO basis by $420,000 on December 31, Year 1, and $730,000 on December 31, Year 2.

Note 5: Condensed financial statements for Burton Credit Corporation, a wholly owned, unconsolidated subsidiary, are shown on page 672.

Note 6: On January 2, Year 1, Kaplan Corporation acquired 80 percent of the outstanding common shares of Heimann Corporation by issuing 20,000 shares of Kaplan Corporation common stock. The Kaplan Corporation shares were selling on

BURTON CREDIT CORPORATION
(amounts in 000's)

	December 31, Year 1	December 31, Year 2
Balance Sheet		
Cash and Marketable Securities	$ 760	$ 840
Accounts Receivable (net)	6,590	7,400
Other Assets	1,050	1,260
Total Assets	$8,400	$9,500
Notes Payable Due Within 1 Year	$3,900	$4,300
Long-Term Note Payable	2,620	3,100
Other Liabilities	1,080	1,170
Common Stock	100	100
Additional Paid-in Capital	300	300
Retained Earnings	400	530
Total Equities	$8,400	$9,500

	Year 2
Statement of Income and Retained Earnings	
Revenues	$680
Expenses	520
Net Income	$160
Less: Dividends	(30)
Retained Earnings, December 31, Year 1	400
Retained Earnings, December 31, Year 2	$530

January 2, Year 1, for $40 a share. Any difference between the acquisition price and the book value of the net assets acquired was considered goodwill and is being amortized over a period of 10 years from the date of acquisition.

Note 7: The note payable included under current liabilities is a 1-year note due on January 2, Year 3. The note requires annual interest payments on December 31 of each year.

Note 8: Bonds payable are the following:

	December 31, Year 1	December 31, Year 2
4 Percent, $2,000,000 Bonds Due Dec. 31, Year 7, with Interest Payable Semiannually . . .	$1,800,920	$1,829,390
10 Percent, $3,000,000 Bonds Due Dec. 31, Year 11, with Interest Payable Semiannually . . .	3,407,720	3,379,790
8 Percent, $1,000,000 Bonds Due on Dec. 31, Year 17, with Interest Payable Semiannually . . .	1,000,000	1,000,000
Total	$6,208,640	$6,209,180

a. Marketable securities costing $180,000 were sold during Year 2. Ascertain the price at which these securities were sold.

b. Refer to part **a**. Compute the cost of marketable securities purchased during Year 2.

c. What was the amount of specific customers' accounts written off as uncollectible during Year 2?

d. Assume that all sales are made on account. Compute the amount of cash collected from customers during the year.

e. Compute the cost of units completed and transferred to the finished goods inventory during Year 2.

f. Direct labor and overhead costs incurred in manufacturing during the year totaled $4,500,000. Determine the cost of raw materials purchased during Year 2.

g. Assume that the amounts disclosed in Note 4 for the current cost of inventories represent the amounts that would be obtained from using a first-in, first-out (FIFO) cost flow assumption. What would cost of goods sold have been if FIFO rather than LIFO had been used?

h. Prepare an analysis that explains the causes of the changes in each of the three intercorporate investment accounts.

i. Assume that Burton Credit Corporation had been consolidated with Kaplan Corporation instead of being treated as an unconsolidated subsidiary. Prepare a condensed consolidated balance sheet on December 31, Year 2, and a condensed consolidated income statement for Year 2 for Kaplan Corporation and Burton Credit Corporation.

j. Prepare an analysis that explains the change in each of the following four accounts during Year 2: Land, Building, Equipment, and Accumulated Depreciation.

k. Give the journal entry made on Kaplan Corporation's books on January 2, Year 1, when it acquired Heimann Corporation.

l. Compute the book value of the net assets of Heimann Corporation on January 2, Year 1.

m. Compute the total amount of dividends declared by Heimann Corporation during Year 2.

n. The 4 percent bonds payable were initially priced to yield 6 percent compounded semiannually. The 10 percent bonds were initially priced to yield 8 percent compounded semiannually. Using the appropriate present value tables at the back of the book, demonstrate that $1,800,920 and $3,407,720 (see Note 8) were the correct valuations of these two bond issues on December 31, Year 1.

o. Calculate the amount of interest expense and any change in the valuation of the bond liability for Year 2 on each of the three long-term bond issues (see Note 8).

p. Compute the amount of income taxes actually paid during Year 2.

q. On July 1, Year 2, Kaplan Corporation sold 10,000 shares of its common stock on the open market for $50 a share. Prepare an analysis explaining the change during Year 2 in each of the following accounts: Common Shares, Additional Paid-in Capital, Retained Earnings, Treasury Shares.

Suggested Solution

a.

Cost of Marketable Securities Sold	$180,000
Gain on Sale (from Income Statement)	30,000
Selling Price	$210,000

b.

Marketable Securities at Cost on December 31, Year 1 ($450,000 + $50,000)	$500,000
Plus Purchases	?
Less Cost of Marketable Securities Sold	(180,000)
Marketable Securities at Cost on December 31, Year 2 ($550,000 + $70,000)	$620,000

The cost of marketable securities purchased during Year 2 was $300,000.

c.

Allowance for Uncollectible Accounts, December 31, Year 1	$200,000
Plus Provision for Uncollectible Accounts During Year 2	120,000
Less Specific Customers' Accounts Written Off as Uncollectible During Year 2	(?)
Allowance for Uncollectible Accounts, December 31, Year 2	$250,000

Specific customers' accounts written off as uncollectible during Year 2 totaled $70,000.

d.

Gross Accounts Receivable December 31, Year 1[a]	$ 2,500
Plus Sales During the Year	12,000
Less Gross Accounts Receivable December 31, Year 2[b]	(3,100)
Accounts Collected or Written Off	$11,400
Less Write-offs	(70)
Cash Collected During Year	$11,330

[a]$2,300 + $200.
[b]$2,850 + $250.

e.

Finished Goods Inventory, December 31, Year 1	$1,800,000
Plus Cost of Units Completed During the Year	?
Less Cost of Units Sold During the Year	(7,200,000)
Finished Goods Inventory, December 31, Year 2	$2,200,000

The cost of units completed was $7,600,000.

f.

Work in Process Inventory, December 31, Year 1	$ 460,000
Plus Cost of Raw Materials Used.	?
Plus Direct Labor and Manufacturing Overhead Costs Incurred	4,500,000
Less Cost of Units Completed	(7,600,000)
Work-in-Process Inventory, December 31, Year 2	$ 530,000

The cost of raw materials used during Year 2 was $3,170,000.

Raw Materials Inventory, December 31, Year 1	$ 330,000
Plus Cost of Raw Materials Purchased	?
Less Cost of Raw Materials Used	(3,170,000)
Raw Materials Inventory, December 31, Year 2	$ 380,000

The cost of raw materials purchased was $3,220,000.

g.

	LIFO	Difference	FIFO
Inventory, December 31, Year 1	$ 2,590,000	$420,000	$ 3,010,000
Purchases Plus Costs Incurred	7,720,000	—	7,720,000
Goods Available.	$10,310,000	$420,000	$10,730,000
Less Inventory, December 31, Year 2 . .	3,110,000	730,000	3,840,000
Cost of Goods Sold	$ 7,200,000	($310,000)	$ 6,890,000

Cost of goods sold under FIFO would have been $6,890,000.

h. Investment in Maher Corporation (lower-of-cost-or-market method)

Balance, December 31, Year 1	$200,000
Plus Additional Investments	-0-
Less Sale of Investments	-0-
Less Increase in Unrealized Loss on Valuation of Investments	15,000
Balance, December 31, Year 2	$185,000

Investment in Johnson Corporation (equity method)

Balance, December 31, Year 1	$310,000
Plus Additional Investments	50,000
Plus Equity in Earnings (total equity in earnings of $300,000 from income statement minus equity in earnings of Burton Credit Corporation of $160,000)	140,000
Less Sale of Investments	-0-
Less Dividend Received (plug).	(90,000)
Balance, December 31, Year 2	$410,000

Investment in Burton Credit Corporation (equity method)

Balance, December 31, Year 1	$800,000
Plus Additional Investments	-0-
Plus Equity in Earnings	160,000
Less Sale of Investments	-0-
Less Dividends Received	(30,000)
Balance, December 31, Year 2	$930,000

i.

Balance Sheet	Kaplan Corp.	Burton Credit Corp.	Eliminations		Consolidated
Cash and Marketable Securities	$ 3,289	$ 840			$ 4,129
Accounts Receivable .	2,850	7,400			10,250
Investment in Burton Credit Corporation .	930	—	$930		—
Other Assets	9,065	1,260			10,325
Total Assets	$16,134	$9,500			$24,704
Notes Payable:					
Due Within 1 Year .	$ 1,000	$4,300			$ 5,300
Long-Term	6,209	3,100			9,309
Other Liabilities	4,740	1,170			5,910
Minority Interest . . .	214				214
Common Shares . . .	600	100	$100		600
Additional Paid-in Capital.	1,205	300	300		1,205
Unrealized Loss on Valuation of Investments	(40)	—			(40)
Retained Earnings . .	2,226	530	530		2,226
Treasury Shares . . .	(20)	—			(20)
Total Equities. . . .	$16,134	$9,500	$930	$930	$24,704
Income Statement					
Revenues	$11,930	$ 680			$12,610
Equity in Earnings of Unconsolidated Affiliates	300	—	$160[a]		140
Expenses	(11,190)	(520)			(11,710)
Net Income	$ 1,040	$ 160			$ 1,040

[a]The credit entry for $160 would be made to the Investment account in Burton Credit Corporation. Because the entry above—to eliminate the investment account—was made to *post-closing* trial balance data, this $160 debit is implicitly included in the debit of $530 made to the Retained Earnings account.

j.   Land

Balance, December 31, Year 1.	$ 400,000
Plus Acquisitions	100,000
Less Disposals	-0-
Balance, December 31, Year 2.	$ 500,000

Building

Balance, December 31, Year 1	$ 800,000
Plus Acquisition	300,000
Less Retirements (plug)	(160,000)
Balance, December 31, Year 2	$ 940,000

Equipment

Balance, December 31, Year 1	$3,300,000
Plus Acquisitions	1,400,000
Less Disposals (plug)	(900,000)
Balance, December 31, Year 2	$3,800,000

Accumulated Depreciation

Balance, December 31, Year 1	$1,200,000
Plus Depreciation for Year 2	560,000
Less Accumulated Depreciation on Building Retired (plug)	(160,000)
Less Accumulated Depreciation on Equipment Sold (see below)	(670,000)
Balance, December 31, Year 2	$ 930,000
Selling Price of Equipment Sold	$ 150,000
Loss on Sale of Equipment	80,000
Book Value of Equipment Sold	$ 230,000
Cost of Equipment Sold (from above)	$ 900,000
Less Accumulated Depreciation on Equipment Sold	(670,000)
Book Value of Equipment Sold	$ 230,000

k.

Investment in Heimann Corporation	800,000	
Common Stock (20,000 × $10)		200,000
Additional Paid-in Capital (20,000 × $30)		600,000

l.

Cost of Investment in Heimann Corporation	$ 800,000
Goodwill $80,000 + (2 × $10,000)	(100,000)
Book Value of Net Assets Acquired	$ 700,000

80 percent acquired; so book value of Heimann on date of acquisition is $700,000/.80 = $875,000.

m.

Minority Interest in Heimann Corporation, January 2, Year 2	$180,000
Plus Minority Interest in Earnings of Heimann Corporation (from income statement)	40,000
Less Minority Interest in Dividends of Heimann Corporation (plug)	(6,000)
Minority Interest in Heimann Corporation, December 31, Year 2 (from balance sheet)	$214,000

Total dividends declared were $30,000 (= $6,000/.20).

n. 4 Percent Bond Issue

$40,000 × 9.9540	$ 398,160
$2,000,000 × .70138	1,402,760
Total	$1,800,920

10 Percent Bond Issue

$150,000 × 13.59033	$2,038,550
$3,000,000 × .45639	1,369,170
Total	$3,407,720

	Liability Beginning of the Period	Market Interest Rate	Interest Expense	Interest Payable	Addition to or Reduction in Liability	Liability End of the Period
o. 4 Percent Bond Issue						
January 1, Year 2.	$1,800,920	.03	$ 54,028	$ 40,000	$14,028	$1,814,948
July 1, Year 2	1,814,948	.03	54,448	40,000	14,448	1,829,396
Total			$108,476	$ 80,000	$28,476	
10 Percent Bond Issue						
January 1, Year 2.	3,407,720	.04	$136,309	$150,000	$13,691	$3,394,029
July 1, Year 2	3,394,029	.04	135,761	150,000	14,239	3,379,790
Total			$272,070	$300,000	$27,930	
8 Percent Bond Issue						
January 1, Year 2.	1,000,000	.04	$ 40,000	$ 40,000	$ 0	$1,000,000
July 1, Year 2	1,000,000	.04	40,000	40,000	0	1,000,000
Total			$ 80,000	$ 80,000	$ 0	

p.

Income Taxes Payable, December 31, Year 1	$250,000
Plus Current Income Tax Expense for Year 2 (see below)	600,000
Less Cash Payment During Year 2.	?
Income Taxes Payable, December 31, Year 2	$375,000
Total Income Tax Expense	$720,000
Less Increase in Deferred Income Taxes	(120,000)
Current Income Tax Expense	$600,000

Cash payments for income taxes totaled $475,000 during Year 2.

| | Common Shares | | Additional Paid-in Capital | Retained Earnings | Treasury Shares |
	Number of Shares	Amount			
q. Balance, December 31, Year 1	50,000	$500,000	$ 800,000	$1,436,000	$30,000
Common Stock Issued on the Open Market .	10,000	100,000	400,000	—	—
Treasury Stock Sold . .	—	—	5,000	—	(10,000)
Net Income	—	—	—	1,040,000	—
Dividends (plug)[a] . . .	—	—	—	(250,000)	—
Balance, December 31, Year 2	60,000	$600,000	$1,205,000	$2,226,000	$20,000

[a]Or, see statement of changes in financial position.

Questions, Exercises, Problems and Cases

Questions

1. Review the meaning of the following concepts or terms discussed in this chapter.
- **a.** Generally accepted accounting principles.
- **b.** Accurate presentation.
- **c.** Fair presentation.
- **d.** Conservatism.
- **e.** Profit maximization.
- **f.** Income smoothing.
- **g.** Least and latest rule.
- **h.** Statement of accounting policies.
- **i.** Development of accounting principles is a political process.

2. A critic of accounting stated: "The financial statements are virtually useless because firms have too much latitude in selecting from among generally accepted accounting methods." Another critic of accounting reacted: "I agree that the financial statements are useless, but it is because there is too little latitude in the way certain transactions are accounted for under generally accepted accounting principles." Respond to these statements.

3. "The controversy over alternative generally accepted accounting principles could be solved by requiring all firms to use the same methods of accounting in their financial statements that they use in their tax return." Respond to this proposal.

4. If net income over long enough time periods is equal to cash-in minus cash-out, why not allow the timing of cash flows to dictate revenue and expense recognition and eliminate alternative generally accepted accounting principles?

5. "The total reported net income over long enough time periods will be the same regardless of whether a firm follows a conservative strategy or a profit-maximizing strategy in selecting its accounting methods." Explain.

6. "The statement of changes in financial position is affected less by the use of alternative accounting principles than the balance sheet and income statement." Explain.

7. If capital markets react quickly and in an unbiased manner to the release of information, including information contained in the financial statements, what is the benefit of analyzing a set of financial statements?

Exercises

8. *Identifying generally accepted accounting principles.* Indicate the generally accepted accounting principle, or method, described in each of the following statements. Explain your reasoning.

    a. This inventory cost flow assumption results in reporting the largest net income during periods of rising prices.

    b. This method of accounting for uncollectible accounts recognizes the implied income reduction in the period of sale.

    c. This method of accounting for long-term investments in the securities of unconsolidated subsidiaries or other corporations usually requires an adjustment to net income to calculate cash provided by operations in the statement of changes in financial position.

    d. This method of accounting for long-term leases by the lessee gives rise to a noncurrent liability.

    e. This inventory cost flow assumption results in approximately the same balance sheet amount as the FIFO flow assumption.

    f. This method of recognizing interest expense on bonds provides a uniform annual rate of interest expense over the life of the bond.

    g. During periods of rising prices, this inventory valuation basis produces approximately the same results as the acquisition cost valuation basis.

    h. When specific customers' accounts are deemed uncollectible and written off, this method of accounting results in a decrease in the current ratio.

    i. This method of depreciation generally provides the largest amounts of depreciation expense during the first several years of an asset's life.

    j. This method of accounting for intercorporate investments in securities can result in a decrease in the investor's total shareholders' equity without affecting retained earnings.

    k. This method of recognizing income from long-term contracts generally results in the least fluctuation in earnings over several periods.

    l. When specific customers' accounts are deemed uncollectible and are written off, this method of accounting has no effect on working capital.

    m. When used in calculating taxable income, this inventory cost flow assumption must generally also be used in calculating net income reported to shareholders.

    n. Under this method of accounting for long-term leases of equipment by the lessor, an amount for depreciation expense on the leased equipment will appear on the income statement.

o. This method of recognizing interest expense on bonds provides a uniform annual amount of interest expense over the life of the bonds.

9. *Identifying generally accepted accounting principles.* Indicate the accounting principle, or procedure, apparently being used to record each of the following independent transactions. Indicate your reasoning.

a. Bad Debt Expense	X	
Accounts Receivable		X
b. Cash	X	
Dividend Income		X
c. Income Taxes Payable—Current	X	
Deferred Investment Tax Credits		X
d. Unrealized Loss from Price Declines in Marketable Securities	X	
Allowance to Reduce Marketable Securities to Market		X
e. Cash	X	
Investment in Unconsolidated Subsidiary		X
Dividend declared and received from unconsolidated subsidiary.		
f. Bad Debt Expense	X	
Allowance for Uncollectible Accounts		X

10. *Identifying generally accepted accounting principles.* Indicate the accounting principle, or procedure, apparently being used to record each of the following independent transactions. Give your reasoning.

a. Rent Expense (for Lease Contract)	X	
Cash		X
b. Advertising Expense	X	
Deferred Advertising Costs		X
c. Investment in Unconsolidated Subsidiary	X	
Equity in Earnings of Unconsolidated Subsidiary		X
d. Allowance for Uncollectible Accounts	X	
Accounts Receivable		X
e. Loss from Price Decline for Inventories	X	
Merchandise Inventories		X
f. Income Taxes Payable—Current	X	
Income Tax Expense (from Investment Credit)		X
g. Liability Under Long-Term Lease	X	
Interest Expense	X	
Cash		X

11. *Identifying effects of generally accepted accounting principles on reported income.* Indicate the accounting principle that provides the smallest amount of earnings in each of the following cases.

a. FIFO, LIFO, or weighted-average cost flow assumption for inventories during periods of rising prices.

b. FIFO, LIFO, or weighted-average cost flow assumption for inventories during periods of declining prices.

c. Lower-of-cost-or-market or equity method of accounting for long-term investments in the securities of unconsolidated subsidiaries where dividends declared by the subsidiary are less than its earnings.

d. Sum-of-the-years'-digits or straight-line depreciation method during the first one-third of an asset's life.

e. Sum-of-the-years'-digits or straight-line depreciation method during the last one-third of an asset's life.

f. Deferral or flow-through method of accounting for the investment tax credit in the year qualifying assets are acquired.

g. The valuation of inventories at acquisition cost or lower of cost or market.

h. Lower-of-cost-or-market or equity method of accounting for long-term investments in the securities of unconsolidated subsidiaries where the investee realizes net losses and does not pay dividends.

i. Effective interest or straight-line method of recognizing interest expense on bonds in the first year that bonds originally issued at a discount are outstanding.

j. Effective interest or straight-line method of recognizing interest expense on bonds in the last year that bonds originally issued at a discount are outstanding.

Problems and Cases

12. *Impact of capitalizing and amortizing versus expensing when incurred.* South Company and North Company incur $50,000 of advertising costs each year. South Company expenses these costs immediately, whereas North Company capitalizes the costs and amortizes them over 5 years.

a. Compute the amount of advertising expense and deferred advertising costs each firm would report beginning in the first year that advertising costs are incurred and continuing for 6 years.

b. For this part, assume that the amount of advertising costs incurred by each firm increases by $10,000 each year. Repeat part **a**.

c. Comment on the differences noted in parts **a** and **b**.

13. *Impact of alternative accounting principles on two firms.* On January 1, Year 1, two corporations are formed to operate merchandising businesses. The firms are alike in all respects except for their methods of accounting. Ruzicka Company chooses the accounting principles that will minimize its reported net income. Murphy Company chooses the accounting principles that will maximize its reported net income but, where different procedures are permitted, will use accounting methods that minimize its taxable income. The following events occur during Year 1.

(1) Both companies issue 500,000 shares of $1-par-value common shares for $6 per share on January 2, Year 1.

(2) Both firms acquire equipment on January 2, Year 1, for $1,650,000 cash. The equipment is estimated to have a 10-year life and zero salvage value. An investment tax credit of 10 percent is applicable to this equipment.

(3) Both firms engage in extensive sales promotion activities during Year 1, incurring costs of $400,000.

(4) The two firms make the following purchases of merchandise inventory.

Date	Units Purchased	Unit Price	Cost of Purchase
January 2	50,000	$6.00	$ 300,000
April 1	60,000	6.20	372,000
August 15	40,000	6.25	250,000
November 30	50,000	6.50	325,000
Total	200,000		$1,247,000

(5) During the year, both firms sell 140,000 units at an average price of $15 each.

(6) Selling, general, and administrative expenses, other than advertising, total $100,000 during the year.

The Ruzicka Company uses the following accounting methods (for both book and tax purposes): LIFO inventory cost flow assumption, accelerated depreciation method, immediate expensing of the costs of sales promotion, and the deferral method of accounting for the investment credit. The sum-of-the-years'-digits depreciation method is used for financial reporting and Accelerated Cost Recovery System depreciation is used for tax purposes. Depreciation for tax purposes on this equipment is $247,500 for Year 1.

The Murphy Company uses the following accounting methods: FIFO inventory cost flow assumption for both book and tax purposes, the straight-line depreciation method for book and Accelerated Cost Recovery System depreciation for tax purposes, capitalization and amortization of the costs of the sales promotion campaign over 4 years for book and immediate expensing for tax purposes, and the flow-through method of accounting for the investment credit.

a. Prepare comparative income statements for the two firms for Year 1. Include separate computations of income tax expense. The income tax rate is 46 percent.

b. Prepare comparative balance sheets for the two firms as of December 31, Year 1. Both firms have $1 million of outstanding accounts receivable on this date and a single current liability for income taxes payable for the year.

c. Prepare comparative statements of changes in financial position for the two firms for Year 1, defining funds as cash.

14. *Impact of two sets of alternative accounting principles on net income and cash flows.* The Langston Corporation is formed on January 2, Year 1, with the issuance at par of 100,000 shares of $10-par-value common stock for cash. During Year 1, the following transactions occur.

(1) The assets of the Dee's Department Store are acquired on January 2, Year 1, for $800,000 cash. The market values of the identifiable assets received are as

follows: accounts receivable, $200,000; merchandise inventory, $400,000 (200,000 units); store equipment, $150,000; goodwill, $50,000.

(2) Merchandise inventory is purchased during Year 1 as follows:

Date	Units Purchased	Unit Price	Cost of Purchase
April 1	30,000	$2.10	$ 63,000
August 1	20,000	2.20	44,000
October 1	50,000	2.40	120,000
Total	100,000		$227,000

(3) During the year, 210,000 units are sold at an average price of $3.20.

(4) Extensive training programs are held during the year to acquaint previous employees of Dee's Department Store with the merchandising policies and procedures of Langston Corporation. The costs incurred in the training programs total $50,000.

(5) Selling, general, and administrative costs incurred and recognized as an expense during Year 1 are $80,000.

(6) The store equipment is estimated to have a 5-year useful life and zero salvage value.

(7) The income tax rate is 46 percent. Goodwill arising from a corporate acquisition is not deductible in computing taxable income and the difference is a permanent difference, not a timing difference. Ignore investment tax credit provisions in this problem.

The management of Langston Corporation is uncertain about the accounting methods that should be used in preparing its financial statements. The choice has been narrowed to two sets of accounting methods, and you have been asked to determine net income for Year 1 using each set.

Set A consists of the following accounting methods (for book and tax purposes): LIFO inventory cost flow assumption, an accelerated depreciation method, immediate expensing of the costs of the training program, and amortization of goodwill over 10 years. Depreciation will be computed using the double-declining-balance method for book and accelerated cost recovery system depreciation for tax. Depreciation for tax purposes will be $22,500.

Set B consists of the following accounting methods: FIFO inventory costing assumption, straight-line depreciation for book and Accelerated Cost Recovery System depreciation for tax purposes, capitalization and amortization of the costs of the training program over 5 years for book and immediate expensing for tax purposes, and amortization of goodwill over 40 years.

    a. Calculate net income for Year 2 under each set of accounting methods.

    b. Calculate cash flow from operations under each set of accounting methods. Assume that accounts receivable at year end total $160,000.

15. *Impact of alternative accounting principles on net income, Year 2.* Net income of Miller Corporation for the year ending December 31, Year 2, is $600,000 based on the accounting methods actually used by the firm. You have been asked to calculate the amount of net income that would have been reported under several alternative accounting methods. The income tax rate is 40 percent, and the same accounting methods are used for financial reporting and income tax purposes unless otherwise indicated. Each of the following questions should be considered independently.

   a. Miller Corporation acquired a machine costing $300,000 on January 1, Year 2. The machine was depreciated during Year 2 using the straight-line method based on a 5-year useful life and zero salvage value. What would net income have been if the sum-of-the-years'-digits depreciation method had been used? Ignore the investment tax credit.

   b. Miller Corporation obtained an investment tax credit of $10,000 on the machine acquired in part **a**. It accounted for the investment credit using the flow-through method. What would net income have been if the deferral method had been used? In responding to this question, assume that the machine was depreciated using the straight-line method based on a 5-year life and zero salvage value. Also assume that this is the first year that investment tax credits have been realized by Miller Corporation.

   c. Miller Corporation used the lower-of-cost-or-market method of accounting for its 18 percent investment in the common shares of General Tools Corporation. During Year 2, General Tools Corporation earned $200,000 and paid dividends of $50,000. The market value of General Tools Corporation was the same at the end of Year 2 as it was at the beginning of Year 2. What would net income have been during Year 2 if Miller Corporation continued to account for the investment under the lower-of-cost-or-market method for income tax purposes but used the equity method for financial reporting purposes?

   d. Miller Corporation used the FIFO inventory cost flow assumption. Under FIFO, the January 1, Year 2, inventory was $300,000, and the December 31, Year 2, inventory was $320,000. Under LIFO, the January 1, Year 2, inventory would have been $240,000 and the December 31, Year 2, inventory would have been $230,000. What would net income have been if the LIFO inventory costing assumption had been used?

16. *Computation of cash provided by operations.* The income statement of Garrett Corporation for Year 5 appears in Exhibit 15.7. An analysis of changes in working capital accounts appears in Exhibit 15.8. Notes to these statements follow.

Note 1: Garrett Corporation owns 10 percent of the outstanding common shares of Williams Corporation. During Year 5, Williams Corporation earned $2,000,000 and declared dividends of $600,000.

Note 2: Garrett Corporation owns 30 percent of the outstanding common shares of Knowles Corporation. During Year 5, Knowles Corporation earned $1,000,000 and declared dividends of $400,000.

Note 3: Depreciation charges of $200,000 and $100,000 are included in Cost of Goods Sold and Selling and Administrative Expenses, respectively.

Note 4: Income Tax Expense is composed of the following:

(Note 4 continued)

Current.	$500,000
Deferred	200,000
Total	$700,000

Exhibit 15.7
GARRETT CORPORATION
Income Statement for Year 5
(Problem 16)

Revenues:

Sales.	$5,000,000
Interest	100,000
Dividends (Note 1).	60,000
Equity in Earnings of Unconsolidated Affiliate (Note 2).	300,000
Recovery of Loss on Valuation of Marketable Equity Securities	30,000
Total Revenue	$5,490,000

Expenses:

Cost of Goods Sold (Note 3)	$3,000,000
Selling and Administrative (Note 3)	800,000
Interest	200,000
Total Expenses	$4,000,000
Income Before Income Taxes	$1,490,000
Income Tax Expense (Note 4)	700,000
Income Before Minority Interest	$ 790,000
Less Minority Interest in Earnings of Consolidated Subsidiary	160,000
Net Income	$ 630,000

Exhibit 15.8
GARRETT CORPORATION
Analysis of Changes in Working Capital Accounts for Year 5
(Problem 16)

Increase (Decrease) in Current Assets:

Cash	$ 70,000
Marketable Securities	30,000
Accounts Receivable	430,000
Merchandise Inventories.	370,000

Decrease (Increase) in Current Liabilities:

Accounts Payable	(320,000)
Income Taxes Payable	(120,000)
Increase in Working Capital	$460,000

Current income tax expense has been reduced by $40,000 for amortization of deferred investment tax credits. The investment credit realized during Year 5 and added to the Deferred Investment Tax Credit account on the balance sheet is $60,000.

Compute the amount of cash provided by operations for Garrett Corporation during Year 5. Your analysis should begin with net income of $630,000.

17. *Preparation of income statement and balance sheet from comprehensive data.* The data in Exhibit 15.9 are taken from the adjusted trial balances of the Hickory Merchandising Company as of December 31, Year 1 and Year 2. The brackets indicate amounts to be found in the solution of the problem.
Additional data:

(1) Preferred shares: 6 percent, cumulative, $100 par value; 2,000 shares authorized.
(2) Common shares: $1 par value; 150,000 shares authorized.
(3) On January 10, Year 2, a 10 percent stock dividend was declared on common stock, issuable in common stock. The market price per share was $10 and the dividend was capitalized at $10 per share.
(4) On March 31 and September 30, Year 2, dividends of 25 cents per share were declared. The dividends were payable on April 20 and October 20, Year 2, respectively. On December 31, Year 2, an extra dividend of 12½ cents per share was declared payable on January 20, Year 3. Note that all dividends, in cash and in shares, have been debited to Dividends accounts, not to Retained Earnings.
(5) Plant and equipment items having a cost of $39,240 and accumulated depreciation of $32,570 were retired and sold for $15,000. Acquisitions during Year 2 amounted to $71,500.
(6) The bonds are 30-year bonds and mature on June 30, Year 14. All bonds issued remain outstanding; straight-line amortization is used.
  a. Prepare a well-organized comparative statement of income and retained earnings.
  b. Prepare a well-organized comparative balance sheet.
  c. Prepare a well-organized statement of changes in financial position for Year 2, defining funds as cash.

18. *Preparation of three principal financial statements from comprehensive data.* The data in Exhibit 15.10 are taken from the records of the Barr Sales Company.
 Additional information:

(1) During the year the company retired fully depreciated fixtures that had cost $2,000. These were the only dispositions of furniture and fixtures.
(2) Furniture and fixtures acquired on May 10, Year 2, were financed one-third down, one-third due May 10, Year 3, and one-third due May 10, Year 4.
(3) On December 9, Year 2, the company sold a parcel of land it had purchased on January 14, Year 2, at a cost of $8,000.

Exhibit 15.9
HICKORY MERCHANDISING COMPANY
Adjusted Trial Balance
(Problem 17)

	December 31, Year 1		December 31, Year 2	
Accounts Payable		$ 97,320		$ 98,715
Accounts Receivable—Net	$ 580,335		$ 617,530	
Accruals and Withholdings Payable		99,800		99,700
Administrative Expenses	449,160		447,260	
Bonds Payable (6 percent)		275,000		277,000
Cash	114,080		149,485	
Common Stock		100,000		[ ]
Cost of Goods Sold	3,207,840		3,220,390	
Depreciation Expense	45,710		48,825	
Dividends on Common Shares—Cash and Stock	50,000		[ ]	
Dividends on Preferred Shares—Cash	6,000		6,000	
Dividends Payable		—		[ ]
Federal and State Income Tax Expense	104,975		122,675	
Federal and State Income Tax Payable		104,975		111,675
Gain on Sale of Plant		—		[ ]
Interest Expense on Notes	2,900		3,100	
Interest Expense on Bonds	20,000		[ ]	
Interest and Dividend Revenue		16,010		18,070
Inventories	616,120		633,690	
Investments in Subsidiaries	162,000		162,000	
Notes Payable		51,500		53,400
Notes Receivable	65,600		68,400	
Plant and Equipment—Net	391,880		[ ]	
Preferred Stock		100,000		100,000
Premium on Common Stock		700,000		[ ]
Prepaid Insurance	8,240		7,640	
Retained Earnings		[ ]		[ ]
Royalties Revenue		37,020		44,285
Sales		4,552,320		4,605,275
Selling Expenses	642,530		656,230	
	$6,467,370	$6,467,370	$6,739,860	$6,739,860

(4) On June 15, Year 2, the company purchased additional investments at a cost of $3,200. This was the only acquisition during the year. All investments are shown at cost, since market value exceeds cost.

(5) Merchandise was delivered during the year on customers' deposits in the amount of $1,200. All other deliveries were on account.

(6) On January 2, Year 2, the board of directors declared a 5 percent stock dividend. The dividend was capitalized at $11 per share.

(7) On June 20, Year 2, and December 20, Year 2, the board of directors declared the regular semiannual cash dividends of $0.50 per share.

(8) On June 30, Year 2, the company issued 250 shares of stock for cash.

Exhibit 15.10
BARR SALES COMPANY
Trial Balance Data
(Problem 18)

	December 31	
	Year 2 Adjusted Trial Balance	Year 1 Post-closing Trial Balance
Accounts Payable—Merchandise	$ 8,400	$ 9,160
Accounts Receivable.	25,100	25,900
Accumulated Depreciation	4,600	5,600
Allowance for Uncollectible Accounts	400	430
Bad Debt Expense	800	
Cash	27,802	21,810
Common Stock ($10 par value)	55,000	50,000
Cost of Goods Sold	155,000	
Deposits by Customers	420	
Depreciation	1,000	
Dividends on Common Shares (both in cash and in shares)	8,125	
Dividends Payable.	2,750	2,500
Federal Income Tax Expense	3,600	
Federal Income Tax Payable	3,600	2,400
Furniture and Fixtures	21,000	20,000
Gain on Sale of Land	1,500	
Installment Contracts Payable.	2,000	
Interest Expense on Mortgage	482	
Interest Revenue on Investments	500	
Interest Payable on Mortgage.	50	
Interest Receivable	50	30
Investments.	14,000	15,000
Loss on Sale of Investments	300	
Merchandise Inventory	33,450	31,150
Mortgage Payable (5 percent)	10,122	10,140
Other Expenses	26,293	
Premium on Common Shares.	4,500	4,000
Prepaid Rent	300	
Rent Expense.	3,600	
Retained Earnings.	28,860	28,860
Sales	210,000	
Sales Commissions	12,400	
Sales Commissions Payable	600	800

(9) Note that all dividends, both in cash and in shares, were debited to Dividends on Common Shares, not to Retained Earnings.

   a. Prepare a well-organized statement of income and retained earnings for Year 2.

   b. Prepare a well-organized comparative balance sheet.

19. *Chrysler discussion case of costly switch from LIFO to FIFO.* In the 1960s, Chrysler switched its inventory cost flow assumption from FIFO to LIFO. It was the only one of the Big Three auto makers to do so at that time. By 1970, Chrysler's inventories had grown and prices of its acquisition for inventory had increased so much that it had saved over $50 million in income taxes by using LIFO. Then, in the 1970s, Chrysler switched from LIFO back to FIFO. To comply with government tax regulations on inventory accounting, Chrysler paid to the government all of the taxes that it had saved from using LIFO over the entire time it had used LIFO. Chrysler paid the federal government more than $50 million for the privilege of switching from LIFO back to FIFO.

Investigation of why Chrysler would send the government $50 million for the privilege of switching back to FIFO suggests that Chrysler was in danger of violating a covenant in some of its bond indentures with respect to the debt-equity ratio. If the debt-equity ratio rose above a critical value, certain bonds would become due immediately that otherwise would not mature for a decade or more.

Under what conditions would a company not want its old bonds suddenly to come due for immediate payment? Explain. Under what conditions would switching from LIFO to FIFO and incurring an immediate $50 million liability improve Chrysler's position? Explain. What is the purpose of bond indentures such as the one to which Chrysler had agreed? Were the bondholders made better off by Chrysler's actions? Discuss.

20. *Impact of alternative accounting principles on debt ratio.* Two conventional calculations of the debt-equity ratio were introduced in Chapter 6. In this problem we focus on the following definition:

$$\text{Debt Ratio} = \frac{\text{Total Long-Term External Financing}}{\text{Owners' Equity}}.$$

Many analysts use this ratio to assess the risk in the financial structure of a corporation. The higher the debt-equity ratio, other things being equal, the greater the risk. Many analysts construct ratios from the conventional, historical cost financial statements without adjustment. This problem illustrates how the assessment of the relative risk of companies can change as more sophisticated analysis of the financial statements is undertaken. In this problem, various adjustments to the conventional financial statements are made and new versions of the debt-equity ratio are compared.

The problem may be worked all at once at the end of the course as a review, or it may be worked part by part as the various topics in the course are covered. Each part contains guidance as to when in the course the reader should be ready to work that part.

Data for four companies are presented in Exhibit 15.11. The methods are illustrated with the data for General Products Company (from Appendix A). The reader is to prepare answers for the three other companies. All data are taken from the financial statements of the various companies for the same year. All dollar amounts are in millions. Income tax effects are ignored, except where noted.

Exhibit 15.11
(dollar amounts in millions)
(Problem 20)

	General Products Company	Eastman Kodak	General Motors	Zenith
1. Long-Term Debt	$1,000	$ 152.4	$ 1,668.7	$ 50.0
2. Deferred Tax Credits (balance sheet)	—[a]	144.0	472.5	18.3
3. Owners' Equity	8,200	4,026.3	14,385.2	292.4
4. Excess of Current (FIFO) Cost over LIFO Cost of Ending Inventory	2,240	330.3	299.5	9.2
5. Unrecognized Pension Cost (unamortized prior service costs or unfunded vested costs, if larger)	964	520.0	3,000.0[b]	None
6. Long-Term Debt of Financing Subsidiary	2,384	None	6,509.2[b]	None

[a]General Products Company reports only deferred tax debits (assets).
[b]Excludes $2 billion of unfunded pension obligations of subsidiary.

a. (After Chapter 6.) Compute the debt ratio for each of the companies. Include deferred income taxes with long-term financing in the numerator. For General Products Company the debt ratio is

$$\frac{\$1,000 + \$0}{\$8,200} = 12.2 \text{ percent.}$$

Which companies appear to be significantly different from the others in terms of financial structure and risk? Discuss.

b. (After Chapter 8.) Chapter 8 pointed out that LIFO companies show old, out-of-date inventory amounts on their balance sheets. The LIFO cost flow assumption has the effect of understating total assets and understating owners' equity. (Owners' equity is understated because the unrealized holding gains on the inventory are not included in the balance sheet.) The financial statements can be made more realistic by adjusting them with the following entry, which ignores income tax effects:

Inventory	2,240	
Owners' Equity		2,240

$2,240 million is the amount shown in General Products Company's notes as the excess of current cost, or FIFO cost, over the balance sheet amount of ending inventory.

The debt-equity ratio for General Products Company after making this inventory adjustment is

$$\frac{\$1,000 + \$0}{\$8,200 + \$2,240} = \frac{\$1,000}{\$10,440} = 9.6 \text{ percent.}$$

Compute the debt ratio for each of the companies and the percentage change in the ratio from part **a** for each of the firms. On which companies did this adjustment have the most impact?

c. (After Chapter 11.) Chapter 11 suggests that certain items shown as liabilities should not be, whereas certain other items not shown as liabilities should be. These two "errors" do not necessarily cancel each other out.

   (i) First, note that in most cases Deferred Income Taxes are not likely even to be paid and should perhaps be reclassified as owners' equity. This reclassification can be reflected in the financial statements by making the following entry:

Deferred Income Taxes (Balance Sheet) . . . .   a
   Owners' Equity . . . .   a
Amount is that shown in line 2 of Exhibit 15.11. The
amount for General Products Company is zero because
Deferred Income Taxes has a debit, or asset, balance.

Case-by-case analysis might be required in practice to find out if some of the companies' timing differences are likely to reverse in the foreseeable future. An analysis of these companies' reported items does not reveal any such significant potential reversals.

   (ii) The unrecognized prior service cost for pension plans meets all of the criteria to be a (long-term) liability, but is not shown as such. The amount is merely disclosed in the notes. To bring this number onto the balance sheet, the financial statements are adjusted with the following entry, which ignores income tax effects:

Deferred Pension Costs   964
   Pension Liability.   964
$964 million is the amount shown in General Products
Company's notes to the financial statements for unamor-
tized prior service costs.

After adjusting for the pension liability only, General Products Company's debt-equity ratio is

$$\frac{\$1,000 + \$0 + \$964}{\$8,200} = \frac{\$1,964}{\$8,200} = 24.0 \text{ percent.}$$

If all adjustments in parts **a**, **b**, and **c** are made, General Products Company's debt-equity ratio is

$$\frac{\$1,000 + \$964}{\$8,200 + \$0 + \$2,240} = \frac{\$1,964}{\$10,440} = 18.8 \text{ percent.}$$

Make the adjustments suggested above and recompute the debt ratio for each of the other three companies. Compute the ratios on a cumulative and noncumulative basis; that is, compute the debt ratio after making each individual adjustment to the ratios computed in part **a**, and then after taking all the adjustments together, compute the percentage change in the ratio for each company. On which of the companies did each of these adjustments have the most impact?

d. (After Chapter 13.) Chapter 13 illustrated that various companies use different consolidation policies with respect to a wholly owned subsidiary engaged in the financing of customer purchases of the company's goods. For example (see Chapter 13, Problem **32**), Sears consolidates its financial subsidiary, but J. C. Penney does not. To make comparisons of debt ratios more valid, the same consolidation policy should be used for all companies. The following entry has the effect of consolidating an unconsolidated, but 100 percent-owned, subsidiary:

Assets of Subsidiary	9,344	
Investment of Parent in Subsidiary		931
Liabilities of Subsidiary		8,413

See Note 12 of General Products Company's financial statements. $9,344 million represents the total amount of the subsidiary's assets; $931 million represents General Products Company's investment in the subsidiary (which is equal to the subsidiary's total owners' equity); $8,413 million represents the subsidiary's total liabilities.

Once this entry is made, there may be another entry eliminating intercompany receivables and payables, if any. These eliminating entries are immaterial, and their effect has been taken into account in showing the data above.

For purposes of this problem, we are interested in examining the effect of bringing the financing subsidiary's long-term liabilities onto the parent company's balance sheet. The effect of the preceding entry on long-term liabilities can be accomplished with the following entry:

Assets	2,384	
Long-Term Liabilities		2,384

$2,384 million represents the amount of General Products Company's financial subsidiary's total long-term liabilities.

After consolidating General Products Company's financing subsidiary, the debt ratio becomes

$$\frac{\$1,000 + \$0 + \$2,384}{\$8,200} = \frac{\$3,384}{\$8,200} = 41.3 \text{ percent.}$$

If all adjustments to General Products Company's balance sheet are taken into account, the debt ratio is

$$\frac{\$1,000 + \$964 + \$2,384}{\$8,200 + \$0 + \$2,240} = \frac{\$4,348}{\$10,440} = 41.6 \text{ percent.}$$

Make the adjustments suggested here for General Motors, the only company of the three that does not consolidate its financing subsidiary. Recompute the debt ratio for this company both cumulatively and noncumulatively. Calculate the percentage change in the debt ratio. Comment on any apparent changes in the debt ratio from those computed in parts **a**, **b**, and **c**.

e. What can you infer from this exercise about the debt ratio computed from published financial statements?

21. *Comprehensive review problem.* The principal objective of this book has been to help you develop a sufficient understanding of the accounting process that generates financial statements for external users so that the resulting statements can then be (1) interpreted, (2) analyzed, and (3) evaluated. This problem has been designed partly as a review of the material covered in the book and partly as a means of assessing your progress toward this objective. A partial set of financial statements of Calmes Corporation for Year 2, including consolidated comparative balance sheets at December 31, Year 1 and Year 2 and a consolidated statement of income and retained earnings for Year 2, is presented in Exhibits 15.12 and 15.13. A series of discussion questions and short problems relating to the financial statements of Calmes Corporation are then presented. It is suggested that you study the financial statements before responding to these questions and problems. The following additional information may be helpful.

(1) Machinery and equipment costing $500,000, and with a book value of $100,000, were sold for cash during Year 2.

(2) The only transaction affecting common or preferred stocks during Year 2 was the sale of treasury stock.

(3) The bonds payable have a maturity value of $2 million.

Part I—Financial Statement Interpretation

For each of the accounts or items listed below and appearing on the consolidated balance sheets and income statement of the Calmes Corporation, describe (1) the nature of the account or item (that is, the transaction or conditions that resulted in its recognition) and (2) the valuation method used in determining its amount. Respond in descriptive terms rather than using specific numbers from the financial statements of the Calmes Corporation. The first one is provided as an example.

a. Accumulated Costs Under Contracts in Progress in Excess of Progress Billings— The Calmes Corporation is providing services of some type to specific customers under contract. All costs incurred under the contracts are accumulated in this current asset account. When customers are billed periodically for a portion of the contract price, this account is credited. The account, therefore, reflects the excess of costs incurred to date on uncompleted contracts over the amounts billed to customers. Since the account does not include any income or profit from the contracts (that is, "accumulated costs"), the firm is apparently using the completed contract method rather than the percentage-of-completion method of recognizing revenues.

Exhibit 15.12
CALMES CORPORATION
Consolidated Statement of Income and Retained Earnings for Year 2
(Problem 21)

Revenues:

Sales		$6,000,000
Gain on Sale of Machinery and Equipment		100,000
Income from Completed Contracts		960,000
Equity in Earnings of Unconsolidated Subsidiaries and Affiliates:		
Calmes Finance Corporation	$900,000	
Richardson Company	50,000	
Anthony Corporation	50,000	1,000,000
Total Revenues		$8,060,000

Expenses:

Cost of Goods Sold	$2,500,000
Employee Payroll	1,500,000
Depreciation of Plant and Equipment and Amortization of Leased Property Rights	500,000
Amortization of Intangibles	100,000
Bad Debt Expense	60,000
Interest	300,000
General Corporate	100,000
Income Taxes—Current	700,000
Income Taxes—Deferred	100,000
Total Expenses	$5,860,000
Net Income Before Minority Interest	$2,200,000
Minority Interest in Earnings	200,000
Net Income	$2,000,000
Less: Dividends on Preferred Shares	60,000
Dividends on Common Shares	840,000
Increase in Retained Earnings	$1,100,000
Retained Earnings, January 1, Year 2	1,400,000
Retained Earnings, December 31, Year 2	$2,500,000
Primary Earnings per Common Share (based on 1,000,000 average shares outstanding)	$1.94
Fully Diluted Earnings per Share (assuming conversion of preferred stock)	$1.25

b. Investment in Calmes Finance Corporation.
c. Property Rights Acquired Under Lease.
d. Goodwill.
e. Rent Received in Advance.
f. Deferred Income Taxes (Balance Sheet).
g. Minority Interest in Subsidiary (Balance Sheet).
h. Treasury Shares.
i. Bad Debt Expense (Income Statement).

Exhibit 15.13
CALMES CORPORATION
Consolidated Balance Sheets
December 31
(Problem 21)

	Year 2	Year 1
Assets		
Current Assets:		
Cash	$ 50,000	$ 100,000
Marketable Securities at Lower of Cost of Market (market value, $160,000)	150,000	—
Accounts Receivable (net of estimated uncollectibles of $80,000 in Year 2 and $50,000 in Year 1)	300,000	250,000
Merchandise Inventory	700,000	600,000
Accumulated Costs Under Contracts in Process in Excess of Progress Billings	200,000	150,000
Prepayments	100,000	100,000
Total Current Assets	$ 1,500,000	$1,200,000
Investments (at equity):		
Calmes Finance Corporation (100 percent owned)	$ 2,000,000	$1,100,000
Richardson Company (50 percent owned)	500,000	450,000
Anthony Company (25 percent owned)	100,000	50,000
Total Investments	$ 2,600,000	$1,600,000
Property, Plant, and Equipment:		
Land	$ 250,000	$ 200,000
Building	2,000,000	2,000,000
Machinery and Equipment	4,000,000	3,650,000
Property Rights Acquired Under Lease	750,000	750,000
Total	$ 7,000,000	$6,600,000
Less Accumulated Depreciation and Amortization	(2,000,000)	(1,900,000)
Total Property, Plant, and Equipment	$ 5,000,000	$4,700,000
Intangibles (at net book value):		
Patent	$ 200,000	$ 250,000
Goodwill	700,000	750,000
Total Intangibles	$ 900,000	$1,000,000
Total Assets	$10,000,000	$8,500,000

Part II—Financial Statement Analysis

a. Compute the amount of specific customers' accounts written off as uncollectible during Year 2, assuming that there were no recoveries during Year 2 of accounts written off in years prior to Year 2.

b. The Calmes Corporation used the LIFO cost flow assumption in computing its cost of goods sold and beginning and ending merchandise inventory amounts. If the FIFO cost flow assumption had been used, the beginning inventory would have been $900,000 and the ending inventory would have been $850,000. Compute the actual gross profit (net sales less cost of goods sold) of the Calmes

Exhibit 15.13 *(continued)*
CALMES CORPORATION
Consolidated Balance Sheets
December 31
(Problem 21)

	Year 2	Year 1
Liabilities and Shareholders' Equity		
Current Liabilities:		
Notes Payable	$ 250,000	$ 200,000
Accounts Payable	350,000	330,000
Salaries Payable	150,000	120,000
Income Taxes Payable	200,000	150,000
Rent Received in Advance	50,000	—
Other Current Liabilities	200,000	100,000
Total Current Liabilities	$ 1,200,000	$ 900,000
Long-Term Debt:		
Bonds Payable	$ 1,824,000	$1,800,000
Equipment Mortgage Indebtedness	176,000	650,000
Capitalized Lease Obligations	500,000	550,000
Total Long-Term Debt	$ 2,500,000	$3,000,000
Deferred Income Taxes	$ 800,000	$ 700,000
Minority Interest in Subsidiary	$ 500,000	$ 300,000
Shareholders' Equity:		
Convertible Preferred Stock	$ 1,000,000	$1,000,000
Common Stock	1,000,000	1,000,000
Additional Paid-in Capital	1,000,000	900,000
Retained Earnings	2,500,000	1,400,000
Total	$ 5,500,000	$4,300,000
Less Cost of Treasury Shares	(500,000)	(700,000)
Total Shareholders' Equity	$ 5,000,000	$3,600,000
Total Liabilities and Shareholders' Equity	$10,000,000	$8,500,000

Corporation for Year 2 under LIFO and the corresponding amount of gross profit if FIFO had been used (ignore income tax effects). Calmes Corporation used the periodic inventory method.

c. Refer to part **b**. What can be said about the quantity of merchandise inventory at the beginning and end of Year 2 and the direction of price changes during Year 2? Explain.

d. The Calmes Corporation accounts for its three intercorporate investments in unconsolidated subsidiaries using the equity method. The shares in each of these companies were acquired at book value at the time of acquisition. What were the total dividends declared by these three companies during Year 2? How can you tell?

e. The Calmes Corporation accounts for its three intercorporate investments in unconsolidated subsidiaries using the equity method. The shares in each of these companies were acquired at book value at the time of acquisition. Give the journal entry (entries) that was (were) made during Year 2 in applying the equity method.

f. The building was acquired on January 1, Year 1. It was estimated to have a 40-year useful life and zero salvage value at that time. Calculate the amount of depreciation expense on this building for Year 2, assuming that the double-declining-balance method is used.

g. Machinery and equipment costing $500,000, and with a book value of $100,000, were sold for cash during Year 2. Give the journal entry to record the disposition.

h. The bonds payable carry 6 percent annual coupons. Interest is paid on December 31 of each year. Give the journal entry made on December 31, Year 2, to recognize interest expense for Year 2, assuming that Calmes Corporation uses the effective interest method.

i. Refer to part **h**. What was the effective or market interest rate on these bonds on the date they were issued? Explain.

j. The only timing difference between net income and taxable income during Year 2 was in the amount of depreciation expense. If the income tax rate was 40 percent, calculate the difference between the depreciation deduction reported on the tax return and the depreciation expense reported on the income statement.

k. Give the journal entry that explains the change in the treasury shares account, assuming that there were no other transactions affecting common or preferred shares during Year 2.

l. If the original amount of the patent acquired was $500,000 and the patent is being amortized on a straight-line basis, how long ago was the patent acquired?

m. The stock of the Anthony Company was acquired on December 31, Year 1. If the same amount of stock in the Anthony Company were held during the year, but the amount represented only *15 percent* ownership of the Anthony Company, how would the financial statements have differed? Disregard income tax effects and assume the shares' market price exceeds their cost.

n. During Year 2, Calmes paid $85,000 to the lessor of property represented on the balance sheet by "Property Rights Acquired Under Lease." Property rights acquired under lease have a 10-year life and are being amortized on a straight-line basis. What was the total expense reported by Calmes Corporation during Year 2 from using the leased property?

o. How would the financial statements have differed if the Calmes Corporation accounted for marketable securities on the lower-of-cost-or-market basis and the market value of these securities had been $130,000 instead of $160,000 at the end of Year 2? Disregard income tax effects.

p. If the Minority Interest in Subsidiary represents a 20 percent interest in Calmes Corporation's only consolidated subsidiary, what was the *total* amount of dividends declared by this subsidiary during Year 2? How can you tell?

q. Refer to the earnings-per-share amounts in the income statement of Calmes Corporation. How many shares of common stock would be issued if all of the outstanding shares of preferred stock were converted into common stock?

r. Insert the missing items of information numbered **(3)–(27)** in the statement of changes in financial position of the Calmes Corporation in Exhibit 15.14. Be

Exhibit 15.14
CALMES CORPORATION
Consolidated Statement of Changes in Financial Position for Year 2
(Problem 21)

Sources of Cash

Operations:

(3)_____ . . . . . $_____

Add Expenses and Deductions Not Using Cash:

(4)_____ . . . . . _____

(5)_____ . . . . . _____

(6)_____ . . . . . _____

(7)_____ . . . . . _____

(8)_____ . . . . . _____

Add Credit Changes in Operating Current Asset
and Current Liability Accounts:

(9)_____ . . . . . _____

(10)_____ . . . . . _____

(11)_____ . . . . . _____

(12)_____ . . . . . _____

(13)_____ . . . . . _____

(14)_____ . . . . . _____

Subtract Revenues and Additions Not Providing
Cash:

(15)_____ . . . . . _____

(16)_____ . . . . . _____

Subtract Debit Changes in Operating Current
Asset and Current Liability Accounts:

(17)_____ . . . . . _____

(18)_____ . . . . . _____

(19)_____ . . . . . _____

(20)_____ . . . . . _____

Cash Provided by Operations $1,774,000

New Financing:

(21)_____ . . . . . _____

(22)_____ . . . . . _____

    Total Sources of Cash. $2,274,000

Uses of Cash

Reduction in Financing:

(23)_____ . . . . . _____

(24)_____ . . . . . _____

(25)_____ . . . . . _____

Acquisition of Assets:

(26)_____ . . . . . _____

(27)_____ . . . . . _____

    Total Uses of Cash $2,324,000

Decrease in Cash . . . . $ 50,000 sure to include both descriptions of the missing items and their amounts. Provide supporting calculations for each of the missing items in the statement.

s. On January 2, Year 3, the Calmes Corporation requested its bank to grant a 6-month loan for $300,000. If approved, the loan would be granted on January 10, Year 3. As the bank's senior credit analyst, you have been asked to assess the liquidity of the Calmes Corporation and present a memorandum summarizing your conclusions. Include any ratios and any other information from the financial statements that you feel are relevant. Also include a summary of information not disclosed in the financial statements that you feel the loan officer should consider before making a final decision.

Part III—Financial Statement Evaluation

a. The treasurer of the Calmes Corporation recently remarked, "The value or worth of our company on December 31, Year 2, is $5,000,000, as measured by total shareholders' equity." Describe briefly at least three reasons why the difference between recorded total assets and recorded total liabilities on the balance sheet does not represent the firm's value or worth.

b. The accounting profession has been criticized for permitting several "generally accepted accounting principles" for the same or similar transactions. What are the major arguments for **(1)** narrowing the range of acceptable and **(2)** continuing the present system of permitting business firms some degree of flexibility in selecting their accounting methods?

22. *Comprehensive review problem.* Partial financial statements of Tuck Corporation for Year 2 are presented in Exhibit 15.15 (consolidated statement of income and retained earnings) and Exhibit 15.16 (consolidated balance sheet). Also shown are a statement of accounting policies and a set of notes to the financial statements. After studying these financial statements and notes, respond to each of the following questions.

   a. Prepare an analysis that explains the change in Marketable Equity Securities—Net account during Year 2.

   b. Calculate the proceeds from sales of marketable equity securities classified as a current asset during Year 2.

   c. Calculate the amount of the provision for estimated uncollectible accounts made during Year 2.

   d. Calculate the amount of cost of goods sold assuming a FIFO cost flow assumption had been used.

   e. Give the journal entry(s) to account for the change in the Investment in Thayer Corporation—Net account during Year 2.

   f. Calculate the amount of income or loss from the Investment in Thayer Corporation during Year 2.

   g. Give the journal entry(s) to account for the change in the Investment in Tuck Credit Corporation account during Year 2.

   h. Assume that Tuck Credit Corporation had been consolidated with Tuck Corporation on December 31, Year 2. Calculate the amount of (1) Total Assets, (2) Total Liabilities, and (3) Net Income.

Exhibit 15.15
TUCK CORPORATION
Consolidated Statement of Income and Retained Earnings for Year 2
(Problem 22)

Revenues and Gains:

Sales	$4,000,000	
Gain on Sale of Equipment	3,000	
Recovery of Unrealized Loss on Valuation of Marketable Equity Securities	4,000	
Rental Revenue	240,000	
Dividend Revenue	8,000	
Equity in Earnings of Unconsolidated Subsidiary and Affiliate	102,000	
Total Revenues and Gains		$4,357,000

Expenses, Losses, and Deductions:

Cost of Goods Sold (including depreciation and amortization)	$2,530,000	
Selling and Administrative Expenses (including depreciation and amortization).	1,096,205	
Warranty Expense	46,800	
Interest Expense.	165,995	
Loss on Sale of Marketable Equity Securities	8,000	
Income Tax Expense.	200,000	
Minority Interest in Earnings of Consolidated Subsidiary . . .	10,000	
Total Expenses, Losses, and Deductions		4,057,000
Consolidated Net Income		$ 300,000
Less Dividends Declared		(120,000)
Increase in Retained Earnings for Year 2.		$ 180,000
Retained Earnings, December 31, Year 1		220,000
Retained Earnings, December 31, Year 2		$ 400,000

i. Prepare an analysis that identifies the factors and the amounts that explain the change in the Minority Interest in Subsidiary account on the balance sheet.

j. Calculate the balance in the Investment in Harvard Corporation account on Tuck Corporation's books on December 31, Year 2, assuming that the equity method had been used.

k. Calculate the amount of cash received during Year 2 for rental fees.

l. Calculate the actual cost of goods and services required to service customers' warranties during Year 2.

m. Refer to Note 7. Calculate the amount of interest expense on the $1 million, 6 percent bonds for Year 2.

n. Give the journal entry(s) that accounts for the change in the Mortgage Payable account during Year 2.

o. The income tax rate is 40 percent. Calculate the difference between the amount of depreciation recognized for financial reporting purposes and the amount recognized for tax reporting.

Exhibit 15.16
TUCK CORPORATION
Consolidated Comparative Balance Sheet
(Problem 22)

	December 31, Year 1	December 31, Year 2
Assets		
Current Assets:		
Cash.	$ 240,000	$ 280,000
Marketable Equity Securities—Net (Note 1)	125,000	141,000
Accounts Receivable—Net (Note 2).	1,431,200	1,509,600
Inventories (Note 3)	1,257,261	1,525,315
Prepayments	28,000	32,000
Total Current Assets.	$3,081,461	$3,487,915
Investments (Note 4):		
Investment in Thayer Corporation—Net (15 percent owned)	$ 92,000	$ 87,000
Investment in Hitchcock Corporation (30 percent owned)	120,000	135,000
Investment in Tuck Credit Corporation (100 percent owned)	215,000	298,000
Total Investments	$ 427,000	$ 520,000
Property, Plant, and Equipment (Note 5):		
Land	$ 82,000	$ 82,000
Building	843,000	843,000
Equipment	497,818	1,848,418
Leasehold	98,182	98,182
Total Plant Assets at Cost	$1,521,000	$2,871,600
Less Accumulated Depreciation and Amortization	(376,000)	(413,000)
Total Plant Assets—Net	$1,145,000	$2,458,600
Intangibles:		
Goodwill—Net	$ 36,000	$ 34,000
Total Assets	$4,689,461	$6,500,515

continued

p. Give the journal entry made on July 1, Year 2, upon conversion of the preferred stock.

q. Give the journal entry(s) to account for the change in the Treasury Stock account during Year 2.

r. Prepare a T-account work sheet for the preparation of a statement of changes in financial position, defining funds as cash.

Statement of Accounting Policies

Basis of consolidation. The financial statements of Tuck Corporation are consolidated with Harvard Corporation, a 90 percent-owned subsidiary acquired on January 2, Year 0.

Exhibit 15.16 *(continued)*
TUCK CORPORATION
Consolidated Comparative Balance Sheet
(Problem 22)

	Year 1	Year 2
Liabilities and Shareholders' Equity		
Current Liabilities:		
Note Payable (Note 6)	$ 100,000	$ 200,000
Accounts Payable	666,100	723,700
Rental Fees Received in Advance	46,000	58,000
Estimated Warranty Liability	75,200	78,600
Interest Payable on Notes	1,500	2,000
Dividends Payable	25,000	30,000
Income Taxes Payable—Current	140,000	160,000
Total Current Liabilities	$1,053,800	$1,252,300
Noncurrent Liabilities:		
Bonds Payable (Note 7)	$1,104,650	$1,931,143
Mortgage Payable (Note 8)	299,947	280,943
Capitalized Lease Obligation (Note 9)	62,064	56,229
Deferred Income Taxes	130,000	145,000
Total Noncurrent Liabilities	$1,596,661	$2,413,315
Total Liabilities	$2,650,461	$3,665,615
Shareholders' Equity:		
Minority Interest in Subsidiary	$ 32,000	$ 36,500
Convertible Preferred Stock, $100 par Value (Note 10) . . .	700,000	200,000
Common Stock, $10 par Value (Note 11)	1,000,000	1,650,000
Additional Paid-in Capital—Common	130,000	583,600
Unrealized Loss from Price Declines of Marketable Equity Investments	(16,000)	(21,000)
Retained Earnings	220,000	400,000
Total	$2,066,000	$2,849,100
Less Cost of Treasury Stock (Note 12)	(27,000)	(14,200)
Total Shareholders' Equity	$2,039,000	$2,834,900
Total Liabilities and Shareholders' Equity	$4,689,461	$6,500,515

Marketable equity securities. Marketable equity securities are stated at lower of acquisition cost or market.

Accounts receivable. Uncollectible accounts of customers are accounted for using the allowance method.

Inventories. Inventories are measured using a last-in, first-out cost flow assumption.

Investments. Investments of less than 20 percent of the outstanding common stock of other companies are accounted for using the lower-of-cost-or-market method. Investments of greater than or equal to 20 percent of the outstanding common stock of unconsolidated affiliates and subsidiaries are accounted for using the equity method.

Building, equipment, and leaseholds. Depreciation for financial reporting purposes is calculated using the straight-line method. For income tax purposes, ACRS depreciation is used.

Goodwill. Goodwill arising from investments in Harvard Corporation is amortized over a period of 20 years.

Interest expense on long-term debt. Interest expense on long-term debt is recognized using the effective interest method.

Deferred income taxes. Deferred income taxes are provided for timing differences between book and taxable income. All timing differences relate to depreciation.

Notes to the Financial Statements

Note 1: Marketable equity securities are shown net of an allowance for price declines below acquisition cost of $25,000 on December 31, Year 1, and $21,000 on December 31, Year 2. Marketable equity securities costing $35,000 were sold during Year 2. No dividends were received from marketable equity securities during Year 2.

Note 2: Accounts receivable are shown net of an allowance for uncollectible accounts of $128,800 on December 31, Year 1, and $210,400 on December 31, Year 2. A total of $63,000 of accounts were written off as uncollectible during Year 2.

Note 3: The valuation of inventories on a FIFO basis exceeded the amounts on a LIFO basis by $430,000 on December 31, Year 1, and by $410,000 on December 31, Year 2.

Note 4: Condensed balance sheet data for Tuck Credit Corporation, a wholly owned, unconsolidated credit subsidiary, are shown below:

	December 31, Year 1	December 31, Year 2
Total Assets	$375,000	$478,000
Total Liabilities	$160,000	$180,000
Shareholders' Equity	$215,000	$298,000

Net income of Tuck Credit Corporation for Year 2 was $87,000. Dividends declared and paid during Year 2 totaled $24,000.

Note 5: Equipment with a cost of $23,000 and a book value of $4,000 was sold during Year 2. This was the only disposition of property, plant, or equipment during the year.

Note 6: A 90-day, 9 percent note with a face amount of $100,000 was paid with interest at maturity on January 30, Year 2. On December 1, Year 2, Tuck Corporation borrowed $200,000 from its local bank, promising to repay the principal plus interest at 12 percent in 6 months.

Note 7: Bonds Payable on the balance sheet is composed of the following:

	December 31, Year 1	December 31, Year 2
$1,000,000, 6 Percent 20-Year Semiannual Coupon Bonds, Due Dec. 31, Year 16, Priced at $1,125,510 to Yield 5 Percent, Compounded Semiannually, at the Time of Issue.	$1,104,650	$1,099,823
$1,000,000, 8 Percent 20-Year Semiannual Coupon Bonds, Due Dec. 31, Year 21, Priced at $828,409 to Yield 10 Percent, Compounded Semiannually, at the Time of Issue.	—	831,320
Total	$1,104,650	$1,931,143

Note 8: Mortgage Payable represents a mortgage on buildings requiring equal installment payments of $40,000 on December 31 of each year. The loan underlying the mortgage bears interest of 7 percent, compounded annually. The final installment payment is due on December 31, Year 12.

Note 9: The Capitalized Lease Obligation represents a 20-year, noncancelable lease on certain equipment. The lease requires annual payments in advance of $10,000 on January 2 of each year. The last lease payment will be made on January 2, Year 8. The lease is capitalized at the lessee's borrowing rate (at the inception of the lease) of 8 percent.

Note 10: Each share of preferred stock is convertible into 5 shares of common stock. On July 1, Year 2, holders of 5,000 shares of preferred stock exercised their options. The conversion was recorded using book values.

Note 11: On October 1, Year 2, 40,000 shares of common stock were issued on the open market for $15 per share.

Note 12: Treasury Stock is composed of the following:

Dec. 31, Year 1: 2,250 Shares at $12 per Share	$27,000
Dec. 31, Year 2: 450 Shares at $12 per Share	$ 5,400
550 Shares at $16 per Share	8,800
	$14,200

During Year 2, 1,800 shares of treasury stock were sold and 550 shares were acquired.

23. *Selecting accounting methods.* Champion Clothiers, Inc., owns and operates 80 retailing establishments throughout New England, specializing in quality men's and women's clothing. The company was established many years ago by James

Champion and has been run by a member of the Champion family ever since. Currently, Ronald Champion, grandson of the founder, is president and chief executive officer. The company's shares are held by members of the Champion family.

The setting for this case is March of 1985. The following conversation takes place between Ronald Champion and the company's accountant, Tom Morrissey.

Champion (President): "Tom, you said on the telephone that the financial statements for 1984 were now complete. How much did we earn last year?"

Morrissey (Accountant): "Net income was $800,000, with earnings per share at $1.60. With the $1.20 per share earned in 1982 and $1.38 earned in 1983, we have maintained our 15 percent growth rate in profits."

Champion: "That sounds great! Tom, at our board meeting next week I am going to announce that the Champion family has decided to take the company public. We will be issuing shares equal to a 40 percent stake in the company early in 1986. It is important that our earnings for 1985 continue to reflect the growth rate we have been experiencing. By my calculations, we need an earnings per share for 1985 in the neighborhood of $1.84. Does this seem likely?"

Morrissey: "I'm afraid not. Our current projections indicate an earnings per share around $1.65 for this year. Major unexpected style changes earlier this year have left us with obsolete inventory that will have to be written off. In addition, increased competition in several of our major markets is putting a squeeze on margins. Even the acquisition of Green Trucking Company in June of this year will not help earnings that much."

Champion: "I know you accountants have all kinds of games you can play to doctor up the numbers. There must be something we can do to increase earnings to the desired level. What about our use of LIFO for inventories?"

Morrissey: "We have been using LIFO in the past because it reduces income and saves taxes during a period of rising prices. The more recent, higher acquisition costs of inventory items are used in computing cost of goods sold in the income statement. The older, lower acquisition prices are used in the valuation of inventory on the balance sheet. We could switch to FIFO for 1985. That would add about $.21 to earnings per share. However, we would probably have to use FIFO for tax purposes as well, increasing our taxes for the year by about $50,000."

Champion: "I don't like paying more taxes, but FIFO certainly more closely approximates the physical flow of our goods. If we decide to stay on LIFO, is there anything we can do in applying the LIFO method that would prop up earnings?"

Morrissey: "We now classify our inventory very broadly into two LIFO groups, or pools: one for men's clothing and one for women's clothing. We do this to minimize the possibility of dipping into an old LIFO layer. As you will recall, if we sell more than we purchase during a given period, we dip into an old LIFO layer. These LIFO layers are valued using acquisition costs of the year the layer was added. Some of these layers reflect costs of the mid-50s. When we dip into one of these layers, we have to use these old, lower costs in figuring cost of goods sold and net income. By defining our LIFO pools broadly to include our dollar investment in men's clothing and our dollar investment in women's clothing, we minimize the probability of liquidating an old LIFO layer. We could define our LIFO pools more narrowly to increase the possibility of dipping. We could then let the inventory of particular items run down at the end of the year, dip into the LIFO layer to increase earnings, and then rebuild the inventory early in the next year. I suspect we could add about $.02 a share to 1985 earnings if we went with narrower pools.''

Champion: ''We own all of our store buildings and display counters. Is there anything we can do with depreciation expense?''

Morrissey: ''We now depreciate these items using the shortest lives allowed and the fastest write-off permitted by tax law. However, unlike LIFO, we do not have to calculate depreciation for financial reporting the same as we do for tax reporting. We could depreciate these items over the expected economic life of each asset, which would be longer than the tax life. That should add about $.04 to earnings per share for 1985. We could also use the straight-line depreciation method for financial reporting. While our depreciable assets probably decrease in value faster than the straight-line method would indicate, we would be using the depreciation method that most of our competitors use for financial reporting. The use of straight-line depreciation would add another $.08.''

Champion: ''Now you're talking. What else can we do?''

Morrissey: ''There are some possibilities with respect to the acquisition of Green Trucking later this year. We currently plan to account for this acquisition using the purchase method. Under the purchase method, we will record the assets (and liabilities) of Green Trucking on our books at their market value on the date of acquisition. Since we expect to pay a price higher than the market value of Green's identifiable assets, there will also be some goodwill recorded.''

Champion: ''How does the acquisition impact earnings for 1985?''

Morrissey: ''On the plus side, we will include the earnings of Green Trucking from the date of acquisition in June until the end of the year. However, cost of goods sold and depreciation expense must be based on the higher current market values recorded on our books for Green's assets rather than the lower recorded amounts on Green's books. In addition, we will have to amortize the goodwill. I expect to pick up $.08 per share in earnings for 1985 from the Green acquisition, but this is already reflected in my $1.65 estimate for the year.''

Champion: ''Can we account for the acquisition any differently?''

Morrissey: ''If we can qualify, we may be able to use the pooling-of-interests method. Under the pooling method, we would record Green's assets (and liabilities) on our books at the amounts at which they are stated on Green's books. That is, the older, lower book values would be carried over. This means that cost of goods sold and depreciation expense will be lower this year and in the future than if we used the purchase method. In addition, no goodwill would be recognized and therefore no goodwill amortization would have to be recorded. Also, we would reflect in our earnings for 1985 the earnings of Green Trucking for all of 1985, not just that portion after June. Using the pooling method, earnings per share should increase $.10 more than the purchase method.''

Champion: ''That sounds great, but what do we have to do to qualify?''

Morrissey: ''To justify carrying over the old book values of Green Trucking, we have to show that we are merely combining the predecessor companies *and their shareholders*. The shareholders of Green Trucking must receive common stock of Champion Clothiers in exchange for their shares in Green Trucking. The shareholders in each of the predecessor companies then become shareholders in the new combined company (which will carry the Champion name). The Green shareholders

Exhibit 15.17
CHAMPION CLOTHIERS, INC.
Alternative Strategies for Managing Earnings per Share
(Problem 23)

Alternative	Impact on Earnings per Share			
	1982	1983	1984	1985
Actual or Anticipated	$1.20	$1.38	$1.60	$1.65
Adoption of FIFO	+.15	+.17	+.20	+.21
Use of Narrower LIFO Pools	+.02	+.03	+.02	+.02
Use of Longer Depreciable Lives	—	—	—	+.04
Adoption of Straight-Line Depreciation	+.05	+.06	+.07	+.08
Adoption of Pooling of Interests	+.02	+.04	+.06	+.10
Amortization of Pension Obligation over 30 Years	—	—	—	+.05
Deferral of Maintenance	—	—	—	+.02
Deferral of Advertising	—	—	—	+.03
Acceleration of Capital Expenditures	—	—	—	+.04
Sale of Marketable Securities	—	—	—	+.02
Sale of Land	—	—	—	+.04

would own 10 percent of Champion after the acquisition. Accountants view such a transaction as a change in form rather than in substance and permit the carryover of the old book values of Green.''

Champion: ''My family may not be too happy about this arrangement, but let's move on.''

Morrissey: ''Well, there is one thing we can do very easily with our pension plan to improve earnings. When we adopted the pension plan 2 years ago, we gave all employees credit for their service prior to adoption. This created an immediate obligation for past service. We are amortizing this obligation as a charge against earnings over a 15-year period, which is the average remaining work life of our employees. Generally accepted accounting principles permit us to use 30 years instead of 15 years as the amortization period; that switch would increase earnings per share by $.05 for 1985.''

Champion: ''All of the things you have suggested deal with the selection or application of accounting methods. Can we do anything with the timing of expenditures to help 1985's earnings?''

Morrissey: ''Well, painting and other maintenance of our stores scheduled for the last quarter of this year could be postponed until the first quarter of next year. That would add $.02 to earnings per share. In addition, we anticipate running a major advertising campaign just after Christmas. While the advertising expenditure will be made in 1985 and will reduce earnings per share by $.03, all of the benefits of the campaign will be realized in greater sales early in 1986. Finally, capital expenditures scheduled for the first quarter of 1985 could be moved back to the fourth quarter of this year. We realize a tax saving from the investment tax credit on these expenditures. By realizing these credits this year, we could increase earnings per share by $.04.''

Champion: ''I hadn't realized how much flexibility we had for managing our earnings. Before we decide which choices to make, can you think of any other avenues open to us?''

Morrissey: ''We could always sell off assets on which we have potential gain. For example, we hold some marketable securities that we purchased last year. Selling those securities would net us an additional $.02 in earnings per share. In addition, we own two parcels of land that we hope to use some day for new stores. These parcels could be sold at a gain of $.04 per share.''

Champion: ''It strikes me that these alternatives could increase earnings per share for 1985 to the $2.00-plus range. This level is a lot more appealing than the $1.65 per share anticipated for the year. Will we have to do anything to earnings per share for prior years if we adopt any of these alternatives?''

Morrissey: ''I have set out in Exhibit 15.17 the impact of each of the choices on earnings per share for 1985, as well as any retroactive adjustment required for prior years. This summary should be helpful as we decide our strategy.''

How much do you think Champion Clothiers should report as earnings per share for 1985?

Appendix A Corporate Financial Statements Illustrated and Annotated

This appendix illustrates current financial reporting with a comprehensive set of corporate financial statements prepared in accordance with generally accepted accounting principles.

The financial statements for the General Products Company, shown here, are adapted from those of the General Electric Company. General Electric will send you a copy of its actual, current annual report. Write Investor Relations, General Electric Company, Fairfield, Connecticut 06431.

This appendix is organized as follows. The annual report of General Products Company appears in four exhibits, numbered Exhibit A.1 to A.4. These exhibits generally appear on the left-hand pages that follow. In the margins of those exhibits are bracketed numbers (which do not appear in the original). Authors' comments that explain various features of the accounting appearing in the financial statements are on nearby pages. Questions and problems appear at the end of the appendix.

Exhibit A.1
GENERAL PRODUCTS COMPANY
and consolidated affiliates
Statement of Income and Retained Earnings

For the years ended December 31 (In millions)	1985	1984	1983
Sales Sales of products and services to customers (note 1)	$24,959	$22,461	$19,654
Operating Cost of goods sold	17,751	15,991	13,915
expenses Selling, general and administrative expense	4,258	3,716	3,205
Depreciation, depletion and amortization	707	624	576
Operating expenses (notes 2 and 3)	22,716	20,331	17,696
Operating margin	2,243	2,130	1,958
Other income (note 4)	564	519	419
Interest and other financial charges (note 5)	(314)	(258)	(224)
Earnings Earnings before income taxes and minority interest	2,493	2,391	2,153
[1] Provision for income taxes (note 6)	(958)	(953)	(894)
[2] Minority interest in earnings of consolidated affiliates	(21)	(29)	(29)
Net income applicable to common stock	$ 1,514	$ 1,409	$ 1,230
[3] Earnings per common share (in dollars) (note 7)	$6.65	$6.20	$5.39
Dividends declared per common share (in dollars)	$2.95	$2.75	$2.50
Operating margin as a percentage of sales	9.0%	9.5%	10.0%
Net earnings as a percentage of sales	6.1%	6.3%	6.3%
For the years ended December 31 (In millions)	1985	1984	1983
Retained Balance January 1	$6,307	$5,522	$4,862
earnings Net earnings	1,514	1,409	1,230
Dividends declared on common stock	(670)	(624)	(570)
Balance December 31	$7,151	$6,307	$5,522

[4]

The information in the notes is an integral part of these statements.

[5] ## Report of Independent Certified Public Accountants

To Share Owners and Board of Directors of General Products Company

We have examined the statement of financial position of General Products Company and consolidated affiliates as of December 31, 1985 and 1984, and the related statements of earnings, retained earnings and changes in financial position for each of the three years in the period ended December 31, 1985. Our examinations were made in accordance with generally accepted auditing standards, and accordingly included such tests of the accounting records and such other auditing procedures as we considered necessary in the circumstances.

In our opinion, the aforementioned financial statements present fairly the financial position of General Products Company and consolidated affiliates at December 31, 1985 and 1984, and the results of their operations and the changes in their financial position for each of the three years in the period ended December 31, 1985, in conformity with generally accepted accounting principles applied on a consistent basis.

Stuckey, Wells & Co.
1101 E. 58th Street
Chicago, IL 60637

Stuckey Wells & Co.

February 20, 1986

Authors' Comments

[1] Provision usually means "estimated expense" in this country; see the Glossary at *provision* for the contrast in this word's meanings in the U.S. and the U.K.

[2] GP does not own all the shares in all of its consolidated subsidiaries. Some of the shares belong to outsiders, called the *minority interest*. The minority interest's share of the earnings of the subsidiary companies does not belong to GP's shareholders. Hence, in deriving income to GP's shareholders, the minority interest's share in earnings is subtracted from the earnings of the consolidated group of companies. Note, however, that this reduction in income uses no cash or other funds, so that there is an adjustment on the statement of changes in financial position for this charge against income. See Comment **[15]**.

[3] This is primary earnings per share, as called for by APB *Opinion No. 15*. See GP's note 7 for a discussion of fully diluted earnings per share. Fully diluted earnings per share is not shown separately here because the amount is within 1 percent of the primary earnings-per-share amount. (In general, fully diluted earnings per share need not be shown separately if it is within 3 percent of primary earnings per share.)

[4] Generally accepted accounting principles require a reconciliation of changes in all of the owners' equity accounts during the year. The only major changes in GP's retained earnings account are caused by the earning of income and the declaration of dividends. GP's note 18 explains other changes in owners' equity.

[5] This is the auditor's report. This particular report is both nonqualified ("clean") and in standard format. The first paragraph of the auditor's report is the scope paragraph—telling the work done—and the last paragraph is the opinion. The auditor's report usually precedes or follows the annual report, but is reproduced here for convenience.

[6] GP uses the completed contract method of recognizing revenue from long-term construction contracts; see GP's Summary of Significant Accounting Policies at "Sales." As GP incurs costs on these contracts it makes journal entries such as:

Work-in-Process Inventory for Long-Term Contracts	X	
Various Assets and Liabilities		X
To record cost of construction activity.		

Some of GP's long-term construction contracts provide that the customer shall make progress payments to GP as the work is done. GP does not recognize revenue until the work is completed, so the journal entry made at the time cash is received is one such as:

Exhibit A.2
GENERAL PRODUCTS COMPANY
and consolidated affiliates
Statement of Financial Position

At December 31 (In millions)		1985	1984
Assets	Cash (note 8)	$ 2,201	$ 2,576
	Current receivables (note 9)	4,339	3,647
	Inventories (note 10)	3,343	3,161
	Current assets	9,883	9,384
	Property, plant, and equipment—net (note 11) . . .	5,780	4,613
	Investments (note 12)	1,820	1,691
	Other assets (note 13)	1,028	956
	Total assets	$18,511	$16,644
Liabilities	Short-term borrowings (note 14)	$ 1,093	$ 871
and equity	Accounts payable (note 15)	1,671	1,477
[6]	Progress collections and price adjustments accrued .	2,084	1,957
	Dividends payable.	170	159
	Taxes payable	628	655
	Other payables (note 16)	1,946	1,753
	Current liabilities	7,592	6,872
	Long-term borrowings (note 17)	1,000	947
	Other liabilities	1,565	1,311
	Total liabilities	10,157	9,130
[7]	Minority interest in equity of consolidated affiliates	154	152
	Preferred stock ($1 par value; 2,000,000 shares authorized; none issued)	—	—
	Common stock ($2.50 par value; 251,500,000 shares authorized; 231,463,949 shares issued 1985 and 1984)	579	579
	Amounts received for stock in excess of par value .	659	656
	Retained earnings.	7,151	6,307
		8,389	7,542
[8]	Deduct common stock held in treasury	(189)	(180)
	Total share owners' equity (notes 18, 19, and 20)	8,200	7,362
	Total liabilities and equity	$18,511	$16,644
	Commitments and contingent liabilities (note 21)		

The information in the notes is an integral part of this statement.

Cash	Y	
Advances from Customers on Long-Term Contracts		Y
To record cash received and to set up the corresponding liability.		

When the balance sheet is prepared, the amounts in the inventory accounts, X (debit balance), are netted against the amounts in the liability accounts, Y (credit balance). If there is a net credit balance, as here, with Y greater than X, then the difference, $Y - X$, is reported as a liability. GP shows this liability under the title "Progress collections." On contracts where the amounts in the inventory account exceed the cash collections, then the difference, $X - Y$, is shown as an asset under a title such as "Costs Incurred on Long-Term Contracts in Excess of Billings." This netting of costs incurred against cash collections and the separate showing of the excesses are required by *Accounting Research Bulletin No. 45*.

On many of GP's contracts the only cash collected before completion of construction is for engineering costs incurred in preparing to undertake construction. GP expenses these engineering costs, rather than accumulating them in Work-in-Process inventory accounts. Thus, there is no asset account to net against the liability. The "Progress collections" title is appropriate because it tends to represent gross "advances from customers," rather than a netting of work-in-process inventory against advances from customers.

[7] (Refer to Comment [2] for a description of "minority interest" on the income statement.) This account represents the equity of the minority shareholders in the consolidated affiliates. From the point of view of GP's shareholders, this equity belonging to the minority is a liability. From the point of view of the consolidated entity, the minority shareholders' interest is part of total owners' equity. Thus whether one believes that minority interest is a liability or an item of owners' equity depends on whether one views the financial statements as being prepared for the shareholders of GP (the proprietorship theory) or for all potential readers (the entity theory). Note that GP avoids the issue by not classifying "minority interest" either with liabilities or with owners' equity.

[8] GP uses the cost method of accounting for treasury stock and shows the cost of its own shares acquired on the market as contra to all of owners' equity. Refer to Comment [69].

[9] Some companies define funds as working capital = current assets − current liabilities. GP uses a more restrictive definition of funds; for GP, funds = cash (which includes a small amount of nonequity marketable securities). See Comment [59].

Exhibit A.3
GENERAL PRODUCTS COMPANY
and consolidated affiliates
Statement of Changes in Financial Position

For the years ended December 31 (In millions)			1985	1984	1983
[9]	**Source of**	*From operations* [10]			
	Cash	Net earnings.	$1,514	$1,409	$1,230
		Items of income not requiring (or producing) cash from operating activities:			
	[11]	Depreciation, depletion and amortization	707	624	576
	[12]	Investment tax credit deferred—net	56	45	25
	[13]	Income tax timing differences	63	(37)	32
	[14]	Earnings retained by nonconsolidated finance affiliate .	(22)	(18)	(15)
	[15]	Minority interest in earnings of consolidated affiliates. .	21	29	29
		Other operating sources and (uses) of cash:			
	[16]	(Increase) in current receivables	(692)	(358)	(306)
	[17]	(Increase) in inventories	(182)	(158)	(399)
	[18]	Increase (decrease) in short-term borrowings	222	(89)	188
	[18]	Increase in current payables other than short-term borrowings	498	786	570
		Cash provided by operations	$2,185	$2,233	$1,930
	[19]	Increase in long-term borrowings	122	50	96
		Newly issued common stock	—	—	3
		Disposition of treasury shares	136	148	190
		Decrease in investments	—	—	24
		Other—net	143	102	149
		Total sources of cash.	$2,586	$2,533	$2,392
	Application	Additions to property, plant, and equipment	1,948	1,262	1,055
	of Cash	Dividends declared on common stock	670	624	570
		Increase in investments.	129	281	—
	[19]	Reduction in long-term borrowings	69	97	386
		Purchase of treasury shares.	145	156	196
		Total application of funds	$2,961	$2,420	$2,207
	Net change	Net increase (decrease) in cash [20]	$ (375)	$ 113	$ 185

The information in the notes is an integral part of this statement.

[10] This statement, as is customary, starts with net income as shown in the income statement in Exhibit A.1. The next few lines show subtractions for revenues and other credits to income that did not produce cash, and additions for expenses and other charges against income that did not use cash. Then appear operating sources of cash from increases in current liabilities and operating uses of cash for increases in current assets. Total cash produced by operations appears after these adjustments to income and changes in current assets and liabilities.

[11] Depreciation is *not* a source of cash. Rather, it is an expense that reduces net income without using any cash. The cash was used some time in the past when the depreciable assets were acquired.

[12] See Comment **[48]**. GP earns investment credits in the year it acquires new qualifying assets. Because it uses the conservative deferral method for investment credits, it recognizes the effect on income over the lives of the assets acquired. More cash is provided by the investment credit than is recognized in income in the year of acquisition. On the other hand, income is increased somewhat because of the effect of amounts deferred in prior years that are used to reduce reported tax expense in the current year. The net difference is added to net income in deriving cash provided by operations.

[13] In 1985 and 1983, income tax expense for the year exceeded the amount of income taxes payable. See the discussion at GP's note 6 and Comments **[49]**– **[53]**. Because less cash was used for income taxes than was reported as income tax expense, there has to be an addition for the amount of expense not using cash in deriving funds from operations. The results for 1984 show that taxes payable exceeded tax expense.

[14] All earnings of the GP Credit Corporation ($115 million in 1985) are included in income under the equity method. See "Other income," GP's note 4. Only $93 million of dividends were declared by the Credit Corporation; see the "Current and retained earnings statement" of the Credit Company in GP's note 12. The difference, $22 (= $115 − $93) million, provided no cash to GP (but was added to GP's Investment account) and must be subtracted from net income to derive GP's funds from operations. That is, the entire $115 million is included in the $1,514 million shown as net earnings by GP, but dividend declarations of the Credit Corporation provided funds of only $93 million.

[15] See Comment **[2]**. The charge on the income statement for the minority's interest in earnings (of $21 million in 1985) reduces the income reported to GP's shareholders, but does not reduce the amount of cash provided by operations of the consolidated entity. Thus, there is an addback to net income for $21 million in 1985 in deriving cash produced by operations.

[16] GP's definition of funds does not include current receivables. Thus, an increase in current receivables is an operating use of cash. Some would classify the increase in receivables as nonoperating. Then, an increase in receivables would use cash just as any increase in investments uses cash.

[21] **Exhibit A.4**
Summary of significant
accounting policies

[22] **Basis of consolidation**

The financial statements consolidate the accounts of the parent General Products Company and those of all majority-owned and controlled companies ("affiliated companies"),
[23] except the finance company whose operations are not similar to those of the consolidated
group. All significant items relating to transactions among the parent and affiliated compa-
[24] nies are eliminated from the consolidated statements.

The nonconsolidated finance company is included in the statement of financial position
[25] under investments and is valued at equity plus advances. In addition, companies in which
GP and/or its consolidated affiliates own 20% to 50% of the voting stock ("associated
companies") are included under investments, valued at the appropriate share of equity
plus advances. After-tax earnings of nonconsolidated finance companies and associated
companies are included in the statement of earnings under other income.

[26] **Sales**

The Company and its consolidated affiliates record a transaction as a sale only when title
to products passes to the customer.

[27] **Vacation expense**

Most employees earn credits during the current year for vacations to be taken in the
following year. The expense for this liability is accrued during the year vacations are
earned rather than in the year vacations are taken.

Pensions

Investments of the General Products Pension Trust, which funds the obligations of the
General Products Pension Plan, are carried at amortized cost plus programmed apprecia-
[28] tion in the common stock portfolio. The funding program and Company cost determination
for the Pension Plan use 6% as the estimated rate of future Trust income. Trust income
includes recognition of appreciation in the common stock portfolio on a systematic basis
which does not give undue weight to short-term market fluctuations. Programmed appreciation will not be recognized if average carrying value exceeds average market value,
calculated on a moving basis over a multiyear period.

Changes in accrued actuarial liabilities for prior service are amortized over 20 years. Net
actuarial gains and losses are amortized over 15 years.

Costs of a separate, supplementary pension plan, primarily affecting long-service professional and managerial employees, are not funded. Current service costs and amortization of actuarial liabilities for prior service over a period of 20 years are being charged to
operating expenses currently.

Investment tax credit

[29] The investment tax credit is recorded by the "deferral method" and is amortized as a
reduction of the provision for taxes over the lives of the facilities to which the credit applies,
rather than being "flowed through" to income in the year the asset is acquired.

Inventories

Substantially all manufacturing inventories located in the U.S. are valued on a last-in
[30] first-out, or LIFO, basis. Manufacturing inventories outside the U.S. are generally valued
on a first-in first-out, or FIFO, basis. Valuations are based on the cost of material, direct
[31] labor and manufacturing overhead, and do not exceed net realizable values. Certain indirect manufacturing expenses are charged directly to operating costs during the period
incurred, rather than being inventoried.

Mining inventories, which include principally mined ore and coal, metal concentrates
and mining supplies, are stated at the lower of average cost or market. The cost of mining
inventories includes both direct and indirect costs consisting of labor, purchased supplies
and services, and depreciation, depletion and amortization of property, plant and equipment.

[17] GP's definition of funds does not include inventories. Increases in inventories use cash. Some might call this a nonoperating use of funds.

[18] GP's definition of funds does not include current payables. Although GP classifies this as an operating source, some would classify it as nonoperating. Then, an increase in current payables would provide cash just as new long-term borrowing provides cash.

[19] As is preferable, GP shows separately cash provided by new borrowings and cash used to reduce old borrowings. Some companies show only the net effect either as a source or as an application of cash; they provide no information about the amount of actual borrowings and repayments during the period.

[20] Some firms would add the opening balance of cash to the amount shown here in order to reconcile the change in the balance sheet amount of cash. For 1985, for example, note from the balance sheet that the beginning balance of cash was $2,576 and the decrease in cash for the year was $375. Thus, the ending balance of cash is derived as $2,201 (= $2,576 − $375) and the amount appears on the end-of-1985 balance sheet as the cash balance.

[21] APB *Opinion No. 22* requires that all annual reports include a summary of significant accounting principles used so that the reader can know which accounting alternatives have been chosen by the company.

[22] A parent, such as GP, usually consolidates a subsidiary when all three of the following criteria are met:

(i) The parent owns more than 50 percent of the voting shares of the subsidiary.
(ii) There are no important restrictions on the ability of the parent to exercise control of the subsidiary.
(iii) The asset and equity structure of the subsidiary is not significantly different from that of the parent.

[23] GP reports here that it consolidates all "majority-owned" (greater than 50 percent) and "controlled" companies except the finance company, which is not similar to the others in the consolidated group. Instead, the finance affiliate is accounted for using the equity method. As can be seen from GP Credit Corporation's balance sheet in note 12, most (90 percent at year end 1985) of the Credit Corporation's assets are receivables and most (80 percent) of its equities are debt, rather than owners' equity. In this sense, the operations of the finance affiliate "are not similar to those of the consolidated group." As Comment [61] points out, the nonconsolidation of the finance company makes GP's balance sheet differ substantially from its appearance if the finance affiliates were consolidated. Although there is no effect on final net income, the components of income differ.

[24] Consolidated financial statements present information about a group of affiliated companies as if the group were one economic entity. Consequently, gains or losses on sales of assets between companies in the consolidated group must be eliminated from reported financial statements. The recognition of such

Property, plant, and equipment

Manufacturing plant and equipment includes the original cost of land, buildings and equipment less depreciation, which is the estimated cost consumed by wear and obsolescence. An accelerated depreciation method, based principally on a sum-of-the-years'-digits formula, is used to record depreciation of the original cost of manufacturing plant and equipment purchased and installed in the U.S. subsequent to 1960. Most manufacturing plant and equipment located outside the U.S. is depreciated on a straight-line basis. If manufacturing plant and equipment is subject to abnormal economic conditions or obsolescence, additional depreciation is provided. Expenditures for maintenance and repairs of manufacturing plant and equipment are charged to operations as incurred.

The cost of mining properties includes initial expenditures and cost of major rebuilding projects which substantially increase the useful lives of existing assets. The cost of mining properties is depreciated, depleted or amortized over the useful lives of the related assets by use of unit-of-production, straight-line or declining-balance methods.

Mining exploration costs are expensed until it is determined that the development of a mineral deposit is likely to be economically feasible. After this determination is made, all costs related to further development are capitalized. Amortization of such costs begins upon commencement of production and is over ten years or the productive life of the property, whichever is less.

[32]   Oil and gas properties are accounted for by use of the full-cost method.

Notes to financial statements

1 Sales

[33] Approximately one-eighth of sales were to agencies of the U.S. government, which is the Company's largest single customer. The principal source of these sales was the Technical Systems and Materials segment of the Company's business.

2 Operating expenses

Operating costs by major categories are shown below: (In millions)	1985	1984	1983
Employee compensation, including benefits . . .	$ 9,196	$ 8,286	$ 7,401
Materials, supplies, services, and other costs . .	12,696	11,320	9,867
Depreciation, depletion, and amortization	707	624	576
Taxes, except Social Security and those on income	299	259	251
[34] Increase in inventories during the year	(182)	(158)	(399)
Operating expenses.	$22,716	$20,331	$17,696

Supplemental details are as follows: (In millions)	1985	1984	1983
Maintenance and repairs	$784	$775	$672
[35] Company-funded research and development . .	760	640	521
Social Security taxes	484	471	397
Advertising.	315	282	247
Mineral royalties and export duties	80	82	79

[36] Foreign currency translation gains, after recognizing related income tax effects and minority interest share, were $40 million in 1985 and $12 million in 1984 and 1983.

gains or losses is postponed until the assets are sold by one company of the consolidated group to a buyer outside the consolidated group.

[25] GP reports that it uses the equity method for the nonconsolidated finance affiliate. Under the equity method, GP's earnings include its share of the earnings, not just the dividends, of this company. See Comment [14].

[26] GP uses the completed contract method of recognizing revenue on long-term construction projects. See Comment [6].

[27] GP reports that (as required by *SFAS No. 43*) it charges vacation pay to expense (or product cost) accounts as employees earn vacations, rather than charging income when employees take their vacations. These amounts include fringe benefits on the base pay.

[28] That is, in computing future values of pension fund investments and interest on unfunded obligations for prior service costs, a 6 percent rate is used. GP's note 3 indicates that the rate earned in 1985 was 8.4 percent.

[29] See Comment [48] for a discussion of the investment credit and the effect of GP's using the conservative deferral method.

[30] Most foreign governments do not allow LIFO for tax purposes.

[31] GP reports that it will not show an item of inventory on the balance sheet at an amount greater than net realizable value; one can deduce that GP must be using a lower-of-cost-or-market valuation basis.

[32] GP uses ''full cost'' accounting for its oil and gas operations. See the Glossary at *reserve recognition accounting* for discussion of the options. The U.S. Congress passed a law that required the SEC (and FASB) to set uniform accounting in the petroleum industry by the end of 1977. FASB *Statement No. 19* was issued in 1977 to comply. The statement required successful efforts accounting and forbade full cost accounting. In 1978, the SEC said it would allow either successful efforts or full cost accounting until it could write rules for ''reserve recognition accounting.'' In 1979, the FASB issued *SFAS No. 25*, rescinding *SFAS No. 19*, so that both full cost accounting and successful efforts accounting may be used. In 1981, the SEC indicated that it was delaying indefinitely use of reserve recognition accounting in the principal financial statements; either successful efforts or full cost continue to be used. GP's reported income is probably slightly larger because it uses full cost accounting rather than successful efforts accounting.

[33] *SFAS No. 14* requires disclosure of this information about customers whose purchases represent 10 percent or more of a firm's revenues.

[34] All manufacturing costs incurred during the year are shown as components of operating costs. If inventories have increased (ending inventory > beginning inventory), then some of those costs have not expired and are not expenses. Hence, the increase in inventories is deducted from total operating costs to derive operating *expenses*.

3 Pensions

Total pension costs of General Products and consolidated affiliates were $478 million in 1985, $413 million in 1984, and $381 million in 1983. General Products and its affiliates have a number of pension plans. The most significant of these plans is the General Products Pension Plan (the "Plan"), in which substantially all employees in the U.S. are participating. Approximately 80,800 persons were receiving benefits at year-end 1985 (75,700 and 72,100 at year-end 1984 and 1983, respectively).

Pension benefits under the Plan are funded through the General Products Pension Trust. Earnings of the Trust, including the programmed recognition of common stock appreciation, as a percentage of the carrying value of the portfolio, were 8.4% for 1985 and 1984, and 7.8% for 1983. The limitation on recognition of programmed appreciation of common stock was not exceeded in any year.

Condensed information for the General Products Pension Trust appears below.

General Products Pension Trust
Change in net assets at current value
(In millions)

For the year	1985	1984	1983
Net assets at January 1	$4,968	$4,202	$3,734
Company contributions	404	341	317
Employee contributions	86	94	83
Investment income	435	383	312
Pensions paid	(254)	(225)	(201)
[37] Unrecognized portion of change in current value	779	173	(43)
Net assets at December 31	$6,418	$4,968	$4,202

Net assets at current value
(In millions)

December 31	1985	1984	1983
U.S. government obligations and guarantees	$ 44	$ 118	$ 93
Corporate bonds and notes	727	496	340
Real estate and mortgages	825	713	725
Common stocks and other equity securities	4,181	3,193	2,726
	5,777	4,520	3,884
Cash and short-term investments	553	371	240
Other assets—net	88	77	78
Current value of net assets	$6,418	$4,968	$4,202
Carrying value of net assets	$5,593	$4,922	$4,329

The actuarial present value of accumulated plan benefits for the General Products Pension Plan and the supplementary pension plan together represent over 90% of accumulated pension plan benefits for General Products and its consolidated affiliates. These present values have been calculated using a 6% interest rate assumption as of December 31 for each of the years in the table below. The table also sets forth the total of the current value of Pension Trust assets and the relevant accruals in the Company's accounts.

[35] *SFAS No. 2* requires the expensing of research and development costs, and the disclosure, such as GP's here, of the costs incurred during the year for R&D. *SFAS No. 2* allows the capitalizing of R&D costs that are incurred under contract and that are reimbursable. GP is making clear that these costs ($760 million in 1985) do not qualify for capitalization.

[36] *SFAS No. 8* requires separate disclosure of these amounts.

[37] The "unrecognized portion of changes in current value" is analogous to unrealized holding gains.

[38] **General Products Pension Plan
and Supplementary Pension Plan
(In millions)**

December 31	1985	1984	1983
Estimated actuarial present value of accumulated plan benefits:			
Vested benefits	$6,027	$5,426	$4,732
Nonvested benefits.	415	382	331
Total benefits	$6,442	$5,808	$5,063
Current value of trust assets plus accruals	$6,580	$5,075	$4,273

For pension plans not included above, there was no significant difference between accumulated benefits and the relevant fund assets plus accruals.

[39]   The forgoing amounts are based on FASB standards which differ from those used by the Company for funding and cost determination purposes. Based on the actuarial method used by the Company, and with assets at carrying value, unfunded and unamortized liabilities for the two principal pension plans totaled $964 million, $1,082 million, and $882 million at year-end 1985, 1984, and 1983, respectively.

An increase in pensions of retired employees effective February 1, 1986, will increase the actuarial present value of accumulated vested benefits by an estimated $196 million.

4 Other income

(In millions)	1985	1984	1983
[40] Net earnings of General Products Credit Corporation	$115	$ 90	$ 77
Income from:			
Marketable securities and bank deposits.	229	229	140
[41] Customer financing	72	70	49
Royalty and technical agreements	52	50	44
Associated companies and nonconsolidated uranium mining affiliate	22	11	34
Other investments:			
Interest	21	20	19
Dividends	13	11	10
Other sundry items	40	38	46
	$564	$519	$419

[42] **5 Interest and other financial charges**

Interest capitalized on major property, plant, and equipment projects was $21 million, $18 million, and $15 million in 1985, 1984, and 1983, respectively.

[38] *SFAS No. 36* requires that the assets and liabilities of the pension plan be disclosed in notes to the employer's financial statements. *SFAS No. 36* requires that the same actuarial cost method be used by all companies in their disclosures about their pension plans. See Chapter 11. In the paragraph following the schedule, GP discloses the results of applying the more conservative actuarial cost method it uses for its own purposes.

[39] GP discloses that the present value of the expected payments to current and retired employees exceeds the carrying value ($5,593 million in 1984) of pension plan assets by $964 million at the end of 1985.

[40] GP uses the equity method of accounting for its 100 percent ownership of the GP Credit Corporation. Hence it shows 100 percent of the earnings of the Credit Corporation as "Other income." See Comments **[14]** and **[61]**.

[41] "Customer financing" is interest on receivables held by GP arising from some of its sales.

[42] *SFAS No. 34* requires separate disclosure of amounts of interest capitalized into plant under construction. See the discussion in Chapter 9.

[43] This first schedule shows the details of income tax expense, called a "provision." The bottom line of the first schedule is the total expense reported on the statement of earnings. It is the sum of U.S. federal, foreign, and other income tax expenses. The U.S. federal and foreign income tax expense amounts are derived in essentially two steps: First is shown the amount of taxes payable; then there is an adjustment for timing differences. GP also shows the effect of the investment credit, which is discussed in Comment **[48]**.

[44] In 1985, income tax expense exceeded income taxes payable because of timing differences. The details of the U.S. federal timing differences are shown in the next schedule.

[45] GP uses the deferral method of accounting for the investment credit; see Chapter 9.

[46] The Internal Revenue Service has not completed its audit of GP's tax returns for years after 1977.

[47] APB *Opinion No. 23* says that income of affiliates that is expected to be indefinitely reinvested in the affiliate need not be subject to income tax provisions by the parent. If the parent expects to receive dividends from the affiliate in the foreseeable future, then the parent must make an income tax provision.

[48] GP uses the deferral method of accounting for the investment credit, rather than the less conservative flow-through method. (Most U.S. corporations use the flow-through method.) GP earned $92 million of investment credits during 1985. A portion (which cannot be computed from the published data) of this $92 million reduced reported tax expense in 1985; the remainder is shown as a deferred investment credit on the balance sheet (under "Other liabilities"). A portion of previous years' investment credits, which had been deferred, also served to reduce 1985 reported tax expense. The total of these two reductions

[43]   6 Provision for income taxes

(In millions)	1985	1984	1983
U.S. federal income taxes:			
Estimated amount payable	$574	$599	$590
[44] Effect of timing differences	14	(31)	(13)
[45] Investment credit deferred—net	56	45	25
	644	613	602
Foreign income taxes:			
Estimated amount payable	238	323	221
[44] Effect of timing differences	39	(6)	45
	277	317	266
Other (principally state and local income taxes)	37	23	26
	$958	$953	$894

[46] All General Products consolidated U.S. federal income tax returns have been closed through 1977.

[47]   Provision has been made for federal income taxes to be paid on that portion of the undistributed earnings of affiliates and associated companies expected to be remitted to the parent company. Undistributed earnings intended to be reinvested indefinitely in affiliates and associated companies totaled $1,111 million at the end of 1985, $944 million at the end of 1984, and $815 million at the end of 1983.

Changes in estimated foreign income taxes payable and in the effect of timing differences result principally from fluctuations in foreign earnings and tax rates, and from recognizing in the current year for tax payment purposes the results of transactions in Australia recorded for financial reporting purposes in other years.

[48]   Investment credit amounted to $92 million in 1985, compared with $76 million in 1984 and $51 million in 1983. In 1985, $36 million were included in net earnings, compared with $31 million in 1984 and $26 million in 1983. At the end of 1985, the amount still deferred and to be included in net earnings in future years was $262 million.

[49]   Effect of timing differences on U.S.
federal income taxes
(In millions)

Increase (decrease) in provision for income taxes	1985	1984	1983
[50] Tax over book depreciation	$ 48	$ 23	$ 26
[51] Undistributed earnings of affiliates and associated companies.	29	(2)	8
[52] Margin on installment sales	1	(10)	(10)
[53] Provision for warranties	(46)	(36)	(31)
Other—net	(18)	(6)	(6)
	$ 14	$(31)	$(13)

[54] The cumulative net effect of timing differences has resulted in a deferred-tax asset which is shown under other assets.

of reported tax expense in 1985 was $36 million. If GP had used the flow-through method, income tax expense would have been reduced by an additional $56 (= $92 − $36) million and 1985 net income would have been $56 million larger. Under the flow-through method, retained earnings at the end of 1985 would have been $262 million larger. Total deferred investment credits of $262 million are part of "Other liabilities" on the balance sheet.

[49] This schedule shows the components of the timing differences on U.S. federal income taxes.

[50] Depreciation on the tax return exceeded the amount included in cost of goods sold and other expenses on the financial statements. For most companies, tax depreciation exceeds book depreciation because the accelerated methods of ACRS are used for taxes and the straight-line method is used for financial reporting. GP, however, uses an accelerated method (based on the sum-of-the-years' digits) in its financial statements; see the Summary of Significant Accounting Policies. The excess of tax deductions for depreciation over book depreciation expenses for GP arises from GP's using shorter depreciable lives for tax than for book calculations. See the Glossary at ACRS. We can compute the excess of tax depreciation deductions over the book depreciation expense reported in the financial statements by using the $48 million timing difference shown here for 1985. If income tax expense exceeds income taxes payable by $48 million because of depreciation timing differences and if the marginal income tax rate is 46 percent of pretax income, then depreciation on the tax return must have exceeded depreciation on the financial statements by x, where

$$.46x = \$48 \text{ million}$$
$$x = \frac{\$48 \text{ million}}{.46}$$
$$= \$104 \text{ million.}$$

[51] Revenues from subsidiaries ("affiliates") shown on the financial statements under the equity method exceeded taxable revenue from these subsidiaries. Taxable revenue from this source is based primarily on the amount of dividends received. (Note that 85 percent of dividends received by one corporation from another corporation are not taxed. This is, however, a permanent difference that would not appear here.)

[52] GP makes sales on credit, with cash payments from the customer to GP spread over time. Such sales are called "installment sales." APB *Opinion No. 10* requires that revenue from most such sales be recognized in the financial statements for the period of sale. For tax purposes, GP recognizes revenue when the cash payments are collected. This creates a timing difference. The amount shown here for GP is relatively small because GP tends not to have large percentages of its sales on the installment method.

[53] Estimated warranty expense recognized by the "allowance method" does not qualify as a tax deduction. GP uses the "allowance method" of recognizing warranty expense for financial reporting. As products carrying warranties are

[55] **Reconciliation from statutory to effective income tax rates**	1985	1984	1983
U.S. federal statutory rate	46.0%	46.0%	46.0%
Reduction in taxes resulting from:			
Varying tax rates of consolidated affiliates (including DISC)	(4.7)	(3.3)	(2.4)
Inclusion of earnings of the Credit Corporation in before-tax income on an after-tax basis	(2.1)	(1.7)	(1.5)
Investment credit	(1.5)	(1.3)	(1.2)
Income tax at capital gains rate	(0.1)	—	(0.6)
Other—net	0.8	0.2	1.2
Effective tax rate	38.4%	39.9%	41.5%

[56] Based on the location of the component furnishing goods or services, domestic income before taxes was $1,854 million in 1985 ($1,706 million in 1984, and $1,592 million in 1983). The corresponding amounts for foreign-based operations were $639 million, $685 million and $561 million in each of the last three years, respectively. Provision for income taxes is determined on the basis of the jurisdiction imposing the tax liability. Therefore, U.S. and foreign taxes shown do not compare directly with these segregations.

[57] **7 Earnings per common share**

Earnings per share are based on the average number of shares outstanding. Any dilution which would result from the potential exercise or conversion of such items as stock options or convertible debt outstanding is insignificant (less than 1% in 1985, 1984, and 1983).

8 Cash

[58] Deposits restricted as to usage and withdrawal or used as partial compensation for short-term borrowing arrangements were not material.

[59] Included in this caption are small amounts of marketable securities (none of which are equity securities) carried at the lower of amortized cost or market value. Carrying value was substantially the same as market value at year-end 1985 and 1984.

9 Current receivables

(In millions) December 31	1985	1984
Customers' accounts and notes	$3,816	$3,254
Associated companies	25	36
Nonconsolidated affiliates	17	7
Other	584	439
	4,442	3,736
Less allowances for uncollectibles	(103)	(89)
	$4,339	$3,647

sold, GP makes the following entry recognizing the estimated liability for future repairs and replacements:

Estimated Warranty Expense (Provision)   X
   Estimated Warranty Liability   X
Entry made in the period of sale for expected warranty costs.

Later, when repairs are made, and warranty costs are incurred, the entry is

---

Estimated Warranty Liability . . . . :   Y
   Assets Used and Liabilities Incurred . . . .   Y
To recognize cost of actual repairs and replacements.

The repair and, therefore, the second entry often occur in a year subsequent to the year of sale. The cost of providing the warranty services does not become a tax deduction until the repair is actually made. Thus timing differences are created: An expense is subtracted on the financial statements in one year but is deducted on the tax return in a later year. The following inference about all 3 years reported on can be made. The provision for warranties (the estimated expense) results in income taxes payable being larger than income tax expense. Therefore, it must be true that the estimated expense of rendering warranty service in future years for sales in the current year is greater than the actual costs of warranty repairs made in current years, most of which related to sales of earlier years.

[54] Primarily because of the accounting (explained just above) for warranties, GP's cumulative income tax payments have exceeded cumulative income tax expense reported in the financial statements although this cumulative excess was reduced in 1985. This has resulted in a "deferred tax debit" (whereas most companies have the reverse situation and a "deferred tax credit"), which GP reports among its "Other assets"; see GP's note 13.

[55] Most readers of financial statements are aware that the U.S. federal tax rate on most corporate income is 46 percent of pretax income. The SEC requires that companies report in their notes why the reported income tax expense rate differs from 46 percent. The $115 million of income in 1985 for GP Credit reported in GP's note 4 is after taxes. Yet it appears in GP's income statement before the income tax calculation. GP need pay no further taxes on the income from GP Credit; this accounts for part of the difference between GP's effective tax rate on "pretax income," 38.4 percent in 1985, and the statutory rate, 46 percent. The investment credit reduces taxes otherwise payable, and this accounts for another part of the difference.

[56] The SEC requires disclosure of the disaggregation of pretax income into domestic and foreign sources.

10 Inventories

(In millions) December 31	1985	1984
Raw materials and work in process	$2,082	$1,943
Finished goods	961	966
Unbilled shipments	300	252
	$3,343	$3,161

[60] About 84% of total inventories are valued using the LIFO method of inventory accounting. If the FIFO method of inventory accounting had been used to value all inventories, they would have been $2,240 million higher than reported at December 31, 1985 ($1,950 million higher at year-end 1984).

11 Property, plant, and equipment

(In millions)	1985	1984
Major classes at December 31:		
Manufacturing plant and equipment		
Land and improvements	$ 139	$ 125
Buildings, structures and related equipment	2,329	2,098
Machinery and equipment	6,197	5,324
Leasehold costs and manufacturing plant under construction	453	372
Mineral property, plant and equipment	1,917	1,456
	$11,035	$9,365
Cost at January 1	$ 9,365	$8,328
Additions	1,948	1,262
Dispositions	(278)	(225)
Cost at December 31	$11,035	$9,365
Accumulated depreciation, depletion, and amortization		
Balance at January 1	$ 4,752	$4,305
Current-year provision	707	624
Dispositions	(214)	(188)
Other changes	10	11
Balance at December 31	$ 5,255	$4,752
Property, plant, and equipment less depreciation, depletion, and amortization at December 31	$ 5,780	$4,613

[57] GP reports only primary earnings per share. Because it has so few dilutive securities outstanding, fully diluted earnings per share would be less than 1 percent below the primary earnings per share. A dual presentation of earnings per share is required only when fully diluted earnings per share are 97 percent or less of primary earnings per share.

[58] See *compensating balance* in the Glossary. Compensating balances increase the stated cost of borrowing; accordingly, the SEC requires disclosure of such amounts, if they are significant. GP states that its compensating balances are not significant.

[59] The inclusion of nonequity, marketable securities with cash is a common practice, at least when the amounts are immaterial. *ARB No. 43* requires disclosure of aggregate cost and aggregate market value of nonequity, marketable securities.

[60] GP provides information that allows us to calculate what the operating income would have been if a FIFO cost flow assumption had been used. (Chapter 8 explains why LIFO leads to lower reported net income in periods of rising prices.) The IRS does not allow companies using LIFO for tax purposes to disclose directly on the income statement what income would have been under FIFO. The SEC requires the disclosure of beginning and ending inventories as they would have been under FIFO, if these amounts are significantly different from the LIFO amounts. The SEC's required disclosure of inventory differences allows the reader to compute the income difference. As of December 31, 1985, cumulative pretax income is $2,240 million less than it would have been under FIFO. As of January 1, 1985, cumulative pretax income is $1,950 million less than it would have been under FIFO. This difference increased by $290 (= $2,240 − $1,950) million during the year 1985. Hence 1985 pretax income would have been $290 million, or about 19 percent, larger if FIFO had been used.

This calculation may be seen more clearly in Exhibit 8.6 on page 345.

12 Investments

(In millions) December 31	1985	1984
Nonconsolidated finance affiliate.	$ 931	$ 817
Nonconsolidated uranium mining affiliate	188	157
Miscellaneous investments (at cost):		
Government and government guaranteed securities	187	233
Other.	143	155
	330	388
Marketable equity securities.	44	44
Associated companies	342	301
Less allowance for losses	(15)	(16)
	$1,820	$1,691

Condensed consolidated financial statements for the nonconsolidated finance affiliate, General Products Credit Corporation (GPCC), follow. During the normal course of business, GPCC has transactions with the parent General Products Company and certain of its consolidated affiliates, and GPCC results are included in General Products' consolidated U.S. federal income tax return. However, virtually all products financed by GPCC are manufactured by companies other than General Products.

General Products Credit Corporation **Current and retained earnings** **(In millions)** **For the year**	1985	1984	1983
Earned income	$1,389	$1,102	$813
Expenses:			
Interest and discount.	719	528	337
Operating and administrative	451	396	315
Provision for losses			
—receivables	75	69	56
—other assets	3	(2)	8
Provision for income taxes	26	21	20
	1,274	1,012	736
Net earnings	115	90	77
[61] Less dividends	(93)	(72)	(62)
Retained earnings at January 1	239	221	206
Retained earnings at December 31	$ 261	$ 239	$221

[61] Note that the following two events both occurred during 1985:

   (i) GP required GPCC to declare dividends (payable to GP) in the amount of $93 million, and

   (ii) GP invested an additional $92 (= $658 − $566) million in GPCC through the purchase of "Capital stock."

One might wonder why the parent bothers to have the subsidiary declare dividends and then turn right around and reinvest that cash in the same subsidiary. The executive compensation plan for the top managers of GP contains bonus clauses tying total pay to the reported income of the parent company as computed with a special formula. In that formula, the income from the Credit Company is based on accounting using the cost method, not the equity method. (One of the questions at the end of this Appendix explores why this fact might explain the otherwise puzzling phenomenon.)

General Products Credit Corporation
Financial position
(In millions)

December 31	1985	1984
Cash and marketable securities	$ 531	$ 374
Receivables:		
Time sales and loans	8,159	7,480
Deferred income	(1,380)	(1,124)
	6,779	6,356
Sundry receivables	1,643	1,207
Investment in leases	197	141
Total receivables	8,619	7,704
Allowance for losses	(249)	(231)
Net receivables	8,370	7,473
Other assets	443	321
[62] Total assets	$9,344	$8,168
Notes payable:		
Due within one year	$4,425	$3,921
Long-term—senior	1,984	1,743
—subordinated	400	325
Other liabilities	707	631
Total liabilities	7,516	6,620
Deferred income taxes	876	718
Deferred investment tax credit	21	13
[61] Capital stock	658	566
Additional paid-in capital	12	12
Retained earnings	261	239
Equity	931	817
Total liabilities, deferred tax items, and equity	$9,344	$8,168

The nonconsolidated uranium mining company is valued at lower of cost or equity, plus advances.

[63]   The estimated realizable value of miscellaneous investments was $287 million at December 31, 1985 ($350 million at December 31, 1984).

Marketable equity securities are valued at the lower of cost or market. Aggregate market
[64] value of marketable equity securities was $242 million and $181 million at year-end 1985 and 1984, respectively. At December 31, 1985, gross unrealized gains on marketable equity securities were $198 million.

Investments in nonconsolidated affiliates and associated companies included advances of $180 million at December 31, 1985 ($123 million at December 31, 1984).

[62] If the Credit Corporation were consolidated, rather than accounted for on the equity method, all these assets, liabilities, and deferred credits would be shown on GP's balance sheet. GP's consolidated retained earnings would be no different, however, because the equity method records income of unconsolidated subsidiaries as earned. The $931 (= $9,344 − $7,516 − $876 − $21) million of net assets added to GP's balance sheet would be offset with the elimination of $931 shown on the balance sheet and detailed in GP's note 12.

Exhibit A.5
General Products and GP Credit Corporation, 1985
(for Comment [62])

Income Statement	Equity Method (as reported)	Adjustment Debit	Adjustment Credit	Consolidated
Revenues (other than from Credit Corporation)[a] . . .	$25,408	$	$ 1,389 (1)	$26,797
Equity Method Revenues from Credit Corporation. . .	115	115 (1)		
Total Revenues[b]	$25,523			
Total Expenses[c].	24,009	1,274 (1)		25,283
Net Income	$ 1,514			$ 1,514
Balance Sheet				
All Assets Except Investment in Credit Corporation . .	$17,580	9,344 (2)		$26,924
Investment in Credit Corporation	931		931 (2)	
Total Assets	$18,511			$26,924
Liabilities (including minority interest)	$10,311		8,413[d] (2)	$18,724
Owners' Equity	8,200			8,200
Total Equities	$18,511	$10,733	$10,733	$26,924

Rate of Return on Assets:

$$\frac{\$1,514 + \$21^e + (.54 \times \$314^f)}{\$18,511}$$ $$\frac{\$1,514 + \$21^e + .54 \times (\$314^f + \$719^g)}{\$26,924}$$

$$= \frac{\$1,705}{\$18,511} = 9.2\%$$ $$= \frac{\$2,093}{\$26,924} = 7.8\%$$

Debt-Equity Ratio:

$$\frac{\$10,311}{\$18,511} = 56\%$$ $$\frac{\$18,724}{\$26,924} = 68\%$$

[a]$24,959 + $564 − $115; a plug.

[b]$24,959 shown as Sales in Exhibit A.1 plus $564 of Other income.

[c]$22,716 (operating expense) + $314 (interest) + $958 (income taxes) + $21 (minority interest).

[d]GP Credit's "liabilities" ($7,516) plus "deferred income taxes" ($876) plus "deferred investment credit" ($21).

[e]Minority interest in net income from income statement.

[f]GP's interest expense. Multiply by 0.54 to state on aftertax basis.

[g]GP Credit's interest expense. Multiply by 0.54 to state on aftertax basis.

Adjusting entry (1) adds the revenues and expenses of the Credit Corporation to the consolidated totals, while removing the equity method revenue reported by GP.

Adjusting entry (2) adds the assets and liabilities of the Credit Corporation to the consolidated totals, while removing GP's net investment from the asset account for Investments.

13 Other assets

(In millions) December 31	1985	1984
Long-term receivables	$ 340	$307
Deferred charges	198	145
Real estate development projects	132	81
Recoverable engineering costs on government contracts	113	121
Customer financing	103	107
[65] Licenses and other intangibles—net	75	52
[66] Deferred income taxes	21	98
Other	46	45
	$1,028	$956

Licenses and other intangibles acquired after October 1970 are being amortized over appropriate periods of time.

14 Short-term borrowings

The average balance of short-term borrowings, excluding the current portion of long-term borrowings, was $822 million during 1985 (calculated by averaging all month-end balances for the year) compared with an average balance of $705 million in 1984. The maximum balance included in these calculations was $962 million and $727 million at the end of October 1985 and March 1984, respectively. The average effective interest rate for the year 1985 was 14.9%, and for 1984 was 13.6%. These average rates represent total short-term interest incurred divided by the average balance outstanding. A summary of short-term borrowings and the applicable interest rates is shown below.

Short-term borrowings (In millions) December 31	1985		1984	
	Amount	Average rate at Dec. 31	Amount	Average rate at Dec. 31
Parent notes with trust departments . .	$ 353	15.05%	$290	12.62%
Consolidated affiliate bank borrowings .	539	21.83	389	18.10
Other, including current portion of long-term borrowings.	201		192	
	$1,093		$871	

Parent borrowings are from U.S. sources. Borrowings of consolidated affiliated companies are primarily from foreign sources. Other borrowings include amounts from nonconsolidated affiliate of $95 million in 1985 ($65 million in 1984).

Although the total unused credit available to the Company through banks and commercial credit markets is not readily quantifiable, informal credit lines in excess of $1 billion had been extended by approximately 100 U.S. banks at year end.

If GP were to consolidate GP Credit Corporation, the results would be as shown in the Exhibit A.5. It shows the income statement and balance sheet as reported and as they would appear if GP Credit Corporation were consolidated. Two key financial ratios, as they would be calculated from year-end account balances, also appear. The consolidation policy with respect to GP Credit Corporation affects the amounts in the financial statements. For an even larger effect, refer to the financial statements of General Motors Corporation and go through the exercise of consolidating GMAC (General Motors Acceptance Corporation), which GM accounts for by the equity method.

[63] The disclosure of both historical cost and current market values follows the requirement of *SFAS No. 12*. The net realizable value of these securities at year-end 1985 is \$287 million; the cost (see GP's note 12) was \$330 million. Thus GP has an unrealized holding loss on these securities of \$43 (= \$287 value − \$330 cost) million at year-end 1985. At year-end 1984, the unrealized holding loss was \$38 (= \$350 − \$388) million. Thus the unrealized holding loss increased during the year by \$5 million, from \$38 million to \$43 million. GP therefore had unrealized holding loss during 1985 of \$5 million on these securities.

[64] The aggregate market value of these securities at year-end 1985 is \$242 million; the cost is \$44 million. Thus, the unrealized holding gain at the end of 1985 is \$198 (= \$242 − \$44) million. At year-end 1984, the unrealized holding gain was \$137 (= \$181 value − \$44 cost) million. Thus, the unrealized holding gain increased by \$61 (= \$198 − \$137) million during the year 1985. GP had an increase in wealth of \$61 million that is not reported in the conventional financial statements, which are based on historical costs.

[65] Licenses and other intangibles acquired before October 1970 need not be amortized. APB *Opinion No. 17* requires that licenses and intangibles acquired after October 1970 be amortized over a period of not more than 40 years.

[66] See Comments [53] and [54].

15 Accounts payable

(In millions) December 31	1985	1984
Trade accounts	$1,402	$1,259
Collected for the account of others	203	172
Nonconsolidated affiliates	66	46
	$1,671	$1,477

16 Other payables

The balances at year-end 1985 and 1984 included compensation and benefit costs accrued of $703 million and $641 million, respectively.

17 Long-term borrowings

(In millions) Outstanding December 31	1985	1984	Due date	Sinking fund prepayment period
General Products Company:				
5¾% notes	$ 62	$ 69	1996	1977–95
5.30% debentures	70	80	1997	1978–96
7½% debentures	135	149	2001	1982–00
8½% debentures	288	295	2009	1990–06
Coal International Inc.:				
Notes with banks	37	5	1998	1986–98
8% guaranteed sinking fund debentures	15	17	1992	1982–92
7.6% notes	28	32	1993	1979–93
Other	32	25		
General Products Overseas				
Capital Corporation:				
4¼% bonds	23	24	1990	1981–89
4¼% debentures	50	50	1992	None
5½% sterling/dollar guaranteed loan stock	9	8	1998	None
Other	34	37		
All other	217	156		
	$1,000	$947		

The amounts shown above are after deduction of the face value of securities held in treasury as shown below.

Face value of long-term borrowings in treasury
(In millions)

December 31	1985	1984
General Products Company:		
5.30% debentures	$50	$50
$7\frac{1}{2}$% debentures	35	29
$8\frac{1}{2}$% debentures	12	5
General Products Overseas Capital Corporation:		
$4\frac{1}{4}$% bonds.	6	7

Coal International Inc. notes with banks were subject to average interest rates at year-end 1985 and 1984 of 11.3% and 7.9%, respectively.

Borrowings of General Products Overseas Capital Corporation are unconditionally guaranteed by General Products as to payment of principal, premium if any, and interest. This Corporation primarily assists in financing capital requirements of foreign companies in which General Products has an equity interest, as well as financing certain customer purchases.

Borrowings include $4\frac{1}{4}$% Guaranteed Debentures due in 1992, which are convertible into General Products common stock at $80.75 a share, and $5\frac{1}{2}$% Sterling/Dollar Guaranteed Loan Stock due in 1998 in the amount of £3.6 million ($9 million), convertible into GP common stock at $73.50 a share. During 1985 and 1984, General Products Overseas Capital Corporation $4\frac{1}{4}$% Guaranteed Bonds having a face value and a reacquired cost of $2 million were retired in accordance with sinking fund provisions.

All other long-term borrowings were largely by foreign and real estate development affiliates with various interest rates and maturities and included amounts due to nonconsolidated affiliate of $7 million in 1985 and 1984.

[67]   Long-term borrowing maturities during the next five years, including the portion classified as current, are $91 million in 1986, $130 million in 1987, $62 million in 1988, $42 million in 1989, and $68 million in 1990. These amounts are after deducting reacquired debentures held in treasury for sinking fund requirements.

[68] **18 Common stock**

At December 31, 1985 and December 31, 1984, respectively, 227,765,000 and 227,839,000 common shares were outstanding. Common stock held in treasury at December 31, 1985, included 1,921,706 shares for the deferred compensation provisions of incentive compensation plans (1,785,656 shares at December 31, 1984). These shares are carried at market value at the time of allotment, which amounted to $96 million and $88 million at December 31, 1985 and 1984, respectively. The liability is recorded under other liabilities.

Other common stock in treasury, which is carried at cost, aggregated 1,777,382 and 1,839,762 shares at December 31, 1985 and 1984, respectively. These shares are held for future corporate requirements, including distributions under employee savings plans, incentive compensation awards and possible conversion of General Products Overseas Capital Corporation convertible indebtedness. The maximum number of shares required for conversions was 736,079 at December 3, 1985 (737,725 at December 31, 1984). Corporate requirements of shares for benefit plans and conversions may be met either from unissued shares or from shares in treasury.

	1985	1984	1985	1984
	(In millions)		(Thousands of shares)	
Common stock issued				
Balance January 1 and December 31 . . .	$579	$579	231,464	231,464
Amounts received for stock in excess of par value				
Balance January 1	$656	$658		
[69] Gain/(loss) on disposition of treasury stock.	3	(2)		
Balance December 31	$659	$656		
Common stock held in treasury				
Balance January 1	$180	$172	3,625	3,428
Purchases	145	156	2,684	3,155
Dispositions:				
Employee savings plans	(99)	(124)	(1,879)	(2,492)
Employee stock ownership plan. . . .	(16)	(11)	(296)	(213)
Incentive compensation plans.	(7)	(8)	(158)	(152)
Stock options and appreciation rights	(14)	(5)	(275)	(101)
Conversion of Overseas Capital Corporation loan stock	—	—	(2)	—
Balance December 31	$189	$180	3,699	3,625

During 1983, the balance in common stock issued did not change, amounts received for common stock in excess of par value decreased by $10 million, and the balance of common stock held in treasury increased by $6 million.

19 Retained earnings

[70] Retained earnings at year-end 1985 included approximately $251 million ($246 million at December 31, 1984), representing the excess of earnings of nonconsolidated affiliates over dividends received since their formation. In addition, retained earnings have been increased by $10 million ($5 million reduction at December 31, 1984), which represents the change in equity in associated companies since acquisition.

[71] 20 Stock option information

Stock option plans, appreciation rights and performance units are described in the Company's current Proxy Statement. A summary of stock option transactions during the last two years is shown below.

[67] GP's note 14 gives the details of its short-term borrowings. GP's note 16 gives the details of its long-term borrowings. This paragraph helps the analyst to understand GP's intermediate-term borrowings. From these data, the analyst can estimate cash requirements for debt retirement over the next several years.

[68] APB *Opinion No. 12* (1966) requires the disclosure of all changes in owners' equity accounts. GP shows the sources of the changes in the retained earnings account below the income statement, in Exhibit A.1. The schedule in note 18 shows the sources of the changes in the other owners' equity accounts.

[69] Neither gain nor loss can be recognized on transactions by a company in its own shares (called *treasury shares*). GP's accounting is correct, but the use of the terms *gain* and *loss* may be misleading. When GP reissues previously acquired treasury shares, the adjustment to achieve equal debits and credits is not to a gain or loss account (to appear on the income statement), but to the account "Amounts Received for Stock in Excess of Par Value." If treasury shares are acquired for an outlay of $1,000 and then are reissued for $1,200, the entries would be

Common Stock Held in Treasury	1,000	
Cash		1,000
To record acquisition of treasury shares.		
Cash	1,200	
Common Stock Held in Treasury		1,000
Amounts Received for Stock in Excess of Par Value (not Gain on Disposition of Treasury Shares)		200
To record reissue of treasury shares for an amount greater than outlay to acquire them.		

If proceeds of reissue are $800, not $1,200, then in the second entry the $200 is debited, not credited, to the account "Amounts Received for Stock in Excess of Par Value."

[70] Associated companies are 20 percent to 50 percent owned by GP. APB *Opinion No. 18* requires GP to use the equity method for its investment in those companies.

[71] *Accounting Research Bulletin No. 43* (1953) requires the disclosure of the details of stock option plans and of the currently outstanding options. At the end of 1985, the market price of a share of GP common stock was $61.25. The average price of the 4,303,322 options exercisable at the end of 1985 was $51.56. Thus, if all the options were exercised, the present owners' equity would be diluted by approximately $42 million [= ($61.25 − $51.56) × 4,303,322 shares] in comparison to the issue of new shares at the current market price.

Stock options	Shares subject to option	Average per share	
		Option price	Market price
Balance at January 1, 1984	4,088,853	$51.37	$47.13
Options granted.	1,023,122	46.25	46.25
Options exercised	(98,145)	40.63	50.14
Options surrendered on exercise of appreciation rights	(68,834)	40.52	49.17
Options terminated	(186,068)	50.77	—
Balance at December 31, 1984.	4,758,928	50.67	50.63
Options granted.	98,100	61.50	61.50
Options exercised	(273,193)	44.13	56.16
Options surrendered on exercise of appreciation rights	(123,350)	41.93	54.92
Options terminated	(157,163)	51.02	—
Balance at December 31, 1985.	4,303,322	51.56	61.25

The number of shares available for granting additional options at the end of 1985 was 1,862,756 (1,831,456 at the end of 1984).

21 Commitments and contingent liabilities

[72] Lease commitments and contingent liabilities, consisting of guarantees, pending litigation, taxes and other claims, in the opinion of management, are not considered to be material in relation to the Company's financial position.

[73] Industry segment information

Consumer Products and Services consists of major appliances, air conditioning equipment, lighting products, housewares and audio products, television receivers, and broadcasting and cablevision services. It also includes service operations for major appliances, air conditioners, TV receivers, and housewares and audio products.

General Products Credit Corporation, a wholly owned nonconsolidated finance affiliate, engages primarily in consumer, commercial and industrial financing, principally in the U.S. It also participates, to a lesser degree, in life insurance and fire and casualty insurance activities. Products of companies other than GP constitute virtually all products financed by GPCC.

Industrial Products and Components includes components (appliance controls, small motors and electronic components); industrial capital equipment (construction, automation and transportation); maintenance, inspection, repair and rebuilding of electric, electronic and mechanical apparatus; and a network of supply houses offering products of General Products and other manufacturers.

Power Systems includes steam turbine-generators, gas turbines, nuclear power reactors and nuclear fuel assemblies, transformers, switchgear, meters, and installation and maintenance engineering services.

Technical Systems and Materials consists of jet engines for aircraft, industrial and marine applications; electronic and other high-technology products and services primarily for aerospace applications and defense; materials (engineered plastics, silicones, industrial cutting materials, laminated and insulating materials, and batteries); medical and communications equipment, and time sharing, computing, and remote data processing.

Natural Resources includes the mining of coking coal (principally in Australia), uranium, steam coal, iron and copper. In addition, it includes oil and natural gas production, ocean shipping (primarily in support of mining operations) and land acquisition and development.

(In millions) — Revenues for the years ended December 31

	Total revenues			Intersegment sales			External sales and other income		
	1985	1984	1983	1985	1984	1983	1985	1984	1983
Consumer products and services. . .	$ 5,599	$ 5,358	$ 4,788	$ 201	$ 199	$ 188	$ 5,398	$ 5,159	$ 4,600
Net earnings of GP Credit Corp. . .	115	90	77	—	—	—	115	90	77
Total consumer products and services	5,714	5,448	4,865	201	199	188	5,513	5,249	4,677
Industrial products and components .	5,157	4,803	4,124	565	508	468	4,592	4,295	3,656
Power systems	4,023	3,564	3,486	175	210	174	3,848	3,354	3,312
Technical systems and materials . . .	7,128	6,061	4,745	258	255	190	6,870	5,806	4,555
Natural resources	1,374	1,260	1,032	—	—	—	1,374	1,260	1,032
Foreign multi-industry operations . . .	3,234	2,901	2,767	75	64	55	3,159	2,837	2,712
Corporate items and eliminations. . .	(1,107)	(1,057)	(946)	(1,274)	(1,236)	(1,075)	167	179	129
Total	$25,523	$22,980	$20,073	$ —	$ —	$ —	$25,523	$22,980	$20,073

[74]

	Operating profit For the years ended December 31			Net earnings For the years ended December 31		
	1985	1984	1983	1985	1984	1983
Consumer products and services. . .	$ 558	$ 568	$ 574	$ 292	$ 311	$ 300
Net earnings of GP Credit Corp. . .	115	90	77	115	90	77
Total consumer products and services	673	658	651	407	401	377
Industrial products and components .	568	485	426	315	272	223
Power systems	194	174	196	141	114	93
Technical systems and materials . . .	774	672	545	373	356	278
Natural resources	404	431	372	224	208	180
Foreign multi-industry operations . . .	285	241	245	68	65	76
Total segment operating profit . . .	2,898	2,661	2,435			
Interest and other financial charges .	(314)	(258)	(224)			
Corporate items and eliminations. . .	(91)	(12)	(58)	(14)	(7)	3
Total	$ 2,493	$ 2,391	$ 2,153	$ 1,514	$ 1,409	$ 1,230

[74]

	Assets At December 31			Property, plant, and equipment for the years ended December 31					
				Additions			Depreciation, depletion and amortization		
	1985	1984	1983	1985	1984	1983	1985	1984	1983
Consumer products and services. . .	$ 2,325	$ 2,157	$ 2,018	$ 238	$ 208	$ 169	$ 133	$ 115	$ 104
Investment in GP Credit Corp. . . .	931	817	677	—	—	—	—	—	—
Total consumer products and services	3,256	2,974	2,695	238	208	169	133	115	104
Industrial products and components .	2,595	2,329	2,125	224	176	166	109	106	91
Power systems	2,289	2,135	2,105	129	101	84	91	84	79
Technical systems and materials . . .	4,475	3,422	2,683	693	444	289	200	163	150
Natural resources	2,109	1,679	1,489	446	201	212	94	83	77
Foreign multi-industry operations . . .	2,564	2,259	2,100	161	109	119	66	61	64
Corporate items and eliminations. . .	1,223	1,846	1,839	57	23	16	14	12	11
Total	$18,511	$16,644	$15,036	$ 1,948	$ 1,262	$ 1,055	$ 707	$ 624	$ 576

Foreign Multi-industry Operations consists principally of foreign affiliates which manufacture products primarily for sale in their respective home markets.

[75] **Net earnings for industry segments** include allocation of corporate interest income, expense and other financial charges to parent company components based on change in individual component average nonfixed investment. Interest and other financial charges of affiliated companies recognize that such companies generally service their own debt.

General corporate expenses are allocated principally on the basis of cost of operations, with certain exceptions and reductions which recognize the varying degrees to which affiliated companies maintain their own corporate structures.

In addition, provision for income taxes ($958 million in 1985, $953 million in 1984, and $894 million in 1983) is allocated based on the total corporate effective tax rate, except for GPCC and Natural Resources, whose income taxes are calculated separately.

Minority interest ($21 million in 1985 and $29 million in both 1984 and 1983) is allocated to operating components having responsibility for investments in consolidated affiliates.

In general, it is GP's policy to price internal sales as nearly as practicable to equivalent commercial selling prices.

(In millions)	Revenues for the years ended December 31								
	Total revenues			Intersegment sales			External sales and other income		
	1985	1984	1983	1985	1984	1983	1985	1984	1983
United States	$20,750	$18,859	$16,443	$ 484	$ 467	$ 362	$20,266	$18,392	$16,081
Far East including Australia . .	1,277	1,183	1,109	355	280	242	922	903	867
Other areas of the world. . . .	4,459	3,814	3,270	124	129	145	4,335	3,685	3,125
Elimination of intracompany transactions	(963)	(876)	(749)	(963)	(876)	(749)	—	—	—
Total	$25,523	$22,980	$20,073	$ —	$ —	$ —	$25,523	$22,980	$20,073

	Net Earnings For the years ended December 31			Assets At December 31		
	1985	1984	1983	1985	1984	1983
United States	$ 1,175	$ 1,120	$ 961	$13,732	$12,693	$11,410
Far East including Australia . .	169	174	170	1,090	842	889
Other areas of the world. . . .	181	120	104	3,808	3,207	2,827
Elimination of intracompany transactions	(11)	(5)	(5)	(119)	(98)	(90)
Total	$ 1,514	$ 1,409	$ 1,230	$18,511	$16,644	$15,036

Geographic segment information (including allocation of income taxes and minority interest in earnings of consolidated affiliates) is based on the location of the operation furnishing goods or services. Included in United States revenues were export sales to unaffiliated customers of $3,781 million in 1985, $2,772 million in 1984, and $2,571 million in 1983. Of such sales, $2,089 million in 1985 ($1,581 million in 1984 and $1,662 million in 1983) were to customers in Europe, Africa, and the Middle East; and $926 million in 1985 ($741 million in 1984 and $498 million in 1983) were to customers in the Far East including Australia. U.S. revenues also include royalty and licensing income from unaffiliated foreign sources.

Revenues, net earnings and assets associated with foreign operations are shown in the tabulations above. At December 31, 1985, foreign operation liabilities, minority interest in equity, and GP interest in equity were $2,562 million, $141 million, and $2,195 million, respectively. On a comparable basis, the amounts were $2,101 million, $139 million, and $1,809 million, respectively, at December 31, 1984, and $1,910 million, $150 million, and $1,656 million, respectively, at December 31, 1983.

[72] Both the SEC and the FASB (*SFAS No. 13*) require disclosure of material commitments under long-term noncancelable leases. GP has no such material commitments. In general, the disclosures must include the effects on both the income statement and the balance sheet of capitalizing such leases.

[73] *SFAS 14* requires disclosure of segment data. Segments are required to be defined both by kind of operation (consumer products, industrial power, etc.) and by location (United States, Far East, etc.).

[74] Earnings of the individual segments sum to an amount larger than net income for 1985 of $1,514 by $14 million. Assets of the individual segments sum to an amount smaller than total assets by $1,223 million. Hence rates of return computed for individual segments will overstate true rate of return. If a "true" rate of return for the company as a whole is defined to be net income over total assets, then GP's rate of return is 8.2 percent (= $1,514/18,511). The incomes of the individual segments total $1,528 million and the sum of the segments assets is $17,288 (= $18,511 − $1,223) million. If one were computing rates of return for individual segments, then, the aggregate rate of return might be computed as 8.8 percent (= $1,528/$17,288). For GP, the resulting overstatement of the combined segment rates of return is not as dramatic as it is for some other companies. Some who criticize segment reporting have in mind the misleading inferences the unwary analyst (or politician or government regulator) might draw from computing rates of return for individual segments.

[75] The major difficulty in constructing meaningful and useful segment reports is the allocation of these "corporate items" to the major categories. They are truly common or joint costs of running the entire corporation but must be allocated to the various segments in order to present subtotals for segment earnings that add up to the total earnings, $1,514 million for 1985.

[76] The detail shown here by GP goes beyond that required by the SEC in its 1980 *ASR Nos. 279–281*. GP shows 6 years of data so that one can construct time-series analysis for at least 5 years in all cases. Note that if only five columns are shown, then growth rates for items like sales can be computed for only 4 years.

[77] During 1976 the SEC defined a new class of footnotes with which the auditor is "associated" (to use the SEC's term), but which are not audited.

[78] During the year, GP (and other companies) are required to send quarterly (interim) financial statements to shareholders. The SEC requires companies to show in the annual statements the amounts of the interim earnings *after* all information for the year is available. If there is a difference, the company must explain why its interim reported numbers differ from the corresponding numbers shown in the annual report.

[79] *SFAS No. 33* requires these disclosures, which are discussed in Chapter 14.

[76] Six-year summary (a)
Selected financial data

(Dollar amounts in millions; per-share amounts in dollars)	1985	1984	1983	1982	1981	1980
Summary of operations						
Sales of products and services to customers	$24,959	$22,461	$19,654	$17,519	$15,697	$14,105
Cost of goods sold.	17,751	15,991	13,915	12,288	11,048	10,210
Selling, general and administrative expense	4,258	3,716	3,205	3,011	2,635	2,238
Depreciation, depletion and amortization	707	624	576	522	486	470
Operating costs	22,716	20,331	17,696	15,821	14,169	12,918
Operating margin	2,243	2,130	1,958	1,698	1,528	1,187
Other income	564	519	419	390	274	174
Interest and other financial charges	(314)	(258)	(224)	(199)	(175)	(187)
Earnings before income taxes and minority interest	2,493	2,391	2,153	1,889	1,627	1,174
Provision for income taxes	(958)	(953)	(894)	(773)	(668)	(460)
Minority interest	(21)	(29)	(29)	(28)	(28)	(26)
Net earnings	$ 1,514	$ 1,409	$ 1,230	$ 1,088	$ 931	$ 688
Earnings per common share (b)	$ 6.65	$ 6.20	$ 5.39	$ 4.79	$ 4.12	$ 3.07
Dividends declared per common share (c)	$ 2.95	$ 2.75	$ 2.50	$ 2.10	$ 1.70	$ 1.60
Earnings as a percentage of sales	6.1%	6.3%	6.3%	6.2%	5.9%	4.9%
Earned on average share owners' equity	19.5%	20.2%	19.6%	19.4%	18.9%	15.7%
Dividends—General Products	$ 670	$ 624	$ 570	$ 477	$ 333	$ 293
Dividends—Coal International Inc. (d)	—	—	—	—	$ 28	$ 33
Shares outstanding—average (in thousands) (e) . . .	227,541	227,173	227,985	227,154	225,791	224,262
Share owner accounts—average	524,000	540,000	552,000	553,000	566,000	582,000
Market price range per share (c)	63–44	55⅛–45	57⅞–43⅜	57¼–47⅞	59¼–46	52⅞–32⅜
Price/earnings ratio range (c)	9–7	9–7	11–8	12–10	14–11	17–10
Current assets	$ 9,883	$ 9,384	$ 8,755	$ 7,865	$ 6,685	$ 5,750
Current liabilities	7,592	6,872	6,175	5,417	4,605	4,163
Working capital	$ 2,291	$ 2,512	$ 2,580	$ 2,448	$ 2,080	$ 1,587
Short-term borrowings	$ 1,093	$ 871	$ 960	$ 772	$ 611	$ 667
Long-term borrowings	1,000	947	994	1,284	1,322	1,239
Minority interest in equity of consolidated affiliates . .	154	152	151	132	119	105
Share owners' equity	8,200	7,362	6,587	5,943	5,253	4,617
Total capital invested.	$10,447	$ 9,332	$ 8,692	$ 8,131	$ 7,305	$ 6,628
Earned on average total capital invested	17.3%	17.6%	16.3%	15.8%	15.1%	12.5%
Share owners' equity per common share— year end (b).	$ 36.00	$ 32.31	$ 28.88	$ 26.05	$ 23.18	$ 20.49
Total assets	$18,511	$16,644	$15,036	$13,697	$12,050	$10,741
Property, plant and equipment additions	$ 1,948	$ 1,262	$ 1,055	$ 823	$ 740	$ 588
Employees—average worldwide.	402,000	405,000	401,000	384,000	380,000	380,000

(a) Unless specifically noted, all years are adjusted to include Coal International Inc., which became a wholly owned affiliate of General Products on December 20, 1981, through the exchange of 41,002,034 shares of General Products common stock for all of the outstanding shares of Coal.
(b) Computed using outstanding shares as described in note (e).
(c) For General Products common stock as reported in the years shown.
(d) Reflects transactions prior to merger date.
(e) Includes General Products outstanding average shares or year-end shares as appropriate, plus, in 1981 and prior years, outstanding shares previously reported by Coal multiplied by 1.3. Adjustments have been made for the two-for-one Coal stock split effected in the form of stock dividends in 1981.

[77] Other information (unaudited)

Quarterly dividend and stock market information

	Dividends declared		Common stock market price range	
	1985	**1984**	**1985**	**1984**
First quarter	70¢	65¢	$57½–$44	$50¾–$45½
Second quarter	75	70	52 – 44½	51⅝– 46⅞
Third quarter	75	70	58⅛– 51⅛	55⅛– 49⅜
Fourth quarter	75	70	63 – 51½	52¼– 45

The New York Stock Exchange is the principal market on which GP common stock is traded and, as of December 8, 1985, there were approximately 512,282 share owners of record.

[78] **Operations by quarter for 1985 and 1984** **(Dollar amounts in millions; per-share amounts in dollars)**	**First quarter**	**Second quarter**	**Third quarter**	**Fourth quarter**
1985				
Sales of products and services to customers	$5,881	$6,197	$5,963	$6,918
Operating margin	527	556	513	647
Net earnings	342	403	358	411
Net earnings per common share . . .	1.50	1.77	1.58	1.80
1984				
Sales of products and services to customers	$5,082	$5,642	$5,609	$6,128
Operating margin	470	598	511	551
Net earnings	303	382	341	383
Net earnings per common share . . .	1.33	1.69	1.50	1.68

[79] **Changing Prices**

Your Company's financial results are not immune to the distorting effects of inflation. Financial data elsewhere in this Annual Report, including the audited financial statements, are presented using the traditional basis of financial reporting which does not fully identify the effects of inflation. The following table presents information which supplements the traditional financial statements in order to gauge the effect of changing prices on results for 1985.

[80] **Supplementary Information**
Effect of Changing Prices

For the year
ended December 31, 1985

| (in millions; except per-share amounts) | As reported | Adjusted for (a) | |
		General inflation	Current costs
Sales of products and services to customers .	$24,959	C$24,959	C$24,959
Cost of goods sold.	17,751	17,904	17,892
Selling, general and administrative expense .	4,258	4,258	4,258
Depreciation, depletion and amortization . . .	707	1,052	1,092
Operating costs	22,716	23,214	23,242
Operating margin	2,243	1,745	1,717
Other income	564	564	564
Interest and other financial charges	(314)	(314)	(314)
Earnings before income taxes.	2,493	1,995	1,967
Provision for income taxes	(958)	(958)	(958)
Minority interest	(21)	(8)	(8)
Net earnings	$ 1,514	C$ 1,029	C$ 1,001
Earnings per share	$ 6.65	C$ 4.52	C$ 4.40
Effective tax rate	38.4%	48.0%	48.7%
Share owners' equity at Dec. 31	$ 8,200	C$12,377	C$12,913

[81] (a) In dollars of average 1985 purchasing
power based on the CPI–H   [82]   [83]

This table shows two different ways of attempting to remove inflationary impacts from
financial results as traditionally reported. In both "adjusted for" columns, restatements are
[82] made to (1) cost of goods sold for the current cost of replacing inventories, and (2) depreciation for the current cost of plant and equipment. The column headed "general inflation"
uses only a broad index to calculate the restatement, while the column headed "current
[83] costs" uses data more specifically applicable to GP.
     The restatements to cost of goods sold are relatively small for GP because extensive
use of last-in, first-out inventory accounting already largely reflects current costs in the
traditional earnings statement. However, restatements to depreciation, which allocates
plant and equipment costs to expenses over time, are relatively large because of the high
rate of inflation, particularly in the last three years. This is because traditional reporting of
depreciation based on original cost does not adequately reflect higher prices for replacement of productive capacity of fixed assets which were purchased a number of years ago.
Both of these methods of adjusting for inflation result in lower earnings than traditionally
reported.
     *Significantly, because inflation adjustments are not allowable for tax purposes, the
"real" tax rate was about 10 points higher than in traditional statements.*
Your management believes the "current cost" method is more representative of GP's
results, but emphasizes the considerable subjectivity involved in the calculations. These
types of adjusted data are likely to be more useful in reviewing trends over a period of time,
rather than in making comparisons of restatements for any one period or in specific analyses of one period compared with another. GP's after-tax earnings on the traditional basis
of accounting have been higher each year from 1981 through 1985. Since 1980, the
average annual growth rate for earnings as reported was about 16%. Using the "current
cost" method of removing the effects of inflation, earnings grew at an average annual rate
since 1980 of about 24%. However, the purchasing power of a dollar in 1985 had dimin-
ished by more than one-third since 1980. To reflect this deterioration of the dollar's purchasing power, current-cost earnings for the years since 1980 can be expressed in dollars
of 1980 purchasing power. On this basis, the data indicate a real average annual growth
rate in earnings since 1980 of about 14%.

[80] The first column of the supplementary income statement shows the conventional financial statements based on nominal dollar measures of historical cost. The second column shows constant dollar measures of historical cost. The third column shows current costs. The measuring unit in the third column can be interpreted either as nominal dollars or as constant dollars of 1985 year-average purchasing power. One of the reasons that the FASB allows using year-average dollars as the measuring unit is that the numbers that appear in the third column of this statement will be essentially the same whether the current costs are measured using constant average-year dollars or nominal dollars. The FASB requires supplementary data on income from continuing operations only; GP's disclosure for individual revenues and expenses goes beyond the minimum requirement.

[81] Note that there is no such price index as the CPI–H (which stands for CPI–Hypothetical). The FASB requires use of the CPI–U (Consumer *Price Index* for all *Urban* consumers). Because the price index for 1985 cannot be known until after the end of 1985 and this book goes to press before then, we have constructed a hypothetical price index for use in this example disclosure.

[82] *Constant Dollar Accounting Disclosures.* The numbers shown in the middle column are based on historical costs measured in constant dollars of general purchasing power. The notation ''C$'' denotes constant dollars. The FASB allows use of the notation ''$'' and most companies use the simpler, if less precise, ''$'' symbol.

[83] *Current Cost Accounting Disclosures.* The items in the current cost column are measured in constant dollars (of mid-year purchasing power of the specific items), but because these appear the same as when they are measured in nominal dollars, *SFAS No. 33* allows the symbol ''$'' to be used in the third column instead of ''C$.''

[84] *Multiyear Summary.* The FASB requires a 5-year summary. GP shows data for 6 years so that trends can be seen for 5 years of operations. The summary shows data in a format useful for following the trend of items over time. *SFAS No. 33* permits the use in this summary of either current 1985 dollars or dollars of some base period, such as 1970, which is the base period for the CPI–H. Using current dollars expresses the data in units that reflect current experience, but it requires the data of the earlier years in the summary to be restated each year to reflect the change in the measuring unit. When the summary is stated in base-period dollars, there is no need for annual revision of those data.

Excerpts from the constant dollar summary and from the nominal dollar 6-year summary on page 746 are instructive. Observe, for example, that the market price of a share of GP common stock is shown as C$68 for 1980. Its actual market price at the end of 1980 was $44.40. (The amount shown is derived from C$68 = $44.40 × 308.5/201.5.) Whereas the nominal dollar amount of a share has increased more than 34 percent (from $44 to $59) over the 5-year period from the end of 1980 to the end of 1985, the general purchasing power represented by an investment in that share has declined by about 13 percent, from C$68 to C$59. Similarly, although nominal dollar sales have

[84] **Current cost information in average dollars of 1985 purchasing power (a) (In millions except per-share amounts)**

	Sales	Net earn- ings (b)	Share owners' equity Dec. 31 (b)	Per common share Earn- ings (b)	Per common share Divi- dends	Per common share Market price Dec. 31	Pur- chasing power gain (loss) (c)
1985	C$24,959	C$1,001	C$12,913	C$4.40	C$2.95	C$59	C$(198)
1984	25,493	1,119	12,659	4.93	3.12	54	(237)
1983	24,819	1,092	12,508	4.79	3.16	57	(145)
1982	23,817	1,001	12,095	4.40	2.86	66	(69)
1981	22,717	885	11,947	3.92	2.46	79	(23)
1980	21,590	479	11,414	2.13	2.45	68	22

(a) Average 1985 dollars, using the U.S. Consumer Price Index–Hypothetical (1970 = 100): 1980—201.5; 1981—213.1; 1982—226.9; 1983—244.3; 1984—271.8; and 1985—308.5.

(b) Current cost basis.

(c) On net monetary items.

Proper use of supplementary information concerning the effect of changing prices requires an understanding of certain basic concepts and definitions.

In the table showing details for 1985, "as reported" refers to information drawn directly from the financial statements and notes. This information is prepared using generally accepted accounting principles which render an accounting based on the number of actual dollars involved in transactions, with no recognition given to the fact that the value of the dollar changes over time.

"Adjusted for general inflation" refers to information prepared using a different approach to transactions involving inventory and property, plant and equipment assets. Under this procedure, the number of dollars involved in transactions at different dates are all restated to equivalent amounts in terms of the general purchasing power of the dollar as it is measured by the Consumer Price Index–Hypothetical (CPI–H). For example, $1,000 invested in a building in 1970 would be restated to its 1985 dollar purchasing power equivalent of $3,085 to value the asset and calculate depreciation charges. Similarly, the 1984 purchases of non-LIFO inventory sold in 1985 would be accounted for at their equivalent in terms of 1985 dollars, rather than in terms of the actual number of dollars spent. Using this method, earnings for 1984 in 1985 dollars were $1,208 million ($5.31 per share) and share owners' equity at December 31, 1984, was $11,845 million.

"Adjusted for current costs" refers to information prepared using a third approach to inventory and property, plant and equipment transactions. In this case, rather than restating to dollars of the same general purchasing power, estimates of specific current costs of the assets are used. Principal types of information used to adjust for changes in specific prices (current costs) are: for inventory costs, GP-generated indices of price changes for specific goods and services; and for property, plant and equipment, externally generated indices of price changes for major classes of assets. Data for mineral resource assets have been adjusted by applying internally generated indices to reflect current costs. Adjustments for oil and gas properties are based on industry indices.

[85]   At December 31, 1985, the current cost of inventory was $5,701 million, and of property, plant and equipment was $8,797 million ($5,251 million and $7,004 million, respectively, at December 31, 1984). In dollars of average 1985 purchasing power, estimated current costs applicable to such assets increased during 1985, or during the part of the year the assets were held, by approximately $1,356 million, which was $196 million less than the $1,552 million increase which could be expected because of general inflation. The comparable increase for 1984 in dollars of average 1985 purchasing power was approximately $1,261 million, which was $373 million less than the $1,634 million increase which could be expected because of general inflation.

In presenting results of either of the supplementary accounting methods for more than one year, real trends are more evident when results for all years are expressed in terms of the general purchasing power of the dollar for a designated period. Results of such restatements are generally called "constant dollar" presentations. In the six-year presentations shown here, dollar results for earlier periods have been restated to their equivalent number of constant dollars of 1985 general purchasing power (CPI–H basis).

increased over the years shown at about 12 percent per year, from $14 billion to nearly $25 billion, sales measured in constant dollars have risen by only 3 percent per year, from C$21.6 to C$25.0 billion.

Note in the last column of the multiyear summary that GP reports purchasing power losses on net monetary items for each of the years 1981 through 1985 and a gain only for 1980. From this we can infer that GP's average balance of monetary assets exceeded the average balance of monetary liabilities in each of the years 1981 through 1985.

[85] Exhibit A.6 summarizes some of the information in this paragraph. Exhibit A.6 derives the total holding gain for 1985 in nominal dollars of $1,420 million. GP reports the total holding gains as $1,356 million. The difference between the two amounts of $64 (= $1,420 − $1,356) million reflects the increase in current cost of inventories and plant between mid-year and December 31.

Exhibit A.6
Summary of Data on Realized and Unrealized Holding Gains for 1985 in Nominal Dollars
(for Comment [85])

	Inventory and Cost of Goods Sold	Property, Plant, Equipment, and Depreciation
Asset Balances		
December 31, 1985		
Current Cost[a]	$ 5,701	$ 8,797
Historical Cost[b]	(3,343)	(5,780)
Unrealized Holding Gain, End of Year . . . . (1)	$ 2,358	$ 3,017
December 31, 1984		
Current Cost[a]	$ 5,251	$ 7,004
Historical Cost[b]	(3,161)	(4,613)
Unrealized Holding Gain, Start of Year . . . . . . (2)	2,090	2,391
Unrealized Holding Gain		
During 1985 = (2) − (1)	$ 268	$ 626
Expense Totals:		
Based on		
Current Cost[c]	$17,892	$ 1,092
Historical Costs[d]	(17,751)	(707)
Realized Holding Gains.	141	385
Total Holding Gains of $1,420 (= $409 + $1,011)	$ 409	$ 1,011

[a]See Exhibit A.4 at Comment [85].
[b]From Statement of Financial Position, Exhibit A.2.
[c]See Exhibit A.4 at Comment [80].
[d]From Statement of Income and Retained Earnings, Exhibit A.1.

Because none of these restatements is allowable for tax purposes under existing laws, income tax amounts are the same as in the traditional statements (but expressed in constant dollars).

All average annual growth rates in this Report use the "least squares" method of calculation.

[86] Form 10-K and other supplemental information

The financial information in this Report, in the opinion of management, substantially conforms with or exceeds the information required in the "10-K Report" submitted to the Securities and Exchange Commission. Certain supplemental information, considered non-substantive, is included in that report, however, and copies will be available without charge, on or about May 1.

[86] The SEC requires that firms make the Form 10-K available to shareholders and tell them of its availability.

Questions and Problems

1. Review the meaning of the following concepts or terms discussed in this appendix.
  a. Allowance method.
  b. Central corporate expenses and central corporate assets hinder measures of segment rates of return.
  c. Compensating balance.
  d. Consolidated financial statements.
  e. Deferred income tax debit.
  f. Installment sales.
  g. Minority interest on income statement versus minority interest on balance sheet.
  h. Progress billings.
  i. Provision.
  j. Statutory versus effective income tax rate.

2. Assume that all sales of General Products Company and consolidated affiliates for the year 1985 were made on account. How much cash was collected from customers?

3. What amount of cash was disbursed during 1985 by GP and consolidated affiliates for dividends?

4. Refer to note 9 of the GP annual report. Observe, there, receivables labeled "Associated companies" and "Nonconsolidated affiliates." Are these receivables more likely to represent amounts owed to GP by these "Associated companies" and "Nonconsolidated affiliates" or are they amounts owed by customers to "Associated companies" and "Nonconsolidated affiliates?" Explain your reasoning.

5. Refer to the data in GP's note 15 on accounts payable. Are the amounts shown for "nonconsolidated affiliates" more likely amounts owed by GP to these "nonconsolidated affiliates" or amounts owed by them to others? Explain your reasoning.

6. Refer to the data in GP's note 14 on short-term borrowings. Compute the dollar amount of interest expense on these borrowings for 1985.

7. Assume that GP prepared the statement of changes in financial position using funds defined as working capital, rather than as cash. Prepare an analysis of changes in net change in funds for the year 1985.

8. Refer to GP's note 19 on retained earnings. What are the retained earnings of the nonconsolidated affiliates *other* than those of GP Credit Company at the end of 1985?

9. Assuming a marginal income tax rate of 46 percent, by what amount did depreciation claimed on the tax return for 1984 differ from the depreciation expense reported in the financial statements for 1984?

10. Refer to Comment **[62]**. Explain why the compensation agreement described there might help one understand the simultaneous dividend declaration and common stock issue of GP Credit Company.

11. Assume that GP Credit Corporation were consolidated, rather than accounted for on the equity method.
   a. By how much would GP's consolidated revenue and other income for 1984 differ from the amounts reported?
   b. By how much would GP's consolidated expenses for 1984 differ from the amounts reported?
   c. By how much would GP's consolidated income for 1984 differ from the amount reported?
   d. By how much would GP's consolidated assets differ from the amount reported?
   e. By how much would GP's consolidated owners' equity differ from the amount reported?

12. Refer to GP's multiyear summary of data on the effects of changing prices. What was market price per share in nominal dollars of a share of GP's stock at the end of 1981?

Appendix B   Compound Interest Concepts and Applications

Money is a scarce resource, which its owner can use to command other resources. Like owners of other scarce resources, owners of money can permit borrowers to rent the use of their money for a period of time. Payment for the use of money differs little from other rental payments, such as those made to a landlord for the use of property or to a car rental agency for the use of a car. Payment for the use of money is called *interest*. Accounting is concerned with interest because it must record transactions in which the use of money is bought and sold.

Accountants and managers are concerned with interest calculations for another, equally important, reason. Expenditures for an asset most often do not occur at the same time as the receipts for services produced by that asset. Money received sooner is more valuable than money received later. The difference in timing can affect whether acquiring an asset is profitable. Amounts of money received at different times are different commodities. Managers use interest calculations to make amounts of money to be paid or received at different times comparable. For example, an analyst might compare two amounts to be received at two different times by using interest calculations to find the cash equivalent value of one amount at the time the other is due.

Contracts involving a series of money payments over time, such as bonds, mortgages, notes, and leases, are evaluated by finding the *present value* of the stream of payments. The present value of a stream of payments is a single amount of money at the present time that is the economic equivalent of the entire stream.

Compound Interest Concepts

The quotation of interest "cost" is typically specified as a percentage of the amount borrowed per unit of time. Examples are 12 percent per year and 1 percent per month, which are not the same. Another example occurs in the context of discounts on purchases. The terms of sale "2/10, net/30" are equivalent to 2 percent for 20 days because if the discount is not taken, payment can be delayed and the money can be used for up to an extra 20 (= 30 − 10) days.

The amount borrowed or loaned is called the *principal*. To *compound* interest means that the amount of interest earned during a period is added to the principal and the principal for the next interest period is larger.

For example, if you deposit $1,000 in a savings account that pays compound interest at the rate of 6 percent per year, you will earn $60 by the end of 1 year. If you do not withdraw the $60, then $1,060 will be earning interest during the second year. During the second year your principal of $1,060 will earn $63.60 interest, $60 on the initial deposit of $1,000 and $3.60 on the $60 earned the first year. By the end of the second year, you will have $1,123.60.

When only the original principal earns interest during the entire life of the loan, the interest due at the time the loan is repaid is called *simple* interest. In simple interest calculations, interest on previously earned interest is ignored.[1] The use of simple interest calculations in accounting arises in the following way. If you borrow $10,000 at a rate of 12 percent per year, but compute interest for any month as $100 (= $10,000 × .12 × $\frac{1}{12}$), then you are using a simple interest calculation. Nearly all economic calculations involve compound interest.

The "force," or effect, of compound interest is more substantial than many people realize. For example, compounded annually at 8 percent, money "doubles itself" in 9 years. Put another way, if you invest $100 at 8 percent compounded annually, you will have $200 in 9 years.

Problems involving compound interest generally fall into two groups with respect to time: First, there are the problems for which we want to know the future value of money invested or loaned today; second, there are the problems for which we want to know the present value, or today's value, of money to be received or paid at later dates. In addition, the accountant must sometimes compute the interest rate implicit in certain payment streams.

Future Value

When $1.00 is invested today at 12 percent compounded annually, it will grow to $1.12000 at the end of 1 year, $1.25440 at the end of 2 years, $1.40493 at the end of 3 years, and so on according to the formula

$$F_n = P(1 + r)^n,$$

where

F_n represents the accumulation or future value,

P represents the one-time investment today,

r is the interest rate per period, and

n is the number of periods from today.

The amount F_n is the future value of the present payment, P, compounded at r percent per period for n periods. Table 1, following this section of the book, shows the future values of $P = \$1$ for various numbers of periods and for various interest rates. Extracts from that table appear here in Table B.1.

Example Problems in Computing Future Value

Example 1 How much will $1,000 deposited today at 8 percent compounded annually be worth 10 years from now?

One dollar deposited today at 8 percent will grow to $2.15892; therefore $1,000 will grow to $1,000 $(1.08)^{10}$ = $1,000 × 2.15892 = $2,158.92.

---

[1]If interest earned may be withdrawn, then compound interest techniques are relevant. The withdrawn interest can be invested elsewhere to earn additional interest.

Table B.1
(Excerpt from Table 1)
Future Value of $1 at 8 Percent
and 12 Percent per Period
$F_n = (1 + r)^n$

Number of Periods = n	Rate = r	
	8 Percent	12 Percent
1	1.08000	1.12000
2	1.16640	1.25440
3	1.25971	1.40493
10	2.15892	3.10585
20	4.66096	9.64629

Example 2 Macaulay Corporation deposits $10,000 in an expansion fund today. The fund will earn 12 percent per year. How much will the $10,000 grow to in 20 years if the entire fund and all interest earned on it are left on deposit in the fund?

One dollar deposited today at 12 percent will grow to $9.64629 in 20 years. Therefore, $10,000 will grow to $96,463 (= $10,000 × 9.64629) in 20 years.

Present Value

The preceding section developed the tools for computing the future value, F_n, of a sum of money, P, deposited or invested today. P is known; F_n is calculated. This section deals with the problems of calculating how much principal, P, has to be invested today in order to have a specified amount, F_n, at the end of n periods. The future amount, F_n, the interest rate, r, and the number of periods, n, are known; P is to be found. In order to have $1 one year from today when interest is earned at 8 percent, P of .92593 must be invested today. That is, $F_1 = P(1.08)^1$ or $1 = $.92593 × 1.08. Because $F_n = P(1 + r)^n$, dividing both sides of the equation by $(1 + r)^n$ yields

$$\frac{F_n}{(1 + r)^n} = P,$$

or

$$P = \frac{F_n}{(1 + r)^n} = F_n(1 + r)^{-n}.$$

Present Value Terminology

The number $(1 + r)^{-n}$ is the present value of $1 to be received after n periods when interest is earned at r percent per period. The term *discount* is used in this context as follows: The *discounted* present value of $1 to be received n periods in the future is $(1 + r)^{-n}$ when the *discount* rate is r percent per period for n periods. The number r

is the discount *rate* and the number $(1 + r)^{-n}$ is the discount *factor* for *n* periods. A discount factor $(1 + r)^{-n}$ is merely the reciprocal, or inverse, of a number, $(1 + r)^n$, in Table B.1. Therefore, tables of discount factors are not necessary for present value calculations if tables of future values are at hand. But present value calculations are so frequently needed, and division is so onerous, that tables of discount factors are as widely available as tables of future values. Portions of Table 2, which shows discount factors or, equivalently, present values of $1 for various interest (or discount) rates for various numbers of periods, appear in Table B.2.

Example Problems in Determining Present Values

Example 3 What is the present value of $1 due 10 years from now if the interest (equivalently, the discount) rate *r* is 8 percent per year?

From Table B.2, 8 percent column, 10-period row, the present value of $1 to be received 10 periods hence at 8 percent is $.46319.

Example 4 (This example is used in Chapter 11.) You issue a non-interest-bearing note that promises to pay $16,000 three years from today in exchange for used equipment. How much is that promise worth today if the discount rate appropriate for such notes is 12 percent per period?

One dollar paid 3 years hence discounted at 12 percent has a present value of $.71178. Thus, the promise is worth $16,000 \times .71178 = $11,388.

Changing the Compounding Period: Nominal and Effective Rates

"Twelve percent, compounded annually" is the price for a loan; this means that interest is added to or *converted* into principal once a year at the rate of 12 percent. Often, however, the price for a loan states that compounding is to take place more than once a year. A savings bank may advertise that it pays 6 percent, compounded quarterly. This means that at the end of each quarter the bank credits savings accounts with interest calculated at the rate 1.5 percent (= 6 percent/4). The interest payment can be withdrawn or left on deposit to earn more interest.

If $10,000 is invested today at 12 percent compounded annually, its future value 1 year later is $11,200. If the rate of interest is stated as 12 percent compounded semiannually, then 6 percent interest is added to the principal every 6 months. At the end of the first 6 months, $10,000 will have grown to $10,600, so that the accumulation will be $10,600 \times 1.06 = $11,236 by the end of the year. Notice that 12 percent compounded *semiannually* is equivalent to 12.36 percent compounded *annually*.

Suppose that the price is quoted as 12 percent, compounded quarterly. Then an additional 3 percent of the principal will be added to, or converted into, principal every 3 months. By the end of the year, $10,000 will grow to $10,000 \times

Table B.2
(Excerpt from Table 2)
Present Value of $1 at 8 Percent
and 12 Percent per Period
$P = F_n(1 + r)^{-n}$

Number of Periods = n	Rate = r	
	8 Percent	12 Percent
1	.92593	.89286
2	.85734	.79719
3	.79383	.71178
10	.46319	.32197
20	.21455	.10367

$(1.03)^4 = \$10,000 \times 1.12551 = \$11,255$. Twelve percent compounded quarterly is equivalent to 12.55 percent compounded annually. If 12 percent is compounded monthly, then $1 will grow to $\$1 \times (1.01)^{12} = \$1.12683$ and $10,000 will grow to $11,268. Thus, 12 percent compounded monthly is equivalent to 12.68 percent compounded annually.

For a given *nominal* rate, such as the 12 percent in the examples above, the more often interest is compounded or converted into principal, the higher the *effective* rate of interest paid. If a nominal rate, r, is compounded m times per year, then the effective rate is equal to $(1 + r/m)^m - 1$.

In practice, to solve problems that require computation of interest quoted at a nominal rate of r percent per period compounded m times per period for n periods, merely use the tables for rate r/m and $m \times n$ periods. For example, 12 percent compounded quarterly for 5 years is equivalent to the rate found in the interest tables for $r = 12/4 = 3$ percent for $m \times n = 4 \times 5 = 20$ periods.

Some savings banks advertise that they compound interest daily or even continuously. The mathematics of calculus provides a mechanism for finding the effective rate when interest is compounded continuously. If interest is compounded continuously at nominal rate r per year, then the effective annual rate is $e^r - 1$, where e is the base of the natural logarithms. Tables of values of e^r are widely available.[2] Six percent per year compounded continuously is equivalent to 6.1837 percent compounded annually; 12 percent per year compounded continuously is equivalent to 12.75 percent compounded annually. Do not confuse the compounding period with the payment period. Some banks, for example, compound interest daily but pay interest quarterly. You can be sure that such banks do not employ clerks or even computers to calculate interest every day. They merely use tables to derive an equivalent effective rate to apply at the end of each quarter.

---

[2]See, for example, *Handbook of Modern Accounting,* 3rd ed. edited by Sidney Davidson and Roman L. Weil, McGraw-Hill Book Company, New York, 1983, chap. 9, Exhibit 1.

Example Problems in Changing the Compounding Period

Example 5 What is the future value 5 years hence of $600 invested at 16 percent compounded semiannually?

Sixteen percent compounded two times per year for 5 years is equivalent to 8 percent per period compounded for 10 periods. Table B.1 shows the value of $F_{10} = (1.08)^{10}$ to be 2.15892. Six hundred dollars, then, would grow to $600 $\times$ 2.15892 = $1,295.35.

Example 6 How much money must be invested today at 16 percent compounded semiannually in order to have $10,000 ten years from today?

Sixteen percent compounded two times a year for 10 years is equivalent to 8 percent per period compounded for 20 periods. The *present* value, Table B.2, of $1 received 20 periods hence at 8 percent per period is $.21455. That is, $.21455 invested today for 20 periods at an interest rate of 8 percent per period will grow to $1. To have $10,000 in 20 periods (10 years), $2,146 (= $10,000 $\times$ $.21455) must be invested today.

Example 7 A local department store offers its customers credit and advertises its interest rate at 18 percent per year, compounded monthly at the rate of $1\frac{1}{2}$ percent per month. What is the effective annual interest rate?

One and one-half percent per month for 12 months is equivalent to $(1.015)^{12} - 1 = 19.562$ percent per year. See Table 1, 12-period row, $1\frac{1}{2}$ percent column where the factor is 1.19562.

Example 8 If prices increased at the rate of 6 percent during each of two consecutive 6-month periods, how much did prices increase during the entire year?

If a price index is 100.00 at the start of the year, it will be 100.00 $\times$ $(1.06)^2 = 112.36$ at the end of the year. The price change for the entire year is $(112.36/100.00) - 1 = 12.36$ percent.

Annuities

An *annuity* is a series of equal payments made at the beginning or end of equal periods of time. Examples of annuities include monthly rental payments, semiannual corporate bond coupon (or interest) payments, and annual payments to a lessor under a lease contract. Armed with an understanding of the tables for future and present values, you can solve any annuity problem. Annuities arise so often, however, and their solution is so tedious without special tables, that annuity problems warrant special study and the use of special tables.

Terminology for Annuities

The terminology used for annuities can be confusing because not all writers use the same terms. Definitions of the terms used in this text follow.

An annuity whose payments occur at the *end* of each period is called an *ordinary annuity* or an *annuity in arrears*. Semiannual corporate bond coupon payments are usually paid in arrears or, equivalently, the first payment does not occur until after the bond has been outstanding for 6 months.

An annuity whose payments occur at the *beginning* of each period is called an *annuity due* or an *annuity in advance*. Rent is usually paid in advance, so a series of rental payments is an annuity due.

A *deferred* annuity is one whose first payment is at some time later than the end of the first period.

Annuities can be paid forever. Such annuities are called *perpetuities*. Bonds that promise payments forever are called *consols*. The British and Canadian governments have, from time to time, issued consols. A perpetuity can be in arrears or in advance. The only difference between the two is the timing of the first payment.

Annuities can be confusing. Their study is made easier with a *time line* such as the one shown below.

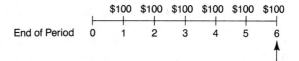

A time line marks the end of each period, numbers the period, shows the payments to be received or paid, and shows the time at which the annuity is valued. The time line just pictured represents an ordinary annuity (in arrears) for six periods of $100 to be valued at the end of period 6. The end of period 0 is "now." The first payment is to be received one period from now.

Ordinary Annuities (Annuities in Arrears)

The future values of ordinary annuities appear in the back of the book in Table 3, portions of which Table B.3 reproduces.

Table B.3
(Excerpt from Table 3)
Future Value of an Ordinary Annuity of
$1 per Period at 8 Percent and 12 Percent

$$F_A = \frac{[(1 + r)^n - 1]}{r}$$

Number of Periods = n	Rate = r	
	8 Percent	12 Percent
1	1.00000	1.00000
2	2.08000	2.12000
3	3.24640	3.37440
5	5.86660	6.35285
10	14.48656	17.54874
20	45.76196	72.05244

Consider an ordinary annuity for three periods at 12 percent. The time line for the future value of such an annuity is

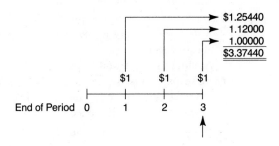

The $1 received at the end of the first period earns interest for two periods, so it is worth $1.25440 at the end of period 3. (See Table B.1.) The $1 received at the end of the second period grows to $1.12000 by the end of period 3, and the $1 received at the end of period 3 is, of course, worth $1.00000 at the end of period 3. The entire annuity is worth $3.37440 at the end of period 3. This is the amount shown in Table B.3 for the future value of an ordinary annuity for three periods at 12 percent. Factors for the future value of an annuity for a particular number of periods are merely the sum of the factors for the future value of $1 for each of the periods. The future value of an ordinary annuity is calculated as follows:

$$\begin{matrix} \text{Future Value of} \\ \text{Ordinary Annuity} \end{matrix} = \begin{matrix} \text{Periodic} \\ \text{Payment} \end{matrix} \times \begin{matrix} \text{Factor for} \\ \text{the Future} \\ \text{Value of an} \\ \text{Ordinary Annuity.} \end{matrix}$$

Thus,

$$\$3.37440 \quad = \quad \$1 \quad \times \quad 3.37440.$$

Table 4 at the end of this Appendix shows the present value of ordinary annuities. Table B.4 reproduces excerpts from Table 4.

The time line for the present value of an ordinary annuity of $1 per period for three periods, discounted at 12 percent, is

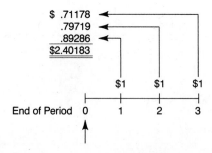

Table B.4
(Excerpt from Table 4)
Present Value of an Ordinary Annuity of
$1 per Period at 8 Percent and 12 Percent

$$P_A = \frac{[1 - (1 + r)^{-n}]}{r}$$

Number of Periods = n	Rate = r	
	8 Percent	12 Percent
1.	.92593	.89286
2.	1.78326	1.69005
3.	2.57710	2.40183
5.	3.99271	3.60478
10.	6.71008	5.65022
20.	9.81815	7.46944

The $1 to be received at the end of period 1 has a present value of $.89286, the $1 to be received at the end of period 2 has a present value of $.79719, and the dollar to be received at the end of the third period has a present value of $.71178. Each of these numbers comes from Table B.2. The present value of the annuity is the sum of these individual present values, $2.40183, shown in Table B.4.

The present value of an ordinary annuity for n periods is the sum of the present value of $1 received 1 period from now plus the present value of $1 received 2 periods from now, and so on until we add on the present value of $1 received n periods from now. The present value of an ordinary annuity is calculated as follows:

$$\begin{array}{ccc} \text{Present Value} & & \text{Factor for} \\ \text{of an} & = \text{Periodic} \times & \text{the Present} \\ \text{Ordinary Annuity} & \text{Payment} & \text{Value of an} \\ & & \text{Ordinary Annuity.} \end{array}$$

Thus,

$$\$2.40183 \quad = \quad \$1 \quad \times \quad 2.40183.$$

Example Problems Involving Ordinary Annuities

Example 9 An individual plans to invest $1,000 at the end of each of the next 10 years in a savings account. The savings account accumulates interest of 12 percent compounded annually. What will be the balance in the savings account at the end of 10 years?

The time line for this problem is

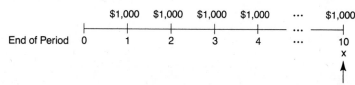

The symbol x denotes the amount to be calculated. Table B.3 indicates that the factor for the future value of an annuity at 12 percent for ten periods is 17.54874. Thus,

$$\begin{array}{l}\text{Future Value} \\ \text{of an} \\ \text{Ordinary Annuity}\end{array} = \begin{array}{l}\text{Periodic} \\ \text{Payment}\end{array} \times \begin{array}{l}\text{Factor for} \\ \text{the Future} \\ \text{Value of an} \\ \text{Ordinary Annuity}\end{array}$$

$$x = \$1,000 \times 17.54874$$
$$x = \$17,549.$$

Example 10 An individual wishes to receive $60 every 6 months, starting 6 months hence, for the next 5 years. How much must be invested today if the interest rate is 12 percent compounded semiannually?

The time line is

```
       $60  $60  $60  $60  ···  $60
   ├────┼────┼────┼────┼──  ··· ──┤
   0    1    2    3    4   ···    10
   x
   ▲
   │
```

The factor from Table 4 for the present value of an annuity at 6 percent (= 12 percent per year/2 semiannual periods per year) for 10 (= 2 periods per year × 5 years) periods is 7.36009. Thus,

$$\begin{array}{l}\text{Present Value} \\ \text{of an} \\ \text{Ordinary Annuity}\end{array} = \begin{array}{l}\text{Periodic} \\ \text{Payment}\end{array} \times \begin{array}{l}\text{Factor for} \\ \text{the Present} \\ \text{Value of an} \\ \text{Ordinary Annuity}\end{array}$$

$$x = \$60 \times 7.36009$$
$$x = \$441.61.$$

If $441.61 is invested today, the principal plus interest compounded on the principal will provide sufficient funds so that $60 can be withdrawn every 6 months for the next 5 years.

Example 11 (Western Company mortgage example, from Chapter 10.) A company borrows $125,000 from a savings-and-loan association. The interest rate on the loan is 12 percent compounded semiannually. The company agrees to repay the loan in equal semiannual installments over the next 5 years. The first payment is to be made 6 months from now. What is the amount of the required semiannual payment?

The time line is

```
                  x    x    x    x   ···   x
              ├────┼────┼────┼────┼──  ··· ──┤
End of Period 0    1    2    3    4   ···    10
        $125,000
```

This problem is similar to Example 10 because both involve periodic payments in the future that are discounted to today. In Example 10, the periodic payments were given and the present value was computed. In Example 11, the present value is given and the periodic payment is computed. Table 4 indicates that the present value of annuity at 6 percent (= 12 percent per year/2 semiannual periods per year) for 10 (= 2 periods per year × 5 years) periods is 7.36009. Thus,

$$\begin{array}{ccc}
\text{Present Value} & & \text{Factor for} \\
\text{of an} & = \text{Periodic} \times & \text{the Present} \\
\text{Ordinary Annuity} & \text{Payment} & \text{Value of an} \\
& & \text{Ordinary Annuity}
\end{array}$$

$$\$125{,}000 = x \times 7.36009$$

$$x = \frac{\$125{,}000}{7.36009}$$

$$x = \$16{,}983.$$

Because the periodic payment is being calculated, the present value amount of $125,000 must be divided by the present value factor. (You may wish to turn to Exhibit 10.2 to study the amortization table for this loan. The amount of each semiannual payment shown here is $17,000 rather than $16,983, but the last payment is less than $17,000.)

Example 12 (Myers Company lease example, from Chapter 11.) A company signs a lease acquiring the right to use property for 3 years. Lease payments of $19,709 are to be made annually at the end of this and the next 2 years. The discount, or interest, rate is 15 percent per year. What is the present value of the lease payments?
    The time line is

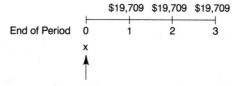

The factor from Table 4 for the present value of an annuity at 15 percent for three periods is 2.28323. Thus,

$$\begin{array}{ccc}
\text{Present Value} & & \text{Factor for} \\
\text{of an} & = \text{Periodic} \times & \text{the Present} \\
\text{Ordinary Annuity} & \text{Payment} & \text{Value of an} \\
& & \text{Ordinary Annuity}
\end{array}$$

$$x = \$19{,}709 \times 2.28323$$

$$x = \$45{,}000.$$

In the Myers Company example in Chapter 11 the cost of the equipment is given at $45,000 and the periodic rental payment is computed with an annuity factor. Thus,

$$\begin{array}{ccc}
\text{Present Value} & & \text{Factor for} \\
\text{of an} & = \text{Periodic} \times & \text{the Present} \\
\text{Ordinary Annuity} & \text{Payment} & \text{Value of} \\
& & \text{an Annuity}
\end{array}$$

$$\$45{,}000 = x \times 2.28323$$

$$x = \frac{\$45{,}000}{2.28323}$$

$$x = \$19{,}709.$$

Example 13 (Pension funding example.) A company is obligated to make annual payments to a pension fund at the end of each of the next 30 years. The present value of those payments is to be $100,000. What must the annual payment be if the fund is projected to earn interest at the rate of 8 percent per year?

The time line is

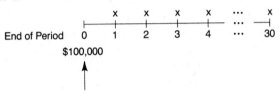

Table 4 indicates that the factor for the present value of $1 paid at the end of the next 30 periods at 8 percent per period is 11.25778. Thus,

$$\begin{array}{ccc}
\text{Present Value} & & \text{Factor for} \\
\text{of an} & = \text{Periodic} \times & \text{the Present} \\
\text{Ordinary Annuity} & \text{Payment} & \text{Value of an} \\
& & \text{Ordinary Annuity}
\end{array}$$

$$\$100{,}000 = x \times 11.25778$$

$$x = \frac{\$100{,}000}{11.25778}$$

$$x = \$8{,}883.$$

Example 14 Mr. Mason is 62 years old. He wishes to invest equal amounts on his sixty-third, sixty-fourth, and sixty-fifth birthdays so that starting on his sixty-sixth birthday he can withdraw $5,000 on each birthday for 10 years. His investments will earn 8 percent per year. How much should be invested on the sixty-third through sixty-fifth birthdays?

The time line for this problem is

On his sixty-fifth birthday, Mr. Mason needs to have accumulated a fund equal to the present value of an annuity of $5,000 per period for 10 periods, discounted at 8

percent per period. The factor from Table B.4 for 8 percent and 10 periods is 6.71008. Thus,

$$
\begin{array}{lcl}
\begin{array}{c}\text{Present Value}\\\text{of an}\\\text{Ordinary Annuity}\end{array} & = \begin{array}{c}\text{Periodic}\\\text{Payment}\end{array} \times & \begin{array}{c}\text{Factor for}\\\text{the Present}\\\text{Value of an}\\\text{Ordinary Annuity}\end{array}\\
x & = \$\,5{,}000 \times & 6.71008\\
x & = \$33{,}550. &
\end{array}
$$

The time line now appears as follows:

The question now becomes: How much must be invested on Mr. Mason's sixty-third, sixty-fourth, and sixty-fifth birthdays to accumulate to a fund of $33,550 on his sixty-fifth birthday? The factor for the future value of an annuity for three periods at 8 percent is 3.24640. Thus,

$$
\begin{array}{lcl}
\begin{array}{c}\text{Future Value}\\\text{of an}\\\text{Ordinary Annuity}\end{array} & = \begin{array}{c}\text{Periodic}\\\text{Payment}\end{array} \times & \begin{array}{c}\text{Factor for}\\\text{the Future}\\\text{Value of an}\\\text{Ordinary Annuity}\end{array}\\
\$33{,}550 & = \quad x \quad \times & 3.24640\\
x & = \dfrac{\$33{,}550}{3.24640} &\\
x & = \$10{,}335. &
\end{array}
$$

In the solution above, all calculations are expressed in terms of equivalent amounts on Mr. Mason's sixty-fifth birthday. That is, the present value of an annuity of $5,000 per period for 10 periods at 8 percent is equal to the future value of an annuity of $10,335 per period for 3 periods at 8 percent and both of these amounts are equal to $33,550. The problem could have been worked by selecting any common time period between Mr. Mason's sixty-second and seventy-fifth birthdays.

One possibility would be to express all calculations in terms of equivalent amounts on Mr. Mason's sixty-second birthday. To solve the problem in this way, first find the present value on Mr. Mason's *sixty-fifth* birthday of an annuity of $5,000 per period for 10 periods ($33,550 = $5,000 × 6.71008). Discount $33,550 back three periods using Table 2 for the present value of $1 ($26,633 = $33,550 × .79383). The result is the present value of the payments to be made to Mr. Mason *measured as of his sixty-second birthday.* Then find the amounts that must be invested by Mr. Mason on his sixty-third, sixty-fourth, and sixty-fifth birthdays that have a *present value* on his sixty-second birthday equal to $26,633. The calculation is as follows:

$$\begin{array}{ccc}
\begin{array}{c}\text{Present Value}\\ \text{of an}\\ \text{Ordinary Annuity}\end{array} & = & \begin{array}{c}\text{Periodic}\\ \text{Payment}\end{array} \times & \begin{array}{c}\text{Factor for}\\ \text{the Present}\\ \text{Value of an}\\ \text{Ordinary Annuity}\end{array}
\end{array}$$

$$\$26{,}633 \;\; = \;\; x \;\; \times \;\; 2.57710$$
$$x \;\; = \$10{,}335.$$

The amount $10,335 is the same as that found above.

Perpetuities

A periodic payment to be received forever is called a *perpetuity*. Future values of perpetuities are undefined. If $1 is to be received at the end of every period and the discount rate is r percent, then the present value of the perpetuity is $1/r$. This expression can be derived with algebra or by observing what happens in the expression for the present value of an ordinary annuity of $A per payment as n, the number of payments, approaches infinity:

$$P_A = \frac{A[1 - (1 + r)^{-n}]}{r}.$$

As n approaches infinity, $(1 + r)^{-n}$ approaches zero, so that P_A approaches $A(1/r)$. If the first payment of the perpetuity occurs now, the present value is $A[1 + 1/r]$.

Examples of Perpetuities

Example 15 The Canadian government offers to pay $30 every 6 months forever in the form of a perpetual bond. What is that bond worth if the discount rate is 15 percent compounded semiannually?

Fifteen percent compounded semiannually is equivalent to 7.5 percent per 6-month period. If the first payment occurs 6 months from now, the present value is $30/.075 = $400. If the first payment occurs today, the present value is $30 + $400 = $430.

Example 16 Every 2 years, Ms. Young gives $20,000 to the University to provide a scholarship for an entering student in a 2-year business administration course. If the University credits 6 percent per year to its investment accounts, how much must Ms. Young give to the University to provide such a scholarship every 2 years forever, starting 2 years hence?

A perpetuity in arrears assumes one payment at the end of each period. Here, the period is 2 years; 6 percent compounded once a year over 2 years is equivalent to a rate of $(1.06)^2 - 1 = .12360$ or 12.36 percent compounded once per 2-year period. Consequently, the present value of the perpetuity paid in arrears every 2 years is $161,812 (= $20,000/.12360). A gift of $161,812 will be sufficient to provide a $20,000 scholarship forever. If the first scholarship is to be awarded now, the gift must be $181,812 (= $161,812 + $20,000).

Implicit Interest Rates: Finding Internal Rates of Return

In the preceding examples, given the interest rate and stated cash payments, a future value or a present value was computed. Or the required payments were computed given their known future value or their known present value. In some calculations, the present or future value and the periodic payments are known; the implicit interest rate is to be found. For example, Chapter 11 illustrates a case in which the cash price of some equipment is known to be $10,500 and the asset was acquired using a note. The note is non-interest-bearing, has a face value of $16,000, and matures in 3 years. In order to compute interest expense over the 3-year period, the implicit interest rate must be found. The time line for this problem is

$$
\begin{array}{ccccc}
+\$10,500 & 0 & 0 & -\$16,000 \\
\vdash & \quad + & \quad + & \dashv \\
\text{End of Year} \quad 0 & 1 & 2 & 3
\end{array}
$$

The implicit interest rate is r, such that

(I)
$$0 = \$10,500 - \frac{\$16,000}{(1 + r)^3}.$$

(II)
$$\$10,500 = \frac{\$16,000}{(1 + r)^3}.$$

That is, the present value of $16,000 discounted three periods at r percent per period is $10,500. The present value of all current and future cash flows nets to zero when future flows are discounted at r per period. In general, the only way to find such an r is a trial-and-error procedure. In cases where r appears only in one term, as here, r can be found analytically. Here, $r = (\$16,000/\$10,500)^{1/3} - 1 = .1507 = 15.1$ percent.

The general procedure is called "finding the internal rate of return" of a series of cash flows. The *internal rate of return* of a series of cash flows is the discount rate that equates the net present value of that series of cash flows to zero. The steps in finding the internal rate of return are as follows:

1. Make an educated guess, called the "trial rate," at the internal rate of return. If you have no idea what to guess, try zero.
2. Calculate the present value of all the cash flows (including the one at the end of Year 0).
3. If the present value of the cash flows is zero, stop. The current trial rate is the internal rate of return.
4. If the amount found in step 2 is less than zero, try a larger interest rate as the trial rate and go back to step 2.
5. If the amount found in step 2 is greater than zero, try a smaller interest rate as the new trial rate and go back to step 2.

The iterations below illustrate the process for the example in equation (I).

Iteration Number	Trial Rate = r	Net Present Value: Right-Hand Side of (I)
1	0.0%	−$5,500
2	10.0	− 1,521
3	15.0	− 20
4	15.5	116
5	15.2	34
6	15.1	7

With a trial rate of 15.1 percent, the right-hand side is close enough to zero so that 15.1 percent can be used as the implicit interest rate. Continued iterations would find trial rates even closer to the true rate, which is about 15.0739 percent.

Finding the internal rate of return for a series of cash flows can be tedious and should not be attempted unless one has at least a desk calculator. An exponential feature, the feature that allows the computation of $(1 + r)$ raised to various powers, helps.[3]

Example Problem Involving Implicit Interest Rates

Example 17 The Alexis Company acquires a machine with a cash price of $10,500. It pays for the machine by giving a note promising to make payments equal to 7 percent of the face value, $840, at the end of each of the next 3 years and a single payment of $12,000 in 3 years. What is the implicit interest rate in the loan?

The time line for this problem is

	$10,500	−$840	−$840	−$12,840
End of Period	0	1	2	3

The implicit interest rate is r, such that[4]

(III)
$$\$10,500 = \frac{\$840}{(1 + r)} + \frac{\$840}{(1 + r)^2} + \frac{\$12,840}{(1 + r)^3}.$$

---

[3]There are ways to guess the trial rate that will approximate the true rate in fewer iterations than the method described here. If you want to find internal rates of return efficiently with successive trial rates, refer to a mathematical reference book to learn about the "Newton search" method, sometimes called the "method of false position."

[4]Compare this formulation to that in equation (I). Note that the left-hand side is zero in one case but not in the other. The left-hand side can be either a nonzero number or zero, depending on what seems convenient for the particular context.

The internal rate of return is found to the nearest tenth of 1 percent to be 12.2 percent:

Iteration Number	Trial Rate	Right-Hand Side of (III)
1	7.0%	$12,000
2	15.0	9,808
3	11.0	10,827
4	13.0	10,300
5	12.0	10,559
6	12.5	10,428
7	12.3	10,480
8	12.2	10,506
9	12.1	10,532

Summary

Accountants typically use one of four kinds of compound interest calculations: the present or future value of a single payment or of a series of payments. In working annuity problems, a time line helps in deciding which particular kind of annuity is involved.

Questions, Exercises, Problems and Cases

Questions

1. Review the following concepts or terms discussed in this appendix.

    a. Compound interest.
    b. Principal.
    c. Simple interest.
    d. Future value.
    e. Present value.
    f. Discounted value.
    g. Discount factor.

    h. Discount rate.
    i. Ordinary annuity (annuity in arrears).
    j. Perpetuity.
    k. Deferred annuity.
    l. Implicit interest rate (internal rate of return).

2. What is interest?

3. Distinguish between simple and compound interest.

4. Distinguish between the discounted present value of a stream of future payments and their net present value. If there is no distinction, then so state.

5. Distinguish between an annuity due and an ordinary annuity.

6. Describe the "implicit interest rate" for a series of cash flows and a procedure for finding it.

7. Does the present value of a given amount to be paid in 10 years increase or decrease if the interest rate increases? Suppose that the amount were due in 5 years? 20 years? Does the present value of an annuity to be paid for 10 years increase or decrease if the discount rate decreases? Suppose that the annuity were for 5 years? 20 years?

8. Rather than pay you $100 a month for the next 20 years, the person who injured you in an automobile accident is willing to pay a single amount now to settle your claim for injuries. Would you rather an interest rate of 6 percent or 12 percent be used in computing the present value of the lump-sum settlement? Comment or explain.

Exercises

9. *Effective interest rates.* State the rate per period and the number of periods, in each of the following:
   a. 12 percent per annum, for 5 years, compounded annually.
   b. 12 percent per annum, for 5 years, compounded semiannually.
   c. 12 percent per annum, for 5 years, compounded quarterly.
   d. 12 percent per annum, for 5 years, compounded monthly.

Exercises 10 through 26 involve calculations of present and future value for single payments and for annuities, both ordinary and in arrears. To make the exercises more realistic, specific guidance is not given with each individual exercise.

10. Compute the future value of:
   a. $100 invested for 5 years at 4 percent compounded annually.
   b. $500 invested for 15 periods at 2 percent compounded once per period.
   c. $200 invested for 8 years at 3 percent compounded semiannually.
   d. $2,500 invested for 14 years at 8 percent compounded quarterly.
   e. $600 invested for 3 years at 12 percent compounded monthly.

11. Compute the present value of:
   a. $100 due in 30 years at 4 percent compounded annually.
   b. $250 due in 8 years at 8 percent compounded quarterly.
   c. $1,000 due in 2 years at 12 percent compounded monthly.

12. Compute the amount (future value) of an ordinary annuity (an annuity in arrears) of:
   a. 13 rents of $100 at $1\frac{1}{2}$ percent per period.
   b. 8 rents of $850 at 6 percent per period.
   c. 28 rents of $400 at 4 percent per period.

13. Mr. Adams has $500 to invest. He wishes to know how much it will amount to if he invests it at
   a. 6 percent per year for 21 years.
   b. 8 percent per year for 33 years.

14. Ms. Black wishes to have $15,000 at the end of 8 years. How much must she invest today to accomplish this purpose if the interest rate is

   a. 6 percent per year?
   b. 8 percent per year?

15. Mr. Case plans to set aside $4,000 each year, the first payment to be made on January 1, 1982, and the last on January 1, 1987. How much will he have accumulated by January 1, 1987 if the interest rate is
   a. 6 percent per year?
   b. 8 percent per year?

16. Ms. David wants to have $450,000 on her sixty-fifth birthday. She asks you to tell her how much she must deposit on each birthday from her fifty-eighth to sixty-fifth, inclusive, in order to receive this amount. Assume an interest rate of
   a. 8 percent per year.
   b. 12 percent per year.

17. If Mr. Edwards invests $900 on June 1 of each year from 1982 to 1992, inclusive, how much will he have accumulated on June 1, 1993 (note that 1 year elapses after last payment) if the interest rate is
   a. 5 percent per year?
   b. 10 percent per year?

18. Mr. Frank has $145,000 with which he purchases an annuity on February 1, 1982. The annuity consists of six annual payments, the first to be made on February 1, 1983. How much will he receive in each payment? Assume an interest rate of
   a. 8 percent per year.
   b. 12 percent per year.

19. In the preceding Exercises 10–18, you have been asked to compute a number. First you must decide what factor from the tables is appropriate and then you use that factor in the appropriate calculation. Notice that the last step could be omitted. You could write an arithmetic expression showing the factor you want to use without actually copying down the number and doing the arithmetic. For example, define the following notation: $T(i, p, r)$ means Table i (1, 2, 3, or 4), row p (periods 1 to 20, 22, 24, . . ., 40, 45, 50, 100), and column r (interest rates from $\frac{1}{2}$ percent up to 20 percent). Thus, $T(3, 16, 12)$ would be the factor in Table 3 for 16 periods and an interest rate of 12 percent per period, which is 42.75328. Using this notation, you can write an expression for any compound interest problem. Any clerk can evaluate the expression.

   You can check that you understand this notation by observing that the following are true statements:

$T(1, 20, 8)$ =   4.66096
$T(2, 12, 5)$ =   0.55684
$T(3, 16, 12)$ = 42.75328
$T(4, 10, 20)$ =   4.19247.

In the following questions, write an expression for the correct answer using the notation introduced here, but do not attempt to evaluate the expression.
   a. Work the **a** parts of Exercises 10–14.
   b. Work the **b** parts of Exercises 15–18.

c. How might the use of this notation make it easier for your instructor to write examination questions on compound interest?

20. Ms. Grady agrees to lease a certain property for 10 years, at the following annual rentals, payable in advance:

Years 1 and 2—$1,000 per year.

Years 3 to 6—$2,000 per year.

Years 7 to 10—$2,500 per year.

What single immediate sum will pay all of these rents if they are discounted at
    a. 6 percent per year?
    b. 8 percent per year?
    c. 10 percent per year?

21. In order to establish a fund that will provide a scholarship of $3,000 a year indefinitely, with the first award to occur now, how much must be deposited if the fund earns:
    a. 6 percent per period?
    b. 8 percent per period?

22. Consider the scholarship fund in the preceding question. Suppose that the first scholarship is not to be awarded until 1 year from now. How much should be deposited if the fund earns:
    a. 6 percent per period?
    b. 8 percent per period?

Suppose that the first scholarship is not to be awarded until 5 years from now. How much should be deposited if the fund earns:
    c. 6 percent per year?
    d. 8 percent per year?

23. The state helps a rural county maintain a bridge and has agreed to pay $6,000 now and every 2 years thereafter forever toward the expenses. The state wishes to discharge its obligation by paying a single sum to the county now in lieu of the payment due and all future payments. How much should the state pay the county if the discount rate is
    a. 8 percent per year?
    b. 12 percent per year?

24. Find the interest rate implicit in a loan of $100,000 that is discharged with the two annual installments of $55,307 each paid at the ends of Years 1 and 2.

25. A single-payment note has a face value of $140,493, to be paid in 3 years. The note is exchanged for equipment having a fair market value of $100,000 three years before the maturity date on the note.

What interest rate will be imputed in accounting for the single-payment note?

26. A single-payment note has a face value of $67,280, due on maturity of the note. The note is exchanged for land with a fair market value of $50,000 two years before the maturity date on the note.

a. What interest rate will be imputed in accounting for this single-payment note?

b. Construct an amortization schedule for the note using the interest rate imputed. Show book value of the note at the start of each year, interest for each year, amount reducing or increasing book value each year, and book value at the end of the year.

27. *Finding implicit interest rates; constructing amortization schedules.* Berman Company purchased a plot of land for possible future development. The land had fair market value of $86,000. Berman Company gave a 3-year interest-bearing note. The note had face value of $100,000 and provided for interest at a stated rate of 8 percent—payments of $8,000 were due at the end of each of 3 years, the last payment coinciding with the maturity of the note's face value of $100,000.

a. What is the interest rate implicit in the note accurate to the nearest tenth of one percent?

b. Construct an amortization schedule for the note for each year, showing the book value of the note at the start of the year, interest for the year, payment for the year, amount reducing or increasing the book value of the note for each payment, and the book value of the note at the end of each year. Use the interest rate found in part **a**. See Exhibit 10.2 for an example of an amortization schedule.

28. The terms of sale "2/10, net/30" mean that a discount of 2 percent from gross invoice price can be taken if the invoice is paid within 10 days and that otherwise the full amount is due within 30 days.

a. Write an expression for the implied annual rate of interest being offered, if the entire discount is viewed as being interest for funds received sooner rather than later. (Note that 98 percent of the gross invoice price is being borrowed for 20 days.)

b. The tables at the back of the book do not permit the exact evaluation of the expression derived in part **a**. The rate of interest implied is 44.59 percent per year. Use the tables to convince yourself that this astounding (to some) answer must be close to correct.

Problems and Cases

29. *Present value of a perpetuity.* An oil-drilling company figures that $300 must be spent for an initial supply of drill bits and that $100 must be spent every month to replace the worn-out bits. What is the present value of the cost of the bits if the company plans to be in business indefinitely and discounts payments at 1 percent per month?

The following problems involve using future value and present value techniques to solve a variety of realistic problems. No hints as to the specific calculation are given with the problems.

30. If you promise to leave $35,000 on deposit at the Quarter Savings Bank for 4 years, the bank will give you a new car today and your $35,000 back at the end of

4 years. How much are you, in effect, paying today for the car if the bank pays 8 percent interest compounded quarterly (2 percent paid four times per year)?

31. When Mr. Shafer died, his estate after taxes amounted to $300,000. His will provided that Widow Shafer would receive $24,000 per year starting immediately from the principal of the estate and that the balance of the principal would pass to the Shafers' children upon Widow Shafer's death. The state law governing this estate provided for a *dower* option. If Widow Shafer elects the dower option, she renounces the will and can have one-third of the estate in cash now. The remainder will then pass immediately to their children. Widow Shafer wants to maximize the present value of her bequest. Should she take the annuity or elect the dower option if she will receive five payments and discounts payments at:
   a. 8 percent per year?
   b. 12 percent per year?

32. Mrs. Heileman occasionally drinks beer. She consumes one case in 20 weeks. She can buy beer in disposable bottles for $12.60 per case or for $12.00 a case of returnable bottles if a $1.50 refundable deposit is paid at the time of purchase. If her discount rate is $\frac{1}{4}$ percent per week, how much in present value dollars does she save by buying the returnables and thereby losing the use of the $1.50 deposit for 20 weeks?

33. When the General Electric Company first introduced the Lucalox ceramic, screw-in light bulb, the bulb cost three-and-one-half times as much as an ordinary bulb but lasted five times as long. An ordinary bulb cost $.50 and lasted about 8 months. If a firm has a discount rate of 12 percent compounded three times a year, how much would it save in present value dollars by using one Lucalox bulb?

34. The Roberts Dairy Company switched from delivery trucks with regular gasoline engines to ones with diesel engines. The diesel trucks cost $2,000 more than the ordinary gasoline trucks, but $600 per year less to operate. Assume that the operating costs are saved at the end of each month. If Roberts Dairy uses a discount rate of 1 percent per month, approximately how many months, at a minimum, must the diesel trucks remain in service for the switch to save money?

35. On January 1, Year 1, Outergarments, Inc., opened a new textile plant for the production of synthetic fabrics. The plant is on leased land; 20 years remain on the nonrenewable lease.

The cost of the plant was $2 million. Net cash flow to be derived from the project is estimated to be $300,000 per year. The company does not normally invest in such projects unless the anticipated yield is at least 12 percent.

On December 31, Year 1, the company finds cash flows from the plant to be $280,000 for the year. On the same day, farm experts predict cotton production to be unusually low for the next 2 years. Outergarments estimates the resulting increase in demand for synthetic fabrics to boost cash flows to $350,000 for each of the next 2 years. Subsequent years' estimates remain unchanged. Ignore tax considerations.

   a. Calculate the present value of the future expected cash flows from the plant when it was opened.

b. What is the present value of the plant on January 1, Year 2, immediately after the reestimation of future incomes?

c. On January 2, Year 2, the day following the cotton production news release, Overalls Company announces plans to build a synthetic fabrics plant to be opened in 3 years. Outergarments, Inc., keeps its Year 2–Year 4 estimates, but reduces the estimated annual cash flows for subsequent years to $200,000. What is the value of the Outergarments' present plant on January 1, Year 2, after the new projections?

d. On January 2, Year 2, an investor contacts Outergarments about purchasing a 20 percent share of the plant. If the investor expects to earn at least a 12 percent annual return on the investment, what is the maximum amount that the investor can pay? Assume that the investor and Outergarments, Inc., both know all relevant information and use the same estimates of annual cash flows.

36. *Finding implicit interest rates (truth-in-lending laws reduce the type of deception suggested by this problem).* The Friendly Loan Company advertises that it is willing to lend money for 5 years at the low rate of 8 percent per year. A potential borrower discovers that a 5-year, $10,000 loan requires that the 8 percent interest be paid in advance, with interest deducted from the loan proceeds. The borrower will collect $6,000 [= $10,000 − (5 × .08 × $10,000)] cash and must repay the ''$10,000'' loan in five annual installments of $2,000, one each at the end of the next 5 years.

Compute the effective interest rate implied by these loan terms.

37. *Deriving net present value of cash flows for decision to dispose of asset.* The Wisher Washer Company purchased a made-to-order machine tool for grinding washing machine parts. The machine cost $100,000 and was installed yesterday. Today, a machine tool is offered that will do exactly the same work but costs only $50,000. Assume that the discount rate is 12 percent, that both machines will last for 5 years, that both machines will be depreciated on a straight-line basis for tax purposes with no salvage value, that the income tax rate is and will continue to be 40 percent, and that Wisher Washer Company earns sufficient income that any loss from disposing of or depreciating the ''old'' machine can be used to offset other taxable income. Ignore the investment credit.

How much, at a minimum, must the ''old'' machine fetch on resale at this time to make purchasing the new machine worthwhile?

38. *Computation of present value of cash flows; untaxed acquisition, no change in tax basis of assets.* The balance sheet of Lynch Company shows assets of $100,000, net, and owners' equity of $100,000. The assets are all depreciable assets with remaining lives of 20 years. The income statement for the year shows revenues of $700,000, depreciation of $50,000 (= $100,000/20 years), no other expenses, income taxes of $260,000 (40 percent of pretax income of $650,000), and net income of $390,000.

Zeff Company is considering purchasing all of the stock of Lynch Company. It is willing to pay an amount equal to the present value of the cash flows from operations for the next 20 years discounted at a rate of 10 percent per year.

The transaction will not be taxable; that is, after the purchase, the tax basis of the assets of Lynch Company will remain unchanged, so that depreciation charges will remain at $50,000 per year and income taxes will remain at $260,000 per year. Revenues will be $700,000 per year for the next 20 years.

    a. Compute the annual cash flows produced by Lynch Company.

    b. Compute the maximum amount Zeff Company should be willing to pay.

39. *Computation of present value of cash flows; taxable acquisition, changing tax basis of assets.* Refer to the data in the preceding problem. Assume now that the acquisition is taxable, so that the tax basis of the assets acquired changes after the purchase. If the purchase price is $V, then depreciation charges will be $V/20$ per year for 20 years. Income taxes will be 40 percent of pretax income.

What is the maximum Zeff Company should be willing to pay for Lynch Company?

Compound Interest, Annuity, and Bond Tables

Table 1
Future Value of $1
$$F_n = P(1 + r)^n$$
r = interest rate; n = number of periods until valuation; P = $1

Periods = n	½%	1%	1½%	2%	3%	4%	5%	6%	7%	8%	10%	12%	15%	20%	25%
1	1.00500	1.01000	1.01500	1.02000	1.03000	1.04000	1.05000	1.06000	1.07000	1.08000	1.10000	1.12000	1.15000	1.20000	1.25000
2	1.01003	1.02010	1.03023	1.04040	1.06090	1.08160	1.10250	1.12360	1.14490	1.16640	1.21000	1.25440	1.32250	1.44000	1.56250
3	1.01508	1.03030	1.04568	1.06121	1.09273	1.12486	1.15763	1.19102	1.22504	1.25971	1.33100	1.40493	1.52088	1.72800	1.95313
4	1.02015	1.04060	1.06136	1.08243	1.12551	1.16986	1.21551	1.26248	1.31080	1.36049	1.46410	1.57352	1.74901	2.07360	2.44141
5	1.02525	1.05101	1.07728	1.10408	1.15927	1.21665	1.27628	1.33823	1.40255	1.46933	1.61051	1.76234	2.01136	2.48832	3.05176
6	1.03038	1.06152	1.09344	1.12616	1.19405	1.26532	1.34010	1.41852	1.50073	1.58687	1.77156	1.97382	2.31306	2.98598	3.81470
7	1.03553	1.07214	1.10984	1.14869	1.22987	1.31593	1.40710	1.50363	1.60578	1.71382	1.94872	2.21068	2.66002	3.58318	4.76837
8	1.04071	1.08286	1.12649	1.17166	1.26677	1.36857	1.47746	1.59385	1.71819	1.85093	2.14359	2.47596	3.05902	4.29982	5.96046
9	1.04591	1.09369	1.14339	1.19509	1.30477	1.42331	1.55133	1.68948	1.83846	1.99900	2.35795	2.77308	3.51788	5.15978	7.45058
10	1.05114	1.10462	1.16054	1.21899	1.34392	1.48024	1.62889	1.79085	1.96715	2.15892	2.59374	3.10585	4.04556	6.19174	9.31323
11	1.05640	1.11567	1.17795	1.24337	1.38423	1.53945	1.71034	1.89830	2.10485	2.33164	2.85312	3.47855	4.65239	7.43008	11.64153
12	1.06168	1.12683	1.19562	1.26824	1.42576	1.60103	1.79586	2.01220	2.25219	2.51817	3.13843	3.89598	5.35025	8.91610	14.55192
13	1.06699	1.13809	1.21355	1.29361	1.46853	1.66507	1.88565	2.13293	2.40985	2.71962	3.45227	4.36349	6.15279	10.69932	18.18989
14	1.07232	1.14947	1.23176	1.31948	1.51259	1.73168	1.97993	2.26090	2.57853	2.93719	3.79750	4.88711	7.07571	12.83918	22.73737
15	1.07768	1.16097	1.25023	1.34587	1.55797	1.80094	2.07893	2.39656	2.75903	3.17217	4.17725	5.47357	8.13706	15.40702	28.42171
16	1.08307	1.17258	1.26899	1.37279	1.60471	1.87298	2.18287	2.54035	2.95216	3.42594	4.59497	6.13039	9.35762	18.48843	35.52714
17	1.08849	1.18430	1.28802	1.40024	1.65285	1.94790	2.29202	2.69277	3.15882	3.70002	5.05447	6.86604	10.76126	22.1861	44.40892
18	1.09393	1.19615	1.30734	1.42825	1.70243	2.02582	2.40662	2.85434	3.37993	3.99602	5.55992	7.68997	12.37545	26.62333	55.51115
19	1.09940	1.20811	1.32695	1.45681	1.75351	2.10685	2.52695	3.02560	3.61653	4.31570	6.11591	8.61276	14.23177	31.94800	69.38894
20	1.10490	1.22019	1.34686	1.48595	1.80611	2.19112	2.65330	3.20714	3.86968	4.66096	6.72750	9.64629	16.36654	38.33760	86.73617
22	1.11597	1.24472	1.38756	1.54598	1.91610	2.36992	2.92526	3.60354	4.43040	5.43654	8.14027	12.10031	21.64475	55.20614	135.5253
24	1.12716	1.26973	1.42950	1.60844	2.03279	2.56330	3.22510	4.04893	5.07237	6.34118	9.84973	15.17863	28.62518	79.49685	211.7582
26	1.13846	1.29526	1.47271	1.67342	2.15659	2.77247	3.55567	4.54938	5.80735	7.39635	11.91818	19.04007	37.85680	114.4755	330.8722
28	1.14987	1.32129	1.51722	1.74102	2.28793	2.99870	3.92013	5.11169	6.64884	8.62711	14.42099	23.88382	50.06561	164.8447	516.9879
30	1.16140	1.34785	1.56308	1.81136	2.42726	3.24340	4.32194	5.74349	7.61226	10.06266	17.44940	29.95992	66.21177	237.3763	807.7936
32	1.17304	1.37494	1.61032	1.88454	2.57508	3.50806	4.76494	6.45339	8.71527	11.73708	21.11378	37.58173	87.56507	341.8219	1262.177
34	1.18480	1.40258	1.65900	1.96068	2.73191	3.79432	5.25335	7.25103	9.97811	13.69013	25.54767	47.14252	115.80480	492.2235	1972.152
36	1.19668	1.43077	1.70914	2.03989	2.89828	4.10393	5.79182	8.14726	11.42394	15.96817	30.91268	59.13557	153.15185	708.8019	3081.488
38	1.20868	1.45953	1.76080	2.12230	3.07478	4.43881	6.38548	9.15425	13.07927	18.62528	37.40434	74.17966	202.54332	1020.675	4814.825
40	1.22079	1.48886	1.81402	2.20804	3.26204	4.80102	7.03999	10.28572	14.97446	21.72452	45.25926	93.05097	267.86355	1469.772	7523.164
45	1.25162	1.56481	1.95421	2.43785	3.78160	5.84118	8.98501	13.76461	21.00245	31.92045	72.89048	163.9876	538.76927	3657.262	22958.87
50	1.28323	1.64463	2.10524	2.69159	4.38391	7.10668	11.46740	18.42015	29.45703	46.90161	117.3909	289.0022	1083.65744	9100.438	70064.92
100	1.64667	2.70481	4.43205	7.24465	19.21863	50.50495	131.5013	339.3021	867.7163	2199.761	13780.61	83522.27	117×10^4	828×10^5	491×10^7

Table 2
Present Value of $1

$$P = F_n(1 + r)^{-n}$$

r = discount rate; n = number of periods until payment; F_n = \$1

Periods = n	½%	1%	1½%	2%	3%	4%	5%	6%	7%	8%	10%	12%	15%	20%	25%
1	.99502	.99010	.98522	.98039	.97087	.96154	.95238	.94340	.93458	.92593	.90909	.89286	.86957	.83333	.80000
2	.99007	.98030	.97066	.96117	.94260	.92456	.90703	.89000	.87344	.85734	.82645	.79719	.75614	.69444	.64000
3	.98515	.97059	.95632	.94232	.91514	.88900	.86384	.83962	.81630	.79383	.75131	.71178	.65752	.57870	.51200
4	.98025	.96098	.94218	.92385	.88849	.85480	.82270	.79209	.76290	.73503	.68301	.63552	.57175	.48225	.40960
5	.97537	.95147	.92826	.90573	.86261	.82193	.78353	.74726	.71299	.68058	.62092	.56743	.49718	.40188	.32768
6	.97052	.94205	.91454	.88797	.83748	.79031	.74622	.70496	.66634	.63017	.56447	.50663	.43233	.33490	.26214
7	.96569	.93272	.90103	.87056	.81309	.75992	.71068	.66506	.62275	.58349	.51316	.45235	.37594	.27908	.20972
8	.96089	.92348	.88771	.85349	.78941	.73069	.67684	.62741	.58201	.54027	.46651	.40388	.32690	.23257	.16777
9	.95610	.91434	.87459	.83676	.76642	.70259	.64461	.59190	.54393	.50025	.42410	.36061	.28426	.19381	.13422
10	.95135	.90529	.86167	.82035	.74409	.67556	.61391	.55839	.50835	.46319	.38554	.32197	.24718	.16151	.10737
11	.94661	.89632	.84893	.80426	.72242	.64958	.58468	.52679	.47509	.42888	.35049	.28748	.21494	.13459	.08590
12	.94191	.88745	.83639	.78849	.70138	.62460	.55684	.49697	.44401	.39711	.31863	.25668	.18691	.11216	.06872
13	.93722	.87866	.82403	.77303	.68095	.60057	.53032	.46884	.41496	.36770	.28966	.22917	.16253	.09346	.05498
14	.93256	.86996	.81185	.75788	.66112	.57748	.50507	.44230	.38782	.34046	.26333	.20462	.14133	.07789	.04398
15	.92792	.86135	.79985	.74301	.64186	.55526	.48102	.41727	.36245	.31524	.23939	.18270	.12289	.06491	.03518
16	.92330	.85282	.78803	.72845	.62317	.53391	.45811	.39365	.33873	.29189	.21763	.16312	.10686	.05409	.02815
17	.91871	.84438	.77639	.71416	.60502	.51337	.43630	.37136	.31657	.27027	.19784	.14564	.09293	.04507	.02252
18	.91414	.83602	.76491	.70016	.58739	.49363	.41552	.35034	.29586	.25025	.17986	.13004	.08081	.03756	.01801
19	.90959	.82774	.75361	.68643	.57029	.47464	.39573	.33051	.27651	.23171	.16351	.11611	.07027	.03130	.01441
20	.90506	.81954	.74247	.67297	.55368	.45639	.37689	.31180	.25842	.21455	.14864	.10367	.06110	.02608	.01153
22	.89608	.80340	.72069	.64684	.52189	.42196	.34185	.27751	.22571	.18394	.12285	.08264	.04620	.01811	.00738
24	.88719	.78757	.69954	.62172	.49193	.39012	.31007	.24698	.19715	.15770	.10153	.06588	.03493	.01258	.00472
26	.87838	.77205	.67902	.59758	.46369	.36069	.28124	.21981	.17220	.13520	.08391	.05252	.02642	.00874	.00302
28	.86966	.75684	.65910	.57437	.43708	.33348	.25509	.19563	.15040	.11591	.06934	.04187	.01997	.00607	.00193
30	.86103	.74192	.63976	.55207	.41199	.30832	.23138	.17411	.13137	.09938	.05731	.03338	.01510	.00421	.00124
32	.85248	.72730	.62099	.53063	.38834	.28506	.20987	.15496	.11474	.08520	.04736	.02661	.01142	.00293	.00079
34	.84402	.71297	.60277	.51003	.36604	.26355	.19035	.13791	.10022	.07305	.03914	.02121	.00864	.00203	.00051
36	.83564	.69892	.58509	.49022	.34503	.24367	.17266	.12274	.08754	.06262	.03235	.01691	.00653	.00141	.00032
38	.82735	.68515	.56792	.47119	.32523	.22529	.15661	.10924	.07646	.05369	.02673	.01348	.00494	.00098	.00021
40	.81914	.67165	.55126	.45289	.30656	.20829	.14205	.09722	.06678	.04603	.02209	.01075	.00373	.00068	.00013
45	.79896	.63905	.51171	.41020	.26444	.17120	.11130	.07265	.04761	.03133	.01372	.00610	.00186	.00027	.00004
50	.77929	.60804	.47500	.37153	.22811	.14071	.08720	.05429	.03395	.02132	.00852	.00346	.00092	.00011	.00001
100	.60729	.36971	.22563	.13803	.05203	.01980	.00760	.00295	.00115	.00045	.00007	.00001	.00000	.00000	.00000

Table 3
Future Value of Annuity of $1 in Arrears

$$F = \frac{(1+r)^n - 1}{r}$$

r = interest rate; n = number of payments

No. of Payments = n	½%	1%	1½%	2%	3%	4%	5%	6%	7%	8%	10%	12%	15%	20%	25%
1	1.00000	1.00000	1.00000	1.00000	1.00000	1.00000	1.00000	1.00000	1.00000	1.00000	1.00000	1.00000	1.00000	1.00000	1.00000
2	2.00500	2.01000	2.01500	2.02000	2.03000	2.04000	2.05000	2.06000	2.07000	2.08000	2.10000	2.12000	2.15000	2.20000	2.25000
3	3.01503	3.03010	3.04523	3.06040	3.09090	3.12160	3.15250	3.18360	3.21490	3.24640	3.31000	3.37440	3.47250	3.64000	3.81250
4	4.03010	4.06040	4.09090	4.12161	4.18363	4.24646	4.31013	4.37462	4.43994	4.50611	4.64100	4.77933	4.99338	5.36800	5.76563
5	5.05025	5.10101	5.15227	5.20404	5.30914	5.41632	5.52563	5.63709	5.75074	5.86660	6.10510	6.35285	6.74238	7.44160	8.20703
6	6.07550	6.15202	6.22955	6.30812	6.46841	6.63298	6.80191	6.97532	7.15329	7.33593	7.71561	8.11519	8.75374	9.92992	11.25879
7	7.10588	7.21354	7.32299	7.43428	7.66246	7.89829	8.14201	8.39384	8.65402	8.92280	9.48717	10.08901	11.06680	12.91590	15.07349
8	8.14141	8.28567	8.43284	8.58297	8.89234	9.21423	9.54911	9.89747	10.25980	10.63663	11.43589	12.29969	13.72682	16.49908	19.84186
9	9.18212	9.36853	9.55933	9.75463	10.15911	10.58280	11.02656	11.49132	11.97799	12.48756	13.57948	14.77566	16.78584	20.79890	25.80232
10	10.22803	10.46221	10.70272	10.94972	11.46388	12.00611	12.57789	13.18079	13.81645	14.48656	15.93742	17.54874	20.30372	25.95868	33.25290
11	11.27917	11.56683	11.86326	12.16872	12.80780	13.48635	14.20679	14.97164	15.78360	16.64549	18.53117	20.65458	24.34928	32.15042	42.56613
12	12.33556	12.68250	13.04121	13.41209	14.19203	15.02581	15.91713	16.86994	17.88845	18.97713	21.38428	24.13313	29.00167	39.58050	54.20766
13	13.39724	13.80933	14.23683	14.68033	15.61779	16.62684	17.71298	18.88214	20.14064	21.49530	24.52271	28.02911	34.35192	48.49660	68.75958
14	14.46423	14.94742	15.45038	15.97394	17.08632	18.29191	19.59863	21.01507	22.55049	24.21492	27.97498	32.39260	40.50471	59.19592	86.94947
15	15.53655	16.09690	16.68214	17.29342	18.59891	20.02359	21.57856	23.27597	25.12902	27.15211	31.72248	37.27971	47.58041	72.03511	109.6868
16	16.61423	17.25786	17.93237	18.63929	20.15688	21.82453	23.65749	25.67253	27.88805	30.32428	35.94973	42.75328	55.71747	87.44213	138.1085
17	17.69730	18.43044	19.20136	20.01207	21.76159	23.69751	25.84037	28.21288	30.84022	33.75023	40.54470	48.88367	65.07509	105.9306	173.6357
18	18.78579	19.61475	20.48938	21.41231	23.41444	25.64541	28.13238	30.90565	33.99903	37.45024	45.59917	55.74971	75.83636	128.1167	218.0446
19	19.87972	20.81090	21.79672	22.84056	25.11687	27.67123	30.53900	33.75999	37.37896	41.44626	51.15909	63.43968	88.21181	154.7400	273.5558
20	20.97912	22.01900	23.12367	24.29737	26.87037	29.77808	33.06595	36.78559	40.99549	45.76196	57.27500	72.05244	102.44358	186.6880	342.9447
22	23.19443	24.47159	25.83758	27.29898	30.53678	34.24797	38.50521	43.39229	49.00574	55.45676	71.40275	92.50258	137.63164	271.0307	538.1011
24	25.43196	26.97346	28.63352	30.42186	34.42647	39.08260	44.50200	50.81558	58.17667	66.76476	88.49733	118.1552	184.16784	392.4842	843.0329
26	27.69191	29.52563	31.51397	33.67091	38.55304	44.31174	51.11345	59.15638	68.67647	79.95442	109.1818	150.3339	245.71197	567.3773	1319.489
28	29.97452	32.12910	34.48148	37.05121	42.93092	49.96758	58.40258	68.52811	80.69769	95.33883	134.2099	190.6989	327.10408	819.2233	2063.952
30	32.28002	34.78489	37.53868	40.56808	47.57542	56.08494	66.43885	79.05819	94.46079	113.2832	164.4940	241.3327	434.74515	1181.881	3227.174
32	34.60862	37.49407	40.68829	44.22703	52.50276	62.70147	75.29883	90.88978	110.2181	134.2135	201.1378	304.8477	577.10046	1704.109	5044.710
34	36.96058	40.25770	43.93309	48.03380	57.73018	69.85791	85.06696	104.1838	128.2588	158.6267	245.4767	384.5210	765.36535	2456.118	7884.609
36	39.33610	43.07688	47.27597	51.99437	63.27594	77.59831	95.83632	119.1209	148.9135	187.1022	299.1268	484.4631	1014.34568	3539.009	12321.95
38	41.73545	45.95272	50.71989	56.11494	69.15945	85.97034	107.7095	135.9042	172.5610	220.3159	364.0434	609.8305	1343.62216	5098.373	19255.30
40	44.15885	48.88637	54.26789	60.40198	75.40126	95.02552	120.7998	154.7620	199.6351	259.0565	442.5926	767.0914	1779.09031	7343.858	30088.66
45	50.32416	56.48107	63.61420	71.89271	92.71986	121.0294	159.7002	212.7435	285.7493	386.5056	718.9048	1358.230	3585.12846	18281.31	91831.50
50	56.64516	64.46318	73.68283	84.57940	112.7969	152.6671	209.3480	290.3359	406.5289	573.7702	1163.909	2400.018	7217.71628	45497.19	280255.7
100	129.33370	170.4814	228.8030	312.2323	607.2877	1237.624	2610.025	5638.368	12381.66	27484.52	137796.1	696010.5	783×10^4	414×10^6	196×10^8

Note: To convert from this table to values of an annuity in advance, determine the annuity in arrears above for one more period and subtract 1.00000.

Table 4
Present Value of an Annuity of $1 in Arrears

$$P_A = \frac{1 - (1 + r)^{-n}}{r}$$

r = discount rate; n = number of payments

No. of Payments = n	½%	1%	1½%	2%	3%	4%	5%	6%	7%	8%	10%	12%	15%	20%	25%
1	.99502	.99010	.98522	.98039	.97087	.96154	.95238	.94340	.93458	.92593	.90909	.89286	.86957	.83333	.80000
2	1.98510	1.97040	1.95588	1.94156	1.91347	1.88609	1.85941	1.83339	1.80802	1.78326	1.73554	1.69005	1.62571	1.52778	1.44000
3	2.97025	2.94099	2.91220	2.88388	2.82861	2.77509	2.72325	2.67301	2.62432	2.57710	2.48685	2.40183	2.28323	2.10648	1.95200
4	3.95050	3.90197	3.85438	3.80773	3.71710	3.62990	3.54595	3.46511	3.38721	3.31213	3.16987	3.03735	2.85498	2.58873	2.36160
5	4.92587	4.85343	4.78264	4.71346	4.57971	4.45182	4.32948	4.21236	4.10020	3.99271	3.79079	3.60478	3.35216	2.99061	2.68928
6	5.89638	5.79548	5.69719	5.60143	5.41719	5.24212	5.07569	4.91732	4.76654	4.62288	4.35526	4.11141	3.78448	3.32551	2.95142
7	6.86207	6.72819	6.59821	6.47199	6.23028	6.00205	5.78637	5.58238	5.38929	5.20637	4.86842	4.56376	4.16042	3.60459	3.16114
8	7.82296	7.65168	7.48593	7.32548	7.01969	6.73274	6.46321	6.20979	5.97130	5.74664	5.33493	4.96764	4.48732	3.83716	3.32891
9	8.77906	8.56602	8.36052	8.16224	7.78611	7.43533	7.10782	6.80169	6.51523	6.24689	5.75902	5.32825	4.77158	4.03097	3.46313
10	9.73041	9.47130	9.22218	8.98259	8.53020	8.11090	7.72173	7.36009	7.02358	6.71008	6.14457	5.65022	5.01877	4.19247	3.57050
11	10.67703	10.36763	10.07112	9.78685	9.25262	8.76048	8.30641	7.88687	7.49867	7.13896	6.49506	5.93770	5.23371	4.32706	3.65640
12	11.61893	11.25508	10.90751	10.57534	9.95400	9.38507	8.86325	8.38384	7.94269	7.53608	6.81369	6.19437	5.42062	4.43922	3.72512
13	12.55615	12.13374	11.73153	11.34837	10.63496	9.98565	9.39357	8.85268	8.35765	7.90378	7.10336	6.42355	5.58315	4.53268	3.78010
14	13.48871	13.00370	12.54338	12.10625	11.29607	10.56312	9.89864	9.29498	8.74547	8.24424	7.36669	6.62817	5.72448	4.61057	3.82408
15	14.41662	13.86505	13.34323	12.84926	11.93794	11.11839	10.37966	9.71225	9.10791	8.55948	7.60608	6.81086	5.84737	4.67547	3.85926
16	15.33993	14.71787	14.13126	13.57771	12.56110	11.65230	10.83777	10.10590	9.44665	8.85137	7.82371	6.97399	5.95423	4.72956	3.88741
17	16.25863	15.56225	14.90765	14.29187	13.16612	12.16567	11.27407	10.47726	9.76322	9.12164	8.02155	7.11963	6.04716	4.77463	3.90993
18	17.17277	16.39827	15.67256	14.99203	13.75351	12.65930	11.68959	10.82760	10.05909	9.37189	8.20141	7.24967	6.12797	4.81219	3.92794
19	18.08236	17.22601	16.42617	15.67846	14.32380	13.13394	12.08532	11.15812	10.33560	9.60360	8.36492	7.36578	6.19823	4.84350	3.94235
20	18.98742	18.04555	17.16864	16.35143	14.87747	13.59033	12.46221	11.46992	10.59401	9.81815	8.51356	7.46944	6.25933	4.86958	3.95388
22	20.78406	19.66038	18.62082	17.65805	15.93692	14.45112	13.16300	12.04158	11.06124	10.20074	8.77154	7.64465	6.35866	4.90943	3.97049
24	22.56287	21.24339	20.03041	18.91393	16.93554	15.24696	13.79864	12.55036	11.46933	10.52876	8.98474	7.78432	6.43377	4.93710	3.98111
26	24.32402	22.79520	21.39863	20.12104	17.87684	15.98277	14.37519	13.00317	11.82578	10.80998	9.16095	7.89566	6.49056	4.95632	3.98791
28	26.06769	24.31644	22.72672	21.28127	18.76411	16.66306	14.89813	13.40616	12.13711	11.05108	9.30657	7.98442	6.53351	4.96967	3.99226
30	27.79405	25.80771	24.01584	22.39646	19.60044	17.29203	15.37245	13.76483	12.40904	11.25778	9.42691	8.05518	6.56598	4.97894	3.99505
32	29.50328	27.26959	25.26714	23.46833	20.38877	17.87355	15.80268	14.08404	12.64656	11.43500	9.52638	8.11159	6.59053	4.98537	3.99683
34	31.19555	28.70267	26.48173	24.49959	21.13184	18.41120	16.19290	14.36814	12.85401	11.58693	9.60857	8.15656	6.60910	4.98984	3.99797
36	32.87102	30.10751	27.66068	25.48884	21.83225	18.90828	16.54685	14.62099	13.03521	11.71719	9.67651	8.19241	6.62314	4.99295	3.99870
38	34.52985	31.48466	28.80505	26.44064	22.49246	19.36786	16.86789	14.84602	13.19347	11.82887	9.73265	8.22099	6.63375	4.99510	3.99917
40	36.17223	32.83469	29.91585	27.35548	23.11477	19.79277	17.15909	15.04630	13.33171	11.92461	9.77905	8.24378	6.64178	4.99660	3.99947
45	40.20720	36.09451	32.55234	29.49016	24.51871	20.72004	17.77407	15.45583	13.60552	12.10840	9.86281	8.28252	6.65429	4.99863	3.99983
50	44.14279	39.19612	34.99969	31.42361	25.72976	21.48218	18.25593	15.76186	13.80075	12.23348	9.91481	8.30450	6.66051	4.99945	3.99994
100	78.54264	63.02888	51.62470	43.09835	31.59891	24.50500	19.84791	16.61755	14.26925	12.49432	9.99927	8.33323	6.66666	5.00000	4.00000

Note: To convert from this table to values of an annuity in advance, determine the annuity in arrears above for one less period and add 1.00000.

Table 5
Bond Values in Percent of Par:
10 Percent Semiannual Coupons
Bond value $= 10/r + (100 - 10/r)(1 + r/2)^{-2n}$
r = yield to maturity; n = years to maturity

Years to Maturity	Market Yield Percent per Year Compounded Semiannually										
	8.0	9.0	9.5	10.0	10.5	11.0	12.0	13.0	14.0	15.0	20.0
0.5	100.9615	100.4785	100.2387	100.0	99.7625	99.5261	99.0566	98.5915	98.1308	97.6744	95.4545
1.0	101.8861	100.9363	100.4665	100.0	99.5368	99.0768	98.1666	97.2691	96.3840	95.5111	91.3223
1.5	102.7751	101.3745	100.6840	100.0	99.3224	98.6510	97.3270	96.0273	94.7514	93.4987	87.5657
2.0	103.6299	101.7938	100.8917	100.0	99.1186	98.2474	96.5349	94.8613	93.3256	91.6267	84.1507
2.5	104.4518	102.1950	101.0899	100.0	98.9251	97.8649	95.7876	93.7665	91.7996	89.8853	81.0461
5.0	108.1109	103.9564	101.9541	100.0	98.0928	96.2312	92.6399	89.2168	85.9528	82.8398	69.2772
9.0	112.6593	106.0800	102.9803	100.0	97.1339	94.3770	89.1724	84.3513	79.8818	75.7350	58.9929
9.5	113.1339	106.2966	103.0838	100.0	97.0393	94.1962	88.8419	83.8979	79.3288	75.1023	58.1754
10.0	113.5903	106.5040	103.1827	100.0	96.9494	94.0248	88.5301	83.4722	78.8120	74.5138	57.4322
15.0	117.2920	108.1444	103.9551	100.0	96.2640	92.7331	86.2352	80.4120	75.1819	70.4740	52.8654
19.0	119.3679	109.0250	104.3608	100.0	95.9194	92.0976	85.1540	79.0312	73.6131	68.8015	51.3367
19.5	119.5845	109.1148	104.4017	100.0	95.8854	92.0357	85.0509	78.9025	73.4701	68.6525	51.2152
20.0	119.7928	109.2008	104.4408	100.0	95.8531	91.9769	84.9537	78.7817	73.3366	68.5140	51.1047
25.0	121.4822	109.8810	104.7461	100.0	95.6068	91.5342	84.2381	77.9132	72.3985	67.5630	50.4259
30.0	122.6235	110.3190	104.9381	100.0	95.4591	91.2751	83.8386	77.4506	71.9216	67.1015	50.1642
40.0	123.9154	110.7827	105.1347	100.0	95.3175	91.0345	83.4909	77.0728	71.5560	66.7690	50.0244
50.0	124.5050	110.9749	105.2124	100.0	95.2666	90.9521	83.3825	76.9656	71.4615	66.6908	50.0036

Table 6
Bond Values in Percent of Par:
12 Percent Semiannual Coupons
Bond value $= 12/r + (100 - 12/r)(1 + r/2)^{-2n}$
$r =$ yield to maturity; $n =$ years to maturity

Market Yield Percent per Year Compounded Semiannually

Years to Maturity	8.0	9.0	10.0	11.0	11.5	12.0	12.5	13.0	14.0	15.0	20.0
0.5	101.9231	101.4354	100.9524	100.4739	100.2364	100.0	99.7647	99.5305	99.0654	98.6047	96.3636
1.0	103.7722	102.8090	101.8594	100.9232	100.4600	100.0	99.5433	99.0897	98.1920	97.3067	93.0579
1.5	105.5502	104.1234	102.7232	101.3490	100.6714	100.0	99.3348	98.6758	97.3757	96.0992	90.0526
2.0	107.2598	105.3813	103.5459	101.7526	100.8713	100.0	99.1387	98.2871	96.6128	94.9760	87.3205
2.5	108.9036	106.5850	104.3295	102.1351	101.0603	100.0	98.9540	97.9222	95.8998	93.9312	84.8369
5.0	116.2218	111.8691	107.7217	103.7688	101.8620	100.0	98.1816	96.4056	92.9764	89.7039	75.4217
9.0	125.3186	118.2400	111.6896	105.6230	102.7585	100.0	97.3432	94.7838	89.9409	85.4410	67.1944
9.5	126.2679	118.8899	112.0853	105.8038	102.8449	100.0	97.2642	94.6326	89.6644	85.0614	66.5403
10.0	127.1807	119.5119	112.4622	105.9752	102.9266	100.0	97.1898	94.4907	89.4060	84.7083	65.9457
15.0	134.5841	124.4333	115.3724	107.2669	103.5353	100.0	96.6489	93.4707	87.5910	82.2844	62.2923
19.0	138.7357	127.0750	116.8679	107.9024	103.8283	100.0	96.3995	93.0104	86.8065	81.2809	61.0694
19.5	139.1690	127.3445	117.0170	107.9643	103.8565	100.0	96.3760	92.9675	86.7351	81.1915	60.9722
20.0	139.5855	127.6024	117.1591	108.0231	103.8832	100.0	96.3539	92.9272	86.6683	81.1084	60.8838
25.0	142.9644	129.6430	118.2559	108.4658	104.0822	100.0	96.1930	92.6377	86.1993	80.5378	60.3407
30.0	145.2470	130.9570	118.9293	108.7249	104.1960	100.0	96.1053	92.4835	85.9608	80.2609	60.1314
40.0	147.8308	132.3480	119.5965	108.9655	104.2982	100.0	96.0313	92.3576	85.7780	80.0614	60.0195
50.0	149.0100	132.9248	119.8479	109.0479	104.3316	100.0	96.0093	92.3219	85.7307	80.0145	60.0029

Glossary[1]

A

AAA. *American Accounting Association.*

Abacus. A scholarly journal containing articles on theoretical aspects of accounting. Published twice a year by the Sydney University Press, Sydney, Australia.

abatement. A complete or partial cancellation of a levy imposed by a government unit.

abnormal spoilage. Actual spoilage exceeding that expected to occur if operations are normally efficient. Usual practice treats this cost as an *expense* of the period rather than as a *product cost.* Contrast with *normal spoilage.*

aboriginal cost. In public utility accounting, the *acquisition cost* of an *asset* incurred by the first *entity* devoting that asset to public use. Most public utility regulation is based on aboriginal cost. If it were not, then public utilities could exchange assets among themselves at ever-increasing prices in order to raise the rate base and, then, prices based thereon.

absorbed overhead. *Overhead* costs allocated to individual products at some *overhead rate.*

absorption costing. The generally accepted method of *costing* that assigns all types of *manufacturing costs* (direct material and labor as well as fixed and variable overhead) to units produced. Sometimes called "full costing." Contrast with *direct costing.*

Accelerated Cost Recovery System. ACRS. A form of *accelerated depreciation* enacted by the Congress in 1981. The system provides percentages of the asset's cost to be depreciated each year for tax purposes. *Salvage value* is ignored. For income tax purposes, almost all *depreciable assets* are grouped into one of four classes: those to be depreciated for tax purposes over 3 years (such as automobiles), those to be depreciated for tax purposes over 5 years (such as most machinery and equipment), those to be depreciated over 10 years (such as railroad

tankcars), and those to be depreciated over 15 years (such as most plant assets owned by public utilities). For financial reporting, the depreciable life is chosen as the best estimate of its useful life. Income tax *timing differences* for depreciation are created when a shorter life is used for tax reporting than for financial reporting.

accelerated depreciation. Any method of calculating *depreciation* charges where the charges become progressively smaller each period. Examples are *double-declining-balance* and *sum-of-the-years'-digits* methods.

acceptance. A written promise to pay that is equivalent to a *promissory note.*

account. Any device for accumulating additions and subtractions relating to a single *asset, liability,* or *owners' equity* item, including *revenues* and *expenses.*

account form. The form of *balance sheet* where *assets* are shown on the left and *equities* are shown on the right. Contrast with *report form.* See also *T-account.*

account payable. A *liability* representing an amount owed to a *creditor,* usually arising from purchase of *merchandise* or materials and supplies; not necessarily due or past due. Normally, a *current* liability.

account receivable. A claim against a *debtor* usually arising from sales or services rendered; not necessarily due or past due. Normally, a *current* asset.

accountability center. *Responsibility center.*

accountancy. The British word for *accounting.* In the United States, it means the theory and practice of accounting.

Accountants' Index. A publication of the *AICPA* that indexes, in detail, the accounting literature of the period.

accountant's opinion. *Auditor's report.*

accountant's report. *Auditor's report.*

accounting. An *information system* conveying information about a specific *entity.* The information is in financial

---

[1]Many words and phrases in the Glossary are defined in terms of other words and phrases. Terms in a given definition that are themselves explained elsewhere under their own listings are *italicized.*

terms and is restricted to information that can be made reasonably precise. The *AICPA* defines accounting as a service activity whose "function is to provide quantitative information, primarily financial in nature, about economic entities that is intended to be useful in making economic decisions."

accounting changes. As defined by *APB Opinion* No. 20, a change in (1) an *accounting principle* (such as a switch from *FIFO* to *LIFO* or from *sum-of-the-years'-digits* to *straight-line depreciation*), (2) an accounting estimate (such as estimated useful lives or salvage value of depreciable assets and estimates of *warranty* costs or *uncollectible accounts*), and (3) the reporting *entity*. Changes of type (1) should be disclosed. The cumulative effect of the change on *retained earnings* at the start of the period during which the change was made should be included in reported earnings for the period of change. Changes of type (2) should be treated as affecting only the period of change and, if necessary, future periods. The reasons for changes of type (3) should be disclosed and, in statements reporting on operations of the period of the change, the effect of the change on all other periods reported on for comparative purposes should also be shown. In some cases (such as a change from *LIFO* to another inventory *flow assumption* or in the method of accounting for long-term construction contracts), changes of type (1) are treated like changes of type (3). That is, for these changes all statements shown for prior periods must be restated to show the effect of adopting the change for those periods as well. See *all-inclusive concept* and *accounting errors*.

accounting conventions. Methods or procedures used in accounting. This term tends to be used when the method or procedure has not been given official authoritative sanction by a pronouncement of a group such as the *APB*, *FASB*, or *SEC*. Contrast with *accounting principles*.

accounting cycle. The sequence of accounting procedures starting with *journal entries* for various transactions and events and ending with the *financial statements* or, perhaps, the *post-closing trial balance*.

accounting entity. See *entity*.

accounting equation. *Assets* = Equities. Assets = Liabilities + Owners' Equity.

accounting errors. Arithmetic errors and misapplications of *accounting principles* in previously published financial statements that are corrected in the current period with direct *debits* or *credits* to *retained earnings*. In this regard, they are treated like *prior-period adjustments*, but, technically, they are not classified by *APB Opinion* No. 9 as prior-period adjustments. See *accounting changes* and contrast with changes in accounting estimates as described there.

accounting event. Any occurrence that is recorded in the accounting records.

accounting methods. *Accounting principles*. Procedures for carrying out accounting principles.

accounting period. The time period for which *financial statements* that measure *flows*, such as the *income statement* and the *statement of changes in financial position*, are prepared. Should be clearly identified on the financial statements. See *interim statements*.

accounting policies. *Accounting principles* adopted by a specific *entity*.

accounting principles. The methods or procedures used in accounting for events reported in the *financial statements*. This term tends to be used when the method or procedure has been given official authoritative sanction by a pronouncement of a group such as the *APB*, *FASB*, or *SEC*. Contrast with *accounting conventions* and *conceptual framework*.

Accounting Principles Board. See *APB*.

accounting procedures. See *accounting principles*, but usually this term refers to the methods for implementing accounting principles.

accounting rate of return. Income for a period divided by average investment during the period. Based on income, rather than discounted cash flows and, hence, a poor decision-making aid or tool. See *ratio*.

Accounting Research Bulletin. ARB. The name of the official pronouncements of the former *Committee on Accounting Procedure* of the *AICPA*. Fifty-one bulletins were issued between 1939 and 1959. *ARB No. 43* summarizes the first 42 bulletins.

Accounting Research Study. ARS. One of a series of studies published by the Director of Accounting Research of the *AICPA* "designed to provide professional accountants and others interested in the development of accounting with a discussion and documentation of accounting problems." Fifteen such studies were published between 1961 and 1974.

The Accounting Review. Scholarly publication of the *American Accounting Association*.

Accounting Series Release. ASR. See *SEC*.

accounting standards. *Accounting principles*.

Accounting Standards Executive Committee. AcSEC. The senior technical committee of the *AICPA*, authorized to speak for the AICPA in the areas of *financial accounting* and reporting as well as *cost accounting*.

accounting system. The procedures for collecting and summarizing financial data in a firm.

Accounting Terminology Bulletin. ATB. One of four releases of the Committee on Terminology of the *AICPA* issued in the period 1953-1957.

Accounting Trends and Techniques. An annual publication of the *AICPA* that surveys the reporting practices of 600 large corporations. It presents tabulations of specific practices, terminology, and disclosures along with illustrations taken from individual annual reports.

accounts receivable turnover. *Net sales* on account for a period divided by the average balance of net accounts receivable. See *ratio.*

accretion. Increase in economic worth through physical change, usually said of a natural resource such as an orchard, caused by natural growth. Contrast with *appreciation.*

accrual. Recognition of an *expense (or revenue)* and the related *liability (or asset)* that is caused by an *accounting event,* frequently by the passage of time, and that is not signaled by an explicit cash transaction. For example, the recognition of interest expense or revenue (or wages, salaries, or rent) at the end of a period even though no explicit cash transaction is made at that time. Cash flow occurs after accounting recognition; contrast with *deferral.*

accrual basis of accounting. The method of recognizing *revenues* as *goods* are sold (or delivered) and as *services* are rendered, independent of the time when cash is received. *Expenses* are recognized in the period when the related revenue is recognized, independent of the time when cash is paid out. *SFAC No. 1* says that "accrual accounting attempts to record the financial effects on an enterprise of transactions and other events and circumstances that have cash consequences for the enterprise in the periods in which those transactions, events, and circumstances occur rather than only in the periods in which cash is received or paid by the enterprise." Contrast with the *cash basis of accounting.* See *accrual* and *deferral.* The basis would more correctly be called "accrual/deferral" accounting.

accrued. Said of a *revenue (expense)* that has been earned (recognized) even though the related *receivable (payable)* is not yet due. This adjective should not be used as part of an account title. Thus, we prefer to use Interest Receivable (Payable) as the account title, rather than Accrued Interest Receivable (Payable). See *matching convention.* See *accrual.*

accrued depreciation. An incorrect term for *accumulated depreciation.* Acquiring an asset with cash, capitalizing it, and then amortizing its cost over periods of use is a process of *deferral* and allocation, not of *accrual.*

accrued payable. A *payable* usually resulting from the passage of time. For example, *salaries* and *interest* accrue as time passes. See *accrued.*

accrued receivable. A *receivable* usually resulting from the passage of time. See *accrued.*

accumulated depreciation. A preferred title for the *contra-asset* account that shows the sum of *depreciation* charges on an asset since it was acquired. Other titles used are *allowance* for *depreciation* (acceptable term) and *reserve* for *depreciation* (unacceptable term).

accurate presentation. The qualitative accounting objective suggesting that information reported in financial statements should correspond as precisely as possible with the economic effects underlying transactions and events. See *fair presentation* and *full disclosure.*

acid test ratio. *Quick ratio.*

acquisition cost. Of an *asset,* the net *invoice* price plus all *expenditures* to place and ready the asset for its intended use. The other expenditures might include legal fees, transportation charges, and installation costs.

ACRS. *Accelerated Cost Recovery System.*

AcSEC. *Accounting Standards Executive Committee* of the *AICPA.*

activity accounting. *Responsibility accounting.*

activity-based depreciation. *Production method of depreciation.*

actual cost (basis). *Acquisition* or *historical cost.* Contrast with *standard* cost.

actual costing. Method of allocating costs to products using actual *direct materials,* actual *direct labor,* and actual *factory overhead.* Contrast with *normal costing* and *standard cost system.*

actuarial. Usually said of computations or analyses that involve both *compound interest* and probabilities, such as the computation of the *present value* of a life-contingent *annuity.* Sometimes the term is used if only one of the two is involved.

actuarial accrued liability. A 1981 *report* of the Joint Committee on Pension Terminology (of various actuarial societies) stated that the terms "supplemental actuarial value," "past service cost," and "prior service cost" are no longer recommended and that this term be used instead. It will take a few years for this term to become standard in accounting. The Joint Committee defines this term as "the portion . . . of the actuarial present value of pension plan benefits . . . not provided for by future normal costs." *Present value* at a given time of a *pension plan's* unrecognized benefits assigned to employees for their service before that given time. Called "prior service cost" in *APB Opinion* No. 8 and supplemental actuarial value in *SFAS No. 35;* includes *past service cost.* Such obligations are not recognized as liabilities in the accounting records but must be disclosed in the notes to the financial statements; contrast with *normal cost.*

additional paid-in capital. An acceptable alternative title for the *capital contributed in excess of par (or stated) value account.*

adequate disclosure. *Fair presentation* of *financial statements* requires *disclosure* of *material* items. This *auditing standard* does not, however, require publicizing all information detrimental to a company. For example, the company may be threatened with a lawsuit and disclosure might seem to require a *debit* to a *loss* account and a *credit* to an *estimated liability* account. But the mere making of this entry might adversely affect the actual outcome of the suit. Such entries need not be made, although impending suits should be disclosed.

adjunct account. An *account* that accumulates additions to another account. For example, Premium on Bonds Payable is adjunct to the liability Bonds Payable; the effective liability is the sum of the two account balances at a given date. Contrast with *contra account*.

adjusted acquisition (historical) cost. Cost adjusted to a *constant dollar amount* to reflect *general price level changes*. See also *book value*.

adjusted bank balance of cash. The *balance* shown on the statement from the bank plus or minus amounts, such as for unrecorded deposits or outstanding checks, to reconcile the bank's balance with the correct cash balance. See *adjusted book balance of cash*.

adjusted basis. The *basis* used to compute gain or loss for tax purposes upon disposition of an *asset*. See also *book value*.

adjusted book balance of cash. The *balance* shown in the firm's account for cash in the bank plus or minus amounts, such as for *notes* collected by the bank or bank service charges, to reconcile the account balance with the correct cash balance. See *adjusted book balance of cash*.

adjusted trial balance. *Trial balance* taken after *adjusting entries* but before *closing entries*. Contrast with *pre-* and *post-closing trial balances*. See *unadjusted trial balance* and *post-closing trial balance*. See also *work sheet*.

adjusting entry. An entry made at the end of an *accounting period* to record a *transaction* or other *accounting event*, which for some reason has not been recorded or has been improperly recorded during the accounting period. An entry to update the accounts. See *work sheet*.

adjustment. A change in an *account* produced by an *adjusting* entry. Sometimes the term is used to refer to the process of restating *financial statement* amounts to *constant dollars*.

administrative expense. An *expense* related to the enterprise as a whole, as contrasted to expenses related to more specific functions such as manufacturing or selling.

admission of partner. Legally, when a new partner joins a *partnership*, the old partnership is dissolved and a new one comes into being. In practice, however, the old accounting records may be kept in use and the accounting entries reflect the manner in which the new partner joined the firm. If the new partner merely purchases the interest of another partner, the only accounting is to change the name for one capital account. If the new partner contributes *assets* and *liabilities* to the partnership, then the new assets must be recognized with debits and the liabilities and other sources of capital with credits. See *bonus method*.

ADR. See *asset depreciation range*.

advances from (by) customers. A preferred title for the *liability* account representing *receipts* of *cash* in advance of delivering the *goods* or rendering the *service* (that will cause *revenue* to be recognized). Sometimes called "deferred revenue" or "deferred income."

advances to affiliates. *Loans* by a parent company to a *subsidiary*. Frequently combined with "investment in subsidiary" as "investments and advances to subsidiary" and shown as a *noncurrent asset* on the parent's *balance sheet*. These advances are eliminated in *consolidated financial statements*.

advances to suppliers. A preferred term for *disbursements* of cash in advance of receiving *assets* or *services*.

adverse opinion. An *auditor's report* stating that the financial statements are not fair or are not in accord with *GAAP*.

affiliated company. Said of a company controlling or controlled by another company.

after closing. *Post-closing trial balance*; said of a *trial balance* at the end of the period.

aftercost. Said of *expenditures* to be made subsequent to *revenue* recognition. For example, *expenditures* for *repairs* under warranty are aftercosts. Proper recognition of aftercosts involves a debit to expense at the time of the sale and a credit to an *estimated liability*. When the liability is discharged, the debit is to the estimated liability and the credit is to the assets consumed.

agency fund. An account for *assets* received by governmental units in the capacity of trustee or agent.

agency theory. A branch of economics relating the behavior of principals (such as owner nonmanagers or bosses) and their *agents* (such as nonowner managers or subordinates). The principal assigns responsibility and authority to the agent, but the agent has his or her own risks and preferences different from those of the principal. The principal is unable to observe all activities of the agent. Thus the principal must be careful about the kinds of observations of or reports sought from the agent, perhaps through an independent *auditor,* and the sorts of incentive contracts that the principal makes with the agent.

agent. One authorized to transact business, including executing contracts, for another.

aging accounts receivable. The process of classifying *accounts receivable* by the time elapsed since the claim came into existence for the purpose of estimating the amount of uncollectible accounts receivable as of a given date. See *sales contra, estimated uncollectibles*, and *allowance for uncollectibles*.

aging schedule. A listing of *accounts receivable*, classified by age, used in *aging accounts receivable*.

AICPA. American Institute of Certified Public Accountants. The national organization that represents *CPAs*. See *AcSEC*. It oversees the writing and grading of the Uniform CPA Examination. Each state, however, sets its own requirements for becoming a CPA in that state. See *certified public accountant*.

all financial resources. All *assets* less all *liabilities*. Sometimes the *statement of changes in financial position* explains the changes in all financial resources rather than only the changes in *working capital*.

all-capital earnings rate. *Rate of return on assets*.

all-inclusive (income) concept. Under this concept, no distinction is drawn between *operating* and *nonoperating revenues* and *expenses*; thus, the only entries to retained earnings are for *net income* and *dividends*. Under this concept all *income, gains*, and *losses* are reported in the *income statement*; thus, events usually reported as *prior-period adjustments* and as *corrections of errors* are included in net income. This concept in its pure form is not the basis of *GAAP*, but *APB Opinions* No. 9 and 30 move very far in this direction. They do permit retained earnings entries for prior-period adjustments and correction of errors.

allocate. To spread a *cost* from one *account* to several accounts, to several products or activities, or to several periods.

allocation of income taxes. See *deferred income tax*.

allowance. A balance sheet *contra account* generally used for *receivables* and depreciable assets. See *sales (or purchase) allowance* for another use of this term.

allowance for funds used during construction. One principle of public utility regulation and rate setting is that customers should pay the full costs of producing the services (e.g., electricity) that they use—nothing more and nothing less. Thus an electric utility is even more careful than other businesses to capitalize into an *asset account* the full costs, but no more, of producing a new electric power generating plant. One of the costs of building a new plant is the *interest* cost on money tied up during construction. If *funds* are explicitly borrowed by an ordinary business, the journal entry for interest of $1,000 is typically:

Interest Expense	1,000	
Interest Payable		1,000

Interest expense for the period.

If the firm is constructing a new plant, then another entry would be made capitalizing interest into the plant-under-construction account:

Construction Work in Progress	750	
Interest Expense		750

Capitalize relevant portion of interest relating to construction work in progress into the asset account.

The cost of the *plant asset* is increased; when the plant is used, *depreciation* is charged; the interest will become an expense through the depreciation process in the later periods of use, not currently as the interest is paid. Thus the full cost of the electricity generated during a given period is reported as expense in that period.

But suppose, as is common, that the electric utility does not explicitly borrow the funds, but uses some of its own funds, including funds raised from equity shares as well as from debt. Even though there is not explicit interest expense, there is the *opportunity cost* of the funds. Put another way, the cost of the plant under construction is not less in an economic sense just because the firm used its own cash rather than borrowing. The public utility using its own funds, on which $750 of interest would be payable if the funds had been explicitly borrowed, will make the following entry:

Construction Work in Progress	750	
Allowance for Funds Used During Construction		750

Recognition of interest, an opportunity cost, on own funds used.

The allowance account is a form of *revenue*, to appear on the income statement, and will be closed to Retained Earnings, increasing it. On the *funds statement*, it is an income or revenue item not producing funds and so must be subtracted from net income in deriving *funds provided by operations*. SFAS No. 34 specifically prohibits nonutility companies from capitalizing the opportunity cost (interest) on own funds used into plant under construction.

allowance for uncollectibles (accounts receivable). A *contra* to Accounts Receivable that shows the estimated amount of *accounts receivable* that will not be collected. When such an allowance is used, the actual *write-off* of specific accounts receivable (*debit* allowance, *credit* specific account) does not affect *revenue* or *expense* at the time of the write-off. The revenue reduction is recognized when the allowance is credited; the amount of the credit to the allowance may be based on a percentage of sales on account for a period of time or computed from *aging accounts receivable*. This contra account enables an estimate to be shown of the amount of receivables that will be collected without identifying specific uncollectible accounts. See *allowance method*.

allowance method. A method of attempting to *match* all *expenses* of a transaction with its associated *revenues*. Usually involves a debit to expense and a credit to an *estimated liability*, such as for estimated warranty expenditures, or a debit to a revenue (*contra*) account and a credit to an asset (*contra*) account, such as for uncollectible accounts. See *allowance for uncollectibles* for further explanation. When the allowance method is used for *sales discounts*, sales are recorded at *gross invoice* prices (not reduced by the amounts of discounts made available). An estimate of the amount of discounts to be taken is debited to a *revenue contra account* and *credited* to an allowance account, shown contra to *accounts receivable*.

American Accounting Association. AAA. An organization primarily for academic accountants, but open to all interested in accounting. It publishes *The Accounting Review*.

American Institute of Certified Public Accountants. See *AICPA*.

American Stock Exchange. AMEX. ASE. A public market where various corporate *securities* are traded.

AMEX. *American Stock Exchange.*

amortization. Strictly speaking, the process of liquidating or extinguishing ("bringing to death") a *debt* with a series of payments to the *creditor* (or to a *sinking fund*). From that usage has evolved a related use involving the accounting for the payments themselves: an "amortization schedule" for a mortgage, which is a table showing the allocation between *interest* and *principal*. The term has come to mean writing off ("liquidating") the cost of an asset. In this context it means the general process of *allocating acquisition cost* of an asset to either the periods of benefit as *expenses* or to *inventory* accounts as *product costs*. Called *depreciation* for *plant assets, depletion* for *wasting assets* (natural resources), and "amortization" for *intangibles. SFAC No. 3* refers to amortization as "the accounting process of reducing an amount by periodic payments or write-downs." The expressions "unamortized debt discount or premium" and "to amortize debt discount or premium" relate to *accruals*, not to *deferrals*. The expressions "amortization of long-term assets" and "to amortize long-term assets" refer to deferrals, not accruals.

analysis of changes in working capital accounts. The *statement of changes in financial position* explains the causes of the changes in *working capital* during a period. This part of the statement, which may appear in footnotes, shows the net changes in the specific working capital accounts that have been explained in the main section of the statement.

analysis of variances. See *variance analysis*.

annual report. A report for shareholders and other interested parties prepared once a year; includes a *balance sheet*, an *income statement*, a *statement of changes in financial position*, a reconciliation of changes in *owners' equity* accounts, a *summary of significant accounting principles*, other explanatory *notes*, the *auditor's report*, and comments from management about the year's events. See *10-K* and *financial statements*.

annuitant. One who receives an *annuity*.

annuity. A series of payments, usually made at equally spaced time intervals.

annuity certain. An *annuity* payable for a definite number of periods. Contrast with *contingent annuity*.

annuity due. An *annuity* whose first payment is made at the start of period 1 (or at the end of period 0). Contrast with *annuity in arrears*.

annuity in advance. An *annuity due*.

annuity in arrears. An *ordinary annuity* whose first payment occurs at the end of the first period.

annuity method of depreciation. See *compound interest depreciation*.

antidilutive. Said of a *potentially dilutive security* that will increase *earnings per share* if it is *exercised* or *converted* into common stock. In computing *primary* and *fully diluted earnings per share*, antidilutive securities may not be assumed to be exercised or converted and hence do not affect reported earnings per share in a given period.

APB. Accounting Principles Board of the *AICPA*. It set *accounting principles* from 1959 through 1973, issuing 31 *APB Opinions*. It was superseded by the *FASB*.

APB Opinion. The name given to pronouncements of the *APB* that make up much of *generally accepted accounting principles*; there are 31 *APB Opinions*, issued from 1962 through 1973.

APB Statement. The *APB* issued four *Statements* between 1962 and 1970. The *Statements* were approved by at least two-thirds of the board, but they are recommendations, not requirements. For example, *Statement* No. 3 (1969) suggested the publication of *constant dollar financial statements* but did not require them.

APBs. An abbreviation used for *APB Opinions*.

application of funds. Any transaction that reduces *funds* (however "funds" is defined). A *use of funds*.

applied cost. A *cost* that has been *allocated* to a department, product, or activity; need not be based on actual costs incurred.

applied overhead. *Overhead costs* charged to departments, products, or activities.

appraisal. The process of obtaining a valuation for an *asset* or *liability* that involves expert opinion rather than evaluation of explicit market transactions.

appraisal method of depreciation. The periodic *depreciation* charge is the difference between the beginning- and end-of-period appraised values of the *asset* if that difference is positive. If negative, there is no charge. Not generally accepted.

appreciation. An increase in economic worth caused by rising market prices for an *asset*. Contrast with *accretion*.

appropriated retained earnings. See *retained earnings, appropriated*.

appropriation. In governmental accounting, an *expenditure* authorized for a specified amount, purpose, and time.

appropriation account. In governmental accounting, an account set up to record specific authorizations to spend; it is credited with appropriation amounts. *Expenditures* during the period and *encumbrances* outstanding at the end of the period are closed (debited) to this account at the end of the period.

ARB. Accounting Research Bulletin.

arbitrage. Strictly speaking, the simultaneous purchase in one market and sale in another of a *security* or commodity in hope of making a *profit* on price differences in the different markets. Often this term is used loosely when the item sold is somewhat different from the item purchased; for example, the sale of shares of *common stock* and the simultaneous purchase of a *convertible bond* that is convertible into identical common shares.

arm's length. Said of a transaction negotiated by unrelated parties, each acting in his or her own self-interest; the basis for a *fair market value* determination.

arrears. Said of *cumulative preferred stock dividends* that have not been declared up to the current date. See *annuity in arrears* for another context.

ARS. Accounting Research Study.

articles of incorporation. Document filed with state authorities by persons forming a corporation. When the document is returned with a certificate of incorporation, it becomes the corporation's *charter*.

articulate. Said of the relationship between any operating statement (for example, *income statement* or *statement of changes in financial position*) and *comparative balance sheets*, where the operating statement explains (or reconciles) the change in some major balance sheet category (for example, *retained earnings* or *working capital*).

ASE. *American Stock Exchange*.

ASR. Accounting Series Release. See *SEC*.

assess. To value property for the purpose of property taxation; the assessment is computed by the taxing authority. To levy a charge on the owner of property for improvements thereto, such as for sewers or sidewalks.

assessed valuation. A dollar amount for real estate or other property used by a government as a basis for levying taxes. The amount may or may not bear some relation to *market value*.

asset. *SFAC No. 3* defines assets as "probable future economic benefits obtained or controlled by a particular entity as a result of past transactions. An asset has three essential characteristics: (a) it embodies a probable future benefit that involves a capacity, singly or in combination with other assets, to contribute directly or indirectly to future net cash inflows, (b) a particular enterprise can obtain the benefit and control others' access to it, and (c) the transaction or other event giving rise to the enterprise's right to or control of the benefit has already occurred." A footnote points out that "probable" means that which can be reasonably expected or believed but is neither certain nor proved. May be *tangible* or *intangible*, *short-term* (current) or *long-term* (noncurrent).

asset depreciation range. ADR. The range of *depreciable lives* allowed by the *Internal Revenue Service* before the adoption of *ACRS* for a specific depreciable *asset*.

asset turnover. Net sales divided by average assets. See *ratio*.

assignment of accounts receivable. Transfer of the legal ownership of an *account receivable* through its sale. Contrast with *pledging* accounts receivable, where the receivables serve as *collateral* for a *loan*.

ATB. Accounting Terminology Bulletin.

at par. Said of a *bond* or *preferred stock* issued or selling at its *face amount*.

attachment. The laying claim to the *assets* of a borrower or debtor by a lender or creditor when the borrower has failed to pay debts on time.

attest. Rendering of an *opinion* by an auditor that the *financial statements* are fair. This procedure is called the "attest function" of the CPA. See *fair presentation*.

attribute measured. When making physical measurements, such as of a person, one needs to decide the units with which to measure, such as inches or centimeters or pounds or grams. One chooses the attribute—height or weight—independently of the measuring unit—English or metric. In conventional accounting the attribute measured is *historical cost* and the measuring unit is *nominal dollars*. Some theorists argue that accounting is more useful when the attribute measured is *current cost*. Others argue that accounting is more useful when the measuring unit is *constant dollars*. Some, including us, think both changes from conventional accounting should be made. The attribute historical cost can be measured in nominal dollars or in constant dollars. The attribute current cost can also be measured in nominal dollars or constant dollars. Choosing between two attributes and two measuring units implies four different accounting systems. Each of these four has its uses.

audit. Systematic inspection of accounting records involving analyses, tests, and *confirmations*. See *internal audit*.

audit committee. A committee of the board of directors of a *corporation*, usually consisting of outside directors who nominate the independent auditors and discuss the auditors' work with them. If the auditors believe that certain matters should be brought to the attention of shareholders, the auditors first bring these matters to the attention of the audit committee.

Audit Guides. See *Industry Audit Guides*.

audit program. The procedures followed by the *auditor* in carrying out the *audit*.

audit trail. A reference accompanying an *entry*, or *posting*, to an underlying source record or document. A good audit trail is essential for efficiently checking the accuracy of accounting entries. See *cross-reference*.

Auditing Research Monograph. Publication series of the *AICPA*.

auditing standards. A set of 10 standards promulgated by the *AICPA*, including three general standards, three standards of field work, and four standards of reporting. According to the *AICPA*, these standards "deal with the measures of the quality of the performance and the objectives to be attained," rather than with specific auditing procedures.

Auditing Standards Advisory Council. An *AICPA* committee.

Auditing Standards Board. Operating committee of the *AICPA* promulgating auditing rules.

auditor. One who checks the accuracy, fairness, and general acceptability of accounting records and statements, and then *attests* to them.

auditor's opinion. *Auditor's report*.

auditor's report. The auditor's statement of the work done and an opinion of the *financial statements*. Opinions are usually unqualified ("clean"), but may be *qualified*, or the auditor may disclaim an opinion in the report. Often called the "accountant's report." See *adverse opinion*.

AudSEC. The former Auditing Standards Executive Committee of the *AICPA*, now functioning as the *Auditing Standards Board*.

authorized capital stock. The number of *shares* of stock that can be issued by a corporation; specified by the *articles of incorporation*.

average. The arithmetic mean of a set of numbers; obtained by summing the items and dividing by the number of items.

average collection period of receivables. See *ratio*.

average tax rate. The rate found by dividing *income tax expense* by *net income* before taxes. Contrast with *marginal tax rate, statutory tax rate*.

average-cost flow assumption. An *inventory flow assumption* where the cost of units is the *weighted average* cost of the *beginning inventory* and purchases. See *inventory equation*.

avoidable cost. A *cost* that will cease if an activity is discontinued. An *incremental* or *variable cost*. See *programmed cost*.

B

backlog. Orders for which insufficient *inventory* is on hand for current delivery and which will be filled in a later period.

backlog depreciation. In *current cost accounting*, a problem arising for the *accumulated depreciation* on *plant assets*. Consider an *asset* costing $10,000 with a 10-year life depreciated with the *straight-line method*. Assume that a similar asset has a current cost of $10,000 at the end of the first year but $12,000 at the end of the second year. Assume that the depreciation charge is based on the average current cost during the year, $10,000 for the first year and $11,000 for the second. The depreciation charge for the first year is $1,000 and for the second is $1,100 $(=.10 \times \$11,000)$, so the *accumulated depreciation account* is $2,100 after 2 years. Note that at the end of the second year, 20 percent of the asset's future benefits have been used, so the accounting records based on current costs must show a *net book value* of $9,600 $(=.80 \times \$12,000)$, which would result if accumulated depreciation of $2,400 were subtracted from a current cost of $12,000. But the sum of the depreciation charges has been only $2,100. The *journal entry* to increase the accumulated depreciation account requires a *credit* to that account of $300. The question arises, what account is to be debited? That is the problem of backlog depreciation. Some theorists would *debit* an *income* account and others would *debit* a *balance sheet owners' equity* account without reducing current-period earnings. The answer to the question of what to do with the debit is closely tied to the problem of how *holding gains* are recorded. When the asset account is debited for $2,000 to increase the recorded amount from $10,000 to $12,000, a holding gain or $2,000 must be recorded with a credit. Many theorists believe that whatever account is credited for the holding gains is the same account that should be debited for backlog depreciation. Sometimes called "catch-up depreciation."

bad debt. An *uncollectible account receivable*; see *sales contra, estimated uncollectibles*.

bad debt expense. See *sales contra, estimated uncollectibles*.

bad debt recovery. Collection, perhaps partial, of a specific account receivable previously written off as uncollectible. If the *allowance method* is used, the *credit* is usually to the *allowance* account. If the direct write-off method is used, the credit is to a *revenue account*.

bailout period. In a *capital budgeting* context, the total time that must elapse before net accumulated cash inflows from a project, including potential *salvage value* of assets at various times, equal or exceed the accumulated cash outflows. Contrast with *payback period*, which assumes completion of the project and uses terminal salvage value. Bailout is superior to payback because bailout takes into account, at least to some degree, the *present value* of the cash flows after the termination date being considered. The potential salvage value at any time includes some estimate of the flows that can occur after that time.

balance. The sum of *debit* entries minus the sum of *credit* entries in an *account*. If positive, the difference is called a debit balance; if negative, a credit balance.

balance sheet. Statement of financial position that shows *Total Assets* = Total Liabilities + Owners' Equity.

balance sheet account. An account that can appear on a balance sheet. A *permanent account*; contrast with *temporary account*.

bank balance. The amount of the balance in a checking account shown on a *bank statement*. Compare with *adjusted bank balance* and see *bank reconciliation schedule*.

bank prime rate. See *prime rate*.

bank reconciliation schedule. A schedule that shows how the difference between the book balance of the cash

in a bank account and the bank's statement can be explained. Takes into account the amount of such items as checks issued that have not cleared or deposits that have not been recorded by the bank, as well as errors made by the bank or the firm.

bank statement. A statement sent by the bank to a checking account customer showing deposits, checks cleared, and service charges for a period, usually 1 month.

bankrupt. Said of a company whose *liabilities* exceed its *assets* where a legal petition has been filed and accepted under the bankruptcy law. A bankrupt firm is usually, but need not be, *insolvent*.

base stock method. A method of inventory valuation that assumes that there is a minimum normal or base stock of goods that must be kept on hand at all times for effective continuity of operations. This base quantity is valued at *acquisition cost* of the inventory on hand in the earliest period when inventory was on hand. The method is not allowable for income tax purposes and is no longer used, but is generally considered to be the forerunner of the *LIFO* method.

basic accounting equation. *Accounting equation*.

basis. *Acquisition cost*, or some substitute therefor, of an asset used in computing gain or loss upon disposition or retirement. *Attribute measured*.

basket purchase. Purchase of a group of assets for a single price; *costs* must be assigned to each of the assets so that the individual items can be recorded in the *accounts*.

bear. One who believes that security prices will fall. A "bear market" refers to a time when stock prices are generally declining. Contrast with *bull*.

bearer bond. See *registered bond* for contrast and definition.

beginning inventory. Valuation of *inventory* on hand at the beginning of the accounting period.

betterment. An *improvement*, usually *capitalized*.

bid. An offer to purchase, or the amount of the offer.

big bath. A *write off* of a substantial amount of costs previously treated as *assets*. Usually caused when a corporation drops a line of business that required a large investment but that proved to be unprofitable. Sometimes used to describe a situation where a corporation takes a large write off in one period in order to free later periods of gradual write offs of those amounts. In this sense, it frequently occurs when there is a change in top management.

Big Eight. Eight large *public accounting (CPA)* partnerships; in alphabetical order: Arthur Andersen & Co.; Coopers & Lybrand; Deloitte Haskins & Sells; Ernst & Whinney; Peat, Marwick, Mitchell & Co.; Price Waterhouse & Co.; Touche Ross & Co.; and Arthur Young & Company. Klynveld Main Goerdeler (KMG) is actually larger than many of these when worldwide operations are measured. An international firm, KMG's U.S. affiliate is Main Hurdman.

Big Nine. See *Big Eight*.

bill. An *invoice* of charges and *terms of sale* for *goods and services*. Also, a piece of currency.

bill of materials. A specification of the quantities of *direct materials* expected to be used to produce a given job or quantity of output.

board of directors. The governing body of a corporation elected by the shareholders.

bond. A certificate to show evidence of debt. The *par value* is the *principal* or face amount of the bond payable at maturity. The *coupon rate* is the amount of interest payable in 1 year divided by the principal amount. Coupon bonds have attached to them coupons that can be redeemed at stated dates for interest payments. Normally, bonds carry semiannual coupons.

bond conversion. The act of exchanging *convertible bonds* for *preferred* or *common stock*.

bond discount. From the standpoint of the issuer of a *bond* at the issue date, the excess of the *par value* of a bond over its initial sales price; at later dates the excess of par over the sum of initial issue price plus the portion of discount already amortized. From the standpoint of a bondholder, the difference between par value and selling price when the bond sells below par.

bond indenture. The contract between an issuer of *bonds* and the bondholders.

bond premium. Exactly parallel to *bond discount* except that the issue price (or current selling price) is higher than *par value*.

bond ratings. Ratings of corporate and *municipal bond* issues by Moody's Investors Service and by Standard & Poor's Corporation, based on the issuer's existing *debt* level, its previous record of payment, the *coupon rate* on the bonds, and the safety of the *assets* or *revenues* that are committed to paying off *principal* and *interest*. Moody's top rating is Aaa; Standard & Poor's is AAA.

bond redemption. Retirement of *bonds*. A *corporation* acquires its *bonds* from the *bondholders*. Bonds can be retired at *maturity* or before, either by paying *cash*, exchanging *shares* of *stock* (if the bond is *convertible*), by serial retirement (for *serial bonds*), by setting up a *sinking fund*, or by replacing one bond issue with another (*bond refunding*).

bond refunding. To incur *debt*, usually through the issue of new *bonds*, intending to use the proceeds to retire an *outstanding* bond issue.

bond sinking fund. See *sinking fund*.

bond table. A table showing the current price of a *bond* as a function of the *coupon rate*, years to *maturity*, and effective *yield to maturity* (or *effective rate*).

bonus. Premium over normal *wage* or *salary*, paid usually for meritorious performance.

bonus method. When a new partner is admitted to a *partnership* and the new partner is to be credited with *capital* in excess proportion to the amount of *tangible* assets he or she contributes, two methods may be used to recognize this excess, say, $10,000. First, $10,000 may be transferred from the old partners to the new one. This is the bonus method. Second, goodwill in the amount of $10,000 may be recognized as an asset, with the credit to the new partner's capital account. This is the *goodwill method*. (Notice that the new partner's percentage of total ownership is not the same under the two methods.) If the new partner is to be credited with capital in smaller proportion than the amount of contribution, then there will be bonus or goodwill for the old partners.

book. As a verb, to record a transaction. As a noun, usually plural, the *journals* and *ledgers*. As an adjective, see *book value*.

book inventory. An *inventory* amount that results, not from physical count, but from the amount of beginning inventory plus *invoice* amounts of net purchases less invoice amounts of *requisitions* or withdrawals; implies a *perpetual* method.

book of original entry. A *journal*.

book value. The amount shown in the books or in the *accounts* for an *asset*, *liability*, or *owners' equity* item. Generally used to refer to the net amount of an *asset* or group of assets shown in the account that records the asset and reductions, such as for *amortization*, in its cost. Of a firm, the excess of total assets over total liabilities. *Net assets*.

book value per share of common stock. Common *shareholders' equity* divided by the number of shares of *common stock outstanding*. See *ratio*.

bookkeeping. The process of analyzing and recording transactions in the accounting records.

boot. The additional money paid or received along with a used item in a trade-in or exchange transaction for another item. See *trade-in transaction*.

borrower. See *loan*.

branch. A sales office or other unit of an enterprise physically separated from the home office of the enterprise but not organized as a legally separate *subsidiary*. The term is rarely used to refer to manufacturing units.

branch accounting. An accounting procedure that enables the financial position and operations of each *branch* to be reported separately but later combined for published statements.

breakeven analysis. See *breakeven chart*.

breakeven chart. Two kinds of breakeven charts are shown here. The charts are based on the information for a month shown below. Revenue is $30 per unit.

Cost Classification	Variable Cost, per Unit	Fixed Cost, per Month
Manufacturing costs:		
Direct material	$ 4	—
Direct labor	9	—
Overhead	4	$3,060
Total manufacturing costs	$17	$3,060
Selling, general, and administrative costs.	5	1,740
Total cost	$22	$4,800

The cost-volume-profit graph presents the relationship of changes in volume to the amount of *profit*, or *income*. On such a graph, total *revenue* and total *costs* for each volume level are indicated and profit or loss at any volume can be read directly from the chart. The profit-volume graph does not show revenues and costs but more readily indicates profit (or loss) at various output levels.

Two caveats should be kept in mind about these graphs. Although the curve depicting *variable cost* and total cost is shown as being a straight line for its entire length, it is likely that at very low or very high levels of output, variable cost would probably be different from $22 per unit. The variable cost figure was probably established by studies of operations at some broad central area of production, called the *relevant range*. For very low (or very high) levels of activity, the chart may not be applicable. For this reason, the total cost and profit-loss curves are sometimes shown as dotted lines at lower (or higher) volume levels. Second, this chart is simplified because it assumes a single-product firm. For a multiproduct firm, the horizontal axis would have to be stated in dollars rather than in physical units of output. Breakeven charts for multiproduct firms necessarily assume that constant proportions of the several products are sold, and changes in this mixture as well as in costs or selling prices would invalidate such a chart.

breakeven point. The volume of sales required so that total *revenues* and total *costs* are equal. May be expressed in units (*fixed costs/contribution per unit*) or in sales dollars [selling price per unit × (fixed costs/contribution per unit)].

A. Cost-Volume-Profit Graph

B. Profit-Volume Graph

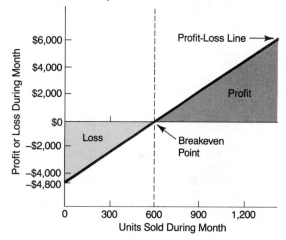

budget. A financial plan used to estimate the results of future operations. Frequently used to help control future operations. In governmental operations, budgets often become the law.

budgetary accounts. In governmental accounting, the accounts that reflect estimated operations and financial condition, as affected by estimated *revenues, appropriations*, and *encumbrances*. Contrast to *proprietary accounts*, which record the transactions.

budgetary control. Management of a governmental (nongovernmental) unit in accordance with an official (approved) *budget* in order to keep total expenditures within authorized (planned) limits.

budgeted cost. See *standard cost* for definition and contrast.

budgeted statements. *Pro forma* statements prepared before the event or period occurs.

bull. One who believes that security prices will rise. A "bull market" refers to a time when stock prices are generally rising. Contrast with *bear*.

burden. See *overhead costs*.

business combination. As defined in *APB Opinion* No. 16, the bringing together into a single accounting *entity* of two or more incorporated or unincorporated businesses. The *merger* will be accounted for either with the *purchase method* or the *pooling-of-interests method*. See *conglomerate*.

business entity. *Entity*. *Accounting entity*.

bylaws. The rules adopted by the shareholders of a corporation that specify the general methods for carrying out the functions of the corporation.

by-product. A *joint product* whose sales value is so small relative to the sales value of the other joint product(s) that it does not receive normal accounting treatment. The costs assigned to by-products reduce the costs of the main product(s). By-products are allocated a share of joint costs such that the expected gain or loss upon their sale is zero. Thus, by-products are shown in the *accounts* at *net realizable value*.

C

CA. *Chartered accountant*.

call. An option to buy *shares* of a publicly-traded corporation at a fixed price during a fixed time span. Contrast with *put*.

call premium. See *callable bond*.

call price. See *callable bond*.

callable bond. A *bond* for which the issuer reserves the right to pay a specific amount, the call price, to retire the obligation before *maturity* date. If the issuer agrees to pay more than the *face amount* of the bond when called, the excess of the payment over the face amount is the "call premium."

Canadian Institute of Chartered Accountants. The national organization that represents *chartered accountants* in Canada.

cancelable lease. See *lease*.

capacity. Stated in units of product, the amount that can be produced per unit of time. Stated in units of input, such as *direct labor* hours, the amount of input that can be used in production per unit of time. This measure of output or input is used in allocating *fixed costs* if the amounts producible are normal, rather than maximum, amounts.

capacity costs. A *fixed cost* incurred to provide a firm with the capacity to produce or to sell. Consists of *standby costs* and *enabling costs*. Contrast with *programmed costs*.

capacity variance. Standard fixed *overhead* rate per unit of normal *capacity* (or base activity) times (units of base activity budgeted or planned for a period minus actual units of base activity worked or assigned to product during the period). Often called a "volume variance."

capital. *Owners' equity* in a business. Often used, equally correctly, to mean the total assets of a business. Sometimes used to mean *capital assets*. Sometimes used to mean *cash* or *funds*.

capital asset. Properly used, a designation for income tax purposes that describes property held by a taxpayer, except *cash*, inventoriable *assets*, goods held primarily for sale, most depreciable property, *real estate, receivables*, certain *intangibles*, and a few other items. Sometimes this term is used imprecisely to describe *plant* and *equipment*, which are clearly not capital assets under the income tax definition. Often the term is used to refer to an *investment* in *securities*.

capital budget. Plan of proposed outlays for acquiring long-term *assets* and the means of *financing* the acquisition.

capital budgeting. The process of choosing *investment* projects for an enterprise by considering the *present value* of cash flows and deciding how to raise the funds required by the investment.

capital consumption allowance. The term used for *depreciation expense* in national income accounting and the reporting of funds in the economy.

capital contributed in excess of par (or stated) value. A preferred title for the account that shows the amount received by the issuer for *capital stock* in excess of *par (or stated) value*.

capital expenditure (outlay). An *expenditure* to acquire long-term *assets*.

capital gain. The excess of proceeds over *cost*, or other *basis*, from the sale of a *capital asset* as defined by the Internal Revenue Code. If the capital asset has been held for a sufficiently long time before sale, then the tax on the gain is computed at a rate lower than is used for other gains and ordinary income.

capital lease. A *lease* treated by the *lessee* as both the borrowing of funds and the acquisition of an *asset* to be *amortized*. Both the *liability* and the asset are recognized on the balance sheet. Expenses consist of *interest* on the *debt* and *amortization* of the asset. The *lessor* treats the lease as the sale of the asset in return for a series of future cash receipts. Contrast with *operating lease*.

capital loss. A negative capital gain; see *capital gain*.

capital rationing. In a *capital budgeting* context, the imposing of constraints on the amounts of total capital expenditures in each period.

capital stock. The ownership shares of a corporation. Consists of all classes of *common* and *preferred stock*.

capital structure. The composition of a corporation's equities; the relative proportions of *short-term debt, long-term debt*, and *owners' equity*.

capital surplus. An inferior term for *capital contributed in excess of par (or stated) value*.

capitalization of a corporation. A term used by investment analysts to indicate *shareholders' equity* plus *bonds outstanding*.

capitalization of earnings. The process of estimating the economic worth of a firm by computing the *net present value* of the predicted *net income* (not *cash flows*) of the firm for the future.

capitalization rate. An *interest rate* used to convert a series of payments or receipts or earnings into a single *present value*.

capitalize. To record an *expenditure* that may benefit a future period as an *asset* rather than to treat the expenditure as an *expense* of the period of its occurrence. Whether or not expenditures for advertising or for research and development should be capitalized is controversial, but *SFAS No. 2* requires expensing of *R&D* costs. We believe that expenditures should be capitalized if they lead to future benefits and thus meet the criterion to be an asset.

carryback, carryforward, carryover. The use of losses or tax credits in one period to reduce income taxes payable in other periods. There are three common kinds of carrybacks: for net operating losses, for *capital losses*, and for the *investment credit*. The first two are applied against taxable income and the third against the actual tax. In general, carrybacks are for 3 years, with the earliest year first. Operating losses and the investment credit can be carried forward for 15 years. Corporate capital loss carryforwards are for 5 years. The capital loss for individuals can be carried forward indefinitely.

carrying cost. Costs (such as property taxes and insurance) of holding, or storing, *inventory* from the time of purchase until the time of sale or use.

carrying value (amount). *Book value*.

CASB. Cost Accounting Standards Board. A board of five members authorized by the U.S. Congress to "promulgate cost-accounting standards designed to achieve uniformity and consistency in the cost-accounting principles followed by defense contractors and subcontractors under federal contracts." The *principles* promulgated by the CASB are likely to have considerable weight in practice where the *FASB* has not established a standard. The CASB started work in 1970; although it ceased operations in 1980, its standards have the same force as before.

cash. Currency and coins, negotiable checks, and balances in bank accounts.

cash basis of accounting. In contrast to the *accrual basis of accounting*, a system of accounting in which *revenues* are recognized when *cash* is received and *expenses* are recognized as *disbursements* are made. No attempt is made to *match revenues* and *expenses* in determining *income*. See *modified cash basis*.

cash budget. A schedule of expected cash *receipts* and *disbursements*.

cash collection basis. The *installment method* for recognizing *revenue*. Not to be confused with the *cash basis of accounting*.

cash cycle. The period of time that elapses during which *cash* is converted into *inventories*, inventories are converted into *accounts receivable*, and receivables are converted back into cash. *Earnings cycle*.

cash disbursements journal. A specialized *journal* used to record *expenditures* by *cash* and by *check*. If a *check register* is also used, a cash disbursements journal records only expenditures of currency and coins.

cash discount. A reduction in sales or purchase price allowed for prompt payment.

cash dividend. See *dividend*.

cash equivalent value. A term used to describe the amount for which an *asset* could be sold. *Market value. Fair market price (value)*.

cash flow. Cash *receipts* minus *disbursements* from a given *asset*, or group of assets, for a given period. A term used imprecisely by financial analysts to mean *net income* plus *depreciation changes* as an approximation to *funds* from *operations*.

cash flow statement. A statement similar to the typical *statement of changes in financial position* where the flows of cash, rather than of *working capital*, are explained.

cash receipts journal. A specialized *journal* used to record all *receipts* of *cash*.

cash (surrender) value of life insurance. An amount equal, not to the face value of the policy to be paid in event of death, but to the amount that could be realized if the policy were immediately canceled and traded with the insurance company for cash. If a firm owns a life insurance policy, the policy is reported as an asset at an amount equal to this value.

cash yield. See *yield*.

cashier's check. A bank's own *check* drawn on itself and signed by the cashier or other authorized official. It is a direct obligation of the bank. Compare with *certified check*.

catch-up depreciation. *Backlog depreciation*.

CCA. *Current cost accounting; current value accounting*.

central corporate expenses. General *overhead expenses* incurred in running the corporate headquarters and related supporting activities of a corporation. These expenses are treated as *period expenses*. Contrast with *manufacturing overhead*. A major problem in *line-of-business reporting* is the treatment of these expenses.

certificate. The document that is the physical embodiment of a *bond* or a *share of stock*. A term sometimes used for the *auditor's report*.

Certificate in Management Accounting. *CMA*.

certificate of deposit. Federal law constrains the *rate of interest* that banks can pay. Under current law, banks are allowed to pay a rate higher than the one allowed on a *time deposit* if the depositor promises to leave funds on deposit for several months or more. When the bank receives such funds, it issues a certificate of deposit. The depositor can withdraw the funds before maturity if a penalty is paid.

certified check. The *check* of a depositor drawn on a bank on the face of which the bank has inserted the words "accepted" or "certified" with the date and signature of a bank official. The check then becomes an obligation of the bank. Compare with *cashier's check*.

certified financial statement. A financial statement attested to by an independent *auditor* who is a *CPA*.

certified internal auditor. See *CIA*.

certified public accountant. CPA. An accountant who has satisfied the statutory and administrative requirements of his or her jurisdiction to be registered or licensed as a public accountant. In addition to passing the Uniform CPA Examination administered by the *AICPA*, the CPA must meet certain educational, experience, and moral requirements that differ from jurisdiction to jurisdiction. The jurisdictions are the 50 states, the District of Columbia, Guam, Puerto Rico, and the Virgin Islands.

chain discount. A series of *discount* percentages; for example, if a chain discount of 10 and 5 percent is quoted, then the actual, or *invoice*, price is the nominal, or list, price times .90 times .95, or 85.5 percent of invoice price.

change fund. Coins and currency issued to cashiers, delivery drivers, and so on.

changes, accounting. See *accounting changes*.

changes in financial position. See *statement of changes in financial position*.

charge. As a noun, a *debit* to an account; as a verb, to debit.

charge off. To treat as a *loss* or *expense* an amount originally recorded as an *asset*; use of this term implies that the charge is not in accord with original expectations.

chart of accounts. A list of names and numbers of *accounts* organized systematically.

charter. Document issued by a state government authorizing the creation of a corporation.

chartered accountant. CA. The title used in Australia, Canada, and the United Kingdom for an accountant who has satisfied the requirements of the institute of his or her jurisdiction to be qualified to serve as a *public accountant*. In Canada, each provincial institute or order has the right to administer the examination and set the standards of performance and ethics for Chartered Accountants in its province. For a number of years, however, the provincial organizations have pooled their rights to qualify new members through the Inter-provincial Education Committee and the result is that there are nationally set and graded examinations given in English and French. The pass/fail grade awarded by the Board of Examiners (a subcommittee of the Inter-provincial Education Committee) is rarely deviated from.

check. The Federal Reserve Board defines a check as "a *draft* or order upon a bank or banking house purporting to be drawn upon a deposit of funds for the payment at all events of a certain sum of money to a certain person therein named or to him or his order or to bearer and payable instantly on demand." It must contain the phrase "pay to the order of." The amount shown on the check's face must be clearly readable, and it must have the signature of the drawer. Checks need not be dated, although they usually are. The *balance* in the *cash account* is usually reduced when a check is issued, not later when it clears the bank and reduces cash in bank.

check register. A *journal* to record *checks* issued.

CIA. Certified Internal Auditor. One who has satisfied certain requirements of the *Institute of Internal Auditors* including experience, ethics, education, and passing examinations.

CICA. *Canadian Institute of Chartered Accountants*.

CIF. Cost, insurance, and freight; a term used in contracts along with the name of a given port to indicate that the quoted price includes insurance, handling, and freight charges up to delivery by the seller at the given port.

circulating capital. *Working capital*.

clean opinion. See *auditor's report.*

clean surplus concept. The notion that the only entries to the *retained earnings* account are to record *net income* and *dividends.* See *comprehensive income.* Contrast with *current operating performance concept.* This concept, with minor exceptions, is now controlling in *GAAP.* (See *APB Opinions* Nos. 9 and 30.)

clearing account. An account containing amounts to be transferred to another account(s) before the end of the *accounting period.* Examples are the *income summary* account (whose balance is transferred to *retained earnings*) and the purchases account (whose balance is transferred to *inventory* or to *cost of goods sold*).

close. As a verb, to transfer the *balance* of a *temporary* or *contra* or *adjunct* account to the main account to which it relates; for example, to transfer *revenue* and *expense* accounts directly, or through the *income summary* account, to an *owners' equity* account, or to transfer *purchase discounts* to purchases.

closed account. An account with equal debits and credits, usually as a result of a closing entry. See *ruling an account.*

closing entries. The entries that accomplish the transfer of balances in temporary accounts to the related balance sheet accounts. See *work sheet.*

closing inventory. *Ending inventory.*

CMA. Certificate in Management Accounting. Awarded by the Institute of Management Accounting of the *National Association of Accountants* to those who pass a set of examinations and meet certain experience and continuing education requirements.

CoCoA. *Continuously Contemporary Accounting.*

coding of accounts. The numbering of *accounts*, as for a *chart of accounts*, which is particularly necessary for computerized accounting.

coinsurance. Insurance policies that protect against hazards such as fire or water damage often specify that the owner of the property may not collect the full amount of insurance for a loss unless the insurance policy covers at least some specified "coinsurance" percentage, usually about 80 percent, of the *replacement cost* of the property. Coinsurance clauses induce the owner to carry full, or nearly full, coverage.

COLA. Cost-of-living adjustment. See *indexation.*

collateral. Assets pledged by a *borrower* that will be given up if the *loan* is not paid.

collectible. Capable of being converted into cash; now, if due; later, otherwise.

combination. See *business combination.*

commercial paper. *Short-term notes* issued by corporate borrowers.

commission. Remuneration, usually expressed as a percentage, to employees based on an activity rate, such as sales.

committed costs. *Capacity costs.*

Committee on Accounting Procedure. CAP. Predecessor of the *APB.* The *AICPA's* principles-promulgating body from 1939 through 1959. Its 51 pronouncements are called *Accounting Research Bulletins.*

common cost. *Cost* resulting from use of *raw materials*, a facility (for example, plant or machines), or a service (for example, fire insurance) that benefits several products or departments and must be allocated to those products or departments. Common costs result when multiple products are produced together although they could be produced separately; joint costs occur when multiple products are of necessity produced together. Many writers use common costs and *joint costs* synonymously. See *joint costs, indirect costs,* and *overhead.* See *sterilized allocation.*

common dollar accounting. *Constant dollar accounting.*

common monetary measuring unit. For U.S. corporations, the dollar. See also *stable monetary unit assumption* and *constant dollar accounting.*

common shares. *Shares* representing the class of owners who have residual claims on the assets and earnings of a corporation after all debt and preferred shareholders' claims have been met.

common stock equivalent. A *security* whose primary value arises from its ability to be exchanged for *common shares*; includes *stock options, warrants,* and also *convertible bonds* or *convertible preferred stock* whose cash *yield* for any year within 5 years of issue is less than two-thirds the *prime rate* at the time of issue.

common-size statement. A *percentage statement* usually based on total *assets* or *net sales* or *revenues.*

company-wide control. See *control system.*

comparative (financial) statements. Financial statements showing information for the same company for different times, usually two successive years. Nearly all published financial statements are in this form. Contrast with *historical summary.*

compensating balance. When a bank lends funds to a customer, it often requires that the customer keep on deposit in his or her checking account an amount equal to some percentage—say, 20 percent—of the loan. The amount required to be left on deposit is the compensating balance. Such amounts effectively increase the *interest rate*. The amounts of such balances must be disclosed in *notes* to the *financial statements*.

completed contract method. Recognizing *revenues* and *expenses* for a job or order only when it is finished, except that when a loss on the contract is expected, revenues and expenses are recognized in the period when the loss is first forecast. This term is generally used only for long-term contracts. It is otherwise equivalent to the *sales basis* of *revenue recognition*.

completed sales basis. See *sales basis of revenue recognition*.

compliance audit. Objectively obtaining and evaluating evidence regarding assertions, actions, and events to ascertain the degree of correspondence between them and established performance criteria.

composite depreciation. *Group depreciation* of dissimilar items.

composite life method. *Group depreciation*, which see, for items of unlike kind. The term may be used when a single item, such as a crane, which consists of separate units with differing service lives, such as the chassis, the motor, the lifting mechanism, and so on, is depreciated as a whole rather than treating each of the components separately.

compound entry. A *journal entry* with more than one *debit* or more than one *credit*, or both. See *trade-in transaction* for an example.

compound interest. *Interest* calculated on *principal* plus previously undistributed interest.

compound interest depreciation. A method designed to hold the *rate of return* on an asset constant. First find the *internal rate of return* on the cash inflows and outflows of the asset. The periodic depreciation charge is the cash flow for the period less the internal rate of return multiplied by the asset's book value at the beginning of the period. When the cash flows from the asset are constant over time, the method is sometimes called the "annuity method" of depreciation.

compounding period. The time period for which *interest* is calculated. At the end of the period, the interest may be paid to the lender or added (that is, converted) to principal for the next interest-earning period, which is usually a year or some portion of a year.

comprehensive budget. *Master budget*.

comprehensive income. Defined in *SFAS No. 3* as "the change in equity (net assets) of an entity during a period from transactions and other events and circumstances from nonowner sources. It includes all changes in equity during a period except those resulting from investments by owners and distributions to owners." In this definition, "equity" means *owners' equity*.

comptroller. Same meaning and pronunciation as *controller*.

conceptual framework. A coherent system of interrelated objectives and fundamentals, promulgated by the *FASB* primarily through its *SFAC* publications, expected to lead to consistent standards for *financial accounting* and reporting.

confirmation. A formal memorandum delivered by the customers or suppliers of a company to its independent *auditor* verifying the amounts shown as receivable or payable. The confirmation document is originally sent by the auditor to the customer. If the auditor asks that the document be returned whether the *balance* is correct or incorrect, then it is called a "positive confirmation." If the auditor asks that the document be returned only if there is an error, it is called a "negative confirmation."

conglomerate. *Holding company*. This term is used when the owned companies are in dissimilar lines of business.

conservatism. A *reporting objective* that calls for anticipation of all *losses* and *expenses* but defers recognition of *gains* or *profits* until they are *realized* in *arm's-length* transactions. In the absence of certainty, events are to be reported in a way that tends to minimize cumulative income.

consignee. See *on consignment*.

consignment. See *on consignment*.

consignor. See *on consignment*.

consistency. Treatment of like *transactions* in the same way in consecutive periods so that financial statements will be more comparable than otherwise. The reporting policy implying that procedures, once adopted, should be followed from period to period by a reporting *entity*. See *accounting changes* for the treatment of inconsistencies.

consol. A *bond* that never matures; a *perpetuity* in the form of a bond. Originally issued by Great Britain after the Napoleonic wars to consolidate debt issues of that period. The term arose as an abbreviation for "consolidated annuities."

consolidated financial statements. Statements issued by legally separate companies that show financial position and income as they would appear if the companies were one economic *entity*.

constant dollar. A hypothetical unit of *general purchasing power*, denoted "C$" by the *FASB*.

constant dollar accounting. Accounting where items are measured in *constant dollars*. See *historical cost/constant* *dollar accounting* and *current cost/nominal dollar accounting*.

constant dollar date. The time at which the *general purchasing power* of one *constant dollar* is exactly equal to the *general purchasing power* of one *nominal dollar*; that is, the date when C$1 = $1. When the constant dollar date is mid-period, then the nominal amounts of *revenues* and *expenses* spread evenly throughout the period are equal to their constant dollar amounts, but end-of-period *balance sheet* amounts measured in constant mid-period dollars differ from their nominal dollar amounts. When the constant dollar date is at the end of the period, then the constant dollar and nominal dollar amounts on a balance sheet for that date are identical.

constructive receipt. An item is included in taxable income when the taxpayer can control funds whether or not cash has been received. For example, *interest* added to *principal* in a savings account is deemed by the *IRS* to be constructively received.

Consumer Price Index. CPI. A *price index* computed and issued monthly by the Bureau of Labor Statistics of the U.S. Department of Labor. The index attempts to track the price level of a group of goods and services purchased by the average consumer. The *FASB* requires use of the CPI in *constant dollar accounting*. Contrast with *GNP Implicit Price Deflator*.

contingency. A potential *liability*; if a specified event were to occur, such as losing a lawsuit, a liability would be recognized. The contingency is merely disclosed in notes, rather than shown in the balance sheet. *SFAS No. 5* requires treatment as a contingency until the outcome is "probable" and the amount of payment can be reasonably estimated, perhaps within a range. When the outcome becomes probable (the future event is "likely" to occur) and the amount can be reasonably estimated (using the lower end of a range if only a range can be estimated), then the liability is recognized in the accounts, rather than being disclosed in the notes. A *material* contingency may lead to a qualified, "subject to," auditor's opinion. *Gain* contingencies are not recorded in the accounts, but are merely disclosed in notes.

contingent annuity. An *annuity* whose number of payments depends on the outcome of an event whose timing is uncertain at the time the annuity is set up; for example, an annuity payable for the life of the *annuitant*. Contrast with *annuity certain*.

contingent issue (securities). Securities issuable to specific individuals upon the occurrence of some event, such as the firm's attaining a specified level of earnings.

contingent liability. *Contingency*. This term is to be avoided because it refers to something that is not a *liability* on the *balance sheet*.

continuing appropriation. A governmental *appropriation* automatically renewed without further legislative action until it is altered or revoked or expended.

continuing operations. See *income from continuing operations*.

continuity of operations. The assumption in accounting that the business *entity* will continue to operate long enough for current plans to be carried out. The *going-concern assumption*.

continuous budget. A *budget* that perpetually adds a month in the future as the month just ended is dropped.

continuous compounding. *Compound interest* where the *compounding period* is every instant of time. See *e* for the computation of the equivalent annual or periodic rate.

continuous inventory method. The *perpetual inventory* method.

Continuously Contemporary Accounting. CoCoA. A name coined by the Australian theorist, Raymond J. Chambers, to indicate a combination of *current value accounting* where amounts are measured in *constant dollars* and based on exit values.

contra account. An *account*, such as *accumulated depreciation*, that accumulates subtractions from another account, such as machinery. Contrast with *adjunct account*.

contributed capital. The sum of the balances in *capital stock* accounts plus *capital contributed in excess of par (or stated) value* accounts. Contrast with *donated capital*.

contributed surplus. An inferior term for *capital contributed in excess of par value*.

contribution approach. Method of preparing *income statements* that separates *variable costs* from *fixed costs* in order to emphasize the importance of cost behavior patterns for purposes of planning and control.

contribution margin. *Revenue* from *sales* less all variable *expenses*. See *gross margin*.

contribution per unit. Selling price less *variable costs* per unit.

contributory. Said of a *pension plan* where employees, as well as employers, make payments to a pension *fund*. Note that the provisions for *vesting* are applicable only to the employer's payments. Whatever the degree of vesting of the employer's payments, the employee typically gets back all of his or her payments, with interest, in case of death, or other cessation of employment, before retirement.

control (controlling) account. A summary *account* with totals equal to those of entries and balances that appear in individual accounts in a *subsidiary ledger*. Accounts Receivable is a control account backed up with an account for each customer. The balance in a control account should not be changed unless a corresponding change is made in the subsidiary accounts.

control system. A device for ensuring that actions are carried out according to plan or for safeguarding *assets*. A system for ensuring that actions are carried out according to plan can be designed for a single function within the firm, called "operational control"; for autonomous segments within the firm that generally have responsibility for both revenues and costs, called "divisional control"; or for activities of the firm as a whole, called "company-wide control." Systems designed for safeguarding *assets* are called "internal control" systems.

controllable cost. A *cost* whose amount can be influenced by the way in which operations are carried out, such as advertising costs. These costs can be *fixed* or *variable*. See *programmed costs* and *managed costs*.

controlled company. A company, a majority of whose voting stock is held by an individual or corporation. Effective control can sometimes be exercised when less than 50 percent of the stock is owned.

controller. The title often used for the chief accountant of an organization. Often spelled *comptroller*.

conversion. The act of exchanging a convertible security for another security.

conversion cost. *Direct labor* costs plus factory *overhead* costs incurred in producing a product. That is, the cost to convert raw materials to finished products. *Manufacturing cost*.

conversion period. *Compounding period*. Period during which a *convertible bond* or *convertible preferred stock* can be converted into *common stock*.

convertible bond. A *bond* that may be converted into a specified number of shares of *capital stock* during the *conversion period*.

convertible preferred stock. *Preferred shares* that may be converted into a specified number of shares of *common stock*.

co-product. A product sharing production facilities with another product. For example, if an apparel manufacturer produces shirts and jeans on the same line, these are co-products. Co-products are distinguished from *joint products* and *by-products*, which by their very nature must be produced together, such as the various grades of wood produced in a lumber factory.

copyright. Exclusive right granted by the government to an individual author, composer, playwright, and the like for the life of the individual plus 50 years. If the copyright is granted to a firm, then the right extends 75 years after the original publication. The *economic life* of a copyright may be considerably less than the legal life as, for example, the copyright of this book.

corporation. A legal entity authorized by a state to operate under the rules of the entity's *charter*.

correcting entry. An *adjusting entry* where an improperly recorded *transaction* is properly recorded. Not to be confused with entries that correct *accounting errors*.

correction of errors. See *accounting errors*.

cost. The sacrifice, measured by the *price* paid or required to be paid, to acquire *goods* or *services*. See *acquisition cost* and *replacement cost*. The term "cost" is often used when referring to the valuation of a good or service acquired. When "cost" is used in this sense, a cost is an *asset*. When the benefits of the acquisition (the goods or services acquired) expire, the cost becomes an *expense* or *loss*. Some writers, however, use cost and expense as synonyms. Contrast with *expense*.

cost accounting. Classifying, summarizing, recording, reporting, and allocating current or predicted *costs*. A subset of *managerial accounting*.

Cost Accounting Standards Board. See *CASB*.

cost accumulation. Bringing together, usually in a single *account*, all *costs* of a specified activity. Contrast with *cost allocation*.

cost allocation. Assigning *costs* to individual products or time periods. Contrast with *cost accumulation*.

cost behavior. The functional relation between changes in activity and changes in *cost*. For example, *fixed* versus *variable costs*; *linear* versus *curvilinear cost*.

cost center. A unit of activity for which *expenditures* and *expenses* are accumulated.

cost effective. Among alternatives, the one whose benefit, or payoff, per unit of cost is highest. Sometimes said of an action whose expected benefits exceed expected costs whether or not there are other alternatives with larger benefit/cost ratios.

cost estimation. The process of measuring the functional relation between changes in activity levels and changes in cost.

cost flow assumption. See *flow assumption*.

cost flows. Costs passing through various classifications within an entity. See *flow of costs* for a diagram.

cost method (for investments). Accounting for an investment in the *capital stock* or *bonds* of another company where the investment is shown at *acquisition cost*, and only *dividends* declared or *interest receivable* is treated as *revenue*.

cost method (for treasury stock). The method of showing *treasury stock* as a *contra* to all other items of *shareholders' equity* in an amount equal to that paid to reacquire the stock.

cost objective. Any activity for which a separate measurement of costs is desired. Examples include departments, products, and territories.

cost of capital. *Opportunity cost* of funds invested in a business. The rate of return required to be earned on an asset before the rational owner will devote that asset to a particular purpose. Sometimes measured as the average rate per year a company must pay for its *equities*. In efficient capital markets, the *discount rate* that equates the expected *present value* of all future cash flows to common shareholders with the market value of common stock at a given time.

cost of goods manufactured. The sum of all costs allocated to products completed during a period; includes materials, labor, and *overhead*.

cost of goods purchased. Net purchase price of goods acquired plus costs of storage and delivery to the place where the items can be productively used.

cost of goods sold. Inventoriable *costs* that are expensed because the units are sold; equals beginning inventory plus *cost of goods purchased* or *manufactured* minus *ending inventory*.

cost of sales. Generally refers to *cost of goods sold*; occasionally, to *selling expenses*.

cost or market, whichever is lower. See *lower of cost or market*.

cost percentage. One less *markup percentage*. *Cost* of *goods available for sale* divided by selling prices of goods available for sale (when *FIFO* is used). With *LIFO, cost* of *purchases* divided by selling price of purchases. See *markup* for further detail on inclusions in calculation of cost percentage.

cost pool. *Indirect cost pool.*

cost principle. The *principle* that requires reporting *assets* at *historical* or *acquisition cost*, less accumulated *amortization*. This principle is based on the assumption that cost is equal to *fair market value* at the date of acquisition and that subsequent changes are not likely to be significant.

cost sheet. Statement that shows all the elements comprising the total cost of an item.

cost terminology. The word ''cost'' appears in many accounting terms. The accompanying exhibit classifies some of these by the distinctions the terms are used to make. Joel Dean was, to our knowledge, the first to attempt such distinctions; we have used some of his ideas here. Some terms have more detailed discussion under their own listings.

cost-recovery-first method. A method of *revenue* recognition that *credits inventory* as collections are received until all costs are recovered. Only after costs are completely recovered is *income* recognized. To be used in financial reporting only when the total amount of collections is highly uncertain. Can never be used in income tax reporting. Contrast with the *installment method*, where *constant proportions* of each collection are credited both to cost and to income.

cost-to-cost. The *percentage-of-completion method,* where the estimate of completion is the ratio of costs incurred to date divided by total costs expected to be incurred for the entire project.

cost-volume-profit graph (chart). A graph that shows the relation between *fixed costs, contribution per unit, breakeven point*, and *sales*. See *breakeven chart*.

costing. The process of calculating the cost of activities, products, or services. The British word for *cost accounting*.

coupon. That portion of a *bond* document redeemable at a specified date for *interest* payments. Its physical form is much like a ticket; each coupon is dated and is deposited at a bank, just like a check, for collection or is mailed to the issuer's agent for collection.

coupon rate. Of a *bond*, the amount of annual coupons divided by par value. Contrast with *effective rate*.

covenant. A promise with legal validity.

CPA. See *certified public accountant*. The *AICPA* suggests that no periods be shown in the abbreviation.

CPI. *Consumer Price Index.*

CPP. Current purchasing power; usually used as an adjective modifying the word ''accounting'' to mean the accounting that produces *constant dollar financial statements*.

Cr. Abbreviation for *credit*.

credit. As a noun, an entry on the right-hand side of an *account*. As a verb, to make an entry on the right-hand side of an account. Records increases in *liabilities, owners' equity, revenues*, and *gains*; records decreases in *assets* and *expenses*. See *debit and credit conventions*. Also the ability or right to buy or borrow in return for a promise to pay later.

credit loss. The amount of *accounts receivable* that is, or is expected to become, *uncollectible*.

credit memorandum. A document used by a seller to inform a buyer that the buyer's *account receivable* is being credited (reduced) because of *errors, returns*, or *allowances*. Also, the document provided by a bank to a depositor to indicate that the depositor's balance is being increased because of some event other than a deposit, such as the collection by the bank of the depositor's *note receivable*.

Cost Terminology: Distinctions Among Terms Containing the Word "Cost"

Terms (Synonyms Given in Parentheses)			Distinctions and Comments
			1. The following pairs of terms distinguish the "attribute" or "basis" measured in accounting.
Historical Cost (Acquisition Cost)	vs.	Current Cost	A distinction used in financial accounting. Current cost can be used more specifically to mean replacement cost, net realizable value, or present value of cash flows. "Current cost" is often used narrowly to mean replacement cost.
Historical Cost (Actual Cost)	vs.	Standard Cost	The distinction between historical and standard costs arises in product costing for inventory valuation. Some systems record actual costs while others record the standard costs.
			2. The following pairs of terms denote various distinctions among historical costs. For each pair of terms, the sum of the two kinds of costs equals total historical cost used in financial reporting.
Variable Cost	vs.	Fixed Cost (Constant Cost)	Distinction used in breakeven analysis and in designing cost accounting systems, particularly for product costing. See (4), below, for a further subdivision of fixed costs and (5), below, for an economic distinction closely paralleling this one.
Traceable Cost	vs.	Common Cost (Joint Cost)	Distinction arises in allocating manufacturing costs to product. Common costs are allocated to product, but the allocations are more-or-less arbitrary. The distinction also arises in segment reporting and in separating manufacturing from nonmanufacturing costs.
Direct Cost	vs.	Indirect Cost	Distinction arises in designing cost accounting systems and in product costing. The distinction generally applies only to manufacturing costs.
Out-of-Pocket Cost (Outlay Cost; Cash Cost)	vs.	Book Cost	Virtually all costs recorded in financial statements require a cash outlay at one time or another. The distinction here separates expenditures to occur in the future from those already made and is used in making decisions. Book costs, such as for depreciation, reduce income without requiring a future outlay of cash. The cash has already been spent. See future vs. past costs in (5), below.
Incremental Cost (Marginal Cost) (Differential Cost)	vs.	Sunk Cost	Distinction used in making decisions. Incremental costs will be incurred (or saved) if a decision is made to go ahead (or to stop) some activity, but not otherwise. Sunk costs will be reported in financial statements whether the decision is made to go ahead or not, because cash has already been spent or committed. Not all sunk costs are book costs, as, for example, a salary promised but not yet earned, that will be paid even if a no-go decision is made.
			The economist restricts the term marginal cost to the cost of producing one more unit. Thus the next unit has a marginal cost; the next week's output has an incremental cost. If a firm produces and sells a new product the related new costs would properly be called incremental, not marginal. If a factory is closed, the costs saved are incremental, not marginal.
Escapable Cost	vs.	Inescapable Cost (Unavoidable Cost)	Same distinction as incremental vs. sunk costs, but this pair is used only when the decision maker is considering stopping something—ceasing to produce a product, closing a factory, or the like. See next pair.
Avoidable Cost	vs.	Unavoidable Cost	A distinction sometimes used in discussing the merits of variable and absorption costing. Avoidable costs are treated as product cost and unavoidable costs are treated as period expenses under variable costing.
Controllable Cost	vs.	Uncontrollable Cost	The distinction here is used in allocating responsibility and in setting bonus or incentive plans. All costs can be affected by someone in the entity; those who design incentive schemes attempt to hold a person responsible for a cost only if that person can influence the amount of the cost.

Terms (Synonyms Given in Parentheses)			Distinctions and Comments

3. In each of the following pairs, used in historical cost accounting, the word "cost" appears in one of the terms where "expense" is meant.

Expired Cost	vs.	Unexpired Cost	The distinction is between *expense* and *asset*.
Product Cost	vs.	Period Cost	The terms distinguish product cost from period expense. When a given asset is used, is its cost converted into work in process and then finished goods on the balance sheet until the goods are sold or is it an expense shown on this period's income statement? Product costs appear on the income statement as part of cost of goods sold in the period when the goods are sold. Period expenses appear on the income statement with an appropriate caption for the item in the period when the cost is incurred or recognized.

4. The following subdivisions of fixed (historical) costs are used in analyzing operations. The relation between the components of fixed costs is:

$$\underbrace{\begin{array}{c} \text{Fixed} \\ \text{Costs} \end{array}}_{\substack{\text{Semifixed} + \text{Fixed} \\ \text{Costs} \quad \text{Portions} \\ + \quad \text{of} \\ \text{"Pure"} \quad \text{Semivariable} \\ \text{Fixed Costs Costs}}} = \underbrace{\begin{array}{c} \text{Capacity} \\ \text{Costs} \end{array}}_{\substack{\text{Standby} + \text{Enabling} \\ \text{Costs} \quad \text{Costs}}} + \begin{array}{c} \text{Programmed} \\ \text{Costs} \end{array}$$

Capacity Cost (Committed Cost)	vs.	Programmed Cost (Managed Cost; Discretionary Cost)	Capacity costs give a firm the capability to produce or to sell. Programmed costs, such as for advertising or research and development, may not be essential, but once a decision to incur them is made, they become fixed costs.
Standby Cost	vs.	Enabling Cost	Standby costs will be incurred whether capacity, once acquired, is used or not, such as property taxes and depreciation on a factory. Enabling costs, such as for security force, can be avoided if the capacity is unused.
Semifixed Cost	vs.	Semivariable Cost	A cost fixed over a wide range but that can change at various levels is a semifixed cost or "step cost." An example is the cost of rail lines from the factory to the main rail line where fixed cost depends on whether there are one or two parallel lines, but are independent of the number of trains run per day. Semivariable costs combine a strictly fixed component cost plus a variable component. Telephone charges usually have a fixed monthly component plus a charge related to usage.

5. The following pairs of terms distinguish among economic uses or decision making uses or regulatory uses of cost terms.

Fully Absorbed Cost (Full Cost)	vs.	Variable Cost (Direct Cost)	Fully absorbed costs refer to costs where fixed costs have been allocated to units or departments as required by generally accepted accounting principles. Variable costs, in contrast, may be more relevant for making decisions, such as in setting prices.
Opportunity Cost	vs.	Outlay Cost (Out-of-Pocket Cost)	Opportunity cost refers to the economic benefit foregone by using a resource for one purpose instead of for another. The outlay cost of the resource will be recorded in financial records. The distinction arises because a resource is already in the possession of the entity with a recorded historical cost. Its economic value to the firm, opportunity cost, generally differs from the historical cost; it can be either larger or smaller.
Future Cost	vs.	Past Cost	Effective decision making analyzes only present and future outlay costs, or out-of-pocket costs. Opportunity costs are relevant for profit maximizing; past costs are used in financial reporting.

Terms (Synonyms Given in Parentheses)			Distinctions and Comments
Short-Run Cost	vs.	Long-Run Cost	Short-run costs vary as output is varied for a given configuration of plant and equipment. Long-run costs can be incurred to change that configuration. This pair of terms is the economic analog of the accounting pair, see (2) above, variable and fixed costs. The analogy is not perfect because some short-run costs are fixed, such as property taxes on the factory, from the point of view of breakeven analysis.
Imputed Cost	vs.	Book Cost	In a regulatory setting some costs, for example the cost of owners' equity capital, are calculated and used for various purposes. Imputed costs are not recorded in the historical cost accounting records for financial reporting. Book costs are recorded.
Average Cost	vs.	Marginal Cost	The economic distinction equivalent to fully absorbed cost of product and direct cost of product. Average cost is total cost divided by number of units. Marginal cost is the cost to produce the next unit (or the last unit).

creditor. One who lends.

cross-reference (index). A number placed by each *account* in a *journal entry* indicating the *ledger* account to which the entry is posted and placing in the ledger the page number of the journal where the entry was made. Used to link the *debit* and *credit* parts of an entry in the ledger accounts back to the original entry in the journal. See *audit trail*.

cross-section analysis. Analysis of *financial statements* of various firms for a single period of time, as opposed to time-series analysis, where statements of a given firm are analyzed over several periods of time.

cumulative dividend. Preferred stock *dividends* that, if not paid, accrue as a commitment that must be paid before dividends to common shareholders can be declared.

cumulative preferred shares. *Preferred* shares with *cumulative dividend* rights.

current asset. *Cash* and other *assets* that are expected to be turned into cash, sold, or exchanged within the normal operating cycle of the firm, usually 1 year. Current assets include *cash, marketable securities, receivables, inventory*, and *current prepayments*.

current cost. *Cost* stated in terms of current values (of *productive capacity*) rather than in terms of *acquisition cost*. See *net realizable value, current selling price*.

current cost accounting. The *FASB's* term for *financial statements* where the *attribute measured* is *current cost*.

current cost/nominal dollar accounting. Accounting based on *current cost* valuations measured in *nominal dollars*. Components of *income* include an *operating margin* and *holding gains and losses*.

current exit value. *Exit value*.

current fund. In governmental accounting, a synonym for general fund.

current funds. *Cash* and other assets readily convertible into cash. In governmental accounting, funds spent for operating purposes during the current period. Includes *general, special revenue, debt service*, and *enterprise funds*.

current liability. A debt or other obligation that must be discharged within a short time, usually the *earnings cycle* or 1 year, normally by expending *current assets*.

current (gross) margin. See *operating margin (based on current costs)*.

current operating performance concept. The notion that reported *income* for a period ought to reflect only ordinary, normal, and recurring operations of that period. A consequence is that *extraordinary* and nonrecurring items are entered directly in the Retained Earnings account. Contrast with *clean surplus concept*. This concept is no longer acceptable. (See *APB Opinions* Nos. 9 and 30.)

current ratio. Sum of *current assets* divided by sum of *current liabilities*. See *ratio*.

current realizable value. *Realizable value*.

current replacement cost. Of an *asset*, the amount currently required to acquire an identical asset (in the same condition and with the same service potential) or an asset capable of rendering the same service at a current *fair market price*. If these two amounts differ, the lower is usually used. Contrast with *reproduction cost*.

current selling price. The amount for which an *asset* could be sold as of a given time in an *arm's-length* transaction, rather than in a forced sale.

current value accounting. The form of accounting where all assets are shown at *current replacement cost (entry value)* or *current selling price* or *net realizable value (exit value)* and all *liabilities* are shown at *present value*. Entry and exit values may be quite different from each other, so there is no general agreement on the precise meaning of current value accounting.

current yield. Of a *bond*, the annual amount of *interest coupons* divided by the current market price of the bond. Contrast with *yield to maturity*.

currently attainable standard cost. *Normal standard cost*.

curvilinear (variable) cost. A continuous, but not necessarily linear (straight-line), functional relation between activity levels and *costs*.

customers' ledger. The *ledger* that shows accounts receivable of individual customers. It is the *subsidiary ledger* for the *controlling account*, Accounts Receivable.

D

days of average inventory on hand. See *ratio*.

DCF. *Discounted cash flow*.

DDB. *Double-declining-balance depreciation*.

debenture bond. A *bond* not secured with *collateral*.

debit. As a noun, an entry on the left-hand side of an *account*. As a verb, to make an entry on the left-hand side of an account. Records increases in *assets* and *expenses*; records decreases in *liabilities*, *owners' equity*, and *revenues*. See *debit and credit conventions*.

debit and credit conventions. The equality of the two sides of the *accounting equation* is maintained by recording equal amounts of *debits* and *credits* for each *transaction*. The conventional use of the *T-account* form and the rules for debit and credit in *balance sheet accounts* are summarized as follows.

Any Asset Account

Opening Balance Increase + Dr. Ending Balance	Decrease − Cr.

Any Liability Account

Decrease − Dr.	Opening Balance Increase + Cr. Ending Balance

Any Owners' Equity Account

Decrease − Dr.	Opening Balance Increase + Cr. Ending Balance

Revenue and expense accounts belong to the owner's equity group. The relationship and the rules for debit and credit in these accounts can be expressed as follows.

Owners' Equity

Decrease − Dr. Expenses		Increase + Cr. Revenues	
Dr. + *	Cr. −	Dr. −	Cr. + *

*Normal balance prior to closing.

debit memorandum. A document used by a seller to inform a buyer that the seller is debiting (increasing) the amount of the buyer's *account receivable*. Also, the document provided by a bank to a depositor to indicate that the depositor's *balance* is being decreased because of some event other than payment for a *check*, such as monthly service charges or the printing of checks.

debt. An amount owed. The general name for *notes, bonds, mortgages*, and the like that are evidence of amounts owed and have definite payment dates.

debt capital. *Noncurrent liabilities*. See *debt financing* and contrast with *equity financing*.

debt financing. Raising *funds* by issuing *bonds, mortgages*, or *notes*. Contrast with *equity financing*. *Leverage*.

debt guarantee. See *guarantee*.

debt ratio. *Debt-equity ratio*.

debt service fund. In governmental accounting, a *fund* established to account for payment of *interest* and *princi-*

pal on all general-obligation *debt* other than that payable from special *assessments*.

debt service requirement. The amount of cash required for payments of *interest*, current maturities of *principal* on outstanding *debt*, and payments to *sinking funds* (corporations) or to the *debt service fund* (governmental).

debt-equity ratio. Total *liabilities* divided by total equities. See *ratio*. Sometimes the denominator is merely total shareholders' equity. Sometimes the numerator is restricted to *noncurrent debt*.

debtor. One who borrows.

declaration date. Time when a *dividend* is declared by the *board of directors*.

declining-balance depreciation. The method of calculating the periodic *depreciation* charge by multiplying the *book value* at the start of the period by a constant percentage. In pure declining-balance depreciation the constant percentage is $1 - \sqrt[n]{s/c}$, where n is the *depreciable life*, s is *salvage value*, and c is *acquisition cost*. See *double-declining-balance depreciation*.

deep discount bonds. Said of *bonds* selling much below (exactly how much is not clear) *par value*.

defalcation. Embezzlement.

default. Failure to pay *interest* or *principal* on a *debt* when due.

defensive interval. A financial *ratio* equal to the number of days of normal cash *expenditures* covered by *quick assets*. It is defined as

$$\frac{\text{Quick Assets}}{\text{(All Expenses Except Amortization and Others Not Using Funds/365)}}.$$

The denominator of the ratio is the cash expenditure per day. This ratio has been found useful in predicting *bankruptcy*.

deferral. The accounting process concerned with past *cash receipts* and *payments*; in contrast to *accrual*. Recognizing a liability resulting from a current cash receipt (as for magazines to be delivered) or recognizing an asset from a current cash payment (or for prepaid insurance or a long-term depreciable asset).

deferral method. See *flow-through method* (of accounting for the *investment credit*) for definition and contrast.

deferred annuity. An *annuity* whose first payment is made sometime after the end of the first period.

deferred asset. *Deferred charge.*

deferred charge. *Expenditure* not recognized as an *expense* of the period when made but carried forward as an *asset* to be *written off* in future periods, such as for advance rent payments or insurance premiums. See *deferral*.

deferred cost. *Deferred charge.*

deferred credit. Sometimes used to indicate *advances from customers*. Also sometimes used to describe the *deferred income tax liability*.

deferred debit. *Deferred charge.*

deferred expense. *Deferred charge.*

deferred gross margin. *Unrealized gross margin.*

deferred income. *Advances from customers.*

deferred income tax (liability). Generally a *credit* balance on the *balance sheet* that arises when the pretax income shown on the tax return is less than what it would have been had the same *accounting principles* been used in tax returns as used for financial reporting. *APB Opinion No. 11* requires that the firm debit income tax *expense* and credit deferred income tax with the amount of the taxes delayed by using different accounting principles in tax returns from those used in financial reports. See *timing difference* and *permanent difference*. See *installment sales*. Although the item is often reported as a *liability* on the balance sheet, there is no obligation to pay. If, as a result of timing differences, cumulative taxable income exceeds cumulative reported income before taxes, the deferred income tax account will have a *debit* balance and will be reported as a *deferred charge*.

deferred performance liability. *Estimated liability* that arises under product *warranty*. Sometimes used to mean *advances from customers*.

deferred revenue. Sometimes used to indicate *advances from customers*.

deferred tax. See *deferred income tax*.

deficit. A *debit balance* in the Retained Earnings account; presented on the balance sheet as a *contra* to shareholders' equity. Sometimes used to mean negative *net income* for a period.

defined-benefit plan. A *pension plan* where the employer promises specific dollar amounts to each eligible employee; the amounts usually depend on a formula that takes into account such things as the employee's earnings, years of employment, and age. The employer's cash contributions and pension expense are adjusted in relation to *actuarial* experience in the eligible employee group and investment performance of the pension *fund*. Sometimes called a "fixed-benefit" pension plan. Contrast with *money purchase plan*.

defined-contribution plan. A *money purchase (pension) plan* or other arrangement, based on formula or discretion, where the employer makes cash contributions to eligible individual employee *accounts* under the terms of a written plan document.

deflation. A period of declining *general price changes*.

demand deposit. *Funds* in a *checking account* at a bank.

demand loan. See *term loan* for definition and contrast.

denominator volume. Capacity measured in expected number of units to be produced this period; divided into *budgeted fixed costs* to obtain fixed costs applied per unit of product.

depletion. Exhaustion or *amortization* of a *wasting asset* or natural resource. See also *percentage depletion*.

depletion allowance. See *percentage depletion*.

deposit method (of revenue recognition). This method of *revenue* recognition is not distinct from the *completed sale* or *completed contract method*. In some contexts such as retail land sales, the customer must make substantial payments while still having the right to back out of the deal and receive a refund. When there is uncertainty about whether the deal will be completed but a cash collection is made by the seller, the seller must *credit* deposits, a *liability account*, rather than *revenue*. (In this regard, the accounting differs from the completed contract method, where the account credited is offset against the *work-in-process inventory* account.) When the *sale* becomes complete, a revenue account is credited and the deposit account is *debited*.

deposit, sinking fund. Payments made to a *sinking fund*.

deposits (by customers). A *liability* arising upon receipt of *cash* (as in a bank, or in a grocery store when the customer pays cash for sodapop bottles to be repaid when the bottles are returned).

deposits in transit. Deposits made by a firm but not yet reflected on the *bank statement*.

depreciable cost. That part of the *cost* of an asset, usually *acquisition cost* less *salvage value*, that is to be charged off over the life of the asset through the process of *depreciation*.

depreciable life. For an *asset*, the time period or units of activity (such as miles driven for a truck) over which *depreciable cost* is to be allocated. For tax returns, depreciable life may be shorter than estimated *service life*.

depreciation. *Amortization of plant assets*; the process of allocating the cost of an asset to the periods of benefit— the *depreciable life*. Classified as a *production cost* or a *period expense*, depending on the asset and whether *absorption* or *direct costing* is used. Depreciation terms described in this glossary include the *annuity method*, *appraisal method, backlog depreciation, composite de-*

preciation, compound interest depreciation, declining-balance depreciation, double-declining-balance depreciation, production method, replacement cost method, retirement method, sinking fund method, straight-line depreciation, and *sum-of-the-years'-digits depreciation*.

depreciation reserve. An inferior term for *accumulated depreciation*. See *reserve*. Do not confuse with a replacement *fund*.

Descartes' rule of signs. In a *capital budgeting* context, the rule says that a series of cash flows will have a non-negative number of *internal rates of return*. The number is equal to the number of variations in the sign of the cash flow series or is less than that number by an even integer. Consider the following series of cash flows, the first occurring now and the others at subsequent yearly intervals: $-100, -100, +50, +175, -50, +100$. The internal rates of return are the numbers for r that satisfy the equation

$$-100 - \frac{100}{(1+r)} + \frac{50}{(1+r)^2} + \frac{175}{(1+r)^3}$$
$$- \frac{50}{(1+r)^4} + \frac{100}{(1+r)^5} = 0.$$

The series of cash flows has three variations in sign: a change from minus to plus, a change from plus to minus, and a change from minus to plus. The rule says that this series must have either one or three internal rates of return; in fact, it has only one, about 12 percent. But see also *reinvestment rate*.

determination. See *determine*.

determine. The verb "determine" and the noun "determination" are often used (in our opinion, overused) by accountants and those who describe the accounting process. A leading dictionary associates the following meanings with the verb "determine": settle, decide, conclude, ascertain, cause, affect, control, impel, terminate, and decide upon. In addition, accounting writers can mean any one of the following: measure, allocate, report, calculate, compute, observe, choose, and legislate. In accounting, there are two distinct sets of meanings—those encompassed by the synonym "cause or legislate" and those encompassed by the synonym "measure." The first set of uses conveys the active notion of causing something to happen and the second set of uses conveys the more passive notion of observing something that someone else has caused to happen. An accountant who writes of cost or income "determination" generally means measurement or observation, not causation; management and economic conditions cause costs or income to be what they are. One who writes of accounting principles "determination" can mean choosing or applying (as in "determining depreciation charges" from an allowable set) or causing to be acceptable (as in the FASB "determining" the accounting for *leases*). In the long run, income is cash in less cash out, so management and economic conditions "determine" (cause) income to be what it is. In the short run, reported income is a function of accounting principles chosen and applied, so the accountant "determines" (measures) income. A question such as ''Who determines income?'' has, therefore, no unambiguous answer. The meaning of ''an accountant determining acceptable accounting principles'' is also vague. Does the clause mean merely choosing one from the set of generally acceptable principles, or does it mean using professional judgment to decide that some of the generally accepted principles are not correct under the current circumstances? We try never to use ''determine'' unless we mean ''cause.'' Otherwise we use ''measure,'' ''report,'' ''calculate,'' ''compute,'' or whatever specific verb seems appropriate. We suggest that careful writers will always ''determine'' to use the most specific verb to convey meaning. ''Determine'' is seldom the best choice to convey specifity in describing a process where those who make decisions often differ from those who apply technique.

development-stage enterprise. As defined in *SFAS No. 7*, a firm whose planned principal *operations* have not commenced or, having commenced, have not generated significant *revenue*. Such enterprises should be so identified, but no special *accounting principles* apply to them.

differential analysis. Analysis of *incremental costs*.

differential cost. *Incremental cost*.

dilution. A potential reduction in *earnings per share* or *book value* per share by the potential *conversion* of securities or by the potential exercise of *warrants* or *options*.

dilutive. Said of a *security* that would reduce *earnings per share* if it were exchanged for *common stock*.

dipping into LIFO layers. See *LIFO inventory layer*.

direct cost. Cost of *direct material* and *direct labor* incurred in producing a product. See *prime cost*. In some accounting literature, this term is used to mean the same thing as *variable cost*.

direct costing. This method of allocating costs assigns only *variable manufacturing costs* to product and treats *fixed manufacturing costs* as *period* expenses. A better term for this concept is ''variable costing.'' Contrast with *absorption costing*.

direct labor (material) cost. Cost of labor (material) applied and assigned directly to a product; contrast with *indirect labor (material)*.

direct posting. A method of bookkeeping where *entries* are made directly in *ledger accounts*, without the use of a *journal*.

direct write-off method. See *write-off method*.

disbursement. Payment by *cash* or by *check*. See *expenditure*.

DISC. Domestic International Sales Corporation. A U.S. *corporation*, usually a *subsidiary*, whose *income* is attributable primarily to exports. *Income tax* on 50 percent of a DISC's income is usually deferred for a long period. Generally, this results in a lower overall corporate tax for the *parent* than would otherwise be incurred.

disclaimer of opinion. An *auditor's report* stating that an opinion cannot be given on the *financial statements*. Usually results from *material* restrictions on the scope of the audit or from material uncertainties about the accounts that cannot be resolved at the time of the audit.

disclosure. The showing of facts in *financial statements*, *notes* thereto, or the *auditor's report*.

discontinued operations. See *income from discontinued operations*.

discount. In the context of *compound interest*, *bonds*, and *notes*, the difference between *face* or *future value* and *present value* of a payment. In the context of *sales* and *purchases*, a reduction in price granted for prompt payment. See also *chain discount*, *quantity discount*, and *trade discount*.

discount factor. The reciprocal of 1 plus the *discount rate*. If the discount rate is 10 percent per period, the discount factor for three periods is $(1.10)^{-3} = 0.75131$.

discount rate. *Interest rate* used to convert future payments to *present values*.

discounted bailout period. In a *capital budgeting* context, the total time that must elapse before discounted value of net accumulated cash flows from a project, including potential *salvage value* at various times of assets, equals or exceeds the *present value* of net accumulated cash outflows. Contrast with *discounted payback period*.

discounted cash flow. DCF. Using either the *net present value* or the *internal rate of return* in an analysis to measure the value of future expected cash *expenditures* and *receipts* at a common date.

discounted payback period. Amount of time over which the discounted present value of cash inflows from a project, excluding potential *salvage value* at various times of assets, equals the discounted *present value* of the cash outflows.

discounting a note. See *note receivable discounted* and *factoring*.

discounts lapsed (lost). The sum of *discounts* offered for prompt payment that were not taken (or allowed) because of expiration of the discount period. See *terms of sale*.

discovery value accounting. See *reserve recognition accounting*.

Discussion Memorandum. A neutral discussion of all the issues concerning an accounting problem of current concern to the *FASB*. The publication of such a document usually implies that the FASB is considering issuing an *SFAS* or *SFAC* on this particular problem. The Discussion Memorandum brings together material about the particular problem to facilitate interaction and comment by those interested in the matter. It may lead to an *Exposure Draft*.

dishonored note. A *promissory note* whose maker does not repay the loan at *maturity* for a *term loan*, or on demand, for a *demand loan*.

disintermediation. Federal law regulates the maximum *interest rate* that both banks and savings and loan associations can pay for *time deposits*. When free-market interest rates exceed the regulated interest ceiling for such time deposits, some depositors withdraw their funds and invest them elsewhere at a higher interest rate. This process is known as "disintermediation."

distributable income. The portion of conventional accounting net income that can be distributed to owners (usually in the form of *dividends*) without impairing the physical capacity of the firm to continue operations at current levels. Pretax distributable income is conventional pretax income less the excess of *current cost* of goods sold and *depreciation* charges based on the replacement cost of *productive capacity* over cost of goods sold and depreciation on an *acquisition cost basis*. Contrast with *sustainable income*. See *inventory profit*.

distribution expense. *Expense* of selling, advertising, and delivery activities.

dividend. A distribution of assets generated from *earnings* to owners of a corporation; it may be paid in cash (cash dividend), with stock (stock dividend), with property, or with other securities (dividend in kind). Dividends, except stock dividends, become a legal liability of the corporation when they are declared. Hence, the owner of stock ordinarily recognizes *revenue* when a dividend, other than a stock dividend, is declared. See also *liquidating dividend* and *stock dividend*.

dividend yield. *Dividends* declared for the year divided by market price of the stock as of a given time of the year.

dividends in arrears. Dividends on *cumulative preferred stock* that have not been declared in accordance with the preferred stock contract. Such arrearages must usually be cleared before dividends on *common stock* can be declared.

dividends in kind. See *dividend*.

divisional control. See *control system*.

divisional reporting. *Line-of-business reporting*.

dollar sign rules. In presenting accounting statements or schedules, place a dollar sign beside the first figure in each column and beside any figure below a horizontal line drawn under the preceding figure.

dollar-value LIFO method. A form of *LIFO* inventory accounting with inventory quantities *(layers)* measured in dollar, rather than physical, terms. Adjustments to account for changing prices are made by use of specific price indexes appropriate for the kinds of items in the inventory.

Domestic International Sales Corporation. See *DISC*.

donated capital. A *shareholders' equity* account credited when contributions, such as land or buildings, are freely given to the company. Do not confuse with *contributed capital*.

double entry. The system of recording transactions that maintains the equality of the accounting equation; each entry results in recording equal amounts of *debits* and *credits*.

double T-account. *T-account* with an extra horizontal line showing a change in the account balance to be explained by the subsequent entries into the account, such as:

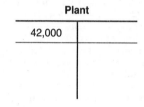

Plant

42,000

This account shows an increase in the asset account, plant, of $42,000 to be explained. Such accounts are useful in preparing the *statement of changes in financial position*; they are not a part of the formal record-keeping process.

double taxation. Corporate income is subject to the corporate income tax, and the aftertax income, when distributed to owners, is subject to the personal income tax.

double-declining-balance depreciation. DDB. *Declining-balance depreciation*, which see, where the constant percentage used to multiply by book value in determining the depreciation charge for the year is $2/n$ and n is the *depreciable life* in periods. Maximum declining-balance rate permitted in the *income tax* laws. *Salvage value* is omitted from the depreciable amount. Thus if the asset cost $100 and has a depreciable life of 5 years, the depreciation in the first year would be $40 = 2/5 \times \$100$, in the second would be $24 = 2/5 \times (\$100 - \$40)$, and in the third year would be $14.40 = 2/5 \times (\$100 - \$40 - \$24)$. By the fourth year, the remaining undepreciated cost could be depreciated under the straight-line method at $10.80 = 1/2 \times (\$100 - \$40 - \$24 - \$14.40)$ per year for tax purposes.

doubtful accounts. *Accounts receivable* estimated to be *uncollectible*.

Dr. The abbreviation for *debit*.

draft. A written order by the first party, called the drawer, instructing a second party, called the drawee (such as a bank) to pay a third party, called the payee. See also *check, cashier's check, certified check, NOW account, sight draft*, and *trade acceptance*.

drawee. See *draft*.

drawer. See *draft*.

drawing account. A *temporary account* used in *sole proprietorships* and *partnerships* to record payments to owners or partners during a period. At the end of the period, the drawing account is closed by crediting it and debiting the owner's or partner's share of income or, perhaps, his or her capital account.

drawings. Payments made to a *sole proprietor* or to a *partner* during a period. See *drawing account*.

dry-hole accounting. See *reserve recognition accounting* for definition and contrast.

dual transactions assumption (fiction). In presenting the *statement of changes in financial position*, some transactions not involving *working capital* accounts are reported as though working capital was generated and then used. For example, the issue of *capital stock* in return for the *asset*, land, is reported in the statement of changes in financial position as though stock were issued for *cash* and cash were used to acquire land. Other examples of transactions that require the dual transaction fiction are the issue of the *mortgage* in return for a noncurrent asset and the issue of stock to bondholders upon *conversion* of their *convertible bonds*.

duality. The axiom of *double-entry* record keeping that every *transaction* is broken down into equal *debit* and *credit* amounts.

E

e. The base of natural logarithms; 2.71828182846. . . . If *interest* is compounded continuously during a period at a stated rate of r per period, then the effective *interest rate* is equivalent to interest compounded once per period at rate i, where $i = e^r - 1$. Tables of e^r are widely available. If 12 percent annual interest is compounded continuously, the effective rate is $e^{.12} - 1 = 12.75$ percent.

earned surplus. A term once used, but no longer considered proper, for *retained earnings*.

earnings. *Income*, or sometimes *profit*.

earnings cycle. The period of time that elapses for a given firm, or the series of transactions, during which *cash* is converted into *goods* and *services*, goods and services are sold to customers, and customers pay for their purchases with cash. *Cash cycle*.

earnings per share (of common stock). *Net income* to common shareholders (net income minus *preferred dividends*) divided by the weighted average number of *common shares* outstanding; see also *primary earnings per share* and *fully diluted earnings per share*. See *ratio*.

earnings per share (of preferred stock). *Net income* divided by the weighted average number of *preferred shares* outstanding during the period. This ratio indicates how well the preferred dividends are covered or protected; it does not indicate a legal share of *earnings*. See *ratio*.

earnings, retained. See *retained earnings*.

earnings statement. *Income statement*.

earn-out. An agreement between two merging firms under which the amount of payment by the acquiring firm to the acquired firm's shareholders depends on the future earnings of the *consolidated entity*.

easement. The acquired right or privilege of one person to use, or have access to, certain property of another. For example, a public utility's right to lay pipes or lines under property of another and to service those facilities.

economic depreciation. Decline in *current cost* of an *asset* during a period.

economic entity. See *entity*.

economic life. The time span over which the benefits of an *asset* are expected to be received. The economic life of a *patent, copyright*, or *franchise* may be less than the legal life. *Service life*.

economic order quantity. In mathematical *inventory* analysis, the optimal amount of stock to order when inventory is reduced to a level called the "reorder point." If A represents the *incremental cost* of placing a single order, D represents the total demand for a period of time in units, and H represents the incremental holding cost during the period per unit of inventory, then the economic order quantity $Q = \sqrt{2AD/H}$. Q is sometimes called the "optimal lot size."

ED. *Exposure Draft*.

effective interest method. A systematic method for computing *interest expense* (or *revenue*) that makes the interest expense for each period divided by the amount of the net *liability (asset)* at the beginning of the period equal to the *yield rate* on the bond at the time of issue (acquisition). Interest for a period is the yield rate (at time of issue) multiplied by the net liability (asset) at the start of the period. The *amortization* of discount or premium is the *plug* to give equal *debits* and *credits*. (Interest expense is a debit and the amount of coupon payments is a credit.)

effective (interest) rate. Of a bond, the *internal rate of return* or *yield to maturity* at the time of issue. Contrast with *coupon rate*. If the bond is issued for a price below *par*, the effective rate is higher than the coupon rate; if it is issued for a price greater than par, then the effective rate is lower than the coupon rate. In the context of *compound interest*, when the *compounding period* on a *loan* is different from 1 year, such as a nominal interest rate of 12 percent compounded monthly, then the single rate that could be applied at the end of a year to the beginning balance is economically equivalent to the series of compound interest calculations. If 12 percent per year is compounded monthly, the effective interest rate is 12.683 percent. In general, if the nominal rate is r percent per year and is compounded m times per year, then the effective rate is $(1 + r/m)^m - 1$.

efficiency variance. A term used for the *quantity variance* for labor or *variable overhead* in a *standard cost system*.

efficient market hypothesis. The supposition in finance that securities' prices reflect all available information and react nearly instantaneously and in an unbiased fashion to new information.

eliminations. *Work sheet* entries to prepare *consolidated statements* that are made to avoid duplicating the amounts of *assets*, *liabilities*, *owners' equity*, *revenues*, and *expenses* of the consolidated *entity* when the accounts of the *parent* and *subsidiaries* are summed.

Employee Retirement Income Security Act. See *ERISA*.

employee stock option. See *stock option*.

Employee Stock Ownership Trust (or Plan). See *ESOT*.

employer, employee payroll taxes. See *payroll*.

enabling costs. A type of *capacity cost* that will stop being incurred if operations are shut down completely but must be incurred in full if operations are carried out at any level. Costs of a security force or of a quality control inspector for an assembly line might be examples. Contrast with *standby costs*.

encumbrance. In governmental accounting, an anticipated *expenditure*, or *funds* restricted for an anticipated expenditure, such as for outstanding purchase orders. *Appropriations* less expenditures less outstanding encumbrances yields unencumbered balance.

ending inventory. The *cost of inventory* on hand at the end of the *accounting period*, often called ''closing inventory.'' The dollar amount of inventory to be carried to the subsequent period.

endorsee. See *endorser*.

endorsement. See *draft*. The *payee* signs the draft and transfers it to a fourth party, such as the payee's bank.

endorser. The *payee* of a *note* or *draft* signs it, after writing ''Pay to the order of X,'' transfers the note to person X, and presumably receives some benefit, such as cash, in return. The payee who signs over the note is called the endorser and person X is called the endorsee. The endorsee then has the rights of the payee and may in turn become an endorser by endorsing the note to another endorsee.

enterprise. Any business organization, usually defining the accounting *entity*.

enterprise fund. A *fund* established by a governmental unit to account for acquisition, operation, and maintenance of governmental services that are supposed to be self-supporting from user charges, such as for water or airports.

entity. A person, *partnership*, *corporation*, or other organization. The *accounting entity* for which accounting statements are prepared may not be the same as the entity defined by law. For example, a *sole proprietorship* is an accounting entity, but the individual's combined business and personal assets are the legal entity in most jurisdictions. Several affiliated corporations may be separate legal entities although *consolidated financial statements* are prepared for the group of companies operating as a single economic entity.

entity theory. The view of the corporation that emphasizes the form of the *accounting equation* that says *assets = equities*. Contrast with *proprietorship theory*. The entity theory is less concerned with a distinct line between *liabilities* and *shareholders' equity* than is the proprietorship theory. Rather, all equities are provided to the corporation by outsiders who merely have claims of differing legal standings. The entity theory implies using a *multiple-step* income statement.

entry value. The *current cost* of acquiring an asset or service at a *fair market price*. *Replacement cost*.

EOQ. *Economic order quantity*.

EPS. *Earnings per share*.

EPVI. *Excess present value index*.

equalization reserve. An inferior title for the allowance account when the *allowance method* is used for such things as maintenance expenses. Periodically, maintenance *expense* is debited and the allowance is credited. As maintenance *expenditures* are actually incurred, the allowance is debited and cash or the other asset expended is credited.

equities. *Liabilities* plus *owners' equity*. See, however, *equity*.

equity. A claim to *assets*; a source of assets. *SFAS No. 3* defines equity as ''the residual interest in the assets of an entity that remains after deducting its liabilities.'' Usage may be changing so that ''equity'' will exclude liabilities. We prefer to keep the broader definition, including liabilities, because there is no other single word that serves this useful purpose.

equity financing. Raising *funds* by issuance of *capital stock*. Contrast with *debt financing*.

equity method. A method of accounting for an *investment* in the stock of another company in which the proportionate share of the earnings of the other company is debited to the investment account and credited to a *revenue* account as earned. When *dividends* are received, *cash* is debited and the investment account is credited. Used in reporting when the investor owns sufficient shares of stock of an unconsolidated company to exercise significant control over the actions of that company. One of the few instances where revenue is recognized without a change in *working capital*.

equity ratio. *Shareholders' equity* divided by total *assets*. See *ratio*.

equivalent production. *Equivalent units*.

equivalent units (of work). The number of units of completed output that would require the same costs as were actually incurred for production of completed and partially completed units during a period. Used primarily in *process costing* calculations to measure in uniform terms the output of a continuous process.

ERISA. Employee Retirement Income Security Act of 1974. The federal law that sets *pension plan* requirements.

error accounting. See *accounting errors*.

ESOP. Employee Stock Ownership Plan. See *ESOT*.

ESOT. Employee stock ownership trust. A trust *fund* created by a corporate employer that can provide certain tax benefits to the corporation while providing for employee stock ownership. The corporate employer can contribute up to 25 percent of its payroll per year to the trust. The contributions are *deductions* from otherwise taxable income for federal *income tax* purposes. The assets of the trust must be used for the benefit of employees—for example, to fund death or retirement benefits. The assets of the trust are usually the *common stock*, sometimes nonvoting, of the corporate employer. As an example of the potential *tax shelter*, consider the case of a corporation with $1 million of *debt* outstanding, which it wishes to retire, and an annual payroll of $2 million. The corporation sells $1 million of common stock to the ESOT. The ESOT borrows $1 million with the loan guaranteed by, and therefore a *contingency* of, the corporation. The corporation uses the $1 million proceeds of the stock issue to retire its outstanding debt. (The debt of the corporation has been replaced with the debt of the ESOT.) The corporation can contribute $500,000 (= .25 × $2 million payroll) to ESOT each year and treat the contribution as a deduction

for tax purposes. After a little more than 2 years, the ESOT has received sufficient funds to retire its loan. The corporation has effectively repaid its original $1 million debt with pretax dollars. Assuming an income tax rate of 40 percent, it has saved $400,000 (= .40 × $1 million) of aftertax dollars *if* the $500,000 expense for the contribution to the ESOT for the pension benefits of employees would have been made, in one form or another, anyway. Observe that the corporation could use the proceeds ($1 million in the example) of the stock issue to the ESOT for any of several different purposes: financing expansion, replacing plant assets, or acquiring another company.

Basically this same form of pretax dollar financing through pensions is ''almost'' available with any corporate pension plan, but with one important exception. The trustees of an ordinary pension trust must invest the assets ''prudently''; if they do not, they are personally liable to employees. Current judgment about ''prudent'' investment requires diversification—pension trust assets should be invested in a wide variety of investment opportunities. (Not more than 10 percent of a pension trust's assets can ordinarily be invested in the parent's common stock.) Thus the ordinary pension trust cannot, in practice, invest all, or even most, of its assets in the parent corporation's stock. This constraint does not apply to the investments of an ESOT. All ESOT assets may be invested in the parent company's stock.

The ESOT also provides a means for closely held corporations to achieve wider ownership of shares without *going public*. The laws enabling ESOTs provide for independent professional appraisal of shares not traded in public markets and for transactions between the corporation and the ESOT or between the ESOT and the employees to be based on the appraised values of the shares.

estimated expenses. See *aftercost*.

estimated liability. The preferred terminology for estimated costs to be incurred for such uncertain things as repairs under *warranty*. An estimated liability is shown in the *balance sheet*. Contrast with *contingency*.

estimated revenue. A term used in governmental accounting to designate revenue expected to accrue during a period whether or not it will be collected during the period. A *budgetary account* is usually established at the beginning of the budget period.

estimated salvage value. Synonymous with *salvage value* of an *asset* before its retirement.

estimates, changes in. See *accounting changes*.

except for. Qualification in an *auditor's report*, usually caused by a change, approved by the auditor, from one acceptable accounting principle or procedure to another.

excess present value. In a *capital budgeting* context, *present value* of anticipated net cash inflows minus cash outflows, including initial cash outflow for a project.

excess present value index. *Present value* of future *cash* inflows divided by initial cash outlay.

exchange. The generic term for a transaction (or, more technically, a reciprocal transfer) between one entity and another. In another context, the name for a market, such as the New York Stock Exchange.

exchange gain or loss. The phrase used by the *FASB* for *foreign exchange gain or loss*.

exchange rate. The *price* of one country's currency in terms of another country's currency. For example, the British pound might be worth $1.50 at a given time. The exchange rate would be stated as "one pound is worth one dollar fifty cents" or "one dollar is worth .67 (= £ 1/ $1.50) pounds."

excise tax. Tax on the manufacture, sale, or consumption of a commodity.

ex-dividend. Said of a stock at the time when the declared *dividend* becomes the property of the person who owned the stock on the *record date*. The payment date follows the ex-dividend date.

executory contract. An agreement providing for payment by a payor to a payee upon the performance of an act or service by the payee, such as a labor contract. Obligations under such contracts generally are not recognized as *liabilities*. Some contracts are partially executory; these give rise to an *asset* or *liability* to the extent of partial performance. An example is the downpayment on a purchase.

exemption. A term used for various amounts subtracted from gross income in computing taxable income. Not all such subtractions are called "exemptions." See *tax deduction*.

exercise. When the owner of an *option* or *warrant* purchases the security that the option entitles him or her to purchase, he or she has exercised the option or warrant.

exercise price. See *option*.

exit value. The proceeds that would be received if assets were disposed of in an *arm's-length transaction. Current selling price. Net realizable value.*

expected value. The mean or arithmetic *average* of a statistical distribution or series of numbers.

expendable fund. In governmental accounting, a *fund* whose resources, *principal*, and earnings may be distributed.

expenditure. Payment of *cash* for goods or services received. Payment may be made either at the time the goods or services are received or at a later time. Virtually synonymous with *disbursement* except that disbursement is a broader term and includes all payments for goods or services. Contrast with *expense*.

expense. As a noun, a decrease in *owners' equity* caused by the using up of *assets* in producing *revenue* or carrying out other activities that are part of the entity's *operations*. A "gone" asset; an expired cost. The amount is the *cost* of the assets used up. Do not confuse with *expenditure* or *disbursement*, which may occur before, when, or after the related expense is recognized. Use the word "cost" to refer to an item that still has service potential and is an asset. Use the word "expense" after the asset's service potential has been used. As a verb, to designate a past or current expenditure as a current expense.

expense account. An *account* to accumulate *expenses*; such accounts are closed at the end of the accounting period. A *temporary owners' equity* account. Also used to describe a listing of expenses by an employee submitted to the employer for reimbursement.

expense center. *Cost center.*

experience rating. A term used in insurance, particularly unemployment insurance, to denote changes from ordinary rates to reflect extraordinarily large or small amounts of claims over time by the insured.

expired cost. An *expense* or a *loss*.

Exposure Draft. ED. A preliminary statement of the *FASB* (or *APB* between 1962 and 1973) that shows the contents of a pronouncement the board is considering making effective.

external reporting. Reporting to shareholders and the public, as opposed to internal reporting for management's benefit. See *financial accounting* and contrast with *managerial accounting*.

extraordinary item. A *material expense* or *revenue* item characterized both by its unusual nature and infrequency of occurrence that is shown along with its income tax effects separately from ordinary income and *income from discontinued operations* on the *income statement*. A *loss* from an earthquake would probably be classified as an extraordinary item. Gain (or loss) upon retirement of *bonds* is treated as an extraordinary item under the terms of *SFAS No. 4*.

F

face amount (value). The nominal amount due at *maturity* from a *bond* or *note* not including contractual interest that may also be due on the same date. The corresponding amount of a stock certificate is best called the *par* or *stated value*, whichever is applicable.

factoring. The process of buying *notes* or *accounts receivable* at a *discount* from the holder to whom the debt is owed; from the holder's point of view, the selling of such notes or accounts. When a single note is involved, the process is called "discounting a note."

factory. Used synonymously with *manufacturing* as an adjective.

factory burden. *Manufacturing overhead.*

factory cost. *Manufacturing cost.*

factory expense. *Manufacturing overhead. Expense* is a poor term in this context because the item is a *product cost.*

factory overhead. Usually an item of *manufacturing cost* other than *direct labor* or *direct materials.*

fair market price (value). Price (value) negotiated at *arm's length* between a willing buyer and a willing seller, each acting rationally in his or her own self-interest. May be estimated in the absence of a monetary transaction.

fair presentation (fairness). When the *auditor's report* says that the *financial statements* "present fairly. . . ," the auditor means that the accounting alternatives used by the entity are all in accordance with *GAAP.* In recent years, however, courts are finding that conformity with *generally accepted accounting principles* may be insufficient grounds for an opinion that the statements are fair. *SAS No. 5* requires that the auditor judge the accounting principles used "appropriate in the circumstances" before attesting to fair presentation.

FASB. Financial Accounting Standards Board. An independent board responsible, since 1973, for establishing *generally accepted accounting principles.* Its official pronouncements are called *Statements of Financial Accounting Concepts (SFAC), Statements of Financial Accounting Standards (SFAS),* and *Interpretations of Financial Accounting Standards.* See also *Discussion Memorandum* and *Technical Bulletin.*

FASB Interpretation. An official statement of the *FASB* interpreting the meaning of *Accounting Research Bulletins, APB Opinions,* and *Statements of Financial Accounting Standards.*

FASB Technical Bulletin. See *Technical Bulletin.*

favorable variance. An excess of actual *revenues* over expected revenues. An excess of *standard cost* over actual cost.

federal income tax. *Income tax* levied by the U.S. government on individuals and corporations.

Federal Insurance Contribution Act. *FICA.*

Federal Unemployment Tax Act. See *FUTA.*

feedback. The process of informing employees about how their actual performance compares with the expected or desired level of performance in the hope that the information will reinforce desired behavior and reduce unproductive behavior.

FEI. *Financial Executives Institute.*

FICA. Federal Insurance Contributions Act. The law that sets *Social Security taxes* and benefits.

fiduciary. Someone responsible for the custody or administration of property belonging to another, such as an executor (of an estate), agent, receiver (in *bankruptcy*), or trustee (of a trust).

FIFO. First in, first out; the *inventory flow assumption* by which *ending inventory* cost is computed from most recent purchases and *cost of goods sold* is computed from oldest purchases including beginning inventory. See *LISH.* Contrast with *LIFO.*

finance. As a verb, to supply with *funds* through the *issue* of stocks, bonds, notes, or mortgages, or through the retention of earnings.

financial accounting. The accounting for *assets, equities, revenues,* and *expenses* of a business. Concerned primarily with the historical reporting of the *financial position* and operations of an *entity* to external users on a regular, periodic basis. Contrast with *managerial accounting.*

Financial Accounting Foundation. The independent foundation (board of trustees) that raises funds to support the *FASB,* appoints its members, approves its operating policies and procedures, and appoints members of the *Financial Accounting Standards Advisory Council.*

Financial Accounting Standards Advisory Council. A committee giving advice to the *FASB* on matters of strategy and emerging issues.

Financial Accounting Standards Board. *FASB.*

Financial Executives Institute. An organization of financial executives, such as chief accountants, *controllers,* and treasurers, of large businesses.

financial expense. An *expense* incurred in raising or managing *funds.*

financial position (condition). Statement of the *assets* and *equities* of a firm displayed as a *balance sheet.*

financial ratio. See *ratio.*

financial reporting objectives. FASB *Statement of Financial Accounting Concepts No. 1* sets out the broad objectives of financial reporting that are intended to guide the development of specific *accounting standards.*

Financial Reporting Release. New series of releases, issued by the SEC, since 1982. Replaces the *Accounting Series Releases.* See *SEC.*

financial statements. The *balance sheet, income statement, statement of retained earnings, statement of changes in financial position,* statement of changes in *owners' equity accounts,* and *notes* thereto.

financial structure. *Capital structure*.

financial year. The term for *fiscal year* in Australia and Britain.

financing lease. *Capital lease*.

finished goods. Manufactured product ready for sale; a *current asset (inventory) account*.

firm. Informally, any business entity. (Strictly speaking, a firm is a *partnership*.)

first in, first out. See *FIFO*.

fiscal year. A period of 12 consecutive months chosen by a business as the *accounting period* for annual reports. May or may not be a *natural business year* or a calendar year. Called *financial year* in Australia and Britain.

FISH. An acronym, conceived by George H. Sorter, for *first in, still here*. FISH is the same cost flow assumption as *LIFO*. Many readers of accounting statements find it easier to think about inventory questions in terms of items still on hand. Think of LIFO in connection with *cost of goods sold* but of FISH in connection with *ending inventory*. See *LISH*.

fixed assets. *Plant assets*.

fixed assets turnover. *Sales* divided by average total *fixed assets*.

fixed benefit plan. A *defined-benefit (pension) plan*.

fixed budget. A plan that provides for specified amounts of *expenditures* and *receipts* that do not vary with activity levels. Sometimes called a "static budget." Contrast with *flexible budget*.

fixed charges earned (coverage) ratio. *Income* before *interest expense* and *income tax expense* divided by interest expense.

fixed cost (expense). An *expenditure* or *expense* that does not vary with volume of activity, at least in the short run. See *capacity costs*, which include *enabling costs* and *standby costs*, and *programmed costs* for various subdivisions of fixed costs. See *cost terminology*.

fixed liability. *Long-term* liability.

fixed manufacturing overhead applied. The portion of *fixed manufacturing overhead cost* allocated to units produced during a period.

flexible budget. *Budget* that projects receipts and expenditures as a function of activity levels. Contrast with *fixed budget*.

flexible budget allowance. With respect to manufacturing overhead, the total cost that should have been incurred at the level of activity actually experienced during the period.

float. *Checks* whose amounts have been *added* to the depositor's bank account, but not yet subtracted from the *drawer's* bank account.

flow. The change in the amount of an item over time. Contrast with *stock*.

flow assumption. When a *withdrawal* is made from *inventory*, the cost of the withdrawal must be computed by a flow assumption if *specific identification* of units is not used. The usual flow assumptions are *FIFO, LIFO,* and *weighted-average*.

flow of costs. *Costs* passing through various classifications within an *entity*. See the diagram on page 820 for a summary of *product* and *period cost* flows.

flow-through method. Accounting for the *investment credit* to show all income statement benefits of the credit in the year of acquisition, rather than spreading them over the life of the asset acquired, called the "deferral method." The *APB* preferred the deferral method in *Opinion* No. 2 (1962) but accepted the flow-through method in *Opinion* No. 4 (1964). The term is also used in connection with *depreciation* accounting, where the *straight-line method* is used for financial reporting and an *accelerated* method for tax reporting. Followers of the flow-through method would not recognize a *deferred tax liability*. APB *Opinion* No. 11 prohibits the use of the flow-through approach in financial reporting, although it has been used by some regulatory commissions.

FOB. Free on board some location (for example, FOB shipping point; FOB destination); the *invoice* price includes delivery at seller's expense to that location. Title to goods usually passes from seller to buyer at the FOB location.

footing. Adding a column of figures.

footnotes. More detailed information than that provided in the *income statement, balance sheet, statement of retained earnings,* and *statement of changes in financial position*; these are considered an integral part of the statements and are covered by the *auditor's report*. Sometimes called "notes."

forecast. An estimate or projection of costs or revenues or both.

foreclosure. The borrower fails to make a required payment on a *mortgage*; the lender takes possession of the property for his or her own use or sale. Assume that the lender sells the property but the proceeds of sale are insufficient to cover the outstanding balance on the loan at the time of foreclosure. Under the terms of most mortgages, the lender becomes an unsecured creditor of the borrower for the still-unrecovered balance of the loan.

Flow of Costs (and Sales Revenue)

*The credit in the entry to record these items is usually to a payable; for all others, the credit is usually to an asset, or to an asset contra account.
**When sales to customers are recorded, the Sales account is credited. The debit is usually to Cash or Accounts Receivable.

foreign currency. For *financial statements* prepared in a given currency, any other currency.

foreign exchange gain or loss. Gain or loss from holding *net* foreign *monetary items* during a period when the *exchange rate* changes.

Form 10-K. See *10-K*.

forward exchange contract. An agreement to exchange at a specified future date currencies of different countries at a specified rate called the "forward rate."

franchise. A privilege granted or sold, such as to use a name or to sell products or services.

free on board. *FOB*.

freight-in. The *cost* of freight or shipping incurred in acquiring *inventory*, preferably treated as a part of the cost of *inventory*. Often shown temporarily in an *adjunct account* that is closed at the end of the period with other purchase accounts to the inventory account by the acquirer.

freight-out. The *cost* of freight or shipping incurred in selling *inventory*, treated by the seller as a selling *expense* in the period of sale.

full (aborption) costing. *Absorption costing*; the "full" is not necessary, but is often used for emphasis. See *reserve recognition accounting* for another definition in the context of accounting for natural resources.

full disclosure. The reporting policy requiring that all significant or *material* information is to be presented in the financial statements. See *fair presentation*.

fully diluted earnings per share. Smallest *earnings per-share* figure on *common stock* that can be obtained by computing earnings per share for all possible combinations of assumed *exercise* or *conversion* of *potentially dilutive securities*. Must be reported on the *income statement* if it is 97 percent or less of earnings available to common shareholders divided by the average number of common shares outstanding during the period.

fully vested. Said of a *pension plan* when an employee (or his or her estate) has rights to all the benefits purchased with the employer's contributions to the plan even if the employee is not employed by this employer at the time of death or retirement.

function. In governmental accounting, said of a group of related activities for accomplishing a service or regulatory program for which the governmental unit is responsible. In mathematics, a rule for associating a number, called the dependent variable, with another number or numbers, called independent variable(s).

functional classification. *Income statement* reporting form in which *expenses* are reported by functions, that is,

cost of goods sold, administrative expenses, financing expenses, selling expenses; contrast with *natural classification*.

fund. An *asset* or group of assets set aside for a specific purpose. See also *fund accounting*.

fund accounting. The accounting for resources, obligations, and *capital* balances, usually of a not-for-profit or governmental *entity*, which have been segregated into *accounts* representing logical groupings based on legal, donor, or administrative restrictions or requirements. The groupings are described as "funds." The accounts of each fund are *self-balancing* and from them a *balance sheet* and an operating statement for each fund can be prepared. See *fund* and *fund balance*.

fund balance. In governmental accounting, the excess of assets of a *fund* over its liabilities and reserves; the not-for-profit equivalent of *owners' equity*.

funded. Said of a *pension plan* or other obligation when *funds* have been set aside to meet the obligation when it becomes due. The federal law for pension plans requires that all *normal costs* be funded as recognized. In addition, *actuarial accrued liability* of pension plans must be funded over 30 or over 40 years, depending on the circumstances.

funding. Replacing *short-term* liabilities with *long-term* debt.

funds. Generally *working capital*; current assets less current liabilities. Sometimes used to refer to *cash* or to cash and *marketable securities*.

funds provided by operations. An important subtotal in the *statement of changes in financial position*. This amount is the total of revenues producing *funds* less *expenses requiring funds*. Often, the amount is shown as *net income* plus expenses not requiring funds (such as depreciation charges) minus revenues not producing funds (such as revenues recognized under the *equity method* of accounting for a long-term investment). The statement of changes in financial position maintains the same distinctions between *continuing operations, discontinued operations*, and *income* or *loss* from *extraordinary items* as does the *income statement*.

funds statement. An informal name often used for the *statement of changes in financial position*.

funny money. Said of securities such as *convertible preferred stock, convertible bonds, options*, and *warrants* that have aspects of *common stock* equity but that did not reduce reported *earnings per share* prior to the issuance of *APB Opinions* No. 9, in 1967, and No. 15, in 1969.

FUTA. Federal Unemployment Tax Act, which provides for taxes to be collected at the federal level to help subsidize the individual states' administration of their unemployment compensation programs.

future value. Value at a specified future date of a sum increased at a specified *interest rate*.

G

GAAP. *Generally accepted accounting principles*. A plural noun.

gain. Increase in *owners' equity* caused by a transaction not part of a firm's typical, day-to-day operations and not part of owners' *investment* or *withdrawals*. The term "gain" (or "*loss*") is distinguished in two separate ways from related terms. First, gains (and losses) are generally used for nonoperating, incidental, peripheral, or nonroutine transactions: gain on sale of land in contrast to *gross margin* on *sale* of *inventory*. Second, gains and losses are *net* concepts, not gross concepts: gain or loss results from subtracting some measure of *cost* from the measure of inflow. *Revenues* and *expenses*, on the other hand, are gross concepts; their difference is a net concept. Gain is nonroutine and net, *profit* or *margin* is routine and net; revenue is routine and gross. Loss is net but can be either routine ("loss on sale of inventory") or not ("loss on disposal of segment of business").

gain contingency. See *contingency*.

gearing. British term for *financial leverage*.

gearing adjustment. Consider a firm, part of whose assets are *noncurrent liabilities* and who has experience *holding gains* on its *assets* during a period. All of the increase in wealth caused by the holding gains belongs to the owners; none typically belongs to the lenders. Some British accounting authorities believe that published *income statements* should show the part of the holding gain as financed with debt in *income* for the period. That part is called the "gearing adjustment."

general debt. Debt of a governmental unit legally payable from general revenues and backed by the full faith and credit of the governmental unit.

general expenses. *Operating expenses* other than those specifically assigned to cost of goods sold, selling, and administration.

general fixed asset (group of accounts). Accounts showing those long-term assets of a governmental unit not accounted for in *enterprise, trust,* or intragovernmental service funds.

general fund. Assets and liabilities of a nonprofit entity not specifically earmarked for other purposes; the primary operating fund of a governmental unit.

general journal. The formal record where transactions, or summaries of similar transactions, are recorded in *journal entry* form as they occur. Use of the adjective "general" usually implies only two columns for cash amounts or that there are also various *special journals*, such as a *check register* or *sales journal*, in use.

general ledger. The name for the formal *ledger* containing all of the financial statement accounts. It has equal debits and credits as evidenced by the *trial balance*. Some of the accounts in the general ledger may be *controlling accounts*, supported by details contained in *subsidiary ledgers*.

general partner. Member of *partnership* personally liable for all debts of the partnership; contrast with *limited partner*.

general price index. A measure of the aggregate prices of a wide range of goods and services in the economy at one time relative to the prices during a base period. See *Consumer Price Index* and *GNP Implicit Price Deflator*. Contrast with *specific price index*.

general price level changes. Changes in the aggregate prices of a wide range of goods and services in the economy. These price changes are measured using a *general price index*. Contrast with *specific price changes*.

general price level-adjusted statements. See *constant dollar accounting*.

general purchasing power. The command of the dollar over a wide range of goods and services in the economy. The general purchasing power of the dollar is inversely related to changes in a general price index. See *general price index*.

general purchasing power accounting. See *constant dollar accounting*.

generally accepted accounting principles. GAAP. As previously defined by the *APB* and now by the *FASB*, the conventions, rules, and procedures necessary to define accepted accounting practice at a particular time; includes both broad guidelines and relatively detailed practices and procedures.

generally accepted auditing standards. The standards, as opposed to particular procedures, promulgated by the *AICPA* (in *Statements on Auditing Standards*) that concern "the auditor's professional quantities" and "the judgment exercised by him in the performance of his examination and in his report." Currently, there are 10 such standards: three general ones (concerned with proficiency, independence, and degree of care to be exercised), three standards of field work, and four standards of reporting. The first standard of reporting requires that the *auditor's report* state whether or not the *financial statements* are prepared in accordance with *generally accepted accounting principles*. Thus, the typical auditor's report says that the examination was conducted in accordance with generally accepted auditing standards and that the statements are prepared in accordance with generally accepted accounting principles. See *auditor's report*.

GNP Implicit Price Deflator (Index). A *price index* issued quarterly by the Office of Business Economics of the U.S. Department of Commerce. This index attempts to trace the price level of all *goods and services* comprising the *gross national product*. Contrast with *Consumer Price Index*.

going public. Said of a business when its *shares* become widely traded, rather than being closely held by relatively few shareholders. Issuing shares to the general investing public.

going-concern assumption. For accounting purposes a business is assumed to remain in operation long enough for all its current plans to be carried out. This assumption is part of the justification for the *acquisition cost* basis, rather than a *liquidation* or *exit value* basis, of accounting.

goods. Items of merchandise, supplies, raw materials, or finished goods. Sometimes the meaning of "goods" is extended to include all *tangible* items, as in the phrase "goods and services."

goods available for sale. The sum of *beginning inventory* plus all acquisitions of merchandise or finished goods during an *accounting period*.

goods in process. *Work in process*.

goodwill. The excess of cost of an acquired firm (or operating unit) over the current *fair market value* of the separately identifiable *net assets* of the acquired unit. Before goodwill is recognized, all identifiable assets, whether or not on the books of the acquired unit, must be given a *fair market value*. For example, a firm has developed a *patent* that is not recognized on its books because of *SFAS No. 2*. If another company acquires the firm, the acquirer will recognize the patent at an amount equal to its estimated fair market value. Informally, the term is used to indicate the value of good customer relations, high employee morale, a well-respected business name, and so on, that are expected to result in greater than normal earning power.

goodwill method. A method of accounting for the *admission* of a new partner to a *partnership* when the new partner is to be credited with a portion of capital different from the value of the *tangible* assets contributed as a fraction of tangible assets on the partnership. See *bonus method* for a description and contrast.

GPL. General price level; usually used as an adjective modifying the word "accounting" to mean *constant dollar accounting*.

GPLA. General price level-adjusted accounting; *constant dollar accounting*.

GPP. General purchasing power; usually used as an adjective modifying the word "accounting" to mean *constant dollar accounting*.

graded vesting. Said of a *pension plan* where not all employee benefits are currently *vested*. By law, the benefits must become vested according to one of several formulas as time passes.

grandfather clause. An exemption in new accounting *pronouncements* exempting transactions that occurred before a given date from the new accounting treatment. For example, *APB Opinion* No. 17, adopted in 1970, exempted *goodwill* acquired before 1970 from required *amortization*. The term "grandfather" appears in the title to *SFAS No. 10*.

gross. Not adjusted or reduced by deductions or subtractions. Contrast with *net*.

gross margin. *Net sales* minus *cost of goods sold*.

gross margin percent. $100 \times (1 - cost\ of\ goods\ sold/net\ sales) = 100 \times (gross\ margin/net\ sales)$.

gross national product. GNP. The market value within a nation for a year of all goods and services produced as measured by final sales of goods and services to individuals, corporations, and governments plus the excess of exports over imports.

gross price method (of recording purchase or sales discounts). The *purchase* (or *sale*) is recorded at its *invoice price*, not deducting the amounts of *discounts* available. Discounts taken are recorded in a *contra* account to purchases (or sales). Information on discounts lapsed is not made available, and for this reason, most firms prefer the *net price method* of recording purchase discounts.

gross profit. *Gross margin*.

gross profit method. A method of estimating *ending inventory* amounts. *Cost of goods sold* is measured as some fraction of sales; the *inventory equation* is then used to value *ending inventory*.

gross profit ratio. *Gross margin* divided by *net sales*.

gross sales. All *sales* at *invoice* prices, not reduced by *discounts, allowances, returns*, or other adjustments.

group depreciation. A method of calculating *depreciation* charges where similar assets are combined rather than depreciated separately. No gain or loss is recognized upon retirement of items from the group until the last item in the group is sold or retired. See *composite life method*.

guarantee. A promise to answer for payment of debt or performance of some obligation if the person liable for the debt or obligation fails to perform. A guarantee is a *contingency* of the *entity* making the promise. Often, the words "guarantee" and "warranty" are used to mean the same thing. In precise usage, however, "guarantee" means a promise to fulfill the promise of some person to perform a contractual obligation such as to pay a sum of money, whereas ''warranty'' is most often used to refer to promises about pieces of machinery or other products. See *warranty*.

H

half-year convention. An assumption used in *tax accounting* under *ACRS*, and sometimes in *financial accounting*, that *depreciable assets* were acquired at mid-year of the year of acquisition. When this convention is used, the *depreciation charge* for the year is computed as one-half the charge that would be used if the assets had been acquired at the beginning of the year.

hidden reserve. The term refers to an amount by which *owners' equity* has been understated, perhaps deliberately. The understatement arises from an undervaluation of *assets* or overvaluation of *liabilities*. By undervaluing assets on this period's *balance sheet*, *net income* in some future period can be made to look artificially high by disposing of the asset: Actual *revenues* less artificially low cost of assets sold yields artificially high net income. There is no *account* that has this title.

historical cost. *Acquisition cost; original cost; a sunk cost.*

historical cost/constant dollar accounting. Accounting based on *historical cost* valuations measured in *constant dollars*. *Nonmonetary items* are restated to reflect changes in the *general purchasing power* of the dollar since the time the specific *assets* were acquired or *liabilities* were incurred. A *gain* or *loss* is recognized on *monetary items* as they are held over time periods when the general purchasing power of the dollar changes.

historical summary. A part of the *annual report* to shareholders that shows important items, such as *net income, revenues, expenses, asset* and *equity* totals, *earnings per share*, and the like, for 5 or 10 periods including the current one. Usually not as much detail is shown in the historical summary as in *comparative statements*, which typically report as much detail for the two preceding years as for the current year. Annual reports may contain both comparative statements and a historical summary.

holding company. A company that confines its activities to owning *stock* in, and supervising management of, other companies. A holding company usually owns a controlling interest in, that is, more than 50 percent of the voting stock of, the companies whose stock it holds. Contrast with *mutual fund*. See *conglomerate*. In British usage, the term refers to any company with controlling interest in another company.

holding gain or loss. Difference between end-of-period price and beginning-of-period price of an asset held during the period. Realized holding gains and losses are not ordinarily separately reported in financial statements. Unrealized gains are not usually reflected in income at all. Some unrealized losses, such as on inventory or marketable securities, are reflected in income or *owners' equity* as the losses occur; see *lower of cost or market*. See *inventory profit* for further refinement, including *gains* on *assets* sold during the period. See also *backlog depreciation*.

holding gain or loss net of inflation. Increase or decrease in the *current cost* of an asset while it is held measured in units of *constant dollars*.

holding period. The time between acquisition and disposition of an *asset*. The length of the holding period can affect the tax rate applied to the *gain* or *loss* upon sale.

horizontal analysis. *Time-series analysis.*

human resource accounting. A term used to describe a variety of proposals that seek to report and emphasize the importance of human resources—knowledgeable, trained, and loyal employees—in a company's earning process and total assets.

hurdle rate. Required rate of return in a *discounted cash flow* analysis.

hybrid security. *Security*, such as a *convertible bond*, containing elements of both *debt* and *owners' equity*.

hypothecation. The *pledging* of property, without transfer of title or possession, to secure a loan.

I

I. *Identity matrix.*

IAA. *Interamerican Accounting Association.*

ideal standard costs. *Standard costs* set equal to those that would be incurred under the best possible conditions.

identity matrix. A square *matrix* with ones on the main diagonal and zeros elsewhere; a matrix **I** such that for any other matrix **A**, **IA** = **AI** = **A**. The matrix equivalent to the number one.

IIA. *Institute of Internal Auditors.*

IMA. Institute of Management Accounting. See *CMA* and *National Association of Accountants*.

implicit interest. *Interest* not paid or received. See *interest, imputed*. All transactions involving the deferred payment or receipt of cash involve interest, whether explicitly mentioned or not. The implicit interest on a single-payment *note* is the difference between the amount collected at maturity less the amount lent at the start of the loan. The implicit *interest rate* per year can be computed from

$$\frac{\text{Cash Received at Maturity}}{\text{Cash Lent}}^{(1/t)} - 1$$

where t is the term of the loan in years; t need not be an integer.

imprest fund. *Petty cash fund.*

improvement. An *expenditure* to extend the useful life of an *asset* or to improve its performance (rate of output, cost) over that of the original asset. Such expenditures are *capitalized* as part of the asset's cost. Sometimes called "betterment." Contrast with *maintenance* and *repair*.

imputed cost. A cost that does not appear in accounting records, such as the *interest* that could be earned on cash spent to acquire inventories rather than, say, government bonds. Or, consider a firm that owns the buildings it occupies. This firm has an imputed cost for rent in an amount equal to what it would have to pay to use similar buildings owned by another.

imputed interest. See *interest, imputed*.

in the black (red). Operating at a profit (loss).

income. *Excess of revenues* and *gains* over *expenses* and *losses* for a period; *net income*. Sometimes used with an appropriate modifier to refer to the various intermediate amounts shown in a *multiple-step income statement*. Sometimes used to refer to revenues, as in "rental income." See *comprehensive income*.

income accounts. *Revenue* and *expense accounts*.

income before taxes. On the *income statement*, the difference between all *revenues* and *expenses* except *income tax* expense. Contrast with *net income* and *taxable income*.

income (revenue) bond. See *special revenue debt*.

income determination. See *determine*.

income distribution account. *Temporary account* sometimes debited when *dividends* are declared; closed to *retained earnings*.

income from continuing operations. As defined by *APB Opinion No. 30*, all *revenues* less all *expenses* except for the following: results of operations (including income tax effects) that have been or will be discontinued; *gains* or *losses*, including income tax effects, on disposal of segments of the business; gains or losses, including income tax effects, from *extraordinary items*; and the cumulative effect of *accounting changes*.

income from discontinued operations. *Income*, net of tax effects, from parts of the business that have been discontinued during the period or are to be discontinued in the near future. Such items are reported on a separate line of the *income statement* after *income from continuing operations* but before *extraordinary items*.

income smoothing. A method of timing business *transactions* or choosing *accounting principles* so that variations in reported *income* from year to year are reduced from what they would otherwise be. Although income smooth-ing is an objective of some managements, it is not an official *accounting principle* or *reporting objective*.

income statement. The statement of *revenues, expenses, gains*, and *losses* for the period, ending with *net income* for the period. The *earnings-per-share* amount is usually shown on the income statement; the *reconciliation* of beginning and ending balances of *retained earnings* may also be shown in a combined statement of income and retained earnings. See *income from continuing operations, income from discontinued operations, extraordinary items, multiple-step, single-step*.

income summary. An *account* used in problem solving that serves as a surrogate for the *income statement*. All *revenues* are closed to the income summary account as *credits*, and all *expenses* as *debits*. The *balance* in the account, after all other *closing entries* are made, is then closed to the retained earnings or other *owners' equity* account and represents *net income* for the period.

income tax. An annual tax levied by the federal and other governments on the income of an entity.

income tax allocation. See *deferred tax liability* and *tax allocation: intrastatement*.

incremental. An adjective used to describe the change in *cost, expense, investment, cash flow, revenue, profit*, and the like if one or more units are produced or sold or if an activity is undertaken.

indenture. See *bond indenture*.

independence. The mental attitude required of the *CPA* in performing the *attest* function. It implies impartiality and that the members of the auditing CPA firm own no stock in the corporation being audited.

independent accountant. The *CPA* who performs the *attest* function for a firm.

indeterminate-term liability. An obligation not due at a definite time. This term is our own coinage to encompass the *deferred income tax credit* and *minority interest*.

indexation. An attempt by lawmakers or parties to a contract to cope with the effects of *inflation*. Amounts fixed in law or contracts are "indexed" when these amounts change as a given measure of price changes. For example, a so-called escalator clause (*COLA*) in a labor contract might provide that hourly wages will be increased as the *Consumer Price Index* increases. Many economists have suggested the indexation of numbers fixed in the *income tax* laws. If, for example, the personal *exemption* is $1,000 at the start of the period, prices rise by 10 percent during the period, and the personal exemption is indexed, then the personal exemption would automatically rise to $1,100 (= $1,000 + .10 \times 1,000$) at the end of the period.

indirect cost pool. Any grouping of individual costs that are not identified with a *cost objective*.

indirect costs. Costs of production not easily associated with the production of specific goods and services; *overhead costs*. May be *allocated* on some arbitrary basis to specific products or departments.

indirect labor (material) cost. An *indirect cost* for labor (material), such as for supervisors (supplies).

individual proprietorship. *Sole proprietorship*.

Industry Audit Guide. A series of publications by the *AICPA* providing specific *accounting* and *auditing principles* for specialized situations. Audit guides have been issued covering government contractors, state and local government units, investment companies, finance companies, brokers and dealers in securities, and many others.

inflation. A time of generally rising prices.

inflation accounting. Strictly speaking, *constant dollar accounting*. Some writers use the term, incorrectly, to mean *current cost accounting*.

information system. A system, sometimes formal and sometimes informal, for collecting, processing, and communicating data that are useful for the managerial functions of decision making, planning, and control, and for financial reporting under the *attest* requirement.

insolvent. Unable to pay debts when due. Said of a company even though *assets* exceed *liabilities*.

installment. Partial payment of a debt or collection of a receivable, usually according to a contract.

installment contracts receivable. The name used for *accounts receivable* when the *installment method* of recognizing revenue is used. Its *contra, unrealized gross margin*, is shown on the balance sheet as a subtraction from the amount receivable.

installment (sales) method. Recognizing *revenue* and *expense* (or *gross margin*) from a sales transaction in proportion to the fraction of the selling price collected during a period. Allowed by the *IRS* for income tax reporting, but acceptable in *GAAP (APB Opinion* No. 10*)* only when cash collections are reasonably uncertain. See *realized* (and *unrealized*) *gross margin*.

installment sales. Sales on account where the buyer promises to pay in several separate payments, called *installments*. Sometimes are, but need not be, accounted for on the *installment method*. If installment sales are accounted for with the sales *basis of revenue recognition* for financial reporting, but with the installment method for income tax returns, then a *deferred income tax liability* arises.

Institute of Internal Auditors. IIA. The national association of accountants who are engaged in internal auditing and are employed by business firms. Administers a comprehensive professional examination; those who pass qualify to be designated CIA, certified internal auditor.

Institute of Management Accounting. See *CMA*.

insurance. A contract for reimbursement of specific losses; purchased with insurance premiums. Self-insurance is not insurance but merely the willingness to assume risk of incurring losses while saving the premium.

intangible asset. A nonphysical, *noncurrent* right that gives a firm an exclusive or preferred position in the marketplace. Examples are a *copyright, patent, trademark, goodwill, organization costs, capitalized* advertising cost, computer programs, licenses for any of the preceding, government licenses (e.g., broadcasting or the right to sell liquor), *leases*, franchises, mailing lists, exploration permits, import and export permits, construction permits, and marketing quotas.

Interamerican Accounting Association. An organization, headquartered in Mexico City, devoted to facilitating interaction among accounting practitioners in Central America, North America, and South America.

intercompany elimination. See *eliminations*.

intercompany profit. If one *affiliated company* sells to another, and the goods remain in the second company's *inventory* at the end of the period, then the first company's *profit* has not been realized by a sale to an outsider. That profit is called "intercompany profit" and is eliminated from net *income* in *consolidated income statements* or when the *equity method* is used.

intercompany transaction. *Transaction* between *parent company* and *subsidiary* or between subsidiaries in a *consolidated entity* whose effects are eliminated in preparing *consolidated financial statements*. See *intercompany profit*.

intercorporate investment. A given *corporation* owns *shares* or *debt* issued by another.

interest. The charge or cost for using money; the earnings from lending money; expressed as a rate per period, usually 1 year, called the interest rate. See *effective interest rate* and *nominal interest rate*.

interest, imputed. If a borrower merely promises to pay a single amount, sometime later than the present, then the present value (computed at a *fair market* interest rate, called the "imputed interest rate") of the promise is less than the *face amount* to be paid at *maturity*. The difference between the face amount and the present value of a promise is called imputed interest. See also *imputed cost*.

interest factor. One plus the *interest* rate.

interest method. See *effective interest method*.

interest rate. See *interest*.

interfund accounts. In governmental accounting, the accounts that show transactions between funds, especially interfund receivables and payables.

interim statements. Statements issued for periods less than the regular, annual *accounting period*. Most corporations are required to issue interim statements on a quarterly basis. The basic issue in preparing interim reports is whether their purpose is to report on the interim period (1) as a self-contained accounting period, or (2) as an integral part of the year of which they are a part so that forecasts of annual performance can be made. *APB Opinion* No. 28 and the *SEC* require that interim reports be constructed largely to satisfy the second purpose.

internal audit. An *audit* conducted by employees to ascertain whether or not *internal control* procedures are working, as opposed to an external audit conducted by a *CPA*.

internal control. See *control system*.

internal rate of return. The discount rate that equates the net *present value* of a stream of cash outflows and inflows to zero.

internal reporting. Reporting for management's use in planning and control; contrast with *external reporting* for financial statement users.

Internal Revenue Service. IRS. Agency of the U.S. Treasury Department responsible for administering the Internal Revenue Code and collecting income, and certain other, taxes.

International Accounting Standards Committee. An organization that promotes the establishment of international accounting standards.

interperiod tax allocation. *Income tax expense* is assigned to the period when *income* is earned for *financial reporting* purposes rather than to the period when an obligation to pay *income taxes* is generated. This process is sometimes called "normalization" of income tax expense. See *deferred income tax liability*.

interpolation. The estimation of an unknown number intermediate between two (or more) known numbers.

***Interpretations of Statements of Financial Accounting Standards*.** See *FASB Interpretations*.

intrastatement tax allocation. See *tax allocation: intrastatement*.

inventoriable costs. *Costs* incurred that are added to the cost of manufactured products. *Product costs (assets)* as opposed to *period expenses*.

inventory. As a noun, the *balance* in an asset *account* such as raw materials, supplies, work in process, and finished goods. As a verb, to calculate the *cost* of goods on hand at a given time or physically to count items on hand.

inventory equation. *Beginning inventory* + net additions − withdrawals = ending inventory. Ordinarily, additions are net purchases and withdrawals are *cost of goods sold*. Notice that ending inventory, to be shown on the balance sheet, and cost of goods sold, to be shown on the income statement, are not independent of each other. The larger is one, the smaller must be the other. In valuing inventories, beginning inventory and net purchases are usually known. In some inventory methods (for example, some applications of the *retail inventory method*), costs of goods sold is measured and the equation is used to find the cost of ending inventory. In most methods, cost of ending inventory is measured and the equation is used to find the cost of goods sold (withdrawals). In *current cost* (in contrast to *historical cost*) accounting, *additions* (in the equation) include holding gains, whether realized or not. Thus the current cost inventory equation is: Beginning Inventory (at Current Cost) + Purchases (Where Current Cost Is Historical Cost) + Holding Gains (Whether Realized or Not) − Ending Inventory (at Current Cost) = Cost of Goods Sold (Current Cost).

inventory flow assumption. *Flow assumption* for measuring *inventory* and *cost of goods sold*.

inventory holding gains. See *inventory profit*.

inventory layer. See *LIFO inventory layer*.

inventory profit. This term has several possible meanings. Consider the data in the accompanying illustration. The *historical cost* data are derived in the conventional manner; the firm uses a *FIFO cost flow assumption*. The *current cost* data are assumed, but are of the kind that the *FASB* requires in *SFAS No. 33*.

The term *income from continuing operations* refers to revenues less expenses based on current, rather than historical, costs. To that subtotal add realized holding gains to arrive at realized (conventional) income. To that, add unrealized holding gains to arrive at *economic income*.

The term "inventory profit" often refers (for example, in some *SEC* releases) to the realized holding gain, $110 in the illustration. The amount of inventory profit will usually be material when FIFO is used and prices are rising.

Others, including ourselves, prefer to use the term "inventory profit" to refer to the total *holding gain*, $300 (=$110 + $190, both realized and unrealized), but this appears to be a lost cause.

In periods of rising prices and increasing inventories, the realized holding gains under a FIFO cost flow assumption will be substantially larger than under LIFO. In the illustration, for example, assume under LIFO that the historical cost of goods sold is $4,800, that historical LIFO cost of beginning inventory is $600, and that historical LIFO cost of ending inventory is $800. Then income from

Inventory Profit Illustration

	(Historical) Acquisition Cost Assuming FIFO	Current Cost
Assumed Data		
Inventory, 1/1/82	$ 900	$1,100
Inventory, 12/31/82	1,160	1,550
Cost of Goods Sold for 1982 . .	4,740	4,850
Sales for 1982	$5,200	$5,200
INCOME STATEMENT FOR 1982		
Sales	$5,200	$5,200
Cost of Goods Sold.	4,740	4,850
(1) Income from Continuing Operations		$ 350
Realized Holding Gains		110[a]
(2) Realized Income = Conventional Net Income (under FIFO)	$ 460	$ 460
Unrealized Holding Gain		190[b]
(3) Economic income		$ 650

[a]Realized holding gain during a period is current cost of goods sold less historical cost of goods sold; for 1982 the realized holding gain under FIFO is $110 = $4,850 − $4,740. Some refer to this as ''inventory profit.''
[b]The total unrealized holding gain at any time is current cost of inventory on hand at that time less historical cost of that inventory. The unrealized holding gain during a period is unrealized holding gain at the end of the period less the unrealized holding gain at the beginning of the period. Unrealized holding gain prior to 1982 is $200 = $1,100 − $900. Unrealized holding gain during 1982 = ($1,550 − $1,160) − ($1,100 − $900) = $390 − $200 = $190.

continuing operations, based on current costs, remains $350 (=$5,200 − $4,850), realized holding gains are $50 (=$4,850 − $4,800), realized income is $400 (=$350 + $50), the unrealized holding gain for the year is $250 [=($1,550 − $800) − ($1,100 − $600)], and economic income is $650 (=$350 + $50 + $250). Because the only real effect of the cost flow assumption is to split the total holding gain into realized and unrealized portions, economic income is the same, independent of the cost flow assumption. The total of holding gains is $300 in the illustration. The choice of cost flow assumption merely determines the portion reported as realized.

inventory turnover. Number of times the average *inventory* has been sold during a period; *cost of goods sold* for a period divided by average inventory for the period. See *ratio*.

invested capital. *Contributed capital*.

investee. A company whose *stock* is owned by another.

investment. An *expenditure* to acquire property or other assets in order to produce *revenue;* the *asset* so acquired; hence a *current* expenditure made in anticipation of future income. Said of *securities* of other companies held for the long term and shown in a separate section of the *balance sheet;* in this context, contrast with *marketable securities*.

investment credit. A reduction in income tax liability granted by the federal government to firms that buy new equipment. This item is a credit, in that it is deducted from the tax bill, not from pretax income. The tax credit has been a given percentage of the purchase price of certain assets purchased. The actual rules and rates have changed over the years. See *flow-through method* and *carryforward*.

investment tax credit. *Investment credit*.

invoice. A document showing the details of a sale or purchase transaction.

IRR. *Internal rate of return*.

IRS. *Internal Revenue Service*.

issue. When a corporation exchanges its stock (or bonds) for cash or other assets, the corporation is said to issue, not sell, that stock (or bonds). Also used in the context of withdrawing supplies or materials from inventory for use in operations and drawing of a *check*.

issued shares. Those shares of *authorized capital stock* of a *corporation* that have been distributed to the shareholders. See *issue*. Shares of *treasury stock* are legally issued but are not considered to be *outstanding* for the purpose of voting, *dividend declarations*, and *earnings-per-share* calculations.

J

job cost sheet. A schedule showing actual or budgeted inputs for a special order.

job development credit. The name used for the *investment credit* in the 1971 tax law on this subject.

job-order costing. Accumulation of *costs* for a particular identifiable batch of product, known as a job, as it moves through production.

joint cost. Cost of simultaneously producing or otherwise acquiring two or more products, called joint products, that must, by the nature of the process, be produced or acquired together, such as the cost of beef and hides of cattle. Generally, the joint costs of production are allocated to the individual products in proportion to their respective sales value at the *splitoff point*. Other examples include central *corporate expenses, overhead* of a department when several products are manufactured, and *basket purchases*. See *common cost*. See *sterilized allocation*.

joint product. One of two or more outputs with significant value produced by a process that must be produced or acquired simultaneously. See *by-product* and *joint cost*.

journal. The place where transactions are recorded as they occur. The book of original entry.

journal entry. A recording in a *journal*, of equal *debits* and *credits*, with an explanation of the *transaction*, if necessary.

Journal of Accountancy. A monthly publication of the *AICPA*.

Journal of Accounting Research. Scholarly journal containing articles on theoretical and empirical aspects of accounting. Published three times a year by the Graduate School of Business of the University of Chicago.

journal voucher. A *voucher* documenting (and sometimes authorizing) a transaction, leading to an entry in the *journal*.

journalize. To make an entry in a *journal*.

K

kiting. This term means slightly different things in banking and auditing contexts. In both, however, it refers to the wrongful practice of taking advantage of the *float*, the time that elapses between the deposit of a *check* in one bank and its collection at another. In the banking context, an individual deposits in Bank A a check written on Bank B. He (or she) then writes checks against the deposit created in Bank A. Several days later, he deposits in Bank B a check written on Bank A, to cover the original check written on Bank B. Still later, he deposits in Bank A a check written on Bank B. The process of covering the deposit in Bank A with a check written on Bank B and vice versa is continued until an actual deposit of cash can be arranged. In the auditing context, kiting refers to a form of *window dressing* where the amount of the account Cash in Bank is made to appear larger than it actually is by depositing in Bank A a check written on Bank B without recording the check written on Bank B in the *check register* until after the close of the *accounting period*.

know-how. Technical or business information of the type defined under *trade secret*, but that is not maintained as a secret. The rules of accounting for this asset are the same as for other *intangibles*.

L

labor variances. The *price* (or *rate*) and *quantity* (or *usage*) *variances* for *direct labor* inputs in a *standard cost system*.

land. An *asset shown at acquisition cost* plus the *cost* of any nondepreciable *improvements*. In accounting, implies use as a plant or office site, rather than as a *natural resource*, such as timber land or farm land.

lapping (accounts receivable). The theft, by an employee, of cash sent in by a customer to discharge the latter's *payable*. The theft from the first customer is concealed by using cash received from a second customer. The theft from the second customer is concealed by using the cash received from a third customer, and so on. The process is continued until the thief returns the funds or can make the theft permanent by creating a fictitious *expense* or receivable write-off, or until the fraud is discovered.

lapse. To expire; said of, for example, an insurance policy or discounts made available for prompt payment that are not taken.

last in, first out. See *LIFO*.

layer. See *LIFO inventory layer*.

lead time. The time that elapses between placing an order and receipt of the *goods* or *services* ordered.

learning curve. A mathematical expression of the phenomenon that incremental unit costs to produce decrease as managers and labor gain experience from practice.

lease. A contract calling for the lessee (user) to pay the lessor (owner) for the use of an asset. A cancelable lease is one the lessee can cancel at any time. A noncancelable lease requires payments from the lessee for the life of the lease and usually has many of the economic characteristics of *debt financing*. Most long-term noncancelable leases meet the usual criteria to be classified as a *liability*, but some leases entered into before 1977 need not be shown as a liability. *SFAS No. 13* and the *SEC* require disclosure in notes to the financial statements of the commitments for long-term noncancelable leases. See *capital lease* and *operating lease*.

leasehold. The *asset* representing the right of the *lessee* to use leased property. See *lease* and *leasehold improvement*.

leasehold improvement. An *improvement* to leased property. Should be *amortized* over *service life* or the life of the lease, whichever is shorter.

least and latest rule. Pay the least amount of taxes as late as possible within the law to minimize the *present value* of tax payments for a given set of operations.

ledger. A book of accounts. See *general ledger* and *subsidiary ledger*; contrast with *journal*. Book of final entry.

legal capital. The amount of *contributed capital* that, according to state law, must remain permanently in the firm as protection for creditors.

legal entity. See *entity*.

lender. See *loan.*

lessee. See *lease.*

lessor. See *lease.*

letter stock. Privately placed *common shares*; so called because the *SEC* requires the purchaser to sign a letter of intent not to resell the shares.

leverage. "Operating leverage" refers to the tendency of *net income* to rise at a faster rate than sales when there are *fixed costs.* A doubling of sales, for example, usually implies a more than doubling of net income. "Financial leverage" (or "capital leverage") refers to the increased rate of return on *owners' equity* (see *ratio*) when an investment earns a return larger than the *interest rate* paid for *debt* financing. Because the interest charges on debt are usually fixed, any *incremental* income benefits owners and none explicitly benefits debtors. When "leverage" is used without a qualifying adjective, it usually refers to financial leverage and means the use of *long-term* debt in securing *funds* for the *entity.*

leveraged lease. A special form of *lease* involving three parties—a *lender,* a *lessor,* and a *lessee.* The lender, such as a bank or insurance company, lends a portion, say, 80 percent, of the cash required to acquire the *asset.* The lessor puts up the remainder, 20 percent, of the cash required. The lessor acquires the asset with the cash, using the asset as security for the loan, and leases it to the lessee on a *noncancelable* basis. The lessee makes periodic lease payments to the lessor, who in turn makes payments on the loan to the lender. Typically, the lessor has no obligation for the debt to the lender other than transferring a portion of the receipts from the lessee. If the lessee should default on required lease payments, then the lender can repossess the leased asset. The lessor is usually entitled to deductions for tax purposes for depreciation on the asset, for interest expense on the loan from the lender, and for any investment credit. The lease is leveraged in the sense that the lessor, who enjoys most of the risks and rewards of ownership, usually borrows most of the funds needed to acquire the asset. See *leverage.*

liability. A probable future sacrifice of economic benefits arising from present obligations of a particular *entity* to *transfer assets* or to provide services to other entities in the future as a result of past *transactions* or events. *SFAC No. 3* says that "probable" refers to that which can reasonably be expected or believed but is neither certain nor proved. A liability has three essential characteristics: (1) transfer of assets or services at a specified or determinable date; (2) the entity has little or no discretion to avoid the transfer; and (3) the event causing the obligation has already happened.

lien. The right of person A to satisfy a claim against person B by holding B's property as security or by seizing B's property.

life annuity. A *contingent annuity* in which payments cease at death of a specified person(s), usually the *annuitant(s).*

LIFO. *Last in, first out.* An *inventory* flow assumption where the *cost of goods sold* is the cost of the most recently acquired units and the *ending inventory cost* is computed from costs of the oldest units; contrast with *FIFO.* In periods of rising prices and increasing inventories, LIFO leads to higher reported expenses and therefore lower reported income and lower balance sheet inventories than does FIFO. See also *FISH* and *inventory profit.*

LIFO conformity rule. The *IRS* requires that companies which use a *LIFO cost flow assumption* for *income taxes* also use LIFO in computing *income* reported in *financial statements* and forbids disclosure of *pro forma* results from using any other cost flow assumption. During 1981, this rule was challenged by a federal court decision in the Insilco case.

LIFO, dollar-value method. See *dollar-value LIFO method.*

LIFO inventory layer. The *ending inventory* for a period is likely to be larger than the *beginning inventory.* Under a *LIFO cost flow assumption,* this increase in physical quantities is given a value computed by the prices of the earliest purchases during the year. The LIFO inventory then consists of layers, sometimes called "slices," which typically consist of relatively small amounts of physical quantities from each of the past several years. Each layer carries the prices from near the beginning of the period when it was acquired. The earliest layers will typically (in periods of rising prices) have prices very much less than current prices. If inventory quantities should decline in a subsequent period, the latest layers enter cost of goods sold first.

LIFO reserve. *Unrealized holding gain* in *ending inventory*: current or *FIFO historical* cost of ending inventory less LIFO *historical cost.* See *reserve.*

limited liability. Shareholders of corporations are not personally liable for debts of the company.

limited partner. Member of a *partnership* not personally liable for debts of the partnership; every partnership must have at least one *general partner* who is fully liable.

line of credit. An agreement with a bank or set of banks for short-term borrowings on demand.

line-of-business reporting. See *segment reporting.*

liquid. Said of a business with a substantial amount (the amount is unspecified) of *working capital,* especially *quick assets.*

liquid assets. *Cash, current marketable securities,* and, sometimes, *current receivables.*

liquidating dividend. *Dividend* declared in the winding up of a business to distribute the assets of the company to the shareholders. Usually treated by recipient as a return of *investment*, not as *revenue*.

liquidation. Payment of a debt. Sale of assets in closing down a business or a segment thereof.

liquidation value per share. The amount each *share* of stock will receive if the corporation is dissolved. For *preferred stock* with a *liquidation preference*, a stated amount per share.

liquidity. Refers to the availability of *cash*, or near cash resources, for meeting a firm's obligations.

LISH. An acronym, conceived by George H. Sorter, for *last in, still here.* LISH is the same cost flow assumption as *FIFO.* Many readers of accounting statements find it easier to think about inventory questions in terms of items still on hand. Think of FIFO in connection with *cost of goods sold* but of LISH in connection with *ending inventory.* See *FISH.*

list price. The published or nominally quoted price for goods.

list price method. See *trade-in transaction.*

loan. An arrangement where the owner of property, called the lender, allows someone else, called the borrower, the use of the property for a period of time that is usually specified in the agreement setting up the loan. The borrower promises to return the property to the lender and, often, to make a payment for use of the property. Generally used when the property is *cash* and the payment for its use is *interest.*

long-lived (term) asset. An asset whose benefits are expected to be received over several years. A *noncurrent* asset; usually includes *investments, plant assets,* and *intangibles.*

long-term (construction) contract accounting. The *percentage-of-completion method* of *revenue* recognition. Sometimes used to mean the *completed contract method.*

long-term liability (debt). *Noncurrent liability.*

loss. Excess of *cost* over net proceeds for a single transaction; negative *income* for a period. A cost expiration that produced no *revenue.* See *gain* for a discussion of related and contrasting terms.

loss contingency. See *contingency.*

lower of cost or market. A basis for valuation of *inventory* or *marketable equity securities.* The inventory value is set at the lower of *acquisition cost* or *current replacement cost* (market), subject to the following constraints: First, the market value of an item used in the computation

cannot exceed its *net realizable value*—an amount equal to selling price less reasonable costs to complete production and to sell the item. Second, the market value of an item used in the computation cannot be less than the net realizable value minus the normal *profit* ordinarily realized on disposition of completed items of this type. The lower-of-cost-or-market valuation is chosen as the lower of acquisition *cost* or replacement cost *(market)* subject to the upper and lower bounds on replacement cost established in the first two steps. Thus,

Market Value = Midvalue of (Replacement Cost, Net Realizable Value, Net Realizable Value Less Normal Profit Margin)

Lower-of-Cost-or-Market Valuation = Minimum of (Acquisition Cost, Market Value)

The accompanying exhibit illustrates the calculation of the lower-of-cost-or-market valuation for four inventory items. Notice that each of the four possible outcomes occurs once in determining lower of cost or market. Item 1 uses acquisition cost; item 2 uses net realizable value; item 3 uses replacement cost; and item 4 uses net realizable value less normal profit.

	Item			
	1	**2**	**3**	**4**
Calculation of Market Value				
(a) Replacement Cost	$92	$96	$92	$96
(b) Net Realizable Value	95	95	95	95
(c) Net Realizable Value Less Normal Profit Margin [= (b) − $9]	86	86	86	86
(d) Market = Midvalue [(a), (b), (c)]	92	95	92	86
Calculation of Lower of Cost or Market				
(e) Acquisition Cost............	90	97	96	90
(f) Market [= (d)]	92	95	92	86
(g) Lower of Cost or Market = Minimum [(e), (f)]	90	95	92	86

Lower of cost or market cannot be used for inventory on tax returns in combination with a *LIFO* flow assumption.

In the context of inventory, once the asset is written down, a new "original cost" basis is established and subsequent increases in market value are ignored in the accounts.

In the context of *marketable equity securities*, the method is applied separately to short-term and long-term portfolios of securities. Losses in market value on the short-term portfolio (and any subsequent recoveries in value up to original cost) are reported as part of *income from continuing operations* for the period. For the long-term portfolio, the losses (and subsequent recoveries, if any) are *debited* (or *credited*) directly to an *owners' equity contra account*.

Note that hyphens are not used when the term is used as a noun but hyphens are used when the term is used as an adjectival phrase.

lump-sum acquisition. *Basket purchase.*

M

maintenance. *Expenditures* undertaken to preserve an *asset's* service potential for its originally intended life; these expenditures are treated as *period expenses* or *product costs*; contrast with *improvement*. See *repair*.

make-or-buy decision. A managerial decision about whether the firm should produce a product internally or purchase it from others. Proper make-or-buy decisions in the short run result when *opportunity costs* are the only costs considered in decision making.

maker (of note) (of check). One who signs a *note* to borrow. One who signs a *check*; in this context synonymous with drawer; see *draft*.

management. Executive authority that operates a business.

Management Accounting. Monthly publication of the *NAA*.

management (managerial) accounting. Reporting designed to enhance the ability of management to do its job of decision making, planning, and control; contrast with *financial accounting*.

management audit. An audit conducted to ascertain whether the objectives, policies, and procedures for a firm or one of its operating units are properly carried out. Generally applies only to activities for which qualitative standards can be specified. See *audit* and *internal audit*.

management by exception. A principle of management where attention is focused only on performance that is significantly different from that expected.

managerial accounting. See *management accounting*.

manufacturing cost. Cost of producing goods, usually in a factory.

manufacturing expense. An imprecise, and generally incorrect, alternative title for *manufacturing overhead*.

manufacturing overhead. General manufacturing *costs* incurred in providing a capacity to carry on productive activities but that are not directly associated with identifiable units of product. *Fixed* manufacturing overhead costs are treated as a *product cost* under *absorption costing* but as an *expense* of the period under *direct costing*.

margin. *Revenue* less specified expenses. See *contribution margin, gross margin*, and *current margin*.

margin of safety. Excess of actual, or budgeted, sales over *breakeven* sales. Usually expressed in dollars; may be expressed in units of product.

marginal cost. The *incremental cost* or *differential cost* of the last unit added to production or the first unit subtracted from production. See *cost terminology*.

marginal costing. *Direct costing*.

marginal revenue. The increment in *revenue* from sale of one additional unit of product.

marginal tax rate. The tax imposed on the next dollar of taxable income generated; contrast with *average tax rate*.

markdown. See *markup* for definition and contrast.

markdown cancellation. See *markup* for definition and contrast.

market price. See *fair market price*.

market rate. The rate of *interest* a company must pay to borrow *funds* currently. See *effective rate*.

marketable equity securities. *Marketable securities* representing *owners' equity* interest in other companies, rather than *loans* to them.

marketable securities. *Stocks* and *bonds* of other companies held that can be readily sold on stock exchanges or over-the-counter markets and that the company plans to sell as cash is needed. Classified as *current assets* and as part of *working capital*. The same securities held for *long-term* purposes would be classified as *noncurrent assets*. *SFAS No. 12* requires the *lower-of-cost-or-market* valuation basis for all marketable equity securities but different accounting treatments (with differing effect on income) depending on whether the security is a *current* or a *noncurrent asset*.

markon. See *markup* for definition and contrast.

markup. When a retailer acquires items for *inventory*, the items are given a selling price. The difference between the original selling price and cost is most precisely called "markon," although many business people use the term "markup," and because of confusion of this use of "markup" with its precise definition (see below), "original markup'' is sometimes used. If the originally established retail price is increased, the precise term for the amount of price increase is ''markup,'' although ''additional markup'' is sometimes used. If a selling price is lowered, the terms ''markdown'' and ''markup cancellation'' are used. ''Markup cancellation'' refers to reduction in price following ''additional markups'' and can, by definition, be no more than the amount of the additional markup; ''cancellation of additional markup,'' although not used, is descriptive. ''Markdown'' refers to price reductions from the original retail price. A price increase after a markdown is a ''markdown cancellation.'' If original cost is $12 and original selling price is $20, then markon (original markup) is $8; if the price is later increased to $24, the $4 increase is markup (additional markup); if the price is later lowered to $21, the $3 reduction is markup cancellation; if price is lowered further to $17, the $4 reduction is $1 markup cancellation and $3 markdown; if price is later increased to $22, the $5 increase is $3 of markdown cancellation and $2 of markup (additional markup). Markup cancellations and markdowns are counted separately because the former are deducted (whereas the latter are not) in computing the selling prices of goods available for sale for the denominator of the *cost percentage* used in the conventional *retail inventory method*.

markup cancellation. See *markup* for definition and contrast.

markup percentage. *Markup* divided by (acquisition cost plus *markup*).

master budget. A *budget* projecting all *financial statements* and their components.

matching convention. The concept of recognizing cost expirations *(expenses)* in the same accounting period when the related *revenues* are recognized. Combining or simultaneously recognizing the revenues and expenses that jointly result from the same *transactions* or other events.

material. As an adjective, it means relatively important. See *materiality*. Currently, no operational definition exists. As a noun, *raw material*.

material variances. *Price* and *quantity variances* for *direct materials* in *standard cost systems*. Sometimes used to mean variances that are significant; see *materiality*.

materiality. The concept that accounting should disclose separately only those events that are relatively important (no operable definition yet exists) for the business or for understanding its statements. *SFAC No. 2* suggests that accounting information is material if ''the judgment of a reasonable person relying on the information would have been changed or influenced by the omission or misstatement.''

matrix. A rectangular array of numbers or mathematical symbols.

matrix inverse. For a given square *matrix* **A**, the square matrix inverse is the matrix, $\mathbf{A}^{-1}$, such that $\mathbf{AA}^{-1} = \mathbf{A}^{-1}\mathbf{A} = \mathbf{I}$, the *identity matrix*. Not all square matrices have inverses. Those that do not are called singular; those that do are nonsingular.

maturity. The date at which an obligation, such as the *principal* of a *bond* or a *note*, becomes due.

maturity value. The amount expected to be collected when a loan reaches *maturity*. Depending on the context, the amount may be *principal* or principal and *interest*.

measuring unit. See *attribute measured* for definition and contrast.

merchandise. *Finished goods* bought by a retailer or wholesaler for resale; contrast with finished goods of a manufacturing business.

merchandise turnover. *Inventory turnover* for merchandise; see *ratio*.

merchandising business. As opposed to a manufacturing or service business, one that purchases (rather than manufactures) *finished goods* for resale.

merger. The joining of two or more businesses into a single *economic entity*. See *holding company*.

minority interest. A *balance sheet account* on *consolidated statements* showing the *equity* in a less-than-100-percent-owned *subsidiary* company allocable to those who are not part of the controlling (majority) interest. May be classified either as shareholders' equity or as a liability of indeterminate term on the consolidated balance sheet. On the *income statement*, the minority's interest in the current period's income of the less-than-100-percent-owned subsidiary must be subtracted to arrive at consolidated *net income* for the period.

minority investment. A holding of 50 percent or less of the *voting stock* in another corporation. Accounted for with the *equity method* when sufficient shares are owned so that the investor can exercise ''significant influence,'' and with the *lower-of-cost-or-market* method otherwise. See *mutual fund*.

minutes book. A record of all actions authorized at corporate *board of directors'* or shareholders' meetings.

mixed cost. A *semifixed* or a *semivariable* cost.

modified cash basis. The *cash basis of accounting* with long-term assets accounted for with the *accrual basis of accounting*. Most uses of the term ''cash basis of accounting'' actually mean ''modified cash basis.''

monetary assets, liabilities. See *monetary items*.

monetary gain or loss. The *gain* or loss in general purchasing power as a result of holding *monetary assets* or liabilities during a period when the *general purchasing power of the dollar* changes. During periods of *inflation*, holders of net monetary assets lose, and holders of net monetary liabilities gain, general purchasing power. During periods of *deflation*, holders of net monetary assets gain, and holders of net monetary liabilities lose, general purchasing power. Explicitly reported in *constant dollar accounting*.

monetary items. Amounts fixed in terms of dollars by statute or contract. *Cash, accounts receivable, accounts payable,* and *debt.* The distinction between monetary and nonmonetary items is important for *constant dollar accounting* and for *foreign exchange gain* or *loss* computations. In the foreign exchange context, account amounts denominated in dollars are not monetary items, whereas amounts denominated in any other currency are monetary.

money. A word seldom used with precision in accounting, at least in part because economists have not yet agreed on its definition. Economists use the term to refer to both a medium of exchange and a unit of value. See *cash* and *monetary items.*

money purchase plan. A *pension plan* where the employer contributes a specified amount of cash each year to each employee's pension fund. Benefits ultimately received by the employee are not specifically defined but depend on the rate of return on the cash invested. Sometimes called a "defined-contribution" pension plan; contrast with *defined-benefit plan.* As of the mid-1980s, most corporate pension plans were defined-benefit plans because both the law and *generally accepted accounting principles* for pensions made defined-benefit plans more attractive than money purchase plans. *ERISA* makes money purchase plans relatively more attractive than they had been. We expect the relative number of money purchase plans to increase.

mortality table. Data of life expectancies or probabilities of death for persons of specified ages and sex.

mortgage. A claim given by the borrower (mortgagor) to the lender (mortgagee) against the borrower's property in return for a loan.

moving average. An *average* computed on observations over time. As a new observation becomes available, the oldest one is dropped so that the average is always computed for the same number of observations and only the most recent ones. Sometimes, however, this term is used synonymously with *weighted average.*

moving average method. *Weighted-average inventory method.*

multiple-step. Said of an *income statement* where various classes of *expenses* and *losses* are subtracted from *revenues* to show intermediate items such as *operating income,* income of the enterprise (operating income plus *interest* income), income to investors (income of the enterprise less *income taxes*), net income to shareholders (income to investors less interest charges), and income retained (income to shareholders less dividends). See *entity theory.*

municipal bond. A *bond* issued by a village, town, or city. *Interest* on such bonds is generally exempt from federal *income taxes* and from some state income taxes. Because bonds issued by state and county governments often have these characteristics, such bonds are often called "municipals" as well. Sometimes referred to as "tax exempts."

mutual fund. An investment company that issues its own stock to the public and uses the proceeds to invest in securities of other companies. A mutual fund usually owns less than 5 or 10 percent of the stock of any one company and accounts for its investments using current *market values;* contrast with *holding company.*

mutually exclusive projects. Competing investment projects, where accepting one project eliminates the possibility of undertaking the remaining projects.

N

NAARS. *National Automated Accounting Research System.*

National Association of Accountants. NAA. A national society generally open to all engaged in activities closely associated with *managerial accounting.* Oversees the administration of the *CMA* Examinations through the Institute of Management Accounting.

National Automated Accounting Research System. NAARS. A computer-based information retrieval system containing, among other things, the complete text of most public corporate annual reports and *Forms 10-K.* The system is available to users through the *AICPA.*

natural business year. A 12-month period chosen as the reporting period so that the end of the period coincides with a low point in activity or inventories. See *ratio* for a discussion of analyses of financial statements of companies using a natural business year.

natural classification. *Income statement* reporting form in which *expenses* are classified by nature of items as acquired, that is, materials, wages, salaries, insurance, and taxes, as well as depreciation; contrast with *functional classification.*

natural resources. Timber land, oil and gas wells, ore deposits, and other products of nature that have economic value. The cost of natural resources is subject to *depletion.* Natural resources are "nonrenewable" (for example, oil, coal, gas, ore deposits) or "renewable" (timber land, sod fields); the former are often called "wasting assets." See also *reserve recognition accounting* and *percentage depletion.*

negative confirmation. See *confirmation*.

negative goodwill. Refer to *goodwill*. When the purchase price of the company acquired is less than the sum of the *fair market value* of the *net assets* acquired, *APB Opinion* No. 16 requires that the valuation of noncurrent assets (except long-term *investments* in *marketable securities*) acquired be reduced proportionately until the purchase price equals the adjusted valuation of the fair market value of net assets acquired. If, after the adjusted valuation of noncurrent assets is reduced to zero, the purchase price is still less than the net assets acquired, then the difference is shown as a credit balance in the balance sheet as negative goodwill and is amortized to income over a period not to exceed 40 years. For negative goodwill to exist, someone must be willing to sell a company for less than the fair market value of net current assets and marketable securities. Because such a bargain purchase is rare, negative goodwill is rarely found in the financial statements; when it does appear, it generally signals unrecorded obligations, such as for *pensions*.

negotiable. Legally capable of being transferred by endorsement. Usually said of *checks* and *notes* and sometimes of *stocks* and *bearer bonds*.

net. Reduced by all relevant deductions.

net assets. *Owners' equity*; total *assets* minus total *liabilities*.

net bank position. From a firm's point of view, *cash* in a specific bank less *loans* payable to that bank.

net book value. *Book value*.

net current asset value (per share). *Working capital* divided by the number of common shares outstanding. Many security analysts think that when a common share trades in the market for an amount less than net current asset value, then the share is undervalued and should be purchased. We find this view naive because it ignores the efficiency of capital markets generally and, specifically, unrecorded obligations such as for *pension plans*, not currently reported as liabilities in the *balance sheet* under *GAAP*.

net current assets. *Working capital* = current assets − current liabilities.

net income. The excess of all *revenues* and *gains* for a period over all *expenses* and *losses* of the period. See *comprehensive income*.

net loss. The excess of all *expenses* and *losses* for a period over all *revenues* and *gains* of the period. Negative *net income*.

net markup. In the context of *retail inventory methods*, *markups* less markup cancellations; a figure that usually ignores *markdowns* and markdown cancellations.

net of tax method. A nonsanctioned method for dealing with the problem of income tax allocation; described in *APB Opinion* No 11. Deferred tax credit items are subtracted from specific asset amounts rather than being shown as a deferred credit or liability.

net of tax reporting. Reporting, such as for *income from discontinued operations, extraordinary items*, and *prior-period adjustments*, where the amounts presented in *financial statements* have been adjusted for all income tax effects. For example, if an extraordinary loss amounted to $10,000 and the marginal tax rate were 40 percent, then the extraordinary item would be reported "net of taxes" as a $6,000 loss. Hence, all income taxes may not be reported on one line of the income statement. The taxes will be allocated to *income from continuing operations, income from discontinued operations, extraordinary items*, cumulative effects of *accounting changes*, and *prior-period adjustments*.

net operating profit. Income from *continuing operations*.

net present value. Discounted or *present value* of all cash inflows and outflows of a project or from an *investment* at a given *discount rate*.

net price method (of recording purchase or sales discounts). The *purchase* (or *sale*) is recorded at its *invoice* price less all *discounts* made available under the assumption that nearly all discounts will be taken. Discounts lapsed through failure to pay promptly are recorded in an *adjunct account* to purchases (or sales) or, in the purchasing context, to an *expense* account. For purchases, management usually prefers to know about the amount of discounts lost because of inefficient operations, not the amounts taken, so that most managers prefer the net price method to the *gross price method*.

net realizable value. Selling price of an item less reasonable further costs to make the item ready for sale and to sell it. See *lower of cost or market*.

net sales. Sales (at gross invoice amount) less *returns, allowances*, freight paid for customers, and *discounts* taken.

net working capital. *Working capital;* the "net" is redundant in accounting. Financial analysts sometimes mean *current assets* when they speak of working capital, so for them the "net" is not redundant.

net worth. A misleading term, to be avoided, that means the same as *owners' equity*.

New York Stock Exchange. NYSE. A public market where various corporate *securities* are traded.

next in, first out. See *NIFO*.

NIFO. Next *in, first out*. In making decisions, many managers consider *replacement costs* (rather than *historical costs*) and refer to them as NIFO costs.

no par. Said of *stock* without a *par value*.

nominal accounts. *Temporary accounts* as opposed to *balance sheet accounts*. All nominal accounts are *closed* at the end of each *accounting period*.

nominal amount (value). An amount stated in dollars, in contrast to an amount stated in *constant dollars*. Contrast with *real amount (value)*.

nominal dollars. The measuring unit giving no consideration to differences in the *general purchasing power of the dollar* over time. The face amount of currency or coin, a *bond*, an *invoice*, a *receivable* is a nominal dollar amount. When that amount is adjusted for changes in *general purchasing power*, it is converted into a *constant dollar* amount.

nominal interest rate. A rate specified on a *debt* instrument, which usually differs from the market or *effective rate*. Also, a rate of *interest* quoted for a year. If the interest is compounded more often than annually, then the *effective interest rate* is higher than the nominal rate.

noncancelable. See *lease*.

nonconsolidated subsidiary. An *intercorporate investment* where more than 50 percent of the shares of the *subsidiary* are owned but the investment is accounted for with the *equity method* or, in some rare circumstances, the *cost method*.

noncontributory. Said of a *pension plan* where only the employer makes payments to a pension *fund*; contrast with *contributory*.

noncurrent. Due more than 1 year (or more than one *operating cycle*) hence.

nonexpendable fund. A governmental fund, whose *principal*, and sometimes earnings, may not be spent.

non-interest-bearing note. A *note* that bears no explicit interest. The *present value* of such a note at any time before *maturity* is less than the *face value* so long as *interest rates* are positive. *APB Opinion* No. 21 requires that the present value, not face value, of long-term non-interest-bearing notes be reported as the *asset* or *liability* amount in financial statements. See *interest, imputed*.

nonmanufacturing costs. All *costs* incurred other than those to produce goods.

nonmonetary items. All items that are not monetary; see *monetary items*.

nonoperating. In the *income statement* context, said of revenues and expenses arising from transactions incidental to the company's main line(s) of business. In the *statement of changes in financial position* context, said of all sources or uses of *working capital* other than working capital provided by operations. See *operations*.

nonprofit corporation. An incorporated *entity*, such as a hospital, with owners who do not share in the earnings. It usually emphasizes providing services rather than maximizing income.

nonrecurring. Said of an event that is not expected to happen often for a given firm. Under *APB Opinion* No 30, the effects of such events should be disclosed separately, but as part of *ordinary* items unless the event is also unusual. See *extraordinary* item.

normal cost. *Pension plan expenses* incurred during an *accounting period* for employment services performed during that period; contrast with *actuarial accrued liability* and see *funded*.

normal costing. Method of charging costs to products using actual *direct materials*, actual *direct labor*, and predetermined *factory overheard* rates.

normal spoilage. Costs incurred because of ordinary amounts of spoilage; such costs should be prorated to units produced as *product costs*; contrast with *abnormal spoilage*.

normal standard cost. The *cost* expected to be incurred under reasonably efficient operating conditions with adequate provision for an average amount of rework, spoilage, and the like.

normal volume. The level of production over a time span, usually 1 year, that will satisfy demand by purchasers.

normalization. See *interperiod tax allocation*.

note. An unconditional written promise by the maker (borrower) to pay a certain amount on demand or at a certain future time. See *footnotes* for another context.

note receivable discounted. A *note* assigned by the holder to another. If the note is assigned with recourse, it is the *contingent liability* of the assignor until the debt is paid. See *factoring*.

NOW account. Negotiable order of withdrawal. A *savings account* on which orders to pay, much like *checks* but technically not checks, can be drawn and given to others who can redeem the orders at the savings institution.

number of days sales in inventory (or receivables). Days of average inventory on hand (or average collection period for receivables). See *ratio*.

NYSE. *New York Stock Exchange*.

O

OASD(H)I. *Old Age, Survivors, Disability, and (Hospital) Insurance*.

objective. See *reporting objectives* and *objectivity*.

objectivity. The reporting policy implying that formal recognition will not be given to an event in financial statements until the magnitude of the events can be measured with reasonable accuracy and is subject to independent verification.

obsolescence. A decline in *market value* of an *asset* caused by improved alternatives becoming available that will be more *cost effective*; the decline in market value is unrelated to physical changes in the asset itself. See *partial obsolescence*.

Occupational Safety and Health Act. *OSHA.*

off-balance-sheet financing. A description often used for a *long-term, noncancelable lease* accounted for as an *operating lease* and other means of borrowing that do not qualify as *liabilities*.

Old Age, Survivors, Disability, and (Hospital) Insurance. The technical name for Social Security under the Federal Insurance Contribution Act (FICA).

on (open) account. Said of a *purchase* or *sale* when payment is expected sometime after delivery and no *note* evidencing the *debt* is given or received. The purchaser has generally signed an agreement sometime in the past promising to pay for such purchases according to an agreed time schedule. When a sale (purchase) is made on open account, *Accounts Receivable (Payable)* is *debited (credited)*.

on consignment. Said of goods delivered by the owner (the consignor) to another (the consignee) to be sold by the consignee; the owner is entitled to the return of the property or payment of an amount agreed upon in advance. The goods are assets of the consignor.

one-line consolidation. Said of an *intercorporate investment* accounted for with the *equity method*. The effects of this method on reported *income* and *balance sheet* total *assets* and *equities* are identical to those that would appear if the investee firm were consolidated, even though the income from the investment appears on a single line of the income statement and the net investment appears on a single line in the assets section of the balance sheet.

open account. Any *account* with a nonzero *debit* or *credit balance*. See *on (open) account*.

operating. An adjective used to refer to *revenue* and *expense* items relating to the company's main line(s) of business. See *operations*.

operating accounts. *Revenue, expense*, and *production cost accounts*; contrast with *balance sheet accounts*.

operating cycle. *Earnings cycle.*

operating expenses. *Expenses* incurred in the course of *ordinary* activities of an *entity*. Frequently, a classification including only *selling, general*, and *administrative* *expenses*, thereby excluding *cost of goods sold, interest*, and *income tax* expenses. See *operations*.

operating income. *Income from continuing operations.*

operating lease. A *lease* accounted for by the *lessee* without showing an *asset* for the lease rights *(leasehold)* or a *liability* for the lease payment obligations. Rental payments of the lessee are merely shown as *expenses* of the period. The asset remains on the lessor's *books*, where rental collections appear as *revenues*; contrast with *capital lease*.

operating leverage. Usually said of a firm with a large proportion of *fixed costs* in its *total costs*. Consider a book publisher or a railroad; the *incremental costs* of producing another book or transporting another freight car are much less than *average cost*, so the *gross margin* upon sale of the unit is relatively large. Contrast, for example, a grocery store, where the *cost of goods sold* is usually more than 95 percent of the selling price. For firms with equal profitability, however defined, the one with the larger percentage increase in income from a given percentage increase in unit sales is said to have the larger operating leverage. See *leverage* for contrast of this term with "financial leverage." See *cost terminology* for definition of terms involving the word "cost."

operating margin (based on current costs). *Revenues* from *sales* minus *current cost* of goods sold. A measure of operating efficiency that is independent of the *cost flow assumption* for *inventory*. Sometimes called "current (gross) margin." See *inventory profit* for illustrative computations.

operating ratio. See *ratio*.

operational control. See *control system*.

operations. A word not precisely defined in *accounting*. Generally, operating activities (producing and selling *goods* or *services*) are distinguished from financing activities (raising funds). Acquiring goods on account and then paying for them in one month, though generally classified as an operating activity, has the characteristics of a financing activity. Or consider the transaction of selling plant assets for a price in excess of book value. On the *income statement*, the gain is part of income from operations (continuing operations or discontinued operations, depending on the circumstances), but on the *statement of changes in financial position*, all of the funds received on disposition are reported below the "funds from operations" section, as a nonoperating source of funds, disposition of noncurrent assets. In income tax accounting an "operating loss" results whenever deductions are greater than taxable revenues.

opinion. The *auditor's report* containing an attestation or lack thereof. Also, *APB Opinion*.

opinion paragraph. Section of *auditor's report*, generally following the *scope paragraph*, giving the auditor's conclusion that the *financial statements* are (rarely, are not) in accordance with *GAAP* and present fairly the *financial position*, changes in financial position, and the results of *operations*.

opportunity cost. The *present value* of the *income* (or *costs*) that could be earned (or saved) from using an *asset* in its best alternative use to the one being considered.

option. The legal right to buy something during a specified period at a specified price, called the *exercise* price. Employee stock options should not be confused with put and call options traded in various public markets.

ordinary annuity. An *annuity in arrears*.

ordinary income. For income tax purposes, reportable *income* not qualifying as *capital gains*.

organization costs. The *costs* incurred in planning and establishing an *entity*; example of an *intangible* asset. Often, since the amounts are not *material*, the costs are treated as *expenses* in the period incurred even though the *expenditures* clearly provide future benefits and should be treated as *assets*.

original cost. *Acquisition cost*. In public utility accounting, the acquisition cost of the *entity* first devoting the asset to public use.

original entry. Entry in a *journal*.

OSHA. Occupational Safety and Health Act. The federal law that governs working conditions in commerce and industry.

outlay. The amount of an *expenditure*.

out-of-pocket. Said of an *expenditure* usually paid for with cash. An *incremental* cost.

out-of-stock cost. The estimated decrease in future *profit* as a result of losing customers because insufficient quantities of *inventory* are currently on hand to meet customers' demands.

output. Physical quantity or monetary measurement of *goods* and *services* produced.

outside director. A member of a corporate board of directors who is not a company officer and does not participate in the corporation's day-to-day management.

outstanding. Unpaid or uncollected. When said of *stock*, the shares issued less *treasury stock*. When said of checks, it means a check issued that did not clear the *drawer's* bank prior to the *bank statement* date.

over-and-short. Title for an *expense account* used to account for small differences between book balances of cash and actual cash and vouchers or receipts in *petty cash* or *change funds*.

overapplied (overabsorbed) overhead. An excess of costs applied, or *charged*, to product for a period over actual *overhead* costs during the period. A *credit balance* in an overhead account after overhead is assigned to product.

overdraft. A check written on a checking account that contains funds less than the amount of the check.

overhead costs. Any *cost* not associated directly with the production or sale of identifiable goods and services. Sometimes called ''burden'' or ''indirect costs'' and, in Britain, ''oncosts.'' Frequently limited to manufacturing overhead. See *central corporate expenses* and *manufacturing overhead*.

overhead rate. Standard, or other predetermined rate at which *overhead costs* are applied to products or to services.

over-the-counter. Said of a *security* traded in a negotiated transaction, rather than in an auctioned one on an organized stock exchange, such as the *New York Stock Exchange*.

owners' equity. *Proprietorship; assets* minus *liabilities; paid-in capital* plus *retained earnings* of a corporation; partners' capital accounts in a *partnership*; owner's capital account in a *sole proprietorship*.

P

P&L. Profit and loss statement; *income statement*.

paid-in capital. Sum of balances in *capital stock* and *capital contributed in excess of par (or stated) value* accounts. Same as *contributed capital* (minus *donated capital*). Some use the term to mean only *capital contributed in excess of par (or stated) value*.

paid-in surplus. See *surplus*.

paper profit. A *gain* not yet realized through a *transaction*. An *unrealized holding gain*.

par. See *at par* and *face amount*.

par value. *Face amount* of a *security*.

par value method. The method of accounting for *treasury stock* that *debits* a common stock account with the *par value* of the shares required and allocates the remaining debits between the *additional paid-in capital* and *retained earnings* accounts; contrast with *cost method*.

parent company. Company owning more than 50 percent of the voting shares of another company, called the *subsidiary*.

partial obsolescence. As technology improves, the economic value of existing *assets* declines. In many cases, however, it will not pay a firm to replace the existing asset with a new one even though the new type, rather than the old, would be acquired if the acquisition were to be made currently. In these cases, the accountant should theoretically recognize a loss from partial obsolescence from the firm's owning an old, out-of-date asset, but *GAAP* does not permit recognition of partial obsolescence. The old asset will be carried at *cost* less *accumulated depreciation* until it is retired from service. See *obsolescence*.

partially funded. Said of a *pension plan* where not all earned benefits have been funded. See *funded* for funding requirements.

partially vested. Said of a *pension plan* where not all employee benefits are *vested*. See *graded vesting*.

participating dividend. *Dividend* paid to preferred shareholders in addition to the minimum preferred dividends when the *preferred stock* contract allows such sharing in earnings. Usually applied after dividends on *common stock* have reached a certain level.

participating preferred stock. *Preferred stock* with rights to *participating dividends*.

partner's drawing. A payment to a partner to be charged against his or her share of income or capital. The name of a *temporary account* to record such payments.

partnership. Contractual arrangement between individuals to share resources and operations in a jointly run business. See *general* and *limited partner* and *Uniform Partnership Act*.

past service cost. *Present value* at a given time of a *pension plan's* unrecognized, and usually unfunded, benefits assigned to employees for their service before the inception of the plan. A part of *actuarial accrued liability*. See *funded*; contrast with *normal cost*.

patent. A right granted for up to 17 years by the federal government to exclude others from manufacturing, using, or selling a claimed design, product, or plant (e.g., a new breed of rose) or from using a claimed process or method of manufacture. An asset if acquired by purchase. If developed internally, the development costs are *expensed* when incurred under current *GAAP*.

pay as you go. Said of an *income tax* scheme where periodic payments of income taxes are made during the period when the income to be taxed is being earned; in contrast to a scheme where no payments are due until the end of, or after, the period whose income is being taxed. (Called PAYE—pay as you earn—in Britain.) Sometimes used to describe an *unfunded pension plan*, where payments to pension plan beneficiaries are made from general corporate funds, not from cash previously contributed to a pension fund. Not acceptable as a method of accounting for pension plans.

payable. Unpaid but not necessarily due or past due.

payback period. Amount of time that must elapse before the cash inflows from a project equal the cash outflows.

payback reciprocal. One divided by the *payback period*. This number approximates the *internal rate of return* on a project when the project life is more than twice the payback period and the cash inflows are identical in every period after the initial period.

PAYE. See *pay as you go*.

payee. The person or entity to whom a cash payment is made or who will receive the stated amount of money on a check. See *draft*.

payout ratio. *Common stock dividends* declared for a year divided by net *income* to common stock for the year. A term used by financial analysts; contrast with *dividend yield*.

payroll taxes. Taxes levied because salaries or wages are paid; for example, *FICA* and unemployment compensation insurance taxes. Typically, the employer pays a portion and withholds part of the employee's wage fund.

P/E ratio. *Price-earnings ratio*.

Pension Benefit Guarantee Corporation. PBGC. A federal corporation established under *ERISA* to administer terminated pension plans and impose *liens* on corporate assets for certain unfunded pension liabilities.

pension fund. *Fund*, the assets of which are to be paid to retired ex-employees, usually as a *life annuity*. Usually held by an independent trustee and thus not an *asset* of the employer.

pension plan. Details or provisions of employer's contract with employees for paying retirement *annuities* or other benefits. See *funded, vested, normal cost, past service cost, prior service cost, actuarial accrued liability, money purchase plan*, and *defined-benefit plan*.

per books. An expression used to refer to the *book value* of an item at a specific time.

percent. Any number, expressed as a decimal, multiplied by 100.

percentage depletion (allowance). Deductible *expense* allowed in some cases by the federal *income tax* regulations; computed as a percentage of gross income from a *natural resource* independent of the unamortized cost of the asset. Because the amount of the total deductions for tax purposes is usually greater than the cost of the asset being *depleted*, many people think the deduction is an unfair tax advantage or "loophole."

percentage statement. A statement containing, in addition to (or instead of) dollar amounts, ratios of dollar amounts to some base. In a percentage *income statement*, the base is usually either *net sales* or total *revenues*; in a percentage *balance sheet*, the base is usually total *assets*.

percentage-of-completion method. Recognizing *revenues* and *expenses* on a job, order, or contract (1) in proportion to the *costs* incurred for the period divided by total costs expected to be incurred for the job or order ("cost-to-cost"), or (2) in proportion to engineers' or architects' estimates of the incremental degree of completion of the job, order, or contract during the period. Contrast with *completed contract method*.

period. *Accounting period*.

period cost. An inferior term for *period expense*.

period expense (charge). *Expenditure*, usually based on the passage of time, charged to operations of the accounting period rather than *capitalized* as an asset; contrast with *product cost*.

periodic inventory. A method of recording *inventory* that uses data on beginning inventory, additions to inventories, and ending inventory to find the cost of withdrawals from inventory.

periodic procedures. The process of making *adjusting entries*, *closing entries*, and preparing the *financial statements*, usually by use of *trial balances* and *work sheets*.

permanent account. An account that appears on the *balance sheet*; contrast with *temporary account*.

permanent capital. *Noncurrent liabilities* and *owners' equity*.

permanent difference. Difference between reported income and taxable income that will never be reversed and, hence, requires no entry in the *deferred income tax (liability)* account. An example is the difference between taxable and reportable income from interest earned on state and municipal bonds; contrast with *timing difference* and see *deferred income tax liability*.

perpetual annuity. *Perpetuity*.

perpetual inventory. Records on quantities and amounts of *inventory* that are changed or made current with each physical addition to or withdrawal from the stock of goods; an inventory so recorded. The records will show the physical quantities and, frequently, the dollar valuations that should be on hand at any time. Because *cost of goods sold* is computed explicitly, the *inventory equation* can be used to compute *ending inventory*. The computed amount of ending inventory can be compared to the actual amount of ending inventory as a *control* device. Contrast with *periodic inventory*.

perpetuity. An *annuity* whose payments continue forever. The *present value* of a perpetuity in *arrears* is *p/r* where *p* is the periodic payment and *r* is the *interest rate* per period. If $100 is promised each year, in arrears, forever and the interest rate is 20 percent per year, then the value of the perpetuity is $500 = $100/.20.

personal account. *Drawing account*.

petty cash fund. Currency and coins maintained for expenditures that are made with cash on hand.

physical verification. *Verification*, by an *auditor*, performed by actually inspecting items in *inventory, plant assets*, and the like; may be based on statistical sampling procedures; in contrast to mere checking of written records.

plant. *Plant assets*.

plant asset turnover. Number of dollars of *sales* generated per dollar of *plant assets*. Equal to sales divided by average *plant assets*.

plant assets. Buildings, machinery, equipment, land, and natural resources. The phrase "property, plant, and equipment" is, therefore, a redundancy. In this context, "plant" means buildings.

pledging. The borrower assigns *assets* as security or *collateral* for repayment of a loan.

pledging of receivables. The process of using expected collections on accounts receivable as *collateral* for a loan. The borrower remains responsible for collecting the receivable but promises to use the proceeds to repay the debt.

plow back. To retain assets generated by earnings for continued investment in the business.

plug. For any *account*, beginning balance + additions − deductions = ending balance; if any three of the four items are known, the fourth can be found by plugging. In making a *journal entry*, often all *debits* are known, as are all but one of the *credits* (or vice versa). Because *double-entry* bookkeeping requires equal debits and credits, the unknown quantity can be computed by subtracting the sum of the known credits from the sum of all the debits (or vice versa). This process is also known as plugging. The unknown found is called the plug. For example, if a *discount* on *bonds payable* is being *amortized* with the *straight-line method*, then *interest expense* is a plug: interest expense = interest payable + discount amortization. See *trade-in transaction* for an example.

pooling-of-interests method. Accounting for a *business combination* by merely adding together the *book value* of the *assets* and *equities* of the combined firms. Contrast with *purchase method*. Generally leads to a higher reported *net income* for the combined firms than would be reported had the business combination been accounted for as a purchase, because the *market values* of the merged assets are generally larger than their book values. See *APB Opinion* No. 16 for the conditions that must be met before the pooling-of-interests treatment is acceptable.

positive confirmation. See *confirmation*.

post. To record entries in an *account* in a *ledger*; usually the entries are transferred from a *journal*.

post-closing trial balance. *Trial balance* taken after all *temporary accounts* have been closed.

post-statement events. Events with *material* impact that occur between the end of the *accounting period* and the formal publication of the *financial statements*. Such events must be disclosed in notes for the auditor to give a *clean opinion*, even though the events are subsequent to the period being reported on.

potentially dilutive. A *security* that may be converted into, or exchanged for, common stock and thereby reduce reported *earnings per share: options, warrants, convertible bonds*, and *convertible preferred stock*.

PPB. *Program budgeting;* the second "P" means "plan."

practical capacity. Maximum level at which the plant or department can operate efficiently.

preclosing trial balance. *Trial balance* taken at the end of the period before *closing entries*. In this sense an *adjusted trial balance*. Sometimes taken before *adjusting entries* and then synonymous with *unadjusted trial balance*.

predetermined (factory) overhead rate. Rate used in applying *overhead* to products or departments developed at the start of a period by dividing estimated overhead cost by the estimated number of units of the overhead allocation base (or *denominator volume*) activity.

preemptive right. The privilege of a shareholder to maintain a proportionate share of ownership by purchasing a proportionate share of any new stock issues.

preference as to assets. The rights of *preferred shareholders* to receive certain payments in case of dissolution before common shareholders receive payments.

preferred shares. *Capital stock* with a claim to *income* or *assets* after *bondholders* but before *common shares*. *Dividends* on preferred shares are *income distributions*, not *expenses*. See *cumulative preferred stock*.

premium. The excess of issue (or market) price over *par value*. For a different context, see *insurance*.

premium on capital stock. Alternative but inferior title for *capital contributed in excess of (par) or stated value*.

prepaid expense. An *expenditure* that leads to a *deferred charge* or *prepayment*; strictly speaking, a contradiction in terms, for an *expense* is a gone asset and this title refers to past *expenditures*, such as for rent or insurance premiums, that still have future benefits and thus are *assets*.

prepaid income. An inferior alternative title for *advances from customers*. An item should not be called *revenue* or *income* until earned, when goods are delivered or services are rendered.

prepayments. *Deferred charges. Assets* representing *expenditures* for future benefits. Rent and insurance premiums paid in advance are usually classified as *current* prepayments.

present value. Value today of an amount or amounts to be paid or received later, discounted at some *interest* or *discount rate*.

price. The quantity of one *good* or *service*, usually *cash*, asked in return for a unit of another good or service. See *fair market price*.

price index. A series of numbers, one for each period, that purports to represent some *average* of prices for a series of periods, relative to a base period.

price level. The number from a *price index* series for a given period or date.

price level-adjusted statements. *Financial statements* expressed in terms of dollars of uniform purchasing power. *Nonmonetary* items are restated to reflect changes in general *price levels* since the time specific *assets* were acquired and *liabilities* were incurred. A *gain* or *loss* is recognized on *monetary items* as they are held over time periods when the general *price level changes*. Conventional financial statements show *historical costs* and ignore differences in purchasing power in different periods.

price variance. In accounting for *standard costs* (actual cost per unit − standard cost per unit) times quantity purchased.

price-earnings ratio. At a given time, the market value of a company's *common stock*, per share, divided by the *earnings per* common *share* for the past year. See *ratio*.

primary earnings per share. Net *income* to *common shareholders* plus *interest (net of tax* effects*)* or *dividends* paid on *common stock equivalents* divided by (weighted average of common shares outstanding plus net increase in the number of common shares that would become *outstanding* if all common stock equivalents were exchanged for common shares, with cash proceeds, if any, used to retire common shares).

prime cost. Sum of *direct materials* plus *direct labor* costs assigned to product.

prime rate. The rate for loans charged by commercial banks to their most preferred risks. For the purpose of deciding whether a security is or is not a *common stock equivalent* in calculating *earnings per share*, the corporation should use the rate in effect at the bank at which it does business or an average of such rates if the corporation does business with more than one bank. The *Federal Reserve Bulletin* is considered the authoritative source of information about historical prime rates.

principal. An amount on which *interest* is charged or earned.

principle. See *generally accepted accounting principles*.

prior service cost. *Actuarial accrued liability*.

prior-period adjustment. A *debit* or *credit* made directly to *retained earnings* (which does not affect *income* for the period) to adjust earnings as calculated for prior periods. Such adjustments are now extremely rare. Theory might suggest that corrections of errors in accounting estimates (such as the *depreciable life* or *salvage value* of an asset) should be treated as adjustments to retained earnings. But *GAAP* require that corrections of such estimates flow through current, and perhaps future, *income statements*. See *accounting changes* and *accounting errors*.

pro forma statements. Hypothetical statements. Financial statements as they would appear if some event, such as a *merger* or increased production and sales had occurred or were to occur. Pro forma is often spelled as one word.

proceeds. The *funds* received from disposition of assets or from the issue of securities.

process costing. A method of *cost accounting* based on average costs (total cost divided by the *equivalent units* of work done in a period). Typically used for assembly lines or for products that are produced in a series of steps that are more continuous than discrete.

product. *Goods* or *services* produced.

product cost. Any *manufacturing cost* that can be inventoried. See *flow of costs* for example and contrast with *period expenses*.

production cost. *Manufacturing cost*.

production cost account. A *temporary account* for collecting *manufacturing costs* during a period.

production department. A department producing salable *goods* or *services*; contrast with *service department*.

production method (depreciation). The depreciable asset is given a *depreciable life* measured, not in elapsed time, but in units of output or perhaps in units of time of expected use. Then the *depreciation* charge for a period is a portion of depreciable cost equal to a fraction computed by dividing the actual output produced during the period by the expected total output to be produced over the life of the asset. Sometimes called the "units-of-production (or output) method."

production method (revenue recognition). *Percentage-of-completion method* for recognizing *revenue*.

productive capacity. In computing *current cost* of *long-term assets*, we are interested in the cost of reproducing the productive capacity (for example, the ability to manufacture 1 million units a year), not the cost of reproducing the actual physical assets currently used (see *reproduction cost*). Replacement cost of productive capacity will be the same as reproduction cost of assets only in the unusual case when there has been no technological improvement in production processes and the relative prices of goods and services used in production have remained approximately the same as when the currently used ones were acquired.

profit. Excess of *revenues* over *expenses* for a *transaction*; sometimes used synonymously with *net income* for the period.

profit and loss sharing ratio. The fraction of *net income* or loss allocable to a partner in a *partnership*. Need not be the same fraction as the partner's share of capital.

profit and loss statement. *Income statement*.

profit center. A unit of activity for which both *revenue* and *expenses* are accumulated; contrast with *cost center*.

profit margin. *Sales* minus all *expenses* as a single amount. Frequently used to mean ratio of sales minus all *operating* expenses divided by sales.

profit maximization. The doctrine that a given set of operations should be accounted for so as to make reported *net income* as large as possible; contrast with *conservatism*. This concept in accounting is slightly different from the profit-maximizing concept in economics, where the doctrine states that operations should be managed to maximize the present value of the firm's wealth, generally by equating *marginal costs* and *marginal revenues*.

profitability accounting. *Responsibility accounting*.

profit-volume graph. See *breakeven chart*.

profit-volume ratio. *Net income* divided by net sales in dollars.

program budgeting. Specification and analysis of inputs, outputs, costs, and alternatives that link plans to *budgets*.

programmed costs. A *fixed cost* not essential for carrying out operations. Research and development and advertising designed to generate new business are controllable, but once a commitment is made to incur them, they become fixed costs. Sometimes called *managed costs* or *discretionary costs*; contrast with *capacity costs*.

progressive tax. Tax for which the rate increases as the taxed base, such as income, increases; contrast with *regressive tax*.

project financing arrangement. As defined by *SFAS No. 47*, the financing of an investment project in which the lender looks principally to the *cash flows* and *earnings* of the project as the source of funds for repayment and to the *assets* of the project as *collateral* for the loan. The general *credit* of the project entity is usually not a significant factor, either because the entity is a *corporation* without other assets or because the financing is without direct *recourse* to the entity's owners.

projected financial statement. *Pro forma* financial statement.

promissory note. An unconditional written promise to pay a specified sum of money on demand or at a specified date.

proof of journal. The process of checking arithmetic accuracy of *journal entries* by testing for the equality of all *debits* with all *credits* since the last previous proof.

property dividend. A *dividend in kind*.

proprietary accounts. See *budgetary accounts* for contrast in context of governmental accounting.

proprietorship. *Assets* minus *liabilities* of an *entity*; equals *contributed capital* plus *retained earnings*.

proprietorship theory. The view of the corporation that emphasizes the form of the *accounting equation* that says *assets* − liabilities = owners' equity; contrast with *entity theory*. The major implication of a choice between these theories deals with the treatment of *subsidiaries*. For example, the view that *minority interest* is an *indeterminate-term liability* is based on the proprietorship theory. The proprietorship theory implies using a *single-step income statement*.

prorate. To *allocate* in proportion to some base; for example, allocate *service department* costs in proportion to hours of service used by the benefited department.

prospectus. Formal written document describing *securities* to be issued. See *proxy*.

protest fee. Fee charged by banks or other financial agencies when items (such as checks) presented for collection cannot be collected.

provision. Often the exact amount of an *expense* is uncertain, but must be recognized currently anyway. The entry for the estimated expense, such as for *income taxes* or expected costs under *warranty*, is

Expense (Estimated)	X
Liability (Estimated)	X

In American usage, the term "provision" is often used in the expense account title of the above entry. Thus, Provision for Income Taxes is used to mean the estimate of income tax expense. (In British usage, the term "provision" is used in the title for the estimated liability of the above entry, so that Provision for Income Taxes is a balance sheet account.)

proxy. Written authorization given by one person to another so that the second person can act for the first, such as to vote shares of stock. Of particular significance to accountants because the *SEC* presumes that financial information is distributed by management along with its proxy solicitations.

public accountant. Generally, this term is synonymous with *certified public accountant*. In some jurisdictions, individuals have been licensed as public accountants without being CPAs.

public accounting. That portion of accounting primarily involving the *attest* function, culminating in the *auditor's report*.

PuPU. An acronym for *pu*rchasing *p*ower *u*nit conceived by John C. Burton, former Chief Accountant of the *SEC*. Those who think *constant dollar accounting* is not particularly useful poke fun at it by calling it "PuPU accounting."

purchase allowance. A reduction in sales *invoice price* usually granted because the *goods* received by the purchaser were not exactly as ordered. The goods are not returned to the seller, but are purchased at a price lower than originally agreed upon.

purchase discount. A reduction in purchase *invoice price* granted for prompt payment. See *sales discount* and *terms of sale*.

purchase method. Accounting for a *business combination* by adding the acquired company's assets at the price paid for them to the acquiring company's assets. Contrast with *pooling-of-interests method*. The acquired assets are put on the books at current values, rather than original costs, the *amortization expenses* are usually larger (and reported income, smaller) than for the same business combination accounted for as a pooling of interests. The purchase method is required unless all criteria to be a pooling are met.

purchase order. Document authorizing a seller to deliver goods, with payment to be made later.

purchasing power gain or loss. *Monetary gain or loss*.

push-down accounting. Assume that Company A purchases substantially all of the *common shares* of Company B but that Company B must still issue its own *financial statements*. The question arises, shall the *basis* for Company B's *assets* and *equities* be changed on its own books to the same updated amounts at which they are shown on Company A's *consolidated* statements. When Company B shows the new asset and equity bases reflecting Company A's purchase, Company B is using "push-down accounting," because the new bases are "pushed down" from Company A (where they are required in *GAAP* to Company B (where the new bases would not appear in *historical cost accounting*). Since 1983, the *SEC* has required push-down accounting under some circumstances.

put. An option to sell *shares* of a publicly-traded corporation at a fixed price during a fixed time span. Contrast with *call*.

Q

qualified report (opinion). *Auditor's report* containing a statement that the auditor was unable to complete a satisfactory examination of all things considered relevant or that the auditor has doubts about the financial impact of some material item reported in the financial statements. See *except for* and *subject to*.

quantity discount. A reduction in purchase price as quantity purchased increases; amount of the discount is constrained by law (Robinson-Patman Act). Not to be confused with *purchase discount*.

quantity variance. In *standard cost* systems, the standard price per unit times (actual quantity used minus standard quantity that should be used).

quasi-reorganization. A *reorganization* where no new company is formed or no court has intervened, as would happen in *bankruptcy*. The primary purpose is to absorb a *deficit* and get a "fresh start."

quick assets. *Assets* readily convertible into *cash*; includes cash, *current marketable securities,* and *current receivables*.

quick ratio. Sum of (*cash, current marketable securities*, and *receivables*) divided by *current liabilities*. Some nonliquid receivables may be excluded from the numerator. Often called the "acid test ratio." See *ratio*.

R

R&D. See *research* and *development*.

Railroad Accounting Principles Board. RAPB. A board brought into existence by the Staggers Rail Act of 1980 to advise the Interstate Commerce Commission on matters of accounting affecting railroads. The RAPB had not started work by the time this book went to press.

RAPB. *Railroad Accounting Principles Board*.

rate of return (on total capital). See *ratio* and *rate of return on assets*.

rate of return on assets. *Net income* plus aftertax *interest charges* plus *minority interest* in income divided by average total *assets*. Perhaps the single most useful ratio for assessing management's overall operating performance. See *ratio*.

rate of return on common stock equity. See *ratio*.

rate of return on shareholders' (owners') equity. See *ratio*.

rate variance. *Price variance*, usually for *direct labor costs*.

ratio. The number resulting when one number is divided by another. Ratios are generally used to assess aspects of profitability, solvency, and liquidity. The commonly used financial ratios are of three kinds:

1. Those that summarize some aspect of *operations* for a period, usually a year.
2. Those that summarize some aspect of *financial position* at a given moment—the moment for which a balance sheet has been prepared.
3. Those that relate some aspect of operations to some aspect of financial position.

Exhibit 6.11 lists the most common financial ratios and shows separately both the numerator and denominator used to calculate the ratio.

For all ratios that require an average balance during the period, the average is most often derived as one-half the sum of the beginning and ending balances. Sophisticated analysts recognize, however, that when companies use a fiscal year different from the calendar year, this averaging of beginning and ending balances may be misleading. Consider, for example, the *rate of return on assets* of a retailing firm, such as J.C. Penney, which chooses a fiscal year to end in late January. It chooses a late January closing date at least in part because inventories are at a low level and are therefore easy to count—the Christmas merchandise has been sold and the Easter merchandise has not yet all been received. Furthermore, by January 31, most Christmas sales have been collected or returned, so receivable amounts are not unusually large. Thus at January 31, the amount of total assets is lower than at many other times during the year. Consequently, the denominator of the rate of return on assets, total assets, for the retailing firm is more likely to represent a smaller amount of total assets on hand during the year than the average amount. The rate of return on assets for companies that choose a fiscal year-end to coincide with low points in the inventory cycle is likely to be larger than if a more accurate estimate of the average amounts of total assets were used.

raw material. Goods purchased for use in manufacturing a product.

reacquired stock. *Treasury stock.*

real accounts. *Balance sheet accounts;* as opposed to *nominal accounts.* See *permanent accounts.*

real amount (value). An amount stated in *constant dollars.* For example, if an investment costing $100 is sold for $130 after a period of 10 percent general *inflation*, the *nominal amount* of gain is $30 (= $130 − $100) but the real amount of gain is C$ 20 (= $130 − 1.10 × $100), where "C$" denotes constant dollars of purchasing power on the date of sale.

real estate. *Land* and its *improvements*, such as landscaping and roads, but not buildings.

realizable value. *Market value* or, sometimes, *net realizable value.*

realization convention. The accounting practice of delaying the recognition of *gains* and *losses* from changes in the market price of *assets* until the assets are sold. However, unrealized losses on *inventory* and *marketable securities* classified as *current assets* are recognized prior to sale when the *lower-of-cost-or-market* valuation basis is used.

realize. To convert into *funds.* When applied to a *gain* or *loss*, implies that an *arm's-length transaction* has taken place. Contrast with *recognize*; a loss (as for example on *marketable equity securities*) may be recognized in the financial statements even though it has not yet been realized in a transaction.

realized gain (or loss) on marketable equity securities. An income statement account title for the difference between the proceeds of disposition and the *original cost* of *marketable equity securities.*

realized holding gain. See *inventory profit* for definition and an example.

rearrangement costs. Costs of reinstalling assets, perhaps in a different location. May be *capitalized* as part of the assets cost, just as is original installation cost.

recapitalization. *Reorganization.*

recapture. Various provisions of the *income tax* rules require refund by the taxpayer (recapture by the government) of various tax advantages under certain conditions. For example, the tax savings provided by the *investment credit* or by *accelerated depreciation* must be repaid if the item providing the tax savings is retired prematurely.

receipt. Acquisition of *cash.*

receivable. Any *collectible*, whether or not it is currently due.

receivable turnover. See *ratio.*

reciprocal holdings. Company A owns stock of Company B and Company B owns stock of Company A.

recognize. To enter a transaction in the accounts. Not synonymous with *realize.*

reconciliation. A calculation that shows how one balance or figure is derived systematically from another, such as a *reconciliation of retained earnings* or a *bank reconciliation schedule.* See *articulate.*

record date. *Dividends* are paid on payment date to those who own the stock on the record date.

recourse. See *note receivable discounted.*

recovery of unrealized loss on marketable securities. An *income statement account title* for the *gain* during the current period on the current asset portfolio of *marketable equity securities.* This gain will be *recognized* only to the extent that net losses have been recognized in preceding periods in amounts no smaller than the current gain. (The Allowance for Declines in Marketable Equity Securities account can never have a *debit balance.*)

redemption. Retirement by the issuer, usually by a purchase or *call*, of *stocks* or *bonds.*

redemption premium. *Call premium.*

redemption value. The price to be paid by a corporation to retire *bonds* or *preferred stock* if called before *maturity.*

refunding bond issue. Said of a *bond* issue whose proceeds are used to retire bonds already *outstanding.*

register. Collection of consecutive entries, or other information, in chronological order, such as a check register or an insurance register, which lists all insurance policies owned. If entries are recorded, it may serve as a *journal.*

registered bond. *Principal* of such a *bond* and *interest*, if registered as to interest, is paid to the owner listed on the books of the issuer. As opposed to a bearer bond, where the possessor of the bond is entitled to interest and principal.

registrar. An *agent*, usually a bank or trust company, appointed by a corporation to keep track of the names of shareholders and distributions of earnings.

registration statement. Statement required by the Securities Act of 1933 of most companies wishing to have their securities traded in public markets. The statement discloses financial data and other items of interest to potential investors.

regression analysis. A method of *cost estimates* based on statistical techniques for fitting a line (or its equivalent in higher mathematical dimensions) to an observed series of data points, usually by minimizing the sum of squared deviations of the observed data from the fitted line.

regressive tax. Tax for which the rate decreases as the taxed base, such as income, increases. Contrast with *progressive tax*.

Regulation S-X. The *SEC*'s regulation specifying the form and content of financial reports to the SEC.

rehabilitation. The improving of a used *asset* via an extensive repair. Ordinary *repairs* and *maintenance* restore or maintain expected *service potential* of an asset and are treated as *expenses*. A rehabilitation improves the asset beyond its current service potential, restoring the service potential to a significantly higher level than before the rehabilitation. Once rehabilitated, the asset may be better, but need not be, than it was when new. *Expenditures* for rehabilitation, like those for *betterments* and *improvements*, are *capitalized*.

reinvestment rate. In a *capital budgeting* context, the rate at which cash inflows from a project occurring before the project's completion are invested. Once such a rate is assumed, there will never be multiple *internal rates of return*. See *Descartes' rule of signs*.

relative sales value method. A method for *allocating joint costs* in proportion to *realizable values* of the joint products. For example, joint products A and B together cost $100; A sells for $60, whereas B sells for $90. Then A would be allocated $(60/\$150) \times \$100 = .40 \times \$100 = \$40$ of cost, whereas B would be allocated $(\$90/\$150) \times \$100 = \$60$ of cost.

relevant cost. *Incremental cost. Opportunity cost.*

relevant range. Activity levels over which costs are linear or for which *flexible budget* estimates and *breakeven charts* will remain valid.

remittance advice. Information on a *check* stub, or on a document attached to a check by the *drawer*, which tells the *payee* why a payment is being made.

rent. A charge for use of land, buildings, or other assets.

reorganization. A major change in the *capital structure* of a corporation that leads to changes in the rights, interests, and implied ownership of the various security owners. Usually results from a *merger* or agreement by senior security holders to take action to forestall *bankruptcy*.

repair. An *expenditure* to restore an *asset's* service potential after damage or after prolonged use. In the second sense, after prolonged use, the difference between repairs and maintenance is one of degree and not of kind. Treated as an *expense* of the period when incurred. Because repairs and maintenance are treated similarly in this regard, the distinction is not important. A repair helps to maintain capacity intact at levels planned when the *asset* was acquired; contrast with *improvement*.

replacement cost. For an asset, the current fair market price to purchase another, similar asset (with the same future benefit or service potential). *Current cost*. See *reproduction cost* and *productive capacity*. See also *distributable income* and *inventory profit*.

replacement cost method of depreciation. The original-cost *depreciation* charge is augmented by an amount based on a portion of the difference between the *current replacement cost* of the asset and its *original cost*.

replacement system of depreciation. See *retirement method of depreciation* for definition and contrast.

replacement value accounting. The Dutch term for *current cost accounting*.

report. *Financial statement; auditor's report.*

report form. This form of *balance sheet* typically shows *assets* minus *liabilities* as one total. Then, below that it shows the components of *owners' equity* summing to the same total. Often, the top section shows *current* assets less current liabilities before *noncurrent assets* less noncurrent liabilities. Contrast with *account form*.

reporting objectives (policies). The general purposes for which financial statements are prepared. The FASB has discussed these in *SFAC* No. 1.

reproduction cost. The *cost* necessary to acquire an *asset* similar in all physical respects to another asset for which a *current value* is wanted. See *replacement cost* and *productive capacity* for further contrast.

required rate of return. The opportunity *cost of capital*.

requisition. A formal written order or request, such as for withdrawal of supplies from the storeroom.

resale value. *Exit value. Net realizable value.*

research and development. Research is activity aimed at discovering new knowledge in hopes that such activity will be useful in creating a new product, process, or service or improving a present product, process, or service. Development is the translation of research findings or other knowledge into a new or improved product, process, or service. *SFAS No. 2* requires that costs of such activities be *expensed* as incurred, on the grounds that the future benefits are too uncertain to warrant *capitalization* as an asset. This treatment seems questionable to us, because we wonder why firms would continue to undertake R&D if there were no expectation of future benefit; if future benefits exist, then the *costs* should be assets.

reserve. When properly used in accounting, the term refers to an account that appropriates *retained earnings* and restricts dividend declarations. Appropriating retained earnings is itself a poor and vanishing practice, so the word should seldom be used in accounting. In addition, used in the past to indicate an *asset contra* (for example, "reserve for depreciation") or an *estimated liability* (for example, "*reserve for warranty costs*"). In any case, re-

retail terminology. See *markup*.

retained earnings. Net *income* over the life of a corporation less all *dividends* (including capitalization through *stock dividends*); *owners' equity* less *contributed capital*.

retained earnings, appropriated. An *account* set up by crediting it and debiting *retained earnings*. Used to indicate that a portion of retained earnings is not available for dividends. The practice of appropriating retained earnings is misleading unless all capital is earmarked with its use, which is not practicable. Use of formal retained earnings appropriations is declining.

retained earnings statement. *Generally accepted accounting principles* require that whenever *comparative balance sheets* and an *income statement* are presented, there must also be presented a *reconciliation* of the beginning and ending balances in the *retained earnings account*. This reconciliation can appear in a separate statement, in a combined statement of income and retained earnings, or in the balance sheet.

retirement method of depreciation. No entry is recorded for *depreciation expense* until an *asset* is retired from service. Then, an entry is made *debiting* depreciation expense and *crediting* the asset account for the cost of the asset retired. If the retired asset has a *salvage value*, the amount of the debit to depreciation expense is reduced by the amount of salvage value with a corresponding debit to cash, receivables, or salvaged materials. The "replacement system of depreciation" is similar, except that the debit to depreciation expense equals the cost of the new asset less the salvage value, if any, of the old asset. These methods were used by some public utilities. For example, if 10 telephone poles are acquired in Year 1 for $60 each and are replaced in Year 10 for $100 each, when the salvage value of the old poles is $5 each, then the accounting would be as follows:

Retirement Method.

Plant Assets.	600	
Cash		600

To acquire assets in Year 1.

Depreciation Expense	550	
Salvage Receivable	50	
Plant Assets.		600

To record retirement and depreciation in Year 10.

Plant Assets.	1,000	
Cash		1,000

To record acquisition of new assets in Year 10.

Replacement Method.

Plant Assets.	600	
Cash		600

To acquire assets in Year 1.

Depreciation Expense	950	
Salvage Receivable	50	
Cash		1,000

To record depreciation on old asset in amount quantified by net cost of replacement asset in Year 10.

The retirement method is like *FIFO* in that the cost of the first asset is recorded as depreciation and the cost of the second asset is put on the balance sheet. The replacement method is like *LIFO* in that the cost of the second asset determines the depreciation expense and the cost of the first asset remains on the balance sheet.

retirement plan. *Pension plan.*

return. A schedule of information required by governmental bodies, such as the tax return required by the *Internal Revenue Service*. Also the physical return of merchandise. See also *return on investment*.

return on investment. return on capital. *Income* (before distributions to suppliers of capital) for a period. As a rate, this amount divided by average total assets. *Interest*, net of tax effects, should be added back to *net income* for the numerator. See *ratio*.

revenue. The increase in *owners' equity* caused by a service rendered or the sale of goods. The monetary measure of a service rendered. *Sales* of products, merchandise, and services, and earnings from *interest*, *dividends*, rents, and the like. The amount of revenue is the expected *net present value* of the *net assets* received. Do not confuse with *receipt* of *funds*, which may occur before, when, or after revenue is recognized. Contrast with *gain* and *income*. See also *holding gain*. Some writers use the term *gross income* synonymously with *revenue*; such usage is to be avoided.

revenue center. A *responsibility center* within a firm that has control only over revenues generated; contrast with *cost center*. See *profit center*.

revenue expenditure. A phrase sometimes used to mean an *expense*, in contrast to a capital *expenditure* to acquire an *asset* or to discharge a *liability*. Avoid using this phrase; use *period expense* instead.

revenue received in advance. An inferior term for *advances from customers*.

serve accounts have *credit* balances and are not pools of *funds*, as the unwary reader might infer. If a company has set aside a pool of *cash* or *marketable securities*, then that cash will be called a *fund*. No other word in accounting is so misunderstood and misused, even by "experts" who should know better. A leading unabridged dictionary defines *reserve* as "Cash, or assets readily convertible into cash, held aside, as by a corporation, bank, state or national government, etc., to meet expected or unexpected demands." This definition is absolutely wrong in accounting. Reserves are not funds. For example, a contingency fund of $10,000 is created by depositing cash in a fund, and this entry is made:

Dr. Contingency Fund	10,000	
Cr. Cash.		10,000

The following entry may accompany this entry if retained earnings are to be appropriated:

Dr. Retained Earnings.	10,000	
Cr. Reserve for Contingencies . .		10,000

The transaction leading to the first entry is an event of economic significance. The second entry has little economic impact for most firms. The problem with the word "reserve" arises because the second entry can be made without the first—a company can create a reserve, that is, appropriate retained earnings, without creating a fund. The problem is caused at least in part by the fact that, in common usage, "reserve" means a pool of assets, as in the phrase "oil reserves." The *Internal Revenue Service* does not help in dispelling confusion about the term *reserves*. The federal *income tax* return for corporations uses the title "Reserve for Bad Debts" to mean the "Allowance for Uncollectible Accounts" and speaks of the "Reserve Method" in referring to the *allowance method* for estimating *revenue* or *income* reductions from estimated *uncollectibles*. *Accounting Terminology Bulletin No. 1*, issued in 1953, suggested that the word should seldom be used.

reserve recognition accounting. In exploration for natural resources, there is the problem of what to do with the expenditures for exploration. Suppose that $10 million is spent to drill 10 holes ($1 million each) and that nine of them are dry, whereas one is a gusher containing oil with a *net realizable value* of $40 million. Dry hole, or *successful efforts*, accounting would *expense* $9 million and *capitalize* $1 million to be *depleted* as the oil was lifted from the ground. *SFAS No. 19*, now suspended, requires successful efforts accounting. Full costing would expense nothing but capitalize the $10 million of drilling costs to be depleted as the oil is lifted from the single productive well. Reserve recognition accounting would capitalize $40 million to be depleted as the oil is lifted, with a $30 million *credit* to *income* or *contributed capital*. The *balance sheet* shows the *net realizable value* of proven oil

and gas reserves. The *income statement* has thre[e] items: (1) current income resulting from prod[ ] "lifting profit," which is the *revenue* from sales [ ] gas less the expense based on the current valuatio[n] at which these items had been carried on the balan[ce] (2) profit or loss from exploration efforts, where [ ] rent value of new discoveries is revenue and all the [explo]ration cost is expense; and (3) gain or loss on char[ge] current value during the year, which is in other c[ ] called a *holding gain or loss*.

residual income. In an external reporting context, [ ] term refers to *net income* available for *common sh[ ]* (= net income less *preferred stock dividends*). In man[age]rial accounting, this term refers to the excess of inc[ome] for a division or *segment* of a company over the produc[t] the *cost of capital* for the company multiplied by the av[er]age amount of capital invested in the division during t[he] period over which the income was earned.

residual security. A *potentially dilutive security*. Op[-]tions, warrants, convertible bonds, and convertible pre-ferred stock.

residual value. At any time, the estimated or actual, *net realizable value* (that is, proceeds less removal costs) of an *asset*, usually a depreciable *plant asset*. In the context of depreciation accounting, this term is equivalent to *salvage value* and is preferable to *scrap value*, because the asset need not be scrapped. Sometimes used to mean net *book value*. In the context of a *noncancelable* lease, the estimated value of the leased asset at the end of the lease period. See *lease*.

responsibility accounting. Accounting for a business by considering various units as separate entities, or *profit centers*, giving management of each unit responsibility for the unit's *revenues* and *expenses*. Sometimes called "activity accounting." See *transfer price*.

responsibility center. Part or *segment* of an organizatio[n] that is accountable for a specified set of activities. Als[o] called "*accountability center*."

restricted assets. Governmental resources restricted [by] legal or contractual requirements for specific purpos[es.]

restricted retained earnings. That part of *retained e[arn]ings* not legally available for *dividends*. See *retained e[arn]ings, appropriated*. Bond indentures and other loan [con]tracts can curtail the legal ability of the corporati[on to] declare dividends without formally requiring a re[tained] earnings appropriation, but disclosure is required.

retail inventory method. Ascertaining cost amo[unt of] *ending inventory* as follows (assuming *FIFO*): cos[t of end]ing inventory = (selling price of *goods avail[able for]* *sale − sales*) × *cost percentage*. Cost of good[s sold is] then computed from the *inventory equation*; co[st of be]ginning inventory, purchases, and ending invent[ory are] known. (When *LIFO* is used, the method is si[milar to the] *dollar-value LIFO method*). See *markup*.

reversal (reversing) entry. An *entry* in which all *debits* and *credits* are the credits and debits, respectively, of another entry, and in the same amounts. It is usually made on the first day of an *accounting period* to reverse a previous *adjusting entry*, usually an *accrual*. The purpose of such entries is to make the bookkeeper's tasks easier. Suppose that salaries are paid every other Friday, with paychecks compensating employees for the 2 weeks just ended. Total salaries accrue at the rate of $5,000 per 5-day work week. The bookkeeper is accustomed to making the following entry every other Friday:

(1) Salary Expense	10,000	
Cash		10,000

To record salary expense and salary payments.

If paychecks are delivered to employees on Friday, June 25, then the *adjusting entry* made on June 30 (or, perhaps, later) to record accrued salaries for June 28, 29, and 30 would be

(2) Salary Expense	3,000	
Salaries Payable		3,000

To charge second-quarter operations with all salaries earned in second quarter.

The Salary Expense account would be closed as part of the June 30 *closing entries*. On the next payday, July 9, the salary entry would have to be

(3) Salary Expense	7,000	
Salaries Payable	3,000	
Cash		10,000

To record salary payments split between expense for the third quarter (7 days) and liability carried over from the second quarter.

To make entry (3), the bookkeeper must look back into the records to see how much of the debit is to Salaries Payable accrued from the previous quarter so that total debits are properly split between third-quarter expense and the liability carried over from the second quarter. Notice that this entry forces the bookkeeper both (a) to refer to balances in old accounts and (b) to make an entry different from the one customarily made, entry (1).

The reversing entry, made just after the books have been closed for the second quarter, makes the salary entry for July 9, the same as that made on all other Friday paydays. The reversing entry merely *reverses* the adjusting entry (2):

(4) Salaries Payable	3,000	
Salary Expense		3,000

To reverse the adjusting entry.

This entry results in a zero balance in the Salaries Payable account and a *credit* balance in the Salary Expense account. If entry (4) is made just after the books are closed for the second quarter, then the entry on July 9 will be the customary entry (1). Entries (4) and (1) together have exactly the same effect as entry (3).

The procedure for using reversal entries is as follows: The required adjustment to record an accrual (*payable* or *receivable*) is made at the end of an *accounting period*; the closing entry is made as usual; as of the first day of the following period, an entry is made reversing the adjusting entry; when a payment is made (or received), the entry is recorded as though no adjusting entry had been recorded. Whether or not reversal entries are used affects the recordkeeping procedures, but not the financial statements.

Also used to describe the entry reversing an incorrect entry before recording the correct entry.

reverse stock split. A stock split in which the number of shares *outstanding* is decreased. See *stock split.*

revolving fund. A *fund* whose amounts are continually expended and then replenished; for example, a *petty cash fund.*

revolving loan. A *loan* that is expected to be renewed at *maturity.*

right. The privilege to subscribe to new *stock* issues or to purchase stock. Usually, rights are contained in securities called *warrants,* and the warrants may be sold to others. See also *preemptive right.*

risk. A measure of the variability of the *return on investment.* For a given expected amount of return, most people prefer less risk to more risk. Therefore, in rational markets, investments with more risk usually promise, or are expected to yield, a higher rate of return than investments with lower risk. Most people use "risk" and "uncertainty" as synonyms. In technical language, however, these terms have different meanings. "Risk" is used when the probabilities attached to the various outcomes are known, such as the probabilities of heads or tails in the flip of a fair coin. "Uncertainty" refers to an event where the probabilities of the outcomes, such as winning or losing a lawsuit, can only be estimated.

An Open Account, Ruled and Balanced

(Steps indicated in parentheses correspond to steps described in "ruling an account.")

Date 1985	Explanation	Ref.	Debit (1)		Date 1985	Explanation	Ref.	Credit (2)		
Jan. 1	Balance	✓	100	00						
Jan. 13		VR	121	37	Sept. 15		J		42	
Mar. 20		VR	56	42	Nov. 12		J	413	15	
June 5		J	1,138	09	Dec. 31	Balance	✓	1,050	59	(3)
Aug. 18		J	1	21						
Nov. 20		VR	38	43						
Dec. 7		VR	8	64						
(4) 1986			1,464	16	1986			1,464	16	(4)
(5) Jan. 1	Balance	✓	1,050	59						

risk premium. Extra compensation paid to an employee or extra interest paid to a lender, over amounts usually considered normal, in return for their undertaking to engage in activities more risky than normal.

risk-adjusted discount rate. In a *capital budgeting* context, a decision maker compares projects by comparing their *net present values* for a given *interest* rate, usually the *cost of capital*. If a given project's outcome is considered to be much more or much less risky than the normal undertakings of the company, then the interest rate will be increased (if the project is more risky) or decreased (if less risky) and the rate used is said to be risk-adjusted.

ROI. *Return on investment*, but usually used to refer to a single project and expressed as a ratio: *income* divided by average *cost* of *assets* devoted to the project.

royalty. Compensation for the use of property, usually a patent, copyrighted material, or natural resources. The amount is often expressed as a percentage of receipts from using the property or as an amount per unit produced.

RRA. See *Reserve recognition accounting*.

RRR. Required rate of return.

rule of 69. An amount of money invested at r percent per period will double in $69/r + .35$ periods. This approximation is accurate to one-tenth of a period for interest rates between $r\frac{1}{4}$ and 100 percent per period. For example, at 10 percent per period, the rule says that a given sum will double in $69/10 + .35 = 7.25$ periods. At 10 percent per period, a given sum actually doubles in $7.27+$ periods.

rule of 72. An amount of money invested at r percent per period will double in $72/r$ periods. A reasonable approxi-

mation but not nearly as accurate as the *rule of 69*. For example, at 10 percent per period, the rule says that a given sum will double in $72/10 = 7.2$ periods.

rule of 78. The rule followed by many finance companies for allocating earnings on *loans* among the months of a year on the sum-of-the-months'-digits basis when equal monthly payments from the borrower are to be received. The sum of the digits from 1 through 12 is 78, so 12/78 of the year's earnings are allocated to the first month, 11/78 to the second month, and so on. See *sum-of-the-years' digits depreciation*.

ruling (and balancing) an account. The process of summarizing a series of entries in an *account* by computing a new *balance* and drawing double lines to indicate that the information above the double lines has been summarized in the new balance. The process is illustrated below. The steps are as follows. (1) Compute the sum of all *debit* entries including opening debit balance, if any—$1,464.16. (2) Compute the sum of all credit entries including opening credit balance, if any—$413.57. (3) If the amount in (1) is larger than the amount in (2), write the excess as a credit with a check mark—$1,464.16 − $413.57 = $1,050.59. (4) Add both debit and credit columns, which should both now sum to the same amount, and show that identical total at the foot of both columns. (5) Draw double lines under those numbers and write the excess of debits over credits as the new debit balance with a check mark. (6) If the amount in (2) is larger than the amount in (1), write the excess as a debit with a check mark. (7) Do steps (4) and (5) except that the excess becomes the new credit balance. (8) If the amount in (1) is equal to the amount in (2), the balance is zero and only the totals with the double lines beneath them need be shown. This process is illustrated in the figure above.

S

SAB. *Staff Accounting Bulletin* of the *SEC*.

safe-harbor lease. See *tax-transfer lease*.

salary. Compensation earned by managers, administrators, and professionals, not based on an hourly rate. Contrast with *wage*.

sale. A *revenue* transaction where *goods* or *services* are delivered to a customer in return for cash or a contractual obligation to pay.

sale and leaseback. Phrase used to describe a *financing* transaction where improved property is sold but is taken back for use on a long-term *lease*. Such transactions often have advantageous income tax effects, but usually have no effect on *financial statement income*.

sales allowance. A reduction in sales *invoice* price usually given because the goods received by the buyer are not exactly what was ordered. The amounts of such adjustments are often accumulated by the seller in a temporary *revenue contra account* having this, or a similar, title. See *sales discount*.

sales basis of revenue recognition. *Revenue* is recognized, not as goods are produced nor as orders are received, but only when the sale (delivery) has been consummated and cash or a legal receivable obtained. Most revenue is recognized on this basis. Compare with the *percentage-of-completion method* and the *installment method*. Identical with the *completed contract method*, but this latter term is ordinarily used only for *long-term* construction projects.

sales contra, estimated uncollectibles. A title for the *contra-revenue account* to recognize estimated reductions in income caused by accounts receivable that will not be collected. See *allowance for uncollectibles* and *allowance method*.

sales discount. Reduction in sales *invoice* price usually offered for prompt payment. See *terms of sale* and *2/10, n/30*.

sales return. The physical return of merchandise; the amounts of such returns are often accumulated by the seller in a temporary *revenue contra account*.

sales value method. *Relative sales value method*.

salvage value. Actual or estimated selling price, net of removal or disposal costs, of a used *plant asset* to be sold or otherwise retired. See *residual value*.

SAS. *Statement on Auditing Standards* of the *AICPA*.

SAV. *Supplemental actuarial value*.

schedule. Supporting set of calculations that show how figures in a statement or tax return are derived.

scientific method. *Effective interest method* of *amortizing bond discount* or *premium*.

scope paragraph. Section of *auditor's report* containing a description of the work done by the auditor.

scrap value. *Salvage value* assuming that item is to be junked. A *net realizable value*. *Residual value*.

SEC. Securities and Exchange Commission, an agency authorized by the U.S. Congress to regulate, among other things, the financial reporting practices of most public corporations. The SEC has indicated that it will usually allow the *FASB* to set accounting principles but it reserves the right to require more disclosure than required by the FASB. The SEC's accounting requirements are stated in its *Financial Reporting Releases* (formerly called *Accounting Series Releases, ASRs*) and *Regulation S-X*. See also *registration statement* and *10-K*.

secret reserve. *Hidden reserve*.

Securities and Exchange Commission. *SEC*.

security. Document that indicates ownership or indebtedness or potential ownership, such as an *option* or *warrant*.

segment (of a business). As defined by *APB Opinion No. 30*, "a component of an *entity* whose activities represent a separate major line of business or class of customer. . . . [It may be] a *subsidiary*, a division, or a department, . . . provided that its *assets*, results of *operations*, and activities can be clearly distinguished, physically and operationally for financial reporting purposes, from the other assets, results of operations, and activities of the entity." In *SFAS No. 14* a segment is defined as "A component of an enterprise engaged in promoting a product or service or a group of related products and services primarily to unaffiliated customers . . . for a profit."

segment reporting. Reporting of *sales, income,* and *assets* by *segments of a business*, usually classified by nature of products sold but sometimes by geographic area where goods are produced or sold, or by type of customers. Sometimes called "line-of-business reporting." *Central corporate expenses* are not allocated to the segments.

self-balancing. A set of records with equal *debits* and *credits*, such as the *ledger* (but not individual accounts), the *balance sheet*, and a *fund* in nonprofit accounting.

self-insurance. See *insurance*.

selling and administrative expenses. *Expenses* not specifically identifiable with, nor assigned to, production

semifixed costs. *Costs* that increase with ac step function.

semivariable costs. *Costs* that increase strictly linearly with activity but that are positive at zero activity level. Royalty fees of 2 percent of sales are variable; royalty fees of $1,000 per year plus 2 percent of sales are semivariable.

senior securities. *Bonds* as opposed to *preferred stock; preferred stock* as opposed to *common stock*. The senior security has a claim against *earnings* or *assets* that must be met before the claim of less senior securities.

serial bonds. An *issue* of *bonds* that mature in part at one date, another part on another date, and so on; the various maturity dates usually are equally spaced; contrast them with *term bonds*.

service basis of depreciation. *Production method*.

service department. A department, such as the personnel or computer department, that provides services to other departments, rather than direct work on a salable product; contrast with *production department*. Costs of service departments whose services benefit manufacturing operations must be *allocated* to *product costs* under *absorption costing*.

service life. Period of expected usefulness of an asset; may not coincide with *depreciable life* for income tax purposes.

service potential. The future benefits embodied in an item that cause the item to be classified as an *asset*. Without service potential, there are no future benefits and the item should not be classified as an asset. *SFAS No. 3* suggests that the primary characteristic of service potential is the ability to generate future net cash inflows.

services. Useful work done by a person, a machine, or an organization. See *goods and services*.

setup. The time or costs required to prepare production equipment for doing a job.

SFAC. *Statement of Financial Accounting Concepts* from the *FASB*.

SFAS. *Statement of Financial Accounting Standards* from the *FASB*.

share. A unit of *stock* representing ownership in a corporation.

shareholders' equity. *Proprietorship* or *owners' equity* of a corporation. Because *stock* means inventory in Australian, British, and Canadian usage, the term "shareholders' equity" is usually used by Australian, British, and Canadian writers.

short-term. Current; ordinarily, due within 1 year.

shrinkage. An excess of *inventory* shown on the *books* over actual physical quantities on hand. Can result from theft or shoplifting as well as from evaporation or general wear and tear.

sight draft. A demand for payment drawn by a person to whom money is owed. The *draft* is presented to the borrower's (the debtor's) bank in expectation that the borrower will authorize its bank to disburse the funds. Such drafts are often used when a seller sells goods to a new customer in a different city. The seller is not sure whether the buyer will pay the bill. The seller sends the *bill* of lading, or other evidence of ownership of the goods, along with a sight draft to the buyer's bank. Before the goods can be released to the buyer, the buyer must instruct its bank to honor the sight draft by withdrawing funds from the buyer's account. Once the sight draft is honored, the bill of lading or other document evidencing ownership is handed over to the buyer and the goods become the property of the buyer.

simple interest. *Interest* calculated on *principal* where interest earned during periods before maturity of the loan is neither added to the principal nor paid to the lender. *Interest* = principal × interest rate × time. Seldom used in economic calculations except for periods less than 1 year; contrast with *compound interest*.

single proprietorship. *Sole proprietorship*.

single-entry accounting. Accounting that is neither *self-balancing* nor *articulated*; that is, it does not rely on equal *debits* and *credits*. No *journal entries* are made. *Plugging* is required to derive *owners' equity* for the *balance sheet*.

single-step. Said of an *income statement* where *ordinary revenue* and *gain* items are shown first and totaled. Then all ordinary *expenses* and *losses* are totaled. Their difference, plus the effect of *income from discontinued operations* and *extraordinary items*, is shown as *net income*; contrast with *multiple-step* and see *proprietorship theory*.

sinking fund. *Assets* and their earnings earmarked for the retirement of bonds or other long-term obligations. Earnings of sinking fund investments are taxable income of the company.

sinking fund method of depreciation. The periodic charge is an amount such that when the charges are considered to be an *annuity*, the value of the annuity at the end of its depreciable life is equal to the *acquisition cost* of the asset. In theory, the charge for a period ought to include interest on the accumulated depreciation at the start of the period as well. A *fund* of cash is not necessarily, or even usually, accumulated. This method is rarely used.

skeleton account. *T-account*.

slide. The name of the error made by a bookkeeper in recording the digits of a number correctly with the decimal point misplaced, for example, recording $123.40 as $1,234.00 or as $12.34.

soak-up method. The *equity method*.

Social Security taxes. Taxes levied by the federal government on both employers and employees to provide *funds* to pay retired persons (or their survivors) who are entitled to receive such payments, either because they paid Social Security taxes themselves or because the Congress has declared them eligible. See *Old Age, Survivors, Disability*, and *(Hospital) Insurance*.

sole proprietorship. All *owners' equity* belongs to one person.

solvent. Able to meet debts when due.

SOP. Statement of Position (of *AcSEC* of the *AICPA*).

sound value. A phrase used mainly in appraisals of *fixed assets* to mean *fair market value* or *replacement cost* in present condition.

source of funds. Any *transaction* that increases *working capital*.

sources and uses statement. *Statement of changes in financial position*.

SOYD. *Sum-of-the-years'-digits depreciation*.

special assessment. A compulsory levy made by a governmental unit on property to pay the costs of a specific improvement, or service, presumed not to benefit the general public but only the owners of the property so assessed. Accounted for in a special assessment fund.

special journal. A *journal*, such as a sales journal or cash disbursements journal, to record *transactions* of a similar nature that occur frequently.

special revenue debt. Debt of a governmental unit backed only by revenues from specific sources such as tolls from a bridge.

specific identification method. Method for valuing *ending inventory* and *cost of goods sold* by identifying actual units sold and in inventory and summing the actual costs of those individual units. Usually used for items with large unit value, such as jewelry, automobiles, and fur coats.

specific price changes. Changes in the market prices of specific *goods and services*; contrast with *general price level changes*.

specific price index. A measure of the price of a specific good or service, or a small group of similar goods or services, at one time relative to the price during a base period; contrast with *general price index*. See *dollar-value LIFO method*.

spending variance. In *standard cost systems*, the difference between *budgeted overhead* (for a given production plan) and actual *overhead costs* incurred.

split. *Stock split*. Sometimes called "splitup."

splitoff point. The point where all costs are no longer *joint costs* but can be identified with individual products or perhaps with a smaller number of *joint products*.

spoilage. See *abnormal spoilage* and *normal spoilage*.

spread sheet. A *work sheet* organized like a *matrix* that provides a two-way classification of accounting data. The rows and columns are both labeled with *account* titles. An entry in a row represents a *debit*, whereas an entry in a column represents a *credit*. Thus, the number "100" in the "cash" row and the "accounts receivable" column records an entry debiting cash and crediting accounts receivable for $100. A given row total indicates all debit entries to the account represented by that row, and a given column total indicates the sum of all credit entries to the account represented by the column.

squeeze. A term sometimes used for *plug*.

SSARS. See *Statement on Standards for Accounting and Review Services*.

stabilized accounting. *Constant dollar accounting*.

stable monetary unit assumption. In spite of *inflation* that appears to be a way of life, the assumption that underlies *historical cost/nominal dollar accounting*—namely, that current dollars and dollars of previous years can be meaningfully added together. No specific recognition is given to changing values of the dollar in the usual *financial statements*. See *constant dollar accounting*.

Staff Accounting Bulletin. An interpretation issued by the Staff of the Chief Accountant of the *SEC* "suggesting" how the various *Accounting Series Releases* should be applied in practice.

standard cost. Anticipated *cost* of producing a unit of output; a predetermined cost to be assigned to products produced. Standard cost implies a norm: what costs should be. Budgeted cost implies a forecast: something likely, but not necessarily a "should," as implied by a norm. Standard costs are used as the benchmark for gauging good and bad performance. While a budget may be used similarly, it need not be. A budget may be simply a planning document, subject to changes whenever plans change, whereas standard costs are usually not changed until technology changes or costs of labor and materials change.

standard cost system. *Product costing* using *standard costs* rather than actual costs. May be based on either *absorption* or *direct costing* principles.

standard manufacturing overhead. *Overhead costs* expected to be incurred per unit of time and per unit produced.

standard price (rate). Unit price established for materials or labor used in *standard cost systems*.

standard quantity allowed. The quantity of direct material or direct labor (inputs) that should have been used if the units of output had been produced in accordance with preset *standards*.

standby costs. A type of *capacity cost*, such as property taxes, incurred even if operations are shut down completely. Contrast with *enabling costs*.

stated capital. Amount of capital contributed by shareholders. Sometimes used to mean *legal capital*.

stated value. A term sometimes used for the *face amount of capital stock*, when no *par value* is indicated. Where there is a stated value per share, it may be set by the directors (in which case, capital *contributed in excess of stated value* may come into being).

statement of affairs. A *balance sheet* showing immediate *liquidation* amounts, rather than *historical costs*, usually prepared when *insolvency* or *bankruptcy* is imminent. The *going-concern assumption* is not used.

statement of changes in financial position. As defined by *APB Opinion No. 19,* a statement that explains the changes in *working capital* (or cash) balances during a period and shows the changes in the working capital (or cash) accounts themselves. Sometimes called the "funds statement." See *dual transactions assumption* and *all financial resources*.

Statement of Financial Accounting Concepts. **SFAC**. One of a series of *FASB* publications in its *conceptual framework* for *financial accounting* and reporting. Such statements set forth objectives and fundamentals to be the basis for specific financial accounting and reporting standards.

Statement of Financial Accounting Standards. **SFAS**. See *FASB*.

statement of financial position. *Balance sheet*.

Statement of Position. **SOP**. A recommendation on an emerging accounting problem issued by the *AcSEC* of the *AICPA*. The AICPA's Code of Professional Ethics specifically states that *CPAs* need not treat *SOPs* as they do rules from the FASB, but a CPA would be wary of departing from the recommendations of a *SOP*.

statement of retained earnings (income). A statement that reconciles the beginning-of-period and end-of-period balances in the *retained earnings* account. It shows the effects of *earnings, dividend declarations*, and *prior-period adjustments*.

Statement on Auditing Standards. **SAS**. *No. 1* of this series (1973) codifies all statements on auditing standards previously promulgated by the AICPA. Later numbers deal with specific auditing standards and procedures.

Statement on Standards for Accounting and Review Services. **SSARS**. Pronouncements issued by the *AICPA* on

unaudited financial statements and unaudited financial information of nonpublic entities.

static budget. *Fixed budget*.

statutory tax rate. The tax rate specified in the *income tax* law for each type of income (for example, *ordinary income, capital gain or loss*).

step cost. *Semifixed cost*.

step-down method. The method for *allocating service department* costs that starts by allocating one service department's costs to *production departments* and to all other service departments. Then a second service department's costs, including costs allocated from the first, are allocated to production departments and to all other service departments except the first one. In this fashion, the costs of all service departments, including previous allocations, are allocated to production departments and to those service departments whose costs have not yet been allocated.

sterilized allocation. Optimal decisions result from considering *incremental costs*, only. *Allocations* of *joint* or *common costs* are never required for optimal decisions. An allocation of these costs that causes the optimal decision choice not to differ from the one that occurs when joint or common costs are unallocated is "sterilized" with respect to that decision. The term was first used in this context by Arthur L. Thomas. Because *absorption costing* requires that all manufacturing costs be allocated to product, and because some allocations can lead to bad decisions, Thomas (and we) advocate that the allocation scheme chosen lead to sterilized allocations that do not alter the otherwise optimal decision. There is, however, no single allocation scheme that is always sterilized with respect to all decisions. Thus, Thomas (and we) advocate that decisions be made on the basis of incremental costs before any allocations.

stock. *Inventory. Capital stock.* A measure of the amount of something on hand at a specific time; in this sense, contrast with *flow*.

stock appreciation rights. The employer promises to pay to the employee an amount of *cash* on a certain future date. The amount of cash is the difference between the *market value* of a certain number of *shares* of *stock* in the employer's company on a given future date and some base price set on the date the rights are granted. This is a form of compensation used because both changes in tax laws in recent years and stock market performance have made *stock options* relatively less attractive. *GAAP* computes compensation based on the difference between market value of the shares and the base price set at the time of the grant. *Expense* is recognized as the holder of the rights performs the services required for the rights to be exercised.

stock dividend. A so-called *dividend* where additional *shares* of *capital stock* are distributed, without cash payments, to existing shareholders. It results in a *debit* to *retained earnings* in the amount of the market value of the shares issued and a *credit to capital stock* accounts. It is ordinarily used to indicate that earnings retained have been permanently reinvested in the business; contrast with a *stock split*, which requires no entry in the capital stock accounts other than a notation that the *par* or *stated value* per share has been changed.

stock option. The right to purchase a specified number of shares of *stock* for a specified price at specified times, usually granted to employees; contrast with *warrant*.

stock right. See *right*.

stock split. Increase in the number of common shares outstanding resulting from the issuance of additional shares to existing shareholders without additional capital contributions by them. Does not increase the total *par* (or *stated*) *value of common stock* outstanding because par (or stated) value per share is reduced in inverse proportion. A three-for-one stock split reduces par (or stated) value per share to one-third of its former amount. Stock splits are usually limited to distributions that increase the number of shares outstanding by 20 percent or more; compare with *stock dividend*.

stock subscriptions. See *subscription* and *subscribed stock*.

stock warrant. See *warrant*.

stockholders' equity. See *shareholders' equity*.

stores. *Raw materials*, parts, and supplies.

straight-debt value. An estimate of what the *market value* of a *convertible bond* would be if the bond did not contain a conversion privilege.

straight-line depreciation. If the *depreciable life* is *n* periods, then the periodic *depreciation* charge is $1/n$ of the *depreciable cost*. Results in equal periodic charges and is sometimes called "straight-time depreciation."

Subchapter S Corporation. A firm legally organized as a *corporation* but taxed as if it were a *partnership*.

subject to. Qualifications in an *auditor's report* usually caused by a *material* uncertainty in the valuation of an item, such as future promised payments from a foreign government or outcome of pending litigation.

subordinated. Said of *debt* whose claim on income or assets is junior to, or comes after, claims of other debt.

subscribed stock. A *shareholders' equity* account showing the capital that will be contributed as soon as the subscription price is collected. A subscription is a legal contract, so an entry is made debiting an owners' equity contra account and crediting subscribed stock as soon as the stock is subscribed.

subscription. Agreement to buy a *security*, or to purchase periodicals such as magazines.

subsequent events. *Post-statement events*.

subsidiary. Said of a company more than 50 percent of whose voting stock is owned by another.

subsidiary (ledger) accounts. The *accounts* in a *subsidiary ledger*.

subsidiary ledger. The *ledger* that contains the detailed accounts whose total is shown in a *controlling account* of the *general ledger*.

successful efforts accounting. In petroleum accounting, the *capitalization* of the drilling costs of only those wells that contain oil. See *reserve recognition accounting* for an example.

summary of significant accounting principles. *APB Opinion* No. 22 requires that every *annual report* summarize the significant *accounting principles* used in compiling the annual report. This summary may be a separate exhibit or the first *note* to the financial statements.

sum-of-the-years'-digits depreciation. SYD. SOYD. An *accelerated depreciation* method for an asset with *depreciable life* of *n* years, where the charge in period *i* $(i = 1, \ldots, n)$ is the fraction $(n + 1 - i)/[n(n + 1)/2]$ of the *depreciable cost*. If an asset has a depreciable cost of \$15,000 and a 5-year depreciable life, for example, the depreciation charges would be \$5,000 (= $5/15 \times$ \$15,000) in the first year, \$4,000 in the second, \$3,000 in the third, \$2,000 in the fourth, and \$1,000 in the fifth.

sunk costs. *Costs* incurred in the past that are not affected by, and hence irrelevant for, current decisions, aside from *income tax* effects; contrast with *incremental costs* and *imputed costs*. For example, the *acquisition cost* of machinery is irrelevant to a decision of whether or not to scrap the machinery. The current *exit value* of the machine is the imputed cost of continuing to own it, and the cost of, say, electricity to run the machine is an incremental cost of its operation. Sunk costs become relevant for decision making when *income taxes* (*gain* or *loss* on disposal of asset) are taken into account because the cash payment for income taxes depends on the tax basis of the asset.

supplemental actuarial value. Actuarial accrued liability.

supplementary statements (schedules). Statements (schedules) in addition to the four basic *financial statements* (including the retained earnings reconciliation as a basic statement).

surplus. A word once used but now considered poor terminology; prefaced by "earned" to mean *retained earnings* and prefaced by "capital" to mean *capital contributed in excess of par* (or *stated*) *value*.

surplus reserves. Of all the words in accounting, *reserve* is the most objectionable and *surplus* is the second most objectionable. This phrase, then, has nothing to recommend it. It means, simply, *appropriated retained earnings*.

suspense account. A *temporary account* used to record part of a transaction prior to final analysis of that transaction. For example, if a business regularly classifies all sales into a dozen or more different categories but wants to deposit the proceeds of cash sales every day, it may credit a sales suspense account pending detailed classification of all sales into sales, type 1; sales, type 2; and so on.

sustainable income. The part of *distributable income* (computed from *current cost* data) that the firm can be expected to earn in the next accounting period if operations are continued at the same levels as during the current period. *Income from discontinued operations*, for example, may be distributable but not sustainable.

S-X. See *Regulation S-X.*

SYD. *Sum-of-the-years'-digits depreciation. SOYD.*

syndicate. A group of *underwriters*, who have joined together to market a particular *issue* of *securities*.

T

T-account. Account form shaped like the letter T with the title above the horizontal line. *Debits* are shown to the left of the vertical line, *credits* to the right.

take-home pay. The amount of a paycheck; earned wages or *salary* reduced by deductions for *income taxes, Social Security taxes,* contributions to fringe benefit plans, union dues, and so on. Take-home pay might be as little as 60 percent of earned compensation.

take-or-pay contract. As defined by *SFAS No. 47,* an agreement between a purchaser and a seller that provides for the purchaser to pay specified amounts periodically in return for products or services. The purchaser must make specified minimum payments even if it does not take delivery of the contracted products or services.

taking a bath. To incur a large loss. See *big bath.*

tangible. Having physical form. Accounting has never satisfactorily defined the distinction between tangible and *intangible assets*. Typically, intangibles are defined by giving an exhaustive list and everything not on the list is defined as tangible.

target cost. *Standard cost.*

tax. A nonpenal, but compulsory, charge levied by a government on income, consumption, wealth, or other basis for the benefit of all those governed. The term does not include fines or specific charges for benefits accruing only to those paying the charges, such as licenses, permits, special assessments, admissions fees, and tolls.

tax accounting. tax reporting. Process of measuring *taxable income* according to regulations of the *IRS*. Contrast with *financial accounting* and *managerial accounting.*

tax allocation: interperiod. See *deferred income tax liability.*

tax allocation: intrastatement. The showing of income tax effects on *extraordinary items, income from discontinued operations,* and *prior-period adjustments* along with these items, separately from income taxes on other income. See *net-of-tax reporting.*

tax avoidance. See *tax shelter.*

tax credit. A subtraction from taxes otherwise payable; contrast with *tax deduction.*

tax deduction. A subtraction from *revenues* and *gains* to arrive at taxable income. Tax deductions are technically different from tax *exemptions*, but the effect of both is to reduce gross income in computing taxable income. Both are different from *tax credits*, which are subtracted from the computed tax itself in determining taxes payable. If the tax rate is the fraction t of pretax income, then a *tax credit* of \$1 is worth \$1/t of *tax deductions.*

tax evasion. The fraudulent understatement of taxable revenues or overstatement of deductions and expenses or both; contrast with *tax shelter.*

tax exempts. See *municipal bonds.*

tax shelter. The legal avoidance of, or reduction in, *income taxes* resulting from a careful reading of the complex income tax regulations and the subsequent rearrangement of financial affairs to take advantage of the regulations. Often the term is used pejoratively, but the courts have long held that an individual or corporation has no obligation to pay taxes any larger than the legal minimum. If the public concludes that a given tax shelter is "unfair," then the laws and regulations can be changed. Sometimes used to refer to the investment that permits tax avoidance.

tax shield. The amount of an *expense* that reduces taxable income but does not require *working capital*, such as *depreciation*. Sometimes this term is expanded to include expenses that reduce taxable income and use working capital. A depreciation deduction (or *R&D expense* in the expanded sense) of \$10,000 provides a tax shield of \$4,600 when the marginal tax rate is 46 percent.

taxable income. *Income* computed according to *IRS* regulations and subject to *income taxes*. Contrast with *income, net income, income before taxes* (in the *income statement*), and *comprehensive income* (a *financial reporting* concept).

tax-transfer lease. The Congress has provided business with an incentive to invest in qualifying *plant and equipment* by granting an *investment credit*, which though it occurs as a reduction in *income taxes* otherwise payable, is effectively a reduction in the purchase price of the assets. Similarly, the Congress has granted an incentive to acquire such assets by allowing *Accelerated Cost Recovery* (*ACRS*, a form of unusually *accelerated depreciation*). Accelerating depreciation for tax purposes allows a reduction of taxes paid in early years of an asset's life, which provides the firm with an increased *net present value* of *cash flows*. Both of these incentives are administered by the *IRS* through the income tax laws, rather than being granted as an outright cash payment by some other government agency. A business with no taxable income in many cases had difficulty reaping the benefits of the investment credit or of accelerated depreciation because the Congress had not provided for tax refunds to those who acquire qualifying assets but who have no taxable income. In principle, a company without taxable income could lease from another firm with taxable income an asset that would otherwise have been purchased by the first company. The second firm acquires the asset, gets the tax reduction benefits from the acquisition, and becomes a lessor, leasing the asset (presumably at a lower price reflecting its own costs lowered by the tax reductions) to the unprofitable company. Such leases were discouraged by the tax laws prior to 1981. That is, although firms could enter into such leases, the tax benefits could not be legally transferred. Under certain conditions, the tax law allows a profitable firm to earn tax credits and take deductions while leasing to the firm without tax liability in such leases. These leases have sometimes been called "safe-harbor leases."

Technical Bulletin. The *FASB* has authorized its staff to issue bulletins to provide guidance on financial accounting and reporting problems. Although the FASB does not formally approve the contents of the bulletins, their contents are presumed to be part of *GAAP*.

technology. The sum of a firm's technical *trade secrets* and *know-how*, as distinct from its *patents*.

temporary account. *Account* that does not appear on the *balance sheet. Revenue* and *expense* accounts, their *adjuncts* and *contras, production cost accounts, dividend distribution accounts*, and purchases-related accounts (which are closed to the various inventories). Sometimes called a "nominal account."

temporary difference. See *timing difference.*

temporary investments. Investments in *marketable securities* that the owner intends to sell within a short time, usually 1 year, and hence classified as *current assets*.

10-K. The name of the annual report required by the *SEC* of nearly all publicly held corporations.

term bonds. A *bond issue* whose component bonds all mature at the same time; contrast with *serial bonds.*

term loan. A loan with a *maturity* date, as opposed to a demand loan, which is due whenever the lender requests payment. In practice, bankers and auditors use this phrase only for loans for a year or more.

terms of sale. The conditions governing payment for a sale. For example, the terms *2/10, n(et)/30* mean that if payment is made within 10 days of the invoice date, a *discount* of 2 percent from *invoice* price can be taken; the invoice amount must be paid, in any event, within 30 days or it becomes overdue.

throughput contract. As defined by *SFAS No. 47*, an agreement between a shipper (processor) and the owner of a transportation facility (such as an oil or natural gas pipeline or a ship) or a manufacturing facility that provides for the shipper (processor) to pay specified amounts periodically in return for the transportation (processing) of a product. The shipper (processor) is obligated to make cash payments even if it does not ship (process) the contracted quantities.

tickler file. A collection of vouchers or other memoranda arranged chronologically to remind the person in charge of certain duties to make payments (or to do other tasks) as scheduled.

time cost. *Period cost.*

time deposit. Cash in bank earning interest; contrast with *demand deposit.*

time-adjusted rate of return. *Internal rate of return.*

time-series analysis. See *cross-section analysis* for definition and contrast.

times-interest earned. Ratio of pretax *income* plus *interest* charges to interest charges. See *ratio.*

timing difference. A difference between taxable income and pretax income reported to shareholders that will be reversed in a subsequent period and requires an entry in the *deferred income tax* account. For example, the use of *accelerated depreciation* for tax returns and *straight-line depreciation* for financial reporting. Contrast with *permanent difference.*

total assets turnover. *Sales* divided by average total *assets*. Contrast with *permanent difference.*

total overhead variance. Difference between total *overhead* costs and *absorbed overhead.*

trade acceptance. A *draft* drawn by a seller that is presented for signature (acceptance) to the buyer at the time goods are purchased and that then becomes the equivalent of a *note receivable* of the seller and the *note payable* of the buyer.

trade credit. One business allows another to buy from it in return for a promise to pay later. As contrasted with consumer credit, where a business extends the privilege of paying later to a retail customer.

trade discount. A *discount* from *list price* offered to all customers of a given type; contrast with a *discount* offered for prompt payment and *quantity discount.*

trade payables (receivables). *Payables (receivables)* arising in the ordinary course of business transactions. Most accounts payable (receivable) are of this kind.

trade secret. Technical or business information such as formulas, recipes, computer programs, and marketing data not generally known by competitors and maintained by the firm as a secret. A famous example is the secret formula for *Coca-Cola* (a registered *trademark* of the company). Compare with *know-how.* Theoretically capable of having an infinite life, this intangible asset is capitalized only if purchased and then amortized over a period not to exceed 40 years. If it is developed internally, then no asset will be shown.

trade-in. Acquiring a new *asset* in exchange for a used one and perhaps additional cash. See *boot* and *trade-in transaction.*

trade-in transaction. The accounting for a trade-in depends on whether or not the asset received is "similar" to the asset traded in and whether the accounting is for *financial statements* or for *income tax* returns. Assume that an old asset cost $5,000, has $3,000 of *accumulated depreciation* (after recording depreciation to the date of the trade in), and hence has a *book value* of $2,000. The old asset appears to have a market value of $1,500, according to price quotations in used-asset markets. The old asset is traded in on a new asset with a list price of $10,000. The old asset and $5,500 cash *(boot)* are given for the new asset. The generic entry for the trade-in transaction is

New Asset.	A		
Accumulated Depreciation			
(Old Asset)	3,000		
Adjustment on Exchange of Asset .	B	or	B
Old Asset			5,000
Cash			5,500

1. The *list price* method of accounting for trade-ins rests on the assumption that the list price of the new asset closely approximates its market value. The new asset is recorded at its list price (A = $10,000 in the example); B is a *plug* (= $2,500 credit in the example). If B requires a *debit* plug, the Adjustment on Exchange of Asset is a *loss*; if a *credit* plug is required (as in the example), the adjustment is a *gain.*

2. Another theoretically sound method of accounting for trade-ins rests on the assumption that the price quota-

tion from used-asset markets gives a more reliable measure of the market value of the old asset than is the list price a reliable measure of the market value of the new asset. This method uses the *fair market value* of the old asset, $1,500 in the example, to determine B (= $2,000 book value − $1,500 assumed proceeds on disposition = $500 debit or loss). The exchange results in a loss if the book value of the old asset exceeds its market value and in a gain if the market value exceeds the book value. The new asset is recorded on the books by plugging for A (= $7,000 in the example).

3. For income tax reporting, no gain or loss may be recognized on the trade-in. Thus the new asset is recorded on the books by assuming that B is zero and plugging for A (= $7,500 in the example). In practice, firms that wish to recognize the loss currently will sell the old asset directly, rather than trading it in, and acquire the new asset entirely for cash.

4. *Generally accepted accounting principles (APB Opinion No. 29)* require a variant of these methods. The basic method is (1) or (2), depending on whether the list price of the new asset (1) or the quotation of the old asset's market value (2) is the more reliable indication of market value. If, when applying the basic method, a debit entry, or loss, is required for the Adjustment on Exchange of Asset, then the trade-in is recorded as described in (1) or (2) and the full amount of the loss is recognized currently. If, however, a credit entry, or gain, is required for the Adjustment on Exchange of Asset, then the amount of gain recognized currently depends on whether or not the old asset and the new asset are "similar." If the assets are not similar, then the entire gain is recognized currently. If the assets are similar and cash is not received by the party trading in, then no gain is recognized and the treatment is like that in (3): that is, B = 0, plug for A. If the assets are similar and cash is received by the party trading in—a rare case—then a portion of the gain is recognized currently. The portion of the gain recognized currently is the fraction *cash received/fair market value of total consideration received.* [When the list price method (1) is used, the market value of the old asset is assumed to be the list price of the new asset plus the amount of cash received by the party trading in.]

The results of applying *GAAP* to the example can be summarized as follows:

More Reliable Information as to Fair Market Value	Old Asset Compared with New Asset	
	Similar	Not Similar
New Asset List . . . A = $7,500		A = $10,000
Price . . . . . B = 0		B = 2,500 gain
Old Asset Market . . A = $7,000		A = $ 7,000
Price . . . . . B = 500 loss		B = 500 loss

trademark. A distinctive word or symbol affixed to a product, its package, or dispenser, which uniquely identifies the firm's products and services. See *trademark right*.

trademark right. The right to exclude competitors in sales or advertising from using words or symbols that may be confusingly similar to the firm's *trademarks*. Trademark rights last as long as the firm continues to use the trademarks in question. In the United States, trademark rights arise from use and not from government registration. They therefore have a legal life independent of the life of a registration. Registrations last 20 years and are renewable as long as the trademark is being used. Thus, as an asset, purchased trademark rights might, like land, not be subject to amortization if management believes that the life of the trademark is indefinite. In practice, accountants amortize a trademark right over some estimate of its life, not to exceed 40 years. Under *SFAS No. 2*, internally developed trademark rights must be *expensed*.

trading on the equity. Said of a firm engaging in *debt financing*; frequently said of a firm doing so to a degree considered abnormal for a firm of its kind. *Leverage*.

transaction. A *transfer* between the accounting *entity* and another party, or parties.

transfer. *SFAC No. 3* distinguishes "reciprocal" and "nonreciprocal" transfers. In a reciprocal transfer, or "exchange," the entity both receives and sacrifices. In a nonreciprocal transfer, the entity sacrifices but does not receive (examples include gifts, distributions to owners) or receives but does not sacrifice (investment by owner in entity). *SFAC No. 3* suggests that the term "internal transfer" is self-contradictory and that the term "internal event" be used instead.

transfer agent. Usually a bank or trust company designated by a corporation to make legal transfers of *stock (bonds)* and, perhaps, to pay *dividends (coupons)*.

transfer price. A substitute for a *market*, or *arm's-length*, *price* used in *profit center*, or *responsibility*, *accounting* when one segment of the business "sells" to another segment. Incentives of profit center managers will not coincide with the best interests of the entire business unless transfer prices are properly set.

translation gain (or loss). *Foreign exchange gain (or loss)*.

transportation-in. *Freight-in*.

transposition error. An error in record keeping resulting from reversing the order of digits in a number, such as recording "32" for "23." If an error of this sort has been made in a number added in a total, then the incorrect total will differ from the correct total by a number divisible by nine. Thus if *trial balance* sums differ by a number divisible by nine, one might search for a transposition error.

treasury bond. A bond issued by a corporation and then reacquired; such bonds are treated as retired when reacquired and an *extraordinary gain or loss* on reacquisition is recognized. Also, a *bond* issued by the U.S. Treasury Department.

treasury shares. *Capital stock* issued and then reacquired by the corporation. Such reacquisitions result in a reduction of *shareholders' equity*, and are usually shown on the balance sheet as *contra* to shareholders' equity. Neither *gain* nor *loss* is recognized on transactions involving treasury stock. Any difference between the amounts paid and received for treasury stock transactions is debited (if positive) or credited (if negative) to *additional paid-in capital*. See *cost method* and *par value method*.

treasury stock. *Treasury shares*.

trial balance. A listing of *account balances*; all accounts with *debit* balances are totaled separately from accounts with *credit* balances. The two totals should be equal. Trial balances are taken as a partial check of the arithmetic accuracy of the entries previously made. See *adjusted, preclosing, post-closing, unadjusted trial balance*.

troubled debt restructuring. As defined in *SFAS No. 15*, a concession (changing of the terms of a *debt*) granted by a *creditor* for economic or legal reasons related to the *debtor's* financial difficulty that the creditor would not otherwise consider.

turnover. The number of times that *assets*, such as *inventory* or *accounts receivable*, are replaced on average during the period. Accounts receivable turnover, for example, is total sales on account for a period divided by average accounts receivable balance for the period. See *ratio*.

turnover of plant and equipment. See *ratio*.

two-T-account method. A method for computing either (1) *foreign exchange gains and losses* or (2) monetary gains or *losses* for *constant dollar accounting statements*. The left-hand *T-account* shows actual net balances of *monetary items* and the right-hand T-account shows implied *(common) dollar* amounts.

2/10, *n*(et)/30. See *terms of sale*.

U

unadjusted trial balance. *Trial balance* before *adjusting* and *closing entries* are made at the end of the period.

unappropriated retained earnings. *Retained earnings* not appropriated and therefore against which *dividends* can be charged in the absence of retained earnings restrictions. See *restricted retained earnings*.

uncertainty. See *risk* for definition and contrast.

uncollectible account. An *account receivable* that will not be paid by the *debtor*. If the preferable *allowance method* is used, the entry upon judging a specific account to be uncollectible is to *debit* the allowance for uncollectible accounts and to *credit* the specific account receivable. See *sales contra, estimated uncollectibles*.

unconsolidated subsidiary. A *subsidiary* not consolidated and, hence, accounted for on the *equity method*.

uncontrollable cost. The opposite of *controllable cost*.

underapplied (underabsorbed) overhead. An excess of actual *overhead costs* for a period over costs applied, or charged, to products produced during the period. A *debit balance* remaining in an overhead account after overhead is assigned to product.

underlying document. The record, memorandum, *voucher*, or other signal that is the authority for making an *entry* into a *journal*.

underwriter. One who agrees to purchase an entire *security issue* for a specified price, usually for resale to others.

undistributed earnings. *Retained earnings*; typically, this term refers to that amount retained for a given year.

unearned income (revenue). *Advances from customers*; strictly speaking, a contradiction in terms.

unemployment tax. See *FUTA*.

unencumbered appropriation. In governmental accounting, portion of an *appropriation* not yet spent or *encumbered*.

unexpired cost. An *asset*.

unfavorable variance. In *standard cost* accounting, an excess of actual cost over standard cost assigned to product.

unfunded. Not *funded*. An obligation or *liability*, usually for *pension costs*, exists but no *funds* have been set aside to discharge the obligation or liability.

Uniform Partnership Act. A model law, enacted by many states, to govern the relations between partners where the *partnership* agreement fails to specify the agreed-upon treatment.

unissued capital stock. *Stock* authorized but not yet issued.

unitary taxation. Many states believe that *corporations* unfairly avoid paying *income taxes* in their state by using artificially concocted *transfer prices* to show high income in locations with low income tax rates and low income in locations with high income tax rates. Unitary taxation is a method used by some states to *allocate* worldwide corporate income so that income taxes can be levied. The allo-cation formulas take into account *revenues, plant assets,* and employment in various locations.

units-of-production method. The *production method of depreciation*.

unlimited liability. The liability of *general partners* or the sole proprietor for all debts of the *partnership* or sole proprietorship.

unqualified opinion. See *auditor's report*.

unrealized appreciation. An *unrealized holding gain*; frequently used in the context of *marketable securities*.

unrealized gross margin (profit). A *contra* account to *installment accounts receivable* used with the *installment method* of revenue recognition. Shows the amount of profit that will eventually be realized when the receivable is collected. Some accountants show this account as a *liability*.

unrealized holding gain. See *inventory profit* for definition and an example.

unrealized loss on marketable securities. An *income statement account* title for the amount of *loss* during the current period on the portfolio of *marketable securities* below the beginning-of-period *book value* of that portfolio. *SFAS No. 12* requires that losses caused by declines in price below market be *recognized* in the income statement, even though they have not been *realized*.

unrecovered cost. *Book value* of an *asset*.

usage variance. *Quantity variance*.

use of funds. Any transaction that reduces funds (however funds is defined).

useful life. *Service life*.

V

valuation account. A *contra account* or *adjunct account*. When *marketable securities* are reported at *lower of cost or market*, any declines in market value below cost will be credited to a valuation account. In this way, the acquisition cost and the amount of price declines below cost can both be shown. *SFAS No. 3* says that a valuation account is "a separate item that reduces and increases the carrying amount" of an asset (or liability). The accounts are part of the related assets (or liabilities) and are neither assets (nor liabilities) in their own right.

value. Monetary worth; the term is usually so subjective that it ought not to be used without a modifying adjective unless most people would agree on the amount; not to be confused with *cost*. See *fair market value, entry value, exit value*.

value added. *Cost* of a product or *work in process*, minus the cost of the material purchased for the product or work in process.

value variance. *Price variance.*

variable annuity. An *annuity* whose periodic payments depend on some uncertain outcome, such as stock market prices.

variable budget. *Flexible budget.*

variable costing. *Direct costing.* Contrast with *absorption costing.*

variable costs. *Costs* that change as activity levels change. Strictly speaking, variable costs are zero when the activity level is zero. See *semivariable costs.* In accounting, this term most often means the sum of *direct costs* and variable *overhead.*

variance. Difference between actual and *standard costs* or between *budgeted* and actual *expenditures* or, sometimes, *expenses.* The word has completely different meanings in accounting and statistics, where it is a measure of dispersion of a distribution.

variance analysis. The investigation of the causes of *variances* in a *standard cost system.* This term has a different meaning in statistics.

variation analysis. Analysis of the causes of changes in items of interest in financial statements such as net *income* or *gross margin.*

vendor. A seller. Sometimes spelled "vender."

verifiable. A qualitative *objective* of financial reporting specifying that items in *financial statements* can be checked by tracing back to *underlying documents*—supporting *invoices*, canceled *checks*, and other physical pieces of evidence.

verification. The auditor's act of reviewing or checking items in *financial statements* by tracing back to *underlying documents*—supporting *invoices*, canceled *checks*, and other business documents—or sending out *confirmations* to be returned. Compare with *physical verification.*

vertical analysis. Analysis of the financial statements of a single firm or across several firms for a particular time, as opposed to *horizontal* or time-series analysis, where items are compared over time for a single firm or across firms.

vested. Said of an employee's *pension plan* benefits that are not contingent on the employee continuing to work for the employer.

volume variance. *Capacity variance.*

voucher. A document that signals recognition of a *liability* and authorizes the disbursement of cash. Sometimes used to refer to the written evidence documenting an *accounting entry*, as in the term *journal voucher.*

voucher system. A method for controlling *cash*, that requires each *check* to be authorized with an approved *voucher.* No cash *disbursements* are made except from *petty cash funds.*

W

wage. Compensation of employees based on time worked or output of product for manual labor. But see *take-home pay.*

warrant. A certificate entitling the owner to buy a specified number of shares at a specified time(s) for a specified price. Differs from a *stock option* only in that options are granted to employees and warrants are issued to the public. See *right.*

warranty. A promise by a seller to correct deficiencies in products sold. When warranties are given, proper accounting practice recognizes an estimate of warranty *expense* and an *estimated liability* at the time of sale. See *guarantee* for contrast in proper usage.

wash sale. The sale and purchase of the same or similar *asset* within a short time period. For *income tax* purposes, *losses* on a sale of stock may not be recognized if equivalent stock is purchased within 30 days before or 30 days after the date of sale.

waste. Residue of material from manufacturing operations with no sale value. Frequently, it has negative value because additional costs must be incurred for disposal.

wasting asset. A *natural resource* having a limited *useful life* and, hence, subject to *amortization*, called *depletion.* Examples are timber land, oil and gas wells, and ore deposits.

watered stock. *Shares* issued for *assets* with *fair market value* less than *par* or *stated value.* The assets are put onto the books at the overstated values. In the law, for shares to be considered watered, the *board of directors* must have acted in bad faith or fraudulently in issuing the shares under these circumstances. The term originated from a former practice of cattlemen who fed cattle ("stock") large quantities of salt to make them thirsty. The cattle then drank a lot of water before being taken to market. This was done to make the cattle appear heavier and more valuable than otherwise.

weighted average. An average computed by counting each occurrence of each value, not merely a single occurrence of each value. For example, if one unit is purchased for $1 and two units are purchased for $2 each, then the simple average of the purchase prices is $1.50 but the weighted average price per unit is $5/3 = $1.67. Contrast with *moving average.*

weighted-average inventory method. Valuing either *withdrawals* or *ending inventory* at the *weighted-average* purchase price of all units on hand at the time of withdrawal or of computing ending inventory. The *inventory equation* is used to calculate the other quantity. If the *perpetual inventory* method is in use, often called the "moving average method."

where-got, where-gone statement. A term used by W. M. Cole for a statement much like the *statement of changes in financial position*.

window dressing. The attempt to make financial statements show *operating* results, or *financial position*, more favorable than would otherwise be shown.

with recourse. See *note receivable discounted*.

withdrawals. *Assets* distributed to an owner. *Partner's drawings*. See *inventory equation* for another context.

withheld income taxes. See *withholding*.

withholding. Deductions from *salaries* or *wages*, usually for *income taxes*, to be remitted by the employer, in the employee's name, to the taxing authority.

without recourse. See *note receivable discounted*.

work in process. Partially completed product; an *asset* that is classified as *inventory*.

work sheet. A tabular schedule for convenient summary of *adjusting* and *closing entries*. The work sheet usually begins with an *unadjusted trial balance*. Adjusting entries are shown in the next two columns, one for *debits* and one for *credits*. The horizontal sum of each line is then carried to the right into either the *income statement* or *balance sheet* column, as appropriate. The *plug* to equate the income statement column totals is the income, if a debit plug is required, or loss, if a credit plug is required, for the period. That income will be closed to retained earnings on the balance sheet. The income statement credit columns are the revenues for the period and the debit columns are the expenses (and revenue *contras*) to be shown on the income statement.

Work sheet is also used to refer to *schedules* for computing other items appearing on the *financial statements* that require adjustment or compilation.

working capital. *Current assets* minus *current liabilities*. The *statement of changes in financial position* usually explains the changes in working capital for a period.

working capital equation. The *balance sheet* states that *assets* = equities. The information in comparative balance sheets from the start and end of a period can be restated as:

$$\text{Change in Assets} = \text{Change in Equities}$$

This equation can be further broken down to say that

$$\begin{array}{l}\text{Change in Current} \\ \text{Assets Plus Change} \\ \text{in Noncurrent Assets}\end{array} = \begin{array}{l}\text{Change in Current} \\ \text{Liabilities Plus Change} \\ \text{in Noncurrent Equities}\end{array}$$

which is equivalent to

$$\begin{array}{l}\text{Change in Current} \\ \text{Assets Less Change} \\ \text{in Current Liabilities}\end{array} = \begin{array}{l}\text{Change in Noncurrent} \\ \text{Equities Less Change} \\ \text{in Noncurrent Assets}\end{array}$$

The left-hand side of this equation is the change in *working capital* for the period. The items on the right-hand side cause the change in working capital during the period. The *statement of changes in financial position* typically shows the causes of the changes (right-hand side of the equation) at the top of the statement and the way working capital has changed (left-hand side of the equation) at the bottom of the statement.

working capital provided by operations. See *funds provided by operations*.

working papers. The schedules and analyses prepared by the *auditor* in carrying out investigations prior to issuing an *opinion* on *financial statements*.

worth. *Value*. See *net worth*.

worth-debt ratio. Reciprocal of the *debt-equity ratio*. See *ratio*.

write down. *Write off*, except that not all the assets' cost is charged to expense or *loss*. Generally used for nonrecurring items.

write off. *Charge* an *asset* to *expense* or *loss*; that is, *debit* expense (or loss) and *credit* asset.

write up. To increase the recorded *cost* of an *asset* with no corresponding *disbursement* of *funds*; that is, *debit* asset and *credit revenue*, or perhaps, *owners' equity*. Seldom done because currently accepted accounting principles are based on actual transactions. When a portfolio of *marketable equity securities* increases in market value subsequent to a previously recognized decrease, the *book value* of the portfolio is written up—the debit is to the *contra account*.

write-off method. A method for treating *uncollectible accounts* that charges *bad debt expense* and credits accounts receivable of specific customers as uncollectible amounts are identified. May not be used when uncollectible amounts are significant and can be estimated. See *sales contra*, *estimated uncollectibles*, and the *allowance method* for contrast.

Y

yield. *Internal rate of return* of a stream of cash flows. Cash yield is cash flow divided by book value. See also *dividend yield*.

yield to maturity. At a given time, the *internal rate of return* of a series of cash flows, usually said of a *bond*. Sometimes called the "effective rate."

Z

zero salvage value. If the *salvage value* of a *depreciable asset* is estimated to be less than 10 percent of its *cost*, the tax regulations permit an assumption of zero salvage value in computing *depreciation* for federal *income tax* purposes. This convention is often used in financial reporting as well, but seldom in textbooks.

zero-base(d) budgeting. ZBB. In preparing an ordinary *budget* for the next period, a manager starts with the budget for the current period and makes adjustments as seem necessary, because of changed conditions for the next period. Because most managers like to increase the scope of the activities managed and because most prices increase most of the time, amounts in budgets prepared in the ordinary, incremental way seem to increase period after period. The authority approving the budget assumes that operations will be carried out in the same way as in the past and that next period's expenditures will have to be at least as large as the current period's. Thus, this authority tends to study only the increments to the current period's budget. In ZBB, the authority questions the process for carrying out a program and the entire budget for the next period. Every dollar in the budget is studied, not just the dollars incremental to the previous period's amounts. The advocates of ZBB claim that in this way: (1) programs or divisions of marginal benefit to the business or governmental unit will more likely be deleted from the program, rather than being continued with costs at least as large as the present ones; and (2) alternative, more cost-effective, ways of carrying out programs are more likely to be discovered and implemented. ZBB implies questioning the existence of programs, and the fundamental nature of the way they are carried out, not merely the amounts used to fund them. Experts appear to be evenly divided as to whether the middle word should be "base" or "based."

Index